OXFORD MEDICAL PUBLICA

C000173476

TEXTBOOK OF
DENTAL PHARMACOLOGY AND THERAPEUTICS

TEXTBOOK OF
DENTAL PHARMACOLOGY
AND THERAPEUTICS

•

JOHN G. WALTON
JOHN W. THOMPSON
AND
ROBIN A. SEYMOUR

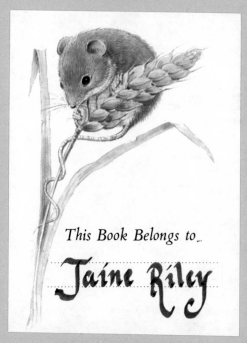

This Book Belongs to
Jaine Riley

Oxford   New York   Tokyo
OXFORD UNIVERSITY PRESS

Oxford University Press, Walton Street, Oxford OX2 6DP

Oxford New York Toronto
Delhi Bombay Calcutta Madras Karachi
Petaling Jaya Singapore Hong Kong Tokyo
Nairobi Dar es Salaam Cape Town
Melbourne Auckland

and associated companies in
Berlin Ibadan

Oxford is a trade mark of Oxford University Press

Published in the United States
by Oxford University Press, New York

British Library Cataloguing in Publication Data
Walton, J.G.
Textbook of dental pharmacology and
therapeutics
1. Dentistry
I. Title. II. Thompson, John W.
III. Seymour, Robin A.
617.6
ISBN 0-19-261823-7
ISBN 0-19-261235-2 (Pbk)

Library of Congress Cataloging in Publication Data
Walton, J. G.
Textbook of dental pharmacology and therapeutics/J.G. Walton,
John W. Thompson, and Robin A. Seymour.
(Oxford medical publications)
Includes bibliographies and index.
1. Pharmacology. 2. Dentistry. I. Thompson, John W. (John Warburton)
II. Seymour, R. A. III. Title. IV. Series.
[DNLM: 1. Dentistry. 2. Pharmacology. QV 50 W239t]
RM300.W36 1989 615'.1—dc19 88-28909 CIP
ISBN 0-19-261823-7
ISBN-0-19-261235-2 (pbk.)

Printed in Great Britain by
Bookcraft Ltd, Midsomer Norton, Avon

FOREWORD

ROY STORER

Dean of Dentistry, University of Newcastle upon Tyne

THOSE conversant with the publications on Dental Pharmacology will recall the highly successful British Dental Journal booklet entitled *Pharmacology for the Dental Practitioner* by Mr John Walton and Professor John Thompson. They have been joined by Dr Robin Seymour in this textbook which is an expansion of that earlier publication. John Walton has been lecturing to dental students on pharmacology since 1960 and John Thompson began his academic career in medical pharmacology by presenting a course to dental students. Robin Seymour is a more recent addition to the Newcastle team and he has developed a particular interest in analgesics. The three authors have encouraged others in the Sub-Faculty of Dentistry at Newcastle to participate in research in the pharmacological field and the projects will be a valuable contribution to pharmacology in relation to dentistry, which is emerging as a specialist subject within the dental curriculum.

In this book, the authors have not only dealt with, in appropriate detail, those drugs used by the dentist but also those the dentist is likely to encounter in patients who are receiving medication from their medical practitioners.

As an increasing proportion of the population move into the elderly category, it is likely that more of those who seek dental health care will be on long-term medication. Therefore it is very important that the dental practitioner should have 'a thorough understanding of the principles of pharmacology so that he can anticipate drug interactions, allergies, incompatibilities, side effects, and other dangers.' (An Inquiry into Dental Education—A Report to the Nuffield Foundation, 1980, The Nuffield Foundation, London).

The chapter on Emergencies in Dental Practice is based on the authors' annual postgraduate course for dental practitioners in the Northern Region, which must be one of the most successful of its kind.

This book will be appreciated by undergraduates, by those studying for higher diplomas, and, not least, by general dental practitioners who, in the provision of whole mouth care for their patients, will be better able to deal with those who are on complex medication.

March 1988

PREFACE

Over the past 30 years or so the subject of pharmacology has developed explosively with the result that there are now many groups of potent drugs used for the treatment of disease. This has had two important consequences for dentistry. First, a number of the newer drugs have found important roles in dental treatment. Second, many patients who attend for dental treatment are taking drugs for the treatment of medical conditions and it is therefore important for the dentist to be aware of this fact and to be fully conversant with the pharmacology and rationale behind the use of these drugs. Furthermore, it is obviously important for the dentist to be aware of the unwanted effects that may be produced by the drugs prescribed, some directly concerned with the mouth. Of equal importance is the need to know about possible interactions that might occur (and must therefore be avoided) in the event that the dental practitioner prescribes one or more drugs for dental treatment that have the potential to interact with those already being taken by the patient for medical reasons. Thus the need for the present-day dental student and dental practitioner to have a sound working knowledge of pharmacology and therapeutics is a pressing one, and this book has been written to meet these needs.

The book is divided into two sections. The first deals with general pharmacological principles together with those drugs that are part of the day-to-day pharmacological armamentarium of the dental practitioner. The second part deals with the pharmacology and therapeutics related to drugs which, although unlikely to be prescribed by the dental practitioner, are nevertheless of considerable importance for reasons already given.

This book is based on an earlier and much shorter book entitled *Pharmacology for the Dental Practitioner*, which was written by two of the authors of the present book (J.G.W. and J.W.T.). That original book has now been expanded into a comprehensive textbook for dental students and dental practitioners and, in tackling this difficult and lengthy task, the original authors have had the good fortune to acquire the invaluable help of Dr Robin Seymour, who has for some time assisted his colleagues in the teaching of pharmacology to dental students.

The authors are grateful to many colleagues and others who have willingly helped in various ways, and the names of these individuals are listed in the Acknowledgements. However, the authors alone are responsible for any errors of omission or commission that are to be found in this book. Furthermore, they would be most grateful to any reader who takes the trouble to point out mistakes or to make suggestions for a further edition.

Newcastle upon Tyne   J.G.W.
February 1988   J.W.T.
                                                                               R.A.S.

ACKNOWLEDGEMENTS

The authors gratefully acknowledge the generous help and assistance they have had from colleagues in the preparation of this book. Those who have kindly read, and constructively criticized various chapters or sections of the text include Dr Heather Ashton, Professor R. W. F. Campbell, Dr T. S. J. Elliott, Professor B. T. Golding, Professor C. J. Hull, Professor M. D. Rawlins, Dr P. A. Routledge, and Mr A. K. Watson (Astra Laboratories). They also wish to acknowledge the valuable help given by the Audio Visual Centre and the Medical and Dental Library of the University of Newcastle upon Tyne. They are deeply indebted to Mrs Margaret Cheek for her tireless work in typing the seemingly endless drafts and also for her conscientious and painstaking labours concerned with the bibliography of this book. The help and forbearance of the staff of Oxford University Press is gratefully acknowledged. Finally, the authors wish to thank Mrs Judith Thompson for her help in preparing the index.

FIGURE AND TABLE ACKNOWLEDGEMENTS

The authors of this book wish to thank the following authors, editors, and publishers for kindly granting permission to reproduce published material as indicated.

Fig. 1.1: Adapted from Fig. 1.1 on p. 5, Grahame-Smith, D. G. and Aronson, J. K. (1984). *Oxford Textbook of Clinical Pharmacology and Drug Therapy*. Oxford University Press, Oxford. **Fig. 1.4**: Redrawn from Fig. 1, p. 201, Brodie, B. B. (1964). *Absorption and Distribution of Drugs*, (ed. T. B. Binns). Livingstone, Edinburgh. **Figs. 1.5 and 1.6**: Based partly on Fig. 2, p. 37, Gillette, J. R. (1967). In, *Drug Responses in Man*. (eds. G. Wolstenholme and R. Porter). Churchill, London. Based partly on Fig. 1, p. 17, Brodie, B. B. (1964). *Absorption and Distribution of Drugs*, (ed. T. B. Binns). Livingstone, Edinburgh. **Fig. 1.7(b)**: Fig. 1, p. 995, Drew, G. C., Colquhoun, W. P., and Long, H. A. (1958). Effects of small doses of alcohol on skill resembling driving. *British Medical Journal*, **2**, 993–9. **Fig. 1.9**: Fig. 2.2, p. 22, Creasey, W. A. (1979). *Drug Disposition in Humans*. Oxford University Press, Oxford. **Fig. 1.10(a and b)**: Fig. 13.8, p. 189, Rowland, M. and Tozer, T. N. (1980). *Clinical Pharmacokinetics: Concepts and Applications*. Lea and Febiger, Philadelphia. **Fig. 1.12**: Fig. 3–10, p. 27, Schild, H. O. (1980). *Applied Pharmacology*. Churchill Livingstone, Edinburgh. **Tables 1.3 and 1.4**: Adapted from Table I, p. 453. Lefkowitz, R. J. (1979). Direct binding studies of adrenergic receptors: biochemical, physiologic and clinical implications. *Annals of Internal Medicine*, **91**, 450–8. Table II, pp. 68 and 88. Lefkowitz, R. J. and Hoffman, B. B. (1981). New directions in adrenergic receptor research. Parts I and II. In, *Towards Understanding Receptors*, (ed. J. W. Lamble). Elsevier/North Holland, Amsterdam. **Table 1.5**: Adapted from Fig. 1, p. 228, Koch-Weser, J. (1972). Serum drug concentrations as therapeutic guides. *New England Journal of Medicine*, **287**, 227–31. **Fig. 6.1**: Thompson, J. W. (1984). Pain: mechanisms and principles of management. In, *Advanced Geriatric Medicine 4* (ed. J. Grimley Evans). Pitman, London. **Fig. 13.1**: Adapted from Fig. 8–16, p. 25, Schmidt, R. F. (ed.) (1978). *Neurophysiology*. Springer-Verlag, New York, Heidelberg, Berlin. **Fig. 13.3**: Wilson, A. and Schild, H. O. (1968) *Applied*

Pharmacology, (10th edn), p. 77. Churchill, London. **Fig. 13.5**: After Axelrod, J. (1960). *Proceedings of the 2nd International Pharmacology Meeting.* Churchill Livingstone, Edinburgh. **Figs. 15.1 and 15.2**: Adapted from Fig. 11.1, p. 141. Noble, D. (1975). *The initiation of the heart beat.* Oxford University Press, Oxford. **Fig. 21.3**: Drawn from data of Kalow, W. and Gunn, D. R. (1957). *Journal of Pharmacology,* **120**, 203.

CONTENTS

PART II · GENERAL DRUGS

1

General principles of drug action

THE word 'pharmacology' means nothing more nor less than the study of the effects of chemical substances upon living tissues; it is derived from two Greek words; *pharmakon*, drug; *logos*, study. Living cells, tissues, and organs consist of biological systems and a chemical substance that is capable of modifying a biological system in a relatively selective way is known as a drug. Whilst many chemical substances could be said to fall into this category, only a small proportion of them are sufficiently selective and safe to use for the prevention or treatment of disease or, in other words, as therapeutic agents. For example, phenol and many other chemical substances when applied to nerves can block impulse transmission but cannot be used for this purpose routinely because they cause irreversible damage to nerve tissue. The actual number of clinically acceptable local anaesthetics used by the average dental practitioner can be counted on the fingers of one hand.

The rapid increase in the number of new drugs during the past quarter century has been aptly described as the 'drug explosion'. Prior to this, the number of drugs of real value was very small; there were many virtually useless preparations but they did not do much harm even if they did not do much good! Today, the situation is vastly different; a bewildering and ever-increasing number of new and powerful drugs is available for therapeutic use. The subject of pharmacology has developed at a phenomenal pace, particularly when one considers that it was only in the 1930s that it crystallized out as a separate subject from related disciplines such as physiology and chemistry (Paton 1963). Pharmacology has received its greatest impetus from progress made in the field of synthetic organic chemistry and the momentum has been maintained by the ever-present need for chemical substances that can be used to prevent or control disease.

The dental practitioner, in the same way as the medical practitioner, is faced with the problem of keeping abreast of developments in pharmacology and therapeutics. In order to use drugs rationally, it is important to understand the basic principles of drug action. The clarification of old ideas of drug action coupled with the discovery of new mechanisms have made it possible to begin to interpret the effects of drugs in terms of molecular events governed by physico-chemical laws. The stage has therefore been reached when it is now possible to enumerate the different processes involved in the absorption, distribution, mechanism of action, fate, and excretion of drugs. Furthermore, it is in the study of the mechanism of drug action that major progress has been achieved. Sufficient knowledge is now available to make it possible, in many instances, to present a coherent account of the action of a drug. It is the authors' fervent belief that the administration of any drug, irrespective of type and route, should always be carried out with these principles constantly in mind. Drugs will come and drugs will go; but basic principles will always remain even though these may be modified and extended as new knowledge becomes available.

The dental practitioner most commonly applies drugs locally; much less often is he or she concerned with their systemic administration, with the exception of analgesics, antibiotics, and drugs used for sedation. Nevertheless, many of the same pharmacological principles apply whether the drugs are used systemically or locally. When a drug is given locally, some proportion of the total dose will be absorbed into the general circulation, the amount depending upon the drug, the dose, and the area to which it is applied. It is possible therefore that under certain conditions, local application of a drug may be followed by undesirable systemic effects. Today, many patients who come to the dental surgery are already taking drugs prescribed by their medical practitioners or even by themselves. The dental surgeon should always be aware of the risk of a drug interaction between the drug(s) to be prescribed and those the patient is already taking. Thus, the problem of drug interaction is another reason why the dental practitioner needs to be conversant with the general principles of drug action. This is also an appropriate moment to remind ourselves of a particularly important point, namely, that to the layman the word 'drug' usually means something different from that understood by the prescriber. Furthermore, in the mind of the average patient, there is often a vast difference between the meanings of the words 'drug', 'pill', 'tablet', 'medicine', and 'mixture'. If this is not appreciated by the practitioner the fact that a particular patient is under the influence of a powerful drug may be missed to their possible detriment.

SOURCE OF DRUGS

In the past, drugs were obtained from natural sources and some of the most important drugs are still derived in this way. For example, insulin is obtained from the pancreas of cattle or pigs; digitalis from certain species of the foxglove plant; and iron, commonly used in the form of ferrous sulphate, is derived from mineral sources. Nevertheless, today, the majority of drugs are synthesized by chemists and every year many thousands of new compounds are made and screened for possible use as drugs. Table 1.1 indicates the stages involved in the development of a drug (Thompson 1967; Goldberg and Griffin 1984; M. D. Rawlins, personal communication). It also shows the points at which the Committee on Safety of Medicines operate in order to weigh the evidence about new drugs submitted to it by the pharmaceutical industry and by the dental and medical professions, so that

Table 1.1. Development of a drug

Principal individual(s) concerned	Stages in the development of a drug	Regulatory involvement
Various	Ideas	
Chemist	Natural or synthetic chemical compounds	
Pharmacologist Biochemist	Pharmacological tests including: pharmacodynamics ⎫ pharmacokinetics ⎭ in animals	
Toxicologist	Acute toxicity (e.g. LD_{50}) Chronic toxicity tests including: studies on two species of animals, one rodent and the other non-rodent Reproduction toxicity (fertility and reproduction teratogenesis, fetal and embryological toxicology) Mutagenicity Carcinogenicity	
Pharmacist	Pharmaceutical formulation Clinical trials	
Clinical pharmacologist Normal volunteers	Phase 1: a pilot investigation made in a small number of normal volunteers	
Dentist/Doctor Clinical pharmacologist Nurse Patients Statistician	Phase 2: an 'open' clinical trial carried out in a small number of patients Phase 3: large-scale clinical trial (double blind)	Clinical trial certificate (or clinical trial exemption) required
Practising dentists/doctors and their patients	Phase 4: monitored release and post-marketing surveillance of new drug Accepted drug	Product licence required Post-marketing surveillance For unforeseen reasons, usually toxicological, it may prove necessary to withdraw a drug at any time

it can act as an independent assessor. As can be seen from Table 1.1, the development of a drug is a long and complicated process involving many stages and many individuals.

CLASSIFICATION OF DRUGS

The most logical way to classify drugs would be according to their mechanism of action, but this is not yet feasible because for many drugs this information is still incomplete. One of the largest areas where knowledge is lacking concerns drugs which act on the central nervous system, a situation which is slowly improving as new knowledge becomes available about the biochemistry and pharmacology of the brain.

At present, the most practical way to classify drugs is according to their main site(s) of action and this is the method adopted by (see Chapter 3) the *British National Formulary* and also by the *Dental Practitioner's Formulary* (a joint publication of the British Dental Association, the British Medical Association, and The Pharmaceutical Society of Great Britain).

MODE OF ACTION OF DRUGS

The subject of pharmacology exists because a large number of substances exert a selective action, so modifying the behaviour of some cells or tissues more than others. Indeed, were it not for selective action, it would be impossible to use chemical substances therapeutically. Unfortunately, with many of the drugs at present available, the degree of selective action is less than is desirable, so that in order to produce the required effect it may be necessary to use a dose that also gives rise to certain unwanted actions. In some instances these are of trivial inconvenience to the patient but in others, unwanted effects of a more serious nature may occur. Pharmacologists, particularly those in the pharmaceutical industry, are constantly striving to produce drugs that exert a higher degree of selective action than existing drugs of the same type. However, it is likely to be a long time before the majority of drugs available exert such a high degree of selective action that they are incapable of producing any unwanted effects.

THE PROCESSES OF DRUG THERAPY

Four main processes are involved in drug therapy:

(1) the pharmaceutical process;

(2) the pharmacokinetic process;

(3) the pharmacodynamic process;

(4) the therapeutic process.

As has been pointed out by Grahame-Smith and Aronson (1984), each of these four processes can be formulated as a simple question:

(1) Is the drug getting into the patient?

(2) Is the drug getting to its site of action?

(3) Is the drug producing the required pharmacological effect?

(4) Is the pharmacological effect being translated into a therapeutic effect?

These closely interrelated processes will now be discussed in detail and Fig. 1.1 illustrates them diagrammatically.

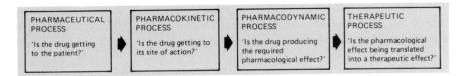

PHARMACEUTICAL PROCESS	PHARMACOKINETIC PROCESS	PHARMACODYNAMIC PROCESS	THERAPEUTIC PROCESS
'Is the drug getting to the patient?'	'Is the drug getting to its site of action?'	'Is the drug producing the required pharmacological effect?'	'Is the pharmacological effect being translated into a therapeutic effect?'

Fig. 1.1. Processes involved in drug therapy. (Grahame-Smith and Aronson 1984.)

THE PHARMACEUTICAL PROCESS: IS THE DRUG GETTING INTO THE PATIENT?

The fundamental importance of the pharmaceutical formulation and presentation of a drug is often insufficiently appreciated. Thus, an oral preparation of the most powerful drug would be useless if, through a faulty formulation, it failed to disintegrate on contact with the gastro-intestinal contents and therefore was not absorbed. Likewise, the injection of a preparation of local anaesthetic would be not only fruitless but positively dangerous if it had been formulated in an insoluble form. Scant attention and thought is given to the enormous amount of time and effort taken to produce a formulation and presentation that meets, as far as possible, the needs of the patient and of the clinician. Although the pharmaceutical process is mainly the concern of the pharmaceutical chemist and the pharmacist, the dental practitioner should take an intelligent interest in the subject for the good of the patient. Occasionally, therapeutic problems arise with respect to a particular drug or patient and these may be due to a formulation problem concerned with the particle size, excipients, and coating materials used in the preparation of a drug. The outbreaks of toxicity from digoxin and phenytoin in the late 1960s and early 1970s are striking and important examples of this type of problem (for further details see Tyrer *et al.* 1970; Smith and Dodd 1982).

Drug compliance

It should be remembered that the simplest cause of an apparent therapeutic failure is because the patient has failed to take an adequate quantity of the drug! This may be unintentional, for example, where they have misunderstood the directions; or it may be due to a wilful determination on their part not to take the drug. It should also be noted that for a given patient the greater the number of drugs prescribed the less likely are these to be taken correctly.

THE PHARMACOKINETIC PROCESS: IS THE DRUG GETTING TO ITS SITE OF ACTION?

Pharmacokinetics is concerned with the absorption, distribution, and elimination (by means of metabolism and excretion) of drugs. The term 'pharmacokinetics' was introduced by Dost (1953) and is concerned with the mathematical analysis of the time course of drug absorption, distribution, metabolism, and excretion. After oral administration of a drug, a given fraction is absorbed and the amount of drug in the body at any moment depends upon the balance between the rate of absorption and the rate of elimination.

Factors governing the fate of a drug in the body

Whether a drug is applied locally or is administered systemically, there are four main factors that determine its subsequent fate in the body:

(1) molecular weight;

(2) chemical stability;

(3) lipid solubility;

(4) degree of ionization.

Each drug has its own characteristic profile of these factors, which may be conveniently termed its physico-chemical profile. This topic will now be discussed in more detail.

Molecular weight (MW)

Substances with a high molecular weight are not usually absorbed intact except in minute quantities. Moreover, they may be altered by enzymatic action so that following oral administration, proteins, for example, will be broken down to their constituent amino acids. Thus insulin, which is a protein, undergoes enzymatic breakdown in the gastro-intestinal tract and is, for practical purposes, not absorbed.

Chemical stability

Unstable drugs may be inactivated in the gastro-intestinal tract. Benzylpenicillin is unstable in an acid medium and therefore cannot be relied upon to produce satisfactory results if given by mouth because a high proportion of the original dose is rendered inactive by the acid contents of the stomach. Phenoxymethyl-penicillin is more stable in an acid medium than benzylpenicillin so that adequate doses given by mouth are therapeutically effective.

Lipid solubility

If a drug is to be absorbed from any part of the gastro-intestinal tract, including the mouth, it is necessary for it to pass through cell membranes. Thus, it must first pass through the cells of the mucous membrane of the gastro-intestinal tract and thence into the circulation either directly via the capillary walls or indirectly via the lymphatic drainage of the area. As cell membranes are lipid in nature, the degree and rate of penetration of them by a drug is dependent to a large extent on its lipid solubility (for a more detailed discussion on this topic see below and Chapter 7).

Degree of ionization

Under physiological conditions some substances, such as ethanol (ethyl alcohol), are un-ionized whilst others, for example acetylcholine, are highly ionized. The important fact is that the majority of drugs are weak bases or weak acids so that at a physiological pH (7.4) they exist partly in the un-ionized form and partly in the ionized form, the proportion of each form varying with the environmental pH. At a particular pH, the proportion of un-ionized to ionized molecules of a drug depends upon its dissociation constant $(K_a; -\log K_a = pK_a)$. The pH, pK_a, and ratio of un-ionized to ionized molecules are related by the Henderson–Hasselbach equation as follows:

$$\text{For acids, pH} = pK_a - \log_{10} \frac{\text{un-ionized acid}}{\text{ionized acid}}$$

$$= pK_a - \log_{10} \frac{[AH]}{[A^-]}.$$

$$\text{For bases, pH} = pK_a - \log_{10} \frac{\text{ionized base}}{\text{un-ionized base}}$$

$$= pK_a - \log_{10} \frac{[BH^+]}{[B]}.$$

Where pK_a is the dissociation constant expressed as its negative logarithm to base 10; pH, the concentration of hydrogen ions in the solution expressed as the negative logarithm to base 10; [AH], concentration of un-ionized acid; [A$^-$], concentration of ionized acid; [BH$^+$] concentration of ionized base; [B] concentration of un-ionized base.

The fundamental and important relationship between the degree of drug ionization and drug absorption is that the un-ionized portion of a drug is lipid soluble and so readily absorbed (see later under Cell membranes) whereas the ionized portion is lipid insoluble and so very poorly absorbed.

The physico-chemical profile of a drug (i.e. the molecular weight (MW), chemical stability, lipid solubility, and degree of ionization) principally governs its fate in the body. We must now consider the processes involved in the absorption of drugs. This can be put in the form of a question: how do drugs cross the cell membrane? In order to answer this question the structure of cell membrane itself must first be examined.

The cell membrane

Various studies have shown that the plasma membrane of mammalian cells consists of three principal organic components, which are arranged as shown in Fig. 1.2. The major part of the plasma membrane consists of a double-layer of lipid

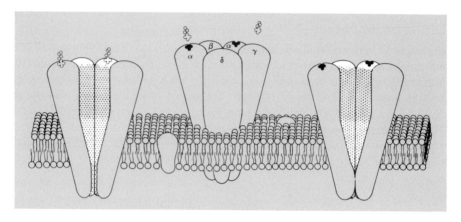

Fig. 1.2. Model of cell membrane with acetylcholine receptor (nicotinic type). Note the following: (i) The cell membrane consists of a double layer of lipid molecules orientated with hydrophilic groups situated at inner and outer surfaces, and hydrophobic portions occupying the inner and central part. (ii) Integral protein occupies the full width of the membrane. (iii) Middle of figure shows reconstruction of acetylcholine receptor and associated ion channel consisting of five protein subunits: alpha (α) (two), beta (β), gamma (γ), and delta (δ), which surround a central pore. Acetylcholine binds to the α subunits and two molecules of acetylcholine must bind in order to open the channel. *Right channel:* closed because two molecules of acetylcholine have not yet occupied the receptors. *Left channel:* open in response to occupation of both receptors by molecules of acetylcholine.

molecules orientated so that their hydrophilic groups are situated at the inner and outer surfaces of the membrane, whilst their hydrophobic portions, which consist of hydrocarbon chains, occupy the inner and central part.

Proteins also form an important component of the plasma membrane and are present in two forms:

(1) integral protein, which occupies the full width of the cell membrane;

(2) peripheral protein, which is attached either to the integral protein on the inner aspect of the membrane or attached to the hydrophilic ends of the lipids at the external or internal surfaces.

In addition, several varieties of glycoproteins or glycolipids may be attached to the integral protein or hydrophilic lipid, respectively, on the external surface of the plasma membrane.

It is important to note that the cell plasma membrane is not a fixed structure but a dynamic one in which the various components are mobile. The membrane contains membrane-bound water that interacts with ionized groups and thus forms a barrier to the diffusion of water-soluble agents. The membrane is asymmetrical both structurally and electrically; it also contains pores formed both within the membrane of an individual cell and between the membranes of adjacent cells. As a consequence, substances (including drugs) with a molecular weight not exceeding 100 daltons are able to diffuse freely across the membrane (see next section). The external surface of the membrane also contains pharmacological receptors (described later). These are linked with intracellular mechanisms that can thus be switched on or off by the interaction of appropriate drug molecules with the membrane receptors. For general references on the structure of the cell membrane see Houslay and Stanley (1982).

The principal mechanisms involved in the passage of drugs across cell membranes

A drug is unlikely to be absorbed unless it is able to go into solution. For example, barium ions are very poisonous but barium sulphate can be used safely in radiology as a contrast agent because it is highly *insoluble*.

Pharmaceutical formulations of a drug can greatly influence the amount and rate at which it is absorbed. The rate at which acetylsalicylic acid (aspirin) is absorbed and the maximum plasma concentration attained varies widely according to the formulation used. In one study (Leonards 1963), effervescent aspirin (0.6 g) caused more than double the plasma level produced by an equivalent dose of ordinary aspirin (both measured after 30 minutes). However, when the same dose of ordinary aspirin was given in hot water it resulted in a plasma concentration almost as high as that attained with the effervescent preparation. Sometimes tablets or capsules may fail to disintegrate so that absorption cannot take place. Under these circumstances, the absence of a therapeutic effect may be wrongly attributed to other factors such as too small a dose or failure of the patient to take the medicine.

Lipid diffusion

Figure 1.3 illustrates diagrammatically the principal mechanisms involved in absorption of drugs, for example from the gastro-intestinal tract (Brodie 1964; Smyth 1964; Gillette 1967). The majority of drugs cross membranes by lipid diffusion (simple diffusion) at a rate related to their lipid solubility or, to be more exact, to their lipid/water partition coefficient. The rate can be expressed by Fick's law, which states that:

$$m = \frac{PA(C_o - C_i)t}{W}.$$

Where m = amount of unchanged molecule diffusing passively through an area; A = area of cell membrane over which diffusion is under consideration; t = time over which diffusion takes place; C_o = concentration of solute on outer side of membrane; C_i = concentration of solute on inner side of membrane; P = permeability constant; W = thickness of cell membrane.

A lipid-soluble non-electrolyte is readily absorbed whilst a lipid-insoluble non-electrolyte will only be absorbed exceedingly slowly. As noted earlier, the

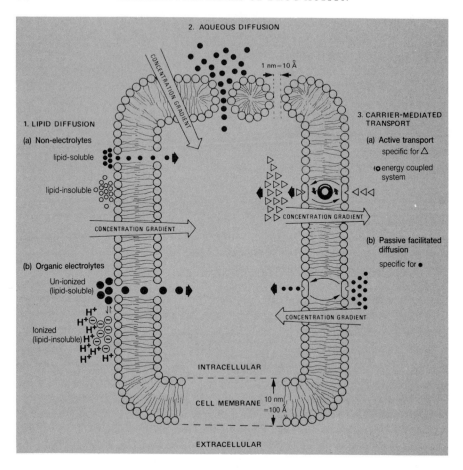

Fig. 1.3. Illustration of the principal mechanisms of (1) lipid diffusion, (2) aqueous diffusion, and (3) carrier-mediated transport ((a) active transport and (b) passive facilitated diffusion) by which drugs and other substances cross cell membranes. Note that the direction of molecular movement is down the concentration gradient with the exception of active transport, where it is distinguished by molecular movement *against* the concentration gradient. See text for further details.

majority of drugs are weak organic electrolytes that exist partly un-ionized and party ionized, the proportion of each depending on the dissociation constant (pK_a) of the particular drug and the pH of its environment. The un-ionized form is lipid-soluble, whereas the ionized form is not (see Fig. 1.3), so any factors which tend to increase the un-ionized fraction will also increase the rate of absorption; the converse is also true.

Diffusion can take place either:

(1) directly via the lipoprotein membrane or;

(2) through the paracellular spaces (as indicated earlier).

Lipid diffusion is the most common mechanism by which drugs cross cell membranes to enter the body, and also the mechanism by which they are subsequently distributed around it and ultimately excreted.

Aqueous diffusion (filtration through pores)

Water-soluble (lipid-insoluble) drugs of sufficiently small molecular size (MW less than 100 daltons) are able to cross cell membranes by passing through the polar pores or spaces between membranes of adjacent cells (see Fig. 1.3). Ethanol (MW = 46) and urea (MW = 60) are believed to pass through membranes by this means. The size of the drug molecule relative to the size of the pore is of considerable importance in determining the ease or difficulty with which the drug can pass through pores (see Fig. 1.3). Moreover, pore size differs in the cell membranes of different tissues (Lindemann and Solomon 1962). Pores found in the capillaries and the renal glomeruli are probably the largest (50–100 nm diameter) and offer greater ease of passage than those available in other tissues.

Active transport (specific carrier-mediated transport systems)

A number of substances essential to the body but too lipid-insoluble to dissolve in the cell membrane (lipid diffusion) and too large to flow through pores (aqueous diffusion) are nevertheless readily transported across cell membranes. Important examples are sodium, potassium, calcium, and chloride ions; others are iron, amino acids, and glucose; for each of these substances, there are highly specific carrier-mediated transport systems (see Fig. 1.3). Three features distinguish these active transport systems from the other mechanisms involved in passage of drugs across cell membranes. These are:

(1) Ability to work against concentration, osmotic, electrical, or hydrostatic gradients.

(2) Specificity, such that these systems have the ability to concentrate a selected substance on one side of the cell membrane.

(3) Each system requires an energy source, usually adenosine triphosphate (ATP), to which it is directly coupled.

The actual transport is carried out by large proteins that lie within the substance of the membrane and act as a two-state gated pore passing the specific substrate in one direction only. This is a saturable system but only at high substrate concentrations. Although active transport systems possess high specificity they will often transport substances that are closely related chemically to their natural substrates. For example, the system for aromatic amino acids in the gut wall will also transport the chemically related drugs, L-dopa and α-methyl dopa.

The kidney also has at least three special transport mechanisms. The proximal renal tubule contains a mechanism for the transport of acids and another for the

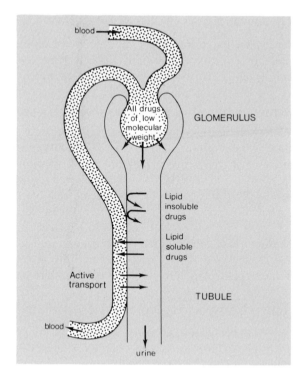

Fig. 1.4. The excretion of drugs by the kidneys. (After Brodie 1964.) (See text for details.)

transport of bases. The third is located in the distal tubule, which actively transports the cardiac drug, digoxin. Benzylpenicillin is actively transported into the renal tubules through the acidic transport system (see Fig. 1.4) and, as it also passes into the glomerular filtrate, this dual channel of excretion accounts for the rapid removal of this drug from the body. The half-life of benzylpenicillin is less than an hour (the half-life is the time taken for the original amount of drug in the body to be reduced by half; see later sections of this chapter).

Facilitated diffusion

This is a passive process whereby drugs can move across membranes more rapidly than by simple diffusion; it involves the action of a specific but saturable carrier system. However, it differs from active transport in that it *can only work in the presence of an appropriate concentration gradient* and so, for example, can only move drugs into a cell provided that their extracellular concentration is higher than their intracellular concentration.

Distribution of drugs

The principal factors concerned in the distribution of drugs in the body are indicated in Fig. 1.5 (after Brodie 1964; Gillette 1967). If a drug is taken by

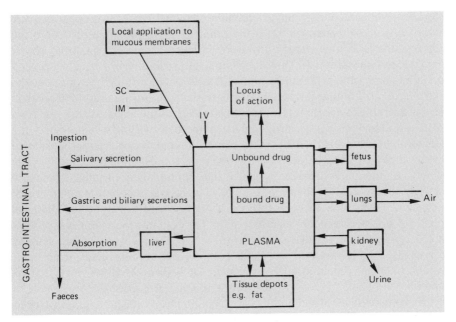

Fig. 1.5. Factors concerned in the distribution of a drug in the body. (Adapted from Brodie 1964, and Gillette 1967.) An arrow represents the direction of movement of the drug in question. Double arrows indicate that a drug and/or its metabolites move in both directions between the points indicated. (SC = subcutaneous; IM = intramuscular; IV = intravenous.)

mouth it will become mixed with the various secretions associated with the gastro-intestinal tract and a varying proportion of the total dose will be absorbed (depending on factors already discussed). The faeces may contain only unabsorbed drug or may also include a certain amount of drug that was originally absorbed and subsequently excreted into the gut either unchanged or partly metabolized. After absorption, the drug passes first into the portal circulation and thence via the liver enters the general circulation. It is important to note that some drugs are extensively metabolized during their first passage through the liver (so-called 'first pass metabolism') such that only a small proportion of the original drug is available to enter the general circulation and thereby produce an effect. Such a drug is referred to as undergoing 'high first pass metabolism', and an example is the β-adrenoceptor antagonist, propranolol (see Chapter 13).

Drugs may be administered parenterally by subcutaneous (SC), intramuscular (IM) or intravenous (IV) injections (Fig. 1.5), or may be applied to mucous membranes, such as in the mouth, where drugs with an appropriate physico-chemical profile may be absorbed with great rapidity.

Once a drug has entered the blood, it is carried to all the vascular tissues in the body. It may be retained within the blood (e.g. heparin) or may pass through the capillary wall and enter the extracellular fluid where it is then principally confined (e.g. D-tubocurarine). On the other hand, it may then pass from the extracellular fluid and enter the intracellular fluid of some or the majority of cells (e.g. thiopentone, ethanol). Thus, the volume of distribution of a drug will depend upon its compartmental distribution; if it is widely distributed throughout the extra- and intracellular fluid compartments, the concentration in the blood will be considerably lower than if it is confined solely to the blood.

In the kidney (Fig. 1.4), drugs of low molecular weight will pass into the glomerular filtrate and thence into the urine, although a significant proportion of lipid-soluble drugs will be reabsorbed by the renal tubules and thus leave the body slowly. As mentioned earlier, certain drugs, such as benzylpenicillin, may be actively transported by the renal tubules, which largely accounts for the rapid excretion of this antibiotic from the body. Thus, once again, the physico-chemical profile of a drug determines its distribution. Drugs of low molecular weight that are lipid-soluble and exist largely in the un-ionized form will be distributed freely across cell membranes and will enter both the extracellular and intracellular compartments. In addition, such drugs will readily cross the blood–brain barrier, and they are liable to cross the placenta and reach the fetus.

There are two special additional factors, binding to plasma proteins and to cells, which must be taken into account when considering the distribution of drugs in the body.

Binding to plasma proteins

Most drugs to varying extents become reversibly bound to various constituents of the tissues and especially to plasma proteins. Thus, acidic drugs (e.g. salicylic acid, warfarin) bind to albumin whereas some basic drugs (e.g. propranolol, diazepam) bind to α_1-acid glycoproteins and also to lipoproteins. As a result, a state of equilibrium becomes established between the bound and unbound portions according to the law of mass action. Figure 1.6 illustrates this effect in relation to the distribution of a drug between plasma and cerebrospinal fluid.

The plasma binding of drugs has several important consequences. First, it is only the unbound portion that is pharmacologically active, and free to leave the

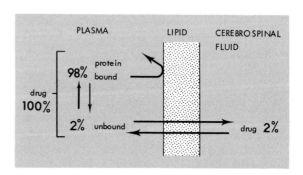

Fig. 1.6. The effect of protein binding of a drug on its distribution between plasma and cerebrospinal fluid. Only the unbound portion equilibrates across the membrane. (Brodie 1964.)

circulation and reach those cells on which it is to act. Second, although the plasma protein–drug complex is pharmacologically inactive, it is a means whereby the total plasma concentration can often exceed the aqueous solubility of the drug and thereby assist in distribution to the tissues. Third, the plasma protein–drug complex forms a reservoir that dissociates to release more free drug as soon as the existing level of free drug falls because of redistribution or elimination, e.g. at the site of action. It thus smooths out any fluctuations in concentration that would otherwise occur. Fourth, acidic drugs compete for binding sites on the plasma albumin such that drugs with a high affinity displace those with a lower affinity. However, when this happens it causes only a transient increase in the concentration of free drug because the effect is followed by an increase in its elimination so that its concentration returns to its previous value. Thus, although it was originally thought that this mechanism might be responsible for the potentiation of, for example, the anticoagulant effect of warfarin by aspirin, it is now clear that this is not so and that aspirin potentiates warfarin by other mechanisms including inhibition of its metabolism (Park and Breckenridge 1981; Routledge 1986; see also Chapters 5 and 22).

Binding in cells

Some drugs become bound onto the surface or inside of cells with the result that a high concentration is slowly built up. For example, the amount of the anti-malarial drug, chloroquine, that becomes bound in the liver, spleen, lung, kidney, and retina may be several hundred times greater than that present in the plasma. If a drug binds reversibly with some intracellular protein, this drug–protein complex will act as a depot from which the drug will be slowly released into the circulation, thus giving rise to a prolonged effect.

Inactivation of drugs: drug metabolism

The statement of Brodie that 'the action of a drug would probably last a lifetime if the body did not have ways of limiting its duration' (Brodie 1956) is certainly not sufficiently appreciated. Moreover, it is rather surprising that when the body is presented, as it increasingly is, with new drugs having chemical structures entirely foreign to any of its constituents, it is apparently able to deal with these compounds in a relatively restricted number of ways. Here again, the physico-chemical profile of any compound plays a major role in determining the eventual outcome. Thus one, or more of two main events may occur namely, excretion in its original form and transformation into one or into several metabolites.

Excretion in the original form

There are very few drugs which are not at least partially metabolized in the body or, in other words, are excreted entirely unchanged. Hexamethonium, a highly ionized ganglion blocker and the first antihypertensive compound, although no longer in clinical use, illustrates certain principles well. As a consequence of being highly ionized it is poorly and erratically absorbed, it is not metabolized to any significant extent, and it is therefore excreted in the urine unchanged. Its variable absorption resulted, not surprisingly, in an unpredictable lowering of the blood pressure in hypertensive patients. It was therefore abandoned as soon as a reliable oral drug had been developed. Most drugs undergo extensive metabolism although a small proportion of the original dose may be excreted unchanged. For example, approximately 15 per cent of a therapeutic dose of acetylsalicylic acid (aspirin) is excreted unchanged whilst the remainder is metabolized in a variety of ways (see Chapter 5).

Transformation to one or more metabolites

Many drugs are metabolized and their metabolites excreted in the urine or bile, or both. The main organ of drug metabolism is the liver, but many other tissues have a limited ability to metabolize drugs and other foreign substances, for example, the gastro-intestinal tract, lung, kidney, skin, and placenta. Biotransformation of drugs has two effects:

1. It alters the pharmacological activity, usually decreasing it but sometimes converting the drug to a compound with similar or greater activity (potency) than the original. Occasionally it converts an inactive compound (a pro-drug) to an active one. A good example is the anticancer drug, cyclophosphamide, which is inactive until it is converted into 4-hydroxycyclophosphamide, and which in turn is converted via two further steps into phosphoramide mustard. Sometimes the metabolism of an active drug will result in a compound with a longer plasma half-life ($T_{0.5}$) than the parent compound. For example, diazepam ($T_{0.5}$ about 30 hours) is converted to desmethyldiazepam ($T_{0.5}$ of 100 hours).

2. It usually results in metabolites that are more water-soluble and less lipid-soluble than the parent compounds and therefore more readily excreted in the urine.

There are two phases of drug metabolism, phase I and phase II.

Phase I metabolism
The drug molecules undergo chemical changes which lead to the exposure or addition of chemically reactive groups. These changes include:

(1) oxidation (requiring NADPH, oxygen, and cytochrome P_{450}), e.g. diazepam, warfarin;

(2) reduction, e.g. nitrazepam, cortisone;

(3) hydrolysis, e.g. suxamethonium, amethocaine.

Phase II reactions
These either replace phase I reactions or form a consecutive step after them. The molecules formed as a result of Phase II conjugation are almost always less

pharmacologically active and less lipid-soluble, i.e. more water-soluble, than the molecule before conjugation. Thus the conjugates are more readily excreted especially in the urine.

Phase II reactions involve conjugation to form one or more of the following:

(1) glucuronide, e.g. morphine, paracetamol;

(2) sulphate, e.g. isoprenaline;

(3) acetate, e.g. isoniazid, hydralazine;

(4) glutathione, e.g. paracetamol.

Sites of drug metabolism

The major site of drug metabolism is in the liver although some occurs at other sites such as the kidney (vitamin D), wall of intestine (tyramine), plasma (suxamethonium), lung (5-hydroxytryptamine = serotonin), skin (vitamin D), and placenta (a large range of drugs).

Types of enzymatic reaction

The metabolic changes described above may be due to enzymes located in the endoplasmic reticulum ('microsomes') or at non-microsomal sites.

Factors affecting drug metabolism

It is important to note that the following factors affect drug metabolism and therefore should always be taken into account when prescribing a drug.

Age

The ability to metabolize drugs is reduced at the extremes of age. Thus, children under the age of 6 months and especially premature babies show impaired drug metabolism due to a reduced capacity of hepatic enzyme activity. An example of an unwanted effect of this impairment is the well-documented 'grey syndrome' in which chloramphenicol causes peripheral circulatory collapse when given to young babies. In a similar way, an elderly patient may show intolerance to a normal therapeutic dose of a drug, for example, a tricyclic antidepressant, due to impaired metabolism. Evidence available (Rawlins *et al.* 1987) suggests that this altered response in the elderly is due to a reduced amount of normal enzyme coupled with a reduction in liver blood flow. This problem is easily overcome by ensuring that when a drug is prescribed to an elderly patient the dose chosen is smaller than usual. In practice it is easiest to start off with a dose that is half (or less) than the normal therapeutic one and then to increase it slowly until the desired therapeutic effect is achieved.

Sex

In rodents, drug metabolism appears to be faster in the male than in the female. In humans such an overall difference between the sexes does not seem to occur although several clinical reports suggest that benzodiazepines, salicylates, and oestrogens are metabolized faster in the male than in the female (Katzung 1984). However, in general these differences are not clinically significant and, other things being equal, drugs are prescribed in the same dosage to males and females.

Liver disease

The capacity of the liver to metabolize drugs is very great and as a consequence liver disease needs to be extensive before it is likely to produce a significant effect on the action of normal therapeutic doses of drugs. Thus, for example, chronic alcoholism can greatly reduce hepatic metabolism with obvious consequences. The decreased liver blood flow in heart failure may result in a significant reduction of drug metabolism.

Environmental factors

The presence of other drugs, differences in nutrition, the use of alcohol (see under Liver Disease above), smoking, and exposure to pesticides can all influence drug metabolism. Benzpyrene from heavy cigarette smoking and occupational exposure to chlorinated hydrocarbon insecticides can induce certain drug-metabolizing pathways and thereby modify the response to drugs (Alvares 1978; Jusko 1978). In heavy cigarette smokers the metabolism of theophylline is increased and such patients may therefore need above average doses as compared with non-smokers (Ogilvie 1978). Heavy smokers may also require higher doses of analgesics such dextropropoxyphene. For further details the interested reader should consult Sjöqvist et al. (1980), and Rawlins and Thompson (1985).

Genetic factors (pharmacogenetics)

Pharmacogenetics is concerned with the modification of the responses to drugs by hereditary influences (Kalow 1962). The importance of pharmacogenetics to therapeutics is best illustrated by reference to the antituberculous drug, isoniazid. The major route of metabolism of this drug is under the action of acetylation by the enzyme N-acetyltransferase in the liver. The ability to acetylate isoniazid is inherited as an autosomal recessive trait. When the rate of metabolism of isoniazid is studied in groups of patients it is found that the rate of acetylation may be fast or slow. In Europe and North America approximately half of the population acetylate isoniazid slowly, whereas in other populations the proportion of slow acetylators may be as small as 20 per cent or as high as 90 per cent. This variation is due to a gene which controls the synthesis of hepatic N-acetyltransferase. The abnormal gene controls the synthesis of an *atypical* form of N-acetyltransferase, which acetylates isoniazid more slowly than the typical (normal) enzyme. There are three possible genotypes, namely (i) those with two normal genes (rapid–rapid); (ii) those with one abnormal and one normal gene (slow–rapid or rapid–slow); and (iii) those in whom both genes are of the slow type (slow–slow). As the inheritance is autosomal recessive it was assumed that these three genotypes would give rise to two phenotypes namely rapid acetylators ((i) and (ii)) and slow acetylators (iii). However, more recent and refined work (Lee and Lee 1982) has demonstrated that it is possible to separate the heterozygous rapid phenotype (ii) from the homozygous rapid phenotype (i). Thus, three groups—rapid, intermediate, and slow acetylators—can be identified. The important therapeutic point is that when isoniazid is given in normal doses to a slow acetylator, it is likely to accumulate to toxic levels and thereby produce adverse effects, particularly peripheral neuropathy. The same problem will arise when other drugs that are primarily inactivated by acetylation are given to such patients and these include phenelzine (a monoamine oxidase inhibitor (MAOI)), nitrazepam (a benzodiazepine hypnotic), and sulphasalazine (a complex of a sulphonamide with a salicylic-acid derivative), which is used for the treatment of ulcerative colitis.

The administration of the short-acting neuromuscular blocking drug, suxamethonium, is occasionally followed by prolonged apnoea (see Chapter 8). This effect is likely to be due to an atypical form of the enzyme non-specific cholinesterase (pseudocholinesterase). Here again the abnormality is due to a single gene but with the difference that the type of inheritance involved here is known as autosomal autonomous so that in heterozygotes the trait is partially expressed. Thus, in the population there is a trimodal distribution with one group showing normal enzyme activity, another group with abnormally slow activity of the enzyme, and a third intermediate group. Individuals can be identified by means of the 'dibucaine' test.

Another genetic disorder is the rare condition of malignant hyperthermia (hyperpyrexia), which is due to an abnormality of calcium binding in muscle. As a consequence of this abnormality the general anaesthetic, halothane, and the depolarizing neuromuscular blocking drug, suxamethonium, may, due to depolarization, trigger the intracellular release of calcium which then gives rise to a long, muscle contracture (not contraction) associated with the production of increased heat and lactic acid. Malignant hyperthermia is inherited as an autosomal dominant, as is hereditary porphyria, which is due to an abnormality in haem metabolism. Compounds likely to trigger an attack of acute porphyria (abdominal pain, neuritis, mental changes, and the urinary excretion of porphyrins) are griseofulvin, phenytoin, barbiturates, sulphonamides, and also oral hypoglycaemic drugs.

Excretion of drugs

Drugs are mainly excreted by the kidney, so appearing in the urine. To a lesser extent they are excreted via the bile, skin (sweat), lungs (expired air), saliva, and milk. With the inhalation anaesthetics the expired air is the main route of excretion.

The excretion of a drug by the kidney is best expressed in terms of the renal plasma clearance. This is the volume of plasma effectively cleared of the drug by the kidney in unit time. Thus it is that portion of the apparent volume of distribution (AVD) to be cleared of the drug in unit time (with units of flow i.e. ml/min or litres/h). Therefore, drug clearance (Cl) may be expressed as follows:

$$\text{Clearance (Cl)} = \text{AVD} \times K = \frac{\text{AVD} \times 0.693}{T_{0.5}}.$$

where AVD = apparent volume of distribution; K = elimination rate constant; $0.693 = \log_e 2$; $T_{0.5}$ = half life of drug.

The excretion of a drug by the kidney involves several processes, each of which is now considered.

Glomerular filtration

Under normal conditions the glomerular filtration rate (GFR) is about 125 ml/min. Thus, the rate of drug filtration will depend upon the plasma concentration of drug and also upon its molecular weight (MW). The glomerular capillary membrane contains a pore size approaching the molecular dimensions of albumin (MW approx. 68 000 daltons). Therefore all but a very few drugs can be filtered easily at the glomerulus provided that the drug is free, i.e. not bound to plasma protein. When it is partially bound to plasma protein then it is only the unbound fraction that is available for filtration. It should be noted that the rate of filtration is not dependent on either the lipid solubility or on the degree of ionization of the drug.

Drug excretion in the presence of renal impairment

When glomerular filtration is impaired this will have potentially serious implications for the excretion of any drug that is eliminated predominantly by the renal route. The clearance of creatinine (Cl_{cr}) is commonly used to measure GFR. Creatinine is a breakdown product derived from the amino acids of muscle and is eliminated by glomerular filtration at a rate equivalent to GFR. Thus, in a healthy adult, the Cl_{cr} is approximately 125 ml/min. In a patient suffering from renal impairment this figure will be reduced, and the prescriber will need to make appropriate allowance for this fact when calculating the dosage of a drug that depends mainly upon renal excretion. The simplest way to calculate the appropriate amended dosage is by means of nomograms, which are available in appropriate texts on clinical pharmacology.

Tubular reabsorption

The function of the renal tubules is to reabsorb appropriate amounts of selected ions, particularly sodium and chloride, along with water. Any molecules of drug that are present in the filtrate will be reabsorbed in accordance with their physico-chemical profile in just the same way as this profile determined their absorption. Thus, highly ionized drugs entering the glomerular filtrate will be excreted in the urine without significant reabsorption by the renal tubules. On the other hand, a drug that arrives in the filtrate in an un-ionized and therefore lipid-soluble form will be partially reabsorbed by the renal tubules and so re-enter the circulation. Non-polar lipid-soluble drugs (for example, thiopentone, inhalational anaesthetics, and phenytoin) will be almost completely reabsorbed from the tubular urine. Acidic drugs that have a pK_a ranging from 2 to 8 (for example, salicylic acid) will be excreted in a pH-dependent fashion. Thus, the ionized (lipid-insoluble) moiety will not be reabsorbed by the tubules whereas the un-ionized (lipid-soluble) moiety will readily pass through the tubular cell membrane and thus be reabsorbed. When it is desired to expedite excretion of acidic drugs this can be achieved by alkalinizing the urine to a pH of approximately 8, which is why the urine is alkalinized as part of the treatment of aspirin poisoning (see Chapter 5). Basic drugs with a pK_a ranging from 6–12 also exhibit pH-dependent excretion but, of course, in the opposite direction. Thus, the excretion of amphetamine can be expedited by acidyifying the urine through administration of ascorbic acid to the lowest attainable pH, which is usually about 5.

Tubular secretion

As we have outlined above, the renal tubules contain three secretory systems, two in the proximal tubule of low specificity and the third in the distal tubule, which appears to be concerned with the secretion of digoxin. Of the two systems in the proximal tubule, one is for anions—for example, benzylpenicillin ($pK_a = 2.8$), acetylsalicylic acid (aspirin $pK_a = 3.5$), hydrochlorothiazide ($pK_a = 7.9$)—and also conjugates of drugs with glucuronic acid, glycine, and sulphuric acid. Probenecid is a competitive antagonist to this transport system and can thereby slow the excretion of a drug such as benzylpenicillin. The other low-specificity system is for cations and is concerned with the secretion of bases such as morphine ($pK_a = 8$), atropine ($pK_a = 9.7$), and neostigmine ($pK_a = 12$).

Drugs that undergo tubular secretion have a renal clearance which usually is in excess of the GFR because this process occurs *in addition* to elimination via glomerular filtration. The sum of the two clearances may be as large as the renal plasma flow.

Pharmacokinetics of drug elimination

For a given unit of time, drug elimination occurs at either a constant rate or at a constant fraction. We must now consider these in a little more detail.

Constant rate elimination (zero-order kinetics)

Under these conditions a drug is eliminated at a constant rate irrespective of any changes in the rate of absorption and is therefore independent of the amount of drug in the body at any one time (Fig. 1.7(a)).

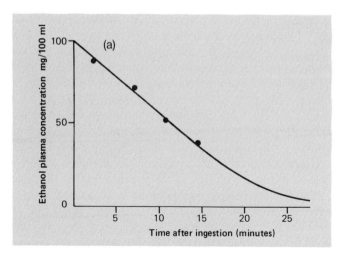

Fig. 1.7(a). Graph of zero-order kinetics as illustrated by the elimination of ethyl alcohol (ethanol). Note the linear relationship between time (abscissa) and concentration in plasma (ordinate) indicating a constant rate of elimination independent of plasma concentration (cf. first-order kinetics).

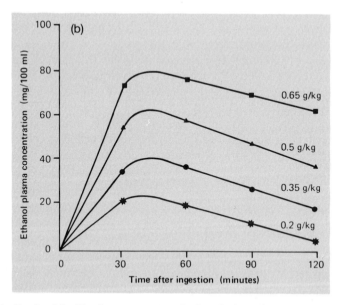

Fig. 1.7(b). Graph of the blood concentration of ethanol after taking four different doses of ethanol; each point is the mean of 40 subjects. Note that the curves are virtually parallel indicating that the rate of fall of blood concentration is the same and independent of the dose. The lowest dose is equivalent to about $\frac{3}{4}$ pint of beer or 1.5 whiskies and the largest dose to 3 pints of beer or 6 whiskies. (Reproduced from Drew *et al.* 1958 with permission.)

Mathematically, constant rate elimination (zero-order kinetics), for example mg/h, may be represented by the mathematical expression:

$$\text{Rate of movement} = K.$$

Thus the amount of drug in the body will decline at a constant rate, i.e. linear rate. If the rate of absorption exceeds the rate of elimination then the plasma concentration will increase, i.e. it will never reach a plateau. Drugs metabolized by readily saturable enzyme systems are likely to be treated in this way by the body. Thus, ethanol (ethyl alcohol) is metabolized by the enzyme, alcohol dehydrogenase, to acetaldehyde and subsequently to acetic acid. Figure 1.7(b) shows a family of blood concentrations of alcohol after taking four different doses of alcohol (Drew *et al.* 1958). The lowest dose (0.2 g/kg) is equivalent to about three-quarters of a pint of beer or 1.5 whiskies whilst the largest does (0.65 g/kg) is equivalent to 3 pints of beer or 6 whiskies. It should be noted that a graph plotted with linear coordinates (Fig. 1.7(b)) shows a series of virtually parallel curves thus indicating that the rate of elimination is constant and independent of the magnitude of the blood alcohol concentration. Although the rate of oxidation of ethyl alcohol varies in different individuals, the average value in a man of 70 kg body weight is 10 g or 12.5 ml per hour. The zero-order kinetics of ethanol explains why this drug readily accumulates if the rate of intake exceeds the rate of elimination.

The metabolism of certain other drugs may be initially first-order kinetics (see next section) but at therapeutic concentrations their metabolism is principally zero-order kinetics; examples of these are acetylsalicylic acid (aspirin) and the anticonvulsant drug, phenytoin. As a consequence of the saturation of first-order kinetics of such a drug, there is a switch to zero-order kinetics with the *clinically important result* that for a relatively small increase in the dose of the drug there may be a large increase in plasma concentration.

Constant fraction elimination (first-order kinetics)

Under these conditions the rate of elimination of the drug is proportional to the quantity of drug to be transferred. This process of elimination applies to the majority of drugs and it means that for any regular dosage a plateau is reached when the rate of clearance of the drug equals the rate of its entry; this is known as the steady state. Mathematically, the process can be expressed as:

$$\text{Rate} = K \times D.$$

where K = elimination rate constant with units of reciprocal time i.e. hours^{-1} or days^{-1} (for example, 0.1 h^{-1} = a tenth or 10 per cent of the drug eliminated per h); D = amount of drug to be transferred.

Figure 1.8(a) shows a graph of first-order kinetics plotted on linear coordinates, from which it can be seen that the slope of the curve is initially steep but becomes less so as elimination proceeds. If these data are now plotted semi-logarithmically, i.e. time against the *logarithm* of the dose, the result is a straight line (Fig. 1.8(b)).

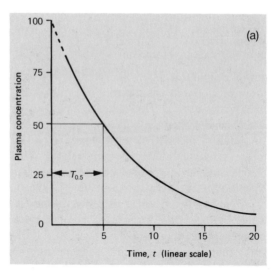

Fig. 1.8(a). Graph of first-order kinetics illustrating the elimination pattern typical for most drugs. Note (i) the exponential curve indicating that a constant fraction of drug is eliminated in unit time and (ii) the half-life which represents the time taken for the amount in the plasma to fall by half ($T_{0.5}$).

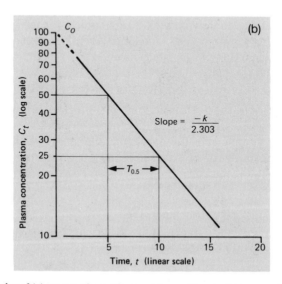

Fig. 1.8(b). Re-plot of (a) on semi-logarithmic scale resulting in linear graph thus confirming log-linear (exponential) relationship between coordinates. The half-life ($T_{0.5}$) can be measured between any two points that correspond to a change of plasma concentration of one-half.

If this is extrapolated backwards to time zero then the theoretical concentration of drug at zero time can be read from the graph.

Half-life

The half-life is the time required for the concentration of drug to decline to half of its original value. In Figs. 1.8(a) and (b) we are concerned with plasma concentration of a drug so, in this context, the half-life ($T_{0.5}$) is the time taken for the concentration in the plasma to decline to half of its original value. The measurement of $T_{0.5}$ from the graph can be made over any part of it (most conveniently from the semi-log plot).

The half-life may also be calculated from K (elimination rate constant) by the equation:

$$T_{0.5} = \frac{\log_e 2}{K} = \frac{0.693}{K}$$

where $K =$ elimination rate constant.

The half-lives of drugs vary greatly from less than an hour to many hours or even days. The following is a list of half-lives of drugs in common use:

Name	$T_{0.5}$ (h)	
	[Very short to short half-life]	
Tubocurarine	0.1	
Acetylsalicylic acid (aspirin)	0.3	(i) hydrolysis with deacetylation to salicylate
	2.0–4.5	(ii) salicylate
Benzylpenicillin	0.5	
Ampicillin	1.0–1.5	
Erythromycin	1.5–2.0	
Cortisol (hydrocortisone)	1.7	
Paracetamol	2.0	
	[Intermediate half-life]	
Pethidine	2.5	
Morphine	3.0	
Tetracycline	6–10	
Phenytoin	10–42	

Name	$T_{0.5}$ (h)
	[*Long to very long half-life*]
Warfarin	35–45
Nortriptyline	15–90
Digoxin	30–40
Desmethyldiazepam	36–200
(active metabolite of diazepam which has a $T_{0.5}$ of 20–100 h i.e. longer than the parent drug)	
Phenylbutazone	30–175

(Main source of data: Avery 1980)

Drug clearance

This is a more accurate measure of the efficiency with which a drug is eliminated by the body. It is based upon the apparent volume of distribution (AVD), and may be defined as the theoretical portion of the AVD that is cleared of the drug in unit time. Therefore, the clearance is the product of the volume of distribution (AVD) and the elimination rate constant. Thus it may be expressed as:

$$\text{Clearance} = \text{AVD} \times K = \frac{\text{AVD} \times 0.693}{T_{0.5}},$$

where K = elimination rate constant.

It is expressed in units of time, for example, ml/min, and where necessary this may be corrected for body weight, for example ml/kg. Clearance may be considered in relation to one organ (e.g. liver) or to the whole body (total body clearance). The total body clearance is equal to the sum of the clearances by the different routes of elimination involved for a particular drug. For practical purposes this may be divided into renal and non-renal clearance.

The advantage of measuring drug elimination in terms of clearance rather than half-life ($T_{0.5}$) is that unlike half-life it is unaffected by a change in the volume of distribution of the drug.

Routes of administration

Drugs may be administered locally in order to apply a high concentration to a particular site of action or may be administered systemically and thereby rely on the circulation to carry them to the required site of action.

Local

Local methods of administration include:

topical	intranasal	intra-articular
intradermal	intraconjunctival	intra-arterial
intrathecal	intra-oral	other special routes
	vaginal	

It is of particular importance for dental practitioners to note that locally administered drugs may be absorbed at a rate and to an extent sufficient to result in the production of systemic effects. This is even more likely to occur when the drug has been applied to diseased tissues where the natural barriers have been damaged and the blood supply increased by inflammatory changes.

Systemic

These routes are enteral or parenteral. The major enteral routes are sublingual, gastro-intestinal, and rectal.

Sublingual   administration is useful for the absorption of drugs that are given in small amounts and are relatively lipid-soluble. The high vascularity of the oral mucosa ensures rapid absorption directly into the general circulation and bypasses the liver. This route is thus particularly useful for drugs that undergo high 'first pass' metabolism by destruction in the gastro-intestinal tract and liver before reaching the general circulation.

The rate of absorption of ingested drugs (*gastro-intestinal* route) depends on a number of factors, particularly the rate of gastric emptying, which is itself dependent on both physiological and psychological factors.

Rectal   administration by means of a suppository is utilized when the oral route is unsuitable or unavailable, for example in a patient unable to take food by mouth or who is vomiting. The absorption of drugs from the rectum is slow and may be incomplete but can nevertheless be most useful in certain circumstances, such as when opioid suppositories are used in the treatment of terminal cancer patients.

The parenteral routes are subcutaneous, intramuscular, and intravenous.

The rate of absorption after *subcutaneous* or *intramuscular* administration depends on the local blood flow and also on whether vasoconstrictor substance has been added to the injection or not. It also depends upon the physico-chemical profile of the drug.

A drug administered by the *intravenous* route is obviously absorbed immediately and for this reason the rate of an intravenous injection should be slow enough for the injected bolus not to result in an excessively high plasma concentration, as this might produce undesirable local and systemic effects, particularly on the cardiovascular and central nervous systems.

It should be noted that the results of an intramuscular injection are inconstant and may give a pattern of absorption varying between that of a subcutaneous and an intravenous injection.

Plasma concentrations and clinical effects

The plasma concentrations (levels) achieved in different patients receiving the same oral dose of a given drug vary greatly. This is due mainly to intrinsic differences between individuals. The relationship between plasma concentration and clinical effect is less variable and has been studied in considerable detail for a large number of drugs. For drugs with a low therapeutic index (see page 40) the therapeutic range of plasma concentration and the toxicological range are in close proximity. Table 1.2 is a list of drugs and their plasma concentrations commonly associated with a therapeutic effect or likely to be associated with unwanted effects. It shows that with some drugs the gap between the two concentrations is very narrow whilst for others it is considerably wider.

Table 1.2. Therapeutic and toxic plasma concentrations of some drugs

Drugs	Normal half-life (hours)	Therapeutic range		Toxic level		Usual route of elimination[4]
Amitriptyline[2]	15–60	<200	µg/l	>200	µg/l	M
Carbamazepine	30–40	5–10	mg/l	>10	mg/l	M
Digoxin	30–40	1–2	µg/l	>2	µg/l	R
Disopyramide	4–8	3–6	mg/l	>8	mg/l	R
Lignocaine	2–4	2–5	mg/l	>8	mg/l	M
Lithium	7–20	0.8–1.3	mmol/l	>1.5	mmol/l	R
Mexiletine	4–8	1–2	mg/l	>3	mg/l	M&R
Nortriptyline	15–90	50–150	µg/l	>180	µg/l	M
Phenobarbitone						
plasma	20–100	15–40	mg/l	>40	mg/l	M
saliva	20–100	8–20	mg/l	>20	mg/l	
Phenytoin[1,3]						
plasma	10–42	10–20	mg/l	>20	mg/l	M
saliva	10–42	1–2	mg/l	>2	mg/l	
Procainamide	2–6	4–8	mg/l	>8	mg/l	M
Propranolol	2–4	>100	µg/l	—		M
Quinidine	3–6	3–6	mg/l	>6	mg/l	M
Salicylate[3]	2–4.5	150–300	mg/l	>400	mg/l	M&R
Theophylline[3]	8–20	5–20	mg/l	>20	mg/l	M
Valproate	6–12	>50	mg/l(?)	?		M

1. Phenytoin binding (normally 90%) is reduced substantially in uraemia and the 'therapeutic' and 'toxic' ranges of plasma concentrations are reduced. Alternatively, monitor salivary levels (which correspond to unbound levels) and aim for a therapeutic range of 1–2 mg/l.

2. Amitriptyline is metabolized to nortriptyline. The sum of the two concentrations should be added to yield the therapeutic range for amitriptyline.

3. These drugs have 'non-linear' kinetics and increasing the dose is likely to produce a more than proportional increase in plasma levels.

4. M = eliminated by metabolism; R = eliminated by renal excretion.

N.B. In the International System of Units (Système International d'Unités; SI) concentrations may be expressed either as mass concentration, e.g. mg/l, µg/l, as in this table, or as 'amount of substance' concentration, e.g. mmol/l, µmol/l. The two ways of expressing each concentration are readily interconverted by using the value of the appropriate molecular weight (MW) as follows: $mmol/l = \dfrac{mg/l}{MW}$ and conversely, mg/l = mmol/l × MW. Example: phenytoin (MW = 252), 10 mg/l $= \dfrac{10}{252} = 0.04$ mmol/l = 40 µmol/l; m = milli; µ = micro; 1 m = 1000 µ.

Plasma concentration–time curve

Plasma concentration–time curves obviously vary with the route of administration of a drug. Figure 1.9 illustrates the different shaped curves following the administration of penicillin by oral, intramuscular, and intravenous routes. With the oral route the peak plasma concentration is the lowest, with the intravenous route it is the highest, and with the intramuscular it is intermediate.

The effects of regular dosing as in normal therapeutic use are shown in Fig. 1.10(a) for the intravenous route and Fig. 1.10(b) for the oral route. In each case a dose is followed by a peak plasma concentration, which then falls to a trough to be followed by another peak plasma concentration, which then falls to a trough to be followed by another peak and trough and so on until a plateau is reached, i.e. the steady state. The major difference between these two routes is that with the intravenous route the rise of the plasma concentration is steeper and reaches a higher peak. It should be noted that the graphs (Fig. 1.10) have been drawn for the situation where each dose is given at intervals (6-hourly) equal to one-half of the half-life of the drug (12 h), and that it takes approximately five doses to reach steady state. Where there is a close correlation between the plasma concentration of a drug and its effect—for example, with the use of phenytoin for the control of epilepsy—it is essential to arrange that the doses are given at regular intervals so that not only the peak but also the trough concentrations are within the therapeutic range. If they are not, then as the plasma concentration falls between doses, the risk of a fit is increased. This is an important example of the application of the relationship between the plasma concentration and therapeutic effect of drugs (see Table 1.2). The same principle applies to the use of aspirin for the relief of dental pain.

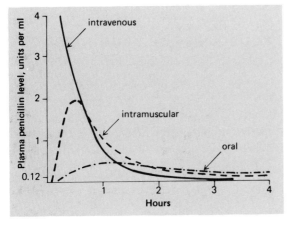

Fig. 1.9. Plasma concentration curves in a human subject after administration of 100 000 units = 60 mg benzylpenicillin by intravenous, intramuscular, and oral routes. (Reproduced from Creasey 1979 with permission of the publisher.)

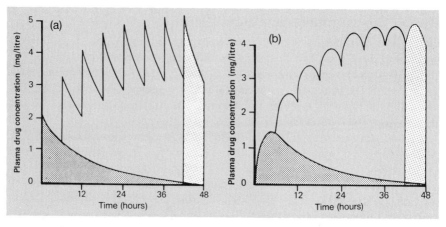

Fig. 1.10. Plasma concentrations of a drug given (a) intravenously and (b) orally on a fixed dose of 50 mg and fixed dosing interval of 6 hours. The half-life is 12 hours. Note that the area under the plasma concentration-time curve during a dosing interval *at steady state* is equal to the total area under the curve for a single dose. The fluctuation of the concentration is diminished when given orally (half-life of absorption is 1.4 hours) but the average steady-state concentration is the same as that after intravenous administration because the absorption of this drug is assumed to be complete.

Cumulation

This results when the intake of a drug exceeds its clearance from the body. It is obviously more likely to occur when drugs with long half-lives are used. It also occurs when the mechanisms for elimination are affected by disease, for example, renal failure. Thus the dose of the cardiac stimulant, digoxin, must be reduced when given to a patient who suffers from renal failure. If this step is not taken then the drug may accumulate and reach dangerously high concentrations in the body.

THE PHARMACODYNAMIC PROCESS: IS THE DRUG PRODUCING THE REQUIRED PHARMACOLOGICAL EFFECT?

Drugs modify the function of living cells. When a drug produces an effect on a certain tissue this is the end-result of an interaction between its molecules and some part of the cells of which that tissue is composed. It is now clear that drugs can be divided into two main types according as to whether or not they act on pharmacological receptors, special receptive sites situated on or within cells.

Drugs which act via pharmacological receptors:

(1) act at *low* concentrations;

(2) react with *specific* receptors;

(3) show *structure–activity relationships*;

(4) can be antagonized by *specific antagonists*.

Examples are acetylcholine, noradrenaline, adrenaline, and histamine.

Drugs which do **NOT** *act via pharmacological receptors:*

(1) act at *higher* concentrations;

(2) do *not* react with specific receptors;

(3) *tend not* to show structure–activity relationships;

(4) do *not* have specific antagonists.

Examples of drugs which belong to this group are general anaesthetics, e.g. diethyl ether, halothane; diuretics, e.g. thiazides; and non-specific destructants of cell membranes, e.g. detergents.

Drugs which act on specific pharmacological receptors

Historical

The concept of receptors grew out of the work of Paul Ehrlich (1854–1915), who was Director of the Institute for Experimental Therapy in Frankfurt from 1899 to 1915. He believed living matter was composed of large protoplasmic molecules that possessed side chains. He developed a side-chain theory of immunity, enzyme action, and drug action. The proposal that drugs may act upon special sites or 'receptive substances' was first made in 1905 by J. N. Langley (1852–1925), who was Professor of Physiology at Cambridge (Langley 1905). Over the ensuing 75 years, evidence for the existence of 'receptive substances', now renamed 'pharmacological receptors', grew steadily. Mathematical theories to explain the relationship between the dose of a drug and the response or effect produced were developed by other workers, especially A. J. Clark (1885–1941), who was Professor of Pharmacology at Edinburgh University, and also by J. H. Gaddum, E. J. Ariens, and H. Schild. More recently, with the development of new techniques, attempts have been made to visualize and to isolate receptors. The development of various binding techniques has made it possible to map out and to measure the density of receptors for drugs, hormones, and neurotransmitters on various tissues, including changes that take place during various disease processes.

Drug–receptor interaction

A pharmacological receptor is a macromolecule with special sites to which specific substances, i.e. drugs (sometimes called ligands) bind. Drug–receptor (ligand–receptor) binding leads to a change in the macromolecule, which in turn triggers a train of events resulting in the response of the tissue or organ—for example, contraction of smooth muscle, secretion of a gland, and stimulation (or inhibition) of nerve cells leading to release (or inhibition of release) of the chemical transmitter from their endings. In this context, we must now define other important terms relating to drugs and receptors.

An *agonist* is a drug (or hormone, or neurotransmitter) which combines with its specific receptor, activates it, and initiates a sequence of effects.

An *antagonist* is a drug which interferes with the action of an agonist. A *pure* antagonist has no action of its own but only by virtue of the fact that it interferes with the action of an agonist. An example of such a drug is the opioid antagonist, naloxone.

A *partial agonist* is a drug that acts on a receptor with an intrinsic activity or efficacy of < 1. In practical terms an activity of 1 means the ability of a drug to elicit a maximal response. By definition it follows that the largest response obtainable from a partial agonist is less than the maximum that can be achieved by a complete agonist acting on the same receptor. It will be appreciated that the term partial agonist is a comparative one; the degree of agonism is measured by comparing the maximum responses obtainable from a whole series of compounds acting on the same receptor. The one that produces the largest response is said to have an intrinsic activity or efficacy of 1 (the symbol α (alpha) is commonly used for this purpose so that in this case $\alpha = 1$) and the other compounds are ranked accordingly.

Mixed agonist–antagonist is a relatively new term that we must also mention. It is frequently confused (and thereby abused) with the term partial agonist. A mixed agonist–antagonist is a drug that acts simultaneously on a mixed group of receptors with an agonist action on one set and with an antagonist action on another set. There are two corollaries of this definition:

(1) The agonist action of such a drug may be complete or partial.

(2) With multiple receptor systems upon which this type of drug may act, numerous combinations of agonist or antagonist actions are theoretically possible.

At the present time, drugs with mixed agonist–antagonist activity are most likely to be found among the opioids (see Chapter 6).

Distribution of pharmacological receptors

Pharmacological receptors are found in two main sites and are named according to either (a) the principal endogenous agonist that activates them (adrenoceptors, cholinoceptors, glucocorticoid receptors, etc.) or (b) the first exogenous agonist found to activate them (for example, opioid receptors, benzodiazepine receptors, and so on) whether or not an endogenous agonist is subsequently discovered (Bowman *et al.* 1986).

The sites in which drug receptors are found are as follows:

(1) *On or within cell membranes*: these may be one of two types, those that:

    (i) act on membrane permeability to alter it with a very fast response time measured in milliseconds such as produced by the nicotinic acetylcholine receptor, or;

   (ii) act on intracellular second messenger with a fast response time of seconds or minutes such as is produced by adrenaline or noradrenaline.

(2) *Inside cells*: alter DNA transcription with a slow response time of hours such as that produced by steroids.

Evidence for the existence of pharmacological receptors

A substantial body of evidence now exists to support the concept of pharmacological receptors. This may be listed as follows:

1. Many drugs act in low concentrations (= high dilutions), for example, 10^{-3} to 10^{-5} mols per litre. For a drug with a molecular weight = 200 daltons this represents 200 μg per ml to 2 μg per ml. Some drugs, for example atropine, are active in very low concentrations (10^{-8} and 10^{-9} mols per litre).

2. The rate of the frog heart can be slowed 50 per cent by 0.02 μg of acetylcholine per gram of tissue. This dose of acetylcholine contains about 10^{14} molecules and Clark (1937) calculated that this amount would cover approximately 1/6000th of the total cell surface i.e. less than 0.02 per cent. This implies that only *part* of each cell needs to be covered with drug molecules in order to produce an effect.

3. In some tissues certain cells appear to possess areas specially sensitive to particular drugs: for example, the end plate of skeletal muscle normally only responds to acetylcholine.

4. Chemical alteration of many drugs alters their pharmacological activity (structure–activity relationship).

5. Where a drug exists in optically isomeric forms, the pharmacological activity of the isomeric forms usually differs greatly. Thus, L(R)-noradrenaline is more active than D(S)-noradrenaline, the ratio of activities depending upon the tissue under consideration.

6. Pharmacologically active substances produced in the body—for example acetylcholine, catecholamines (i.e. dopamine, noradrenaline, and adrenaline), histamine, 5-hydroxytryptamine (serotonin)—are found to act as endogenous ligands at their own specific receptors located on certain cells.

7. Not all cells in the body have a complete set of specific receptors for all endogenously produced pharmacological ligands. However, in cells where more than one type of receptor co-exists, the effects of activating them may produce the same or opposite effects depending upon the particular tissue.

8. Some endogenous ligands and drugs act on more than one type of receptor for a particular ligand. For example, adrenaline acts on both α- and β-adrenoceptors; histamine acts on H_1 and H_2 (histamine)-receptors.

9. The use of radio-ligand techniques has helped greatly to plot the distribution of receptors in tissues.

10. New techniques have made it possible to isolate certain receptors and to determine their chemical structures. Furthermore, some receptors have been isolated from cell membranes and then inserted into artificial membranes.

Some features of the receptor system

As indicated earlier, drugs that act on receptors, the neurotransmitters, and some hormones all exert their effects without entering the cell upon which they act. They interact with specific receptors that are coupled to various effector or amplifier systems, which then generate internal signals or so-called second messengers. The detailed mechanisms are still being worked out but the main components of the system, together with two examples, may be represented as follows (Berridge 1981):

(1) Agonist (drug, hormone, or neurotrans- mitter)	(2) Receptor	(3) Transducer	(4) Effector	(5) Second messenger	(6) Effect
		EXAMPLES			
Acetylcholine (Ach)	Ach receptor	Phospholipase C	Calcium gate	Ca^{2+}	Contraction of smooth muscle
Noradrenaline (NAd)	NAd receptor	Guanosine triphosphate (GTP)	Adenylate cyclase	Cyclic adenosine monophos- phate (cyclicAMP)	Metabolic changes

From the above it can be seen that there is a cascade of events that links the interaction of an agonist with its receptor and with the ultimate biological effect. This multi-stage system is analogous to an amplifier in that the initial molecular interaction leads to progressively larger numbers of interactions at each of the stages involved. Thus, just as a small signal from a microphone can be amplified in stages so that the output is capable of driving powerful loudspeakers, so small molecules of acetylcholine acting upon muscle endplate can ultimately result in powerful contraction of a large skeletal muscle. Although theoretically the complexity of receptor–response coupling mechanisms is very great, in reality the number of mechanisms is limited to three as follows:

1. *Receptor–ion channel coupling* The interaction between agonist and receptor causes the cell membrane to undergo a conformational change with the result that an ion channel opens to allow the passage of a particular ion. An example (already referred to earlier) is the action of acetylcholine on nicotinic cholinoceptors, which results in an influx of sodium ions. This leads to depolarization of the muscle endplate, which in turn triggers off an action

potential. This brings about the release of calcium ions, which in its turn leads to a contraction of the muscle fibres.

2. *Receptor–enzyme coupling* Here the interaction between agonist and receptor leads to a conformational change in an enzyme. An example is the activation of β-adrenoceptors that are coupled to the enzyme adenylate cyclase in the cell membrane. Activation of this enzyme leads to the formation of cyclic AMP, which then phosphorylates a protein kinase and which in turn phosphorylates intracellular proteins so modifying the activity of the cell.

3. *Intracellular steroid receptor–protein synthesis coupling* Steroid hormones, which are highly lipid-soluble and therefore penetrate cell membranes with ease, combine with specific receptor-binding proteins in the cytosol. The hormone–receptor complex then enters the cell nucleus and triggers changes that are transcribed into messenger RNAs. These in turn signal the synthesis of specific proteins and by this means cellular activity is modified.

Receptor regulation

There is abundant evidence to show that neither the density nor the affinity of receptors are fixed quantities. Tissues normally innervated by the autonomic nervous system, for example, vascular smooth muscle, after sympathetic denervation show supersensitivity to the catecholamines, noradrenaline and adrenaline. This phenomenon is known as Cannon's Law of Denervation (Cannon and Rosenblueth 1949). The use of modern techniques has shown that the density and affinity of receptors are in a dynamic state subject to various physiological and pathological factors. Thus, alterations in the receptors will modify the effects produced by agonists (drugs, neurotransmitters, or hormones) acting on these receptors, and may play a role in the pathology of various diseases and in their therapy (Lefkowitz 1979; Lefkowitz and Hoffman 1981). Table 1.3

Table 1.3. Factors regulating α- and β-adrenoceptors

Regulatory agent or condition	Effect on number of receptors
α-adrenoceptors	
α-adrenergic catecholamines	Decrease
Denervation	Increase
Hyperthyroidism	Decrease (also decrease affinity)
β-adrenoceptors	
β-adrenergic catecholamines	Decrease
Propranolol	Increase
Denervation (chemical, pharmacological, or surgical)	Increase
Hyperthyroidism	Increase
Hypothyroidism	Decrease

(Lefkowitz 1979; Lefkowitz and Hoffman 1981.)

Table 1.4. Clinical implications of receptors (for drugs, hormones, and neurotransmitters

Disease	Receptor involved
Diabetes mellitus	Insulin
Male pseudohermaphrodism:	
Testicular feminization syndrome	Androgen
Reifenstein syndrome	Androgen
Vitamin D-resistant rickets	1,25-dihydroxy Vitamin D_3 (1,25-dihydroxy cholecalciferol; calcitriol)
Asthma, including desensitization to β-agonists	β-adrenoceptor
Hypothyroidism	β-adrenoceptor
Myasthenia gravis	Acetylcholine (nicotinic)

(Lefkowitz 1979; Lefkowitz and Hoffman 1981.)

lists some factors regulating α- and β-adrenoceptors. Table 1.4 indicates the clinical implications of receptors by listing those diseases in which receptor abnormalities are known to be involved. Thus, the subject of pharmacological receptors is not only of academic interest to pharmacologists but has become of great practical importance in the pathology, diagnosis, and treatment of disease.

Relationships between the dose of a drug and the effect (response) it produces

Two types of relationship need to be considered.

1. Quantitative (= graded) responses or effects

Consider the situation where increasing doses of a drug are applied to a piece of isolated tissue—for example, small intestine. With the smallest doses no effect is seen until a certain threshold dose is reached when a detectable effect is recorded. Thereafter the effect increases as the dose is increased until a maximum is reached. Beyond this point any further increase in dose is not accompanied by an increase in the size of the response. When the relationship between the dose and effect is plotted as a graph it produces a hyperbolic shaped curve; see Fig. 1.11(a). Pharmacologists find it more useful to plot the logarithm of the dose of agonist (instead of the dose) against the effect because this transforms the hyperbolic curve (Fig. 1.11(a)) into a sigmoid curve; see Fig. 1.11(b). It can be seen that over the range 25–75 per cent maximum response the graph is a straight line and this is much more convenient to handle than the hyperbolic curve. This is particularly so when comparing a series of dose–effect curves that have been constructed from the results of testing varying concentrations of a drug in the presence of a series of fixed concentrations of a specific antagonist to that drug.

    It is not necessary for the dental student or practitioner to be conversant with the detailed mathematical analysis of dose–effect curves. However, the present availability of personal microcomputers has encouraged many individuals to

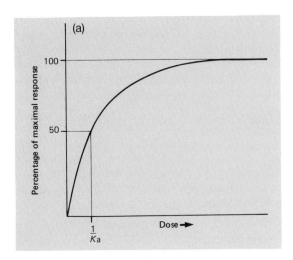

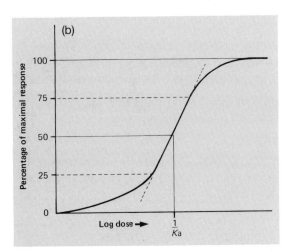

Fig. 1.11. Quantitative (graded responses: dose–response (dose–effect) curves. (a) Graph showing relationship between concentration of a drug and response (effect) plotted linearly. (b) Same data as in (a) but plotted semi-logarithmically. Note: (i) Hyperbolic curve in (a) transformed by semi-logarithmic plot into sigmoid curve (b), which is conveniently linear over the range 25–75% maximal response. (ii) Both curves have same maxima. (iii) If it is assumed that a half-maximal contraction occurs when 50% of receptors are occupied, then from equation 2 (see text)

$$(A) = \frac{1}{Ka}.$$

The Figure shows how the value of (A) is measured from the dose–response curve and from which the affinity constant (Ka) is obtained by calculating the reciprocal. Thus, the lower the concentration required to elicit a half-maximal response, the greater the affinity of the drug and the larger the numerical value of Ka.

become mathematically inquisitive. It thus seems appropriate to indicate that the relationship between the dose of a drug and the effect it produces can be represented by a mathematical equation:

$$Y = \frac{(A)Ka}{1+(A)Ka}.$$
Equation (1)

where Y = proportion of receptors occupied; (A) = molar concentration of drug; Ka = affinity (association) constant.

Thus, if it is assumed that the effect produced by a drug is related to the number of receptors occupied (Y) then it follows from this equation that:

(1) With no drug (i.e. when $(A)=0$) there is no effect (because the expression on the right-hand side of the equation reduces to zero).

(2) As the concentration of drug (A) is increased, so the effect increases until it reaches a *limiting maximum*.
    Note: this statement may be verified by substituting the term $(A)Ka$ (which appears in both the numerator and denominator of the equation) with increasing numerical values, e.g. 1, 10, 100, 1000, etc.

(3) When 50 per cent of receptors are occupied:

$$(A) = \frac{1}{Ka}.$$
Equation (2)

The affinity constant (Ka) for a drug can be readily determined by carrying out a laboratory experiment in which sufficient doses are given to span the full range of the dose–response curve. The curve is then plotted and from this the dose required to produce 50 per cent of maximum response is read off and the reciprocal calculated; this value represents the Ka of the drug (see Fig. 1.11). This method can be used to determine the relative affinities of a series of drugs acting on the same receptor—for example, a group of β-adrenoceptor blocking drugs.

2. Quantal (all or nothing) responses or effects

In many situations the response to a drug is all or none. For example, in a toxicity test a dose of a drug will either kill or not, so that an animal is either alive or dead. When such a test is carried out, the animals are first divided into several groups. The dosage *within* groups is the same (on a dose for body weight basis) whereas the dose *between* groups is different. For example, there might be five groups of animals each containing six animals. The doses given to each group might be 2.5, 5, 10, 20, and 40 mg/kg (i.e. distributed logarithmically) and each animal in a particular group would receive the dose for that group adjusted for body weight. The percentage responding in each group is recorded and a graph is plotted of these values against the dose used for each group.

Similarly, the dose of an hypnotic needed to produce drowsiness can be expressed graphically. Figure 1.12 shows the results of a study in which amylobarbitone (a barbiturate) was used to produce drowsiness (given by slow intravenous injection) in 55 obstetric patients, and shows that these kind of data can be plotted in two ways. Figure 1.12(a) shows the data as a frequency histogram, and Fig. 1.12(b) shows them in the form of a cumulative distribution curve. Note that the data in Fig. 1.12(b) have been plotted linearly, i.e. it has not been necessary to carry out a semi-logarithmic transformation (although this may be necessary when data turns out to be skewed). From the foregoing it can be seen that quantal data can be treated in the same way as data representing quantitative (= graded) effects. When, as mentioned earlier in this section, the experiment concerns the measurement of drug toxicity in animals, the amount required to kill 50 per cent of animals can be determined, and this is known as the LD_{50} (lethal dose to kill 50 per cent). An analogous term used to describe the dose required to produce a given effect in 50 per cent of the population of animals is known as the ED_{50} (effective dose in 50 per cent of animals).

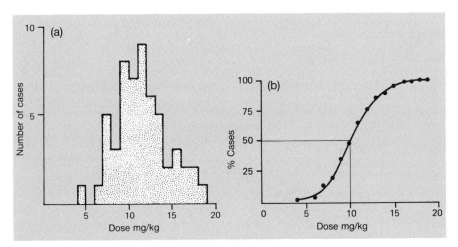

Fig. 1.12. Quantal (all or nothing) responses. Graphs showing the dosage of amylobarbitone sodium needed to produce drowsiness when given by slow intravenous injection to 55 obstetric patients. (a) The data have been expressed as a frequency histogram. (b) The same results plotted as a cumulative frequency distribution. Note: effective dose for 50% of patients (ED_{50}) is 10 mg/kg with a four-fold range extending from 4–19 mg/kg for all patients.

Therapeutic index

An 'ideal' drug would cure all patients in a dose that kills none. The therapeutic index gives a measure of the safety margin available, although it does not take into account the possible occurrence of an abnormal response, such as an allergic response or idiosyncracy (see Chapter 21). Figure 1.13 shows quantal responses

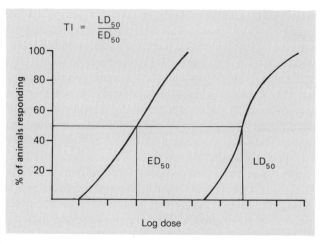

Fig. 1.13. Illustration of the concept of therapeutic index (TI). Abscissa shows the dose of drug (mg/kg) and ordinate shows percentage of animals responding. The left-hand curve indicates the percentage of animals that respond to various doses of drug from which the dose needed to produce the desired pharmacological effect in 50% of animals is found. The right-hand curve shows the relationship between the dose of drug and the number of animals that die from it, from which the dose required to kill 50% is then found.

$$\text{The Therapeutic Index (TI)} = LD_{50}/ED_{50}. \text{ For example: } \frac{6.6}{3} = 2.2.$$

The drug that has the same pharmacological action but a higher TI than the one illustrated would (other things being equal) be a safer drug and vice versa. Graphically the TI is represented by the distance between the two curves, provided they are tolerably parallel. (Reproduced by permission from Clark, W. G., Brater, D. C., and Johnson, A. R. (1988). *Goth's Medical Pharmacology*, (12th edn). The C.V. Mosby Co., St Louis, MO, USA.)

for a therapeutic effect (for example, hypnosis) and a toxic effect (death) from which it can be seen that:

$$\text{Therapeutic index} = \frac{LD_{50}}{ED_{50}}$$

which in this case is 6.6 divided by 3 = 2.2. The higher the numerical value of the therapeutic index, the safer the drug is likely to be.

Clinical implications

Whilst there is no such thing as a 'safe' drug, some are safer than others, i.e. have a higher therapeutic index than others. For example, if lignocaine is taken as a reference compound with a therapeutic index = 1, then cocaine has a therapeutic index of 0.6 whereas prilocaine has a therapeutic index of 1.18. This means that, all other things being equal, cocaine is substantially more toxic than lignocaine whereas prilocaine is about as toxic as the reference compound. When it is proposed to prescribe any drug its toxicity should always be taken into consideration and the risk of treatment weighed against the risk of the disease (risk: benefit ratio). An example of the application of this principle in practice is the use of a known highly toxic drug for the treatment of cancer.

Drug antagonism

Antagonism between two drugs can be said to occur when their biological effect is less than the expected sum of their individual effects. Therapeutically, drug action is commonly employed in order to reduce (or sometimes abolish) the action of (i) some endogenous compound—for example, a neurotransmitter or hormone; or (ii) another drug—for example, to counteract an unwanted effect or to treat an overdose effect. There are some five types of drug antagonism classified as follows:

Pharmacological antagonism

By convention the term 'pharmacological antagonism' implies antagonism by receptor blockade and is of two main types:

1. *Reversible competitive (equilibrium competitive) antagonism* This occurs when the action of an agonist is interfered with by an antagonist because both substances are competing dynamically for the same pharmacological receptor (see Fig. 1.14). A key feature, and one of both academic and clinical importance, is that of surmountability of the block by the addition of agonist. An example is atropine antagonizing the muscarinic actions of acetylcholine. As indicated earlier, with this type of antagonism the concentration of the agonist (in this example, acetylcholine) is not altered by the presence of atropine; but the effect of the atropine is to reduce the probability that a given molecule of acetylcholine will be successful in arriving at and activating a receptor. This will be because it has been prevented from so doing by a molecule of atropine that, having united with the receptor, is unable to inactivate it. This concept can be verified both experimentally and in certain clinical situations, where an existing degree of pharmacological block can be increased or decreased at will by administering additional doses of the appropriate antagonist or agonist (within reasonable limits). Other examples are H_1 and H_2 blockers antagonizing the actions of histamine; α- and β-adrenoceptors blocking the actions of noradrenaline and adrenaline.

2. *Irreversible competitive (non-equilibrium competitive) antagonism* Some drugs act as antagonists by forming very strong bonds—for example, covalent bonds with receptors—thereby occluding them for long periods of time (see Fig. 1.14). Thus the molecules of antagonist dissociate very slowly or not at all. Examples are: phenoxybenzamine which antagonizes the actions of noradrenaline and adrenaline.

Clinical implications

A reversible competitive antagonist has much greater clinical acceptability than an irreversible competitive antagonist because its action can, if necessary, be reversed (theoretically, if not in practice) by administering a dose of an

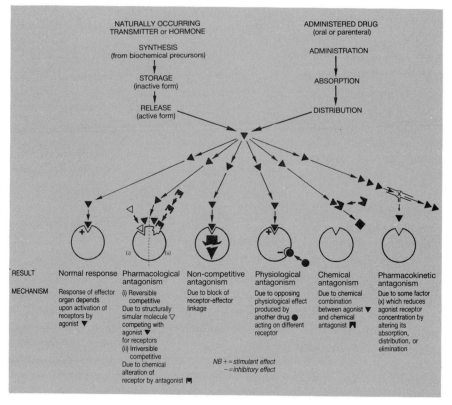

Fig. 1.14. Diagram to illustrate the different types of drug antagonism. The molecules of agonist are shown arising from alternative sources. Top left, endogenous: the stages in the synthesis of a naturally occurring transmitter or hormone are indicated. Top right, exogenous: the stages that follow the oral or parenteral administration of a drug are indicated. The action of agonist molecules on a single receptor of an effector organ under normal conditions is depicted as well as in the presence of pharmacological (reversible competitive or irreversible competitive), non-competitive, physiological, chemical, or pharmacokinetic antagonists. Note: in order to simplify the diagram, it has been assumed that the naturally occurring substance and the administered drug act on the same receptor and that all four types of antagonist exist for the same agonist. Reversible pharmacological antagonism occurs commonly; the second and third are uncommon, and the fourth is rare. Physiological antagonism and pharmacokinetic antagonism are less common, whilst the others are uncommon.

appropriate agonist. This cannot be done with an irreversible competitive antagonist because it binds on to the receptors tenaciously and remains static. Therefore if the patient is given too large a dose of an irreversible competitive antagonist no amount of agonist (which normally acts on the same receptor) can reverse the effect, although it may be possible to reverse it by using a physiological antagonist (see below).

Non-competitive antagonism

Some antagonists block the action of an agonist NOT at the receptor level *but* by interfering, in a non-specific way, with some point in the critical link between receptor and effector that normally leads to the action of the agonist. A good example is that of a calcium channel blocker, which will interfere with the action of any agonist that normally activates a response in which calcium ions (Ca^{2+}) play a critical role.

Physiological antagonism

This occurs when two drugs that act on *different* receptors produce opposite effects. A good example is when adrenaline antagonizes the constrictor effects of histamine on bronchial smooth muscle. Physiological antagonism is of clinical importance and can be life-saving in the treatment of bronchial asthma (due to endogenous bronchoconstrictor substances) with drugs such as adrenaline, isoprenaline, or salbutamol (the latter two given as inhalations). Physiological antagonism can also be used to deal with a clinical situation where an excessive dose of an irreversible competitive antagonist (see above) has been given.

Chemical antagonism

This occurs when one drug combines chemically with another to produce an inactive product; for example, as when dimercaprol (British Anti-Lewisite) forms relatively non-toxic complexes with compounds of mercury, arsenic, antimony, and gold and so can be used to treat poisoning with these substances. Thus, with sodium arsenite (a trivalent arsenical compound), dimercaprol, forms a cyclic thioarsenite by means of coupling with sulphydryl (SH) groups:

$$\text{NaOAs}=0 \quad + \quad \begin{array}{c} \text{HS—CH}_2 \\ | \\ \text{HS—CH} \\ | \\ \text{HO—CH}_2 \end{array} \rightarrow \text{NaOAs} \begin{array}{c} \text{S—CH}_2 \\ | \\ \text{S—CH} \\ | \\ \text{HO—CH}_2 \end{array} + \quad \text{H}_2\text{O}$$

Chemical antagonists that combine chemically with another substance (endogenous or exogenous) are also known as chelating agents (Gk. *khele* = claw). Other important examples are D-penicillamine (chelates Cu, cystine) and ethylenediamine tetra-acetic acid (EDTA) (chelates Ca).

Pharmacokinetic antagonism

This occurs when one drug effectively reduces the concentration of another at its site of action by altering its absorption, distribution, or elimination. For example, the effect of warfarin (an anticoagulant) may be reduced by certain drugs (e.g. phenobarbitone) that increase its rate of metabolism in the body.

Drugs which do NOT act on specific receptors

As indicated earlier, members of this group (i) act at higher concentrations; (ii) tend NOT to show structure–activity relationships; and (iii) do not have specific antagonists. Examples include general anaesthetics, e.g. halothane; diuretics, e.g. thiazides; and non-specific destructants of cell membranes, e.g. detergents.

Drugs in this group act by causing some change in cell membranes by virtue of their physico-chemical properties. It seems likely that general anaesthetics perturb cell membranes in such a way that they interfere with the normal passage of ions and other essential substances across these vital structures. Although general anaesthetic agents produce the same type of effect on all cells membranes, brain cells are more susceptible and can thus be reversibly depressed by these agents at concentrations that do not produce serious effects on cells of other tissues. Also of importance is the fact that cells within the vital centres of the brain (respiration, blood pressure) are more resistant than those in certain other parts of the nervous system. This produces a useful differential effect resulting in general anaesthesia without the loss of function of vital centres, except in overdose. (For further discussion on the mode of action of general anaesthetics see Chapter 8.)

THE THERAPEUTIC PROCESS: IS THE PHARMACOLOGICAL EFFECT BEING TRANSLATED INTO A DESIRED THERAPEUTIC EFFECT?

When drugs are used to treat disease it is important to try to understand the way in which the drug and its effects interact with the pathological processes

Table 1.5. Factors that determine the relationship between prescribed drug dosage and drug effect

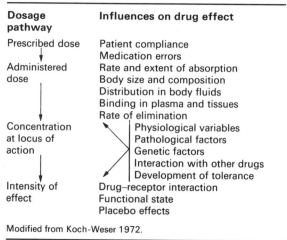

Dosage pathway	Influences on drug effect
Prescribed dose	Patient compliance
	Medication errors
Administered dose	Rate and extent of absorption
	Body size and composition
	Distribution in body fluids
	Binding in plasma and tissues
	Rate of elimination
Concentration at locus of action	Physiological variables
	Pathological factors
	Genetic factors
	Interaction with other drugs
	Development of tolerance
Intensity of effect	Drug–receptor interaction
	Functional state
	Placebo effects

Modified from Koch-Weser 1972.

underlying the disease. In some instances this is fairly obvious whilst in others it is far from clear. There are many factors concerned with the drug and with the patient that influence the final result and these vary from drug to drug and from patient to patient. The use of particular drugs for the treatment of particular diseases encountered by the dental practitioner are dealt with elsewhere within the appropriate chapters of this book. Nevertheless, each time a drug is prescribed the dental practitioner should bear in mind the main steps that lead from the prescription of the drug(s) to the end result. It is useful and important to have in mind a check list of the various stages involved and the factors that determine the relationship between prescribed drug dosage and drug effect. These have been usefully summarized by Koch-Weser (1972) in the form of a flow chart (Table 1.5).

REFERENCES

Alvares, A. P. [1978]. Interactions between environmental chemicals and drug biotransformation in man. *Clinical Pharmacokinetics*, **3**, 462.

Avery, G. S. (1980). *Drug treatment* (2nd edn). Adis Press, Sydney and New York.

Berridge, M. J. (1981). Receptors and calcium signalling. In *Towards understanding receptors* (ed. J. W. Lamble). Elsevier/North Holland, Amsterdam.

Bowman, W. C., Bowman, A., and Bowman, A. (1986). *Dictionary of pharmacology*. Blackwell Scientific Publications, Oxford.

Brodie, B. B. (1956). Review Article. Pathways of drug metabolism. *Journal of Pharmacy and Pharmacology*, **8**, 1–17.

Brodie, B. B. (1964). Physico-chemical factors in drug absorption. In *Absorption and distribution of drugs*. (ed. T. B. Binns). Livingstone, Edinburgh.

Cannon, W. S. and Rosenblueth, A. (1949). *The supersensitivity of denervated structures: law of denervation*. The Macmillan Company, New York.

Clark, A. J. (1937). General pharmacology. In *Handbuch der experimentelle Pharmakologie Vol. 4* (ed. A. Heffter and H. Henbner). Springer, Berlin.

Clark, W. G., Brater, D. C., and Johnson, A. R. (1988). *Goths Medical Pharmacology*, (12th edn). The C. V. Mosly Co., St Louis, MO, USA.

Creasy, W. A. (1979). *Drug disposition in humans*. Oxford Univesity Press.

Dost, F. H. (1953). *Der blutspiegel kinetik der konzentraztion-sablaufe in der kreislauffussigkeit*. Thieme, Leipzig.

Drew, G. C., Colquhoun, W. P., and Long, H. A. (1958). Effects of small doses of alcohol on a skill resembling driving. *British Medical Journal*, **2**, 993–9.

Gillette, J. R. (1967). In *Drug responses in man*. (ed. G. Wolstenholme and R. Porter). Churchill, London.

Goldberg, A. and Griffin, J. P. (1984). Functions of the Committee on Safety of Medicines. *Update* July 1984, 29–33.

Grahame-Smith, P. G. and Aronson, J. K. (1984). *Oxford textbook of clinical pharmacology and drug therapy*. Oxford University Press, Oxford.

Houslay, M. D. and Stanley, K. K. (1982). *Dynamics of biological membranes*. John Wiley and Sons, Chichester and New York.

Jusko, W. J. (1978). Role of tobacco smoking in pharmacokinetics. *Journal of Pharmacokinetics and Biopharmaceutics*, **6**, 7.

Kalow, W. (1962). *Pharmacogenetics: heredity and the response to drugs.* Saunders, Philadelphia.

Katzung, B. G. (1984). *Basic and clinical pharmacology* (2nd edn), Lange Medical Publications, Los Altos, CA.

Koch-Weser, J. (1972). Serum drug concentrations as therapeutic guides. *New England Journal of Medicine,* **287,** 227–31.

Langley, J. N. (1905). On the reaction of cells and of nerve-endings to certain poisons chiefly as regards the reaction of striated muscle to nicotine and to curari. *Journal of Physiology,* **33,** 374–413.

Lee, E. J. D. and Lee, L. K. H. (1982). A simple pharmacokinetic method for separating the three acetylation phenotypes: a preliminary report. *British Journal of Clinical Pharmacology,* **3,** 375–8.

Lefkowitz, R. J. (1979). Direct binding studies of adrenergic receptors: biochemical, physiologic and clinical implications. *Annals of Internal Medicine,* **91,** 450–8.

Lefkowitz, R. J. and Hoffman, B. B. (1981). New directions in adrenergic receptor research. Parts I & II. In *Towards understanding receptors.* (ed. J. W. Lamble). Elsevier/North Holland, Amsterdam.

Leonards, J. R. (1963). The influence of solubility on the rate of gastrointestinal absorption of aspirin. *Clinical Pharmacology and Therapeutics,* **4,** 476–9.

Lindemann, B. and Solomon, A. K. (1962). Permeability of luminal surface of intestinal mucosal cells. *Journal of General Physiology,* **45,** 801–10.

Ogilvie, R. I. (1978). Clinical pharmacokinetics of theophylline. *Clinical Pharmacokinetics,* **3,** 267.

Park, B. K. and Breckenridge, A. M. (1981). Clinical implications of enzyme induction and enzyme inhibition. *Clinical Pharmacokinetics,* **6,** 1–24.

Paton, W. D. M. (1963). *The early days of pharmacology.* In *Chemistry the service of medicine* (ed. F. N. L. Paynter). Pitman Medical, London.

Rawlins, M. D., James, O. F. W., Williams, F. M., Wynne, H., and Woodhouse, K. W. (1987). Age and the metabolism of drugs. *Quarterly Journal of Medicine, New Series,* **64,** 243, 545–7.

Rawlins, M. D. and Thompson, J. W. (1985). Mechanisms of adverse drug reactions. In *Textbook of adverse drug reactions.* (3rd edn) (ed. D. M. Davies). Oxford University Press, Oxford.

Routledge, P. A. (1986). Interactions that matter: 6. Warfarin. *Prescriber's Journal,* **26**(3), 71–5.

Schild, H. O. (1980). *Applied pharmacology.* Churchill Livingstone, Edinburgh.

Sjöqvist, B., Borga, A., and Orme, M. L'E. (1980). Fundamentals of Clinical Pharmacology. In *Drug treatment* (ed. G. S. Avery). Adis Press, Sydney and New York.

Smith, J. M. and Dodd, T. R. P. (1982). Adverse reactions to pharmaceutical excipients. *Adverse Drug Reactions and Acute Poisoning Review,* **i,** 93–142.

Smyth, D. H. (1964). In *Absorption and distribution of drugs.* (ed. T. B. Binns). Livingstone, Edinburgh.

Thompson, J. W. (1967). Pharmacology in perspective. An inaugural lecture, University of Newcastle upon Tyne.

Tyrer, J. H., Eadie, M. J., Sutherland, J. M., and Hooper, W. D. (1970). Outbreak of anticonvulsant intoxication in an Australian city. *British Medical Journal,* **iv,** 271–3.

2

The administration of drugs: the routes of administration

In broad terms, the administration of drugs has already been considered in Chapter 1 under two headings: (a) local or topical administration; and (b) systemic administration. The purpose here is consider detail of these routes, their advantages and disadvantages.

LOCAL ADMINISTRATION

This route includes applications to the oral mucous membranes, the skin, and other epithelial surfaces. Topical application is instituted to obtain a local drug effect, such as the use of a local anaesthetic spray prior to insertion of a needle, or of a caustic stick to remove a wart from the skin. The intention behind such local applications is to restrict the activity of that drug to the point of application.

There is some danger in thinking of drugs in this static way for, although most drugs do not penetrate the unbroken skin, this is not universally true. However, many potentially toxic drugs may be applied topically to the skin without the worry of them causing general unwanted effects throughout the body. A good example of this are the potent synthetic corticosteroids, which have revolutionized the treatment of many skin diseases. Corticosteroid creams and ointments when applied locally to skin disorders will provide relief in properly selected cases. Some of the steroid drug may be absorbed into the body but fortunately the plasma levels so obtained are usually insufficient to produce systemic effects. Of course, if the skin is broken then drugs can be quickly absorbed from such damaged surfaces. In a child with extensive eczema there could be significant absorption of the applied steroid. An infant's skin is more permeable and in them steroids penetrate more completely.

The mucous membranes of the oral cavity differ from the skin in that they provide excellent surfaces for the *absorption* of a wide variety of substances. Indeed absorption may be very rapid and this fact has not always been utilized to advantage in pharmacy. Nevertheless, mucous absorption (see below) is made use of (e.g. sublingual glyceryl trinitrate for angina) as one of the enteral, systemic routes. What must be made clear is that when a drug is applied to the mucous membranes with the intention of producing a local effect, it may not only produce a local action but may also be rapidly absorbed (e.g. xylodase paste).

SYSTEMIC ADMINISTRATION

When a drug is given with the intention of being absorbed it is said to have been administered systemically. The systemic routes can conveniently be classified (see Chapter 1) as (a) enteral; and (b) parenteral.

Enteral routes

By these oral and rectal routes a drug is placed directly into the gastro-intestinal tract from where absorption occurs.

Oral route

This is probably the safest, most convenient, and economical method of administering drugs systemically. Drugs given by mouth are, for the most part, absorbed from the small intestine but alcohol is appreciably absorbed through the stomach—almost an unique substance. The ways of drug absorption have been discussed in Chapter 1. The oral route is probably the safest way because, if the patient is allergic to the drug, the reaction is likely to be less severe if administration is by this route than by some other routes. This does not imply that this route is absolutely safe; drugs given orally can produce some very severe reactions. However, it is a more convenient method for obvious reasons and much more economical, for patients can always take the dose themselves, and tablets and capsules are much less costly than an injection, which often has to be given by a nurse or doctor.

There are several disadvantages to the oral ingestion of drugs:

1. Irritant drugs cannot always be given by mouth for they may cause sickness, e.g. large doses (over 1.5 g) of erythromycin will hardly be tolerated. Often the irritant effect can be mitigated by giving such a drug just before or with food, when absorption may be delayed, e.g. iron preparations on an empty stomach.

2. It is not feasible to give drugs by this route to patients who are vomiting or who are moribund.

3. Many drugs are destroyed by the action of the digestive ferments before they can be absorbed, e.g. benzylpenicillin.

4. Intestinal absorption may, at times, be somewhat irregular due to the influences of other substances in the gastro-intestinal tract. The timing of drug administration in relation to food, for instance, can influence the effectiveness of that drug. There may be enhanced absorption or reduced absorption. Generally speaking oral antibiotics should be given on an empty stomach to avoid impairment of absorption when food is present. On the other hand, oral hypoglycaemic agents should be taken with or just before meals in order that they can exert optimal control of blood sugar.

Rectal route

Drugs are sometimes given via the rectum, in a solid form as suppositories or in a liquid form as enemata. It is a route which can be used if the patient is unable to swallow, and it also avoids the acidity and enzymes of the gastric juice.

Parenteral routes

Parenteral administration is generally chosen when speed or reliability are especially desired.

Injection

In some instances injection of the drug is essential if the drug is to be absorbed in active form, e.g. streptomycin. Absorption is usually more predictable and more rapid than when the oral route is used. Injections have some obvious disadvantages:

(1) It can be difficult for patients to perform the injection themselves.

(2) Strict asepsis must be maintained if infection is to be avoided.

(3) Parenteral administration is usually more costly than oral administration and is generally less safe.

(4) Injections can cause pain whereas swallowing a tablet is usually an innocuous business.

Injections can be made into subcutaneous, intramuscular, and intravenous sites.

Subcutaneous (SC)   The subcutaneous route can only be used for drugs which are not irritant to tissues, otherwise a slough could be caused. It is a common way of giving such drugs as morphine sulphate, adrenaline, and insulin. The volume of most subcutaneous injections is usually 1 ml or less, and should seldom exceed 2 ml. Cutaneous blood flow is much slower than in muscle and so absorption is that much slower. Sustained effects can be obtained from drugs by the implantation of a pellet subcutaneously.

Intramuscular (IM)   The blood supply to muscle is good. Lipid-soluble drugs are able to diffuse rapidly through capillary walls and so absorption from this route is good. Even completely lipid-insoluble drugs can be rapidly absorbed provided their molecular weight is low enough for them to pass through the pores in the capillary membrane.

Strangely enough the intramuscular route can be more dangerous than the intravenous route. If an adverse effect occurs during intravenous injection, then the injection can be immediately discontinued but, if such an effect develops after an intramuscular injection, there is no way in which further absorption can be prevented. Larger volumes can be injected intramuscularly than subcutaneously, and the route is also better for irritant substances.

Occasionally, long acting depot preparations are used by deep intra-muscular injection, e.g. norethisterone ocnanthate. This is an oily preparation providing contraception for 8 weeks.

Intravenous (IV)   The advantages of this route are:

(1) Rapid action: the desired blood concentration is reached with an immediacy not obtained by any other route.

(2) It can be used for drugs which are irritant by intramuscular injection.

Disadvantages are:

(1) Once introduced, the drug cannot be recalled.

(2) Intravenous injections tend to produce more immediate unfavourable reactions.

(3) If injected rapidly a too high concentration of the drug is readily obtained.

(4) The chance of getting into an artery instead of a vein is a possibility.

Other routes of administration include (a) buccal and sublingual; (b) inhalation.

Buccal and sublingual

This enteral route is used infrequently but, as explained in Chapter 1, is useful in the case of a drug which has pronounced 'first-pass' hepatic metabolism. For example, glyceryl trinitrate is of proven use in an angina attack but if swallowed it is likely to be totally ineffective as its first-pass metabolism approaches 100 per cent. So it is used by sublingual administration, when there is no such effect.

Inhalation

Inhalant anaesthetics are the best example of this route of administration and are discussed in Chapter 8.

Aerosol inhalation has been used extensively in the treatment of obstructive airway disease, such as asthma. Inhalation is via the mouth; absorption will occur in the small bronchioles. An example is the use of disodium cromoglycate for inhalation via a 'Spinhaler'.

Other, less common sites of parenteral administration include intrathecal injection. Antimicrobials are sometimes given by this route in meningeal infections in order to by-pass the blood–brain barrier.

3

Prescribing and the law

THE dental surgeon does not prescribe a wide variety of drugs, but he must have knowledge of the regulations that govern prescribing. At one time pharmacists made up elaborate prescriptions to the order of the doctor; today most drugs are conveniently prepared in various forms (tablets, capsules, etc.). Drugs have chemical names, official/approved names, and proprietary names—the brand names provided by a manufacturer. Wherever possible it is sensible to use the official name rather than the proprietary name. If the proprietary name is used, then the pharmacist must supply that particular brand. If the official name is used, then the pharmacist is able to dispense whichever brand is available. After all, there may be many proprietary names and it would be impossible for any pharmacist to stock all of them. The official name is spelt with a small initial letter, and the proprietary name with an initial capital e.g. erythromycin (Erythrocin, Erycen, Erythroped).

Prescribing is governed by a number of regulations made under the Medicines Act of 1968 and the Misuse of Drugs Act of 1971.

THE MEDICINES ACT 1968

This Act deals with the manufacture, distribution, and importation of medicines for human use and of medicines for administration to animals. It also deals with things like the advertising and promotion of drugs, the registration of pharmacies, homeopathic medicines, containers and packages for drugs, labelling regulations, pharmacopoeias, formularies, and much else.

The Medicines Act is an enabling Act that allows, or enables, the appropriate Ministers (Health Ministers) to make orders or regulations interpreting the spirit of the Act in practical terms. The Health Ministers are advised by The Medicines Commission, which is a body appointed to advise them on matters related to medicines. The orders that are promulgated from time to time to interpret the meaning of the Act are known as Statutory Instruments (SI).

The Medicines Act is intended to ensure the safety, quality, and efficacy of medicines to be prescribed. The products subject to the Act are those which fall within the definition of a medicinal product, together with certain other articles and substances incorporated in an animal feeding stuff for a medicinal purpose, or brought within the licensing provision by statutory orders under the Act.

A basic principle of the Act is that it only applies when substances are used as medicinal products or as ingredients of medicinal products. A medicinal product is defined as a substance or article sold or supplied for administration to human beings or animals for a medicinal purpose, or as an ingredient for use in a preparation in a pharmacy or in a hospital, or by a practitioner, or in the course of a retail herbal remedy business.

There are three classes of medicinal products:

1. *General Sales List (GSL) Medicines*   This is really a list of substances that can be sold or supplied other than under the direction of a pharmacist. This list includes such things as aspirin, paracetamol, liquid paraffin, honeysuckle flowers, rock water, rose water, and much else. Such substances do not have to be sold in a pharmacy, although there may be a limit on the quantity supplied if sold other than in a pharmacy.

2. *Prescription Only Medicines (POM)*   These are medicinal products that can only be sold or supplied from pharmacies in accordance with a prescription given by an appropriate practitioner. For the purposes of the Act, a dental surgeon is regarded as an 'appropriate practitioner', as is a doctor and veterinary surgeon. The order that specifies such medicines includes things like lignocaine, antimicrobials, psychotropic drugs, and many other substances.

3. *Pharmacy Medicines (P)*   There is a host of substances, ill-defined, which are called pharmacy medicines. These are medicinal products that are not listed as General Sales List Medicines or as Prescription Only Medicines. These are substances which can be sold over the counter to the general public without prescription but which have to be sold from a pharmacy and with the pharmacist present at the time of the sale.

The prescription for a Prescription Only Medicine

This has to follow certain rules, for example:

(1) It must be written in indelible ink, or be typewritten.

(2) It must contain the following particulars:

    (i) the address and usual signature of the practitioner giving it

    (ii) the appropriate date on which it was signed by the practitioner giving it

    (iii) such particulars as indicate whether the practitioner giving it is a dentist, a doctor, or a veterinary surgeon

    (iv) where the practitioner is a dentist or a doctor, the name, address, and the age (if under 12) of the person for whose treatment it is given.

(3) The prescription shall not be dispensed later than 6 months after the appropriate date.

The form of the prescription

Prescriptions should be written clearly in English. There are a number of abbreviations that have commonly been used and may still be used—for example,

IM(i.m.) = intramuscular injection; IV (i.v.) = intravenous injection; SC (s.c.) = subcutaneous injection. Many other abbreviations are best discarded— such as o.m. = every morning; o.n. = every night; t.d.s. = three times a day; q.d.s. = four times a day. Multiplicity of abbreviations leads to confusion and error.

Doses of drugs are to be found in official books of reference, such as the *Dental Practitioners' Formulary* (DPF). The recommendations contained in these guides are not binding on the prescriber but are obviously sensible indications based on experience and deliberation. A prescription is the authority for a pharmacist to supply specified drugs to any particular patient. A sample of a completed prescription is shown in Fig. 3.1.

The general form of the prescription should be clear from the sample provided. The main body of the prescription refers to the actual drugs to be prescribed, in this instance erythromycin. The name and strength of the drug is first indicated (e.g. erythromycin tablets 250 mg), and this is followed by the amount of the

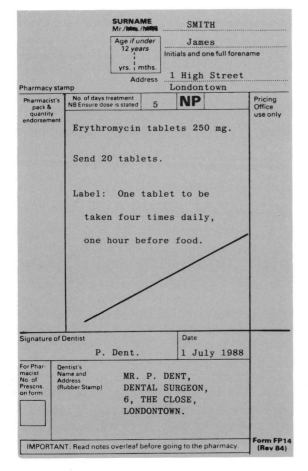

Fig. 3.1. Prescription writing. Layout for a prescription only medicine (POM).

supplied (e.g. 20 tablets). This information is immediately followed by instructions to the pharmacist as to what information is to be written on the labelled medicine and, on the prescription form, follows the word 'Label'. Such directions should be written in English without abbreviation and it is of the utmost importance that these instructions are clear. There must be no possibility of confusion on the part of the dispenser, for it is these instructions that are transcribed by the dispenser to the label on the package to be received by the patient. A phrase like 'as directed' should never appear as this is far too vague and open to misinterpretation.

It is not always necessary to give the strength of the drug to be supplied, prescribing can be by 'title'. Drugs that are of fixed composition and are included in the *British National Formulary* (BNF) or the *Dental Practitioners' Formulary* (DPF) may be prescribed by title. For example, instead of writing penicillin V tablets, 250 mg, it is in order to write penicillin V tablets DPF. Here the amount in each tablet is not specified because the inclusion of the abbreviation DPF indicates a standard preparation. Prescriptions for other and non-standard preparations must be written out in full.

Although the dental surgeon may issue a prescription for such drugs, he may wish to keep some in his surgery for supply to the patients as needed. The dental surgeon is a person who is able to purchase such medicines. In this case, the seller, i.e. the chemist, has to keep a record of supply of Prescription Only Medicines (POM) in his Prescription Only Register. The following details are required:

(1) the date on which the Prescription Only Medicine was sold or supplied

(2) the name, quantity, and pharmaceutical form and strength of the medicine

(3) the name and address, trade, business, or profession of the person to whom the medicine is sold or supplied.

No entry is required in the Prescription Only Register where the drug is a 'controlled drug' (see Misuse of Drugs Act below) as a separate entry has then to be made in another register.

The dental practitioner is able to prescribe drugs listed in the *Dental Practitioners' Formulary* as a charge to the Health Service. For this purpose Form F.P.14 is used in England and Wales, and Form E.C.14 in Scotland. Prescribing is not limited to those drugs listed in the *Formulary* but if a drug is prescribed which is not so listed it will have to be prescribed privately. A prescription must be signed by the prescribing practitioner and an assistant must also add the name of the practitioner by whom he or she is employed.

SOME FACTORS INFLUENCING PRESCRIBING

Age

The dose of a drug should bear some relationship to body weight. The reaction to drugs is markedly different in children, especially in the new born, to that of adults. In the very early days of life there is limited renal filtration and detoxification of drugs is inadequate. Although doses for children based on body weight or body surface area are to be preferred, an age-related dosage can be used when prescribing drugs with a high therapeutic index (see Chapter 1).

Age	Percentage of adult dose
Birth	12–13
1 year	25
3 years	33
7 years	50
10 years	60
14 years and over	Adult dose

Dosage for the in-between years can be adjusted accordingly. An important point to remember is that drugs should not be prescribed in liquid preparations containing sucrose, particularly if this is to be over a long period. Clearly the presence of sucrose will encourage dental caries.

The elderly also present a problem for the prescriber. In old age many factors may be changed, for instance the speed of absorption of drugs may be altered, and so may the metabolism and excretion. These were explained in Chapter 1 but bear repetition here. Of especial importance is the decrease in renal clearance which occurs from mid-life onwards. This will invariably increase the concentration of the drug in the body because of the reduction in the rate of elimination. At the same time the liver may not be so efficient in metabolizing drugs as it is in earlier life. The *British National Formulary* suggests that 'when prescribing drugs in the elderly, it is a sensible policy to limit the range of drugs used to a minimum' and that 'it is good practice to initiate treatment in aged patients with doses of little more than half that recommended for younger subjects'.

Prescribing in pregnancy and during breast-feeding

Care must be exercised in prescribing drugs to the pregnant patient because of the possibility of fetal damage. In fact, it is better not to prescribe drugs to the pregnant patient at all unless this is absolutely imperative, and new drugs should be viewed with extreme caution. This subject is extensively reviewed in the combined *National Formulary*, which should be possessed by all dental practitioners. Prescribing during breast-feeding is also reviewed in the combined *Formulary*.

The letters NP appear on National Health Service prescription forms. NP (*nomen proprium*) means that the drug(s) listed in the prescription will be named on the label automatically. This is invaluable in that it makes for ready identification of the drug(s). If, for any reason, the prescriber does not want the drugs so labelled, then the NP must be crossed out.

Prescribing in renal disease

Some drugs should be avoided when the patient has reduced renal function, whilst others should be prescribed at reduced dosage (Table 3.1). In the presence of renal impairment a drug, or its metabolites, may not be excreted and the accumulation of the drug may produce a toxic effect.

Table 3.1. Drugs in the DPF to be avoided or used with caution in renal impairment

Drugs	Dosage recommendations	Comments
Central nervous system		
Anti-inflammatory analgesics	Avoid if possible	Fluid retention and deterioration in renal function
Aspirin	Avoid	As above. Also increased risk of gastro-intestinal bleeding
Diflunisal	Avoid	Excreted by kidney
Hypnotics and anxiolytics	Start with small doses	Increased cerebral sensitivity
Narcotic analgesics		
Codeine, dihydrocodeine	Avoid	Increased and prolonged effect
Pethidine	Avoid	Increased CNS toxicity
Infections		
Acyclovir	Reduce dose	May produce transient increase in plasma urea
Amphotericin	Use only if no alternative	Nephrotoxic
Cephalosporins		
Cephalexin	Max. 500 mg daily when GFR<10	
Cephradine	Reduce dose	
Co-trimoxazole	Max. 960 mg daily when GFR<10	Rashes and blood disorders
Lincomycin	Use clindamycin instead	
Penicillins		
Amoxycillin	Reduce dose	Rashes more common
Ampicillin	Reduce dose	Rashes more common
Benzylpenicillin	Max. 6 g daily when GFR<10	Neurotoxicity
Tetracyclines (except doxycyline and minocycline)	Avoid	Anti-anabolic effect, increased plasma urea, further deterioration in renal function

Source: Dental Practitioners' Formulary 1986–8. (Published by kind permission of The Pharmaceutical Society of Great Britain.)

Prescribing in liver disease

Many factors may alter the patient's response to drugs in liver disease. Although metabolism by the liver is probably the principal route whereby drugs are metabolized (see Chapter 1), liver disease has to be very severe before significant effects are produced on drug metabolism. Prothrombin and fibrinogen are formed in the liver and, in the presence of liver disease, there may be reduced synthesis of such clotting factors, which may lead to overactivity of oral anticoagulants such as warfarin. Furthermore, some drugs are hepatotoxic, and this may be dose-related or idiosyncratic. Drugs that should be used with caution or avoided in liver disease, and which are drugs listed in the DPF, include anti-inflammatory analgesics (e.g. aspirin, paracetamol), opioid analgesics, psychotropic drugs, and antimicrobials such as clindamycin, metronidazole, and i.v. tetracyclines.

Cardiovascular disease

The problems associated with the use of vasoconstrictors in cardiovascular disease will be dealt with elsewhere (see Chapter 7).

STANDARD REFERENCE BOOKS AND DATA SHEETS

The Dental Practioners' Formulary (DPF)

This is perhaps the most useful book of reference for the dental surgeon. It is revised every 2 years and comes out as a supplement to the *British National Formulary*, which is itself issued every 6 months. The *Dental Practitioners' Formulary* is issued free to all practising dentists and lists all those preparations that the dental surgeon can prescribe as a charge to the Health Service. Information is provided on each drug listed, on adverse effects of drugs used in dentistry, and on medical problems.

Dental surgeons are not limited in their prescribing to those drugs listed in the *Formulary*—they can prescribe other drugs provided that they observe the appropriate regulations. The patient will have to bear the full cost of the prescription. The hospital dental surgeon is not limited to the DPF in NHS prescribing.

The British National Formulary (BNF)

This is an index of preparations in common use in medicine. It contains useful information on the actions and adverse effects of important drugs. It is a useful publication for the dental practitioner because identification of a drug that the patient is taking on medical prescription, and details about that drug, provide information about the nature of the disease from which the patient is suffering.

MIMS (Monthly Index of Medical Specialties)

A quote from the cover of MIMS (July 1988) reads: 'MIMS is designed as a reference and prescribing guide for doctors in general practice and lists proprietary preparations which may be prescribed or recommended. The inclusion of products in the index does not necessarily mean that they are available at NHS expense.'

MIMS is a useful reference booklet because of its monthly revision. It is sent free of charge to all general medical practitioners, heads of hospital pharmacy departments, and on rotation to selected doctors and consultants in the UK. It is not supplied free of charge to dental practitioners and all payments and enquiries about subscriptions should be addressed to: MIMS Subscriptions, 12–14 Ansdell Street, London, W8 5TR.

Data sheets

Before an advertisement is forwarded to a practitioner (dental or medical), or any representation made to him about a medicinal product, a data sheet relating to the product must have been provided. A data sheet is simply an information sheet about a drug, which has to conform to certain particulars as regards size, printing, etc. The data sheet must contain the following information about the product:

(1) name of the product
(2) presentation: e.g. a description of appearance and pharmaceutical form of the medicinal product;
(3) uses: the main action of the medicinal product and the purpose for which it is to be recommended in treatments;
(4) dosage and administration; methods and routes of administration must be specified,
(5) contraindications and warnings.

There is other information that must be contained on the sheet, but the above indicates the main categories. The data sheet is produced for each product of a manufacturer and the information contained must be factual and not promotional.

Data Sheet Compendium

Data sheets are prepared by the individual pharmaceutical manufacturers. A *Data Sheet Compendium* is compiled each year and is published by Datapharm Publications Limited in association with the Association of the British Pharmaceutical Industry (ABPI). This joint compendium is prepared other than by persons or organizations concerned with manufacturing medicinal products. The individual data sheets are prepared by the companies concerned and participation in this joint compendium is open to all producing medicinal products for use under medical or dental supervision.

THE MISUSE OF DRUGS ACT 1971

Prior to 1971 drugs that were regarded as subject to abuse were regulated by the Dangerous Drugs Act in particular. The present legislation has tidied up what had become a somewhat confused legislation.

The Misuse of Drugs Act of 1971 and its associated orders control those drugs that are liable to abuse, e.g. morphine, amphetamines, etc. These are described as 'controlled' drugs, whereas at one time they would have been referred to as 'dangerous' drugs.

Under this Act an Advisory Council has been set up to advise the appropriate Minister (in this instance, the Secretary of State for the Home Office) on those drugs that are, or appear likely to be, misused and that may thereby cause a social problem. The Council consists of 20 members representing various interested parties, including dentistry and medicine.

Controlled drugs are classified in the Act as 'Class A drugs', 'Class B drugs', and 'Class C drugs', and this division refers to the penalties for misuse awarded under the Act. Penalties for illegal use or possession of Class A drugs tend to be more severe than for the other two classes. Class A drugs (over 100 preparations) include substances such as cocaine, diamorphine, lysergide, methadone, opium, pethidine. Class B drugs include oral amphetamines, barbiturates, cannabis, codeine, and pentazocine, for example. Class C drugs include most benzodiazepines.

The Misuse of Drugs Regulations, which interpret the spirit of the Act, allow certain persons or classes of persons (e.g. dentists) to possess, supply, prescribe, or administer controlled drugs in the *practice of their profession*. They also apply selective controls in relation to record-keeping, custody of drugs, and prescription writing. The regulations to the Act were originally stated in 1973 and have been revised in 1985, Statutory Instrument No. 2066. These regulations include five schedules listing different categories of drugs to which varying requirements as to supply, prescribing, and record-keeping apply. A further schedule, Schedule 6, is simply a form of register indicating details to be kept when drugs listed under Schedules 1 and 2 are received or supplied (see p. 61 later).

Schedule 1 includes such drugs as cannabis, lysergide, and mescaline. A licence from the Home Secretary is required to possess, supply, administer, or cause to be administered, any drugs specified in this Schedule.

Schedule 2 lists those drugs that are used medicinally and are subject to the strictest controls. The list includes amphetamine, cocaine, codeine, dihydrocodeine, dextropropoxyphene, methadone, morphine, pethidine, and many others.

Unless exempted in Schedule 5, these drugs are subject to the full control exercised by the regulations regarding prescriptions, safe custody, and record-keeping.

Schedule 3   includes the barbiturates and pentazocine. These drugs must fulfil the special prescription requirements for controlled drugs, but not the special requirements for safe custody. The Schedule 6 type of register need not be kept for drugs so listed.

Schedule 4   includes over 30 benzodiazepines, which are not subject to the strict controls regarding prescriptions, safe custody, or record-keeping indicated for drugs in the previous schedules. The benzodiazepines are Prescription Only Medicines (POM) and the form of prescription is as indicated on p. 53.

Schedule 5   includes preparations that, because of their strength, are exempt from nearly all the Controlled Drug requirements. The substances so exempt are not preparations for injection. Included in this list are certain preparations of dihydrocodeine or codeine. For instance, dihydrocodeine tartrate 30 mg tablet, because of the strength used, is classed simply as a Prescription Only Medicine (POM), whereas dihydrocodeine for injection is a Schedule 2 drug and therefore strictly controlled. Similarly, codeine, as contained in Codis tablets, has even less control than does dihydrocodeine tartrate tablets, being classified as a Pharmacy Medicine (P). On the other hand, codeine phosphate injection would come under the strict regulations governing Schedule 2 drugs.

A doctor or dentist may administer to a patient any drug specified in Schedule 2, 3, or 4. Furthermore, the dentist may direct another person, other than a doctor or a dentist, to administer such a drug to a patient under his/her care. Any person may administer to another any drug specified in Schedule 5.

The form of the prescription for a Schedule 2 or 3 drug

A prescription containing a controlled drug listed in Schedule 2 or 3, and issued by a dentist or doctor, must be written in ink or otherwise indelible material. Its layout is shown in Fig. 3.2. The whole of the prescription must be in the handwriting of the prescriber and it must be signed by him/her with his/her usual signature and be dated by him/her. Except in the case of a NHS prescription, the address of the person issuing the prescription must be given, but this need not be in handwriting. To minimize the possibility of forgery or alteration of the prescription, the following details should be in the dentist's or doctor's own handwriting:

(1) the name and address of the person for whose treatment the prescription is issued;

(2) the dose to be taken and, in the case of a prescription that is a preparation, the form, e.g. tablet, capsule, etc.;

(3) the total quantity of the drug to be supplied must be stated in both words and figures;

Schedule 6

THE MISUSE OF DRUGS REGULATIONS 1985

'FORM OF REGISTER'

PART 1
Entries to be made in case of obtaining

Date on which supply received	NAME ADDRESS of person or firm from whom obtained	Amount obtained	Form in which obtained

PART 2
Entries to be made in case of supply

Date on which the transaction was effected	NAME ADDRESS of person or firm supplied	Particulars as to licence or authority of person or firm supplied to be in possession	Amount supplied	Form in which supplied

Fig. **3.2.** Prescription writing.
Layout for a controlled drug
(CD).

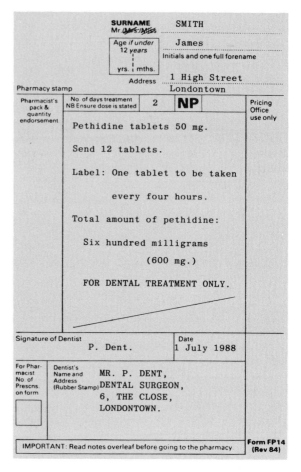

(4) a dental prescription for Schedule 2 or 3 drugs must be endorsed with the
    words 'for dental treatment only'.

It must be seen that the requirement of providing a prescription in the
handwriting of the prescriber, and the necessity of writing the total quantity of
the drug in both words and figures, is to prevent alterations of the prescription.
This elaboration is only required for drugs listed in Schedules 1, 2, and 3, and
even here there is some modification in that phenobarbitone is exempt from the
handwriting requirement, other than for the prescriber's usual signature.

A dental surgeon working in a general hospital may wish to instruct staff to
administer a fully controlled drug to a patient under his/her care. Any such drug
prescribed to an in-patient in a NHS hospital must conform to standard
prescribing procedures of the ward.

Requisition of controlled drugs

In order to obtain supplies of such drugs for use in practice, the practitioner must provide the supplier (pharmacist) with a signed requisition form giving the practitioner's name, address, profession or occupation, the purpose for which the drug is required, and the total quantity of the drug to be supplied.

The supplier must be satisfied that the signature on the requisition form is genuine and that the signatory is engaged in the profession or occupation stated.

Registers for controlled drugs (Schedule 6)

Registers must be kept for all drugs specified in Schedules 1 and 2 of the Regulations. A register must be kept for receipt of drugs and another for the issue of these drugs. The 'Form of Register' is shown on p. 61. The register must be a bound book, loose-leaf books will not do. All entries must be in chronological order giving particulars of every quantity of a drug received and every quantity of a drug supplied, whether by way of administration or otherwise.

Entries must be made on the day the drugs are obtained or supplied and, if this is not possible, then the entries must be made not later than the next day. Entries must be made with some indelible material and must not be erased or changed in any way. If a correction is necessary, then this must be made by means of marginal or footnote, and the date of correction indicated. A separate part of the Register must be used for each substance specified in the Act.

The Registers must be kept on the premises to which they relate, in other words separate Registers must be maintained for each set of premises. The record must be preserved for 2 years from the date of the final entry, and the Registers must be available for scrutiny by appropriate authority when required.

Storage of controlled drugs

A controlled drug must be kept in a locked receptacle, the key of which is in the possession of the dentist.

It will be seen that the acquiring, possession, and storage of Schedule 1 and 2 drugs does pose problems and it is unlikely that many dentists will feel the effort is worthwhile. The use of opioids and like drugs in hospital practice is, of course, another matter.

LIMITED LIST REGULATIONS

From 1 April 1985 the range of drugs available for prescription on the NHS was limited (The 'Selected List Scheme'). The Government had concluded that there were two areas in which action should be taken. Firstly, action concerning simple remedies for the relief of minor ailments and self-limiting complaints which were often bought over the counter by patients, without recourse to the medical practitioner, e.g. antacids, laxatives, analgesics. Secondly, action over the use of benzodiazepines, which had escalated in recent years, very often with expensive proprietary preparations being prescribed rather than generic compounds. The limitation was introduced to deal with these two areas and the categories of drugs involved were listed as:

laxatives
antacids
mild analgesics
cough and cold remedies
vitamins
benzodiazepines

So there came into being what has come to be known as a 'white list' and a 'black list' of drugs. The list of drugs available for the medical practitioner to prescribe under the NHS is the 'white list' and the 'black list' comprises those drugs no longer prescribable under the NHS, as shown above. Doctors and pharmacists were provided with a complete list of drugs not prescribable as from 1 July 1986. This list is amended from time to time.

FURTHER READING

Anon. (1978). The Medicines Act 1968 and other legislation. *British Dental Journal,* **145,** 174–7.

Duxbury, A. J., Leach, F. N., and Duxbury, J. T. (1984). Common prescribing problems. *Dental Update,* **11,** 101–10.

Dental Practitioners' Formulary 1986–8. British Dental Association, the British Medical Association and the Pharmaceutical Society of Great Britain.

Medicines Act, 1968. HMSO, London.

Misuse of Drugs Act, 1971. HMSO, London.

The Misuse of Drugs Regulations, 1985. Statutory Instrument 1985 No. 2066. HMSO, London.

The Medicines (General Sale List) Order, 1977. Statutory Instrument 1977 No. 2129. HMSO, London.

The Medicines (Prescription Only) Order, 1977. Statutory Instrument 1977 No. 2127. HMSO, London.

The Medicines (Prescription Only) Amendment Order, 1978. Statutory Instrument 1978 No. 189. HMSO, London.

PART I

DRUGS USED IN DENTISTRY

4

Pharmacology of inflammation

INFLAMMATION is a complex process that can be defined as 'the reaction of the vascular and supporting elements of a tissue to injury, and results in the formation of a protein-rich exudate, provided the injury has not been so severe as to destroy the area' (Walter and Israel 1980).

The clinical features that accompany inflammation have been known since antiquity; they include swelling (tumor), redness (rubor), hotness (calor), and pain (dolor). Inflammation is under the control of a variety of endogenous biochemical mediators produced at or near the site of injury. The biochemical and pharmacological properties of these mediators will be considered in this chapter, together with drugs that can affect the inflammatory response.

CHEMICAL MEDIATORS OF INFLAMMATION

Histamine

This vasocative amine is found in most tissues of the body, but the major source is in the granules of mast cells. Histamine is formed by the decarboxylation of the amino acid, histidine. Trauma, either mechanical or chemical, causes the release of histamine from the mast cells into the extracellular fluid. Once released, histamine is rapidly metabolized by one of two enzyme systems (histamine-N-methyltransferase and diamine oxidase) to metabolites with little or no pharmacological activity (Fig. 4.1).

Pharmacological properties

Many of the properties of histamine are related to its action on smooth muscles, including relaxation of the vascular smooth muscle and contraction of the bronchi and gut wall. It is also a very potent stimulus to secretion of the exocrine glands, particularly those in the gastric mucosa. Histamine also has a direct effect on free nerve endings and is important in the production of pain and itch.

H_1 and H_2-receptors

There are two types of histamine receptors termed H_1 and H_2. H_1-receptors are

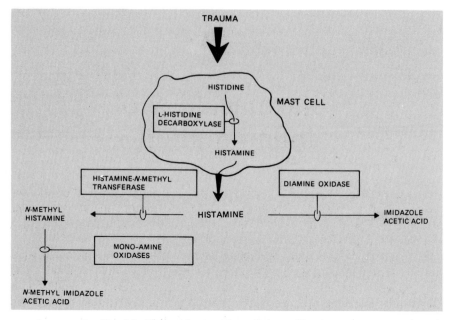

Fig. 4.1. The synthesis and metabolism of histamine.

primarily related to smooth muscle activity, i.e. vasodilatation and bronchial constriction (Ash and Schild 1966). H_2-receptors are mainly involved with the stimulation of gastric secretion (Black et al. 1972).

Cardiovascular effects

Histamine causes dilation of the small blood vessels, an effect mediated principally by the H_1-receptor, that leads to flushing, a lowered peripheral resistance, and a drop in blood pressure. The vasodilatation is accompanied by an increase in capillary permeability that results in oedema. The effect of histamine on the vasculature is best demonstrated by the 'triple response' described by Lewis and Grant in 1924.

The effect of histamine on the heart is variable: the response depends, in part, upon concentration, the simultaneous release of catecholamines, or the reduction in blood pressure causing stimulation of the baroreceptor reflex. Cardiac effects include an increase in heart rate and force of contraction, which result in an increase in cardiac output. Higher concentrations of histamine may cause arrhythmias due to slowing of the A-V conduction.

Smooth muscles

The bronchial muscles are the most important group of smooth muscles affected by histamine. Bronchoconstriction results from activation of the H_1-receptor. Patients who suffer from asthma are particularly sensitive to the action of histamine on the bronchial musculature. However, antihistamines are of no value in the treatment of asthma because histamine is not the principal causative agent in this condition.

Gastric secretion

The gastric secretory cells are very sensitive to the action of histamine, with even low concentrations causing a copious secretion of the gastric juices. This effect is mediated by the H_2-receptor.

Pain and itch

Histamine directly stimulates free nerve endings, which accounts for its ability to produce pain and itch when injected into the skin. A subcutaneous injection of histamine causes a sharp pain of short duration, similar to a wasp's sting. When injected into the more superficial layers of the skin, histamine causes itching.

Anaphylaxis and allergy

The release of histamine from mast cells plays a crucial role in both anaphylactic and allergic reactions. The active release is due to an antigen combining with a specific antibody attached to the surface of the mast cell. The combination of antigen with antibody causes the extrusion of histamine from the secretory granules in the mast cells (degranulation). Histamine release is accompanied by the liberation of many other endogenous substances (see below) that contribute to the varied responses seen in such reactions.

Many substances can act as antigens and cause anaphylactic or allergic reactions. Common examples include penicillin, animal fur, and pollen. Anaphylactic reactions can be fatal; their management is discussed in Chapter 21.

The eicosanoids

The term eicosanoids has been used to denote the metabolites of certain 20-carbon polyunsaturated fatty acids, mainly arachidonic acid. These precursors can be converted into a range of compounds that have a variety of effects as regulators and mediators of the functions of various cells.

A considerable number of different products of arachidonic-acid metabolism have been identified, but they can all be conveniently divided into two main groups on the basis that they are ultimately derived from the action of one of two enzymes (cyclo-oxygenase or lipoxygenase enzyme systems) on arachidonic acid. Thus they may all be considered as either cyclo-oxygenase products or lipoxygenase products.

Cyclo-oxygenase products can be further subdivided into three groups, the prostaglandins, the thromboxanes, and prostacyclin. Lipoxygenase products consist mainly of the leukotrienes and various compounds based on eicosatetrae-noic acid. The synthesis of the eicosanoids is illustrated in Fig. 4.2.

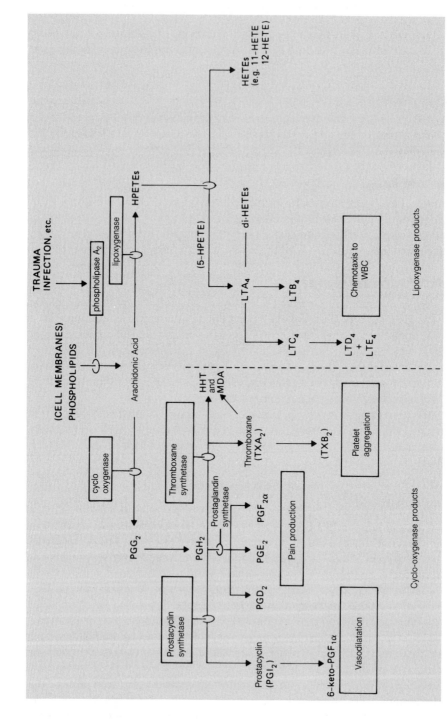

Fig. 4.2. The metabolic pathways of arachidonic acid and the synthesis of the eicosanoids. (WBC = white blood cells; other abbreviations, see text.)

Arachidonic acid

This is a 20-carbon polyunsaturated fatty acid. It has been suggested that there are two sources, the metabolic pool and the cell membrane pool (Crawford 1983). The endogenous synthesis of arachidonic acid appears to be from the metabolic pool by metabolism of dietary linoleic acid, whereas stimulated synthesis (e.g. from trauma) comes from the cell membrane pool. The membrane pool would seem to be the major source of the eicosanoid precursor in inflammation.

In most cells and tissues it is thought that the phosphatide fraction constitutes the major source of arachidonic acid (Blackwell and Flower 1983), and therefore the first step in eicosanoid synthesis is the liberation of arachidonic acid from that fraction. Arachidonic acid is liberated from cell membrane phospholipids (phosphate fraction) by the action of a group of enzymes collectively known as the phospholipases. In particular, the action of phospholipase A_2 is responsible for the bulk of arachidonic-acid synthesis.

Cyclo-oxygenase products

The next step in the formation of cyclo-oxygenase products is the action of the enzyme cyclo-oxygenase on free arachidonic acid. This action results in the insertion of two oxygen molecules into the fatty-acid carbon chain to form PGG_2, which is rapidly transformed by the peroxidase-like activity of cyclo-oxygenase into the hydroxyperoxide, PGH_2 (Bakhle 1983). Following this, and depending on the particular cell and circumstances involved, one or more of the three main groups mentioned earlier may be formed—the prostaglandins, thromboxane, or prostacyclin.

Prostaglandins

These were first identified in 1930, but it was not until the 1960s that their structure and function were elucidated. Prostaglandins occur in every tissue and body fluid; their pharmacological properties are listed later.

Thromboxane and prostacyclin

As we have seen, cyclo-oxygenase activity converts arachidonic acid to an intermediate compound, PGH_2. Further enzyme activity (thromboxane and prostacyclin synthetase) on PGH_2 results in the formation of thromboxane (TXA_2) and prostacyclin (PGI_2). The main synthesis of thromboxane occurs in platelets, whereas prostacyclin is synthesized in vessel walls. Thromboxane A_2 plays an important role in platelet aggregation. Prostacyclin is a potent vasodilator and acts as an antagonist of platelet aggregation. It would appear that thromboxane A_2 and prostacyclin represent biologically opposite poles of the mechanism for regulating the platelet–vessel wall interaction and the formation of a haemostatic plug (Moncada and Vane 1978). Both thromboxane A_2 and prostacyclin are unstable with very short half-lives. Thromboxane A_2 is broken down to thromboxane B_2 whereas prostacyclin is further metabolized to 6-keto-PGF$_1$ (Fig. 4.2). Further details of the mechanisms of haemostasis are given in Chapter 12.

Lipoxygenase products (leukotrienes)

The pathways resulting in the synthesis of lipoxygenase products have only recently been elucidated (Samuelsson 1981). The action of the lipoxygenase enzyme system on arachidonic acid forms a range of hydroperoxyeicosatetrae-noic acids (HPETEs), which may then be reduced to form the corresponding hydroxyeicosatetraenoic acids (HETEs). The leukotrienes are derived from 5-lipoxygenase acting on arachidonic acid to form 5-HPETE, which may then be reduced to 5-HETE or rearranged to form LTA$_4$ (Taylor and Morris 1983). The LTA$_4$ can be hydrolysed enzymatically to produce LTB$_4$, or non-enzymatically to produce various di-HETEs. Alternatively, LTA$_4$ may undergo nucleophillic attack by glutathione to produce LTC$_4$ from which LTD$_4$ and LTE$_4$ are generated.

The role of the leukotrienes in inflammation has not been fully elucidated. Lipoxygenase products have potent chemotactic properties and are probably involved in the process of cellular infiltration that accompanies inflammation.

Pharmacological properties of prostaglandins

Cardiovascular system

The prostaglandins are potent vasodilators and hence cause a fall in blood pressure (Robinson et al. 1973). Cardiac output is increased by prostaglandins E and F.

Smooth muscles

Prostaglandins of the F series contract bronchial muscles, whereas prostaglan-dins of the E series relax them (Cuthbert 1973). An intravenous infusion of PGE$_2$ or PGF$_{2\alpha}$ causes severe contractions of the uterus.

Inflammation and immune response

Prostaglandins play an important role in the inflammatory process and the immune response (Larsen and Henson 1983). Prostaglandins of the E series cause a long-lasting vasodilatation accompanied by an increase in vascular permeabil-ity. PGE$_1$ appears to regulate the function of the B-lymphocyte and the activity of the T-lymphocyte by inhibiting the production and release of lymphokines from sensitized T-cells (Goldyne 1977).

Pain

Prostaglandins contribute to the pain that often accompanies inflammation, either by directly stimulating sensory nerve endings or by sensitizing the nerve endings to other stimuli. They also produce pain when given either intravenously or intramuscularly (Vane 1976). The intradermal administration of histamine, bradykinin (see below), and PGE$_2$ produces pain of short duration, but hyperalgesia is only produced by PGE_2 (Ferreira 1972). Histamine, bradykinin, or PGE_2, when given singularly via the subcutaneous route, produce slight pain of short duration. However, the effect of the addition of PGE_2 to bradykinin or to histamine is overtly painful, whereas the further addition of bradykinin or histamine is not. In areas already 'sensitized' by prostaglandins, subsequent infusions of bradykinins or histamine cause pain. It would appear that prostaglandins, particularly of the E series, are able to sensitize pain receptors (free nerve endings) to mechanical and chemical stimulation.

Bradykinin

Bradykinin is a polypeptide formed from $alpha_2$-globulins in plasma by a complex series of proteolytic reactions. Trauma, in particular cell damage, causes the release of proteolytic enzymes that act on plasma kininogen to form bradykinin. The half-life of bradykinin is very short (30 s), with the compound being rapidly inactivated by carboxypeptidases (Fig. 4.3).

Pharmacological properties

Bradykinin is a very potent vasodilator and increases capillary permeability leading to oedema. In this respect, bradykinin, on a molar basis, is approximately ten times more active than histamine. The role of bradykinin in pain has been discussed under 'Pain' above.

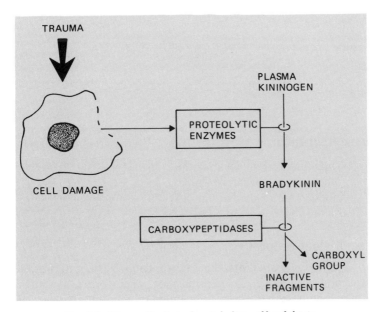

Fig. 4.3. The synthesis and metabolism of bradykinin.

Fig. 4.4. The synthesis and metabolism of 5-hydroxytryptamine (serotonin).

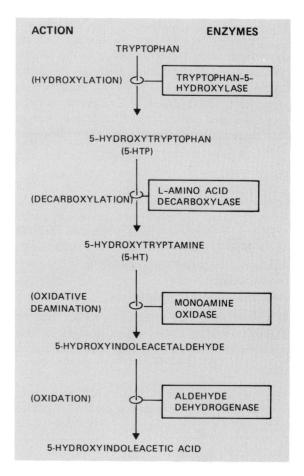

5-Hydroxytryptamine (serotonin)

5-Hydroxytryptamine (5-HT) is an amine formed by the hydroxylation of tryptophan, which is then decarboxylated to form 5-HT. After release, 5-HT is oxidized by monoamine oxidases (Fig. 4.4). The enterochromaffin cells of the gastric mucosa are the main storage site of 5-HT.

Pharmacological properties

The role of 5-HT in inflammation is uncertain and may be insignificant. However, it has a wide and variable range of pharmacological properties that not only vary between species but also in the same individual. An important property of 5-HT is its effect on blood vessels—dilatation of arteries and constriction of veins.

Complement

The complement system consists of a series of proteins that react in a cascade fashion (Fig. 4.5). One stimulus for the cascade reaction is the combination of antigen with antibody on a cell surface (this is known as the 'classical pathway'). An 'alternate' pathway can be triggered by bacterial toxins or large polysaccharides.

Fragments produced during the complement cascade are important in the inflammatory process. Fragments C3a and C5a induce the release of histamine from mast cells which, as described earlier, causes increased capillary permeability. Other components of the complement cascade are chemotactic to white blood cells (C5a, C5b, C567 complex) and enhance phagocytosis (C3b, C5b). Damage to cell membranes, followed by cell lysis, occurs when factors C8 and C9 are activated.

Lymphokines

These are a series of factors, presumably proteins, produced by the sensitized T-lymphocyte and to a lesser extent by the B-lymphocyte. The stimulus for

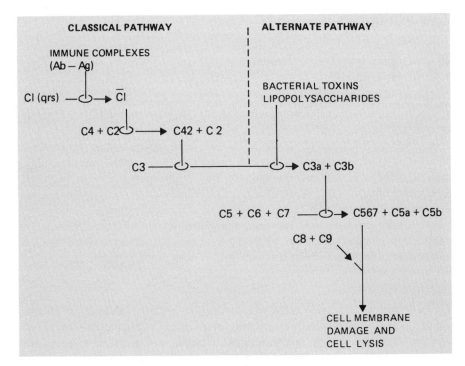

Fig. 4.5. The complement cascase.

production is antigenic challenge. The functions of lymphokines in inflammation are as follows:

(1) chemotactic for macrophages;

(2) macrophage activation;

(3) macrophage inhibition—promotes accumulation of macrophages at the site of inflammation;

(4) chemotactic for other mononuclear white blood cells;

(5) mitogenic for other lymphocytes;

(6) increases vascular permeability;

(7) activates osteoclasts.

ANTIHISTAMINES

These competitively antagonize histamine at the receptor sites: they do not alter the formation or release of histamine from tissues or mast cells. Antihistamines are conveniently classified as H_1- or H_2-receptor blockers.

H_1-blocking agents

These are sometimes referred to as the classical antihistamines and examples are chlorpheniramine and promethazine.

Pharmacological properties

H_1-blockers are competitive antagonists, that is they interact with H_1-receptors on cell membranes, which results in a decrease in the availability of these receptors for the actions of histamine. Hence, H_1-blockers will antagonize the action of histamine on smooth muscles, vasodilatation, capillary permeability, and the flare and itch components of the 'triple response'. Furthermore, H_1-blockers have central effects, including sedation and the reduction of nausea and vomiting, that are not related to the antagonism of histamine.

H_1-blockers are well-absorbed from the gastro-intestinal tract. Therapeutic effects can be observed within 15 to 30 minutes after dosage. The drugs are widely distributed throughout the body and broken down in the liver.

Therapeutic uses

H_1-blockers are widely used in the treatment (prevention) of a variety of allergic conditions, for example rhinitis, hay fever, and certain allergic dermatoses such as acute urticaria. Topical application of H_1-blockers is useful in relieving the itching associated with insect bites, but such application is not without problems (see below). H_1-blockers are widely used in common cold remedies—usually combined with a decongestant (e.g. Actifed). However, there is no evidence to suggest that H_1-blockers prevent or shorten the duration of the common cold.

The central effects of H_1-blockers make them useful in the prophylaxis of motion sickness and as a sedative, especially in children.

H_1-blockers have no effect on bronchospasm or the severe hypotension associated with anaphylactic shock. Similarly, this group of drugs is of no value in the treatment of asthma.

Unwanted effects

Sedation is the major unwanted effect associated with the H_1-blockers, but the degree of sedation does vary between different preparations, and indeed some may cause stimulation (e.g. Thephorin). Alcohol should be avoided whilst taking H_1-blockers as it will enhance the sedative effect. Other unwanted effects include xerostomia (dryness of the mouth) and a variety of gastro-intestinal disturbances. The incidence of these disturbances can be reduced by taking the H_1-blockers with meals.

Topical application of antihistamines

Antihistamine creams and lotions are widely used to relieve itching in skin conditions and after insect bites. However, these preparations are liable to produce a contact dermatitis (Type IV reaction) (see Chapter 21) and their use is contra-indicated. Under these conditions, topical antihistamines act as haptens and probably conjugate with some protein of epidermal origin. If these drugs were to be applied topically in certain oral conditions, a similar sensitization might occur. Such sensitization to antihistamines is not only highly undesirable but may be fatal because at some future time a patient so sensitized might be in urgent need of systemic treatment with antihistamines. If it were known that the patient was hypersensitive to antihistamines, they could not be treated with systemic antihistamine; if this vital fact were not known, treatment with antihistamines would be potentially dangerous.

H_2-blocking agents

These competitively antagonize the action of histamine at the H_2-receptor. The two most widely used H_2-blockers are cimetidine and ranitidine.

Pharmacological properties and therapeutic uses

The most important property of H_2-blockers is their ability to reduce gastric secretion in both volume and hydrogen ion concentration. Hence their main therapeutic use is in the treatment of duodenal ulcers and gastric hypersecretion such as occurs in the Zollinger–Ellison syndrome. Unwanted effects are slight and include headache, dizziness, constipation or diarrhoea, and skin rashes.

Dental applications of antihistamines

Only H_1-blocking agents have any dental applications, and it is rather for their central actions that they are used in dentistry. Promethazine has both sedative and weak atropine-like properties, and is used as a pre-operative sedative, particularly in children. H_1-blockers may be of some value in the treatment of allergic lesions on the face and lips.

Antihistamines have been evaluated in the control of pain, swelling, and other sequelae of oral surgery, but appear to be of little value in this application (Seymour and Walton 1984).

5-HT ANTAGONISTS

The ergot alkaloids are a group of related compounds that are antagonists for 5-HT. Ergotamine is the most widely used of the ergot alkaloids and is an important drug in the relief of migraine. The treatment of migraine is discussed in more detail in Chapter 14.

STEROIDS

Corticosteroids and synthetic steroids have potent anti-inflammatory properties. The general pharmacology and physiology of the steroids is discussed in Chapter 18.

Anti-inflammatory properties

Steroids inhibit many of the processes associated with inflammation. In its early stages they reduce the capillary permeability caused by histamine and bradykinin, which in turn reduces oedema. They also inhibit both bradykinin formation and the migration of white blood cells into the site of inflammation. In its later stages, steroids reduce granulation-tissue formation by inhibiting the proliferation of fibroblasts and blood vessels. There is also evidence that steroids can affect eicosanoid synthesis by inhibiting the conversion of fatty acids to arachidonic acid (see above). It is suggested that steroids induce the formation of an intermediate protein (macrocortin) that inhibits the phospholipase A_2 enzyme system. We have seen that this system acts on cell membrane phospholipids to form arachidonic acid, which in turn serves as a substrate for the precursor of prostaglandins and leukotrienes (Blackwell et al. 1980; Hirata et al. 1980).

When steroids are used to suppress inflammation, such therapy is palliative for the underlying cause of the inflammation still remains. Steroids should not be used where an infection is suspected.

Topical corticosteroid therapy

Such topical application is extensively used in the treatment of most dermatological conditions. However, this use of corticosteroids is not without unwanted effects, the most common of which, atrophy of the skin, can occur as early as three to four weeks after commencement of treatment. Atrophy is especially common on the face where the skin is normally thin. Both epidermis and dermis are affected: in the epidermis there is a reduction in cell size and number, and in the dermis there is decreased fibroblast activity and collagen synthesis. These latter two decreases give rise to a loss of dermal support, which in turn leads to dilatation of small blood vessels and to telangiectasia; the telangiectactic vessels rupture easily and produce ecchymosis.

Absorption of topical corticosteroids may lead to adrenal suppression (see Chapter 18). The extent of suppression is dependent upon the steroid potency, the duration of treatment, the amount used, and the skin area treated. Although isolated cases of severe adrenocortico-suppression have been reported (Miyachi 1982), the suppressive effect of topical steroids on cortisol levels is of little clinical significance with normal usage (Munro and Clift 1973). As a general rule, little adverse effect on cortisol production is likely to occur with the application of up to 50 g weekly for an adult or 15 g weekly for a child of a potent steroid ointment (Dahl 1985).

Allergic contact dermatitis due to topical steroids is very rare and is more commonly due to a constituent of the base (e.g. lanolin).

Use of steroids in dentistry

Oral ulceration and oral mucosal lesions

Steroids are widely used in the treatment of recurrent oral ulceration and other oral mucosal lesions such as erosive lichen planus, erythema multiforme, and pemphigus. Many of these conditions are treated by topical applications and optimal results are achieved when the period of contact between steroid and lesion is maximal. Severe oral ulceration may require systemic steroids. In some instances, injection of a steroid into the lesion may be of benefit. Topical steroid preparations include triamcinolone acetonide 0.1 per cent; hydrocortisone sodium succinate 2.5 mg; betamethasone 17-valerate (topical spray). Intra-lesional steroids are triamcinolone hexacetonide and hydrocortisone acetate. Prednisolone is the most widely used systemic steroid.

Pulpal inflammation

Steroids are often applied over a carious exposure of the dental pulp. One such preparation, Ledermix, contains triamcinolone and a tetracycline (demeclocycline hydrochloride); however, its efficacy is not established.

Temperomandibular-joint pain

Intra-articular injections of hydrocortisone or prednisolone have been shown to be of value in certain inflammatory joint conditions. However, such use can cause deterioration of the articular surface of the joint and it is unwise to repeat the procedure more than twice (Toller 1977).

Bell's palsy

This is a unilateral facial paralysis affecting one or more branches of the facial nerve. It is of unknown aetiology but may accompany a viral infection. Prednisolone is the treatment of choice and therapy must be started within five to six days of onset of the paralysis. It is usual to start off steroid administration with a high dose, tailing this off over 10 days.

Postoperative pain and swelling after dental surgery

There has been much interest in the use of steroids to reduce pain, swelling, and other sequelae after removal of impacted lower third molars and after orthognathic surgery (Lyuk *et al.* 1985). For this, a course of steroids is usually short so unwanted effects are minimized. Methylprednisolone and betamethasone are used for this purpose and, for optimal effect, the steroids are given intramuscularly just before surgery.

Anaphylactic and allergic reactions

The use of steroids in the treatment of anaphylacic and allergic reactions is dealt with in Chapter 21.

REFERENCES

Ash, A. S. F. and Schild, H. O. (1966). Receptors mediating some actions of histamine. *British Journal of Pharmacology,* **27,** 427–39.

Bakhle, Y. S. (1983). Synthesis and catabolism of cyclo-oxygenase products. *British Medical Bulletin,* **39,** 214–18.

Black, J. W., Duncan, W. A. M., Durant, C. J., Ganellin, C. R., and Parsons, E. M. (1972). Definition and antagonism of histamine H_2-receptors. *Nature,* **236,** 385–90.

Blackwell, G. J., Carnuccio, R., Dirosa, M., Flower, R. J., Parente, L., and Persico, P. (1980). Macrocortin: a polypeptide causing the anti-phospholipase effects of glucocorticoids. *Nature,* **287,** 1147–9.

Blackwell, G. J. and Flower, R. J. (1983). Inhibition of Phospholipase. *British Medical Bulletin,* **39,** 260–4.

Crawford, M. A. (1983). Background to essential fatty acids and their prostanoids derivatives. *British Medical Bulletin,* **39,** 210–13.

Cuthbert, M. F. (1973). Prostaglandins and respiratory smooth muscle. In *The prostaglandins: pharmacological and therapeutic advances* (ed. M. F. Cuthbert), pp. 253–86. Lippincott, Philadelphia.

Dahl, M. G. C. (1985). Hazards of topical steroid cream. *Adverse Drug Reactions Bulletin,* **115,** 428–31.

Ferreira, S. H. (1972). Prostaglandins, aspirin-like drugs and analgesia. *Nature New Biology,* **240,** 200–3.

Goldyne, M. E. (1977). Prostaglandins and the modulation of the immune responses. *International Journal of Dermatology,* **16,** 701–12.

Hirata, F., Schiffmann, E., Venkatasubamanian, K., Salomon, D., and Axelrod, J. (1980). A phospholipase A_2 inhibitory protein in rabbit neutrophils induced by glucorticoids. *Proceedings of the National Academy of Sciences U.S.A.,* **77,** 2533–6.

Larsen, G. L. and Henson, P. M. (1983). Mediators of inflammation. *Annual Review of Immunology,* **1,** 335–59

Lewis, T. and Grant, R. T. (1924). Vascular reactions of the skin to injury; the liberation of histamine-like substance to injured skin; the underlying cause of factitious urticaria and of weals produced by burning; and observations upon the nervous control of certain skin reactions. *Heart,* **11,** 209–18.

Luyk, N. H., Anderson, J., and Ward-Booth, P. W. (1985). Corticosteroid therapy and the dental patient. *British Dental Journal,* **159,** 12–17.

Miyachi, Y. (1982). Adrenal axis suppression caused by a small dose of a potent topical corticosteroid. *Archives of Dermatologoly,* **118,** 451–2.

Moncada, S. and Vane, J. R. (1978). Unstable metabolites of arachidonic acid and their role in haemostasis and thrombosis. *British Medical Bulletin,* **34,** 129–36.

Munro, D. D. and Clift, D. C. (1973). Pituitary–adrenal function after prolonged use of topical corticosteroids. *British Journal of Dermatology,* **88,** 381–7.

Robinson, B. F., Collier, J. G., Karim, S. M. M., and Somers, K. (1973). Effect of prostaglandins A_1, A_2, B_1, E_2 and F_2 on forearm arterial bed and superficial hand veins in man. *Clinical Science,* **44,** 367–76.

Samuelsson, B. (1981). Prostaglandins, thromboxane and leukotrienes: formation and biological roles. *Harvey Lectures,* **75,** 1–40.

Seymour, R. A. and Walton, J. G. (1984). Pain control after third molar surgery. *International Journal of Oral Surgery,* **13,** 457–85.

Taylor, G. W. and Morris, H. R. (1983). Lipoxygenase pathways. *British Medical Bulletin,* **39,** 219–22.

Toller, P. A. (1977). Use and misuse of intra-articular corticosteroids in treatment of temporomandibular joint pain. *Proceedings of the Royal Society of Medicine,* **70,** 461–3.

Vane, J. R. (1976). Prostaglandins as mediators of inflammation. *Advances in Prostaglandin and Thromboxane Research,* **2,** 797–801.

Walter, J. B. and Israel, M. S. (1980). *General pathology* (5th edn). Churchill Livingstone, Edinburgh.

5

Aspirin and other non-steroidal anti-inflammatory drugs

THIS group of analgesics, the non-steroidal anti-inflammatory drugs (NSAIDs) or aspirin-like drugs, acts at the site of inflammation by interfering with the biochemical mediators of inflammation (Chapter 4), especially those associated with pain. Most of these drugs, as described later, inhibit the synthesis of the prostaglandins by blocking the cyclo-oxygenase enzyme system (Vane 1971) and they have, in addition to their analgesic properties, anti-inflammatory and central antipyretic activity. All these properties are important in the treatment of dental pain.

The prostaglandins, particularly PGE_2 and $PGF_{2\alpha}$, sensitize free nerve endings to the nociceptive properties of histamine and bradykinin, which produce pain (see Chapter 4). Therefore any analgesic that inhibits the production of prostaglandins will primarily reduce pain occurring at the site of inflammation.

ASPIRIN

Aspirin (acetylsalicylic acid) is the most wisely used medicinal agent in the Western world. It is a weak organic acid structurally related to salacin, a natural product found in willow bark (*Salix alba*). The drug is nearly always taken orally and soluble preparations are more efficacious than tablet formulations (Seymour *et al.* 1986).

Pharmacokinetics

Aspirin is rapidly absorbed from the gastro-intestinal tract, partly from the stomach, but mainly from the upper small intestine. On absorption, it is quickly hydrolyzed to salicylate by esterase enzymes (aspirin esterases) in the gut wall, blood, and liver. The half-life of aspirin in man is 20 to 30 minutes, whereas that of salicylate is two to three hours.

Salicylate is excreted in the urine mainly as salicyluric acid and glucuronides. In the liver, salicylate is conjugated with glycine and glucuronic acid to form

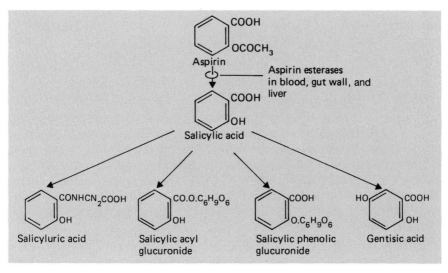

Fig. 5.1. The metabolism of aspirin.

salicyluric acid, and acyl and phenolic glucuronides, respectively. A very small fraction of salicylic acid is converted to gentisic acid. The metabolism of aspirin is illustrated in Fig. 5.1.

Pharmacodynamics

There is now convincing evidence that many of aspirin's pharmacological properties come from its ability to inhibit the synthesis of the important chemical mediators—the eicosanoids (prostaglandins, prostacyclin, thromboxane, and the leukotrienes). The eicosanoids, formed from fatty acids, have been discussed in Chapter 4. Aspirin is an irreversible inhibitor of the cyclo-oxygenase system by acetylating the active site of the enzyme (Roth *et al.* 1975), thus reducing its activity.

Pharmacological properties

Analgesia

Aspirin is usually classified as a mild analgesic and is effective against pain associated with inflammation, such as dental and rheumatic pain. The drug is also widely used to relieve headaches, migraines, and dysmenorrhoea. Aspirin's analgesic properties are mainly due to the inhibition of the synthesis of prostaglandins PGE_2 and $PGE_{2\alpha}$. Suitable dose regimes for aspirin are in the range 600–1200 mg every four to six hours.

Anti-inflammatory

These properties are again related to its ability to inhibit eicosanoid synthesis. In addition, salicylate, the major metabolite of aspirin, blocks the lipoxygenase enzyme system, the products of which are important mediators of the inflammatory response (Siegel *et al.* 1979). Thus, aspirin may have a dual action whereby acetylsalicylic acid blocks the synthesis of cyclo-oxygenase products and salicylate blocks the synthesis of lipoxygenase products.

Antipyretic

Aspirin effectively and rapidly lowers an elevated body temperature but has no effect on normal body temperature. Pyrexia, of course, usually accompanies an acute infection or acute inflammation. Many bacterial endotoxins can cause the synthesis and release of pyrogens from neutrophils. These pyrogens are proteins with a large molecular weight that stimulate the release of prostaglandins within the brain (particularly in the hypothalamic area). Prostaglandins PGE_2 and $PGE_{2\alpha}$ are pyrogenic and hence cause fever. The antipyretic properties of aspirin are therefore due to its inhibition of the synthesis of prostaglandins as stimulated by pyrogens.

Unwanted effects

Aspirin has many of these and they show marked individual variation; some of them are related to dosage and chronic usage.

Gastro-intestinal

Aspirin causes a high incidence of gastro-intestinal disturbances including epigastric pain, nausea, and gastric erosions leading to blood loss. Faecal blood loss is often related to dose and can be in the range of 3–10 ml per day. Because of these effects, aspirin should not be given to patients who suffer from peptic ulceration or inflammatory disease of the gut.

Haemostatic effects

Aspirin causes a prolongation of bleeding time (O'Brien 1969; Weiss *et al.* 1968) and this effect can occur after ingestion of a single aspirin tablet (300 mg). The prolonged bleeding time is due to impaired platelet aggregation caused by aspirin inhibiting the synthesis of platelet thromboxane (Roth and Majerus 1975). The increase in bleeding time will continue until the platelet population has been replaced (7–10 days), because platelets are incapable of regenerating the cyclo-oxygenase enzyme (see Chapter 12).

   High doses of aspirin (i.e. 4–6 g/day), over a long time, will reduce plasma prothrombin levels and cause an increase in clotting time. This effect can be reversed by Vitamin K. Aspirin should be avoided in any patient with a haemorrhagic disorder (e.g. haemophiliacs) and in patients taking anticoagulants, as it may potentiate the anticoagulant effect.

Tinnitus
High doses of aspirin cause tinnitus and hearing loss due to a rise in labyrinthine pressure. Reducing the dose of aspirin reverses this problem in 2 to 3 days.

Uricosuric effect
Aspirin at the dosage of 1–2 g per day decreases uric acid secretion, which results in an increase in plasma uric-acid concentrations. Aspirin should not be given to patients suffering from gout, a disorder of uric-acid metabolism.

Metabolic effects

Oxidative phosphorylation
Aspirin causes the uncoupling of oxidative phosphorylation, which results in the inhibition of a number of ATP-dependent reactions. At normal therapeutic doses, this uncoupling has little untoward effect, but becomes serious in overdose (see below).

Carbohydrate metabolism
Aspirin in high doses (> 5 g/day) may cause hypoglycaemia and was indeed once used as a treatment of diabetes. In even higher doses (> 10 g/day) aspirin depletes the liver of its glycogen stores and causes hyperglycaemia.

Aspirin hypersensitivity
True hypersensitivity is rare as many patients confuse unwanted effects such as nausea and tinnitus with an allergic response. In a true hypersensitivity reaction, clinical manifestations occur within minutes of ingestion of aspirin and may range from a rhinitis to life-threatening laryngeal oedema. The management of aspirin hypersensitivity and other drug hypersensitivity reactions is discussed in Chapter 21. The underlying mechanism for hypersensitivity to aspirin is unknown. Although the response resembles anaphylaxis, it does not appear to be immunological in nature. However, the incidence of aspirin hypersensitivity is much higher in patients who suffer from general allergic conditions such as asthma and hay fever, hence aspirin should be avoided in such subjects (Settipane *et al.* 1974). Other drugs that inhibit the cyclo-oxygenase enzyme (e.g. ibuprofen and mefenamic acid) may cause a hypersensitivity reaction in patients allergic to aspirin.

Drug interactions
Aspirin binds firmly to plasma proteins and so may displace other drugs from the binding sites, especially warfarin (Pullar and Cappell 1983), methotrexate, and

sulphonylureas. If such drugs are displaced, then their pharmacological properties will be enhanced. The problem with warfarin can be further compounded by the antihaemostatic properties of aspirin, which can lead to a fatal haemorrhage.

Aspirin overdose

As aspirin is widely used and readily available to the public, it is not surprising that it is one of the most common drugs for attempted suicide and is so often a cause of accidental poisoning in children. Doses of 10 to 30 g can be fatal.

Overdose of aspirin will cause an increase in CO_2 production in skeletal muscles due to deranged metabolism. Initially, this increase will stimulate respiration and cause some degree of hyperventilation. However, CO_2 production then outstrips its alveolar excretion causing a rise in plasma P_{CO_2} and hence blood pH falls; this is referred to as metabolic acidosis. The acidosis is further compounded by the high plasma concentrations of aspirin metabolites being themselves acidic, and also causing impairment of renal function, which will lead to the accumulation of acidic waste products. Hyperthermia and dehydration accompany the aspirin intoxication. If left untreated, death will occur as a result of coma and respiratory depression. Treatment is aimed at preventing further absorption of aspirin by gastric lavage and at restoring blood pH by intravenous infusion of bicarbonate.

Aspirin and Reye's Syndrome

Reye's syndrome is a rare disorder, occurring in childhood, that comprises an acute encephalopathic illness and fatty degeneration of the viscera, especially the liver. Its main feature is that it arises after an infectious illness, often chickenpox or influenza. The precise aetiology is unknown, but there is now accumulating evidence of a link between aspirin consumption during the course of the viral infection and the syndrome (Tarlow 1986). As a result of this association, paediatric aspirin preparations are no longer available to the public.

Aspirin in dentistry

Aspirin is widely used as an analgesic in postoperative dental pain, and many studies support the efficacy of this drug (Seymour 1983). Furthermore, the efficacy of aspirin is dose-related, with 1000 to 1200 mg providing greater analgesia than 500 to 600 mg (Seymour and Rawlins 1982) and related to the rate at which an individual hydrolyses aspirin to salicylate (Seymour *et al*. 1984). Postoperative dental pain is of short duration and usually patients only take analgesics for the first 24 to 48 hours after surgery (Seymour *et al*. 1983; 1985). As analgesics are only required for a short duration, it is unlikely that certain unwanted effects, for example, tinnitus, will occur.

If a patient has taken even a single dose of aspirin or an aspirin-containing analgesic *before* tooth extraction or other dental surgical procedure, then there is the real risk of postoperative haemorrhage (Lemkin *et al*. 1974; McGaul 1978). It would be a wise precaution to pack and suture extraction sockets in such patients. However, when aspirin is given postoperatively, there is little risk of haemorrhage as the haemostatic mechanism will be well-established.

Some toothache sufferers may try and relieve their pain by placing an aspirin tablet in the buccal sulcus against the offending tooth. This practice is of no value for pain relief, but will cause severe sloughing and ulceration of the buccal mucosa.

PARA-AMINOPHENOLS

These so-called coal-tar analgesics are all analine derivatives. Phenacetin and acetanalid were first introduced in 1887 but, in 1949, it was realized that the active metabolite of both these drugs is N-acetyl-p-aminophenol or paracetamol, which is now the most widely used of this group of analgesics.

Pharmacokinetics

Paracetamol is well-absorbed from the small intestine after oral ingestion. Peak plasma concentrations usually occur between 30 and 60 minutes after dosage, and the half-life is approximately 2 hours. Paracetamol is conjugated in the liver and the conjugates excreted in the urine.

Pharmacodynamics and pharmacological properties

Paracetamol has both analgesic and antipyretic properties similar to those of aspirin; however, the drug has little or no anti-inflammatory action, for which there is no satisfactory explanation. Neither the site nor the mechanisms of the analgesic action of paracetamol have been clearly established. Different workers have concluded that the site of action is purely peripheral, purely central, or both (Koch-Weser 1976). It is very much less effective than aspirin as a peripheral cyclo-oxygenase inhibitor, but has the same potency as aspirin in inhibiting brain prostaglandin synthetase (Ferreira and Vane 1974). The antipyretic property of paracetamol probably has a similar mechanism to that of aspirin.

Unwanted effects and overdose

Paracetamol has remarkably few unwanted effects and at normal therapeutic doses is probably the safest analgesic. Skin rashes and white blood-cell disorders have occasionally been reported. However, the most serious problem with paracetamol is hepatotoxicity after overdose (Prescott et al. 1971). At normal doses, paracetamol is broken down in the liver to metabolites that are normally innocuous. In overdose, one of the metabolites (probably N-acetyl-p-benzoqui-none), which is usually reduced by glutathione and eliminated, accumulates and renders liver cells incapable of synthesizing protein. Acute liver damage can occur after a single dose of 10 to 15 g; a dose of 25 g is invariably fatal. The problem of paracetamol overdose is further compounded by the absence of untoward effects in the first 24 hours after overdose, during which time serious and perhaps fatal liver damage will have occurred. Hence the overdose victim may take further tablets but, more seriously, their relations or friends will have seen little obvious signs of illness and so may not seek help. Signs and symptoms of liver damage manifest themselves between 2 to 6 days after overdose. Jaundice and coagulation disorders accompany the hepatotoxicity, which leads to coma and death.

Early treatment is essential for success in paracetamol overdose. Gastric lavage will prevent further absorption, provided it is in the first hour after dosage. If less than 12 hours has elapsed, then N-acetylcysteine is the treatment of choice. This drug can be given orally and treatment should persist until there is a significant reduction of plasma paracetamol concentrations. N-acetylcysteine will conjugate with the metabolite and thus protect the liver cells from further damage (Prescott et al. 1979).

If the patient is seen after 24 hours, then the success of treatment will depend upon the magnitude of the initital overdose. If large quantities of paracetamol have been consumed, then they will invariably suffer a slow and often distressing death.

Use in dentistry

Paracetamol is a useful analgesic in patients where aspirin is contraindicated (e.g. those with a haemorrhagic diathesis). The efficacy of paracetamol in postoperative dental pain has not been shown to be dose-related, therefore increasing the dosage may not cause an equivalent increase in analgesia.

Paracetamol elixir is extensively used in the treatment of 'teething', although its efficacy in this poorly defined condition has not been established. Teething is often accompanied by systemic disturbances, particularly pyrexia, which may be due to some other infection. The combined antipyretic and analgesic properties of paracetamol, together with its few unwanted effects, thus make this drug popular for the relief of teething problems although it may be the symptoms of the underlying infection that are palliated and this may require medical attention. Paracetamol elixir also contains a high proportion of sugar, and its regular use may increase the incidence of dental caries. The problem of caries is compounded because the medicine is often given last thing at night.

OTHER NSAIDS

This group of analgesics is sometimes referred to as aspirin-like drugs, for they share many of aspirin's pharmacological properties. Like aspirin, they are anti-inflammatory and analgesic because they can inhibit the synthesis of the eicosanoids (see Chapter 4). However, many NSAIDs will produce unwanted effects similar to those of aspirin, such as gastro-intestinal disturbances and impaired platelet aggregation. The incidence of unwanted effects varies markedly between the different groups of these analgesics. Furthermore, a patient who is hypersensitive to aspirin is likely to have a similar reaction when given another NSAID. These analgesics are mainly used in rheumatic and other musculo-skeletal disorders. However, because of their combined analgesic and anti-inflammatory properties, they are becoming widely used for the treatment of dental pain.

Propionic-acid derivatives

Examples of these include ibuprofen, naproxen, and fenoprofen. Ibuprofen is the most widely used analgesic in this group and is becoming increasingly popular in dentistry.

Pharmacological properties and unwanted effects

Ibuprofen is rapidly absorbed following oral administration; peak plasma concentrations occur within 1.5 hours after dosage, and the plasma half-life is 2 hours. The drug is broken down in the liver and the metabolites excreted in the urine.

Ibuprofen has similar unwanted effects to those of aspirin. About 15 per cent of patients taking it find these effects so severe that they have to discontinue the drug (Davies and Avery 1971). Ibuprofen and other propionic-acid derivatives should be avoided in patients with a gastro-intestinal disorder, haemostatic problems, or a history of hypersensitivity to aspirin.

The fenamates

Mefenamic acid (Ponstan) is the only member of this group of drugs that is used in dentistry.

Pharmacological properties and unwanted effects

Mefenamic acid is rapidly absorbed after oral dose and peak plasma concentrations occur after two hours; the half-life is three to four hours. The drug is metabolized in the liver; half of the metabolites are excreted in the urine, and the other half in the faeces. Mefenamic acid is about as active as aspirin as an analgesic and anti-inflammatory agent. However, the incidence of unwanted effects, especially gastro-intestinal disturbances, is high. Troublesome diarrhoea occurs in 25 per cent of patients on this drug (Chadwick *et al.* 1976; Marks and Gleeson 1975). As with other NSAIDs, mefenamic acid should not be given to a patient for whom aspirin is contra-indicated.

Indomethacin (Indocid)

This is an indole derivative developed in 1963. The use of this drug in dentistry is limited because of the high incidence of unwanted effects.

Pharmacological properties and unwanted effects

Indomethacin is one of the most potent inhibitors of the cyclo-oxygenase enzyme, and a powerful anti-inflammatory agent. A high proportion of patients (30–50 per cent) receiving this drug experience unwanted effects; these include gastro-intestinal complaints, and central nervous system disturbances such as dizziness, headache, confusion, and vertigo. The precise mechanism of these central actions is unknown, but they may be due to prostaglandin inhibition within brain tissue, or to salt and water retention (Carney 1977). Severe depression of the activity of the bone marrow and hypersensitivity reactions have been associated with this drug.

Diflunisal

This is a difluorophenyl derivative of salicylic acid with similar pharmacological properties to aspirin. The main advantage of this drug is its long plasma half-life (approx. 8 h) so the dose regime is only twice a day. Diflunisal is a comparatively new analgesic with a low incidence of unwanted effects, but it has not been established if this low incidence persists with chronic usage.

Efficacy of NSAIDs in dental pain

This group of analgesics has been extensively evaluated in postoperative dental pain and many trials support their efficacy (for review, see Seymour and Walton 1984). However, the incidence and severity of unwanted effects sometimes outweighs the advantages of analgesia obtained from these drugs. Ibuprofen and diflunisal appear to have the lowest incidence of unwanted effects. It has not been established whether these two analgesics offer any advantage over 1 g aspirin in the treatment of postoperative dental pain.

REFERENCES

Carney, M. W. P. (1977). Paranoid psychoses with indomethacin. *British Medical Journal*, **2**, 994.

Chadwick, R. G., Hossenbocus, A., and Colin-Jones, D. G. (1976). Steatorrhoea complicating therapy with mefenamic acid. *British Medical Journal*, **1**, 397.

Davies, E. F. and Avery, G. S. (1971). Ibuprofen, a review of its pharmacological properties and therapeutic efficacy in rheumatic disorders. *Drugs*, **2**, 416–34.

Ferreira, S. H. and Vane, J. R. (1974). New aspects of the mode of nonsteroidal anti-inflammatory drugs. *Annual Review of Pharmacology*, **14**, 57–73.

Koch-Weser, J. (1976). Drug therapy—acetaminophen. *New England Journal of Medicine,* **295**, 1297–300.

Lemkin, S. R., Billesdon, J. E., Davee, S. S., Leake, D. L., and Kattlove, H. E. (1974). Aspirin-induced oral bleeding: correction with platelet transfusion: a reminder. *Oral Surgery,* **37**, 498–501.

McGaul, T. (1978). Postoperative bleeding caused by aspirin. *Journal of Dentistry,* **6**, 207–9.

Marks, J. S. and Gleeson, M. H. (1975). Steatorrhoea complicating therapy with mefenamic acid. *British Medical Journal,* **4**, 442.

O'Brien, J. R. (1968). Effects of salicylates on human platelets. *Lancet,* **1**, 779–83.

Prescott, L. F., Wright, N., Roscoe, P., and Brown, S. S. (1971). Plasma-paracetamol half-life and hepatic necrosis in patients with paracetamol overdosage. *Lancet,* **1**, 519–22.

Prescott, L. F., Illingworth, R. N., Critchley, J. A. H. J., Stewart, M. J., Adam, R. D., and Proudfoot, A. T. (1979). Intravenous N-acetylcysteine; the treatment of choice for paracetamol poisoning. *British Medical Journal,* **2**, 1097–100.

Pullar, T. and Capell, H. A. (1983). Interaction between oral anticoagulant drugs and non-steroidal anti-inflammatory agents: a review. *Scottish Medical Journal,* **28**, 42–7.

Roth, G. J. and Majerus, P. W. (1975). The mechanism of the effect of aspirin on human platelets. I Acetylation of a particular fraction protein. *Journal of Clinical Investigation,* **56**, 624–32.

Roth, G. J., Stanford, N., and Majerus, P. W. (1975). Acetylation of prostaglandin synthetase by aspirin. *Proceedings of the National Academy of Sciences U.S.A.,* **72**, 3073–6.

Settipane, G. A., Chafee, F. H., and Klein, D. E. (1974). Aspirin intolerance—a prospective study in an atopic and normal population. *Journal of Allergy and Clinical Immunology,* **53**, 200–4.

Seymour, R. A. (1983). Aspirin in dentistry. *Australian Journal of Pharmacology,* **16**, 19–21.

Seymour, R. A. and Rawlins, M. D. (1982). The efficacy and pharmacokinetics of aspirin in postoperative dental pain. *British Journal of Clinical Pharmacology,* **13**, 807–10.

Seymour, R. A. and Walton, J. G. (1984). Pain control after third molar surgery. *International Journal of Oral Surgery,* **13**, 457–85.

Seymour, R. A., BLair, G. S., and Wyatt, F. A. R. (1983). Postoperative dental pain and analgesic efficacy. II Analgesic usage and efficacy after dental surgery. *British Journal of Oral Surgery,* **21**, 298–303.

Seymour, R. A., Williams, F. M., Ward, A., and Rawlins, M. D. (1984). Aspirin metabolism and analgesic efficacy in postoperative dental pain. *British Journal of Clinical Pharmacology,* **17**, 697–701.

Seymour, R. A., Meechan, J. G., and Blair, G. S. (1985). An investigation into postoperative pain after third molar surgery under local anaesthesia. *British Journal of Oral and Maxillofacial Surgery,* **23**, 410–18.

Seymour, R. A., Williams, F. M., Luyk, N., Boyle, M. A., Whitfield, P. M., Nicholson, E., Ward-Booth, P., and Rawlins, M. D. (1986). Comparative efficacy of soluble aspirin and aspirin tablets in postoperative dental pain. *European Journal of Clinical Pharmacology,* **30**, 495–8.

Siegel, M. I., McConnell, R. T., and Cuatrecasas, P. (1979). Aspirin-like drugs interfere with arachidonic acid metabolism by inhibition of the 12-hydroperoxy-5,8,10,14-eicosatetraenoic acid peroxidase activity of the lipoxygenase pathway. *Proceedings of the National Academy of Sciencies,* **76**, 3774–8.

Tarlow, M. (1986). Reye's syndrome and aspirin. *British Medical Journal,* **292**, 1543.

Vane, J. R. (1971). Inhibition of prostaglandin synthesis as a mechanism of action for aspirin-like drugs. *Nature New Biology*, **231**, 232–5.

Weiss, H. J., Aledort, L. M., and Kochwa, S. (1968). The effect of salicylates on the haemostatic properties of platelets in man. *Journal of Clinical Investigation*, **47**, 2169–80.

6

Opioids and opiates

OPIOIDS and opiates exert their analgesic effect within the central nervous system by modifying neural activity associated with pain, hence they are sometimes referred to as centrally acting analgesics.

The therapeutic properties of the milky exudate obtained from the seed pod of the white poppy *Papaver somniferum* have been known since the third century BC. The exudate is dried and is known as opium, which contains the alkaloids morphine and codeine. These drugs, together with many synthetic compounds, are known as opioids, that is they have an opium- or morphine-like activity. The opioids are mainly used as analgesics through their interaction with specific opioid receptors within the central nervous system (CNS). Their other important therapeutic properties are the suppression of cough, and the reduction of gastro-intestinal mobility.

TERMINOLOGY

The term 'opiate' is used to designate drugs derived from opium, i.e. essentially morphine and codeine, although it has been loosely applied to morphine derivatives. The term 'opioid' refers to any directly acting compound, the effects of which are antagonized by naloxone. Narcotics and major analgesics are now obsolete terms that have been used to describe this group of drugs.

OPIOID RECEPTORS

These were first isolated in 1973 (Pert and Snyder 1973), and four types have been described, μ (mu), κ (kappa), δ (delta) and σ (sigma), but there are also sub-types of these receptors. The effects of stimulating the various opioid receptors together with the endogenous ligands are summarized in Table 6.1.

Morphine and related compounds appear to have different affinities for the three types of receptors, which may account for many of the differing pharmacological properties of this group of drugs. Opioid receptors are found throughout the central nervous system; there are high concentrations in the limbic system, the substantia gelatinosa, the spinal nucleus of the fifth cranial nerve (V), and the thalamus. The receptors appear to be the site of action of the endogenous opioids (opioid peptides)—the enkephalins, dynorphins, and endorphins (Chang and Cuatrecasas 1981; Martin 1983).

Table 6.1. Opioid receptors, endogenous ligands and the effect of receptor stimulation

Receptor	Endogenous ligand	Effect of receptor stimulation
μ (mu)	Endorphin	Analgesia (μ_1) Dependence (μ_2) Miosis (μ_2) Respiratory depression (μ_2) Constipation (μ_2)
κ (kappa)	Dynorphin	Spinal analgesia Sedation
δ (delta)	Enkephalins	Respiratory depression
σ (sigma)	Unknown	Dysphoria

PAIN-RELATED NEUROTRANSMITTERS AND NEUROHORMONES

Enkephalins

These are a series of peptides originally identified from pig brain extracts by Hughes *et al.* (1975). Two structurally similar peptides were found—methionine enkephalin (met-enkephalin) and leucine enkephalin (leu-enkaphalin)—each of which is derived by enzyme cleavage from a larger and independent precursor, proenkephalin A. The identification of the enkephalins was followed by the realization that the met-enkephalin amino-acid sequence was present in the pituitary peptide, β-lipotropin, as residues 61 to 65. Soon afterwards, it was shown that the C-fragment of β-lipotropin (residues 61 to 91) interacts specifically with opioid receptors; this is now known as β-endorphin.

All of these peptides have properties in common with morphine, such as production of analgesia, physical dependence and tolerance, and the contraction of smooth muscle. Their actions can be reversed or blocked by the specific opioid antagonist, naloxone (see Terminology above). There is now evidence that the enkephalins are neurotransmitters of specific nerve fibres in the brain that modulate sensory information pertaining to pain and emotional behaviour. Regional variations in enkephalin levels parallel the distribution of opioid receptors. The highest levels of enkephalins are found in brain fractions containing nerve terminals, the distribution of which is likewise similar to that of the opioid receptor (Akil *et al.* 1984).

The dynorphins

These may act as neurotransmitters or neurohormones; they are produced by enzyme cleavage from the precursor, prodynorphin. The dynorphins are larger peptides than the enkephalins but their physiological role is uncertain.

The endorphins

These comprise at least four different peptides designated α-, β-, γ-, and δ-endorphins, of which β-endorphin is the most significant. All are derived by enzyme cleavage from the precursor pro-opiomelancortin, which also serves as the precursor for β-lipotropin (see Enkephalins above) and corticotropin.

The endorphins appear to be neurohormones that are released into the blood stream and have a variable duration of action. They are found mainly in the anterior pituitary gland, in the same cells as corticotropin and β-lipotropin. All of these hormones are secreted in parallel during stress, possibly as an adaptive mechanism: the endorphins may help to relieve any pain the individual might then incur.

β-endorphin has potent and long-lasting analgesic activity (Oyama *et al.* 1980). The analgesia produced by β-endorphin was also shown to be reversed by the opioid antagonist, naloxone. It was thus anticipated that the long-sought, non-addictive analgesic had finally been found, as it appeared a reasonable assumption that man is not likely to become addicted to endogenously produced substances. However, in experimental animals, repeated injections of β-endorphin have produced symptoms of tolerance and dependence.

If there is such a pain-suppressing system, why is it that the human being experiences pain? The answer may be connected with the fact that a painful stimulus activates both A-delta and C-fibres. Pain transmitted by A-delta fibres (first pain) acts as a warning system; this type of pain is hardly affected by morphine or other opioids. C-fibre-induced pain is perhaps the more clinically relevant, and it is affected by morphine. It may be inferred that pain of a protracted nature (suffering) is more likely to be modulated by endorphin release than warning pain. It is not difficult to conceive that suppression of protracted post-traumatic pain may serve a sensible purpose.

Further properties of the endorphins

The human placenta produces β-endorphin (Houck *et al.* 1980), which may be distributed to the fetus, so exposing it to high perinatal endorphin levels, but the significance of this is unclear. From behavioural investigations, it has been shown that pain sensitivity in the new-born child is relatively low, although pain reactions can be evoked, and that the sensitivity becomes much greater after a few days of life. This pattern of reaction to pain in neonates may be related to residual maternal levels of β-endorphin in the central nervous system.

Pain sensitivity varies between many ethnic groups. Research has demonstrated certain correlations between experimental measures of pain and β-endorphin levels in the cerebrospinal fluid (CSF). Patients with high endorphin levels have high pain thresholds and pain tolerance levels. At the risk of over-simplification, it would seem as if constitutional differences in response to pain, and differences in attitude to potentially painful or other noxious stimuli, may be related to endorphin activity (von Knorring *et al.* 1978).

Certain pathological conditions are characterized by abnormal insensitivity to pain. One such is congenital analgesia, in which there may be a central defect, and two cases have been reported of patients who responded to naloxone, with a lowering of pain threshold and return of pain responsiveness (Dehen *et al.* 1978; Yanagida 1978). This response suggests that these patients may have excessive endorphin production and activity. Patients with schizophrenia seldom complain during venepuncture, lumbar puncture, or other painful diagnostic procedures. Furthermore, their pain sensitivity increases after they have received naloxone. Various studies have shown that schizophrenics, as well as patients with endogenous depression, frequently show elevated CSF levels of endorphins (Bellenger *et al.* 1979; Geschwind 1975).

Placebo analgesia, acupuncture, hypnosis, and the endorphin system

It is a well-known clinical observation that psychological and emotional factors are important in the control of pain. Placebos are pharmacologically inert substances and it is estimated that some 30 to 40 per cent of the population will show a therapeutic response when, unknown to them, they are given placebo. Such subjects are known as 'placebo responders'. The placebo effect is prominent in the testing of any analgesics and its magnitude seems to be related to the potency of the analgesic drug under evaluation. Levine *et al.* (1978) have studied the effect of naloxone on the placebo response in patients undergoing removal of their impacted lower third molars. Postoperatively, these received intravenously either an analgesic or placebo in random, double-blind order. One-third of those who received placebo reported a significant reduction in pain. When these 'placebo-responders' were subsequently given naloxone, their pain returned to its original pre-injection level. The remaining patients, who did not respond to the placebo injection, failed to show any response after naloxone. These findings would suggest a link between endorphin production and activity, and the placebo response.

The derivation of the analgesia that may be induced by hypnosis is controversial. There have been conflicting reports of the effect of naloxone on hypnosis-induced analgesia (Barber and Mayer 1977; Goldstein and Hilgard 1975; Nasrallah *et al.* 1979; Stephenson 1978). However, the overwhelming impression from the literature is that naloxone does not appear to reverse hypnotic analgesia. But this may not be true for every type of hypnotherapy and it has not yet been ruled out that purely mental activation of a neuronal process could lead to endorphin release. If mental control over endorphin production and activation could be proven, this might lead to methods for the self-regulation of pain.

Acupuncture analgesia has been used for centuries in China, and recent studies have confirmed that it does induce an increase in the pain threshold in man. How acupuncture works remains uncertain, but the finding that naloxone can reverse the analgesia induced by acupuncture suggests that release of endorphins may be a factor (Mayer *et al.* 1977; Sjölund *et al.* 1977). Both the time delay before the onset of acupuncture analgesia, and the prolonged effect afterwards, indicate the release of some hormonal factor.

Closely related to acupuncture are electrical stimulation methods for controlling pain. Essentially, two procedures are in use. The first is high-frequency (100–200 Hz) stimulation, which is apparently not endorphin-mediated, but may work by activating the gate-control (see below) mechanisms. The second is low-frequency (1–2 Hz) stimulation, which is associated with a rise in CSF endorphin levels and is reversed by naloxone (Sjölund *et al.* 1977; 1979).

The detection of an endogenous opioid system (the opioid receptors, endorphins, dynorphins, and enkephalins) has created a great deal of interest in pain mechanisms. Furthermore these findings have given a rational background for the understanding and use of various stimulation techniques for pain relief.

Substance P

Substance P (so-called because it was a 'P'owder) is a polypeptide, originally discovered by von Euler and Gaddum (1931). The evidence suggests that substance P is a neurotransmitter in small-diameter fibres, particularly C-fibres. Staining techniques have shown that substance P is found in the following areas related to pain:

(1) cell bodies of posterior root ganglia projecting to the substantia gelatinosa of the spinal cord;

(2) caudal division of the trigeminal (V) spinal nucleus;

(3) nucleus raphe pallidus and magnus;

(4) periaqueductal grey area.

That substance P is specifically related to pain is indicated by the disappearance of nerve endings containing it (sited in the caudal division of the trigeminal nerve) after removal of tooth pulps in cats. The tooth pulp is innervated almost exclusively by pain fibres.

In general, endogenous opioid peptides suppress pain, whereas substance P promotes it (Sweet 1980). However, application of substance P to the exposed tooth pulp does not excite sensory neurones and its role in the pulp is still obscure (Gazelius *et al.* 1977). Substance P and enkephalins (see above) do interact: the release of substance P is inhibited not only by met-enkephalin, but also by β-endorphin and morphine.

The role of substance P and enkephalins in pain transmission

The discovery of the interaction between substance P, enkephalins, and opioid receptors (Jessel and Iversen 1977) can, in part, help to explain neuropharmacological aspects of Melzack and Wall's gate-control theory of pain (Melzack and Wall 1965).

Within the substantia gelatinosa, a nociceptive impulse transmitted via small C-fibres causes release of substance P at the synapse (Fig. 6.1). Substance P binds with specific receptors postsynaptically and the impulse is further transmitted. Synapsing with the small C-fibre terminal is an enkephalinergic fibre that, on excitation, releases met-enkephalin. The met-enkaphalin binds to opioid receptors on the terminal of the C-fibre, depolarizes the membrane, and inhibits the release of substance P. Consequently, the nerve impulse carrying nociceptive sensations does not progress beyond the synapse.

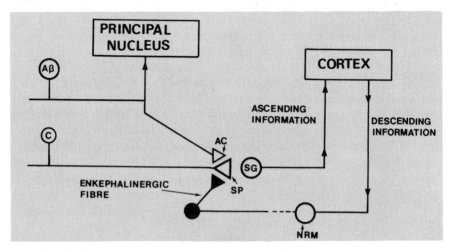

Fig. 6.1. Schematic representation of the organization of inhibition in the substantia gelatinosa (AC = acetyl-choline; SG = substantia gelatinosa; SP = substance P; NRM = nucleus raphe magnus; C = cell body of C-fibre; Aβ = cell body of a beta fibre).

The enkephalinergic fibres are, in turn, connected to the cortex via the nucleus raphe magnus. The transmitter substance in raphe neurones is not enkephalin, but 5-hydroxytryptamine. Their terminals synapse with and activate enkephalinergic interneurones in the substantia gelatinosa (Fig. 6.2). Activity in the nucleus raphe magnus is under the descending control of the cortex.

In addition to the pain-suppressing system brought about by activity in the enkephalinergic fibres, activity in the large sensory A-beta fibres can cause presynaptic inhibition (depolarization) of activity in small-fibre (C-fibre) terminals. This mechanism constitutes the gate-control. Clinically, it can be applied in the form of transcutaneous nerve stimulation, which consists of high-frequency, low-intensity electrical pulses passing through pad electrodes. Analgesia brought about by such stimulation is not naloxone-reversible.

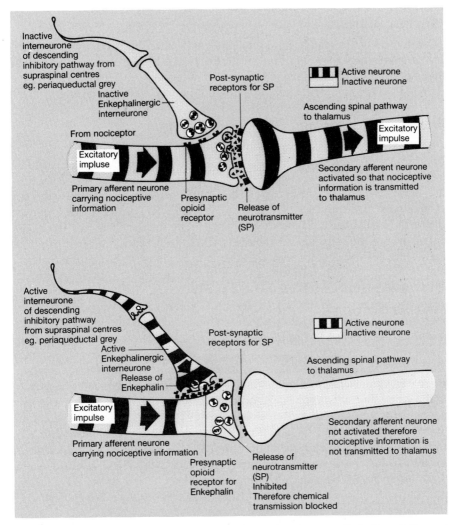

Fig. 6.2. Diagrammatic representation of the interaction between an enkephalinergic fibre and a C-fibre.

SPECIFIC OPIOIDS AND OPIOID ANTAGONISTS

Morphine

Morphine, named after Morpheus, the Greek god of dreams, was first isolated in 1803. This drug is the most widely used of the opioids and is considered to be the most potent analgesic in use for the relief of pain.

Pharmacokinetics

As with most of the opioids, morphine undergoes extensive first pass metabolism in the liver when given via the oral route. Hence for optimal use, it is given parenterally. Morphine is conjugated with glucuronic acid in the liver and is excreted via the kidney; its half-life in man is approximately three hours.

Pharmacodynamic and pharmacological properties

Analgesia

Understanding of how morphine works as an analgesic must be accompanied by more detailed information about the pain experience. This experience comprises the initial sensation together with emotional, psychological, and suffering components that the sensation evokes. For example, coronary chest pain or cancer pain will have a different significance to the sufferer than, say, toothache or pain from a fractured limb. Morphine is particularly effective against pain that has a large suffering component. In addition to its analgesic properties, the drug also produces other central effects, such as drowsiness, sedation, and euphoria, all of which add to the general comfort of a patient in pain. Morphine does not alter other sensations such as touch, pressure, vision, or hearing. Those given morphine will feel a pinprick as normal though it may be less unpleasant. Also, morphine is considered to be more effective against continuous, dull pain than against sharp, intermittent pain.

Although the precise mechanism of morphine-induced analgesia is uncertain, there is much evidence to suggest that the drug combines with opioid receptors (μ and κ) in the substantia gelatinosa, the spinal nucleus of V, and the periaqueductal and periventricular grey matter. By activating these receptors, morphine alters the central release of neurotransmitters (probably substance P) from nerve fibres transmitting painful stimuli. A 10 mg dose of morphine given intramuscularly will provide adequate pain relief within 30 minutes and a duration of effect of four to five hours.

Gastro-intestinal tract

Opium has been used for centuries to treat diarrhoea and dysentery. All the opioids produce a degree of constipation and some are used solely for this purpose (e.g. loperamide hydrochloride and diphenoxylate hydrochloride). These drugs act on the smooth muscles of the gastro-intestinal tract by increasing muscle and sphincter tone. This results in delayed emptying of the gut, diminished peristalsis, and a decrease in propulsive motility. The constipating properties of the opioids show marked variation between patients, with some experiencing painful muscle spasms, particularly of the smooth muscles of the biliary tract.

Cough suppression

Morphine and many of the opioids, especially codeine (see below), are effective antitussives. The opioids have a direct effect on the cough centre in the medulla. Cough suppression occurs with low doses of morphine.

Cardiovascular effects
Morphine at therapeutic doses has an insignificant effect on blood pressure, cardiac output, and heart rate. However, it does cause the release of histamine, which produces vasodilatation of the peripheral vessels and causes the sensation of warmth that many experience after receiving morphine.

Unwanted effects

Respiratory depression
Morphine and many of the other opioids depress respiration by a direct effect on the respiratory centres in the brain stem. Some degree of respiratory depression occurs with normal therapeutic doses but, in overdose, the respiratory depression can be life-threatening. Morphine decreases the response of the respiratory centre to the concentration of CO_2 (P_{CO_2}) levels in the blood; it also depresses the pontine and medullary centres that control respiratory rhythm. Thus, after morphine, there is a reduction in respiratory rate, minute volume, and tidal exchange.

Dependence
One of the main draw-backs of the opioids is the development of tolerance and physical dependence with repeated use. The problem of drug abuse is dealt with in more detail in Chapter 23. Tolerance develops to the depressant actions of the opioids—analgesia, euphoria, drowsiness, and respiratory depression. Both physical dependence and tolerance will depend upon the dose and frequency of administration. Similarly, the degree of physical dependence will determine the intensity of the withdrawal syndrome.

Nauseant and emetic effects
Nausea and vomiting are common unwanted effects associated with morphine and many of the other opioids. This is due to a direct stimulation of the chemoreceptor trigger zone in the medulla. The incidence of nausea and vomiting is much higher in ambulatory patients, which suggests that a vestibular component is active. The administration of an anti-emetic, such as cyclizine tartrate or prochlorperazine, may reduce this problem.

Effects on the pupil
Morphine, together with many of the more potent opioids, causes a constriction of the pupil (miosis), due to an excitatory action on the autonomic segment of the nucleus of the oculomotor nerve (Edinger–Westphal nucleus). Because of the miosis, it is unwise to give morphine to patients with a suspected head injury as the drug will mask the pupillary constriction reflex, which is an important indicator of brain damage.

Overdose

Death from overdose of the opioids is due to respiratory depression. The subject who has taken an overdose, either accidentally or intentionally, will invariably be asleep and difficult to arouse. The respiratory rate will be very low; there will be a drop in blood pressure; the pupils will be constricted and show no response to light. The skin will be cold and clammy, and all skeletal muscles will be flaccid, including the tongue, which may fall back and block the airway.

Treatment is to establish and maintain an airway and then administer an opioid antagonist such as naloxone. The usual dose of naloxone is 0.4 mg intravenously, which can be repeated after two to three minutes if required. The half-life of naloxone is short (about 1 h) and further repeated doses may be necessary to avoid a relapse into a coma state.

Uses of morphine

Although morphine is widely used in the treatment of postoperative pain after general surgery, its main use is in the relief of cancer pain and other pains of terminal illness. The combined analgesic, euphoriant, and sedative properties of morphine are a considerable advantage in reducing the pain and suffering that often accompany a terminal illness. A variety of other opioids are used for this purpose, particularly those that are effective by mouth, thus avoiding repeated injections in frail patients.

As morphine suppresses the cough reflex and respiratory activity, the drug should not be used indiscriminately in postoperative pain after general surgery, where such suppression can lead to pneumonia.

Codeine

Codeine, or methyl morphine, is a naturally occurring alkaloid present in opium; like all the opioids, it binds to opioid receptors within the central nervous system. The drug is metabolized in the liver to form nor-codeine and morphine, so morphine may acount for codeine's analgesic properties. About half the drug is excreted in the urine unchanged or conjugated with glucuronide; about 10 per cent is excreted as morphine glucuronide and the remainder as nor-codeine glucuronide.

Pharmacological properties

Codeine is one of the few opioids that is effective when taken by mouth, but it is only useful in treating mild to moderate pain. Peak plasma concentrations occur one hour after oral dosage, and the duration of analgesia is two to four hours. On a dose per dose basis, codeine has about one-twelfth the potency of morphine, but it is appreciably more effective than morphine when given by mouth. There are many proprietary analgesics that contain mixtures of codeine and either paracetamol or aspirin. Combining both a peripherally and a centrally acting analgesic appears to enhance the efficacy of the combination—an effect that is often more than additive.

Codeine is a very effective antitussive, and so is contained in many proprietary cough medicines.

Unwanted effects

Codeine is capable of producing all the unwanted effects of the opioids as a group, such as nausea, vomiting, sedation, and dizziness. As with morphine, these effects are more often observed in ambulatory patients than those in bed. When the drug is administered orally in the usual therapeutic doses (30–60 mg), the incidence of unwanted effects is low, and those that do occur are annoying rather than serious. Codeine can depress respiration to a measurable extent, but the degree of respiratory depression is of little clinical significance except in overdose. Constipation is frequently noted when repeated doses are administered, and so the drug has been used as an antidiarrhoeal.

The risk of dependence or addiction to codeine is small. The usual dose regime of codeine (30–60 mg × 4 daily), even when given for several months, does not induce significant dependence. Most addicts who have resorted to codeine have done so because nothing better was available.

Pethidine

This is a synthetic opioid, first manufactured in 1939. It can be given orally, but optimal analgesia is obtained when given intramuscularly. Pethidine is hydrolysed in the liver to meperidinic acid, which is conjugated and excreted in the urine. The half-life of pethidine is about three hours.

Pharmacological properties

Pethidine provides rapid analgesia when given via the parenteral route, with the maximum analgesic effect occurring one hour after dosage. The duration of analgesia obtained from 50 mg is approximately two to four hours; this is slightly less than that obtained from morphine. It has been estimated that 80–100 mg pethidine have the same potency as 10 mg morphine.

Unwanted effects

These are similar to those of morphine and include respiratory depression, dependence, and pupillary constriction. The effect of pethidine on the muscles of the gastro-intestine tract is considerably less than that of morphine or codeine. At normal therapeutic doses, it has little effect on the cardiovascular system but intravenous administration causes an alarming increase in heart rate. In overdose, pethidine sometimes produces excitation of the central nervous system resulting in tremors, muscle twitching, seizures, and an atropine-like action causing an increase in heart rate.

Drug interactions

Pethidine should not be given to patients receiving monoamine oxidase inhibitors as this may cause convulsions, hypothermia, hyperpyrexia, and severe

respiratory depression. These reactions are totally unlike the normal pharmacological effects of pethidine and are therefore of the Type B reactions (see Chapter
22).

Concurrent administration of pethidine with either tricyclic antidepressants or
chlorpromazine will enhance its sedative properties.

Pentazocine

This is a benzomorphan derivative that has both agonistic and weak opioid
antagonistic activity. The drug acts as an antagonist on the μ-receptor, but as an
agonist on the κ- and σ-receptors. This agonism accounts for the high incidence of
hallucinations associated with pentazocine. Because of the antagonistic action on
the μ-receptor, pentazocine should not be used with an opioid agonist. It was
originally thought that it would have little or no abuse potential but, with
widespread use, physical dependence and abuse have become apparent.
Pentazocine can be administered both orally and parenterally; however, repeated
injections should be avoided as the drug causes a local irritation and extensive
fibrosis. Pentazocine is well absorbed from the site of administration and
undergoes extensive first pass metabolism (80 per cent). The drug is metabolized
in the liver and the metabolites are excreted in the kidney; the rate of metabolism
shows marked individual variation, which may account for inter-individual
differences in pharmacological properties (Beckett *et al.* 1970). The half-life of
pentazocine is two to three hours. An intramuscular dose of 30–50 mg
pentazocine is approximately equivalent to 10 mg morphine. When given orally,
50 mg pentazocine produces analgesia equivalent to 60 mg codeine.

Unwanted effects.

There is a high incidence of these (Forrest 1974)—including hallucinations,
nightmares, sedation, dizziness, sweating, and nausea—and their frequency
increases with dose. High doses of pentazocine cause an increase in blood
pressure and heart rate. The effect on blood pressure may be due to an increase in
plasma concentration of catecholamines (Tammisto *et al.* 1971). The effects of
pentazocine on the gastro-intestinal tract and respiration are similar to those of
the other opioids. Pentazocine raises pulmonary artery pressure (Alderman *et al.*
1972) and therefore should not be used to reduce chest pain following a
myocardial infarction.

Dihydrocodeine

This is considered to be a moderately potent analgesic and is in wide clinical use. It
is derived from codeine and was first manufactured in 1911. Structurally,
dihydrocodeine is related to both codeine and morphine and so may be expected
to share some of the properties of either or both of these drugs. It can be given

orally or parenterally and has a half-life of three to four hours. When given orally, the drug undergoes extensive first pass metabolism. Dihydrocodeine is metabolized in the liver to dihydromorphine, which is further conjugated with glucuronide and excreted via the kidneys. Dose regimes of dihydrocodeine are 30 mg every four to six hours.

Unwanted effects

Dihydrocodeine is associated with a high incidence of such effects, which include nausea, dizziness, and constipation. It is estimated that 25 per cent of patients who take dihydrocodeine experience side-effects of sufficient unpleasantness to prevent them from taking further doses (Langdon 1969).

Dextropropoxyphene

This is a tertiary amine ester, both chemically and pharmacologically related to methadone and other opioids. However, its efficacy as an analgesic agent is questionable, and as an individual compound the drug is not used in dentistry. However, co-proxamol, which is a combination of dextropropoxyphene (32.5 mg) and paracetamol (325 mg), is the most widely prescribed analgesic preparation in the UK (Skegg et al. 1977).

The toxicity of co-proxamol presents a serious problem in overdose, and death has been reported from as few as 15 tablets taken with alcohol (Whittington 1977). The effects of overdose of dextropropoxyphene are similar to those of other opioids, but a particularly worrying feature is the rapid onset of respiratory depression. Patients surviving the effects of dextropropoxyphene in co-proxamol may develop hepatic necrosis from the paracetamol. The continuing popularity of preparations containing dextropropoxyphene is difficult to understand; controlled studies have failed to show that dextropropoxyphene is any more effective than paracetamol or aspirin alone. (Hopkinson et al. 1976).

Combination analgesics

Combination analgesics (see co-proxamol above) contain both a peripherally acting (e.g. aspirin or paracetamol) and a centrally acting (e.g. codeine or dextropropoxyphene) analgesic. The rationale for combined analgesics is that they will block pain at the site of the injury as well as alter the transmission of pain within the central nervous system.

Evidence from clinical trials would suggest that combined analgesics are more effective than when the individual constituents are used singularly. The efficacy of the preparations is often more than additive. Although combined analgesics are widely used, there is also a high incidence of unwanted effects; this may be due to a synergistic effect of the two component drugs (Parkhouse 1975).

Naloxone

This is a competitive opioid antagonist, mainly used to treat opioid overdose, and in particular to reverse the effect of an opioid on respiration. In the treatment of opioid-induced respiratory depression, naloxone must be given intravenously (0.4–0.8 mg) for immediate effect. If the depression is not reversed, the dose is repeated after two minutes. The half-life of naloxone is only one hour and further repeated administration may be required. Naloxone can also be used if there is a problem in diagnosing physical dependence or addiction to the opioids for, in such subjects, naloxone will induce symptoms of withdrawal.

Buprenorphine

This is a semi-synthetic opioid derived from thebaine. An intramuscular dose of 0.4 mg buprenorphine has an analgesic potency equivalent to 10 mg of intramuscular morphine; the duration of analgesia with this dose of buprenorphine is about six hours. The drug is particularly well-absorbed when given sublingually. Buprenorphine is extensively bound to plasma protein (96 per cent) and has a plasma half-life of about three hours. Most of the drug is excreted unchanged in the faeces.

Receptor binding studies suggest that buprenorphine is a partial agonist for the μ-receptor but may well act as an antagonist at other opioid receptors.

Unwanted effects of buprenorphine are similar to those of morphine and include sedation, nausea, vomiting, dizziness, sweating, and dependence (Heel *et al.* 1980).

Methadone

This is a synthetic opioid, first manufactured during the early 1940s. It is well absorbed from all routes of administration, and is effective when given orally. Methadone is broken down in the liver and the metabolites are excreted in the urine; the plasma half-life is one to one-and-a-half days. Methadone is a μ-agonist and on a dose per dose basis is as effective an analgesic as morphine. However, the advantages of methadone over morphine are its longer duration of action and efficacy when given orally. The main uses of methadone are relief of pain, treatment of opioid abstinence syndrome, and treatment (by substitution) of heroin users.

USE OF OPIOIDS IN DENTISTRY

Although morphine and related analgesics are widely used in relieving pain, their dental application is limited. Most types of dental pain, such as in pulpitis, dry socket, or pericoronitis, can be effectively treated by local measures, and the dental surgeon is unlikely to prescribe opioids for these conditions.

Postoperative pain after a dental surgical procedure is the main indication for recommending or prescribing analgesics. Such pain has a major inflammatory component, and as the opioids possess no anti-inflammatory action, their efficacy is doubtful in this context. Clinical trials to evaluate codeine, dextropropoxyphene, and pentazocine, have all shown that the efficacy of these drugs in relieving pain after removal of impacted lower third molars is poor (Seymour and Walton 1984). One study (Seymour *et al.* 1982) showed that dihydrocodeine, when given intravenously, increased the severity of postoperative dental pain when compared to a placebo.

Critical reappraisal of evidence supporting the efficacy of opioids in dental pain indicates that these drugs are of virtually no value. However, the opioids are particularly effective in the treatment of postoperative pain after general surgery, and of cancer pain. Cancer pain, as described earlier, has emotional and suffering components that would be alleviated by the euphoriant properties of the opioids together with alteration of the pain reaction. Pain after general surgery, as after dental surgery, will have a similar, but greater, inflammatory element, but the patient's reaction to their pain may differ because of their own expectations: for example one undergoing major abdominal surgery as an in-patient is likely to have a different view of their circumstances from one who has had impacted lower third molars removed in an out-patient clinic. The difference between out-patient and in-patient surgery may be reflected in different levels of anxiety, particularly if the surgery has been undertaken for a life-threatening condition. The apparent lack of pain relief afforded by the opioids after dental surgery may be accounted for by the relative absence of any significant emotional component of the pain, a factor likely to be present after major in-patient surgery.

Thus analgesics with an established anti-inflammatory property (such as aspirin) appear to offer more advantages in the treatment of dental pain than the opioids.

REFERENCES

Akil, H., Watson, S. J., Young, E., Lewis, M. E., Khachaturian, H., and Walker, J. M. (1984). Endogenous opioids: biology and function. *Annual Review of Neuroscience*, **7**, 223–55.

Alderman, E. L., Barry, W. H., Graham, A. F., and Harrison, D. C. (1972). Haemodynamic effects of morphine and pentazocine differ in cardiac patients. *New England Journal of Medicine*, **287**, 623–7.

Barber, J. and Mayer, D. (1977). Evaluation of the efficacy and neural mechanisms of a hypnotic analgesia procedure in experimental and clinical dental pain. *Pain*, **4**, 41–8.

Beckett, A. H., Taylor, J. F., and Kourounakis, P. (1970). The absorption, distribution and excretion of pentazocine in man after oral and intravenous administration. *Journal of Pharmacy and Pharmacology*, **22**, 123–8.

Bellenger, J. C., Post, R. M., Sternberg, D. E., Kammen, D. P., Cowdry, R. W., and Goodwin F. K. (1979). Headaches after lumbar puncture and insensitivity to pain in psychiatric patients. *New England Journal of Medicine*, **30**, 110.

Chang, K. W. and Cuatrecasas, P. (1981). Heterogeneity and properties of opiate receptors. *Federation Proceedings*, **40**, 2729–34.

Dehen, H., Willer, J. G., Prier, S., Boureau, F., and Chambier, J. (1978). Congenital insensitivity to pain and the morphine-like analgesic system. *Pain*, **5**, 351–8.

Forrest, W. H. (1974). Oral pentazocine. *Annals of Internal Medicine*, **8**, 644–6.

Gazelius, B., Olgart, L., Edwall, L., and Trowbridge, H. O. (1977). Effects of substance P on sensory nerves and blood flow in the feline dental pulp. In *Pain in the trigeminal region* (ed. D. J. Anderson and B. Matthews) pp. 95–101. Elsevier, Amseterdam.

Geschwind, N. (1975). Insensitivity to pain in psychotic patients. *New England Journal of Medicine*, **296**, 1480.

Goldstein, A. and Hilgard, E. R. (1975). Failure of the opiate antagonist naloxone to modify hypnotic analgesia. *Proceedings of the National Academy of Sciences U.S.A.*, **72**, 2041–43.

Heel, R. C., Brogden, R. N., Speight, T. M., and Avery, G. S. (1980). Buprenorphine: a review of its pharmacological properties and therapeutic efficacy. *Drugs*, **17**, 81–110.

Hopkinson, J. H., Blatt, G., and Cooper, M. (1976) Effective pain relief: comparative results with acetaminophen in a new formulation, propoxyphene, a napsylate–acetaminophen combination and placebo. *Current Therapeutic Research*, **19**, 622–30.

Houck, J. C., Kimball, C., Chang, G., Pedigo, N. W. Y., and Yamamuraz, H. I. (1980). Placental β-endorphin-like peptides. *Science*, **207**, 78–9.

Hughes, J. H., Smith, T. W., Kosterlitz, H. W., Fothergill, I. A., Morgan, B., and Morris, H. R. (1975). Identification of two related pentapeptides from the brain with patient opiate agonist activity. *Nature*, **258**, 577–9.

Jessel, T. M. and Iversen, L. L. (1977). Opiate analgesics inhibit substance P release from rat trigeminal nucleus. *Nature*, **268**, 549–51.

Langdon, K. (1969). Adverse effects of dihydrocodeine. *British Dental Journal*, **126**, 494.

Levine, J. D., Gordon, N. C., and Fields, H. L. (1978). The mechanisms of placebo analgesia. *Lancet*, **ii**, 654–7.

Martin, W. R. (1983). Pharmacology of opioids. *Pharmacology Review*, **35**, 283–323.

Mayer, D. J., Price, D. D., and Rafii, A. (1977). Antagonism of acupuncture analgesia in man by the narcotic antagonist naloxone. *Brain Research*, **121**, 368–72.

Melzack, R. and Wall, P. (1965). Pain mechanisms: a new theory. *Science*, **150**, 971–9.

Nasrallah, H. A., Holley, T., and Janowsky, D. S. (1979). Opiate antagonism fails to reverse hypnotic-induced analgesia. *Lancet*, **i**, 1355.

Omaya, T., Jin, T., Yamaya, R., Ling, N., and Guillemin, R. (1980). Profound analgesic effects of β-endorphin in man. *Lancet*, **i**, 122–6.

Parkhouse, J. (1975). Simple analgesics. *Drugs*, **10**, 366–93.

Pert, C. B. and Snyder, S. H. (1973). Opiate receptor: demonstration in nervous tissue. *Science*, **179**, 101–14.

Seymour, R. A. and Walton, J. G. (1984). Pain control after third molar surgery—a review. *International Journal of Oral Surgery*, **13**, 457–85.

Seymour, R. A., Rawlins, M. D., and Rowell, F. J. (1982). Dihydrocodeine-induced hyperalgesia in postoperative dental pain. *Lancet*, **i**, 1425–6.

Sjölund, B. H. and Eriksson, M. B. E. (1979). The influence of naloxone on analgesia produced by peripheral conditioning stimulation. *Brain Research*, **173**, 295–301.

Sjölund, B. H., Terenius, L., and Eriksson, M. B. E. (1977). Increased cerebrospinal fluid levels of endorphins after electro-acupuncture. *Acta Physiologica Scandinavica*, **100**, 382–4.

Skegg, D. G., Doll, R., and Perry, J. (1977). Use of medicines in general practice. *British Medical Journal*, **ii**, 1561–3.

Stephenson, J. B. P. (1978). Reversal of hypnosis-induced analgesia by naloxone. *Lancet*, **ii**, 991–2.

Sweet, W. H. (1980). Neuropeptides and monoaminergic neurotransmitters: their relation to pain. *Journal of the Royal Society of Medicine*, **73**, 482–91.

Tammisto, T., Jaatela, A., Nikki, P., and Takki, S. (1971). Effects of pentazocine and pethidine on plasma catecholamine levels. *Annals of Clinical Research*, **3**, 22–9.

von Euller, U. S. and Gaddum, J. H. (1931). Unidentified depressor substance in certain tissue extracts. *Journal of Physiology*, **72**, 74–87.

von Knorring L., Almay, B. G. L., Johansson, F., and Terenius, L. (1978). Pain perception and endorphin levels in cerebrospinal fluid. *Pain*, **5**, 359–67.

Whittington, R. M. (1977). Dextropropoxyphene (Distalgesic) overdose in the West Midlands. *British Medical Journal*, **ii**, 172–3.

Yanagida, H. (1978). Congenital insensitivity and naloxone. *Lancet*, **ii**, 520–1.

7

Local anaesthetics (local analgesics)

LOCAL anaesthesia may be produced by four methods:

(1) by the application of cold;

(2) by the application of pressure to nerve trunks;

(3) by rendering the tissues anaemic;

(4) by paralysing sensory nerve endings or nerve fibres with drugs.

The last of these methods is the most important therapeutically; method (1) has a limited application whilst (2) and (3) are unsafe for therapeutic use. Many different substances can interfere with the transmission of nerve impulses (method (4)), but for a drug to be clinically acceptable as a local anaesthetic, it must be able to produce a fully reversible block of nerve conduction at concentrations that do not damage the tissues. For example, procaine or lignocaine satisfy these criteria, whereas phenol abolishes the transmission of nerve impulses by causing irreversible damage to nerve fibres. Since 1884 when Karl Koller first introduced cocaine into clinical use (for historical review, see Koller 1928), much effort has been expended in trying to produce better and safer local anaesthetics. The perfect local anaesthetic does not exist and all of those in clinical use are capable of producing a variety of unwanted effects, which are discussed later.

CHEMISTRY

As a group, local anaesthetics are organic bases and as such are insoluble in water; but they can be converted into soluble salts, for example hydrochlorides, and these are the form in which they are used clinically. Their detailed chemical structures vary, but as Löfgren (1948) points out, the formulae of most local anaesthetics are built on a common plan, which is composed of three parts, as explained by the list and formula below:

(1) an aromatic residue with an acidic group (lipophilic); (R_1 where R = radical);

(2) a connecting intermediate aliphatic chain (with ester or amide link), usually an amino-alcohol; (R_2);

(3) a terminal substituted amino group (hydrophilic); (R_3 and R_4).

Thus a general formula may be written as follows, the three parts being numbered as in the preceding list:

$$R_1CO—R_2—N\begin{array}{c}R_3\\R_4\end{array}$$

$$(1)\quad (2)\quad (3)$$

Note that R_3 and R_4 may form part of a cyclic system as in mepivacaine and bupivacaine, two of the agents included in Fig. 7.1, which shows the structure of some common local anaesthetics according to the common plan described above.

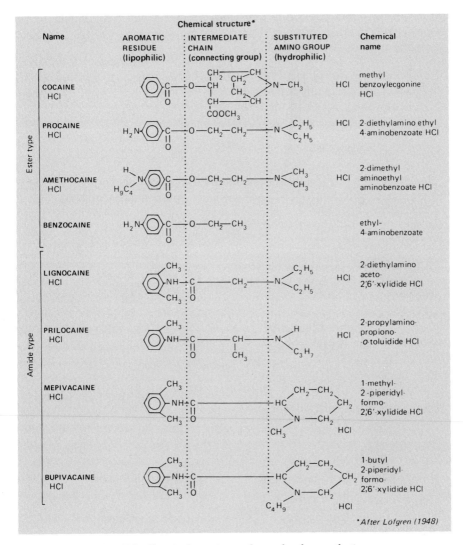

Fig. 7.1. Chemical structures of some local anaesthetics.

Physico-chemical properties

There are three that need to be considered, namely ionization, the partition coefficient, and protein binding.

Ionization

As local anaesthetics are weak bases, it follows that they will exist partly in an un-ionized form and partly in an ionized form, the proportion of each depending upon the pK_a or dissociation constant of the particular drug (i.e. the pH at which the ionized and non-ionized forms of the drug are present in equal amounts), and the pH of the surrounding medium (see Table 7.1 below and also Chapter 1). For example, procaine (as procaine hydrochloride) with a pK_a of 9.0 will ionize according to the following equation:

un-ionized form   ionized form

The proportion of procaine that is un-ionized at the physiological pH of 7.4 can be calculated from the Henderson–Hasselbach equation (see Chapter 1):

$$\text{For procaine, } pK_a = 9.0$$

$$pH = 7.4$$

$$\text{For bases, } pH = pK_a - \log_{10} \frac{\text{ionized base}}{\text{un-ionized base}},$$

$$\text{so re-writing, } \log_{10} \frac{\text{ionized base}}{\text{un-ionized base}} = pK_a - pH$$

$$= 9.0 - 7.4$$

$$= 1.6.$$

Taking antilogs on both sides of the equation,

$$\frac{\text{ionized base}}{\text{un-ionized base}} = \frac{39.8}{1.0}$$

$$\text{i.e. approximately} = \frac{40.0}{1.0}.$$

Therefore, the percentage ratio of ionized/un-ionized molecules ($= 40$) within a total of $40 + 1$ molecules ($= 41$) is:

$$\frac{40}{41} \times 100 = 97.6\%.$$

Expressed the opposite way round, the ratio of un-ionized/ionized molecules is 1/41 (2.4 per cent). Thus, at pH 7.4 only a small proportion of a dose of injected procaine will be present in the un-ionized form that is lipid-soluble and readily crosses the lipid-containing sheaths of nerves. At one time it was believed that the un-ionized form of a local anaesthetic was responsible for producing the local anaesthetic effect, but the work of Ritchie and his colleagues (see Ritchie and Greengard 1966; Ritchie 1975) has indicated it is the *ionized* form that is able to block nerve conduction (see later). However, it is now clear that *both* the un-ionized and ionized forms are important if a local anaesthetic effect is to be achieved. Thus, the un-ionized form, being lipid-soluble, is able to cross the fatty sheath of nerves and gain ready access inside the nerve fibres; having gained entry to the cytoplasm of the nerve cell it is the ionized form that is able to block conduction (see later under 'Mechanism of action of local anaesthetics'). As these two forms of a local anaesthetic are in equilibrium it follows that as soon as some un-ionized molecules arrive inside the cell, some will become ionized, the proportion depending upon the pK_a of the drug and the intracellular pH, which is normally lower (e.g. pH 7 or less) than the extracellular pH of 7.4; see Fig. 7.3, p. 119).

Table 7.1 lists the pK_a of those local anaesthetics commonly used in dentistry (together with some others), and also indicates the percentage of each drug in the un-ionized and ionized forms at pH 7.4. It can be seen that in general the amide types have a lower pK_a than the ester types (with the exception of benzocaine, which does not form soluble salts and can therefore only be used as a surface local anaesthetic). This means that the proportion of the lipid-soluble (i.e. un-ionized) form present in solution at physiological pH (7.4) is considerably greater with the amides (e.g. for lignocaine, 25 per cent) as compared with the ester type (e.g. for procaine, 2.4 per cent). This accounts for the faster onset of action of lignocaine (1–2 min) compared with procaine (2–5 min).

Partition coefficient

The partition coefficient measures lipid solubility or, to be more precise, the relative solubilities of an agent in fat and water—so that the more fat-soluble and the less water-soluble a compound is, the higher the numerical value (compare procaine = 0.6 with lignocaine = 3; see Table 7.1). All other things being equal, the greater the fat solubility, the greater the ease and rapidity with which a compound will cross a lipid barrier such as a nerve sheath.

Protein binding

Most drugs bind to plasma proteins in varying degrees (see Chapter 1) and local anesthetics are no exception (see Table 7.1). The two proteins chiefly involved are

Table 7.1. Pharmacokinetic data for certain local anaesthetics

Drug[a] (MW)	pK_a[a]	% un-ionized[b] (pH 7.4)	% ionized[b] (pH 7.4)	Partition[c] coefficient	Plasma[d] protein binding %	Toxicity	Vol. of[d] distribution (litres)	Estimated[d] hepatic extraction ratio	Clearance[d] (l min⁻¹)	$T_{0.5}$[d]
Ester type										
Cocaine (303)	8.6	6	94	?	?	V. high	118	?	0.71–3.08	0.7–1.5
Procaine (236)	9.0	2.4	97.6	0.6	5.8	Low	?	?	?	<1
Amethocaine (264)	8.5	7	93	80	75.6	High	?	?	?	?
Benzocaine (165)	2.5	—	—	?	—	Low	—	—	—	—
Amide type										
Lignocaine (234)	7.9	25	75	3	64	Medium	91	0.65	0.95	1.6
Prilocaine (220)	7.9	25	75	1	50	Low/ medium	191	?	2.37	1.6
Mepivacaine (283)	7.6	33	67	1	77	Medium	84	0.52	0.78	1.9
Bupivacaine (302)	8.1	17	83	28	96	Medium	73	0.38	0.58	2.7

Abbreviations: pK_a = dissociation constant; ? = data not available; — = not applicable; MW = Molecular weight; $T_{0.5}$ = systemic; $T_{0.5}$ i.e. the time (hours) take for the amount of drug absorbed into the circulation to fall by one half.
Partition coefficient = lipid/water solubility ratio.
Vol. of distribution = effective volume (litres) into which, after absorption, the drug is finally distributed.
Clearance (l min⁻¹) = number of litres of plasma cleared of the drug per minute.
Hepatic extraction ratio = fraction of drug removed from the blood during a single passage through the liver (NB: high >0.7).
[a]Martindale (1982) [b]calculated from Henderson–Hasselbach equation (see text) [c]Wildsmith (1986) [d]Tucker and Mather (1979), and Arthur *et al.* (1979).)

α-1 acid glycoprotein, which has high affinity but low capacity, and albumin, which has low affinity but high capacity. The binding is a simple reversible one and tends to increase in proportion to the number of side chains of the molecule; for example, lignocaine 64 per cent binding compared with bupivacaine 96 per cent. In general the degree of protein binding is related to the duration of action of the local anaesthetic. This is because the bound portion acts as a reservoir from which free drug can be released in order to replace that which has left the site either due to diffusion or metabolism. Thus, we may compare the duration of action of lignocaine (plain), which is 15 to 45 minutes, with that of bupivacaine (plain), which is six hours. However, it should be noted that other factors may alter this relationship. Thus, prilocaine is less protein-bound (50 per cent) than lignocaine (64 per cent) and yet has a longer duration of action because it does not have the vasodilator action of lignocaine, and this more than compensates for its physico-chemical disadvantages (Wildsmith 1986).

Relevance of chemical structure to clinical use

Local anaesthetics form one of the most important groups of drugs used by the dental practitioner, who should therefore have some general awareness of their chemical structure. There are also at least four special categories in which some knowledge of this structure is relevant to clinical use; these are now detailed.

Local anaesthetic activity of amines

Figure 7.1 (above) shows that although the chemical structures of those local anaesthetics in clinical use have general features in common, there is considerable variation between the different formulae. Many drugs in other groups that are amines also possess local anaesthetic activity—for example, mepyramine (H_1-blocker), atropine (antimuscarinic), pethidine (opioid), and quinidine (anti-arrhythmic). However, this action is not made use of clinically because, of course, these drugs have other actions as well, and some are irritant on injection into the tissues. Knowledge of this action explains some of their side effects, such as the numbing effect on the tongue produced by some antihistamines (H_1-blockers). Similarly, it accounts for the fact that the inadvertent intravenous administration of a sufficiently large dose of an H_1-blocker may interfere with the normal conduction processes within the heart (see Chapter 15).

Biotransformation of local anaesthetics

The presence or absence of an esteratic link in the intermediate chain determines whether or not a compound is susceptible to attack by the cholinesterase group of enzymes. Thus, the ester link in procaine is susceptible to the ubiquitous pseudocholinesterase (plasma esterases), and this is an important reason why procaine is rapidly inactivated after injection (see later). By contrast, the amide link in lignocaine can only be broken by amidases located in the liver, so accounting in part for the longer systemic half-life of this drug (see Table 7.1 above).

Hypersensitivity

Drug allergy due to a local anaesthetic is obviously important, and the main features and underlying mechanism of it are dealt with in Chapter 21. In this context, a direct consequence of chemical structure is that if a patient is known to be hypersensitive to a certain local anaesthetic with a formula based on p-aminobenzoic acid (e.g. procaine) it is almost certain that they will show cross-hypersensitivity to any other local anaesthetic based on that acid (e.g. amethocaine). On the other hand, they might well not show cross-hypersensitivity to lignocaine or prilocaine because these compounds are not derivatives of p-aminobenzoic acid (see Fig. 7.1). Nevertheless, it would be unwise to make this assumption in the absence of specific tests for hypersensitivity to lignocaine or prilocaine, tests that are not without their own risks and should be carried out by a specialist in this field.

Drug interactions

Local anaesthetics that are derivatives of p-aminobenzoic acid (e.g. procaine and amethocaine) can under certain conditions interfere with the bacteriostatic action of sulphonamides (see Chapter 10). This is because sulphonamides act as competitive antagonists to p-aminobenzoic acid, which is normally an essential growth factor for micro-organisms sensitive to the sulphonamide group of drugs. The presence of these local anaesthetics during sulphonamide therapy would make available p-aminobenzoic acid and so redress the balance in favour of the bacteria. In practice, however, as Laurence and Bennett (1987) have pointed out: '. . . with wounds, or when local anaesthesia is being used for lumbar puncture or other exploration in sulphonamide-treated patients, local sulphonamide antagonism followed by infection is a theoretical risk.' It is noteworthy that local anaesthetics with no p-aminobenzoic acid moiety (e.g. lignocaine, prilocaine) do not antagnoize sulphonamides.

PHARMACOLOGICAL ACTIONS OF LOCAL ANAESTHETICS

These may be listed as follows:

(1) reversible block of conduction in nerve endings and nerve trunks;
(2) muscle: (i) direct relaxation of smooth muscle (e.g. vasodilatation via vascular smooth muscle; (ii) interference with neuromuscular transmission (i.e. in skeletal muscle)—usually not clinically significant;

(3) quinidine-like action on the heart (see Chapter 15);

(4) stimulation and/or depression of the CNS.

These apparently different actions of local anaesthetics are due largely, if not entirely, to a common mechanism of action on excitable cell membranes, as is now described.

Nerve conduction and the mechanism of action of local anaesthetics

The conduction of a nerve impulse along a nerve fibre depends critically upon the movement of certain ions across the nerve cell membrane. In the resting state (i.e. in the absence of a nerve impulse) this membrane is permeable to potassium ions but only very slightly permeable to sodium ions (Fig. 7.2); the result is a difference of electrical potential, such that the inside of the nerve cell is approximately 80 millivolts negative to the outside. The intracellular concentration of sodium ions is normally kept low by means of an active extrusion process known as the sodium pump. During conduction of a nerve impulse, sodium permeability transiently increases by several hundred times and, as the concentration of sodium ions outside the nerve cell is more than ten times that inside the fibre (i.e. there is a concentration gradient of sodium ions from outside to inside the cell), these ions diffuse rapidly into the cell. As a result, there is a temporary reversal of electrical polarity across the cell membrane (Fig. 7.2), and this permits an outflow of potassium ions down their concentration gradient (which is opposite to that of sodium, i.e. from within to without the cell). The outward movement of potassium ions brings about a repolarization during which a short-lived hyperpolarization (i.e. reversal or overshoot) occurs (Fig. 7.2b). The sodium pump, which is temporarily overwhelmed during the momentary inward rush of sodium ions, then extrudes the excess of sodium ions and this is accompanied by a re-entry of potassium ions with recovery of the membrane potential to the resting value (Fig. 7.2c). Those who elucidated these mechanisms (see, for example, Hodgkin and Huxley 1945) have shown that if these ionic movements are prevented, especially the inward entry of sodium ions, then nerve conduction no longer takes place.

There is much evidence to support the contention that local anaesthetics prevent the inward entry of sodium ions, which is essential for normal impulse transmission. As a result they prevent the generation and conduction of action potentials. Voltage clamp experiments, and other studies using radioactive neurotoxins and antibodies, have revealed the presence of sodium channels with several sites at which local anaesthetics could interfere with the normal changes in sodium permeability (Hille et al. 1975; Cahalan and Almers 1979). Thus blocking agents may act at specific receptor sites on the external or internal part of the sodium channels located in the nerve cell membrane. The biotoxins, tetrodotoxin and saxitoxin, are both potent local anaesthetics; they bind to a

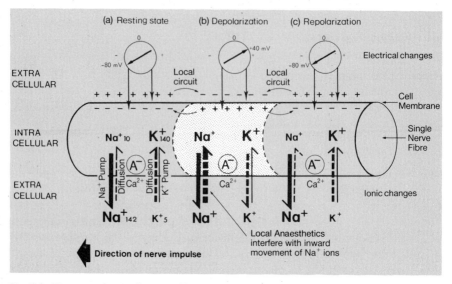

Fig. 7.2. Diagram of a single nerve fibre to illustrate the electrical (upper surface) and ionic (lower surface) changes that occur during the conduction of a nerve impulse (central shaded area) passing in the direction from right to left (i.e. (c) to (a)). (a) Resting state: the extracellular concentration of sodium ions (Na^+) greatly exceeds the intracellular concentration, whilst the opposite is true for potassium ions (K^+). (Indicated by relative size of symbols; the actual amounts in mmol/l are also shown). Active transport of ions is indicated by continuous arrows ($\rightarrow$) and diffusion by broken arrows ($--\rightarrow$). The presence of intracellular indiffusible and negatively charged protein anions (A^-) and extracellular calcium ions (Ca^{2+}), which are essential components, is also shown. (b) Depolarization: the reversal of membrane polarity caused by the transient inward rush of Na^+ is followed by the outward movement of K^+. (c) Repolarization: the sodium pump extrudes the excess of intracellular Na^+ and this is rapidly followed by the inward movement of K^+. The presence of local electrical circuits at the junctions between normal and depolarized segments of nerve are indicated by semicircular arrows. Local anaesthetics are believed to block nerve conduction by interfering with the inward movement of Na^+ which is essential for normal transmission. (This diagram is an oversimplification of a complicated process; for further details see text.)

receptor on the external aspect of the sodium channel and thereby block the pore. Unfortunately they are unsuitable for clinical use. By contrast, local anaesthetics in common clinical use act at receptors situated on the internal or intracellular aspect of the sodium channel. It also seems likely that local anaesthetics can alter the membrane structure of the nerve to distort and close the sodium channels. Thus, local anaesthetics probably act by both mechanisms.

Sodium channels

The available evidence suggests that the sodium channel involves at least two 'gates'. One of these is a barrier and is named an 'activation' or 'm' gate, whereas the other is an 'inactivation' or 'h' gate (see Fig. 7.3). The depolarization that occurs with the arrival of a nerve impulse opens the 'm' gate and sodium ions are

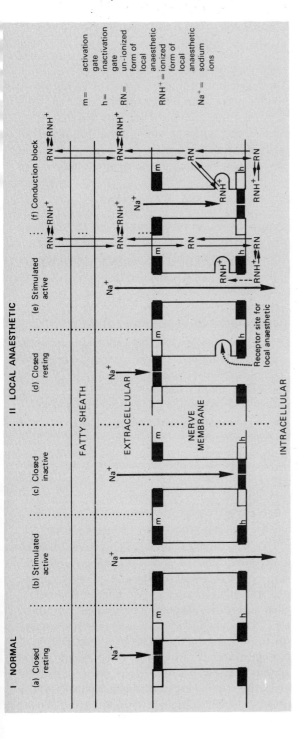

Fig. 7.3. Diagram to illustrate mechanism of action of a local anaesthetic. A section of nerve cell membrane is shown containing sodium channels with the m and h gates that control them. A length of accompanying fatty nerve sheath is also shown. I. NORMAL. The nerve cell membrane may be in one of three phases. (a) Closed resting: m closed, h open, sodium channel closed. (b) Stimulated active: m and h open, sodium channel open with inward movement of sodium ions. (c) Closed inactive: m open, h closed, sodium channel closed and remains so until full repolarization has taken place (thus accounting for refractory period). Note carefully that stages (a), (b), and (c) in this diagram correspond to stages (a), (b), and (c) in Fig. 7.2. II. LOCAL ANAESTHETIC. (d) Closed resting as in (a) but includes proposed receptor site for local anaesthetic which is linked to the h gate. (e) Local anesthetic has been applied outside the nerve sheath where it exists partly in the unionized (lipid soluble) form and partly in the ionized (lipid insoluble) form. The unionized form has diffused across the nerve sheath where it exists partly in the unionized (lipid soluble) form and partly in the ionized (lipid insoluble) form. The unionized form has diffused across the nerve sheath to the space beneath it and thence across the nerve membrane to enter the nerve cell where it partially reionizes (according to the Henderson–Hasselbach equation: see text). The ionized moiety then enters the internal end of the sodium channel to occupy and activate the local anaesthetic receptor site which closes the h gate: the situation depicted in (e) is just prior to the closure of the h gate by the local anaesthetic. (f) The h gate has now been activated and the membrane is held in the closed inactive state as in (c). Note: it seems probable that when the h gate has been closed by the presence of local anaesthetic, the latter can continue to gain access to the receptor site by diffusing to it directly from within the nerve membrane, as indicated by the pair of diagonal arrows. RN represents unionized form of local anaesthetic, RNH⁺ represents ionized form of local anaesthetic.)

able to move through the membranes, but this is soon stopped by the operation of the 'h' gate, which closes the channel. Once closed, it cannot re-open until full repolarization has taken place, thus explaining the phenomenon of the refractory period after excitation during which a nerve cannot be excited however large the stimulus. Local anaesthetics first traverse the sodium channel and then bind to an intracellular receptor, thereby interfering with the gate mechanism described above. They may also gain access by diffusing through the lipophilic membrane of the axon and then enter the intracellular opening of the sodium channel (see Fig. 7.3).

Role of calcium

An adequate extracellular concentration of calcium is essential for normal nerve transmission. Thus, reducing this concentration can potentiate the action of a local anaesthetic because both agents compete for the same phospholipid receptor. Nevertheless it seems clear that calcium is not involved in the primary nerve-blocking action of local anaesthetics.

Differential sensitivity of nerve fibres to local anaesthetics

As a general rule the susceptibility of nerve fibres to local anaesthetics is inversely proportional to their diameter, so that smaller nerve fibres are more sensitive to their blocking action than larger diameter fibres (Gasser and Erlanger 1929). This appears to be related to the greater susceptibility of smaller nerve fibres to sodium lack (Nathan and Sears 1962). As sensory information is carried by nerve fibres smaller than those that carry motor information, sensation is lost before motor activity is blocked. In general terms, pain is the first sensation to disappear followed by temperature, touch, and pressure.

Measurement of local anaesthetic activity

There are many different methods for the estimation of local anaesthetic activity, which include the measurement of variables such as minimal effective concentration, latency of onset of anaesthesia, or duration of effect. Unfortunately, there is no standard method available so that it is difficult or inappropriate to compare the results obtained from different tests. One particularly useful method by which the relative potency of two local anaesthetics can be determined in man is that devised by Mongar (1955). in which local anaesthetic is applied to an exposed area of dermis on the flexor aspect of the forearm. A modification of this method, using intradermal injections of drug or placebo (saline), also produces informative and useful results (see Fig. 7.4, p. 124). However, it must be appreciated that results obtained by this method are not directly applicable to the use of local anaesthetics in dentistry; in this context, an elegant and relevant method is that of Bjorn (1946), in which local anaesthetics are tested on teeth subjected to electrical stimulation.

FATE AND METABOLISM OF LOCAL ANAESTHETICS

Local anaesthetics are not absorbed from intact skin but many of them, when applied to mucous membranes (or *damaged* skin), or injected into tissues, are absorbed into the blood stream. The rate at which absorption takes place depends principally upon:

(1) the particular drug and its concentration;

(2) the vascularity of the tissues, the rate of absorption being faster the more vascular the part;

(3) whether or not a vasoconstrictor drug has been added in order to prolong the action of the local anaesthetic (discussed later).

All local anaesthetics undergo metabolism in the liver to inactive metabolites. In addition, as we have seen, those which contain an ester link in their chemical structure are also broken down by plasma cholinesterase (pseudocholinesterase) so that procaine is split into its constituents namely, p-aminobenzoic acid (sometimes abbrev. PABA) and diethylaminoethanol (see Fig. 7.1). Kalow (1952) and Brodie *et al.* (1948) have shown that procaine is broken down by this enzyme at about 20 mg per minute. Amethocaine, which also contains an ester linkage, is hydrolysed by plasma cholinesterase at about one quarter the rate of procaine. By contrast, lignocaine and prilocaine contain amide and not ester linkages and so are not susceptible to plasma cholinesterase; these molecules are split by amidases in the liver.

Thus, there are two ways in which the liver is of importance in the metabolism of local anaesthetics: (i) it is the major site of metabolism of many of them, and (ii) it is the source of plasma cholinesterase, which is important in the metabolism of those that contain an ester linkage. For these reasons, a normal dose of local anaesthetic given to a patient suffering from impaired liver function could result in relative overdosage (see Chapter 21).

THE PROPERTIES OF THE 'IDEAL' LOCAL ANAESTHETIC

Although no such compound exists, consideration of these properties is a convenient way to highlight the advantages and disadvantages of those local anaesthetics that are available for clinical use. It also leads us into the discussion of some of the important problems associated with the unwanted effects of this group of drugs.

The 'ideal' local anaesthetic should have the following properties:

1. The drug should exert a specific and fully reversible paralytic action on nerves and nerve endings in concentrations that do not injure or irritate the tissues. Surprisingly, there is no standard method to compare the potency of local

anaesthetics. As noted earlier, methods for undertaking this in man are those devised by Bjorn (1946) and Mongar (1955).

2. The drug should produce rapid onset of anaesthesia without preliminary excitation. One of the disadvantages of cinchocaine is that local anaesthesia takes from five to ten minutes to develop, whereas with lignocaine the onset of action is very rapid (see Table 7.2 below).

3. The drug should be soluble, chemically stable, and capable of sterilization by heat. Whereas cocaine is unstable when heated, lignocaine is very stable and can be sterilized by this means.

4. The drug should have penetrating properties so that it can be used for topical anaesthesia. In this respect, procaine is useless whereas lignocaine is effective.

5. The drug should have a high safety margin or therapeutic ratio. As discussed in Chapter 1, the therapeutic ratio is commonly expressed as:

$$\frac{LD_{50}}{ED_{50}}$$

where LD_{50} = dose that kills 50 per cent of a group of animals; ED_{50} = dose that produces a desired effect in 50 per cent of a group of animals.

The higher the value of this ratio, the greater the safety margin, i.e. the less toxic the drug. (The use of the term 'toxic(ity)' is in general undesirable; but in relation to testing the safety of a drug, particularly with reference to LD_{50} estimations in animals, the term 'toxicity' is established by long usage.)

Unfortunately, for local anaesthetics the problem of drug safety is more complex than hitherto realized and many of the data recorded in the literature are of doubtful clinical relevance. This is because most of the testing of local anaesthetics has been carried out by administering them to animals by the subcutaneous route. In *clinical practice*, the chief danger is inadvertent *intravenous* administration and, as Weatherby (1964) has pointed out, the '... maximal potential hazard associated with the use of an anaesthetic can therefore be expressed most accurately in terms of the LD_{50} obtained by *rapid intravenous injection*. With rapid intravenous injection, sufficient time is not available for the elimination of an appreciable fraction of the dose, and susceptible structures are exposed to the maximal concentration almost immediately.'

Ideally, estimates of potency should be performed on man although, at the present time, initial measurements must be done by means of animal tests. Purely objective tests on the isolated sciatic nerve of the frog can be carried out using complicated electronic stimulating and recording apparatus, as described by Rud (1961). On the other hand, available tests in man depend upon subjective assessment and utilize experimentally induced pain, which is vastly different from that of pathological origin. Thus, the measurement of therapeutic ratios for local anaesthetics is at present a compromise; in Table 7.2 below, these ratios for the drugs listed have been calculated using acute IV LD_{50} values in the rabbit and relative potencies obtained from isolated frog sciatic-nerve experiments (data from Truant and Takman 1965). On the basis of these calculations, procaine has the highest therapeutic ratio, followed (in descending order) by mepivacaine, prilocaine, lignocaine, cocaine, amethocaine, and bupivacaine.

6. When necessary, the drug should allow combination with a vasoconstrictor agent. The reasons usually given for the desirability of adding such an agent are threefold:

  (i) in order to prolong the duration of local anaesthesia by delaying absorption of the drug into the general circulation;

 (ii) in order to reduce the risk of an unwanted effect by reducing the rate of absorption of the drug into the general circulation;

(iii) in order to produce a relatively bloodless field to facilitate surgery.

It seems clear that the addition of a vasoconstrictor achieves number (i) of these listed objectives; Fig. 7.4 shows the results of a class experiment in which the time course of the local anaesthetic effect produced by procaine in the presence and absence of adrenaline was compared using Mongar's method (Mongar 1955). From common experience it is known that objective number (iii) is also attained, but the results of experiments in animals suggest that the objective number (ii) may not always be achieved with all local anaesthetics. Thus, when Avant and Weatherby (1960) compared the effect of the presence and absence of adrenaline on the LD_{50} values of five local anaesthetics, they found that only with amethocaine was the addition of a vasoconstrictor accompanied by a highly significant reduction in toxicity; with the four other compounds there was no appreciable difference, whilst procaine containing adrenaline 1:50 000 appeared more toxic than procaine alone. The trend toward a reduction in the amount of vasoconstrictor added without loss of effect (Gangarosa and Halik 1967), coupled with Avant and Weatherby's findings, make it important to ensure that the amount of vasoconstrictor added to any local anaesthetic is the minimum required.

In this context it should be noted, as pointed out by Cawson (1984), that mere psychological stress can raise plasma catecholamine levels by a factor of from five to ten (Dimsdale and Moss 1980), which is greater than that resulting from the use of a local anaesthetic with added vasoconstrictor.

UNWANTED EFFECTS OF LOCAL ANAESTHETICS

From time to time, the administration of a local anaesthetic is followed by some unfavourable response of the patient (see, for examples, Cawson et al. 1983). It appears that the majority of adverse reactions are due to inadvertent overdosage rather than to other causes (Moore and Bridenbaugh 1960). In such an event, it is important for the dental practitioner to have available a plan that will enable the possible causes and treatment of an adverse reaction to be considered quickly.

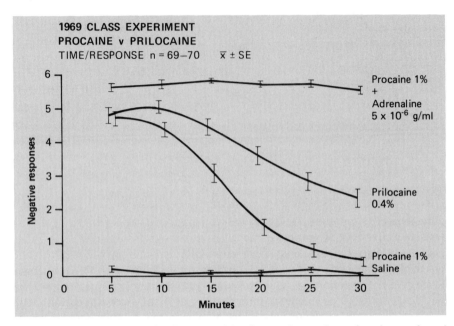

Fig. 7.4. Graph comparing the duration of local anaesthesia obtained with intradermal injections of procaine 1 per cent, procaine 1 per cent with adrenaline 5×10^{-6} g/ml ($= 1:200\,000$), prilocaine (Citanest) 0.4 per cent and physiological saline solution, using the method of Mongar (1955). The figures plotted are the mean results $\bar{x}$ ($\pm$standard error) obtained by 69–70 medical students during a class experiment in pharmacology. The experiment was designed as a 'double-blind' trial and the intradermal weals containing the four different doses were made in a random order to allow for differences in sensitivity along the flexor surface of the forearm. Each weal was tested for anaesthesia by pricking with a pin six times in different parts of the weal, using a standardized stimulus. The test was repeated every five minutes for half an hour and the total number of pricks not felt gave a measure of anaesthetic activity. The highly significant potentiation of the duration of action of procaine by the addition of adrenaline is shown. The longer duration of action of prilocaine 0.4 per cent compared with procaine 1 per cent is also illustrated; the saline control produced a trivial effect.

The first important decision to be made is whether the unwanted effect is due to the local anaesthetic or to some other factor. The second decision concerns the institution of the correct treatment.

The following classification is based on that of Sadove *et al.* (1952); its correspondence with the Type A/B classification (Rawlins and Thompson 1985) is indicated.

I. Unwanted effects that are due to the local anaesthetic agent

    (1) In normal individuals (Type A reactions):

        A. *Central nervous system*

            (i) Stimulation   (a) Cerebral cortex

    (ii) Depression   (b) Medulla

                   (i) respiratory centre;

                   (ii) vasomotor centre;

                   (iii) others.

    B. *Cardiovascular system*

       (i) Direct action on the heart

       (ii) Action on the vascular bed

(2) In intolerant individuals: effects include those in (1) above that follow a standard (or even sub-standard) dose.

(3) In abnormal individuals (Type B reactions):

    (i) hypersensitivity (drug allergy);

    (ii) idiosyncrasy.

II. Unwanted effects that are *not* due to the local anaesthetic

    (i) psychomotor;

    (ii) vasopressor (Type A).

Each of these problems will now be discussed in the format given in the list above.

Unwanted effects that are due to the local anaesthetic

In normal individuals (Type A reactions)

Central nervous system

All local anaesthetics are potential central stimulants (possibly through interference with central inhibitory mechanisms) and may produce apprehension, confusion, excitement, or frank euphoria. The patient may complain of giddiness, tinnitus, a metallic taste in the mouth, headache, nausea, and sometimes a feeling of coldness (Horton 1966). This stage may be followed by muscle twitchings and convulsions, the latter severe enough to require intravenous thiopentone to control them, administered as increments of 50 mg in 2.5 per cent solution (Horton 1966). Alternatively, midazolam (2.5–7 mg) can be given intravenously or 5 mg intramuscularly; if necessary, a further dose can be given half to one hour later.

Initial central stimulation may be followed by central depression, which leads to a fall in blood pressure with consequent loss of consciousness and respiratory depression. If this occurs it will be necessary to start artificial respiration. Occasionally the excitatory onset is absent and the clinical picture begins with sudden collapse due to depression of the respiratory, vasomotor, and other centres in the brain. In any collapse, the patient should be laid flat (on the floor if necessary), ideally with the head down, and steps should be taken to ensure that artificial respiration and cardiac massage can be instituted if needed. As pointed out by Moore and Bridenbaugh (1960), oxygen is the most important factor in the treatment of this emergency.

Although large doses of local anaesthetics are contra-indicated in epileptics, the relatively small amounts used in most dental procedures would seem to carry little risk of provoking a fit (E. A. Cooper, personal communication).

Cardiovascular system

If a dose of local anaesthetic is administered intravenously by accident it may cause cardiac arrest due to the direct depressant action of the drug on the heart and, in particular. on its conduction system. If this occurs it is vital to give external cardiac massage combined with artificial respiration immediately. On the other hand, the quantity of local anaesthetic inadvertently injected into a vein may instead be distributed in the body so that its effects are exerted mainly on the peripheral vasculature. When this happens, the clinical picture will be one of peripheral vascular collapse, which may require the administration of vasopressor drugs to restore the blood pressure.

In abnormal individuals (Type B)

Hypersensitivity

In certain individuals, the administration of a local anaesthetic is followed rapidly by anaphylactic shock or, after a latency of minutes or hours, by asthma, rhinitis, angio(neurotic) oedema, or urticaria. These responses are due to hypersensitivity and are the result of an antigen–antibody reaction in which the offending local anaesthetic has acted as a hapten (for details see Chapter 21). The majority of hypersensitivity reactions to local anaesthetics have been produced by procaine, or by a drug chemically related to procaine in which the acidic group is p-aminobenzoic acid (Hanauer 1955). By contrast, lignocaine, which is widely used, appears to be remarkably safe; one case of an anaphylactic reaction to lignocaine has been reported by Holti and Hood (1965), whose paper contains three references to other cases of suspected hypersensitivity to this drug (Noble and Pierce 1961; Kirkler 1962; Gregg et al. 1963). (See also a reference quoted by Trimble 1962). An unusual hyperpigmentation caused by lignocaine has been reported by Curley et al. (1987).

As discussed above, if a patient is found to be sensitive to one local anaesthetic, for example procaine, it is highly probable that they will exhibit cross-hypersensitivity to others that are chemically related to the offending one. On the other hand, it is less likely that they will be hypersensitive to any chemically unrelated local anaesthetic, such as, in this example, lignocaine, although it will be necessary to arrange for special sensitivity tests to be performed (by an expert).

In spite of the foregoing comments it should be noted that with those local anaesthetics in common use in dentistry, the incidence of allergy as a cause of adverse effects is very low (Cawson et al. 1983). The subject of local anaesthetics and allergic reactions is reviewed by Giovannitti and Bennett (1979), and by Reynolds (1987), to whom the reader is referred for further details.

In dentists and others, contact dermatitis due to application of ointments containing local anaesthetics or due to constant handling of these drugs may occur. Contact dermatitis is an example of delayed-type hypersensitivity (see Chapter 21); the use of ointments and creams containing local anaesthetics always carries risk of this hazard and these preparations should therefore be avoided wherever possible (see later).

Intolerance

For any given drug the population contains a very small minority of individuals whose response to the standard dose is exaggerated (see Chapter 21). Thus, if a very small dose of local anaesthetic is followed by one (or more) of the central nervous-system and/or cardiovascular responses classified under IA or IB in the list above (and is clearly not due to hypersensitivity or idiosyncrasy), it is most probably due to intolerance.

Idiosyncrasy

This unwanted effect comprises very rare reactions of a bizarre nature that cannot be explained by any of the other known mechanisms. When such an event occurs with a local anaesthetic containing an ester link, it is worthwhile considering the possibility that the patient's plasma may contain an atypical pseudocholinesterase, such as would also be revealed by an idiosyncratic response to suxamethonium (Downs 1966; see also p. 413).

Unwanted effects *not* due to the local anaesthetic

Psychomotor

This group includes effects in patients who faint at the sight of a needle, or whose psychological reaction is abnormal and may take the form of hysterical behaviour. This situation calls for sympathetic but firm handling; difficult cases may require appropriate sedation (see Chapter 8).

Vasopressor

The addition of vasoconstrictor substances, such as adrenaline or other sympathomimetic amines, to local anaesthetic solutions may produce local or general unwanted effects (see also earlier).

Local adverse effects include a change from initial vasoconstriction with pallor to local cyanosis accompanied by a local reduction in oxygen tension (Klingenstrom and Westermark 1964). This state of affairs can be followed by a reactive hyperaemia, which may increase the risk of postoperative bleeding.

General adverse effects of adrenaline in the concentrations and amounts used in dentistry do not commonly occur, although it should be noted that entry of adrenaline from local anaesthetic solutions into the circulation is known to be rapid (Tolas *et al.* 1982). However, if the solution is injected inadvertently into a vein, or undergoes rapid absorption, adverse effects could include tachycardia (interpreted by the patient as palpitations), apprehension, and a rise of blood pressure that may be dangerous in subjects with cardiovascular disease; these effects may also occur with other sympathomimetic amines. It is thus essential that all local anaesthetic administration in dentistry should be with an aspirating technique. It is just conceivable that in an exceptional case of adverse reaction to adrenaline, specific therapy in the form of an adrenergic α-receptor blocking drug, e.g. phentolamine, might be needed (see Chapters 13 to 15); under these circumstances medical aid should be sought immediately.

Recently it has been shown that adrenaline in amounts commonly injected with local anaesthetic during dental anaesthesia reduces plasma potassium concentrations within 10 minutes (Meechan and Rawlins 1987). Although this is unlikely to be a hazard in healthy individuals, it might predispose to cardiac arrhythmias in patients with incipient hypokalaemia caused by prolonged medication with potassium-losing diuretics (see Chapter 15).

SPECIFIC LOCAL ANAESTHETICS: 1. ESTER TYPE

(Throughout see Fig. 7.1 above for chemistry; see Table 7.2 for details of preparations including doses.)

Cocaine

In addition to being a local anaesthetic, this alkaloid, which is obtained from the leaves of the coca plant (*Coca erythroxolon*), has sympathomimetic properties, and also powerful stimulant actions on the central nervous system including the ability to induce psychic dependence. Consequently, cocaine is too dangerous to use by injection but, in special circumstances, can be employed topically, for example in dental apicectomies. Its sympathomimetic properties, at one time thought to be due to inhibition of amine oxidase, are now known to be due to its ability to block the uptake by the amine pump of noradrenaline released from adrenergic nerve endings (see Chapter 13). The use of cocaine is now restricted to topical application. The smallest effective dose should be used and never in higher concentration than 10 per cent. It is metabolized in the liver and also by plasma esterases, the plasma route being probably the more important in man (Van Dyke *et al.* 1976).

Procaine

Until the advent of lignocaine, procaine was for 50 years the nearest to the 'ideal' local anaesthetic. The fact that it is rapidly metabolized by the readily available plasma esterases is no doubt an important factor in its safety. However, this drug is useless topically and, as it is an active vasodilator, it is essential to add vasoconstrictor agents to solutions for injection. Although it is certainly one of the safest local anaesthetics, it may produce adverse reactions, including death, in patients hypersensitive to it (Criep and Ribeiro 1953). An additional hazard for the dental practitioner is contact dermatitis (see above). These disadvantages, coupled with the availability of better agents, mean that procaine is now used rarely in dentistry, and only occasionally for very special reasons in medicine.

Amethocaine

This local anaesthetic was first synthesized by O. Eisleb in Germany in 1928. It is the most potent (9.5 times the potency of lignocaine) of the ester type to be used clinically. It is rather unstable to heat and inactivated by alkalis. Amethocaine is an excellent topical anaesthetic although its onset of action is slow. As better and safer local anaesthetics (of the amide type; see below) are available, it is rarely used in dentistry and then only by topical application, such as to anaesthetize the gum prior to injection of another local anaesthetic.

Pharmacokinetics

Amethocaine is hydrolysed by plasma cholinesterase but about four times more slowly than procaine (see earlier 'Fate and metabolism of local anaesthetics'). Although its rate of onset is slow it is rapidly absorbed from mucous membrane because of its very high lipid solubility, as shown by a partition coefficient of 80 (see Table 7.1).

Unwanted effects

Amethocaine is particularly liable to produce the unwanted effects that characterize local anaesthetics as a group, including hypersensitivity. For this reason it is only occasionally used in dentistry (see above).

Benzocaine

Unlike all other local anaesthetics used in dentistry, benzocaine does not contain the hydrophilic amine group common to the others (see Fig. 7.1). It is therefore unable to ionize (at a physiological pH) and, as a consequence, can neither form water soluble salts nor be used for injection. It is thus restricted to topical use. Its inability to ionize raises the question as to how it acts as a local anaesthetic. The answer is that it diffuses directly across the nerve cell membrane and gains access to the gating mechanism of the sodium channel via the lipid component (i.e. without passing through the sodium channel as do the ionized anaesthetics; see Fig. 7.3). It has limited use in dentistry (see Table 7.2).

Table 7.2. Some local anaesthetics used in dentistry

Chemical class	Name (and synonyms)	(a) Relative potency (isolated nerve)	(b) Relative toxicity IV LD$_{50}$ rabbit	(a/b) Therapeutic ratio	Preparations type	Description	Contents Local anaesthetic	vasoconstrictor (if present)	Onset of action min	Duration of action	Maximum 'safe' dose mg	Indications	Comments (stability refers to plain local anaesthetic unless stated otherwise)
Ester type	Cocaine HCl	2.5	1.5	0.6	Topical only	Cocaine hydrochloride 10%	Cocaine HCl 10%	—	rapid	1 h	100	Applied to floor of nose to facilitate supraperiosteal injections in maxillary incisor region.	Decomposes on boiling. Stimulates CNS and causes vasoconstriction and mydriasis. Dependence. Restricted to topical use due to toxicity.
	Procaine HCl	0.26	0.47	1.8	Injection only	Procaine and adrenaline injection	Procaine HCl 2%	Adrenaline acid tartrate 1:50,000	2–5	1 h	500	Seldom used now, but may be useful for patient hypersensitive to anilide derivatives, e.g. lignocaine.	Moderately heat stable. Active vasodilator therefore added vasoconstrictor essential. Useless topically. Sulphonamide antagonism a theoretical risk.
	Benzocaine	insoluble			Topical only	Benzocaine lozenges DPF / Benzocaine compound lozenges BPC	Benzocaine 10 mg / Benzocaine 100 mg + menthol 3 mg	—	rapid	duration of contact	—	To help patients otherwise unable to tolerate an impression or new dentures. Occasionally to relieve pain of severe ulceration.	Insoluble. Stable, but protect from light.
Amide type	Lignocaine HCl (lidocaine)	1.0	1.0	1.0	Injection	Xylocaine 2% plain	Lignocaine HCl 2%	—	1–2	15–45 min	200	Indicated when use of adrenaline dangerous, e.g. patients with severe cardiovascular disease or uncontrolled hyperthyroidism. More usual alternative prilocaine with felypressin (see below).	
						Xylocaine 2% with adrenaline	ditto	Adrenaline Acid tartrate 1:80,000	1–2 infiltration	2–4 h	500	Most commonly used local anaesthetic solutions	WARNING (see below)
						Xylocaine 2% with noradrenaline (all three preparations available in 2 ml cartridges)	ditto	l-noradrenaline* 1:– 80,000	4–5 nerve block	2–4 hr	500		
					Topical	Xylocaine spray	lignocaine 10 mg per spray dose	—	0.25	25–30 min	200 (=20 spray-doses)	Useful topical preparations.	
						Xylodase (a cream)	lignocaine 5% hyaluronidase 0.015%	—	1–2	25–30 min	200 (=4 g cream)		

Drug				Route	Preparation	Local anaesthetic	Vasoconstrictor		Duration	Max dose	Indications	Properties
Prilocaine hydrochloride (Citanest)	0.65	0.77	1.18	Injection	Citanest 4% plain (2 ml cartridge)	Prilocaine	—	2–5	30 min	400	For use when adrenaline or noradrenaline contra-indicated, e.g. patients with cardiovascular disease, hyperthyroidism. Note: In doses higher than those recommended, prilocaine causes cyanosis due to methaemoglobinaemia. In a healthy patient this is usually of little account, but in one unable to compensate for reduced oxygen-carrying capacity, e.g. anaemia, it would be prudent to choose an alternative drug.	Stable and heat-resistant. Solutions with vasoconstrictors are stable for 2 years if stored away from light and at a temperature not exceeding 15°C (to preserve vasoconstrictor). Methaemoglobinaemia due to prilocaine can be prevented or reversed with the aid of the reducing agent, methylene blue, 1 mg/kg IV
					Citanest 3% + Octapressin 0.03 I.U./ml (2 ml cartridge)	Prilocaine HC1 3%	felypressin 0.03 I.U./ml (1 I.U. = 0.018 mg) 0.54 µg/ml		2.5 hr	600	For use when longer acting preparation required and when adrenaline contra-indicated, e.g. patients with cardiovascular disease, hyperthyroidism.	
Mepivacaine HCl	0.55	0.81	1.47	Injection	3% (1.8 ml cartridge)	Mepivacaine HCl 3%	—	1–2	Upper jaw 15–30 min lower jaw 30–40 min	400	Short-acting local anaesthetic	Stable and heat-resistant
Bupivacaine hydrochloride (Marcain)	4	7.8†	1.95	Injection	Marcain	Bupivacaine HCl 0.25% 0.5% 0.25% 0.5%	— — Adrenaline acid tartrate 1:200,000 (=5µg/ml) 1:200,000 (=5µg/ml)	4	6 hr 6+ hr	2 mg/kg 2 mg/kg	Situations where there is likely to be immediate severe postoperative pain; reduces postoperative analgesic requirements.	Prolonged anaesthesia increases risk of trauma due to biting or hot drinks; some patients find prolonged dental anaesthesia unpleasant.

*The use of noradrenaline as an added vasoconstrictor to local anaesthetics is not advised because:
1. It is a very potent pressor agent and is potentially dangerous, especially in patients with cardiovascular disease.
2. Adrenaline is normally satisfactory as an added vasoconstrictor and is much less potentially hazardous.
3. If it is essential to AVOID the administration of adrenaline then either
   (i) a local anaesthetic without any added vasoconstrictor can be used or, alternatively
   (ii) felypressin (Octapressin), a polypeptide vasoconstrictor (a derivative of vasopressin) can be used; a suitable preparation is Citanest 3% + Octapressin 0.03 i.u./ml.

†IV LD$_{50}$ mice (Reynolds 1987)

N.B. Measurement of strength of solutions: It is traditional, although illogical, to employ one system of units to measure the strength of a solution of local anaesthetic and another system to measure the strength of vasoconstrictor contained within the same solution! Nevertheless it is obviously important for every dental practitioner to be thoroughly familiar with this dual system.

1. The strength of a local anaesthetic solution is usually expressed as a *percentage concentration* so that, for example, a 2 per cent solution is one that contains 2 g of the particular local anaesthetic per 100 ml of solution.

2. The amount of vasoconstrictor added to a solution of local anaesthetic is expressed as a *dilution*. Thus a solution labelled 1:200 000 indicates that it contains 1 g of the particular vasoconstrictor dissolved in 200 000 ml of local anaesthetic solution. As this system indicates dilution it follows that a dilution of 1:400 000 is twice as dilute (half as concentrated) as a dilution of 1:200 000. Dilution values can be converted to concentration values (and vice versa) by using the following relationship:

$$\text{a dilution of } 1:y = \text{a concentration of } \frac{100}{y} \text{ mg/ml;}$$

$$\text{conversely, a concentration of } x \text{ mg/ml} = \text{dilution of 1 in } \frac{1000}{x}.$$

In this Table the strength of vasoconstrictor has been expressed in both systems.

Pharmacokinetics

Benzocaine is hydrolysed very rapidly by plasma esterases to para-aminobenzoic acid, and this presumably accounts for its low toxicity.

Unwanted effects

The metabolite, para-aminobenzoic acid, is liable to act as a hapten and to cause allergic responses. Thus, of 887 patients with dermatitis or eczema patch tested with 5 per cent benzocaine in yellow soft paraffin, nearly 6 per cent gave a positive reaction (Rudzki and Kleniewska 1970). It is therefore particularly important for dentists to exercise great care so as not to come into skin contact with benzocaine (or any other local anaesthetic for that matter).

SPECIFIC LOCAL ANAESTHETICS: 2. AMIDE TYPE

Lignocaine (Xylocaine, Lidocaine)

Lignocaine (Löfgren 1948) was introduced in the early 1950s and soon replaced procaine, being more potent than it and also effective topically. According to which method of comparison is used, lignocaine is between one to four times as active as procaine for infiltration anaesthesia, and two to four times as active as procaine in nerve block (Wiedling 1964). Although lignocaine can be used without the addition of vasoconstrictor (plain), this is generally not very successful in producing dental anaesthesia. It may be used for minor surgical procedures but, again, adequate anaesthesia is unpredictable and it is better to use prilocaine with felypressin (see later) if adrenaline is thought to be contraindicated.

Lignocaine 2 per cent *with* adrenaline 1:80 000 (= 12.5 μg/ml) is certainly the most useful local anaesthetic available for dentistry at the present time. In dental outpatients injected with lignocaine 2 per cent plus 1:100 000 adrenaline, the outcome was effective infiltration anaesthesia in 91 to 100 per cent of injections (Cowan 1968; Brown and Ward 1969; Epstein 1969; Chilton 1971). Other important properties of lignocaine are: (i) rapidity of onset of analgesia; (ii) useful duration of action when combined with adrenaline 1:80 000 (2–4 hours); and (iii) very low incidence of toxic effects.

Pharmacokinetics

Lignocaine is highly lipophilic (partition coefficient = 3; see Table 7.1) and so is rapidly absorbed. It undergoes virtually complete biotransformation in the liver and has a systemic $T_{0.5}$ of approximately 100 minutes. Figure 7.5 shows that lignocaine is subject to three metabolic transformations, namely oxidative-N-dealkylation, hydrolysis, and hydroxylation. Thus, it is first dealkylated to the monoethyl derivative, after which the amide link is broken by hydrolysis yielding

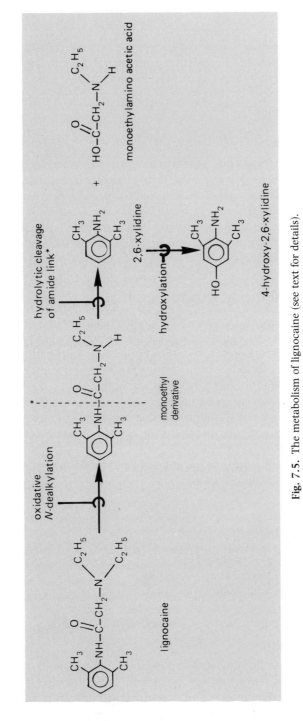

Fig. 7.5. The metabolism of lignocaine (see text for details).

2,6-dimethylxylidine and monoethyl aminoacetic acid. Finally, the dimethylxylidine undergoes hydroxylation to 4-hydroxy-2,6-dimethylxylidine. It seems that only the first metabolite (monoethyl aminoacetyl-2,6-xylidide) possesses local anaesthetic properties, and all of the metabolites have longer half-lives and are less toxic than the parent drug. Only negligible amounts of unchanged drug are excreted in the urine.

Unwanted effects

When used in the correct dosage and in the correct way, the toxicity of lignocaine is low. Nevertheless, adverse reactions involving the central nervous system or cardiovascular system can occur, as have been described earlier in this chapter. Allergy to lignocaine is also rare (Rood 1973; Cawson *et al.* 1983); it is most likely to occur following repeated application to the skin either in the form of a cream or ointment (allergy in the patient), or during recurrent careless handling by an operator (allergy in the dentist, doctor, etc.).

Prilocaine (Citanest, propitocaine)

This is a more recent and important addition to the range of local anaesthetics. It is equipotent with lignocaine and has the lowest toxicity of the amide drugs (see Table 7.2). A comparison made between prilocaine 3 per cent with adrenaline 1:300 000 and lignocaine 2 per cent with 1:80 000 adrenaline has shown that the drugs are similar although, two hours after injection, a higher proportion of the soft tissues had recovered from prilocaine anaesthesia (Goldman and Gray 1963). Thus, the shorter duration of action combined with the reduced amount of adrenaline required is a distinct advantage of prilocaine during the average dental session.

The following compares the duration of anaesthesia in soft tissue and dental pulp for lignocaine and prilocaine:

Preparation	Duration of anaesthesia (hours) Soft tissue	Pulp
Lignocaine 2% + adrenaline 1:50 000	3 +	3/4
Prilocaine 3% + adrenaline 1:300 000	2 +	1/3
Prilocaine 3% + felypressin 0.03 IU/ml	2	1/2–3/4

Pharmacokinetics

Prilocaine has a similar profile to that of lignocaine, although it differs from it in several important ways that account for its lower toxicity. Thus it does not produce any vasodilatation (or vasoconstriction); it is distributed more rapidly and has a larger volume of distribution (see Chapter 1) than lignocaine; and its rate of clearance (2.37 l min^{-1}) is higher than that of all other amide local anaesthetics, suggesting (Tucker 1986) that it may undergo extensive extrahepatic metabolism (see Table 7.1), so resulting in relatively low blood concentrations. These reasons account for the maximum 'safe' dose of prilocaine (400 mg) being twice that of lignocaine.

In the liver, prilocaine is acted on by amidases (Geddes 1965), which cause hydrolytic cleavage of the molecule into α-propyl-aminopropionic acid and o-toluidine (Fig. 7.6), the latter then undergoing oxidation to nitrosotoluidine. The metabolite o-toluidine is capable of causing methaemoglobinaemia but this is only likely to be significant when more than 600 mg of prilocaine have been administered. It must be remembered that under normal circumstances methaemoglobin is being formed continuously during red cell metabolism but does not exceed about 1 per cent of the total haemoglobin. Cyanosis does not occur until more than 1.5 per cent of haemoglobin is present as methaemoglobin. If a dose of prilocaine sufficient to cause cyanosis is given, the condition is likely to disappear spontaneously within 24 hours and is not likely to be clinically significant, except in a patient who already suffers from anaemia or an impaired circulation (see next section; unwanted effects).

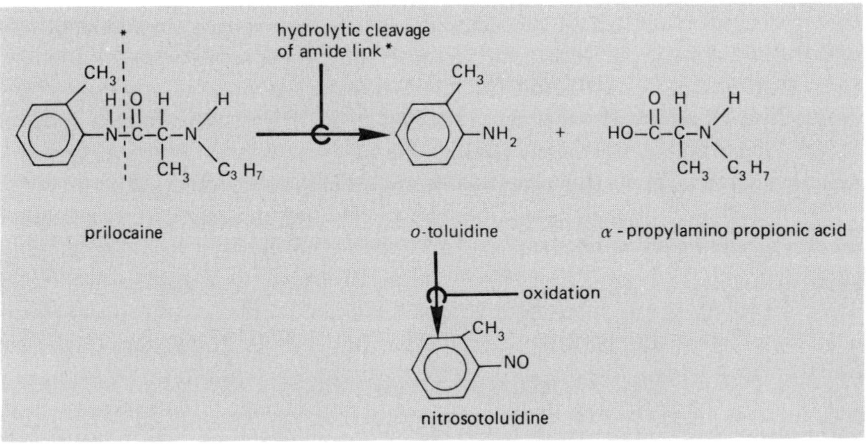

Fig. 7.6. The metabolism of prilocaine (see text for details).

Unwanted effects

Since its introduction, prilocaine appears to have been remarkably free from such effects, apart from occasional cyanosis (described above) due to mild methaemoglobinaemia, which usually occurs only with dosage above that recommended. This form of systemic toxicity is unique to prilocaine, is dosage-related and, as has been explained, is not directly due to the parent substance but to its metabolite, o-toluidine. Although cyanosis will occur in the presence of small amounts of methaemoglobinaemia. It seldom causes any embarrassment to the patient unless the oxygen-carrying capacity and/or the oxygen requirements are already compromised. When necessary the methaemoglobinaemia may be rapidly reversed by intravenous injection of methylene blue 1 mg/kg, the normal haemoglobin levels being restored in 15 to 20 minutes.

Problems associated with the use of adrenaline in local anaesthetic solutions

In the past, the need to add adrenaline to prilocaine, or indeed to any other local anaesthetic used in dentistry, was considered to be a disadvantage in treating patients already taking tricyclic antidepressants (see Chapter 14). There are theoretical reasons why an interaction might occur between adrenaline and tricyclic antidepressant but, in practice, this interaction has not occurred and it would therefore seem that the anticipated risk has been overestimated (Cawson *et al.* 1983). Nevertheless, it was not unreasonable to anticipate the possibility of such an interaction, particularly in view of the evidence obtained from experimental studies (Boakes *et al.* 1973). In passing, it should be said that it has been better to err on the side of caution rather than to ignore such evidence, as was the case for the dangerous interaction that can occur between monoamine oxidase inhibitors (MAOI) and the indirect-acting sympathomimetic amines, particularly tyramine, found in fermented foods, e.g. cheese (see Chapter 22). The MAOI interaction was entirely predictable and could have been prevented if available knowledge in this area had been carefully considered at the time.

The use of adrenaline in local anaesthetic solutions has been discussed above, where it was seen that there is little risk from its use in patients with cardiovascular problems if aspirating injection techniques are used. However, for those dental surgeons who have reservations about its use, an alternative is available; this is the synthetic vasopressor polypeptide known as felypressin (Octapressin), which is related chemically to vasopressin (antidiuretic hormone, ADH) from the posterior lobe of the pituitary gland. It differs only from vasopressin in that phenylalanine replaces the molecule of tyrosine normally located at position 2. When present in a final concentration of 0.03 IU/ml (1 IU = 0.018 mg), this vasoconstrictor, which is less potent than adrenaline, nevertheless resulted in a marginal increase in the duration of anaesthesia produced by prilocaine 3 per cent compared with the same strength of local anaesthetic combined with adrenaline 1:300 000 (Goldman and Evers 1969). These authors also observed that 0.03 IU/ml felypressin appeared to be an optimal concentration; lower and higher concentrations decreased the duration of pulpal analgesia, suggesting that vasoconstriction may not be the only factor in the prolongation of analgesic effect by this substance.

It should be noted that felypressin does not necessarily limit the level of prilocaine in the plasma (Cannell and Whelpton, 1986), and that it causes prolonged coronary vasoconstriction *in animals*, although the evidence for this in patients is controversial (see Cannel, 1983).

Mepivacaine (Carbocaine)

This drug resembles lignocaine pharmacologically but is distinguished from it chemically in that the hydrophilic end of the molecule consists of a ring structure (an N-methylated pyridine) instead of a diethyl amino group as in lignocaine (see Fig. 7.1). It is chemically stable, being resistant to acid and alkaline hydrolysis. It is not a vasodilator. It is a short-acting anaesthetic and is only available as a 3 per cent solution without vasoconstrictor. It does not appear to be widely used, and the interested reader should consult Mumford and Geddes (1961), and Goebel *et al.* (1980) for further information.

Pharmacokinetics

Mepivacaine, like lignocaine, is metabolized in the liver where the amide link is cleaved to yield pipecolylxylidine and monoethylamino acetic acid, with some unchanged drug excreted in the urine. However, unlike lignocaine, in neonates it is not metabolized but eliminated by the kidneys. In adults the maximum dose is 5 mg/kg or 400 mg.

Unwanted effects

It is claimed that mepivacaine is a little less toxic than lignocaine. One case of an acute anaphylactic reaction has been reported (Seskin 1978) following a mandibular block with mepivacaine 3 per cent without vasoconstrictor. As mepivacaine has a chemical structure similar to the other amide local anaesthetics, cross-hypersensitivity may be expected to occur.

Bupivacaine

Bupivacaine (0.25–0.5 per cent with or without adrenaline) is a long-acting local anaesthetic, similar in chemical structure to mepivacaine (see Fig. 7.1). It was introduced for use where prolonged local anaesthesia is required, such as in orthopaedic and accident work, and including epidural administration and intravenous regional analgesia. Thus, it was not originally designed for dental use but it has found a use in dentistry where there is likely to be immediate and severe postoperative pain, such as in patients undergoing removal of impacted third molars (Moore and Dunsky 1983; Wilson *et al.* 1986). Under these conditions it has been found valuable and, as a consequence of the prolonged analgesia, it reduces the need for postoperative analgesic medication. However, the disadvantage of such prolonged dental analgesia (six to eight hrs) is the risk of trauma, which occurs as a result of self-biting or the ingestion of hot drinks.

Furthermore, some patients find prolonged dental analgesia an unpleasant experience.

Pharmacokinetics

The major part of a dose of bupivacaine is metabolized in the liver where, after dealkylation and cleavage of the amide link, the metabolite, pipecolylxylidine, is excreted in the urine. Bupivacaine is absorbed into the systemic circulation from the site of injection more slowly than the shorter-acting amide local anaesthetics (lignocaine, prilocaine, and mepivacaine). An important factor here is the greater binding of this drug to plasma and tissue proteins (Tucker 1986).

Unwanted effects

The risk of an adverse reaction with bupivacaine does not appear to be any greater than with lignocaine, provided that it is given in the correct dosage and inadvertent intravenous injection is carefully avoided. The main experience with this drug is outside dentistry, where it has been found to have a wide therapeutic margin when used correctly (Reynolds 1987). Thus, primary ventricular fibrillation has developed after the injection of excessive amounts of bupivacaine into the general circulation (Covino 1984). As bupivacaine is chemically similar to lignocaine, prilocaine, and mepivacaine, there is likely to be cross-hypersensitivity between these agents.

INTRALIGAMENTARY INJECTION OF A LOCAL ANAESTHETIC SOLUTION

The periodontal ligament provides the attachment between the root surface and alveolar bone, and comprises a series of well-organized collagen bundles and a rich blood supply. The width of the ligament in health is 0.1 to 0.25 mm. The nerve supply to teeth must traverse the ligament to reach the apical foramen, and thus an injection of local anaesthetic solution into the ligament will anaesthetize the nerve supply to that tooth. This technique is known as intraligamentary anaesthesia and has been practiced by dental surgeons for many years. The recent introduction of high-pressure syringes with ultra-fine needles (Ligmaject and Peri-press) has renewed interest in this method of administering a local anaesthetic. The advantages and disadvantages of this technique are listed below:

Advantages

1. Rapid onset of anaesthesia (15–45 seconds).

2. Less of the local anaesthetic solution is administered when compared with conventional local anaesthesia. This reduces the risk of unwanted effects.

3. Lower teeth are anaesthetized without the need of an inferior dental nerve block, thereby reducing the risk of tongue and lip trauma. Hence, intraligamen-

tary anaesthesia may be especially useful in children. The technique also allows for bilateral anaesthesia of mandibular teeth, thus avoiding bilateral inferior-dental nerve block.

Disadvantages

1. The technique is destructive to the periodontal ligament and can cause resorption of the crestal bone (Walton and Garnick 1982). It is not advisable to use this technique in patients with periodontal disease.

2. Postoperative discomfort: the incidence of this is uncertain, and depends upon whether the injection was given for restorative procedures or tooth extraction (Jones 1981; Faulkner 1983). If intraligamentary anaesthesia is used for restorative procedures, the tooth may be tender to bite on for up to 24 hours. The injection may introduce infection into the periodontal ligament but the incidence of this can be reduced by swabbing the gingiva with 0.2 per cent chlorhexidine solution prior to injection.

3. It is reported that there is a higher incidence of dry socket (alveolar osteitis) after teeth have been extracted with intraligamentary anaesthesia than after conventional anaesthesia (J. G. Meechan, personal communication). This may be attributable to the direct action of the vasoconstrictor in inhibiting haemorrhage and thus the formation of the necessary blood clot in the socket.

Evidence now suggests that intraligamentary anaesthesia may be useful as an adjunct to conventional anaesthesia for restorative procedures. Its use in routine extractions is yet to be evaluated.

THE USE AND ABUSE OF TOPICALLY APPLIED LOCAL ANAESTHETICS

In dental practice, local anaesthetics can be applied topically in the form of solutions, aerosols, ointments, or lozenges (see Table 7.2). Thus, the use of a topical preparation to facilitate a subsequent injection of local anaesthetic is an example of a reasonable use of topical anaesthesia. However, this use should be restricted to a minimum because of the risks involved. These may be listed as follows:

1. Absorption of local anaesthetics from mucous membranes can be rapid and substantial. Adriani and Campbell (1956) measured blood levels of amethocaine in dogs: they found that a quantity of drug, which when injected subcutaneously failed to produce detectable blood levels, if applied topically produced blood levels similar to those achieved by one-third to one-half the same dose given intravenously. Thus the risk of producing unwanted effects due to overdosage may be considerable when local anaesthetics are applied topically.

2. Excessive use of topical preparations, particularly lozenges, may lead to a

dangerous degree of anaesthesia in the oropharynx with consequent inhalation of food into the respiratory tract during eating.

3. Prolonged use of topical preparations carries the risk of inducing hypersensitivity, with the development of severe swelling of the mouth. Subsequent exposure of the patient to the same or a chemically related local anaesthetic could lead to renewed hypersensitivity responses, including the possibility of anaphylactic shock.

4. The dental practitioner should take great care in handling topical preparations because of the risk of becoming hypersensitive to them, as described earlier.

REFERENCES

Adriani, J. and Campbell, D. (1956). Fatalities following topical application of local anaesthetics to mucous membranes. *Journal of the American Medical Association*, **162**, 1527–30.

Arthur, G. R., Scott, D. H. T., Boyes, R. N., and Scott, D. B. (1979). Pharmacokinetic and clinical pharmacological studies with mepivacaine and prilocaine. *British Journal of Anaesthesia*, **51**, 481–5.

Avant, W. E. and Weatherby, J. H. (1960). Effects of epinephrine on toxicities of several local anaesthetic agents. *Proceedings of the Society for Experimental Biology (N.Y.)*, **102**, 353–6.

Bjorn, H. (1946). Electrical excitation of teeth. *Svensk tandlakaretidskrift*, **39**, suppl.

Boakes, A. J., Laurence, D. R., Teoh, P. C., Barer, F. S. K., Benedikter, L. T., and Prichard, B. N. C. (1973). Interactions between sympathomimetic amines and antidepressant agents in man. *British Medical Journal*, i, 311–15.

Brodie, B. B., Lief, P. A., and Poet, R. (1948). Fate of procaine in man following its intravenous administration and methods for estimation of procaine and diethylaminoethanol. *J. Pharmacology and Experimental Therapeutics*, **94**, 359–66.

Brown, G. and Ward, N. L. (1969). Prilocaine and lignocaine plus adrenaline. A clinical comparison. *British Dental Journal*, **126**, 557–62.

Cahalan, M. D. and Almers, W. (1979). Interactions between quaternary lidocaine, the sodium channel gates and tetrodotoxin. *Biophysical Journal*, **27**, 39–56.

Cannell, H. (1983). The hazards of dental local anaesthetics. *British Dental Journal*, **155**, 6.

Cannell, H. and Whelpton, R. (1986). Systemic uptake of prilocaine after injection of various formulations of the drug. *British Dental Journal*, **160**, 47–9.

Cawson, R. A. (1984). Vasoconstrictor preference (letter). *Journal of the American Dental Association*, **109**, 542–3.

Cawson, R. A., Curson, I., and Whittington, D. R. (1983). The hazards of dental local anaesthetics. *British Dental Journal*, **154**, 253–8.

Chilton, N. W. (1971). Clinical evaluation of prilocaine hydrochloride 4 per cent solution with and without epinephrine. *Journal of the American Dental Association*, **83**, 149–54.

Covino, B. G. (1984). Current controversies in local anaesthetics. In *Regional anaesthesia 1884–1984*. (ed. D. B. Scott, J. H. McClure, and J. A. W. Wildsmith), pp. 74–81. ICM, Södertälje.

Cowan, A. (1968). Further clinical evaluation of prilocaine (Citanest) with and without epinephrine. *Oral Surgery*, **26**, 304–11.

Criep, L. H. and Ribeiro, C. de C. (1953). Allergy to procaine hydrochloride with 3 fatalities. *Journal of the American Medical Association*, **151**, 1185–7.

Curley, R. K., Baxter, P. W., and Tyldesley, W. R. (1987). An unusual cutaneous reaction to lignocaine. *British Dental Journal*, **162**, 113–14.

Dimsdale, J. E. and Moss, J. (1980). Short-term catecholamine response to psychological stress. *Psychosomatic Medicine*, **42**, 493–7.

Downs, J. R. (1966). Atypical cholinesterase activity: its importance in dentistry. *Journal of Oral Surgery*, **24**, 256–7.

Epstein, S. (1969). Clinical study of prilocaine with varying concentrations of epinephrine. *Journal of the American Dental Association*, **78**, 85–90.

Faulkner, R. K. (1983). The high pressure periodontal ligament injection. *British Dental Journal*, **154**, 103–5.

Gangarosa, L. P. and Halik, F. J. (1967). A clinical evaluation of local anaesthetic solutions containing graded epinephrine concentrations. *Archives of Oral Biology*, **12**, 611–21.

Gasser, H. S. and Erlanger, J. (1929). The role of fiber size in the establishment of a nerve block by pressure or cocaine. *American Journal of Physiology*, **88**, 581–92.

Geddes, I. C. (1965). Studies of the metabolism of Citanest C114. *Acta Anaesthesia Scandinavica*, (suppl.) **16**, 37–41.

Giovannitti, J. A. and Bennett, C. R. (1979). Assessment of allergy to local anaesthetics. *Journal of the American Dental Association*, **98**, 701–6.

Goebel, W. M., Allen, G., and Randall, F. (1980). Comparative circulatory serum levels of 2 per cent mepivacaine and 2 per cent lignocaine. *British Dental Journal*, **148**, 261–4.

Goldman, V. and Evers, H. (1969). Prilocaine felypressin: a new combination for dental analgesia. *Dental Practitioner*, **19**, 225–31.

Goldman, V. and Gray, W. (1963). A clinical trial of a new local anaesthetic agent. *British Dental Journal*, **115**, 59–65.

Gregg, J. B., Barnett, G. L., and Ensberg, D. L. (1963). Mucosal slough reactions to topical anesthetic agent, lidocaine. *Archives of Otolaryngology*, **77**, 1–2.

Hanauer, A. (1955). Gruppensensibilisierung gegenuber anasthetika chemotherapeutika under antibiotika. *Deutsche Medizinische Wochenschrift*, **80**, 1175.

Hille, B., Courtney, K., and Dunn, R. (1975). Rate and site of action of local anesthetics in myelinated nerve. In *Molecular mechanisms of anesthesia*, (ed. B. R. Fink), pp. 13–20. Raven Press, New York.

Hodgkin, A. L. and Huxley, A. F. (1945). Resting and action potentials in single nerve fibres. *Journal of Physiology*, **104**, 176–95.

Holti, G. and Hood, F. J. C. (1965). An anaphylactoid reaction to lignocaine. *Dental Practitioner*, **15**, 294–6.

Horton, J. A. G. (1966) The complications of local anaesthetics. *Newcastle Medical Journal*, **29**, 125–30.

Jones, P. C. (1981). *Dental Advertiser*, (August), 26–9.

Kalow, W. (1952). Hydrolysis of local anaesthetics by human serum cholinesterase. *Journal of Pharmacology and Experimental Therapeutics*, **104**, 122–34.

Kirkler, D. M. (1962). Allergy to lignocaine. *Lancet*, **i**, 159.

Klingenstrom, P. and Westermark, L. (1964). Local tissue-oxygen tension after adrenaline, noradrenaline & octapressin in local anaesthesia. *Acta Anaesthesia Scandinavica*, **8**, 261–6.

Koller, C. (1928). Historical notes on the beginning of local anaesthesia. *Journal of the American Medical Association*, 90, 1742–3.

Laurence, D. R. and Bennett, P. (1987). *Clinical pharmacology*, (6th edn.), p. 451. Churchill Livingstone, Edinburgh.

Löfgren, N. (1948). *Studies on local anaesthetics—Xylocaine.* Hoegstroms, Stockholm.

Martindale: The Extra Pharmacopoeia (1982) 28th edn. (ed. J. E. F. Reynolds and A. B. Prasad). The Pharmaceutical Press, London.

Meechan, J. G. and Rawlins, M. D. (1987). A comparison of the effect of two different dental local anaesthetic solutions on plasma potassium concentration. *British Dental Journal*, 163, 191–3.

Mongar, J. L. (1955). Study of 2 methods for testing local anaesthetics in man. *British Journal of Pharmacology*, 10, 240–6.

Moore, D. C. and Bridenbaugh, L. D. (1960). Oxygen: the antidote for systemic toxic reactions from local anaesthetic drugs. *Journal of the American Medical Association*, 174, 842–7.

Moore, P. A. and Dunsky, J. L. (1983). Bupivacaine anesthesia—a clinical trial for endodontic therapy. *Oral Surgery*, 55, 176–9.

Mumford, J. M. and Geddes, I. C. (1961). Trial of carbamazepine in conservative dentistry. *British Dental Journal*, 110, 92–4.

Nathan, P. W. and Sears, T. A. (1962). Differential nerve block by sodium-free and sodium-deficient solutions. *Journal of Physiology. (Lond.)*, 164, 375–94.

Noble, D. S. and Pierce, G. F. M. (1961). Allergy to lignocaine: a case history. *Lancet*, ii, 1436.

Rawlins, M. D. and Thompson, J. W. (1985). Mechanisms of adverse drug reactions. In *Textbook of adverse drug reactions*, (ed. D. M. Davies), pp. 12–38. Oxford University Press.

Reynolds, F. (1987). Adverse effects of local anaesthetics. *British Journal of Anaesthesia*, 59, 78–95.

Ritchie, J. M. (1975). Mechanism of action of local anesthetic agents and biotoxins. *British Journal of Anaesthesia*, 47, 191.

Ritchie, J. M. and Greengard, P. (1966). On the mode of action of local anaesthetics. *Annual Review of Pharmacology*, 6, 405.

Rood, J. P. (1973). A case of lignocaine hypersensitivity. *British Dental Journal*, 135, 411–12.

Rud, J. (1961). Local anaesthetics. An electrophysiological investigation of local anaesthesia of peripheral nerves with special reference to xylocaine. *Acta Physiologica Scandinavica*, 51 (suppl. 178), 1–171.

Rudzki, E. and Kleniewska, D. (1970). The epidemiology of contact dermatitis in Poland. *British Journal of Dermatology*, 83, 543–5.

Sadove, M. S., Wyant, G. M., Gittelson, L. A., and Kretchmer, H. E. (1952). Classification and management of reactions to local anaesthetic agents. *Journal of the American Medical Association*, 148, 17–22.

Seskin, L. (1978). Anaphylaxis due to local anaesthesia hypersensitivity: report of case. *Journal of the American Dental Association*, 96, 841–3.

Tolas, A. G., Pflug, A. E., and Halter, J. B. (1982). Arterial plasma epinephrine concentrations and haemodynamic responses after dental injection of local anaesthetic with epinephrine. *Journal of the American Dental Association*, 104, 41–3.

Trimble, G. (1962). Allergy to lignocaine. *Lancet*, i, 435, quotes *U.S. Armed Forces Medical Journal* (1957) 8, 740.

Truant, A. P. and Takman, B. (1965). Local anaesthetics. In *Drill's pharmacology in medicine*, (3rd edn), pp. 133–56. McGraw-Hill, New York.

Tucker, G. T. (1986). Pharmacokinetics of local anaesthetics. *British Journal of Anaesthesia*, **58**, 717–31.

Tucker, G. T. and Mather, L. E. (1979). Clinical pharmacokinetics of local anaesthetics. *Clinical Pharmacokinetics*, **4**, 241–78.

Van Dyke, C., Barash, B. G., Tatlow, P., and Byck, R. (1976). Cocaine: plasma concentration after intranasal application in man. *Science*, **191**, 859–61.

Walton, R. E. and Garnick, J. J. (1982). The periodontal ligament injection. Histologic effects on the periodontium in monkeys. *Journal of Endodontics*, **8**, 22–6.

Weatherby, J. H. (1964). Local anaesthetics. In *Evaluation of drug activities: pharmacometrics*, Vol. 1. (ed. D. R. Laurence and A. L. Bacharach), pp. 205–14. Academic Press, London.

Wiedling, S. (1964). *Xylocaine*, (2nd edn.). Almqvist and Wiksell, Stockholm.

Wildsmith, J. A. W. (1986). Peripheral nerve and local anaesthetic drugs. *British Journal of Anaesthesia*, **58**, 692–700.

Wilson, I. H., Richmond, M. N., and Strike, P. W. (1986). Regional analgesia with bupivacaine in dental anaesthesia. *British Journal of Anaesthesia*, **58**, 401–5.

8

General anaesthesia and sedation

INTRODUCTION

GENERAL anaesthesia is the drug-induced absence of the perception of all sensation thus allowing surgery or other painful procedures to be carried out. This state is usually achieved by inhalation agents. Several other drugs are used in conjunction with general anaesthetic agents to ensure a safe, smooth, and uneventful operative procedure. These include drugs used to premedicate the patient, neuromuscular blocking agents, induction agents, and inhalation anaesthetic agents.

PREMEDICATION AGENTS

Premedication may be defined as the administration of drugs before an anaesthetic with a view to facilitating the operation and anaesthetic. Drugs used for this purpose are divided into (a) those used for their sedative effects, and (b) those used for their anticholinergic effects. The features required of premedication agents are as follows:

(1) to alleviate pre-operative anxiety;

(2) to provide some degree of postoperative amnesia, especially in children; so that a possible unpleasant experience is not remembered;

(3) to make the induction and maintenance of anaesthesia easier;

(4) to reduce the amount of anaesthetic agents required by enhancing their effects;

(5) to provide additional analgesia during surgery and in the postoperative period;

(6) to reduce salivary and bronchial secretions;

(7) to reduce activity in the parasympathetic nervous system, especially in the vagal plexus.

Opioids, anxiolytics, neuroleptics, and anticholinergic drugs are used as premedication agents.

Opioids

Morphine, pethidine, and papaveretum (a mixture of opium alkaloids) are the main opioids used in this way. Their pharmacological properties and mode of action have been discussed in Chapter 6. Their analgesic, sedative, and euphoriant properties make them popular as premedication agents. The dose regimes are shown in Table 8.1. Morphine does produce certain unwanted effects, in particular, nausea and vomiting. The incidence of postoperative vomiting with morphine is about 20 per cent, but this increases if the patient is ambulatory. Postoperative vomiting and nausea can be reduced by use of an anti-emetic such as cyclizine or prochlorperazine. The incidence of these effects is less after papaveretum. Pethidine is a less powerful analgesic than either morphine or papaveretum, but has a lower incidence of unwanted effects.

All the opioids produce a degree of respiratory depression and suppression of the cough reflex, which is important after abdominal and chest surgery where coughing is essential to clear the lungs of excessive secretions, thus reducing the risk of pneumonia.

Table 8.1. Dosage and routes of administration of opioids used as premedication agents

Drug	Route	Adult Dose	Child Dose	Times of administration
Pethidine hydrochloride	IM	50–100 mg	1–2 mg/kg	1 hour before operation
Morphine sulphate	IM	10 mg	150 μg/kg	1–1.5 hours before operation
Papaveretum	IM	10–20 mg	1–5 years: 2.5–5 mg 6–12 years: 5–10 mg	45–60 mins before operation

Anxiolytics

The benzodiazepines (diazepam, lorazepam, and temazepam) may be used orally to provide pre-operative sedation. Their use is discussed below in the section 'Oral sedation' (p. 165).

Antipsychotics (neuroleptics)

Phenothiazine derivatives, such as promethazine and trimeprazine, are sometimes used as premedication agents. These drugs are effective as pre-anaesthetic sedatives and they have a powerful potentiating effect on general anaesthetics. Phenothiazine derivatives also have important anti-emetic properties and are valuable in patients who fear or who have a predisposition to postoperative

Table 8.2. Dosages and routes of administration of neuroleptic drugs used as premedication agents

Drug	Route	Adult Dose	Child Dose	Time of administration
Promethazine hydrochloride	Oral	—	6–12 months: 10 mg 1–5 years: 15–20 mg 6–10 years: 20–25 mg	1–2 hours before operation
"	IM	25–50 mg	6.25–12.5 mg	1 hour before operation
Trimeprazine tartrate	IM	3–4.5 mg/kg	2–4 mg/kg	1–2 hours before operation
Chlorpromazine hydrochloride	IM	20–50 mg	—	1 hour before operation

vomiting. They also depress respiration and cause a varying amount of hypotension. Dose regimes are shown in Table 8.2.

Anticholinergic premedication agents

Most gaseous anaesthetic agents cause an increase in salivary and bronchial secretions during induction and light anaesthesia. This excessive production of saliva and mucus may cause respiratory obstruction, which will interfere with the smooth course of the anaesthetic but, more seriously, may put the patient's life at risk. The need to depress salivary secretion during anaesthesia is even more important in children than in adults: the larynx and trachea are so small that a minimal quantity of secretion may seriously impair respiration. It is thus essential that every patient, except those having the briefest of anaesthetics, should receive a drug that reduces these secretions. Anticholinergic drugs also prevent overactivity of the parasympathetic nervous system especially in the vagus nerve. Drugs used to reduce salivary and bronchial secretions are atropine sulphate, hyoscine, and glycopyrolate.

Atropine sulphate

Atropine is commonly used to reduce salivary and bronchial secretions during anaesthesia. It produces these effects by antagonizing the actions of acetylcholine at muscarinic receptors (see Chapter 13). Atropine can be given intravenously immediately before anaesthesia, the adult dose being 300 to 600 micrograms (μg). The same dose can be given intramuscularly 30 to 60 minutes before induction.

Hyoscine

Like atropine, this antagonizes the effect of endogenous acetylcholine at muscarinic receptors. In order to dry up salivary and bronchial secretions, the adult dose of hyoscine is 200 to 600 μg given subcutaneously 30 to 60 minutes before induction of anaesthesia. Unlike atropine, hyoscine is a central nervous-system depressant, and causes a varying amount of drowsiness and depression of the vomiting centre; hence it is anti-emetic. Atropine, at high doses, may act as a stimulant of the central nervous system. Elderly people are sometimes confused by hyoscine and it is therefore best avoided in their premedication.

Both atropine and hyoscine depress vagal nerve endings in the heart. This gives some protection against the vagal stimulation that occurs with anaesthetic agents like trichlorethylene.

Glycopyrolate

This is a quaternary ammonium anticholinergic agent. It is highly ionized at physiological pH and thus penetrates poorly the blood–brain barrier and the placenta. Glycopyrolate produces prolonged and good control of salivary and pharyngeal secretions at doses that do not produce marked changes in heart rate. It has less effect on the cardiovascular system than atropine.

Glycopyrolate is also used as a preoperative or intra-operative antimuscarinic to attenuate or prevent the intra-operative bradycardia sometimes associated with the use of suxamethonium, or due to cardiac vagal reflexes. The usual adult does of glycopyrolate is 0.2 to 0.4 mg intravenously or intramuscularly before the induction of anaesthesia. For children, the dose is 0.004 to 0.008 mg/kg up to a maximum of 0.2 mg.

NEUROMUSCULAR BLOCKING AGENTS

These are widely used in anaesthetic practice because, by specific blockage of the neuromuscular junction, they enable light levels of anaesthesia to be achieved yet with adequate relaxation of the muscles of the abdomen and diaphragm. Neuromuscular blocking agents produce relaxation of abdominal muscles and paralysis of respiratory muscles. Prior to their introduction into anaesthetic practice, anaesthesia had to be very deep indeed to achieve the same degree of relaxation. They also relax the vocal cords, so allowing the passage of a tracheal tube.

There are two types of neuromuscular blocking agents depending on their mechanisms of action: (1) non-depolarizing (competitive) muscle relaxants, and (2) depolarizing muscle relaxants. These are detailed below, but to understand their action it is necessary to review the events of muscle contraction.

Muscle contraction

Acetylcholine bridges the gap between a motor nerve terminal and the motor/muscle end-plate or postsynaptic membrane. The sequence of events leading up to muscle contraction is as follows:

1. An action potential travels down the motor nerve and causes release of packets or 'quanta' of acetylcholine. Each quantum consists of many millions of acetylcholine molecules.

2. The released acetylcholine crosses the synaptic cleft and interacts with cholinergic receptors on the end-plate of a muscle fibre.

3. In the resting phase the muscle cell membrane is polarized, the interior being electronegative to the exterior. The surge of released acetylcholine impinging upon the end-plate receptor of the muscle brings about a massive increase in the permeability of the postsynaptic membrane to sodium ions and, to a lesser extent, potassium ions. Sodium ions enter and generate a local end-plate potential. When this depolarization of the end-plate potential reaches a critical threshold, this triggers off a muscle action potential that is propagated along the muscle fibre, so that a wave of depolarization is also propagated along the fibre, causing it to contract.

4. Acetylcholine is very rapidly broken down by cholinesterases in the neuromuscular junction; the motor end-plate repolarizes and is then ready to be stimulated again.

Non-depolarizing muscle relaxants

Tubocurarine

At one time natives of South America used to smear their arrows with curare to paralyse their victims. The active principle of curare is D-tubocurarine.

Tubocurarine is highly ionized and ineffective by mouth, so it is therefore given intravenously. In man it produces paralysis of all voluntary muscles, including those of respiration, so patients should always have their respiration controlled until the drug has been inactivated. Its action commences about 3 to 4 minutes after injection and lasts up to 40 minutes.

Tubocurarine produces its action by occupying acetylcholine receptors on a muscle end-plate, so preventing the occurrence of an end-plate potential. It competes with acetylcholine for the motor-end-plate and prevents the access of acetylcholine to the receptor so that the depolarization necessary for muscular contraction does not occur. Tubocurarine is therefore a competitive neuromuscular blocking agent.

Tubocurarine is largely used as an adjunct to general anaesthesia. To produce deep muscular relaxation by means of a general anaesthetic substance the depth of anaesthesia has to be profound, and this may cause serious depression of the medullary centres of respiration and circulation. Tubocurarine will produce a profound muscular relaxation of about 30 to 45 minutes duration and, at the same time, only a minimal amount of the general anaesthetic agent will be required. It does not in itself affect consciousness.

The actions of tubocurarine can be reversed by the administration of neostigmine, which is an anticholinesterase. The competitive antagonism between acetylcholine and tubocurarine for the same receptor sites is a quantitative phenomenon. Neostigmine prevents the destruction of acetylcholine by cholinesterases and so prolongs its effects with the result that the activity of tubocurarine is overcome. When tubocurarine has been used as an adjunct to general anaesthetic agents it is customary to assist recovery by the intravenous injection of neostigmine. However, before giving neostigmine, it is essential to administer atropine sulphate intravenously to prevent the muscarinic actions of accumulated acetylcholine (e.g. slowing of the heart).

In addition to producing neuromuscular blockade, tubocurarine is a weak ganglion blocker, and it also causes the release of histamine. Peripheral vaso-dilatation caused by the histamine release, together with the sympathetic ganglia blockade, will lower the blood pressure. In fact, if tubocurarine is rapidly injected intravenously, there is likely to be a severe drop in blood pressure. The release of histamine may also cause flushing of the skin and bronchospasm.

Tubocurarine does not cross the blood–brain barrier or the placenta.

Pancuronium

This is more potent than tubocurarine but has a shorter period of action. It acts in the same way by competitive block but, unlike tubocurarine, it does not normally block transmission in autonomic ganglia and so does not significantly alter the blood pressure. However, if rapidly injected intravenously, the drug may actually cause ganglionic stimulation with a rise in blood pressure. Pancuronium does not cause histamine to be released from mast cells and so is unlikely to induce bronchospasm. It thus has obvious advantages and is widely used to produce relaxation in clinical anaesthesia.

In addition to producing muscular relaxation during anaesthesia, such agents may be used to produce relaxation in a number of pathological conditions, e.g. tetanus.

Atracuronium and vecuronium

These are the neuromuscular blocking agents most likely to be used at the present time. They have little effect on the cardiovascular system and so there is relatively little change in blood pressure. Atracuronium (but not vecuronium) may produce histamine release but this is much less marked that with tubocurarine. Neither drug produces sympathetic blockade.

Depolarizing muscle relaxants

Suxamethonium

This depolarizes the postsynaptic membrane and maintains this state so that the adjacent muscle fibres are electrically inexcitable. Although suxamethonium is fairly quickly hydrolysed by pseudocholinesterase its action is long enough (5 minutes) to be clinically useful. It is the ideal agent for use when passing an endotracheal tube. The drug is injected intravenously and within half a minute it produces complete muscular relaxation. Its rather short duration of action makes it useful in preventing muscular movements during electroconvulsive therapy. If longer procedures are required then the drug can be used in repeated dosage.

The action of suxamethonium may be prolonged in patients with low pseudocholinesterase levels due to liver disease. On the other hand, the prolonged apnoea that may occasionally follow the administration of suxamethonium could prove to be due to the presence of an abnormal cholinesterase. It has been estimated that about 1 to 2 800 persons have this atypical esterase, which hydrolyses suxamethonium more slowly than pseudocholinesterase so that the duration of neuromuscular block is prolonged (this is an example of an unwanted effect—idiosyncrasy).

Suxamethonium promotes release of intracellular potassium and this may be important in patients taking digoxin and/or diuretics, because digoxin may itself promote intracellular depletion of potassium, and many diuretics increase the excretion of potassium. The drug has a number of muscarinic actions, which include increased salivary secretion. Muscle injury may occasionally occur with suxamethonium; this may be due to a direct action of the drug on muscle or follow on potassium depletion from muscles. Occasionally, malignant hyper-pyrexia has followed the use of halothane with suxamethonium; it is fairly certain that this condition is genetically based, and it is a very serious one, as the mortality rate is in the region of 60 to 70 per cent.

INDUCTION AGENTS
(INTRAVENOUS ANAESTHETIC AGENTS)

These are widely used to induce anaesthesia. They are very potent drugs and, once injected, little can be done to terminate their action. Some can be used for short, painful operations such as reduction of a dislocation. The most widely used intravenous anaesthetic agents are sodium thiopentone, methohexitone, etomidate, and propofol. Ketamine is sometimes used for intravenous induction.

Sodium thiopentone

Sodium thiopentone is an ultrashort-acting barbiturate (ethyl thiobarbiturate). The sodium salt is water-soluble and the anaesthetic dose is 4 mg/kg of body weight.

Pharmacokinetics

Sodium thiopentone is given intravenously and produces loss of consciousness in 10 to 20 seconds. The maximum depth of anaesthesia occurs at 40 seconds after dosage and the patient becomes conscious some 2 to 3 minutes after dosage. The drug rapidly enters the brain because of its high lipid solubility. Its short action is attributable to the rapid fall in plasma concentration that is due to distribution into the tissues (especially into muscles, followed by adipose tissue). About 85 per cent of sodium thiopentone is bound to plasma protein, and the drug is metabolized in the liver, the metabolites being excreted via the kidney.

Pharmacological properties

Sodium thiopentone depresses many of the functions of the CNS (see Chapter 14), resulting in sedation, anaesthesia, and a dose-related respiratory depression. Like other barbiturates, it has no analgesic properties and low doses may even increase sensitivity to pain (Dundee 1960). It is also an anticonvulsant and can be used in emergency for status epilepticus.

Anaesthetic doses of sodium thiopentone produce a reduction in cardiac output and force of cardiac contraction. There is also a transient drop in blood pressure. Administration of thiopentone is often associated with laryngospasm and even bronchospasm, but the mechanism of these reactions is unknown. It has no effect on the uterus, but it does cross the placenta and can depress the fetal cardiovascular system.

Uses

Sodium thiopentone is used to induce unconsciousness prior to inhalation anaesthesia, and to provide anaesthesia for short operative procedures, such as reduction of a dislocation, and in electroconvulsive therapy.

Unwanted effects

Cough, laryngospasm, and bronchospasm are the more common of these. Because of the high incidence of laryngospasm and bronchospasm, thiopentone should not be used in asthmatics. An extravascular injection of sodium thiopentone will cause pain and, if the concentration of the solution is greater than 2.5 per cent, then tissue necrosis may occur. If it is inadvertently injected into an artery, the endothelial and deeper layers are immediately damaged, followed by an endarteritis and sometimes thrombosis. This damage is caused by the drug crystallizing out of solution due to reduced dilution in blood. If untreated, ischaemia and even gangrene may result. Damage to the arterial wall is instantaneous and treatment should be rapid. The needle should be left *in situ* and the artery infused with 5 to 10 ml of 1 per cent procaine, which will reduce the pain and arteriospasm. Heparin should then be administered to inhibit thrombus formation, and a regional block of the sympathetic nerves performed, to cause arterial dilatation. The damage from intra-arterial injections of sodium thiopentone is greatly reduced if the concentration of the solution does not exceed 2.5 per cent.

Sodium thiopentone, together with other barbiturates, must not be given to patients with porphyria, a condition which has a high incidence in South Africans of Afrikaaner descent. If a porphyria sufferer is given barbiturates, they will cause widespread demyelination of the peripheral and cranial nerves and disseminated lesions throughout the central nervous system, resulting in pain, weakness, and paralysis; these may be life-threatening.

Methohexitone

Like sodium thiopentone, this is also a short-acting barbiturate (sodium oxybarbiturate), and consequently both drugs have similar pharmacological properties. Anaesthesia is induced with a dose of 1 mg/kg of body weight, and recovery is rapid. Intra-arterial injection of methohexitone is very dangerous. The drug is not an anticonvulsant and can possible induce fits during anaesthesia.

Etomidate

This is a relatively new intravenous anaesthetic agent; chemically it is a carboxylated imidazole derivative. For induction purposes it is used at a dose of 0.3 mg/kg of body weight. Its main advantage over the short-acting barbiturates is the rapid recovery with no 'hangover' effect. Both these properties may be due to the short plasma half-life (approx. one hour). Intravenous injections of etomidate are painful and cause extraneous muscle movements. It does not cause histamine release, and so it can be used as an induction agent in asthmatics and in patients with a history of drug hypersensitivity. Etomidate has little or no effect on the cardiovascular system and is therefore mainly used for patients with cardiac disease.

Ketamine

This soluble anaesthetic agent is usually given intravenously, but can be given intramuscularly. It is used as either a 1, 5, or 10 per cent solution. Ketamine has high lipid solubility and rapidly passes the blood-brain barrier. An intravenous dose of 12 mg/kg of body weight produces anaesthesia within 30 seconds that lasts for 5 to 10 minutes. Unlike the short-acting barbiturates, ketamine administration is associated with profound sedation and analgesia. The main unwanted effect of ketamine is vivid hallucinations and nightmares. The drug also raises blood pressure and pulse rate, and so should not be used in hypertensive patients. Ketamine, an anaesthetic induction agent, is particularly useful in the management of mass casualties, especially for anaesthesia of trapped patients to carry out amputations or the like.

Propofol

This is a new phenolic (diisopropylphenol) intravenous anaesthetic induction agent. The drug is also licensed for use in maintenance of anaesthesia, provided the surgical procedure does not exceed one hour. The dose needed for induction is 2 to 2.5 mg/kg of body weight. Light general anaesthesia can be maintained by repeated bolus injections of between 25 to 50 mg. Recovery from such an anaesthesia is usually rapid and uneventful.

Pharmacokinetics

Propofol is highly lipophilic and, following an intravenous dose, there is a rapid decline in blood concentrations, indicating a swift distribution into the tissues. The pharmacokinetic profile is best described as a three-phase sequence:

(1) a very rapid distribution from blood ($T_{0.5}$ about 2 to 4 minutes);

(2) a rapid intermediate phase reflecting metabolic clearance ($T_{0.5}$, 35 to 45 minutes).

(3) a slower final phase, representing the slow return of drug to the blood from a poorly perfused deep compartment, probably body fat ($T_{0.5}$, 200 to 300 minutes).

The drug is mainly metabolized in the liver, and the metabolites are excreted via the kidney.

Unwanted effects

Cardio-respiratory depression is the main one of these; apnoea occurs on induction and the drug has a marked hypotensive effect. Another frequent unwanted effect is pain on injection, and this is particularly marked when propofol is injected into a small vein. Accidental extravasation does not produce any tissue damage.

Propofol is more expensive than existing intravenous induction agents, but its recovery characteristics make it particularly suitable for day-case procedures.

INHALATION ANAESTHESIA

This is the most widely used form of anaesthesia in the UK.

The various stages of anaesthesia were first described by Guedel (1937) with reference to ether. Hence the guidelines listed below must be subject to careful interpretation, and are clearly modified by modern anaesthetic techniques and agents. Many of the widely used anaesthetic agents bring the patient to Stage III very rapidly, and the subtle differences between the stages of anaesthesia may not be distinguishable. Furthermore, the depth of anaesthesia cannot be judged by the degree of muscular relaxation if a neuromuscular blocking agent has been used.

In the classical description, inhalation anaesthesia occurs in four stages, as listed next.

Stage I—analgesia stage

During this stage, the patient is still conscious and can talk, but feels giddy and sleepy. There is a progressive decrease in reaction to painful stimuli, and an increase in respiratory and pulse rate. The eyelash reflex is gradually lost.

Stage II—excitement stage

Although the patient is unconscious, this stage is known as the excitement stage because during it they may be agitated and struggle. Alternatively, they may be quiet, and much of this variable response may depend on the type of patient, the presence or absence of stimuli, and the skill of the anaesthetist. During the excitement stage, conscious control is removed, and the patient may struggle from a fear that has been concealed during Stage I or because they are being subjected to some stimulus, such as a premature attempt to extract teeth. In stage II, the pupils dilate, the pulse is rapid and strong, but respiration is irregular.

Stage III—surgical anaesthesia

The characteristic features of surgical anaesthesia concern eye signs and the muscles of respiration. There is a decrease in the range and activity of the movements of the eyeballs until eventually the eye comes to rest in the central position and remains there. In the early phase of surgical anaesthesia there is complete functioning of the intercostal muscles and diaphragm.

Stage IV—respiratory paralysis

At the stage of respiratory paralysis, the heart still beats and the patient may be kept alive if adequately oxygenated by artificial means. If such support is not given, the pulse will be rapid, there will be a drop in blood pressure, and the pupils will dilate. This will be followed by complete respiratory and circulatory collapse, and the patient will die.

The depth of anaesthesia will depend upon the type of operation. Most dental procedures can be carried out during the early phases of Stage III.

INHALATION ANAESTHETIC AGENTS

The properties of an ideal inhalation anaesthetic agent are:

(1) a rapid and pleasant induction of, and recovery from anaesthesia;

(2) the ability to produce rapid changes in the depth of anaesthesia;

(3) the ability to produce adequate relaxation of skeletal muscles;

(4) a wide margin of safety;

(5) no unwanted effects or other adverse properties in normal use.

Inhalation anaesthetic agents can be classified into two groups, gaseous agents (nitrous oxide and cyclopropane) and volatile liquids (halothane, enflurane, isoflurane, trichlorethylene, and ether).

Nitrous oxide

This colourless, odourless gas was the first agent to be used as an anaesthetic. It is stored as a liquid under pressure in metal cylinders, and evaporates when released. The gas is not flammable but supports combustion. Nitrous oxide has a very low solubility in blood (but not as low as nitrogen), and a state of equilibrium between alveolar and arterial tension is quickly reached. It is excreted unchanged in the expired gases.

Pharmacological properties

Nitrous oxide is a weak anaesthetic agent, mainly used as an adjunct to other agents (e.g. halothane). Surgical anaesthesia can be obtained in a minority of patients with nitrous oxide alone at concentrations in excess of 80 per cent. However, at these concentrations there is every danger of hypoxia. The mechanism for nitrous oxide-induced anaesthesia remains uncertain. It is an excellent analgesic agent, and may exert its analgesic properties by initiating the release of the endogenous opioids (see Chapter 6 and Berkowitz *et al.* 1977). When nitrous oxide is mixed with an adequate amount of oxygen (30 per cent), the mixture has little or no significant effect on the cardiovascular or respiratory system. However, it is a direct myocardial depressant, and also stimulates the sympathetic nervous system. As a result of these two actions, cardiac output remains unchanged.

Unwanted effects

The incidence of nausea and vomiting after administration of nitrous oxide alone is approximately 15 per cent, which compares unfavourably with halothane. *In vitro* studies have shown that nitrous oxide interrupts cell division in the presynthetic (G-1) phase of the DNA-synthesis cycle (Brinkley and Rao 1973; see also Chapter 17). Excessive use of nitrous oxide may suppress spermatogenesis and the production of white and red blood cells in the bone marrow (Kripke *et al.* 1976). However, this problem does not appear to arise in normal clinical use (Ames *et al.* 1978).

In experimental animals, nitrous oxide can cause megaloblastic anaemia and neuropathy through oxidation of the cobalt ion of vitamin B_{12}. This finding may be significant to personnel repeatedly exposed to nitrous oxide, such as anaesthetic and operating-theatre staff. Scavenger systems should be fitted to all systems where nitrous oxide is used to ensure that the atmosphere does not contain more than 50 p.p.m. A neuropathy similar to that of vitamin B_{12} deficiency has been observed in dental surgeons who regularly use nitrous oxide (Layzer 1978). Nitrous oxide may have a deleterious effect if used in patients who have an air-containing closed space in their bodies as the gas diffuses into such a space with a resulting build-up of pressure. This effect may be dangerous in cases of pneumothorax, which lesion may enlarge and so compromise respiration.

Uses

Nitrous oxide is used as an adjunct to other inhalation anaesthetic agents such as halothane or enflurane. Low doses are used in sedation and are discussed later. 'Entonox' is a commercially available mixture of 50 per cent nitrous oxide and 50 per cent oxygen; it is widely used to produce analgesia without loss of consciousness, and is especially useful in obstetric practice, for changing painful dressings, as an aid to postoperative physiotherapy, and in emergency ambulances. In ambulance emergencies, the mixture is very efficacious at reducing the pain of myocardial infarction. Cylinders containing 'Entonox' must always be stored in a warm room because, at low temperatures, the gaseous mixture separates out and the less dense nitrous oxide rises to the top of the cylinder. When such separation has occurred, the next patient will be exposed to 100 per cent nitrous oxide.

Halothane

This halogenated hydrocarbon is the most widely used anaesthetic agent. At room temperature, it is a colourless liquid that decomposes on contact with light. The liquid has a pleasant smell and readily vapourizes with a boiling point of 50°C. It is not inflammable and is non-explosive. Halothane can be used to induce anaesthesia at a concentration of 2 to 4 per cent, and anaesthesia can be maintained with a concentration of 1 to 2 per cent. Although intravenous anaesthetic agents are commonly used to induce anaesthesia (see p. 150), induction can be achieved with halothane. The vapour does not irritate the larynx so induction is smooth and a rapid depth of anaesthesia can readily be achieved.

Pharmacokinetics

Sixty to eighty per cent of halothane is eliminated unchanged in the expired gases. That portion absorbed is biotransformed in the liver, and the metabolites excreted via the kidney.

Pharmacological properties

Halothane has a marked effect on the cardiovascular system causing a dose-related reduction in blood pressure. The hypotension is due to a reduction both in cardiac output and in the baroreceptor response. Halothane also causes a slowing of the heart rate mediated by the vagus nerve and, more importantly, sensitizes the myocardium to catecholamines, which can provoke severe dysrhythmia. Such sensitization can be a problem in certain dental surgical procedures where injections of a local anaesthetic solution containing adrenaline may be used to maintain a relatively bloodless field. It is recommended that the amount of adrenaline should not exceed 0.1 mg in 10 minutes or 0.3 mg in 1 hour (Katz *et al.* 1962).

Halothane depresses respiration causing a reduction in gaseous exchange. However, it also produces bronchodilatation, thus making it a suitable agent for use in asthmatics and bronchitics. Halothane does not have any analgesic properties but does produce a degree of muscle relaxation, although rarely enough for most types of surgery.

Unwanted effects

Hepatic necrosis has been associated with halothane anaesthesia at an incidence of 1:10 000 anaesthetic administrations. However, the incidence increases with repeated halothane anaesthesia (Summary of the National Halothane Study 1966). Clinical signs and symptoms of a halothane-induced hepatic necrosis usually arise 2 to 5 days after administration. The patient becomes pyrexic, and complains of nausea and vomiting. Death occurs in 50 per cent of these patients. The mechanism of hepatic necrosis is uncertain: any residual halothane that is not expired is likely to be metabolized in the liver; however, a metabolite may induce an immune response resulting in hepatitis. Although halothane hepatitis is serious, other complications of general anaesthesia occur with much greater frequency.

A rare, unwanted effect of halothane is the syndrome of malignant hyperpyrexia, characterized by a rapid rise in body temperature, and a massive increase in both oxygen consumption and production of carbon dioxide. This condition can be fatal unless treated.

Enflurane

This is a halogenated ether; at room temperature it is a colourless, non-inflammable liquid with a mild, sweet odour. Anaesthesia can be smoothly induced with enflurane 4 per cent, and maintained with concentrations of 1.5 to 3 per cent. Induction is associated with mild stimulation of salivary flow and tracheobronchial secretions, but these are not usually troublesome. Enflurane also alters certain types of electrical activity in the brain that may be epileptogenic. Therefore, this agent should not be used in patients with a history of epilepsy.

Pharmacokinetics

About 80 per cent of enflurane is excreted unchanged in the expired gases. Of the remainder, only 2 to 5 per cent is metabolized in the liver; metabolites are excreted via the kidney.

Pharmacological properties

Enflurane produces a dose-dependent reduction in blood pressure in a manner similar to halothane. Its effect on the heart is also similar to that produced by halothane, but there is a smaller incidence of arrhythmias. Adrenaline-containing local anaesthetic solutions can be used safely with it.

Enflurane causes respiratory depression, and patients are usually ventilated when this agent is being used. Deep anaesthesia with enflurane is associated with muscle twitching of the limbs, jaw, face, and neck. These muscular movements are usually self-limiting, and are prevented by reducing the depth of anaesthesia. Because of this unwanted effect, enflurane should be avoided in epileptic patients. It has no significant effect on the liver and is often used in preference to halothane when repeated anaesthesia is required.

Isoflurane

This is an isomer of enflurane; chemically, it is a halogenated methyl ethyl ether. Its physical properties are similar to those of enflurane. Induction of anaesthesia with isoflurane is smooth and rapid, and can be achieved with a concentration of 3 per cent; maintenance is achieved with 1.5 to 2.5 per cent.

Pharmacological properties

Like the other halogenated volatile liquids, isoflurane causes a reduction in blood pressure, but has little or no effect on cardiac output. Administration is associated with an increase in heart rate but no arrhythmias. It does not sensitize the heart to catecholamines so adrenaline-containing local anaesthetic solutions can be used safely with this agent. Respiration is depressed with isoflurane, which may also stimulate airway reflexes, causing increased secretion, coughing, and laryngospasm. The incidence of nausea and vomiting is similar to that produced by the other halogenated compounds, and hepatotoxicity does not appear to be a problem

Trichlorethylene

This is a weak anaesthetic agent and a poor muscle relaxant, but a potent analgesic. It is rarely used as an anaesthetic agent because of slow induction and long recovery, due to its poor solubility.

Ether (diethyl ether)

This was one of the earliest and safest volatile liquids to be used in anaesthetic practice. Liquid ether is very pungent, irritating to the mucous membrane, inflammable, and explosive. Induction with ether was slow and unpleasant, and recovery was often associated with nausea and vomiting. Because of these unwanted effects, ether is now rarely used.

ASSESSMENT, AND ANAESTHETIC PROBLEMS OF THE MEDICALLY COMPROMISED PATIENT

Before any general anaesthetic is administered it is essential to check that the patient has had nothing to eat or drink for a period of six hours before induction. If possible, the patient's bladder should be empty. Where anaesthetics are being administered to out-patients, the patient must be accompanied by a responsible adult.

The medical conditions listed below can cause complications during anaesthesia and, where possible, such patients should be treated under local anaesthesia. If a general anaesthetic has to be used then they should be referred to hospital, and the anaesthetic should always be administered by an experienced anaesthetist.

Pregnancy

During the first trimester, drugs employed in anaesthetic practice could impair the development of the fetus and placenta. The middle trimester is probably the optimal time for a general anaesthetic if this is definitely required. In the final trimester, the bulky uterus will cause a reduction in gastric emptying, and it may impair venous return from the lower extremities, which will also cause a reduction in cardiac output.

Cardiovascular problems

Any disorders of this, the body's main transport system, will have serious implications during general anaesthesia.

Patients with angina pectoris should have a percutaneous preparation of glyceryl trinitrate (Transiderm-Nitro) applied to their skin before an anaesthetic. Those with ischaemic heart disease are already suffering from some degree of oxygen deprivation and any additional deprivation may produce an infarct.

All antihypertensive drugs are potentiated by general anaesthetic agents, especially the barbiturates and halothane, and a severe hypotensive attack could result from this interaction. Halothane may have some ganglion-blocking activity, and could also enhance the antihypertensive effects of other drugs.

Respiratory disorders

General anaesthesia should be postponed in patients with acute diseases of the upper respiratory tract (i.e. the common cold). Those with disease of the lower respiratory tract are prone to excessive mucus production, and such patients should be referred for a medical opinion before a general anaesthetic is administered.

Haematological disorders

All types of anaemia can affect the course of a general anaesthetic, but the two most serious forms are sickle cell disease and thalassaemia.

Sickle cell disease is an inherited disease found in about 10 per cent of people of African or West Indian origin. There are two types, a homozygous form (sickle cell disease) and a heterozygous form (sickle cell trait). In homozygous sickle cell disease, the red blood cells contain an abnormal haemoglobin (Hb_S). When such cells are exposed to a reduced oxygen tension, or a rise in blood pH, they become sickle-shaped (sickling) and haemolysis occurs. Dehydration, stasis of the circulation, and pyrexia also predispose to sickling. Patients with the heterozygous sickle cell trait may have some Hb_S in their red blood cells and the amount needs to be determined before a general anaesthetic is administered.

Thalassaemia is a rare inherited anaemia that occurs mainly in mid- and southern Europeans. The red blood cells in thalassaemia have a short life-span and contain fetal haemoglobin. Sufferers usually have a severe hypochronic anaemia.

Endocrine disorders

The problem of administering a general anaesthetic to patients suffering from diabetes or who have adrenocortical suppression is discussed in Chapter 18.

Hyperthyroidism causes tachycardia, and disturbances such as arrhythmias or even cardiac failure. Therefore the hyperthyroid patient is at risk when a general anaesthetic is administered because of the possible precipitation of dangerous arrhythmias.

Neurological disorders

Methohexitone should not be used as an intravenous anaesthetic agent in patients with a history of epilepsy (see p. 152). In such a patient, methohexitone could result in status epilepticus under general anaesthesia.

Patients with a history of spasticity, myasthenia gravis, and multiple sclerosis are a special anaesthetic risk and should be be anaesthetized in hospital.

Drug therapy

Patients taking mono-amine oxidase inhibitors should not be given pethidine as a premedication, as severe and life-threatening interactions occur between them (see Chapter 22).

ANAESTHETIC EMERGENCIES

The two emergencies to be discussed in this section are respiratory obstruction and hypersensitivity reactions. Other emergencies can occur at any phase of general anaesthesia, i.e. cardiac arrest, syncope, etc., and these are discussed in Chapter 24.

Respiratory obstruction

Obstruction of the airway during anaesthesia can be caused by the several factors listed below:

(1) *Anatomical:* large tongue, retrognathic mandible, enlarged adenoids and tonsils;

(2) *Operative problems:* obstructing the airway by applying too much back pressure during extraction, or too much flexion of the head;

(3) *Pathological problems:* upper respiratory tract infection, blocked nasal airway;

(4) *Laryngeal spasm:* caused by blood, saliva, mucus, pus, vomit, or foreign bodies touching the vocal cords;

(5) *Obstruction below vocal cords:* caused by inhaled foreign body, or broncho-spasm.

Signs and symptoms

If respiratory sounds can still be heard, this is an indication of only *partial* blockage of the airway; no respiratory sounds means *total obstruction.* With complete obstruction there is alternate indentation of the intercostal spaces and jerking movements of the abdominal wall because of the efforts of the diaphragm, which is the most powerful muscle of respiration. Respiratory obstruction, if not urgently treated, will lead to circulatory collapse.

Treatment

In the first instance, try and find the cause of the obstruction: the cervical spine should be extended to open the pharynx and the mandible lifted forward. With a laryngoscope, inspect the larynx for foreign material such as blood, saliva, and mucus; remove with suction. This, however, can be an extremely difficult procedure even for an experienced anaesthetist. Foreign bodies, such as tooth fragments, should be removed with McGill's forceps. Respiratory obstruction in small children can usually be cleared by holding them upside down and thumping their back.

If the condition does not improve with these measures, then a cricothyrotomy should be carried out. For this technique, the neck is extended and a cricothyroid cannula inserted through the cricothyroid membrane. If a cricothyroid needle is not available, then a large venepuncture needle could allow sufficient air (200 ml) to pass into the lungs. Oxygen should be administered through the cannula. If circulatory collapse has occurred, resuscitation techniques described in Chapter 24 should be employed.

Hypersensitivity reactions

Any of the drugs used in general anaesthesia are capable of causing a hypersensitivity reaction. However, such reactions are more likely to occur with the intravenous anaesthetic agents, and this was especially true of Althesin and propanidid, which contain the solvent, cremophor E-L. These two drugs are no longer used, but other compounds may still cause a problem. The signs, symptoms, and treatment of hypersensitivity reactions are discussed in Chapter 21.

SEDATION

Introduction

Fear of dental treatment is a common reason for failure to seek regular dental care; all dentists encounter apprehensive patients and are aware of the problems of managing their anxiety so that treatment can be carried out. Sedation is one of the most widely used methods for reducing such axiety. The Wylie Report (1978) defines sedation as '. . . a technique in which the use of a drug or drugs produces a state of depression of the central nervous system enabling treatment to be carried out, but during which verbal contact with the patient is maintained throughout the period of sedation. The drugs and techniques used should carry a margin of safety wide enough to render unintended loss of consciousness unlikely.'

Hill and Morris (1983) list the ideal properties of a sedation agent as follows:

(1) alleviation of fear and anxiety;

(2) production of a degree of amnesia and analgesia;

(3) suppression of vomiting reflexes, but not of protective reflexes;

(4) prolongation of potential operating time;

(5) readily effective;

(6) having a sufficiently long effect but which then quickly wears off;

(7) no side effects;

(8) safety and easily administered by the operator;

(9) not requiring special procedures or precautions before or after use;

(10) the associated techniques and equipment should be simple and the drugs inexpensive.

Sedation techniques used in dentistry can be categorized into three types depending on the route of administration—these being inhalation, oral, and intravenous. Whatever sedation technique is used, local anaesthesia must be also employed. Sedation techniques on their own are not sufficient to reduce painful impulses arising from dental procedures.

Inhalation methods of producing sedation

Nitrous oxide is the main inhalation agent used to provide sedation in dentistry, although the efficacy of low concentrations of enflurane and isoflurane is also being evaluated. After its introduction as an anaesthetic agent, it was soon recognized that low concentrations (20 to 25 per cent) of nitrous oxide could produce sedation. This property has been incorporated into two sedation techniques, inhalation sedation and relative analgesia.

Nitrous oxide, in the concentrations required for sedation, is a very safe drug producing very little systemic disturbance. The gaseous mixture (see below) can be rapidly cleared from the blood stream in the lungs within five minutes of breathing normal air. There are a few patients who are very sensitive to nitrous oxide and these may become anaesthetized with the concentrations used for sedation.

Inhalation sedation

This method involves the administration of a fixed concentration of 25 per cent nitrous oxide in an oxygen-enriched (25 per cent) air mixture at a flow rate in excess of the patient's anticipated minute volume. With the concentration of nitrous oxide fixed at 25 per cent, loss of consciousness cannot occur; thus this technique is safe for single operators. The gaseous mixture is administered via a nasal mask, and the level of sedation is determined by the amount of nose or mouth breathing, with nose breathing producing deeper sedation and mouth breathing recovery, whereby the level of sedation is controlled by the patient.

The mixture of nitrous oxide and oxygen-enriched air, when supplied at a flow rate above the normal minute volume, causes a small positive pressure in the breathing circuit. This minimizes the problem of dilution of the inspired gas mixture by air in a leaky breathing circuit.

Relative analgesia

In this method of sedation, the gas flow from the machine is below the minute-volume requirements and, to compensate, the air dilution valve on the nosepiece is partially opened to admit additional volumes of air. This results in a variable and unpredictable dilution of the inspired gases according to changes in the partial pressure in the system. Such changes result from the inspiratory effort, which can vary from breath to breath. Consequently, the level of sedation must be monitored by the operator by altering the flow rate of the gases.

Patient preparation and administration of inhalation sedation

The patient does not need to starve before inhalation sedation. Patients must be accompanied, and should not be permitted to drive or to place themselves in a situation where they might be a hazard either to themselves or others. Lingering, subtle effects on judgement or co-ordination cannot be completely excluded in the aftermath of sedation. Furthermore, one who is approaching a dental appointment in a state of anxiety and fear is not fully rational at the time and is at a greater hazard than the normal population. The euphoria commonly experienced after sedation may also interfere with judgement and responses; this is apart from any possible effects of the drug.

Prior to the appointment, the patient should be given details of the sedative technique and its likely effects. At the appointment, they should be placed in the supine position and allowed to familiarize themselves with the nosepiece, making adjustments for comfort. When the nosepiece is in position, the gaseous mixture is turned on and the patient instructed to breath slowly and regularly. During induction, quiet and reassuring verbal contact should be maintained between operator and patient, which produces a state of semi-hypnosis.

Signs of sedation

The signs and symptoms of inhalation sedation produced by nitrous oxide are listed by Edmunds and Rosen (1983), and categorized as either objective or subjective.

Objective signs

The patient remains awake, follows instructions, and responds to questions. There is a reduced response to painful stimuli, and the patient appears drowsy and relaxed. The respiratory rate is normal and smooth with little or no gagging or coughing. There is no excessive movement of the limbs; the pupil size, eye reactions, pulse, and blood pressure are normal.

Subjective signs

These are:

(1) mental and physical relaxation, and relief of anxiety;
(2) euphoria, headiness, and a feeling of floating;
(3) an indifference to surroundings and to the passage of time;
(4) feelings of warmth and tingling of extremities;
(5) buzzing or ringing in ears;
(6) sounds seeming distant.

Once the patient is sedated, the local anaesthetic can be injected and the operative procedure carried out. On completion of treatment, the patient breathes 100 per cent oxygen for 2 minutes, and within 10 minutes they should be fit to leave the surgery.

Contra-indications to inhalation sedation

This technique should not be used during pregnancy. In the early stages of pregnancy there is the possibility of teratogenicity from nitrous oxide and, in the later stages, there is the risk of relaxation of the uterus, although this is most unlikely if the concentration of nitrous oxide stays below 25 per cent. Inhalation sedation techniques are not suitable for patients with acute or chronic nasal obstruction: these include upper respiratory tract infections, chronic bronchitis, or an attack of hay fever. The obese may be intolerant of the supine position because of difficulties in breathing due to diaphragm compression. Psychiatrically disturbed patients are best treated in hospital after consultation with their psychiatrist.

Summary

Inhalation sedation techniques are safe and usually well-tolerated by most anxious patients. The administration of nitrous oxide by the inhalation sedation method has the advantage over relative analgesia by allowing a fixed dose of the gas to be given. Thus the operator is not distracted by having to adjust the nitrous-oxide level, being left free to concentrate on the dental procedure. Inhalation sedation techniques also appear to 'cure' dental anxiety, and it is then possible to 'wean' patients off sedation onto conventional treatment under local anaesthesia.

Oral sedation

The oral administration of drugs to produce sedation has the advantage of relative safety and acceptability. Oral sedation is particularly useful in children. The disadvantages of the oral route are the delayed onset of action, unreliable drug absorption, inability to regulate easily the intensity of the drug effect, and often a prolonged duration of action. For these reasons, oral sedative agents are mainly used to ensure that patients have a restful night before a dental procedure and to provide some degree of sedation in the period before the appointment. Drugs used for this purpose include the benzodiazepines, antihistamines, and triclofos.

Benzodiazepines

Diazepam, temazepam, and lorazepam are the main benzodiazepines used for oral sedation. The general pharmacology of these drugs is dealt with in Chapter 14, and dose regimes are shown in Table 8.3. Elderly patients are unusually sensitive to diazepam and, if this drug is to be used in them, then the normal adult dose should be halved. Conversely, children show a degree of resistance to diazepam and should be prescribed a dose regime of 0.2 to 0.5 mg/kg of body weight (Trapp 1981). Unwanted effects of diazepam include dizziness, an

Table 8.3. Dose regimes of drugs used for oral sedation.

Drug	Adult Dose	Child Dose	Time of administration
Diazepam	5 mg	5–10 mg	5 mg at night 5 mg on wakening 5 mg 2 hours before dental procedure
Temazepam	10–30 mg	—	40–60 minutes prior to dental procedure
Lorazepam	1–5 mg	—	1–3 mg at night 1–5 mg, 2–6 hours before dental procedure
Trimeprazine tartrate	3–4.5 mg/kg	2–4 mg/kg	1–2 hours before dental procedure
Promethazine hydrochloride	—	6–12 months: 10 mg 1–5 years: 15–20 mg	1–2 hours prior to dental procedure
Triclofos sodium	1–2 g	1 year: 100–250 mg 1–5 years: 250–500 mg 6–12 years: 0.5–1 g	30 minutes before retiring to bed

increased awareness of painful stimuli, ataxia, and prolonged postoperative drowsiness.

Temazepam and lorazepam are both classified as sedative-hypnotics. They are especially useful in the anxious patient for ensuring undisturbed sleep before a dental appointment. Both drugs have a short half-life and there is little hangover effect.

Antihistamines

Some antihistamines (H$_1$-antagonists; see Chapter 4) cause drowsiness and sedation as unwanted effects, but they can also be used therapeutically for this purpose. Trimeprazine and promethazine are widely used as sedative agents especially in children; dosages are shown in Table 8.2. Both drugs also have anti-emetic properties. Trimeprazine is especially useful for out-patient sedation, but unwanted effects include persistent drowsiness, disturbed dreams, nasal stuffiness, and headache. Promethazine is less effective than trimeprazine as a sedative agent and may produce restlessness, irritability, and hallucinations.

Triclofos sodium

This is chemically related to chloral hydrate, both of which are discussed in Chapter 14. It is mainly used as a sedative/hypnotic in children, and dosages are shown in Table 8.2. Unwanted effects from triclofos sodium include drowsiness, dizziness, headache, and gastro-intestinal disturbances.

Intravenous sedation agents

The administration of sedative agents via the intravenous route is probably the most reliable and effective method of producing sedation. Furthermore, this route provides a rapid onset of action, and the dose of agent used can be titrated to each patient's needs. The disadvantage of intravenous sedation is the inability to reverse the actions of the drug once administered. The recent availability of the benzodiazepine antagonist, flumazenil, may be helpful in this context. The technique also requires a certain amount of patient co-operation to allow venepuncture, hence this method is not suitable for young children. Intravenous sedation is particularly useful for the moderate to very anxious patient, and the physically and mentally handicapped.

Early pioneers of intravenous sedation were Jorgenson (see Jorgenson 1976) and Drummond-Jackson (see Drummond-Jackson 1967). Jorgenson's technique involved the intravenous administration of an incremental dose of pentobarbitone, followed by pethidine and hyoscine. Not only did the patients become sedated, but many fell asleep. This technique is rarely used now because it is slow and requires skilled training. When patients are asleep their protective reflexes may be reduced. Recovery from this sedation technique is very slow and so it is not suitable for out-patients.

Drummond-Jackson advocated the intravenous administration of incremental doses of methohexitone producing ultra-light anaesthesia. Much controversy surrounded the safety and efficacy of this technique, especially the use of the same person acting as operator/anaesthetist. This technique is condemned by anaesthetists as dangerous; it has been replaced with the advent of the benzodiazepines. Diazepam and midazolam are the most widely used intravenous sedation agents used in dentistry. As well as producing sedation, both drugs produce amnesia, which is especially useful for certain dental procedures (Greg *et al.* 1974).

Diazepam

Diazepam is available as a 5 mg/ml viscous solution, and as an emulsion preparation (Diazemuls[R]) for intravenous sedation. The drug is administered into a vein usually in the antecubital fossa. The solution should be injected slowly (5 mg/min) until the required level of sedation is achieved. During the period of injection, the patient's speech becomes slurred and there is ptosis of the upper eyelid (Verril's sign). Apnoea may occur during the onset of sedation and oxygen must always be available in case this problem presents. Normal adults usually require 5 to 20 mg; the duration of sedation is usually 45 to 60 minutes. Most patients can usually leave the dental surgery about 1 to 1.5 hrs after administration, but there is a rebound effect, where the patient may feel drowsy, which occurs 6 to 8 hours after dosage. This is probably due to the release of an active metabolite, desmethyl diazepam. Consequently, patients should always be accompanied and escorted home. They should not be allowed to drive or operate machinery during the 24 hours after intravenous diazepam.

Other unwanted effects arising from intravenous diazepam are pain at the site of injection, and sometimes thrombosis (Olesen and Huttel 1980) because the solution is irritant to the vein. This problem can be overcome by preparing the drug in an emulsified oil solvent (Diazemuls[R]; Rosenbaum 1982).

Midazolam

This is a new benzodiazepine that is water-soluble and may well replace diazepam as an intravenous sedation agent. The water solubility means there is less tendency for pain on injection and thrombophlebitis. In comparison to diazepam, midazolam has a shorter half-life (1.7 hours) and a shorter duration of action. Midazolam is 50 per cent more potent that diazepam and has a superior amnesic effect (Maisel 1980; see Chapter 14).

Combined intravenous preparations for sedation in dentistry

Over the years, it has become the practice of some operators to supplement intravenous sedation with benzodiazepines by adding a centrally acting analgesic such as pentazocine or pethidine. The rationale for this procedure is two-fold. Firstly, the opioids will potentiate the sedative properties of the benzodiazepines and the patient will therefore require a reduced dose of the latter. Secondly, when this sedation mixture is used for dental surgical procedures, the opioids may provide some degree of postoperative pain relief.

Opioids and benzodiazepines produce respiratory depression and deaths have occurred following the use of this sedation technique. It should also be noted that the efficacy of the opioids in postoperative dental pain is uncertain (Seymour and Walton 1982; 1984), and their use for this purpose is very questionable. With the new generation of benzodiazepines, there seems little point in supplementing sedation with other drugs that could be life-threatening.

Conclusions

Sedation techniques have had a tremendous impact on the practice of dentistry and patients' perception of dental treatment. There are some practitioners who never attempt sedation techniques and others who employ them all the time, whether they are required or not. It is important to realize that all sedation techniques have potential problems, and the drugs, if misused, can be life-threatening. A practitioner may consider him or herself competent at administering various sedation techniques, but must always have respect for the agents used. In all instances, emergency resuscitation equipment and drugs must be available to treat any unforeseen problem.

REFERENCES

Ames, J. A. L., Burman, J. F., Rees, G. M., Nancekievill, D. G., and Mollin, D. L. (1978). Megablastic hemopoiesis in patients receiving nitrous oxide. *Lancet*, **2**, 339–41.

Berkowitz, B. A., Fink, A. D., and Nga, S. H. (1977). Nitrous oxide analgesia: reversal by naloxone and development of tolerance. *Journal of Pharmacology and Experimental Therapeutics*, **203**, 539–47.

Brinkley, B. R. and Rao, P. N. (1973). Nitrous oxide: effects on the mitotic apparatus and chromosome movement in Hela cells. *Journal of Cell Biology*, **58**, 96–106.

Drummond-Jackson, S. L. (1967). Minimal incremental methohexitone in intravenous anaesthesia. In *Society for the Advancement of Anaesthesia in Dentistry* (3rd edn), p. 143. London.

Dundee, J. W. (1960). Alterations in response to somatic pain associated with anaesthesia. II. The effect of thiopentone and pentobarbitone. *British Journal of Anaesthesia*, **32**, 407–14.

Edmunds, D. H. and Rosen, M. (1983). Inhalation sedation. *Dental Update*, **10**, 469–76.

Greg, J. M., Ryan, D. E., and Levin, K. H. (1974). The amnesic actions of diazepam. *Journal of Oral Surgery*, **32**, 651–64.

Guedel, A. E. (1937). *Inhalation anaesthesia: a fundamental guide*. Macmillan, New York.

Hill, C. M. and Morris, P. J. (1983). *General anaesthesia and sedation in dentistry*. Wright, Bristol.

Jorgensen, N. B. (1976). Local anaesthesia and intravenous pre-medication. *Anaesthesia Progress*, **13**, 168–76.

Katz, R. L., Matteo, R. S., and Papper, E. M. (1962). The injection of epinephrine during general anaesthesia. II. Halothane. *Anaesthesiology*, **23**, 597–600.

Kripke, B. J., Kelman, A. D., Shah, N. K., Balogh, K., and Handler, A. H. (1976). Testicular reaction to prolonged exposure to nitrous oxide. *Anaesthesiology*, **44**, 104–13.

Layzer, R. B. (1978). Myeloneuropathy after prolonged exposure to nitrous oxide. *Lancet*, **ii**, 1222–30.

Maisel, G. M. (1980). Midazolam: second generation of benzodiazepines. *Anaesthesia Progress*, **27**, 159–60.

Olesen, A. S. and Huttel, M. S. (1980). Local reactions to I.V. diazepam in different formulations. *British Journal of Anaesthesia*, **52**, 609–11.

Rosenbaum, N. L. (1982). A new formulation of diazepam for intravenous sedation in dentistry: a clinical evaluation. *British Dental Journal*, **153**, 192–3.

Seymour, R. A. and Walton, J. G. (1982). Analgesic efficacy in dental pain. *British Dental Journal*, **153**, 291–7.

Seymour, R. A. and Walton, J. G. (1984). Pain control after third molar surgery. *International Journal of Oral Surgery*, **13**, 457–85.

Summary of the National Halothane Study. (1966). *Journal of the American Medical Association*, **197**, 775–88.

Trapp, L. D. (1981). Pharmacological management of pain and anxiety. In *Pediatric Dentristry* (ed. R. E. Stewart, T. K. Barber, K. C. Troutman and S. H. Y. Wei). Mosby. St. Louis.

The Wylie Report (1978). Report of the working party on training of dental anaesthetists. *British Dental Journal*, **151**, 385–7.

9

Antiseptics and disinfectants

AT one time antiseptics and disinfectants formed a major part of the dental students' teaching in dental pharmacology. Today they play a lesser role, but nevertheless an important one. Some of these substances are of great use in medicine and dentistry; the dental surgeon should be able to choose, from all those available, those with real advantages and, at the same time, appreciate their limitations. The prevention of cross-infection, and the use of antiseptics for this purpose, are referred to later in this chapter.

Many chemical substances kill bacteria. The use of phenol in operating theatres, associated historically with the name of Lister, introduced a new era into antisepsis. The trouble with most chemical agents is that in concentrations destructive to micro-organisms, they are also destructive to other living tissue.

TERMINOLOGY

Antiseptics are substances that kill or prevent the growth of micro-organisms; the term is generally applied to substances used on living tissues. In contrast, the term disinfectant is usually applied to substances used on inanimate objects. Disinfectants prevent infection by the destruction of pathogenic organisms, and are generally regarded as being bactericidal. The distinction between antiseptics and disinfectants is not so much that one group is bacteriostatic and the other bactericidal, but that the distinction is implicit in the way they are used. For instance, antiseptics are applied to living surfaces and, by preventing the growth and multiplication of organisms, they assist the natural defence mechanisms of the body. If the vitality of the micro-organisms can be reduced below a certain level, then these natural mechanisms will have a chance to repel the microbial invasion. Usually disinfectants are too toxic to be applied to living tissues; they not only kill off bacteria but also they kill healthy living tissue. Disinfectants are therefore used on objects, e.g. instruments—when, for instance, heat sterilization is not possible.

INDIVIDUAL ANTISEPTICS AND DISINFECTANTS

These will be considered under separate headings, those with similar chemical structures being grouped together.

Alcohols

Alcohol is a protoplasmic poison; it acts by precipitating the proteins of the protoplasm.

Ethyl alcohol and isopropyl alcohol are effective antibacterial agents and are used for disinfection of the skin, but alcohol is ineffective when applied to the oral mucosa. The curious thing is that alcohols are effective in concentrations of 50 to 70 per cent by weight, but higher concentrations are useless. The activity of other antiseptics, e.g. chlorhexidine, iodine (see later), is increased in the presence of alcohol.

Surgical spirit, which is a mixture of ethyl and methyl alcohols, is used for cleaning surgical surfaces.

Aldehydes

Formaldehyde

This has bactericidal activity against bacteria, fungi, and viruses. However, its action is very slow—in 0.5 per cent concentrations it would take about 12 hours to kill bacteria. Formaldehyde is usually used in 2 to 8 per cent concentrations as a means of disinfecting inanimate objects.

Glutaraldehyde

This aldehyde is much superior to formaldehyde as a sterilizing agent and acts against all micro-organisms, including viruses. It is much less volatile than formaldehyde and causes less odour. It is marketed as a useful preparation in a 2 per cent concentration. This is used for 'cold sterilization' of instruments. It is recommended for the treatment of articles that have been contaminated by hepatitis B virus (see below), and that cannot be heat sterilized. Exposure should be for at least 1 hour, but preferably for a longer period, e.g. up to 12 hours.

Chlorhexidine

Chlorhexidine (Hibitane) finds extensive use in medicine and in dentistry as an antiseptic and disinfectant. Many preparations are available, and a few are now listed:

1. *Hibiscrub ICI*—chlorhexidine gluconate 4 per cent in non-ionic detergent base. The solution is used for pre-operative preparation of skin, and for hand disinfection.

2. *Hibisol ICI*—chlorhexidine gluconate 0.5 per cent in isopropyl alcohol. This solution is used for disinfection of the skin and hands. It should be applied to clean dry skin/hands and rubbed briskly until dry.

3. *Corsodyl ICI*—chlorhexidine gluconate 1 per cent: dental gel (red). There is

also a Corsodyl Mouthwash, which is a chlorhexidine gluconate 0.2 per cent solution.

4. *Hibitane ICI*—chlorhexidine gluconate 1 per cent cream. Pre-operative preparation of hands and skin.

5. *Hibitane Concentrate*—chlorhexidine gluconate 5 per cent; used as a general purpose antiseptic.

Chlorhexidine is a highly effective agent against a wide variety of organisms, both Gram-positive and Gram-negative, but more particularly Gram-positive. It is especially effective when in alcoholic solution. It is non-irritant to the tissues in the recommended concentration, and is non-toxic. Chlorhexidine 0.5 per cent in 70 per cent alcohol is a useful solution for pre-operative skin preparation of both surgeons and patients. 'Hibiscrub' is also used for the same purposes. Chlorhexidine may also be used for storing sterile instruments.

A particular use for chlorhexidine has been found in dentistry (see Chapter 11). In 0.5 per cent solution in 70 per cent alcohol it is useful for sterilizing the mucosa prior to local anaesthetic injection. More importantly, the aqueous solution has been found to inhibit dental plaque formation. Daily mouth rinsing with a 0.2 per cent solution has been shown to inhibit the deposition of plaque, and this leads to a reduction in the amount of gingival inflammation. Unwanted effects, seemingly few, include some disturbance of taste, perhaps due to the unpleasant taste of the mouthwash. It also produces a staining of the teeth that is not all that easy to remove. Occasionally it is said to have induced swellings of the parotid glands. Although the long-term use of chlorhexidine does not seem to be accompanied by problems of a serious nature, perhaps its use would best be limited to short courses associated with current periodontal treatment. The reader is referred to modern textbooks on preventive dentistry for further information.

Dyes

These are complex organic substances, which are all derived in some way from coal tar, and they include the aniline dyes, gentian violet, and brilliant green. Also included are the acridine dyes, acriflavin and proflavine.

Gentian violet and brilliant green are effective against some Gram-positive organisms, but Gram-negative organisms are very resistant. Their effectiveness is decreased by the presence of pus and serum. Gentian violet is a fungicide and, prior to the introduction of the antifungal antimicrobials, was used in the treatment of oral thrush (acute candidiasis). It stains the tissues blue and is messy; with newer agents now available, it is no longer used.

Acriflavine and proflavine differ considerably from the aniline dyes in that they are active against Gram-negative as well as Gram-positive organisms, and they are not inactivated to any extent by organic matter. They may be used for application to superficial wounds.

Halogens

These substances are effective because they unite with proteins of bacteria and this chemical action is toxic.

Chlorine

This halogen is bactericidal, used in the disinfection of water and for disinfecting drains. In practice it is the hypochlorites that find particular use, and they exert their effect by liberating chlorine. Chlorine is inactivated by organic matter: it combines with the proteins of the tissues as well as with those of bacteria, with consequent rapid loss of its activity. In dentistry, a 2 per cent solution of sodium hypochlorite is used as an antiseptic irrigant of root canals, and is an effective solvent of necrotic tissues, e.g. the dead pulp. At one time this syringing was alternated with 5 to 10 volumes hydrogen peroxide and the final syringing done with saline solution. Care must be exercised to ensure that neither the hypochlorite solution nor the hydrogen peroxide get through the root apex where they would cause irritation, and hydrogen peroxide must not be sealed into a canal. Today, irrigation is generally by sodium hypochlorite alone.

Iodine

This acts as an antiseptic in much the same way as chlorine; it is bactericidal and is also a fungicide, but one difference is that it is not readily inactivated by organic matter. It is an effective agent in sterilization of the skin prior to surgery, when it is used in the form of weak iodine solution, 2.5 per cent iodine in potassium iodine, water, and alcohol. When painted on the skin this solution is said to produce a sterile area, in about five minutes, that lasts some time. Unfortunately, it does discolour the skin and just very occasionally causes hypersensitivity reactions. Weak solution of iodine was sometimes painted on inflamed gums when, supposedly, it acted as a counter-irritant.

Iodoform

This is mildly antiseptic due to slow liberation of iodine when applied to tissues. A number of preparations containing iodoform have been, or are still, used in dentistry; all have a strong, persistent, and characteristic smell. One such preparation is Whitehead's Varnish, which contains 10 per cent iodoform with benzoin, storax, and balsam of tolu in solvent ether. Whitehead's Varnish, usually incorporated into ribbon gauge, is used to treat infected sockets, and as a dressing after surgical removal of third molars and cysts. Another iodoform preparation, once very popular in dentistry, is Kri-Paste, which consists of Kri Liquid (40 per cent) and iodoform (60 per cent). Kri Liquid contains (approx.) parachlorphenol, 45 parts; camphor, 49 parts; and methanol, 6 parts. It was frequently used as a medicament to sterilize root canals, and the paste as a root-canal filler.

Iodophors

Are combinations of iodine and surface-active detergents, e.g. povidone–iodine. Povidone is a water-soluble polymer that seems to prolong the activity of many drugs, and does so with iodine by liberating it slowly from the complex. Such combinations are probably effective against most Gram-positive and Gram-negative organisms after about 15 seconds contact. They do not irritate or stain the skin. Povidone–iodine mouthwash (povidone–iodine, 1 per cent) is available, and may be used either undiluted or diluted with an equal volume of warm water as a mouthwash for mucosal infections.

Oxidizing agents

These act by liberating oxygen, which unites with proteins of bacteria, and also with tissue proteins. All the available oxygen is soon used up and the antiseptic action quickly exhausted.

Hydrogen peroxide

This oxidizing agent is a weak antiseptic; when brought into contact with living tissue it is decomposed into water and oxygen but it gives off its oxygen rapidly and so its germicidal action is limited. It has been used as a mild antiseptic mouthwash in the treatment of acute ulcerative gingivitis (15 ml of the 20 volume solution (approx 6 per cent) to a half tumbler full of warm water). Its use in this form of gingivitis was advocated because of the anaerobic nature of the infection. Apart from its antiseptic properties, hydrogen peroxide exerts a mechanical cleansing action through the effervescence produced by the liberation of the oxygen. A stronger solution of hydrogen peroxide (30 per cent aqueous solution) is used to bleach discoloured root-filled teeth.

Sodium perborate

In solution this may also be used in the treatment of acute ulcerative gingivitis, for it too liberates oxygen when in contact with organic matter. 'Bocasan' (buffered sodium peroxyborate monohydrate) is said by the manufacturers to release far more effervescent oxygen than ordinary sodium perborate.

Phenols, cresols, and their derivatives

Phenol

As mentioned in the Introduction to this chapter, phenol is associated with the pioneering work of Lister in the field of antiseptics. As an antiseptic it has now been largely superseded by less toxic chemicals. It was often used as liquified phenol, which is phenol 80 per cent in water. Its action on micro-organisms is largely due to the fact that it is more soluble in lipids and proteins than in water.

Consequently it leaves a watery medium and concentrates on the microbial bodies. There is significance in this differential solubility, for oily phenolic preparations are virtually valueless as antiseptics. When applied to the skin or mucous membranes in weak or moderately weak solutions, phenol produces some feeling of anaesthesia as it does have a depolarizing local anaesthetic action. It is this 'anaesthetic' property that made it popular as an ingredient of mouthwashes. If a strong solution is applied to the skin it is irritant and caustic, producing a burning pain. The area of skin will show a white slough if the application of the strong phenol is prolonged; this local action is due to the precipitation of proteins. Phenol is not firmly held in the protein precipitate and is thus capable of quite deep percutaneous penetration.

Camphorated paramonochlorphenol (CMCP)

This is a 35 per cent solution of parachlorphenol in camphor and has been widely used as a medicament in root canals. The pronounced disinfectant property of this preparation depends on the liberation of chlorine in the presence of phenol, the chlorine replacing one of the hydrogen atoms in phenol. It is comparatively non-irritant. A commonly used antiseptic today is a 1 per cent aqueous parachlorphenol solution.

Cresol

This has about three times the bactericidal potency of phenol and is about as toxic. However, metacresyl acetate (Cresatin) is a cresol that is used as a chemical antiseptic for the irrigation of root canals. It is not irritant to the periapical tissues and has an anodyne effect on residual pulp tissue.

Chloroxylenols

These are less effective against microbes than other phenolic agents and what activity they do have is considerably reduced in the presence of organic matter. Dettol (about 5 per cent chloroxylenol) is a well-known preparation. Solutions of chloroxylenol are often so ineffective that they are liable to be contaminated by one pathogen, namely *Pseudomonas pyocyanea*; indeed the growth of this organism may be encouraged by such solutions.

Hexachlorophane

This is very effective against Gram-positive cocci and is an excellent surface disinfectant. Preparations containing hexachlorophane are used on the skin prior to surgery, and as a pre-surgical hand cream. Hexachlorophane is not very irritant to the tissues but neurotoxic effects have been reported as a result of absorption following its application to babies in dusting powders. This problem may have related to the widespread application of the powder, particularly on raw skin surfaces.

Surface-acting agents

These alter surface tension; they have both fat- and water-soluble groups in the same molecule. They are variously classified, the classification depending on the electric charge on the water-soluble group—cationic, positive charge; anionic, negative charge; amphoteric, positive and negative charges; and non-ionic, that is un-ionized. Non-ionic forms have little activity, but the others all have some degree of antibacterial activity, the cationic agents being the most effective. These substances are very active detergents, but are really only weak antiseptics.

Some cationic surface-active agents have attracted interest; these are the quaternary ammonium compounds, a few examples of which include:

(1) *cetrimide (Cetavlon)*—used as an aqueous or as an alcoholic solution for skin disinfection and cleansing of wounds;
(2) *Benzalkonium chloride (Roccal)*—1 per cent solution used as pre-operative skin preparation.

The quaternary ammonium compounds are incompatible with soaps and are inhibited by organic matter. Sometimes these agents are combined with other substances: for instance, chlorhexidine gluconate 1.5 per cent and cetrimide 15 per cent in a solution called Savlon Concentrate, which is used for general antisepsis. They are poor antiseptics, but are used as anti-plaque agents in dentistry (see Chapter 11).

THE DENTAL USES OF ANTISEPTICS

These can be summarized as follows:

(1) skin preparation before surgery or injection;
(2) pre-operative preparation of the oral mucosa;
(3) sometimes as an ingredient of dentifrices;
(4) inhibition of dental plaque;
(5) cleaning of operating areas;
(6) the 'cold' sterilization of instruments and equipment (where 'heat' sterilization is impractical);
(7) storage of sterilized surgical equipment;
(8) preparation of the surgeon's hands;
(9) irrigation of root canals in endodontics.

ASTRINGENTS

These are substances that are said to precipitate proteins in superficial cells and thereby form a protective layer against irritants and bacterial invasion. This layer is also supposed to inhibit exudation of leucocytes and serum. There is much doubt about the efficacy of astringents; their effect is mainly subjective, merely causing the mucous membranes to feel shrunken and shrivelled.

Astringents are classified into two groups:

(1) the soluble salts of heavy metals, e.g. iron, lead, zinc, copper, aluminium, silver, and mercury;

(2) the vegetable astringents.

Metallic astringents

The zinc salts are the main components of this group; for example, zinc sulphate and zinc chloride mouthwash. It has been suggested that although the so-called astringent action of zinc mouthwashes may have little or no value, perhaps zinc salts themselves are helpful in promoting healing. Although such mouthwashes have been used in the healing of ulcers, their value is doubtful.

Silver nitrate is an astringent antiseptic that found much favour in dentistry at one time. Its astringent action is powerful but superficial, so concentrated solutions are caustic but not penetrating. A 10 per cent solution of silver nitrate has been used to reduce the sensitivity of dentine exposed at the necks of teeth. The solution is burnished into the exposed tissue by means of a plastic instrument. Even if this is effective, the solution stains and is not suitable for anterior teeth.

Vegetable astringents

Tannic acid is the example of a vegetable astringent. At one time it was used in dentistry in powder form as a haemostatic, the powder being applied to the bleeding tooth socket and covered with a gauze pack. It was also a constituent of some mouthwashes, but this substances no longer finds favour in dentistry as it is ineffective.

CAUSTICS

A number of substances, when concentrated, act as caustics, e.g. zinc chloride, zinc sulphate, silver nitrate, phenol, chromic acid. Trichloracetic acid is perhaps still of some interest in dentistry as a caustic. Sometimes a small amount placed beneath a gum flap with college tweezers will relieve the discomfort of a mild pericoronitis. It does so by simply destroying sensory nerve endings.

HEPATITIS AND AIDS

It seems appropriate to discuss these two diseases together and within this Chapter on antiseptics because the use of certain antiseptics is recommended in precautionary procedures when treating such patients.

Hepatitis B (serum hepatitis)

The hepatitis B virus (HBV) produces a number of serological markers; for instance the Dane particle is composed of, amongst other things, a surface antigen designated as HBsAG. This is detectable in patients with acute hepatitis and has usually disappeared from the serum in about six weeks from the onset of clinical jaundice. However, in some 4 to 5 per cent of patients, the HBsAG antigen can be detected many months after the onset of the illness, and these patients become chronic carriers. Another antigen from hepatitis B is the e antigen designated as HBeAG, and this is only found in HBsAG-positive serum.

Another group infected with the virus do not develop overt symptoms and the subclinical picture is not associated with jaundice; the majority so infected fall into this group. The carrier state is more likely to develop in those with a subclinical infection rather than in those who have had an acute infection.

Most patients with acute hepatitis B recover within a few weeks without ill consequences, but some may develop cirrhosis of the liver and a small percentage may eventually develop hepatocellular carcinoma.

Certain patients (and staff) are predisposed to become carriers of this disease and form a 'risk' group; these include:

(1) those frequently receiving blood products, e.g. haemophiliacs;

(2) those who, for whatever reason, have a defective immune response, e.g. on immunosuppressive drugs (including transplant patients) or who are immunodeficient;

(3) intravenous drug abusers;

(4) patients or staff in long-stay institutions, especially for the mentally handicapped;

(5) those undergoing haemodialysis;

(6) staff in renal dialysis units;

(7) the sexually promiscuous, particularly male homosexuals;

(8) patients from certain parts of the world where there is a high incidence of the disease, e.g. Asia and Africa;

(9) the tattooed individual.

Serum hepatitis is more likely to occur in those constantly exposed to blood or blood products, a category which must include dental surgeons. The disease is transmitted by blood and saliva. Most carriers of the virus will be unaware that they are carriers. The British Dental Association (BDA) suggests that all dental clinical staff should be immunized against hepatitis B, as an effective vaccine is available, which can be provided by a General Medical Practitioner under the National Health Service.

AIDS (acquired immunodeficiency syndrome)

A great deal of attention has been given to this disease, and to those who are infected with the human immunodeficiency virus (HIV). The public are alarmed about AIDS and, considering the likely mortality produced by the infection, this is understandable. AIDS is the name given to a group of disorders in which there is a serious cell-mediated immunodeficiency. Because of this deficiency, it is not surprising that sufferers tend to acquire various opportunistic infections, such as candidosis(-iasis) and, particularly, the otherwise rare *Pneumocystis carinii* pneumonia.

A characteristic of the disease is the long incubation period, varying from a few months to perhaps years. The full-blown picture of AIDS is often preceded by various syndromes, the most common being a persistent generalized lympha-denopathy accompanied by malaise, low-grade pyrexia, and weight loss. Oral candidosis may be an early feature, and the dental surgeon must recognize that this may be a pointer to the presence of the disease. Once AIDS is fully manifest, then opportunistic infections and/or malignant neoplasms are characteristic. A high percentage of patients have *Pneumocystis* pneumonia and Kaposi's sarcoma, a rare, usually cutaneous, tumour which may also be an early oral manifestation of AIDS, forming a red patch or nodule, often on the hard palate. Herpes simplex infections are often present, and are persistent and severe. The AIDS virus infects the brain and this may well lead to dementia.

The risk groups for AIDS are not dissimilar to those for hepatitis B. Throughout Britain, at the time of writing, the main risk groups are promiscuous homosexual or bisexual men, intravenous drug abusers, and haemophiliacs. The risk of transmitting AIDS appears to be low, the disease being less readily acquired than hepatitis B. Although the virus is present in saliva, transmission of the disease from this source is uncertain. Transmission is essentially through receptive anal intercourse, and by the administration of infected blood or blood products.

For both hepatitus B and AIDS, the practical aim in dentistry is to avoid cross-infection in the surgery, and to provide a safe environment for both patient and dental personnel. 'The Problems of Cross-infection in Dentistry' were considered by a BDA workshop convened on 27 November 1985 to look at the whole problem. The recommendations of the working party were considered under two headings: Appendix 1—Control of Cross Infection in Routine Dental Practice; and Appendix 2—Dental Treatment of Patients Carrying Blood-borne Viruses including Hepatitis B and HTLV III (AIDS). These BDA workshop recommendations are stated below. (Published by kind permission of the Editor of the British Dental Journal).

Control of cross-infection in routine dental practice (Appendix 1)

Every member of the dental team has a duty to ensure that all necessary steps are taken to prevent cross-infection to protect both their patients and themselves.

While special precautions are recommended when treating patients known to be carrying blood-borne diseases such as hepatitis B and HTLV III, many patients will not have been identified and the only safe approach is to assume that any patient may be a carrier. It is necessary to strike a balance between cumbersome 'perfect' procedures and a reasonable approach which is practical while minimizing the hazards to a point where they present a negligible risk.

The following recommendations for procedures in routine dental practice are made in the light of current knowledge and may be subject to alteration and updating as further information becomes available.

1. Medical history

A thorough medical history should be taken for all patients and up-dated at subsequent examinations. The use of medical history sheets and questionnaires is recommended but they must be supported by direct questioning and discussion with the patient.

2. Cleaning of instruments

All instruments should be cleaned thoroughly before sterilization and all visible deposits must be removed. Ultrasonic cleaners are recommended for small instruments.

Gloves of the heavy duty ('kitchen') type should be worn. Great care should be taken when handling sharp instruments.

3. Sterilization of instruments

Sterilization procedures must be effective against all known pathogens. The method of choice for all instruments is an autoclave which reaches a temperature of 134°C for a minimum of 3 min. Hot air ovens may also be used at a temperature of 160°C for a minimum of 60 min. Hot air ovens should be of the type which ensures an uninterrupted timed cycle with an automatic locking device on the door. Boiling water is *not* an effective method for sterilizing instruments in dental practice. Its use should be discontinued.

Cold sterilizing solutions are not suitable for routine use and should only be employed when the instrument cannot be exposed to heat. The instrument must be scrupulously clean and the manufacturer's instructions followed precisely.

All instruments and equipment likely to be contaminated with blood should be sterilized, including aspirator tips and beakers where these are not disposable.

Some dental instruments, including handpieces, have been difficult to sterilize. Handpieces which can be autoclaved are now available and should be used.

4. Disposables

The general use of disposables, including aspirator tips, impression trays and beakers, is recommended whenever possible.

Disposable needles should always be used. They must *never* be re-used for another patient. Similarly, part-used local anaesthetic cartridges may contain blood from the patient and they must *never* be used for a second patient. Towels for hand drying should be disposable or of the roller type which presents a fresh section of towel each time it is used.

5. Surgery surfaces

The bracket table or similar working surface may accumulate infective material. The best solution is to use a system of sterilizable trays or, failing that, a disposable covering. Work surfaces should be cleaned and dried with a solution of 70 per cent isopropyl alcohol. If there is visible blood or pus, the surface should be cleaned with a disposable cloth and disinfected with hypochlorite solution containing 1 per cent available chlorine or, if the surface is metal, with 2 per cent glutaraldehyde. The solution should be left for a minimum of 3 minutes and the surface rinsed and dried. This routine should be followed at the end of each working session even in the absence of a spillage of blood. Equipment should be chosen which is easy to clean.

6. Personal protection

The dental profession has been unique in not taking precautions to prevent contact between patients' blood and unprotected skin. There is much to recommend the routine use of operating gloves for all dentists and close-support dental surgery assistants. They should certainly be worn whenever there is any likelihood of the hands coming into contact with blood. The gloved hands may be washed between patients using a proprietary handwash.

Cuts and abrasions should be kept covered with waterproof dressings at all times even if gloves are worn.

Protective glasses should be worn by operators, close-support dental surgery assistants and patients to protect the eyes against the splatter which may occur during cavity preparation, scaling and the cleaning of instruments.

It is recommended that a well-fitting face mask is worn during high-speed cavity preparation, when using an ultrasonic scaler or undertaking surgical procedures.

Particular care should be taken to avoid needlestick injuries, especially if local anaesthetic needles are resheathed.

Vaccination gives safe and effective protection against hepatitis B and it is recommended for all dental staff.

7. Aspiration and ventilation

The use of efficient high-speed aspirators which exhaust externally will reduce the risk of cross-infection from aerosols. This risk is further reduced by good ventilation. Aspirators should be cleaned regularly in accordance with the manufacturers instructions.

8. Disposal of waste

Sharp items, including needles and scalpels, and local anaesthetic cartridges should be placed in a rigid 'safe' container. Great care should be taken to avoid needlestick injuries. Other items, such as napkins and cotton wool rolls, should be consigned to stout plastic bags which are sealed before disposal.

Heavy duty gloves should be worn.

The collection and incineration of surgical waste should be arranged locally.

Needles, local anaesthetic cartridges and other surgical waste must *never* be dumped on a normal refuse tip.

9. Laboratory items

Impressions and appliances should be rinsed thoroughly before sending to the laboratory. Disposable impression trays are recommended. Technicians should be encouraged to wear gloves when handling impressions and pouring models.

10. Training

All dental staff should be trained thoroughly and should understand the policies adopted in the practice for the prevention of cross-infection. Particular attention should be given to the training of new members of staff. All procedures should be reviewed from time to time to ensure that they are being carried out correctly.

Dental treatment for patients carrying blood-borne viruses including Hepatitis B and HTLV III (Appendix 2)

Patients who are ill with hepatitis B or AIDS should normally receive dental treatment under hospital conditions.

Patients who are known, or may be presumed, to be infectious but are otherwise well may be treated in normal dental practice. The majority of carriers of these and other blood-borne viral diseases are not identified and many receive routine dental treatment each day. The treatment of known carriers would not add materially to the hazards of practice, and they should therefore be treated by general dental practitioners as a matter of course. It should be remembered that the transmissibility of HTLV III is low and there is little risk to health-care workers. It is not necessary to make any special arrangements for waiting rooms or other non-clinical areas.

It is unlikely to be possible for dentists to be informed of the names of all patients who may be carriers, and in some cases the passage of this information is further constrained by the need for confidentiality which is a legal requirement in the case of sexually transmitted diseases. It is therefore essential that a careful history is taken and that the approach to patients enables them to disclose sensitive information. Known carriers are counselled to inform their dentist and the response they receive will determine whether or not they continue to disclose their carrier state. A dentist should regard it as a privilege to be informed and should express gratitude for the information. Any unsympathetic response or a failure to provide treatment is likely to lead to concealment in the future. Confidentiality must be preserved and the information restricted to those members of staff who need to know.

Clinical procedures that minimize exposure to actually or potentially infectious material, including blood, must be employed routinely and all dentists should follow the guidelines in Appendix 1. The following additional precautions are recommended when treating patients known to be carriers of hepatitis B and HTLV III.

1. The appointment should normally be arranged at the end of the day. All the procedures for the control of cross-infection and for personal protection listed in Appendix 1 *must* be used. Protective eyewear, masks and gloves are essential

during treatment and when handling contaminated instruments and materials. Gowns, preferably disposable, should be worn.

2. All instruments, including handpieces, must be sterilizable or disposable. Freshly prepared 2% glutaraldehyde can be used, if necessary, for instruments which cannot be autoclaved. They should be soaked in glutaraldehyde for 1 hour before thorough cleaning and then left in fresh glutaraldehyde for a further period of 3 hours.

3. Aerosols should be minimized by the use of a high-volume aspirator which vents externally. Ultrasonic scalers should be avoided.

High-speed drills should not be used for patients known to be HBeAG positive unless the staff involved in providing treatment have been vaccinated. There is no evidence to suggest an infection risk from the use of high-speed drills when treating carriers of HTLV III.

4. Contaminated working surfaces or blood splashes elsewhere should be physically cleaned and swabbed with hypochlorite solution (1% available chlorine) left in contact for 30 minutes or, if metal, with 2% glutaraldehyde which is left in contact with the surface for 3 hours. The surface should then be rinsed and dried.

5. Aspirators should be flushed with 2% glutaraldehyde and the solution left in the system collector for 3 hours.

6. Impressions should be taken in a silicone-based material. These and any appliances should be placed in 2% glutaraldehyde for 1 hour. They should be rinsed and soaked in fresh solution for at least 3 hours before being sent to the laboratory.

7. Great care must be taken to avoid needlestick injuries. In the event of accidental innoculation or contamination of the eyes or mouth, the affected part should be washed with running water. The accident should be reported immediately and medical advice sought. The District Medical or Dental Officer will be able to provide information on the appropriate local contacts.

8. All disposable materials must be placed in plastic bags (sharp items in rigid 'safe' containers), labelled in accordance with local practice and incinerated.

9. Non-disposable laundry items such as towels may be safely washed in a washing machine with a cycle which holds the temperature at 90°C for a period of 10 minutes.

10. General anaesthetics should be avoided if at all possible. If general anaesthesia is essential, reference should be made to the guidance to anaesthetists provided by the Department of Health.

11. *Further information* The British Dental Journal book *Viral Hepatitis, AIDS and Dental Treatment* by R. C. W. Dinsdale is recommended as a source of more detailed information and advice. It contains many references to other published reports on the subject and may be obtained from Professional and Scientific Publications at BMA House, Tavistock Square, London WC1H 9JR, price £2.50.

Further advice is contained in:

1. Report of the Expert Group on Hepatitis in Dentistry London, HMSO, 1979.

2. Acquired Immune Deficiency Syndrome. London: DHSS

  (i) General Information for Doctors, 1985;

  (ii) Information for Doctors concerning the Introduction of the HTLV III Antibody Test, 1985;

  (iii) Guidance for Surgeons, Anaesthetists and Dentists, 1986.

The real point at issue is that many patients who are carriers of the blood-borne infections discussed above will not be identified as carriers. The recommendations of the working party as contained under Appendix 1 are aimed at making routine treatments in dental practice as safe as possible, without creating too burdensome surgery procedures.

FURTHER READING

Babajews, A., Poswillo, D. E., and Griffin, G. E. (1985). Acquired immune deficiency syndrome presenting as recalcitrant Candida. *British Dental Journal,* **159,** 106–8.

BDA Dental Health and Science Committee Workshop (1986). The problems of cross-infection in dentistry. *British Dental Journal,* **160,** 131–4.

Bystrom, A. and Sundqvist, G. (1985). The antibacterial action of sodium hypochlorite and EDTA in 60 cases of endodontic therapy. *International Endodontic Journal,* **18,** 35–40.

Field, A. E. and Martin, M. V. (1986). Handwashing: soap or disinfectant. *British Dental Journal,* **160,** 278–80.

Greenspan, D., Greenspan, J. S., Pindborg, J. J., and Schiodt, M. (1986). *AIDS and the Dental Team,* (1st edn). Munksgaard, Copenhagen.

Howell, R. A. (1980). Bleaching discoloured root-filled teeth. *British Dental Journal,* **148,** 159–62.

Leading article (1985). AIDS: safeguards, not Panic. *British Dental Journal,* **158,** 195.

Leading article (1986). Infection Control—changes Needed. *British Dental Journal,* **160,** 109.

MacFarlane, T. W. and Follett, E. A. C. (1986). Serum hepatitis: a significant risk in the dental care of the mentally handicapped. *British Dental Journal,* **160,** 386–8.

Matthews, R. (1987). Cross-infection—the phoney war? *Dental Practice,* **25,** 1–3.

Matthews, R. W., Hislop, W. S., and Scully, C. (1986). The prevalence of hepatitis B markers in high-risk dental out-patients. *British Dental Journal,* **161,** 294–6.

Matthews, R. W., Scully, C., and Dowell, T. B. (1986). Acceptance of hepatitis B vaccine by dental practitioners in the United Kingdom. *British Dental Journal,* **161,** 371–3.

Mentz, T. C. F. (1982). The use of sodium hypochlorite as a general endodontic medicament. *International Endodontic Journal,* **15,** 132–6.

Richards, J. M. (1985). Notes on AIDS. *British Dental Journal,* **158,** 199–201.

Samaranayake, L. P. and Lewis, M. A. O. (1985). AIDS and the dental practitioner. *Dental Update,* **12,** 551–62.

Scully, C. (1985). Hepatitis B: an update in relation to dentistry. *British Dental Journal,* **159,** 321–8.

Scully, C., Cawson, R. A., and Porter, S. R. (1986). Acquired immune deficiency syndrome: a review. *British Dental Journal*, **161**, 53–60.

Wray, D., Moody, G. H., and McMillan, A. (1986). Oral 'Hairy' Leukoplakia in a male homosexual with persistent lymphadenopathy syndrome: report of two cases. *British Dental Journal*, **161**, 338–9.

10

Antimicrobials

INTRODUCTION

CHEMOTHERAPEUTIC agents are substances that are used to kill micro-organisms or neoplastic cells. This chapter will be concerned with antimicrobial drugs, which are agents used against micro-organisms, and with the principles underlying their use. The term antibiotic refers to substances produced by micro-organisms that, in high dilution, will prevent the growth of, or kill, other micro-organisms. As many antibiotics are now synthesized, this restricted meaning may be somewhat academic.

Until the advent of the sulphonamides in 1935, the search for systemic chemotherapeutic agents to treat infection had met with little success. The sulphonamides heralded an era that has been prolific in the discovery of new substances capable of acting against infective organisms. Great successes can be claimed for the use of penicillin in the treatment of infections with haemolytic streptococci. On the other hand, the number of substances available for use against viral agents is somewhat limited.

The object of chemotherapy is to kill or to prevent the multiplication of invading organisms, with minimal damage to the host. Valuable though powerful chemotherapeutic agents are, they can also produce unwanted effects in the individual and the community. It is clearly important that they be used with discrimination. Although it is impossible to make definitive rules for the prescribing of chemotherapeutic agents, there are certain guiding principles.

GENERAL PRINCIPLES OF TREATMENT

Diagnosis

There must be some clear indication that chemotherapy is necessary. It is indefensible to prescribe antimicrobials for conditions not due to infection; nor indeed should trivial and self-limiting infections be treated with antimicrobial drugs.

Choice of drug

Ideally this should depend on bacteriological identification of the causative organisms, and sensitivity tests to establish the susceptibility of the particular organism to the antimicrobial of obvious choice. In dental practice, such specialist services are not usually available and are mostly unnecessary. Clinical experience has shown that most acute infections in dentistry respond to a limited range of antimicrobial agents, e.g. penicillin, and so the choice is dictated through clinical experience. Exceptions to this general statement will be discussed later. It should be kept in mind that severe infections should not be treated without bacteriological assistance, a position that has been well summed up by O'Grady (1973) in the following words:

Blind treatment of severe infections without bacteriological assistance, and delay of treatment while the wheels of the bacteriological machine slowly turn, are both wrong. Adequate specimens should always be obtained before therapy of dangerous infections begins. However, treatment should then be instituted with what appears to be the most appropriate agent.

Dosage and route of administration

The object of treatment is to maintain a sufficiently high concentration of the drug in the infected tissues for as long as is required to overcome the infection. The actual concentration in the blood may not be so directly important except in the case of septicaemia, endocarditis, or osteomyelitis, when blood levels need to be high. In order to achieve effective tissue levels it may be necessary, when a drug is excreted rapidly, to administer it frequently so that tissue levels can equilibrate with blood levels. A good example of this is the use of benzylpenicillin, which has a half-life of less than one hour. On the other hand, some antimicrobials, e.g. gentamicin, may accumulate and dose intervals should be altered appropriately.

The duration of therapy depends on several factors, not least being the precise nature of the infection and the response to treatment. Patients should be impressed with the importance of adhering to the therapeutic regime advocated and of not discontinuing treatment at their own discretion. Treatment should be continued until the infection is overcome, and the early response should be monitored. In general terms, in dentistry, if there is no response to treatment within 48 to 72 hours, the antibacterial substance is unlikely to prove effective. This would suggest wrong diagnosis or the choice of the wrong antimicrobial.

In dentistry, systemic antimicrobials are usually given orally or by intramuscular injection. In hospitals, antimicrobials are often administered by the intravenous route, either by slow injection or infusion. Where there is a choice, administration by injection is to be preferred in severe infections as absorption is likely to be more certain and it produces a more immediate effect. Sometimes treatment, or prophylaxis, is started by injection and followed up by oral administration.

Use of antimicrobial agents in renal failure

When it is essential to prescribe an antimicrobial agent in the presence of renal disease, it is mandatory to consider what effect any impairment of renal function may have on the dose regime to be employed. For those drugs that are excreted predominantly by the kidney it may be necessary to modify therapy under these circumstances. If such a problem is encountered by the dental surgeon the matter should be discussed with the medical practitioner. Some antimicrobials should be avoided altogether in the presence of renal impairment.

Antimicrobials to be avoided wherever possible, or where their dosage should be monitored carefully, include cephaloridine, chloramphenicol, neomycin, nalidixic acid, nitrofurantoin, sulphadiazine, tetracyclines (except doxycycline and minocycline), and parenterally administered vancomycin.

Antimicrobials (detailed later) where dosage should be reduced include cephalosporins, cotrimoxazole, amoxycillin, ampicillin, trimethoprim, and others. Examples where a major dosage adjustment (reduction) will be required, and where serum concentrations need to be monitored, include gentamicin, kanamycin, streptomycin, and amphotericin B (if used systemically).

Antimicrobials (detailed below) listed in the *Dental Practitioners' Formulary 1986–88* should be modified as follows:

Acyclovir	—reduce dosage
Amoxycillin	—reduce dosage
Ampicillin	—reduce dosage
Benzylpenicillin	—max. 6 g daily when GFR < 10
Cephalexin	—max. 500 mg daily when GFR < 10
Cephadrine	—reduce dosage
Co-trimoxazole	—max. 960 mg daily when GFR < 10
Lincomycin	—use clindamycin instead
Tetracyclines (except doxycycline and minocycline)	—avoid

GFR = Glomerular filtration rate; this indicates the degree of renal impairment.

Published by kind permission of The Pharmaceutical Society of Great Britain.

The reason why the plasma levels of some drugs should be monitored is simply to keep them within safe limits, especially when there is a very serious risk of ototoxicity, as may occur with streptomycin, for example.

Use of antimicrobial agents in liver disease

As many drugs are metabolized in the liver, prescribing of drugs in general should be kept to a minimum in the presence of liver disease. Clindamycin is the only antimicrobial listed in the *Dental Practitioners' Formulary* where the dose should be reduced. This is not to imply that other antimicrobials outside of that Formulary would not similarly require modification. For instance, the use of a particular preparation of erythromycin (see below), namely the estolate, is liable to cause idiosyncratic hepatotoxicity, and may cause jaundice in the absence of liver disease when used for a long period.

Accompanying treatment

Antimicrobials are not a substitute for necessary surgery; where pus is present, drainage should be established. It is unjustifiable to rely on antibiotics alone when drainage is obviously required; to do so may cause the formation of a tumour-like cold abscess surrounded by fibrous tissue. In many instances, drainage of an infected area will suffice in itself without recourse to antimicrobials.

Combination of drugs

Antimicrobial drugs are basically classified as bacteriostatic or bactericidal: bacteriostatic drugs inhibit the multiplication of organisms, and bactericidal drugs kill them. Some bacteriostatic drugs exhibit bactericidal activity when used in high concentrations, e.g. erythromycin. Drug combinations can sometimes reduce the development of resistant strains of organisms, a well-known example being the use of streptomycin and isoniazid together in the treatment of tuberculosis. Used alone, resistance quickly develops to either of these drugs, but is much reduced when they are combined. However, combined drug therapy is not always beneficial, and may indeed be harmful. For example, many bactericidal drugs only kill rapidly multiplying cells and, in the presence of a bacteriostatic agent, their killing effect is antagonized (e.g. penicillin in the presence of tetracyclines). Such combinations should be avoided.

Topical administration

The principal arguments against the topical use of antibiotics are:

(1) the risk of sensitizing the patient;
(2) the risk of development of resistant strains.

It is generally agreed that antimicrobials for topical use should be selected from those that are unlikely to be used systemically, possibly because they are not absorbed or because they are liable to produce unwanted effects. Common examples are neomycin and polymyxin B. Nevertheless, the topical use of antifungal agents (e.g. nystatin) has proved most valuable in dentistry; their usage will be considered later.

Previous hypersensitivity

If a patient gives a history of hypersensitivity to any particular antimicrobial agent, then drugs of similar structure should not be administered because of the likelihood of cross-allergenicity. Some patients provide doubtful evidence of previous reactions, but it would be unwise to ignore the history however seemingly improbable. Drug hypersensitivity reactions are more likely to occur in patients with an allergic diathesis.

INDICATIONS FOR THE USE OF SYSTEMIC CHEMOTHERAPEUTIC AGENTS IN DENTISTRY

Treatment of infections

Chemotherapeutic agents should not be used in the normally healthy patient for minor infections that are likely to respond to treatment by other means, or are self-limiting. Needless to say, if local measures appear to be inadequate, or in the presence of severe infection, antimicrobial therapy should be instituted. A number of indications for the use of antimicrobials in dental practice are indicated below:

(1) In severe acute ulcerative gingivitis, especially if there are signs of systemic involvement (e.g. pyrexia and lymphadenopathy). In less severe cases, but where systemic chemotherapy is deemed necessary, metronidazole is the drug of choice.

(2) In severe infections of dental origin, e.g. cellulitis, acute osteomyelitis, severe pericoronitis, and deep infections implanted by local anaesthesia.

(3) In sinus infection complicating oro-antral fistula.

General prophylaxis

Antimicrobials may be used prophylactically in an attempt to prevent infection following surgery. There is no overwhelming evidence to suggest that such prophylaxis will prevent postoperative infection, although there are circumstances where it is generally agreed that such chemoprophylaxis should be provided. Of course, the situation is different when the patient has some underlying medical condition, but even then the exact position of chemoprophylaxis is uncertain. However, prophylactic antimicrobials may be considered for:

(1) Debilitated patients who are to have surgery, e.g. those with severe anaemia, blood dyscrasias, or diabetes—some diabetic patients show a lessened resistance to infection, and this is especially true of uncontrolled diabetes mellitus;

(2) Patients who have had radiation to the jaws and for whom, unfortunately, oral surgical procedures are required—any irradiated area must be considered as having lowered vitality and poor resistance to infection;

(3) Patients on prolonged steroid therapy for whom surgery is to be undertaken—prolonged steroid therapy weakens natural defence mechanisms against infection (see Chapter 18) but antimicrobial cover is certainly not

required for all such patients, and much will depend on circumstances at the time (e.g. the extent of the operation);

(4) transplant patients who require oral surgical procedures, as they will be receiving an immunosuppressant drug, e.g. cyclosporin, steroids, or azathioprine, and could therefore be liable to infection.

It must be emphasized that the prophylactic use of antimicrobials to prevent postoperative infection is an uncertain measure, even in the conditions listed above. If used, the agent of choice should be given just prior to surgery in order to allow peak plasma concentrations to be reached at the time of operation. The cover should be continued for three to seven days; exactly how long must depend on the clinical judgement of the operator.

DRUG RESISTANCE

Antimicrobial drugs are not active against all micro-organisms; each has its own spectrum of activity that depends to a large degree on its mechanism of action. The phenomenon whereby certain micro-organisms are resistant to a particular antimicrobial agent, referred to as drug resistance, is an important and complex one. Various mechanisms may be concerned with the development of drug resistance in the therapeutic use of antimicrobial agents. These will be considered under three main headings—selection, mutation, and transmission.

Therapeutic selection

In certain instances a bacterial population will consist of some strains that are naturally resistant to a particular drug and others that are sensitive. In the course of therapy the sensitive strains are eliminated leaving the resistant strains to flourish. The strains may be resistant because they are drug-tolerant or drug-destroying. Drug-tolerant bacteria are able to grow in the presence of an antibiotic; sometimes these may actually become physically dependent upon the antimicrobial. Drug-destroying bacteria are able to grow in the presence of the drug because they possess mechanisms that inactivate it. The main example of this type is the penicillinase-producing staphylococcus.

Mutation

It seems beyond dispute that the exposure of certain organisms to certain antimicrobials leads to a degree of drug resistance. In the early days of antimicrobial therapy it was generally believed that the development of drug resistance was due to mutation, and the best-known evidence to support this notion comes from the method of replica plating. This method involves successive plating of a particular culture, followed by sensitivity testing, and it shows that organisms never before exposed to a particular antibiotic nevertheless contained some insensitive cells. Other evidence indicates that drug-resistant bacteria can arise by adaptive mechanisms. Whatever the final mechanism, one fact seems clear, namely, that with some antibiotics, for example polymyxin, drug resistance does not seem to develop. On the other hand, when it is liable to occur, for example with streptomycin, then special steps must be taken to reduce the risk to a minimum, e.g. (see above) by combination therapy. Some organisms may develop drug resistance within a matter of hours (to streptomycin) or days (to erythromycin) but fortunately, in the majority of organisms, resistance develops more slowly.

Transmission of genetic material from one organism to another

The genetic control of cell activity may be altered if the genetic composition of a bacterial cell is changed. This composition may be modified by the arrival of genetic material from external sources, mainly in one of two ways—transduction or conjugation.

Transduction

In transduction, plasmids, which are extra-chromosomal particles of genetic material, are transferred to the micro-organism by means of bacteriophage (a virus that infects bacteria). If the material so transferred contains a gene for drug resistance, the bacterial cell newly infected by the virus may become resistant to the antimicrobial agent. This mechanism was first demonstrated in a staphylococcus that originally had been sensitive to penicillin and was transduced to produce penicillinase and thereby became resistant. It has since been shown that simultaneous transduction of resistance to more than one chemotherapeutic agent may occur. However, the mechanism depends on the existence of a suitable host for the bacteriophage, which, because of its fastidiousness, in general confines the transduction to organisms of the same species.

Conjugation

In episomal transference by conjugation (infectious resistance) it has been found that transfer of drug resistance can occur between organisms of all genera of the Enterobacteriaceae. What conjugation really consists of is the passage of genes from cell to cell by direct contact. As with transduction, the genetic material so transferred consists of plasmids or episomes, which themselves comprise extra-chromosomal genetic particles. In contrast to the more selective transfer of drug resistance, such particles can be passed from one species to another. However, it appears that this type of transference is mainly confined to Gram-negative species. Bacteria capable of transmitting drug resistance by this mechanism can only do so when a second factor is present, known as the 'resistance transfer factor'.

The mechanism whereby an organism, previously drug-sensitive, becomes drug-resistant as a result of episomal transference by conjugation is the formation of an enzyme that inactivates the drug (antibiotic).

It is, of course, of fundamental importance to know whether infectious drug resistance is a permanent feature or whether it is reversible. Fortunately, it appears that provided the affected organism is removed from further exposure to the antimicrobial agent, infectious resistance disappears within a matter of weeks or months. Indeed, if this were not so it would be difficult to understand how the organisms concerned could have retained any sensitivity to the drugs commonly used to treat the infections they cause. It is alarming to find that a high percentage of cultures tested have been shown to exhibit resistance. This finding obviously demands that the greatest care be taken in deciding to use any antimcrobial drug, and also in the prevention of cross-infection between patients.

PENICILLINS

Many types of penicillins are now available. Of those originally isolated, benzylpenicillin was found to be the most suitable for use and its basic properties will now be described, together with the general pharmacodynamics of the group.

Benzylpenicillin

This has a relatively narrow spectrum of antibacterial activity. It is effective against many species of Gram-negative cocci, and also against *Treponema pallidum* and other treponemata. Most Gram-negative bacilli are resistant (e.g. *Escherichia coli; Salmonella typhi; Bacteroides fragilis*); *Bacteroides melaninogenicus* is sensitive.

Amongst susceptible organisms, naturally occurring resistant strains are found. Such strains of viridans streptococci may occur in the mouth together with a majority of sensitive strains, and this poses a hazard for patients with valvular defects of the heart (see p. 213).

There are resistant strains of *Staphylococcus aureus*, resistance being due to their action in forming beta-lactamase (penicillinase), which destroys penicillin. These strains existed before the era of antimicrobials but, in the early days of penicillin, were probably few compared to those staphylococci sensitive to the antibiotic. Today the position is different: the sensitivity of *Staph. aureus* to benzylpenicillin is very variable, with most strains being resistant. In some hospitals there is a high proportion of mutliple resistant *Staph. aureus* strains (MRSA), and this has caused a serious problem.

Pharmacodynamics

Penicillins are bactericidal and interfere with biosynthesis of the bacterial cell wall in susceptible organisms. It is important to realize that there is a striking difference between the cell walls of bacteria and those of mammalian cells. Unlike the mammalian cell wall, the bacterial cell wall is a tough, thick structure, situated external to the cytoplasmic membrane and so acting as a rigid external casing to the organism; this accounts for its remarkable resistance to osmotic damage. If there existed an antimicrobial agent that acted exclusively on the bacterial cell wall, it would have no effect on the mammalian host since there is no counterpart to the bacterial cell wall in the mammal; the nearest to this ideal is penicillin.

A further important factor is the difference between the composition of the cell wall of Gram-positive and Gram-negative organisms, a fact that accounts, in some instances, for the different sensitivities of these main groups of organisms to particular antibiotics. Gram-positive organisms have a thick cell wall that contains a rigid envelope of peptidoglycan, which represents at least 60 per cent of the structure. The cell wall may also contain teichoic and teichuronic acids. Gram-negative organisms have a thin layer of peptidoglycan, which represents not more than 10 per cent of the cell wall, the main components of the wall being lipopolysaccharides and lipoproteins.

Peptidoglycan is synthesized in stages that involve amino acids and the sugar, acetylmuramic acid, which is characteristically found in the bacterial cell wall. The complex is coupled to a molecule of acetylglucosamine and together these form a glycan unit, which is the building brick of the wall. The glycan units are then carried across the cytoplasmic membrane of the bacterial cell by means of a lipid carrier and then incorporated into the cell wall.

The final stage involves the joining of peptides of one layer to the peptides of the next via a peptide link. Penicillins and also cephalosporins prevent the cross-linking of peptide strands, which is the last and vital step in the story of the cell wall. This was once thought to be achieved by blocking the transpeptidase enzyme responsible for this final stage. However, the actual mechanism of penicillin activity is more complex. It is now recognized that there are several penicillin-binding proteins associated with the bacterial cell membrane, which serve different functions, including the final cell wall cross-linking reactions. Each of these penicillin-binding proteins may be involved in the mode of action of this antimicrobial.

Pharmacokinetics

Benzylpenicillin is unstable in acidic conditions, and therefore cannot be relied upon to produce satisfactory clinical results if given by mouth because a high proportion of the original drug is rendered inactive by the acid contents of the stomach. When given by intramuscular injection it is quickly absorbed, the maximum concentration being reached within half an hour and then rapidly falls. In order to maintain a satisfactory plasma concentration, at least 300 mg of benzylpenicillin should be administered intramuscularly every four to six hours. It should also be remembered that tissue concentrations take time to equilibrate with those of plasma.

It is partially bound to plasma protein (46 to 58 per cent) and, although it passes into serous cavities, the concentration is low, especially in the cerebrospinal fluid and joint cavities. When the meninges are inflamed there is increased penetration of the penicillin into the cerebrospinal fluid providing adequate concentrations. The half-life of benzylpenicillin is less than an hour.

The major part (80 per cent) of any dose is excreted rapidly by the kidney due to extensive tubular secretion, and the remaining 20 per cent being via glomerular filtration. This excretion can be delayed by the administration of substances that compete with penicillin for active tubular secretion. Such a drug is probenecid and, by delaying excretion, it prolongs therapeutic plasma concentrations. Benzylpenicillin readily diffuses from the maternal to the fetal circulation.

Less soluble compounds of penicillin delay absorption from the site of injection; an example is procaine penicillin, prepared by the interaction of procaine hydrochloride and benzylpenicillin. The peak concentration of procaine penicillin is reached in 4 hours and thereafter falls over the next 24 hours. Even less soluble compounds are available, such as benethamine penicillin and benzathine penicillin, the effects of which are prolonged up to days or weeks. Unfortunately, the less soluble compounds produce lower plasma concentrations than benzylpenicillin.

Phenoxymethylpenicillin (penicillin V)

This is an oral penicillin that resists destruction in gastric juice and is absorbed from the upper part of the small intestine, although incompletely. Maximum blood concentration is reached in one hour and excretion is as rapid as benzylpenicillin. Administration every four to six hours is necessary to maintain therapeutic concentrations. The range of antibacterial activity is similar to that of benzylpenicillin, but it is somewhat less active against streptococci.

Other acid-resistant penicillins have been introduced, such as phenethicillin. Although more completely absorbed than phenoxymethylpenicillin, they do not seem to offer any real advantages. Phenoxymethylpenicillin is less protein-bound than these later penicillins and consequently there is more antibiotic freely available to diffuse to the site of infection. Phenoxymethylpenicillin remains the acid-resistant penicillin of choice.

Unwanted effects of the penicillins

Penicillin therapy is remarkably free from unwanted effects except for the production of hypersensitivity reactions. Sensitization is often produced by previous treatment but sometimes a history of such contact cannot be established. However, previous exposure to penicillin may not be obvious; an example of occult exposure is the drinking of milk from cows treated with the drug. Penicillin is though to be the most common cause of drug allergy, but this must be considered against the background of its extensive usage. The allergic reactions range from a mild urticaria to a serious anaphylactic shock, which, although rare, may be fatal. The estimated incidence of allergic reactions to penicillin in various areas of the world ranges from 0.7 to 10 per cent.

All preparations of penicillin can bring about hypersensitivity reactions. Although oral preparations are thought to produce reactions much less frequently than parenterally administered penicillin, it must be emphasized that serious reactions have occurred following oral administration. Procaine penicillin is probably the most common offender. All patients who are to receive penicillin, by whatever route, should be questioned as to any previous untoward experience with this drug and offered an alternative antibiotic when necessary.

The penicillins have minimal toxicity. However, intrathecal injection of penicillin G may produce a severe encephalopathy.

Uses

Extremely serious infections of dental origin should be treated by means of benzylpenicillin intramuscularly, 300 to 600 mg every four to six hours, and continued until the infection is overcome. Such a regime would require in-patient care, and usually a dose of 300 mg six-hourly will be found to be adequate.

Most susceptible infections of dental origin can be controlled by the intramuscular injection of 1 ml of fortified procaine penicillin, once or twice daily, followed by the daily injection of a similar amount for four to five days. (Fortified procaine penicillin injection contains both procaine penicillin and benzylpenicillin.) Benzylpenicillin provides a maximal concentration of the antibiotic in the blood within 30 minutes, and the procaine penicillin sustains a therapeutic level over a period of 12 to 24 hours.

For the less severe infections, an oral penicillin, i.e. phenoxymethylpenicillin, 250 mg, four to six-hourly will often suffice. It has been suggested that absorption after a meal is better. Because of the incomplete absorption of the oral penicillins, parenterally administered penicillin is more certain in its effects and should be used for severe infections. As a rule, if the patient treated with penicillin is showing no response within 48 to 72 hours, continued use of the drug is unlikely to be effective in most dental infections.

Penicillinase-resistant penicillins
(e.g. methicillin, cloxacillin, and flucloxacillin)

These are reserved for the treatment of staphylococcal infections, and treatment of such infections should be started with one of these drugs unless the antibiotic sensitivity of the strain is known. However, a staphylococcal infection in dental practice is likely to be rare but serious, calling for supervision in a hospital environment. Methicillin was the first of the penicillinase-resistant penicillins, and it must be administered by injection as it is not acid-resistant. It is probably less active against staphylococci than are cloxacillin or flucloxicillin, and has been implicated in a number of unwanted effects, e.g. granulocytopenia. It finds little use in clinical practice today, having been superseded by the other penicillinase-resistant penicillins. Flucloxacillin is better absorbed from the gut and is to be preferred to cloxacillin for oral therapy.

Broad-spectrum penicillins
(e.g. ampicillin, amoxycillin, becampicillin, ciclacillin, mezlocillin, piperacillin, pivam-picillin, talampicillin)

Ampicillin is effective against Gram-positive organisms, although slightly less so than benzylpenicillin. However, it has much greater activity against Gram-negative bacteria. It is destroyed by penicillinases and should not, therefore, be used to treat resistant staphylococcal infections. Ampicillin is acid-resistant and can be administered orally, but for maximal effect it should be given parenterally. Its main use seems to be in the treatment of bronchitis and urinary infections, although many urinary isolates, e.g. *E. coli,* are now resistant to ampicillin.

Skin rashes appear to be more common with ampicillin than with other penicillins, with an incidence of about seven per cent. Most of these rashes are of the maculopapular type and seem unrelated to those of true penicillin allergy. The rashes may develop during the course of treatment or sometimes days after treatment has stopped. Ampicillin rashes tend to occur more frequently in patients suffering from infectious mononucleosis, and the drug should not be administered to such patients. Cross-hypersensitivity probably exists between all penicillins in the susceptible patient. However, the maculopapular rash of ampicillin does not necessarily contra-indicate later treatment with other penicillins.

Amoxycillin has the same spectrum of antibacterial activity as ampicillin. It is related to ampicillin but is more rapidly and completely absorbed from the gastro-intestinal tract. Peak concentrations in plasma are about twice as high as attained by ampicillin after oral administration of the same dose. Another advantage is that absorption does not appear to be affected by food. The half-life of the drug is in the region of six hours. In dentistry, it finds particular use as a prophylactic agent in the prevention of infective endocarditis (see later). Its unwanted effects are similar to those of ampicillin.

Clavulanate

Clavulanate is a beta-lactamase inhibitor, and is combined with amoxycillin in the preparation Augmentin. Clavulanate is not, in itself, antimicrobial but, by preventing the destructiveness of penicillinases, allows amoxycillin to act against resistant staphylococci, which it would otherwise not do.

Other penicillins

Ticarcillin, carbenicillin, azlocillin, and carfecillin are used in infections due to *Pseudomonas aeruginosa*. Others, such as mecillinam and pivmecillinam, are broad-spectrum penicillins, active against a wide variety of Gram-negative bacilli, such as *E. coli, Proteus mirabilis*, and salmonellae. These have no activity against *P. aeruginosa*, penicillinase-producing staphylococci, or enterococci and much less activity against Gram-positive organisms. Mecillinam must be given by injection. Pivmecillinam is an ester of mecillinam and is well-absorbed when given orally. After absorption it is hydrolysed to the active agent, mecillinam. Pivmecillinam has a local irritant effect on the oesophageal mucosa and occasionally causes oesophagitis. These drugs may be indicated in severe infections due to enterobacteria, e.g. *E. coli*, which account for a high proportion of urinary tract infections.

None of these drugs has a place in dentistry.

Cephalosporins

These are closely related chemically to penicillin. They are broad-spectrum antimicrobials with activity against a wide range of Gram-positive and Gram-negative bacteria. The first of the series to be used in Britain was cephaloridine, and it was thought to be resistant to beta-lactamase producing staphylococci, but this is now known not to be the case. It was also nephrotoxic.

The cephalosporins have been divided into three generations, as follows:

(1) first generation—cephalothin, cephalexin, cephazolin, cephradine;

(2) second generation—cefuroxime, cephamandole, cefoxitin, cefaclor;

(2) third generation—cefotaxime, ceftazidine, ceftizomine, and latamoxef.

The first generation has good activity against Gram-positive and Gram-negative bacteria including streptococci, *Neisseria gonorrhoea, Strep. pneumoniae*, and *Corynebacterium diphtheriae*. Their activity against some Gram-negative organisms is variable. They have no activity against *Ps. aeruginosa, Strep. faecalis, Bact. fragilis*, and most of the Enterobacteria.

The second generation of cephalosporins is largely resistant to beta-lactames, and they are much more active against almost all Gram-negative bacilli. Cephamandole is very active against the Enterobacteria and staphylococci.

The third generation of cephalosporins is more active than either of the other two generations against certain Gram-negative bacteria.

Pharmacodynamics

The cephalosporins act in the same way as the penicillins by interfering with the biosynthesis of the bacterial cell wall in susceptible organisms, thereby exerting a bactericidal effect.

Pharmacokinetics

The first cephalosporins, cephaloridine and cephalothin, both had to be administered parenterally. Newer preparations include cephradine (oral and parenteral administration); cephazolin (parenteral); cefuroxime (parenteral); cephamandole (parenteral). Cefadroxil is a new oral cephalosporin. Once absorbed into the circulation the cephalosporins exhibit variable binding to plasma proteins from 20 to 90 per cent (e.g. cephaloridine, 20 per cent; cephalothin, 70 per cent). The cephalosporins are mainly excreted by the kidney, some unchanged and others as metabolites.

Unwanted effects

It seems that the incidence of allergic reactions to cephalosporins is lower than that of the penicillins, the reactions which occur being similar to those caused by the penicillins.

In penicillin-sensitive subjects the use of cephalosporins should be viewed with caution as there is clinical evidence of partial cross-allergenicity between the penicillins and the cephalosporins. It seems that patients with a history of penicillin allergy are predisposed to accelerated reactions to cephalosporins; such reactions suggest that the underlying mechanism is likely to be due to cross-allergenicity, rather than to a generalized and unspecific tendency to drug hypersensitivity. Patients with a history of mild urticaria to penicillins do not seem to be at a great risk of an allergic reaction when given cephalosporins, but a patient with a severe, immediate reaction to penicillin should not be given a cephalosporin. About 10 per cent of patients who are allergic to penicillins react in some way to the cephalosporins.

Cephalosporins have been implicated in renal damage, but this was most commonly due to the original cephaloridine.

Uses

In general terms there appear to be few absolute indications for the use of the cephalosporins, especially in dentistry. Perhaps they can be regarded as 'second line of defence' antimicrobials.

TETRACYCLINES

(e.g. tetracycline, chlortetracycline, clomocycline, demeclocycline, doxycycline, lyme-cycline, methacycline, minocycline, and oxytetracycline)

The tetracyclines comprise a group of closely related, bacteriostatic antimicro-bials that provide a 'broad spectrum' of activity against organisms. Susceptible species include Gram-positive organisms, which are also sensitive to penicillin, and many Gram-negative organisms insensitive to penicillin. Tetracyclines are also active against rickettsia (e.g. typhus), brucella, and diseases due to *Chlamydia trachomatis*, causing lymphogranuloma venereum. They are also effective against treponemata and *H. influenzae*. Initially the tetracyclines were effective against aerobic Gram-negative bacilli, but now many species are resistant.

Pharmacodynamics

The majority of the broad-spectrum antimicrobials act by interfering with the synthesis of protein by bacteria. They achieve this by interrupting one or more of the critical synthetic steps in a process which depends upon the sequential coupling of amino acids, brought about through the beautifully co-ordinated activities of messenger RNA (mRNA), ribosomal RNA (rRNA), and transfer RNA (tRNA). In order to describe the various ways in which different antimicrobials interfere with protein synthesis, it is necessary to review briefly the normal mechanisms of bacterial protein synthesis.

The primary information for protein synthesis is stored by DNA, and is transmitted to mRNA during transcription. The actual process of protein synthesis takes place on ribosomes, which consist of rRNA and protein, and which either lie free in the cytoplasm or attached to the cytoplasmic membrane. The cytoplasmic membrane of bacteria corresponds to the membrane of mammalian cells. Each bacterial ribosome, which consists of a 30 S and a 50 S component (the 'S' refers to Svedberg unit, a measure of the relative density as determined by speed of centrifugation), threads itself on to the end of a strand of mRNA where it contains two attachment sites for amino acids. At the same time, the available amino acids become temporarily attached to tRNA, each amino acid having its own specific tRNA, thus ensuring the correct assembling of the amino acids to form the peptide chain. Thus mRNA consists of a long chain of four nucleotides joined in such a way as to provide a codon triplet, each one of which represents a code for a specific amino acid. Similarly, each amino acid is 'recognized' by its specific anticodon triplet, which couples to it and transports it to the appropriate codon triplet site on mRNA when the appropriate acceptor site becomes available. Transpeptidation then takes place, whereby the peptide chain already attached (by means of tRNA) is transferred to the next amino acid thus freeing the carrier tRNA. Translocation of the ribosome now takes place and it moves along mRNA and opens up a new acceptor site, which contains another codon for the next amino acid in the chain. The whole process is then repeated.

The tetracyclines interfere with the transfer of amino acids because they bind to the 30 S component of the ribosome and thus prevent polypeptide synthesis.

Pharmacokinetics

The tetracyclines are generally administered orally, but occasionally by intravenous or intramuscular injection.

Absorption from the gastro-intestinal tract is fairly rapid, but significant amounts are retained in the bowel. Absorption is reduced if the drug is taken with milk or with substances containing calcium, magnesium, iron, or aluminium, all of which chelate with tetracyclines.

The original tetracyclines, i.e. tetracycline, chlortetracycline, and oxytetra-cycline, produce adequate and maintained plasma concentrations by the administration of 250 mg at six-hourly intervals. They have a half-life of about 6 to 10 hours; the maximal concentration in the plasma is reached in 2 to 4 hours after oral administration, and gradually falls to about half this amount in 9 to 12 hours, and to a very low concentration at 24 hours.

Demeclocycline and methacycline, on the other hand, have half-lives of about 16 hours, and satisfactory plasma concentrations may persist for 24 hours or more.

Doxycycline and minocycline have longer half-lives, being in the region of 16 to 18 hours. Doxycycline, for instance, is given in an initial dose of 200 mg— maximum plasma concentration being reached in two hours—and this is followed by a daily dose of 100 mg.

Tetracyclines are widely distributed in the tissues and they also enter the cerebrospinal fluid. As they chelate with calcium ions, they are localized in bone and teeth. Excretion of the tetracyclines is in the urine and the faeces, but mainly via the kidneys. Clearly, in general terms, the exceretion of these drugs will be affected by the state of renal function. The exceptions are doxycycline and minocycline, where excretion is in the faeces.

Unwanted effects

Hypersensitivity reactions are rarely encountered with the tetracyclines but, where they are, cross-hypersensitivity between the various members of the group will be present. Large doses of tetracyclines given parenterally can damage the liver; pregnant women appear to be particularly susceptible.

Immediately after absorption tetracyclines are built into calcifying tissues and this becomes a permanent, discolouring feature in the teeth. The use of tetracyclines should be avoided during the formative period of the crowns of the teeth. There is a clear linear relationship between the number of courses of treatment with tetracyclines and the discolouration of developing teeth (0 to 12 years). Of the original tetracyclines it appeared that chlortetracycline produced a grey-brown discolouration; yellow staining of varying intensity occurred in patients who had taken tetracycline, oxytetracycline, or demethylchlortetracyc-line. The third type, a brownish-yellow discolouration, was of mixed origin. Of the earlier tetracyclines the least objectionable staining was produced by oxytetra-cycline.

In infants, increased intracranial pressure with bulging fontanelles has been observed with tetracycline therapy. This is not a common occurrence and all signs clear up on cessation of treatment.

Gastro-intestinal disturbances may complicate therapy with tetracyclines: some patients complain of abdominal discomfort or a feeling of nausea, and there may even be vomiting or diarrhoea. these effects may result from the direct irritant action of the drug on the intestinal mucosa, or may occur because of an alteration of the gut flora. All antimicrobials have the ability to alter the normal microbial flora of the upper respiratory tract, intestinal tract, and genito-urinary tract, and probably do so to some extent in every individual. Pseudomembranous colitis is a rare, but serious, complication of tetracycline therapy. The colitis is characterized by severe diarrhoea and mucus-containing stools. The cause of this condition is the colonization and multiplication of the organism *Clostridium difficile* in the colon, a process encouraged by the alteration of the normal gut flora by the antimicrobial. *Cl. difficile* produces a toxin that is damaging to the gastro-intestinal mucosa. Tetracyclines are not the only antimicrobials which can produce this serious condition; it may occur with others, e.g. ampicillin, amoxycillin, lincomycin, and clindamycin (see below). The treatment of the colitis is to stop the drug immediately and to administer oral vancomycin or metronidazole, to which *Cl. difficile* is sensitive.

Candida albicans is a normal commensal of mucous membranes. The fungus may cause disease in certain predisposed patients, e.g. diabetics; those with leukaemias or lymphomas; those who have received lengthy treatment with cytotoxic drugs, immunosuppressive drugs, or broad spectrum antimicrobials. Patients who have received a long course of treatment with broad-spectrum antimicrobials, e.g. tetracyclines, may develop an oral candidal infection that has been named 'antibiotic stomatitis'. This condition may follow the use of topical antimicrobials in the mouth. The surface proliferation of *C. albicans*, which is known to occur with the administration of broad-spectrum antimicrobials, increases the chances of it invading the tissues and thereby causing infection. A tetracycline mouthbath is listed in the *Dental Practitioners' Formulary 1986–88,* * and its use is recommended for no longer than three days, to be followed by a break of three days before the treatment is recommenced. This recommendation is made to avoid the occurrence of an antibiotic induced oral thrush.

Tetracyclines may cause end-stage renal failure when administered to patients with chronic renal disease. These antimicrobials cause a rise in blood urea, which is often accompanied by deterioration in renal function. While the normal half-life of the original tetracyclines is in the region of 6 to 12 hours, this may be increased to 57 to 108 hours in patients with renal failure. Tetracyclines should not, therefore, be given to patients with impaired renal function. Doxycycline and minocycline are possible exceptions to this general statement. The serum half-life of these preparations is in the region of 18 hours and is not significantly changed in patients with chronic renal failure.

Severe liver damage can occur after very large doses, and this may follow the accumulation of tetracyclines in renal failure. It is also likely to occur following parenteral administration in the third trimester of pregnancy.

* Not listed in 1988–90 DPF.

Uses

At one time tetracylines were regarded as second-choice antimicrobials to the penicillins in dental practice. This is no longer the case. Indeed, there are few indications for the use of tetracyclines in dentistry. A tetracycline mouthwash is sometimes useful in relieving the painful ulcerations of severe recurrent aphthae, the erosions of lichen planus, and especially for oral hepetic ulceration. For this purpose 10 ml of tetracycline mouthbath* is held in the mouth for two to three minutes, three times daily for no longer than three days. The rationale of this treatment is obscure; possibly it is effective in reducing any secondary infection. If the treatment is continued for more than three days consecutively, then there is the danger of superinfection with *C. albicans* in susceptible patients.

More recently, tetracyclines have found use in periodontal treatments (see Chapter 11).

ERYTHROMYCIN

This has a narrow spectrum of activity, similar to that of benzylpenicillin, but is more active against *Staph. aureus*. It is a bacteriostatic drug but bactericidal in high concentrations.

Pharmacodynamics

Erythromycin blocks translocation (see mode of action of tetracyclines for information on protein synthesis in bacteria). It binds to the bacterial ribosomal units and prevents translocation, with subsequent blocking of polypeptide synthesis. It is, then, a drug that interferes with protein synthesis within the bacterial cell. Drugs that affect translocation are, for some reason, liable to give rise to resistant mutants. In general, Gram-positive organisms are more sensitive than Gram-negative organisms because their cell walls are more readily permeable to such drugs. The Gram-negative enterobacteria, e.g. *E. coli*, salmonella, are resistant to erythromycin. On the other hand some of the Parvobacteria, such as *H. influenzae* and *Bordetella pertussis* are sensitive to erythromycin. The Gram-negative *Legionella pneumophilia* is also sensitive.

Pharmacokinetics

Erythromycin base is destroyed by acid gastric juices and so is administered in enteric coated tablets. It is absorbed from the upper part of the small intestine. Peak plasma concentrations are reached in about four hours and, to achieve this,

* Not listed in 1988–90 DPF.

the tablets should be taken in the absence of food. However, erythromycin estolate is more acid-stable and is usually given in the form of capsules. It is absorbed to a greater extent than any other oral preparation of erythromycin, and gives peak plasma concentrations within about two hours. Higher concentrations of erythromycin can be achieved by intravenous administration. The half-life of erythromycin is in the order of 1.5 to 2 hours.

Erythromycin is widely distributed throughout the body tissues and two to five per cent of the orally administered drug is excreted in its active form in the urine. Although a proportion of the drug is also excreted in the bile, of which some is reabsorbed, the greater part of it seems to be broken down in the body.

Unwanted effects

In general terms, erythromycin may be counted as one of the safest antimicrobials. All preparations of erythromycin can cause gastro-intestinal upsets such as nausea, vomiting, and diarrhoea; epigastric discomfort is not infrequent. This latter symptom is likely to be very marked if large doses are given.

Hypersensitivity reactions are rare with the base, but the estolate produces a high incidence of cholestatic hepatitis, which is thought to be due to hypersensitivity. This condition starts about 10 to 12 days after the commencement of treatment, and is manifested by abdominal pain, jaundice, and fever. On stopping the drug the symptoms and signs disappear, but re-exposure to the preparation may cause an immediate recurrence of the hepatitis.

Uses

Erythromycin is a useful alternative to penicillin when the patient is known to be hypersensitive to the latter and can, perhaps, be regarded as a second-choice antimicrobial to penicillin. It is generally administered orally and, for most dental infections, a five days course will suffice, the dose being 250 mg six-hourly. Erythromycin stearate should be used for treating infections especially if the course of treatment is to last more than a week. The use of the estolate in dentistry is unlikely to cause hepatitis as a course of treatment is usually not prolonged. Erythromycin also finds a use as a prophylactic agent against infective endocarditis, a subject discussed later in this chapter.

Although erythromycin is a useful drug, it is the drug of choice in relatively few diseases, but is recommended for the treatment of infections caused by *L. pneumophilia* (Legionnaire's disease).

Cross-resistance to other commonly used antimicrobials does not occur readily, but erythromycin has the disadvantage that some sensitive organisms (e.g. staphylococci and even haemolytic streptococci) may become resistant to it during prolonged therapy.

METRONIDAZOLE

This, given orally, is effective in the treatment of trichomonal infections of the genital tract, and coincidentally, it has been found to be successful in the treatment of acute ulcerative gingivitis and other dental infections (see below). Metronidazole exhibits activity against anaerobic cocci and against anaerobic Gram-negative bacilli, including Bacteroides species.

Pharmacodynamics

The drug inhibits DNA synthesis in organisms. When metronidazole is used in infections, it is reduced to form an extremely unstable and reactive intermediate that is thought to bind to DNA and interfere with further cell replication. This results in very rapid killing of obligate anaerobes.

Pharmacokinetics

Metronidazole is available as tablets and for intravenous infusion. The drug is well-absorbed after oral administration and a mean peak plasma concentration is produced in about 1 to 2 hours; the plasma half-life is about 8 hours. The drug penetrates into body tissues and fluids, and is metabolized in the liver; unchanged drug and metabolites are excreted in the urine.

Unwanted effects

Numerous unwanted effects have been recorded, and these are commonly related to the gastro-intestinal tract, e.g. nausea, vomiting, indigestion, diarrhoea, or constipation. Dizziness and headaches have also been reported. It is not unusual for the patient to complain of a bitter, metallic taste in the mouth. Occasionally skin rashes have occurred. Fortunately, the drug is well tolerated and the untoward effects are not often serious. When metronidazole is prescribed, patients should be instructed not to take alcohol as the drug may produce similar reactions to that of disulfiram (Antabuse) when combined with alcohol, e.g. it will inhibit the alcohol metabolism. Metronidazole also potentiates the effects of warfarin and the other coumarin anticoagulants.

Metronidazole has been shown to be carcinogenic in rodents fed on high doses for a prolonged period, but there does not seem to be evidence that there is such a risk in man. Although there appears to be no risk in administering metronidazole in pregnancy, as with all other drugs it should be avoided if possible, especially in the first trimester.

Uses

In medical practice, metronidazole is used in the treatment of genital infections with *Trichomonas vaginalis*. It is also effective in the treatment of *Giardia lamblia* infections (giardiasis). Addditionally it is used in the treatment of amoebic infections, and in the treatment of anaerobic infections due to Bacteroides species, including *fragilis*. In dentistry, the efficacy of metronidazole in the treatment of acute ulcerative gingivitis is well-established. Metronidazole is the first choice of drugs in the treatment of this condition and is dispensed as 200 mg and 400 mg tablets. One 200 mg tablet is swallowed thrice daily for three days. Discomfort usually decreases after 24 hours and ulcerations are beginning to heal after 48 hours.

As yet, sensitive organisms have not been found to develop resistance to metronidazole, and its use in the treatment of oral conditions does not, therefore, prejudice its efficacy against infections occurring in medical practice.

Metronidazole is probably as effective as penicillin in the treatment of acute pericoronitis, and it may also have wider usages in dentistry. A variety of bacterial species are found in dental abscesses, including a high proportion of obligate anaerobes of which *Bact. melaninogenicus* may well be important. This organism is known to produce tissue-active toxins such as collagenase, hyaluronidase, proteinase, and heparinase. It is possible that these may be concerned in the considerable and extensive inflammatory response which characterizes some acute dental infections. Obligate anaerobes are sensitive to both penicillin and metronidazole and, if they are the cause of a lot of dental infections, a rapid response to either of these antimicrobial agents would be expected. There is evidence that both are equally effective. Perhaps the true nature of many dental infections has not been appreciated because of the problems associated in the past with the isolation of anaerobes. Metronidazole may well be a satisfactory alternative to penicillin in patients with acute dental infections. In acute apical infections, 400 mg tablets should be considered rather than the 200 mg tablets, 400 mg being given twice daily. If as effective as penicillin, metronidazole may be preferred as it produces fewer hypersensitivity reactions. *Bact. fragilis* is not found in dental infections for, although it would respond to treatment with metranidazole, it is penicillin-resistant.

LINCOMYCIN AND CLINDAMYCIN

Clindamycin is a derivative of lincomycin, which it has replaced. Both are active against Gram-positive bacteria, including penicillinase-producing strains of staphylococci. Aerobic Gram-negative bacilli are resistant, but the Gram-negative aerobic *Bact. fragilis*, and *melaninogenicus*, are sensitive. Neisseria and enterococci are resistant to these drugs.

Pharmacodynamics

Lincomycin and clindamycin bind to ribosomal units and prevent translocation with subsequent blocking of polypeptide synthesis in organisms (see Pharmacodynamics of the tetracyclines).

Pharmacokinetics

Clindamycin is available for intramuscular injection or slow intravenous infusion; it is also presented as capsules and as a paediatric mixture. Clindamycin is rapidly and almost completely absorbed after oral administration, and its absorption does not seem to be significantly affected by the presence of food in the gut. It produces peak blood concentrations in about 45 minutes. The half-life of the drug is approximately three hours. After intramuscular injection of the phosphate form, peak plasma concentrations are not achieved until three hours in the adult, and somewhat more swiftly in children. Clindamycin is widely distributed throughout the body and penetrates well into bone.

Most of the drug is metabolized and is excreted as metabolites in the urine and bile. A small amount (10 per cent) is excreted unchanged in the urine and an even smaller amount is found in the faeces.

Unwanted effects

Diarrhoea is the most likely unwanted effect, and incidence of this has been suggested as being anything from as low as 2 per cent to well over 20 per cent. It is likely to be much higher with lincomycin. Unfortunately some patients have developed pseudomembranous colitis, a condition described earlier under Unwanted Effects of Tetracycline, with which it is also rarely associated. This can be a very serious problem and, before the mechanism producing this syndrome was understood, the treatment could even extend to colostomy. Although this condition, often referred to as antibiotic-associated colitis, can occur with other antimicrobials, it seems particularly associated with clindamycin, whether used orally or parenterally. Its occurrence seems to be unrelated to dosage, and it can arise any time during treatment or even after discontinuation of treatment. If it does occur, then the drug should be stopped and the condition treated with oral vancomycin or metronidazole to which *Cl. difficile*, the causative organism, is sensitive.

Allergic reactions may occur, and skin rashes are observed in a number of patients. There are more and rare serious reactions, such as Stevens–Johnson syndrome (severe, febrile erythema multiforme; see Sulphonamides below). Interestingly, clindamycin is an antimicrobial that inhibits, or interferes with, neuromuscular transmission and could, therefore, potentiate the effect of certain neuromuscular block agents, e.g. tubocurarine.

Uses

Clindamycin is a very effective drug in many infections, but the high incidence of diarrhoea and the possible occurrence of antibiotic-associated colitis must limit its use. It is especially useful in the treatment of infections caused by Bacteroides species, and in particular those due to *Bact. fragilis*. It should be reserved for infections caused by such organisms and, occasionally, for staphylococcal bone infections after bacteriological identification. The drug of first choice for such bone infections is likely to be flucloxacillin, and there appears to be very little indication for the use of clindamycin in dentistry.

ANTIFUNGAL ANTIMICROBIALS
(e.g. nystatin, amphotericin, imidazole agents)

Fungi are not sensitive to the antimicrobials used against bacterial infections, e.g. penicillin, tetracyclines, erythromycin, and others. Fortunately, up to now, systemic fungal infections have been rare in Britain, for they are serious diseases and difficult to treat. On the other hand, superficial infections by *C. albicans* are not uncommon and are usually trivial, but they tend to persist and may be troublesome in susceptible patients. As we have seen, oral candidiasis may occur as a response to treatment with certain drugs; for example corticosteroids, antibiotics (especially tetracyclines), and immunosuppressive agents.

A number of antifungal drugs are now available for local or systemic use, and one or two have found favour in dentistry; these are now described.

Nystatin

This is effective against *C. albicans* and some other fungi.

Pharmacodynamics

Nystatin is active against yeasts and fungi but inactive against bacteria. This selective toxicity is due to the presence of ergosterol in the cytoplasmic membrane of fungi and yeasts, which is not present in bacterial membranes. A hydrophobic interaction between nystatin and the membrane ergosterol molecule disrupts the osmotic function of the membrane, with consequent death of the fungi.

Pharmacokinetics

Nystatin is not absorbed from the skin or mucous membranes. It is, therefore, used for its local effect in the treatment of candidiasis on the skin or any part of the alimentary tract.

Unwanted effects

These are exceedingly rare. The occasional patient feels nauseated after oral administration. There have been no reports of hypersensitivity reactions. The drug has a very unpleasant taste.

Uses

Nystatin is used primarily to treat fungal infections caused by *C. albicans*, which produces thrush, denture stomatitis, antibiotic stomatitis, and some forms of mucocutaneous candidiasis(-osis).

In treating most oral candidal infections, one pastille of nystatin (100 000 units) is allowed to dissolve in the mouth, and four pastilles are prescribed each day for periods varying from one week to four weeks (e.g. denture stomatitis and angular cheilitis, two to four weeks; thrush and conditions following drug therapy, one to two weeks). In treating candidal leukoplakia, a chronic lesion, the daily regime advocated may have to be continued for many months.

Patients who have denture stomatitis should be advised to leave out their dentures as much as possible and to keep them in a cleansing agent such as sodium hypochlorite solution (Milton). It is understandable that many patients are reluctant to leave out their dentures for any length of time, so a compromise is to smear the fitting surface of the denture with an antifungal ointment (such as nystatin ointment, or amphotericin ointment) before insertion of the denture.

Persistent candidiasis, in spite of treatment, may point to some underlying predisposition. For instance, oral candidiasis is a common complication of leukaemias, especially where immunosuppressive drugs have been used.

Candidal vaginitis is a commonly transmitted sexual disease and generally responds to treatment with local applications of nystatin.

Amphotericin B

This is effective against a number of fungi, including Candida species. Its mode of action is thought to be like that of nystatin, and it has no effect on bacteria.

Pharmacokinetics

Amphotericin is little absorbed from the gastro-intestinal tract and probably not at all from the unbroken skin. It is used locally for the treatment of conditions for which nystatin could be used. Amphotericin B is available for intravenous injection, when it can be used for the treatment of systemic fungal infections, e.g. candidal septicaemia, histoplasmosis. The metabolism of the intravenously administered drug seems to be unknown, but the drug is excreted in an inactive form in the urine, and there is also biliary excretion.

Unwanted effects

The parenteral use of the drug is associated with a host of unwanted effects; these include fever, nausea, and vomiting. Some undesirable effects on the kidney are almost inevitable; a rise in blood urea may occur.

Uses

Amphotericin B is one of the relatively few antimicrobials effective against systemic fungal infections and is, therefore, a valuable weapon in the medical armamentarium, particularly as nystatin is too toxic to be used systemically. In dentistry, it is used for the same purposes as nystatin, so amphotericin B (10 mg) lozenges may be used locally in the mouth as an alternative to nystatin. In severe infections the dose may be doubled. Amphotericin B ointment can be substituted for nystatin ointment.

Imidazole agents
(e.g. miconazole, ketoconazole, clotrimazole)

The particular drug used in dentistry is miconazole. Miconazole and clotrimazole may be used topically; miconazole and ketoconazole may be used systemically. Their mode of action is similar to nystatin, and these drugs alter the permeability of the cytoplasmic membrane.

Pharmacokinetics

Miconazole is available for oral and parenteral administration. It has a lot of unwanted effects when given intravenously and is not the drug of choice as an antifungal for systemic use.

Ketoconazole is available for oral administration, and peak plasma concentrations appear about two hours after an oral dose of 400 mg. Metabolism of the drug occurs in the liver, and most is excreted as metabolites in the urine.

Unwanted effects

Although the most commonly encountered unwanted effects with parenteral ketoconazole are nausea and vomiting, other untoward effects have occurred, e.g. headache, photophobia, rash, and thrombocytopenia. Hepatic toxicity occasionally produces hepatic dysfunction. Unwanted effects when miconazole is used intravenously are frequent, e.g. anaemia, anaphylactoid reactions, central nervous-system involvement (hallucinations, blurred vision).

Uses

Ketoconazole finds a use in the treatment of systemic fungal infections and candidiasis. It is also useful as a prophylaxis in patients who are on immunosuppressive therapy and also in the treatment of such patients who have chronic candidal leukoplakia. A once-daily dose of ketoconazole (200 mg tablet) is taken with food, and the treatment is continued for one to two weeks after symptoms have disappeared and cultures are negative.

Miconazole has found a place in dentistry, and its primary use is topical. Miconazole tablets (250 mg) are available, and the dose regimen is 250 mg six-hourly. The drug is also presented as a sugar-free oral gel (25 mg/ml). The application of the gel is thought to be useful in the treatment of candidal leukoplakia or chronic mucocutaneous candidiasis.

OTHER ANTIMICROBIAL AGENTS

There are many of these, some carefully reserved for the treatment of particular infections. For example, *streptomycin* finds its principal use in the management of tuberculosis (see below), whilst *chloramphenicol* is one of the drugs of choice in typhoid fever, where the seriousness of the complaint overrides the dangers of its use. Chloramphenicol is a dangerous drug because it can produce irreversible bone marrow aplasia; it has no place in general dental practice.

Neomycin sulphate

This is a member of a group of drugs collectively referred to as aminoglycosides. This group also includes gentamicin, kanamycin, netilmicin, streptomycin, and tobramycin. They are particularly effective against many Gram-negative bacillary organisms but, in addition, streptomycin is effective against *Mycobacterium tuberculosis*. Neomycin is not a drug that is used parenterally because it may cause renal damage and is liable to produce deafness; auditory changes may even occur after topical administration. Nevertheless, neomycin alone, or in combination with other drugs, did once achieve some popularity in dermatological preparations. This era seems to have passed and few preparations are listed in the *British National Formulary*. Neomycin combined with a steroid as a cream or ointment was sometimes suggested as being helpful in treating the symptoms of herpes labialis. Various combinations of neomycin with other drugs have been used in dentistry; for example, Cicatrin powder (essentially neomycin and zinc bacitracin) on wounds to prevent postoperative infection. The topical use of neomycin is not without its dangers and it is a fairly frequent cause of allergic sensitization, usually in the form of skin reactions of the delayed type. Such preparations are no longer used in dentistry.

Sodium fusidate (fusidic acid)

This is a drug that is effective against staphylococci, although resistant strains do emerge *in vivo*, if rather slowly. Sodium fusidate ointment is listed in the *Dental Practitioners' Formulary*, and it is suggested that this be used in the fissures of angular cheilitis where *Staph. aureus* has been isolated.

Vancomycin

This antimicrobial is mainly active against Gram-positive bacteria. Clostridia species are inhibited by it. It is available for intravenous use and also as a powder for oral use. It is not absorbed from the gut, and so when given orally its use is really as a topical application. By oral administration it may treat antibiotic-associated colitis (500 mg as a loading dose followed by 125 mg six-hourly). It is painful on intravenous injection and should, therefore, be given by slow intravenous infusion. Vancomycin is only used to treat serious infections, such as certain staphylococcal infections (e.g. septicaemia, endocarditis), where the patient is allergic to penicillinase-resistant penicillins. It is also recommended as a prophylaxis against infective endocarditis in special circumstances (see later).

Quinolones

These comprise a group of drugs that act by inhibiting the bacterial enzyme DNA gyrase. The group includes nalidixic acid and cinoxacin. Both of these drugs are active against most Gram-negative bacteria but excluding *P. aeruginosa*. Gram-positive bacteria are predominantly resistant. The main use of quinolones has been in the treatment of urinary infections. More recently a new quinolone, ciprofloxacin, has been introduced, which is a broad-spectrum antimicrobial with activity against both Gram-positive and Gram-negative aerobes. It would appear to have a low incidence of unwanted effects. Like other quinolones, its most common unwanted effects are gastro-intestinal disturbances, e.g. abdominal discomfort and nausea. Concomitant administration of ciprofloxacin with theophylline may lead to elevated plasma concentrations of the latter, with an increased risk of adverse reactions related to theophylline, i.e. CNS stimulant effects. The earlier quinolones had no place in dentistry, but ciprofloxacin could well find a use because of its wider range of activity. Experience with this drug will surely establish its significance, if any, for dental practice.

Anti-tuberculous drugs

These include streptomycin, isoniazid, rifampicin, ethambutol, and pyrazinamide. An important point about rifampicin is that it is an enzyme inducer, and so hastens the metabolism of many other drugs, including prednisone, digoxin, propranolol, the oral contraceptives, and the oral anticoagulants. Clearly the effectiveness of these drugs may be reduced. Oral contraceptives may also be affected by other antimicrobials, e.g. ampicillin and tetracyclines, but perhaps not by enzyme induction; this subject is discussed in Chapter 22.

PROPHYLAXIS: THE PREVENTION OF INFECTIVE ENDOCARDITIS

The dental treatment of patients with valvular defects of the heart poses a special problem. Patients with congenital heart defects, with a history of rheumatic fever or chorea, or those who have undergone valvular cardiac surgery, may all be predisposed to infective endocarditis. Those with a past history of infective endocarditis should be regarded as a special high-risk group. The disease is caused by direct infection from the blood stream with bacteria colonizing the heart valves. Before the era of antimicrobials, infective endocarditis was almost invariably fatal; even today mortality is about 30 per cent, and patients are left with severely damaged hearts in spite of prolonged treatment with antimicrobials. There is a changing pattern in the disease, as now the older patient is affected rather than the young. Rheumatic fever causing residual heart lesions is no longer the main scourge in the young patient, but rather congenital heart defects. In the pre-antimicrobial era a high percentage of cases of infective endocarditis were caused by viridans Streptococci, organisms found in the mouth, and today such streptococci are still heavily implicated.

Transient bacteraemias follow many dental procedures. In the normal patient these are of little moment, for the bacteria are quickly removed from the bloodstream by the body's defences. However, in the predisposed patient, organisms may be implanted on an abnormal heart valve with perpetuation of the bacteraemia from an endocardial focus. The dental treatment of such patients should be undertaken as follows.

History

All patients attending for dental treatment should be questioned for any history of heart disease, previous rheumatic fever, or chorea. There is not complete agreement as to which patients should be considered at risk; not all would accept that one with a history of rheumatic fever, but with no apparent residual heart defects, should be so regarded. If such a patient attends for elective treatment it would be desirable to have the opinion of a cardiologist as to whether antimicrobial cover was required or not. If the same patient attends for emergency treatment, then they should be regarded as 'at risk' until vouchsafed otherwise by a cardiologist. It is important, anyway, to establish a positive history of rheumatic fever, for an indefinite history could have the patient being recorded as a potential risk without justification.

A patient who has had a myocardial infarction or coronary by-pass surgery is not regarded as 'at risk'.

Treatment plan

Those at risk should be encouraged to maintain a high standard of oral care. The teeth must be restored where necessary and periodontal disease prevented. If this state cannot be achieved, either because of indifference on the part of the patient, or because of the inherent quality of the dental tissues, extractions should be contemplated. It must be remembered that dental tissues may be the source of bacteraemias even in the absence of dental procedures. It must also be emphasized that the edentulous patient is not free from risk of infective endocarditis. Ulcers due to ill-fitting dentures may be the cause of a bacteraemia, and such ulcers should receive early attention.

Although it is agreed that any dental procedures may cause a bacteraemia, the emphasis must be on what should be regarded as a 'significant bacteraemia'. After all, chewing and toothbrushing could cause bacteraemias!

The use of antimicrobial agents

In order to prevent the occurrence of infective endocarditis in those patients considered to be at risk, antimicrobial cover should be provided when certain dental procedures are undertaken. A Working Party of the British Society for Antimicrobial Chemotherapy produced a report, published in the *Lancet* of 11 December 1982, on the subject of 'The Antibiotic Prophylaxis of Infective Endocarditis'. This report was not merely concerned with dental problems but a summary of the report, appertaining to the practice of dentistry, was published in the *British Dental Journal* (Cawson 1983). The Working Party report indicated that 'a risk of infective endocarditis appears to be associated only with extractions or scaling or surgery involving the gingival tissues'. This is a positive statement, but there are bound to be 'grey' areas in which clinical judgement will have to be exercised. For instance, in endodontic treatment it seems that a bacteraemia will not be produced so long as instrumentation is contained within the root canal. Instrumentation beyond the apex is likely to produce a bacteraemia and, in spite of the apparent margin of safety, many—perhaps most—endodontists would consider that root canal therapy should be undertaken under antimicrobial cover, and preferably completed at one visit.

The fact is that relatively few patients with infective endocarditis will give a recent history of dental treatment. Furthermore, it is impossible to know how effective are prophylactic antimicrobial regimens in preventing the occurrence of infective endocarditis. Nevertheless, in spite of all the ignorance surrounding the subject, the occurrence of the disease is so serious that it is generally agreed that prophylaxis must be provided for some patients.

The antimicrobial regimens for patients predisposed to infective endocarditis are as follows:

1. Dental treatment under local anaesthesia:
    (a) patients not allergic to penicillin.

Adults—3 g amoxycillin orally one hour before the operation. The drug should be given with either the dentist or the dental nurse present. This is done simply to ensure that the antimicrobial is taken by the patient. For *children* under ten years, half the adult dose; and for children under five years, quarter of the adult dose. For children over ten years, the dosage is as for the adult.

This regimen applies to patients with prosthetic heart valves as well as those with natural valvular disease. The patient who has a properly functioning prosthetic valve is no more likely to get infective endocarditis following on dental procedures than one with damaged natural valves. However, if the patient with prosthetic valves does have an attack of infective endocarditis then it is likely to be severe with a poorer prognosis.

(b) Patients allergic to penicillin.

Adults—1.5 g erythromycin stearate given orally under supervision, 1 to 1.5 hours before the dental procedure, followed by a second dose of 500 mg orally 6 hours later. For *children* under ten years, half the adult dose; for children under five, quarter of the adult dose; and for children over ten years, the dosage is as for the adult.

These regimens will cover most problems faced in general dental practice. The 3 g of amoxycillin is a high dosage and seems to provide adequate plasma concentrations for the critical period of 10 hours following the dental procedure. The reason why two doses of erythromycin are recommended is because absorption of erythromycin is less predictable and the initial dose, although quite large in itself, is not equivalent to the 3 g dose of amoxycillin. However, a 1.5 g dose of erythromycin is about the maximum that can be tolerated by patients without causing nausea.

At one time an alternative to amoxycillin was suggested if the patient had been taking a penicillin recently. It is now thought that high-dose (3 g) regimens of amoxycillin are appropriate, even for patients who have recently taken a penicillin.

2. Dental treatment under general anaesthesia:
   (a) patients not allergic to penicillin.

Adults—1 g of amoxycillin intramuscularly before induction and 500 mg of oral amoxycillin, six hours later. *Children* under 10 years, half the adult dose. Amoxycillin given intramuscularly is painful, and 1 g is about the maximum that can be tolerated. An alternative is to give 3 g of oral amoxycillin, four hours prior to induction, followed by another 3 g of oral amoxycillin as soon as possible after the dental treatment.

These regimens are not suitable for patients with prosthetic heart valves.

(b) patients who are allergic to penicillin.

Intravenous vancomycin and intravenous gentamicin are recommended for these patients, but these drugs are not available to dental practitioners under the *Dental Practitioners' Formulary.* Such patients should be referred to hospital.

A special problem exists for patients with prosthetic heart valves who require a general anaesthetic, and for patients who have had endocarditis. For those with prosthetic valves, a regimen using intramuscular amoxycillin (1 g) and intramuscular gentamicin (1.5 mg/kg) is recommended immediately before induction, followed by oral amoxycillin (500 mg), six hours later. For the patient who has had a previous attack of endocarditis, whether attending for local or general anaesthesia, a similar regimen of intramuscular amoxycillin and intramuscular gentamicin is recommended. All such patients should be referred to hospital for dental treatment, for these are at special risk. Whenever particular problems present themselves, the patient's physician should be consulted.

As the onset of endocarditis may be insidious, patients should be advised to report any untoward symptoms of signs to their medical practitioner. Endocarditis may develop in spite of prophylaxis and the position has been summed up in the *British Medical Journal* (Leading Article) of 20 October 1973:

Infective endocarditis presents a complex problem both in temperate and tropical countries. The role of immunological and other factors in the patient is uncertain. When we consider the large number of people at risk who have dental extractions or other procedures without any antibiotic cover, the incidence of the disease must be remarkably small. In two-thirds of patients no precipitating cause is detectable. The host's immunological response is probably more important than the infection, but in our present state of ignorance it remains obligatory to give prophylactic antibiotics for those at risk.

SULPHONAMIDES

These were discovered in Germany in 1935, where it was shown that a red dye, prontosil, would cure streptococcal infections in mice. Within a short period, researchers in France and England found that this substance was broken down in the body to two components, one of which, sulphanilimide, was therapeutically active. This was the real beginning of antibacterial chemotherapy and since that time many improvements have been made. Sulphonamides have a wide range of activity against both Gram-positive and Gram-negative organisms, for example streptococci. pneumococci, *H. influenzae*, *Vibrio cholerae*, *N. meningitidis*, *E. coli*, *N. gonorrhoeae*. Unfortunately, many organisms have become resistant to the sulphonamides and this, at one time, included the gonococci. However, in recent years there has been a gradual re-emergence of sensitive strains of gonococci due to the fact that the drug has not been used for some time in the treatment of gonorrhoea. On the other hand, there has been a gradual emergence of resistant strains of meningococci, and sulphonamides cannot be relied upon to treat meningococcal meningitis.

Pharmacodynamics

The sulphonamides are bacteriostatic drugs, inhibiting the growth and multiplication of sensitive organisms, thus allowing the natural defence mechanisms of the body to deal with the existing infection without being overwhelmed.

Para-aminobenzoid acid (PABA) is an essential metabolite of bacterial cells and sulphonamides are competitive antagonists of PABA. Para-aminobenzoic acid is required for the synthesis of folic acid; the sulphonamides inhibit competitively the enzyme responsible for the incorporation of PABA into the precursor of folic acid. The organisms affected by sulphonamides are those which synthesize their own PABA; those which utilize pre-formed PABA are not affected. Fortunately the mammalian cell, which also requires PABA, utilizes preformed PABA.

Local anaesthetics that are derivatives of PABA, e.g. procaine, amethocaine, could, in theory, interfere with the antibacterial action of the sulphonamides. As discussed in Chapter 7, the presence of such local anaesthetics could make available the PABA and so redress the balance in favour of the bacteria. However, local anaesthetics with formulae that do not have a PABA moiety, e.g. lignocaine, prilocaine, do not antagonize the sulphonamides even theoretically.

Pharmacokinetics

Most sulphonamides are readily absorbed from the gastro-intestinal tract after oral administration, the small intestine being the main site of absorption. There are exceptions to this general statement, for there are some sulphonamides that are not absorbed and are used topically in the bowel.

The sulphonamides are widely distributed throughout the body and they cross the blood-brain barrier to enter the cerebrospinal fluid, more so when the meninges are inflamed. They also readily cross the placenta and enter the fetal circulation. The sulphonamides are mainly metabolized in the liver to acetylated forms. The drug is excreted in the urine unchanged or as metabolites.

Unwanted effects

The sulphonamides produce a high incidence of these, and this was especially marked with the earlier products. Nausea, with or without vomiting, headache, and malaise were all quite common with the earlier sulphonamides but are rarely seen today.

The most serious effects of the sulphonamides are on the bone marrow. A degree of polymorphonuclear leucopenia is not uncommon but is of little importance in itself. However, agranulocytosis does occasionally arise and sometimes, although very rarely, an haemolytic anaemia. The mechanism of these is not fully understood; they may be manifestations of hypersensitivity. Probably there is very little danger if the treatment is not continued for more than 10 days, although this is not an absolute. After withdrawal of the drug, it may take weeks or months for the granulocytes to return to normal levels; nevertheless, recovery does normally occur. Aplastic anaemia, where all functions of the bone marrow are depressed, is a very rare occurrence indeed.

There are hypersensitivity reactions with the sulphonamides, and their incidence tends to vary with the preparation used; the long-acting sulphonamides are particularly implicated. Skin rashes of various sorts may appear— urticarial, pemphigoid, purpuric, and petechial rashes are all possibilities. Serum sickness-type syndrome may occur after some days of treatment, with fever, joint pains, and rashes. Stevens–Johnson syndrome, a severe form of erythema multiforme, may occur and may present with blisters in the mouth and on the skin. The long-acting sulphonamides e.g. sulfametopyrazine, sulphadimethox-ine, and sulphamethoxypyridazine, are most likely to be those concerned. Toxic effects due to accumulation are likely to occur with these preparations. Cawson and Spector (1985) describe the essentials of the syndrome in this way: 'the most striking and characteristic feature is the swollen, cracked, bleeding and crusted lips'. There may be ocular involvement. Although an extremely unpleasant condition, it is rarely fatal.

Renal damage from sulphonamides is likely to be rare these days but was not so in the past, when preparations, particularly the acetylated forms, tended to be less soluble than those used today. These insoluble forms appeared as crystals in the urine (crystalluria), and deposition of crystals in the kidney, ureters, or bladder could lead to obstruction and renal failure. Sulphadiazine, though still used, is poorly soluble, and may cause crystalluria.

Uses

A number of groups of sulphonamides can be described; namely, those that are:

(1) readily absorbed, widely distributed, and quickly excreted, e.g. sulphaurea, sulphafurazole, sulphadiazine, sulphadimadine;

(2) readily absorbed, widely distributed, and slowly excreted (long-acting), which include sulfametopyrazine and sulphadimethoxine;

(3) poorly absorbed, e.g. phthalylsulphathiazole, calcium sulphaloxate, sulpha-gaunidine;

(4) for topical application, e.g. sulphacetamide.

Urinary infections may be treated with sulphadimidine, sulphaurea, or sulphafurazole, being rapidly absorbed and excreted. However, these are less commonly used today because superior antimicrobials are available. Sulfameto-pyrazine and sulphadimethoxine are used for the treatment of chronic bronchitis. Indeed, the main usage for the sulphonamides is in the treatment of urinary infections and bronchitis.

The poorly absorbed sulphonamides have been used for preoperative bowel sterilization and for the treatment of some intestinal infections, but they are no longer recommended for these purposes.

Sulphadiazine is not available in Britain in tablet form except in combination with other drugs. However, it is available for intramuscular or intravenous injection and has been used prophylactically to prevent the occurrence of meningitis in patients at risk who have had maxillofacial injuries with leakage of cerebrospinal fluid. As pointed out previously, many strains of meningococci are now resistant to the sulphonamides. Benzylpenicillin is probably the first-choice antimicrobial for treating meningococcal meningitis. In patients allergic to penicillin, chloramphenicol may be the drug of choice.

Sulphacetamide, as eye drops, is used locally for the treatment of infections.

Trimethoprim-sulphamethoxazole (co-trimoxazole)

Trimethoprim is an antibacterial agent and has a range of activity similar to that of the sulphonamides. Like the sulphonamides, it inhibits bacteria by metabolic deprivation but at a later stage in their metabolism. When trimethoprim is combined with a sulphonamide (sulphamethoxazole) as in the preparation co-trimoxazole, it exerts a bactericidal effect.

A high proportion of the unwanted effects that occur with this combination are due to the sulphonamide element and the majority of unwanted effects refer to skin. Nevertheless there may be various haematological reactions, e.g. aplastic, haemolytic anaemias, as may also occur with sulphonamides. Theoretically, co-trimoxazole could cause a folic-acid deficiency with consequent anaemia, but this is most unlikely to occur in the normal healthy patient given therapeutic doses.

Trimethoprim-sulphamethoxazole is used to treat lower urinary tract infections and is very effective. The combination appears to be particularly useful in the management of chronic and recurrent infections; it is also used for the treatment of exacerbations of chronic bronchitis. It is one of the drugs of choice for the treatment of dysentry (shigellosis) as many of the causative organisms are now resistant to the broad-spectrum penicillins. The combination is useful in the treatment of typhoid and paratyphoid fevers because it seems to be as active as chloramphenicol but with less risk of producing such serious unwanted effects. It may also be useful in the management of the S. typhi carrier state.

Co-trimoxazole may be useful in the treatment of severe dental infections, and in sinusitis and sialadenitis. Co-trimoxazole comes in tablet form (480 mg in each tablet), and the dose is 960 mg every 12 hours, although this may be increased to 1.44 g in severe infections. Although the risk of crystalluria is slight, it is desirable when taking this preparation to increase the fluid intake (water).

Sulphasalazine

This preparation is worthy of mention as it is used in the treatment of mild ulcerative colitis, and is a useful prophylactic agent in that condition, maintaining clinical remissions for many patients. Sulphasalazine is broken down in the gut to sulphapyridine and 5-aminosalicylate. It is the salicylate that seems to act as an anti-inflammatory agent in both ulcerative colitis and Crohn's disease.

ANTIVIRAL AGENTS

Introduction

Viral infections differ from other types of infection because viruses are obligate intracellular parasites that require for their survival the active participation of the metabolic processes of the invaded cell. Thus, agents used to destroy viruses may also damage the invaded cell. Few therapeutic measures have been developed that are clinically acceptable; those applicable to dentistry are described in this section.

Acyclovir

This is an analogue of the nucleotide, purine, and its antiviral activity is essentially confined to the herpes virus. The drug can be given orally (200 mg), intravenously, and topically (5 per cent cream).

Acyclovir has a greater affinity (over 200 fold) for viral enzymes than for cellular enzymes. Viral enzymes phosphorylate acyclovir to form the compound acyclo-GMP, which is then further catalysed by cellular enzymes to acyclo-GTP. The latter is a potent inhibitor of viral DNA synthesis, thus inhibiting replication of the virus. (Fig. 10.1).

When given orally, acyclovir has a half-life of 2.5 hours and is poorly bound to plasma protein (15 per cent). The drug crosses the blood–brain barrier and is eliminated by the kidneys.

Unwanted effects arising from oral administration are few, and include nausea and headache. Topical application of acyclovir to mucous membrane can cause a transient burning sensation but this may be due to the polyethylene base.

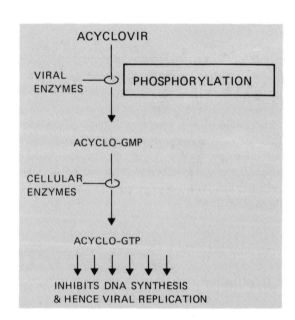

Fig. 10.1. Mode of action of acyclovir.

Uses

Acyclovir is used to treat the following viral infections.

1. *Herpes simplex type I virus:* acyclovir is effective at reducing the symptoms of the mucocutaneous lesions of the face and oropharynx associated with this viral infection.

2. *Herpes simplex type II virus:* this virus causes genital herpes and may also be responsible for meningitis. Primary genital herpes responds to acyclovir, but does not prevent recurrence. The drug is currently being tested for viral meningitis.

3. *Varicella-zoster virus:* Shingles is the principal disease caused by this virus and, in some patients, this is followed by post-herpetic neuralgia. Acyclovir has been shown to reduce the symptoms of the initial attack of shingles, but is of little value in the treatment of the neuralgia.

Idoxuridine

This is an antiviral agent structurally related to thymidine. It is phosphorylated within cells and the triphosphate so formed is incorporated into viral DNA synthesis. The synthesized viral DNA is more susceptible to breakage, and altered viral proteins may result from faulty transcription. Hence idoxuridine is mainly used against DNA viruses (herpes simplex type I, vaccinia, varicella, and cytomegalovirus). Idoxuridine is too toxic for systemic administration and is therefore only used topically.

For management of acute herpetic gingivostomatitis, a 0.1 per cent solution should be used. In young children, the solution should be painted on lesions four to five times a day. Older children and adults can apply a few ml of the solution as a mouthwash, allowing the solution to have maximum contact with the lesions for at least two to three minutes, three times a day.

Idoxuridine is effective in the treatment of herpes labialis, provided it is applied as early as possible. Established cases may respond to idoxuridine 5 per cent in dimethyl sulphoxide solution. The solvent aids the penetration of the antiviral agent into the skin. The solution is applied to the lesions every two hours until they resolve.

Herpes zoster infections may also respond to idoxuridine 5 per cent in dimethyl sulphoxide, provided the solution is applied early in the illness or as soon as the first skin lesions appear. Idoxuridine will reduce the pain associated with herpes zoster and accelerate healing.

Unwanted effects from topically applied idoxuridine are few. The solution has an unpleasant taste and patients may experience stinging when the solution is first applied. Excessive use of idoxuridine in dimethyl sulphoxide may cause maceration of the skin.

Table 10.1. Antimicrobials

Group	Official or approved name	Other names	Spectrum	Drug resistance	Adult dosage	Unwanted effects	Comments
Benzylpenicillin	Benzylpenicillin	Penicillin G Crystapen			300–600 mg, IM, 2–4 times daily	An innocuous drug even in high dosages, apart from hypersensitivity reactions. Hypersensitivity reactions are the most serious hazard—including anaphylactic shock.	Used for treating severe infections and/or relatively insensitive organisms, when high blood levels are required. Rapidly excreted.
	Procaine penicillin	Procaine penicillin G, Depocillin	C+, B+, C−, S. Proteus mirabilis and other Proteus often sensitive.	Many strains of Staphylococcus aureus.	300 mg. IM, 1–2 daily	Procaine penicillin appears to produce a higher incidence of allergic reactions; phenoxymethylpenicillin a low incidence of reactions.	Effective in all but relatively severe/resistant infections. Lower blood levels maintained for 24 h.
Acid resistant	Phenoxymethyl penicillin	Penicillin V, Apsin VK, Crystapen V, Distaquaine V-K, Stabillin V-K V-Cil-K			250 mg, orally, 4–6 hourly	N.B. Cross allergenicity is likely to exist between the penicillins.	Acid resistant. For oral administration. Unsuitable for serious infections because irregular absorption may produce inadequate blood levels. N.B. Penicillin is usually regarded as first choice antimicrobial in dentistry. Metronidazole may be an alternative (see text).
Penicillins resistant to penicillinase	Methicillin	Celbenin			1 g. IM, 4–6 hourly.	Have the same low order of unwanted effects as benzylpenicillin. It has been suggested that methicillin may cause permanent renal damage.	Although active against penicillin sensitive and penicillinase producing strains of Staphylococcus aureus, much less active than benzylpenicillin against other penicillin sensitive species. None of these penicillins is effective against infections due to Gram− bacilli. Reserved for the treatment of serious infections due to resistant staphylococci.
	Cloxacillin	Orbenin	Penicillinase resistant penicillins reserved for the treatment of staphylococcal infections	A few strains of Staphylococcus aureus.	500 mg orally, 6 hourly. 250 mg. IM, 4–6 hourly		
	Flucloxacillin	Floxapen			250 mg orally, or IM. 6 hourly		
Broad spectrum penicillins	Ampicillin*	Amfipen Ampilar Penbritin Vidopen	C+, B+, C−, B−, S. Slightly inferior to benzylpenicillin against most Gram+ bacteria.	Many strains of Staphylococcus aureus.	250 mg–1 g orally, 6 hourly.	Ampicillin produces a higher incidence of skin rashes than other penicillins. The rash is usually of the maculopapular type and may be unrelated to the usual type of penicillin hypersensitivity. The rash...	These penicillins are active against Gram+ bacteria, but are especially effective against Gram− bacteria. In dentistry these drugs should be reserved for infections caused by identified Gram− organisms. In ...
	Amoxycillin	Amoxidin			250–500 mg orally, 8 hourly.		

Class	Drug	Proprietary names	Microbiology	Dosage	Side effects	Comments
				(about 5) after the discontinuation of treatment.		has been used for a wide variety of infections, especially urinary tract infections. Amoxycillin used as prophylactic agent.
Carboxypenicillins	Carbenicillin	Pyopen	Pseudomonas infections and infections with Proteus species.	5 g, 4–6 hourly. Slow IV injection. 15–20 g daily in divided doses. IM or slow IV injection.	As for benzylpenicillin	These penicillins are of importance because of their activity against Pseudomonas aeruginosa and certain Proteus species. Ticarcillin is more active against Ps. aeruginosa than is carbenicillin.
	Ticarcillin	Ticar				
Cephalosporins	Cephalothin	Keflin	A degree of susceptibility to staphylococcal penicillinase	1 g, IV, every 4–6 hours.	The incidence of allergic reactions may be lower than that for the penicillins. There is a degree of cross allergenicity between the cephalosporins and the penicillins. Cephalothin, and possibly other cephalosporins, may be nephrotoxic in patients with renal impairment.	A useful alternative to penicillin when the latter cannot be used, other than because of hypersensitivity. Not, as at first hoped, the answer to staphylococcal infections, being susceptible to penicillinase. The second generation cephalosporins (cefuroxime and cephamandole) are less susceptible to inactivation by penicillinases. A third generation (e.g. cefotaxime, ceftazidime, etc.) are more active against certain Gram− bacilli. Cephalosporins find little place in dentistry.
	Cephradine	Velosef	Similar to ampicillin	250–500 mg, orally, 6 hourly. 0.5–1 g. IM, 6 hourly.		
	Cephalexin	Ceporex Keflex		250 mg, orally, 6 hourly.		
	Cefuroxime Cephamandole	Zinacef Kefadol	Less susceptible to penicillinase.			
	Oxytetracycline	Chemocycline Galenomycin Imperacin Oxymycin Terramycin Unimycin	B−, S, R, V. Often inactive against Proteus species and Pseudomonas aeruginosa.	orally, 6 hourly is the dose reange for most preparations. Exceptions: Sustamycin, Tetrabid. Doses for individual preparations should be checked prior to administration. Preparations are available for injection.	Nausea, vomiting and diarrhoea may occur. Super-infection with resistant strains of Staphylococcus aureus can cause a fatal enterocolitis. Overgrowth of Candida albicans may lead to thrush, glossitis, pruritis ani, etc. Staining of the teeth if administered during the period of calcification of the dental tissues, if given over a long period. May cause terminal renal failure in a stabilized renal failure. Tetracyclines should not be given to patients with renal disease with the exception of doxycycline and minocycline. N.B. Cross hypersensitivity is likely to exist between the tetracyclines.	The development of bacterial resistance has reduced the general usefulness of the tetracyclines. However, they are valuable agents in rickettsia, in some infections produced by mycoplasma and in infections caused by chlamydia (e.g. psittacosis, urethritis). Tetracyclines are also useful in treating exacerbations of chronic bronchitis. They find little place in dentistry but are useful in the management of juvenile periodontitis. Whenever possible tetracyclines should be avoided during the period of calcification of the teeth because of the staining produced in developing teeth. Tetracyclines should be avoided in patients with ulcerative colitis.
	Tetracycline	Achromycin Economycin Sustamycin Tetrabid Tetrachel Tetrex	development of resistance but many Streptococci are resistant and there is an emerging resistance of Pneumococci. Cross resistance between the tetracyclines.			
	Doxycycline	Doxatet Doxylar Nordox Vibramycin		200 mg orally on first day. Then 100 mg daily.		
	Minocycline	Minocin		Initially 200 mg orally. Then 100 mg 12 hourly.		

Table 10.1. Antimicrobials

Group	Official or approved name	Other names	Spectrum	Drug resistance	Adult dosage	Unwanted effects	Comments
Erythromycin group (Macrolides)	Erythromycin	Erycen Erymax Erythrocin Erythrolar Erythromid Ilotycin Retcin	Legionnaire's disease C+, B+, C−, S	Develops rapidly; may occur during treatment	250–500 mg orally, 6 hourly	Gastrointestinal upsets (nausea, vomiting, epigastric discomfort, diarrhoea) not uncommon. Hypersensitivity reactions are rare except that erythromycin estolate produces a high incidence of cholestatic hepatitis if given for more than 10 days. In this instance the hepatitis is thought to be due to hypersensitivity.	Similar range of activity to benzylpenicillin. In low concentration it is mainly bacteriostatic, but in higher concentration it exerts a bactericidal effect. It is another alternative in the treatment of infections when the patient is allergic to penicillin, or when prophylaxis is required. It may be useful in the treatment of infections due to penicillin resistant strains of *Staphylococcus aureus*, if sensitivity is established.
	Erythromycin estolate	Ilosone			250–500 mg, orally, 6 hourly		
Lincomycin	Lincomycin	Lincocin			500 mg orally, 3–4 times daily. 600 mg, IM (every 24 h in mild to moderate infections; every 12 h in severe infections).	Hypersensitivity reactions appear to be rare. Diarrhoea is common with both drugs, possibly less so with clindamycin. Cases of pseudomembranous colitis have been reported following the use of both drugs. N.B. Cross allergenicity is likely to exist between lincomycin and clindamycin.	Probably best reserved for the treatment of osteomyelitis as they are thought to penetrate well into bone. It is recommended that these drugs be used with extreme caution, and only where no suitable alternative is available, because of the possibility of pseudomembranous colitis. The colitis is due to a toxin produced by *Clostridium difficile* which is resistant to lincomycin and clindamycin. If diarrhoea colitis occurs the drug should be stopped at once. Treatment of the colitis is by vancomycin or metronidazole, the anaerobic *Cl. difficile* being sensitive to these drugs.
	Clindamycin	Dalacin C	Similar to that of erythromycin	Some strains of *Staphylococcus aureus*.	150–300 mg, orally, 6 hourly. 0.6–2.7 g, IM daily in 2–4 divided doses.		

Anti-fungals							
	Nystatin	Nystan	Candida albicans. (No antibacterial activity).	Strains of Candida albicans serially subcultured become resistant. Resistant Candida albicans not yet found clinically.	Nystatin pastilles (100 000 i.u. per pastille) 1 pastille sucked 4 times daily. Nystatin tablets (500 000 units per tablet) 1–2 tablets 4 times daily Nystatin ointment. Applied to lesions 4 times daily.	Occasionally produces nausea and vomiting.	It is used locally in the management of candidiasis of the alimentary tract. In treating oral candidiasis (e.g. denture stomatitis, thrush) 1 nystan pastille is allowed to dissolve in the mouth, 4 times daily, for a period of from 1–4 weeks. Dentures should preferably be removed and disinfected. (Tablets are swallowed to treat intestinal infection and the local treatment should be combined with this to help combat the generalized gastrointestinal infection.) If angular cheilitis is present, nystan ointment may be applied to the lesions. Sometimes nystatin is combined with tetracyclines to prevent overgrowth of Candida albicans.
	Amphotericin B	Fungizone (for infusion) Fungilin lozengers, Fungilin tablets, Fungilin ointment.	Candida species. Coccidioides immitis. Blastomyces dermatidis. Cryptococcus neoformans.	Strains of Candida albicans serially subcultured become resistant. Resistant Candida albicans not yet found clinically.	1 lozenge (10 mg) to be dissolved in the mouth 4 times/day for 1–4 weeks. 1–2 tablets (each containing 100 mg), 4 times daily. Amphotericin ointment 3%, applied 4 times/day.	Parenterally administered amphotericin B is associated with a large number of unwanted effects, e.g. hypersensitivity reactions, chills, fever, local thrombophlebitis, decreased renal function, and, rarely, irreversible renal failure.	Amphotericin B (Fungizone) is available when it is administered intravenously for the treatment of severe, systemic mycotic disease. Amphotericin B (Fungilin) lozenges and ointment are used for the same purpose as nystatin tablets and ointment, in the treatment of oral candidiasis. Amphotericin tablets are used to combat gut candidiasis. Amphotericin B does not have the unpleasant taste of nystatin.

Table 10.1. Antimicrobials

Group	Official or approved name	Other names	Spectrum	Drug resistance	Adult dosage	Unwanted effects	Comments
Anti-fungals	Miconazole nitrate	Daktarin tablets Daktarin injection Daktarin oral gel	Active against a broad spectrum of fungi.		250 mg. orally, 6 hourly. 600 mg. 3 times daily, by slow IV infusion. Miconazole: Oral Gel 25 mg/ml, 5–10 ml placed in mouth near lesions. Retain and then swallow. 4 times daily.	Unwanted effects are frequent after systemic administration. These include nausea, vomiting, anaemia, hypersensitivity reactions, CNS toxicity. The vehicle carrying the active agent is cremophorel which also produces unwanted effects.	Miconazole is essentially a drug for topical use, it is too toxic for parenteral administration, except in special circumstances. The oral gel seems to be effective in the treatment of denture stomatitis and angular cheilitis. The gel is lightly smeared over the fitting surface of the upper denture and this is done 4 times daily. The fitting surface should be clean and dry prior to the application of the gel. Similarly, the gel may be applied to lesions at the angle of the mouth. Treatment may have to be carried out for a number of weeks.
Nitroimidazoles	Metronidazole	Flagyl	Anaerobic bacteria e.g. *Bacteroides* species (including *Bacteroides fragilis*). Protozoa, e.g. *Giardia lamblia*, *Trichomonas vaginalis*.	Primary resistance is very unusual in sensitive species of anaerobes.	Anaerobic infections: 400 mg orally, 3 times daily. A.U.G.: 200 mg. orally, 3 times daily. Giardiasis: by mouth, 2 g. daily for 3 days. Trichomoniasis: by mouth, 200 mg. every 8 h for 7 days.	Nausea, vomiting, diarrhoea in about 3% of patients. Occasional metallic taste. Dizziness and ataxia may occur, and transient epileptiform seizures with high doses. Peripheral neuropathy may occur after prolonged treatment. A reversible neutropenia sometimes occurs. Disulfiram-like effect with alcohol.	Metronidazole is a very safe drug overall. No teratogenic effects have been noted after the administration of the drug at various stages of pregnancy. Nevertheless the manufacturer recommends avoidance of high-dose regimens during pregnancy and breast feeding. Such regimens are unlikely in dentistry. Alcohol must be avoided when taking metronidazole as the concurrent use will cause some patients to have vomiting and/or headache. Other nitroimidazoles are available, e.g. tinidazole, nimorazole. Metronidazole is useful in the treatment of antibiotic associated colitis (due to *Clostridia difficile*.)

*The ampicillin esters, bacampicillin (Ambaxin), pivampicillin (Pondocillin), and talampicillin (Talpen), produce higher plasma concentrations than ampicillin, and absorption is little affected by the presence of food.
Code: C+ = Gram+cocci. C− = Gram−cocci. B+ = Gram+bacilli. B− = Gram−bacilli. R = Rickettsiae. V = Chlamydiae, e.g. Chlamydia trachomatis. S = Treponema pallidum.
N.B.: Doses of older penicillins were originally expressed in units, but it is now customary to express doses in mg (or g). e.g. Benzylpenicillin, 250 000 units=150 mg: Procaine penicillin, 100 000 units = 100 mg.

Interferon

Interferons are glycoproteins produced by the body in response to a viral infection. Their properties include the induction of resistance to viral infections and the regulation of other cell functions. *In vitro* studies have shown that interferon has a broad-spectrum antiviral activity. However, preliminary results from clinical trials suggest that interferon is not as efficacious in viral infections as initially hoped.

REFERENCES AND FURTHER READING

Admadsyah, I. and Salim, A. (1985). Treatment of tetanus: an open study to compare the efficacy of procaine penicillin and metronidazole. *British Medical Journal*, **291**, 648–50.

Bain, R. J. I. *et al.* (1985). Failure of single dose amoxycillin as prophylaxis against endocarditis. *British Medical Journal*, **290**, 316–17.

Ball, A. P. (1982). Clinical uses of penicillins. *Lancet*, **ii**, 197.

Cafferkey, M. T. *et al.* (1985). Occasional Survey: methicillin-resistant *Staphylococcus aureus* in Dublin 1971–1984. *Lancet*, **ii**: 705–8.

Cawson, R. A. (1981). Infective endocarditis as a complication of dental treatment. *British Dental Journal*, **151**, 409.

Cawson, R. A. (1983). A summary of the BSAC Working Party Report: the antibiotic prophylaxis of infective endocarditis. *British Dental Journal*, **154**: 183–4.

Cawson, R. A. (1986). Update on antiviral chemotherapy: the advent of acyclovir. *British Dental Journal*, **161**, 245–52.

Cawson, R. A. and Spector, R. G. (1985). *Clinical pharmacology in dentistry*, (4th edn), p. 344. Churchill Livingstone, Edinburgh.

Clinical Pharmacy, In *The Pharmaceutical Journal* (1987), **238**, No. 6418, p. 198.

Cohen, J. (1982). Antifungal chemotherapy. *Lancet*, **ii**: 532–7.

Davies, A. J. and Lewis, D. A. (1984). Rifampicin in non-tuberculous infections. *British Medical Journal*, **289**, 3–4.

Eggleston, D. J. (1980). Procaine penicillin psychosis. *British Dental Journal*, **148**, 73–4.

Gallagher, D. M. and Sinn, D. P. (1983). Penicillin-induced anaphylaxis in a patient under hypotensive anaesthesia. *Oral Surgery*, **56**, 361–4.

Goldberg, A. (1985). Co-trimoxazole toxicity. *British Medical Journal*, **291**, 673.

Gould, I. M. and Wise, R. (1985). Third generation cephalosporins. *British Medical Journal*, **290**, 878–9.

Hay, R. J. (1985). Ketoconazole: a reappraisal. *British Medical Journal*, **290**, 260–1.

Holbrook, W. P., Willey, R. F., and Shaw, T. R. D. (1983). Prophylaxis of infective endocarditis. *British Dental Journal*, **154**, 36–9.

Hood, F. J. C. (1978). The place of metronidazole in the treatment of acute oro-facial infection. *Journal of Antimicrobial Chemotherapy*, **4**, (suppl. C), 71–3.

Kucers, A. (1982). Good antimicrobial prescribing. *Lancet*, **ii**, 425–9.

Lacey, R. W. Hawkey, P. M., Devaraj, S. K., Millar, M. R., Inglis, I. J. J., and Goodwin, P. G. R. (1985). Co-trimoxazole toxicity. *British Medical Journal*, **291**, 481.

Leading article (1985). Fifty years of sulphonamides. *Lancet*, **i**, 378.

Leading article (1985). Born-again vancomycin. *Lancet*, **i**, 677–8.

Leading article (1985). What's to be done about resistant staphylococci? *Lancet,* **ii,** 189–90.

Leading article (1985). A nasty shock from antibiotics? *Lancet,* **ii,** 594.

Leading article (1985). Decline in rheumatic fever. *Lancet,* **ii,** 647–8.

Leading article (1985). Antibiotic care for cardiac surgery. *Lancet,* **ii,** 701–2.

Leading article (1985). Antibiotic-induced neutropenia. *Lancet,* **ii,** 814.

Levy, S. B. (1982). Microbial resistance to antibiotics. *Lancet,* **ii,** 83–8.

Martin, M. V., Farrelly, P. J., and Hardy, P. (1986). An investigation of the efficacy of nystatin for the treatment of chronic atrophic candidosis (denture sore mouth). *British Dental Journal,* **160,** 201–4.

McGowan, D. A. and Hendry, M. L. (1985). Is antibiotic prophylaxis required for dental patients with joint replacements? *British Dental Journal,* **158,** 336–8.

McGowan, D. A. Nair, S., MacFarlane, T. W., and MacKenzie, D. (1983). Prophylaxis of experimental endocarditis in rabbits using one or two doses of amoxycyllin. *British Dental Journal,* **155,** 88–90.

Mitchell, D. A. (1986). A controlled clinical trial of prophylactic tinidazole for chemoprophylaxis in third molar surgery. *British Dental Journal,* **160,** 284–6.

Mitchell, L. (1984). Topical metronidazole in the treatment of 'dry socket'. *British Dental Journal,* **156,** 132–4.

Morell, P., Hey, E., Mackee, I. W., Rutter, N., and Lewis, M. (1985). Deafness in preterm baby associated with topical antibiotic spray containing neomycin. *Lancet,* **i,** 1167–8.

Morris, G. K. (1985). Infective endocarditis: a preventable disease? *British Medical Journal,* **290,** 1532–3.

Neu, H. C. (1982). Clinical uses of cephalosporins. *Lancet,* **ii,** 252–5.

O'Grady, F. (1973). *Current antibiotic therapy,* p. 7. Churchill Livingstone, Edinburgh and London.

Orme, M. L'E. and Black, D. J. (1986). Drug interactions between oral contraceptive steroids and antibiotics. *British Dental Journal,* **160,** 169–70.

Phillips, I. (1982). Aminoglycosides. *Lancet,* **ii,** 311–15.

Reeves, D. (1982). Sulphonamides and trimethoprim. *Lancet,* **ii,** 370–3.

Renson, C. E. (1983). Infective endocarditis—prophylaxis and prevention. *Dental Update,* **10,** 254–8.

Roberts, J. Bianco, M. M., and Fine, J. (1985). Report of a case: fatal anaphylactic reaction to oral penicillin. *Journal of the American Dental Association,* **110,** 505–6.

Roe, F. J. (1977). Metronidazole: review of uses and toxicity. *Journal of Antimicrobial Chemotherapy,* **3,** 205–12.

Sanderson, P. J. (1984). Common bacterial pathogens and resistance to antibiotics. *British Medical Journal,* **289,** 638–9.

Schifter, S., Agaard, M. T., and Jensen, L. (1985). Adverse reactions to vancomycin. *Lancet,* **ii,** 499.

Sterry, A. K., Langeroudi, M., and Dolby, A. E. (1985). Metronidazole as an adjunct to periodontal therapy with sub-gingival curettage. *British Dental Journal,* **158,** 176–8.

Therapeutics (1985). Antibiotic treatment of streptococcal and staphylococcal endocarditis. Report of a Working Party of the British Society of Antimicrobial Chemotherapy. *Lancet,* **ii,** 815–17.

Walker, D. M., Stafford, G. D., Huggett, R., and Newcombe, R. G. (1981). The treatment of denture-induced stomatitis. *British Dental Journal,* **151,** 416–19.

Watson, C. J., Walker, D. M., Bates, J. F., and Newcombe, R. G. (1982). The efficacy of topical miconazole in the treatment of denture stomatitis. *British Dental Journal*, **152**, 403–6.

Wheeley, M. St.G. (1986). Effect of antibiotics on oral contraception. *British Medical Journal*, **292**, 903.

Wise, R. (1982). Penicillins and cephalosporins: antimicrobial and pharmacological properties. *Lancet*, **ii**, 140–3.

Wroblewski, B. A., Singer, W. D., and Whyte, J. (1986). Carbamazepine–erythromycin interaction. *Journal of the American Medical Association*, **255**, 1165–7.

11

Pharmacological control of dental caries and periodontal disease

INTRODUCTION

DENTAL caries and periodontal disease are the two principal diseases that affect the morbidity of the dentition. Microbial plaque is the main aetiological factor in both diseases, although diet and the host response play vital roles. The incidence of dental caries can be considerably reduced by fluoride; more recently, attention has focused on the development of a vaccine against dental caries. Mechanical removal of plaque is the basis for controlling periodontal disease but, although desirable, this is often impracticable because of the high degree of motivation and dexterity required to make a mouth plaque-free. Research has been concentrated on the development of chemical methods for inhibiting plaque formation. This chapter discusses the various pharmacological methods for controlling dental caries and periodontal disease.

DENTAL CARIES

This is caused by a biological interaction between bacteria, diet, and the tooth surface. There is now overwhelming evidence that refined carbohydrates are broken down by acid-producing bacteria, which in turn produce further acid causing demineralization of the enamel surface. Streptococci of the *mutans* type are the main bacteria implicated in dental caries, which produce lactic acid from dietary carbohydrates.

The relationship between fluoride and dental caries was first realized in the early part of this century. Since then many epidemiological studies have demonstrated unequivocally the role of fluoride in preventing dental caries (for review see Murray and Rugg-Gunn 1982).

Mode of action of fluoride in reducing dental decay

The precise mode of action is uncertain; fluoride probably acts via several mechanisms including an effect on enamel structure, an alteration in tooth morphology, and an action on bacterial plaque.

Fluoride and enamal structure

Enamel is mainly composed of crystals of hydroxyapatite, which readily loses its hydroxyl group in the presence of fluoride to form fluorapatite. Hydroxyapatite crystals dissolve more easily than fluorapatite in acid due to the presence of voids caused by disordered arrangement of the hydroxyl group. Fluoride thus makes apatite crystals less soluble in acid by two mechanisms. Firstly, crystals of fluorapatite have less voids than crystals of hydroxyapatite, thus reducing solubility (Gron et al. 1963). Secondly, fluoride displaces carbon and magnesium ions from apatite crystals; such displacement improves the crystalline structure. There is a greater concentration of fluorapatite on the surface of enamel, which further reduces enamel solubility (Weatherell et al. 1972).

Fluoride also has an effect on the remineralization of enamel after acid attack, causing an increase in the formation of the more stable fluorapatite. Thus the enamel surface will be more resistant to future acid attack (Brown et al. 1977; Koulourides et al. 1980).

Fluoride and tooth morphology

It has been shown that fluoride ingested during dental development slightly alters the shape of teeth resulting in wider fissures and more rounded cusps (Forrest 1956). Enamel and dentine are also thinner due to altered matrix formation caused by impaired protein synthesis (Kruger 1970). However, it is unlikely that these actions of fluoride are of any great clinical significance and may only have a slight effect on the incidence of pit and fissure caries.

Fluoride and plaque

Research has shown that fluoride has a dual effect on plaque, causing an inhibition of formation and a reduction of enzymic action within formed plaque. The early phase of plaque formation depends upon the integrity of the dental pellicle, which is derived from salivary protein. Fluoride reduces the precipitation of protein from saliva on the enamel surface. However, the value of this mode of action of fluoride for causing a reduction in caries is uncertain (Jenkins 1978).

Much interest has been focused on the action of fluoride on plaque metabolism, in particular anaerobic glycolysis. Low concentrations of fluoride (1 to 2 p.p.m.) are capable of inhibiting acid production in plaque. Furthermore, plaque can concentrate fluoride, although it is easily leached out. Repeated exposure of plaque to fluoride (either in toothpastes or rinses) maintains the concentration of fluoride in the plaque (Birkeland et al. 1971).

Pharmacokinetics of fluoride

Fluoride is passively absorbed from the stomach, stored in skeletal tissue, and excess is excreted via the kidney, sweat, and faeces. The placenta acts as a partial barrier to fluoride, which depends upon the maternal concentration of fluoride. Thus, the efficacy of therapeutic fluoride given to the pregnant mother to enhance the baby's teeth is uncertain.

Fluoride administration

Fluoride can be administered systemically via the water supply, tablets, drops, milk, and salt, or topically in the form of solutions, gels, varnishes, and toothpastes.

Water fluoridation

Early epidemiological studies in areas with natural fluoride in the water supply clearly demonstrated its anticaries effect. In areas with no natural fluoride in their water supply, the addition of fluoride up to 1 p.p.m. causes a significant reduction in the incidence of dental caries. Fluoride so added has the additional benefit of serving a large population at minimal cost.

Fluoride tablets and drops

These are either the sodium or calcium salt, or the acidulated phosphate salt of fluoride; dosage is between 0.5 to 1 mg per day. The effectiveness of fluoride tablets depends upon the age at which the child commences treatment; the earlier, the greater the percentage reduction in caries. Overall results from several studies indicate that this form of fluoride therapy produces a 40 to 80 per cent reduction in the incidence of dental caries (Murray and Rugg-Gunn 1982). Compliance with home-administered fluoride is poor but school-based programmes might overcome this problem.

Fluoridized milk

Milk is widely dispensed in schools and would thus seem a good vehicle for delivering fluoride. Furthermore, absorption of fluoride is not affected by the Ca^{2+} present in milk (Ericsson 1958). There have been few studies to support the effectiveness of fluoridized milk in controlling dental caries, and other methods of fluoride delivery may be more acceptable. The amount of fluoride added to milk, in the form of sodium fluoride, is the equivalent of receiving 1 mg F/per day.

Fluoridated table salt

Salt, like water and milk, is another excellent vehicle for dispensing fluoride. Concentrations of fluoride in salt vary between 200 to 350 mg F/kg salt. Although widely used on the continent of Europe, there have been few studies of the efficacy of this method of fluoride delivery for controlling dental caries. However, what findings there are suggest that fluoridated salt is an effective method for controlling dental caries, but not as good as fluoride in the water supply (Murray and Rugg-Gunn 1982).

Fluoride solutions

These can be classified into two types: aqueous solutions of sodium or stannous fluoride, or the acidulated phosphate fluoride system.

Sodium and stannous fluoride

Sodium fluoride was the first topically applied fluoride solution. In clinical use, a 2 per cent solution is applied to dried teeth for three minutes, usually three to four times per year. The long-term efficacy (over four years or more) of this method of fluoride application is uncertain, but short-term results indicate a caries reduction of between 30 to 50 per cent.

Stannous fluoride has been shown to be more effective than sodium fluoride at reducing enamel dissolution by acid. In clinical practice, an 8 to 10 per cent stannous fluoride solution is used, but such a solution is unstable and each new application requires a fresh solution. A further disadvantage of stannous fluoride is the staining of teeth, especially at the margins of restorations.

Acidulated phosphate fluoride

This system was developed after studies had shown that the uptake of fluoride by enamel was enhanced by reducing the pH (Bibby 1947). Clinical trials have demonstrated that a 1.23 per cent acidulated phosphofluoride solution causes a 20 to 40 per cent reduction in caries activity. The acidulated solution has to be applied to dried teeth for four minutes, usually twice a year. Application of the solution can present a problem with young children who have a copious salivary flow. Acidulated fluoride solutions cause nausea and sometimes vomiting if swallowed. This problem can be overcome by applying the solution in the form of a gel or by using a tray that fits closely to the teeth.

Fluoride varnishes

Fluoride applied in the form of a varnish allows of longer contact between the enamel surface and fluoride ions. Proprietary fluoride varnishes include Duraphat, Elmex, Protector, and Epoxylite 9070, which are usually applied twice a year. The effectiveness of this mode of applying fluoride is uncertain, and claims of caries reduction show marked variation between studies. Evidence suggests that this method of applying fluoride is the least effective (Hodge *et al.* 1980; Mainwaring and Naylor, 1983).

Fluoride toothpastes

Fluoride in toothpaste is the commonest and easiest method of applying topical fluoride. Nearly all brands of toothpaste sold in the UK contain fluoride, usually sodium monofluorophosphate. Regular use of a fluoride toothpaste causes a 30 per cent reduction in the incidence of dental caries. Recently, the effectiveness of sodium monofluorophosphate has been enhanced by the addition of either sodium fluoride or calcium glycerophosphate to the toothpaste.

Mouth rinses

A sodium fluoride solution at a concentration of 100 to 200 p.p.m. is widely used as a mouth rinse. The efficacy of this method of applying fluoride depends upon the frequency of rinsing, which is usually recommended once a week. Supervision at schools offers an ideal opportunity to carry out such a programme.

Unwanted effects of fluoride therapy

These can be classified as effects on skeletal tissue and effects on the teeth.

Effects of skeletal tissue

A high regular intake of fluoride (greater than 8 p.p.m.) can lead to skeletal fluorosis, which is characterized by an increase in bone density, especially in the lumbar spine and pelvis, and an increase in the thickness of long bones. In severe cases, calcification of the ligaments occurs. Histologically, skeletal fluorosis resembles osteomalacia but, biochemically, the plasma calcium and phosphate levels are normal. The strength of fluorotic bone is poor, and spontaneous fractures are common (Nordin 1973).

Effect on teeth

Excessive fluoride intake will cause dental fluorosis. The clinical appearance can range from white patches in the enamel to severe hypoplasia of the whole tooth. Dental fluorosis can develop if the daily fluoride intake exceeds 2 p.p.m.

Fluoride overdose

The various fluoride preparations are readily available to the public and overdose can arise, especially in young children consuming excess tablets or drops. The lethal dose of sodium fluoride for man is 5 g. Signs and symptoms of overdose include abdominal pain, vomiting, and diarrhoea. Fluoride overdose is treated by gastric lavage to reduce further absorption.

PHARMACOLOGICAL CONTROL OF PERIODONTAL DISEASE

Introduction

Periodontal disease is caused by bacterial plaque, although various systemic factors can modify the inflammatory response of the periodontal tissues to bacterial toxins. The disease can be prevented by either inhibiting the formation of plaque on the tooth surface or by complete plaque removal before inflammatory changes occur in the gingival tissues. Complete plaque removal by mechanical means may be possible in well-motivated individuals, but the majority of people leave plaque on some part of the tooth surface after brushing. Much attention has, therefore, been focused on chemical means to inhibit plaque formation; inhibitory agents can be categorized into the following groups: enzymes, antiseptics, antibiotics, oxygen-releasing agents, and fluoride.

Enzymes

The major part of bacterial plaque (70 per cent) comprises micro-organisms, and the remainder is an intermicrobial matrix of protein and carbohydrate. Enzymes are utilized to break down the plaque matrix and disperse micro-organisms. Enzymes that have been used to 'destroy' plaque include mucinases, extracts from dried pancreas (containing trypsin, chymotrypsin, carboxypeptidase, amylase, lipase, and nuclease), and dextranase. These have to be incorporated into chewing gum and toothpastes. However, their efficacy in plaque control is poor, and although *in vitro* findings showed promise, clinical trials produced indifferent results and a high incidence of unwanted effects. The present consensus of opinion does not favour the use of enzymes as a method for controlling plaque formation and periodontal disease (Hull 1980).

Antiseptics

Many antiseptic mouthwashes can affect the bacterial flora in the mouth and the development of plaque. However, their inhibitory effect is often short, and repeated use is required. Antiseptics used for controlling plaque are the biguanides and the quarternary ammonium compounds.

Biguanides

The main biguanide used for controlling plaque is chlorhexidine (see Chapter 9); alexidine is also used. Biguanides are effective against both Gram-positive and Gram-negative micro-organisms. Chlorhexidine destroys bacteria by being adsorbed onto the cell wall, which leads to damage of the permeability barriers. High concentrations cause precipitation and coagulation of the bacterial cytoplasmic contents. It is used as a mouthwash (0.2 per cent aqueous solution), with 10 ml being applied twice daily, or as a toothpaste gel (0.5 to 1 per cent).

Regular twice-daily rinsing with 10 ml chlorhexidine causes an 85 to 95 per cent reduction in salivary bacteria. Bacterial counts return to normal within 48 hours after cessation of the rinses (Loe and Schiott 1970).

Chlorhexidine, although used for inhibiting plaque formation, has no effect on subgingival plaque except by direct irrigation into periodontal pockets (Flotra *et al.* 1971). An important property of chlorhexidine is its ability to bind to various oral surfaces, including tooth enamel, the pellicle, and salivary protein.

Chlorhexidine is mainly used after periodontal surgery where mechanical plaque-control methods may be difficult to achieve until final healing has occurred (Davies 1976). Chlorhexidine mouthwash has also been shown to be useful in the management of aphthous ulceration and denture stomatitis (Addy 1977; Budtz-Jorgensen and Loe 1972).

Unwanted effects

Chlorhexidine has been used for 20 years; as outlined in Chapter 9, most of its unwanted effects are of a local nature. Many patients find the initial taste of this compound unpleasant and repeated use often produces a disturbance in taste, which may last for several hours. Occasional cases of desquamative lesions of the oral mucosa and parotid swelling have been reported, but the incidence is low. The main unwanted effect of chlorhexidine mouthwash or gel is a brown staining of the teeth. Three possible mechanisms may account for this staining; these are as follows—all three mechanisms may contribute to this problem (Eriksen et al. 1985):

1. Non-enzymatic browning reactions (Maillard reactions). Carbohydrates and amino acids can act as substrates for the Maillard reaction. These food substances undergo a series of condensation and polymerization reactions leading to the formation of brown pigmented substances known as melanoids. Melanoid production is catalysed by a high pH and by chlorhexidine (Nordbo 1979). The glycoprotein of the acquired pellicle covering the tooth surface may well serve as a substrate for the Maillard reaction.

2. Formation of pigmented metal sulphides. The glycoprotein molecules of the tooth pellicle contains many disulphide bridges. When the glycoprotein is denatured, these bridges split, yielding free sulphydryl groups. These free groups will react with ferric or stannous ions in the diet to form the corresponding brown or yellow metallic sulphides. Chlorhexidine causes denaturation of the pellicle glycoprotein, which may contribute towards the staining potential (Hjeljord et al. 1973).

3. Reaction between chlorhexidine and factors in the diet. Many factors may be involved in this reaction (Addy et al. 1979). It has been shown that aldehydes and ketones react with chlorhexidine to form coloured products that would attach to a tooth surface. Staining from chlorhexidine is accentuated if there is a heavy consumption of tea, coffee, and red wine, which all contain tannin. Wine causes denaturation of the pellicle glycoprotein; red wine also contains a high amount of iron.

Regular use of chlorhexidine causes thickening of the pellicle, which provides a larger than usual surface area for stain absorption. The thickened pellicle also predisposes towards supragingival calculus formation, which may counteract the benefit of chlorhexidine (Leach and Appleton 1981).

Although staining from chlorhexidine is troublesome, the stain can be removed with a rubber cup and pumice paste.

Quaternary ammonium compounds

Mouthwashes containing either benethonium chloride or cetylpyridinium chloride are the main quaternary ammonium compounds used to control plaque. These compounds have chemical and antibacterial properties, and unwanted effects, similar to those of chlorhexidine. However, they are less effective than chlorhexidine as plaque-inhibiting agents (Hull 1980). This difference in efficacy may be due to the poor adsorption of quaternary ammonium compounds.

Antibiotics

As plaque mainly comprises bacteria, many antibiotics have been evaluated as anti-plaque agents. Two widely used for this purpose are tetracycline and metronidazole. However, it must be stressed that antibiotics should only be used for a short time to support conventional periodontal treatment. Continuous prophylactic use of antibiotics in the treatment of periodontal disease is not recommended.

Tetracycline

The pharmacological properties and unwanted effects of this broad-spectrum antibiotic were discussed in Chapter 10. The drug has been administered either systemically, as a mouthwash, or by direct delivery into periodontal pockets as methods of controlling bacterial plaque. Direct irrigation has the advantage of reducing the amount of tetracycline administered (Lindhe *et al.* 1979). Clinical studies have shown that tetracycline therapy significantly reduces bacterial colonization of teeth and periodontal pockets. The drug is particularly useful in cases of juvenile periodontitis where it reduces the micro-organisms *Actinobacillus actinomycetemcomitans* and Capnocytophaga.

Metronidazole

This is effective against obligate anaerobes (see Chapter 10), and studies have shown that systemic administration retards plaque accumulation and the development of gingivitis. The drug has also been used in the treatment of progressive periodontal disease, where it is effective against *Bact. asacharolyticus*, and in juvenile periodontitis against *A. actinomycetemcomitans* and Capnocytophaga (Mitchell 1984).

Oxygen-releasing agents

Hydrogen peroxide and sodium peroxyborate (Bocasan) are the main oxygen-releasing agents used in the treatment of periodontal disease. Both are restricted to the treatment of acute ulcerative gingivitis, which is thought to be caused by anaerobic bacteria. It is doubtful if the amount of oxygen released has a significant action on the metabolism of anaerobic organisms during the short period of exposure.

DENTINE SENSITIVITY

Painful symptoms arising from exposed dentine are a common finding in the adult population, with an incidence of 1:7. Exposure of dentine can arise from either removal of enamel or denudation of the root surface. Loss of enamel occurs in attrition, erosion, toothbrush abrasion, or caries. Several factors can cause denudation of the root surface including gingival recession with increasing age, chronic peridontal disease, periodontal surgery, incorrect toothbrushing, and trauma (Dowell and Addy 1983).

Dentine sensitivity (erroneously termed hypersensitivity) is characterized by pain, elicited by various stimuli and disappearing when the stimulus is removed. Some people are sensitive to cold alone; others to touch, sweet, or sour foods, and some to a combination of any of these stimuli. The pain may be so severe that they find eating difficult.

Theories of dentine sensitivity

Precisely how external stimuli are transmitted through dentine to the pulp is not established and, although evidence suggests that dentine is innervated, the extent or magnitude of this innervation is uncertain. There are three theories of dentine sensitivity: (a) the dentinal receptor mechanism; (b) the hydrodynamic mechanism; (c) the modulation of nerve impulses by polypeptides.

Dentinal receptor mechanism

This theory suggests that the odontoblast has a sensory function, perhaps serving as a transducer between external stimuli and the nearby pulpal nerve plexus. Certainly, when there is disruption of odontoblasts, the dentine becomes very sensitive (Brannstrom and Astrom 1964). However, pain-inducing substances, such as potassium chloride, 5-hydroxytryptamine, and histamine, have failed to evoke pain when applied to exposed dentine (Brannstrom 1962). This finding would question the nociceptive role of the odontoblast.

Hydrodynamic mechanism

This is the most widely accepted theory of the cause of dentine sensitivity. Dentinal tubules contain fluid; a blast of air, or hot and cold stimuli, will cause a rapid movement of this within the tubules. this movement will cause deformation of both the odontoblastic process and adjacent nerve fibres. Nerve deformation causes pain (Brannstrom 1966).

Modulation of nerve impulses by polypeptide

Pulpal tissue contains a number of polypeptides that can act as regulators of neural transmission. These include substance P and bradykinin, which may alter the permeability of the odontoblast cell membrane (hyperpolarization). Such hyperpolarization could make the pulp more sensitive to various external stimuli. Thus, substance P and bradykinin may act as modulators of nerve impulses in the pulp (Kroeger 1968).

Desensitizing agents

The ideal properties of a desensitizing agent were postulated by Grossman in 1935, and include:

(1) non-irritant to the pulp;

(2) relatively painless on application;

(3) easily applied;

(4) rapid onset of action;

(5) effective permanently;

(6) should not stain the teeth;

(7) consistently effective.

Many agents have been used against dentine sensitivity, and some are discussed below.

Sodium fluoride

This is conveniently applied as a paste, for example Lukomsky's paste, which contains equal parts by weight of sodium fluoride, kaolin, and glycerin. The paste is burnished into the previously dried sensitive area, and left on for about three minutes before the patient is allowed to rinse. Occasionally, paste application may cause marked but transitory pain. Fluoride from the sodium salt will be taken up by the dentine thus making it more resistant to acid decalcification. The fluoride may also lead to an increase in secondary dentine formation, which will block dentinal tubules. Sodium fluoride either in pastes, gels, or mouthwashes has to be applied frequently for maximum effectiveness.

Stannous fluoride

This also reduces dentine sensitivity. In solution it undergoes spontaneous hydrolysis and oxidation, so it is applied in the form of a gel mixed with carboxymethylcellulose or glycerine. Stannous fluoride acts as an enzyme poison and may inactivate enzymic activity within the odontoblastic process. Like sodium fluoride, stannous fluoride induces mineralization within the dentinal tubules, which creates a calcific barrier on the dentine surface.

Sodium monofluorophosphate

This fluoride salt is widely used in toothpastes, but is of uncertain efficacy as a desensitizing agent. It is suggested that monofluorophosphate is hydrolysed by hydroxyapatite on the surface of enamel and dentine. The hydrolysis releases fluoride ions, which are then incorporated into the lattice work of the apatite crystal.

Calcium hydroxide

Although this compound occludes dentinal tubules, its use as a desensitizing agent is uncertain, probably because of its poor adhesion to exposed dentine.

Tresiolan

This comprises a mixture of two siloxane esters, which are immiscible in water. It is a light yellow liquid, marketed in plastic drip bottles. In the presence of moisture, Tresiolan polymerizes, and when applied to the surface of dentine it forms an organosiloxane resinous skin. This skin is probably superficial, although there may be some penetration of the liquid into the surface of the dentinal tubules before polymerization commences. It would appear that this material seals off or plugs the orifices of the dentinal tubules, forming a mechanical barrier against exogenous stimuli.

Tresiolan is applied to the sensitive area by means of a pledget of cotton-wool. The area must be dried before application, and two minutes allowed for the reaction to be complete. It does not cause pain on application, and is not irritant to the oral mucous membrane. As with other densensitizing agents, the action of Tresiolan is not permanent and several applications are usually necessary to produce complete desensitization. The medicament may prove ineffective for some patients.

Strontium chloride

Strontium ions have a strong affinity for calcified tissues, and they also accelerate the rate of calcification. Thus, strontium salts will obliterate the dentinal tubules. Sensodyne toothpaste contains 10 per cent strontium chloride, but the efficacy of this compound in controlling dentine sensitivity is uncertain (Addy and Dowell 1983).

Formaldehyde

Toothpastes containing 1.3 to 1.4 per cent formalin (e.g. Emoform) are used as desensitizing agents, but their unpleasant taste may limit their use. Formalin is thought to precipitate protein in the dentinal tubules and hence reduce sensitivity.

Resins and adhesives

Various of these can be applied to exposed dentine, sealing off the tubules and hence acting as a mechanical barrier to external stimuli. Tooth preparation, such as acid-etching, is required before some of these materials can be applied, so their use should be restricted to the more persistent cases of dentine sensitivity.

CARIES VACCINATION

Dental caries is now recognized as an infectious disease and there has, in recent years, been a revival of interest concerning the use of the body's own defence mechanisms to reduce both the incidence and severity of caries. These mechanisms can, in general, be mobilized by vaccination. Many of the experimental studies in animals have used a vaccine prepared against *Strep. mutans.* The cell wall of this bacterium has many antigens, especially the enzyme glucosyltransferase (GTF), which is responsible for the synthesis of insoluble extracellular mutan. A caries vaccine prepared from Strep mutans, which contains antibodies to GTF, has provided protection against dental caries in animals.

Human caries vaccine

The findings from animal experiments have given impetus to the development of a caries vaccine that can be used both safely and efficaciously in man. However, there are certain drawbacks. For example, caries in the experimental animal was induced by infection with *Strep. mutans,* thus assuming a direct causal relationship between dental caries and that bacterium. In man, this association is less clear and, if a vaccine were to eliminate *mutans,* other bacteria might take on a cariogenic role. Problems have also been encountered of a possible cross-reaction between antigens from the cell wall of *Strep. mutans* and human heart tissue.

A human caries vaccine could easily be incorporated into the general vaccination programme, but dental caries is not a life-threatening disease, and other preventive methods are available for reducing its incidence. If there is any element of doubt as to the safety of a vaccination, then public opinion would be against such a procedure. The future of a caries vaccine for use in man is still questionable (Sims 1985).

REFERENCES

Addy, M. (1977). Hibitane in the treatment of aphthous ulceration. *Journal of Clinical Periodontology,* **4**, 108–16.

Addy, M. and Dowell, P. (1983). Dentine hypersensitivity—a review. Clinical and *in vitro* evaluation of treatment agents. *Journal of Clinical Periodontology,* **10**, 351–63.

Addy, M., Prayitno, S., Taylor, L., and Codogan, S. (1979). An *in vitro* study of the role of dietary factors in the aetiology of tooth staining associated with the use of chlorhexidine. *Journal of Periodontal Research*, **14**, 403–10.

Bibby, B. G. (1947). A consideration of the effectiveness of various fluoride mixtures. *Journal of the American Dental Association*, **34**, 26.

Birkeland, J. M., Jorkjend, L., and von der Fehr, F. R. (1971). The influence of fluoride rinses on the fluoride content of dental plaque in children. *Caries Research*, **5**, 169–79.

Brannstrom, M. (1962). The elicitation of pain in human dentine and pulp by chemical stimulation. *Archives of Oral Biology*, **7**, 59–62.

Brannstrom, M. (1966). Sensitivity of dentine. *Oral Surgery*, **21**, 517–26.

Brannstrom, M. and Astrom, A. (1964). A study on the mechanisms of pain elicited from the dentine. *Journal of Dental Research*, **43**, 619–25.

Brown, W. E., Gregory, T. M., and Chow, L. C. (1977). Effect of fluoride on enamel solubility and cariostasis. *Caries Research*, **11**(suppl. 1), 118–41.

Budtz-Jorgensen, E. and Loe, H. (1972). Chlorhexidine as a denture disinfectant in the treatment of denture stomatitis. *Scandinavian Journal of Dental Research*, **80**, 457–64.

Davies, R. M. (1976). Use of hibitane following periodontal surgery. *Journal of Clinical Periodontology*, **4**, 129–35.

Dowell, P. and Addy, M. (1983). Dentine hypersensitivity—a review. Aetiology, symptoms and theories of pain production. *Journal of Clinical Periodontology*, **10**, 341–50.

Ericsson, Y. (1958). The state of fluoride in milk. *Acta Odontologica Scandinavica*, **16**, 51–7.

Eriksen, H. M., Nordbo, H., Kantanen, H., and Ellingsen, J. E. (1985). Chemical plaque control and extrinsic tooth discoloration—a review of possible mechanisms. *Journal of Clinical Periodontology*, **12**, 345–50.

Flotra, L., Gjermo, P., Rolla, G. and Waerhaug, J. (1971). Side effects of chlorhexidine mouthwashes. *Scandinavian Journal of Dental Research*, **79**, 119–25.

Forrest, J. R. (1956). Caries incidence and enamel defects in areas with different levels of fluoride in the drinking water. *British Dental Journal*, **100**, 195–200.

Gron, P., Spinelli, M., Trautz, O., and Brudevold, F. (1963). The effect of carbonate on the solubility of hydroxyapatittite. *Archives of Oral Biology*, **8**, 251–63.

Grossmann, L. (1935). A systematic method for the treatment of hypersensitive dentine. *Journal of the American Dental Association*, **22**, 592–602.

Hjeljord, L. G., Sonju, T., and Rolla, G. (1973). Chlorhexidine–protein interactions. *Journal of Periodontal Research*, **8**(suppl. 12), 11–16.

Hodge, H. C., Holloway, P. J., Davies, T. G. H., and Worthington, H. V. (1980). Caries prevention by dentrifices containing a combination of sodium monofluorophosphate and sodium fluoride. *British Dental Journal*, **149**, 193–204.

Hull, P. S. (1980). Chemical inhibition of plaque. *Journal of Clinical Periodontology*, **7**, 431–42.

Jenkins, G. N. (1978). *The physiology and biochemistry of the mouth*, (4th edn). Blackwell, Oxford.

Koulourides, T., Keller, S. E., Manson-Hing, L., and Lilley, V. (1980). Enhancement of fluoride effectiveness by experimental cariogenic priming of human enamel. *Caries Research*, **14**, 32–9.

Kroeger, D. C. (1968). Possible role of neurohormonal substances in the pulp. In *Biology of the dental Pulp organ* (ed. S. B. Finn), pp. 334–46. Alabama Press, Birmingham University, Ill.

Kruger, B. J. (1970). The effect of different levels of fluoride on the ultrastructure of ameloblasts in the rate. *Archives of Oral Biology*, **15**, 109–14.

Leach, S. A. and Appleton, J. (1981). Ultrastructural investigation by energy dispersive X-ray micro-analysis of some of the elements involved in the formation of dental plaque and pellicle. In *Tooth surface interactions and preventitive dentistry*, pp. 65–79. IRL Press, London.

Lindhe, J., Heijil, L., Goodson, J. M., and Socransky, S. S. (1979). Local tetracycline delivery using hollow fibre devices in periodontal therapy. *Journal of Clinical Periodontology*, **6**, 141–49.

Loe, H. and Schiott, C. R. (1970). The effect of mouthrinses and topical application of chlorhexidine on the development of dental plaque and gingivitis in man. *Journal of Periodontal Research*, **5**, 79–83.

Mainwaring, P. J. and Naylor, M. N. (1983). A four-year clinical study to determine the caries inhibiting effect of calcium glycophosphate and sodium fluoride in calcium carbonate base dentifrices containing sodium monofluorophosphate. *Caries Research*, **17**, 267–76.

Mitchell, D. A. (1984). Metronidazole: its use in clinical dentistry. *Journal of Clinical Periodontology*, **11**, 145–58.

Murray, J. J. and Rugg-Gunn, A. J. (1982). *Fluoride in Caries Prevention* (2nd edn). Wright, Bristol.

Nordbo, H. (1979). Ability of chlorhexidine and benzalconium chloride to catalyze browning reactions *in vitro*. *Journal of Dental Research*, **58**, 1429.

Nordin, B. E. C. (1973). *Metabolic bone and stone disease*. Churchill Livingstone, Edinburgh.

Sims, W. (1985). *Streptococcus mutans* and vaccines for dental caries: a personal commentary and critique. *Community Dental Health*, **2**, 129–47.

Weatherell, J. A., Robinson, C., and Hallsworth, A. S. (1972). Changes in the fluoride concentration of the labial enamel surface with age. *Caries Research*, **6**, 312–24.

12

Haemostasis and haemostatic agents

HAEMOSTASIS

SEVERAL factors play an integrated role in the arrest of haemorrhage after a tooth extraction or dental surgery. These include the ability of vessel walls to contract, the adhesion and aggregation of platelets, the ability of blood to coagulate, and the breakdown of blood clot (fibrinolysis). A variety both of diseases and drugs can affect these factors. However, in the context of this Chapter only the effect of drugs will be discussed.

Vessel wall contraction

In the early stages of injury, contraction of the smooth muscles in vessel walls is an important factor in the control of haemorrhage. This vasoconstriction is only of short duration (usually 5 to 20 minutes) but can be prolonged by topical or local infiltration of adrenaline.

Platelets

These are non-nuclear cells with a cytoplasm rich in granules. They are formed by the fragmentation and detachment of delicate processes from the megakaryocyte. The normal platelet count in man is in the range 150 000–400 000 cells/ml, and their half-life is 7 to 10 days. Platelets have an essential role in haemostasis: when a blood vessel is cut or damaged, they rapidly adhere to the exposed sub-endothelial tissues, especially collagen. This platelet adhesion is followed by the release from the platelet granules of adenosine diphosphate (ADP) and the powerful pro-aggregating substance, thromboxane A_2 (TXA_2), (Hamburg *et al.* 1975). Both ADP and thromboxane induce further platelets to stick to each other (platelet aggregation) to form a platelet plug. The plug will arrest haemorrhage, but it must be further stabilized by fibrin. Fibrin formation is stimulated by the exposed cut collagen, platelet membranes, and chemicals released by the platelets themselves, such as 5-hydroxytryptamine and platelet phospholipid (Walsh 1974).

Blood coagulation

This is a complex process that involves the initiation and interaction of several factors in blood and damaged tissues (Fig. 12.1). The basic framework of blood coagulation is the activity of thromboplastin (Factor III) on prothrombin (Factor II) to form thrombin, which in turn converts fibrinogen (Factor I) to fibrin. Fibrin is further polymerized by Factor XIII.

Thromboplastin activity can be generated in two ways—by an intrinsic system (blood thromboplastin), or an extrinsic system (tissue thromboplastin). Activation of the intrinsic system occurs when blood contacts an abnormal surface. This leads to the sequential activation of Factors XII, XI, IX, VIII, and X. Activated Factor X (Xa) together with Factor V and phospholipids derived from platelets result in the formation of thromboplastin (Fig. 12.1). The extrinsic system is

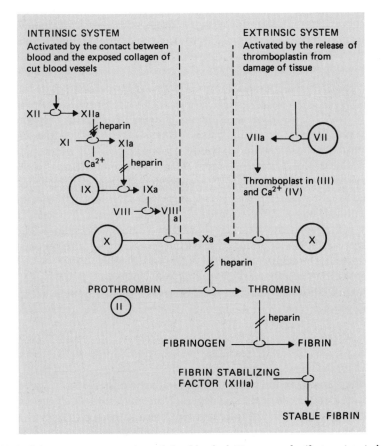

Fig. 12.1. Schematic representation of the blood clotting cascade (factors in circles are dependent on vitamin K for their synthesis, and are affected by warfarin).

activated by tissue damage, which results in the release of a tissue factor rich in phospholipid. The tissue factor, together with Factor VII, activates Factor X. The sequence of events is then the same as in the intrinsic system.

Calcium ions (Factor IV) are essential for many of the stages of blood coagulation and help to accelerate the reaction between thrombin and fibrinogen.

Vitamin K

Vitamin K is a fat-soluble vitamin that is essential for the normal hepatic biosynthesis of several factors required for blood clotting (II, VII, IX, X). The pharmacology of vitamin K is dealt with in more detail in Chapter 19.

The main use of vitamin K is the correction of hypoprothrombinaemia—either congenital, or drug-induced by the coumarin group of anticoagulants (see later). Excessive bleeding from patients on these anticoagulants can be corrected by an intravenous injection of 10 to 20 mg vitamin K. Careful monitoring of the prothrombin time and anticoagulant levels are necessary following this procedure. Vitamin K is also used to treat hypoprothrombinaemia of the newborn.

Fibrinolysis

The final state of haemostasis—the breakdown of blood clot by proteolytic enzymes—is known as fibrinolysis. Extravascularly, as in the case of a haematoma, the proteolytic enzymes are produced by white blood cells. Intravascularly, blood clots are broken down by plasmin, which is derived from the plasma protein, plasminogen. The conversion of plasminogen to plasmin may be caused by either tissue or blood activators (Fig. 12.2). The tissue factor has not been identified, but may be released as a result of tissue damage. The blood activator is formed by the action of kinases on a blood pro-activator. The kinases are liberated from blood, tissues, and certain bacteria (e.g. streptococci produce streptokinase (see later)).

Fibrinolysis can be influenced by a whole range of factors; for example, age, sex, diet, smoking, altitude, and exercise. It can be inhibited by the inactivation of plasmin by the protein, α_2 antiplasmin.

ANTICOAGULANTS

These either directly or indirectly interfere with the normal clotting mechanisms of blood, and thus reduce the incidence of thrombo-embolic disorders. Hence, patients likely to be receiving anticoagulant therapy include those with a history of myocardial infarction, cerebrovascular thrombosis, venous thrombosis, and pulmonary embolism. Those on renal dialysis also receive anticoagulant therapy prior to and during dialysis.

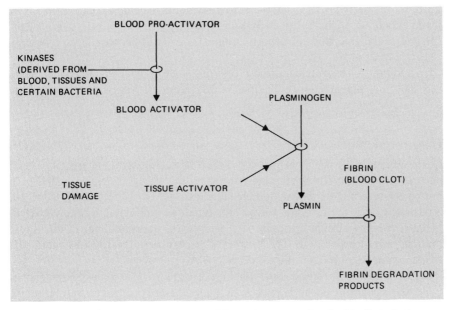

Fig. 12.2. Schematic representation of the various stages involved in fibrinolysis.

Heparin

This glycosaminoglycan occurs in minute amounts in mast cells, but its physiological function is unclear. The drug was 'accidentally' discovered in 1916, although its widespread use as an anticoagulant did not occur until the early 1940s. The synthetic drug is the only effective direct-acting anticoagulant, that is it is immediately effective on fresh blood.

Pharmacodynamics

Heparin interferes with blood coagulation in two ways, both of which are due to the formation of a plasma co-factor (antithrombin III). Firstly, antithrombin III neutralizes several of the activated clotting factors, namely XII, XI, IX, X, II, and XIII. Secondly, antithrombin III inactivates thrombin by forming an irreversible complex with the clotting protein. The activity of antithrombin III is related to the dose of heparin—the lower the dose, the greater the activity particularly against thrombin.

Pharmacological properties

Heparin must be administered parenterally as it is very poorly absorbed from the gut because the drug is highly ionized. It is metabolized in the liver by the enzyme heparinase, and the metabolites excreted via the kidney. After intravenous infusion, the half-life of heparin is one to three hours. Low doses of heparin can be given subcutaneously, but high doses should be given via an intravenous drip. Intramuscular injections of heparin should be avoided because large haematomas can form at the site of injection.

In addition to the anticoagulant properties of heparin, the drug also causes a reduction in plasma concentration of triglycerides. This is of little or no therapeutic value.

Unwanted effects

Haemorrhage is the principle unwanted effect associated with heparin; it usually occurs from the gastro-intestinal or genito-urinary tract. Hence, heparin should not be given to any patient with a bleeding disorder or ulceration of the gastro-intestinal tract. Careful monitoring of the patient's prothrombin time whilst on heparin therapy should minimize the problem of haemorrhage. Prothrombin time is now reported as the British Comparative Ratio (BCR), and the recommended therapeutic range is 2.0 to 4.0.

A mild transient thrombocytopenia is reported to occur in about 25 per cent of patients receiving heparin. However, in a few, thrombocytopenia can be severe and deaths have occurred. Platelet counts should be carried out at regular intervals for all those on heparin therapy.

Commercial preparations of heparin are obtained from animal tissues, and care should be exercised in their use on patients with any history of allergy. Long-term heparin therapy can cause osteoporosis and alopecia.

The anticoagulant effects of heparin can be reversed by the specific antagonist, protamine sulphate, at the dose regime of 1 mg of protamine for every 100 units of heparin. Protamine acts by combining with heparin to form a stable complex that has no anticoagulant properties. This complex is formed through heparin being electronegative and protamine electropositive.

Coumarin anticoagulants

This group, also known as the oral anticoagulants, includes warfarin sodium and phenindione. Coumarin anticoagulants are derived from a substance found in the spoiled sweet clover plant.

Pharmacodynamics

Coumarin anticoagulants are antagonists to vitamin K. Hence they will reduce the synthesis of the vitamin K-dependent clotting factors (II, VII, IX, and X). Because of the varying rate of synthesis of these factors, there is a delay of 8 to 12 hours before a therapeutic response can be obtained after a coumarin anticoagulant. Many factors can affect the activity of these anticoagulants, including diet, small-bowel disease, pyrexia, age, pregnancy, and liver disease.

Pharmacological properties

Warfarin sodium, which is the archetype of the coumarin anticoagulants, is rapidly absorbed and extensively (98 per cent) bound to plasma protein. Its plasma half-life is 35–37 hours. The drug is metabolized in the liver, and the metabolites are excreted in the urine and faeces. Coumarin anticoagulants differ from heparin in that they are effective when given by mouth and have a much longer duration of action.

Unwanted effects

Haemorrhage is the most common unwanted effect, and regular monitoring of the prothrombin (BCR) time (which assesses the efficacy of the anticoagulant) is essential for patients on these drugs. Haemorrhagic problems include haematuria, ecchymosis, epistaxis, and gingival bleeding (O'Reilly 1976). Such problems are treated by withdrawal of the drug, followed by the oral or intravenous administration of vitamin K (10–20 mg) depending on the severity of the haemorrhage. Withdrawal of anticoagulant therapy must be done in consultation with the patient's physician.

Drug interactions

Coumarin anticoagulants are frequently implicated in drug interactions that can either increase or decrease the anticoagulant response. Drugs that increase this response include aspirin, metronidazole, and co-trimoxazole.

Aspirin should not be given to patients on coumarin anticoagulant therapy: as few as one or two aspirin tablets can impair platelet function by blocking the release of ADP and the powerful aggregatory substance, thromboxane A_2 (see earlier). As a consequence of these properties of aspirin, there is a weak and poorly formed platelet plug; the impairment of platelet function, together with the impairment in blood coagulation, can lead to a fatal haemorrhage. Other aspirin-like drugs, such as non-steroidal anti-inflammatory agents (see Chapter 5), may also affect platelet aggregation, and should similarly be avoided in patients on coumarin anticoagulants. Aspirin also displaces warfarin from the plasma-protein binding site, the result being an enhancement of the anticoagulant effect of warfarin.

Metronidazole and co-trimoxazole interfere with the pharmacokinetics of warfarin, resulting in an increase in the drug's half-life. Hence concomitant administration of these antimicrobials with warfarin will enhance the anticoagulant effect.

Barbiturates are the main group of drugs that decrease the anticoagulant response of warfarin. Barbiturates cause an induction of hepatic microsomal enzymes, which increase the metabolism of the anticoagulant. This increase in clearance causes a decrease in hypoprothrombinaemia.

Vitamin C in massive doses can reduce the hypoprothrombinaemic effect of coumarin anticoagulants in some patients. The mechanism of this interaction is unclear, but vitamin C may reduce the absorption of these drugs.

ANTITHROMBOTIC DRUGS

Antithrombotic or antiplatelet drugs decrease thrombin formation. Aspirin has been widely investigated for this purpose; other antithrombotic drugs are dipyridamole and sulphinpyrazone.

Aspirin and platelet aggregation

Aspirin causes an increase in bleeding time by reducing platelet aggregation (O'Brien 1968; Weiss *et al.* 1968). The haemostatic response to aspirin shows marked inter-individual variation (Seymour *et al.* 1984). Aspirin inhibits the release of ADP from platelets and prevents aggregation by irreversibly blocking (acetylating) the platelet cyclo-oxygenase enzyme system (Roth *et al.* 1975). This prevents the formation of the powerful platelet aggregating substance, thromboxane A_2. The anti-aggregatory effect of aspirin lasts for the life-span of the platelet (7 to 10 days), and a single dose of 600 mg may produce detectable effects on platelet aggregation and bleeding time for several days. Normal platelet aggregation is only restored when new platelets are released into the circulation.

In addition to the action on platelet cyclo-oxygenase, aspirin also inhibits the synthesis of vessel-wall prostacyclin (Vane 1978). It is thought that prostacyclin inhibition occurs with higher doses of aspirin (over 1 g per day). Furthermore, vascular endothelial cells are less sensitive to aspirin than are platelets, so cyclo-oxygenase activity in vessel walls can be quickly restored (Preston *et al.* 1981).

Use of aspirin in the prevention of thrombo-embolic disorders

There has been much interest in the use of aspirin in the prevention of thrombo-embolic disorders such as transient ischaemic attacks (TIAs), myocardial infarction, cerebrovascular disease, and venous thrombo-embolism. However, there remains much controversy as to the most suitable dose of aspirin for such conditions. The confusion has arisen from reports claiming that large doses of aspirin inhibit both thromboxane and prostacyclin biosynthesis, whereas low doses of aspirin selectively inhibit platelet thromboxane synthesis.

Aspirin (600 mg per day) has been shown to be effective in reducing the incidence of TIAs (Fields 1983), but its efficacy in preventing myocardial infarction is equivocal (Elwood 1983; Lewis *et al.* 1983). Further studies are therefore required, with perhaps different dose regimes, to determine whether aspirin is of any value in preventing such life-threatening conditions.

DENTAL MANAGEMENT OF PATIENTS WITH HAEMOSTATIC PROBLEMS

Haemostatic problems that the dental surgeon is likely to encounter can be broadly classified into three groups:

(1) impaired platelet function;

(2) vascular defects;

(3) impaired coagulation.

In all patients with haemostatic problems, careful treatment planning and consultation with their physician are essential. When surgery is required, such patients are best treated in a Dental Hospital or Oral Surgery Department. Every attempt should be made to obtain adequate haemostasis during the operative procedure (i.e. by suturing and packing sockets).

Impaired platelet function

This may be due to a reduction in platelet count (thrombocytopenia), or impaired aggregation resulting from drug therapy.

Thrombocytopenia occurs when the normal platelet count (range 150 000–400 000 cells/ml blood) falls below 100 000 cells/ml. It can be caused by a variety of factors such as radiotherapy, connective tissue disease, or leukaemia. In patients with a low platelet count (less than 50 000 cells/ml blood), a platelet transfusion may be necessary just prior to a dental surgical procedure (i.e. tooth extraction or periodontal surgery). If the thrombocytopenia is due to immune destruction of platelets, as occurs in idiopathic thrombocytopenic purpura, then corticosteroids need to be administered, either instead of or with the platelet infusion.

Drugs that cause impairment of platelet aggregation and an increase in bleeding time include aspirin and non-steroidal anti-inflammatory drugs (see above), sodium valproate, and phenytoin. When tooth extractions are carried out on patients taking these drugs it is a wise precaution to suture and pack the socket and hence minimize the risk of post-extraction haemorrhage.

Vascular defects

Those that can cause impairment of naemostasis are associated with vitamin C deficiency (ascorbutic) and long-term corticosteroid therapy. Vitamin C is essential for collagen synthesis and a deficiency causes scurvy. Ascorbutic patients have increased capillary fragility, which can cause bleeding problems after surgery. Long-term corticosteroid therapy can cause both a thrombocytopenia and an inadequate constriction of the small vessels after surgery. Both factors can lead to haemorrhagic problems. Patients undergoing dental surgery with such vascular defects can present with these problems of haemorrhage. Usually this can be controlled by pressure, suturing, and packing.

Impaired coagulation

This can be due to either an inherited coagulation defect (for example, haemophilia, von Willebrand's disease, or Christmas disease) or to anticoagulant therapy.

Haemophilia

This is a sex-linked, inherited coagulation disorder that usually affects only males. Patients have a reduced Factor VIII activity, which can be corrected by replacement therapy of freeze-dried Factor VIII (cryoprecipitate). Any dental procedures that involve haemorrhage, such as extractions or scaling, will put the haemophiliac patient at risk. All dental procedures should be carefully planned and carried out with Factor VIII cover. The dose of Factor VIII is dependent upon the severity of the haemophilia. Factor VIII cover may need to be repeated as it is only effective for 12 hours. Other drugs used in conjunction with Factor VIII include the anti-fibrinolytic agent, epsilon aminocaproic acid, which reduces the Factor VIII requirements. This drug should be started pre-operatively and continued until all risk of haemorrhage has ceased.

Christmas disease

This is associated with a deficiency of Factor IX; clinically, the disease is identical to haemophilia. Factor IX is derived from plasma, but is not present in cryoprecipitate. The half-life of Factor IX is greater than that of Factor VIII, so replacement therapy is given at longer intervals. The dental management of patients with Christmas disease is the same as for haemophiliacs.

Von Willebrand's disease

This is an inherited disorder associated with both a prolonged bleeding time and a deficiency of Factor VIII, although the latter shows marked individual variation. When Factor VIII levels are low, replacement therapy is necessary if surgery is to be carried out on these patients.

Anti-coagulant therapy

Heparin

Heparinized patients are usually confined to hospital; this group will include those with recent thrombo-embolic disorders and those undergoing renal dialysis. The anticoagulant effects of heparin will last for four to six hours after a single dose. If an emergency extraction is needed on a heparinized patient it should be carried out when the anticoagulant effect is minimal. Patients on continuous heparin therapy should be given intravenous protamine sulphate at the dosage of 1 mg per 100 units of heparin. Monitoring the patient's prothrombin time (BCR) is essential.

Coumarin anticoagulants

If elective surgery, such as removal of an impacted lower third molar, is required for patients on coumarin anticoagulants, consultation with the patient's physician is essential, so that dose regimes can be altered. Prothrombin activity should be measured prior to surgery. Usually, vitamin K (5 mg) is given the day before surgery, or 2.5 mg vitamin K given orally for two days before surgery. The 5 mg dose of vitamin K will bring the prothrombin activity from the so-called 'therapeutic range' of 25 per cent of normal, up to the normal range (90–100 per cent activity). The 2.5 mg dose regimen of vitamin K will bring the value to 50 to 60 per cent of normal activity. The prothrombin activity will return to its previous level of 25 per cent in about four days.

Emergency single extractions can be carried out on patients taking coumarin anticoagulants, provided their prothrombin time does not exceed 2 to 2.5 times the normal value. Sockets should be packed and sutured. If haemorrhage does occur, the anticoagulant effect can be reversed by intravenous vitamin K (phytomenadione, 10–20 mg).

FIBRINOLYTIC DRUGS

This group of drugs promotes the breakdown of thrombi by activation of plasminogen to form plasmin. Examples include streptokinase and urokinase. Fibrinolytic drugs have a prolonged effect on haemostasis and can cause extensive problems if not used carefully.

Streptokinase

This is a protein derived from β-haemolytic streptococci, which interacts with the pro-activator of plasminogen. The combination of pro-activator and streptokinase catalyses the conversion of plasminogen to plasmin. Bleeding from the site of injection is a common problem associated with streptokinase administration. Streptokinase is used to treat acute pulmonary embolism and deep vein thrombosis. The drug is extremely expensive, which imposes restrictions on its routine use.

Urokinase

This is a proteolytic enzyme that activates the conversion of plasminogen to plasmin. The drug is as active as streptokinase and is used in patients who are allergic to the streptokinase.

ANTIFIBRINOLYTIC DRUGS

These encourage the stabilization of fibrin by inhibiting plasminogen activation. Examples include epsilon-aminocaproic acid or the more potent, tranexamic acid.

Antifibrinolytic agents may be useful in controlling persistent haemorrhage after tooth extraction, in conjunction with local measures. However, their main use is in haemophiliacs as an adjunct to Factor VIII therapy. Unwanted effects associated with antifibrinolytic drugs include nausea, diarrhoea, and hypotension.

THE MANAGEMENT OF POST-EXTRACTION HAEMORRHAGE

A careful and detailed history should be taken from all patients presenting with a post-extraction haemorrhage. This is essential to ensure that there is no underlying systemic disease or drug therapy (e.g. aspirin or anticoagulant therapy) contributing to the haemorrhage. If the patient has a predisposing problem, then the appropriate treatment should be carried out as previously outlined.

Most cases of post-extraction haemorrhage are due to tears in the mucoperiosteum around the tooth socket. In the majority of such cases, a suture will effectively control the haemorrhage. Further aids to haemostasis can be obtained by placing an absorbable material in the socket. These materials are made of either cellulose, alginate, gelatin, or fibrin, and provide a network that activates the clotting mechanisms.

Surgicel (oxidized regenerated cellulose) is the most widely and easily applied resorbable material. It is available in strips and can be cut and placed in the tooth socket. Surgicel resorbs within 7 to 10 days, and foreign-body reactions are rare.

REFERENCES

Elwood, P. C. (1983). British studies of aspirin and myocardial infarction. *American Journal of Medicine*, **74**, 50–4.

Fields, W. S. (1983). Aspirin for prevention of stroke. *American Journal of Medicine*, **74**, 61–5.

Hamberg, M., Svenson, J., and Samuelsson, B. (1975). Thromboxanes: a new group of biologically active compounds derived from prostaglandin endoperoxides. *Proceedings of the National Academy of Sciences U.S.A.*, **72**, 2994–8.

Lewis, H. D. *et al.* (1983). Protective effects of aspirin against acute myocardial infarction and death in men with unstable angina. *New England Journal of Medicine*, **309**, 396–403.

O'Brien, J. R. (1968). Aspirin and platelet aggregation. *Lancet*, **i**, 204–5.

O'Reilly, R. A. (1976). Vitamin K and the oral anticoagulant drugs. *Annual Review of Medicine*, **27**, 245–61.

Preston, F. E., Whipps, S., Jackson, C. A., French, A. J., Wyld, P. J., and Stoddard, C. J. (1981). Inhibition of prostacyclin and platelet thromboxane A$_2$ after low dose aspirin. *New England Journal of Medicine*, **304**, 76–9.

Roth, G. J. and Majerus, P. W. (1975). The mechanism of the effect of aspirin on human platelets I: acetylation of a particular fraction protein. *Journal of Clinical Investigation*, **56**, 624–32.

Seymour, R. A. *et al.* (1984). A comparative study of the effects of aspirin and paracetamol (acetaminophen) on platelet aggregation and bleeding time. *European Journal of Clinical Pharmacology*, **26**, 567–71.

Vane, J. R. (1978). Inhibitors of prostaglandin, prostacyclin and thromboxane synthesis. *Advances in Prostaglandin and Thromboxane Research*, **4**, 27–44.

Walsh, P. N. (1974). Platelet coagulant activities and haemostasis: a hypothesis. *Blood*, **47**, 597–605.

Weiss, H. J., Aledort, L. M., and Kochwa, S. (1968). The effect of salicylates on the haemostatic properties of platelets in man. *Journal of Clinical Investigation*, **47**, 2169–80.

PART II

GENERAL DRUGS

13

Autonomic nervous system

GENERAL ORGANIZATION

THE autonomic nervous system consists of two main parts:

(1) central

(2) peripheral, which in turn consists of;

    (i) sympathetic (thoracolumbar outflow; lateral horn cells T1–L2);

    (ii) parasympathetic (craniosacral outflow: cranial nuclei 3, 7, 9, and 10; lateral horn cells, sacral 2–4.

Classically, the peripheral autonomic nervous system has been considered to be exclusively efferent. However, it is clear that certain *afferent* nerves form an essential functional part of the system; for example, visceral afferent, vagal afferent, and nociceptive fibres, which travel with specific nerves. These afferent nerves form the afferent arm of various important autonomic reflexes. Thus, the afferent fibres from the viscera consist mainly of non-myelinated fibres and form the primary afferent neurones in autonomic reflex arcs that are concerned with respiratory, vasomotor, and other functions. Integration of these reflexes takes place initially in the spinal cord but their overall integration takes place centrally, particularly in the hypothalamus.

Central autonomic nervous system

The organization of the central autonomic nervous system is illustrated diagrammatically in Fig. 13.1. The 'head' of the central autonomic is the hypothalamus. It receives its input from somatic and visceral afferent fibres and, after functional integration of this information, controls those organs and systems that it supplies via the sympathetic and parasympathetic outflows. The hypothalamus contains many nuclei, of which those located posterolaterally are mainly sympathetic in function, whilst those anteromedially are mainly concerned with the parasympathetic system. The hypothalamus also has important connections with the pituitary gland (hypophysis), limbic system, thalamocortical system, and brain stem. Furthermore, it receives and integrates information about the milieu from receptors sensitive to temperature, ionic concentration (osmolarity), and hormone concentration. Through these interac-

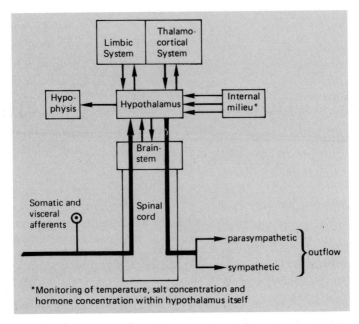

Fig. 13.1 The organization of the central autonomic nervous system

tions it is responsible for the regulation of visceral, metabolic, and endocrine functions, which include the following:

Cardiovascular system	Respiration
Swallowing	Feeding
Vomiting	Metabolism
Temperature	Micturition
Defaecation	Sexual function
Emotions	Sleep
Endocrine mechanisms	

Thus it can be seen that the autonomic nervous system, through its central and peripheral parts, is responsible for controlling those vital body functions that require constant monitoring and adjustment, not only to control the internal milieu but to adapt it to rapidly changing requirements and environmental conditions.

Drugs acting upon the autonomic nervous system may be divided into two broad categories. first, those designed to act upon some part of it; for example, adrenoceptor blocking drugs, antimuscarinic drugs. Second, drugs not designed to act upon the autonomic nervous system but that nevertheless, through lack of specificity, produce various actions upon it that manifest themselves as unwanted effects; for example, antimuscarinic effects of tricyclic antidepressants, hypotensive action of neuroleptics (antipsychotics).

Peripheral efferent parts of the autonomic nervous system

The efferent pathways of the autonomic nervous system, both sympathetic and parasympathetic divisions, transmit impulses to the effector cells from central connections. The peripheral efferent portions of the system comprise preganglionic and postganglionic neurones (Fig. 13.2). The preganglionic neurone arises from cells of central origin and ends at the ganglion. From cell bodies within the ganglion fibres arise that pass to the effector cells, and these fibres comprise the postganglionic neurone.

The sympathetic outflow is limited to the thoracic and upper lumbar segments of the spinal cord. Between the first thoracic and second lumbar segments (inclusive), the grey matter of the spinal cord has lateral horns. The sympathetic neurones have their cell bodies in these horns, and the preganglionic fibres pass out via the anterior nerve roots. These fibres enter the sympathetic chain, which runs on either side of the spinal cord. This chain extends for the whole length of the spinal cord; it has a swelling or ganglion associated with each spinal segment with the exception of the cervical region, where there are only three ganglia (superior, middle, and inferior cervical ganglia). The preganglionic fibres may run up or down the sympathetic chain before synapsing with a postganglionic fibre in one of the ganglia. Each postganglionic fibre leaves the chain and runs to its

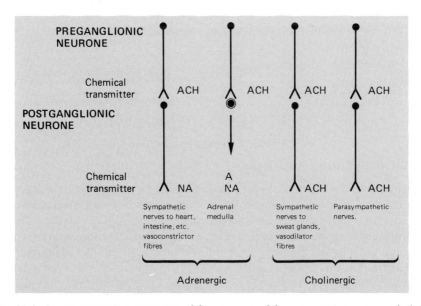

Fig. 13.2. Diagrammatic representation of the neurones of the autonomic nervous with their related chemical transmitters. Left: adrenergic; right: cholinergic. Note that although nerves to the sweat glands are anatomically part of the sympathetic nervous system, pharmacologically they are included with the cholinergic division (ACH = acetylcholine; A = Adrenaline; NA = noradrenaline).

destination in a mixed motor and sensory nerve. The cranial sympathetic fibres run in the outer coat (adventitia) of blood vessels—the internal carotid and external carotid arteries, and their branches.

In the parasympathetic nervous system the nerves leave the central nervous system (CNS) in the spinal region only at the second, third and fourth lumbar segments but, in addition, there is an important outflow in some of the cranial nerves that arise from the brain itself; thus the parasympathetic system has a craniosacral outflow. By far the most widely distributed cranial nerve is the tenth cranial nerve or vagus, which supplies the contents of the thorax and the abdomen.

A gap, called a synapse, exists between the preganglionic and the postganglionic neurones, and a similar junction occurs between the postganglionic neurone and the autonomic effector organ, so that there must be a mechanism for bridging these junctions. It is generally agreed that transmission at synapses is performed by chemical mediators or transmitters. The transmitter liberated at all preganglionic nerve endings, and at parasympathetic post-ganglionic nerve endings, is acetylcholine. Adrenergic transmission, which occurs between post-ganglionic sympathetic nerve endings and the effectors innervated by them, is mediated by noradrenaline. Noradrenaline is important in the maintenance of normal sympathetic tone, not only by virtue of being a chemical transmitter, but also as a result of being released in appropriate amounts from the adrenal medulla into the general circulation.

SYMPATHETIC NERVOUS SYSTEM

The adrenal medulla secretes a number of catecholamines, which are associated with the functioning of the sympathetic nervous system.

Occurrence and synthesis of catecholamines

Three catecholamines occur in the body: these are dopamine, noradrenaline, and adrenaline; a fourth, isoprenaline, is a product of the laboratory. Adrenaline and noradrenaline are secreted by the adrenal medulla; noradrenaline is found concentrated in granules in postganglionic sympathetic neurones; and dopamine is also present in postganglionic sympathetic nerves. Dopamine, noradrenaline, and adrenaline are all found in the brain.

Noradrenaline is synthesized in the neurones from tyrosine through the action of three enzymes (1) tyrosine hydroxylase, (2) dopa decarboxylase, and (3) dopamine-β-hydroxylase. In the neurone, synthesis stops at the stage of noradrenaline formation but, in the adrenal medulla, a further enzymatic step results in the methylation of noradrenaline to become adrenaline (Fig. 13.3).

Fig. 13.3. The intermediate stages in the formation of adrenaline. Note that the last stage, in which noradrenaline is methylated to adrenaline, only occurs in the adrenal medulla. (From A. Wilson and H. O. Schild (1968). *Applied Pharmacology*, (10th edn), p. 77. Churchill, London.)

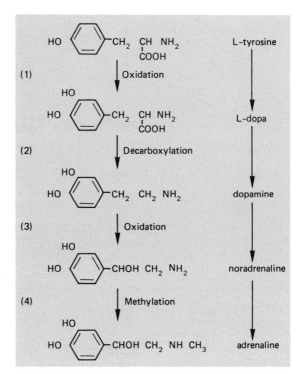

Stages of chemical transmission at synapses

The main stages in synaptic transmission (Fig. 13.4) are as follows:

(1) synthesis of the chemical transmitter from tyrosine;

(2) storage of the chemical transmitter in special granules;

(3) release of the chemical transmitter from storage sites;

(4) activation of post-synaptic receptors leading to stimulation or inhibition of the effector organ;

(5) inactivation of the chemical transmitter, principally through re-uptake into the sympathetic nerve endings.

It is thought that postganglionic sympathetic neurones, adrenal medullary cells, and certain cells in the CNS synthesize catecholamines and store them in granules. The arrival of a nerve impulse at the nerve endings results in the release of the transmitter from the storage granules. The transmitter is released from the postganglionic sympathetic nerve endings and, after diffusing across the synaptic cleft, activates receptors situated on the postsynaptic membrane. This will result

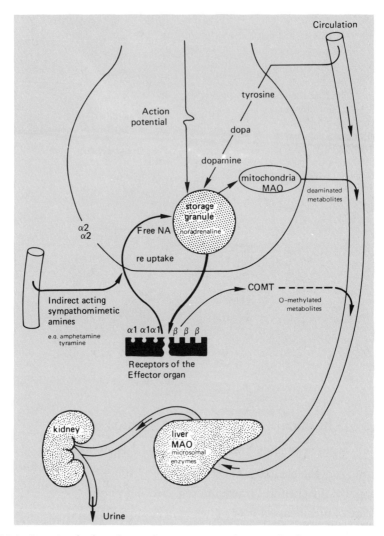

Fig. 13.4. Steps involved in the synthesis, storage, release, and subsequent metabolism of noradrenaline at a postganglionic sympathetic nerve ending (NA = noradrenaline; COMT = catechol-O-methyl transferase; MAO = monoamine oxidase; α = α-receptors; β = β-receptors).

in an action that depends upon the effector organ involved; for example, the contraction of vascular smooth muscle.

There are other amines with actions, like those of the catecholamines, that mimic sympathetic stimulation. At first it was believed that all these drugs acted in the same way as the naturally occurring catecholamines. Later it became clear that, whereas the endogenous adrenaline and noradrenaline act directly upon adrenergic receptors, other drugs (such as amphetamine and tyramine) act indirectly by causing the release of the transmitter substance from the nerve endings. It is now thought that indirectly acting sympathomimetic amines are taken up first by the amine pump (see below), and then by the granule pump, with the result that they displace noradrenaline from its storage sites in the granules (see Fig. 13.4); the noradrenaline so released then acts in the normal way.

Receptors for catecholamines

Postsynaptic receptors for catecholamines are of two types, described as alpha (α) and beta (β) receptors. A number of factors appear to determine the effects produced by a chemical compound that stimulates these receptors. For example, the chemical configuration determines which receptor or receptors will be activated and to what degree. Another factor is the distribution of the α- and β- receptors in the tissues under consideration. For instance, in certain smooth muscles there is a preponderance of β-receptors so that, even if a particular compound is able to stimulate both α- and β-receptors, in these muscles the β effects will predominate. The smooth muscle of blood vessels in skin contains α- receptors, whereas the smooth muscle in vessels supplying the skeletal musculature possesses both α- and β-receptors, although the β-receptors predominate.

Noradrenaline acts mainly on α-receptors whilst isoprenaline acts mainly on β- receptors, whereas adrenaline acts on both. In terms of α- and β-receptor stimulating activity, the relative potencies of noradrenaline, isoprenaline, and adrenaline vary according to the tissue involved, but in general terms are as follows:

	Relative potency on receptors		Selectivity for receptors
	α	β	
Noradrenaline	1	1	α, and β_1, weak β_2
Isoprenaline	1/10–1/50	100	β, slight α
Adrenaline	2–10	10–50	α and β

It should be noted that noradrenaline has a greater selectivity for α-receptors than adrenaline, but weight for weight, adrenaline is the more potent activator of α- receptors.

Distribution of receptors

Alpha receptors (Fig. 13.4) have been subdivided into:

(1) prejunctional receptors, designated as α_2-receptors;

(2) postjunctional receptors, designated as α_1-receptors;

α_1-receptors are mainly located postjunctionally and therefore are responsible for the initiation of postsynaptic events. On the other hand, α_2-receptors are certainly, in part, located on presynaptic nerve terminals; activation of these receptors inhibits the release of noradrenaline. There are also α_2-postjunctional receptors in the CNS, and stimulation of these causes a reduced sympathetic outflow.

Beta receptors have been subdivided into:

(a) β_1-receptors, found chiefly at cardiac sites;

(b) β_2-receptors, found in bronchial smooth muscle, blood vessels of skeletal muscle.

Effects of sympathetic stimulation on various parts

See Table 13.1.

Inactivation of catecholamines

There are at least three ways in which catecholamines are inactivated; by uptake into sympathetic neurones, or by attack from two different enzymes. Sympathetic neurones, as we have seen, have the ability to take up catecholamines, and to bind them within storage granules. This so-called 'amine pump' mechanism is the principal factor in the inactivation of injected catecholamines, and also of noradrenaline released through sympathetic stimulation. The re-uptake mechanism is an example of a very economical use of resources, as noradrenaline released from sympathetic nerve endings is, in the main, re-housed and used again.

At one time the enzyme monoamine oxidase (MAO) was believed to be mainly responsible for the inactivation of catecholamines. Although the main source of the inactivation is re-uptake, it is now clear tht any metabolic degradation is principally through the enzyme catechol-O-methyltransferase. Adrenaline and noradrenaline undergo methylation to become metanephrine and normetanephrine respectively, the reaction being catalysed by catechol-O-methyltransferase. A second step of oxidative deamination is carried out by MAO, to produce 3-methoxy-4-hydroxy-mandelic acid.

A minor route of metabolic degradation of catecholamines involves the same enzymes acting in reverse order—first MAO followed by catechol-O-methyltransferase. These reactions are shown in Fig. 13.5.

Catechol-O-methyltransferase is found outside not within the sympathetic neurone; it also occurs in the liver and kidneys. Monoamine oxidase is widely distributed throughout the body, notably in the mitochondria of sympathetic neurones, the liver, and gastro-intestinal tract. Noradrenaline stored in the granules of sympathetic neurones is not vulnerable to degradation by MAO.

However, noradrenaline that is released, or that leaches out into the neuronal cytoplasm, is metabolized by MOA contained in the mitochondria; thus this enzyme may exert a controlling influence on the total concentration of noradrenaline within the cell.

Table 13.1. The effects of sympathetic stimulation on various parts

	a_1-receptors	a_2-receptors	β_1-receptors	β_2-receptors
Heart				
SA node			Increased heart rate	
AV node and conduction system			Increased conduction	
Atria and Ventricles			Increased strength of contraction. Increased myocardial excitability	
Lungs				
Bronchial musculature (smooth muscle)	Constriction			Relaxation (broncho-dilatation). More evident when muscle is contracted through disease, e.g. bronchial asthma.
Bronchial glands	Secretion decreased			Secretion increased
Arterioles				
Skin and mucosa	Constriction			
Skeletal muscle	Constriction			Dilatation
Coronary	Constriction			Dilatation
Salivary glands	Potassium secretion		Amylase secretion	
Veins	Constriction			Dilatation
Liver	Glycogenolysis— rise in blood sugar			Glycogenolysis
Pancreas				
Islet cells		Decreased secretion		Increased secretion
Stomach				
Sphincters	Contraction			
Motility		Decreased		Decreased
Intestine				
Sphincters	Contraction			
Motility	Decreased		Decreased	Decreased
Eye				
Radial muscle (mydriasis)	Contraction			
Fat cells			Lipolysis	
Uterus (smooth muscle)	Contraction (in pregnancy)			Relaxation
Platelets		Aggregation		

β_1-receptors are predominantly present in the heart and for all practical purposes, the heart has no a-receptors.

As will be seen from Table 13.1 a_1 receptors in blood vessels are concerned with vasoconstriction in the skin and mucosa, coronary vessels, and skeletal musculature. They also mediate the constriction of most sphincters. β_2-receptors are responsible for causing smooth muscle relaxation in many organs, e.g. bronchial, uterine, and intestinal smooth muscle. β_2-receptors are also responsible for vasodilatation in skeletal muscle.

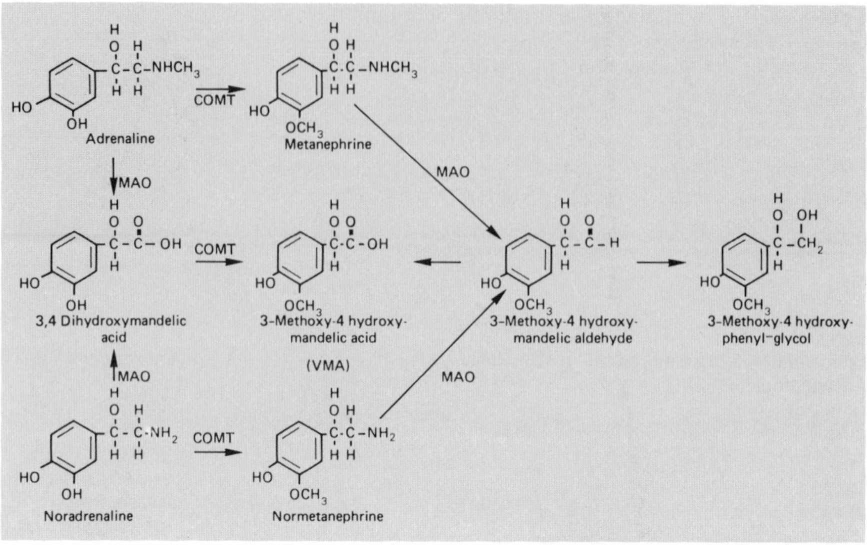

Adrenaline → COMT → Metanephrine

MAO

3,4 Dihydroxymandelic acid — COMT — 3-Methoxy-4 hydroxy-mandelic acid (VMA) — 3-Methoxy-4 hydroxy-mandelic aldehyde — 3-Methoxy-4 hydroxy-phenyl-glycol

MAO

Noradrenaline — COMT — Normetanephrine

Fig. 13.5. Metabolic pathways for adrenaline and noradrenaline in man (COMT = catechol-O-methyl transferase; MAO = monoamine oxidase). (After Axelrod, 1960.)

SYMPATHOMIMETIC DRUGS

These can be classified as:

(1) directly acting sympathomimetics, e.g. adrenaline, noradrenaline, isoprenaline, phenylephrine, salbutamol, and terbutaline;

(2) indirectly acting, e.g. cocaine, amphetamine, tyramine;

(3) directly acting and indirectly acting (mixed), e.g. ephedrine.

Directly acting sympathomimetics

Adrenaline

Pharmacological actions

Adrenaline is formed by the methylation of noradrenaline in the body; both compounds are directly acting amines.

Adrenaline is destroyed by the acid of the stomach and is, therefore, not effective if taken orally. It is usually given by subcutaneous or intramuscular injection, its effects being produced more rapidly from the intramuscular site. Following injection its various actions become apparent within a minute, and they are:

1. Adrenaline is a powerful cardiac stimulant and acts directly on β-receptors.

There is an increase in the force and rate of contraction of the heart, so that the patient may complain of palpitations.

2. There is a rise in systolic blood pressure due to the increased cardiac output. However, the diastolic pressure shows little change as adrenaline produces vasoconstriction only in the skin, whereas peripheral resistance is decreased by the action of adrenaline on the β_2-receptors of muscle vessels causing dilatation.

3. Adrenaline causes an increased coronary flow through stimulation of β_2-receptors.

4. Adrenaline causes relaxation of bronchial muscles (β_2 stimulation). This bronchodilator action is much more noticeable when the bronchial musculature is contracted, as occurs in asthma or hypersensitivity reactions.

5. Adrenaline has a metabolic effect in that it raises blood sugar by mobilizing glucose from the tissues; it decreases the glycogen content of the liver and skeletal muscles. Adrenaline predominantly affects the α-receptors of the pancreas, resulting in a decrease in the secretion of insulin.

The main function of endogenous adrenaline (Goth 1966) '. . . appears to be the great emergency hormone which stimulates metabolism and promotes blood flow to skeletal muscles, preparing the individual for fight or flight'.

Unwanted effects
The rapid injection of adrenaline, or its use in large amounts, may produce ventricular fibrillation, which can be lethal. The intramuscular injection of 1:1000 adrenaline solution in anaphylactic shock is not without hazard and must be undertaken carefully. Intravenous injection of adrenaline has no place in dentistry.

Uses
(1) It is used to relieve many acute hypersensitivity reactions (see chapter 21).

(2) It is used as a vasoconstrictor in many local anaesthetic solutions (see Chapter 7).

(3) It may be used as a topical haemostatic agent, being applied in a 1:250 concentration.

Noradrenaline

Like adrenaline, noradrenaline is a naturally occurring catecholamine and it can also be produced synthetically. It is, as we have seen, the chemical mediator liberated by postganglionic sympathetic nerve endings and acts directly on effector cells.

The actions of adrenaline and noradrenaline on the cardiovascular system are likely to be quite different when both are administered in small doses. The effects are somewhat similar when large, unphysiological doses are administered. Perhaps the most important action of injected noradrenaline is to produce widespread vasoconstriction of the arterioles by stimulation of α_1-receptors. The

β_2-receptors in the vessels of the skeletal musculature are not affected and these vessels are not dilated. There is then an increase in both systolic and diastolic blood pressure, with an increased mean pressure. Intravenous infusions of noradrenaline have been used in the treatment of shock associated with trauma, or haemorrhage. the rationale of this treatment is doubtful, for such shock will already have initiated intense peripheral vasoconstriction.

Noradrenaline is a powerful vasoconstrictor and can cause a reflex bradycardia (except in the presence of an antimuscarinic drug (e.g. atropine), when it can cause a tachycardia). For these reasons its use as a vasoconstrictor in local anaesthetic solutions is contraindicated because of its pressor effects.

'The main function of noradrenaline appears to be the maintenance of normal sympathetic tone and adjustment of circulatory dynamics' (Goth 1966).

Isoprenaline

This is a synthetic catecholamine that has powerful β actions, but is almost devoid of α actions. It is well-absorbed from the buccal mucosa and respiratory tract. Isoprenaline relaxes smooth muscle, including that of the bronchial tree, and so can be used as a bronchodilator. It may be administered by aerosol inhalation, or as a 20 mg tablet sucked until the asthmatic attack is over, when the remainder of the tablet is ejected. Unfortunately, isoprenaline is a non-selective adrenoceptor stimulant and overdosage by inhalation can be dangerous due to the induction of ventricular arrhythmias.

Phenylephrine

This is a non-catecholamine, but is closely related to adrenaline chemically. It acts directly but mainly on α_1-receptors. The drug is a powerful vasoconstrictor and so produces increased peripheral resistance to blood flow with a consequent rise in systolic and diastolic pressures.

Phenylephrine, in nasal drops, is used locally to produce vasoconstriction of the nasal mucous membranes. Such use as a nasal decongestant is not without its hazards. Phenylephrine is a substrate for MAO and so, in the patient taking monoamine oxidase inhibitors (MAOI), phenylephrine will not be metabolized and so may produce a significant rise in blood pressure because of its vasoconstrictor effects.

Salbutamol

Salbutamol is a selective β_2-adrenergic stimulant and so it produces bronchodilatation with considerably fewer cardiovascular effects than, for example, isoprenaline. Nevertheless it may produce tachycardia, but this is seldom a problem when delivered by aerosol inhalation. Its use in asthma is well-established; generally it is taken by mouth as a 4 mg tablet, or administered in an aerosol. It can also be given by slow intravenous injection (250 μg) in severe attacks.

Terbutaline

This is an effective bronchodilator and a selective β_2-adrenoceptor stimulant. It is administered orally or by aerosol inhalation, although it can also be given parenterally.

Indirectly acting sympathomimetics

Amphetamine

This drug acts indirectly in that, following uptake into the sympathetic nerve ending, it causes displacement of noradrenaline from storage sites in the synaptic vesicles. As the actions of noradrenaline are profound on α_1-receptors, but minor on β_2-receptors, the effects of amphetamine, like other indirectly acting sympathomimetics, are marked on receptors related to the peripheral vasculature. Consequently, in human beings, the oral administration of amphetamine raises both systolic and diastolic pressures.

The main interest of amphetamine is its effect on the CNS. It is said to abolish fatigue and restore energy and alertness; it certainly does not improve intelligence or skills. By its stimulant effect, amphetamine may seem to give an elevation of mood. For this reason it has been used in the treatment of depressive illness and can be classified as a psychomotor stimulant. Prolonged use of the drug is invariably followed by mental depression and fatigue. Dependence to amphetamine-like drugs often occurs, and they have little place in medical practice. The amphetamines may be useful in the rare disease called narcolepsy, in which the sufferer has uncontrollable attacks of sleepiness, for these drugs do produce wakefulness. Indeed, taken much after 4.0 p.m. they will usually prevent sleep at night.

Dexamphetamine sulphate combined with amylobarbitone was once used for the treatment of depressive illness, the two drugs potentiating each other. This combination produces the substance called 'Drinamyl', better known as 'purple hearts'.

Apart from their past use in psychiatric medicine, amphetamine-like drugs have been used as appetite suppressants in the treatment of obesity. Such use is hardly justified considering the risks associated with these drugs.

Tyramine

This is an indirectly acting amine, that is it causes the release of noradrenaline from its storage sites and does not itself act directly on receptors. It is to be found in many foodstuffs—mature cheese, broad beans, yeast extracts, yoghourt, and wine—and is a substrate for MAO in the gut and in the liver. It is of interest because when MAOIs are administered, they allow tyramine to reach the systemic circulation, causing noradrenaline release from its storage sites. This release may lead to a dangerous hypertension (the so-called cheese reaction), with cerebrovascular catastrophe and death of the patient if not corrected.

Directly acting and indirectly acting (mixed) sympathomimetics

Ephedrine

This compound occurs naturally in some plants but is prepared synthetically for medical use. Ephedrine stimulates both α- and β-receptors as well as acting indirectly; its actions are, therefore, mixed. In some ways, these actions are similar to those of adrenaline, in other ways most dissimilar. It differs from adrenaline in that it is absorbed from the intestinal tract after oral administration and, although its effects are weaker, they are more prolonged. It has a more marked stimulating effect on the CNS.

Ephedrine increases the systolic and usually the diastolic blood pressure, the effect being mainly due to cardiac stimulation. It also produces a mild degree of bronchial relaxation as compared with adrenaline, but the effect is more prolonged. Consequently, it is useful as a bronchodilator in mild chronic asthma (taken in the form of tablets, 15 to 60 mg orally three times daily), but not in a severe acute attack. It is also used as a nasal decongestant in the form of nasal drops. There is a well-established clinical impression that repeated use of ephedrine over long periods leads to some falling off in its efficacy.

Its stimulant effect on the CNS is not so marked as with the amphetamines. Nevertheless, if it is used for the mild asthmatic it should be remembered that the drug may keep the patient awake at night and, under such circumstances, may have to be combined with a suitable hypnotic drug. Its use should be avoided in those taking a MAOI.

ANTAGONISTS OF ADRENERGIC ACTIVITY
(Drugs used in the treatment of hypertension)

The drugs that oppose adrenergic activity may act peripherally, centrally, or both.

Peripherally acting agents—adrenergic neurone blockers

This group comprises several chemical agents with the common property of interfering with the normal function of adrenergic neurones. They can be divided into subgoups according to their mechanisms of action.

(i) Inhibition of transmitter release
(e.g. guanethidine)

Guanethidine is representative of those drugs that selectively block sympathetic transmission in postganglionic sympathetic neurones by interfering with the release of noradrenaline from the nerve endings. It is taken up into adrenergic nerve endings by the same mechanism that rehouses noradrenaline released from sympathetic nerve endings. This drug also decreases sympathetic activity by depleting the stores of noradrenaline at peripheral nerve endings.

Pharmacokinetics

Absorption of guanethidine from the gastro-intestinal tract is very variable, as little as 3 per cent or as much as 30 per cent may reach the systemic circulation. To some extent this variability must account for the wide variations in dosage required between individuals. The drug is metabolized in the liver, and the metabolites and the parent compound are excreted by the kidney.

Unwanted effects

Guanethidine causes postural hypotension, and this is perhaps the most significant unwanted effect; others include a feeling of weakness, and diarrhoea, which is common.

The action of this drug is inhibited by the tricyclic antidepressants and the phenothiazines, which block the uptake of guanethidine into the sympathetic nerve ending. Guanethidine will only act as a hypotensive if it can reach its site of action within the sympathetic neurone.

Uses

Guanethidine is used to treat a moderate to a severe hypertension, usually in conjunction with a diuretic. It is not often used today because its effect on blood pressure is affected by postural changes, and because better drugs are now available.

Bethanidine and debrisoquine are similar drugs to guanethidine.

(ii) Depletion of noradrenaline stores
(e.g. reserpine)

Reserpine depletes the stores of noradrenaline and 5-hydroxytryptamine centrally, and also produces a depletion of noradrenaline at the sympathetic nerve endings. It causes the release of noradrenaline from the storage granules in the sympathetic nerve endings into the neuronal cytoplasm, where it is metabolized by MAO. The hypotensive effect of this drug may be due to a combination of these central and peripheral actions, which bring about a reduction in the sympathetic outflow to the blood vessels. Reserpine is virtually obsolete today as it tends to produce too many unwanted effects, especially severe mental depression. However, at one time, it was found to be useful in treatment of hypertension.

Centrally acting agents

Methyldopa

At one time it was thought that methyldopa acted peripherally at postganglionic sympathetic nerve endings, but it is now generally agreed that it acts centrally, producing a reduced sympathetic outflow from the brain. It would seem that methyldopa on entering the central nervous system acts as a substrate for dopa decarboxylase with the formation of α-methyldopamine.

Alpha methyldopamine, by a further enzymatic step, is converted to α-methylnoradrenaline. It seems that this α-methylnoradrenaline is an agonist of α_2-receptors in the CNS, and that stimulation of these receptors inhibits the sympathetic outflow.

Pharmacokinetics

The absorption of methyldopa after oral administration is somewhat variable and incomplete. The maximal blood concentrations are reached in about three hours. It is excreted in the urine unchanged in the main, although some is excreted as metabolites.

Unwanted effects

Methyldopa tends to cause drowsiness and sometimes even a depression. The sedative effect is the most common effect and it will tend to wear off with continued use of the drug. A dry mouth may occur with methyldopa but is rarely of any significance.

In about 3 per cent of patients (Rudd and Blaschke, 1985), transient abnormalities of the liver may occur. Usually, on stopping the drug, the liver function returns to normal but the condition may progress to hepatic necrosis.

Drug-related systemic lupus erythematosus has been reported with the use of methyldopa, as have lichenoid eruptions of the oral mucosa (Hay and Reade 1978).

Uses

The drug is used to treat a moderate to mild hypertension in conjunction with a diuretic. It is perhaps less used today than previously because of its unwanted effects.

Clonidine

This antihypertensive, like methyldopa, seems to stimulate central α_2-adrenergic receptors decreasing the sympathetic outflow from the brain. It may also act peripherally on α_2-(prejunctional) receptors.

Pharmacokinetics

Clonidine is much better absorbed than is methyldopa, absorption being rapid and almost complete. Peak plasma concentrations are reached in one to three hours. The half-life of clonidine is about eight to nine hours when administered orally; it is mainly excreted unchanged in the urine. The metabolites produced in the liver by degradation of that fraction which is not passed out in the urine unchanged, are inactive; they, in their turn, are eventually excreted in the urine.

Unwanted effects

The most frequent of these are dry mouth and sedation, both of which may be severe. They may lessen after the drug has been taken for some time, but a proportion of patients have to discontinue its use for these reasons. A so-called rebound hypertension occurs if clonidine is suddenly withdrawn. This is potentially very dangerous and rather suggests that the drug should not be used in those who are unlikely to comply with prescribing instructions. Parotid pain has been recorded in patients treated with clonidine. (Onesti *et al.* 1971).

Uses

Clonidine is hardly ever used for the treatment of hypertension because of its many unwanted effects. However, in low doses it is used for the prophylaxis of migraine, in the form of 'Dixarit' (See Chapter 14).

Adrenergic receptor (adrenoceptor) blockers

Some of the drugs included in this category have found a special place in the treatment of hypertension, these being those drugs that block β-adrenergic receptors. Other drugs, the α-adrenoceptor blocking drugs have not proved particularly useful in this respect, but they have found a place in the treatment of 'hypertensive crises'.

α-adrenoceptor blocking drugs
(e.g. phenoxybenzamine, phentolamine)

These drugs selectively block α-receptors, leaving β-receptors unaffected. Phenoxybenzamine produces an irreversible type of blockade, whereas the blockade produced by phentolamine is competitive. Phenoxybenzamine essentially blocks α_1-receptors whereas phentolamine blocks both α_1- and α_2-receptors.

It might be thought that such drugs would be useful in the management of hypertension but, generally speaking, this has not proved to be the case, and there appear to be few clinical uses for them. However, phentolamine has been found to be useful in the treatment of hypertension crises due to phaeochromocytoma. Phaeochromocytoma is a rare tumour of the adrenal medulla that secretes adrenaline and noradrenaline in excess with a resultant hypertension. The hypertension is often paroxysmal but it may be continuous.

Phentolamine is also used in the treatment of hypertensive crises associated with the sudden withdrawal of clonidine (see above), or with the interaction that sometimes occurs between a MAOI and certain foodstuffs containing pressor amines, e.g. cheese.

β-adrenoceptor blocking drugs

These provide competitive and reversible blockade of β-adrenoceptors in the heart, peripheral vasculature, bronchi, liver, and pancreas. They have many clinical applications and have found a special place in the treatment of hypertension. Their mode of action as hypotensives is uncertain. Some β-blockers are non-selective, e.g. propranolol, nadolol; whereas others are relatively selective having a greater affinity for β_1-receptors (cardiac β-receptors) than for β_2-receptors (bronchial and vascular β-receptors). Some β-adrenoceptor blocking drugs are lipophilic, e.g. propranolol; whereas others are water-soluble, e.g. nadolol, atenolol. Furthermore, some β-adrenoceptor blockers are partial agonists in that they possess a degree of intrinsic sympathomimetic activity, e.g. oxprenolol, acebutolol.

Non-selective β-adrenoceptor blocking drugs
(e.g. propranolol, nadolol, oxprenolol, pindolol, timolol)
Propranolol
This was the first β-blocker of clinical significance. It produces specific blockade of β-receptors but is unselective, blocking both β_1- and β_2-receptors. By blocking cardiac β-receptors it causes a reduction in the rate and force of the heart beat so that cardiac output is lowered; this may account, in part, for the decreased blood pressure. Propranolol may also produce its hypotensive effect by antagonizing the action of noradrenaline released from sympathetic nerve endings. It does so by blocking peripheral adrenoceptors. Some beta-blockers also depress plasma renin secretion, e.g. propranolol (see Chapter 15 for discussion on renin and hypertension).

Pharmacokinetics. When taken orally propranolol is almost completely absorbed. It is a lipophilic drug and is subject to extensive first pass metabolism. The degree of this metabolism varies in different individuals, and the dose regimen has to be adjusted according to individual requirements. Propranolol is extensively bound to plasma proteins (maybe as much as 95 per cent), and ultimately it is almost completely metabolized in the liver before excretion in the urine. Peak plasma concentrations occur in about 90 minutes and the half-life after oral administration is in the order of four hours.

Unwanted effects. The unwanted effects of propranolol are mainly due to actions inherent in the drug itself. They are side-effects resulting from extension of the main action of the drug at sites additional to those required for therapeutic purposes. For instance, the blockade of β-adrenergic receptors in bronchial smooth muscle may lead to increased airway resistance. This is probably of little importance in the normal individual but, in the asthmatic, it may induce a dangerous bronchospasm.

As propranolol is lipophilic, it readily enters the brain and occasionally produces nightmares, hallucinations, and sleeplessness. Such unwanted effects are much less likely to occur with more water-soluble β-blockers, such as nadolol.

Nadolol

This non-selective β-blocker, unlike propranolol, is water-soluble. It is a long-acting drug, and it is taken orally when it has a half-life of perhaps as much as 20 hours. It is not metabolized to any degree and is, therefore, mainly excreted in an unchanged form in the urine. The consequence of the relatively long half-life of nadolol, as compared with propranolol, means that it has only to be administered once a day when used as an antihypertensive.

Selective β-adrenoceptor blocking drugs
(e.g. metoprolol, atenolol, practolol)

These drugs are relatively cardio-selective. The first of them was practolol: this was an extremely effective drug but, when taken by mouth, it produced many serious unwanted effects such as conjunctival scarring and peritoneal fibrosis. Its use is now severely restricted.

Metoprolol and atenolol are relatively selective β_1-receptor blockers. Although they are regarded as cardio-selective, this selectivity does not offer any absolute protection against bronchospasm in patients with obstructive airway disease.

Metoprolol is rapidly absorbed from the gastro-intestinal tract and undergoes extensive first pass metabolism. Little of the drug is excreted unchanged in the urine. On the other hand, atenolol is water-soluble and is excreted by the kidneys mainly in an unchanged form.

Non-selective α- and β-adrenoceptor blocking drugs
(e.g. labetalol)

Labetalol, an antihypertensive drug, is novel in that it blocks α_1-receptors and also β_1- and β_2-receptors. It is sometimes useful for those patients who do not tolerate the unopposed α effects that occur with β-blockers.

Uses of β-adrenoceptor blocking drugs

In the treatment of hypertension

The β-blockers, as we have seen, are effective antihypertensive drugs and they produce relatively few unwanted effects. If they prove inadequate alone in controlling the blood pressure, usually they are combined with a thiazide diuretic. The actions of all the β-blockers are likely to be similar.

In addition to their use as hypotensive agents, β-blockers have other uses.

In the treatment of angina pectoris

Because of their action on β_1-cardiac receptors, these drugs generally diminish sympathetic drive to the heart. They also reduce heart rate and cardiac output, and the force of myocardial contraction is decreased. They reduce the response of the heart to exercise and, because of the effects on the myocardium, myocardial oxygen requirements are reduced. All of these actions are useful in angina as there is already present an impaired blood supply to the myocardium and the patient gets pain in the chest on exercise.

In the treatment of cardiac arrhythmias

Because of the reduction in sympathetic drive brought about by these drugs in general, the excitability of the myocardium is reduced and so there is less likelihood of arrhythmias occurring.

In the treatment of anxiety states

Beta-blockers are useful in treating those people who experience anxiety in particular situations; for example, public performers, examination candidates. They are used in the management of anxiety when the effects of sympathetic overactivity result in troublesome palpitations, tachycardia, and tremor.

As prophylactic agents in the management of migraine (see Chapter 14)

Some β-blockers, e.g. propranolol, possess weak membrane-stabilizing (local anaesthetic) properties but this effect is not seen at the concentrations achieved during therapy. This property has no therapeutic value.

PARASYMPATHETIC NERVOUS SYSTEM

The peripheral parasympathetic system consists of preganglionic and postganglionic neurones. The chemical transmitter at both the ganglion and the effector junction is acetylcholine.

There are two main types of membrane receptors for acetylcholine, and these are named 'muscarinic' and 'nicotinic'. The reason for this terminology is because the substances muscarine and nicotine were found to stimulate these receptors selectively. Muscarine is obtained from a fungus (*Amanita muscaria*); it has the same actions as acetylcholine released from parasympathetic postganglionic fibres. The muscarinic receptor is, therefore, located at the effector junction of postganglionic parasympathetic fibres. Nicotinic receptors are found on the postsynaptic membrane of all autonomic ganglia, both sympathetic and parasympathetic, and also on the neuromuscular junction. Muscarine has no effects at the autonomic ganglia, but here the activity of acetylcholine can be mimicked by low concentrations of nicotine. In high concentrations nicotine blocks transmission.

Synthesis, storage, release and inactivation of acetylcholine

Cholinergic nerves synthesize acetylcholine from choline; this synthesis requires the enzyme, choline acetylase. Choline is found in lecithin, which is widely distributed in all animal and vegetable foodstuffs. Acetylcholine is stored in synaptic vesicles at the nerve endings and is released when there is electrical activity in the nerve fibres. On release from the nerve ending, acetylcholine is quickly hydrolysed by the cholinesterases of the body to form acetic acid. In man there are thought to be two definite cholinesterases, true cholinesterase and pseudocholinesterase, the true form being primarily responsible for the hydrolysis of acetylcholine.

Parasympathomimetic drugs

Acetylcholine is not absorbed from the gastro-intestinal tract and, even if given intravenously, it is so rapidly hydrolysed by the cholinesterases of the body that its effects are transient. Although it is a subject of physiological interest, it is not used in medical treatments. There are a number of other drugs that have similar actions to acetylcholine and find clinical application.

Carbachol

This is a synthetic substance chemically related to acetylcholine. Although its action is predominately on muscarinic receptors, it also has a high level of activity on nicotinic receptors, particularly at autonomic ganglia. It is not hydrolysed by the body cholinesterases and so its actions are more prolonged than those of acetylcholine. In contrast to acetylcholine, carbachol stimulates selectively the urinary and gastro-intestinal tracts, increasing smooth muscle tone. It has been used to overcome urinary retention due to atonic bladder where there was no obstruction to urinary flow.

Carbachol is sometimes used in ophthalmology, often combined with other substances, in an emollient solution as eyedrops to reduce intra-ocular pressure in glaucoma (a condition characterized by increased intra-ocular pressure).

Occasionally the drug produces a slight tachycardia due to stimulation of nicotinic receptors in sympathetic ganglia. Usually, the muscarinic effects predominate and the effects on the ganglia have little or no clinical significance.

Bethanechol chloride

This substance produces only muscarinic effects and, like carbachol, these are relatively selective being related to the smooth muscle of the gut, the ureters, and the bladder. The drug is available as tablets, and is used to stimulate the urinary bladder.

Pilocarpine

This is a naturally occurring alkaloid with mainly muscarinic action. Pilocarpine is used in ophthalmology for the treatment of glaucoma. When applied to the eye it causes pupillary constriction (miosis) and ultimately a fall in intraocular pressure. In fact, reduction of intra-ocular pressure occurs within minutes of application and lasts for up to eight hours.

These substances act directly on the receptors, but there are others that produce their effect by preventing the destruction of acetylcholine by cholinesterases; these are called the *anticholinesterases*.

Physostigmine

This combines reversibly with cholinesterase and prevents the hydrolysis of acetylcholine at nerve terminals throughout the body. The actions of acetylcholine are, therefore, intensified at their three sites of action: (i) parasympathetic nerve endings (muscarinic); (ii) autonomic ganglia (nicotinic); and (iii) the nerve endings in voluntary muscle (nicotinic). The final picture produced by these three groups of actions is likely to be a mixed one, but the action at the parasympathetic nerve endings usually predominates.

Physostigmine is used in the treatment of glaucoma, often being combined with pilocarpine in the form of eyedrops, to produce a constricting (miotic) effect on the pupil. The effects of physostigmine are more prolonged than pilocarpine, lasting 24 hours.

Neostigmine

This is a synthetic anticholinesterase drug, similar to physostigmine, but with much more effect on the neuromuscular junction. Anticholinesterase drugs, such as neostigmine, are used to enhance neuromuscular transmission in conditions such as myasthenia gravis, which is a disease characterized by weakness of voluntary muscles. Repeated stimulation of a motor nerve in a patient suffering from this condition leads to fatigue of the muscles supplied by the particular nerve. By interfering with the breakdown of acetylcholine this weakness can be alleviated. One troublesome problem with the use of neostigmine is that it possesses a marked muscarinic action so that there may be excessive salivation. However, this can be overcome by the simultaneous administration of atropine.

Examples of other drugs used in the treatment of myasthenia gravis are: pyridostigmine, distigmine, edrophonium. Edrophonium has a very brief action and is used simply for diagnostic purposes.

Irreversible anticholinesterases

There are substances that produce an irreversible complex with cholinesterase so that their duration of action is prolonged and depends upon the rate which new cholinesterase is formed. These are the organophosphorus inhibitors; they are used as insecticides and form the basis of 'nerve gases'.

Parasympathetic blocking drugs

Ganglion blocking drugs

Acetylcholine is the chemical transmitter at both sympathetic and parasympathetic ganglia. Ganglion blocking drugs were the first powerful weapons that became available to lower raised blood pressure. These drugs act by competing with the acetylcholine released at preganglionic nerve endings—an example of competitive antagonism. Unfortunately, because of their lack of selectivity, the ganglion blocking drugs readily produced unwanted effects due to their blocking parasympathetic as well as sympathetic ganglia. Because of the parasympathetic blockade there occurs decreased salivation, urinary retention, and constipation.

Atropine

Atropine belongs to the belladona groups of drugs, which are obtained from *Atropa belladonna*, deadly nightshade.

Pharmacokinetics

This drug is well-absorbed from the gastro-intestinal tract, and it can also be given subcutaneously, intramuscularly, or intravenously. It can also be absorbed through broken skin and when applied locally to the mucosal surfaces of the body.

Atropine quickly disappears from the blood and has a half-life of about 2.5 hours. It is distributed throughout the whole body, traces can be found in maternal milk, and it crosses the placental barrier to enter the fetal circulation. The compound is largely broken down by the liver enzymes but a small fraction of it may be excreted in the urine unchanged, mainly within 12 hours.

Pharmacodynamics

Atropine is an antimuscarinic drug, and the major action of all antimuscarinic drugs is competitive antagonism to acetylcholine and drugs like it. To some extent, competitive antagonism is quantitative and can be overcome by increasing the concentration of acetylcholine at the receptor site. Atropine is very selective in its antagonism, acting at receptors of smooth and cardiac muscle and exocrine glands. Atropine does not antagonize the nicotinic action of acetylcholine on skeletal muscle, and only affects autonomic ganglia in very high dosage.

Pharmacological properties

Atropine diminishes cardiac vagal tone and thus leads to an increase in the heart rate. The amount of acceleration produced will depend upon the degree of inhibition present. The influence of atropine on vagal tone is most noticeable in the young, healthy adult; whereas in infancy and old age, it may cause less cardiac acceleration.

Atropine blocks the action of acetylcholine on glands. In therapeutic doses it does not greatly diminish gastric secretion, but it does dry up the copious salivary secretion induced by parasympathetic stimulation.

Sympathetic activity has little control in the regulation of gastro-intestinal tone and motility, parasympathetic nerves being principally involved. Parasympathetic nerves increase both tone and motility and so atropine diminishes these responses, with a decrease in frequency of peristaltic contractions. Atropine has been used to relieve colicky pain.

The administration of atropine leads to a drying up of secretions in the respiratory tract. Although atropine does produce some degree of relaxation of the smooth muscles of the bronchi and bronchioles, it must be remembered that parasympathetic innervation of the bronchi is slight, and cholinergic mechanisms do not seem to play much part in the causation of attacks of bronchial asthma. Other smooth muscle is also relaxed, notably that of the biliary and renal tracts.

When the parasympathetic nerve supply to the eye is blocked there occurs mydriasis (dilation of the pupil) and cycloplegia (paralysis of accommodation) with inability to see near objects. Local administration of atropine to the eye will produce these effects. Mydriasis, for instance, may be necessary for thorough examination of the retina.

Overdosage with atropine leads to an exaggeration of all the actions described, together with a stimulating effect on the CNS with restlessness, hallucinations, and delirium, and finally coma and death.

Uses

1. Atropine (see Chapter 8) is used as part of preanaesthetic medication to dry up salivary and bronchial secretions. Although this is the primary object of such usage, the very fact that secretions are inhibited may reduce the incidence of laryngospasm during general anaesthesia. The administration of atropine also prevents excessive bradycardia and hypotension caused by halothane. The depression of salivary secretion is particularly important in children because the larynx and trachea are so small and any excessive secretion could seriously impair respiration.

2. The drug is used by local application to dilate the pupil so that a proper examination of the retina can take place. Homatropine is often used for the purpose as its effects are not so prolonged as those of atropine.

3. Atropine has been given orally, often as belladonna alkaloids, to treat peptic ulcer; its value here is open to question. The only pharmacological effect that would seem to be beneficial would be if atropine and like drugs suppressed gastric acid secretion. Atropine has a minimal effect on such secretion, but it may be useful in that it relieves spasm of the stomach and duodenal muscles. It also delays gastric emptying so that the action of antacids may be prolonged. Hence, belladonna alkaloids are often combined with other drugs, such as aluminium hydroxide or magnesium trisilicate, both of which are antacids.

Hyoscine

The actions of hyoscine are essentially the same as those of atropine, except for its action on the CNS where, even in small doses, it has a depressant action leading to some degree of sedation, drowsiness, or even sleep. Although a good pre-anaesthetic agent, elderly people tend to be confused by hyoscine and so it is probably best avoided in their premedication. It has a depressant action on the vomiting centre and has been used as a travel sickness remedy.

REFERENCES

Axelrod, J. (1960). The fate of adrenaline and noradrenaline. In *Adrenergic Mechanisms* (ed. J. R. Vane), pp. 28–39. J. and A. Churchill, London.

Goth, A. (1981) Adrenergic drugs. In *Medical Pharmacology*. (12th edn). Mosby, St. Louis.

Hay, K. D. and Reade, P. C. (1978). Methyldopa as a cause of oral mucous membrane reactions. *British Dental Journal*, **145**, 195–203.

Onesti, G., Bock, K. D., Heimsoth, V., Kim, K. E., and Murguet, P. (1971). Clonidine: a new antihypertensive agent. *American Journal of Cardiology*, **28**, 74–83.

Rudd, P. and Blaschke, T. F. (1985). Antihypertensive agents and the drug therapy of hypertension. In *The pharmacological basis of therapeutics* (7th ed) (ed. L. S. Goodman, A. G. Gilman, T. W. Rall, and F. Murad). Macmillan, New York.

FURTHER READING

Beeley, L. (1984). Drug interactions of beta-blockers. (Editorial). *British Medical Journal*, **289**, 1330–1.

Breckenridge, A. (1985). Treating mild hypertension. (Editorial). *British Medical Journal*, **291**, 89–90.

Faldt, R., Liedholm, H., and Aursnes, J. (1984). Beta-blockers and loss of hearing. *British Medical Journal*, **289**, 1490–2.

Kaplan, N. M. (1983). The present and future use of beta-blockers. *Drugs*, **25**, 1.

Leading article (1985). Beta-blockers in situational anxiety. *Lancet*, **ii**, 193.

Leading article (1985). Treatment of hypertension: the 1985 results. *Lancet*, **ii**, 645–7.

Leading article (1985). Treatment of hypertension in the over 60's. *Lancet*, **i**, 1369–70.

Leading article (1985): The functions of adrenaline. *Lancet*, **i**, 561–2.

Michelson, E. L. and Frishman, W. H. (1983). Labetalol: an alpha- and beta-adrenoceptor blocking drug. *Annals of Internal Medicine*, **99**, 553–5.

Ravid, M., Lang, R., and Jutrin, I. (1985). The relative antihypertensive potency of propranolol, oxprenolol, atenolol, and metoprolol given once daily. *Archives of Internal Medicine*, **145**, 1321–3.

Rubin, P. C. and Reid, J. L. (1983). Alpha-blockers and converting enzyme inhibitors. *British Medical Journal*, **286**, 1192–5.

14

The central nervous system

THIS chapter is mainly concerned with disorders of the central nervous system (CNS) and the therapeutic measures used in their treatment. The following disorders will be considered together with their appropriate treatment: psychoses and related disorders, and antipsychotic drugs; depression and antidepressants; hypnotics and anxiolytics; epilepsy, facial neuralgias, and anticonvulsants; migraine, and drugs used in the prophylaxis and treatment of migraine. Many other drugs act on the CNS but are discussed elsewhere; these include opioids (see Chapter 6) and general anaesthetic agents (see Chapter 8).

PSYCHOSES AND RELATED DISORDERS

Psychosis

This major mental illness is characterized by irrational thoughts and loss of contact with reality, and commonly by delusions and/or hallucinations. It can take a number of forms.

Organic

Damage to the brain caused by injury, infection (for example, encephalitis), pharmacological agents (e.g. lysergic acid diethylamide, LSD), toxicological agents (e.g. ethyl alcohol (ethanol); lead), and degenerative changes (Alzheimer's disease; old age) can all lead to temporary or permanent psychotic changes. From what has been said it will be appreciated that organic psychosis is usually accompanied by detectable anatomical, chemical, or pharmacological changes in the brain.

Functional

By contrast to the organic group, this is not accompanied by obvious anatomical changes in the brain. The results of research carried out over the past two decades have shown that some of these conditions appear to be associated with subtle pharmacological changes in various parts of the brain, although whether these are due to cause or effect still remains to be determined. Nevertheless, pharmacological knowledge so obtained has not only made treatment more rational but has also pointed the way to alternative therapeutic approaches.

There are two subdivisions within the functional group.

1. *Schizophrenia*

This term encompasses a group of related disorders that are characterized by such features as withdrawal from reality, regressive behaviour, and delusions that include feelings of persecution, which when intense is known as paranoia. Auditory hallucinations are also common.

2. *Manic–depressive psychosis*

This is characterized by phases of excitement (hypomania) or frank mania; or alternatively by severe depression. When manic–depressive psychosis swings in only one direction i.e. mania or depression, it is often referred to as monopolar, whereas when it may swing from mania to depression it is then referred to as bipolar.

ANTIPSYCHOTIC DRUGS

The term 'antipyschotic' is the now preferred one for a group of drugs that have been previously named 'neuroleptics', and 'major tranquillizers', and also 'ataractics'. The term 'anti-psychotic' is preferred because it indicates the type of disease for which it is used whilst at the same time not attempting to suggest a mechanism of action. The term 'neuroleptic' is not helpful and the term 'major tranquillizers' is liable to be confused with 'minor tranquillizers', which are better named 'anxiolytics'. The term 'ataractic' is obsolete.

Until the early 1950s there was no effective drug treatment of schizophrenia. At that time two new drugs, chlorpromazine and reserpine, arrived upon the pharmacological scene. Chlorpromazine was known to be an antihistamine, whilst reserpine was one of the active principles extracted from *Rauwolfia serpentina*, which had long been used in India for the treatment of high blood pressure, mental illness, and numerous other diseases. Both drugs were found to calm patients suffering from psychiatric illness, and the results of clinical trials soon showed that they produced significant improvement in patients suffering from schizophrenia. Chlorpromazine became the preferred drug because reserpine not only produced undesirable effects on the blood pressure but also induced serious depression in some patients. From then on the pharmaceutical industry decided to concentrate its attention on the phenothiazines, of which chlorpromazine is a member. In spite of many clinical trials of other phenothiazines, chlorpromazine has remained an important therapeutic agent and represents the archetype of antipsychotic drugs.

Classification of antipsychotic drugs

The phenothiazines can be divided into three main groups on the basis of their chemical structure, therapeutic effects, and adverse reaction profiles. This classification is in general use and is also included in the *British National Formulary (BNF)*.

Group 1: chlorpromazine, methotrimeprazine
Characterized by pronounced sedative effects, moderate anticholinergic (antimuscarinic) and extrapyramidal side-effects.

Group 2: pericyazine, pipothiazine, and thioridazine
Characterized by moderate sedative effects, marked anticholinergic (antimuscarinic) effects, but fewer extrapyramidal side-effects than groups 1 or 3.

Group 3: fluphenazine, perphenazine, prochlorperazine, and trifluoperazine
Characterized by fewer sedative effects, fewer anticholinergic (antimuscarinic) effects, but more pronounced extrapyramidal side-effects than groups 1 and 2.

Several other chemical groups of drugs have been found to have pharmacological properties similar to those of the phenothiazines of group 3. These include the following:

  (i) butyrophenones, e.g. benperidol, droperidol, haloperidol, and trifluperidol;
 (ii) diphenylbutylpiperidines, e.g. fluspirilene, pimozide;
(iii) thioxanthenes, e.g. chlorprothixene, flupenthixol, and zuclopenthixol;
(iv) oxypertine;
 (v) benzamide, e.g. sulpiride.

As chlorpromazine is the archetypal anti-psychotic drug, the remainder of this section will describe its properties. Then, where appropriate, some of the other phenothiazines and related compounds will be compared briefly with it.

Chlorpromazine

Phenothiazine is a tricyclic compound that forms the nucleus of chlorpromazine and numerous other phenothiazine derivatives. Chlorpromazine has an aliphatic side-chain (CH_2—CH_2—CH_2—N—$(CH_3)_2$), which is attached to the nitrogen atom (position 10) of the middle ring of the phenothiazine nucleus.

Pharmacodynamics

Chlorpromazine possesses a multiplicity of actions and this is reflected in the original proprietary name of 'Largactil', which signifies a large number of actions. thus, it produces the following effects:

1. Central
The compound is a competitive antagonist to dopamine, and this action may be the mechanism whereby it produces its powerful antipsychotic and tranquillizing effects. However, chlorpromazine (and other phenothiazines) also have anticholinergic (antimuscarinic), α-adrenoceptor blocking, antihistamine (H_1), and

anti-5HT (5-hydroxytryptamine) actions but the contribution of these effects to the central properties is still not clear. Hallucinations can be controlled by chlorpromazine whether they are part of schizophrenia or part of another psychotic illness, including that induced by pharmacological agents such as 'magic mushrooms'. Chlorpromazine's sedative effect is best seen in agitated patients. Through its action on the hypothalamus it reduces sympathetic outflow, reduces temperature control so that the body does not respond adequately to hypothermia, and also increases the release of prolactin with the result that menstrual irregularities may occur in women and gynaecomastia in man (see Unwanted Effects below). The well-known extrapyramidal syndrome is due to its dopamine agonist action on the basal ganglia.

2. Peripheral

These include anticholinergic (antimuscarinic), α-adrenoceptor blockade, quinidine-like action on the heart (Class I anti-arrhythmic effect), weak antihistamine (H_1) effects, and local anaesthetic actions. The peripheral anticholinergic (antimuscarinic) action is responsible for many of the side-effects that may occur with chlorpromazine, particularly in high dosage; these are dry mouth, difficulty in accommodation, the possibility of acute glaucoma, dry skin, constipation, and difficulty in micturition. The α-adrenoceptor blocking action produces postural hypotension, nasal stuffiness, and failure of ejaculation. The quinidine-like action is unlikely to cause problems except in those already suffering from cardiac conduction defects and particularly, of course, if they are already taking other anti-arrhythmic drugs. The weak antihistamine (H_1) action is probably not of clinical relevance, whilst the local anaesthetic action, although potent, is not clinically exploitable because chlorpromazine is too irritant to tissues to permit of its use in this context.

Pharmacokinetics

The metabolism of chlorpromazine starts as soon as it passes through the gut wall and the liver, and thus it undergoes extensive first pass metabolism. Numerous metabolites are formed and these vary in pharmacological activity and also toxicity. There is enterohepatic recirculation with little renal excretion of unchanged drug. The plasma elimination half-life is 16 to 30 hours but, after repeated dosage, the therapeutic effect is more prolonged than the plasma half-life would suggest. This is due to the large volume of distribution of chlorpromazine, which becomes sequestered in many tissues where it can remain for weeks or months.

Therapeutic uses

These are conveniently considered under four headings.

(i) Psychiatric uses

Chlorpromazine is used in the treatment of acute and chronic psychoses, e.g. schizophrenia, hypomania, and mania, where its antipsychotic and sedative effects are of great therapeutic value. It is also useful in the treatment of acute organic psychotic states including those due to pharmacological and toxicological agents.

(ii) Anti-emetic

Chlorpromazine is valuable in the treatment and prevention of nausea and vomiting due to drugs; for example, during cancer chemotherapy and radiotherapy. It should be noted that it is not effective for the treatment of motion sickness for which H_1 blockers (with sedative action) or antimuscarinic drugs are needed.

(iii) Terminal illness

It is occasionally necessary to use chlorpromazine, usually as a sedative, to relieve anxiety and associated mental suffering during terminal illness. However, there has been a tendency to over-prescribe chlorpromazine for this purpose, such that the patient becomes over-sedated and confused. The aim of terminal care, now renamed palliative medicine, is to keep the patient alert and pain-free so that the quality of life is preserved as much as possible for the benefit of them and their carers.

(iv) Surgical uses

Chlorpromazine is sometimes used as part of premedication and, more particularly, in order to permit the induction of surgical hypothermia; it has also been used as the neuroleptic in combination with an opioid for the production of neuroleptanalgesia.

Unwanted effects

In view of the multiplicity of actions of chlorpromazine it is hardly surprising that it can produce a large profile of unwanted effects. Many of these are predictable from its known pharmacology and have already been referred to earlier in this section. From a clinical point of view it is convenient to classify these unwanted effects under three headings.

(i) Central effects

Sedation occurs initially but tolerance to this effect occurs fairly rapidly. With high doses, such as are used for the treatment of schizophrenia, extrapyramidal syndromes are frequent; these include Parkinsonism, akathisia (a most unpleasant form of enforced restlessness), and different forms of acute dystonic reactions (Blain and Stewart-Wynne 1985). The condition known as tardive dyskinesia may become a serious problem either during or after prolonged therapy, or rarely after even a short period of administration. It consists of irregular repetitive involuntary movements, typically abnormal writhing often accompanied by protrusions of the tongue with lip-smacking, chewing movements, and also facial grimaces. In addition, so-called choreo-athetoid movements of the extremities may occur with the orofacial dyskinesia. Tardive dyskinesia is more likely in patients given high doses of chlorpromazine (or related drugs) over prolonged periods of time, following which the condition may not be reversible, especially in those aged 50 years or more. The mechanism of tardive dyskinesia is not altogether clear although it is believed to be related to supersensitivity of dopamine receptors in the corpus striatum, which is the result of continued dopamine-receptor blockade. Unfortunately, withdrawal of drug therapy is not necessarily followed by improvement and sometimes leads to exacerbation of this difficult problem, a discussion of which is beyond the scope of this text. Nevertheless, it is important for the dental practitioner to be aware of this problem because the sufferer will obviously cause major problems in relation to dentistry.

(ii) Peripheral autonomic effects

As indicated earlier, these result from blockade of muscarinic receptors and α-adrenoceptors. Effects due to muscarinic blockade may produce an unacceptable degree of dry mouth, disturbance of accommodation, constipation, and difficulty with micturition. These can only be lessened by reducing the dose of the drug or, alternatively, by prescribing a different phenothiazine or related compound. Postural hypotension due to α-adrenoceptor blockade can be troublesome at least initially, and when the drug is given parenterally. The Class I anti-arrhythmic action may produce changes in the ECG including prolongation of the QT interval and alteration of the T wave.

(iii) Miscellaneous

A variety of other effects may occur, including those due to associated endocrine disturbances and those due to immunological mechanisms.

Dopamine-receptor blockade is followed by increased prolactin secretion and this in turn may give rise to menstrual disturbances, galactorrhoea, and gynaecomastia. Hypersensitivity reactions occur only occasionally, and include skin rashes, photosensitivity, pigmentation, and also cholestatic jaundice, which is a dose-independent reaction reported in about 2 per cent of cases. Blood dyscrasias, including leucopenia and agranulocytosis, occur rarely. Prolonged high doses of chlorpromazine have also been associated with retinopathy and granular deposits in the cornea and lens.

Drug interactions

Concurrent therapy with drugs possessing any of the actions of chlorpromazine are a possible cause of drug interactions. These are most likely to occur with other centrally depressant drugs including ethyl alcohol (ethanol). The effects of hypotensive drugs may be potentiated.

Other antipsychotic drugs

There are several other groups of drugs that are chemically different from but pharmacologically similar to the phenothiazines. These include the butyrophenones (benperidol, droperidol, haloperidol, and trifluperidol), diphenylbutylpiperidines (fluspiriline and pimozide), thioxanthenes (chlorprothixene, flupenthixol, and zuclopenthixol), oxypertine and benzamide (sulpiride). Some of these drugs are less sedative than chlorpromazine (flupenthixol and pimozide) whilst haloperidol is useful for the rapid control of acute psychotic states. One of the problems of the treatment of schizophrenia is that of drug-compliance. In order to surmount this problem, depot preparations of flupenthixol and zuclopenthixol have been formulated as esters (decanoate) that are dissolved in vegetable oil in which form they are given by injection as a depot preparation every two to six weeks. The selection and use of antipsychotic drugs is obviously an area for the psychiatrist but, with such a large number of preparations available, there is the need for even the specialist to become highly selective and competent in the use of this important group of efficacious but potentially dangerous drugs.

LITHIUM

The medical use of lithium is not new and, during the last century, it acquired a therapeutic reputation amongst those who took the waters because it was beneficial for the treatment of gout. Prompted by this fame, some doctors began to prescribe it for gout and other conditions but it soon had to be abandoned because of its serious toxicity. Later it was given a trial for the treatment of epilepsy and also to replace sodium in the preparation of salt-free diets for the treatment of high blood pressure. Unfortunately, both these uses had to be abandoned because of its serious, including fatal, toxic effects. The possible use of lithium as a psychotropic drug came to light when Cade (1949) observed that lithium urate caused guinea-pigs to become sleepy. Clinical trials of lithium soon followed, and it was found to be the only specific drug for the treatment of mania although, not surprisingly, experience showed that the concentration of lithium in the plasma had to be maintained between narrow limits if toxicity was not to ensue.

Pharmacodynamics

When lithium salts are administered there is a slow displacement of sodium ions by lithium ions. It has been observed that in patients suffering from depressive illness the intracellular sodium ion concentration is elevated, especially so in those suffering from mania. It has therefore been suggested that the mechanism of action of lithium is by displacement of intracellular sodium, thus allowing this ion to return towards the normal concentration. In practice, lithium carbonate or lithium citrate are the salts used.

Pharmacokinetics

Lithium salts, like sodium salts, are well-absorbed but the lithium ion crosses cell membranes more slowly than sodium or potassium ions and this has important implications for its toxicity (see Unwanted Effects). Therapeutic plasma concentrations lie between 0.8 and 1.3 mmol/l. Plasma concentrations above 1.5 mmol/l are likely to be associated with unwanted effects and, at concentrations above 3 mmol/l, severe overdose occurs. The $T_{0.5}$ is 7–20 hours but increases to 36 hours with old age.

Uses

As already indicated, lithium salts are used for the treatment of mania and, more particularly, for the treatment of manic depression, where it can prevent the unpleasant and serious mood swings that are the major feature of this condition. It is also used for the treatment of unipolar depression but usually only after this has been controlled by the use of antidepressant drugs such as the tricyclics.

Unwanted effects

Lithium has a low therapeutic index therefore, as explained earlier, it is essential for the plasma concentration to be kept within narrow limits. As it is eliminated entirely through the kidneys then factors that alter fluid balance and renal function are likely to precipitate lithium toxicity. Thus, a reduced fluid intake (for example, vomiting) or an increased fluid loss (for example, vomiting, diarrhoea, fever, or diuretic therapy) may precipitate toxic effects.

The features of lithium intoxication are gastro-intestinal (anorexia, nausea, vomiting, and diarrhoea) and CNS disturbances (drowsiness, giddiness, lethargy, ataxia, tremor, inco-ordination, and dysarthria). Severe intoxication may be associated with a toxic psychosis, convulsions, coma, oliguria, and circulatory failure leading to death. Lithium therapy has been reported to be associated with an increased incidence of dental caries (Rugg-Gunn, 1979).

Drug interactions with lithium

Both pharmacokinetic and pharmacodynamic interactions may occur.

Pharmacokinetics
After glomerular filtration, lithium appears to be reabsorbed in the proximal renal tubule and probably also in the loop of Henle (but unlike sodium not in the distal tubule). Furthermore, reabsorption appears to be linked to that of sodium (Beeley, 1986). Thus, sodium depletion due to any cause stimulates proximal tubular reabsorption of both sodium and lithium with a consequent increase in plasma lithium concentration. The converse effect is produced when the sodium load is increased. Thiazide diuretics increase sodium excretion by inhibiting distal tubular reabsorption; there will be a compensatory increase in proximal tubular reabsorption that will affect lithium as well as sodium and thereby increase plasma lithium concentrations. Thus, thiazide diuretics should be avoided in

patients on lithium; frusemide is less likely to produce this effect. If a patient on lithium requires a diuretic then the dose of lithium must be reduced by 25 to 50 per cent, and the plasma lithium concentration carefully monitored.

Non-steroidal anti-inflammatory drugs (NSAIDs; Chapter 5) reduce lithium excretion and hence increase plasma lithium concentrations. Those known to produce this effect include ibuprofen, naproxen, diclofenac, piroxicam, indometh-acin, and phenylbutazone. Now that ibuprofen is available as an over-the-counter prescription it is important to warn patients on lithium that they should not take this analgesic. Fortunately, aspirin and paracetamol have no effect on lithium excretion.

Theophylline and acetazolamide both increase the excretion of lithium. As indicated earlier, sodium salts also increase in this excretion so that medications containing these substances (sodium bicarbonate, magnesium trisilicate, Gavis-con, Fybogel) are best avoided in these circumstances.

Pharmacodynamics

The antipsychotic drug, haloperidol, may precipitate lithium toxicity as also may the anticonvulsant drug, carbamazepine (see later), particularly when the latter is present in high plasma concentrations. Lithium has neuromuscular blocking properties of its own and may potentiate the effects of both competitive (e.g. tubocurarine) and depolarizing neuromuscular blockers (e.g. suxamethonium). In view of the inevitable disturbances of renal function and fluid balance that are likely to occur during *major* dental surgery, lithium therapy should be temporarily stopped several days before this is undertaken in order to avoid the risk of precipitating lithium intoxication.

DEPRESSION AND ANTIDEPRESSANTS

Mental illness of varying degrees forms a significant part of modern life. Most of us experience, from time to time, swings of moods. These are usually related to the circumstances prevailing at the time. However, some people are prone to recurrent episodes of severe depression during which they become incapacitated and even suicidal. These episodes usually pass, but they may last for weeks, months, or even years unless treated. Some patients have marked swings of mood from depression to the manic state, where there is a marked elevation of mood and the patient becomes agitated. This, as we have seen, is referred to as manic–depressive psychosis (bipolar illness), but more commonly the patient is simply depressed (unipolar illness). The antidepressant drugs are usually divided into the following groups:

(1) tricyclic and related antidepressants;

(2) monoamine oxidase inhibitors (MAOIs);

(3) other antidepressant drugs.

Tricyclic and related (tetracyclic) antidepressants

The tricyclic and related antidepressants can be divided into those with distinct sedative properties in addition to their antidepressant properties, and those with less sedative properties:

(1) tricyclics with sedative properties include: amitriptyline, maprotiline, dothiepin, doxepin, trazodone, and trimipramine;

   (ii) tetracyclics with sedative properties include: mianserin;

(2) tricyclics with less sedative properties include: butriptyline, clomipramine, desipramine, imipramine, iprindole, lofepramine, nortriptyline, and viloxazine.

Protriptyline is also a tricyclic antidepressant but has a stimulant action.

Pharmacodynamics

It has been postulated that mental depression is the result of a disorder of amine metabolism. The tricyclic antidepressants, and related drugs, appear to block the reuptake of noradrenaline into central sympathetic nerve fibres. Normally, noradrenaline released from storage granules within a sympathetic neurone is mainly inactivated by being taken back into sympathetic neurones, where it is housed within storage granules and is ready for reuse. When this reuptake mechanism is interfered with, as occurs with most tricyclic antidepressants and related drugs, then there occurs a concentration of released noradrenaline at central synapses. If a depression is somehow related to a central deficiency of noradrenaline, then it would seem that the increase in concentration produced by the tricyclics centrally will help to correct the disorder. It is unlikely that noradrenaline is the only amine involved; others could be concerned, for instance 5-HT. Furthermore, as this blockage of reuptake occurs immediately but the drugs do not relieve a depression for some weeks, it is clear that this inhibition of reuptake cannot be the only explanation. An additional factor, which supports this reservation, is that iprindole interferes very little with the reuptake of released amines. Possibly this enhancement of noradrenaline concentration in the synaptic cleft is only the beginning of a sequence of events that finally relieve the depression.

Pharmacokinetics

The tricyclic antidepressants are well-absorbed from the gastro-intestinal tract after oral administration, and peak plasma concentrations are reached within two to eight hours. They are lipophilic drugs that are widely distributed and highly bound to plasma proteins. The tricyclics are metabolized in the liver with the production of a number of active metabolites. These are eventually conjugated with glucuronic acid and are excreted in the urine. The half-life of these drugs is very variable, ranging from about 16 hours for amitriptyline to 80 hours for protriptyline (Baldessarini 1985).

Unwanted effects

The tricyclic antidepressants have a marked anticholinergic effect so that the patient may be troubled by dry mouth, constipation, urinary retention, and blurred vision. The dry mouth may be severe and is often very troublesome. In some patients a persistent fine tremor occurs, although these drugs rarely cause the extrapyramidal effects seen with some of the phenothiazines.

Drug interactions may occur in that tricyclic antidepressants can reduce the effect of some hypotensive drugs, e.g. guanethidine, bethanidine, debrisoquine, and clonidine. Guanethidine, bethanidine, and debrisoquine are adrenergic-neurone blocking agents (all rarely used today) and their antihypertensive properties depend on the fact that they reach high concentrations within sympathetic nerve endings. These drugs gain access to the neuronal ending by the same pathway that reuptakes released noradrenaline. When this reuptake mechanism is blocked, as occurs with the tricyclics and the phenothiazines, then the antihypertensive is unable to get into the nerve endings and is ineffective. It seems that in some way the tricyclic antidepressants also block the central effects of the hypotensive drug, clonidine.

Theoretically, the use of adrenaline in local anaesthetic solutions could produce a hypertensive episode because, in the presence of tricyclic antidepressants, the main pathway of inactivation, e.g. reuptake, of catecholamines is blocked. In clinical practice this does not appear to occur and it would seem that with the concentration of adrenaline in the local anaesthetic solution (usually 1:80 000), and in the amounts used in dentistry, there is no problem. (Cawson and Spector 1985).

A common cardiovascular effect of the tricyclics is postural hypotension, especially in the older patient. This is partly due to the blockade of peripheral α-adrenergic receptors. The anticholinergic activity of these drugs may also cause a mild sinus tachycardia. The tricyclic antidepressants have a cardiotoxic effect in predisposed patients, e.g. those with existing cardiac problems.

The tricyclic drugs are extremely toxic in overdosage and are dangerous, especially when used in attempted suicide.

Therapeutic uses

The tricyclic antidepressants are generally regarded as the drugs of first choice for the treatment of mental depression. Unfortunately, their antidepressant action is not immediate but begins in about two to three weeks and is not fully effective until six weeks. Low doses are usually prescribed at first and gradually built up until plasma concentrations are sufficient. For instance, amitriptyline by mouth is given initially in 50 to 75 mg doses (elderly patients and adolescents, 25 to

50 mg) daily, and is often prescribed as a single dose at bedtime. The dose is gradually increased to a maximum of 150 to 200 mg daily. The *BNF* [No. 12 (1986)] suggests that after suppression of symptoms the drug should be maintained at the optimum level for at least another month before any attempt is made to reduce the dosage. The drug should not be stopped prematurely and the patient may be maintained on a much reduced dosage for some months in order to prevent occurrence of a relapse. Perhaps the most widely used of the tricyclics are imipramine and amitriptyline.

The patient should not be given an unlimited quantity of these drugs as depressed patients are potential suicides and, in overdosage, the tricyclic antidepressants are extremely toxic. Their progress should be monitored regularly; the first sign of improvement is usually an improved sleep pattern.

The oxazine, viloxazine, probably produces its antidepressant effect in the same way as the tricyclic drugs. It prevents the reuptake of released noradrenaline and so increases the functional availability of the neurotransmitter. Viloxazine is unlike the tricyclic antidepressants in that it has little anticholinergic activity.

Monoamine oxidase inhibitors (MAOIs)

The monoamine oxidase inhibitors include:

(1) hydrazine MAOIs—iproniazid, isocarboxazid, and phenelzine;

(2) non-hydrazine MAOIs—tranylcypromine.

The story of the discovery of MAOIs as anti-depressive drugs is of interest. In the early 50s isoniazid was developed as an antituberculous drug. It was noticed that patients being treated for tuberculosis with isoniazid appeared to be more euphoric than perhaps their condition warranted. The fact that isoniazid inhibited monoamine oxidase (MAO) supported the theory that depression could be a disorder of amine metabolism.

Pharmacodynamics

Monoamine oxidase inhibitors block the breakdown of naturally occurring amines such as noradrenaline, 5-HT, and dopamine. Consequent upon this failure of metabolism, the concentration of noradrenaline and other amines is increased in the CNS. It has been suggested that this increased availability of amines centrally is the reason for their effectiveness in depression. As with the tricyclic antidepressants, the effect of these drugs on amine inactivation is almost immediate whereas the relief of the depression is delayed for two weeks or more. The way in which amines are concentrated centrally differs between MAOIs and the tricyclic antidepressants. Once again, as with the tricyclics, it would seem that the theory of disordered amine inactivation is not the whole story.

Pharmacokinetics

When given orally the MAOIs are readily absorbed from the gastro-intestinal tract. Not a great deal is known about the pharmacokinetics of these drugs but the hydrazine MAOIs are partly inactivated by acetylation. Furthermore, these produce an irreversible block of MAO and so their activity tends to be prolonged. After cessation of treatment it takes about three weeks before new enzymes are formed in adequate amounts.

The response to these drugs is somewhat varied; for instance with slow acetylators of the hydrazine type, patients may find toxicity occurring.

Unwanted effects

There is a wide variety of these, some relatively trivial and some very serious. The MAOIs affect the autonomic nervous system and hypotension is produced. Other disturbances of that system include dry mouth, water retention, difficulty in micturition, and constipation. A very serious effect, although of low incidence, is the occurrence of diffuse hepatocellular damage with the hydrazine derivatives. Perhaps the most alarming and serious of unwanted effects are those occurring due to interactions with other drugs and substances.

The interaction between MAOIs and sympathomimetic amines is well-known, and is an example of how the absorption of one drug may be increased by another. The gastro-intestinal tract contains large amounts of the enzyme MAO, which normally metabolizes and thereby restricts the absorption of any amines that are substrates for it, for example tyramine or phenylephrine. Certain foods also contain amines, especially cheese, Marmite and other yeast extracts, Bovril, pickled herrings, broad beans (as an amine precursor), yoghourt, strong beer, and some wines. When these agents are taken by a patient who is receiving an MAOI drug, there is a considerable risk that a so-called MAOI crisis may develop. In this condition there is a severe headache with a dangerous rise in blood pressure that, in some cases, has progressed to a cerebral haemorrhage or acute cardiovascular collapse (Blackwell *et al.* 1967). From the practical point of view it is vital that all patients on MAOIs be informed that they must avoid such foods as well as sympathomimetic amines, some of which are concealed within various patent medicines.

It is the indirectly acting sympathomimetics, such as tyramine, that often produce this interaction. These can cause the release of noradrenaline from its storage sites within the granules or synaptic vesicles of sympathetic nerve endings. The released noradrenaline acts on α_1-receptors in the peripheral blood vessels causing vasoconstriction and a rise in blood pressure, noradrenaline being a pressor substance. Normally the amine, tyramine, contained in foods is not absorbed to any extent, being broken down by the gut MAO. However, when the patient is taking an MAOI, tyramine is absorbed, so causing noradrenaline release, with a potentiation of the pressor effect of noradrenaline. The treatment of such an hypertensive crisis is by the use of a short-acting α-adrenergic blocking agent such as phentolamine, 5 mg IV or IM, repeated if necessary.

Another potentially very dangerous interaction may result from the use of the opioid, pethidine, in those taking MAOIs. Pethidine is a recent addition to drugs listed in the *Dental Practitioners' Formulary*. If given to a patient on MAOIs it may cause hyperpyrexia, which can prove to be extremely serious. This is not a reaction that could have been predicted on the known pharmacology of pethidine; it appears to be limited to that opioid but perhaps other opioids should be avoided in those taking MAOIs, simply as a precaution.

It has been suggested in the past that local anaesthetic solutions containing catecholamines should be avoided in patients taking MAOIs as they were thought to interact, possibly producing a hypertensive episode. This view was based on a pharmacological misunderstanding as it was thought, at the time, that the main inactivation of catecholamines was by MAO. This is now known to be untrue and so there is no real contra-indication in dentistry to the use of catecholamine-containing local anaesthetic solutions in patients taking MAOIs.

If a general anaesthetic is absolutely necessary, then this should be administered by a specialist anaesthetist.

Therapeutic uses

The MAOIs were, perhaps, the first drugs of real significance in the treatment of depression. They are no longer the first choice of such drugs, having been generally superseded by the tricyclic antidepressants, and they now have a more limited use because of the wide variety of their unwanted effects. They are used when vigorous treatment with the tricyclics has failed. The *BNF* (1986–8 No. 12) suggests that the '. . . phobic and depressed patient with atypical, hypochondria-cal, or hysterical features are said to respond best to MAOIs.' The delay in improvement of the depression may, as with the tricyclics, be in the order of a few weeks.

In the past, certain of the MAOIs (e.g. the non-hydrazine—pargyline (Eutonyl)) were used as antihypertensive agents as they affected adrenergic activity by neuronal block. Better and safer drugs are now available and pargyline is no longer listed in the *BNF*.

HYPNOTICS AND SEDATIVES

Hypnotics are drugs that induce sleep. Normal sleep has at least two phases, one with regular respiration (called orthodox sleep) alternating with the second phase, which consists of rapid eye movements (REM sleep) associated with irregular breathing. Hypnotics do not produce normal sleep in that, to varying degrees, they tend to reduce the second phase. As the therapeutic effect of the hypnotic begins to wear off before wakening there is an increase in the frequency of REM periods. Nevertheless, in the total sleep period, the proportion occupied by

REM sleep is reduced. When hypnotic drugs are withdrawn, there is an over-compensatory increase in REM sleep and dreaming is excessive. There may even be nightmares associated with the now increased REM activity.

The number of remedies offered to the healing professions and the public suggest that there is a general problem in achieving sleep. Unfortunately the causes of insomnia are as varied as the individuals and the remedies. What is good for one individual is not necessarily good for another. An unduly stuffy room, an overfilled or empty stomach, a distended bladder, pain or discomfort are all frequent causes of insomnia. Such reasons for lack of sleep can usually be tackled without recourse to the use of 'sleeping tablets'. In contrast, insomnia from severe illness or emotional disturbances, such as worry, fear, or bereavement, are different matters altogether. Such cases may require a sleeping tablet, even if only for a short time. As for the elderly, a tot of brandy at night may be as good a remedy as any. Hypnotics should not be prescribed indiscriminately without some good reason and must be under careful supervision. If the cause of lack of sleep is pain then an analgesic should be prescribed, not an hypnotic. Sleep disturbance is very common in psychiatric illnesses, e.g. depression, and it is the illness itself that needs treatment, rather than having recourse to 'sleeping tablets' as an immediate expedient for any sleeplessness.

Hypnotics will be considered under various headings: chloral derivatives, barbiturates, antihistamines, and benzodiazepines. The usual hypnotic drug prescribed today is one of the benzodiazepines. The barbiturates are no longer discussed in the BNF (1986–8) as drugs to be employed for insomnia but, at one time, they were the most commonly used hypnotics (see below).

Chloral hydrate
(0.5 to 1 g, 30 minutes before bedtime)

This was the first of the synthetic hypnotic drugs. It is very irritant to the empty stomach and should be prescribed as a well-diluted solution, preferably with a strong flavouring agent to disguise the unpleasant taste.

Pharmacokinetics

Chloral hydrate is rapidly absorbed from the gastro-intestinal tract and is quickly reduced to trichloroethanol in the liver by alcohol dehydrogenase. Although chloral hydrate itself may possess hypnotic properties, it is believed that the CNS depression that occurs after its ingestion is mainly due to trichloroethanol; in other words, trichloroethanol is the active metabolite. A variable fraction of chloral hydrate is oxidized in the liver to trichloracetic acid (an inactive metabolite). A fraction of trichloroethanol is reduced but the major part is conjugated with glucuronic acid; the conjugate is eventually excreted in the urine, as is trichloroacetic acid.

Unwanted effects

The main one is associated with its irritant effect on the gastric mucosa, causing the patient to feel discomfort. Allergic reactions may occur; these usually take the form of skin rashes. In very large doses, chloral hydrate is a cardiac depressant and is therefore contra-indicated in patients with severe heart disease. It is also to be avoided in those with marked hepatic impairment.

This drug should not be taken together with alcohol as both substances are metabolized by the same enzyme system (alcohol dehydrogenase).

Uses

Chloral is probably still a useful hypnotic drug for, in therapeutic doses, it has little, if any, cardiovascular effect. It appears to be particularly valuable in young children and in the elderly. Hypnotics in general tend to cause post-hypnotic confusion in the elderly, but chloral hydrate seems to cause less.

The BNF (1986–8) refers to chloral hydrate and chloral derivatives as useful hypnotics. It states that dichloralphenazone and triclofos sodium '. . . cause fewer gastro-intestinal upsets than chloral hydrate'. Dichloralphenazone is a popular preparation containing chloral. It is a complex of chloral hydrate with the antipyretic analgesic, phenazone. The phenazone nucleus has been implicated in the production of rashes and agranulocytosis but this white cell effect does not seem to be a problem with dichloralphenazone. It has the advantage that it is available in tablet form and is easier to take than chloral hydrate itself.

The barbiturates

In the past, these were used extensively as sleeping tablets but today they have been displaced by the benzodiazepines. Initially the benzodiazepines were thought less likely to cause dependence problems than did the barbiturates, but sadly this has not proved to be the case (see Benzodiazepines—Unwanted effects, below).

Barbiturates are classified as:

(1) ultra-short acting, e.g. thiopentone, methohexitone (see Chapter 8);
(2) short-acting, e.g. amylobarbitone, pentobarbitone (100 to 200 mg, 30 minutes before bedtime);
(3) long-acting, e.g. phenobarbitone.

Pharmacodynamics

These drugs probably act at many levels in the CNS, but the reticular activating system is particularly sensitive. This system is a complex of neural pathways that extend in the brainstem from the medulla to the thalamus. It is the activity of this system that maintains consciousness and keeps the individual alert. The barbiturates, and other hypnotic drugs, appear to depress transmission of impulses through inhibition of neurotransmitter release.

Pharmacological properties

The effect on the CNS, as indicated above, is inhibition of synaptic transmission.

Therapeutic hypnotic doses of the barbiturates when given orally have few cardiovascular effects in the otherwise healthy patient. They do cause a slight decrease in the blood pressure and heart rate, but these phenomena occur in normal sleep anyway. The barbiturates do, however, inhibit transmission in autonomic ganglia, and intravenous barbiturates may produce a marked fall in blood pressure in the hypertensive patient.

Barbiturates can produce a dose-related depression of respiration. Hypnotic doses usually cause only a minor degree of this, but larger doses cause severe respiratory depression and, in fact, the cause of death in acute barbiturate poisoning is directly attributable to respiratory failure. Another respiratory effect is the production of laryngospasm with the use of the intravenous agents, particularly thiopentone (see Chapter 8).

Barbiturates are enzyme inducers, that is they stimulate the activity of microsomal drug-metabolizing enzymes in the liver. Phenobarbitone is a potent enzyme inducer and the result of such induction is that the half-life of some drugs may be reduced substantially; those so affected include coumarins, phenytoin, and the antifungal drug, griseofulvin. Probably the most dangerous situation that could arise from this effect occurs after the withdrawal of a drug that is an enzyme inducer. Thus, the withdrawal of phenobarbitone during treatment with one of the anticoagulants may lead to a dangerous intensification of the anticoagulant effect. This is due to the reduced rate of metabolism of the anticoagulant.

Pharmacokinetics

For hypnotic use the barbiturates are administered orally. Absorption takes place mainly from the intestine, and food decreases the rate of absorption. The intravenous route is employed for anaesthetic induction.

The barbiturates are bound variously to plasma proteins; the more lipid-soluble the drug, the more binding there is. There exists no impenetrable barrier in the body to the diffusion of the barbiturates. Small amounts of barbiturates may appear in the mother's milk after ingestion of large doses, and they cross the placenta to reach the fetus.

Following absorption the most lipid-soluble barbiturates, that is those used intravenously (ultra-short acting barbiturates), are quickly concentrated in the brain, and so they have a very rapid onset of action. Their duration of action is also very short (see below).

Three processes are responsible for the termination of the CNS-depressant action of the barbiturates:

(1) physical redistribution;

(2) metabolic degradation;

(3) renal excretion.

All these processes reduce the drug's plasma concentration and result in its withdrawal from its site of action in the CNS. The immediate fate of the drug does seem to depend on the degree of its lipid solubility. The most lipid-soluble ultra-short acting barbiturates undergo rapid redistribution to muscle and then to fat. Indeed, it is this early redistribution that accounts for their relatively brief action. Following redistribution, thiopentone is almost completely metabolized in the liver and only a very small fraction is eventually excreted unchanged in the urine. In point of fact, although metabolized, the rate of metabolism is relatively slow— perhaps in the region of 10 to 15 per cent per hour, which is far too slow to account for the very short duration of action. The rapid emergence from sleep after administration of a single dose of thiopentone depends on a shift of the drug from the brain to other tissues and is not a result of metabolic degradation. About 30 minutes after the injection of thiopentone, the brain may have given up as much as 90 per cent of the drug to muscle and fat depots. The same comments apply to methohexitone, although the metabolic degradation of this drug is probably quicker than for thiopentone.

The less lipophilic barbiturates (the short-acting and the long-acting) reach the brain tissues more slowly. These compounds are metabolized in the liver and this is the way in which the activity of a short-acting barbiturate is mainly terminated. The long-acting barbiturate, phenobarbitone, is metabolized in the liver but about 25 per cent may be excreted unchanged in the urine. The metabolites of all the barbiturates are eventually excreted in the urine.

Unwanted effects

1. Drowsiness is a common after-effect of the barbiturates as hypnotics. Headache and nausea may also occur.

2. Hypersensitivity reactions do occur, particularly in subjects with an allergic diathesis. They often take the form of skin rashes or localized swellings.

3. Barbiturates produce both physical and psychological dependence and, for this reason, have been discontinued, with few exceptions (e.g. phenobarbitone in epilepsy, see later).

4. Instead of depressing the CNS, sometimes barbiturates stimulate the subject, who becomes excitable. This curious effect is most likely to be seen in geriatric patients.

5. Interactions with other drugs may occur because of hepatic microsomal enzyme induction (discussed under pharmacological properties above).

6. Porphyrias are inherited diseases in which there is an abnormality of porphyrin synthesis. They are associated with the excretion of large amounts of

porphyrins, or their precursors, in the urine. Barbiturates enhance porphyrin synthesis and must not be given to a patient with porphyria; to do so may precipitate a serious crisis with lower motor-neurone paralysis.

Uses

The short-acting barbiturates were popular at one time as hypnotics but, as we have seen, they are now virtually obsolete. Furthermore, these short-acting compounds, e.g. amylobarbitone, butobarbitone, cyclobarbitone, pentobarbitone, quinalbarbitone, are now classified as 'controlled drugs' and the prescription must be written in the form ordered for such drugs (see Chapter 3). This requirement has further discouraged their use.

The long-acting barbiturate, phenobarbitone, finds a place in the management of epilepsy but it is also now listed as a 'controlled drug'. However, the actual form of the prescription is not as demanding as for the short-acting barbiturates in that, although the prescription must be signed and dated by the prescriber, other details required need not be in the practitioner's handwriting.

The ultra short-acting agents, thiopentone and methohexitone, have been discussed in Chapter 8. Although thiopentone is a drug that will control status epilepticus, it must be remembered that methohexitone has convulsant properties and should not be used in patients with a history of epilepsy (Goldman 1966).

Benzodiazepines

These comprise a group of drugs with useful hypnotic, anxiolytic, anticonvulsant, and skeletal-muscle relaxant properties. The use of benzodiazepines as hypnotics will be discussed first, although some of the general properties of these drugs (e.g. pharmacodynamics, unwanted effects) will also be considered at this stage. Examples of the benzodiazepine hypnotics include:

nitrazepam (5 to 10 mg, 30 minutes before bedtime—the dose should be halved for elderly patients);

flurazepam (15 to 30 mg, 30 minutes before bedtime—elderly patients, 15 mg);

lormetazepam (1 mg at bedtime—elderly patients, 500 µg);

temazepam (10 to 30 mg immediately before bedtime—elderly patients, half the dose);

triazolam (250 µg, 15 to 30 minutes before bedtime—elderly patients, half the dose).

Pharmacodynamics

The benzodiazepines probably work centrally in a similar way to older hypnotic–sedative drugs, such as the barbiturates. It does appear, however, that the benzodiazepines are different in that they have a specific anti-anxiety action, which is lacking in drugs such as the barbiturates. The benzodiazepines depress the reticular system, but they also depress the limbic system at much lower doses and this system is associated with emotions. This is not the case with the barbiturates which, as we have seen, depress the reticular system preferentially. It seems that the benzodiazepines potentiate the inhibitory action of the neurotransmitter gamma(γ)-aminobutyric acid (GABA) on neurones. Although the benzodiazepines diminish REM sleep, they do not seem to do so to the same extent as barbiturates.

Pharmacological properties

The effects on the CNS are those of sedation to hypnosis. They also have anticonvulsant properties as well as the anti-anxiety effect. The cardiovascular effect of the benzodiazepines is small although, in large doses, they all decrease blood pressure. A similar picture applies to respiration; the usual hypnotic dose does not affect the normal individual. The benzodiazepines are not inducers of hepatic microsomal enzymes to any extent.

Pharmacokinetics

The benzodiazepines are generally well-absorbed when given orally. Some do not reach the circulation intact, but produce their effects through clinically active metabolites; one such is flurazepam. When the benzodiazepines are given orally, the peak plasma concentration is variably reached within a period of 0.5 to 8 hours (Harvey 1985). The half-life of a preparation does not necessarily give an indication of the drug's duration of action as it may produce metabolites that have their own half-lives. This is illustrated in the list below.

Drug	Half-life (h)		Active metabolite
Nitrazepam	15–38		
Flurazepam		[40–250]	N-desalkylflurazepam
Lormetazepam	10–12		
Temazepam	8–22		
Triazolam	2		

(Figures in brackets are the half-life of the major active metabolite.)

Flurazepam and lormetazepam are no longer available on the NHS.

As with the barbiturates, there is a phase of redistribution to muscle and fat especially with the most lipid-soluble benzodiazepines. This may account for the duration of an hypnotic effect just as much as may metabolism. The benzodiazepines are extensively metabolized in the liver by microsomal enzymes and, in general terms, the metabolites are conjugated with glucuronic acid and excreted in the urine.

Unwanted effects

1. Without doubt the most common unwanted effect of the benzodiazepines, when used as sedatives or anxiolytics, is drowsiness. This is also associated with a decrease in reaction time, which is likely to affect driving ability. Judgment and concentration may both be impaired.

2. Occasionally, in doses that relieve anxiety, there is a paradoxical effect in which excitement is seen, rather than depression. This arises more often in the young and the elderly; occasionally a patient may even become aggressive.

3. These drugs are not so innocuous as they were first thought to be. Treatment for anxiety should be limited to short periods as tolerance may develop within about 4 months of continuous use, and there is also the danger of the development of dependence, which is something thought not to occur when they were first introduced. There is evidence that medication with benzodiazepines for some weeks or more can lead to both physical and psychological dependence, and that cessation of treatment can lead to definite withdrawal symptoms (Drug Newsletter 1985). The withdrawal symptoms may sometimes hardly be distinguishable from the original anxiety state. Symptoms of withdrawal include insomnia; restlessness; lack of concentration; delusions; visual and auditory hallucinations; altered sensations in the skin, mouth, jaw, and tongue—and even toothache.

4. The combination of the benzodiazepines with other drugs that act on the CNS may potentiate depressant effects. Thus they must be used cautiously with, for instance, alcohol.

5. Hypersensitivity reactions may occur but their incidence is low.

Uses

The benzodiazepines are useful in the treatment of insomnia. The prescription of hypnotics is justifiable for short periods (1–3 weeks) to cover a time of stress but it is undesirable that patients should become used to hypnotics and so take them regularly year in and year out.

For those who find difficulty in getting off to sleep, but who sleep well once sleep has ensued, a drug like temazepam should be used; this has a relatively short half-life and no active metabolites. On the other hand, for the patient who readily gets off to sleep, but who wakens early in the morning, a longer-acting preparation may be desirable. Flurazepam is quickly converted to active metabolites and these have a half-life up to many days. Nitrazepam has a half-life in the range 15–38 hours and, unlike flurazepam, its metabolites are inactive. Both of these drugs may be useful for the early waker but they can produce residual effects in the following day, e.g. drowsiness. Flurazepam is no longer prescribable on the NHS.

Antihistamines (H$_1$-blockers)
(e.g. promethazine)

These produce CNS depression when used in therapeutic doses and so the patient is not alert and may feel drowsy. The various preparations provide differing degrees of sedation and the patient's reaction to them is individualized. Promethazine is a popular sedative/hypnotic for children but is not recommended for those under 6 months of age. Its dosage regimen is:

By mouth: adults, 25 to 75 mg at bedtime; children of 6 to 12 months—10 mg, of 1 to 5 years—15 to 20 mg, of 6 to 10 years—20 to 25 mg, at bedtime; or, for daytime sedation, once or twice daily using the lower dose.

ANXIETY AND ANXIOLYTICS

Benzodiazepines

As outlined earlier, the benzodiazepine drugs have specific anti-anxiety properties. Anxiety is a state where the individual feels uneasy and apprehensive, where there is also a feeling of tension accompanied by many bodily complaints e.g. palpitations, headache, dizziness, flushing, sweating, tense muscles. Anxiety may also be a feature of other psychological illnesses, e.g. depression. Appropriate anxiolytic dosages are:

chlordiazepoxide (orally, 10 mg three times daily);

diazepam (orally, 2 mg three times daily increased in severe anxiety to 15 to 30 mg daily in divided doses);

oxazepam (15 to 30 mg (elderly patients 10 to 20 mg) three to four times daily; increased in severe anxiety to 60 mg three times daily as a maximum);

lorazepam (orally, 1 to 4 mg daily in divided doses, increased to 10 mg in severe anxiety).

Pharmacokinetics

Chlordiazepoxide and diazepam were amongst the early benzodiazepines to be prescribed for anxiety. Chlordiazepoxide is rather slowly absorbed after oral administration and it takes several hours for peak plasma concentrations to be reached. On the other hand, diazepam, which is highly lipid-soluble, is quickly absorbed producing a peak plasma concentration in about one hour. Some of these anxiolytic benzodiazepines e.g. chlordiazepoxide and diazepam, are metabolized to produce active metabolites, whereas oxazepam and lorazepam are converted to inactive metabolites. The half-life of these drugs and their metabolites is indicated in the following list, which may be compared with that shown in the section on the Pharmacokinetics of benzodiazepine hypnotics above:

Drug	Half-life (h)	Active metabolite(s)
Chlordiazepoxide	5–30 [36–200]	Desmethylchlordiazepoxide→ demoxepam→nordiazepam
Diazepam	20–100 [36–200]	Nordiazepam
Oxazepam	4–15	
Lorazepam	10–20	

(Figures in brackets are the active half-life of metabolites.)

The metabolites eventually undergo glucuronidation and are excreted in the urine.

Uses (general)

These drugs are used in both chronic and acute anxiety states. All of us will have experienced anxiety at some time or another, and most of us will not have required medication. However, when anxiety persists and interferes with the daily functioning of life, it is then that the use of the benzodiazepines may be considered. Again it must be emphasized that treatment should be limited to short periods as tolerance may occur and dependence may develop within four months or less of continuous usage. Dependence is more likely in patients who have a background of alcohol or drug abuse, and in those with an unstable background.

Drugs such as chlordiazepoxide and diazepam are useful in managing chronic anxiety. They have a long half-life and consequently provide a sustained action. It must be emphasized that such patients require psychiatric treatment.

Other benzodiazepines recommended for anxiety, e.g. oxazepam and lorazepam, have relatively short half-lives and so do not provide such a sustained activity and are more useful for short acute episodic anxiety.

Uses in dentistry

1. Their anxiolytic effect makes the benzodiazepines useful drugs in pre-anaesthetic medication (see Chapter 8).

2. Intravenous diazepam or midazolam are used to provide sedation as an adjunct to local anaesthesia; the sedation achieved often lasts up to an hour. A useful and characteristic feature of such sedation is the anterograde amnesia produced in over 50 per cent of patients given diazepam, and in nearly 85 per cent of those given midazolam (see Chapter 8).

3. A benzodiazepine is a recommended part of an emergency kit in case of the occurrence of status epilepticus (see Chapter 24). In this situation the anticonvulsant properties of the benzodiazepines are utilized.

4. The muscle relaxant property of the benzodiazepines may be useful in the

management of temporo-mandibular joint pain and dysfunction, which could well be due to tension in the muscles of mastication.

5. The use of oral benzodiazepines to produce sedation before dental procedures, the day before and again just prior to dental treatment, is recommended by some. It is certainly not as sure a method as providing intravenous administration at the time of treatment (see Chapter 8).

General comments on the benzodiazepines

These anxiolytic drugs are sometimes referred to as 'minor tranquillizers' to distinguish them from antipsychotic drugs, which have been called 'major tranquillizers' or neuroleptics. The terms minor and major tranquillizers should not be used as they do not best describe the actions of drugs to which they refer and, in any case, the benzodiazepines can hardly be regarded as 'minor' drugs.

Although certain benzodiazepines are advised for use as hypnotics, and others as anti-anxiety agents, they all serve the same purpose and perhaps the distinction is somewhat artificial.

Propranolol

The use of propranolol for somatic anxiety, as distinct from central anxiety as discussed above, is referred to in Chapter 13.

ANTICONVULSANTS

The treatment of epilepsy and facial neuralgias

Epilepsy is a term used for a group of CNS disorders having in common the occurrence of sudden and transitory episodes (seizures) of abnormal phenomena of motor (convulsions), sensory, autonomic, or psychic origin. The seizures are nearly always associated with abnormal and excessive discharges from neurones within the brain.

Epilepsy can be classified into partial seizures, which are either focal or local, and generalized seizures, which can be of the convulsive or non-convulsive type (International League Against Epilepsy 1981). Epilepsy has an incidence in the range 3–6 per 1,000 population (Hauser 1978).

Generalized epilepsy is by far the most common type of convulsive disorder and two aspects can be recognized, the petit mal attack and the grand mal attack.

The petit mal attack commonly occurs in childhood and is characterized by a very brief loss of consciousness (5 to 10 seconds), sometimes accompanied by facial twitching. Frequent petit mal attacks may well be a warning sign that a grand mal attack is soon to occur. Petit mal responds to therapy.

The grand mal attack is usually of sudden onset, but is often preceded by an aura. The attack is characterized by loss of consciousness, postural tone, and contraction of skeletal muscles. There is often loss of sphincter control causing urination and defaecation. The attacks usually last from a few seconds to a few minutes, but can progress to the life-threatening status epilepticus (see Chapter 24). After the convulsions the patient regains consciousness, but is very drowsy and disorientated; they often complain of a severe headache and usually want to sleep. The management of a grand mal attack in the dental surgery is discussed in Chapter 24.

Drugs used in the treatment of epilepsy include phenytoin, barbiturates, carbamazepine, ethosuximide, valproic acid, and the benzodiazepines.

Phenytoin

This is probably the anticonvulsant of choice to treat most types of epilepsy. Its anticonvulsant properties are thought to be due to a stabilizing effect on neuronal membranes to the action of sodium, potassium, and calcium ions (Woodbury *et al.* 1982).

Pharmacokinetics

Phenytoin is mainly given orally, but can be given intramuscularly or intravenously. The usual oral dose in adults is approximately 300 mg daily. Absorption of phenytoin from the gastro-intestinal tract is often slow and shows marked inter-individual variation. Absorption is affected by age, body weight, sex, and rate of phenytoin metabolism. Once absorbed, the drug is rapidly distributed through all tissues of the body. Phenytoin is highly protein-bound (90 per cent), mainly to albumin. About 5 per cent of phenytoin is excreted unchanged in the urine; the remainder is metabolized in the liver, and the metabolites are excreted initially in the bile and subsequently in the urine.

Unwanted effect

Phenytoin therapy is associated with a high incidence of these, mainly involving the CNS and gastro-intestinal tract. High plasma concentrations of phenytoin can produce ataxia, nystagmus, tremors, and drowsiness. Behavioural effects can occur, including hyperactivity, confusion, and hallucinations. The gastro-intestinal disturbances include nausea, vomiting, epigastric pain, and anorexia; their incidence can be reduced by taking the drug with meals. Hirsutism is a common problem in young female patients taking the drug. Hypersensitivity reactions occur in two to five per cent of patients taking phenytoin and range from skin rashes to the Stevens–Johnson syndrome. Haematological changes have been also reported and include leucopenia, agranulocytosis, thrombocytopenia, and a megaloblastic anaemia due to folic acid deficiency (Waxman *et al.* 1970).

Of particular interest to the dental surgeon is the effect of phenytoin on the gingival tissues. Approximately 50 per cent of those taking phenytoin experience enlargement (hyperplasia) of their gingival tissues (Angelopoulos and Goaz 1972). The pathogenesis of this problem is still uncertain. The hyperplasia occurs more commonly in the anterior part of the mouth and begins as an overgrowth of the interdental papillae, followed by a spread to other gingival regions. The gingiva usually retain their pink colour and their firm consistency. Histopathologically, the hyperplastic tissue comprises dense bundles of collagen fibres (Hassel et al. 1978).

There is some correlation between the degree of gingival hyperplasia and oral hygiene (King et al. 1976; the incidence of gingival hyperplasia can be reduced by maintaining good plaque control. Severe cases can be treated with surgical excision (gingivectomy). Some epileptic patients on phenytoin therapy have recurrent problems with gingival hyperplasia and often undergo repeated gingival surgery. For these, it may be appropriate to consider changing their anticonvulsant therapy through consultation with their physician (Seymour et al. 1985).

Uses

Phenytoin is the most widely used anticonvulsant; it is occasionally used in the treatment of certain facial neuralgias.

Barbiturates

Phenobarbitone is the only barbiturate used in the treatment of epilepsy. The general pharmacological properties of the barbiturates have been discussed earlier. Most have anticonvulsant properties by limiting the spread of seizure activity and elevating seizure threshold. The usual adult dose of phenobarbitone is 60 to 100 mg daily.

Pharmacokinetics

Phenobarbitone is slowly absorbed from the gastro-intestinal tract, with peak plasma concentrations occurring six hours after dosage. The drug is partly bound to plasma protein (50 per cent). About 25 per cent of phenobarbitone is excreted unchanged in the urine; the remainder is metabolized in the liver and the metabolites excreted in the urine. The plasma half-life of phenobarbitone in adults is about 100 hours.

Unwanted effects

Sedation is the main unwanted effect associated with phenobarbitone, especially in the early stages of therapy; however, tolerance soon develops. In children, the drug can produce hyperactivity and irritability, whilst in the elderly it frequently produces agitation and confusion. Occasional skin rashes and haematological problems are associated with it..

Uses

Phenobarbitone is an effective agent for generalized tonic–clonic seizures.

Carbamazepine

This has anticonvulsant properties, although how they are achieved is uncertain. The drug is structurally related to the tricyclic antidepressants and is particularly effective in controlling grand mal seizures, but not petit mal attacks. Carbamazepine is also used to treat trigeminal, glossopharyngeal, and post-herpetic neuralgia (see later). For the treatment of epilepsy, initial therapy is with a dose of 100 to 200 mg twice daily, which can be increased up to 1200 mg daily until seizures are controlled.

Pharmacokinetics

Carbamazepine is absorbed slowly from the gastro-intestinal tract with peak concentrations occurring four to eight hours after dosage. About 75 per cent of the drug is protein-bound. The main metabolite of carbamazepine is the 10,11-epoxide, which also possesses anticonvulsant properties; this is further metabolized to inactive compounds, which are excreted in the urine.

Unwanted effects

The common ones include drowsiness, visual disturbances, nausea, and vomiting. Serious haematological effects may occur with carbamazepine therapy, and include aplastic anaemia and agranulocytosis; routine haematological screening (every three months) is therefore required for all patients on this drug. Chronic usage of carbamazepine is associated with water retention, which may cause problems in elderly patients with cardiac disease.

Ethosuximide

This anticonvulsant is used primarily for the treatment of petit mal seizures. Its action is due to an elevation of the threshold for electro-shock seizures.

Pharmacokinetics

Ethosuximide is well-absorbed following oral administration, and peak plasma concentrations occur three hours after dosage. The plasma half-life is approximately 45 hours. Twenty-five per cent of the drug is excreted unchanged in the urine; the remainder is metabolized in the liver and the metabolites excreted in the urine. The usual dose of ethosuximide is 20 to 40 mg/kg of body weight.

Unwanted effects

Like other anticonvulsants, the main unwanted effects of ethosuximide are related to the CNS and the gastro-intestinal tract; they include drowsiness, lethargy, euphoria, dizziness, headache, nausea, vomiting, and anorexia. Skin rashes and haematological problems have also been reported with this drug.

Valproic acid

This comparatively new anticonvulsant is structurally related to carboxylic acid. Its mechanism of action is uncertain; it may interact with the central neurotransmitter, GABA, by preventing its uptake in nerve fibres.

Pharmacokinetics

Valproic acid is rapidly absorbed from the gastro-intestinal tract and peak plasma concentrations occur one to four hours after dosage. About 90 per cent of the drug is bound to plasma protein, and it has a half-life of 15 hours. Less than three per cent of valproic acid is excreted unchanged in the urine and faeces; the remainder is metabolized in the liver.

Unwanted effects

About 15 per cent of patients experience gastro-intestinal problems such as nausea, vomiting, and anorexia. The drug also has unwanted effects in the CNS including sedation, ataxia, and tremors. Hepatitis is the most serious problem associated with valproic acid therapy, and the incidence of hepatic failure is 1:20 000–40 000 patients taking the drug. Skin rashes and alopecia have been reported, but these are transitory. Of particular concern to the dental surgeon is the effect of valproic acid on haemostasis. The drug may cause thrombocytopenia, impairment of the secondary phase of platelet aggregation, and an increase in prothrombin (BCR) time (Hassell et al. 1979). Thus, some patients taking valproic acid may be at risk from a post-extraction or postoperative haemorrhage. Aspirin should be avoided in those taking valproic acid because it also affects platelet aggregation.

Benzodiazepines

Diazepam, lorazepam, and clonazepam have anticonvulsant properties, but they are not the treatment of choice for epilepsy because of the development of tolerance associated with prolonged use. The benzodiazepines are the first line of treatment for the condition of status epilepticus (see Chapter 24), with either intravenous diazepam or midazolam being the drug of choice.

Anticonvulsant osteomalacia

We have noted that many of the anticonvulsants (especially phenytoin, carbamazepime, and phenobarbitone) are hepatic enzyme inducers, i.e., they enhance the activity of certain enzymes, especially the mixed function oxidases. These hepatic oxidases also increase the catabolism of dietary and endogenously produced vitamin D. Therefore, if there is enhancement of the oxidase enzyme system there will be reduced serum concentrations of 25-hydroxycholecalciferol and, in turn, decreased renal production of the active 1,25-dihydroxycholecalciferol (see Chapter 20). Vitamin D deficiency can therefore occur in patients on anticonvulsant therapy and, if severe, may manifest itself as either rickets or osteomalacia. The problem is more common in the institutionalized elderly patient, who may be on a restricted diet and not often exposed to sunlight. Vitamin D deficiency may also increase the tendency for fits. Patients on anticonvulsant therapy should receive dietary advice and be encouraged to enjoy sunlight.

Trigeminal neuralgia (Tic douloureux)

This condition is characterized by unilateral electric shock-like, brief stabbing pains confined to the distribution of the trigeminal nerve. There is little or no associated sensory loss. The pain is triggered by non-nociceptive stimuli; for example, touch or a current of air.

Treatment of trigeminal neuralgia

Trigeminal neuralgia can be treated either surgically or with drugs.

Surgical treatment

This is a highly specialized area of neurosurgery but, in essence, two main types of operative treatment are in vogue. These are (i) gangliolysis and (ii) suboccipital craniectomy with decompression of the trigeminal nerve (Loeser 1977). Gangliolysis is a destructive procedure and the aim is to produce pain relief with minimal loss of sensation in the region affected by pain. The results indicate that 80 per cent patients will obtain pain relief for one year and in over 50 per cent relief will last for five years.

The alternative procedure, suboccipital craniectomy, is based on the observation that in trigeminal neuralgia the trigeminal nerve is often compressed by a blood vessel or very occasionally by some other local anatomical abnormality. The decompression operation is followed by an 85 per cent long-term success rate (Burchiel et al. 1981).

Drug treatment

Two anticonvulsant drugs, carbamazepine and phenytoin (see above), have been shown effective for this condition (Crill 1973). Carbamazepine, a close chemical relative of the tricyclic antidepressant group, controls the lancinating pains in about 70 per cent of patients. It commonly produces unwanted effects including nausea, dizziness, ataxia, somnolence, and slurring of speech; rarely, a fall in the white or red cell count of the blood may occur. The starting dose is 100 mg twice daily; this is increased slowly thereafter until, if necessary, a maximum total daily dose of 1200 mg is reached. It is useful to check the plasma concentration, for which the therapeutic range is 5 to 10 μg/ml (20–40 μmol/l; Tomson *et al.* 1980). As this drug has a long half-life and also produces auto-induction of drug metabolizing enzymes, it is necessary to wait 14 days after any change in dosage before attempting to measure the plasma concentration if meaningful values are to be obtained. In order to detect any bone marrow changes the haematological picture should be examined at monthly intervals during the first three months of treatment and thereafter at regular three-monthly intervals; the plasma concentration can also be measured. Bone marrow suppression is most likely to occur within the first three months of treatment but whenever it occurs it is an absolute indication for immediate withdrawal of the drug.

Phenytoin is the drug of second choice and is usually less effective than carbamazepine. Unwanted effects occur in about 10 per cent of patients, and include somnolence, dizziness, ataxia, slurring of speech, dermatitis, and gingival hyperplasia (see p. 308). The starting dose is 100 mg three times daily and, as with carbamazepine, the plasma concentration should be checked; the therapeutic range is 10 to 20 μg/ml (40–80 μmol/l) and the $T_{0.5}$ is 12 to 24 hours.

When necessary, other anticonvulsant drugs are occasionally used either alone or in combination with carbamazepine or phenytoin.

Post-herpetic neuralgia

This condition follows a herpes zoster infection (shingles). Pain is a feature of the initial infection but usually only lasts for the duration of the rash. However, some patients experience severe pain for many years after the initial infection, the older age groups being especially susceptible. This continuing severe pain is post-herpetic neuralgia; it frequently has a burning quality and may be spontaneous.

Treatment of post-herpetic neuralgia

This can be (1) physical or (2) pharmacological.

(1) Physical

Transcutaneous electrical nerve stimulation (TENS), which involves the application of electrical shocks at either low (5–10 Hz) or high (100–150 Hz) frequencies, may produce very effective analgesia in some patients. A pair of carbon rubber (or other) electrodes are applied either directly on or adjacent to the painful area, and the strength of shocks adjusted to produce a tingling sensation. The patient is instructed how to use this form of treatment and can then treat him- or herself on a regular basis several times daily. For TENS, patients should be referred to a Pain Relief Clinic where the stimulators are likely to be provided on loan by the National Health Service.

(2) Pharmacological

Selected psychotropic drugs, including anticonvulsants, may be used alone or in combination. A well-tried regime is as follows:

First: start carbamazepine 100 mg 12 hourly orally (e.g. 0800 h and 2000 h) increasing at intervals of several days up to a daily maximum of 1600 mg if required. As detailed earlier, the plasma concentration should be measured to confirm that it lies within the therapeutic range of 5 to 10 mg/l. The concentration should then be checked at three-monthly intervals together with the white cell count.

Second: if carbamazepine at a therapeutic plasma concentration fails to control the pain it should be stopped and replaced by amitriptyline, 25 to 75 mg, at night. This may control the pain on its own or may do so only when combined with sodium valproate, 200 mg twice daily. The plasma concentration of these drugs should be checked every three months; amitriptyline (100–200 μg/ml), sodium valproate (50–100 μg/ml). Adverse effects include: amitriptyline—antimuscarinic, CNS (sedation, paraesthesiae) CVS (tachycardia and other disorders of rate and rhythm), and allergic (skin, cholestatic jaundice, agranulocytosis); sodium valproate (see earlier)—nausea, vomiting, diarrhoea, ataxia, tremor, sedation, thrombocytopenia, temporary hearing loss, hepatotoxicity, false positive test for ketones in urine.

Third: if the combination of amitriptyline with sodium valproate fails to relieve post-herpetic neuralgia then the sodium valproate should be withdrawn and replaced by a neuroleptic such as perphenazine, 4 mg three times a day. Adverse effects include sedation, antimuscarinic effects, extrapyramidal signs and symptoms, hypersensitivity reactions, cholestatic jaundice, endocrine disturbances, and blood dyscrasias.

Migraine

This common condition affects about 5 per cent of the adult population. The characteristic features are periodic headaches (typically unilateral) visual disturbances, and vomiting. Attacks are often preceded by visual disturbances (an aura). During a severe migraine attack, sufferers are usually prostrate and photophobic, which necessitates going to bed in a darkened room.

The aetiology of this condition is still obscure. There is clearly some disturbance in cerebral blood flow. In certain patients, individual food substances rich in tyramine or dopamine may precipitate an attack. Recent attention has focused on the role of 5-HT in migrainous headaches. Prophylaxis against migraine can be achieved with drugs that inhibit the reuptake of 5-HT by platelets. Several types of drugs have been tried; these can be classified as those used in acute attacks and those used for prophylactic purposes.

Treatment of migraine

1. Analgesics

Aspirin is frequently used in the treatment of migraine. However, during a migraine attack, there is gastric stasis and absorption of aspirin is poor. This problem can be overcome by the use of metoclopramide, which will increase the rate of gastric emptying. There is no place for the opioids in the treatment of an acute attack of migraine because of the risk of dependence and their action on gastro-intestinal function (see Chapter 6).

2. Anti-emetics

The nausea and vomiting that often accompany an attack of migraine may respond to an anti-emetic. Metoclopramide is the treatment of choice because of the absence of sedative effects.

3. Ergotamine

Ergotamine is an alkaloid derived from ergot, which is produced by a fungus (*Claviceps purpurea*) that grows on rye and other cereals. It is probably the principal drug used to relieve an acute attack of migraine. Ergotamine blocks both α-adrenergic receptors and 5-HT receptors. It can be given orally, parenterally, rectally, sublingually, or by inhalation. The usual dose regime is 2 mg as soon as the headache starts, followed by 2 mg at half-hourly intervals. The total dose per attack should not exceed 10 mg.

Unwanted effects from ergotamine include peripheral vasoconstriction and paraesthesiae. Gangrene of the fingers has occurred in patients taking this drug. Ergotamine should not be used during pregnancy because it causes contraction of the uterus.

4. Cyproheptadine

This is both a potent H_1 and 5-HT antagonist; it also has tranquillizing properties. Although valuable in the treatment of an acute attack of migraine, its mode of action is uncertain. The usual dosage is 4 mg, followed by a further 4 mg 30 minutes later. Cyproheptadine also has mild anticholinergic properties, and causes dry mouth and blurred vision.

Prophylactic treatment of migraine

Methysergide

This drug is a powerful 5-HT antagonist; it also has anti-inflammatory and vasoconstrictor properties. For the prevention of migraine, methysergide 1 to 2 mg should be taken three times a day with meals. The incidence of unwanted effects is high, and includes gastro-intestinal problems, CNS disturbances, weight gain, oedema, and fibrotic changes in the thorax and abdomen. Retroperitoneal fibrosis limits the use of methysergide and it is mainly used if all else fails.

Other drugs used for the prophylaxis of migraine are pizotifen, which is structurally similar to cyproheptadine; clonidine, an antihypertensive, which at low doses reduces the sensitivity of blood vessels to catecholamines; and propranolol, a β-blocker, which prevents vasodilatation of the cerebral arteries.

REFERENCES

Angelopoulos, A. P. and Goaz, P. W. (1972). Incidence of diphenylhydantoin gingival hyperplasia. *Oral Surgery*, **34**, 898–902.
Baldessarini, R. J. (1985). Drugs and the treatment of psychiatric disorders. In *The pharmacological basis of therapeutics*, (7th edn), (eds. A. G. Gilman, L. S. Goodman, T. W. Rall, and F. Murad). Macmillan Publishing Company, New York, London and Toronto.
Beeley, L. (1986). Drug interactions with lithium. *Prescribers Journal*, **26**, 160–3.
Blackwell, B., Marley, E., Price, J., and Taylor, D. (1967). Hypertensive interactions between monoamine oxidase inhibitors and foodstuffs. *British Journal of Psychiatry*, **113**, 349–65.
Blain, P. G. and Stewart-Wynne, E. (1985). Neurological disorders. In *Textbook of adverse drug reactions*, (3rd edn), (ed. D. M. Davies), Oxford University Press.
Burchiel, K. J., Steege, T. D., Howe, J. F., and Loeser, J. D. (1981). Comparison of percutaneous radiofrequency gangliolysis and microvascular decompression for surgical management of tic douloureux. *Neurosurgery*, **9**, 111–19.
Cade, J. F. J. (1949). Lithium salts in the treatment of psychotic excitement. *Medical Journal of Australia*, **36**, 349–52.
Cawson, R. A. and Spector, R. G. (1985). *Clinical pharmacology in dentistry*, (4th edn). Churchill Livingstone, Edinburgh.
Commission on Classification and Terminology of the International League against Epilepsy. (1981). Proposals for revised clinical and electroencephalographic classification of epileptic disorders. *Epilepsia*, **22**, 489–501.
Crill, W. (1973). Carbamazepine. *Annals of Internal Medicine*, **79**, 79–80.
Drug Newsletter. (1985). Benzodiazepine dependence and withdrawal—an update. *Northern Regional Health Authority Drugs Newsletter*, **31**, 125–6.
Goldman, V. (1966). General anaesthesia for children's dentistry. *British Dental Journal*, **121**, 468–9.
Harvey, S. C. (1985). Hypnotics and sedatives. In *Pharmacological basis of therapeutics*, (7th edn), (eds A. G. Gilman, L. S. Goodman, T. W. Rall, and F. Murad). Macmillan Publishing Company, New York, London, Toronto.
Hassell, T. H., Page, R. G., and Lindhe, J. (1978). Histologic evidence for impaired growth control in diphenylhydantoin gingival hyperplasia. *Archives of Oral Biology*, **23**, 381–4.
Hassell, T. H., White, G. C., Jewson, L. G., and Peele, L. C. (1979). Valproic acid: a new antiepileptic drug with potential side effects of dental concern. *Journal of the American Dental Association*, **99**, 983–7.
Hauser, W. A. (1978). Epidemiology of epilepsy. *Advances in Neurology*, **19**, 313–39.
King, D. A., Hawes, R. R., and Bibby, B. G. (1976). The effect of oral physiotherapy on Dilantin gingival hyperplasia. *Journal of Oral Pathology*, **5**, 1–7.
Loeser, J. D. (1977). The management of tic douloureux. *Pain*, **3**, 155–62.
Rugg-Gunn, A. J. (1979). Lithium treatment and dental caries. *British Dental Journal*, **146**, 136–41.

Seymour, R. A., Smith, D. G., and Turnbull, D. N. (1985). The effects of phenytoin and sodium valproate on the periodontal health of adult epileptic patients. *Journal of Clinical Periodontology*, **12**, 413–19.

Tomson, T., Tybring, G., Bertillson, L., Ekblom, K., and Rane, A. (1980). Carbamazepine in trigeminal neuralgia: clinical effects in relation to plasma concentration. *Uppsala Journal of Medical Sciences*, **31**(suppl.), 45–6.

Waxman, S., Corcino, J. J., and Herbert, V. (1970). Drugs, toxins and dietary amino acids affecting vitamin B_{12} or folic acid absorption or utilization. *American Journal of Medicine*, **48**, 599.

Woodbury, D. M., Penry, J. K., and Pippenger, C. E. (1982). *Anti-epileptic drugs* (2nd edn). Raven Press, New York.

FURTHER READING

Ashton, H. (1984). Benzodiazepine withdrawal: an unfinished story. *British Medical Journal*, **288**, 1135–40.

Catalan, J. and Gath, D. H. (1985). Benzodiazepines in general practice: time for a decision. *British Medical Journal*, **290**, 1374–6.

Farmer, R. and Montgomery, S. A. (1984). Antidepressants and heart disease. *British Medical Journal*, **289**, 559.

Godtlibsen, O. B., Jerko, D., Gordeladze, J. O., Bredsen, J. E., and Matheson, I. (1986). Residual effect of single and repeated doses of midazolam and nitrazepam in relation to their plasma concentration. *European Journal of Clinical Pharmacology*, **29**, 595–600.

Higgitt, A. C., Lader, M. M., and Fonagy, P. (1985). Clinical management of benzodiazepine dependence. *British Medical Journal*, **291**, 688–90.

Leading article (1985). Beta-blockers in situational anxiety. *Lancet*, **ii**, 193.

Lindsey, S. J. E. and Yates, J. A. (1985). The effectiveness of oral diazepam in anxious child dental patients. *British Dental Journal*, **155**, 47–50.

McGimpsey, J. G., Kawar, P., Gamble, J. A. S., Browne, E. S., and Dundee, J. W. (1983). Midazolam in dentistry. *British Dental Journal*, **155**, 47–50.

Morgan, H. G. (1984). Do minor affective disorders need medication. (Leading article). *British Medical Journal*, **289**, 783.

Orme, M. L'E. (1984). Antidepressants and heart disease. (Leading article). *British Medical Journal*, **289**, 1–2.

Power, K. G., Jerrom, D. W. A., Simpson, R. J., and Mitchell, M. (1985). Controlled study of withdrawal symptoms and rebound anxiety after six weeks course of diazepam for generalised anxiety. *British Medical Journal*, **290**, 1246–8.

Singh, A. M., Chemij, M., and Jewell, J. (1986). Treatment of triazolam dependence with a tapering withdrawal regimen. *Canadian Medical Association Journal*, **1–34**, 243–5.

Tyrer, P., Murphy, S., Pates, G., and Kingdon, D. (1985). Psychological treatment for benzodiazepine dependence. *Lancet*, **i**, 1042–3.

15

Drugs used in the treatment of cardiovascular disease

Cardiac drugs may act on one or more of the following structures and systems:

1. *Myocardium*   Drugs may affect the force or the rate of the heart beat, or both. Changes in the force of contraction are known as inotropic effects (Gk: *inos*, fibre), and changes in rate are known as chronotropic effects (Gk: *chronos*, time). Drugs that increase the force or rate of the heart beat are said to produce a positive inotropic or chronotropic effect whereas those that produce the opposite effect are said to produce a negative inotropic or chronotropic effect, respectively.

2. *Conducting tissue*   The rate of conduction through the atrioventricular node (AVN) and the bundle of His may be increased or decreased by certain drugs (either directly or indirectly).

3. *Autonomic control*   Activity of the heart may be increased when the output of the sympathetic nervous system is increased; conversely, it may be decreased (inhibited) by activation of the parasympathetic nervous system.

Physiology of the normal heart

Anatomical aspects (see Fig. 15.1)

A normal impulse is transmitted from the sino-atrial node (SAN) to the AVN through atrial muscle. The AVN passes these impulses on over the intraventricular conduction system, which divides into right and left bundle branches. The right bundle runs to the right ventricle, branching only when it reaches the papillary muscles, whilst the left bundle branch divides into three fascicles known as the anterior, posterior, and centroseptal. The terminal branches of the bundle of His reach the myocardium (causing it to contract) via complex Purkinje–myocardial junctions.

Cellular behaviour of cardiac muscle

Fundamental studies, which have elucidated the electrophysiological changes in the heart, have made possible major advances in understanding of cardiac

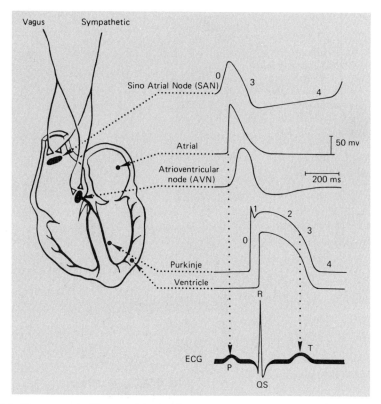

Fig. 15.1. The anatomical layout of the impulse generators and conducting system of the heart, shown in correspondence with an electrocardiogram (ECG).

physiology, both in health and in disease, and also of the effects of cardiac drugs (Noble 1984).

Let us briefly consider the relationship between the action potential (AP), the ionic changes in sodium, potassium and calcium, and the mechanical response of heart muscle (Fig. 15.2).

In cardiac muscle, by contrast with skeletal muscle, the AP lasts as long as the mechanical response, as can be seen by comparing the top and bottom traces in Fig. 15.2. The AP is the result of the movement of sodium, potassium, and calcium ions across the myocardial cell membrane, movements that are dependent upon changes in permeability of cell membrane during the cycle of the AP. Thus, whilst there is an increase in permeability to sodium (second trace), there is a decrease followed by an increase in permeability to potassium ions. There is also an increase in permeability to calcium ions, such that during the plateau of the cardiac AP there is a large influx of calcium ions (slow calcium current). It is for these reasons that the AP in cardiac muscle is so much more prolonged than that in skeletal muscle.

Fig. 15.2. The relationship between electrical and ionic responses of cardiac muscle: from the top downwards the recordings, made from a Purkinje fibre, are of (i) the action potential, (ii) the ionic currents due to sodium (Na^+), potassium (K^+), and calcium (Ca^{2+}); (after Noble 1979).

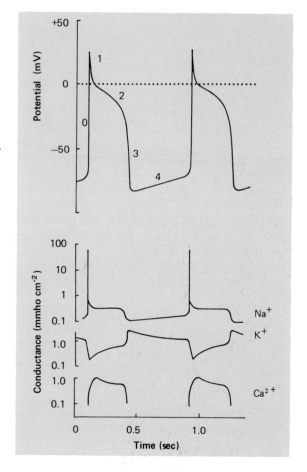

The AP of cardiac muscle, as shown in Fig. 15.2, can be seen to be divided into a number of phases:

Phase 0 is the fast uptake, which represents the rapid depolarization of the membrane potential to a critical threshold of about -60 mV, when the inward current of sodium ions becomes sufficiently large to produce an 'all or nothing' depolarization. It should be noted that the operation of these voltage-dependent sodium channels is transient and, so that they will close again (i.e., become inactivated) within a few milliseconds, the membrane remains depolarized.

Phase 1 consists of partial repolarization, which is a consequence of the inactivation of the sodium current.

Phase 2 consists of a plateau that results from a slow inwards calcium current. The calcium channel, like the sodium channel, is voltage-sensitive but differs from it in that it responds much more slowly. The myocardial contraction is due to the resultant increase in intracellular calcium concentration. It is not quenched by the outward potassium current because the permeability of the muscle cell membrane to potassium is inversely related to the degree of depolarization. Thus, during the plateau of depolarization due to the inward calcium current, the outward potassium current is very small and therefore does not cause any sudden reversal of the membrane depolarization.

Phase 3 is the phase of repolarization and takes place as the calcium current is inactivated. During this phase, potassium permeability rapidly increases with the increase in membrane potential and this accounts for the rapid repolarization (see above under phase 2).

Phase 4 is the so-called pacemaker potential, and differs in various parts of the heart. In nodal and conducting tissues there is a slow depolarization due to an increase in sodium permeability. Furthermore it is most rapid in nodal tissues, and least in the conducting tissues.

In pacemaker cells, such as the SAN and the AVN, the resting potential of the cell is unstable (see Fig. 15.1, phase 4 of recording from SAN), and this accounts for their inherent rhythmicity; as the resting potential rises to the threshold value it fires off another AP, the whole cycle is repeated, and so on indefinitely. In fact, all cardiac cells have some degree of inherent rhythmicity, which is greatest in cells of the SAN and decreases in the order, AVN, His–Purkinje bundle, atrial and ventricular muscle. The result is that if a proximal pacemaker ceases to function or if its impulse is blocked, the next fastest area will take command, usually proximally or distally, in the atrioventricular (AV) junction, or in the bundle of His, or, with more distal disease, in the His-Purkinje system, each with inherently and progressively slower rates.

Autonomic control of the heart

Parasympathetic supply

Parasympathetic cholinergic fibres reach the heart through the vagus to innervate the atrial and nodal tissue. The ventricles are therefore not directly affected by the vagus.

Acetylcholine released at the postganglionic cholinergic nerve endings increases the permeability of the myocardial cell membrane to potassium ions. At the SAN this results in a more negative membrane potential and, therefore, a correspondingly slower rate of rise of the pacemaker potential during diastole, which results in a reduction in heart rate. (NB. The increased potassium permeability allows an increased leak of potassium ions down their concentration gradient out of the cell, which offsets the inward leakage of sodium ions. Excessive vagal activity will stop spontaneous depolarization completely and so stabilize the membrane potential by causing the potassium loss to exceed that of the sodium entry, with the result that the heart stops beating.)

On atrial cells the effect of parasympathetic stimulation is to reduce the duration of the AP by accelerating repolarization. This reduced duration causes a less effective activation of the contractile mechanism of the myocardial cell, which results in a weaker atrial contraction. In addition, there is also a reduction in size of the potentials within the AVN, and the resting membrane potential of the nodal cells may be stabilized. As a consequence, the AV delay is increased and eventually this results in conduction block. It seems likely that all these effects are due to increased potassium permeability of the membrane produced by acetylcholine.

Stimulation of vagal fibres may be produced by such manoeuvres as (i) carotid sinus massage, (ii) eyeball pressure (which can also detach the retina!), (iii) vomiting, and (iv) the Valsalva manoeuvre (forced expiration against a closed glottis and pinched nose). These measures can restore normal sinus rhythm during attacks of paroxysmal supraventricular tachycardia. In the presence of sinus tachycardia these procedures cause a smooth slowing of the pulse but, in atrial flutter (in which the atria contract at approximately 300 per minute and the ventricles follow with a variable degree of AV block), there is a sudden reduction in the ventricular rate as the degree of AV block increases.

Sympathetic nerve supply

Sympathetic nerve fibres running in the cardiac nerves innervate all parts of the heart. Adrenergic stimulation increases the rate of beating of the pacemaker (chronotropic effect) and increases the force of contraction (inotropic effect). There is also an increased conduction rate and ventricular arrhythmia, which may be due to interference with the pattern of repolarization. Adrenaline also increases the force of contraction of the heart and this is associated with an increased concentration of unbound intracellular calcium.

Disorders of cardiac rhythm and anti-arrhythmic drugs

Any such disorder is termed an arrhythmia or a dysrhythmia. An arrhythmia can arise from (i) an abnormality of impulse generation; (ii) an abnormality of conduction; or (iii) a combination of (i) and (ii).

Abnormal impulse generation is caused by an additional pacemaker known as an ectopic focus. Thus, the normal pacemaker for the heart is the SAN, whereas an ectopic focus may arise as a result of a damaged area of muscle or due to the actions of drugs; for example, digoxin or catecholamines. A particular feature of an ectopic focus is an increased liability to depolarize during diastole so giving rise to enhanced automaticity.

Conduction abnormalities occur when some part of the conducting pathway is damaged, resulting in the formation of a unidirectional block. When this occurs in one branch of the bundle, the passage of impulses within it are blocked whereas those in the other branch progress normally; these may then travel via the ventricular muscle to excite that part of the damaged bundle distal to the block and so lead to retrograde impulse conduction. As a consequence, a re-entry or 'circus' mechanism is set up, which is self-perpetuating and so induces arrhythmias.

A large number of drugs can now be used as anti-arrhythmic agents and, whilst a particular drug may be very effective in a particular patient, we do not necessarily know which of the several actions possessed by that drug may be responsible for the beneficial effect. Nevertheless, as Krikler (1974) has pointed out, the target is to control the abnormal process or, in other words: (i) to diminish enhanced automaticity; or (ii) to interrupt a re-entry mechanism.

Enhanced automaticity may be diminished by:

(1) slowing the rate of rise of spontaneous diastolic (phase 4) depolarization

(2) increasing the threshold potential;

(3) lengthening the refractory period, especially in relation to the duration of AP;

(4) lowering the maximum repolarization potential at the end of phase 3.

Re-entry may be broken by prolonging the circuit-time until conduction is too slow to support it (it is only rarely possible to do this in the opposite way by speeding it up).

Classification of anti-arrhythmic agents

As a result of extensive electrophysiological studies carried out by a number of workers—see especially Vaughan Williams (1983), and also Weidmann (1955)—it is now possible to classify anti-arrhythmic agents. Vaughan Williams (1983) classification divides these drugs into four classes (I–IV) as follows:

Class I.   This class is sub-divided into three sub-zones:
Ia: quinidine, procainamide, disopyramide.
These drugs inhibit pacemaker depolarization.
Ib: lignocaine, mexiletine, tocainide.
These drugs do not inhibit pacemaker depolarization but inhibit the inward sodium currents that are associated with the ectopic beats characteristic of ventricular arrhythmias.
Ic: flecainide, encainide (USA), proppafenone (Germany)
Main use: ventricular arrhythmias.

Class II.   Antisympathetic, e.g. β-blockers, bretylium.
These drugs act on sinus nodal tissues.
Main use: supraventricular and ventricular arrhythmias.

Class III.   Prolongation of AP, e.g. amiodarone, bretylium.
This group act on all cardiac tissues.
Main use: supraventricular and ventricular arrhythmias.

Class IV.   Calcium entry blockers (also known as calcium antagonists), e.g. verapamil, diltiazem.
These drugs act on AV nodal conducting tissues.
Main use: supraventricular arrhythmias.

Class I drugs with a direct membrane action

Quinidine and procainamide

Class I drugs produce a slowing in the rate of rise of AP although they may produce other effects as well. One of the oldest anti-arrhythmic drugs is quinidine, which is the D-isomer of quinine, and is the prototype of Class I drugs. It causes decreased excitability, prolonged refractoriness, and decreased conduction velocity. All of these properties might be expected to suppress ectopic foci or 'circus' movements in the heart. The primary effect of quinidine is to slow the rate of rise of depolarization (phase 4); this results in a delay in the firing of an excitable ectopic focus and thus may abolish any arrhythmia due to it.

Procainamide has similar properties to quinidine; both have anticholinergic effects that antagonize vagal activity, thereby reducing their effects with consequent increased conduction and decreased atrial refractory period. Procainamide and quinidine also block conduction; they may therefore, cause conduction disturbances.

Pharmacodynamics

(a) Direct effects

These comprise reduced conduction velocity, prolonged refractory period (atrium greater than ventricle), and reduced excitability.

(b) Electrocardiograph (ECG) changes

Widening of QRS with prolonged PR and QT intervals.

Pharmacokinetics

After absorption, which is complete, distribution of procainamide is extensive with 15 per cent of the drug bound to plasma proteins. The drug is eliminated partly by metabolism (acetylation 30 to 60 per cent) and partly excreted by the kidney (30 to 60 per cent). The N-acetyl metabolite is as active pharmacologically as the parent compound. The half-life is two hours, and frequent four- to six-hourly doses are necessary to maintain adequate plasma concentrations. Slow release preparations may be given eight- to twelve-hourly.

Unwanted effects

Manifestations

Heart block (AV block)

Anorexia, nausea, vomiting, diarrhoea

Hallucinations

Agranulocytosis

Systemic lupus erythematosus-like syndromes with rash, fever, arthralgia, myalgia, pneumonitis, and a positive antinuclear factor (ANF).

Lignocaine

This well-known and versatile local anaesthetic is also a useful anti-arrhythmic agent belonging to Class I. It differs from quinidine and procainamide in that it does not have anticholinergic properties and neither does it affect (or possibly may even increase) conduction velocity. It has been tentatively suggested that the relative lack of toxicity of lignocaine is because, *in the doses used for anti-arrhythmic purposes* (and unlike quinidine and procainamide), it does not block conduction and is therefore less likely to produce conduction disturbances in therapeutic dosage.

Pharmacodynamics

Lignocaine reduces automaticity, modifies and may prevent re-entrant arrhythmias, and produces a slight negative inotropic effect.

Pharmacokinetics

Absorption is complete but the drug undergoes extensive first pass metabolism, which makes oral administration ineffective. After IV or IM administration, the drug is rapidly redistributed to muscle and fat.

Lignocaine is completely metabolized (oxidized) by the liver, where there is a high hepatic clearance of approximately 800 ml per minutes, which means that its elimination is dependent upon the liver blood flow. Impaired elimination is therefore seen in patients with cardiac failure or liver disease.

These pharmacokinetic properties mean that lignocaine must be administered by continuous IV infusion for its effect to be maintained and regulated. Therapeutic effects are observed at plasma concentrations of 2 to 4 μg/ml.

Unwanted effects

These are manifested by paraesthesia around the mouth, and convulsions may occur. Treatment is to stop the infusion and give midazolam for the fits if necessary.

Disopyramide

This is a much more recently introduced drug.

Pharmacodynamics

Conduction is slowed so influencing automatic and re-entrant arrhythmias. As a consequence of its mode of action the QRS interval on ECG is prolonged. It is particularly important for the treatment of a rare form of re-entry arrhythmia that occurs in the Wolff–Parkinson–White syndrome. In this condition, an anatomically abnormal bundle of cardiac muscle fibres joins the atria to the ventricles, thus bypassing the AVN. As a consequence, after normal excitation through the AVN–Purkinje pathway, impulses may pass retrogradely through the abnormal bundle back to the atria and thereby set up a 'circus' excitation.

Pharmacokinetics
Disopyramide is completely absorbed and converted to inactive metabolites. The therapeutic $T_{0.5}$ is 4 to 8 hours, with a therapeutic window in the range 3–6 mg/ml.

Unwanted effects
The drug may induce a metallic taste in the mouth; it may aggravate heart failure and is sometimes associated with arrhythmogenicity.

Class II drugs with antisympathetic effects

This group might be expected to protect against arrhythmias associated with increased sympathetic activity. Thus, the well-known sensitization of the heart to catecholamines, which can occur during anaesthesia with halogenated hydrocarbons (see Chapter 8), can be protected by agents with anti-sympathetic effects. However, this group will also protect against other types of arrhythmias, especially those induced by cardiac glycosides or by ischaemia. The main group of drugs with Class II properties are the β-adrenoceptor blocking agents (β-blockers) and these are dealt with elsewhere (see Chapter 13).

Class III drugs that prolong the duration of the AP

These agents, amiodarone and bretylium, are important because they are active against ventricular arrhythmias.

Amiodarone
This is a remarkable drug because it:

(1) prolongs the duration of the AP;

(2) increases the refractory period;

(3) is active against a variety of arrhythmias, including ventricular fibrillation;

(4) is safe in the presence of severe congestive heart failure;

(5) has a cumulative effect due to an exceptionally long half-life ($T_{0.5} = 4$ weeks).

Pharmacodynamics
(a) Direct effects
Amiodarone prolongs the duration of the AP by slow repolarization (phase 3). It has no effect on phases 4 or 0 and neither does it alter the threshold potential. Thus, it prolongs the refractory period in the SA node, atria, AVN, and conducting system. These effects are similar to those that occur in hypothyroidism.

(b) ECG changes
The QT interval is prolonged.

Pharmacokinetics
This drug has an exceptionally long half-life so that the $T_{0.5}$ is of the order of 4 weeks or longer; its effects thus continue for several weeks after it has been withdrawn. As would be anticipated of a drug with a long $T_{0.5}$, the therapeutic action takes several days to develop.

Unwanted effects
Amiodarone can cause a number of potentially serious unwanted effects. These include photosensitization (ranging from an increased tendency to sunburn to severe erythema); corneal microdeposits of lipofucsin, which are reversible on stopping the drug; interference with thyroid function (probably due to chemical similarity to thyroxine), decreasing the peripheral conversion of thyroxine (T4) to tri-iodothyronine (T3); and, in about 5 per cent of patients, actual hypothyroidism or hyperthyroidism. Other conditions attributed to this drug include a reversible peripheral neuropathy, pneumonitis, and also headache, nausea, vomiting, bradycardia, constipation, nightmares, and tremor.

Drug interactions produced by amiodarone include the potentiation of warfarin, and increase in the plasma concentration of digoxin with enhanced risk of toxicity.

Bretylium

This is an adrenergic neurone blocker, originally used for the treatment of hypertension (see later). After such use was abandoned (because it is poorly absorbed), it made a come back as an anti-arrhythmic drug because it was found to be effective for the treatment of ventricular fibrillation, including that refractory to lignocaine and multiple direct-current (DC) shocks. It is also used to treat other ventricular arrhythmias resistant to lignocaine or procainamide. However, it should be noted that the use of bretylium is steadily declining.

Pharmacodynamics
Bretylium accumulates in adrenergic nerve endings and depresses noradrenaline release thus accounting for its adrenergic neurone-blocking action (although initially it may cause a *release* of catecholamines). However, its anti-arrhythmic action is probably independent of this blocking property and may be due to lengthening of the ventricular (but not the atrial) AP. Although it acts slowly against some ventricular arrhythmias, fortunately it acts quickly against ventricular fibrillation. Experimentally it has been shown to raise the threshold to electrically-induced ventricular fibrillation. However, the initial release of catecholamine may *induce* ventricular arrhythmias, which therefore calls for careful ECG monitoring of therapy.

Pharmacokinetics
Bretylium contains a quaternary nitrogen atom ($-N^+R_4$), thus accounting for its poor absorption, lack of hepatic metabolism, and renal excretion with a $T_{0.5}$ of seven to eight hours.

Unwanted effects
Initial transient hypertension and increased arrhythmias may occur; also hypotension with continued treatment.

Class IV drugs

These are the calcium entry blockers (calcium antagonists; calcium channel blockers).

Calcium is a universal second (or intermediate) messenger responsible for regulating all forms of cellular activity (Berridge 1981; 1985). Intracellular calcium can be increased by one of two mechanisms: (i) extracellular calcium may enter the cell through specific calcium channels; or (ii) calcium may be released from intracellular stores, such as the sarcoplasmic reticulum of cardiac or skeletal muscle, or the endoplasmic reticulum of non-muscle cells. In cardiac muscle, membrane depolarization leads to opening of voltage-dependent calcium channels in the plasma membrane; it is these channels that can be blocked by calcium entry blockers such as nifedipine and verapamil.

Verapamil

This was originally used for the treatment of angina pectoris because of its vasodilator properties (see p. 332). However it has been found to be more useful for the treatment of supraventricular arrhythmias.

Pharmacodynamics
Verapamil blocks the transport of calcium across the cell membrane of cardiac and vascular smooth muscle, thus prolonging phase 2 of the AP (see Fig. 15.2 above) and increasing the effective refractory period. This effect is especially marked in the SAN and AVN so that conduction is slowed, thereby producing a negative inotropic effect. As verapamil also acts on vascular smooth muscle it produces peripheral vasodilatation. The combined effects on cardiac and smooth muscle result in reduced myocardial work and thus reduced myocardial oxygen demand.

Pharmacokinetics
After oral administration, verapamil is well-absorbed and undergoes extensive first pass metabolism. It takes two hours to act, with a peak action at about five hours. It is not clear whether hepatic metabolites are active, but excretion is mainly by the kidneys.

Unwanted effects
The negative inotropic and vasodilatory actions may produce hypotension and also worsen cardiac failure. Verapamil may interact with a β-blocker because both drugs possess negative inotropic and hypotensive actions. This interaction is particularly liable to occur when verapamil is administered intravenously to a patient already taking β-blockers, so this combination is not recommended.

Diltiazem
This recently introduced drug has both anti-arrhythmic and vasodilator effects.

Pharmacokinetics
It has a relative lack of first pass metabolism, which may well suit it better for long-term use than a drug like verapamil.

Cardiac glycosides (digitalis)
Digitalis was introduced into clinical medicine by William Withering over 200 years ago and is remarkable in that it remains the only drug that can be administered to patients over a long time in order to improve myocardial contractility. In addition, it has the important property of being able to control the ventricular rate in arrhythmias arising in the atria.

Pharmacodynamics
Various species of digitalis plant (e.g. foxglove) contain three cardiac glycosides of medicinal importance—digoxin, digitoxin, and ouabain. In the UK, digoxin is used most commonly whereas, in North America, digitoxin is more popular. Chemically, they all consist of an aglycone (or genin) ring structure, which determines their pharmacological activity, coupled to one to four molecules of a sugar, which influence their water solubility and hence determine their pharmacokinetic properties, including penetration into cells.

In essence, cardiac glycosides produce four main effects:

 (i) increased force of myocardial contraction:
 (ii) slowed conduction velocity in the AVN with subsequent increase in AV conduction time (thus lengthening the PR interval on the ECG);
 (iii) decreased refractory period of the myocardium;
 (iv) increased automaticity.

Improved contraction of the myocardium by digitalis leads to reflex vagal stimulation resulting in sinus bradycardia. The ECG reflects these effects so that the increase in AV conduction time produces a lengthening of the PR interval. Other ECG effects are depression of the ST segment followed by the development of a biphasic T wave. Ultimately, the T wave may become inverted whilst the QT interval is shortened by the shortened duration of ventricular systole.

The mechanism of action of cardiac glycosides is to inhibit the enzyme known as sodium–potassium ATPase, which resides in the sarcolemma of cardiac muscle. Sodium-potassium ATPase is responsible for the sodium pump; when this enzyme action is depressed the outcome is an accumulation of intracellular sodium ions, which in turn results in an increase in the concentration of free intracellular calcium ions. This increase leads to improved excitation–contraction coupling of the myocardial cells and thereby increased force of myocardial contraction.

Pharmacokinetics

These are different for digoxin and digitoxin. Digoxin is incompletely absorbed; bioavailability varies between about 65 per cent for tablets and 80 per cent for the elixir. Only about 25 per cent of digoxin is bound to plasma proteins and so the drug becomes widely distributed throughout the body. The concentration in cardiac tissue may reach 30 times that of the plasma concentration. Digoxin is primarily eliminated by the kidney unchanged, with a $T_{0.5}$ of about 40 hours. As a consequence, in renal failure and also in the elderly, renal excretion is slowed and this must be taken into account when calculating the appropriate dose. The therapeutic plasma concentration is in the range 0.8–1.6 μg/l and concentrations above 2.5 μg/l are usually associated with unwanted effects (see later). However, the correlation between plasma concentration and effect is variable.

Digitoxin is by contrast almost completely absorbed after oral administration and highly bound (90 per cent) to plasma proteins. Approximately 70 per cent of the drug is metabolized in the liver, where it undergoes extensive enterohepatic recirculation, with the result that it has a very long $T_{0.5}$ of about seven days.

Uses

Cardiac glycosides have two main uses:

1. The treatment of supraventricular arrhythmias, in which the aim is to slow the heart rate by virtue of the action of digitalis on the conduction system. In atrial fibrillation, digitalis slows the ventricular rate and very occasionally this is followed by restoration of normal rhythm.

2. The treatment of cardiac failure secondary to ischaemic and hypertensive heart disease and also that secondary to valvular disease.

It should be noted that these indications apply with or without the presence of an arrhythmia. By contrast, digitalis is of very limited value in the treatment of heart failure secondary to chronic pulmonary disease.

Unwanted effects

The therapeutic index (safety margin) of cardiac glycosides is very small, as intimated already when discussing the relationship between plasma concentration and therapeutic effect (see p. 28). The commonest signs of overdosage include anorexia, nausea, vomiting, and diarrhoea, and when these symptoms occur in any patient taking cardiac glycosides the possibility of overdose must be considered. Neurological and psychiatric symptoms may also arise; these include headache, confusion, depression, and insomnia. Rarely, visual disturbances including photophobia and disturbances of colour vision occur. Along with these unwanted non-cardiac effects there may be various cardiac ones, especially ventricular ectopic beats. With these there may be coupling so that an ectopic beat immediately follows on a normal contraction. In addition, varying degrees of heart block can occur due to the effect of digitalis on the conducting system. Elderly patients and those with electrolyte disturbances, particularly hypokalaemia, hypercalcaemia, or hypomagnesaemia, are more susceptible to these induced arrhythmias, as are patients already suffering from hypothyroidism. Any simultaneously administered drug that interferes with the renal clearance of digoxin also increases the risk of these unwanted effects. By contrast, those suffering from hyperthyroidism are more resistant to the actions of cardiac glycosides. When it is possible that there are unwanted effects due to cardiac glycosides, measurement of the plasma concentration may well prove helpful in providing diagnostic information, as well as in following the progress of treatment.

DRUGS ACTING ON THE CARDIOVASCULAR SYSTEM: 2. VASODILATORS

Any drug that causes relaxation of smooth muscle in the wall of a blood vessel, thereby increasing its cross-sectional area (and hence decreasing its peripheral resistance), may be called a vasodilator. In the past, the therapeutic approach to heart failure has been to try to 'flog a tired horse' or, in other words, to use drugs to increase the cardiac output. Recently the more logical approach of using vasodilators to reduce the load has gained ground, and this has been applied particularly to the treatment of hypertension and congestive cardiac failure.

Several groups of drugs acting in different ways can produce vasodilatation; these may act predominantly on the arterial (resistance) vessels or on the venous (capacitance) vessels, or on both. Arterial vasodilators, for example hydralazine, primarily lower diastolic blood pressure and are used for the treatment of hypertension. On the other hand, venous vasodilators, for example nitrites, lower systolic pressure but have only a small effect on diastolic pressure and are used therefore to treat congestive cardiac failure.

From Table 15.1 it can be seen that there are at least six mechanisms whereby a drug can produce vasodilatation. Thus it may act directly, via α- or β-adrenoceptors, by blocking the entry of calcium ions, by interference with angiotensin, or by way of diuretic therapy. Some of the groups of vasodilators listed in Table 15.1 are dealt with in this Chapter whilst others are discussed elsewhere in this book as follows:

	Chapter	Page
Direct vasodilators	This	332
α-adrenoceptor antagonists	13	275
β-adrenoceptor agonists	13	270
Calcium entry blockers (calcium antagonists)	This	328
Angiotensin inhibitors	This	335
Diuretics	This	337

Table 15.1. The various groups of vasodilator drugs

Group	Drug	Arterial	Venous	Hypertension	Refractory cardiac failure
1. Direct vasodilator	hydrallazine	++	−	√	√
	nitrites	+	++	0	√
	diazoxide	++	−	√ (acute)	(√)
	minoxidil	++	−	√	(√)
	nitroprusside	++	++	√ (acute)	
2. α-adrenoceptor antagonists					
(i) α₁ vascular receptors	prazosin	++	++	√	√
	indoramin			√	0
	labetalol (also β)			√	0
(ii) α₂ (presynaptic) receptors	phentolamine	++	−	(√)	√
	phenoxybenzamine	++	−	(√)	0
3. β-adrenoceptor agonists	isoprenaline, dopamine, dobutamine, salbutamol	++	++	0	√
4. calcium antagonists	nifedipine	++	+	√	√
	verapamil			(√)	
	diltiazem			?	?
5. angiotensin II inhibitors					
(i) inhibit angiotensin converting enzyme	captopril, teprotide			√	√
(ii) inhibit angiotensin effect on vessel wall	saralasin			√	√
6. diuretics	frusemide			√	√

Key: + mild effect, ++ strong effect, 0 not used, √ used, − insignificant effect, (√) used infrequently, ? may be useful

Direct vasodilators are agents that act through some direct mechanism that varies according to the substance involved. These are exemplified by hydralazine and the nitrates/nitrites.

Hydralazine

This was first introduced many years ago and then abandoned because it induced a reflex tachycardia and rapid tolerance. In some it leads to a condition resembling systemic lupus erythematosus (SLE), now known to occur in those who metabolize (acetylate) the drug slowly. However, it has been introduced successfully in combination with β-blockers, which reduce the reflex tachycardia, so that a maximum daily dose of 200 mg becomes not only an effective hypotensive dose but one at which the likelihood of SLE is greatly reduced. The vascular effects outlast the $T_{0.5}$ of two to four hours, probably due to binding of the drug to vascular tissue.

The commonest adverse effects of hydralazine are nausea, anorexia, headache, palpitations, flushing, sweating, and rarely, peripheral neuropathy and drug fever. As mentioned above, SLE is likely to occur in 10 to 20 per cent of those patients who acetylate the drug slowly but is reversible on withdrawal.

Nitrates and nitrites

It has long been known that inorganic nitrate is pharmacologically inactive whereas organic nitrates, and both inorganic and organic nitrites, are effective direct-acting relaxants of smooth muscle. Thus the vascular smooth muscle of both arteries and veins is relaxed by these agents; the mode of action is direct and does not involve the usual receptor mechanisms, such as those of acetylcholine, histamine, noradrenaline, or 5-HT. The mechanism of action is not yet fully elucidated but two possibilities have been considered. The first is that the compounds are converted into nitric oxide (NO), which interacts with a specific receptor containing a sulphydryl group. The second is that the compounds act by virtue of the nitrite ion, the nitrites acting directly and the nitrates after conversion to nitrites in the tissues.

Organic nitrates, and inorganic and organic nitrites, are predominantly venodilators resulting in venous pooling with consequent reduction in both venous return, and left ventricular and diastolic pressure. The reduction in ventricular-wall tension and consequent reduced oxygen demand lead to the relief of angina.

Nitrates/nitrites are conveniently divided into short- and long-acting.

Short-acting

Amyl nitrite

This volatile liquid is administered from crushable glass ampoules (vitrellae) each containing 0.1 to 0.3 ml. On inhalation, rapid arteriolar dilatation is produced and this leads to a compensatory tachycardia and venoconstriction. This reduces left ventricular afterload. However, amyl nitrite is rarely used now because it is inconvenient and unpleasant, produces a short-lived effect, and is also expensive. Today its main use is for the management of cyanide poisoning.

Glyceryl trinitrate (nitroglycerine, TNT).

This is inactive when swallowed because it undergoes almost complete first pass metabolism. A tablet is therefore placed under the tongue when required. It is rapidly metabolized in the liver to inorganic nitrate; it acts within 2 minutes and lasts up to about 30 minutes.

Patients need to be warned that these tablets may cause headache or a fall of blood pressure and should therefore be taken whilst sitting down.

Unwanted effects are flushing, palpitations, dizziness, headaches, and collapse. Tolerance to the headache may develop but is apparently not associated with loss of circulatory effect.

Long-acting

Several longer-acting preparations of nitrates are available; these include pentaerythritol tetranitrate, isosorbide dinitrate, and also slow-release formulations of glyceryl trinitrate, including Nitrocontin Continus, Suscard, Sustac, and Transiderm-Nitro. The last named is a self-adhesive skin dressing that contains glyceryl trinitrate. The response to these long-acting preparations varies and must be determined by trial and error. Their unwanted effects are similar to those of glyceryl trinitrate.

Diazoxide

This is related chemically to the thiazide diuretics but differs radically from them in that it has sodium-retaining properties, and also hypotensive and hyperglycaemic effects.

Pharmacodynamics

Diazoxide is a direct arterial vasodilator and does not affect venous (capacitance) vessels; neither does it affect cardiovascular reflexes. It is normally employed to treat acute hypertensive emergencies, when it is given intravenously, producing a marked fall in blood pressure, followed by a reflex tachycardia and increased cardiac output. The fall of blood pressure also induces a reflex sympathetic discharge of catecholamines.

In patients with cardiac failure the sodium retention caused by diazoxide may obviously worsen their condition and so a loop diuretic, for example, frusemide, should be given along with the diazoxide. The hyperglycaemic effect is due to (i) a direct inhibitory effect on the release of insulin from the β-cells in the pancreas, and (ii) the release of adrenaline (see above) resulting in an increase in the release of glucose.

Pharmacokinetics

Diazoxide is highly protein-bound (about 90 per cent) and eventually undergoes mainly renal excretion with a long $T_{0.5}$ of about 25 hours.

Uses

Diazoxide is used almost exclusively for the emergency reduction of acute hypertension (intravenous injection). Naturally, once the hypertension has been brought under control it is essential to institute effective oral medication with other appropriate hypotensive drugs (see treatment of hypertension, pp. 352–3).

Unwanted effects

The undesirable effects of sodium retention have been mentioned earlier. The hyperglycaemic effect may produce problems where the ability to excrete excess glucose is impaired, such as in renal failure. Although diazoxide has different pharmacological actions from other thiazides, its close chemical similarity is responsible for hypersensitivity reactions similar to those caused by other thiazides. Furthermore, if a patient is known to be hypersensitive to thiazide diuretics there is likely to be a cross-reaction with diazoxide, which is therefore contra-indicated. As diazoxide is highly bound to plasma proteins it can displace other highly bound drugs from these sites, such as oral anticoagulants, the dose of which may therefore need to be adjusted appropriately.

Nifedipine

Pharmacodynamics

This is a calcium entry blocker and relaxes vascular smooth muscle, resulting in peripheral vasodilatation. It also dilates coronary arteries. However, unlike verapamil (see Section on anti-arrhythmic drugs, p. 322), it does not affect the conducting system in man (Rowland *et al.* 1979) although it does in animals (Endo *et al.* 1978). Thus it is used to treat coronary artery spasm but not supraventricular arrhythmias.

Pharmacokinetics

It is well-absorbed after oral administration (and also sublingually); it undergoes extensive metabolism and has a $T_{0.5}$ of about 5 hours.

Unwanted effects

Headache and flushing, due to vasodilatation, are the main complaints. It has been reported to increase the plasma concentration of digoxin (by some unknown mechanism), and this interaction must therefore be anticipated if these two drugs are used concomitantly. It is of significance to the dental surgeon that patients on nifedipine may experience gingival hyperplasia (Jones 1986).

Angiotensin and its inhibitors

Several polypeptides produce powerful effects on vascular and other smooth muscles and thereby play important roles in the control of local or general blood flow and blood pressure. Thus, vasoconstrictors include angiotensin II and vasopressin, whilst vasodilators include bradykinin, vasoactive intestinal peptide (VIP), substance P, and neurotensin.

Formation of angiotensin
The active form is known as angiotensin II and is formed from the precursor angiotensin I, which is itself formed by the action of the enzyme renin on angiotensinogen, a circulatory protein substance (see Fig. 15.3). Renin is synthesized and stored in the juxtaglomerular apparatus of the kidney and its

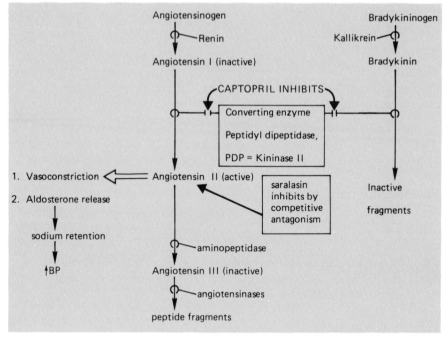

Fig. 15.3. The formation and activation of angiotensin.

release appears to depend upon a number of factors, particularly a vascular stretch receptor in the afferent arteriole of the glomerulus. When this receptor is stretched it leads to a decrease in renin release and vice versa. The sympathetic nervous system also stimulates renin secretion via the release of noradrenaline, which acts on β-adrenoceptors ($?\beta_1$ or β_2).

Relationship to kinins
As the converting enzyme, peptidyl dipeptidase (PDP), is identical with kininase II, which inactivates bradykinin, it is clear that any factors affecting the enzyme will simultaneously affect the production of angiotensin II and the destruction of bradykinin (see Fig. 15.3).

Angiotensin-converting enzyme inhibitors (ACE inhibitors)

Pharmacodynamics
Captopril, a typical ACE inhibitor, is a competitive inhibitor of PDP, so leading to a decrease in the production of angiotensin II (and secondarily, of aldosterone), and also to an accumulation of bradykinin, a vasodilator. These effects are responsible for the therapeutic actions of captopril.

Pharmacokinetics

Captopril is well-absorbed on oral administration but seriously affected by the presence of food, which reduces absorption to 50 per cent. About half of the dose is metabolized in the liver to inactive metabolites, and the $T_{0.5}$ is about two hours.

Therapeutic uses

Until recently, captopril was reserved for the treatment of severe hypertension and severe congestive cardiac failure that had failed to respond to other antihypertensive therapy. However, there is now a move to use captopril for the treatment of patients with lesser degrees of hypertension. Newer ACE inhibitors, such as analapril, with a smoother action are also now available and others are likely to follow.

Unwanted effects

Captopril is a potentially toxic drug. Rashes are common (10 per cent), and may be associated with pyrexia and eosinophilia. Loss of taste, usually transient, occurs in five per cent of patients. Occasionally, there may be proteinuria and haematuria, as also neutropenia, which may progress to agranulocytosis.

DIURETICS

A diuretic is, strictly speaking, any agent that produces an increased output of urine. This can be useful when it is necessary to (i) flush out poisons from the body, (ii) to dilute drug metabolites that might injure the kidney during excretion e.g. cyclophosphamide, or (iii) to prevent the crystallization of substances of low solubility in urine; for example, certain sulphonamides, or uric acid during the treatment of gout.

However, the most important and common use of a diuretic is in order to increase the excretion of sodium, usually with chloride, together with water. A drug with this property is strictly speaking a saluretic but this term is not used as much as it ought to be and, instead, drugs that are saluretics are simply referred to as diuretics, imprecise as this may be.

Normal renal physiology

In order to understand how diuretics (saluretics) work and how they can be used selectively in the treatment of disease, a brief review of normal renal function will be presented first (see Fig. 15.4).

Urine secretion is a two-stage process involving glomerular filtration followed by tubular reabsorption and/or tubular secretion. Thus:

urinary excretion =
glomerular filtration − amount reabsorbed in tubules + tubular secretion.

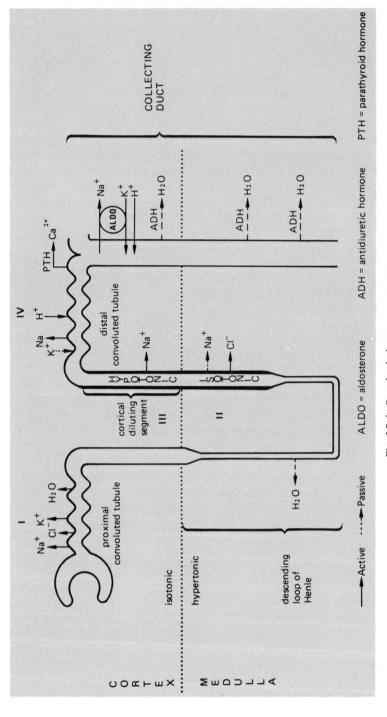

Fig. 15.4. Renal tubular transport systems.

ALDO = aldosterone   ADH = antidiuretic hormone   PTH = parathyroid hormone

→ Active   ---→ Passive

1. The glomerular filtration, which depends on the hydrostatic pressure of the arterial circulation, is normally produced at the rate of 125 ml/min, so that in 24 hours, $125 \times 60 \times 24 = 180\,000$ ml $= 180$ l will be formed, and this contains 25 000 mmol of sodium. However, in 24 hours, only about 1.5 l of urine containing approximately 100 mmol of sodium is voided. This means that $180\,000 - 1500 = 178\,500$ ml or 99.2 per cent of the glomerular filtrate, containing $25\,000 - 100 = 24\,900$ mmol of sodium or 99.6 per cent of sodium is reabsorbed.

2. The reabsorption of water and electrolytes takes place as the result of a number of energy-requiring mechanisms, and these are modified by diuretics. The renal tubule can be divided up into four sites, each of which has its own pattern of reabsorption, and is selectively modified by diuretics (see Fig. 15.5).

Site 1: proximal tubule

At this site about 60 per cent of filtered sodium (Na^+) is actively absorbed accompanied by anions of chloride (Cl^-), two-thirds, and bicarbonate (HCO_3^-), one-third. All filtered potassium (K^+) is absorbed, and the proximal tubule fluid is isosmotic with peritubular fluid.

Site 2: ascending limb of Henle

Here chloride ions are actively reabsorbed together with 25 per cent of filtered sodium (25 per cent of $25\,000 = 6250$ mmol Na^+), which moves passively. This part of the tubule is impermeable to water, as a result of which the concentration of sodium and chloride in the tubular fluid falls whilst *pari passu*, the

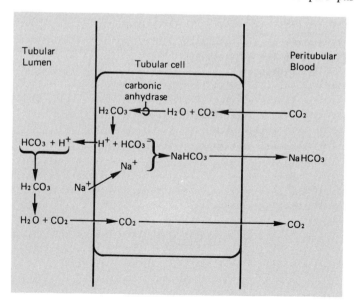

Fig. 15.5. The mechanism of bicarbonate reabsorption in the renal tubule.

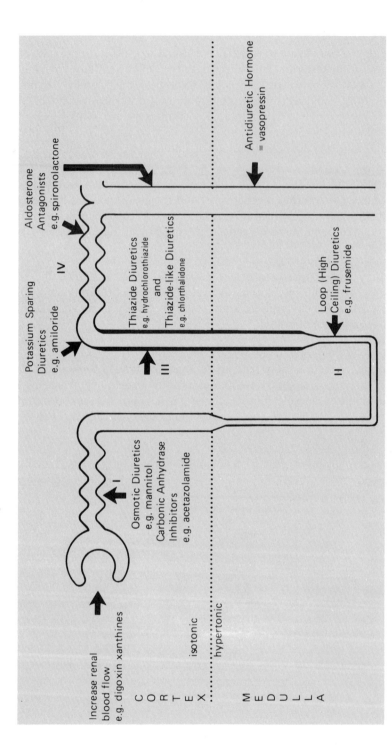

Fig. 15.6. The sites of action of diuretics.

concentration of sodium and chloride ions in the interstitial fluid rises to become hypertonic. The generation of the hypertonic milieu of the interstitium is fundamental in providing the osmotic force needed to produce hypertonic urine in the collecting ducts of the nephron.

Site 3: the cortical segment of the ascending loop of Henle

This is often called the cortical diluting segment, and differs from sites 1 and 2 in that 5 per cent sodium (5 per cent of $25\,000 = 1250$ mmol Na^+) is absorbed *without* water, with the result that the tubular fluid becomes hypotonic. It is important to note that because the reabsorption of sodium from this site takes place within the cortical region (and therefore outside the medullary region) drugs that act on site 3 can reduce cortical diluting ability without affecting the subsequent concentration of urine, which takes place in the collecting duct and depends upon the hypertonic medullary zone (see above).

Site 4: distal convoluted tubule and collecting duct

At this site some additional sodium and chloride reabsorption takes place. In addition, potassium and hydrogen ions are secreted in exchange for sodium ions, the exchange depending upon the amount of sodium delivered to the site and also upon the amount of aldosterone secreted. A diuretic that reduces the amount of sodium reabsorption proximal to Site 4 will result in an increased load of sodium ions being presented to Site 4. As a consequence there will be an increased exchange of sodium ions for potassium and thus an increased loss of potassium ions in the urine.

Site 4 is also important for the reabsorption of water (as mentioned earlier), which takes place under the control of antidiuretic hormone (ADH; vasopressin) and which renders the collecting ducts permeable to water so that it then moves down the osmotic gradient into the interstitium of the medulla. As a result the urine becomes hypertonic.

Control of acid–base balance by the kidney

A major function of the kidney is to control the acid–base balance of the body. The kidney achieves this by:

(1) the tubular reabsorption of bicarbonate ion;
(2) the excretion of hydrogen ions with regeneration of bicarbonate.

These processes, which are illustrated above in Fig. 15.5, operate as follows. Carbon dioxide enters the renal cell from the blood and is hydrated in a reaction that is catalysed by carbonic anhydrase. The carbonic acid so formed then dissociates to form hydrogen ions and bicarbonate ions. The hydrogen ions are then secreted into the tubular lumen where they are exchanged for sodium ions. The sodium ions are then reabsorbed into the tubular cell where they combine with bicarbonate ions (formed from dissociation of carbonic acid) to form sodium bicarbonate, which is reabsorbed into the peritubular blood. At the same time, the hydrogen ions, which were secreted into the lumen and which were exchanged for sodium ions, combine with luminal bicarbonate ions to form carbonic acid, which then dissociates into water and carbon dioxide. The carbon dioxide diffuses back first into the tubular cell and ultimately into the peritubular blood. Thus any drug that is able to inhibit the enzyme, carbonic anhydrase, will interfere with bicarbonate reabsorption and hence acid–base balance (see under carbonic anhydrase).

Mechanism of excretion of organic acids and bases

Secretory systems for naturally occurring organic acids (e.g. uric acid) and organic bases (e.g. creatinine) exist in the proximal tubule. As many drugs are weak organic acids (e.g. aspirin) or weak organic bases (e.g. amitriptyline) (see Chapter 1), they are secreted by these active transport systems. As a consequence, a drug so transported may interact with one of the natural substances, for example, uric acid, being secreted by the same transport system. Furthermore it is possible to block the secretion of a drug that utilizes such a transport system with another that has a high affinity for the same system, e.g. probenecid blocks the secretion of benzylpenicillin (see Chapter 1).

Some drugs are partially reabsorbed from the tubules by non-ionic diffusion and, as the tubule cells are only permeable to the un-ionized fraction, reabsorption is dependent on the pK_a of the drug and the pH of the tubular urine (see Chapter 1). Thus, in the treatment of salicylate poisoning, the urine is made alkaline so that the salicylate will be highly ionized (pK_a of aspirin $= 3.5$) with the result that the amount of diffusion back into the tubular cell, and thence to the circulation via the peritubular blood, will be very small.

Classification of commonly used diuretics (saluretics)

It has already been seen that urinary excretion depends ultimately upon the difference between the amount of glomerular filtrate formed and the amount of the filtrate that is reabsorbed by the tubules. Again, this may be expressed in the form of a simple equation:

urinary excretion = glomerular filtrate − amount reabsorbed in the tubules.

It therefore follows that urinary excretion can be increased either by (i) *increasing* the glomerular filtrate, or (ii) by *decreasing* the reabsorption of the filtered load by the tubules. Diuretics can thus be classified into two groups:

(1) those that act by increasing renal blood flow and glomerular filtration rate;

(2) those that act by inhibiting the reabsorption of sodium by the renal tubules.

Drugs that increase renal blood flow

Digitalis glycosides

Digoxin (and other cardiac glycosides) increase the output of the failing heart (see p. 329) and thereby increase glomerular blood flow. As a consequence glomerular filtration is increased, leading to increased urine production. Digitalis glycosides may therefore be considered to have diuretic activity.

Xanthines

It is a matter of common knowledge that tea, coffee, and other beverages have a diuretic action; this is due to the xanthines (caffeine, theophylline, and theobromine) that they contain. These drugs increase cardiac output by inhibition of the enzyme phosphodiesterase that normally destroys cylicAMP, and hence increase renal blood flow; in addition, they dilate blood vessels in the renal medulla. However, the most potent drug in this group, aminophylline, is not a naturally occurring compound but is made in the laboratory by combining theophylline with ethylene diamine in order to produce a more soluble form of theophylline, suitable for slow intravenous injection.

Drugs that inhibit the reabsorption of sodium

Excess water retention is commonly due to associated sodium retention. It therefore follows that an effective way to reduce an excess of body water should be to increase the excretion of sodium, and this has proved to be the case. As shown earlier (see p. 339), sodium reabsorption takes place along the length of the renal tubule but the major part is reabsorbed in the proximal tubule, whilst sodium is actively reabsorbed without water in the ascending limb of the loop of Henle. In the distal tubule, sodium is exchanged for potassium under the control of aldosterone; as water passes down the collecting tubules it is reabsorbed under the control of ADH.

   Diuretics in this group may be divided into several clinically useful classes based on their mode and/or site of action, and their chemical group. They are listed here in descending order of frequency of use, and then described in turn.

   I Thiazides
  II Loop (high-ceiling)
 III Potassium-sparing
  IV Aldosterone antagonists
   V Osmotic diuretics
  VI Carbonic anhydrase inhibitors

I Thiazides (benzothiadiazines)

These agents were introduced in the mid-1950s and represented a great step forward, being the first orally active diuretics that were effective. They are derived from the sulphonamide structure of carbonic anhydrase inhibitors. The drugs that they replaced were the mercurial diuretics and, whilst they are weaker than these predecessors, they have the great advantage that they are active by mouth. Over 10 thiazide and thiazide-like drugs are now available: bendrofluazide, chlorothiazide, chlorthalidone, clopamide, cyclopenthiazide, hydrochlorothiazide, hydroflumethiazide, mefruside, methylclothiazide, polythiazide, xipamide. No one drug is outstandingly superior to the others.

Pharmacodynamics

1. Diuretic action: they act at site III in the cortical diluting segment and also at site IV, producing an increased output of sodium and water. The increased concentration of sodium ions presented to the distal tubule results in the secondary loss of potassium ions by increased secretion in exchange for the sodium ions.

2. Hypotensive action: thiazides and related compounds produce an antihypertensive effect that is independent of their diuretic action and probably due to a direct action on vascular smooth muscle, possibly by modulating its response to various pressor agents, including catecholamines and angiotensin. The initial reduction of blood volume caused by the diuretic cannot be the primary hypotensive mechanism because the fall in blood pressure continues after homeostatic mechanisms have led to a rise in the blood volume.

Uses

These compounds are used to counter oedema caused by cardiac failure, nephrotic syndrome, and drugs; and to treat hypertension and diabetes insipidus.

Pharmacokinetics

All these drugs are well absorbed by mouth and excreted unchanged in the urine. The $T_{0.5}$ is about four hours, although they act for about three times as long and must therefore be taken in the morning to avoid a disturbed night.

Unwanted effects

All thiazides tend to exhibit the following several unwanted effects. Potassium loss causing hypokalaemia will occur when they are given for a prolonged period. For this reason, potassium supplements should always be taken by those who are on thiazides indefinitely. There may be hyperglycaemia but this is not usually of clinical significance; however, occasionally diabetes mellitus is precipitated in a susceptible patient. In established diabetics being treated with oral hypoglycaemic drugs, increased doses may be needed. Hyperuricaemia occurs due to reduced excretion of uric acid, and this may precipitate an acute attack of gout. Hypercalcaemia may arise due to decreased urinary excretion of calcium. There may be reduced urinary output in patients with nephrogenic diabetes insipidus.

II Loop (high-ceiling) diuretics

This group of drugs includes frusemide, bumetanide, and ethacrynic acid.

Pharmacodynamics

These drugs inhibit sodium and chloride reabsorption in the ascending limb of the loop of Henle and, as a consequence, are much more potent than the thiazides. Because of this action they are also called 'loop diuretics' and 'high-ceiling' diuretics. Although the degree of potassium loss is less than that produced by the thiazides for an equivalent diuresis, they are potent enough to produce substantial potassium loss, so that it is important to administer potassium supplements to patients receiving them. They are readily absorbed from the gut, but can be given intravenously. Their actions persist up to about six hours.

Pharmacokinetics

Frusemide is only 50 per cent absorbed, whereas bumetanide and ethacrynic acid are well absorbed. The $T_{0.5}$ of these drugs are short (1–1.5 hours), and they are mainly secreted unchanged in the urine.

Uses

They are used to treat systemic oedema due to cardiac failure, hepatic disease, and nephrotic syndrome; and acute pulmonary oedema.

Unwanted effects

Their powerful diuretic action can lead to hypokalaemia, hyponatraemia, and dehydration. Hypokalaemia must be prevented by giving adequate potassium supplements (see Pharmacodynamics) or, if appropriate, giving potassium-sparing diuretics, such as spironolactone, triamterene, or amiloride. As hypokalaemia potentiates the effects of cardiac glycosides, particular care must be taken when loop diuretics are given to patients already taking digoxin. Magnesium excretion may also be excessive and result in hypomagnesaemia.

Hyperglycaemia may occur but is not usually of clinical significance except in those suffering from diabetes mellitus, whose dose of oral hypoglycaemic drugs may need to be increased.

There may be hyperuricaemia but it is uncommon for it to precipitate an attack of acute gout. However, the powerful diuretic action of these drugs may precipitate acute urinary retention in those already suffering from prostatic hypertrophy.

III Potassium-sparing diuretics

Pharmacodynamics

Triamterene and amiloride are chemically similar diuretics that act upon the distal convoluted tubule. They cause an increase in sodium and chloride excretion but, in contrast to the diuretics mentioned earlier, they inhibit the exchange of sodium for potassium by an unknown mechanism, which is independent of aldosterone. Consequently, their use is associated with retention of potassium and may thus result in hyperkalaemia.

Pharmacokinetics

Triamterene and amiloride are poorly absorbed by mouth, and almost completely excreted unchanged in the urine with a $T_{0.5}$ of about six hours.

Uses

These drugs are used in combination with other diuretics that cause depletion of potassium; for example, thiazides, frusemide. Moduretic, a proprietary preparation consisting of a combination of hydrochlorothiazide and amiloride, is used when it is necessary to give a diuretic but minimize the risk of hypokalaemia.

Unwanted effects

Hyperkalaemia, dehydration, and hyponatraemia may occur. Both drugs can cause nausea, vomiting, and diarrhoea.

IV Aldosterone antagonists

Pharmacodynamics

Spironolactone is a synthetic steroid that has a structural formula similar to that of aldosterone. It is metabolized to canrenone, which is a competitive antagonist to aldosterone on the distal convoluted tubule. Its effects will clearly depend upon the amount of aldosterone with which it can compete; such competition will cause increased sodium and water excretion, and potassium retention. Furthermore, spironolactone is a weak diuretic because the reabsorption of sodium in the distal convoluted tubule accounts for only a relatively small proportion of the total amount of sodium reabsorbed.

Pharmacokinetics

Spironolactone is absorbed well after oral administration and, although its $T_{0.5}$ is only about 10 minutes, the active metabolite, canrenone, has a much longer half-life ($T_{0.5} = 16$ hours) and, as a consequence, its onset of action is slow.

Uses

Naturally, it is particularly effective when circulating levels of aldosterone are high as may occur in the nephrotic syndrome, hepatic failure, or as a result of intensive diuretic therapy.

Spironolactone can also be used to treat oedema due to cardiac failure, nephrotic syndrome, and liver disease. For reasons given above, it is usually prescribed in combination with a thiazide or one of the high-ceiling diuretics.

Unwanted effects

There may be nausea and vomiting with high doses. Hyperkalaemia may occur even when spironolactone is used in combination with a potassium-losing diuretic, and it is therefore important to be alert to this possibility.

There is chemical similarity between spironolactone (and its active metabolite, canrenone) and the sex hormones, so the drug may act as an agonist at sex hormone receptors. Thus gynaecomastia is common (and often painful); of less frequent occurrence are impotence, testicular atrophy, and menstrual disturbances. For similar reasons the peptic ulcer-healing properties of carbenoxolone may be reversed by spironolactone so that these two drugs should not be given concurrently.

V Osmotic diuretics

Pharmacodynamics

Mannitol is the most important drug in this group; it is a sugar alcohol, which is not metabolized by the body. Under normal circumstances (as has been described earlier) the major reabsorption of sodium from the glomerular filtrate takes place in the proximal convoluted tubule. As the proximal tubule is freely permeable to water, the reabsorption of sodium and water can take place together, with the result that the contents of the tubule remain isosmotic. However, when a substance such as mannitol, which is not reabsorbed by the tubule, is present, this impedes the reabsorption of water in order that the osmotic pressure of the tubular fluid shall remain the same as that of the plasma. As a consequence, the reabsorption of water and, secondarily, of sodium is reduced and a diuresis results. As with other diuretics, the increased sodium load presented to the distal tubule results in an increased exchange of sodium for potassium with consequent increased potassium loss in the urine. It should be noted that for a substance to act as an osmotic diuretic it must (i) enter the glomerular filtrate from the plasma, and (ii) fail either completely or partially to be reabsorbed by the tubule.

Pharmacokinetics

Mannitol is, as might be expected, very poorly absorbed and must therefore be given parenterally. After parenteral administration it remains in the extracellular compartment and depends upon renal excretion for its removal from the body, which takes place rapidly. The intravenous administration of mannitol must be carried out with great care because it can lead to an increase in the circulating volume of blood with a consequent rise in central venous pressure, which in turn may lead to cardiac failure. Furthermore, the increased osmolality of the plasma may then lead to hyponatraemia. It should be noted that if it is given by mouth it will remain within the gastro-intestinal tract and behave as an osmotic laxative.

Uses

Mannitol is used when oedema becomes refractory to other diuretics. It will also improve renal blood flow in certain forms of renal failure (e.g. shock). It may also be employed to produce a forced diuresis in drug poisoning, so as to increase the rate of drug eliminations.

VI Carbonic anhydrase inhibitors

The role of the enzyme carbonic anhydrase has been discussed earlier (see p. 341). Before the advent of the thiazides and the loop diuretics, carbonic anhydrase inhibitors represented a group of orally active but weak diuretic agents. They have since been superseded by the much more potent agents but are occasionally used for special purposes, for example, in the treatment of glaucoma.

Pharmacodynamics
Inhibition of carbonic anhydrase will reduce the supply of hydrogen ions available for exchange with sodium ions (together with bicarbonate ions) with the result that there is an increased excretion of an alkaline urine containing sodium bicarbonate. If this is maintained, the increase in bicarbonate excretion leads to a metabolic acidosis, which unfortunately reduces the further efficacy of the drug. As a consequence the response to subsequent doses rapidly falls off and alternative methods of diuresis must be considered.

Pharmacokinetics
Acetazolamide is well adsorbed after oral administration and is excreted by tubular secretion with a half-life of 2.5–6 hours.

Uses
The increased intra-ocular pressure in chronic glaucoma can be reduced by carbonic anhydrase inhibitors. The enzyme inhibition results in a diminished secretion of aqueous humor into the anterior chamber of the eye, and also a reduced formation of cerebrospinal fluid. Thus, as well as being used for the treatment of glaucoma, carbonic anhydrase inhibitors have also been used as adjuvant therapy for the treatment of epilepsy.

TREATMENT OF SOME CARDIOVASCULAR DISEASES

Treatment of cardiac arrhythmias

The treatment of all but the simplest forms of cardiac arrhythmia fall within the province of the cardiologist. Therefore, the following account attempts only an outline of this complex problem in which it is vital for accurate diagnosis to precede treatment. Furthermore, with the large and bewildering number of anti-arrhythmic drugs now available the selection of the appropriate drug or drugs for a particular patient requires (i) specialized knowledge and experience of this branch of cardiology, and (ii) understanding of the pharmacology of the drugs to be employed. Only an overview of this problem can be given.

Causes of cardiac arrhythmias

There are six main causes of cardiac arrhythmias:

(1) ischaemic heart disease;
(2) valvular heart disease;

(3) cardiomyopathies;

(4) congenital heart disease;

(5) drug induced e.g. cardiac glycosides and other anti-arrhythmic drugs;

(6) metabolic disturbances e.g. hypokalaemia.

When a patient presents with an arrhythmia it is necessary not only to find out the type but also the factor responsible for it. It is not possible to put into reverse changes due to ischaemic heart disease or due to congenital conduction abnormalities. On the other hand, it should be possible to correct drug-induced abnormalities and also to correct metabolic disturbances.

Classification of cardiac arrhythmias

These may arise within the ventricle, above it in the atrium, or in the nodal tissue. Arrhythmias may also be induced by digitalis. It is therefore convenient to consider them under four headings as follows:

(1) sinus node arrhythmias;

(2) supraventricular arrhythmias;

(3) ventricular arrhythmias;

(4) drug-induced arrhythmias.

Some of the more common arrhythmias within each of these groups will now be discussed briefly.

Sinus node arrhythmias

These comprise either sinus tachycardia, in which the heart rate is greater than 100 per minute, or sinus bradycardia, in which the rate is less than 60 per minute. Sinus tachycardia does not require specific treatment, but the underlying cause should be investigated; anxiety or hyperthyroidism are two possible causes.

Chronic sinus bradycardia can be caused by any drug that (i) reduces sympathetic drive to the heart (b-adrenoceptor antagonists); (ii) drugs that increase vagal tone (e.g. acetylcholinesterase inhibitors); (iii) cardiac glycosides. It is also a feature of hypothyroidism. After an acute myocardial infarction, bradycardia is common but does not need treatment unless it results in an unacceptable reduction of cardiac output, in which case the antimuscarinic drug, atropine, is used to antagonize this vagal effect. It should be remembered that sinus bradycardia is a normal occurrence in highly trained athletes. Thus, whilst the cause of sinus bradycardia should always be sought, usually it does not need treatment.

Supraventricular arrhythmias

These comprise (i) atrial flutter, (ii) atrial fibrillation, and (iii) paroxysmal tachycardia.

Atrial flutter

In this condition the atria beat regularly at a rate of 250 to 350 per minute. The precise mechanism is not clear; it may be due to a 'circus movement' in which a self-perpetuating wave of excitation moves in a circle around the orifices of the superior and inferior vena cavae. An alternative view is that it is due to a single, rapidly firing ectopic atrial focus from which impulses spread out over the atrium. However, the high rate of atrial impulses is not usually conducted to the ventricles due to varying degrees of atrioventricular block. Thus, there is usually a 2:1, 3:1, or 4:1 atrioventricular block present, with the result that the ventricular rate is a sub-multiple of the atrial rate; the commonest situation is a 2:1 block with a ventricular rate of 140 to 160 beats per minute. Digitalis (digoxin or digitoxin) is the drug of first choice, with a β-blocker or calcium entry blocker as a second choice. Disopyramide is also useful and should be given in combination with digoxin. However, if digoxin fails it is then usual to attempt direct-current (DC) cardioversion.

Atrial fibrillation

This condition is usually due to acute or chronic myocardial ischaemia, mitral stenosis, or hyperthyroidism, but other less common causes may be responsible. If it is of recent origin an attempt is usually made to convert this completely irregular rhythm to normal rhythm by means of DC cardioversion. However, if the fibrillation has been present for some time then restoration of regular sinus rhythm is unlikely, and the aim then is to use drugs to slow the ventricular rate to the normal range. Once again, digitalis is the drug of first choice but, if this is ineffective on its own, then it may become effective with the addition of a β-adrenoceptor antagonist or calcium entry blocker. Disopyramide is also a useful drug for this problem. Amiodarone, though very effective, should only be considered as a last resort.

Paroxysmal supraventricular tachycardia

This consists of paroxysms of sudden onset during which the heart rate is found to be 140 to 220 per minute although regular in rhythm. Three forms can be identified by means of specialist techniques (Kulbertus 1986; true atrial tachycardia, nodal tachycardia, and pre-excitation tachycardia). The duration of the attacks may be only seconds but, more often they persist for minutes or hours, and occasionally for days. Precipitating factors should be sought (and avoided), and these include dietary (coffee, tobacco, alcohol), psychological (anxiety), or physical (exercise).

During an acute attack, measures designed to increase vagal tone, such as carrying out the Valsalva manoeuvre (see p. 322), swallowing cold water, facial massage, or carotid sinus massage, may be effective. If drug treatment is required, verapamil 10 mg IV slowly (or one of the other calcium entry blockers) is often effective. Alternatively, a β-adrenoceptor blocker can be tried. If these measures fail the patient should be referred to a specialist.

A wide variety of treatments are used in prophylaxis; these include digoxin and/or calcium entry blockers; disopyramide (for true atrial tachycardia or for nodal tachycardia); flecainide, disopyramide, or amiodarone (for pre-excitation tachycardias)

Ventricular arrhythmias

These are most commonly ventricular extrasystoles (premature beats), ventricular tachycardia, and ventricular fibrillation. They are most likely to occur after acute myocardial infarction; they may, however, occur in otherwise healthy individuals, or be caused by ischaemic heart disease or by any drug that has arrhythmogenic properties; for example, digitalis or tricyclic antidepressants.

Ventricular extrasystoles (premature beats) often arise after myocardial infarction and may need treatment. However, the indications for treatment and the best drug for this purpose remain a controversial subject. If treatment is indicated then all anti-arrhythmic drugs (except calcium entry blockers) can be useful and the potential of β-blockers should not be overlooked. For ventricular tachycardia, lignocaine is also considered to be the drug of choice.

Drug-induced arrhythmias

Digitalis is the most likely culprit and commonly produces supraventricular arrhythmias, ectopic ventricular arrhythmias, or heart block, or a combination of these. Sinus bradycardia can be the result of excessive medication with digitalis but only needs treating if it is causing hypotension. As noted earlier, atropine is an effective way of reducing vagal tone and would be an appropriate treatment here if required. The occurrence of atrial tachycardia with heart block might call for treatment with lignocaine or phenytoin, or possibly a combination of a β-adrenoceptor antagonist and the insertion of a cardiac pacemaker. Ventricular arrhythmias would also call for treatment with phenytoin, lignocaine, or a β-adrenoceptor antagonist. It might also be necessary to insert a pacemaker, and DC cardioversion may need to be considered. It should be noted that arrhythmias can be induced by all anti-arrhythmic drugs.

Heart failure and its treatment

There are several different types of heart failure, of which the commonest is due to inadequate contraction of either the right or the left ventricle, or both. If contraction of the right ventricle is inadequate this leads to systemic venous congestion, whilst if the contraction of the left ventricle is inadequate this leads to pulmonary oedema; or there may be a mixture of both. Treatment aims to remove the cause, if this is possible, and to control the signs and symptoms by means of appropriate drugs.

If the underlying cause of heart failure can be removed or modified then this should be done. Thus, if cardiac failure is secondary to valvular disease of the heart it may be possible to deal with this surgically. If the cause is hypertension then this can be treated (see below). Likewise, if cardiac failure is secondary to anaemia or hyperthyroidism these conditions must also be treated (see Chapters 18 and 19). Drugs with negative inotropic properties, such as Class I and Class II anti-arrhythmic agents (see above), may also precipitate cardiac failure, and appropriate modification of the dose or withdrawal of the drug (and possibly replacement by another) would be appropriate treatment here.

When the cause of cardiac failure cannot be removed then drug therapy becomes mandatory and, from earlier sections in this chapter, it will be evident that there are three groups of drugs that can be used to treat the condition.

1. Diuretics are the first drugs of choice because they remove the excess sodium and water that occurs in cardiac failure. Furthermore, if the failure is secondary to hypertension then many of the diuretic agents appear to have an additional and direct action on vascular smooth muscle, which lowers the blood pressure and thereby assists treatment. Thiazides and loop diuretics are most commonly used for this purpose.

2. Digitalis glycosides, which have a positive inotropic action, are also important, and commonly form the mainstay of therapy in patients with congestive cardiac failure.

3. Vasodilators are also important because, as discussed earlier (see p. 331), they reduce the load on the heart and thereby assist it to work more within its reduced capabilities.

The appropriate combination of drugs and their doses calls for careful clinical judgement and continuous review in order that changes in the condition of the patient may be monitored and appropriate modification of drug therapy made.

Treatment of hypertension

Hypertension is a persistently raised blood pressure and, in the early stages, is unlikely to be recognized as it is asymptomatic. Symptomatic recognition may only occur after some considerable time, when damage has already been done to the cardiovascular system. The lesson to be learned from this observation is that regular screening of blood pressure may well be desirable, particularly in patients with a family history of cardiovascular disease.

In the vast majority of patients the reason for the raised blood pressure is unknown, and this is called 'essential' hypertension. Essential hypertension is probably multifactorial in its causation. There is another form of hypertension that arises from a known disorder, such as kidney malfunction, and this is known as 'secondary' hypertension. The discussion here will deal solely with the problem of essential hypertension.

The blood pressure varies as the product of the cardiac output and the resistance to the flow of blood in the peripheral circulation (peripheral resistance).

The smooth muscle in the arteriolar wall is constantly in a state of partial contraction and this state is modified by the vasomotor centre acting by way of the sympathetic nervous system. Increased sympathetic activity causes arteriolar vasoconstriction with a rise in blood pressure, and vice versa. Although many of the drugs used to treat hypertension do so by blocking sympathetic outflow, it is unlikely that excessive activity of the sympathetic nervous system is the sole mechanism causing a raised blood pressure. In recent years, the role played by renin in hypertension has exercized some interest. Renin, as outlined earlier and shown in Fig. 15.3, splits the protein angiotensin to form the peptide angiotensin I, the angiotensin being found in the blood. Angiotensin I is converted to angiotensin II and this, in its turn, is metabolized to angiotensin III. Both angiotensin II and angiotensin III are vasoconstrictors of peripheral arterioles and this can lead to hypertension. Any increased renin activity will lead to excessive production of these angiotensins.

Whatever the cause, essential hypertension is a progressive disease and it will eventually cause damage to the entire cardiovascular system. Treatment is necessary in many instances in order to avoid the consequences of the pressure, e.g. stroke, renal damage, and ischaemic heart disease.

Essential hypertension is an age-related disease, and a pressure in the range 140–150/90 is usually regarded as hypertension in the average patient (Neidle, et al. 1985). There is a wide variety of drugs available for the treatment of essential hypertension and, in general, patients whose average diastolic pressure exceeds 100 should receive antihypertensive treatment. Diuretics are often the first choice of drug for the treatment of hypertension and may suffice in themselves. They will often be quite adequate to control a mild hypertension (Ramsay 1987). Other drugs can be added to diuretics as required in order to produce a satisfactory anyihypertensive effect. It seems that the diuretics potentiate the effects of most other antihypertensive drugs.

The β-adrenoceptor blocking drugs (see Chapter 13) are sometimes used alone to control the blood pressure, and they are also used together with diuretics when either, used separately, have proved inadequate. In more severe hypertension, a third drug, such as a vasodilator, may have to be added, hydralazine being the one normally advocated.

Apart from the use of drugs other remedial factors must be considered. If the patient is overweight, there should be an attempt to reduce this; those who smoke should be encouraged to stop. Alcohol consumption should be moderate.

Treatment of angina pectoris

Angina pectoris is manifested by a sudden and severe pain occurring substernally and this pain often radiates to the left shoulder and arm and, less frequently, to the left mandible and teeth. The pain is typically brought on by exercize, emotion, and cold. This type of angina is referred to as angina of effort and it is a manifestation of myocardial ischaemia, which in itself is caused by atherosclerosis producing narrowing of the coronary arteries. The drugs available for treatment have been considered above; one mainly used to treat an anginal attack is glyceryl trinitrate. The treatment of an acute attack should be prompt and this is best done by placing a tablet of the drug under the tongue from where it is rapidly absorbed. The effects start within about 2 minutes and last up to 30 minutes. Unwanted effects include flushing, headache, and postural hypotension. Glyceryl trinitrate can also be used as a prophylaxis prior to exercize or other factors that tend to bring on an attack.

Amyl nitrite was used at one time but it causes marked vasodilatation of all arterioles with a considerable fall in blood pressure.

Pentaerythritol tetranitrate is a drug that is swallowed; it takes about 10 minutes to become effective and its effects are prolonged over several hours. The drug is used as a prophylactic agent, rather than to treat an acute attack.

Many situations will stimulate the sympathetic nervous system and precipitate an attack of angina, e.g. fear or anxiety. The β-adrenergic antagonists block sympathetic activity to the heart and are effective in reducing the frequency and severity of attacks of angina of effort. They lessen the myocardial oxygen consumption. Beta blockers are taken prophylactically, that is they are taken regularly, and are not used to treat an acute attack of angina. These drugs are not useful if the angina is due to vasospasm.

Calcium entry blockers, e.g. verapamil, nifedipine, are useful in the treatment of angina of effort and of atypical angina. In exertional angina they may produce their effect by reducing myocardial oxygen demands and this, in itself, may be due to the decrease in cardiac contractility produced by these drugs. On the other hand, calcium entry blockers are likely to be effective in the treatment of angina due to vasospasm because they produce vasodilatation in non-atherosclerotic coronary arteries. Nifedipine is particularly valuable in this respect as it is a more potent coronary vasodilator than verapamil.

REFERENCES

Berridge, M. J. (1981). Receptors and calcium signalling. In *Towards understanding receptors* (ed. J. W. Lamble), p. 122. Elsevier, Oxford.

Berridge, M. J. (1985). The molecular basis of communication within the cell. *Scientific American*, **253**, 142–52.

Endo, M., Yanagisawa, T., and Taira, N. (1978). Effects of calcium-antagonist coronary vasodilators, nifedipine and verapamil, on ventricular automaticity of the dog. *Nawnyn-Schimiedeberg's Archiv für Pharmakologie*, **302**: 235–38.

Jones, C. M. (1986). Gingival hyperplasia associated with nifedipine. *British Dental Journal*, **160**, 416–7.

Krikler, D. M. (1974). A fresh look at cardiac arrhythmias IV Theory. *Lancet*, **i**, 1034–7.

Kulbertus, H. E. (ed.) (1986). Management of cardiac arrhythmias. Churchill Livingstone, Edinburgh.

Neidle, A., Kroeger, D. G., and Yagiela, J. A. (1985). *Pharmacology and therapeutics for dentistry*, (2nd ed). Mosby, St. Louis.

Noble, D. (1979). *The initiation of the heart-beat* (2nd edn). Clarendon Press, Oxford.

Noble, D. (1984). The surprising heart: a review of recent progress in cardiac electrophysiology. *Journal of Physiology*, **353**, 1–50.

Ramsay, L. E. (1987). The management of mild hypertension. *Prescribers' Journal*, **27**(2), 1–8.

Rowland, E., Evans, T., and Krikler, D. (1979). Effect of nifedipine on atrioventricular conduction as compared with verapamil. Intracardiac electrophysiological study. *British Heart Journal*, **42**, 124–7.

Vaughan Williams, E. M. (1983). *Antiarrhythmic actions*. Academic Press, London.

Weidmann, S. (1955). The effect of the cardiac membrane potential on the rapid availability of the sodium carrying system. *Journal of Physiology*, **127**, 213–24.

16

Drugs acting on the respiratory system and the gastro-intestinal tract

THIS section will limit itself to those drugs that are used to treat asthma, and that provide some symptomatic relief in respiratory infections, with a brief consideration of respiratory stimulants.

Drugs used to treat bronchial asthma

Bronchial asthma is commonly due to an allergy to some extrinsic factor. Infection may be a precipitating factor and sometimes emotional distress is an important element. The management of acute asthma occurring in an adverse drug reaction is considered in Chapter 21. The asthmatic attack is characterized by acute airway obstruction due to spasm of the bronchiolar smooth muscle (bronchoconstriction). At the same time the bronchial mucosa is oedematous and the lumen contains many mucus plugs. Fortunately the airway obstruction is reversible by certain drugs.

The mechanism of bronchoconstriction is seemingly through release of mediators from sensitized mast cells in the lungs. The substances so released include histamine, slow reacting substance (SRS-A) (now known to be a mixture of leukotrienes C_4 and D_4), 5-hydroxytryptamine (5-HT), and prostaglandins. Although these substances cause bronchoconstriction, histamine is probably little involved for certainly antihistamines (H_1-blockers) are not effective in the management of the disease.

The drugs used in the management of asthma include:

(1) sympathomimetic drugs;

(2) xanthine derivatives;

(3) sodium cromoglycate and ketotifen (mast cell stabilizers);

(4) corticosteroids.

Sympathomimetic drugs

Directly acting sympathomimetic drugs, such as adrenaline and isoprenaline, which stimulate β_2-receptors in the bronchi, will bring about relaxation of the bronchial smooth muscle. Unfortunately, both of these drugs are somewhat unselective and stimulate β_1-receptors in the heart with possible production of tachycardia at the least. Newer drugs are now available, e.g. salbutamol and terbutaline, which are also β_2-stimulants in the bronchi producing relaxation, but which are relatively selective. These drugs have much less effect on cardiac receptors and are to be preferred.

This group has been considered in more detail in Chapter 13.

Xanthine bronchodilators

Theophylline is a xanthine derivative, as is caffeine. Both are CNS stimulants, but caffeine more so. Theophylline is also a mild diuretic (see Chapter 15). It promotes the relaxation of smooth muscle, especially in the bronchi, and in blood vessels other than cerebral vessels. There is no certain agreement on the way theophylline acts to relieve asthma. The mechanism of action was thought to be due to an increase in intracellular cyclic adenosine monophosphate (cAMP) due to the inhibition of the enzyme phosphodiesterase, which metabolises cyclic AMP. It is now thought that the action on bronchial muscles may be due to blockage of adenosine receptors.

Over the years theophylline has proved a very useful drug in relieving bronchial asthma. When administered by mouth it is a gastric irritant. A widely used theophylline compound is called aminophylline; this drug also causes gastric irritation when given orally. Attempts to overcome this problem have been made by various pharmaceutical firms: for instance, aminophylline has been combined with the antacid aluminium hydroxide (aminophylline 195 mg, dried aluminium hydroxide gel 260 mg in each tablet), a preparation which counteracts the gastric acidity so that larger doses of aminophylline can be given with less risk of causing nausea and vomiting. Aminophylline and theophylline are also available as sustained-release preparations that are administered every 12 hours and are thought to cause less gastric irritation.

Aminophylline is also given by slow intravenous injection over a period of at least 10 to 15 minutes, with later maintenance if necessary—by slow intravenous infusion. This regimen is useful in terminating an attack of acute asthma.

Xanthine derivatives may be particularly useful in the treatment of asthma when sympathomimetic drugs have been ineffective.

Sodium cromoglycate

This is a prophylactic drug and is of no use in the treatment of an acute attack of asthma (see Chapter 21). It is administered by inhalation as it is poorly absorbed when given by mouth. It seems to work by stabilizing the mast cell membranes, so preventing the release of the pharmacologically active mediators that cause the bronchospasm. Children seem to respond to the drug better than the older patient. Some patients find that the dry powder inhalations of sodium cromoglycate actually precipitate bronchospasm, although this is usually transient.

Ketotifen, a relatively new drug, is administered orally. Although it is thought to act in the same way as sodium cromoglycate, it is not as effective.

Corticosteroids

The mechanism of action of the corticosteroids in asthma is somewhat uncertain. They are not the first choice of drugs for the treatment of bronchial asthma when the attack can be brought under control by other means. Steroids may occasionally be required when other remedies have failed, and a relatively short course may re-establish the patient's response to drugs such as salbutamol.

Some patients find the use of a steroid inhalant satisfactory. Seemingly the best of the corticosteroids for inhalation is beclomethasone dipropionate. After the inhalation (by aerosol) the drug is deposited in the mouth, nasal passages, and bronchi. In therapeutic doses this steroid does not appear to cause suppression of adrenal function. Such an inhalant can be useful in controlling asthma prophylactically. It must be taken regularly for a prescribed time, and it is not suitable for the treatment of an acute attack. The use of the aerosol inhalant is directed to less severe and more chronic asthma.

One unfortunate, unwanted effect of the use of beclomethasone inhalant is the occurrence of candidiasis of the mouth or throat. This is unlikely to happen unless large doses are used and is rarely seen. A preventitive measure is to rinse the mouth out with water after inhalation of a dose of the steroid.

Patients with severe bronchospasm may be treated with short courses of oral corticosteroids, e.g. prednisolone, for a few days. This dosage is gradually reduced over a week; the regimen may be useful when other remedies have temporarily failed.

In the treatment of an emergency, hydrocortisone is administered intravenously in large doses together with β_2-receptor stimulants.

Nasal decongestants

Ephedrine

This is both a directly and indirectly acting sympathomimetic drug. On the one hand it acts directly on α- and β-receptors and, on the other, it displaces noradrenaline from sympathetic nerve endings, which then acts on the appropriate receptors. Its pharmacological action differs from that of adrenaline in a number of ways: (a) it is absorbed from the intestinal tract after oral administration; (b) its effects are weaker but more prolonged; and (c) it has quite a marked stimulating effect on the CNS.

Ephedrine nasal drops may provide symptomatic relief from the nasal congestion associated with the common cold. The effect is produced by vasoconstriction of the mucosal blood vessels, which reduces the thickness of the nasal mucosa. The use of decongestants should be confined to short periods. All can cause what is termed a 'rebound phenomenon', in this instance, a secondary vasodilation, which occurs as the effects wear off and which, temporarily at least, increases the nasal congestion. This is much less likely to happen with ephedrine than with the more potent sympathomimetic drugs used for the purpose, such as phenylephrine. It should be remembered that indirectly acting sympathomimetics may produce a hypertensive crisis if given to a patient taking a monoamine oxidase inhibitor (see Chapter 13).

Ephedrine also has a mild bronchodilatory effect so ephedrine hydrochloride tablets have been used in the treatment of mild chronic asthma. It produces a more sustained effect than adrenaline. Because of its stimulant effect on the CNS, using it to treat the mild asthmatic may have the disadvantage that it keeps them awake at night.

Steam inhalations

These are useful in the symptomatic treatment of acute infective conditions, e.g. a cold. Volatile substances, such as menthol and eucalyptus, are used for such a purpose. For example, menthol and benzoin inhalation consists of menthol 2 per cent in benzoin inhalation; one teaspoonful of the substance is added to a pint of hot water and the vapour inhaled.

Cough suppressants

These antitussive drugs should be used with discrimination. Coughing is the way of getting rid of excessive secretions and foreign matter and, when the cough is productive, it would be wrong to suppress it. However, the hard non-productive, painful cough is another matter altogether. The opioids (Chapter 6) are cough suppressants and the most commonly used for this purpose is codeine as a linctus. Pholcodine is also a popular preparation. More potent preparations, such as diamorphine hydrochloride linctus, are available for the management of dry or painful cough in terminal illness. All of these drugs are centrally acting.

Expectorants

These are drugs that promote the ejection by spitting of mucus or other fluids from the lungs and trachea. It is very doubtful whether any drug will facilitate the expectoration of bronchial secretions. Ammonium chloride, ipecacuanha, and squill are all used in near emetic doses to promote expectoration. Any effect is probably more that of a placebo than anything else. Expectorants are to be found in compound preparations, with sedatives, for example. One such popular mixture is Benylin Expectorant containing ammonium chloride and the antihistamine sedative, diphenhydramine. There is little evidence of the value of expectorants.

Respiratory stimulants (analeptics)
(e.g. doxapram and nikethamide)

These two respiratory stimulants have a limited use in the treatment of acute respiratory failure in those with chronic obstructive airways disease. Respiratory stimulants are of no value whatsoever in respiratory failure due to drug overdosage. For instance, if the respiratory problem is due to opioid overdosage, a specific antagonist should be given and naloxone is the drug of choice (see Chapter 6). Respiratory depression due to an overdosage of barbiturates will not respond to the respiratory stimulants, nor is naloxone an antidote to such poisoning.

Chronic bronchitis

Respiratory insufficiency may occur due to infection. In some instances, broad-spectrum antimicrobials should be prescribed (tetracyclines, amoxycillin, or co-trimoxazole) although a specimen of sputum should be taken and the organism typed.

THE ALIMENTARY TRACT

This section will contain a brief review of drugs commonly used in treating gastro-intestinal disorders.

Anti-emetic drugs

Anti-emetic drugs can act at the following sites:

(1) vomiting centre in the brain, e.g. hyoscine and some antihistamines;

(2) chemoreceptor trigger zone (CTZ), e.g. metoclopramide, and some phenothiazines, such as chlorpromazine;

(3) stomach, e.g. metoclopramide.

Certain H_1 blockers, such as diphenhydramine and cyclizine, have the ability to counter motion sickness.

Chlorpromazine (see Chapter 14) is a potent anti-emetic under certain circumstances. It does not seem to control motion sickness but is very useful in the treatment of vomiting caused by carcinoma, radiation sickness, and uraemia. The major tranquillizers prevent stimulation of the CTZ by such drugs as morphine, a drug that may well be used in the management of terminal illness.

Metoclopramide acts peripherally to enhance the action of acetylcholine at muscarinic synapses. In the CNS it has an inhibitory effect on the CTZ in the brain, acting in a similar way to the phenothiazines. The CTZ is situated adjacent to and connected with the vomiting centre and so stimulation of the CTZ produces vomiting. Metoclopramide prevents vomiting caused by various agents but is not effective in motion sickness.

The phenothiazine derivatives and metoclopramide occasionally cause dystonic reactions like smacking of lips and even spontaneous temporo-mandibular joint dislocations.

Peptic ulceration

Very often the gastro-duodenal mucosa is subject to erosions rather than to frank ulcerations. Both are caused by the over-production of acid (hyperacidity) secreted by the gastric mucosal cells. Peptic ulceration or erosions may cause a lot of gastric pain, there may be gastro-intestinal bleeding, and there may even be a gastric perforation.

Apart from rest, proper attention to diet, stopping smoking and alcohol, a number of drugs have been used to treat these conditions.

Antacids

The action of these is to neutralize the hydrochloric acid secreted by the stomach. They are effective in many dyspepsias and provide pain relief in conditions such as peptic ulcer. The antacids do not accelerate healing.

Sodium bicarbonate has been used for many years as an antacid; it leaves the stomach quickly so that its action is short-lived. If given in large quantities the excess is absorbed from the intestine and may produce alkalosis. It is not a good antacid because of this problem, but it acts quickly to relieve pain.

Aluminium hydroxide is one of the best antacids. It is usually given as a gel or as a tablet to suck. It combines slowly with the gastric acid to form aluminium chloride and water. After leaving the stomach, aluminium salts are not absorbed and do not lead to alkalosis.

There are other antacids, such as calcium, magnesium, and bismuth salts.

Liquorice derivatives

Liquorice has been a favourite remedy for many years and the older generation will certainly recall liquorice root. However, folk-lore has been translated into two medical preparations containing liquorice, namely carbenoxolone and deglycyrrhizinized liquorice. The use of these substances does seem to promote the healing of gastric ulcers, even without the patient being confined to rest. Carbenoxolone has anti-inflammatory activity and it probably increases the amount of adherent mucus on the gastric mucosa thus providing it with protection. It does not appear to produce any real change in gastric acid secretion.

Carbenoxolone has a number of unwanted effects as it causes sodium retention and oedema, together with hypokalaemia. The potassium depletion leading to hypokalaemia may produce muscle weakness.

Cimetidine and ranitidine

These are histamine- (H_2-)receptor blockers, and they promote the healing of peptic ulcers by a reduction of gastric acid output. These drugs should only be used after a definitive diagnosis of erosions or ulcerations, not simply on a clinical suspicion of their existence. It has been suggested that H_2-receptor blockers allow nitrosamine formation in the stomach and so predispose to gastric carcinoma, but there is no real evidence to suggest that there is such a hazard. These blockers, particularly ranitidine, are relatively free from unwanted effects. Both drugs have revolutionized the management of peptic ulcerations (see Chapter 4).

Pirenzepine

This is an anticholinergic and seems to inhibit gastric acid and pepsin secretion. It is a relatively new drug and requires a long-term assessment.

Diarrhoea

Antidiarrhoeal drugs can be divided into antidiarrhoeal adsorbent mixtures, antidiarrhoeal drugs that reduce motility, and a miscellaneous group of other preparations. Adsorbent mixtures include mixtures of chalk and kaolin. Methylcellulose is also adsorbent.

Diarrhoeas not controlled by an adsorbent mixture may be treated with drugs that reduce motility, such as diphenoxylate, loperamide, or a kaolin and morphine mixture.

Other preparations are used for particular conditions, for instance, sulphasalazine in the treatment of ulcerative colitis, or even the topical use of corticosteroids.

Diarrhoea due to specific infections is treated by the appropriate antimicrobial.

Laxatives

These should be avoided wherever possible, and usually an increase of dietary fibre (bran) will suffice to relieve mild constipation. Laxatives are useful when straining is likely to cause a problem, e.g. in patients with haemorrhoids, and where there has been drug-induced constipation, e.g. with drugs such as codeine or the opioids.

17

Chemotherapeutic agents in neoplastic disease

INTRODUCTION

Chemotherapeutic agents are widely used in the treatment of cancer and other neoplastic conditions. They are often the treatment of choice for some types of neoplasia, such as Hogdkin's disease and acute leukaemia. These agents are either used on their own, or as an adjunct to surgery or radiotherapy. The precise treatment will depend upon the type of neoplasia, its rate of growth, and capacity to metastasize. All chemotherapeutic agents block various stages in the cell cycle through inhibition or blockade of a biochemical or metabolic pathway essential for cell division. Therefore, knowledge of the normal cell-growth cycle is necessary for an understanding of their mechanism of action.

THE CELL CYCLE

Cells progress through stages of development while they are synthesizing, growing, and dividing. However, most cells in the body are fully developed and differentiated, and are no longer cycling or replicating. A portion of normal cells in tissues undergoing cellular turnover are in the process of controlling growth and division (for example, skin, bone marrow, and the lining of the gastrointestinal tract). In contrast, tumour cells continue to grow and divide beyond the normal control of the host.

The stages of cell growth and division are called the cell cycle. Cells begin the cycle in the intermitotic phase (G_1). Substances necessary for cell growth and division are produced in the synthetic phase (S), during which DNA, RNA, and major protein synthesis occurs. At the cessation of S phase, the pre-mitotic or G_2 phase occurs, followed by mitosis (M phase). Cells that are not in the replicating cycle move into the non-proliferating phase (G_0), from which they may return to the active proliferating phase. As the S phase is the period when the cell carries out intensive metabolic and synthetic activities, it is also the phase when it may be most sensitive to agents that interfere with DNA, RNA, and protein synthesis.

PRINCIPLES OF CHEMOTHERAPY

The following factors will govern the success or otherwise of chemotherapy in the treatment of neoplastic disease.

1. *Tumour susceptibility.* Different tumours will respond to different drugs at varying rates. To achieve optimal results, the tumour cells must be susceptible to the chemotherapeutic agent.

2. *Drug/tumour contact.* It is essential that the drug comes into contact with the tumour cells, not only in sufficient concentrations, but also during the critical period of cell division.

3. *Size of tumour.* Chemotherapeutic agents destroy a constant percentage of cells, rather than a constant number. This is referred to as first-order kinetics (see Chapter 1). If a drug destroys 99.99 per cent of tumour cells, this will still leave a substantial numbers of cells especially if the initial tumour mass was large. Even if a few tumour cells remain, there is the possibility of relapse and metastasis.

4. *Tumour cell resistance.* If a tumour becomes unresponsive to a chemotherapeutic agent, it may be due to a build-up of tumour cell resistance. A number of factors can cause this resistance; for example, poor penetration of the tumour due to an impaired blood supply, enzyme alteration, and tumour cell mutation.

5. *Immunotherapy.* The host tissues will possess some measure of defence against the tumour cells. Appropriate immunotherapy may enhance this defence mechanism and, given in conjunction with chemotherapy, may increase the tumour-killing potential of the drugs.

6. *Combination therapy.* Various chemotherapeutic agents act at different stages in the cell cycle. The administration of different drugs will increase their range of activity against the tumour. Furthermore, when combination therapy is used, lower doses are given, which will reduce the incidence of unwanted effects.

7. *Unwanted effects.* The drugs chosen should not cause severe unwanted effects that may prevent the completion of treatment. For a given drug, altering the route of administration may reduce the incidence of these effects.

CLASSIFICATION OF CHEMOTHERAPEUTIC AGENTS

Chemotherapeutic agents can be conveniently divided into five groups:

1. Alkylating agents: these release alkyl radicals that react with organic compounds essential for cell metabolism; they also prevent cell division by cross-linking strands of DNA.

2. Antimetabolites: these act as competitive antagonists for folic acid, purine, and for pyramidine bases, which are essential for the synthesis of DNA, RNA, and certain co-enzymes.

3. Natural products: this group comprises the vinca alkaloids, certain antibiotics, and enzymes.

4. Hormones: those used in the treatment of neoplasia include oestrogen, progesterone, and adrenocorticosteroids.

5. Radioactive isotopes and implants.

Alkylating agents

These were the first drugs to be used in the treatment of neoplastic disease. All alkylating agents are based on the chemical structure of nitrogen mustard, a compound used in chemical warfare; examples include cyclophosphamide, chlorambucil, and mechlorethamine.

Pharmacodynamics and pharmacological properties

Alkylating agents disrupt mitotic activity, cell growth, differentiation, and function. Their primary target is the DNA molecule (Price 1975). They are particularly effective if the tumour cells are rapidly proliferating, but they can also affect tissues with low mitotic activity. Tumour cell resistance can develop against an alkylating agent, which would impart cross-resistance to other drugs in this category.

Unwanted effects

Bone marrow suppression is of rapid onset after administration of an alkylating agent. Lymphocytopenia and thrombocytopenia occur at six to eight days after the start of therapy. Amenorrhoea and impairment of spermatogenesis usually follow a course of treatment. Alopecia, due to damage of the hair follicles, and damage to the epithelial lining of the gastro-intestinal mucosa, are common unwanted effects. Alkylating agents are potent stimulants of the CNS, and nausea and vomiting frequently accompany therapy.

Specific alkylating agents

Mechlorethamine is a nitrogen mustard that can only be given intravenously as it produces local tissue necrosis if given intramuscularly. The drug is mainly used in the treatment of Hodgkin's disease and other lymphomas.

Cyclophosphamide is a cyclic mustard that can be given orally or parenterally. It is probably the most widely used chemotherapeutic agent, either solely or in combination with other drugs. Cyclophosphamide has achieved good results in Hodgkin's disease, lymphosarcoma, leukaemia, and Burkitt's lymphoma.

Chlorambucil is a derivative of mechlorethamine; it is well-absorbed when given orally. The drug is useful in the treatment of chronic lymphocytic leukaemia, Hodgkin's disease, and malignant lymphomas.

Bisulphan an alkyl sulphonate, is the treatment of choice in chronic granulocytic leukaemia.

Nitrosureas are alkylating agents that have attracted special interest because of their high lipid solubility, and hence their ability to cross the blood–brain barrier. These drugs are useful in the treatment of brain tumours and the infiltration of leukaemic cells into the meninges (meningeal leukaemia).

Antimetabolites

These can be calssified according to the substrate they antagonize, i.e. folic acid, pyrimidine, and purine.

Folic acid analogues

Methotrexate is the principal folic acid analogue. *In vivo*, folic acid is metabolized to tetrahydrofolic acid by the enzyme, dihydrofolate reductase. Tetrahydrofolic acid is essential for the synthesis of purines, pyrimides, and nucleic acids. Methotrexate binds irreversibly to dihydrofolate reductase (Osborn *et al.* 1958), and this binding indirectly inhibits such synthesis.

Pharmacological properties and uses

Methotrexate destroys cells during the S phase of the cell cycle. The drug can be given orally, and about 50 per cent is bound to plasma proteins (albumin). Hence other drugs that also bind to albumin, such as salicylates, tetracyclines, and sulphonamides, should be avoided in those already receiving methotrexate therapy.

The binding of methotrexate can be reversed by folinic acid, and normal tissues can be protected from methotrexate by thymidine. Such findings have led to the introduction of 'rescue techniques', which allow the use of very high doses of methotrexate that can subsequently be reversed by folinic acid. These techniques have enabled methotrexate to be used against very resistant tumours.

Methotrexate is useful in the treatment of acute lymphoblastic leukaemia. Other tumours that show a good response are carcinoma of the breast, tongue, and pharynx. The 'rescue technique' has produced effective results in carcinoma of the lung and in osteosarcoma. Methotrexate is also used in the treatment of severe psoriasis (McDonald 1981), Wegener's granulomatosis, hydatidiform moles, and mycosis fungoides.

Unwanted effects

Leukopenia and thrombocytopenia due to aplasia of the bone marrow are the serious unwanted effects associated with methotrexate therapy. Troublesome oral ulceration and diarrhoea may occur in some patients, and often requires an alteration or interruption of dose regimes.

Pyrimidine analogues

These analogues, such as fluorouracil and cytarabine, affect the synthesis of pyrimidine nucleotides and other nucleic acids. Both drugs are usually administered intravenously and are of palliative value in the treatment of a variety of malignant conditions. Topical application of fluorouracil has been shown to be effective in the treatment of both premalignant keratosis and basal cell carcinoma of skin (Klien *et al.* 1972).

Unwanted effects of pyrimidine analogues include anorexia, nausea, diarrhoea, and a severe stomatitis with sloughing and ulceration of the oral mucous membrane. Suppression of bone marrow activity is also very common and produces a neutropenia and thrombocytopenia.

Purine analogues

These are widely used, either as chemotherapeutic agents or as immunosuppressants; examples include mercaptopurine and azathioprine. Their precise mechanism of action in producing cell death is not clearly established. It is suggested that they inhibit purine nucleotide synthesis and alter the synthesis of both DNA and RNA (Elion and Hitchings 1965).

Mercaptopurine is effective when given orally, and is useful in treating most types of leukaemia. It does cause bone marrow suppression, but the onset is gradual.

Azathioprine is widely used as an immunosuppressant in kidney transplant, idiopathic thrombocytopenic purpura, and systemic lupus erythematosus. Infection is a common complication associated with immunosuppressant therapy (see Chapter 10).

Natural products

Vinca alkaloids

These are derived from the periwinkle plant (*Vinca rosea*); examples include vincristine and vinblastine.

Pharmacological properties and uses

Vinca alkaloids block mitosis at the metaphase by binding to tubulin, an essential protein component of cellular microtubules (George *et al.* 1965). Vincristine and vinblastine are given intravenously and, in certain circumstances, they can be infused into the arterial blood supply of a tumour.

These alkaloids are used in a variety of neoplastic conditions, such as Hodgkin's disease, leukaemias, carcinoma of the breast, and tumours of the reproductive system. Vinblastine is also used to treat neuroblastomas and Letterer–Siwe disease (histiocytosis X).

Unwanted effects

Leukopenia is the most serious unwanted effect associated with the vinca alkaloids. Vincristine therapy is accompanied by a high incidence of neurological disturbances, which include muscular weakness, tremors, numbness, and tingling of the extremities. Mood changes can occur on the second or third day of therapy.

Antibiotics

These interfere with bacterial cell division, cell wall synthesis, or intracellular protein synthesis (see Chapter 10); and some have been shown to have antineoplastic properties.

Actinomycin D

This antibiotic is obtained from streptomyces; it binds with DNA, which in turn prevents RNA synthesis (Franklin 1963). It can only be given intravenously and is probably the most potent chemotherapeutic agent in use today. Actinomycin D is used in the treatment of rhabdomyosarcoma, Wilm's tumour, Ewing's sarcoma, and Kaposi's sarcoma.

Unwanted effects include nausea, vomiting, and pancytopenia. Glossitis, cheilitis, and oral ulceration commonly occur one to seven days after completion of treatment.

Bleomycin

This is a fermentation product of *Streptomyces vorticillus*; several different congeners have been prepared. The cytotoxic properties of bleomycin are through its ability to fragment the DNA molecule by chain scission (Suzuki *et al.* 1969). It is usually administered intravenously as oral absorption is poor. This antibiotic is useful in the treatment of squamous cell carcinoma of the head and neck, oesophagus, skin, and genito-urinary tract.

In contrast to other chemotherapeutic agents, bleomycin causes minimal depression of bone marrow activity. Unwanted effects include stomatitis, alopecia, and ulceration and vesiculation of the skin. Pulmonary toxicity, which can be fatal, occurs in five to ten per cent of patients receiving this drug.

Mithramycin

This antibiotic is isolated from *Streptomyces tanashiensis*, it inhibits the synthesis of RNA. Mithramycin has a specific effect on osteoclasts and lowers plasma calcium concentrations (Robins and Jowsey 1973); hence, its main use is in the treatment of bone metastases. Mithramycin has also been used in the treatment of Paget's disease of bone. Haemorrhagic diatheses are the serious unwanted effects associated with this drug, which may limit its use.

Enzymes

The only enzyme that is used as a chemotherapeutic agent is L-asparaginase, which is produced by the bacterium *E. coli*.

L-*Asparaginase.*

L-Asparagine is an amino acid that is essential for cell protein synthesis. The enzyme, L-asparaginase, catalyses the hydrolysis of L-asparagine into aspartic acid and ammonia. Hence, malignant cells are unable to synthesize proteins and die. The main advantage of L-asparaginase is its minimal effect on bone marrow and epithelial tissue, such as the oral mucosa, hair follicles, and the lining of the gut. However, it has unwanted effects on the liver, kidneys, pancreas, and clotting mechanisms, which may limit its use. L-asparaginase is solely used in the treatment of acute lymphoblastic leukaemia.

Hormones

The pharmacological properties of the various hormones are dealt with in Chapter 18; only the use of hormones in the treatment of neoplastic disease will be considered in this section. Adrenocorticosteroids. oestrogen, progesterone, and testosterone are the principal hormones so used.

Adrenocorticosteroids

Of the several synthetic adrenocorticosteroids used to treat neoplastic disease, prednisolone is the most widely deployed. This drug is usually given orally up to dosages of 100 mg/day. Adrenocorticosteroids suppress mitosis in lymphocytes; hence they are extensively used in the treatment of acute leukaemia, particularly in children. These drugs are also used to suppress some of the unwanted effects that accompany other types of cancer therapy. For example, they will suppress oedema associated with radiotherapy, and will reduce pain and fever, and restore appetite. They also produce a feeling of well-being, which is beneficial in the critically ill patient. Unwanted effects of steroid therapy are discussed in Chapter 18.

Progestogens

Progestogens are used for the treatment of carcinoma of the breast in post-menopausal women. If given to women who are still able to menstruate, progestogens may accelerate the neoplastic process. They can be administered orally, and have a slow onset of action. Nausea, vomiting, and diarrhoea are the common unwanted effects; hypercalcaemia and ectopic calcification can occur if progestogens are given together with an adrenocorticosteroid.

Oestrogen

Oestrogen therapy is mainly associated with the treatment of carcinoma of the prostate. Diethylstilboestrol is the oestrogen widely used in this condition, and this drug has greatly improved the life expectancy of patients with this disease. Like adrenocorticosteroids, oestrogen also causes an increase in appetite, weight gain, and an improvement in well-being. Sexual impotence and gynaecomastia are the main unwanted effects.

Radioactive isotopes

Radioactive iodine (^{131}I) and sodium phosphate (^{32}P) are the main isotopes used in the treatment of neoplastic disease.

Radioactive iodine

The half-life of ^{131}I is eight days; the isotope emits both X-rays and β-particles. It is used for a variety of diagnostic procedures related to thyroid function, and also to treat metastatic thyroid cancer. If thyroid metastases accumulate iodine, then therapy with large doses of ^{131}I may prolong life. It is particularly effective in young children (Leeper 1973).

Sodium phosphate

This has a half-life of 14 days, and emits β-particles. The isotope can be given orally or parenterally; ^{32}P will enter those tissues with a high metabolic turnover of phosphate, as in neoplastic cells, bone marrow, spleen, lymph nodes, and bone. However, it has been replaced by other chemotherapeutic agents for, in some instances, the isotope has induced malignant change in bone marrow tissues.

ORAL AND DENTAL PROBLEMS ASSOCIATED WITH CHEMOTHERAPY

Many of the chemotherapeutic agents cause unwanted effects that manifest themselves in the mouth and related structures. The oral epithelium has a rapid cell turnover and is therefore very susceptible to the cell destructive properties of these drugs (Guggenheimer et al. 1977). In addition, the oral bacterial flora is large, and the mouth is important as a potential portal of entry for infective agents in those with suppressed bone-marrow activity.

Common problems that accompany chemotherapy are oral ulceration and stomatitis (due to an atrophic thinning of the oral mucosa), xerostomia, infection, gingivitis, pain, and haemorrhage (Sonis et al. 1978).

Management

Many of these oral and dental problems can be reduced or alleviated by certain pre-treatment measures. Oral hygiene should be meticulous in these patients, which will reduce the incidence of gingival problems (Beck 1979). All potential sources of infection, such as periapical inflammatory lesions, impacted third molars, periodontal pockets, and carious cavities, should be treated. Sharp cusps or restorations should be smoothed to avoid trauma to the oral mucosa.

Stomatitis and oral ulceration

Benzocaine lozenges or lignocaine gel may provide sufficient surface analgesia to make eating more comfortable Secondary infection of the ulcers can be reduced by using a chlorhexidine mouthwash 0.2 per cent. If the ulcers become infected, a tetracycline mouthbath* together with an antifungal agent should be used both topically and then swallowed.

Xerostomia

Saliva substitutes (such as carboxymethylcellulose) may be of some use in those with xerostomia, or regular use of lemon drops may encourage salivary flow. There should be treatment with a topical fluoride to prevent xerostomia-induced dental caries. Angular cheilitis often accompanies xerostomia and should be treated with an appropriate anti-fungal agent, such as nystatin ointment or miconazole cream.

Oral infection

Chemotherapeutic agents used in the treatment of neoplastic disease often produce a neutropenia and subsequent oral infections are common. Candidiasis and herpes labialis are the most frequent of these. Candidiasis should be treated with an antifungal agent, and herpes labialis should respond to an antiviral agent, such as idoxuridine or acyclovir (see Chapter 10).

Gingival and mucosal bleeding

Haemorrhage associated with chemotherapy is invariably due to bone marrow suppression and the resultant thrombocytopenia. Mild cases of bleeding may respond to systemic aminocaproic acid. Severe haemorrhage should be treated by platelet transfusion (Lockhart 1983).

Pain

Patients on chemotherapy often complain of pain in the teeth and jaws. It is essential to eliminate any causative dental factors; if there is no dental cause, the pain will resolve on cessation of treatment. Pain associated with chemotherapy may respond to a peripherally acting analgesic, the type and dosage of which should be tailored to the individual patient.

* Not listed in 1988–90 DPF.

REFERENCES

Beck, S. (1979). Impact of a systematic oral care protocol on stomatitis after chemotherapy. *Cancer Nursing*, **2**, 185–99.
Elion, G. B. and Hitchings, G. H. (1985). Metabolic basis for the actions of analogs of purines and pyrimidines. *Advances in Chemotherapy*, **2**, 91–177.

Franklin, R. M. (1963). The inhibition of ribonucleic acid synthesis in mammalian cells by actinomycin D. *Biochemica et Biophysica Acta*, **72**, 555–65.

George, P., Journey, L. J., and Goldstein, M. N. (1965). Effects of vincristine on the fine structure of Hela cells during mitosis. *Journal of the National Cancer Institute*, **35**, 355–75.

Guggenheimer, J., Verbin, R. S., Appel, B. N., and Schmitz, J. (1977). Clinicopathological effects of cancer chemotherapeutic agents on human buccal mucosa. *Oral Surgery*, **44**, 58–63.

Klein, E., Milgrom, H., Stoll, H. L., Helm, F., Walker, H. J., and Holtermann, O. A. (1972). Topical 5-fluorouracil chemotherapy and malignant epidermal neoplasia. In *Cancer chemotherapy*, II (ed. I. Brodsky and S. G. Kahn), pp. 146–66. Grune and Stratton, New York.

Leeper, R. D. (1973). The effect of ^{131}I therapy on survival of patients with metastatic pupillary or follicular thyroid carcinoma. *Journal of Clinical and Endocrinological Medicine*, **36**, 1143–52.

Lockhart, P. G. (1983). Dental management of patients receiving chemotherapy. In *Oral complications of cancer chemotherapy* (ed. D. E. Peterson and S. T. Sonis), pp. 113–49. Martinus Nijhoff, The Hague.

McDonald, C. J. (1981). The uses of systemic chemotherapeutic agents in psoriasis. *Pharmacology and Therapeutics*, **14**, 1–24.

Osborn, M. J., Freeman, M., and Heunnekens, F. M. (1958). Inhibition of dihydrofolic reductase by aminopterin and amethopterin. *Proceedings of the Society for Experimental Biology and Medicine*, **97**, 429–31.

Price, C. C. (1975). Chemistry of alkylation. In *Antineoplastic and immunosuppressive agents*, part II, (ed. A. C. Sartorelli and D. G. Johns), pp. 1–5. Springer–Verlag, Berlin.

Robins, P. R. and Jowsey, J. (1973). The effect of mithramycin on normal and abnormal bone turnover. *Journal of Laboratory and Clinical Medicine*, **82**, 576–86.

Sonis, S. T., Sonis, A. L., and Lieberman, A. (1978). Oral complications in patients receiving treatment for malignancies other than of the head and neck. *Journal of the American Dental Association*, **97**, 468–72.

Suzuki, H., Nagai, K. Yamaki, H., Tanaka, N., and Umezewa, H. (1969). On the mechanism of action of bleomycin: scission of D.N.A. steroids *in vitro* and *in vivo*. *Journal of Antibiotics*, **22**, 446–8.

18

The endocrine system

INTRODUCTION

Endocrine glands secrete hormones, which regulate cellular metabolism and maintain homeostatis. Hormones are defined as substances secreted by specific tissues and transported to a distant tissue where they exert their effect. The endocrine system is mostly regulated by the pituitary gland, which comprises a glandular component (adenohypophysis) and a neural component (neurohypophysis). Trophic hormones are produced by the adenohypophysis, which in turn regulate the activity of other endocrine glands. The secretion of trophic hormones is controlled by specific releasing factors from the hypothalamus. Production of these factors and of trophic hormones is controlled by a feedback mechanism from circulating hormones. The neurohypophysis stores and releases hormones that are produced in the hypothalamus.

NEUROHYPOPHYSEAL HORMONES

The neurohypophysis secretes two hormones, antidiuretic hormones (ADH; vasopressin) and oxytocin. Both are synthesized in the hypothalamus and transported along nerve fibres to be stored in the posterior lobe of the pituitary gland.

Antidiuretic hormone (ADH)

This affects the distal tubules and collecting ducts of the kidney, and increases water absorption. Secretion of ADH is controlled by hypothalamic neurones that act as osmoreceptors. A high plasma osmotic pressure and a low blood volume stimulate secretion of ADH. Nicotine, alcohol, morphine and physical and emotional stress also influence ADH secretion.

This hormone is used to treat diabetes insipidus. It cannot be given orally because it is destroyed by trypsin in the alimentary tract. It is a potent vasoconstrictor and, at high dose, ADH is sometimes used to arrest haemorrhage from oesophageal varices. A derivative of vasopressin is felypressin, which is used as a vasoconstrictor with the local anaesthetic agent, prilocaine (see Chapter 7).

Oxytocin

This octapeptide is synthesized in the paraventricular nucleus of the hypothalamus. It is released from the posterior pituitary gland following suckling of the breast or uterine stretching. Oxytocin acts on the myoepithelial cells of the mammary glands, causing contraction and milk ejection. The hormone also acts on the smooth muscle of the uterus, initiating contraction; it is widely believed that oxytocin initiates labour and parturition. The main therapeutic use of oxytocin is in obstetrics to stimulate contraction of the uterus and induce labour.

ADENOHYPOPHYSEAL HORMONES

The anterior pituitary gland secretes the following trophic hormones: adrenocorticotrophic hormone (ACTH), thyroid-stimulating hormone (TSH), follicle-stimulating hormone (FSH), and leutenizing hormone (LH). These trophic hormones are discussed under the sections relating to the various glands upon which they act.

Prolactin and growth hormone are also secreted by the anterior pituitary and are discussed now.

Growth hormone

Growth hormone is a peptide that is synthesized and stored in specific cells, known as somatotrophs, in the anterior pituitary gland. The secretion of growth hormone is controlled by two regulating factors produced in the hypothalamus—growth hormone releasing factor and growth hormone inhibiting factor (somatostatin). Plasma concentrations of growth hormone are reduced by food, and increased by fasting, during sleep and physical exercise, and at times of stress and emotional excitement.

Pharmacological and physiological actions

Growth hormone affects growth, protein synthesis, and carbohydrate metabolism.

Growth

The hormone is essential for normal growth and development. A lack of production during the growth period will cause dwarfism; excessive production in a child will cause gigantism and, in an adult, acromegaly. Many of the actions of growth hormone on tissue size are mediated by its effects on sulphation factors or somatomedins. Somatomedins are growth-promoting factors produced by the liver and kidneys. They occur in serum and are activated by growth hormone. Examples of somatomedins are nerve growth factor, epidermal growth factor, fibroblast growth factor, and erythropoietin.

Protein synthesis

Growth hormone increases the transport of amino acids into tissues, and accelerates their incorporation into proteins. This action results in a reduction of blood urea levels due to a diversion of amino acids into anabolic pathways.

Carbohydrate and lipid metabolism

Growth hormone, insulin and, to a lesser extent, corticosteroids, glucagon, and catecholamines, play important roles in carbohydrate and lipid metabolism. Insulin and growth hormone have opposite effects, with insulin utilizing glucose as a source of energy and growth hormone utilizing fat. Hence it may appear that growth hormone has an antagonistic effect with insulin. The increased production of growth hormone during fasting may be an adaptation to lack of food. Growth hormone causes an increase in free fatty acids in the blood due to its lipolytic action on adipose tissue. This action may explain the increased secretion of the hormone that occurs during exercize, which will utilize fat deposits as an alternative source of energy.

Uses

Growth hormone is used to correct pituitary dwarfism.

Prolactin

This has a similar structure to growth hormone and is synthesized, stored, and secreted by lactotrophic cells in the anterior pituitary gland. Its principal action is on the development of the mammary glands and the production of milk. Prolactin is also produced by the placenta. The plasma concentration of prolactin increases throughout pregnancy. During breast feeding, prolactin production is controlled by the sucking stimulus.

Pharmacological and physiological properties

Prolactin is essential for the development of the mammary glands and their preparation for milk production. The hormone promotes proliferation and subsequent differentiation of mammary ductal and alveolar epithelium. In preparation for milk production, prolactin increases the synthesis of RNA, milk proteins, and enzymes necessary for lactose synthesis. Like growth hormone, production of prolactin is influenced by sleep, fasting, and stress.

THYROID HORMONES

The thyroid gland secretes three hormones, thyroxine, tri-iodothyroxine, and calcitonin, which is dealt with in Chapter 20. Secretion of thyroxine and tri-iodothyroxine are under the control of the anterior pituitary peptide, thyroid-stimulating hormone (TSH). Secretion of TSH is stimulated by the hypothalamic peptide, thyrotrophin-releasing hormone (TRH). The pituitary TSH increases the vascularity, cellularity, and size of the thyroid gland, and accelerates the synthesis and release of thyroid hormones. The production of TSH is inhibited by circulating levels of thyroxine and tri-iodothyroxine.

Thyroxine and tri-iodothyroxine

These two thyroid hormones are synthesized and stored as thyroglobulin in the thyroid gland. Synthesis and release of thyroid hormones involve the following processes:

(1) uptake of iodide ions by the gland;
(2) oxidation of iodide and iodination of p-tyrosyl groups of thyroglobulin;
(3) conversion of iodotyrosil to iodothyronyl;
(4) proteolysis of thyroglobulin and release of thyroxine and tri-iodothyronine into the blood stream;
(5) conversion of thyroxine to tri-iodothyronine in the tissues.

Thyroid hormones are strongly bound to plasma proteins (globulin and albumin). They are broken down in the liver, conjugated with glucuronic acid and sulphate, and excreted in the bile. In health, these hormones are slowly eliminated from the body and have a half-life of six to seven days.

Physiological and pharmacological properties

Thyroid hormones have three main functions: they regulate growth and development; they have a calorigenic and a metabolic effect.

Growth and development
They exert their effect on growth and development by controlling protein synthesis. They are also essential for the development of the nervous system, in particular, cell differentiation and proliferation.

Calorigenic effects
Thyroid hormones regulate body temperature (calorigenic effect) by controlling basal metabolic rate. They have a particular effect on the heart, lungs, liver, and kidneys. It is suggested that they exert their calorigenic effect by an action on the enzymes that control the sodium pump.

Metabolic effect
These hormones stimulate the metabolism of cholesterol to bile salts, and accelerate the utilization of carbohydrate for increased calorific demand.

Iodine

This element is essential for the formation of the thyroid hormones. Dietary iodine, in the form of iodide, is absorbed from the stomach and small intestine, transported in the blood, and taken up by the thyroid gland. Within the gland, iodide is oxidized to iodine and utilized to form thyroxine and tri-iodothyroxine. A deficiency of iodine causes non-toxic goitre, which usually responds to potassium iodide. Iodized salt is used to prevent this type of goitre, especially in areas of iodine deficiency.

Disorders of thyroid gland function

Hypofunction of the thyroid gland at birth results in cretinism and, in adults, causes myxoedema. Hypothyroidism is often associated with impairment of the normal immune response and those affected may be susceptible to oral candidiasis. Both cretinism and myxoedema are treated with thyroxine.

Hyperfunction of the thyroid gland (hyperthyroidism) can take the form of a diffuse toxic goitre (Graves' disease) or toxic nodular goitre (Plummer's disease). Signs and symptoms of hyperthyroidism include an intolerance to heat, muscle weakness, tremor, insomnia, anxiety, and an increased heart rate. The cardiovascular changes in hyperthyroidism may be due to an increased sensitivity of the heart to catecholamines. However, the small amount of adrenaline in local anaesthetic solutions is unlikely to cause a problem in those with hyperthyroidism.

Antithyroid drugs

These are used to treat hyperthyroidism; they inhibit the formation of the thyroid hormones by interfering with the incorporation of iodine into thyroxine and tri-iodothyroxine. Examples include carbimazole and propylthiouracil: both drugs can cause a leucopenia, so monitoring of white blood cells is important during therapy.

Potassium perchlorate is also used to treat hyperthyroidism by preventing the uptake and storage of iodine in the thyroid gland.

THE ADRENAL CORTEX

This part of the adrenal gland synthesizes and secretes mainly glucocorticoids and mineralocorticoids, together with small amounts of testosterone, oestrogen, and progesterone. Secretion of glucocorticoids is under the control of ACTH, whereas secretion of mineralocorticoids is controlled by the renin–angiotensin system.

Adrenocorticotrophic hormone (ACTH)

This peptide, secreted by the anterior pituitary gland (adenohypophysis), stimulates the adrenal cortex to secrete glucocorticoids (cortisol and corticosterone). It also stimulates the synthesis of adrenocortical hormones through the agency of the cyclic AMP. The release of ACTH is under dual control. One controlling element is the hypothalamus, which produces a peptide known as corticotrophin-releasing factor (CRF). This travels via the hypophyseal-portal vessel to the anterior pituitary and there stimulates the production of ACTH. The release of CRF is under neural control.

The second element controlling production and secretion of ACTH and CRF is a negative feedback regulatory influence from cortisol and other glucocorticoids. High levels of glucocorticoids suppress the secretion of ACTH and the converse applies with low levels. Production of ACTH also shows diurnal variation, with maximum levels occurring in the early morning and minimal levels at midnight.

This hormone is mainly used as a diagnostic agent in adrenal insufficiency.

Physiological and pharmacological properties of corticosteroids

Two types of steroids are synthesized in the adrenal cortex, the 19-carbon androgens and the 21-carbon corticosteroids; both are derived from cholesterol. The 21-carbon corticosteroids can be further classified into glucocorticoids (cortisol), because of their action on carbohydrate metabolism, and mineralocorticoids (aldosterone), because of their effect on sodium retention. However, the two types of corticosteroids possess both actions.

Aldosterone production is under the control of angiotensin acting on the adrenal cortex. The synthesis and secretion of all other corticosteroids is under control of ACTH. The corticosteroids are continuously synthesized and secreted, hence there is minimal storage in the adrenal cortex.

Corticosteroids have a diverse range of properties and functions. They are involved in carbohydrate, fat, and protein metabolism; they affect electrolyte and water balance; and they are essential for the normal function of the cardiovascular system, kidney, skeletal muscle, and nervous system. They also enable the organism to withstand changes in environment and cope with stressful events. The many different properties of the corticosteroids are due to their action on protein synthesis, especially RNA transcription and the production of specific proteins.

Carbohydrate and protein metabolism

Corticosteroids have the following effect on carbohydrate metabolism: they stimulate the formation of glucose; reduce the utilization of glucose in the peripheral tissues (perhaps by antagonizing the action of insulin); and promote the storage of glucose as glycogen. These actions ensure that the brain always has sufficient glucose for the essential glucose-dependent functions. Corticosteroids act on the liver and stimulate the synthesis of glucose from amino acids. They also inhibit protein synthesis in muscles and connective tissue, thus mobilizing additional amino acids. Therefore, the overall effect of corticosteroids is to cause an increase in blood sugar and liver glycogen content, and an increase in urinary nitrogen excretion. Hence long-term corticosteroid administration (see Other unwanted effects below) or high output from the adrenal cortex will cause protein wasting, resulting in an increase in capillary fragility, muscle wasting, and a reduction in the protein matrix of bone (osteoporosis).

Lipid metabolism

Corticosteroids have several actions on lipid metabolism. They inhibit fatty acid synthesis, but facilitate the mobilization of fatty acids from adipose tissue by lipolytic enzymes. They also have an effect on the distribution of body fat, with excessive production causing an increase in fatty acid deposits in the face (moon face) and on the back of the neck (buffalo hump).

Electrolyte and water balance

Corticosteroids affect this balance through a direct action on the kidney. They cause an increase in the urinary excretion of potassium and hydrogen ions, and enhanced reabsorption of sodium ions from the tubular fluid. These actions result in an increase in sodium retention, hypokalaemia, alkalosis, and an increase in extracellular fluid. Hence, excessive corticosteroid production or long-term use will cause oedema and hypertension. In patients with a pre-existing cardiac problem, long-term corticosteroid therapy will increase the incidence of left ventricular hypertrophy and congestive heart failure. Conversely, a deficiency of endogenous corticosteroids will cause sodium loss, a reduction in extracellular fluid, and cellular hydration.

Effects on blood

Excess corticosteroids cause an increase in red blood cells and their haemoglobin content, and an increase in polymorphs, whereas other white blood cells are reduced in number. A reduction in corticosteroid production will cause a normochromic, normocytic anaemia.

Immune system

Corticosteroids suppress immune reactions (Parillo and Fauci 1979) and are widely used in organ transplants to suppress graft rejection. The precise mechanism of corticosteroid immunosuppression is unknown. Possible modes of action may be an impairment of white blood-cell production and migration, or a reduction in lymphokine production from sensitized T-lymphocytes (see Chapter

21). Alternatively, corticosteroids may act on macrophages by inhibiting their ability to process antigens. The immunosuppressant properties of corticosteroids may also be closely linked to their anti-inflammatory actions (see Chapter 4).

Pharmacokinetics

Synthetic corticosteroids can be administered orally, topically, parenterally, and rectally. Some preparations are given into the synovial fluid. Corticosteroids are well-absorbed from any site of administration, and are transported in the plasma extensively bound to plasma protein. Most are broken down in the liver, conjugated with glucuronic acid, and excreted in the urine as the metabolites, 17-hydroxycorticosteroid and 17-ketohydroxycorticosteroid.

Unwanted effects of corticosteroids

Adrenocortical suppression

Long-term administration of corticosteroids causes suppression of the adeno-hypophysis–adrenal cortex axis, with a reduction in the production and release of ACTH. As a result, there is atrophy of the adrenal cortex, and the cortex cannot produce endogenous corticosteroids to cope with stress, so an adrenal crisis may develop. After cessation of corticosteroids, the return of adrenal function may take nine months (Graber et al. 1965). During this recovery period, and for an additional one to two years, patients with adrenocortical suppression will need to be protected with supplementary corticosteroids during stressful situations, such as dental surgical procedures and severe infections. The features and treatment of an adrenal crisis are dealt with in Chapter 24.

The extent of adrenocortical suppression will depend upon the type of steroid, its potency, dose, and duration of treatment. Adrenocortical suppression is not observed when corticosteroids are used for just a few weeks (Livanou et al. 1967).

Abrupt cessation of corticosteroid therapy can result in acute adrenal insufficiency, characterized by fever, joint and muscle pain, and malaise. Therefore, corticosteroid therapy should be slowly reduced over a long time.

Other unwanted effects

Alterations in carbohydrate metabolism can cause glycosuria, but this is usually controlled by diet. Altered protein metabolism may lead to an increase in capillary fragility causing ecchymosis, muscle wasting, and poor wound healing. Osteoporosis is a common unwanted effect of long-term corticosteroid therapy, especially in the elderly. Steroids produce hypocalcaemia by inhibiting calcium absorption and increasing urinary calcium excretion. The hypocalcaemia causes an increase in parathyroid hormone secretion, which in turn stimulates osteoclastic activity. Thus, there is both an increased resorption and decreased formation of bone (Hahn 1978). Steroid-induced osteoporosis commonly affects the spinal column and sometimes the mandible; spontaneous fractures of these and other bones may occur. The actions of corticosteroids on lipid metabolism will cause the characteristic 'moon face' and 'buffalo hump' (see Lipid metabolism above). Disturbances in electrolyte and water balance will cause hypokalaemia, oedema formation, hypertension, and alkalosis.

Immunosuppressive effects render the patient more susceptible to opportunistic infections, such as candidiasis, and to postoperative infections, the incidence of which can be reduced by prophylactic antibiotic cover prior to surgery. Topical or systemic corticosteroids should not be used for their anti-inflammatory properties if the underlying cause of the inflammation is infective. If corticosteroids are erroneously used in the presence of infection, they will mask its signs and permit it to spread.

Peptic ulceration is an occasional complication of corticosteroid therapy; it may be due to alterations in the mucosal cell's defence mechanisms.

Administration of corticosteroids can cause a feeling of well-being; however, long-term corticosteroid administration can cause certain behavioural disturbances, including insomnia, anxiety, mood changes, and even suicidal tendencies, the mechanisms of which are unknown.

Corticosteroids cause inhibition or arrest of growth in children because these drugs inhibit DNA synthesis and cell division.

Uses

They are particularly used for their anti-inflammatory and anti-allergic properties in various medical conditions exemplified by rheumatoid arthritis, nephrotic syndrome, collagen diseases, allergic states, ocular disease, skin disease, ulcerative colitis, and certain malignancies. Corticosteroids are also for substitution therapy in patients with adrenal insufficiency. Their use in dentistry is discussed in Chapter 4.

PANCREATIC HORMONES

The islets of the pancreas produce two hormones that are essential for glucose metabolism; the β-cells synthesize and secrete insulin, and the α-cells synthesize and secrete glucagon. The secretion of insulin and glucagon is controlled by blood glucose levels. A high glucose concentration stimulates the secretion of insulin, whereas a low concentration stimulates the release of glucagon. Thus both hormones control blood glucose levels and maintain a concentration of 100 mg/ml.

Insulin

This was first isolated in 1921 and used to treat diabetes (see below) in the following year. The insulin molecule is made up of two chains of amino acids, an acidic or A-chain, and a basic or B-chain. Insulin is synthesized in β-islet cells from the precursor, pro-insulin, which in turn is derived from prepro-insulin. Proteolytic enzymes convert the pro-insulin to insulin, which is then released from the Golgi complex together with any unconverted pro-insulin and a superfluous C-peptide. Insulin secretion is stimulated by many factors including carbohydrates, fatty acids, amino acids, growth hormone, ACTH, thyroxine, and glucagon. Secretion of insulin is inhibited by insulin itself, somatostatin, α-adrenergic antagonists, and β-adrenergic blockers.

Pharmacokinetics

Insulin is broken down in the gastro-intestinal tract and hence can only be given parenterally. The hormone has a half-life of six to nine minutes, and is metabolized in both the liver and kidney to inactive peptides. The commercially available insulins show different pharmacokinetic properties, as listed below. All insulin preparations are available in different concentrations.

Soluble insuline This has a short duration of action and is mainly used to treat diabetic emergencies; for example, ketoacidosis and hyperglycaemia.

Protamine zinc insulin A long-acting insulin, which in some diabetics needs only to be administered once a day. However, the long duration of action may have an accumulative effect that could cause hypoglycaemia, especially at night.

Biphasic insulin This contains porcine soluble insulin for an immediate effect, and slow-release bovine insulin, which increases the duration of action. Biphasic insulin is usually given twice a day, but can produce hyperglycaemia because of insufficient amounts of porcine soluble insulin.

Insulin zinc suspension This is prepared either in the amorphous form, which is rapidly absorbed, or the crystalline form, which is slowly absorbed from the site of injection.

Pharmacological and physiological properties

Insulin controls the blood concentration of glucose by acting via receptors on cell membranes. Activation of receptors causes the following:

(1) an increase in the diffusion of glucose through cell membranes;

(2) an increase in the rate of glucose utilization;

(3) an increase in the rate of glycogen deposition;

(4) inhibition of hepatic gluconeogenesis.

Insulin also causes increases in cellular amino acid uptake, DNA and RNA synthesis, and oxidative phosphorylation.

Insulin requirements increase during pregnancy, prolonged exercize, severe infections, and stress.

Unwanted effects of insulin

The most serious of these is hypoglycaemia, which can be fatal if not promptly recognized and treated. The clinical features and management of hypoglycaemia are discussed in Chapter 24.

Insulin is a protein and so antibodies can develop against it, which will give rise to local or systemic allergic reactions. However, the incidence of such reactions is falling due to the development of very pure insulin preparations.

Repeated insulin injections at the same site can cause lipodystrophy and swelling. This problem can be overcome by regularly changing the site of injection.

Diabetes mellitus

This disorder of glucose metabolism is due to insufficient production of insulin or glucagon or both. A lack of insulin will cause a rise in blood glucose levels due to increased gluconeogenesis and decreased glucose uptake. Fat metabolism is also altered with an increase in lipase activity and a decrease in triglyceride synthetase activity. Both altered enzyme activities result in an increase in blood levels of unesterified fatty acids. The excess fatty acids are metabolized by acetyl coenzyme A, which results in the formation of ketone bodies, so causing the metabolic acidosis that often accompanies hyperglycaemia. The increase in blood glucose, fatty acids, and their metabolites contributes to the polyuria and dehydration that is so often an early sign of the disease.

Diabetes, depending upon the severity, can be controlled by diet alone, diet and insulin, or diet and oral hypoglycaemic drugs.

Dental problems associated with diabetic patients

Patients with diabetes are more susceptible to periodontal disease and excessive periodontal destruction (Cohen et al. 1970). White blood cells (especially polymorphs) from diabetics show impaired chemotactic and phagocytic activities, which may enhance periodontal breakdown (McCullen et al. 1981). Poorly controlled diabetics may suffer from xerostomia and candidiasis. Diabetics are more prone to infections and should perhaps receive prophylactic antibiotics prior to a dental surgical procedure.

The main problem with diabetics in dentistry is that dental treatment may interrupt their food intake and insulin requirements, especially if a general anaesthetic is to be administered. Several dental infections may also cause hazards with the insulin-controlled diabetic; such infections should be treated promptly. Monitoring of blood sugar and urine is essential to ensure that diabetics do not become hypo- or hyperglycaemic as a consequence of the infection.

Dental procedures and simple oral surgical procedures under local anaesthesia are usually well-tolerated by diabetic patients. Treatment should ideally be in the morning and not interfere with meal times. Management of diabetic patients prior to a general anaesthetic will depend upon their current therapy. Those controlled by diet alone can usually tolerate a general anaesthetic for minor oral surgical procedures. Regular monitoring of their urine and blood sugar levels is essential, and soluble insulin should be available if hyperglycaemia develops. If the diabetic is controlled by oral hypoglycaemic drugs (see below), they should be admitted to hospital two days before the procedure and placed on insulin. Those on insulin therapy should also be admitted to hospital two days before the procedure and placed on soluble insulin. During surgery, patients are infused with 3 units of soluble insulin per hour and glucose solution at the rate of 6 g/hour. This regime is continued until normal feeding and soluble insulin control can be resumed.

All diabetic patients must be treated in a hospital environment if general anaesthetics are being administered. Changes in their insulin regime should only be made in consultation with their physician. Because diabetics are more prone to infection they should receive prophylactic antibiotic cover for minor oral surgical procedures.

Oral hypoglycaemic drugs

Oral drugs used to control hypoglycaemia are of two types, sulphonylureas and biguanides.

Sulphonylureas

These stimulate islet tissues to secrete insulin by causing degranulation of the β-cells. Their action therefore depends upon the pancreas having some ability to synthesize and secrete insulin. Examples of sulphonylureas are tolbutamide, tolazamide, and chlorpropamide.

Pharmacokinetics

All sulphonylureas are well-absorbed from the gastro-intestinal tract and differences between individual drugs relate to their duration of action. Tolbutamide is taken every six to eight hours whereas chlorpropamide is given only once a day.

Unwanted effects

There is a high incidence of these, the most serious being hypoglycaemia. Other unwanted effects include skin rashes, gastro-intestinal disturbances, jaundice, and haemopoietic changes. Alcohol interacts with the sulphonylureas causing an enhancement of their hypoglycaemic effect. Aspirin reduces the urinary excretion of chlorpropamide and so increases plasma levels, which in turn would enhance the hypoglycaemic effect. Because aspirin also has an effect on blood sugar levels, this analgesic should not be given to patients on chlorpropamide.

Biguanides

It is not clearly established how the biguanides exert their hypoglycaemic effect. They may reduce glucose absorption from the gastro-intestinal tract or facilitate glucose entry into tissues, thus increasing glucose uptake by the peripheral tissues. The biguanides are rarely used as hypoglycaemic agents because of their high incidence of unwanted effects. These include nausea, vomiting, anorexia, and a metallic taste in the mouth. Examples of biguanides include metformin.

Glucagon

This is a single-chain polypeptide secreted by the α-cells of the islets. Secretion is mainly controlled by plasma glucose concentration, with a rise in plasma glucose inhibiting secretion and a fall facilitating secretion. Glucagon is broken down in the plasma, liver, and kidney; it has a plasma half-life of three to six minutes.

Physiological and pharmacological properties

Glucagon antagonizes the actions of insulin: whereas insulin acts as a hormone of glucose storage, glucagon is a hormone of glucose utilization. During fasting or starvation, there is an increase in glucagon secretion and an inhibition of insulin secretion. Glucagon breaks down food substances, which are then stored intracellularly for energy requirements of the brain and other essential tissues. Glucagon secretion is also increased after severe trauma and injury (for example, after burns). In such instances, glucagon stimulates gluconeogenesis and provides an essential supply of glucose.

SEX HORMONES

Hormonal production from the ovaries and testes is under the control of gonadotrophic hormones synthesized and secreted by the adenohypophysis. The gonadotrophic hormones are follicle-stimulating hormone (FSH) and luteinizing hormone (LH). The placenta also produces two gonadotrophins, chorionic gonadotrophin (CG) and chorionic follicle-stimulating hormone (CFSH). The function of CFSH is unknown.

Properties of FSH and LH

These are glycoproteins produced and secreted by cells in the adenohypophysis. The plasma concentrations of these hormones are low in infancy, but increase at puberty. Postpubertal concentrations of gonadotrophins vary in women according to the phase of their menstrual cycle. Gonadotrophins are mainly used for the treatment of infertility.

Action on the ovary

The FSH controls the development of ovarian follicles, stimulates granulosa cell proliferation, and increases oestrogen production; LH induces ovulation and initiates and maintains the corpus luteum.

Action on the testes

The FSH is responsible for spermatogenesis, whereas LH acts on Leydig calls to produce the hormone, testosterone, which is essential for the maturation of spermatocytes and the development of male secondary sexual characteristics.

Chorionic gonadotrophin (CG)

This is produced by syncytiotrophic cells of the placenta shortly after implantation; it maintains the corpus-luteum phase of the ovary, which forestalls the next menstrual cycle.

Female sex hormones

These are produced by the ovaries, and comprise the oestrogens (oestradiol-17β, oestrone, and oestriol) and progesterone. The production and excretion of the female sex hormones is under the control of the gonadotrophins, FSH and LH, with oestrogens exerting a negative feedback control on both these adenohypophyseal hormones.

Oestrogens

These steroids are synthesized in the ovary from acetate and cholesterol. There are three types of oestrogens, oestradiol-17β, oestrone and oestriol. The oestrogens are metabolized in the liver, and excreted as glucuronide and sulphate conjugates in the bile and urine. Oestrone and oestriol are derived from the potent oestradiol-17β by oxidation and hydration respectively.

Physiological and pharmacological properties
Oestrogens control the secondary female sexual characteristics, which occur from puberty onwards. Oestrogen production also plays an essential role in the menstrual cycle, with the cyclic decline in production bringing about menstruation.

High concentrations of oestrogens can cause bone resorption. The osteoporosis sometimes seen in post-menopausal women may be partly due to reduced oestrogen levels.

Many of the actions of oestrogens in the development of secondary sexual characteristics, the menstrual cycle, and pregnancy are often complementary with those of progesterone.

Progesterone

This is structurally similar to oestrogen; it is secreted by the ovary, mainly from the corpus luteum, during the second half of the menstrual cycle. Production of progesterone is under the control of LH.

Properties

Progesterone secretion causes the development of the secretory endometrium; abrupt cessation of progesterone from the corpus luteum determines the onset of menstruation. Progesterone is also important for the maintenance of pregnancy and in preparing the breast for milk production.

Uses

The main use of oestrogens and progesterone is the oral contraceptive pill (see below). Oestrogen is also used for replacement therapy where there is hypofunction of the ovaries. It is also used to treat certain neoplastic conditions, such as carcinoma of the prostate and breast (see Chapter 17). Progesterone is used for certain gynaecological conditions, which are beyond the scope of this book.

Women suffering from menstrually related oral aphthous ulceration have shown an improvement in their symptoms when treated with the contraceptive pill (Carruthers 1977) or progesterone (Ferguson *et al.* 1978).

The contraceptive pill

These usually contain a mixture of an oestrogen (ethinyloestradiol) and a progesterone (norethisterone). The oestrogen component suppresses ovulation by preventing the mid-cycle rise in LH (the trigger of ovulation). Progesterone produces changes in the endometrium that discourage implantation, and has a thickening effect on cervical mucus, thus making it impenetrable to sperm.

The combined pill is taken daily for 21 days, medication is then stopped for 7 days and the withdrawal of oestrogen produces uterine bleeding; the pill is restarted on day 28.

Unwanted effects

It is estimated that some 20 million women take the contraceptive pill, and many epidemiological studies have outlined the risks associated with this very effective method of contraception. The incidence of unwanted effects increases with age (especially in women over the age of 35), the length of time on the pill, and whether there is a history of smoking. Unwanted effects include:

(1) an increased risk of myocardial infarction and cerebral arterial thrombosis (Kaplan 1978; Mann *et al.* 1975);

(2) an increase in blood pressure by increasing renin substrate;

(3) an increase in the incidence of venous thrombosis and thromboembolism, due to an increase in blood clotting factors (Meade 1982);

(4) an increase in migraine attacks;

(5) precipitation of diabetes mellitus;

(6) cancer of the endometrium—this may increase in pill takers (Weiss and Sayvetz 1980; Vessey et al. 1983) but there is a decrease in breast lesions and ovarian cysts—however, the mortality associated with pregnancy and childbirth is greater than the risk of endometrial cancer.

Of dental significance is the effect of the contraceptive pill on the gingival tissues, which causes an enhancement of plaque-induced inflammation and an increase in gingival crevicular fluid (Lindhe and Attstrom 1967; Lindhe and Bjorn 1967). It has also been reported that women taking the contraceptive pill are more susceptible to 'dry socket' after tooth extraction (Catellani et al. 1980). They also have an increased incidence of radiopacities in the mandible (Darzenta and Giunta 1977).

Drug interactions

The widespread use of the contraceptive pill has implicated this drug in a number of interactions. Of concern to the dental surgeon is that between the pill and antibiotics, although there is recent evidence, detailed in Chapter 22, that suggests the problem has been over-stated. Oestrogen and progesterone are conjugated with glucuronide and extensively excreted in the bile. Once excreted, they may in part undergo entero-hepatic circulation, whereby the conjugates are broken down (hydrolyzed) by bacteria in the gut. Oestrogen and progesterone are released from the conjugate and absorbed through the bowel wall. Any antibiotic therapy that destroys the gut flora will subsequently impair the breakdown of the conjugated hormone; hence they will not be absorbed and the conjugate will be excreted in the faeces. Plasma levels of oestrogen and progesterone may be considerably reduced and the pill may be ineffective as a contraceptive.

Those antibiotics implicated in destruction of the gut flora and reduction of the pill's effectiveness include penicillin, ampicillin, co-trimoxazole, and the tetracyclines (Dossetor 1975; Bacon and Shenfield 1980). Thus, when these are prescribed to those on the contraceptive pill, they should be warned of the reduced efficacy of their oral contraceptive and additional alternative forms of contraception should be used.

Rifampicin and anticonvulsants also cause failure of oral contraceptives; both drugs induce hepatic microsomal enzymes, thereby decreasing the plasma concentration of the steroids (Back et al. 1980; Coulam and Annegers 1979).

Other drug interactions associated with the contraceptive pill are between it and coumarin anticoagulants. The pill increases levels of factor VII and reduces the efficacy of this group of anticoagulants. Also, anti-hypertensive and antidepressant therapy becomes less effective in pill takers; the mechanism for this interaction is uncertain.

The effect of female sex hormones on the oral mucosa

It is well-documented that puberty and pregnancy are associated with an increase in the incidence of gingival inflammation (Loe and Silness 1963; Cohen *et al.* 1969). Also, menopausal women frequently complain of sore mouths, which may be due to thinning (atrophy) of the epithelial lining of the oral mucosa.

The gingival changes in puberty and pregnancy may be due to progesterone causing an increase in vascular permeability (Hugoson 1970). The action of progesterone on vessel walls is uncertain. It has been suggested that this hormone affects the nature of the carbohydrate fraction associated with the vessel wall and ground substance. Alternatively, progesterone may enhance pore formation in the vessel wall, causing an increase in permeability and oedema formation. These gingival changes usually resolve after puberty and parturition.

Male sex hormones

The principal male sex hormone is testosterone, produced by the Leydig cells of the testes (90 per cent) and, to a lesser extent, by the adrenal cortex (10 per cent). Secretion of testosterone is stimulated by LH. Testosterone acts on a variety of tissues and, in most target tissues, is converted by the enzyme 5α-reductase to the more active hormone, dihydrotestosterone. Both testosterone and dihydrotestosterone are extensively bound to plasma protein and are inactivated in the liver.

Properties

Testosterone is essential for the development of the male secondary sexual characteristics. The hormone is also required for spermatogenesis, the maturation of sperm, and the production of seminal fluid. Testosterone has marked anabolic effects by causing the retention of nitrogen and an increase in protein synthesis. Hence, this hormone has been used in some sporting activities to encourage muscle development.

Uses

Testosterone is used in replacement therapy in cases of hypogonadism and to initiate puberty in those with a delayed onset of this state. When used injudiciously in women, testosterone will cause the development of male characteristics.

REFERENCES

Back, D. J. *et al.* (1980). The effect of rifampicin on the pharmacokinetics of ethinyloestradiol in women. *Contraception*, **21**, 135–43.

Bacon, J. F. and Shenfield, G. M. (1980). Pregnancy attributable to interaction between tetracycline and oral contraceptive. *British Medical Journal,* 1, 293.

Carruthers, R. (1979). Recurrent aphthous ulcers. *Lancet,* ii, 259.

Catellani, J. E., Harvey, S., Erickson, S. H., and Cherkin, D. (1980). Effect of oral contraceptive cycle on dry socket (local alveolar osteitis). *Journal of the American Dental Association,* 101, 777–80.

Cohen, D. W., Friedman, L., Shapiro, J., and Kyle, G. C. (1969). A longitudinal investigation of the periodontal changes during pregnancy. *Journal of Periodontology,* 40, 563–70.

Cohen, W. D., Friedman, L. A., Shapiro, J., Kyle, C. G. and Franklin, S. (1970). Diabetes mellitus and periodontal disease: two year longitudinal observations. *Journal of Periodontology,* 41, 709–12.

Coulam, C. B. and Annegers, J. F. (1979). Do anticonvulsants reduce the efficacy of oral contraceptives. *Epilepsia,* 20, 519–26.

Darzenta, N. C. and Giunta, J. L. (1977). Radiographic changes of the mandible related to oral contraceptives. *Oral Surgery,* 43, 478–81.

Dossetor, J. (1975). Drug interactions with oral contraceptives. *British Medical Journal,* 4, 467–8.

Ferguson, M. M., McKay, H. D., Lindsay, R., and Stephen, K. W. (1978). Progesterone therapy for menstrually related aphthae. *International Journal of Oral Surgery,* 7, 463–70.

Graber, A. L., Ney, R. L., Nicholson, W. E., Island, D. P., and Liddle, G. W. (1965). Natural history of pituitary-adrenal suppression with corticosteroids. *Journal of Clinical Endocrinology and Metabolism,* 25, 11–6.

Hahn, T. J. (1978). Corticosteroid-induced osteopenia. *Archives of Internal Medicine,* 138, 882–5.

Hugoson, A. (1970). Gingival inflammation and female sex hormones. A clinical investigation of pregnant women and experimental studies in dogs. *Journal of Periodontal Research,* 5 (suppl), 1–18.

Kaplan, N. M. (1978). Cardiovascular complications of oral contraceptives. *Annual Review of Medicine,* 29, 245–76.

Lindhe, J. and Attstrom, R. (1967). Gingival exudation during the menstrual cycle. *Journal of Periodontal Research,* 2, 194–8.

Lindhe, J. and Bjorn, A. L. (1967). Influence of hormonal contraceptives on the gingiva of women. *Journal of Periodontal Research,* 2, 1–6.

Livanou, T., Ferriman, D., and James, V. H. T. (1967). Recovery of hypothalamic pituitary adrenal function after corticosteroid therapy. *Lancet,* ii, 856–9.

Loe, H. and Silness, J. (1963). Periodontal disease in pregnancy. I. Prevalence and severity. *Acta Odontologica Scandinavica,* 21, 533–51.

Mann, J. I., Vessey, M. P., Thorogood, M., and Doll, R. (1975). Myocardial infarction in young women with special reference to oral contraceptive practice. *British Medical Journal,* ii, 241–5.

McCullen, J. A., Van Dyke, T. E., Horoszewicz, H., and Genco, R. J. (1981). Neutrophil chemotaxis in individuals with advanced periodontal disease and a genetic predisposition to diabetes mellitus. *Journal of Periodontology,* 52, 167–73.

Meade, T. W. (1982). Oral contraceptives, clotting factors and thrombosis. *American Journal of Obstetrics and Gynecology,* 142, 758–61.

Parillo, J. E. and Fauci, A. C. (1979). Mechanism of glucocorticoid action on immune processes. *Annual Review of Pharmacology and Toxicology*, **19**, 179–201.

Vessey, M. P., Lawless, M., McPherson, K., and Yeates, D. (1983). Neoplasia of the cervix uteri and contraception: a possible adverse effect of the pill. *Lancet*, **ii**, 930–4.

Weiss, N. S. and Sayvetz, T. A. (1980). Incidence of endometrial cancer in relation to the use of oral contraceptives. *New England Journal of Medicine*, **302**, 551–4.

19

Vitamins and minerals

INTRODUCTION

Vitamins are organic substances that must be provided in small quantities in the diet for the synthesis, by tissues, of co-factors essential for a variety of metabolic reactions. Vitamins can be classified as either water-soluble (B and C) or fat-soluble (A, D, E and K). Normal human requirements and sources of the various vitamins are shown in Table 19.1. Vitamin D is considered in Chapter 20.

Iron is essential for many of the body's functions and occurs in a variety of forms in the earth's crust.

Table 19.1. Daily requirements and food sources of the various vitamins

Vitamin	Daily requirements	Food sources
A	2 mg	Dairy products, fish liver oils,
B_1 (thiamine)	2 mg	Cereals, meat, kidneys, eggs
B_2 (riboflavin	3 mg	Cereal germ, meat, liver, kidney, milk
Nicotinic acid	20 mg	Liver, yeast
B_6 (pyridoxine)		Cereals, liver
Folic acid	5 mg	Green vegetables, salad, yeast
B_{12}	1 μg	Liver, lean meat
C	10–30 mg	Citrus fruits, potatoes, green vegetables
D	500 i.u.	Dairy products.
		Action of sunlight on skin.
K	Adequate supply from gut bacterial flora	Green vegetables, salads

VITAMIN A

A night blindness that could be corrected by diet was first described about 1500 BC; however, it was not until 1923 that this type of night blindness was associated with a deficiency of vitamin A. There are several variants and sources of vitamin A. Vitamin A_1 (retinol) is present in fish and meat. The plant pigment, carotene, is a pro-vitamin that is rapidly converted to vitamin A in the body.

Properties and functions

Vitamin A has many important properties: it is essential for the normal function of the retina; for the growth and differentiation of epithelial tissues; and for bone growth and embryonic development. These different functions are mediated by different forms of the vitamin A molecule, which are collectively known as the retinoids (e.g. retinal, retinol, and retonic acid). Retinal is essential for normal vision, whereas retinol is important in the reproductive process. There has been considerable interest in the apparent ability of the retinoids to interfere with carcinogenesis. Animal experiments have shown that a deficiency of vitamin A can result in marked epithelial hyperplasia and reduced cellular differentiation, changes that may be associated with premalignancy. These changes are reversed when vitamin A is restored to the diet. However, in man, severe toxicity is associated with excessive use of this vitamin.

A variety of food substances contain vitamin A, and ideal sources are shown in Table 19.1. Supplementary doses of vitamin A are given orally in the form of halibut liver-oil capsules. The vitamin is well absorbed from the gastro-intestinal tract, and any excess is stored in the liver. The storage of vitamin A is enhanced by vitamin E.

Deficiency

Dietary deficiency of vitamin A leads to retarded growth and development. The first sign of this is often impaired vision in dim light, a condition known as nyctalopia (night blindness). Other signs include hyperkeratosis of the skin, impaired renal function, and urinary calculi. Severe deficiency results in faulty modelling of bone; diarrhoea also occurs due to alteration in the epithelial lining of the gastro-intestinal tract.

Deficiency of vitamin A is commonly seen in undernourished populations from the Third World. Deficiency also occurs in patients with chronic diseases that affect fat absorption, such as colitis, sprue, and diseases of the biliary tract.

Hypervitaminosis A

Acute poisoning with vitamin A has been reported following consumption of polar bear liver, but is more commonly associated with accidental overdose in children. Signs and symptoms include drowsiness, headache, vomiting, papilloedema, and peeling of the skin. Chronic overdose can result in vomiting, loss of appetite, dryness of the skin, gingivitis, and angular cheilitis. Hyperostoses of the skull can occur with long-term consumption of excess vitamin A. Hypervitaminosis A can be overcome by increasing the intake of vitamin E.

Uses

Vitamin A is used to correct deficiency states and as a prophylaxis during periods of increased requirements, which may occur in pregnancy, lactation, and infancy. Topical retinoic acid is used in the treatment of acne to promote healing.

Large single doses of vitamin A are used to treat certain skin diseases, such as psoriasis and Darier's disease.

THE VITAMIN B COMPLEX

This comprises 11 different chemical compounds, all of which are found in yeast and liver. Dietary deficiency often involves several components of the B complex in the same patient.

Thiamine (vitamin B_1)

This occurs in numerous plants and animal foods (Table 19.1), especially in the husks and coatings of many grain cereals. In the body, thiamine is converted to thiamine pyrophosphate, which then acts as an important co-enzyme in carbohydrate metabolism. Thiamine requirements are directly related to carbohydrate utilization and metabolic rate. The body is unable to store thiamine and a poor diet will lead to signs of deficiency within two weeks.

Deficiency

Thiamine deficiency causes beri-beri, a disease mainly confined to the Far East, where it is due to consumption of polished rice. In Western countries, thiamine deficiency is often seen in alcoholics and, occasionally, in pregnancy and infancy. Early signs of deficiency include a peripheral neuritis with areas of hyperaesthesia and anaesthesia, and a reduction in muscle strength. Severe deficiency will lead to cardiovascular changes, which include dyspnoea on exertion, palpitations, and tachycardia.

Uses

Thiamine is only used to correct deficiency states. If the deficiency is severe, then it should be given intravenously; however most cases can be corrected by giving the vitamin orally.

Riboflavin (vitamin B_2)

This occurs naturally as the yellow respiratory enzyme found in yeast. In the body, riboflavin is converted into two co-enzymes, flavine mononucleotide and flavine dinucleotide, both of which are essential for the respiratory electron transport of protein.

Deficiency

Early signs of riboflavin deficiency include sore throats and angular cheilitis. These are followed by a glossitis and cheilosis (sore and red lips). In extreme cases there is a generalized dermatitis, anaemia, and neuropathy. Deficiency states can be corrected by an oral dose of 5 to 10 mg daily.

Nicotinic acid

This is found mainly in liver and yeast, and functions in the body after conversion to the co-enzymes, nicotinamide adenine dinucleotide or nicotinamide adenine dinucleotide phosphate. Both co-enzymes catalyse a variety of oxidation–reduction reactions that are essential for respiration.

Deficiency

Lack of nicotinic acid causes pellagra, a disease found in countries where large quantities of maize are eaten. Early signs of deficiency include a generalized dermatitis and stomatitis; severe deficiency causes an enteritis and dementia. Deficiency states can be corrected by a daily oral dose of 50 mg of nicotinic acid.

Pyridoxine (vitamin B_6)

Pyridoxine, pyridoxal, and pyridoxamine are the three naturally occurring forms of vitamin B_6. All three forms are converted in the body to pyridoxal phosphate, which acts as a co-enzyme in the various stages of amino acid metabolism. Pyridoxine occurs naturally in various cereals and liver.

Deficiency

Vitamin B_6 deficiency is common in alcoholics, and produces a glossitis, seborrhoea, fits, and peripheral neuropathy. Signs of deficiency can also occur in tuberculosis patients taking isoniazid, and patients taking hydralzine, as both drugs interfere with the pyridoxine metabolism.

Biotin

This organic acid is found in egg yolk and yeast. Like most of the vitamins in the B complex, biotin is also a co-enzyme and catalyses several carboxylation reactions. The co-enzyme also plays an important role in carbon dioxide fixation. Hence biotin is essential for carbohydrate and fat metabolism.

Deficiency

Signs of biotin deficiency include dermatitis, an atrophic glossitis, hyperaesthesia, and muscle pain. Biotin deficiency can occur in new-born babies, and is readily corrected by daily oral doses of 5 to 10 mg.

Vitamin B$_{12}$ and folic acid

These two dietary components are essential for the synthesis of DNA and hence for chromosomal replication and cell division. Tissues with a high cellular turnover, such as haematopoietic tissue, are very sensitive to a deficiency of these two substances.

Vitamin B$_{12}$ represents a group of compounds known as the cobalamins in which the cobalt ion is linked to either cyanide (cyanocobalamin), a hydroxyl group (hydroxycobalamin), or a methyl group (methylcobalamin). Cobalamins are synthesized by micro-organisms in the intestines, but in man they are not absorbed. Hence man depends upon a dietary source of B$_{12}$ to meet requirements. Foods rich in vitamin B$_{12}$ include liver, kidneys, and shell fish.

Properties and functions

Vitamin B$_{12}$ is essential for cell growth and division, and for the normal myelination of nerve fibres. It is necessary for folic acid metabolism, and is also involved in the metabolism of lipids and carbohydrates. Deficiency of vitamin B$_{12}$ causes pernicious anaemia.

Absorption of vitamin B$_{12}$ from dietary sources is dependent upon an intrinsic factor (a glycoprotein) produced by the parietal cells of the stomach. Gastric acid causes the release of dietary B$_{12}$ from proteins. The released vitamin is immediately bound to intrinsic factor, and the combination reaches the ileum, where it combines with specific receptors on the ileal mucosal cell. The vitamin B$_{12}$ and intrinsic factor are then transported into the circulation. Total body stores of vitamin B$_{12}$ are approximately 3 mg.

Deficiency

This affects both the haematopoietic system and the nervous system. Vitamin B$_{12}$ is essential for cell growth and replication, so the high rate of cell turnover in the bone marrow makes it very susceptible to deficiency states of vitamin B$_{12}$. The result is pernicious anaemia, which is characterized by a hypochromic, macrocytic anaemia. Clinical signs of pernicious anaemia include a sore red tongue, angular cheilitis, and premature greying of the hair. Severe vitamin B$_{12}$ deficiency can result in irreversible damage to the nervous system due to demyelination of neurones. Early signs of such changes are paraesthesia of the extremities and decreased tendon reflexes. Those affected can become confused, disorientated, and suffer visual disturbances.

Vitamin B$_{12}$ deficiency can result from poor intake, as could occur in strict vegetarians. More commonly, the deficiency arises in those who lack intrinsic factor, including patients with gastritis or who have undergone gastric surgery. Various types of ileal disease (i.e. Crohn's disease and coeliac disease) can affect the absorption of the vitamin B$_{12}$–intrinsic factor complex, and result in signs and symptoms of deficiency. Certain drugs, for example para-aminosalicylic acid and neomycin, will affect the absorption of vitamin B_{12}. If these drugs are used for prolonged periods, a deficiency state can arise.

Uses

Vitamin B_{12} is used to treat pernicious anaemia and other signs of deficiency. It is usually given by injection, and mild forms of pernicious anaemia usually respond to 500 μg every two months.

Folic acid

This is a weak organic acid (pteroylglutamic acid) that occurs in yeast, liver, and green vegetables. Folic acid is essential for normal production of red blood cells, and a deficiency results in a megaloblastic anaemia. In the body, folic acid is reduced to tetrahydrofolate by the enzyme, dihydrofolate reductase. This enzyme is inhibited by various chemotherapeutic agents (see Chapter 17). Dietary folic acid is absorbed in the small intestines and mainly stored in the liver. These stores will last for about four months.

Deficiency

Folic acid deficiency is a common occurrence in patients with disease of the gastro-intestinal tract, where there is impaired absorption. Deficiency is also found in alcoholics, in pregnancy, and in patients taking phenytoin and phenobarbitone—drugs that affect the absorption of folic acid. Folic acid deficiency causes a megaloblastic anaemia identical to that produced by vitamin B_{12}. However, unlike vitamin B_{12} deficiency, there are no neurological symptoms with folic acid deficiency.

VITAMIN C (ASCORBIC ACID)

The dietary value of fresh lemons in the prevention of scurvy was first established by Lind in 1747. However, the identification of vitamin C and its link with scurvy did not occur until 1907.

Ascorbic acid is structurally related to glucose, and some species can synthesize their own vitamin C from this carbohydrate. Vitamin C is involved in a number of body functions, including the synthesis of collagen, corticosteroids, and lysine chains in certain proteins. The major function of vitamin C is in the synthesis of intercellular substances, including collagen, the matrices of teeth and bone, and the intercellular cement of the capillary endothelium. Vitamin C is well-absorbed when taken orally, and widely distributed throughout all tissues in the body.

Deficiency

This causes scurvy, which is associated with a defect in collagen synthesis. Clinical features include poor healing of wounds, rupture of capillaries leading to petechiae and ecchymoses, loosening of the teeth, and bleeding from the gingival tissues. Scurvy is sometimes seen in alcoholics, drug addicts, children, and the elderly.

Uses

Vitamin C is used in the treatment of scurvy. It is also widely used as a prophylaxis against the common cold. There is no firm evidence to suggest that vitamin C reduces either the chances of catching a cold or shortens its course. Indeed, excessive use of vitamin C can predispose the individual to oxalate renal calculi.

VITAMIN E

This vitamin, which occurs in wheat-germ oil, was first isolated in 1936. Its pharmacological and physiological functions in man are not established. Animal experiments have shown that deficiency of vitamin E causes spontaneous abortion and impaired spermatogenesis. The role of vitamin E in the reproduction system of man is uncertain. Evidence suggests that vitamin E may protect the red blood cell against haemolysis. This vitamin is widely consumed as part of multiple vitamin therapy; fortunately, large doses of vitamin E have no serious unwanted effects.

VITAMIN K

This is essential for the synthesis of several factors required for blood clotting (II, VII, IX, and X). The vitamin is concentrated in chloroplasts and in vegetable oils.

Deficiency of vitamin K causes hypoprothrombinaemia and hence an increased tendency to bleed. Patients will suffer from ecchymoses, epistaxis, haematuria, and gastro-intestinal bleeding. Vitamin K is used to treat symptoms of deficiency, drug-induced hypoprothrombinaemia, and the hypoprothrombinaemia of the new-born (see Chapter 12).

IRON

This is the fourth most abundant element in the earth's crust and is essential for the normal function of many living species. In man, iron is used for the synthesis of haemoglobin, myoglobin, and certain enzymes. Iron not utilized for these purposes is stored as ferretin or haemosiderin. Shortage of iron results in iron-deficiency anaemia.

Pharmacokinetics

Although iron is absorbed throughout the small intestine, the main site of absorption is the duodenum. Absorption of iron, either in the diet or from a variety of iron preparations, can be affected by many factors. Certain foods, particularly cereals, reduce iron absorption. Certain drugs, such as tetracyclines, chelate iron and there is impaired absorption of the chelate. Thus, patients on iron therapy should not be prescribed tetracyclines. Similarly, antacids reduce iron absorption. Iron in the ferrous form is more readily absorbed than ferric iron. In addition, vitamin C and intrinsic factor facilitate iron absorption. Control of absorption appears to be related to the capacity of the intestinal mucosa to transport iron into the blood stream.

On absorption into the mucosal cell, iron combines with the protein apoferritin to form ferritin. However, in patients with iron deficiency the formation of ferritin does not occur and the iron passes straight into the plasma. Free iron in the plasma, or iron released from ferritin, is transported in the bloodstream attached to the glycoprotein, transferrin, from where it is delivered and stored in the bone marrow. Total body stores of iron are 3 to 4 g.

Small quantities of iron are lost via shedding of the mucosal cell in the small intestine, from the bile, and via the kidneys. Iron requirements increase during pregnancy and lactation.

Uses

Iron is given to correct or prevent iron-deficiency anaemia (see below). Usually it is given orally in the form of either ferrous sulphate, gluconate, or fumarate. The response to iron replacement therapy usually occurs 5 to 10 days after commencement of dosage, and treatment should continue for six months after haemoglobin levels have reached the normal range.

Iron can also be given via the parenteral route (in the form of iron dextran), if iron stores are to be rapidly and completely replenished.

Unwanted effects of iron replacement therapy

When given orally, ferrous salts can produce nausea, epigastric pain, constipation, and diarrhoea. Iron dextran can produce staining of the skin.

Iron-deficiency anaemia

This is a common disease, and especially prevalent in the Third World. The incidence is higher in menstruating and pregnant women. The anaemia is either due to an inadequate diet, impaired iron absorption, or chronic blood loss. Thorough investigation of those with iron deficiency is essential in order to elucidate the underlying cause. Early signs of iron deficiency often occur in the mouth; these include ulceration, angular cheilitis, candidiasis, and glossitis. The patients may have cardiovascular problems, such as dyspnoea and angina, and they will appear pale. Their nails may be brittle and spoon-shaped (koilonychia).

Examination of the blood film is a useful diagnostic procedure for confirming iron-deficiency anaemia; the red blood cells are microcytic and hypochromic. The mean corpuscular volume (MCV), mean corpuscular haemoglobin concentration (MCHC), and serum ferritin levels are also significantly reduced.

20

Calcification

SALTS of calcium and phosphate comprise the major inorganic portion of bone. Also both types of compound have several important physiological roles in normal body function. This Chapter deals with the pharmacological and physiological properties of calcium and phosphate, together with the endocrine factors (parathyroid hormone, calcitonin, and vitamin D) that control their metabolism.

CALCIUM

Nearly all the body's calcium is found in the skeletal tissues; small quantities occur in cell cytoplasm and in the extracellular fluid. Ionized calcium is involved in nerve conduction, muscle contraction, cardiac function, and blood clotting. The body's calcium requirements vary with the demands of age, growth spurts, pregnancy, and lactation (dietary requirements are in the range 360–1200 mg/ daily).

Pharmacokinetics

Soluble, ionized calcium is mainly absorbed in the proximal segment of the small bowel; absorption is augmented by vitamin D and parathyroid hormone. Transport of calcium across the gut mucosal cells is probably by means of a calcium-binding protein. Glucocorticoids will depress this transport system. Absorption of calcium is also affected by phytate, oxalate, and phosphate ions in the bowel, which form insoluble salts with calcium. Patients with chronic diarrhoea and steatorrhoea suffer from decreased calcium absorption. Calcium ions are excreted into the gastro-intestinal tract, bile, saliva, and pancreatic juices; calcium is also lost in sweat, and in significant amounts during lactation. Calcium is excreted via the kidney under the control of parathyroid hormone and vitamin D. Parathyroid hormone stimulates calcium reabsorption by an action on the distal tubule, whereas vitamin D stimulates reabsorption from the proximal tubule. Calcitonin inhibits the proximal tubular reabsorption of calcium and thus facilitates excretion.

Pharmacological and physiological properties

Calcium is essential for normal function of the neuromuscular system. A rise in extracellular calcium concentration will cause a rise in the threshold for excitation of nerve fibres and muscle. This will result in muscle weakness, lethargy, and eventually coma. Calcium is involved in the activation of muscle contraction, both in skeletal and cardiac muscle. It is also involved in the release of catecholamines from the adrenal medulla. In addition, calcium ions are essential both for the release of neurotransmitters from synapses and of autocoids from various sites and tissues in the body.

In blood coagulation, Ca^{2+} (Factor V) are essential for the action of thromboplastin on prothrombin to form thrombin (see Chapter 12). Calcium salts, especially calcium chloride, cause irritation and sloughing of tissues if given subcutaneously. Hence this drug should only be given intravenously.

Abnormalities of calcium metabolism

Blood calcium levels can be affected by a variety of factors; these can give rise to either a hypocalcaemic or hypercalcaemic state.

Hypocalcaemia

The signs and symptoms of this include tetany, paraesthesia, laryngospasm, muscle cramps, and convulsions. Hypocalcaemia is associated with the following:

1. Poor intake of calcium and vitamin D: the resultant hypocalcaemia gives rise to an increased production of parathyroid hormone, which mobilizes Ca^{2+} from bone; in adults, this leads to osteomalacia, whereas in infants it causes rickets.
2. Hypoparathyroidism.
3. Renal insufficiency accompanied by hyperphosphatasia: the high plasma concentrations of phosphate inhibit the conversion, in the kidney, of 25-hydroxycholecalciferol to 1,25-dihydroxycholecalciferol.
4. Overdose of sodium fluoride: the fluoride forms a complex with calcium ions thus leading to reduced absorption of them.
5. Massive transfusions with citrated blood: the citrate ions will chelate calcium to form an insoluble complex, thus reducing plasma concentrations of calcium ions.

Hypocalcaemic states are corrected by a dietary increase in calcium. In severe cases of tetany associated with hypocalcaemia, treatment is with intravenous calcium chloride.

Hypercalcaemia

High plasma concentrations of calcium will principally affect the kidney, causing pathological changes in the collecting ducts and distal tubules. The net result is a reduction in renal function if left untreated, and hypercalcaemia will cause renal failure. Hypercalcaemia is associated with the following conditions:

1. Diet, especially the milk-alkali syndrome caused by excessive consumption of milk and antacids, which contain soluble calcium salts—massive amounts of antacids need to be regularly consumed to produce this syndrome.
2. Excessive intake of vitamin D_3.
3. Hyperparathyroidism
4. Sarcoidosis: patients with this granulomatous disorder may have a hypersensitivity to vitamin D.
5. Neoplasms: metastatic deposits in bone can secrete osteoclast activating factor and prostaglandins, which both stimulate bone resorption.
6. Disuse atrophy: as occurs when a limb has been immobilized for a long time.

Hypercalcaemia is usually corrected by the body's homeostatic mechanism. If very severe, it is treated with steroids such as prednisolone.

PHOSPHATE

Phosphate is present in extracellular fluids, collagen, and bone. A balance exists between plasma concentrations of calcium and phosphate. There is also an inverse relationship between plasma phosphate concentration and the rate of renal hydroxylation of 25-hydroxycholecalciferol. Thus, a reduction in plasma phosphate leads to an increase of calcium in the blood, which in turn inhibits the deposition of new bone salts. An increase in plasma phosphate facilitates the effect of calcitonin on the deposition of calcium in bone.

Phosphate ions are absorbed from the bowel, and absorption is enhanced by vitamin D. Large quantities of calcium and aluminium in the bowel will reduce the absorption of phosphate. Like calcium, phosphate requirements vary with age, growth, pregnancy, and lactation.

VITAMIN D (CALCIFEROL)

Although referred to as a vitamin, calciferol (or more precisely the metabolite of 1,25-dihydroxycholecalciferol) is now considered a hormone secreted by the kidney. The metabolism of vitamin D is shown in Fig. 20.1. The precursor of vitamin D is 7-dehydrocholesterol, which is synthesized in the skin. The action of ultraviolet light converts this precursor to cholecalciferol (vitamin D_3). Further

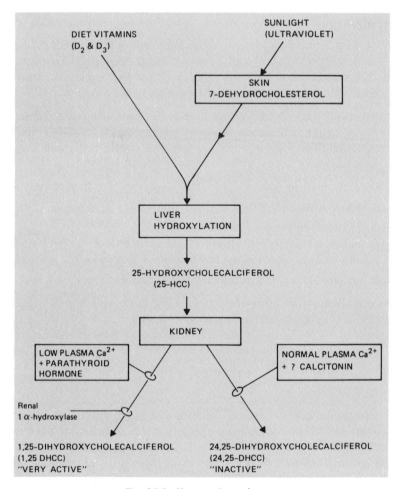

Fig. 20.1. Vitamin D synthesis.

hydroxylation of cholecalciferol occurs in the liver to form the compound 25-hydroxycholecalciferol (25-HCC). This hydroxylation process is controlled by circulating levels of cholecalciferol, with high levels inhibiting the hydroxylation. The 25-HCC is finally activated in the kidneys by the enzyme, renal 1α-hydroxylase, and the product depends upon the calcium needs.

In the presence of low calcium concentrations, 25-HCC is hydroxylated to 1,25-dihydroxycholecalciferol (1,25-DHCC), and the hydroxylation is facilitated by parathyroid hormone. The 1,25-DHCC is highly active, and acts on the intestine to increase the formation of calcium-binding proteins that augment calcium absorption. With normal or high calcium concentrations, 25-HCC is hydroxylated to the relatively inactive 24,25-dihydroxycholecalciferol. This hydroxylation may be facilitated by calcitonin.

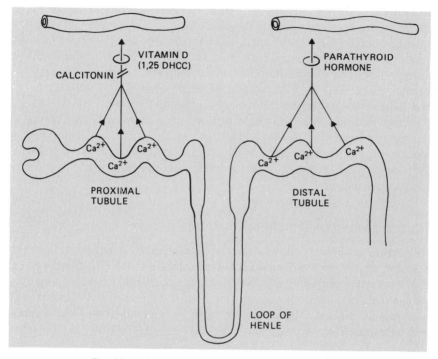

Fig. 20.2. Calcium homeostasis and the renal tubule.

Thus 1,25-DHCC enhances the absorption of calcium from the small intestine, and it also facilitates reabsorption of calcium ions from the proximal tubule (Fig. 20.2). Both 1,25-DHCC and parathyroid hormone mobilize calcium from bone.

Uses

Vitamin D is used to correct deficiency states (see below), and is available in three forms: cholecalciferol, ergocalciferol (vitamin D_2), and dihydrotachysterol. Dihydrotachysterol is more widely used because it bypasses renal regulation.

Unwanted effects

The main adverse effect associated with vitamin D preparations is hypervitaminosis D, characterized by hypercalcaemia, osteoporosis, soft tissue calcification, and renal calculi.

Deficiency

A deficiency of vitamin D, either from dietary sources or lack of sunlight, results in rickets or osteomalacia. Both conditions are characterized by a pathological defect in the mineralization of new bone. Rickets presents clinically during growth, whereas osteomalacia is the adult form of the disease. Oral manifestations of vitamin D deficiency depend upon the severity and age of onset. During growth, vitamin D deficiency will affect the mandibular condylar cartilage, causing retarded development of the mandibular ramus. There is often delayed eruption of the teeth and hypoplasia of tooth enamel. In both rickets and osteomalacia, the jaw bones are weak and prone to fracture.

Patients with chronic renal failure may suffer from renal rickets due to impaired synthesis of 1,25-DHCC. This will result in calcium malabsorption, hypocalcaemia, and a secondary rise in parathyroid hormone production. Hence, such patients will have the signs and symptoms of osteomalacia and (secondary) hyperparathyroidism.

Vitamin D-resistant rickets

This is a rare sex-linked familial disease characterized by a hypophosphataemia associated with a decreased renal tubular reabsorption of PO_4^{3-}. Patients will present with the signs and symptoms of rickets or osteomalacia depending upon their age. This form of rickets appears to respond to a metabolite of vitamin D—1α-hydroxycholecalciferol. This is an example of a disease due to a receptor abnormality (see Chapter 1).

PARATHYROID HORMONE (PTH)

The parathyroids are small, yellow glandular bodies, usually attached to the undersurface of the thyroid gland. They were first discovered in 1880, but their physiological function was not determined until the 1920s. The glands synthesize and secrete PTH.

Physiological functions

The PTH controls calcium metabolism and ensures that the extracellular fluid concentration of Ca^{2+} is kept constant. Hence it will regulate the absorption of Ca^{2+} from the gastro-intestinal tract, the deposition and mobilization of Ca^{2+} in bone, and the excretion of Ca^{2+} via the kidney.

The secretion of PTH is inversely related to the plasma concentration of calcium. When the concentration of Ca^{2+} is low there is an increased secretion of PTH; with normal or high concentrations of Ca^{2+}, secretion is reduced.

Parathyroid hormone increases bone resorption, especially from the older portion of mineralized bone, leading to an increase in the plasma concentration of Ca^{2+}. It acts directly on the osteolytic cells (osteoclasts and osteocytes), and increases the rate of mesenchymal cell differentiation to osteoblasts. Osteoclastic activity is evident some 20 minutes after an infusion of PTH.

The hormone has a dual action in the kidney: it increases tubular reabsorption of Ca^{2+}; and it inhibits tubular reabsorption of PO_4^{3-} (Fig. 20.2), which results in an increased renal excretion of inorganic phosphate. The overall effect of PTH on the kidney is to retain Ca^{2+} and maintain the plasma concentration.

Calcium and phosphate ions, as described earlier, are absorbed in the gastro-intestinal tract, and parathyroid hormone has an indirect effect on their absorption. The absorption of Ca^{2+} is dependent upon the active metabolite of vitamin D (1,25-DHCC); PTH enhances the renal hydroxylation of 25-HCC to 1,25-DHCC. The increase in the production of 1,25-DHCC increases Ca^{2+} absorption.

Disorders of parathyroid function

There are two such disorders, hypo- and hyperparathyroidism.

Hypoparathyroidism

This can result from either hypofunction of the parathyroid glands, surgical removal of the glands following thyroidectomy, or the rare genetic disorder of pseudohypoparathyroidism, in which target organs do not respond to PTH. This genetic disorder is yet another example of disease due to a receptor abnormality (see Chapter 1). In all varieties of hypoparathyroidism, the clinical symptoms are those of hypocalcemia, and include paraesthesia of the extremities, muscle twitching and, if severe, tetany. In chronic cases of hypoparathyroidism, there are various ectodermal changes including loss of hair, grooved and brittle fingernails, and enamel hypoplasia. Hypoparathyroidism is treated with vitamin D and, where necessary, calcium supplements.

Hyperparathyroidism

This is characterized by excessive production of parathyroid hormone. Three forms of the disease are recognized; primary, secondary, and tertiary. Primary hyperparathyroidism is associated with hyperplasia or neoplasia of the para-thyroid glands. In secondary hyperparathyroidism, the underlying cause is a hypocalcaemia associated with chronic renal failure. The hypocalcaemia stimulates excessive production of PTH. Patients with long-standing renal disease and secondary hyperparathyroidism may develop an apparent autonomous hypersecretion of PTH, and this is known as tertiary hyperparathyroidism.

Clinical features

Primary hyperparathyroidism has an incidence of 1:1000 of the population, with females being more affected than males. Excessive PTH activity will cause a hypercalcaemia and hypophosphataemia. The presenting symptoms are those of hypercalcaemia, and include anorexia, thirst, polyuria, renal colic, and renal stones. Approximately one-third of patients show evidence of bone disease, including the bone disorder known as osteitis fibrosa cystica. This condition is characterized by foci of bone destruction leaving spaces filled with vascular and cellular connective tissue containing large numbers of osteoclastic giant cells. Such lesions often occur in the jaws, especially the mandible. Primary hyperparathyroidism is treated by surgical excision of the parathyroid glands. In secondary or tertiary hyperparathyroidism, the underlying renal disease must be corrected.

CALCITONIN

This was first described in 1964, and is a hormone secreted by the parafollicular cells of the thyroid gland. Like PTH, calcitonin secretion is controlled by plasma levels of calcium; it lowers plasma calcium and phosphate levels by an alteration in intracellular cyclic AMP. Calcitonin has two effects on calcium homeostasis. Firstly, it inhibits osteoclastic resorption, thus reducing the release of Ca^{2+} and PO_4^{3-} from the skeletal tissues. This inhibition is more pronounced when there is a high turnover of bone, as occurs in Paget's disease and thyrotoxicosis. Secondly, it has a minor effect on the kidneys, enhancing the excretion of phosphate, calcium, and sodium (Fig. 20.2).

Calcitonin (porcine or salmon varieties) is used to treat Paget's disease, and the hypercalcaemia secondary to malignancy or vitamin D excess. The hormone can only be given parenterally because it is destroyed by gastric secretions. Patients with Paget's disease usually show a response to calcitonin therapy within two months. Unwanted effects are pain at the site of injection, nausea, and flushing of the face. Because of the low doses of calcitonin used in Paget's disease, antibody formation leading to hypersensitivity is unlikely.

21

Unwanted effects of drugs, including immunopharmacology

UNWANTED EFFECTS DUE TO DRUGS

These appear to be fairly common in medical practice, although precise information about their incidence is not available. This is partly because unwanted effects may not be recognized as such either by the patient or by the doctor. Moreover, it will only be possible to calculate the incidence of such effects in relation to a particular drug when accurate information about the numbers of patients exhibiting adverse effects to that drug is available, together with accurate returns that indicate the total number of patients receiving it.

In dental practice, unwanted effects due to drugs would appear to be less common than in medical practice. They are likely to arise in two different ways. The dentist may be the first to observe an unwanted effect produced by a drug prescribed by the patient's medical practitioner; for example, ulceration in the mouth that accompanies agranulocytosis. On the other hand, as part of dental treatment, the dentist may prescribe a drug to which the patient reacts adversely. In order to obtain accurate information about the incidence of unwanted drug effects in dental practice, it is most important for all practitioners to report any suspected unwanted drug effect to the Medical Assessor (Adverse Reactions), Committee on Safety of Medicines, 33/37a Finsbury Square, London EC2B 2ZS. (Special yellow-coloured report cards with prepaid postage are available for this purpose from the Committee on Safety of Medicines).

Classification

It is difficult to classify unwanted effects satisfactorily because very often the mechanism is not clear. However, it is useful to have some form of classification for reference. One broad classification has divided unwanted effects into two classes, Type A Reactions and Type B Reactions (Rawlins and Thompson 1985).

Type A reactions
These are reactions that would be expected, or could be expected, from the known pharmacology of the drug or mixtures of drugs. Such reactions are relatively

common and usually not serious, although they may be unpleasant. An example of this sort of reaction arises from the use of antihistamines (H_1-blockers) to prevent histamine access to receptors involved in allergic responses. In addition to this blocking property the antihistamines have, in general, an intrinsic sedative effect, and this may be unwanted.

Type B reactions

These reactions cannot be predicted or explained by the known pharmacology of the drug. They are relatively uncommon and are often much more serious than the Type A Reaction. Allergic reactions to drugs generally come under this heading.

Another useful classification, a modified version of that proposed by Rosenheim and Moulton (1958), is given below. Both classifications fit well into each other.

(1) overdosage

(2) intolerance

(3) side-effects

(4) secondary effects

(5) idiosyncrasy

(6) teratogenic effects

(7) hypersensitivity

(8) drug interactions

These items are now considered in detail, except for drug interactions, which have been mentioned under individual drugs and will be discussed in Chapter 22.

Overdosage

Unwanted effects due to an excess of drug will be related to the amount of drug in the body. It is important to realize that all drugs are potentially poisonous, although some are relatively more poisonous than others. The safety of a drug will depend upon the size of the margin between the effective dose (ED) and the lethal dose (LD), as discussed in Chapter 1. This cannot be measured in man but can be determined in animals where, in order to allow for biological variation, a series of different doses are given to two groups of animals and two appropriate graphs of the results are drawn, one for effectiveness and one for lethality. From these graphs the amount of drug required to produce the desired effect in 50 per cent of animals (ED_{50}) can be read off, and also the amount required to kill 50 per cent of them (LD_{50}). The safety or, as it is termed, the Therapeutic Index can be obtained by determining the ratio LD_{50}/ED_{50} (see Fig. 1.13). The larger the value of this ratio, the safer is the drug, although it is important to relate the route of administration used in these determinations to that which may be used in man, and also to make allowance for species differences.

Absolute overdosage

This may be (i) immediate, due to the presence of too much drug given in error or taken deliberately with suicidal intent; on the other hand, it may be (ii) cumulative, which is brought about by slow excretion of the drug, with the result that there is a steady increase in the amount of drug in the body over a period of time. For example, digitalis and thyroxine take more than a week to be half-excreted; they therefore accumulate in the body unless steps are taken to reduce the initial dosage when an adequate therapeutic effect has been achieved. By contrast, penicillin is half excreted in less than an hour and is therefore not liable to accumulate.

Relative overdosage

This occurs when the mechanisms for metabolism and/or excretion of a drug are impaired. Under these circumstances, normal or even subnormal doses of the drug may cause signs of overdosage. In hepatic failure, drugs may be metabolized more slowly than normal, with the result that the amount of active drug in the body declines more slowly than usual, so leading to an increased and prolonged effect. For example, the duration of apnoea after a normal dose of the short-acting muscle relaxant, suxamethonium, may be greatly prolonged in patients with low plasma cholinesterase levels due to liver disease (Fig. 21.1). Similarly, renal

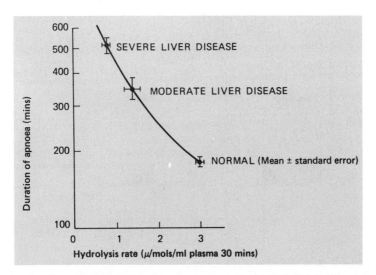

Fig. 21.1. The effect of liver disease on the rate of destruction (by hydrolysis) of the short-acting neuromuscular blocking drug suxamethonium. Plasma cholinesterase which is manufactured by the liver is responsible for the hydrolysis of suxamethonium. Since the presence of liver disease reduces the production of cholinesterase, it also affects the rate of breakdown of suxamethonium and hence the duration of neuromuscular block including apnoea after a dose of this drug. (Drawn from data of Foldes *et al.* 1956.)

failure will result in a diminished rate of excretion of a drug such as digoxin where this is the main route of excretion from the body.

Intolerance

This is said to occur when there is a lowered threshold to the normal pharmacological action of a drug; it is a phenomenon attributable to biological variation. Thus, whereas the normal therapeutic dose produces the desired effect in the majority of individuals, in a minority it may produce too large or too small an effect; the former is due to intolerance, the latter to tolerance. Put the other way round, the dose required to produce the desired effect in an intolerant patient is less than the normal dose, whilst the requisite dose for a tolerant patient is greater than the normal, as illustrated in Fig. 21.2. It follows that it is the intolerant patient who is liable to exhibit unwanted effects when the normal dose is used; the tolerant patient shows little or no effect.

Side-effects

These effects are therapeutically undesirable but pharmacologically unavoidable actions due to a drug. Side-effects can be subdivided into two main groups:

Extension of main action

Some side effects are due to an extension of the main action of the drug at sites additional to those required for therapeutic purposes. For example, atropine given

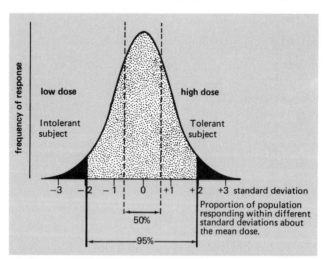

Fig. 21.2. Idealized frequency distribution curve for the responses of a population to a drug. The areas under the curve which represent 50 per cent and 95 per cent of the population are shown and subjects who are considered to be intolerant or tolerant have been arbitrarily shown as belonging to the remaining 5 per cent of the population (black areas). (Standard deviation is a measure of scatter; numerically the value will vary from drug to drug. Where the value is small, the range of doses required about the mean dose will be small, and vice versa.)

in order to produce a dry mouth may also interfere with the accommodation of the eye, and the normal functioning of the bladder and bowels. Although this drug produces widespread effects they are all due to a common mechanism, namely, that atropine competes with acetylcholine released from the postganglionic parasympathetic nerve endings for receptors situated on parasympathetic effector organs. On the other hand, a patient given atropine in order to relieve Parkinsonism may complain of a dry mouth, which under these circumstances becomes the side-effect.

Additional actions

Other side-effects are due to one or more additional actions that are inherent in the particular drug. For example, most antihistamines also possess hypnotic effects. In some circumstances, such as an itching urticarial rash that prevents sleep, these effects may be an added therapeutic benefit; in other situations, such as when used to treat hay fever in a bus driver, they may be highly undesirable. The occurrence of jaundice in patients taking certain of the monoamine oxidase inhibitors or some of the sex hormones is another example.

Secondary effects

These are not due to the direct pharmacological action of a drug but are the indirect consequences of it. For example, the prolonged use of broad-spectrum antibiotics may result in superinfection. Under these conditions, the normal bowel flora is altered by the antibiotic so that pathogenic organisms gain a hold. The result is that a new infection supervenes, and a patient who was originally being treated for a simple infection may contract and possibly die from a very serious one, for example staphylococcal enteritis. Another example is the prolonged use of a tetracycline mouthwash, which leads to a candidal infection of the mouth.

A number of patients treated with the antibiotic, clindamycin, have developed pseudomembranous colitis as a secondary effect; this can be a very dangerous syndrome (see Chapter 10).

Idiosyncrasy

This is a qualitatively abnormal reaction to a drug, which is due to some abnormality of the individual showing the response. For example, the prolonged apnoea that may occur after the administration of the neuromuscular blocking drug, suxamethonium, can be due to the presence of an abnormal cholinesterase, as shown in Fig. 21.3. It has been estimated that about 1 in 2800 persons possess this atypical esterase, which hydrolyses suxamethonium much more slowly than normal cholinesterase with the result that the duration of neuromuscular block is greatly prolonged. Another example is the precipitation of acute porphyria by the administration of barbiturates. This can only occur in patients who are qualitatively different in that they suffer from latent porphyria.

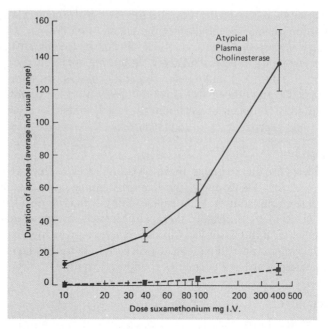

Fig. 21.3. The duration of apnoea after a single intravenous injection of different doses of suxamethonium in adult males with normal and atypical cholinesterase. The greatly reduced rate at which atypical cholinesterase hydrolyses suxamethonium is evident from the prolonged duration of apnoea (upper graph). (Drawn from data of Kalow and Gunn 1957. Reproduced by courtesy of Williams and Wilkins Co, Baltimore.)

Teratogenic effects

Drugs that damage the embryo, but which leave it compatible with prenatal life, and where the abnormalities are observable postnatally, are called teratogens. There are some drugs that have been positively identified as being teratogenic, thalidomide being the obvious example. Others include androgens, and tetracyclines—e.g. producing discoloured teeth. Yet other drugs are suspected as being potentially teratogenic, whilst others are possible teratogenic. For instance, the anticonvulsant, phenytoin, is suspected as a potential teratogen.

Hypersensitivity

Consideration of drug hypersensitivity (allergy) requires some understanding of the immune system; this is discussed now as a separate major section, which leads into the topic of drug allergy and its treatment.

The immune system

This is one of the body's significant defence mechanisms against infection; its functions include the recognition of foreign material (antigen) by various cellular components of the system (macrophages and lymphocytes). Recognition is followed by the production of specific neutralizing chemicals (immunoglobulins or antibodies) or cells (sensitized T-lymphocytes), and the formation of the antibody/antigen complexes. These complexes are finally phagocytosed by polymorphonuclear leucocytes.

The immune system has three important features: memory, specificity, and recognition of non-self. Certain diseases, such as measles, chicken-pox, and mumps, are usually suffered only once. The initial infection stimulates antibody production (primary response) and a memory facility, so that when the infection is encountered again antibodies are readily formed to the infecting agent (secondary response). This is the principle used in immunization. Antibodies raised against the mumps virus are specific for that virus and these antibodies will not render the patient immune to other viral infections. Finally, the immune system must also recognize what is foreign (non-self) and what is self. The failure to discriminate between self and non-self could lead to the synthesis of antibodies directed against tissues of the individual's own body. Such antibodies are referred to as auto-antibodies. The various components of the immune system are considered below.

Immunoglobulins

These are chains of peptides joined together by disulphide bridges. The chains of peptides can be further divided into heavy and light chains. In man, five classes of immunoglobulins can be identified, immunoglobulin G, A, M, D, and E, commonly abbreviated to IgG, IgA, IgM, IgD, and IgE.

Immunoglobulin G

This is the main immunoglobulin formed during the secondary response. It can cross the placenta and hence is essential for the early protection against infection in the new-born child. Immunoglobulin G is found in all cavities of the body where its main function is to neutralize bacterial toxins; such neutralization invariably activates the complement system (see later; and Chapter 4). The various activated complement products are chemotactic for white blood cells and cause an increase in capillary permeability.

Immunoglobulin A

This is referred to as the secretory immunoglobulin for it appears in all secretions produced by the body. Its function is the defence of exposed external body surfaces against infection from micro-organisms. The IgA is synthesized locally by plasma cells, and coats micro-organisms. This coating inhibits their adherence to the surfaces of mucosal cells, thereby preventing entry into the body.

Immunoglobulin M

This is a high molecular-weight immunoglobulin found on the surface of lymphocytes. It appears early in the response to infection and is very efficient at agglutinating bacteria. Hence high concentrations of IgM are associated with bacteraemias.

Immunoglobulin D

This is very susceptible to proteolytic degradation and hence has a short plasma half-life. Like IgM, IgD is found on the surface of lymphocytes and it would seem that both IgM and IgD function as mutually interactive antigen receptors controlling lymphocyte activation and suppression.

Immunoglobulin E

Only small amounts of this are found in serum as IgE is firmly fixed to the surface of mast cells. The combination between antigen and IgE on this surface results in mast cell degranulation, with the release of histamine and other potent chemicals. This is the underlying mechanism for hay fever, asthma, and anaphylaxis. Immunoglobulin E also protects the mucosal surfaces of the body by activating plasma factors and effector cells.

Cellular components of the immune response

Lymphocytes

There are two populations of lymphocytes found in man, thymus-dependent lymphocytes (T-lymphocytes), which are processed by the thymus gland, and bursa-dependent lymphocytes (B-lymphocytes), which are processed by lymphoid tissue equivalent to the structure known as the bursa of Fabricius found in birds. Both types of lymphocyte are derived from bone-marrow stem cells. B-lymphocytes, when stimulated by antigen, develop into plasma cells, which synthesize and release free antibody. T-lymphocytes, when challenged by an antigen, transform to lymphoblasts, which are responsible for cell-mediated immunity.

Macrophages

These are large mononuclear cells; their role in the immune response appears to be the processing and presenting of antigen to lymphocytes. Antigens are partly phagocytosed by macrophages and partly bind to their surface. The processed antigen, or that attached to the cell surface, is then presented to either a T- or B-lymphocyte. Macrophages also produce a chemical mediator, interleukin I, which stimulates T-helper cells (see below).

Cell-mediated response

T-lymphocytes are responsible for the cell-mediated immune response. The surface of the T-lymphocyte contains receptors that are triggered by antigens, which have either been processed by the macrophage or attached to the cell surface. Once the receptor is triggered, the T-lymphocyte undergoes blast transformation to several 'lymphocytes' with different functions. These include lymphokine producers, killer, memory, helper, and suppressor cells. Killer cells, or cytotoxic T-cells, will destroy any cells bearing the antigen that stimulated their formation. Killer cells are particularly involved in viral infections and graft rejection. Helper T-cells are necessary adjuncts to the initial proliferation and differentiation stages of the immune response. Suppressor cells limit the immune response to an antigen, and are important in modulating the immune system.

Lymphokines

These are a group of potent biological substances released from sensitized T-lymphocytes. Lymphokines have a variety of biological activities, as are listed below:

(1) macrophage chemotactic factor: attracts further macrophages to the site of antigen-mediated lymphokine production;

(2) migration inhibition factor: once attracted to the site, the macrophages and other white blood cells are inhibited from leaving;

(3) macrophage activating factor: macrophages are activated into phagocytosis;

(4) skin reactive factor: facilitates movement of macrophages from blood vessels and increases capillary permeability;

(5) interferon: inhibits viral replication;

(6) mitogenic factor and lymphocyte inhibitory factor: both affect the proliferation and suppression of T-lymphocytes;

(7) osteoclast activation factor: stimulates osteoclastic activity (and may be an important factor in bone loss associated with periodontal disease).

Humoral response

When B-lymphocytes are activated by an antigen they differentiate into memory cells and plasma cells. The plasma cells produce antibodies (immunoglobulins), which neutralize the antigen that caused their production. Such antigens are usually bacterial toxins and enzymes. Antibodies will also adhere to bacterial cell walls, often forming a coating on the cell surface. This coating effect enhances the phagocytosis of bacteria. Complement is often activated when antibody combines with an antigen attached to a cell surface (see Chapter 4).

Hypersensitivity (allergy)

Allergy, a term derived from two Greek words (*allos*, other; *ergon*, work or energy), means 'altered reactivity'; it was first introduced by von Pirquet and is concerned with a phenomenon that forms part of the subject of immunology. It is well-known that some unfortunate individuals are unable to eat certain foodstuffs, such as strawberries or lobster, because to do so makes them ill. Similarly, when the majority of people are enjoying summer weather, the pollen in the air causes others to suffer miserably from hay fever. These abnormal responses are examples of allergy and are attributable to an underlying antigen–antibody reaction of a particular type. Likewise, certain patients show abnormal responses to drugs, which are also due to an antigen–antibody reaction, and are examples of drug allergy.

Drug allergy

Incidence

Information about the incidence of drug hypersensitivity reactions is scanty, although it seems clear that whilst minor reactions are fairly frequent, serious or fatal reactions due to drugs are rare.

Antigen

An antigen is a substance that is able to evoke a specific immunological response, namely the production of antibodies. Antigens are substances of large molecular weight (MW), which are usually proteins but sometimes polysaccharides. Simple chemicals with MW of about 1000 or less cannot alone act as antigens. In food allergy, the affected individual reacts immunologically to some macromolecular constituents of the offending food.

Drugs as antigens

The majority of drugs consist of small molecules (MW less than 1000), which alone are unable to act as antigens. When an individual becomes hypersensitive to a drug, for example, acetylsalicylic acid or aspirin, it is believed that the aspirin reacts with a body protein. The aspirin–body protein conjugate is antigenic; substances that combine in this way with proteins and thereby form antigens are known as haptens (or pro-antigens). The hapten, in this case aspirin, confers specificity on the antigen (that is to say the production of antibodies that will react only with aspirin or some closely related chemical compound) whilst the protein confers antigenicity, as indicated below:

$$\text{aspirin} + \text{body protein} \rightarrow \text{aspirin–body protein conjugate.}$$
$$\text{(confers} \qquad \text{(confers antigenicity)}$$
$$\text{specificity)}$$

It appears that readily reversible drug/protein conjugation, which commonly takes place between drugs and plasma proteins, is much less likely to lead to sensitization than is the irreversible conjugation that occurs when covalent bonds link a drug to a protein.

Classification of hypersensitivity reactions

There are various types of hypersensitivity reactions, and these have been classified into types as now described.

Type I—Anaphylactic type reactions

We have seen that initial contact with an antigen causes activation of the various components of the immune system, and that secondary contact with the antigen leads to further boosting of the system (secondary response). However, in some individuals the secondary response may be excessive and lead to gross tissue damage. This excessive response (hypersensitivity) is well-exemplified by the Type I reaction. In Type I reactions, antigen combines with antibody (IgE) on the surface of mast cells, which degranulate bringing about the release of slow reacting substance (SRS), eosinophil chemotactic factor, serotonin, bradykinin, and prostaglandins, as well as histamine. This type of reaction causes systemic anaphylaxis, allergic asthma, rhinitis, and some forms of urticaria, as well as angio-oedema. Some of the chemical mediators of this reaction are now considered:

1. *Histamine* (see Chapter 4), an amine that is normally stored in an inactive form inside cells (in particular, mast cells), is one of the most important pharmacologically active substances released from immunologically damaged cells. It causes contraction of smooth muscle, dilatation and increased permeability of capillaries resulting in a sudden fall of blood pressure, weal formation, and stimulation of glandular secretions, especially those of the oxyntic cells of the stomach, which leads to an outpouring of gastric juice, rich in hydrochloric acid. There are other pharmacologically active substances released under these conditions that may contribute to the overall picture.

2. *Slow reacting substance* is released during anaphylactic shock and produces contractions of human bronchial muscle. It is now believed that this substance is identical to a mixture of the leukotrienes C_4 and D_4 (see Chapter 4).

3. *5-hydroxytryptamine* (5-HT, serotonin), another amine distributed in brain, intestine, and platelets, also stimulates a variety of smooth muscles and nerves.

4. *Bradykinin,* a nonapeptide, also causes a slow contraction of smooth muscle, vasodilatation with increased capillary permeability, and stimulates sensory nerve endings to produce pain.

It seems certain that other pharmacologically active agents are also involved in these reactions, e.g. prostaglandins (see Chapter 4).

The most dramatic and dangerous Type I hypersensitivity reaction is the anaphylactic reaction following the administration of a foreign protein or drug to which the subject has become sensitized. The clinical picture usually starts with flushing and itching of the skin, followed by severe difficulty in breathing due to laryngospasm and bronchospasm, and a severe fall in blood pressure. The pulse is rapid, weak, and may be almost imperceptible. The condition may be rapidly fatal unless immediate steps are taken to administer adrenaline. The earlier the onset of symptoms following administration of the drug allergen, the more severe and dangerous the reaction is likely to be; in fact, dangerous reactions are rare after the first 30 minutes. For this reason a counsel of perfection is to keep all patients who have received injections under observation for at least 30 minutes.

Penicillin is one of the drugs most likely to produce this dangerous reaction, and it has been estimated that in the USA the number of fatal reactions to penicillins may be as high as three hundred per year (Parker 1963). Although anaphylactic reactions are usually associated with injection of a drug or of a foreign protein (skin test, wasp or bee stings), aspirin taken by mouth has produced this reaction in a highly susceptible subject.

Not all reactions are so dramatic; the sort of acute, critical situation outlined above is unlikely to be encountered in ordinary clinical practice. Nevertheless, it must be anticipated and prepared for. What is more likely to occur is a paler version, appearing less dramatically and not causing such concern. The management of the acute and less dramatic event is somewhat different, although the same range of drugs is used, and these should always be available.

Treatment of anaphylactic shock

Treatment of a severe, acute anaphylactic reaction must be immediate, and the necessary drugs should always be at hand, e.g. adrenaline, corticosteroid, and antihistamine (H_1-blocker) (see Fig. 21.4). The patient should be placed horizontally either by appropriate adjustment of the dental chair or by placing them on the floor. If respiratory depression is present, oxygen should be administered or mouth to mouth respiration given.

Then 0.5 ml of 1:1000 (0.1 mg/ml) adrenaline solution should be injected intramuscularly (NEVER INTRAVENOUSLY). This should be followed by hydrocortisone sodium succinate, 100 mg intravenously. Further doses of adrenaline can be given as required at intervals of five minutes until the symptoms begin to subside. The maximum safe does is about 1.5 ml over a period of 15 minutes, a substantial dose that is not without its own risks (see later). Great care must be taken to see that adrenaline is not injected into a blood vessel because it may produce a fatal ventricular fibrillation if given intravenously.

The principal disturbances that occur in anaphylactic shock can be attributed to (a) damage to the endothelial lining of blood vessels with increased permeability and dilatation; and (b) spasm of smooth muscle in the bronchial tree. Adrenaline acts as a physiological antagonist to these effects by virtue of its vasoconstrictor and bronchodilator actions, and so opposes the potentially lethal actions that have been caused by histamine and other pharmacologically active agents explosively released during the anaphylactic reaction.

Although adrenaline is the first line of defence, the intravenous hydrocortisone 100 mg is also important. Glucocorticoids are anti-allergic agents and this dose should ensure that an adequate amount of hydrocortisone (which is normally required and released endogenously under a variety of 'stressful' conditions) is available. Hydrocortisone does not prevent the occurrence of the antigen–antibody reaction, but acts by protecting the cells from the outcome of this

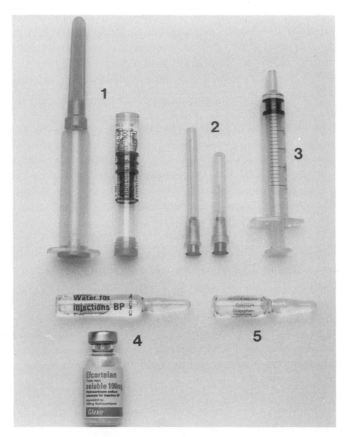

Fig. 21.4. Drugs, needles, and syringes which should always be immediately available for the treatment of drug hypersensitivity reactions.
1. Syringe and cartridge—1 ml, single dose of adrenaline hydrochloride 1:1000 (= 1 mg per ml).
2. Needles for IV, IM, and SC injections; IV = intravenous; IM = intramuscular; SC = subcutaneous.
3. 2 ml syring (removed from sterile wrapper for photograph).
4. Hydrocortisone sodium succinate 100 mg with 2 ml ampoule of water for injection in which it is dissolved.
5. Chlorpheniramine injection BP ('Piriton') 10 mg in 1 ml.

immunological reaction. The reversal of the vasodepressor response by adrenaline is dependent upon the presence of adequate hydrocortisone and if for any reason this is insufficient, for example, in a patient who has an impaired adrenocortical response following prolonged corticosteroid therapy, hydrocortisone is mandatory.

Antihistamines are usually *ineffective* in the treatment of acute anaphylactic shock for at least three reasons. Firstly, histamine is only one of the pharmacologically active agents released; the effects of the other mediators are not antagonized by H_1-blockers. Secondly, these drugs can at best only restore vasomotor tone to its original state and, at worst, may confound the situation due to their own vasodepressor action. Thirdly, in a reaction due to the liberation of histamine, antihistamines work by competing for the same receptor sites. If the receptor sites have already been occupied by histamine, then antihistamines are not likely to be that effective.

If the reaction to the introduction of the drug allergen is not so immediate and acute—the lesser version of what has so far been considered—another line of treatment may be used. In this instance it may suffice to administer hydrocortisone as the first line of defence, followed by an H_1-blocker. The antihistamine could be administered parenterally, e.g. chlorpheniramine 10 to 20 mg IM. Although H_1-blockers are very useful drugs as preventatives, e.g. in hay fever, we have seen that they are not likely to be effective in the very acute reactions where histamine is involved. Nevertheless, in a lesser reaction, antihistamine blockage of receptors may well be useful in preventing further access of histamine. An additional benefit is that antihistamines do have some sedative properties and this is useful as patients are likely to be apprehensive about their condition. Of course, adrenaline should always be available in this lesser situation in case the other remedies prove ineffective.

The question might be asked why adrenaline is not used routinely as it seems to be effective in all situations? The answer resides in the nature of adrenaline itself; it can be a dangerous substance and as such should be reserved for those life-endangering situations when other things won't do.

Other important examples of Type I reactions are asthma, rhinitis, (hay fever), angio-oedema, and urticaria. These are also known as the atopic states, which are usually less severe than acute anaphylaxis.

Asthma

Bronchial asthma has two components, increased tone of the smooth muscle within the bronchial walls (bronchoconstriction), and increased secretion of mucosal glands. In some asthmatic subjects, an attack of bronchoconstriction may be severe and prolonged, enough to cause an emergency almost as grave as that presented by anaphylactic shock. Asthma can be a very dangerous condition; many attacks are relatively mild, but it can kill.

The bronchospasm, as we have seen in Chapter 16, is due to the release of SRS and to a lesser extent, histamine, from sensitized mast cells in the bronchial mucosa. Typically the allergy is due to feathers, animal furs, and dusts. There is a form of asthma that occurs in later life, probably more common in women, where the cause is difficult to pinpoint. Drug-induced asthma is rare except as part of the picture of a systemic anaphylaxis.

Asthma is usually treated with sympathomimetic drugs, which stimulate β_2-receptors with relatively little action on cardiac receptors. Two such drugs are salbutamol and terbutaline; both of these can be used to abate an attack of acute asthma. Salbutamol, for instance, comes in various forms, i.e. as tablets, as a syrup, as an inhaler, as an injection, and as an infusion.

Provided that the airways are adequately open perhaps the best way of delivering the drug is by inhalation direct to the bronchioles. The therapeutic effect is rapid as the drug acts directly on the β_2-receptors of bronchioles and the action persists for four to six hours. Usually it does not adversely affect the cardiovascular system but constant usage can lead to tachycardia and arrhythmias.

Another drug that is useful in abating an acute attack of asthma is aminophylline. It is a xanthine derivative, of which caffeine is another, and is often used by intravenous drip to terminate an acute attack of asthma that has proved resistant to the usual remedies. The place of drugs such as aminophylline in the treatment of asthma has varied from time to time, but there is no doubt that it is effective, although it does have an effect on the heart (e.g. tachycardia), thus providing a cautionary note.

A steroid, beclomethasone, used as an inhalant may be useful in certain situations. For instance, if the attack has not responded to a bronchodilator, a steroid may be required for a short period of treatment to re-establish the activity of the bronchodilator.

Sodium cromoglycate, a drug of relatively recent origin, stabilizes the mast cell and prevents degranulation. This at once implies that it will not terminate an attack of asthma, but may act as a preventative. Sodium cromoglycate is taken prophylactically several times a day and is effective in reducing the frequency and severity of attacks in many asthmatic subjects. It seems to be a very innocuous drug, free of unwanted effects by and large. It is usually prescribed in the form of an inhalant for maintenance therapy.

If an asthmatic attack occurs within the dental surgery, it is likely that the patient will have their remedy with them. It is unlikely that the dental surgeon will have either salbutamol or terbutaline available as part of an emergency kit, although there is no reason why not. However, adrenaline will certainly be part of that kit, and this should abate an attack. The asthma is likely to be relieved by a subcutaneous injection of adrenaline at the rate of about 0.5 ml per minute up to a total dose of 1.0 to 1.5 ml. If the attack is not relieved, an intramuscular injection of a corticosteroid (hydrocortisone 100 mg) should be given, oxygen administered, and medical aid sought. Antihistamines, as we have discussed, are likely to be totally ineffective as the principal mediator in the attack is not histamine.

Angio-oedema

This is a condition where leakage of fluid from vessels causes localized or more general swellings. It is commonly seen in the face, mouth, and upper respiratory tract, and is probably due to the release of histamine from sensitized mast cells. If the condition is very serious, the whole face may become swollen and there may be oedema of the pharynx and larynx to the degree that respiration is jeopardized.

The swelling occurs suddenly and dramatically, and is often preceded by the skin becoming very itchy. Immediate relief of the swelling, especially if the larynx is involved, can be obtained by the subcutaneous injection of adrenaline 1 : 1000 up to a total dose of 1.5 ml. The greatest danger in this condition is respiratory obstruction (more likely to occur in children) and, if the adrenaline fails to bring relief to the oedematous larynx, then it will be necessary to bypass the supralaryngeal airway. The recommended technique is that of laryngotomy, and this is performed by passing a fine-bore tube (cannula), or a large-gauge 'Venflor' between the thyroid and cricoid cartilages (i.e. through the cricothyroid membrane). Oxygen is then introduced through this tube and can be enough to maintain life. An emergency tracheostomy is not advocated; this is an extremely skilled procedure and, in an emergency situation, may prove a problem even to the experienced surgeon, never mind the dental surgeon unskilled in such techniques.

If the attack is less severe, an intramuscular injection of an antihistamine H_1-blocker, for instance chlorpheniramine, 10 to 20 mg, or promethazine, 25 to 50 mg, followed by an adequate oral dosage may suffice.

Rhinitis (hay fever)

This is a localized reaction due to the release of histamine by mast cells in the nasal and conjunctival mucosa. It usually occurs in people sensitized to pollens, and can more or less be regarded as a summer disease. Sneezing, itching and irritation of the nose, running nose, irritation of the eyes, and profuse lachrymation are all symptomatic. Some unfortunate individuals appear to be sensitive to materials of a non-seasonal nature and may show hay fever like symptoms at any time of the year. They are said to suffer from perennial paroxysmal rhinorrhea.

In rhinitis, antihistamines (H_1-blockers) may be the drugs of choice, bringing relief in about 80 per cent of cases. These drugs are effective preventatives rather than curatives. If given continuously to those suffering from hay fever, or at the appropriate season, then by blocking the histamine receptors they will prevent access of the histamine to receptors and may, therefore, prevent the occurrence of an attack.

Hay fever is more troublesome (and it may be very troublesome indeed) than life threatening, and so the problem can be tackled this way, by prevention rather than cure. However, cure can be considered by desensitizing the patient, and this is effective in some cases.

Urticaria

This is due to the release of histamine from sensitized mast cells in the skin. It is commonly known as 'nettle rash', not an inappropriate title, for the lesions are very like those of a nettle sting. In urticaria there is a widespread eruption of firm, pink or white weals, accompanied by intense itching. A very characteristic feature is its evanescent nature, the lesions appearing suddenly and disappearing within hours or even minutes. It is a common manifestation of allergic hypersensitivity to foods and drugs. In many ways, urticaria is an odd phenomenon: it sometimes occurs in people who are apparently not sensitive to any article of diet, but who are under some form of emotional stress; often no apparent cause can be found. The most common things in diet to produce urticaria are the proteins of shellfish, eggs, and milk, and some fruits—especially strawberries.

The best treatment of urticaria may be antihistamines acting as preventatives. Although the response is good, it is perhaps not quite as good as occurs in the subject who has rhinitis.

It will be appreciated that any of these atopic states can be a manifestation of allergy to a drug. All are Type I hypersensitivity reactions and are those most likely to be encountered by the dental practitioner.

Type II—Cytoxic reactions

These are mediated by IgG and IgM antibodies. The antibody combines with an antigen on the cell surface, the complement system is activated, and cell lysis occurs. The principal target cells are those in the circulatory system. An example of a Type II reaction is Rhesus incompatibility in the new-born child where antibodies are produced by a Rhesus negative mother against the Rhesus factor on the red cells of the fetus. The antibodies cross the placenta and cause haemolysis. Another example is sulphonamide-induced granulocytopenia.

Type III—Arthus reactions, serum sickness

These are primarily mediated by IgG; the combination between antigen and antibody forms complexes that subsequently activate complement. The rate of formation of antigen/antibody complexes depends upon the absolute amount of antigen and antibody present and their relative proportions to each other. In the presence of *antibody excess*, antigen/antibody complexes are readily precipitated and are localized at the site of antigen introduction. Complement factors are activated, and the responses occur at the site of antigen introduction. This reaction is known as the Arthus reaction and is characterized by local oedema and necrosis.

When there is *antigen excess*, soluble antigen/antibody complexes are formed that circulate and may become located in vascular endothelium producing a destructive inflammatory response called the serum-sickness syndrome. The clinical symptoms are fever, an urticarial rash, lymphadenopathy, and swelling of the joints (arthralgia). The condition usually lasts for about 6 to 12 days, and subsides on removal of the offending drug (antigen). Sulphonamides, penicillin, streptomycin, as well as other drugs, can cause this syndrome.

The treatment of serum sickness is by steroids; corticosteroids control all its manifestations and are drugs of first choice. Although urticarial and oedematous lesions respond well to H_1-blockers, these drugs often have no effect on the fever or arthralgia.

Type IV—Delayed hypersensitivity reactions

These are mediated by sensitized T-lymphocytes and macrophages, and are therefore cell-mediated reactions (see earlier). When sensitized T-lymphocytes come into contact with antigen, they undergo blast transformation and the resultant cells produce lymphokines (see The Immune System above). Type IV reactions take place one to four days after antigen exposure; examples include contact dermatitis and organ transplant rejection. Many reactions due to drugs, chemicals, and foods belong to this group; for example, contact dermatitis due to procaine, penicillin, or metals such as mercury and nickel. Cell-mediated hypersensitivity is also an important factor in periodontal disease.

These reactions do not respond to sympathomimetic agents or to H_1-blockers; indeed, the blockers, if applied topically, may themselves be responsible for producing delayed hypersensitivity. Corticosteroids are the most useful group of drugs in treatment of this type of reaction, but these cases should be referred to a dermatologist.

It is important for dental surgeons to remember that they themselves are particularly liable to become sensitized to drugs that they handle regularly, such as local anaesthetics and antibiotics, as is discussed in the appropriate Chapters.

Prevention of the unwanted effects due to drugs

A number of points should be noted. firstly, there is an increased incidence of adverse drug reactions in neonates and in the aged. For some unaccountable reason, it seems that women tend to suffer more from adverse drug reactions than do men. Patients with an allergic diathesis are also more prone to adverse reactions, and this may include reactions for which there seems to be no immunological explanation—the asthmatic's reaction to aspirin may be of this nature. Clearly, the presence of renal and hepatic disease can predispose to adverse effects; for example, the metabolism of a drug may be seriously impaired. Certain drugs appear to be especially liable to produce unwanted effects, e.g. anticoagulants, antihypertensive drugs, non-steroidal anti-inflammatory drugs, antimicrobials (penicillin being particularly prone—perhaps because of its extensive usage).

In order to reduce the incidence of adverse reactions, the following points should be considered:

1. Medical history taking must include a drug history; any previous untoward experiences with drugs should be noted and the drug withheld if there is a history of allergy.
2. If a patient is sensitized to one drug, he or she is likely to be sensitized to all drugs in the same group and possibly also to related drugs, e.g. penicillin and the cephalosporins.

3. Has the patient any underlying medical conditions that might predispose to a build-up of the drug and toxicity, e.g. renal failure?
4. Is the drug really necessary at all—is the medical condition self-limiting?
5. Is the safest drug possible being used for the treatment?
6. Is there a possibility of a drug interaction?

In spite of taking into account all factors, no doubt therapeutic misadventures will still occur. However, a proper consideration of all of these factors will minimize the problem.

Oral reactions to drugs

These are relatively rare considering the extent of consumption of drugs. This is a wide subject, and is dealt with fully in specialized textbooks, e.g. *Textbook of Adverse Drug Reactions* (see Further reading). Table 21.1 gives some examples of the sort of reaction that can occur in the mouth, but it makes no pretence to be exhaustive. In general, the mechanisms behind these oral reactions are ill-understood, although in some instances there is an immunlogical basis.

IMMUNOSUPPRESSANTS

When foreign tissue or cells are introduced into the body, the immune system is activated and the foreign material eliminated. Despite the essential protective role of the immune response, the system may need to be suppressed. Immunosuppression is required in organ transplants and in the treatment of certain autoimmune diseases. Cytotoxic drugs and corticosteroids suppress the immune system and these are discussed elsewhere (see Chapters 17 and 18). The main immuno-suppressants used clinically are cyclosporin and azathioprine.

Cyclosporin

Cyclosporin is a relatively new immunosuppressant obtained from the fermentation of two fungi, *Trichoderma polysporum* and *Clindrocarpon lucidum*. Although first developed as an antifungal, and then as an antibiotic, both of these actions proved unsatisfactory. However, it was soon realized that cyclosporin induced a selective type of immunosuppression and the drug is now widely used to prevent the rejection of organ transplants.

Pharmacological properties

Cyclosporin can be administered orally or parenterally. When given orally, the drug is rapidly absorbed from the gastro-intestinal tract and has a half-life of approximately four hours. Cyclosporin is metabolized in the liver, and the metabolites excreted in the bile and elminated in the faeces.

Table 21.1. Unwanted effects of drugs in the orofacial region

Disorder	Drug(s) involved
Xerostomia	Ganglion blockers; atropine and atropine-like antispasmodics, e.g. propantheline bromide; antidepressants—tricyclic and tetracyclic; antiparkinsonian drugs, e.g. benzhexol, biperiden, benztropine, and orphenadrine; antihistamine drugs, H_1-blockers; phenothiazines; clonidine
Disturbances of taste:	
(i) partial or total loss of taste	Penicillamine; clofibrate; carbimazole; lithium carbonate; lincomycin; phenindione; prothionamide; griseofulvin.
(ii) metallic taste	Metronidazole; biguanide antidiabetic drugs, e.g. metformin
Halitosis	Isorbide dinitrate (sublingually); disulfiram
Pain and swelling of the salivary glands	Phenylbutazone and oxyphenbutazone; iodides; bretylium; guanethidine; bethanidine; methyldopa; clonidine; nitrofurantoin; chlorhexidine
Cervical lymphadenopathy	Phenytoin and primidone
Erythema multiforme	Barbiturates; carbamazepine; chlorpropamide; clindamycin; ethambutol; meprobamate; minoxidil;penicillin; phenylbutazone; phenytoin; sulphonamides (long-acting); sulindac; salicylates; rifampicin
Lupus erythematosus (systemic)—SLE	A wide variety of drugs has been implicated in the production of SLE. The oral mucosa is involved in about 25 per cent of patients. Drugs involved range from antihypertensives to anti-infective agents, e.g. penicillin, tetracycline.
Lichenoid eruptions	Chlorpropamide; indomethacin; methyldopa; a-adrenoceptor blocking drugs, e.g. labetalol; chloroquine; mepacrine; gold salts; quinine; quinidine; streptomycin; sodium aminosalicylate
Gingival hyperplasia and hypertrophy	Phenytoin; cyclosporin; oral contraceptives; nifedipine
Discolouration of the oral mucosa and teeth	
(i) mucosal tissues	Lead poisoning; chloroquine; phenothiazines; oral contraceptives; chlorhexidine
(ii) teeth	Tetracyclines; stannous fluoride toothpastes; chlorhexidine
Oral ulcerations	
(i) a number of chemicals can cause 'burns' of the oral mucosa if injudiciously applied	e.g. trichloracetic acid in the treatment of pericoronitis
(ii) Drugs used for other purposes may cause local irritation of the mouth	Aspirin; potassium; isoprenaline (used as sublingual tablets); pancreatin powder or tablets; emepromium bromide; gentian violet; cocaine
(iii) Oral ulceration, either primary or secondary to leucopenia	Antineoplastic agents, such as methotrexate, fluorouracil, actinomycin D, doxorubicin and bleomycin
(iv) Oral ulceration with neutropenia	Naproxen
Oral infections induced or aggravated by drugs	Corticosteroids: given in non-physiological amounts over a long period, these carry an increased risk of bacterial, fungal, or viral infections.

Table 21.1. Unwanted effects of drugs in the orofacial region

Disorder	Drug(s) involved
	Antibiotics: particularly broad-spectrum types, can alter the normal bacterial flora of the mouth, throat and gut, so that resistant organisms may proliferate; overgrowth of *C. albicans* may result, causing oral candidiasis.
	Antimetabolites: topical fluorouracil therapy has been associated with the activation of herpes labialis (and the development of telangiectasia).
	Immunosuppressive drugs: (e.g. azathioprine and prednisone in renal transplants)—bacterial or fungal infections; severe herpes simplex infection has been observed.
	Oral contraceptives: their use has been associated with 'dry socket' after tooth extraction.
Extrapyramidal syndromes	
(i) acute dyskinesia (involuntary movements of the tongue, trismus, and grimacing—together with spontaneous dislocations of the TMJ)	Phenothiazines; butyrophenones; metoclopramide; tricyclic antidepressants; phenytoin; carbamazepine; lithium
(ii) tardive dyskinesia	As above

Pharmacodynamics

An important component of the immune response is the interaction between macrophages and lymphocytes. As a result of this interaction, macrophages produce a chemical mediator called interleukin I, which stimulates T-helper cells. Once stimulated, the T-helper cell produces interleukin II, another chemical transmitter, which activates other uncommitted T-lymphocytes to differentiate into helper, suppressor or killer cells.

Cyclosporin is a selective immunosuppressant, affecting the T-cell or cell-mediated response with little or no effect on the B-cell or humoral response. The action on the cell-mediated system is as follows. Cyclosporin inhibits the priming or 'activation' of macrophages and therefore interferes with the synthesis of interleukin I. Following this action on the macrophage, cyclosporin acts on the T-helper cell by preventing the production of interleukin II. Finally, the drug inhibits the formation of interleukin II receptors on undifferentiated T-cells, which blocks the production of more helper, suppressor, and killer T-cells. It also appears that cyclosporin affects helper cells more than suppressor cells, resulting in a net imbalance in favour of suppressor action.

Unwanted effects

These include nephrotoxicity, hepatotoxicity, mild anaemia, tremors, transient paraesthesia, and excessive hair growth (hirsutism). Of particular interest to the dental surgeon is the action of the drug on the oral structures, causing gingival hyperplasia and transient perioral hyperaesthesia.

Gingival hyperplasia occurs in approximately one-third of those taking cyclosporin. It is more frequent in children than adults, and begins in the interdental papilla. The labial gingiva of the anterior teeth are more commonly affected than the posterior teeth. Local irritants, such as plaque, calculus, faulty restorations, prosthetic and orthodontic appliances, may increase the severity of the hyperplasia.

Many patients experience a perioral tingling sensation when they first start cyclosporin therapy. The sensation usually disappears within a few days; it may be dose-related.

Uses

Cyclosporin is mainly used to prevent rejection of organ transplants, such as kidney, heart, and liver. It has also been used in the treatment of insulin-dependent diabetes, cirrhosis, psoriasis, and rheumatoid arthritis.

Azathioprine

This is a purine derivative with selective immunosuppressant activity against the cell-mediated system. The drug appears to increase T-cell suppressor activity and reduce T-cell helper activity. Azathioprine can be given orally or parenterally.

Unwanted effects

There are many of these, and because of these risks the use of this drug should be balanced against the severity of the patient's condition and the expected clinical effect. The most serious unwanted effect of azathioprine therapy is depression of bone marrow function causing a leucopenia and thrombocytopenia. Routine haematological screening is required for all patients taking azathioprine. Other unwanted effects include gastro-intestinal intolerance, allergic reaction, and skin rashes.

Uses

Azathioprine is mainly used to prevent rejection of organ transplants. The drug is also used as an alternative to corticosteroids in pemphigus, systemic lupus erythematosis, severe rheumatoid arthritis, and thrombocytopenic purpura.

REFERENCES

Foldes, F. F., Swerdlow, M., Lipschitz, E., VanHees, G. R., and Shanor, S. P. (1956). Comparison of the respiratory effects of suxamethonium and suxamethonium in man. *Anaesthesiology*, **17**, 559–68.

Kalow, W., and Gunn, D. R. (1957). The relation between dose of succinylcholine and duration of apnoea in man. *Journal of Pharmacology and Experimental Therapeutics*, **120**, 203–14.

Parker, C. W. (1963). Penicillin allergy. (Editorial). *American Journal of Medicine*, **34**, 747–51.

Rawlins, M. D. and Thompson, J. W. (1985). Mechanisms of adverse drug reactions. In *Textbook of adverse drug reactions*, (3 edn), (ed. D. M. Davies). Oxford University Press.

Rosenheim, M. L. and Moulton, R. L. (ed) (1958). *Sensitivity reactions to drugs*. Blackwell, Oxford.

FURTHER READING

Daley, T. D. and Wysocki, G. P. (1984). Cyclosporin therapy: its significance to the periodontist. *Journal of Periodontology*, **55**, 701–11.

Roitt, I. M. and Lehner, T. (1983). Immunology and oral disease, (2nd edn,). Blackwell, Oxford.

Walton, J. G. and Seymour, R. A. (1985). Dental disorders. In *Textbook of adverse drug reactions*. (3rd edn), (ed. D. M. Davies). Oxford University Press.

22

Drug interactions

INTRODUCTION

It is sometimes necessary to give more than one drug at the same time, and when this is so their effects may be exerted independently or they may interact. It must be made clear at the outset that not all drug interactions are therapeutically undesirable. Thus some interactions may be deliberately planned in order to produce some useful effect that cannot be achieved by means of a single drug; for example, the antimicrobial combination co-trimoxazole (trimethoprim + sulpha-methoxazole), or the combined oral contraceptive (oestrogen + progestogen). On the other hand, the interaction may be undesirable and potentially dangerous (Macgregor 1965; British National Formulary, 1988); one of the earliest and best known examples is that between ethyl alcohol and barbiturates, which can produce a profound depression of the CNS. Other examples are aspirin + warfarin, or a monoamine oxidase inhibitor (MAOI) + cheese (Blackwell *et al.* 1967). The result of the interaction may be the potentiation or antagonism of one drug by another (Type A in the classification of Unwanted effects; Chapter 21), or it may be the production of some different effect that is not readily predictable (Type B in the same classification). Whatever the mechanism, all drug interactions should be reported to the Committee on Safety in Medicines using the special yellow pre-paid postcards that are made available for the report of adverse drug reactions. Clearly the dental surgeon may, in the absence of sufficient knowledge about drug interactions, prescribe a drug to a patient who is already taking another one for some medical condition, and thereby unwittingly precipitate a drug interaction.

INCIDENCE AND IMPORTANCE OF DRUG INTERACTIONS

In theory, many such interactions are possible but in practice only a relatively small number are of clinical importance. An accurate estimate of their incidence amongst out-patients is not available but, for hospital in-patients, it has been estimated to be in the range 0.5–2 per cent. This suggests that adverse drug interactions represent a minor contribution to adverse drug reactions as a whole, and there is little doubt that in the past the potential incidence of drug interactions has been exaggerated. However, for certain drugs the potential for reaction is much higher than it is for others and it is these that must be avoided. For example, in a study of 277 patients taking oral anticoagulants of whom 94 were receiving other drugs with which the anticoagulants might have interacted (33.9 per cent of the total), clinically significant interactions were considered to have developed in 6 patients. This represents an incidence of 6.4 per cent in those taking drug combinations (2.2 per cent in all patients; Williams *et al.* 1976).

Drug interactions of clinical importance

These are likely to be due to two main reasons:

1. *The drug has a steep dose–response curve.* Under these conditions a relatively small quantitative change in the concentration of drug at the target site (receptor, enzyme), or in the tissue, leads to substantial changes in the therapeutic or adverse effect—for example: digoxin, lithium.

2. *The drug has a major effect on a vital process.* Drugs that alter such vital processes as blood pressure, blood coagulation, or control of breathing fall into this category. It will be appreciated that a drug that interacts with another given in a dose carefully determined to produce a particular effect, could produce potentially lethal effects.

In practice, the chief sources of serious clinical interactions are drawn from a short list of drugs that fall into the following classes (Dollery and Brodie, 1980):

(1) oral anticoagulants (coumarins);

(2) oral contraceptives (oestrogen and progestogen);

(3) oral hypoglycaemics (tolbutamide, chlorpropamide, glibenclamide);

(4) cardiovascular: (a) cardiac glycosides, (b) anti-arrhythmics, (c) antihypertensive (hypotensive);

(5) anticonvulsants (phenytoin, phenobarbitone, primidone, carbamazepine);

(6) CNS drugs;

(7) aminoglycoside antibiotics (amikacin, gentamicin, kanamycin, neomycin, netilmicin, streptomycin, and tobramycin);

(8) cytotoxics and immunosuppressants.

CLASSIFICATION OF DRUG INTERACTIONS

Such interactions may be classified into three groups, namely pharmaceutical, pharmacokinetic, and pharmacodynamic.

Pharmaceutical interactions

These are due to the formulation or mixing of chemically incompatible substances. Thus pharmaceutical interactions are most likely to occur when drugs interact in the same infusion solution, e.g. ampicillin with glucose; or when one drug interacts with the solution (e.g. amphotericin is unstable in dextrose–saline solution). Details about the addition of medication to infusion fluids are included in the *British National Formulary* (BNF; see Appendix 2, 1988). This form of interaction is unlikely to occur in dental practice because of the nature of the drugs and the routes of administration normally used. Nevertheless, the dental practitioner should be aware of and alert to this form of interaction.

Pharmacokinetic interactions

These are due to altered absorption, distribution (protein binding), metabolism, or excretion of one drug by another.

Suitable examples will now be given under these headings; Table 22.1 (below) lists other interactions.

Absorption

An example of adverse interactions related to increased absorption are those between MAOIs and sympathomimetic amines (see Chapter 14). Here the drug restricts the action of an intestinal enzyme (monoamine oxidase), allowing the absorption of abnormal quantities of amines, which may have serious effects.

By contrast, an important and useful way in which one drug may decrease the absorption of another is the addition of a vasoconstrictor, usually adrenaline, to solutions of local anaesthetics. This serves a dual purpose: by delaying absorption, it prolongs the duration of anaesthesia; and simultaneously it reduces the rate of increase of the plasma concentration of local anaesthetic and thereby lessens the likelihood of systemic effects.

The absorption of tetracyclines may be reduced as a consequence of interacting chemically with antacids that contain divalent and trivalent cations (e.g. Ca, Al, Mg), dairy products (e.g. milk), oral iron preparations, sucralfate, and zinc sulphate. These combinations of drugs should therefore be avoided otherwise the therapeutic effect of tetracyclines will be reduced.

Distribution

In the context of drug interactions, the factor most likely to affect the distribution of a drug in the body is an alteration in the extent to which it is bound to protein (Brodie, 1964). Thus the displacement of drug X from some of its binding sites on plasma protein by drug Y (which has a stronger affinity) leads to an elevation of the plasma concentration of drug X; and if drug Y is withdrawn the reverse will occur. However, it is important to realize that for a *significant* alteration of the free

1st Agent Prescribed as part of MEDICAL treatment		2nd Agent, which might be prescribed as part of DENTAL (or other) treatment	Clinical result of interaction between 1st and 2nd agent	Course of action and comments	Possible mechanism of interaction
Group	Drug				
1. Gastro-intestinal	Metoclopramide	Antimuscarinic (anticholinergic) e.g. atropine; Opioid (opiate) e.g. morphine	Antagonism—reduced effect of both drugs	Avoid combination	Physiological antagonism
	Antacids containing salts of calcium (Ca), magnesium (Mg), aluminium (Al) Oral iron (Fe)	Tetracyclines	Therapeutic failure (tetracyclines used for treating rapid forms of periodontal destruction see Chapter 11)	Stop antacids that contain Ca, Mg, Al, and oral Fe during therapy with tetracyclines	Chelation
2. Cardiovascular: β-adrenoceptor blocking drugs	Acebutalol Atenolol Metoprolol Nadolol Oxprenolol Penbutolol Pindolol Propranolol Sotalol Timolol	Sympathomimetic amines, e.g. adrenaline phenylephrine (amphetamines), including cold remedies	Severe hypertension, particularly with non-selective β-blockers. Rarely, severe hypertension	Hypertensive crisis should be treated with an α-adrenergic receptor blocking drug (Elis et al. 1967) e.g. phentolamine (Rogitine) 5 mg IV or im, repeated if necessary.	In the presence of β-blockers, the α-agonist actions of the sympathomimetic are exerted unopposed, especially with vasopressor effect.
Antihypertensive drugs	Vasodilators e.g. hydralazine Centrally acting, e.g. methyldopa Adrenergic neurone blockers e.g. bethanidine α-adrenoceptor blockers, e.g. prazosin. Angiotensin-converting enzyme inhibitors e.g. captopril	Hypnotics, sedatives e.g. benzodiazepines, H_1-blockers with sedative property	Potentiates antihypertensive effect	Use combination with care	Hypnotics and sedatives depress vasomotor centre
Anticoagulants	Heparin	Aspirin Compound analgesics containing aspirin	Potentiation of anticoagulant	Avoid combination	Reduced aggregation of platelets. Reduced prothrombin production (chronic use)

Table 22.1. Some drug interactions with which the dental practitioner may be concerned

1st Agent Prescribed as part of MEDICAL treatment		2nd Agent, which might be prescribed as part of DENTAL (or other) treatment	Clinical result of interaction between 1st and 2nd agent	Course of action and comments	Possible mechanism of interaction
Group	**Drug**				
Anticoagulants	Warfarin	Aspirin (D and I) Possibly some other NSAIDs (but ibuprofen and naproxen usually safe) Co-trimoxazole (I) Erythromycin (I) Ketoconazole (I) Metronidazole (I) Paracetamol (regular treatment or high doses)	Potentiation of anticoagulant	Avoid combination: if not possible adjust dose of warfarin appropriately	D = displacement from binding sites, but not clinically significant I = inhibition of warfarin metabolism
3. CNS hypnotics and sedatives	Benzodiazepines: alprazolam chlordiazepoxide clobazam diazepam nitrazepam triazolam	Alcohol Antihistamines (H$_1$-blockers) Narcotic analgesics	Potentiation of hypnotic/sedative effect of benzodiazepine	Avoid combination or adjust dose of 1st or 2nd agent	Synergism of two drugs with central depressant actions
Antidepressants monoamine oxidase inhibitors (MAOIs)	Phenelzine Iproniazid Isocarboxazid Tranylcypromine Pargyline (antihypertensive only)	Indirectly (or mixed) acting sympathomimetic amines: ephedrine phenylephrine Amine-containing foods: cheese pickled herrings Marmite yoghurt Bovril broad beans strong wines and beers	Acute hypertensive crisis with stimulation of CNS Hypertension with headache. Risk of cerebral haemorrhage	Hypertensive crisis should be treated with an α-adrenergic receptor blocking agent, e.g. phentolamine 5 mg IV or IM repeated if necessary. Patients on MAOI must be WARNED not to take these foods	Inhibition of MAO by MAOIs interferes with the biotransformation of those amines which are normally substrates for this enzyme. MAOIs also inhibit other enzyme systems e.g. pethidine demethylase, and this may be responsible for the serious interaction which can occur when a narcotic analgesic such as pethidine is given to a patient taking an MAOI. Many of the other interactions between MAOIs and other drugs

Category	Drug	Interacting drug	Effect	Action	Mechanism
		pethidine morphine codeine barbiturates general anaesthetics	hypotension/ hypertension, CNS stimulation.	repeated as necessary; symptomatic treatment including the use of α-adrenergic receptor blockers for hypertension where necessary; medical aid should be sought immediately. IMPORTANT: These combinations of drugs should not be used. Patients who are receiving MAOIs should *wear a locket* indicating that they are taking these drugs, as well as carrying written evidence from the doctor who prescribed the drug, warning against these dangers. In the event of one of these emergencies hospital treatment should be sought immediately.	
Tricyclic and related compounds	Amitriptyline Butriptyline Clomipramine Desipramine Dothiepin Iprindole Maprotiline Mianserin Nortriptyline Protriptyline Trazodone Trimipramine Viloxazine	Adrenaline noradrenaline (alone or with local anaesthetics)	Hypertension; but it is important to note that the small amount of adrenaline added to a solution of local anaesthetic is usually safe for administration to a patient taking tricyclic antidepressant.	If a hypertensive attack occurs it should be treated with an α-adrenergic receptor blocking agent, e.g. phentolamine 5 mg IV or IM repeated if necessary.	Tricyclic compounds interfere with uptake of adrenaline and noradrenaline (both directly acting sympathomimetic amines) into adrenergic nerve endings.
Anti-epileptics	Phenytoin	Barbiturates (also alcohol, carbamazepine)	Reduced phenytoin effect	Avoid combination or adjust dosage appropriately.	Increased metabolism of phenytoin due to induction of DMES (see text).
Anaesthesia	General anaesthetics	Adrenaline	Arrhythmias with halothane, cyclopropane, trichlorethylene	Avoid combination	Some general anaesthetics sensitize the myocardium to the arrhythmogenic action of adrenaline
4. Infections	Griseofulvin	Barbiturates	Reduced therapeutic effect of griseofulvin	Adjust dose of either drug appropriately	Accelerated inactivation of griseofulvin

Table 22.1. Some drug interactions with which the dental practitioner may be concerned

1st Agent Prescribed as part of MEDICAL treatment		2nd Agent, which might be prescribed as part of DENTAL (or other) treatment	Clinical result of interaction between 1st and 2nd agent	Course of action and comments	Possible mechanism of interaction
Group	**Drug**				
5. Miscellaneous	Ethyl alcohol (ethanol) (most likely to be taken for social reasons)	Barbiturates Benzodiazepines Phenothiazines Antihistamines (H_1-blockers)	Enhanced depression of CNS	Patient must be warned of the risk of these interactions	Additive or synergistic effects due to combination of actions of two centrally depressant drugs
		Metronidazole	May produce unpleasant disulfiram-like effects e.g. flushing, nausea, and epigastric discomfort	Advise patient to avoid use of alcohol during treatment with metronidazole.	Inhibits hepatic metabolism of ethanol causing disulfiram-like ('Antabuse') effects
	Oral contraceptives	Rifampicin, possibly other broad-spectrum antibiotics	Failure of contraception.	Where there may be special concern, alternative methods of contraception should be instituted.	Although there are anecdotal reports of this interaction, convincing evidence is lacking; patient compliance failure is a more likely explanation.

plasma concentration to take place, two conditions must obtain. First, the drug to be displaced (drug X) must be highly bound to plasma protein, e.g. 99 per cent, so that a small change in binding, for example 1 per cent, will result in a doubling of its free plasma concentration (from 1 per cent to 2 per cent of the total). Second, the major part of the total dose of drug X must be distributed in plasma; if the converse is true, then extensive displacement from the plasma binding sites would produce little clinical effect. Three groups of drugs that fulfil these criteria are (i) oral anticoagulants, e.g. warfarin (bound 99 per cent volume of distribution (Vd 9 l)); (ii) oral hypoglycaemics e.g. tolbutamide (bound 96 per cent, Vd 10 l); and (iii) the antiepileptic, phenytoin (bound 90 per cent, Vd 35 l); (Aronson and Grahame-Smith 1981).

The clinical dangers of drug interactions due to displacement from protein-binding sites have turned out to be much less than originally anticipated. This is because for those drugs likely to be involved, the total clearance rate is proportional to the fraction of unbound drug in the plasma. As a consequence, the increase in plasma concentration that follows from binding displacement is offset by a compensatory increase in clearance, so that the plasma *concentration* remains virtually unchanged once the new steady-state has been reached. Nevertheless, until such time as this state has been reached, there will be an increase in the amount of free (i.e. pharmacologically active) drug in the plasma, and this will produce an effect that may result in a potentially adverse reaction; for example, haemorrhage due to excessive anticoagulation (coumarins). In practice this mechanism occurs rarely and other mechanisms are involved, usually inhibition of drug metabolizing enzymes (DMEs; see below and Chapter 1).

Metabolism (biotransformation)

The intensity and duration of effect of many drugs depend largely upon their rate of biotransformation, chiefly in the liver, to less active or inactive metabolites (Gillette, 1967). Therefore, if the rate of metabolism of one drug is altered by another drug, this will substantially modify the effect of the first drug.

Stimulation (induction) of drug-metabolizing enzymes (DMEs)

Certain drugs such as phenobarbitone, phenytoin, primidone, carbamazepine, rifampicin, griseofulvin, and ethanol (ethyl alcohol)—chronic use, as well as cigarette smoking, are powerful inducers of DMEs with the result that the half-life ($T_{0.5}$) of some drugs may be reduced substantially. The enzyme induction develops over several weeks and takes about the same time to disappear after the inducing agent has been withdrawn. Drugs with a metabolism likely to be altered by enzyme inducers are anticoagulants and oral contraceptives. Thus the metabolism of warfarin may be increased, so leading to a diminished anticoagulant effect and the need for an increased dosage. If the inducer is then withdrawn, the subsequent reduced metabolism will lead to an increased effect with possible haemorrhagic complications.

A potentially important interaction belonging to this group is that between oral contraceptive steroids and antibiotics (Dossetor, 1975). Over the past decade there have been sporadic reports of women who have become pregnant whilst taking an antibiotic at the same time as an oral contraceptive steroid. As a consequence, the impression has gained ground that oral contraceptive steroids may fail in the presence of antibiotics. This suggestion received support from the results of animal studies, where there is clear evidence of an entero-hepatic circulation of steroids that can be modulated by broad-spectrum antibiotics. Antibiotics suppress the gut microflora, which normally deconjugate (and therefore reactivate) steroids previously inactivated by conjugation in the liver. However, human studies suggest that in most women entero-hepatic recirculation of contraceptive steroids plays only a minor metabolic role and is therefore most unlikely to account for contraceptive failure in the presence of broad-spectrum antibiotics (Orme and Back 1986). A much more likely explanation is failure of compliance. When there is special concern about the possible effect of an antibiotic on a particular patient already taking contraceptive steroids, then she should be given either co-trimoxazole (because this appears least likely to cause an interaction problem), or she should be advised to use an alternative method of contraception.

Inhibition of drug-metabolizing enzymes (DMEs)

A number of drugs may inhibit DMEs; these include metronidazole, chloramphenicol, phenylbutazone, cimetidine, ethanol (acute intoxication), isoniazid, and MAOIs. The commonest drugs to be affected through this inhibition are phenytoin and anticoagulants; thus the effects of phenytoin are increased in the presence of isoniazid (in slow acetylators) or chloramphenicol.

Unfortunately, despite their name, MAOIs are very unspecific and may also decrease the rate of biotransformation of barbiturates, phenothiazines, and alcohol. It has also been shown in animals that the metabolism of pethidine (and other opioids) is slowed by MAOIs due to inhibition of pethidine demethylase (Clark 1967), the enzyme that demethylates pethidine to norpethidine. The potentially lethal interaction between pethidine and MAOIs that may occur in man could be due to a similar mechanism (Clark and Thompson 1972).

General anaesthetic agents should not be given to any patient receiving an MAOI. If, for the purposes of dental treatment, a general anaesthetic is necessary, the MAOI should be withdrawn, but only after consultation with the patient's medical adviser, and the anaesthetic should not be given until a period of three weeks has elapsed. If it is absolutely essential to give the general anaesthetic in the presence of an MAOI, then the patient must be admitted to hospital and the psychiatrist responsible must, for that patient, vouch that the risk of stopping the MAOI is greater than the risk of a possible interaction.

Excretion

The rate of excretion of drugs that are weak electrolytes can be modified by altering the pH of the urine (see Chapter 1). Thus, the rate of excretion of weak acids, such as salicylates, can be expedited by making the urine alkaline. This increases the proportion of salicylate molecules present in the ionized form; these are more water-soluble (less fat-soluble) than the corresponding un-ionized molecules, which would be reabsorbed by the tubules. This effect is exploited in the treatment of aspirin poisoning, when it is necessary to remove the drug from the body as quickly as possible. Conversely, the excretion of a weak base, such as pethidine, can be hastened by making the urine acid so that once again the drug will be present in the urine predominantly in the ionized and water-soluble form.

The diuretics, frusemide and ethacrynic acid, decrease excretion of gentamicin thus enhancing its potential for ototoxicity and nephrotoxicity. Phenylbutazone reduces the renal clearance of chlorpropamide so increasing the risk of hypoglycaemia. The anti-arrhythmic agent, quinidine, reduces the excretion of digoxin by the kidney and, as it may double the plasma concentration (see Chapter 1), it can precipitate digoxin toxicity.

An alternative form of interaction occurs when two drugs compete for the same transport system in the kidney. It is by this mechanism that probenecid reduces the rate of excretion of the penicillins.

Pharmacodynamic interactions

This type of drug interaction takes place either directly or indirectly at the site of the action of the drug, in other words, in the vicinity of the receptor.

The most common *direct* ones are those that act either on the central or autonomic nervous systems. Thus, many drugs that depress the CNS will produce synergistic effects when given together. A well-known, although not always heeded example, is the danger of drinking ethyl alcohol (ethanol) in the presence of benzodiazepines or antipsychotic drugs. Similarly, antihypertensive drugs may interact in either a useful way (hydralazine and propranolol), or in a potentially harmful way (verapamil and propranolol). There are many other examples; here are some that may have relevance to the dental practitioner:

Potentially hazardous combination	Effect
Frusemide (ethacrynic acid) with gentamicin	Ototoxicity
Competitive neuromuscular with aminoglycoside blockers or antibiotic or quinidine	Increased muscle re- laxation
warfarin with tetracyclines	Increased anticoagu- lant effect

N.B. The interaction warfarin–tetracycline may be due to altered affinity of Vitamin K for clotting factor receptors. Except when there is a dietary deficiency of Vitamin K, antibiotics of the penicillin, cephalosporin, and aminoglycoside groups are safe to use in a patient already taking warfarin (Aronson and Grahame-Smith 1981).

Indirect pharmacodynamic interactions are of two types. In the first, the normal action of a drug is altered as a result of change in fluid or electrolyte balance induced by the interacting drug. An important example (although one unlikely to be of relevance to the dental practitioner) is the potentiation of effect of cardiac glycosides or the antagonism of the anti-arrhythmic drugs, quinidine or lignocaine, as a result of hypokalaemia induced by diuretics.

The second type is of much greater relevance to the dental practitioner. This is the interaction between oral anticoagulants and drugs that either cause gastro-intestinal erosion or ulceration (aspirin and other NSAIDs; corticosteroids), or decrease the aggregation of platelets (aspirin, indomethacin, phenylbutazone). Under these circumstances the tendency to bleed will be increased and, if it occurs, haemostasis may be impaired.

PREDICTION OF DRUG INTERACTIONS

When drugs are being prescribed together, or when an additional drug is prescribed to those already being taken, there are several pointers that should help the prescriber be on the alert to the possibility of a drug interaction (Dollery and Brodie 1980). These are as follows:

1. Does the drug belong to the short list (see p. 433) of those more likely to be involved in drug interactions?
2. Is the drug metabolized in the liver? It is not possible to predict with accuracy the way in which the body will metabolize a particular drug. However, there is a high correlation between the lipid solubility of a drug and its ability to (i) cross the blood–brain barrier and hence have CNS actions, and (ii) enter the hepatocytes and so be metabolized by the liver. The corollary of this is that drugs which gain access to the CNS will be metabolized in the liver, an example being chlorpromazine.
3. Is it highly protein bound? Warfarin is 98 to 99 per cent bound (see Chapter 1) and so can be displaced from its binding site on the plasma proteins by another drug that binds to protein more avidly, for example aspirin.
4. Is it an enzyme inducer? The barbiturates and cimetidine are enzyme inducers; they induce DME systems (see earlier) and hence reduce the half-life of a drug so affected, with potentially serious results.
5. Is it an enzyme inhibitor? The MAOIs are powerful inhibitors of other enzyme systems, including DMEs, and may as a result potentiate the effects of many other drugs (see Chapter 1).
6. Is it excreted unchanged in the urine? Digoxin is excreted unchanged in the urine, so that any drug with the capacity to alter the renal clearance of digoxin can produce potentially dangerous effects.

CONCLUSIONS

It can be seen that drug interactions form a large, heterogeneous, and potentially hazardous group of problems, and it is most important for the dental practitioner to be aware of their existence. Through ignorance of this subject, a dental practitioner may prescribe a drug which interacts with one already being taken by the patient. The list of interactions is growing steadily, and dental practitioners must be prepared to keep themselves informed of them. Table 22.1 has been prepared as a guide to these, and includes those interactions that the dental practitioner is most likely to meet, although it must be pointed out that this Table is not exhaustive. The Table indicates the clinical outcome, the course of action and, wherever possible, the probable mechanism of action for each example.

REFERENCES

Aronson, J. K. and Grahame-Smith, D. G. (1981). Clinical pharmacology: adverse drug interactions. *British Medical Journal*, **282**, 288–91.

Blackwell, B., Marley, E., Price, J., and Taylor, D. (1967). Hypertensive interactions between monoamine oxidase inhibitors and foodstuffs. *British Journal of Psychiatry*, **113**, 349–65.

British National Formulary No. 15 (1988). British Medical Association and The Pharmaceutical Society of Great Britain.

Brodie, B. B. (1964). *Physico-chemical factors in drug absorption* In *absorption and distribution of drugs*, (ed. T. B. Binns). Livingstone, Edinburgh.

Clark, B. (1967). The *in vitro* inhibition of the N-demethylation of pethidine by phenelzine (phenylhydrazine). *Biochemical Pharmacology*, **16**, 2369.

Clark, B. and Thompson, J. W. (1972). Analysis of the inhibition of pethidine N-demethylation by monoamine oxidase inhibitors and some other drugs with special reference to drug interactions in man. *British Journal of Pharmacology*, **44**, 89–99.

Dollery, C. T. and Brodie, M. J. (1980). Drug interactions. *Journal of the Royal College of Physicians, London*, 14, 190–6.

Dossetor, J. (1975). Drug interactions with oral contraceptives. *British Medical Journal*, 467–8.

Elis, J., Laurence, D. R., Mattie, H., and Prichard, B. N. (1967). Modification by monoamine oxidase inhibitors of the effect of some sympathomimetics on blood pressure. *British Medical Journal*, **2**, 75.

Gillette, J. R. (1967). Individually different responses to drugs according to age, sex and functional or pathological state. In *Drug responses in man* (ed. G. Wolstenholme and R. Porter). Churchill, London.

MacGregor, A. G. (1965). Clinical effects of interaction between drugs. Review of points at which drugs can interact. *Proceedings of the Royal Society of Medicine*, **58**, 943–6.

Orme, M. L'E. and Back, D. J. (1986). Drug interactions between oral contraceptive steroids and antibiotics. *British Dental Journal*, **160**, 169–70.

Williams, J. R. B., Griffin, J. P., and Parkins, A. (1976). Effect of concomitantly administered drugs on the control of long term anticoagulant therapy. *Quarterly Journal of Medicine*, **45**, 63–73.

23

Non-medical use of drugs: alcohol and alcoholism

INTRODUCTION

The dental surgeon is most unlikely to be called upon to treat drug dependence or to prescribe drugs in such quantities as would result in dependence. However, the incidence of drug abuse is likely to increase, and dental practitioners are going to encounter this problem amongst their patients. It is therefore important that they be familiar with the problems of common drug abuse. Drug abusers may suffer hallucinations from LSD or withdrawal symptoms from opioids; both problems can occur when abusers attend the dental surgery, and it is thus important that the dental surgeon should recognize their signs and symptoms.

This Chapter defines the non-medical use of drugs (including alcohol), and gives a brief outline of the widely abused drugs and the clinical picture of abuse.

DEFINITIONS

Drug abusage

This is defined as:

the consumption of a drug where there is is no medical indication, or;

the consumption of a drug in therapeutically excessive amounts without medical supervision.

Consequences of drug abusage

1. The effects on the individual, i.e. the action of the drug on the physiological and psychological state of the individual.
2. The effects on society, i.e. the interplay between environmental, sociological, and economic conditions in relation to drugs of dependence.

Drug dependence

Drug dependence is a state of psychic or physical dependence, or both, on a drug, arising in a person following administration of that drug on a periodic of continuous basis. (WHO Expert Committee of Addiction-producing Drugs 1964)

Psychic dependence

In this situation, there is a feeling of satisfaction and a psychic drive that require periodic or continuous administration of the drug to produce pleasure or to avoid discomfort. (WHO 1965)

Physical dependence

Physical dependence is an adaptive state that manifests itself by intensive physical disturbances when the administration of the drug is suspended or when its action is affected by the administration of a specific antagonist. (WHO 1965).

Forces that come into play in drug dependence (Paton 1968)

(1) production of a primary pleasurable reward;

(2) social and environmental factors;

(3) withdrawal or abstinence effects;

(4) drug tolerance.

Motives (WHO 1973)

(1) to satisfy curiosity about drug effects;

(2) to achieve a sense of belonging, to be accepted by others;

(3) to express independence and sometimes hostility;

(4) to have pleasurable, new, thrilling or dangerous experiences;

(5) to gain an improved 'understanding' or 'creativity';

(6) to foster a sense of ease of relaxation;

(7) to escape from something.

ALCOHOL AND ALCOHOLISM

Alcohol (ethanol, ethyl alcohol) is derived from the fermentation of sugars and refined carbohydrates. The compound has little therapeutic usage, but its social significance is enormous.

Pharmacokinetics

Alcohol is rapidly absorbed from the upper part of the gastro-intestinal tract, partly from the stomach, but mainly from the small intestine. Absorption is delayed by food, especially dairy products and fatty foods. Another factor that affects absorption is the concentration of the solution, with strong solutions inhibiting gastric peristalsis. Alcohol is also more rapidly absorbed in habitual drinkers. After absorption, it rapidly diffuses throughout the body fluids and tissues.

Ninety per cent of absorbed alcohol is metabolized (oxidation) by the enzyme system in the liver (alcohol dehydrogenase). The first stage of this metabolism is the formation of acetaldehyde, then acetate, and finally carbon dioxide and water. The remaining 10 per cent is excreted unchanged in the urine, sweat, and breath. The rate of alcohol metabolism varies, but is generally thought to be quicker in heavy drinkers. Alcohol is unusual in that it follows zero-order kinetics (see Chapter 1).

Pharmacological properties

Alcohol has anaesthetic properties and causes depression of the central nervous system (CNS). Hyperactivity, when it occurs, is due to removal of inhibitions. In normal doses, alcohol acts on the brain-stem reticular formation but, with high doses, direct cortical depression occurs. The effect of alcohol on the CNS in relation to consumption is shown in Table 23.1. Alcohol induces peripheral vasodilation by depressing the vasomotor centre; this accounts for the feeling of warmth that people notice after drinking. As a result of the vasodilation there is a loss of body heat, and therefore it is unwise to take alcohol before going out into the cold. There is no firm evidence to suggest that alcohol usefully dilates the coronary arteries, although it does relieve the pain of angina by reducing peripheral resistance through vasodilatation.

In moderate concentrations, alcohol increases the secretion of gastric acid but, at high concentrations, it reduces such secretion. Thus, it is unwise to drink where there is a history of peptic ulceration. The diuretic properties of alcohol are familiar to all drinkers; this property is due to alcohol inhibiting the secretion of antidiuretic hormone (ADH).

Table 23.1. The effect of alcohol on the CNS in relation to alcohol consumption. NB, 1 unit of alcohol is equivalent to 1 measure of spirits, or $\frac{1}{2}$ pint of beer/lager, or 1 glass of wine

Number of units	Effect
1–2	Normal
3–4	Warmth, friendliness, digestive discomfort, lengthening of reaction to visual field
6	Diminished sense of depth, impaired driving
8	Loss of inhibition, euphoria, aggressive behaviour, visual disturbances
10	Deterioration of motor reaction and loss of precision
12	Uncertain movements, reduced ability for adaptation
14	Accommodation disturbances, loss of balance
16	Obvious drunkenness, muscular inco-ordination
18	Irritability, depression, nausea, loss of sphincter control
24–8	Stupor
30–6	Coma
40–60	Paralysis of respiratory centre, death

Alcohol has a dual effect on blood glucose: initially it increases blood glucose due to reduced glucose uptake by the tissues; but this leads to increased insulin output, which will cause hypoglycaemia, an event that is likely to occur if alcohol is taken after severe exercise.

Tolerance develops to alcohol: the more frequently an individual drinks, the more they require to obtain the same effect.

Alcoholism

This can be defined as a chronic disease manifested by repeated drinking so as to cause injury to the drinker's health or to their social and economic functioning. An alcoholic can be defined as an individual who is unable, consistently, to choose whether he/she shall drink or not, and who, if he/she drinks, is unable consistently to choose whether he/she shall stop or not.

Alcoholism has been classified into five types:

(1) alpha: in which the individual drinks as a relief from mental pain, thus using alcohol as a drug;

(2) beta: in which the individual drinks because their position or environment demands it;

(3) epsilon: in which the individual drinks to excess, but only periodically;

(4) gamma: in which the individual cannot control their intake once they have taken their first drink;

(5) delta: in which the individual drinks intermittently without necessarily getting drunk.

The alpha, beta, and epsilon forms of alcoholism demonstrate psychological dependence that can lead into physical dependence. The gamma and delta types demonstrate both psychological and physical dependence.

Thus, alcohol can produce different effects according to the way it is used. It is a drug that can cause psychological dependence when used for the relief of anxiety. It can lead to a strong physical dependence with serious consequences in the physical, psychological, moral, and social senses. In view of this, it is worth noting that whereas we often see drinking, sometimes to excess, and drunkenness, we seldom see alcoholism. This is for two reasons:

Firstly, drinking and drunkenness are physical states and can, therefore, be seen. However, alcoholism is a state of mind, which exists even when it is not showing any symptoms.

Secondly, the drunkard usually gets drunk in public and does not care who sees. The alcoholic is often protected by friends and family, who cover up for deficiencies and do everything possible to prevent the condition from being discovered.

It is necessary to make this distinction between drinking, drunkenness, and alcoholism, not only because of the immediate effects on the drinker, but also because of the long-term ones that influence the drinker and those who come into contact with him or her. This distinction is very much in evidence in the attitudes of society, as well as in the measures taken to deal with the condition. Thus, drunkenness, especially if only occasionally, is often regarded as a temporary lapse that, even if not completely condoned, is looked upon with a certain tolerance. On some occasions, drunkenness is even encouraged and viewed with a certain amount of amusement. This is hardly justifiable in view of the high incidence of alcohol-related driving accidents. The regular drunkard does not enjoy much sympathy from either society or the law. They are usually avoided as an embarrassment by friends and are easily picked up by the police because they are a nuisance. They may run into serious financial difficulties and their family invariably suffers. With help and self-control, the drunkard may be able to overcome their drinking problem.

The picture with alcoholics is very different: they are dependent upon alcohol for their everyday functioning, and all efforts are directed at obtaining drink. They need alcohol to get started in the morning, to keep them going throughout the day, and even more alcohol in the evening before retiring to bed. Alcoholics have to keep themselves continuously topped-up. They may be able to function in society for a time, but eventually their work deteriorates until they are unable to work at all. Their interests become more restricted until they become centred on the one thing that matters—alcohol. Their family and friends desert them, hence alcoholism is often known as the lonely disease.

Stages of alcoholism

It is now recognized that anyone who regularly consumes more than 20 units of alcohol a week is seriously at risk from becoming an alcoholic. (One unit of alcohol is defined as either one glass of wine, one measure of spirits, or half a pint of beer or lager). Four stages of alcoholism can be recognized; these are as follows:

1. *The pre-alcoholic symptomatic phase.* The individual starts drinking socially, but soon realizes that alcohol provides relief from psychological difficulties. At the start he or she seeks relief only occasionally, but soon their tolerance for tension decreases and they resort to alcohol more frequently. Drinking is heavier in the evening and soon becomes noticeable to family and friends.

2. *The prodromal phase.* At this stage, the drinker may consume a considerable quantity of alcohol and still carry on with normal activities, but does not remember anything about them the following morning. The onset of these amnesic episodes (black-outs) may be followed by a change in drinking behaviour, which indicates that alcoholic drinks have ceased to be social pleasure and have become 'drugs of necessity'. The subject may become unduly preoccupied with alcohol, start drinking surreptitiously, and develop guilty

feelings about drinking. The prodromal phase may last anything from six months to five years.

3. *The crucial phase.*   The main feature of this phase is loss of control, which means that as soon as a small quantity of alcohol is taken, then a demand for more alcohol is set up. This is felt as a physical demand by the drinker and lasts until they are too intoxicated or too sick to ingest any more alcohol. At about this time, they begin to rationalize their drinking behaviour by inventive excuses for drinking. Drinking now becomes conspicuous and, as a result, the drinker develops markedly aggressive behaviour and suffers persistent remorse. Both add to his or her tension and provide a further reason for drinking. During the crucial phase, there may be periods of total abstinence or attempts to change the pattern of drinking. The drinker invariably loses his or her job, and family and friends desert them, which leads to the development of unreasonable resentment. They often neglect their food and start drinking at any hour of the day. Progressively, this disease process undermines the morals and physical resistance of the drinker.

4. *The chronic phase.*   At this stage, drinkers begin to find themselves intoxicated during the daytime and continues in this state for several days. Marked ethical deterioration and impairment of thinking occur, and sometimes true alcoholic psychoses. By some strange phenomenon, the drinker becomes less tolerant to alcohol, and undefinable fears and tremors develop.

Table 23.2 lists both the physical and psychological signs and symptoms of the early, the probable, and the certain alcoholic.

Treatment

This can be by aversion therapy, the use of sensitizing drugs, or psychological therapy. Aversion therapy is aimed at creating a conditioned reflex so that the alcoholic feels sick and vomits when they see, smell, or taste alcohol. Drugs used for aversion therapy are emetine and apomorphine. Sensitizing drugs, such as disulfiram, block the metabolism of alcohol by inhibiting the conversion of acetaldehyde to acetate. Thus disulfiram produces a fall in blood pressure, headaches, chest pain, nausea, and vomiting. Psychological therapy, as provided by groups such as Alcoholics Anonymous, has proved to be of tremendous value in the treatment of alcoholism.

VOLATILE SUBSTANCE ABUSE (SOLVENT ABUSE)

The first case of solvent abuse was reported in the UK in 1969. Since that time, there has been a steady increase in the number of fatalities and the age of the abusers has fallen; the range of ages involved is now from 8 to 23 years. It appears that curiosity or peer-group pressure is responsible for the transient indulgence of many teenagers in this activity. Nevertheless, chronic volatile substance abuse does occur, and may lead to hepatic and renal damage, encephalopathy, and

Table 23.2. Physical and psychological signs and symptoms of the early, probable, and certain alcoholic

---

Early alcoholic—physical signs and symptoms
  Chronic gastritis
  Anaemia
  Dimness of vision (amblyopia)
  Vitamin deficiencies (especially vit. C)
  Cardiac irregularities (tachycardias and arrhythmias)
  Flushed face
  Nocturnal sweating
  Bruising on body and limbs
  Cigarette burns
  Increased tolerance to alcohol

Early alcoholic—psychological signs and symptoms
  Gulping drinks
  Person looks for easy employment that offers facilities for drinking
  Frequent car accidents
  Behavioral problems in the family and inexplicable behaviour within it
  Frequent changes of residences
  Changes in social and business relationships
  Major disruption: loss of job
  Feelings of aggression, resentment, and jealousy
  Paranoid attitudes
  Depression and isolation

Probable alcoholic—physical signs and symptoms
  Black-outs
  Increased infections
  Pancreatitis, peripheral neuropathy, alcoholic myopathy, cardiomyopathy
  Constant odour of alcohol on the breath
  Vascular enlargement—characteristic facial appearance

Probable alcoholic—psychological signs and symptoms
  Subjective loss of control
  Surreptitious drinking—morning drinking
  Repeated conscious attempts at abstinence
  Frequent absences from work
  Changing drinks
  Loss of interest
  Outburst of rage and threats of suicide
  Frequent references to alcohol
  Drinking for the relief of anger, insomnia, fatigue, depression, and social discomfort

Certain alcoholic–physical and psychological signs and symptoms
  Withdrawal symptoms when drinking is stopped, i.e. drowsiness, hallucinations, fits, and
    delirium tremens.
  Tolerance—high blood alcohol levels without intoxication
  High consumption of alcohol
  Liver cirrhosis and alcoholic cerebral degeneration
  Blatant indiscriminate use of alcohol
  Drinking continues despite strong medical and social contra-indications

---

peripheral neuropathy, as well as psychological and social problems (Volans and Byatt 1986).

Solvent abuse, now renamed volatile substance abuse (because other substances in addition to glues and solvents are abused), takes the form of deep inhalation from a cloth soaked in the agent or from a plastic bag into which it has been poured.

The clinical picture of solvent abuse is similar to that which follows intoxication with alcohol or volatile anaesthetics. Thus, there is initial stimulation of the CNS followed by depression, but the time-course is different. The onset is rapid, the effects last for minutes and not hours, and the occurrence of disorientation and hallucinations is much more frequent than with alcohol or volatile anaesthetics. The breath smells of the particular solvent used, and there may be evidence of it on the hands and face, including a rash over the muzzle area. It is well-known that solvents can sensitize the heart to catecholamines and hypoxia, so that cardiac arrhythmias may occur during the exposure. There may also be a metabolic acidosis with coma in which the reflexes are exaggerated. Solvent abuse has also precipitated status epilepticus (Allister *et al.* 1981).

Treatment of volatile substance abuse can be difficult and should be left to those experienced in these problems. The treatment includes psychotherapy (listening and talking to the victim; discussing his or her problems), behaviour therapy (retraining to prevent this behaviour when the urge or opportunity arises), and relaxation therapy, including hypnotic techniques (O'Connor 1981).

DENTAL PROBLEMS OF DRUG ABUSERS

All drug abusers will show signs of dental neglect; their oral hygiene will be poor and they often only attend for emergency treatment. Thus, routine dental care is difficult to achieve for such patients. The specific dental problems of the different types of drug abusers are discussed below.

Intravenous drug abusers

Opioids are the common group of drugs taken intravenously. There is a risk of hepatitis B and AIDS amongst intravenous drug abusers, and the dental surgeon should take every precaution to avoid both infection and cross-infection (see Chapter 9). Patients taking opioids may also suffer withdrawal symptoms whilst undergoing dental treatment, and the dental surgeon should be able to recognize this problem. Pentazocine, which is a mixed agonist/antagonist, should not be given to such patients as it may induce withdrawal symptoms.

Alcohol abuse

The chronic alcoholic may suffer from vitamin deficiencies, which will cause oral symptoms such as stomatitis, glossitis, and angular cheilitis. Liver damage following alcohol abuse may result in impaired blood clotting and poor wound healing. General anaesthetics and sedation techniques should be avoided where possible in the alcoholic as they show resistance to the agents used. Other drugs to avoid in alcoholics are aspirin, because of its effect on haemostasis and the gastric mucosa, and metronidazole, which inhibits the metabolism of alcohol.

Smoking

Smoking tobacco results in brown or black stains on the teeth, but does not normally lead to conspicuous changes in the gingiva. In heavy smokers there may be a greyish-white gingival discolouration and, in pipe smokers, the palatal mucosa may be characterized by 'cobblestone' surface, the so-called 'smokers palate', in which the orifices of accessory palatal salivary glands become inflamed and undergo hyperkeratotic change. The degree of bleeding elicited on blunt probing of the gingival crevice may be reduced in smokers with periodontitis (Preber and Bergstrom 1985).

Acute ulcerative gingivitis occurs more frequently in smokers (Kowolik and Nisbet, 1983), and some reports suggest that smoking is associated with an increased prevalence of chronic periodontal disease. Smokers have more dental plaque than non-smokers, but smoking does not appear to increase the rate of plaque formation (Macgregor et al. 1985); the major reason for the increased plaque accumulation in smokers is probably inadequate oral hygiene. It has long been known that smoking causes an increase in salivary flow, and this may partly explain the increased amounts of salivary calculus found in smokers.

Evidence that smoking increases the incidence of 'dry socket' (Sweet and Butler 1978) has not subsequently been confirmed. However, it has been shown that smoking impairs post-extraction socket filling with blood (Rogers et al. 1986); this may impair the healing of tooth sockets.

The generalized keratosis of the normally unkeratinized oral mucosa sometimes seen in heavy smokers appears to be benign, but there is evidence that smoking is a causative factor in leukoplakia (Pindborg 1980), which may be a premalignant lesion. Curiously, smoking seems to have a therapeutic effect on oral aphthous ulceration (Chellemi et al. 1970). Smoking is an important cause of carcinoma of the mouth (Pindborg 1980); the main prospective studies have found that carcinoma of the mouth, pharynx, and oesophagus are all associated with smoking. The risk of developing oral carcinomas has been estimated to be six times greater in smokers than in non-smokers.

Smokeless tobacco

This term is used to describe alternative forms of taking tobacco, which include snuffing, sneezing, dipping, and chewing. Smokeless tobacco consumption is on the increase, especially in school-age children (Schaefer et al. 1985). There is increasing evidence that this form of tobacco consumption is associated with alterations in the oral mucosa and dental tissues. These include gingival recession, periodontal bone loss, leukoplakia, and tooth abrasion. Products from smokeless tobacco have been shown to have the potential for causing carcinoma of the oral mucosa, pharynx, larynx, and oesophagus (Christen 1980). Some smokeless tobacco products have recently been banned in the UK.

REFERENCES

Allister, C., Lush, M., Oliver, J. S., and Watson, J. M. (1981). Status epilepticus caused by solvent abuse. *British Medical Journal*, **283**, 1156.

Chellemi, S. J., Olson, D. L., and Shapiro, S. (1970). The association between smoking and aphthous ulcers. *Oral Surgery*, **29**, 832–6.

Christen, A. G. (1980). The case against smokeless tobacco: five facts for the health professional to consider. *Journal of the American Dental Association*, **101**, 464–9.

Eddy, N. B., Halbach, H., Isbell, H., and Seevers, M. H. (1965). Drug dependence: its significance and characteristics. *Bulletin of World Health Organization*, **32**, 721–33.

Kowolik, M. J. and Nisbet, T. (1983). Smoking and acute ulcerative gingivitis. *British Dental Journal*, **154**, 241–2.

Macgregor, I. D. M., Edgar, W. M., and Greenwood, A. R. (1985). Effects of cigarette smoking on the rate of plaque formation. *Journal of Clinical Periodontology*, **12**, 335–41.

O'Connor, D. J. (1981). Glue sniffing and solvent abuse problems: causes and treatments. *The Police Surgeon, Journal of the Association of Police Surgeons in Great Britain*, **19**, 48–57.

Paton, W. D. M. (1968). Drug dependence—a socio-pharmacological assessment. *Advancement of Science*, **25**, 200–12.

Pindborg, J. J. (1980). *Oral cancer and precancer*. John Wright & Sons, Bristol.

Preber, H. and Bergstrom, J. (1985). Occurrence of gingival bleeding in smokers and non-smoker patients. *Acta Odontologica Scandinavica*, **43**, 315–20.

Rogers, S. N., Meechan, J. G., Macgregor, I. D. M., and Hobson, R. S. (1986). The effect of smoking on immediate post-extraction socket filling with blood and on the incidence of dry socket. *Journal of Dental Research*, **65**, 489.

Schaefer, S. D., Henderson, A. H., Glover, F. D., and Christen, A. G. (1985). Patterns of use and incidence of smokeless tobacco consumption in school-age children. *Archives of Otolaryngology*, **111**, 639–42.

Sweet, J. B. and Butler, D. P. (1978). Predisposing and operative factors. Effect on the incidence of localised osteitis in mandibular third molar surgery. *Oral Surgery*, **46**, 206–15.

Volans, G. N. and Byatt, C. M. (1986). Poisoning from domestic products. *Prescribers' Journal*, **26** (no. 4), 87–97.

WHO Expert Committee on Addiction-producing drugs, Thirteenth Report. (1964). World Health Organization Technical Report Series No. 273.

WHO Technical Report Series. (1973). Youth and drugs. No. 516. Geneva.

24

Emergencies in dental practice

MOST of the emergencies to be considered here are likely to be very rare in dental practice. However, the practitioner must be familiar with methods of dealing with the immediate crisis. The treatment given by the dental practitioner must be as simple as possible, and the emergency kit of drugs (described at the end of the Chapter) as limited as is compatible with need. Too many drugs included in an emergency kit will mean that the practitioner is likely to be familiar with the use of none.

The emergencies will be considered under the following headings:

(1) fainting;

(2) angina and myocardial infarction;

(3) cardiac arrest;

(4) acute allergic reactions;

(5) epilepsy;

(6) hypoglycaemia;

(7) adrenal crisis.

General anaesthetic problems and those associated with bleeding have been dealt with in the appropriate Chapters.

FAINTING

Fainting is likely to be the most common cause of loss of consciousness in the dental surgery. It is due to a transient lack of blood supply to the brain. Very often a fainting attack can be anticipated, and therefore prevented, by careful observation of the patient, particularly at the time of administration of a local anaesthetic. A patient who is pale, sweating, and feels sick and dizzy, is one providing a warning. Such a patient may go quickly into unconsciousness. The pulse is weak at first, slow, and then becomes fuller and bounding.

Fainting in the dental surgery is less common today than in the past, and this is because patients are now treated in the supine position. The sort of patient who is likely to faint is one who is unduly anxious, and the one who has decided not to eat before any dental treatment. If food has not been taken prior to dental treatment, then a glucose drink should be provided.

The treatment for fainting is to lie the patient flat with the head in a dependent position to allow the cerebral blood flow to be maintained.

ANGINA PECTORIS AND MYOCARDIAL INFARCTION

Angina is a symptom of ischaemic heart disease; an attack is characterized by a sudden, very severe substernal pain that often radiates to the left shoulder and arm. Very occasionally the pain may radiate to the left mandible and teeth. The typical anginal attack is often brought on by exercise and by emotion, such as anxiety. Because of the anxiety association, such an attack is a possibility in the dental surgery. The patient may have had anginal attacks for a long time and so will recognize the symptoms; they will be carrying their usual remedy, e.g. glyceryl trinitrate tablets (see Chapter 15). If an attack occurs they should place one tablet under the tongue. If a patient with recurrent angina pectoris happens to develop an acute myocardial infarction, he or she may take several tablets in quick succession in an attempt to relieve the intractable pain. All this will do is to produce a further reduction in myocardial blood flow, and this will clearly have a further adverse effect. Patients should be advised that in the event of very prolonged attacks of pain, when two tablets have not proved helpful, then to take any more will not be effective, but could be harmful.

If the patient has a myocardial infarct, the pain will be similar to that experienced in an attack of angina, the difference being that it will be more severe and persistent. The patient is often breathless and vomiting is common. The pulse will be weak and the blood pressure falls. They may become unconscious for a time, and may suffer cardiac arrest and die.

Once a myocardial infarct has been diagnosed the following steps should be taken:

1. An ambulance must be called for by an assistant.

2. Pain and anxiety must be relieved.

The nature of the pain experienced will provoke acute anxiety. This, in itself, will cause the outpouring of endogenous adrenaline with possible precipitation of cardiac ventricular fibrillation. Fibrillation is a cause of sudden death and should, as far as possible, be prevented by dealing effectively with the pain and anxiety. For this purpose, morphine has been the drug of choice for a long time. Although it is a drug that can be held by dental surgeons, and can be administered by them, it is a controlled drug (see Chapter 3) and is unlikely to be stored in the dental surgery by many practitioners. On the other hand, pentazocine, although also a controlled drug, is more familiar to dental surgeons. It is listed in the *Dental Practitioners' Formulary 1988–90*, and is used in some dental sedative techniques. However, it is *not* recommended for use in the case of myocardial infarction. Even parenterally it is not as good an analgesic as morphine, and unfortunately it cannot be guaranteed to relieve anxiety. Indeed, the reverse may be the case; it may produce anxiety and, in certain instances, hallucinations. When a patient has experienced a myocardial infarction, it is important to maintain their haemodynamic status. Morphine is much more likely to do this than is pentazocine. High doses of pentazocine, unlike morphine, increase the blood pressure and heart rate, and this in itself could put an extra strain on the already overtaxed heart.

The best treatment for myocardial infarction in this context is the use of Entonox, a premixture of gases—50/50 mixture of nitrous oxide and oxygen (see Chapter 8). This gaseous mixture provides more rapid pain relief than morphine. If Entonox is not available, nitrous oxide may be administered with oxygen, but the concentration of nitrous oxide must not exceed 70 per cent, as above this concentration anaesthesia and hypoxia may occur. Nitrous oxide is a weak anaesthetic agent but possesses excellent analgesic properties. In addition it has an euphoriant effect. What is being done should be explained to the patient as the anaesthetic mask may well cause them to feel more anxious.

The patient should be placed in the position that feels most comfortable to them. Pulmonary oedema is a possible consequence of infarction due to left ventricular failure and this causes dyspnoea. To lie the patient flat in these circumstances could cause the lungs to fill with fluid and make breathing virtually impossible. All tight clothing around the neck should be loosened.

CARDIAC ARREST

There are many causes of cardiac arrest, e.g. myocardial infarction, anaesthetic agents, acute anaphylactic reactions, adrenal crisis. Apart from the obvious fact that the patient will be unconscious, there are some signs to look for, namely:

(1) colour of the skin;
(2) absence of arterial pulse.

Pallor indicates under-perfusion of the skin with blood. If the colour is white, then this may indicate a circulatory problem and could be the result of a mild cardiac infarct. If the colour is grey, this would indicate that the remaining oxygen tension in the peripheral vessels has been further reduced. A whitish grey skin suggests circulatory collapse of some duration. Indications of such circulatory collapse would also include lack of pulse. Time is of the essence, and only the radial and carotid pulses should be felt. A stethoscope to listen for heart sounds is worse than useless. Sometimes heart sounds may be difficult to ascertain in this way even in the normal patient; they may be very difficult to find if the patient is obese.

There may also be lack of bleeding from a surgical wound, and the pupils will be dilated. However, eye signs should not be considered an essential feature of early diagnosis because they occur later on in the catastrophe. Do not waste time looking for eye signs!

Cardiopulmonary resuscitation

The brain is the organ most sensitive to oxygen deprivation. If its oxygen supply is cut off for three minutes, then brain death will occur. This presupposes that the patient was in a reasonable condition beforehand. If they were in an agitated state, for example, where the oxygen demand would be raised, then the brain would suffer even more rapidly following cardiac arrest. Such a possibility may arise in the dental chair. So the emergency techniques must be well-known and rehearsed, for no time can be spent reading them up in a book once the emergency has begun. Although a single operator can provide both cardiac and respiratory resuscitation, this is difficult and extremely exhausting.

Procedures

1. *Aid the venous return.*   Place the patient on the floor or onto a firm flat surface. Get their feet up to help the flow of blood back to the heart.

2. *Thump the patient's chest mid-sternum.*   One or two blows with the side of the closed fist may restart the heart. The sole purpose of this is to shock the heart into electrical activity and if two blows produce no response, further ones will be a waste of time for this will not restart the heart.

3. *Start external cardiac massage.*   The operator kneels by the side of the patient and the sternum is depressed 1–1.5 inches. One hand is placed over the other on the lower sternum and a forceful compression started. A rate of 60 to 70 should suffice for an adult. This is a risky business and, in older patients with less elasticity of the rib cage, as many as 50 per cent may suffer fracture of the ribs. In very small children, the compression rate is about 100 and only the thumbs are used to press on the chest.

4. *Artificial ventilation.*   This must be given during the period of cardiac massage. The neck should be extended and the lower jaw held forward in order to keep the airway clear. The ventilation can be accomplished by mouth to mouth respiration or by some sort of face mask and oxygen. The lungs should be inflated after every fifth compression of the chest. During artificial respiration the patient's nose should be closed.

Resuscitation is a very exhausting procedure and where possible one person should attend to the cardiac massage, and another to the respiratory ventilation. If only one person is available, then five compressions to one ventilation is suggested.

Medical help should be sought by an assistant, and the cardiopulmonary resuscitation maintained until there is a return to a good pulse or alternatively until the arrival of expert help. A patient who recovers will be admitted to hospital. It is no part of the dentist's job to try using drugs such as lignocaine to deal with any arrhythmias that may occur.

ACUTE ALLERGIC REACTIONS

See Chapter 21 and the Table at end of this Chapter.

EPILEPSY

Major epilepsy is a convulsive disorder with attacks that are characterized by an aura (a disorder of sensation), a tonic and a clonic phase (see Chapter 14). In the tonic phase the patient is rigid and may stop breathing; in the clonic phase convulsions occur; in either phase the patient may bite their tongue.

If the patient has an attack in the dental surgery, they must be prevented from injuring themselves during the seizure. All appliances should be removed from the mouth as quickly as possible. Recovery is fairly rapid, a matter of a few minutes. Whether or not dental treatment is continued can only be decided by the operator, taking into account the circumstances prevailing at the time. As some patients feel a little drowsy after recovery from a seizure, it is sensible to see they are accompanied home by a responsible adult.

If a patient is known to be an epileptic it is important for them to continue medication before attending for dental treatment.

If the patient does not recover in a matter of minutes, and seizures occur in rapid succession (status epilepticus), then an anticonvulsant drug must be given. The drug of choice is the benzodiazepine, diazepam. The ultrashort-acting barbiturate, thiopentone, will also cut short an attack, but it should be remembered that the ultrashort-acting barbiturate normally used in dental practice, methohexitone, has convulsant properties *and should never be used.* Status epilepticus is a dangerous condition and the patient should be taken into hospital as soon as possible.

HYPOGLYCAEMIA

The diabetic patient's regime can become unbalanced and they may then suffer from too much insulin or too little. Too much will lead to hypoglycaemia, a condition brought about if the diabetic taking insulin has their dietary regime disrupted; too little insulin can produce a state of diabetic ketosis. It is important to distinguish between hypoglycaemia and diabetic ketosis; both can cause the patient to become unconscious. However, it is extemely unlikely that diabetic ketosis would present with unconsciousness in the dental surgery as it takes several days to develop. The differential signs and symptoms are:

Ketosis (lack of insulin)	Hypoglycaemia (excess of insulin)
Weakness	Weakness
Excessive thirst	Hunger
Dehydration (dry skin and mucous membrane)	Sweating
	Blood pressure normal or elevated
Decreased blood pressure	Pulse—full and rapid
Sweet breath—said to be acetone	Patient anxious (adrenaline release)
Deep laboured respirations	Later: coma
Later: coma (unlikely to be seen in dental surgery)	

One characteristic feature of hypoglycaemia is that the patient may become difficult to manage and even aggressive.

Patients experienced in the management of their condition may well be able to distinguish between the onset of a hypoglycaemic attack and ketosis. If there is any doubt about the diagnosis, a few lumps of sugar or sugar sweets will normally rectify the hypoglycaemia fairly rapidly. A hypoglycaemic attack requires urgent treatment and, if the patient is unable to swallow, intravenous dextrose should be administered. If a vein cannot be found, then glucagon should be administered intramuscularly. Glucagon is a hormone secreted by the α-cells of the islets of Langerhans of the pancrease, the β-cells producing insulin. Glucagon raises plasma glucose concentration by mobilizing glycogen stored in the liver (see Chapter 18). Hypoglycaemia must be treated promptly: a prolonged hypoglycaemic coma is likely to lead to irreversible brain damage.

When there is doubt about the diagnosis of whether the coma is hypoglycaemic or hyperglycaemic in origin, insulin must not be administered by the dental surgeon as it can be very dangerous in hypoglycaemic coma. The likelihood is that a coma occurring in the dental surgery in a diabetic patient will be caused by hypoglycaemia.

ADRENAL CRISIS

If the adrenal glands are unable to provide sufficient cortisol to meet the needs of 'stress', an adrenal crisis may occur. This is a state of profound shock, and a warning of such an occurrence would be weakness, vomiting, pallor, perspiration, tachycardia, weak pulse, and hypotension. If surgery is to be carried out on a patient when there is this risk of an inadequate response to 'stress', special precautions should be taken. Adrenocortical function is likely to be depressed if (a) the patient is taking corticosteroids as a prolonged course (month or over), or (b) if the patient has been taking corticosteroids regularly for a month or more during the last year. There is no general agreement on the time taken to restore normal adrenocortical function after prolonged steroid therapy has been discontinued. The approach to prophylactic steroid replacement is shown in Table 24.1.

Table 24.1. Prophylactic steroid replacement for dental procedures

Procedure	Patients currently on a prolonged course of steroid therapy	Patients who have had a prolonged course of steroid therapy during the previous year
Minimal procedures, e.g. an extraction under local anaesthesia	Give 200 mg hydrocortisone orally 2 hours pre-operatively; this is followed by the patient's usual steroid regimen	Give 200 mg hydrocortisone orally 2 hours pre-operatively
Minor oral surgery, e.g. impacted third molar removal and minor procedures under a general anaesthetic	Give 100 mg hydrocortisone intravenously pre-operatively followed by the same dose intramuscularly every 6 hours for a period of 24 hours; this is followed by the patient's usual steroid regimen	Give 100 mg hydrocortisone intravenously pre-operatively followed by the same dose intramuscularly every 6 hours for a period of 24 hours
Major oral surgery	Give 100 mg hydrocortisone intravenously pre-operatively followed by the same dose every 6 hours for a period of 72 hours; this is followed by the patient's usual steroid regimen	Give 100 mg hydrocortisone intravenously pre-operatively followed by the same dose intramuscularly for a period of 72 hours
Routine restorative procedures (other than surgical)	No prophylactic cover required; steroids should be available in case of collapse	No prophylactic cover required; steroids should be available in case of collapse

If, in spite of all the precautions itemized in Table 24.1, the patient shows signs of collapse, hydrocortisone (500 mg) should be given intravenously and immediately. This is a very serious situation and the patient should be admitted to hospital as soon as possible, if not already an in-patient.

Patients who are considered to be vulnerable should have their blood pressure monitored; this may provide a reasonable guide to their general condition. For just how long this should be done, and at what intervals, is not established with any certainty. It is recommended that the blood pressure should be measured in such patients at half-hourly intervals over a period of two hours. If, after this time, the blood pressure is still significantly low, the patient should be referred to hospital.

THE EMERGENCY KIT

Table 24.2 shows the basic emergency drug kit for dental practices, together with recommended dosages for various emergencies.

Table 24.2. The emergency drug kit for dental practice and the dosages for various emergencies

Drug	Dosage	Emergency
Hydrocortisone sodium succinate	100 mg IV or IM (powder in vial plus 2 ml of water for injection)	Anaphylactic shock; adrenal crisis; acute asthma: repeat as required
Adrenaline (1 1000 solution)	0.5 ml IM (MUST NEVER BE GIVEN INTRAVENOUSLY)	Anaphylactic shock
Chlorpheniramine ~piriton chlorpheniramine~	10–20 mg IV or IM	Allergic reactions
Dextrose (10 ml ampoules containing 50% solution)	5–20 ml IV	Hypoglycaemic coma
Glucagon injection	0.5–1 unit IV, IM, or SC	Acute hypoglycaemic reactions
Nitrous oxide and oxygen ideally Entonox 50:50, alternatively a mixture of gases with NOT more than 70% N_2O	inhalation	Myocardial infarction
Morphine sulphate injection BP	8–20 mg IM	Myocardial infarction
Diazepam	by slow intravenous injection: 2.5 mg increments until condition is controlled, up to 20 mg. (2.5 mg increments per 30 s.)	Status epilepticus

25

Therapeutic measures for common dental conditions

LISTED below are some of the common dental conditions that often require treatment. The possible methods of treatment are outlined as being either operative, that is treatment carried out by the dental surgeon, or non-operative, that is the use of medication. In some conditions both types of treatment are necessary. The list of non-operative measures is by no means exhaustive and only serves as a guideline; many of the conditions have been also discussed under various drug treatments. It is beyond the scope of this Chapter to discuss the differential diagnoses of these conditions. For these, the reader is referred to standard texts on oral surgery and medicine for details.

Dentine hypersensitivity

Operative treatment: for cases that do not respond to desensitizing agents, then root canal therapy may have to be carried out.
Non-operative treatment: application of either Lukomasky's paste, stannous fluoride, or Tresiolan to the area of exposed dentine may be of some short-term benefit. Toothpastes containing either strontium chloride or formaldehyde should be used as the regular dentifrice (see Chapter 11).

Pulpal hyperaemia

Operative treatment: remove the cause, either a 'high spot' on a new filling, caries, lack of a lining under a restoration, or a leaky amalgam. The cavity should then be dressed with either a calcium hydroxide base and zinc oxide–eugenol, or just zinc oxide–eugenol.

Acute pulpitis

Operative treatment: remove the pulp or extract the tooth.
Non-operative treatment: Ledermix may be applied to the cavity floor if there is pulpal inflammation causing inadequate anaesthesia. Analgesics are of little value in this common dental condition (see Chapters 5 and 6).

Periapical abscess

Operative treatment: establish drainage via the root canal or extract the tooth.
Non-operative treatment: if the infection is not localized, or treatment has been delayed, antibiotics should be prescribed. Both phenoxymethyl penicillin (250 mg every six hours for five days) and metronidazole (200 mg every eight hours for five days) have been shown to be effective for this condition. For severe infections, the patient should be treated with intramuscular benzylpenicillin (600 mg), followed by oral penicillin. If the patient is allergic to penicillin, a higher dose of metronidazole (400 mg every 12 hours) should be used.

Cellulitis

Operative treatment: if suppuration is present then drainage should be established. The cellulitis may be due to a carious tooth and this should also be removed.
Non-operative treatment: early treatment with antibiotics is essential. If the patient is not allergic to penicillin, then they should be given benzylpenicillin IM, 600 mg every 6 hours for at least 24 hours. If allergic to penicillin they should be treated with intramuscular lincomycin, 600 mg every 12 hours for 24 hours. Any pus obtained during drainage must be sent for culture and antibiotic sensitivity. After the initial course of intramuscular drugs, the patient can usually receive antibiotics orally; the dose regime for oral phenoxymethyl penicillin is 250 mg every six hours for five to seven days, and for clindamycin, 250 mg every six hours, also for five to seven days. Antibiotic therapy may need to be changed depending upon the results of culture and sensitivity.

Osteomyelitis

Operative treatment: if possible, remove the sequestra and any remaining portions of necrotic bone.
Non-operative treatment: initial treatment with intramuscular benzylpenicillin, 600 mg six-hourly, followed by phenoxymethyl penicillin, 250 mg six-hourly. Lincomycin and clindamycin may be useful alternatives to penicillin in this condition. Antibiotic treatment should be continued for 5 to 10 days depending on the severity of the osteomyelitis. Any pus obtained from the wound should be sent for culture and sensitivity, and antibiotic therapy will depend upon these findings.

Pericoronitis

Operative treatment: extract the opposing upper third molar, or reduce the cusps if they are traumatizing the swollen gingival tissue around the erupting lower third molar. Once the pericoronitis has resolved, the lower third molar should be removed.

Non-operative treatment: hot salt-water mouth washes (one teaspoon of salt in a cup of hot water) may be of benefit in pericoronitis. Such mouthwashes should be used every two hours until the inflammation resolves. Trichloracetic acid can be placed under the gingival tissues and then immediately neutralized with glycerine. The efficacy of this treatment is not established and great care should be taken when the caustic is applied. Moderate cases of pericoronitis should be treated with oral antibiotics, either metronidazole, 200 mg every eight hours for five days, or phenoxymethyl penicillin, 250 mg every six hours for five days. Severe cases with trismus, marked buccal swelling, pyrexia, and lymphadeno-pathy should be treated with intramuscular penicillin, 600 mg, or penicillin triple injection, which contains benethamine penicillin 475 mg, procaine penicillin 250 mg, and benzylpenicillin sodium 300 mg.

Acute ulcerative gingivitis

Operative treatment: local debridement of the gingival tissues and removal of a supra-gingival calculus if possible.

Non-operative treatment: If the condition is mild then oxygen-releasing agents, such as hydrogen peroxide or sodium peroxyborate, may be of some benefit. For the moderate to severe cases, oral metronidazole is the treatment of choice (200–400 mg every eight hours for three to five days depending on severity).

Periodontal abscess

Operative treatment: curettage of the pocket to establish drainage and irrigation with 0.2 per cent chlorhexidine.

Non-operative treatment: hot salt-water mouth baths should be prescribed to encourage drainage. Severe cases should be treated with oral antibiotics; penicillin or metronidazole are both efficacious. Where possible, the patient should be instructed to irrigate the periodontal pocket with 0.2 per cent chlorhexidine solution.

Acute herpetic gingivostomatitis

Non-operative treatment: reduce the pyrexia with either aspirin or paracetamol (Aspirin cannot be given to children under 12 years of age because of the risk of Reyes syndrome). The patient should be kept well-hydrated. Idoxuridine 0.1 per cent solution should be painted on the lesions, but this may prove difficult in children. Chlorhexidine 0.2 per cent mouthwash should be used six-hourly to reduce the incidence of secondary infection. Severe or generalized cases may need to be treated with oral acyclovir, 200 mg five times daily for five days.

Teething

Operative treatment: massage the gums over the erupting tooth or allow the baby to chew on something hard.
Non-operative treatment: choline salicylate (Bonjela) rubbed into the gums may be of some benefit. Paracetamol elixir (5–10 ml) should be prescribed to reduce the pyrexia that often accompanies 'teething'.

Herpes labialis

Operative treatment: if patient is prone to herpes labialis, avoid trauma to the lips during dental procedures, and keep the lips coated with vaseline.
Non-operative treatment: idoxuridine 5 per cent in dimethyl sulphoxide should be applied at the earliest opportunity every two hours. Alternatively, acyclovir cream can be used.

Postoperative dental pain

Non-operative treatment: pain after a dental surgical procedure is usually of short duration and responds to aspirin or any of the other NSAIDs. Dosages should be taken every four to six hours. If pain persists after 48 hours, then secondary infection may have occurred and this should be treated with antibiotics. Analgesics recommended are aspirin 1 g, paracetamol 1 g, ibuprofen 400 mg, and diflunisal 500 mg.

Postoperative swelling and trismus

Non-operative treatment: cold compresses applied buccally and hot salt-water mouth baths may be appropriate local measures to reduce swelling. Aspirin or one of the other NSAIDs will help to reduce postoperative swelling and trismus. The pre-operative administration of corticosteroids has been shown to be of some benefit in reducing the incidence and magnitude of swelling after dental surgical procedures (see Chapter 4). Steroids used for this purpose include intramuscular dexamethasone 20 mg, methylprednisolone 80 mg, and hydrocortisone 100 mg. Steroids are administered one to two hours before surgery, and may be repeated six hours after surgery.

Dry socket (alveolar osteitis)

Operative treatment: the socket should be irrigated with warm saline to remove any remains of blood clot.
Non-operative treatment: a sedative dressing should be placed in the socket; examples include ribbon gauze soaked in Whiteheads varnish or bismuth

iodoform paste (BIPP). Alternatively, cotton wool impregnated with zinc oxide and eugenol may help to reduce the pain commonly associated with this condition. Such socket dressings are not without problems and may cause necrosis of bone. Inert cores impregnated with a variety of antibiotics have been tested for reducing the incidence of 'dry socket' after tooth extraction. Of those evaluated, tetracycline appears to be the most efficacious. Patients should be prescribed analgesics, either aspirin or other NSAIDs, to help reduce pain. Prophylactic systemic antibiotics should be considered in patients prone to dry sockets; phenoxymethyl penicillin is the antibiotic of choice.

Sinusitis

Operative treatment: ensure that the antrum is free of foreign bodies, such as root fragments, and that there is no oro-antral fistula present. Recurrent cases should be treated by antral washout.

Non-operative treatment: inhalations with either menthol and benzoin 2 per cent, or menthol and eucalyptus dissolved in hot water. Ephedrine nose drops, 0.5 per cent will produce vasoconstriction of the nasal mucosa and facilitate drainage. Acute cases should be treated with antibiotics; doxycycline 200 mg as an initial dose, followed by 100 mg daily, is particularly effective. Alternatively, any of the broad-spectrum penicillins can be used.

Candidal infections

Thrush

Non-operative treatment: a two-week course of nystatin lozenges, 500 000 units, four times a day; alternatively, amphotericin B lozenges 10 mg, four times a day for two weeks, or miconazole gel, 5–10 ml, four times daily. All preparations are held in the mouth for as long as possible then finally swallowed.

Angular cheilitis

Operative treatment: in edentulous patients, check the vertical height of their dentures. Investigate blood for deficiencies of iron, folate, and vitamin B_{12}.

Non-operative treatment: Sore areas should be treated with a topical antifungal agent, such as nystatin cream, amphotericin cream, or miconazole cream; creams should be applied four times a day.

Denture stomatitis

Operative treatment: leave out dentures as much as possible and keep them in a cleansing agent such as sodium hypochlorite. Dentures should be replaced when the condition resolves. Full haematological investigation should be carried out.

Non-operative treatment: the dentures should be left out, and the patient given nystatin pastilles or amphotericin B lozenges to suck four times a day. However, patients will be reluctant to leave their dentures out for any length of time. When inserted, the denture fitting surface should be coated with miconazole cream.

Candidal leukoplakia

Operative treatment: biopsy or, if small, surgical excision and graft.
Non-operative treatment: miconazole appears to be the antifungal of choice for this condition; treatment may have to be continued for several months.

Minor aphthous ulceration

Operative treatment: remove local causes of irritation, such as sharp edges of teeth and restorations; check that the clasps of appliances or dentures are not traumatizing the oral mucosa. Investigate blood for deficiencies of iron, vitamin B_{12}, and folate.
Non-operative treatment: chlorhexidine mouthwash 0.2 per cent or a tetracycline mouthbath (DPF)* may reduce the incidence of secondary infection associated with aphthous ulceration. Carmellose gelatine paste DPF may provide a mechanical protection of the oral mucosa. Hydrocortisone pellets (2.5 mg) are useful if the patient gets a prodromal symptom, i.e. a tingling sensation in the oral mucosa prior to the ulcers breaking out; the pellets should be applied to the area every six hours and allowed to dissolve. Once ulcers have occurred, triamcinolone acetonide dental paste or betamethasone aerosal spray applied six-hourly may help.

Major aphthous ulceration

Operative treatment: check for haematological deficiencies.
Non-operative treatment: as above for minor aphthous ulceration, but the condition usually requires treatment with systemic corticosteroids. Prednisolone is the treatment of choice, and the dose regime will depend upon the severity of the condition. Very severe cases may need treatment with azathioprine.

Xerostomia

Operative treatment: investigate salivary glands for mechanical obstruction, i.e. calculi.
Non-operative treatment: repeated application of fluoride is necessary to prevent caries, which has a high incidence in dry mouths. Artificial saliva may be of some help. Sugar-free fruit pastilles and chewing gum may promote any residual salivary flow.

* Not listed in 1988–90 DPF.

Index

drugs (*cont.*)
  distribution 12
  excretion 15, 19, 20
  inactivation 15
  mode of action 4
  non-medical use of 444
  source of 2
drugs which act via pharmacological receptors
  30
drugs which do NOT act via pharmacological
  receptors 31
drugs which do NOT act on specific receptors
  44
dry socket (alveolar osteitis) 465
dyes, antiseptics and disinfectants 172

eicosanoids 69, 70, 78, 83
emergencies in dental practice 454
emoform 240
endorphins 95
  acupuncture 96
  hypnosis 96
  placebo analgesia 96
enflurane 157
  pharmacokinetics 157
  pharmacological properties 158
enkephalins 94
  leucine enkephalin (leu-enkephalin) 94
  methionine enkephalin (met-enkephalin)
    94
enzymatic reaction, types of 17
enzymes
  chemotherapeutic use of 368
  in periodontal disese 235
ephedrine 272
  in sinusitis 466
epilepsy
  classification 307
  generalized epilepsy 307
  grand mal 307
  petit mal 307
epsilon aminocaproic acid 254
ergocalciferol (vitamin D$_2$) 406
ergotamine 315
erythromycin ($T_{0.5}$); *see also* antimicrobials 26
ethanol; *see* alcohol
ether (diethyl ether) 158
ethinyloestradiol 387
ethosuximide
  pharmacokinetics 310
  unwanted effects 310
ethyl alchol; *see* alcohol

etomidate 152
excretion of drugs 19
  plasma clearance 19, 20
  in the presence of renal impairment 20
excretion in the original form 15

facilitated diffusion 12
factors governing the fate of a drug in the body
  6
  chemical stability 6
  degree of ionization 6, 7
  lipid solubility 6
  molecular weight 6
felypressin 373
  as vasoconstrictor with local anaesthetic
    131
female sex hormones 386, 389
  effect on oral mucosa 389
fenamates 89
  mefenamic acid 89
    pharmacological properties 89
    unwanted effects 89
ferretin 399
fibrin 244
fibrinogen (Factor I) 245
fibrinolytic drugs 253
Fick's law 9
fluoridated table salt 232
fluoridation, water 232
fluoride 230
  administration 232
  effects on skeletal tissue 234
  effects on teeth 234
  mouth rinses 234
  overdose 234
  pharmacokinetics 231
  solutions 233
  toothpastes 233
  unwanted effects 234
  varnishes 233
fluoride and enamel structures 231
fluoride, mode of action in reducing dental
  decay 230
fluoride and plaque 231
fluoride tablets and drops 232
fluoride and tooth morphology 231
fluoridized milk 232
fluorouracil 366
flupenthixol 289
fluphenazine 286
flurazepam 302
fluspiriline 286, 289

abc civil aircraft markings 2013

Allan S. Wright

Ian Allan
PUBLISHING

Contents

This 64th edition first published 2013

ISBN 978 0 7110 3762 5

All rights reserved. No part of this book may be
reproduced or transmitted in any form or by any
means, electronic or mechanical, including
photocopying, recording, scanning or by any
information storage and retrieval system, on the
internet or elsewhere, without permission from the
Publisher in writing.

© Ian Allan Publishing Ltd 2013

Published by Ian Allan Publishing

an imprint of Ian Allan Publishing Ltd, Hersham,
Surrey KT12 4RG.
Printed in England by Ian Allan Printing Ltd,
Hersham, Surrey KT12 4RG.

Visit the Ian Allan Publishing website at
www.ianallanpublishing.com

Distributed in the United States of America and
Canada by BookMasters Distribution Services

Copyright
Illegal copying and selling of publications deprives
authors, publishers and booksellers of income,
without which there would be no investment in
new publications. Unauthorised versions of
publications are also likely to be inferior in quality
and contain incorrect information. You can help by
reporting copyright infringements and acts of
piracy to the Publisher or the UK Copyright
Service.

Front cover Mark Wagner /
aviation-images.com

Introduction

The familiar 'G' prefixed four-letter registration system was adopted in 1919 after a short-lived spell with serial numbers commencing at K-100. Until July 1928 the UK allocations were issued in the G-Exxx range but, as a result of further international agreements, this series ended at G-EBZZ, the replacement being G-Axxx. From this point registrations were issued in a reasonably orderly manner through to G-AZZZ, the position reached in July 1972. There were, however, two exceptions. In order to prevent possible confusion with signal codes, the G-AQxx sequence was omitted, while G-AUxx was reserved for Australian use originally. In recent years however, individual requests for a mark in the latter range have been granted by the Authorities.

Although the next logical sequence was started at G-Bxxx, it was not long before the strictly applied rules relating to aircraft registration began to be relaxed. Permission was readily given for personalised marks to be issued, incorporating virtually any four-letter combination, while re-registration also became a common feature – a practice almost unheard of in the past. In this book, where this has taken place at some time, all previous UK identities carried appear in parenthesis after the operator's/owner's name. For example, during its career Twin Squirrel G-NTWK has also carried the identities G-BMUS, G-OJOR and G-FTWO.

Some aircraft have also been allowed to wear military markings without displaying their civil identity. In this case the serial number actually carried is shown in parenthesis after the type's name. For example Auster 6A G-ARRX flies in military colours as VF512, its genuine previous identity. As an aid to the identification of such machines, a conversion list is provided.

Other factors caused a sudden acceleration in the number of registrations allocated by the Civil Aviation Authority in the early 1980s. The first surge followed the discovery that it was possible to register plastic bags, and other items even less likely to fly, on payment of the standard fee. This erosion of the main register was checked in early 1982 by the issue of a special sequence for such devices commencing with G-FYAA. Powered hang-gliders provided the second glut of allocations as a result of the decision that these types should be officially registered. Although a few of the early examples penetrated the current in-sequence register, in due course all new applicants were given marks in special ranges, this time G-MBxx, G-MGxx, G-MJxx, G-MMxx, G-MNxx, G-MTxx, G-MVxx, G-MWxx, G-MYxx and G-MZxx. It took some time before all microlights displayed an official mark but gradually the registration was carried, the size and position depending on the dimensions of the component to which it was applied.

There was news of a further change in mid-1998 when the CAA announced that with immediate effect microlights would be issued with registrations in the normal sequence alongside aircraft in other classes. In addition, it meant that owners could also apply for a personalised identity upon payment of the then current fee of £170 from April 1999, a low price for those wishing to display their status symbol. These various changes played their part in exhausting the current G-Bxxx range after some 26 years, with G-BZxx coming into use before the end of 1999. As this batch approached completion the next series to be used began at G-CBxx instead of the anticipated G-CAxx. The reason for this step was to avoid the re-use of marks issued in Canada during the 1920s, although a few have appeared more recently as personalised UK registrations.

Another large increase in the number of aircraft registered has resulted from the EU-inspired changes in glider registration. After many years of self-regulation by the British Gliding Association, new gliders must now comply with EASA regulations and hence receive registrations in the main G-Cxxx sequence. The phasing-in of EASA registration for the existing glider fleet has been a fairly lengthy process but has now come to an end and as at the beginning of 2012 there were over 2,250 examples on the Register.

September 2007 saw the issue of the 50,000th UK aircraft registration with G-MITC being allocated to a Robinson R44 Raven. The total number of aircraft on the Register has risen over the past 25 years from just under 10,000 at the beginning of 1985 to in excess of 21,300 by January 2009. Numbers have fallen back slightly since that time with the figure as at 1st January 2013 standing at 19,939. Of these, 4,045 were microlights, 1,260 were helicopters, 2,248 were gliders and 1,639 were balloons.

Non-airworthy and preserved aircraft are shown with a star (★) after the type.

The three-letter codes used by airlines to prefix flight numbers are included for those carriers most likely to appear in the UK. Radio frequencies for the larger airfields/airports are also listed.

ASW

ACKNOWLEDGEMENTS: Once again thanks are extended to the Registration Department of the Civil Aviation Authority for its assistance and allowing access to its files and thanks are also given to all those who have contributed items for possible use in this edition.

International Civil Aircraft Markings

A2-	Botswana	OB-	Peru
A3-	Tonga	OD-	Lebanon
A4O-	Oman	OE-	Austria
A5-	Bhutan	OH-	Finland
A6-	United Arab Emirates	OK-	Czech Republic
A7-	Qatar	OM-	Slovakia
A8-	Liberia	OO-	Belgium
A9C-	Bahrain	OY-	Denmark
AP-	Pakistan	P-	North Korea
B-	China/Taiwan/Hong Kong/Macao	P2-	Papua New Guinea
C-	Canada	P4-	Aruba
C2-	Nauru	PH-	Netherlands
C3-	Andorra	PJ-	Netherlands Antilles
C5-	Gambia	PK-	Indonesia
C6-	Bahamas	PP-	Brazil
C9-	Mozambique	PR-	Brazil
CC-	Chile	PT-	Brazil
CN-	Morocco	PU-	Brazil
CP-	Bolivia	PZ-	Surinam
CS-	Portugal	RA-	Russia
CU-	Cuba	RDPL-	Laos
CX-	Uruguay	RP-	Philippines
D-	Germany	S2-	Bangladesh
D2-	Angola	S5-	Slovenia
D4-	Cape Verde Islands	S7-	Seychelles
D6-	Comores Islands	S9-	São Tomé
DQ-	Fiji	SE-	Sweden
E3-	Eritrea	SP-	Poland
E5-	Cook Islands	ST-	Sudan
EC-	Spain	SU-	Egypt
EI-	Republic of Ireland	SX-	Greece
EK-	Armenia	T2-	Tuvalu
EP-	Iran	T3-	Kiribati
ER-	Moldova	T7-	San Marino
ES-	Estonia	T8A-	Palau
ET-	Ethiopia	T9-	Bosnia and Herzegovina
EW-	Belarus	TC-	Turkey
EX-	Kyrgyzstan	TF-	Iceland
EY-	Tajikistan	TG-	Guatemala
EZ-	Turkmenistan	TI-	Costa Rica
F-	France, inc Colonies and Protectorates	TJ-	Cameroon
G-	United Kingdom	TL-	Central African Republic
H4-	Solomon Islands	TN-	Republic of Congo
HA-	Hungary	TR-	Gabon
HB-	Switzerland and Liechtenstein	TS-	Tunisia
HC-	Ecuador	TT-	Tchad
HH-	Haiti	TU-	Ivory Coast
HI-	Dominican Republic	TY-	Benin
HK-	Colombia	TZ-	Mali
HL-	South Korea	UK-	Uzbekistan
HP-	Panama	UN-	Kazakhstan
HR-	Honduras	UR-	Ukraine
HS-	Thailand	V2-	Antigua
HZ-	Saudi Arabia	V3-	Belize
I-	Italy	V4	St. Kitts & Nevis
J2-	Djibouti	V5-	Namibia
J3-	Grenada	V6-	Micronesia
J5-	Guinea Bissau	V7-	Marshall Islands
J6-	St. Lucia	V8-	Brunei
J7-	Dominica	VH-	Australia
J8-	St. Vincent	VN-	Vietnam
JA-	Japan	VP-A	Anguilla
JU-	Mongolia	VP-B	Bermuda
JY-	Jordan	VP-C	Cayman Islands
LN-	Norway	VP-F	Falkland Islands
LV-	Argentina	VP-G	Gibraltar
LX-	Luxembourg	VP-L	British Virgin Islands
LY-	Lithuania	VP-M	Montserrat
LZ-	Bulgaria	VQ-B	Bermuda
M-	Isle of Man	VQ-H	Saint Helena/Ascension
N-	United States of America	VQ-T	Turks & Caicos Islands

VT-	India	5B-	Cyprus
XA-	Mexico	5H-	Tanzania
XB-	Mexico	5N-	Nigeria
XC-	Mexico	5R-	Malagasy Republic (Madagascar)
XT-	Burkina Faso	5T-	Mauritania
XU-	Cambodia	5U-	Niger
XW-	Laos	5V-	Togo
XY-	Myanmar	5W-	Western Samoa (Polynesia)
YA-	Afghanistan	5X-	Uganda
YI-	Iraq	5Y-	Kenya
YJ-	Vanuatu	6O-	Somalia
YK-	Syria	6V-	Senegal
YL-	Latvia	6Y-	Jamaica
YN-	Nicaragua	7O-	Yemen
YR-	Romania	7P-	Lesotho
YS-	El Salvador	7Q-	Malawi
YU-	Serbia	7T-	Algeria
YV-	Venezuela	8P-	Barbados
Z-	Zimbabwe	8Q-	Maldives
Z3-	Macedonia	8R-	Guyana
ZA-	Albania	9A-	Croatia
ZK-	New Zealand	9G-	Ghana
ZP-	Paraguay	9H-	Malta
ZS-	South Africa	9J-	Zambia
3A-	Monaco	9K-	Kuwait
3B-	Mauritius	9L-	Sierra Leone
3C-	Equatorial Guinea	9M-	Malaysia
3D-	Swaziland	9N-	Nepal
3X-	Guinea	9Q-	Congo Kinshasa
4K-	Azerbaijan	9U-	Burundi
4L-	Georgia	9V-	Singapore
4O-	Montenegro	9XR-	Rwanda
4R-	Sri Lanka	9Y-	Trinidad and Tobago
4X-	Israel		
5A-	Libya		

Aircraft Type Designations & Abbreviations

(for example PA-28 Piper Type 28)

A.	Beagle, Auster, Airbus
AAC	Army Air Corps
AA-	American Aviation, Grumman American
AB	Agusta-Bell
AESL	Aero Engine Services Ltd
AG	American General
An	Antonov
ANEC	Air Navigation & Engineering Co
ANG	Air National Guard
AS	Aérospatiale
A.S.	Airspeed
A.W.	Armstrong Whitworth
B.	Blackburn, Bristol, Boeing, Beagle
BA	British Airways
BAC	British Aircraft Company
BAC	British Aircraft Corporation
BAe	British Aerospace
BAPC	British Aviation Preservation Council
BAT	British Aerial Transport
B.K.	British Klemm
BN	Britten-Norman
Bo	Bolkow
Bü	Bücker
CAARP	Co-operatives des Ateliers Aéronautiques de la Région Parisienne
CAC	Commonwealth Aircraft Corporation
CAF	Canadian Air Force
CASA	Construcciones Aeronautics SA
CCF	Canadian Car & Foundry Co
CEA	Centre-Est Aviation
CH.	Chrislea
CHABA	Cambridge Hot-Air Ballooning Association
CLA.	Comper
CP.	Piel
CUAS	Cambridge University Air Squadron
Cycl	Cyclone
D.	Druine
DC-	Douglas Commercial
DH.	de Havilland
DHA.	de Havilland Australia
DHC.	de Havilland Canada
DR.	Jodel (Robin-built)
EE	English Electric
EAA	Experimental Aircraft Association
EMB	Embraer Empresa Brasileira de Aeronautica SA
EoN	Elliotts of Newbury
EP	Edgar Percival
ETPS	Empire Test Pilots School
F.	Fairchild, Fokker
F.A.A.	Fleet Air Arm
FFA	Flug und Fahrzeugwerke AG
FH	Fairchild-Hiller
FrAF	French Air Force
FRED	Flying Runabout Experimental Design
Fw	Focke-Wulf
G.	Grumman
GA	Gulfstream American
GAL.	General Aircraft
GC	Globe Aircraft
GECAS	General Electric Capital Aviation Services
GY	Gardan
H	Helio
HM.	Henri Mignet
HP.	Handley Page
HPR.	Handley Page Reading
HR.	Robin
HS.	Hawker Siddeley
ICA	Intreprinderea de Constructii Aeronau
IHM	International Helicopter Museum
I.I.I.	Iniziative Industriali Italiane
IL	Ilyushin
ILFC	International Lease Finance Corporation
IMCO	Intermountain Manufacturing Co
IWM	Imperial War Museum
KR	Rand-Robinson
L.	Lockheed
L.A.	Luton, Lake
LET	Letecky Narodny Podnik
LLP	Limited Liability Partnership
L.V.G.	Luft-Verkehrs Gesellschaft
M.	Miles, Mooney
MBA	Micro Biplane Aviation
MBB	Messerschmitt-Bölkow-Blohm
McD	McDonnell
MDH	McDonnell Douglas Helicopters
MH.	Max Holste
MHCA	Manhole Cover
MJ	Jurca
MS.	Morane-Saulnier
NA	North American
NC	Nord
NE	North East
P.	Hunting (formerly Percival), Piaggio
PA-	Piper
PC.	Pilatus
PZL	Panstwowe Zaklady Lotnicze
QAC	Quickie Aircraft Co
R.	Rockwell
RAF	Rotary Air Force
RAAF	Royal Australian Air Force
RAFGSA	Royal Air Force Gliding & Soaring Association
RCAF	Royal Canadian Air Force
RF	Fournier
R.N.	Royal Navy
S.	Short, Sikorsky
SA,SE,SO	Sud-Aviation, Aérospatiale, Scottish Aviation
SAAB	Svenska Aeroplan Aktiebolag
SC	Short
SCD	Side Cargo Door
SNCAN	Société Nationale de Constructions Aéronautiques du Nord
SOCATA	Société de Construction d'Avions de Tourisme et d'Affaires
SpA	Societa per Azioni
SPP	Strojirny Prvni Petiletky
S.R.	Saunders-Roe, Stinson
SS	Special Shape
ST	SOCATA
SW	Solar Wings
T.	Tipsy
TB	SOCATA
Tu	Tupolev
UH.	United Helicopters (Hiller)
UK	United Kingdom
USAF	United States Air Force
USAAC	United States Army Air Corps
USN	United States Navy
V.	Vickers-Armstrongs
VLM	Vlaamse Luchttransportmaatschappij
VS.	Vickers-Supermarine
WA	Wassmer
WAR	War Aircraft Replicas
WHE	W.H.Ekin
WS	Westland
Z.	Zlin

8

Reg.	Type (†False registration)	Owner or Operator	Notes
G-AAAH†	DH.60G Moth (replica) (BAPC 168) ★	Yorkshire Air Museum/Elvington	
G-AAAH	DH.60G Moth ★	Science Museum Jason/South Kensington	
G-AACA†	Avro 504K (BAPC 177) ★	Brooklands Museum of Aviation/Weybridge	
G-AACN	HP.39 Gugnunc ★	Science Museum/Wroughton	
G-AADR	DH.60GM Moth	E. V. Moffatt	
G-AAEG	DH.60G Gipsy Moth	I. B. Grace	
G-AAHI	DH.60G Moth	Nigel John Western Reid Discretionary Settlement 2008	
G-AAHY	DH.60M Moth	D. J. Elliott	
G-AAIN	Parnall Elf II	The Shuttleworth Collection/Old Warden	
G-AAJT	DH.60G Moth	M. R. Paul	
G-AALY	DH.60G Moth	K. M. Fresson	
G-AAMX	DH.60GM Moth ★	RAF Museum/Hendon	
G-AAMY	DH.60GMW Moth	Totalsure Ltd	
G-AANG	Blériot XI	The Shuttleworth Collection/Old Warden	
G-AANH	Deperdussin Monoplane	The Shuttleworth Collection/Old Warden	
G-AANI	Blackburn Monoplane	The Shuttleworth Collection/Old Warden	
G-AANJ	L.V.G. C VI (7198/18)	Aerospace Museum/Cosford	
G-AANL	DH.60M Moth	R. A. Palmer	
G-AANO	DH.60GMW Moth	A. W. & M. E. Jenkins	
G-AANV	DH.60G Moth	R. A. Seeley	
G-AAOK	Curtiss Wright Travel Air 12Q	Shipping & Airlines Ltd	
G-AAOR	DH.60G Moth	B. R. Cox	
G-AAPZ	Desoutter I (mod.)	The Shuttleworth Collection	
G-AATC	DH.80A Puss Moth	R. A. Palmer	
G-AAUP	Klemm L.25-1A	J. I. Cooper	
G-AAWO	DH.60G Moth	Iain Charles Reid Discretionary Settlement 2009	
G-AAXG	DH 60M Moth	S. H. Kidston	
G-AAXK	Klemm L.25-1A ★	C. C. Russell-Vick (stored)	
G-AAYT	DH.60G Moth	P. Groves	
G-AAYX	Southern Martlet	The Shuttleworth Collection	
G-AAZG	DH.60G Moth	C. C. & J. M. Lovell	
G-AAZP	DH.80A Puss Moth	R. P. Williams	
G-ABAA	Avro 504K ★	Manchester Museum of Science & Industry	
G-ABAG	DH.60G Moth	A. & P. A. Wood	
G-ABBB	B.105A Bulldog IIA (K2227) ★	RAF Museum/Hendon	
G-ABDA	DH.60G Moth	R. A. Palmer	
G-ABDW	DH.80A Puss Moth (VH-UQB) ★	Museum of Flight/East Fortune	
G-ABDX	DH.60G Moth	M. D. Souch	
G-ABEV	DH.60G Moth	S. L. G. Darch	
G-ABHE	Aeronca C.2	N. S. Chittenden	
G-ABLM	Cierva C.24 ★	De Havilland Heritage Museum/London Colney	
G-ABLS	DH.80A Puss Moth	R. A. Seeley	
G-ABMR	Hart 2 (J9941) ★	RAF Museum/Hendon	
G-ABNT	Civilian C.A.C.1 Coupe	Shipping & Airlines Ltd	
G-ABNX	Redwing 2	Redwing Syndicate	
G-ABOI	Wheeler Slymph ★	Midland Air Museum/Coventry	
G-ABOX	Sopwith Pup (N5195)	C. M. D. & A. P. St. Cyrien	
G-ABSD	DHA.60G Moth	M. E. Vaisey	
G-ABUL†	DH.82A Tiger Moth ★	F.A.A. Museum/Yeovilton (G-AOXG)	
G-ABUS	Comper CLA.7 Swift	R. C. F. Bailey	
G-ABVE	Arrow Active 2	Real Aircraft Co	
G-ABWD	DH.83 Fox Moth	R. I. Souch	
G-ABWP	Spartan Arrow	R. T. Blain	
G-ABXL	Granger Archaeopteryx ★	J. R. Granger	
G-ABYA	DH.60G Gipsy Moth	M. J. Saggers	
G-ABZB	DH.60G-III Moth Major	G. M. Turner & N. Child	
G-ACBH	Blackburn B.2 ★	–/Redhill	
G-ACCB	DH.83 Fox Moth	E. A. Gautrey	
G-ACDA	DH.82A Tiger Moth	B. D. Hughes	
G-ACDC	DH.82A Tiger Moth	Tiger Club Ltd	
G-ACDI	DH.82A Tiger Moth	Doublecube Aviation LLP	
G-ACDJ	DH.82A Tiger Moth	R. H. & J. A. Cooper	
G-ACEJ	DH.83 Fox Moth	I. G. Barnett & G. R. Williams	
G-ACET	DH.84 Dragon	G. Cormack	
G-ACGT	Avro 594 Avian IIIA ★	Yorkshire Light Aircraft Ltd/Leeds	

Notes	Reg.	Type	Owner or Operator
	G-ACGZ	DH.60G-III Moth Major	N. H. Lemon
	G-ACIT	DH.84 Dragon ★	Science Museum/Wroughton
	G-ACLL	DH.85 Leopard Moth	V. M & D. C. M. Stiles
	G-ACMA	DH.85 Leopard Moth	P. A. Vacher
	G-ACMD	DH.82A Tiger Moth	M. J. Bonnick
	G-ACMN	DH.85 Leopard Moth	M. R. & K. E. Slack
	G-ACNS	DH.60G-III Moth Major	C. T. Parry
	G-ACOJ	DH.85 Leopard Moth	Norman Aeroplane Trust
	G-ACSP	DH.88 Comet ★	T. M., M. L., D. A. & P. M. Jones
	G-ACSS	DH.88 Comet ★	The Shuttleworth Collection *Grosvenor House*/Old Warden
	G-ACSS†	DH.88 Comet (replica) ★	G. Gayward (BAPC216)
	G-ACSS†	DH.88 Comet (replica) ★	The Galleria Hatfield (BAPC257)
	G-ACTF	Comper CLA.7 Swift ★	The Shuttleworth Collection/Old Warden
	G-ACUS	DH.85 Leopard Moth	R. A. & V. A. Gammons
	G-ACUU	Cierva C.30A (HM580) ★	G. S. Baker/Duxford
	G-ACUX	S.16 Scion (VH-UUP) ★	Ulster Folk & Transport Museum
	G-ACVA	Kay Gyroplane ★	Museum of Flight/East Fortune
	G-ACWM	Cierva C.30A (AP506) ★	IHM/Weston-super-Mare
	G-ACWP	Cierva C.30A (AP507) ★	Science Museum/South Kensington
	G-ACXB	DH.60G-III Moth Major	D. F. Hodgkinson
	G-ACXE	B.K. L-25C Swallow	J. G. Wakeford
	G-ACYK	Spartan Cruiser III ★	Museum of Flight (front fuselage)/East Fortune
	G-ACZE	DH.89A Dragon Rapide	Chewton Glen Aviation Ltd (G-AJGS)
	G-ADAH	DH.89A Dragon Rapide ★	Manchester Museum of Science & Industry *Pioneer*
	G-ADEV	Avro 504K (E3273)	The Shuttleworth Collection/Old Warden (G-ACNB)
	G-ADGP	M.2L Hawk Speed Six	R. A. Mills
	G-ADGT	DH.82A Tiger Moth (BB697)	The Tiger Club 1990 Ltd
	G-ADGV	DH.82A Tiger Moth	M. van Dijk & M. R. Van der Straaten (G-BACW)
	G-ADHD	DH.60G-III Moth Major	M. E. Vaisey
	G-ADIA	DH.82A Tiger Moth	S. J. Beaty
	G-ADJJ	DH.82A Tiger Moth	J. M. Preston
	G-ADKC	DH.87B Hornet Moth	A. J. Davy
	G-ADKK	DH.87B Hornet Moth	R. M. Lee
	G-ADKL	DH.87B Hornet Moth	J. S. & P. R. Johnson
	G-ADKM	DH.87B Hornet Moth	S. G. Collyer
	G-ADLY	DH.87B Hornet Moth	Totalsure Ltd
	G-ADMT	DH.87B Hornet Moth	D. C. Reid
	G-ADMW	M.2H Hawk Major (DG590) ★	RAF Museum Storage & Restoration Centre/RAF Stafford
	G-ADND	DH.87B Hornet Moth (W9385)	D. M. & S. M. Weston
	G-ADNE	DH.87B Hornet Moth	G-ADNE Group
	G-ADNZ	DH.82A Tiger Moth (DE673)	D. C. Wall
	G-ADOT	DH.87B Hornet Moth ★	De Havilland Heritage Museum/London Colney
	G-ADPC	DH.82A Tiger Moth	Baxterley Flying Group
	G-ADPJ	B.A.C. Drone ★	M. J. Aubrey
	G-ADPS	B.A. Swallow 2	J. F. Hopkins
	G-ADRA	Pietenpol Air Camper	A. J. Mason
	G-ADRG†	Mignet HM.14 (replica) ★	Lower Stondon Transport Museum (BAPC77)
	G-ADRR	Aeronca C.3	S. J. Rudkin
	G-ADRX†	Mignet HM.14 (replica) ★	S. Copeland Aviation Group (BAPC231)
	G-ADRY†	Mignet HM.14 (replica) (BAPC29)★	Brooklands Museum of Aviation/Weybridge
	G-ADVU†	Mignet HM.14 (replica) ★	North East Aircraft Museum/Usworth (BAPC211)
	G-ADWJ	DH.82A Tiger Moth	K. F. Crumplin
	G-ADWO	DH.82A Tiger Moth (BB807) ★	Solent Sky, Southampton
	G-ADWT	M.2W Hawk Trainer	R. Earl & B. Morris
	G-ADXS	Mignet HM.14 ★	Thameside Aviation Museum/Shoreham
	G-ADXT	DH.82A Tiger Moth	DH Heritage Flights Ltd
	G-ADYS	Aeronca C.3	E. P. & P. A. Gliddon
	G-ADYV†	Mignet HM.14 (replica) ★	P. Ward (BAPC243)
	G-ADZW†	Mignet HM.14 (replica) ★	Solent Sky/Southampton (BAPC253)
	G-AEBB	Mignet HM.14 ★	The Shuttleworth Collection/Old Warden
	G-AEBJ	Blackburn B-2	BAe Systems (Operations) Ltd
	G-AEDB	B.A.C. Drone 2	M. J. & S. Honeychurch
	G-AEDU	DH.90 Dragonfly	Norman Aeroplane Trust
	G-AEEG	M.3A Falcon Skysport	P. R. Holloway
	G-AEEH	Mignet HM.14 ★	Aerospace Museum/Cosford
	G-AEFG	Mignet HM.14 (BAPC75) ★	N. H. Ponsford/Breighton
	G-AEFT	Aeronca C.3	N. S. Chittenden

Reg.	Type	Owner or Operator	Notes
G-AEGV	Mignet HM.14 ★	Midland Air Museum/Coventry	
G-AEHM	Mignet HM.14 ★	Science Museum/Wroughton	
G-AEJZ	Mignet HM.14 (BAPC120) ★	Aero Venture	
G-AEKR	Mignet HM.14 (BAPC121) ★	Doncaster Museum & Art Gallery	
G-AEKV	Kronfeld Drone ★	Brooklands Museum of Aviation/Weybridge	
G-AEKW	M.12 Mohawk ★	RAF Museum	
G-AELO	DH.87B Hornet Moth	M. J. Miller	
G-AEML	DH.89 Dragon Rapide ★	Fundacion Infante de Orleans/Spain	
G-AENP	Hawker Hind (K5414) (BAPC78)	The Shuttleworth Collection	
G-AEOA	DH.80A Puss Moth	P. & A. Wood/Old Warden	
G-AEOF†	Mignet HM.14 (BAPC22) ★	Aviodrome/Lelystad, Netherlands	
G-AEOF	Rearwin 8500	Shipping & Airlines Ltd	
G-AEPH	Bristol F.2B (D8096)	The Shuttleworth Collection	
G-AERV	M.11A Whitney Straight	R. A. Seeley	
G-AESB	Aeronca C.3	R. J. M. Turnbull	
G-AESE	DH.87B Hornet Moth	B. R. Cox	
G-AESZ	Chilton D.W.1	R. E. Nerou	
G-AETA	Caudron G.3 (3066) ★	RAF Museum/Hendon	
G-AETG	Aeronca 100	J. Teagle and Partners	
G-AEUJ	M.11A Whitney Straight	R. E. Mitchell	
G-AEVS	Aeronca 100	R. A. Fleming	
G-AEXD	Aeronca 100	M. A. & N. Mills	
G-AEXF	P.6 Mew Gull	Real Aircraft Co	
G-AEXT	Dart Kitten II	R. A. Fleming	
G-AEXZ	Piper J-2 Cub	M. & J. R. Dowson	
G-AEZF	S.16 Scion 2 ★	Acebell Aviation/Redhill	
G-AEZJ	P.10 Vega Gull	D. P. H. Hulme	
G-AFAP†	CASA C.352L ★	Aerospace Museum/Cosford	
G-AFBS	M.14A Hawk Trainer 3 ★	G. D. Durbridge-Freeman/Duxford (G-AKKU)	
G-AFCL	B. A. Swallow 2	C. P. Bloxham	
G-AFDO	Piper J-3F-60 Cub	R. Wald	
G-AFDX	Hanriot HD.1 (HD-75) ★	RAF Museum/Hendon	
G-AFEL	Monocoupe 90A	M. Rieser	
G-AFFH	Piper J-2 Cub	M. J. Honeychurch	
G-AFFI†	Mignet HM.14 (replica) (BAPC76) ★	Yorkshire Air Museum/Elvington	
G-AFGD	B. A. Swallow 2	A. T. Williams & ptnrs	
G-AFGE	B. A. Swallow 2	A. A. M. & C. W. N. Huke	
G-AFGH	Chilton D.W.1.	M. L. & G. L. Joseph	
G-AFGI	Chilton D.W.1.	K. A. A. McDonald	
G-AFGM	Piper J-4A Cub Coupé	P. H. Wilkinson	
G-AFGZ	DH.82A Tiger Moth	M. R. Paul (G-AMHI)	
G-AFHA	Mosscraft MA.1. ★	C. V. Butler	
G-AFIN	Chrislea LC.1 Airguard (BAPC203) ★	T. W. J. Carnall	
G-AFIR	Luton LA-4 Minor	J. Cresswell	
G-AFIU	Parker CA-4 Parasol ★	The Aeroplane Collection/Hooton Park	
G-AFJA	Watkinson Dingbat ★	A. T. Christian	
G-AFJB	Foster-Wikner G.M.1. Wicko	J. Dible	
G-AFJR	Tipsy Trainer 1	M. E. Vaisey (stored)	
G-AFJU	M.17 Monarch	Museum of Flight/East Fortune	
G-AFJV	Mosscraft MA.2 ★	C. V. Butler	
G-AFNI	DH.94 Moth Minor	J. Jennings	
G-AFOB	DH.94 Moth Minor	K. Cantwell	
G-AFOJ	DH.94 Moth Minor	A. H. Soper	
G-AFPN	DH.94 Moth Minor	A. A. A. Maitland & R. S. Jones	
G-AFRZ	M.17 Monarch	R. E. Mitchell/Sleap (G-AIDE)	
G-AFSC	Tipsy Trainer 1	D. M. Forshaw	
G-AFSV	Chilton D.W.1A	R. E. Nerou	
G-AFTA	Hawker Tomtit (K1786)	The Shuttleworth Collection	
G-AFTN	Taylorcraft Plus C2 ★	Leicestershire County Council Museums/Snibston	
G-AFUP	Luscombe 8A Silvaire	R. Dispain	
G-AFVE	DH.82A Tiger Moth (T7230)	J. Mainka	
G-AFWH	Piper J-4A Cub Coupé	C. W. Stearn & R. D. W. Norton	
G-AFWI	DH.82A Tiger Moth	P. R. Harvey	
G-AFWT	Tipsy Trainer 1	N. Parkhouse	
G-AFYD	Luscombe 8F Silvaire	J. D. Iliffe	
G-AFYO	Stinson H.W.75	M. Lodge	
G-AFZA	Piper J-4A Cub Coupe	R. A. Benson	
G-AFZK	Luscombe 8A Silvaire	M. G. Byrnes	
G-AFZL	Porterfield CP.50	P. G. Lucas & S. H. Sharpe	
G-AFZN	Luscombe 8A Silvaire	M. Payne	
G-AGAT	Piper J-3F-50 Cub	A. S. Bathgate	
G-AGBN	GAL.42 Cygnet 2 ★	Museum of Flight/East Fortune	

G-AGEG – G-AHVV

Notes	Reg.	Type	Owner or Operator
	G-AGEG	DH.82A Tiger Moth	Norman Aeroplane Trust
	G-AGHY	DH.82A Tiger Moth	P. Groves
	G-AGIV	Piper J-3C-65 Cub	J-3 Cub Group
	G-AGJG	DH.89A Dragon Rapide	M. J. & D. J. T. Miller
	G-AGLK	Auster 5D	C. R. Harris
	G-AGMI	Luscombe 8A Silvaire	Oscar Flying Group
	G-AGNJ	DH.82A Tiger Moth	B. P. Borsberry & ptnrs
	G-AGNV	Avro 685 York (TS798) ★	Aerospace Museum/Cosford
	G-AGOS	R.S.4 Desford Trainer (VZ728) ★	Leicestershire County Council Museums
	G-AGPG	Avro 19 Srs 2 ★	The Aeroplane Collection/Hooton Park
	G-AGPK	DH.82A Tiger Moth	T. K. Butcher
	G-AGRU	V.498 Viking 1A ★	Brooklands Museum of Aviation/Weybridge
	G-AGSH	DH.89A Dragon Rapide 6	Bournemouth Aviation Museum
	G-AGTM	DH.89A Dragon Rapide 6	Air Atlantique Ltd
	G-AGTO	Auster 5 J/1 Autocrat	M. J. Barnett & D. J. T. Miller
	G-AGTT	Auster J/1 Autocrat	C. Norfolk
	G-AGVG	Auster 5 J/1 Autocrat (modified)	P. J. & S. J. Benest
	G-AGXN	Auster J/1N Alpha	Gentleman's Aerial Touring Carriage Group
	G-AGXU	Auster J/1N Alpha	L. J. Kingscott
	G-AGXV	Auster J/1 Autocrat	B. S. Dowsett & I. M. Oliver
	G-AGYD	Auster J/1N Alpha	P. D. Hodson
	G-AGYH	Auster J/1N Alpha	I. M. Staves
	G-AGYK	Auster J/1 Autocrat	Autocrat Syndicate
	G-AGYT	Auster J/1N Alpha	P. J. Barrett
	G-AGYU	DH.82A Tiger Moth (DE208)	S. A. Firth
	G-AGYY	Ryan ST3KR (27)	H. de Vries/Holland
	G-AGZZ	DH.82A Tiger Moth	M. C. Jordan
	G-AHAG	DH.89A Rapide	D. E. Findon
	G-AHAL	Auster J/1N Alpha	Wickenby Aviation
	G-AHAM	Auster J/1 Autocrat	C. P. L. Jenkin
	G-AHAN	DH.82A Tiger Moth	Tiger Associates Ltd
	G-AHAP	Auster J/1 Autocrat	W. D. Hill
	G-AHAT	Auster J/1N Alpha ★	Dumfries & Galloway Aviation Museum
	G-AHAU	Auster 5 J/1 Autocrat	Andreas Auster Group
	G-AHBL	DH.87B Hornet Moth	Shipping and Airlines Ltd
	G-AHBM	DH.87B Hornet Moth	P. A. & E. P. Gliddon
	G-AHCL	Auster J/1N Alpha (modified)	N. Musgrave
	G-AHCN	Auster J/1N Alpha	C. L. Towell & A. G. Boon
	G-AHCR	Gould-Taylorcraft Plus D Special	D. E. H. Balmford & D. R. Shepherd
	G-AHEC	Luscombe 8A Silvaire	C. G. Dodds
	G-AHED	DH.89A Dragon Rapide (RL962) ★	RAF Museum Storage & Restoration Centre/RAF Stafford
	G-AHGD	DH.89A Dragon Rapide (Z7288)	S. G. Jones
	G-AHGW	Taylorcraft Plus D (LB375)	C. V. Butler
	G-AHGZ	Taylorcraft Plus D (LB367)	M. Pocock
	G-AHHH	Auster J/1 Autocrat	H. A. Jones
	G-AHHT	Auster J/1N Alpha	A. C. Barber & N. J. Hudson
	G-AHIP	Piper J-3C-65 Cub	A. D. Pearce
	G-AHIZ	DH.82A Tiger Moth	C.F.G. Flying Ltd
	G-AHKX	Avro 19 Srs 2	The Shuttleworth Collection
	G-AHKY	Miles M.18 Series 2 ★	Museum of Flight/East Fortune
	G-AHLK	Auster 3 (NJ889)	J. H. Powell-Tuck
	G-AHLT	DH.82A Tiger Moth	M. P. Waring
	G-AHNR	Taylorcraft BC-12D	T. M. Buick
	G-AHOO	DH.82A Tiger Moth	J. T. Milsom
	G-AHPZ	DH.82A Tiger Moth	N. J. Wareing
	G-AHRI	DH.104 Dove 1 ★	Newark Air Museum
	G-AHSA	Avro 621 Tutor (K3241)	The Shuttleworth Collection
	G-AHSD	Taylorcraft Plus D (LB323)	A. L. Hall-Carpenter
	G-AHSP	Auster J/1 Autocrat	R. M. Weeks
	G-AHSS	Auster J/1N Alpha	A. M. Roche
	G-AHST	Auster J/1N Alpha	A. C. Frost
	G-AHTE	P.44 Proctor V	D. K. Tregilgas
	G-AHTW	A.S.40 Oxford (V3388) ★	Skyfame Collection/Duxford
	G-AHUF	DH.Tiger Moth	Dream Ventures Ltd
	G-AHUG	Taylorcraft Plus D	D. Nieman
	G-AHUI	M.38 Messenger 2A ★	The Aeroplane Collection/Hooton Park
	G-AHUJ	M.14A Hawk Trainer 3 (R1914) ★	Strathallan Aircraft Collection
	G-AHUN	Globe GC-1B Swift	R. J. Hamlett
	G-AHUV	DH.82A Tiger Moth	A. D. Gordon
	G-AHVU	DH.82A Tiger Moth	J. B. Steel
	G-AHVV	DH.82A Tiger Moth	M. Arter

Reg.	Type	Owner or Operator	Notes
G-AHXE	Taylorcraft Plus D (LB312)	J. M. C. Pothecary	
G-AIBE	Fulmar II (N1854) ★	F.A.A. Museum/Yeovilton	
G-AIBH	Auster J/1N Alpha	M. J. Bonnick	
G-AIBM	Auster J/1 Autocrat	R. Greatrex	
G-AIBR	Auster J/1 Autocrat	P. R. Hodson	
G-AIBW	Auster J/1N Alpha	C. R. Sunter	
G-AIBX	Auster J/1 Autocrat	Wasp Flying Group	
G-AIBY	Auster J/1 Autocrat	D. Morris	
G-AICX	Luscombe 8A Silvaire	N. M. Harwood & M. A. Watts	
G-AIDL	DH.89A Dragon Rapide 6 (TX310)	Air Atlantique Ltd	
G-AIDN	VS.502 Spitfire Tr.VII (MT818)	P. M. Andrews	
G-AIDS	DH.82A Tiger Moth	K. D. Pogmore & T. Dann	
G-AIEK	M.38 Messenger 2A (RG333)	P. E. Beaver	
G-AIFZ	Auster J/1N Alpha	M. D. Ansley	
G-AIGD	Auster V J/1 Autocrat	R. B. Webber	
G-AIGF	Auster J/1N Alpha	D. W. Mathie	
G-AIGT	Auster J/1N Alpha	R. R. Harris	
G-AIIH	Piper J-3C-65 Cub	The G-AIIH Group	
G-AIJI	Auster J/1N Alpha ★	C. J. Baker	
G-AIJM	Auster J/4	N. Huxtable	
G-AIJT	Auster J/4 Srs 100	Aberdeen Auster Flying Group	
G-AIKE	Auster 5	R. H. Cooper & T. K. Rumble	
G-AIPR	Auster J/4	M. A. & N. Mills	
G-AIPV	Auster J/1 Autocrat	W. P. Miller	
G-AIRC	Auster J/1 Autocrat	Z. J. Rockey	
G-AIRK	DH.82A Tiger Moth	J. S. & P. R. Johnson	
G-AISA	Tipsy B Srs 1	S. Slater	
G-AISC	Tipsy B Srs 1	Wagtail Flying Group	
G-AISS	Piper J-3C-65 Cub	K. W. Wood & F. Watson	
G-AIST	VS.300 Spitfire 1A (AR213/PR-D)	Spitfire The One Ltd	
G-AISX	Piper J-3C-65 Cub	Cubfly	
G-AITB	A.S.10 Oxford (MP425) ★	RAF Museum/Hendon	
G-AIUA	M.14A Hawk Trainer 3 (T9768) ★	D. S. Hunt	
G-AIUL	DH.89A Dragon Rapide 6	I. Jones	
G-AIXA	Taylorcraft Plus D (LB264)★	RAF Museum/Hendon	
G-AIXJ	DH.82A Tiger Moth	D. Green	
G-AIXN	Benes-Mraz M.1C Sokol	A. J. Wood	
G-AIYG	SNCAN Stampe SV.4B	J. E. Henny/Belgium	
G-AIYR	DH.89A Dragon Rapide (HG691)	Spectrum Leisure Ltd	
G-AIYS	DH.85 Leopard Moth	R. A. & V. A. Gammons	
G-AIZE	Fairchild F.24W Argus 2 (FS628) ★	Aerospace Museum/Cosford	
G-AIZG	VS.236 Walrus 1 (L2301) ★	F.A.A. Museum/Yeovilton	
G-AIZU	Auster J/1 Autocrat★	C. J. & J. G. B. Morley	
G-AJAD	Piper J-3C-65 Cub	C. R. Shipley	
G-AJAE	Auster J/1N Alpha	J. & B. F. Wolfe	
G-AJAJ	Auster J/1N Alpha	G-AJAJ Group	
G-AJAM	Auster J/2 Arrow	D. A. Porter	
G-AJAP	Luscombe 8A Silvaire	M. Flint	
G-AJAS	Auster J/1N Alpha	P. Ferguson & L. & R. Ferguson-Dalling	
G-AJCP	D.31 Turbulent	B. R. Pearson	
G-AJDW	Auster J/1 Autocrat	D. R. Hunt	
G-AJDY	Auster 5 J/1 Autocrat	W. Bayman	
G-AJEB	Auster J/1N Alpha ★	The Aeroplane Collection/Hooton Park	
G-AJEE	Auster J/1 Autocrat	A. C. Whitehead	
G-AJEH	Auster J/1N Alpha	J. T. Powell-Tuck	
G-AJEI	Auster J/1N Alpha	J. Siddall	
G-AJEM	Auster J/1 Autocrat	A. L. Aish	
G-AJES	Piper J-3C-65 Cub (330485:C-44)	D. E. Jarvis	
G-AJGJ	Auster 5 (RT486)	British Classic Aircraft Restoration Flying Group	
G-AJHS	DH.82A Tiger Moth	Vliegend Museum/Netherlands	
G-AJIH	Auster J/1 Autocrat	A. J. Collins	
G-AJIS	Auster J/1N Alpha	Husthwaite Auster Group	
G-AJIT	Auster J/1 Kingsland Autocrat	G-AJIT Group	
G-AJIU	Auster J/1 Autocrat	M. D. Greenhalgh	
G-AJIW	Auster J/1N Alpha	W. C. Walters	
G-AJJP	Fairey Jet Gyrodyne (XJ389) ★	Museum of Berkshire Aviation/Woodley	
G-AJJS	Cessna 120	Juliet Sierra Group	
G-AJJT	Cessna 120	Juliet Tango Group	
G-AJJU	Luscombe 8E Silvaire	Enstone Luscombe Group	
G-AJKB	Luscombe 8E Silvaire	T. Carter	
G-AJOC	M.38 Messenger 2A ★	Ulster Folk & Transport Museum	

Notes	Reg.	Type	Owner or Operator
	G-AJOE	M.38 Messenger 2A	P. W. Bishop
	G-AJON	Aeronca 7AC Champion	J. M. Gale
	G-AJOV†	Westland WS-51 Dragonfly ★	Aerospace Museum/Cosford
	G-AJOZ	Fairchild F.24W Argus 2 ★	Yorkshire Air Museum/Elvington
	G-AJPI	Fairchild F.24R-41a Argus 3 (314887)	R. Sijben/Netherlands
	G-AJRB	Auster J/1 Autocrat	R. W. Vince
	G-AJRH	Auster J/1N Alpha ★	Charnwood Museum/Loughborough
	G-AJRS	M.14A Hawk Trainer 3 (P6382:C)	The Shuttleworth Collection
	G-AJTW	DH.82A Tiger Moth (N6965:FL-J)	J. A. Barker
	G-AJUE	Auster J/1 Autocrat	P. H. B. Cole
	G-AJUL	Auster J/1N Alpha	M. J. Crees
	G-AJVE	DH.82A Tiger Moth	R. A. Gammons
	G-AJWB	M.38 Messenger 2A	P. W. Bishop
	G-AJXC	Auster 5	R. D. Helliar-Symonds, K. A. & S. E. W. Williams
	G-AJXV	Auster 4 (NJ695)	B. A. Farries
	G-AJXY	Auster 4	X-Ray Yankee Group
	G-AJYB	Auster J/1N Alpha	P. J. Shotbolt
	G-AKAT	M.14A Hawk Trainer 3 (T9738)	R. A. Fleming
	G-AKAZ	Piper J-3C-65 Cub (57-G)	Frazerblades Ltd
	G-AKBO	M.38 Messenger 2A	D. O. Blackburn & P. A. Fenton
	G-AKDF	M.38 Messenger 2A	C. W. P. Turner
	G-AKDK	M.65 Gemini 1A	C. W. P. Turner
	G-AKDN	DHC.1A-1 Chipmunk	P. S. Derry/Canada
	G-AKDW	DH.89A Dragon Rapide ★	De Havilland Heritage Museum/London Colney
	G-AKEL	M.65 Gemini 1A ★	Ulster Folk & Transport Museum
	G-AKEN	M.65 Gemini 1A	C. W. P. Turner
	G-AKEX	Percival Proctor III	M. Biddulph (G-AKIU)
	G-AKGE	M.65 Gemini 3C ★	Ulster Folk & Transport Museum
	G-AKHP	M.65 Gemini 1A	M. A. McCallum
	G-AKHU	M.65 Gemini 1A	C. W. P. Turner
	G-AKHZ	M.65 Gemini 7 ★	The Aeroplane Collection/Hooton Park
	G-AKIB	Piper J-3C-90 Cub (480015:M-44)	R. Horner
	G-AKIF	DH.89A Dragon Rapide	Airborne Taxi Services Ltd
	G-AKIN	M.38 Messenger 2A	Sywell Messenger Group
	G-AKIU	P.44 Proctor V	Air Atlantique Ltd
	G-AKKB	M.65 Gemini 1A	D. R. Gray
	G-AKKH	M.65 Gemini 1A	J. S. Allison
	G-AKKR	M.14A Magister (T9707) ★	Museum of Army Flying/Middle Wallop
	G-AKKY	M.14A Hawk Trainer 3 (L6906)★ (BAPC44)	Museum of Berkshire Aviation/Woodley
	G-AKLW	Short SA.6 Sealand 1 ★	Ulster Folk & Transport Museum
	G-AKOW	Auster 5 (TJ569) ★	Museum of Army Flying/Middle Wallop
	G-AKPF	M.14A Hawk Trainer 3 (N3788)	P. R. Holloway
	G-AKPI	Auster 5	R. H. & J. A. Cooper
	G-AKRA	Piper J-3C-65 Cub	W. R. Savin
	G-AKRP	DH.89A Dragon Rapide 4	Eaglescott Dominie Group
	G-AKSY	Auster 5 (TJ534)	A. Brier
	G-AKSZ	Auster 5D (modified)	P. W. Yates & R. G. Darbyshire
	G-AKTH	Piper J-3C-65 Cub	OFL4 Group
	G-AKTI	Luscombe 8A Silvaire	C. Chambers
	G-AKTO	Aeronca 7BCM Champion	R. M. Davies
	G-AKTP	PA-17 Vagabond	Golf Tango Papa Group
	G-AKTR	Aeronca 7AC Champion	T. White
	G-AKTS	Cessna 120	M. Isterling
	G-AKTT	Luscombe 8A Silvaire	S. J. Charters
	G-AKUE	DH.82A Tiger Moth	D. F. Hodgkinson
	G-AKUF	Luscombe 8E Silvaire	M. O. Loxton
	G-AKUJ	Luscombe 8E Silvaire	P. R. Bentley
	G-AKUK	Luscombe 8A Silvaire	O. R. Watts
	G-AKUL	Luscombe 8A Silvaire	E. A. Taylor
	G-AKUM	Luscombe 8F Silvaire	D. A. Young
	G-AKUN	Piper J-3F-65 Cub	W. R. Savin
	G-AKUO	Aeronca 11AC Chief	L. W. Richardson
	G-AKUP	Luscombe 8E Silvaire	D. A. Young
	G-AKUR	Cessna 140	J. Greenaway & C. A. Davies
	G-AKUW	Chrislea CH.3 Super Ace 2	J. & S. Rickett
	G-AKVF	Chrislea CH.3 Super Ace 2	Aviation Heritage Ltd
	G-AKVM	Cessna 120	N. Wise & S. Walker
	G-AKVN	Aeronca 11AC Chief	P. A. Jackson
	G-AKVO	Taylorcraft BC-12D	A. Weir
	G-AKVP	Luscombe 8A Silvaire	J. M. Edis
	G-AKVR	Chrislea CH.3 Skyjeep 4	R. B. Webber

Reg.	Type	Owner or Operator	Notes
G-AKVZ	M.38 Messenger 4B	Shipping & Airlines Ltd	
G-AKWS	Auster 5A-160 (RT610)	M. C. Hayes	
G-AKWT	Auster 5 ★	C. Baker	
G-AKXP	Auster 5 (NJ633)	M. J. Nicholson	
G-AKXS	DH.82A Tiger Moth	J. & G. J. Eagles	
G-AKZN	P.34A Proctor 3 (Z7197) ★	RAF Museum/Hendon	
G-ALAR	Miles M.38 Messenger 4A	C. W. P. Turner	
G-ALAX	DH.89A Dragon Rapide ★	Durney Aeronautical Collection/Andover	
G-ALBJ	Auster 5 (TW501)	B. M. Vigor	
G-ALBK	Auster 5	J. S. Allison	
G-ALBN	Bristol 173 (XF785) ★	RAF Museum Storage & Restoration Centre/Cardington	
G-ALCK	P.34A Proctor 3 (LZ766) ★	Skyfame Collection/Duxford	
G-ALCU	DH.104 Dove 2 ★	Midland Air Museum/Coventry	
G-ALDG	HP.81 Hermes 4 ★	Duxford Aviation Society (fuselage only)	
G-ALEH	PA-17 Vagabond	A. D. Pearce	
G-ALFA	Auster 5	A. E. Jones	
G-ALFU	DH.104 Dove 6 ★	Duxford Aviation Society	
G-ALGA	PA-15 Vagabond	S. T. Gilbert	
G-ALGT	VS.379 Spitfire F.XIVH (RM689)	Rolls-Royce PLC	
G-ALIJ	PA-17 Vagabond	G-ALIJ Flying Group	
G-ALIW	DH.82A Tiger Moth	F. R. Curry	
G-ALJF	P.34A Proctor 3	J. F. Moore	
G-ALJL	DH.82A Tiger Moth	R. I. & D. Souch	
G-ALJR	Abbott-Baynes Scud III	L. P. Woodage	
G-ALLF	Slingsby T.30A Prefect (ARK)	J. F. Hopkins & K. M. Fresson	
G-ALMA	Piper J3C-65 Cub	M. J. Butler (G-BBXS)	
G-ALNA	DH.82A Tiger Moth	R. J. Doughton	
G-ALND	DH.82A Tiger Moth (N9191)	J. T. Powell-Tuck	
G-ALOD	Cessna 140	H. Merkado	
G-ALSP	Bristol 171 Sycamore (WV783) ★	RAF Museum/Hendon	
G-ALSS	Bristol 171 Sycamore (WA576) ★	Dumfries & Galloway Aviation Museum	
G-ALST	Bristol 171 Sycamore (WA577) ★	North East Aircraft Museum/Usworth	
G-ALSW	Bristol 171 Sycamore (WT933) ★	Newark Air Museum	
G-ALSX	Bristol 171 Sycamore (G-48-1) ★	IHM/Weston-super-Mare	
G-ALTO	Cessna 140	T. M. Jones & ptnrs	
G-ALUC	DH.82A Tiger Moth	Tiger Moth Experience Ltd	
G-ALWB	DHC.1 Chipmunk 22A	D. M. Neville	
G-ALWF	V.701 Viscount ★	Duxford Aviation Society RMA Sir John Franklin	
G-ALWS	DH.82A Tiger Moth	K. F. Crumplin	
G-ALWW	DH.82A Tiger Moth	D. E. Findon	
G-ALXT	DH.89A Dragon Rapide ★	Science Museum/Wroughton	
G-ALXZ	Auster 5-150	G-ALXZ Syndicate	
G-ALYB	Auster 5 (RT520) ★	South Yorkshire Aviation Museum/Doncaster	
G-ALYG	Auster 5D	A. L. Young	
G-ALYW	DH.106 Comet 1 ★	RAF Exhibition Flight (fuselage converted to 'Nimrod')	
G-ALZE	BN-1F ★	M. R. Short/Solent Sky, Southampton	
G-ALZO	A.S.57 Ambassador ★	Duxford Aviation Society	
G-AMAW	Luton LA-4 Minor	The Real Aeroplane Co.Ltd	
G-AMBB	DH.82A Tiger Moth	J. Eagles	
G-AMCK	DH.82A Tiger Moth	Liverpool Flying School Ltd	
G-AMCM	DH.82A Tiger Moth	A. K. & J. I. Cooper	
G-AMDA	Avro 652A Anson 1 (N4877:MK-V) ★	Skyfame Collection/Duxford	
G-AMEN	PA-18 Super Cub 95	The G-AMEN Flying Group	
G-AMHF	DH.82A Tiger Moth	A. J. West	
G-AMHJ	Douglas C-47A Dakota 6 (KG651) ★	Assault Glider Association/Shawbury	
G-AMKU	Auster J/1B Aiglet	P. G. Lipman	
G-AMLZ	P.50 Prince 6E ★	The Jetstream Club	
G-AMMS	Auster J/5K Aiglet Trainer	R. B. Webber	
G-AMNN	DH.82A Tiger Moth	I. J. Perry	
G-AMOG	V.701 Viscount ★	Museum of Flight/East Fortune	
G-AMPG	PA-12 Super Cruiser	A. G. & S. M. Measey	
G-AMPI	SNCAN Stampe SV.4C	T. W. Harris	
G-AMPO	Douglas C-47B (FZ626/YS-DH) ★	(gate guardian)/RAF Lyneham	
G-AMPY	Douglas C-47B (KK116)	Air Atlantique Ltd/Coventry	
G-AMRA	Douglas C-47B	Air Atlantique Ltd	
G-AMRF	Auster J/5F Aiglet Trainer	D. A. Hill	
G-AMRK	G.37 Gladiator I (K7985)	The Shuttleworth Collection	
G-AMSG	SIPA 903	S. W. Markham	
G-AMSN	Douglas C-47B ★	Aceball Aviation/Redhill	

Notes	Reg.	Type	Owner or Operator
	G-AMTA	Auster J/5F Aiglet Trainer	J. D. Manson
	G-AMTF	DH.82A Tiger Moth (T7842)	H. A. D. Monro
	G-AMTK	DH.82A Tiger Moth	S. W. McKay & M. E. Vaisey
	G-AMTM	Auster J/1 Autocrat	R. J. Stobo (G-AJUJ)
	G-AMTV	DH.82A Tiger Moth	G-AMTV Flying Group
	G-AMUF	DHC.1 Chipmunk 21	Redhill Tailwheel Flying Club Ltd
	G-AMUI	Auster J/5F Aiglet Trainer	R. B. Webber
	G-AMVD	Auster 5 (TJ652)	M. Hammond
	G-AMVP	Tipsy Junior	A. R. Wershat
	G-AMVS	DH.82A Tiger Moth	J. T. Powell-Tuck
	G-AMXA	DH.106 Comet 2 (nose only) ★	(stored)
	G-AMYD	Auster J/5L Aiglet Trainer	R. D. Thomasson
	G-AMYJ	Douglas C-47B (KN353) ★	Yorkshire Air Museum/Elvington
	G-AMZI	Auster J/5F Aiglet Trainer	J. F. Moore
	G-AMZT	Auster J/5F Aiglet Trainer	D. Hyde, J. W. Saull & J. C. Hutchinson
	G-ANAF	Douglas C-47B	Air Atlantique Ltd
	G-ANAP	DH.104 Dove 6 ★	Brunel Technical College/Lulsgate
	G-ANCF	B.175 Britannia 308 ★	Bristol Aero Collection (stored)/Kemble
	G-ANCS	DH.82A Tiger Moth	C. E. Edwards & E. A. Higgins
	G-ANCX	DH.82A Tiger Moth	E. N. K. Lison
	G-ANDE	DH.82A Tiger Moth	D. A. Nisbet
	G-ANDM	DH.82A Tiger Moth	N. J. Stagg
	G-ANEH	DH.82A Tiger Moth (N6797)	G. J. Wells
	G-ANEL	DH.82A Tiger Moth	Totalsure Ltd
	G-ANEM	DH.82A Tiger Moth	P. J. Benest
	G-ANEN	DH.82A Tiger Moth	G-ANEN Group
	G-ANEW	DH.82A Tiger Moth	K. F. Crumplin
	G-ANEZ	DH.82A Tiger Moth	C. D. J. Bland
	G-ANFH	Westland WS-55 Whirlwind ★	IHM/Weston-super-Mare
	G-ANFI	DH.82A Tiger Moth (DE623)	G. P. Graham
	G-ANFL	DH.82A Tiger Moth	Felthorpe Tiger Group Ltd
	G-ANFM	DH.82A Tiger Moth	Reading Flying Group
	G-ANFP	DH.82A Tiger Moth	G. D. Horn
	G-ANFU	Auster 5 (NJ719) ★	North East Aircraft Museum/Usworth
	G-ANFV	DH.82A Tiger Moth (DF155)	R. A. L. Falconer
	G-ANGK	Cessna 140A	A T & N T Ltd
	G-ANHK	DH.82A Tiger Moth	J. D. Iliffe
	G-ANHR	Auster 5	H. L. Swallow
	G-ANHS	Auster 4 (MT197)	Mike Tango Group
	G-ANHU	Auster 4	J. Mainka
	G-ANHX	Auster 5D	D. J. Baker
	G-ANIE	Auster 5 (TW467)	R. T. Ingram
	G-ANIJ	Auster 5D (TJ672)	G. M. Rundle
	G-ANIS	Auster 5	J. Clarke-Cockburn
	G-ANJA	DH.82A Tiger Moth	A. D. Hodgkinson
	G-ANJD	DH.82A Tiger Moth	D. O. Lewis
	G-ANKK	DH.82A Tiger Moth (T5854)	Halfpenny Green Tiger Group
	G-ANKT	DH.82A Tiger Moth (K2585)	The Shuttleworth Collection
	G-ANKV	DH.82A Tiger Moth (T7793)	J. A. Cooper
	G-ANKZ	DH.82A Tiger Moth (N6466)	T. D. Le Mesurier
	G-ANLD	DH.82A Tiger Moth	K. Peters
	G-ANLS	DH.82A Tiger Moth	P. A. Gliddon
	G-ANLW	Westland WS-51/2 Widgeon ★	Norfolk & Suffolk Museum/Flixton
	G-ANMO	DH.82A Tiger Moth (K4259:71)	R. J. Moore & B. S. Floodgate
	G-ANMY	DH.82A Tiger Moth (DE470)	Dog Easy Ltd
	G-ANNB	DH.82A Tiger Moth	J. P. Brown
	G-ANNG	DH.82A Tiger Moth	P. F. Walter
	G-ANNI	DH.82A Tiger Moth (T6953)	C. E. Ponsford & ptnrs
	G-ANNK	DH.82A Tiger Moth (T7290)	J. Y. Kaye
	G-ANOA	Hiller UH-12A ★	Redhill Technical College
	G-ANOD	DH.82A Tiger Moth	P. G. Watson
	G-ANOH	DH.82A Tiger Moth	N. Parkhouse
	G-ANOK	SAAB S.91C Safir ★	A. F. Galt & Co (stored)
	G-ANOM	DH.82A Tiger Moth	S. J. Beaty
	G-ANON	DH.82A Tiger Moth (T7909)	M. Kelly
	G-ANOO	DH.82A Tiger Moth	R. K. Packman
	G-ANOV	DH.104 Dove 6 ★	Museum of Flight/East Fortune
	G-ANPE	DH.82A Tiger Moth	T. K. Butcher (G-IESH)
	G-ANPK	DH.82A Tiger Moth	A. D. Hodgkinson
	G-ANPP	P.34A Proctor 3	C. P. A. & J. Jeffrey
	G-ANRF	DH.82A Tiger Moth	C. D. Cyster
	G-ANRM	DH.82A Tiger Moth (DF112)	Spectrum Leisure Ltd

Reg.	Type	Owner or Operator	Notes
G-ANRN	DH.82A Tiger Moth	J. J. V. Elwes	
G-ANRP	Auster 5 (TW439)	S. D. & S. P. Allen	
G-ANRX	DH.82A Tiger Moth ★	De Havilland Heritage Museum/London Colney	
G-ANSM	DH.82A Tiger Moth	Douglas Aviation	
G-ANTE	DH.82A Tiger Moth (T6562)	G-ANTE Flyers Ltd	
G-ANTK	Avro 685 York ★	Duxford Aviation Society	
G-ANUO	DH.114 Heron 2D (G-AOXL) ★	Westmead Business Group/Croydon Airport	
G-ANUW	DH.104 Dove 6 ★	Jet Aviation Preservation Group	
G-ANVY	P.31 Proctor 4	J. W. Tregilgas	
G-ANWB	DHC.1 Chipmunk 21	G. Briggs	
G-ANXB	DH.114 Heron 1B ★	Newark Air Museum	
G-ANXC	Auster J/5R Alpine	Alpine Group	
G-ANXR	P.31C Proctor 4 (RM221)	N. H. T. Cottrell	
G-ANZT	Thruxton Jackaroo (T7798)	D. J. Neville & P. A. Dear	
G-ANZU	DH.82A Tiger Moth	M. I. Lodge	
G-ANZZ	DH.82A Tiger Moth	T. K. Butcher	
G-AOAA	DH.82A Tiger Moth	R. C. P. Brookhouse	
G-AOBG	Somers-Kendall SK.1	P. W. Bishop	
G-AOBH	DH.82A Tiger Moth (NL750)	P. Nutley	
G-AOBJ	DH.82A Tiger Moth	A. D. Hodgkinson	
G-AOBU	P.84 Jet Provost T.1 (XD693)	T. J. Manna	
G-AOBX	DH.82A Tiger Moth	David Ross Flying Group	
G-AOCP	Auster 5 ★	C. J. Baker (stored)	
G-AOCR	Auster 5D (NJ673)	D. A. Hill	
G-AOCU	Auster 5	S. J. Ball	
G-AODA	Westland S-55 Srs 3 ★	IHM/Weston-super-Mare	
G-AODR	DH.82A Tiger Moth	G-AODR Group (G-ISIS)	
G-AODT	DH.82A Tiger Moth (R5250)	R. A. Harrowven	
G-AOEH	Aeronca 7AC Champion	A. Gregori	
G-AOEI	DH.82A Tiger Moth	C.F.G. Flying Ltd	
G-AOEL	DH.82A Tiger Moth ★	Museum of Flight/East Fortune	
G-AOES	DH.82A Tiger Moth	K. A. & A. J. Broomfield	
G-AOET	DH.82A Tiger Moth	Venom Jet Promotions Ltd	
G-AOEX	Thruxton Jackaroo	A. T. Christian	
G-AOFE	DHC.1 Chipmunk 22A (WB702)	W. J. Quinn	
G-AOFS	Auster J/5L Aiglet Trainer	P. N. A. Whitehead	
G-AOGA	M.75 Aries ★	Irish Aviation Museum (stored)	
G-AOGI	DH.82A Tiger Moth	W. J. Taylor	
G-AOGR	DH.82A Tiger Moth (XL714)	R. J. S. G. Clark	
G-AOGV	Auster J/5R Alpine	R. E. Heading	
G-AOHY	DH.82A Tiger Moth (N6537)	S. W. Turley	
G-AOHZ	Auster J/5P Autocar	A. D. Hodgkinson	
G-AOIM	DH.82A Tiger Moth	R. C. P. Brookhouse	
G-AOIR	Thruxton Jackaroo	K. A. & A. J. Broomfield	
G-AOIS	DH.82A Tiger Moth (R5172)	J. K. Ellwood	
G-AOJH	DH.83C Fox Moth	Connect Properties Ltd	
G-AOJJ	DH.82A Tiger Moth (DF128)	JJ Flying Group	
G-AOJK	DH.82A Tiger Moth	R. J. Willies	
G-AOJR	DHC.1 Chipmunk 22	G. J-H. Caubergs & N. Marien/Belgium	
G-AOJT	DH.106 Comet 1 (F-BGNX) ★	De Havilland Heritage Museum (fuselage only)	
G-AOKH	P.40 Prentice 1	J. F. Moore	
G-AOKL	P.40 Prentice 1 (VS610)	The Shuttleworth Collection	
G-AOKO	P.40 Prentice 1 ★	Aero Venture	
G-AOKZ	P.40 Prentice 1 (VS623) ★	Midland Air Museum/Coventry	
G-AOLK	P.40 Prentice 1 ★	RAF Museum	
G-AOLU	P.40 Prentice 1 (VS356)	N. J. Butler	
G-AORG	DH.114 Heron 2	Duchess of Brittany (Jersey) Ltd	
G-AORW	DHC.1 Chipmunk 22A	Skylark Aviation Ltd	
G-AOSK	DHC.1 Chipmunk 22 (WB726)	P. McMillan	
G-AOSY	DHC.1 Chipmunk 22 (WB585:M)	Chippy Sierra Yankee Group	
G-AOTD	DHC.1 Chipmunk 22 (WB588)	S. Piech	
G-AOTF	DHC.1 Chipmunk 23 (Lycoming)	A. C. Darby	
G-AOTI	DH.114 Heron 2D ★	De Havilland Heritage Museum/London Colney	
G-AOTK	D.53 Turbi	J. S. & P. R. Johnson	
G-AOTR	DHC.1 Chipmunk 22	Ace Leasing Ltd	
G-AOTY	DHC.1 Chipmunk 22A (WG472)	A. A. Hodgson	
G-AOUJ	Fairey Ultra-Light ★	IHM/Weston-super-Mare	
G-AOUO	DHC.1 Chipmunk 22 (Lycoming)	M. F. Cuming	
G-AOUP	DHC.1 Chipmunk 22	A. R. Harding	
G-AOUR	DH.82A Tiger Moth ★	Ulster Folk & Transport Museum	
G-AOVF	B.175 Britannia 312F ★	Aerospace Museum/Cosford	
G-AOVS	B.175 Britannia 312F ★	Airport Fire Section/Luton	

Notes	Reg.	Type	Owner or Operator
	G-AOVT	B.175 Britannia 312F ★	Duxford Aviation Society
	G-AOVW	Auster 5	B. Marriott
	G-AOXN	DH.82A Tiger Moth	S. L. G. Darch
	G-AOZH	DH.82A Tiger Moth (K2572)	M. H. Blois-Brooke
	G-AOZL	Auster J/5Q Alpine	R. M. Weeks
	G-AOZP	DHC.1 Chipmunk 22	S. J. Davies
	G-APAF	Auster 5 (TW511)	J. J. J. Mostyn (G-CMAL)
	G-APAH	Auster 5	T. J. Goodwin
	G-APAJ	Thruxton Jackaroo	J. T. H. Page
	G-APAL	DH.82A Tiger Moth (N6847)	P. J. Shotbolt
	G-APAM	DH.82A Tiger Moth	R. P. Williams
	G-APAO	DH.82A Tiger Moth (R4922)	H. J. Maguire
	G-APAP	DH.82A Tiger Moth (R5136)	R. & S. Flanagan
	G-APAS	DH.106 Comet 1XB ★	Aerospace Museum/Cosford
	G-APBE	Auster 5	E. G. & G. R. Woods
	G-APBI	DH.82A Tiger Moth	C. J. Zeal
	G-APBO	D.53 Turbi	R. C. Hibberd
	G-APBW	Auster 5	N. Huxtable
	G-APCB	Auster J/5Q Alpine	A. A. Beswick
	G-APCC	DH.82A Tiger Moth	L. J. Rice/Henstridge
	G-APDB	DH.106 Comet 4 ★	Duxford Aviation Society
	G-APEP	V.953C Merchantman ★	Brooklands Museum of Aviation/Weybridge
	G-APFA	D.54 Turbi	F. J. Keitch
	G-APFJ	Boeing 707-436 ★	Museum of Flight/East Fortune
	G-APFU	DH.82A Tiger Moth	Leisure Assets Ltd
	G-APFV	PA-23-160 Apache	J. L. Thorogood (G-MOLY)
	G-APHV	Avro 19 Srs 2 (VM360) ★	Museum of Flight/East Fortune
	G-APIE	Tipsy Belfair B	D. Beale
	G-APIH	DH.82A Tiger Moth	K. Stewering
	G-APIK	Auster J/1N Alpha	J. H. Powell-Tuck
	G-APIM	V.806 Viscount ★	Brooklands Museum of Aviation/Weybridge
	G-APIT	P.40 Prentice 1 (VR192) ★	WWII Aircraft Preservation Society/Lasham
	G-APIY	P.40 Prentice 1 (VR249) ★	Newark Air Museum
	G-APIZ	D.31 Turbulent	R. G. Meredith
	G-APJB	P.40 Prentice 1 (VR259)	Air Atlantique Ltd
	G-APJJ	Fairey Ultra-light ★	Midland Aircraft Preservation Society
	G-APJZ	Auster J/1N Alpha	P. G. Lipman
	G-APKM	Auster J/1N Alpha	C. M. Tyers
	G-APLG	Auster J/5L Aiglet Trainer ★	Solway Aviation Society
	G-APLO	DHC.1 Chipmunk 22A (WD379)	Lindholme Aircraft Ltd
	G-APLU	DH.82A Tiger Moth	M. E. Vaisey
	G-APMB	DH.106 Comet 4B ★	Gatwick Handling Ltd (ground trainer)
	G-APMH	Auster J/1U Workmaster	M. R. P. Thorogood
	G-APMX	DH.82A Tiger Moth	Foley Farm Flying Group
	G-APMY	PA-23 Apache 160 ★	Aero Venture
	G-APNJ	Cessna 310 ★	Chelsea College/Shoreham
	G-APNT	Currie Wot	B. J. Dunford
	G-APNZ	D.31 Turbulent	J. Knight
	G-APPA	DHC.1 Chipmunk 22	J. Miller
	G-APPL	P.40 Prentice 1	S. J. Saggers
	G-APPM	DHC.1 Chipmunk 22 (WB711)	S. D. Wilch
	G-APRL	AW.650 Argosy 101 ★	Midland Air Museum/Coventry
	G-APRO	Auster 6A	A. F. & H. Wankowski
	G-APRS	SA Twin Pioneer Srs 3	Aviation Heritage Ltd (G-BCWF)
	G-APRT	Taylor JT.1 Monoplane ★	Newark Air Museum
	G-APSA	Douglas DC-6A	G-APSA Ltd
	G-APSR	Auster J/1U Workmaster	D. & K. Aero Services Ltd
	G-APTR	Auster J/1N Alpha	C. R. Shipley
	G-APTU	Auster 5	G-APTU Flying Group
	G-APTW	Westland WS-51/2 Widgeon ★	North East Aircraft Museum/Usworth
	G-APTY	Beech G.35 Bonanza	G. E. Brennand
	G-APTZ	D.31 Turbulent	The Tiger Club (1990) Ltd
	G-APUD	Bensen B.7M (modified) ★	Manchester Museum of Science & Industry
	G-APUE	L.40 Meta Sokol	S. E. & M. J. Aherne
	G-APUP	Sopwith Pup (replica) (N5182) ★	RAF Museum/Hendon
	G-APUR	PA-22 Tri-Pacer 160	S. T. A. Hutchinson
	G-APUW	Auster J/5V-160 Autocar	E. S. E. & P. B. Hibbard
	G-APUY	D.31 Turbulent	C. Jones
	G-APVF	Putzer Elster B (97+04)	A. Wiseman
	G-APVG	Auster J/5L Aiglet Trainer	R. E. Tyers
	G-APVN	D.31 Turbulent	R. Sherwin
	G-APVS	Cessna 170B	N. Simpson Stormin' Norman

Reg.	Type	Owner or Operator	Notes
G-APVU	L.40 Meta Sokol	S. E. & M. J. Aherne	
G-APVZ	D.31 Turbulent	The Tiger Club (1990) Ltd	
G-APWA	HPR.7 Herald 101 ★	Museum of Berkshire Aviation/Woodley	
G-APWJ	HPR.7 Herald 201 ★	Duxford Aviation Society	
G-APWN	Westland WS-55 Whirlwind 3 ★	Midland Air Museum/Coventry	
G-APWY	Piaggio P.166 ★	Science Museum/Wroughton	
G-APXJ	PA-24 Comanche 250	T. Wildsmith	
G-APXR	PA-22 Tri-Pacer 160	A. Troughton	
G-APXT	PA-22 Tri-Pacer 150 (modified)	A. E. Cuttler	
G-APXU	PA-22 Tri-Pacer 125 (modified)	G-APXU Syndicate	
G-APXW	EP.9 Prospector (XM819) ★	Museum of Army Flying/Middle Wallop	
G-APXX	DHA.3 Drover 2 (VH-FDT) ★	WWII Aircraft Preservation Society/Lasham	
G-APYB	Tipsy T.66 Nipper 3	B. O. Smith	
G-APYD	DH.106 Comet 4B ★	Science Museum/Wroughton	
G-APYG	DHC.1 Chipmunk 22	P. A. & J. M. Doyle	
G-APYI	PA-22 Tri-Pacer 135	D. R. Gibby	
G-APYT	Champion 7FC Tri-Traveller	B. J. Anning	
G-APZJ	PA-18 Super Cub 150	S. G. Jones	
G-APZL	PA-22 Tri-Pacer 160	B. Robins	
G-APZX	PA-22 Tri-Pacer 150	V. A. Holliday	
G-ARAD	Luton LA-5 Major ★	North East Aircraft Museum	
G-ARAM	PA-18 Super Cub 150	Skymax (Aviation) Ltd	
G-ARAN	PA-18 Super Cub 150	G-ARAN Group	
G-ARAS	Champion 7FC Tri-Traveller	Alpha Sierra Flying Group	
G-ARAW	Cessna 182C Skylane	Ximango UK	
G-ARAZ	DH.82A Tiger Moth (R4959:59)	D. A. Porter	
G-ARBE	DH.104 Dove 8	M. Whale & M. W. A. Lunn	
G-ARBG	Tipsy T.66 Nipper 2	D. Shrimpton	
G-ARBM	Auster V J1B Aiglet	A. D. Hodgkinson	
G-ARBO	PA-24 Comanche 250	Tatenhill Aviation Ltd	
G-ARBS	PA-22 Tri-Pacer 160 (tailwheel)	S. D. Rowell	
G-ARBV	PA-22 Tri-Pacer 160	L. M. Williams	
G-ARBZ	D.31 Turbulent	G. Richards	
G-ARCF	PA-22 Tri-Pacer 150	M. J. Speakman	
G-ARCS	Auster D6/180	R. J. Fray	
G-ARCT	PA-18 Super Cub 95	A. H. Diver	
G-ARCV	Cessna 175A	R. Francis & C. Campbell	
G-ARCW	PA-23 Apache 160	F. W. Ellis	
G-ARCX	A.W. Meteor 14 ★	Museum of Flight/East Fortune	
G-ARDB	PA-24 Comanche 250	P. Crook	
G-ARDD	CP.301C1 Emeraude	K. N. P. Higgs	
G-ARDE	DH.104 Dove 6 ★	T. E. Evans	
G-ARDJ	Auster D.6/180	P. N. A. Whitehead	
G-ARDO	Jodel D.112	W. R. Prescott	
G-ARDS	PA-22 Caribbean 150	N. P. McGowan & C. A. Donaldson	
G-ARDV	PA-22 Tri-Pacer 160	M. D. N. Fisher	
G-ARDY	Tipsy T.66 Nipper 2	J. K. Davies	
G-ARDZ	Jodel D.140A	M. J. Wright	
G-AREA	DH.104 Dove 8 ★	De Havilland Heritage Museum/London Colney	
G-AREH	DH.82A Tiger Moth	C. D. Cyster & A. J. Hastings	
G-AREI	Auster 3 (MT438)	R. B. Webber	
G-AREL	PA-22 Caribbean 150	The Caribbean Flying Club	
G-AREO	PA-18 Super Cub 150	E. P. Parkin	
G-ARET	PA-22 Tri-Pacer 160	L. A.. Runnalls	
G-AREV	PA-22 Tri-Pacer 160	D. J. Ash	
G-AREX	Aeronca 15AC Sedan	R. J. M. Turnbull	
G-ARFB	PA-22 Caribbean 150	The Tri Pacer Group	
G-ARFD	PA-22 Tri-Pacer 160	N. I. M. Mackintosh	
G-ARFG	Cessna 175°	G. C. Rogers	
G-ARFI	Cessna 150A	J. D. Woodward	
G-ARFO	Cessna 150A	A. P. Amor	
G-ARFT	Jodel DR.1050	R. Shaw	
G-ARFV	Tipsy T.66 Nipper 2	J. J. Austin	
G-ARGG	DHC.1 Chipmunk 22 (WD305)	D. Curtis	
G-ARGO	PA-22 Colt 108	Kauri Group	
G-ARGV	PA-18 Super Cub 180	Wolds Gliding Club Ltd	
G-ARGY	PA-22 Tri-Pacer 160	A. & I. Bazin (G-JEST)	
G-ARGZ	D.31 Turbulent	The Tiger Club (1990) Ltd	
G-ARHB	Forney F-1A Aircoupe	K. J. Peacock & S. F. Turner	
G-ARHC	Forney F-1A Aircoupe	E. G. Girardey	
G-ARHL	PA-23 Aztec 250	C. J. Freeman	
G-ARHM	Auster 6A	R. C. P. Brookhouse	

Notes	Reg.	Type	Owner or Operator
	G-ARHN	PA-22 Caribbean 150	Popham Flying Group
	G-ARHR	PA-22 Caribbean 150	A. R. Wyatt
	G-ARHW	DH.104 Dove 8	Aviation Heritage Ltd
	G-ARHX	DH.104 Dove 8 ★	North East Aircraft Museum
	G-ARHZ	D.62 Condor	E. Shouler
	G-ARID	Cessna 172B	L. M. Edwards
	G-ARIF	Ord-Hume O-H.7 Minor Coupé ★	M. J. Aubrey
	G-ARIH	Auster 6A (TW591)	M. C. Jordan
	G-ARIK	PA-22 Caribbean 150	A. Taylor
	G-ARIL	PA-22 Caribbean 150	S. Eustathiou
	G-ARIM	D.31 Turbulent	S. R. P. Harper & J. C. Holland
	G-ARJB	DH.104 Dove 8	M. Whale & M. W. A. Lunn
	G-ARJE	PA-22 Colt 108	C. I. Fray
	G-ARJH	PA-22 Colt 108	F. Vogels/France
	G-ARJR	PA-23 Apache 160G ★	Instructional airframe/Kidlington
	G-ARJS	PA-23 Apache 160G	Bencray Ltd
	G-ARJT	PA-23 Apache 160G	J. H. Ashcroft
	G-ARJU	PA-23 Apache 160G	F. W. & I. F. Ellis
	G-ARKD	CAC CA-18 Mk.22 Mustang P-51D	Classic Flying Machine Collection Ltd
	G-ARKG	Auster J/5G Autocar (A11-301/931)	A. G. Boon & C. L. Towell
	G-ARKJ	Beech N35 Bonanza	G. D. E. Macdonald
	G-ARKK	PA-22 Colt 108	R. D. Welfare
	G-ARKM	PA-22 Colt 108	Kilo Mike Group
	G-ARKN	PA-22 Colt 108	M. J. Whitwell
	G-ARKP	PA-22 Colt 108	J. P. A. Freeman
	G-ARKS	PA-22 Colt 108	R. A. Nesbitt-Dufort
	G-ARLB	PA-24 Comanche 250	D. Heater (G-BUTL)
	G-ARLG	Auster D.4/108	Auster D4 Group
	G-ARLK	PA-24 Comanche 250	R. P. Jackson
	G-ARLP	Beagle A.61 Terrier 1	Gemini Flying Group
	G-ARLR	Beagle A.61 Terrier 2	M. Palfreman
	G-ARLU	Cessna 172B Skyhawk ★	Instructional airframe/Irish Air Corps
	G-ARLZ	D.31A Turbulent	A. D. Wilson
	G-ARMC	DHC.1 Chipmunk 22A (WB703)	John Henderson Children's Trust
	G-ARMD	DHC.1 Chipmunk 22A	A. L. Grisay
	G-ARMF	DHC.1 Chipmunk 22A (WZ868:H)	J. Miller
	G-ARMG	DHC.1 Chipmunk 22A	M. F. Cuming
	G-ARML	Cessna 175B Skylark	D. Stephens
	G-ARMN	Cessna 175B Skylark	G-ARMN Group
	G-ARMO	Cessna 172B Skyhawk	J. F. Henderson & A. J. Tobias
	G-ARMR	Cessna 172B Skyhawk	Mike Romeo Group
	G-ARMZ	D.31 Turbulent	The Tiger Club (1990) Ltd
	G-ARNB	Auster J/5G Autocar	R. F. Tolhurst
	G-ARND	PA-22 Colt 108	J. L. & J. E. D. Rogerson
	G-ARNE	PA-22 Colt 108	The Shiny Colt Group
	G-ARNG	PA-22 Colt 108	F. B. Rothera
	G-ARNJ	PA-22 Colt 108	R. A. Keech
	G-ARNK	PA-22 Colt 108 (tailwheel)	S. J. Smith
	G-ARNL	PA-22 Colt 108	J. A. Dodsworth
	G-ARNO	Beagle A.61 Terrier 1 (VX113)	R. B. Webber
	G-ARNP	Beagle A.109 Airedale	S. W. & M. Isbister
	G-ARNY	Jodel D.117	G-ARNY Flying Group
	G-ARNZ	D.31 Turbulent	The Tiger Club (1990) Ltd
	G-AROA	Cessna 172B Skyhawk	F. J. L. Kendall
	G-AROC	Cessna 175B	A. J. Symes (G-OTOW)
	G-AROJ	Beagle A.109 Airedale ★	D. J. Shaw (stored)
	G-ARON	PA-22 Colt 108	M. Hayter
	G-AROO	Forney F-1A Aircoupe	K. J. Harron & W. J. McMeekan
	G-AROW	Jodel D.140B	A. R. Crome
	G-AROY	Boeing Stearman A75N.1	I. T. Whitaker-Bethel & J. Mann
	G-ARPH	HS.121 Trident 1C ★	Museum of Flight/East Fortune
	G-ARPK	HS.121 Trident 1C ★	Manchester Airport Authority
	G-ARPO	HS.121 Trident 1C ★	CAA Fire School/Teesside
	G-ARRD	Jodel DR.1050	P. R. Watkins
	G-ARRE	Jodel DR.1050	West of Leicester Flyers
	G-ARRI	Cessna 175B	G-ARRI Partnership
	G-ARRL	Auster J/1N Alpha	A. C. Ladd
	G-ARRM	Beagle B.206-X ★	Bristol Aero Collection (stored)
	G-ARRO	Beagle A.109 Airedale	M. & S. W. Isbister
	G-ARRS	CP.301A Emeraude	J. F. Sully
	G-ARRT	Wallis WA-116-1	K. H. Wallis
	G-ARRU	D.31 Turbulent	D. G. Huck
	G-ARRX	Auster 6A (VF512)	J. E. D. Mackie

Reg.	Type	Owner or Operator	Notes
G-ARRY	Jodel D.140B	C. Thomas	
G-ARRZ	D.31 Turbulent	T. A. Stambach	
G-ARSG	Roe Triplane Type IV (replica)	The Shuttleworth Collection/Old Warden	
G-ARSL	Beagle A.61 Terrier 1 (VF581)	D. J. Colclough	
G-ARSU	PA-22 Colt 108	Sierra Uniform Flying Group	
G-ARTH	PA-12 Super Cruiser	R. I. Souch	
G-ARTJ	Bensen B.8M ★	Museum of Flight/East Fortune	
G-ARTL	DH.82A Tiger Moth (T7281)	F. G. Clacherty	
G-ARTT	MS.880B Rallye Club	R. N. Scott	
G-ARTZ	McCandless M.4 gyroplane	W. R. Partridge	
G-ARUG	Auster J/5G Autocar	D. P. H. Hulme	
G-ARUH	Jodel DR.1050	A. F. Vizoso	
G-ARUI	Beagle A.61 Terrier	T. W. J. Dann	
G-ARUL	LeVier Cosmic Wind	P. G. Kynsey	
G-ARUV	CP.301A Emeraude	D. A. Healey	
G-ARUY	Auster J/1N Alpha	D. Burnham	
G-ARUZ	Cessna 175C	Cardiff Skylark Group	
G-ARVM	V.1101 VC10 ★	Brooklands Museum of Aviation/Weybridge	
G-ARVO	PA-18 Super Cub 95	M. Ali	
G-ARVT	PA-28 Cherokee 160	Red Rose Aviation Ltd	
G-ARVU	PA-28 Cherokee 160	T. W. Mitchell	
G-ARVV	PA-28 Cherokee 160	G. E. Hopkins	
G-ARVZ	D.62B Condor	A. A. M. Huke	
G-ARWB	DHC.1 Chipmunk 22 (WK611)	Thruxton Chipmunk Flying Club	
G-ARWR	Cessna 172C	Devanha Flying Group	
G-ARWS	Cessna 175C	M. D. Fage	
G-ARXB	Beagle A.109 Airedale	S. W. & M. Isbister	
G-ARXD	Beagle A.109 Airedale	D. Howden	
G-ARXG	PA-24 Comanche 250	R. F. Corstin	
G-ARXH	Bell 47G	A. B. Searle	
G-ARXP	Luton LA-4 Minor	R. M. Weeks	
G-ARXT	Jodel DR.1050	CJM Flying Group	
G-ARXU	Auster 6A (VF526)	A. B. Taylor-Roberts and E. M. Le Gresley	
G-ARXW	MS.885 Super Rallye	M. J. Kirk	
G-ARYB	HS.125 Srs 1 ★	Midland Air Museum/Coventry	
G-ARYC	HS.125 Srs 1 ★	De Havilland Heritage Museum/London Colney	
G-ARYD	Auster AOP.6 (WJ358) ★	Museum of Army Flying/Middle Wallop	
G-ARYH	PA-22 Tri-Pacer 160	C. Watt	
G-ARYK	Cessna 172C	M. J. Rubidge	
G-ARYR	PA-28 Cherokee 180	G-ARYR Flying Group	
G-ARYS	Cessna 172C	M. S. Johnston	
G-ARYV	PA-24 Comanche 250	D. C. Hanss	
G-ARYZ	Beagle A.109 Airedale	C. W. Tomkins	
G-ARZB	Wallis WA-116 Srs 1	K. H. Wallis	
G-ARZS	Beagle A.109 Airedale	M. & S. W. Isbister	
G-ARZW	Currie Wot	B. R. Pearson	
G-ASAA	Luton LA-4 Minor	M. J. Aubrey (stored)	
G-ASAI	Beagle A.109 Airedale	K. R. Howden	
G-ASAJ	Beagle A.61 Terrier 2 (WE569)	T. Bailey	
G-ASAL	SA Bulldog Srs 120/124	Pioneer Flying Co Ltd	
G-ASAU	MS.880B Rallye Club	A. C. Bell	
G-ASAX	Beagle A.61 Terrier 2	A. D. Hodgkinson	
G-ASAZ	Hiller UH-12E4 (XS165)	Hields Aviation/Sherburn	
G-ASBA	Phoenix Currie Wot	J. C. Lister	
G-ASBH	Beagle A.109 Airedale	D. T. Smollett	
G-ASCC	Beagle E3 Mk 11 (XP254)	R. Warner	
G-ASCD	Beagle A.61 Terrier 2 (TJ704) ★	Yorkshire Air Museum/Elvington	
G-ASCH	Beagle A.61 Terrier 2	G-ASCH Group	
G-ASCM	Isaacs Fury II (K2050)	R. F. Redknap	
G-ASCZ	CP.301A Emeraude	I. Denham-Brown	
G-ASDF	Edwards Gyrocopter ★	B. King	
G-ASDK	Beagle A.61 Terrier 2	J. Swallow (G-ARLM)	
G-ASDY	Wallis WA-116/F	K. H. Wallis	
G-ASEA	Luton LA-4A Minor	D. Underwood	
G-ASEB	Luton LA-4A Minor	S. R. P. Harper	
G-ASEO	PA-24 Comanche 250	Oxbridge Investments Ltd	
G-ASEP	PA-23 Apache 235	Arrowstate Ltd	
G-ASEU	D.62A Condor	W. M. Grant	
G-ASFA	Cessna 172D	D. Austin	
G-ASFD	L-200A Morava	M. Emery	
G-ASFK	Auster J/5G Autocar	B. C. C. Harrison	
G-ASFL	PA-28 Cherokee 180	G-ASFL Group	
G-ASFR	Bölkow Bö.208A1 Junior	S. T. Dauncey	

Notes	Reg.	Type	Owner or Operator
	G-ASFX	D.31 Turbulent	E. F. Clapham & W. B. S. Dobie
	G-ASGC	V.1151 Super VC10 ★	Duxford Aviation Society
	G-ASHD	Brantly B.2A ★	IHM/Weston-super-Mare
	G-ASHS	SNCAN Stampe SV.4C	J. W. Beaty
	G-ASHT	D.31 Turbulent	C. W. N. Huke
	G-ASHU	PA-15 Vagabond (modified)	The Calybe Flying Group
	G-ASHX	PA-28 Cherokee 180	Powertheme Ltd
	G-ASIB	Cessna F.172D	S. J. Ducker
	G-ASII	PA-28 Cherokee 180	T. N. & T. R. Hart & R. W. S. Matthews
	G-ASIJ	PA-28 Cherokee 180	MK Aero Support Ltd
	G-ASIL	PA-28 Cherokee 180	G. R. Plant & A. D. Harwin
	G-ASIS	Jodel D.112	W. R. Prescott
	G-ASIT	Cessna 180	R. A. Seeley
	G-ASIY	PA-25 Pawnee 235	The Royal Air Force Gliding and Soaring Association
	G-ASJL	Beech H.35 Bonanza	R. L. Dargue
	G-ASJV	VS.361 Spitfire IX (MH434/PK-K)	Merlin Aviation Ltd
	G-ASJZ	Jodel D.117A	M. A. Watts
	G-ASKC	DH.98 Mosquito 35 (TA719) ★	Skyfame Collection/Duxford
	G-ASKK	HPR.7 Herald 211 ★	Norwich Aviation Museum
	G-ASKL	Jodel D.150	J. M. Graty
	G-ASKP	DH.82A Tiger Moth	Tiger Club (1990) Ltd
	G-ASKT	PA-28 Cherokee 180	T. J. Herbert
	G-ASLV	PA-28 Cherokee 235	S. W. Goodswen
	G-ASLX	CP.301A Emeraude	J. J. Reilly
	G-ASMA	PA-30 Twin Comanche 160 C/R	K. Cooper
	G-ASME	Bensen B.8M	R. M. Harris
	G-ASMF	Beech D.95A Travel Air	M. J. A. Hornblower
	G-ASMJ	Cessna F.172E	Aeroscene Ltd
	G-ASML	Luton LA-4A Minor	R. W. Vince
	G-ASMM	D.31 Tubulent	W. J. Browning
	G-ASMS	Cessna 150A	M. & W. Long
	G-ASMT	Fairtravel Linnet 2	P. Harrison
	G-ASMV	CP.1310-C3 Super Emeraude	D. G. Hammersley
	G-ASMW	Cessna 150D	Dukeries Aviation
	G-ASMY	PA-23 Apache 160 ★	R. D. Forster
	G-ASMZ	Beagle A.61 Terrier 2 (VF516)	B. Andrews
	G-ASNC	Beagle D.5/180 Husky	Peterborough & Spalding Gliding Club Ltd
	G-ASNI	CP.1310-C3 Super Emeraude	D. Chapman
	G-ASNK	Cessna 205	Justgold Ltd
	G-ASNW	Cessna F.172E	G-ASNW Group
	G-ASNY	Campbell-Bensen B.8M gyroplane ★	R. Light & T. Smith
	G-ASOH	Beech 95-B55A Baron	G. Davis & C. Middlemiss
	G-ASOI	Beagle A.61 Terrier 2	G.D.B. Delmege
	G-ASOK	Cessna F.172E	D. W. Disney
	G-ASOL	Bell 47D ★	North East Aircraft Museum
	G-ASOM	Beagle A.61 Terrier 2	GASOM.org (G-JETS)
	G-ASOX	Cessna 205A	S. M. C. Harvey
	G-ASPF	Jodel D.120	G. W. Street
	G-ASPP	Bristol Boxkite (replica)	The Shuttleworth Collection/Old Warden
	G-ASPS	Piper J-3C-90 Cub	A. J. Chalkley/Blackbushe
	G-ASPV	DH.82A Tiger Moth (T7794)	P. Zanardo
	G-ASRB	D.62B Condor	B. J. Douglas/Ireland
	G-ASRC	D.62C Condor	C. R. Isbell
	G-ASRK	Beagle A.109 Airedale	Bio Pathica Ltd/Lydd
	G-ASRO	PA-30 Twin Comanche 160	D. W. Blake
	G-ASRT	Jodel 150	P. Turton
	G-ASRW	PA-28 Cherokee 180	G. N. Smith
	G-ASSM	HS.125 Srs 1/522 ★	Science Museum/South Kensington
	G-ASSP	PA-30 Twin Comanche 160	P. H. Tavener
	G-ASSS	Cessna 172E	P. R. March & P. Turner
	G-ASST	Cessna 150D	F. R. H. Parker
	G-ASSV	Kensinger KF	C. I. Jefferson
	G-ASSW	PA-28 Cherokee 140	E. R. Curry
	G-ASSY	D.31 Turbulent	R. C. Bailey
	G-ASTG	Nord 1002 Pingouin II	R. J. Fray
	G-ASTI	Auster 6A	S. J. Partridge
	G-ASTL	Fairey Firefly I (Z2033) ★	F.A. A. Museum/Yeovilton
	G-ASTP	Hiller UH-12C ★	IHM/Weston-super-Mare
	G-ASUB	Mooney M.20E Super 21	S. C. Coulbeck
	G-ASUD	PA-28 Cherokee 180	G-ASUD Group
	G-ASUE	Cessna 150D	D. Huckle
	G-ASUG	Beech E18S ★	Museum of Flight/East Fortune

Reg.	Type	Owner or Operator	Notes
G-ASUI	Beagle A.61 Terrier 2	A. L. Aish	
G-ASUP	Cessna F.172E	GASUP Air	
G-ASUS	Jurca MJ.2B Tempete	M. P. Grimshaw	
G-ASVG	CP.301B Emeraude	K. R. H. Wingate	
G-ASVM	Cessna F.172E	R. H. Bennett	
G-ASVO	HPR.7 Herald 214 ★	Archive Visitor Centre/Shoreham (cockpit section)	
G-ASVP	PA-25 Pawnee 235	Banbury Gliding Club Ltd	
G-ASVZ	PA-28 Cherokee 140	T. D. Jackman	
G-ASWJ	Beagle 206 Srs 1 (8449M) ★	Brunel Technical College/Bristol	
G-ASWN	Bensen B.8M	D. R. Shepherd	
G-ASWX	PA-28 Cherokee 180	Gasworks Flying Group Ltd	
G-ASXC	SIPA 903	A. L. Hall-Carpenter (G-DWEL)	
G-ASXD	Brantly B.2B	Lousada PLC	
G-ASXI	Tipsy T.66 Nipper 3	P. G. Blenkinsopp	
G-ASXS	Jodel DR.1050	R. A. Hunter	
G-ASXU	Jodel D.120A	G-ASXU Group	
G-ASXX	Avro 683 Lancaster 7 (NX611) ★	Panton Family Trust/East Kirkby	
G-ASXZ	Cessna 182G Skylane	Last Refuge Ltd	
G-ASYD	BAC One-Eleven 475 ★	Brooklands Museum of Aviation/Weybridge	
G-ASYG	Beagle A.61 Terrier 2 (VX927)	Terrane Auster Group	
G-ASYJ	Beech D.95A Travel Air	Crosby Aviation (Jersey) Ltd	
G-ASYP	Cessna 150E	Henlow Flying Group	
G-ASYZ	Cessna 150E	R. J. Scott	
G-ASZB	Bölkow Bö.208A2 Junior	M. J. Ayers	
G-ASZE	Beagle A.61 Terrier 2	D. R. Ockleton	
G-ASZR	Fairtravel Linnet 2	R. Hodgson	
G-ASZS	Gardan GY-80 Horizon 160	ZS Group	
G-ASZU	Cessna 150E	L. J. Baker, R. Hall & C. Davies	
G-ASZV	Tipsy T.66 Nipper 2	D. H. Greenwood	
G-ASZX	Beagle A.61 Terrier 1 (WJ368)	R. B. Webber	
G-ATAF	Cessna F.172F	Summit Media Ltd	
G-ATAG	Jodel DR.1050	T. M. Dawes-Gamble	
G-ATAS	PA-28 Cherokee 180	ATAS Group	
G-ATAU	D.62B Condor	M. C. Burlock	
G-ATAV	D.62C Condor	V. A. Holliday	
G-ATBG	Nord 1002 (NJ+C11)	Ardmore Aviation Service	
G-ATBH	Aero 145	P. D. Aberbach	
G-ATBJ	Sikorsky S-61N	British International	
G-ATBL	DH.60G Moth	The R. W. Beaty (Farms) Ltd Unapproved Pension Scheme for Mr. S. J. Beaty	
G-ATBP	Fournier RF-3	D. McNicholl	
G-ATBS	D.31 Turbulent	J. A. Lear	
G-ATBU	Beagle A.61 Terrier 2	T. Jarvis	
G-ATBW	Tipsy T.66 Nipper 2	Stapleford Nipper Group	
G-ATBX	PA-20 Pacer 135	G. D. & P. M. Thomson	
G-ATBZ	Westland WS-58 Wessex 60 ★	IHM/Weston-super-Mare	
G-ATCC	Beagle A.109 Airedale	North East Flight Training Ltd	
G-ATCD	Beagle D.5/180 Husky	T. C. O'Gorman	
G-ATCE	Cessna U.206	A. J. Hickling	
G-ATCJ	Luton LA-4A Minor	Flanders Flyers	
G-ATCL	Victa Airtourer 100	A. D. Goodall	
G-ATCN	Luton LA-4A Minor	The Real Aeroplane Co.Ltd	
G-ATCX	Cessna 182H	Aeramics Ltd	
G-ATDA	PA-28 Cherokee 160	Portway Aviation Ltd	
G-ATDN	Beagle A.61 Terrier 2 (TW641)	S. J. Saggers	
G-ATDO	Bölkow Bö.208C1 Junior	P. Thompson	
G-ATEF	Cessna 150E	Swans Aviation	
G-ATEM	PA-28 Cherokee 180	G. D. Wyles	
G-ATEP	EAA Biplane ★	E. L. Martin (red)/Guernsey	
G-ATEV	Jodel DR.1050	J. C. Carter & J. L. Altrip	
G-ATEW	PA-30 Twin Comanche 160	Air Northumbria (Woolsington) Ltd	
G-ATEZ	PA-28 Cherokee 140	EFI Aviation Ltd	
G-ATFD	Jodel DR.1050	G-ATFD Group	
G-ATFF	PA-23 Aztec 250C	T. J. Wassell	
G-ATFG	Brantly B.2B ★	Museum of Flight/East Fortune	
G-ATFM	Sikorsky S-61N	British International	
G-ATFR	PA-25 Pawnee 150	Borders (Milfield) Gliding Club Ltd	
G-ATFV	Agusta-Bell 47J-2A ★	Caernarfon Air World	
G-ATFY	Cessna F.172G	J. M. Vinall	
G-ATGN	Thorn Coal Gas Balloon	British Balloon Museum/Newbury	
G-ATGP	Jodel DR.1050	Madley Flying Group	
G-ATGY	Gardan GY-80 Horizon	D. H. Mackay	

Notes	Reg.	Type	Owner or Operator
	G-ATHA	PA-23 Apache 235 ★	Brunel Technical College/Bristol
	G-ATHD	DHC.1 Chipmunk 22 (WP971)	Spartan Flying Group Ltd
	G-ATHK	Aeronca 7AC Champion	Chase Flying Group
	G-ATHM	Wallis WA-116 Srs 1	Wallis Autogyros Ltd
	G-ATHN	Nord 1101 Noralpha ★	E. L. Martin (stored)/Guernsey
	G-ATHR	PA-28 Cherokee 180	Azure Flying Club Ltd
	G-ATHT	Victa Airtourer 115	Cotswold Flying Group
	G-ATHU	Beagle A.61 Terrier 1	J. A. L. Irwin
	G-ATHV	Cessna 150F	Cessna Hotel Victor Group
	G-ATHZ	Cessna 150F	R. D. Forster
	G-ATIC	Jodel DR.1050	T. A. Major
	G-ATIG	HPR.7 Herald 214 ★	Norwich Airport towing trainer
	G-ATIN	Jodel D.117	A. Ayre
	G-ATIR	AIA Stampe SV.4C	A. Trueman
	G-ATIS	PA-28 Cherokee 160	D. E. Skertchly
	G-ATIZ	Jodel D.117	R. A. Smith
	G-ATJA	Jodel DR.1050	Bicester Flying Group
	G-ATJC	Victa Airtourer 100 (modified)	Aviation West Ltd
	G-ATJG	PA-28 Cherokee 140	C. A. McGee
	G-ATJL	PA-24 Comanche 260	S. J. Ollier
	G-ATJN	Jodel D.119	J. Upex
	G-ATJV	PA-32 Cherokee Six 260	Wingglider Ltd
	G-ATKF	Cessna 150F	Holdcroft Aviation Services Ltd (G-HPFT)
	G-ATKH	Luton LA-4A Minor	H. E. Jenner
	G-ATKI	Piper J-3C-65 Cub	J. C. Holland
	G-ATKT	Cessna F.172G	R. J. D. Blois
	G-ATKX	Jodel D.140C	Kilo Xray Syndicate
	G-ATLA	Cessna 182J Skylane	J. W. & J. T. Whicher
	G-ATLB	Jodel DR.1050/M1	Le Syndicate du Petit Oiseau
	G-ATLM	Cessna F.172G	Air Fotos Aviation Ltd
	G-ATLP	Bensen B.8M	R. F. G. Moyle
	G-ATLT	Cessna U.206A	Skydive Jersey Ltd
	G-ATLV	Jodel D.120	G. Constantine & A. Y. Leung
	G-ATMC	Cessna F.150F	G. H. Farrah & D. Cunnane
	G-ATMH	Beagle D.5/180 Husky	Dorset Gliding Club Ltd
	G-ATMM	Cessna F.150F	Cranfield Aviation Training School Ltd
	G-ATMT	PA-30 Twin Comanche 160	Montagu-Smith & Co Ltd
	G-ATNB	PA-28 Cherokee 180	Ken Macdonald
	G-ATNE	Cessna F.150F	T. P. Hancock
	G-ATNL	Cessna F.150F	PVI Power Services Ltd
	G-ATNV	PA-24 Comanche 260	K. Powell
	G-ATOH	D.62B Condor	Three Spires Flying Group
	G-ATOI	PA-28 Cherokee 140	R. Ronaldson
	G-ATOJ	PA-28 Cherokee 140	A Flight Aviation Ltd
	G-ATOK	PA-28 Cherokee 140	ILC Flying Group
	G-ATOM	PA-28 Cherokee 140	A. Flight Aviation Ltd
	G-ATON	PA-28 Cherokee 140	Stirling Flying Syndicate
	G-ATOO	PA-28 Cherokee 140	Caralair Aviation
	G-ATOP	PA-28 Cherokee 140	P. R. Coombs
	G-ATOR	PA-28 Cherokee 140	Aligator Group
	G-ATOT	PA-28 Cherokee 180	Sirius Aviation Ltd
	G-ATOU	Mooney M.20E Super 21	DbProf Doo
	G-ATOY	PA-24 Comanche 260 ★	Museum of Flight/East Fortune
	G-ATOZ	Bensen B.8M	C. R. Gordon
	G-ATPN	PA-28 Cherokee 140	M. F. Hatt & ptnrs
	G-ATPT	Cessna 182J Skylane	C. Beer t/a Papa Tango Group
	G-ATPV	JB.01 Minicab	D. H. G. Cotter
	G-ATRG	PA-18 Super Cub 150	Lasham Gliding Society Ltd
	G-ATRK	Cessna F.150F	Falcon Aviation Ltd
	G-ATRL	Cessna F.150F	A. A. W. Stevens
	G-ATRM	Cessna F.150F	J. Redfearn
	G-ATRR	PA-28 Cherokee 140	Blue Sky Investments Ltd
	G-ATRW	PA-32 Cherokee Six 260	Pringle Brandon Architects
	G-ATRX	PA-32 Cherokee Six 260	F. Chakroun
	G-ATSI	Bölkow Bö.208C1 Junior	GATSI Bolkow Ltd
	G-ATSL	Cessna F.172G	C. S. & C. S. Soojeri
	G-ATSR	Beech M.35 Bonanza	C. B. Linton
	G-ATSX	Bölkow Bö.208C1 Junior	Little Bear Ltd
	G-ATSY	Wassmer Wa.41 Super Baladou IV	McLean Aviation
	G-ATSZ	PA-30 Twin Comanche 160B	Sierra Zulu Aviation Ltd
	G-ATTB	Wallis WA-116-1 (XR944)	D. A. Wallis
	G-ATTD	Cessna 182J	M. F. C. Perez
	G-ATTI	PA-28 Cherokee 140	G-ATTI Flying Group

Reg.	Type	Owner or Operator	Notes
G-ATTK	PA-28 Cherokee 140	G-ATTK Flying Group	
G-ATTM	Jodel DR.250-160	C. P. Tomkinson	
G-ATTN	Piccard HA Balloon ★	Science Museum/South Kensington	
G-ATTR	Bölkow Bö.208C1 Junior	S. Luck	
G-ATTV	PA-28 Cherokee 140	G-ATTV Group	
G-ATTX	PA-28 Cherokee 180	IPAC Aviation Ltd	
G-ATUB	PA-28 Cherokee 140	P. Sharpe	
G-ATUF	Cessna F.150F	D. P. Williams	
G-ATUG	D.62B Condor	C. Gill	
G-ATUH	Tipsy T.66 Nipper 1	C. & M. D. Barnard	
G-ATUI	Bölkow Bö.208C1 Junior	M. J. Grundy	
G-ATUL	PA-28 Cherokee 180	Barry Fielding Aviation Ltd	
G-ATVF	DHC.1 Chipmunk 22 (WD327)	The Royal Air Force Gliding and Soaring Association	
G-ATVK	PA-28 Cherokee 140	P. Ratcliffe	
G-ATVO	PA-28 Cherokee 140	Pilot Flying Group	
G-ATVP	Vickers FB.5 Gunbus replica (2345) ★	RAF Museum/Hendon	
G-ATVS	PA-28 Cherokee 180	D. S. Olson	
G-ATVW	D.62B Condor	G. G. Roberts	
G-ATVX	Bölkow Bö.208C1 Junior	A. M. Witt	
G-ATWA	Jodel DR.1050	One Twenty Group	
G-ATWB	Jodel D.117	Andrewsfield Whisky Bravo Group	
G-ATWJ	Cessna F.172F	J. P. A. Freeman	
G-ATXA	PA-22 Tri-Pacer 150	S. Hildrop	
G-ATXD	PA-30 Twin Comanche 160B	C. A. Denovan	
G-ATXJ	HP.137 Jetstream 300 ★	Fire Service training airframe/Cardiff	
G-ATXN	Mitchell-Proctor Kittiwake 1	R. G. Day	
G-ATXO	SIPA 903	C. H. Morris	
G-ATXX	McCandless M.4 gyroplane ★	Ulster Folk & Transport Museum	
G-ATXZ	Bölkow Bö.208C1 Junior	G-ATXZ Group	
G-ATYM	Cessna F.150G	P. W. Fisher	
G-ATYN	Cessna F.150G	J. S. Grant	
G-ATYS	PA-28 Cherokee 180	A. J. Hardy	
G-ATZM	Piper J-3C-90 Cub	N. D. Marshall	
G-ATZS	Wassmer Wa.41 Super Baladou IV	I. R. Siddell	
G-AVAR	Cessna F.150G	J. A. Rees	
G-AVAW	D.62B Condor	Condor Aircraft Group	
G-AVAX	PA-28 Cherokee 180	A. F. Prosser	
G-AVBG	PA-28 Cherokee 180	M. C. Plomer-Roberts	
G-AVBH	PA-28 Cherokee 180	Tenterfield (Holdings) Ltd	
G-AVBS	PA-28 Cherokee 180	Bravo Sierra Flying Group	
G-AVBT	PA-28 Cherokee 180	J. F. Mitchell	
G-AVCM	PA-24 Comanche 260	R. F. Smith	
G-AVCN	BN-2A-8 Islander	Britten-Norman Aircraft Preservation Society	
G-AVCV	Cessna 182J Skylane	University of Manchester, School of Earth, Atmospheric and Environmental Sciences	
G-AVDA	Cessna 182K Skylane	F. W. Ellis	
G-AVDG	Wallis WA-116 Srs 1	K. H. Wallis	
G-AVDS	Beech 65-B80 Queen Air ★	Airport Fire Service/Filton	
G-AVDT	Aeronca 7AC Champion	D. & N. Cheney	
G-AVDV	PA-22-150 Tri-Pacer	P. Bower	
G-AVDY	Luton LA-4A Minor	J. Goodband	
G-AVEC	Cessna F.172 ★	S. M. Furner	
G-AVEF	Jodel 150	Heavy Install Ltd	
G-AVEH	SIAI-Marchetti S.205	EH Aviation	
G-AVEM	Cessna F.150G	N. M. Robinson	
G-AVEN	Cessna F.150G	J. M. Hough	
G-AVEO	Cessna F.150G	Execflyer (G-DENA)	
G-AVER	Cessna F.150G	LAC Flying School	
G-AVEU	Wassmer Wa.41 Baladou IV	The Baladou Flying Group	
G-AVEX	D.62B Condor	C. A. Macleod	
G-AVEY	Currie Super Wot	C. K. Farley	
G-AVEZ	HPR.7 Herald 210 ★	Rescue trainer/Norwich	
G-AVFB	HS.121 Trident 2E ★	Duxford Aviation Society	
G-AVFE	HS.121 Trident 2E ★	Belfast Airport Authority	
G-AVFH	HS.121 Trident 2E ★	De Havilland Heritage Museum (fuselage only)/London Colney	
G-AVFM	HS.121 Trident 2E ★	Brunel Technical College/Bristol	
G-AVFR	PA-28 Cherokee 140	G. Cockerton	
G-AVFU	PA-32 Cherokee Six 300	Trixstar Farms Ltd	
G-AVFX	PA-28 Cherokee 140	A. E. Fielding	
G-AVFZ	PA-28 Cherokee 140	G-AVFZ Flying Group	
G-AVGA	PA-24 Comanche 260	G. McD. Moir	

Notes	Reg.	Type	Owner or Operator
	G-AVGC	PA-28 Cherokee 140	D. Matthews
	G-AVGE	PA-28 Cherokee 140	J. D. C. Lea
	G-AVGI	PA-28 Cherokee 140	Merseyflight Air Training School
	G-AVGU	Cessna F.150G	R. D. Luper
	G-AVGZ	Jodel DR.1050	A. F. & S. Williams
	G-AVHH	Cessna F.172	A. M. Twemlow
	G-AVHL	Jodel DR.105A	Seething Jodel Group
	G-AVHM	Cessna F.150G	D. A. & W. D. Hill
	G-AVHT	Auster AOP.9 (WZ711)	C. W. Romkins LtdSeething Jodel Group
	G-AVHY	Fournier RF.4D	I. G. K. Mitchell
	G-AVIA	Cessna F.150G	American Airplane Breakers
	G-AVIB	Cessna F.150G	Far North Aviation
	G-AVIC	Cessna F.172 ★	Leeside Flying Ltd
	G-AVIL	Alon A.2 Aircoupe (VX147)	G. D. J. Wilson
	G-AVIN	MS.880B Rallye Club	S. L. J. Cook
	G-AVIP	Brantly B.2B	Eaglescott Brantly Group
	G-AVIS	Cessna F.172 ★	J. P. A. Freeman
	G-AVIT	Cessna F.150G	P. Cottrell
	G-AVJF	Cessna F.172H	J. A. & D. T. A. Rees
	G-AVJJ	PA-30 Twin Comanche 160B	A. H. Manser
	G-AVJK	Jodel DR.1050/M1	Juliet Kilo Syndicate
	G-AVJO	Fokker E.III (replica) (422/15)	Flying Aces Movie Aircraft Collection
	G-AVJV	Wallis WA-117 Srs 1	K. H. Wallis (G-ATCV)
	G-AVJW	Wallis WA-118 Srs 2	K. H. Wallis (G-ATPW)
	G-AVKD	Fournier RF-4D	Lasham RF4 Group
	G-AVKE	Gadfly HDW.1 ★	IHM/Weston-super-Mare
	G-AVKG	Cessna F.172H	P. R. Brown-John
	G-AVKI	Slingsby T.66 Nipper 3	Team Nipper
	G-AVKK	Slingsby T.66 Nipper 3	C. Watson
	G-AVKP	Beagle A.109 Airedale	D. R. Williams
	G-AVKR	Bölkow Bö.208C1 Junior	L. Hawkins
	G-AVLB	PA-28 Cherokee 140	M. Wilson
	G-AVLC	PA-28 Cherokee 140	D. P. McCullagh
	G-AVLE	PA-28 Cherokee 140	G. E. Wright
	G-AVLF	PA-28 Cherokee 140	Woodbine Group
	G-AVLG	PA-28 Cherokee 140	R. J. Everett
	G-AVLI	PA-28 Cherokee 140	Lima India Aviation Group
	G-AVLJ	PA-28 Cherokee 140	Cherokee Aviation Holdings Jersey Ltd
	G-AVLM	Beagle B.121 Pup 3	T. M. & D. A. Jones
	G-AVLN	Beagle B.121 Pup 2	Dogs Flying Group
	G-AVLO	Bölkow Bö.208C1 Junior	G. D. Price & P. R. Teager
	G-AVLT	PA-28-140 Cherokee	Transcourt Ltd and Turweston Flying School Ltd (G-KELC)
	G-AVLW	Fournier RF-4D	J. C. A. C. da Silva
	G-AVLY	Jodel D.120A	M. E. Wills & N. V. de Candole
	G-AVMA	Gardan GY-80 Horizon 180	Z. R. Hildick
	G-AVMB	D.62B Condor	L. J. Dray
	G-AVMD	Cessna 150G	Bagby Aviation Flying Group
	G-AVMF	Cessna F. 150G	J. F. Marsh
	G-AVMJ	BAC One-Eleven 510ED ★	European Aviation Ltd (cabin trainer)
	G-AVMK	BAC One-Eleven 510ED ★	Gravesend College (fuselage only)
	G-AVMO	BAC One-Eleven 510ED ★	Museum of Flight/East Fortune
	G-AVMU	BAC One-Eleven 510ED ★	Duxford Aviation Society
	G-AVNC	Cessna F.150G	J. Turner
	G-AVNE	Westland WS-58 Wessex Mk 60 Srs 1 ★	IHM/Weston-super-Mare
	G-AVNN	PA-28 Cherokee 180	G-AVNN Flying Group
	G-AVNO	PA-28 Cherokee 180	November Oscar Flying Group
	G-AVNS	PA-28 Cherokee 180	P. T. Osborne
	G-AVNU	PA-28 Cherokee 180	D. Durrant
	G-AVNW	PA-28 Cherokee 180	Len Smith's (Aviation) Ltd
	G-AVNY	Fournier RF-4D	J. B. Giddins (G-IVEL)
	G-AVNZ	Fournier RF-4D	C. D. Pidler
	G-AVOA	Jodel DR.1050	D. A. Willies
	G-AVOH	D.62B Condor	Condor Group
	G-AVOM	CEA Jodel DR.221	Avon Flying Group
	G-AVOO	PA-18 Super Cub 150	Dublin Gliding Club Ltd
	G-AVOZ	PA-28 Cherokee 180	Oscar Zulu Flying Group
	G-AVPD	Jodel D.9 Bébé ★	S. W. McKay (stored)
	G-AVPI	Cessna F.172H	Air-Tech
	G-AVPJ	DH.82A Tiger Moth	C. C. Silk
	G-AVPM	Jodel D.117	L. B. Clark & J. C. Haynes
	G-AVPN	HPR.7 Herald 213 ★	Yorkshire Air Museum/Elvington

Reg.	Type	Owner or Operator	Notes
G-AVPO	Hindustan HAL-26 Pushpak	B. Johns	
G-AVPV	PA-18 Cherokee 180	K. A. Passmore	
G-AVPY	PA-25 Pawnee 235C	Southdown Gliding Club Ltd	
G-AVRK	PA-28 Cherokee 180	Air Romeo Kilo Ltd	
G-AVRS	Gardan GY-80 Horizon 180	N. M. Robbins	
G-AVRU	PA-28-Cherokee 180	Lanpro	
G-AVRW	Gardan GY-20 Minicab	Kestrel Flying Group	
G-AVRZ	PA-28 Cherokee 180	Mantavia Group Ltd	
G-AVSA	PA-28 Cherokee 180	M. C. Bellamy	
G-AVSB	PA-28 Cherokee 180	D. L. Macdonald	
G-AVSC	PA-28 Cherokee 180	G-AVSC Syndicate	
G-AVSD	PA-28 Cherokee 180	C. B. D. Owen	
G-AVSE	PA-28 Cherokee 180	F. Glendon/Ireland	
G-AVSF	PA-28 Cherokee 180	Monday Club	
G-AVSI	PA-28 Cherokee 140	G-AVSI Flying Group	
G-AVSP	PA-28 Cherokee 180	Internet Search Services Ltd	
G-AVSR	Beagle D.5/180 Husky	G. R. Greenfield & S. D. J. Holwill	
G-AVTC	Slingsby Nipper T.66 RA.45 Srs 3	J. Crawford	
G-AVTP	Cessna F.172H	Tango Papa Group	
G-AVTT	Ercoupe 415D	Wright's Farm Eggs Ltd	
G-AVUG	Cessna F.150H	Skyways Flying Group	
G-AVUH	Cessna F.150H	A. G. McLaren	
G-AVUO	Luton LA4 Minor	M. E. Vaisey	
G-AVUS	PA-28 Cherokee 140	AVUS Group	
G-AVUT	PA-28 Cherokee 140	Bencray Ltd	
G-AVUZ	PA-32 Cherokee Six 300	Ceesix Ltd	
G-AVVC	Cessna F.172H	Babs Flying Group	
G-AVVJ	MS.893A Rallye Commodore	M. Powell	
G-AVVO	Avro 652A Anson 19 (VL348)★	Newark Air Museum	
G-AVWA	PA-28 Cherokee 140	SFG Ltd	
G-AVWD	PA-28 Cherokee 140	M. Howells	
G-AVWI	PA-28 Cherokee 140	L. M. Veitch	
G-AVWJ	PA-28 Cherokee 140	M. R. Booker	
G-AVWL	PA-28 Cherokee 140	G-AVWL Group	
G-AVWM	PA-28 Cherokee 140	P. E. Preston & Partners	
G-AVWO	PA-28R Cherokee Arrow 180	Whiskey Oscar Group	
G-AVWR	PA-28R Cherokee Arrow 180	G-AVWR Flying Group	
G-AVWT	PA-28R Cherokee Arrow 180	O. D. Mihalop	
G-AVWU	PA-28R Cherokee Arrow 180	M. Ali & S. Din	
G-AVWV	PA-28R Cherokee Arrow 180	Strathtay Flying Group	
G-AVWY	Fournier RF-4D	J. P. Marriott	
G-AVXA	PA-25 Pawnee 235	S. Wales Gliding Club Ltd	
G-AVXD	Slingsby T.66 Nipper 3	J. A. Brompton	
G-AVXF	PA-28R Cherokee Arrow 180	G-AVXF Group	
G-AVXW	D.62B Condor	C. Willmott	
G-AVXY	Auster AOP.9	G. J. Siddall	
G-AVXZ	PA-28 Cherokee 140 ★	ATC Hayle (instructional airframe)	
G-AVYB	HS.121 Trident 1E-140 ★	SAS training airframe/Hereford	
G-AVYK	Beagle A.61 Terrier 3	R. Burgun	
G-AVYL	PA-28 Cherokee 180	S. Collins	
G-AVYM	PA-28 Cherokee 180	N. B. Le-Grys	
G-AVYR	PA-28 Cherokee 140	R. M Weeks	
G-AVYS	PA-28R Cherokee Arrow 180	R. J. Schreiber	
G-AVYT	PA-28R Cherokee Arrow 180	M. Bonsall	
G-AVYV	Jodel D.120	L. S. Johnson	
G-AVZB	Aero Z-37 Cmelak ★	Science Museum/Wroughton	
G-AVZI	Bölkow Bö.208C1 Junior	C. F. Rogers	
G-AVZP	Beagle B.121 Pup 1	T. A. White	
G-AVZR	PA-28 Cherokee 180	Lincoln Aero Club Ltd	
G-AVZU	Cessna F.150H	R. D. Forster	
G-AVZV	Cessna F.172H	M. P. Wiseman	
G-AVZW	EAA Biplane Model P	C. Edmondson	
G-AWAC	Gardan GY-80 Horizon 180	P. B. Hodgson	
G-AWAJ	Beech 95-D55 Baron	B. F. Whitworth	
G-AWAT	D.62B Condor	R. E. Matthews	
G-AWAU	Vickers FB.27A Vimy (replica) (F8614) ★	RAF Museum/Hendon	
G-AWAW	Cessna F.150F ★	Science Museum/South Kensington	
G-AWAX	Cessna 150D	G-AWAX Group	
G-AWAZ	PA-28R Cherokee Arrow 180	G-AWAZ Flying Group	
G-AWBB	PA-28R Cherokee Arrow 180	P. J. Young	
G-AWBC	PA-28R Cherokee Arrow 180	Anglo Aviation (UK) Ltd	
G-AWBE	PA-28 Cherokee 140	B. E. Boyle	

Notes	Reg.	Type	Owner or Operator
	G-AWBG	PA-28 Cherokee 140	I. Herdis
	G-AWBJ	Fournier RF-4D	J. B. Giddins & D. M. Hook
	G-AWBM	D.31 Turbulent	D. E. Wood
	G-AWBN	PA-30 Twin Comanche 160B	Stourfield Investments Ltd
	G-AWBS	PA-28 Cherokee 140	R. A. Ballard
	G-AWBT	PA-30 Twin Comanche 160B ★	Instructional airframe/Cranfield
	G-AWBU	Morane-Saulnier N (replica) (MS824)	Flying Aces Movie Aircraft Collection
	G-AWBX	Cessna F.150H	F. B. & J. W. Wolfe
	G-AWCM	Cessna F.150H	R. Garbett
	G-AWCN	Cessna FR.172E	B. & C. Stobart-Hook
	G-AWCP	Cessna F.150H (tailwheel)	C. E. Mason
	G-AWDA	Slingsby T.66 Nipper 3	J. A. Cheesebrough
	G-AWDO	D.31 Turbulent	R. N. Crosland
	G-AWDP	PA-28 Cherokee 180	B. H. & P. M. Illston
	G-AWDR	Cessna FR.172E	B. A. Wallace
	G-AWDU	Brantly B.2B	N. J. M. Freeman
	G-AWEA	Beagle B.121 Pup Srs.1	G. V. Crowe
	G-AWEF	SNCAN Stampe SV.4B	RAF Buchanan
	G-AWEI	D.62B Condor	P. A. Gange
	G-AWEK	Fournier RF-4D	M. P. J. Hill
	G-AWEL	Fournier RF-4D	A. B. Clymo
	G-AWEM	Fournier RF-4D	B. J. Griffin
	G-AWEP	Barritault JB-01 Minicab	R. K. Thomas
	G-AWES	Cessna 150H	D. W. Vincent
	G-AWEV	PA-28 Cherokee 140	Norflight Ltd
	G-AWEX	PA-28 Cherokee 140	Reconnaisance Ventures Ltd
	G-AWEZ	PA-28R Cherokee Arrow 180	R. G. E. Simpson
	G-AWFB	PA-28R Cherokee Arrow 180	J. C. Luke
	G-AWFC	PA-28R Cherokee Arrow 180	A. Simpson
	G-AWFD	PA-28R Cherokee Arrow 180	J. A. Canham
	G-AWFF	Cessna F.150H	R. A. Marven
	G-AWFJ	PA-28R Cherokee Arrow 180	Bavair Ltd
	G-AWFN	D.62B Condor	J. James
	G-AWFO	D.62B Condor	T. A. & R. E. Major
	G-AWFP	D.62B Condor	Blackbushe Flying Club
	G-AWFT	Jodel D.9 Bébé	W. H. Cole
	G-AWFW	Jodel D.117	C. J. Rodwell
	G-AWFZ	Beech A23 Musketeer	Bob Crowe Aircraft Sales Ltd
	G-AWGA	Beagle A.109 Airedale ★	(stored)
	G-AWGD	Cessna F.172H	Rutland Flying School
	G-AWGK	Cessna F.150H	G. E. Allen
	G-AWGN	Fournier RF-4D	R. J. Grimstead
	G-AWGZ	Taylor JT.1 Monoplane	R. L. Sambell
	G-AWHB	CASA 2-111D (6J+PR) ★	Aces High Ltd/North Weald
	G-AWHE	Hispano HA.1112 M1L	Spitfire Ltd
	G-AWHX	Rollason Beta B.2	S. G. Jones
	G-AWHY	Falconar F.11-3	Why Fly Group (G-BDPB)
	G-AWIF	Brookland Mosquito 2	C. A. Reeves
	G-AWII	VS.349 Spitfire VC (AR501)	The Shuttleworth Collection
	G-AWIR	Midget Mustang	E. C. Murgatroyd
	G-AWIT	PA-28 Cherokee 180	G-AWIT Ltd
	G-AWIV	Airmark TSR.3	P. K. Jenkins
	G-AWIW	SNCAN Stampe SV.4B	R. E. Mitchell
	G-AWJE	Slingsby T.66 Nipper 3	K G. G. Howe
	G-AWJV	DH.98 Mosquito TT Mk 35 (TA634) ★	De Havilland Heritage Museum/London Colney
	G-AWJX	Zlin Z.526 Trener Master	P. A. Colman
	G-AWKD	PA-17 Vagabond	C. C. & J. M. Lovell
	G-AWKO	Beagle B.121 Pup 1	J. Martin
	G-AWKP	Jodel DR.253	G-AWKP Group
	G-AWKX	Beech A65 Queen Air ★	(Instructional airframe)/Shoreham
	G-AWLF	Cessna F.172H	Gannet Aviation
	G-AWLG	SIPA 903	S. W. Markham
	G-AWLI	PA-22 Tri-Pacer 150	North Hangar Group
	G-AWLO	Boeing Stearman E75	N. D. Pickard
	G-AWLP	Mooney M.20F	I. C. Lomax
	G-AWLR	Slingsby T.66 Nipper 3	T. D. Reid
	G-AWLS	Slingsby T.66 Nipper 3	G. A. Dunster & B. Gallagher
	G-AWLX	Auster 5 J/2 Arrow	W. J. Taylor
	G-AWLZ	Fournier RF-4D	Nympsfield RF-4 Group
	G-AWMD	Jodel D.11	J. R. Cooper
	G-AWMF	PA-18 Super Cub 150 (modified)	Booker Gliding Club Ltd
	G-AWMN	Luton LA-4A Minor	S. Penfold
	G-AWMR	D.31 Turbulent	J. R. D. Bygraves

Reg.	Type	Owner or Operator	Notes
G-AWMT	Cessna F.150H	Strategic Synergies Ltd	
G-AWNT	BN-2A Islander	Precision Terrain Surveys Ltd	
G-AWOE	Aero Commander 680E	J. M. Houlder	
G-AWOF	PA-15 Vagabond	C. M. Hicks	
G-AWOH	PA-17 Vagabond	A. Lovejoy & K. Downes	
G-AWOT	Cessna F.150H	D. I. Flory	
G-AWOU	Cessna 170B	S. Billington	
G-AWOX	Westland WS-58 Wessex 60 (150225) ★	Paintball Adventure West/Bristol	
G-AWPH	P.56 Provost T.1	J. A. D. Bradshaw	
G-AWPJ	Cessna F.150H	W. J. Greenfield	
G-AWPN	Shield Xyla	J. P. Gilbert	
G-AWPU	Cessna F.150J	LAC Flying School	
G-AWPW	PA-12 Super Cruiser	AK Leasing (Jersey) Ltd	
G-AWPZ	Andreasson BA-4B	J. M. Vening	
G-AWRP	Cierva Rotorcraft ★	IHM/Weston-super-Mare	
G-AWRS	Avro 19 Srs. 2 (TX213) ★	North East Aircraft Museum/Usworth	
G-AWRY	P.56 Provost T.1 (XF836)	A. J. House	
G-AWSA	Avro 652A Anson 19 (VL349) ★	Norfolk & Suffolk Aviation Museum/Flixton	
G-AWSH	Zlin Z.526 Trener Master	P. A. Colman	
G-AWSL	PA-28 Cherokee 180D	A. H. & A. H. Brown	
G-AWSM	PA-28 Cherokee 235	Aviation Projects Ltd	
G-AWSN	D.62B Condor	M. K. A. Blyth	
G-AWSP	D.62B Condor	R. Q. & A. S. Bond	
G-AWSS	D.62A Condor	N. J. & D. Butler	
G-AWST	D.62B Condor	J. R. Bell	
G-AWSV	Skeeter 12 (XM553)	Maj. M. Somerton-Rayner	
G-AWSW	Beagle D.5/180 Husky (XW635)	Windmill Aviation	
G-AWTL	PA-28 Cherokee 180D	G. B. Stevens	
G-AWTP	Schleicher Ka 6E	Papa Victor Syndicate	
G-AWTS	Beech A.23 Musketeer	J. G. Edwards & K. D. Maal	
G-AWTV	Beech 19A Musketeer Sport	J. Whittaker	
G-AWTX	Cessna F.150J	R. D. Forster	
G-AWUB	Gardan GY-201 Minicab	R. A. Hand	
G-AWUE	Jodel DR.1050	K. W. Wood & F. M. Watson	
G-AWUJ	Cessna F.150H	I. M. Ashpole & N. Sutton	
G-AWUL	Cessna F.150H	A. J. Baron	
G-AWUN	Cessna F.150H	G-AWUN Group	
G-AWUT	Cessna F.150J	Aerospace Resources Ltd	
G-AWUU	Cessna F.150J	D. P. Jones	
G-AWUX	Cessna F.172H	G-AWUX Group	
G-AWUZ	Cessna F.172H	Five Percent Flying Group	
G-AWVA	Cessna F.172H	Barton Air Ltd	
G-AWVC	Beagle B.121 Pup 1	J. J. West & M. J. Applewhite	
G-AWVE	Jodel DR.1050/M1	E. A. Taylor	
G-AWVG	AESL Airtourer T.2	C. J. Schofield	
G-AWVN	Aeronca 7AC Champion	Champ Flying Group	
G-AWVZ	Jodel D.112	D. C. Stokes	
G-AWWE	Beagle B.121 Pup 2	Pup Flyers	
G-AWWI	Jodel D.117	T. M. Williams	
G-AWWM	Gardan GY-201 Minicab	P. J. Brayshaw	
G-AWWN	Jodel DR.1050	The G-AWWN Group	
G-AWWO	Jodel DR.1050	W. G. Brooks	
G-AWWP	Aerosport Woody Pusher III	M. S. Bird & R. D. Bird	
G-AWWU	Cessna FR.172F	R. Henderson	
G-AWXR	PA-28 Cherokee 180D	Aero Clube da Costa Verde/Portugal	
G-AWXS	PA-28 Cherokee 180D	C. R. & S. A. Hardiman	
G-AWXX	Westland Wessex 60 Srs 1	D. Brem-Wilson	
G-AWXY	MS.885 Super Rallye	K. Henderson	
G-AWXZ	SNCAN Stampe SV.4C	Bianchi Aviation Film Services Ltd	
G-AWYB	Cessna FR.172F	M.P. & S. T. Barnard & M. S. Macdonald	
G-AWYJ	Beagle B.121 Pup 2	H. C. Taylor	
G-AWYL	Jodel DR.253B	T. C. Van Lonkhuyzen	
G-AWYO	Beagle B.121 Pup 1	B. R. C. Wild	
G-AWYY	Slingsby T.57 Camel replica (B6401) ★	F.A.A. Museum/Yeovilton	
G-AWZI	HS.121 Trident 3B ★	A. Lee/FAST Museum (nose only)/Farnborough	
G-AWZJ	HS.121 Trident 3B ★	Dumfries & Galloway Museum	
G-AWZK	HS.121 Trident 3B ★	Trident Preservation Society/Manchester ✓	
G-AWZM	HS.121 Trident 3B ★	Science Museum/Wroughton	
G-AWZP	HS.121 Trident 3B ★	Manchester Museum of Science & Industry (nose only)	
G-AWZX	HS.121 Trident 3B ★	BAA Airport Fire Services/Gatwick	
G-AXAB	PA-28 Cherokee 140	Bencray Ltd	

Notes	Reg.	Type	Owner or Operator
	G-AXAN	DH.82A Tiger Moth (EM720)	D. & S. A. Firth
	G-AXAS	Wallis WA-116T	K. H. Wallis (G-AVDH)
	G-AXAT	Jodel D.117A	D. Evans
	G-AXBF	Beagle D.5/180 Husky	M. C. R. Wills
	G-AXBJ	Cessna F.172H	Atlantic Bridge Aviation Ltd
	G-AXBW	DH.82A Tiger Moth (T5879:RUC-W)	G-AXBW Ltd
	G-AXBZ	DH.82A Tiger Moth	W. J. de Jong Cleyndert
	G-AXCA	PA-28R Cherokee Arrow 200	W. H. Nelson
	G-AXCG	Jodel D.117	D. J. Millin
	G-AXCM	MS.880B Rallye Club	D. C. Manifold
	G-AXCX	Beagle B.121 Pup 2	L. A. Pink
	G-AXCY	Jodel D.117A	R. S. Marom
	G-AXDI	Cessna F.172H	M. F. & J. R. Leusby
	G-AXDK	Jodel DR.315	R. D. Bennett
	G-AXDN	BAC-Sud Concorde 01 ★	Duxford Aviation Society
	G-AXDV	Beagle B.121 Pup 1	T. A. White
	G-AXDZ	Cassutt Racer IIIM	A. Chadwick
	G-AXED	PA-25 Pawnee 235	Wolds Gliding Club Ltd
	G-AXEH	B.125 Bulldog 1 ★	Museum of Flight/East Fortune
	G-AXEI	Ward Gnome ★	Real Aeroplane Club/Breighton
	G-AXEO	Scheibe SF.25B Falke	P. F. Moffatt
	G-AXEV	Beagle B.121 Pup 2	D. S. Russell & D. G. Benson
	G-AXFG	Cessna 337D	County Garage (Cheltenham) Ltd
	G-AXFN	Jodel D.119	R. Manning & F. J. Wordsworth
	G-AXGE	MS.880B Rallye Club	R. P. Loxton
	G-AXGG	Cessna F.150J	A. J. Simpson
	G-AXGP	Piper J-3C-90 Cub	A. P. Acres
	G-AXGR	Luton LA-4A Minor	B. A. Schlussler
	G-AXGS	D.62B Condor	SAS Flying Group
	G-AXGV	D.62B Condor	Hawkaero Flying Group
	G-AXGZ	D.62B Condor	R. M. Schweitzer
	G-AXHA	Cessna 337A	I. M. Latiff
	G-AXHC	SNCAN Stampe SV.4C	D. L. Webley
	G-AXHO	Beagle B.121 Pup 2	L. W. Grundy
	G-AXHP	Piper J-3C-65 Cub (480636:A-58)	Witham (Specialist) Vehicles Ltd
	G-AXHR	Piper J-3C-65 Cub (329601:D-44)	D. J. Dash
	G-AXHS	MS.880B Rallye Club	B. & A. Swales
	G-AXHT	MS.880B Rallye Club	P. M. Murray
	G-AXHV	Jodel D.117A	Derwent Flying Group
	G-AXIA	Beagle B.121 Pup 1	C. K. Parsons
	G-AXIE	Beagle B.121 Pup 2	J. P. Thomas
	G-AXIO	PA-28 Cherokee 140B	G. W. Mountford
	G-AXIR	PA-28 Cherokee 140B	R. W. Howard
	G-AXIW	Scheibe SF.25B Falke	M. Pedley
	G-AXIX	Glos-Airtourer 150	S. Alexander
	G-AXJB	Omega 84 balloon	Southern Balloon Group
	G-AXJH	Beagle B.121 Pup 2	The Henry Flying Group
	G-AXJI	Beagle B.121 Pup 2	J. J. Sanders & J. A. Walley
	G-AXJJ	Beagle B.121 Pup 2	M. L. Jones & ptnrs
	G-AXJO	Beagle B.121 Pup 2	J. A. D. Bradshaw
	G-AXJR	Scheibe SF.25B Falke	Falke Syndicate
	G-AXJV	PA-28 Cherokee 140B	Seahawk Flying Group
	G-AXJX	PA-28 Cherokee 140B	K. Wilson
	G-AXKH	Luton LA-4A Minor	M. E. Vaisey
	G-AXKJ	Jodel D.9	The Hinton D9 Group
	G-AXKO	Westland-Bell 47G-4A	M. Gallagher
	G-AXKS	Westland Bell 47G-4A ★	Museum of Army Flying/Middle Wallop
	G-AXKX	Westland Bell 47G-4A	R. A. Dale
	G-AXLI	Slingsby T.66 Nipper 3	D. & M. Shrimpton
	G-AXLS	Jodel DR.105A	Axle Flying Club
	G-AXLZ	PA-18 Super Cub 95	R. J. Quantrell
	G-AXMA	PA-24 Comanche 180	B. C. Faulkner
	G-AXMD	Omega O-56 balloon ★	British Balloon Museum/Newbury
	G-AXMT	Bücker Bü 133 Jungmeister	A. J. E. Smith
	G-AXMW	Beagle B.121 Pup 1	DJP Engineering (Knebworth) Ltd
	G-AXMX	Beagle B.121 Pup 2	Bob The Beagle Group
	G-AXNJ	Wassmer Jodel D.120	S. S. M. Turner
	G-AXNN	Beagle B.121 Pup 2	Gabrielle Aviation Ltd
	G-AXNP	Beagle B.121 Pup 2	J. W. Ellis & R. J. Hemmings
	G-AXNR	Beagle B.121 Pup 2	AXNR Group
	G-AXNS	Beagle B.121 Pup 2	Derwent Aero Group
	G-AXNW	SNCAN Stampe SV.4C	C. S. Grace
	G-AXNX	Cessna 182M	T. Latky & C.Csilla

Reg.	Type	Owner or Operator	Notes
G-AXNZ	Pitts S.1C Special	November Zulu Group	
G-AXOG	PA-E23 Aztec 250D	G. H. Nolan	
G-AXOH	MS.894 Rallye Minerva	T. A. D. Crook	
G-AXOJ	Beagle B.121 Pup 2	Pup Flying Group	
G-AXOR	PA-28 Cherokee 180D	Oscar Romeo Aviation Ltd	
G-AXOS	MS.894A Rallye Minerva	R. S. M. Fendt	
G-AXOT	MS.893 Rallye Commodore 180	P. Evans	
G-AXOZ	Beagle B.121 Pup 1	R. J. Ogborn	
G-AXPA	Beagle B.121 Pup 1	Papa-Alpha Group	
G-AXPC	Beagle B.121 Pup 2	T. A. White	
G-AXPF	Cessna F.150K	D. R. Marks	
G-AXPG	Mignet HM.293	W. H. Cole (stored)	
G-AXPZ	Campbell Cricket	W. R. Partridge	
G-AXRC	Campbell Cricket	L. R. Morris	
G-AXRP	SNCAN Stampe SV-4C	C. C. Manning (G-BLOL)	
G-AXRR	Auster AOP.9 (XR241)	R. B. Webber	
G-AXRT	Cessna FA.150K (tailwheel)	C. C. Walley	
G-AXSF	Nash Petrel	Nash Aircraft Ltd	
G-AXSG	PA-28 Cherokee 180	The Tago Island Co Ltd	
G-AXSI	Cessna F.172H	J. B. Cutts (G-SNIP)	
G-AXSM	Jodel DR.1051	T. R. G. & M. S. Barnby	
G-AXSW	Cessna FA.150K	R. J. Whyham	
G-AXSZ	PA-28 Cherokee 140B	White Wings Flying Group	
G-AXTA	PA-28 Cherokee 140B	G-AXTA Aircraft Group	
G-AXTC	PA-28 Cherokee 140B	G-AXTC Group	
G-AXTJ	PA-28 Cherokee 140B	K. Patel	
G-AXTL	PA-28 Cherokee 140B	Bristol and West Aeroplane Club Ltd	
G-AXTO	PA-24 Comanche 260	J. L. Wright	
G-AXTX	Jodel D.112	C. Sawford	
G-AXUA	Beagle B.121 Pup 1	P. Wood	
G-AXUB	BN-2A Islander	Headcorn Parachute Club Ltd	
G-AXUC	PA-12 Super Cruiser	J. J. Bunton	
G-AXUF	Cessna FA.150K	B. T. Walsh	
G-AXUJ	Auster J/1 Autocrat	P. Gill (G-OSTA)	
G-AXUK	Jodel DR.1050	Downland Flying Group	
G-AXUM	HP.137 Jetstream 1 ★	Sodeteg Formation/France	
G-AXVB	Cessna F.172H	R. & J. Turner	
G-AXVK	Campbell Cricket	B. Jones	
G-AXVM	Campbell Cricket	D. M. Organ	
G-AXVN	McCandless M.4	W. R. Partridge	
G-AXWA	Auster AOP.9 (XN437)	C. M. Edwards	
G-AXWT	Jodel D.11	C. S. Jackson	
G-AXWV	Jodel DR.253	R. Friedlander & D. C. Ray	
G-AXWZ	PA-28R Cherokee Arrow 200	Whisky Zulu Group	
G-AXXC	CP.301B Emeraude	J. C. & R. D. P. Cadle	
G-AXXV	DH.82A Tiger Moth (DE992)	C. N. Wookey	
G-AXXW	Jodel D.117	R. K. G. Delve	
G-AXYK	Taylor JT.1 Monoplane	O. C. Pope	
G-AXYU	Jodel D.9 Bébé	P. Turton	
G-AXZD	PA-28 Cherokee 180E	G. M. Whitmore	
G-AXZF	PA-28 Cherokee 180E	D. R. Clyde	
G-AXZH	Glasflugel H201B Standard Libelle	M. C. Gregorie	
G-AXZM	Slingsby T.66 Nipper 3	G. R. Harlow	
G-AXZO	Cessna 180	The Cessna 180 Group	
G-AXZP	PA-E23 Aztec 250D	D. M. Harbottle	
G-AXZT	Jodel D.117	P. Guest	
G-AXZU	Cessna 182N	W. Gollan	
G-AYAB	PA-28 Cherokee 180E	J. R. Green	
G-AYAC	PA-28R Cherokee Arrow 200	Fersfield Flying Group	
G-AYAJ	Cameron O-84 balloon	E. T. Hall	
G-AYAL	Omega 56 balloon ★	British Balloon Museum/Newbury	
G-AYAN	Slingsby Motor Cadet III	G. Hill & R. Moyse	
G-AYAR	PA-28 Cherokee 180E	A. Jahanfar/Southend	
G-AYAT	PA-28 Cherokee 180E	G-AYAT Flying Group	
G-AYAW	PA-28 Cherokee 180E	D. G., P. G. & R. J. Taylor	
G-AYBD	Cessna F.150K	Apollo Aviation Advisory Ltd	
G-AYBG	Scheibe SF.25B Falke	Anglia Sailplanes	
G-AYBO	PA-23 Aztec 250D	A. G. Gutknecht/Austria	
G-AYBP	Jodel D.112	G. J. Langston	
G-AYBR	Jodel D.112	I. S. Parker	
G-AYCC	Campbell Cricket	D. J. M. Charity	
G-AYCF	Cessna FA.150K	E. J. Atkins	

Notes	Reg.	Type	Owner or Operator
	G-AYCG	SNCAN Stampe SV.4C	Tiger Airways
	G-AYCJ	Cessna TP.206D	P. J. Meakin
	G-AYCK	AIA Stampe SV.4C	The Real Flying Co Ltd (G-BUNT)
	G-AYCN	Piper J-3C-65 Cub	W. R. & B. M. Young
	G-AYCO	CEA DR.360	J. D. Boyce & R. Underwood
	G-AYCP	Jodel D.112	J. A. Carey
	G-AYCT	Cessna F.172H	J. R. Benson
	G-AYDI	DH.82A Tiger Moth	E. G. & G. R. Woods
	G-AYDR	SNCAN Stampe SV.4C	D. J. Ashley
	G-AYDV	Coates Swalesong SA11	The Real Aeroplane Co.Ltd
	G-AYDW	Beagle A.61 Terrier 2	A. S. Topen
	G-AYDX	Beagle A.61 Terrier 2	T. S. Lee
	G-AYDY	Luton LA-4A Minor	J. Dible/Ireland
	G-AYDZ	Jodel DR.200	Zero One Group
	G-AYEB	Jodel D.112	Echo Bravo Partnership
	G-AYEC	CP.301A Emeraude	Redwing Flying Group
	G-AYEE	PA-28 Cherokee 180E	Demero Ltd & Transcourt Ltd
	G-AYEF	PA-28 Cherokee 180E	Pegasus Flying Group
	G-AYEG	Falconar F-9	A. L. Smith
	G-AYEH	Jodel DR.1050	H. L. M. Williams
	G-AYEJ	Jodel DR.1050	J. M. Newbold
	G-AYEN	Piper J-3C-65 Cub	P. Warde & C. F. Morris
	G-AYET	MS.892A Rallye Commodore 150	A. T. R. Bingley
	G-AYEW	Jodel DR.1051	J. R. Hope
	G-AYFC	D.62B Condor	A. R. Chadwick
	G-AYFD	D.62B Condor	B. G. Manning
	G-AYFE	D.62C Condor	M. Soulsby
	G-AYFF	D.62B Condor	H. Stuart
	G-AYFJ	MS.880B Rallye Club	Rallye FJ Group
	G-AYFV	Crosby BA-4B	D. W. Mathie
	G-AYGA	Jodel D.117	J. W. Bowes
	G-AYGB	Cessna 310Q ★	Instructional airframe/Perth
	G-AYGC	Cessna F.150K	Alpha Aviation Group
	G-AYGD	Jodel DR.1051	J. F. M. Barlett & J. P. Liber
	G-AYGE	SNCAN Stampe SV.4C	L. J. Proudfoot & ptnrs
	G-AYGG	Jodel D.120	J. M. Dean
	G-AYGX	Cessna FR.172G	Reims Rocket Group
	G-AYHA	AA-1 Yankee	S. J. Carr
	G-AYHX	Jodel D.117A	A. P. Chapman & L. E. Cowling
	G-AYIA	Hughes 369HS ★	G. D. E. Bilton/Sywell
	G-AYIG	PA-28 Cherokee 140C	G. K. Clarkson
	G-AYII	PA-28R Cherokee Arrow 200	Double India Group
	G-AYIJ	SNCAN Stampe SV.4B	D. Savage
	G-AYJA	Jodel DR.1050	D. M. Blair
	G-AYJB	SNCAN Stampe SV.4C	F. J. M. & J. P. Esson
	G-AYJD	Alpavia-Fournier RF-3	Juliet Delta Group
	G-AYJP	PA-28 Cherokee 140C	Transcourt Ltd and Demero Ltd
	G-AYJR	PA-28 Cherokee 140C	Transcourt Ltd and Turweston Flying School
	G-AYJY	Isaacs Fury II	T. E. W. Terrell
	G-AYKD	Jodel DR.1050	J. K. Cook
	G-AYKJ	Jodel D.117A	R. J. Hughes
	G-AYKK	Jodel D.117	J. M. Whitham
	G-AYKS	Leopoldoff L.7 Colibri	W. B. Cooper
	G-AYKT	Jodel D.117	D. I. Walker
	G-AYKW	PA-28 Cherokee 140C	Kilo Whiskey Group
	G-AYKZ	SAI KZ-8	R. E. Mitchell
	G-AYLA	Glos-Airtourer 115	D. S. P. Disney
	G-AYLC	Jodel DR.1051	G-AYLC Flying Group
	G-AYLF	Jodel DR.1051 (modified)	R. Twigg
	G-AYLL	Jodel DR.1050	C. Joly
	G-AYLP	AA-1 Yankee	D. Nairn
	G-AYLV	Jodel D.120	M. R. Henham
	G-AYME	Fournier RF-5	R. D. Goodger
	G-AYMK	PA-28 Cherokee 140C	W. E. Mould
	G-AYMO	PA-23 Aztec 250C	J. A. D. Richardson
	G-AYMP	Currie Wot	R. C. Hibberd
	G-AYMR	Lederlin 380L	P. J. Brayshaw
	G-AYMU	Jodel D.112	M. R. Baker
	G-AYMV	Western 20 balloon	R. G. Turnbull
	G-AYNA	Phoenix Currie Wot	D. R. Partridge
	G-AYND	Cessna 310Q	Source Group Ltd
	G-AYNF	PA-28 Cherokee 140C	BW Aviation Ltd

Reg.	Type	Owner or Operator	Notes
G-AYNJ	PA-28 Cherokee 140C	A. Andreeva	
G-AYNN	Cessna 185B	Bencray Ltd	
G-AYNP	Westland WS-55 Whirlwind Srs 3 ★	IHM/Weston-super-Mare	
G-AYOW	Cessna 182N Skylane	I. F. Ellis, L. M. Hall & C. J. R. Vernon	
G-AYOZ	Cessna FA.150L	P. J. Worrall	
G-AYPE	MBB Bö.209 Monsun	Papa Echo Ltd	
G-AYPG	Cessna F.177RG	D. P. McDermott	
G-AYPH	Cessna F.177RG	M. L. & T. M. Jones	
G-AYPJ	PA-28 Cherokee 180	R. B. Petrie	
G-AYPM	PA-18 Super Cub 95 (115373)	R. Horner	
G-AYPO	PA-18 Super Cub 95	A. W. Knowles	
G-AYPS	PA-18 Super Cub 95	D. Racionzer	
G-AYPU	PA-28R Cherokee Arrow 200	Monalto Investments Ltd	
G-AYPV	PA-28 Cherokee 140D	Ashley Gardner Flying Club Ltd	
G-AYPZ	Campbell Cricket	A. Melody	
G-AYRG	Cessna F.172K	I. G. Harrison	
G-AYRI	PA-28R Cherokee Arrow 200	J. C. Houdret	
G-AYRM	PA-28 Cherokee 140D	M. J. Saggers	
G-AYRO	Cessna FA.150L Aerobat	Fat Boys Flying Club	
G-AYRS	Jodel D.120A	L. R. H. D'Eath	
G-AYRT	Cessna F.172K	P. E. Crees	
G-AYRU	BN-2A-6 Islander	F. G. H. Jensen	
G-AYSB	PA-30 Twin Comanche 160C	M. J. Abbott	
G-AYSH	Taylor JT.1 Monoplane	C. J. Lodge	
G-AYSK	Luton LA-4A Minor	B. A. Schlussler & S. J. Rudkin	
G-AYSX	Cessna F.177RG	A. P. R. Dean	
G-AYSY	Cessna F.177RG	S. A. Tuer	
G-AYTA	SOCATA MS.880B Rallye Club ★	Manchester Museum of Science & Industry	
G-AYTR	CP.301A Emeraude	I. D. Worthington	
G-AYTT	Phoenix PM-3 Duet	R. B. Webber & J. K. Houlgrave	
G-AYTV	Jurca Tempete	C. W. Kirk	
G-AYUB	CEA DR.253B	Rothwell Group	
G-AYUH	PA-28 Cherokee 180F	Broadland Flying Group Ltd	
G-AYUJ	Evans VP-1	T. N. Howard	
G-AYUM	Slingsby T.61A Falke	M. H. Simms	
G-AYUN	Slingsby T.61A Falke	G-AYUN Group	
G-AYUP	Slingsby T.61A Falke	P. R. Williams	
G-AYUR	Slingsby T.61A Falke	R. Hanningan & R. Lingard	
G-AYUS	Taylor JT.1 Monoplane	J. G. W. Newton	
G-AYUT	Jodel DR.1050	G. Bell	
G-AYUV	Cessna F.172H	Justgold Ltd	
G-AYVO	Wallis WA-120 Srs 1	K. H. Wallis	
G-AYVP	Woody Pusher	J. R. Wraight	
G-AYWA	Avro 19 Srs 2 ★	N. K. Geddes	
G-AYWD	Cessna 182N	Wild Dreams Group	
G-AYWH	Jodel D.117A	D. Kynaston	
G-AYWM	Glos-Airtourer Super 150	Star Flying Group	
G-AYWT	AIA Stampe SV.4C	R. A. Palmer	
G-AYXP	Jodel D.117A	G. N. Davies	
G-AYXS	SIAI-Marchetti S205-18R	P. J. Bloore & J. M. Biles	
G-AYXT	WS-55 Whirlwind Srs 2 (XK940:911) ★	IHM/Weston-super-Mare	
G-AYXU	Champion 7KCAB Citabria	E. V. Moffatt & J. S. Peplow	
G-AYYL	Slingsby T.61A Falke	Brightman Industries Ltd	
G-AYYO	Jodel DR.1050/M1	Bustard Flying Club Ltd	
G-AYYT	Jodel DR.1050/M1	R. Warner	
G-AYYU	Beech C23 Musketeer	G-AYYU Group	
G-AYZH	Taylor JT.2 Titch	T. D. Gardner	
G-AYZI	SNCAN Stampe SV.4C	D. M. & P. A. Fenton	
G-AYZJ	Westland WS-55 Whirlwind HAS.7 ★	Newark Air Museum (XM685)	
G-AYZK	Jodel DR.1050/M1	D. G. Hesketh	
G-AYZS	D.62B Condor	M. N. Thrush	
G-AYZU	Slingsby T.61A Falke	A. J. Harpley	
G-AYZW	Slingsby T.61A Falke	Y-ZW Group	
G-AZAB	PA-30 Twin Comanche 160B	Bickertons Aerodromes Ltd	
G-AZAJ	PA-28R Cherokee Arrow 200B	P. Woulfe	
G-AZAW	Gardan GY-80 Horizon 160	J. W. Foley	
G-AZAZ	Bensen B.8M ★	F.A.A. Museum/Yeovilton	
G-AZBB	MBB Bö.209 Monsun 160FV	J. A. Webb	
G-AZBE	Glos-Airtourer Super 150	R. G. Vincent	
G-AZBI	Jodel 150	R. J. Wald	
G-AZBL	Jodel D.9 Bébé	J. Hill	

G-AZBN – G-AZMZ

Notes	Reg.	Type	Owner or Operator
	G-AZBN	Noorduyn AT-16 Harvard IIB (FT391)	Swaygate Ltd
	G-AZBU	Auster AOP.9 (XR246)	Auster Nine Group
	G-AZCB	SNCAN Stampe SV.4C	M. Coward
	G-AZCK	Beagle B.121 Pup 2	P. Crone
	G-AZCL	Beagle B.121 Pup 2	Flew LLP & J. M. Henry
	G-AZCN	Beagle B.121 Pup 2	B. Mahjouri, D. M. Callagham & G. Wildgoose
	G-AZCP	Beagle B.121 Pup 1	M. R. Badmington
	G-AZCT	Beagle B.121 Pup 1	J. Coleman
	G-AZCU	Beagle B.121 Pup 1	A. A. Harris
	G-AZCV	Beagle B.121 Pup 2	N. R. W. Long
	G-AZCZ	Beagle B.121 Pup 2	L. & J. M. Northover
	G-AZDD	MBB Bö.209 Monsun 150FF	Double Delta Flying Group
	G-AZDE	PA-28R Cherokee Arrow 200B	London Elstree Aviation Ltd
	G-AZDG	Beagle B.121 Pup 2	D. J. Sage & J. R. Heaps
	G-AZDJ	PA-32 Cherokee Six 300	K. J. Mansbridge & D. C. Gibbs
	G-AZDX	PA-28 Cherokee 180F	M. Cowan
	G-AZDY	DH.82A Tiger Moth	B. A. Mills
	G-AZEE	MS.880B Rallye Club	J. Shelton
	G-AZEF	Jodel D.120	P. R. Sears
	G-AZEG	PA-28 Cherokee 140D	Ashley Gardner Flying Club Ltd
	G-AZEU	Beagle B.121 Pup 2	G. M. Moir
	G-AZEV	Beagle B.121 Pup 2	G. H. Matthews
	G-AZEW	Beagle B.121 Pup 2	D. Ridley
	G-AZEY	Beagle B.121 Pup 2	B. K. & W. G. Ranger
	G-AZFA	Beagle B.121 Pup 2	J. Smith
	G-AZFC	PA-28 Cherokee 140D	WLS Flying Group
	G-AZFF	Jodel D.112	J. Bolger/Ireland
	G-AZFI	PA-28R Cherokee Arrow 200B	G-AZFI Ltd
	G-AZFM	PA-28R Cherokee Arrow 200B	P. J. Jenness
	G-AZGA	Jodel D.120	A. P. Hatton
	G-AZGC	SNCAN Stampe SV.4C	D. J. Ashley
	G-AZGE	SNCAN Stampe SV.4C	Tiger Airways
	G-AZGF	Beagle B.121 Pup 2	K. Singh
	G-AZGL	MS.894A Rallye Minerva	The Cambridge Aero Club Ltd
	G-AZGY	CP.301B Emeraude	R. H. Braithwaite
	G-AZGZ	DH.82A Tiger Moth (NM181)	R. J. King
	G-AZHB	Robin HR.100/200B	J. F. Gould
	G-AZHC	Jodel D.112	Aerodel Flying Group
	G-AZHD	Slingsby T.61A Falke	R. J. Shallcrass
	G-AZHH	SA 102.5 Cavalier	D. W. Buckle
	G-AZHI	Glos-Airtourer Super 150	Flying Grasshoppers Ltd
	G-AZHK	Robin HR.100/200B	G. I. Applin (G-ILEG)
	G-AZHR	Piccard Ax6 balloon	C. Fisher
	G-AZHT	AESL Airtourer (modified)	Aviation West Ltd
	G-AZHU	Luton LA-4A Minor	C. C. Burton
	G-AZIB	ST-10 Diplomate	W. B. Bateson
	G-AZII	Jodel D.117A	J. S. Brayshaw
	G-AZIJ	Jodel DR.360	F. M. Carter
	G-AZIL	Slingsby T.61A Falke	D. W. Savage
	G-AZIP	Cameron O-65 balloon	Dante Balloon Group
	G-AZJC	Fournier RF-5	Seighford RF5 Group
	G-AZJE	Ord-Hume JB-01 Minicab	Kayee Flyers
	G-AZJN	Robin DR.300/140	C. P. Course
	G-AZJV	Cessna F.172L	G-AZJV Flying Group
	G-AZKE	MS.880B Rallye Club	D. A. Thompson & J. D. Headlam/Germany
	G-AZKO	Cessna F.337F	G. James
	G-AZKP	Jodel D.117	Moray Flying Group
	G-AZKR	PA-24 Comanche	S. J. McGovern
	G-AZKS	AA-1A Trainer	I. R. Matterface
	G-AZKW	Cessna F.172L	D. Stewart
	G-AZKZ	Cessna F.172L	R. D. & E. Forster
	G-AZLE	Boeing N2S-5 Kaydet (1102:102)	A. E. Paulson
	G-AZLF	Jodel D.120	M. S. C. Ball
	G-AZLH	Cessna F.150L	W. Ali
	G-AZLN	PA-28 Cherokee 180F	Enstone Sales & Services Ltd and J. Logan
	G-AZLV	Cessna 172K	G-AZLV Flying Group
	G-AZLY	Cessna F.150L	R. B. McLain
	G-AZMC	Slingsby T.61A Falke	P. J. R. White
	G-AZMD	Slingsby T.61C Falke	Tandem Gliding Syndicate
	G-AZMJ	AA-5 Traveler	W. R. Partridge
	G-AZMX	PA-28 Cherokee 140 ★	NE Wales Institute of Higher Education (Instructional airframe)/Flintshire
	G-AZMZ	MS.893A Rallye Commodore 150	J. Palethorpe

34

Reg.	Type	Owner or Operator	Notes
G-AZNK	SNCAN Stampe SV.4A	November Kilo Group	
G-AZNL	PA-28R Cherokee Arrow 200D	B. P. Liversidge	
G-AZNO	Cessna 182P	M. S. Williams	
G-AZNT	Cameron O-84 balloon	P. Glydon	
G-AZOA	MBB Bö.209 Monsun 150FF	M. W. Hurst	
G-AZOB	MBB Bö.209 Monsun 150FF	J. A. Webb	
G-AZOE	Glos-Airtourer 115	G-AZOE 607 Group	
G-AZOF	Glos-Airtourer Super 150	R. C. Thursby & C. Goldsmith	
G-AZOG	PA-28R Cherokee Arrow 200D	Southend Flying Club	
G-AZOL	PA-34-200 Seneca II	Stapleford Flying Club Ltd	
G-AZOS	Jurca MJ.5-H1 Sirocco	P. J. Tanulak	
G-AZOU	Jodel DR.1050	Horsham Flying Group	
G-AZOZ	Cessna FRA.150L	J. E. Jones	
G-AZPA	PA-25 Pawnee 235	Black Mountains Gliding Club Ltd	
G-AZPC	Slingsby T.61C Falke	D. Heslop & J. R. Kimberley	
G-AZPF	Fournier RF-5	E. C. Mort	
G-AZPH	Craft-Pitts S-1S Special ★	Science Museum/South Kensington	
G-AZPX	Western O-31 balloon	Zebedee Balloon Service Ltd	
G-AZRA	MBB Bö.209 Monsun 150FF	Alpha Flying Ltd	
G-AZRH	PA-28 Cherokee 140D	Trust Flying Group	
G-AZRI	Payne Free Balloon	C. A. Butter & J. J. T. Cooke	
G-AZRK	Fournier RF-5	A. B. Clymo & J. F. Rogers	
G-AZRL	PA-18 Super Cub 95	J. S. & P. R. Johnson	
G-AZRM	Fournier RF-5	Romeo Mike Group	
G-AZRN	Cameron O-84 balloon	C. J. Desmet/Belgium	
G-AZRP	Glos-Airtourer 115	B. F. Strawford	
G-AZRS	PA-22 Tri-Pacer 150	R. H. Hulls	
G-AZRZ	Cessna U.206F	Cornish Parachute Club Ltd	
G-AZSA	Stampe et Renard SV.4B	M. R. Dolman	
G-AZSC	Noorduyn AT-16 Harvard IIB (43:SC)	Goodwood Road Racing Co Ltd	
G-AZSF	PA-28R Cherokee Arrow 200D	Smart People Don't Buy Ltd	
G-AZTA	MBB Bö.209 Monsun 150FF	A. J. Court	
G-AZTF	Cessna F.177RG	R. Burgun	
G-AZTM	AESL Airtourer T2	Victa Restoration Group	
G-AZTS	Cessna F.172L	Eastern Air Executive Ltd	
G-AZTV	Stolp SA.500 Starlet	G. R. Rowland	
G-AZTW	Cessna F.177RG	I. M. Richmond & G. R. Waller	
G-AZUM	Cessna F.172L	Fowlmere Flyers	
G-AZUT	MS.893A Rallye Commodore 180	J. Palethorpe	
G-AZUY	Cessna E.310L	W. B. Bateson	
G-AZUZ	Cessna FRA.150L	D. J. Parker	
G-AZVA	MBB Bö.209 Monsun 150FF	M. P. Brinkmann	
G-AZVB	MBB Bö.209 Monsun 150FF	E. & P. M. L. Cliffe	
G-AZVF	MS.894A Rallye Minerva	Minerva Flying Group	
G-AZVG	AA-5 Traveler	K. M. Whelan	
G-AZVH	MS.894A Rallye Minerva	P. L. Jubb	
G-AZVI	MS.892A Rallye Commodore	G. C. Jarvis	
G-AZVL	Jodel D.119	A. K. & K. B. Raven	
G-AZVP	Cessna F.177RG	L. J. Klarenbeek	
G-AZWB	PA-28 Cherokee 140	G-AZWB Flying Group	
G-AZWD	PA-28 Cherokee 140	BJ Services (Midlands) Ltd	
G-AZWF	SAN Jodel DR.1050	Cawdor Flying Group	
G-AZWS	PA-28R Cherokee Arrow 180	K. M. Turner	
G-AZWT	Westland Lysander IIIA (V9367)	The Shuttleworth Collection	
G-AZWY	PA-24 Comanche 260	Keymer Son & Co Ltd	
G-AZXB	Cameron O-65 balloon	R. J. Mitchener & P. F. Smart	
G-AZXD	Cessna F.172L	R. J. R. Williams & D. Palmer	
G-AZXG	PA-23 Aztec 250D ★	Instructional airframe/Cranfield	
G-AZYA	Gardan GY-80 Horizon 160	R. G. Whyte	
G-AZYB	Bell 47H-1 ★	IHM/Weston-super-Mare	
G-AZYD	MS.893A Rallye Commodore	Staffordshire Gliding Club Ltd	
G-AZYF	PA-28-180 Cherokee D	AZYF Group	
G-AZYS	CP.301C-1 Emeraude	C. G. Ferguson & D. Drew	
G-AZYU	PA-23 Aztec 250E	M. E. & M. H. Cromati & F. & N. P. Samuelson	
G-AZYY	Slingsby T.61A Falke	J. A. Towers	
G-AZYZ	Wassmer Wa.51A Pacific	M. P. Wiseman	
G-AZZR	Cessna F.150L	Zulu Romeo Group	
G-AZZV	Cessna F.172L	Zentelligence Ltd	
G-AZZZ	DH.82A Tiger Moth	S. W. McKay	
G-BAAD	Evans Super VP-1	Breighton VP-1 Group	
G-BAAF	Manning-Flanders MF1 (replica)	Aviation Film Services Ltd	
G-BAAI	MS.893A Rallye Commodore	R. D. Taylor	

Notes	Reg.	Type	Owner or Operator
	G-BAAT	Cessna 182P	T. E. Earl
	G-BAAW	Jodel D.119	Alpha Whiskey Flying Group
	G-BABC	Cessna F.150L	B. B. Singh
	G-BABD	Cessna FRA.150L (modified)	BABD Group
	G-BABE	Taylor JT.2 Titch	T. A. Appleby
	G-BABG	PA-28 Cherokee 180	Mendip Flying Group
	G-BABK	PA-34-200 Seneca II	D. F. J. Flashman
	G-BACB	PA-34-200 Seneca II	Milbrooke Motors
	G-BACE	Fournier RF-5	G-BACE Fournier Group
	G-BACJ	Jodel D.120	Wearside Flying Association
	G-BACL	Jodel 150	G-BACL Flying Group
	G-BACN	Cessna FRA.150L	F. Bundy
	G-BACO	Cessna FRA.150L	C. B. Harmer
	G-BADC	Rollason Beta B.2A	A. P. Grimley
	G-BADH	Slingsby T.61A Falke	M. J. Lake
	G-BADJ	PA-E23 Aztec 250E	C. Papadakis
	G-BADM	D.62B Condor	Delta Mike Condor Group
	G-BADV	Brochet MB50	W. B. Cooper
	G-BADW	Pitts S-2A Special	R. E. Mitchell
	G-BADZ	Aerotek Pitts S-2A Special	R. F. Warner
	G-BAEB	Robin DR.400/160	G. D. Jones
	G-BAEE	Jodel DR.1050/M1	R. Little
	G-BAEM	Robin DR.400/125	M. A. Webb
	G-BAEN	Robin DR.400/180	R. H. & C. R. Partington
	G-BAEO	Cessna F.172M	L. W. Scattergood
	G-BAEP	Cessna FRA.150L (modified)	A. M. Lynn
	G-BAER	Cosmic Wind	A. G. Truman
	G-BAET	Piper J-3C-65 Cub	C. J. Rees
	G-BAEU	Cessna F.150L	Advanced Flight Training Ltd
	G-BAEV	Cessna FRA.L150L	Opex Ltd
	G-BAEW	Cessna F.172M ★	Westley Aircraft
	G-BAEY	Cessna F.172M	Skytrax Aviation Ltd
	G-BAEZ	Cessna FRA.150L	Donair Flying Club Ltd
	G-BAFA	AA-5 Traveler	C. F. Mackley
	G-BAFG	DH.82A Tiger Moth	Spitfire Display Ltd
	G-BAFL	Cessna 182P	R. B. Hopkinson & A. S. Pike
	G-BAFP	Robin DR.400/160	J. C. Bacon
	G-BAFT	PA-18 Super Cub 150	C. A. M. Neidt
	G-BAFU	PA-28 Cherokee 140	C. F. Dukes & W. T. Johnson
	G-BAFV	PA-18 Super Cub 95	T. F. & S. J. Thorpe
	G-BAFW	PA-28 Cherokee 140	A. J. Peters
	G-BAFX	Robin DR.400/140	R. Foster
	G-BAGB	SIAI Marchetti SF.260	V. Balzer
	G-BAGC	Robin DR.400/140	G. Fox & J. R. Roberts
	G-BAGF	Jodel D.92 Bébé	J. Evans
	G-BAGG	PA-32 Cherokee Six 300E	A. D. Hoy
	G-BAGN	Cessna F.177RG	R. W. J. Andrews
	G-BAGR	Robin DR.400/140	J. D. Last
	G-BAGS	Robin DR.400/180 2+2	M. Whale & M. W. A. Lunn
	G-BAGT	Helio H.295 Courier	D. C. Hanss
	G-BAGX	PA-28 Cherokee 140	I. Lwanga
	G-BAGY	Cameron O-84 balloon	P. G. Dunnington
	G-BAHD	Cessna 182P Skylane	Lambley Flying Group
	G-BAHF	PA-28 Cherokee 140	Warwickshire Aviation Ltd
	G-BAHH	Wallis WA-121	K. H. Wallis
	G-BAHI	Cessna F.150H	MJP Aviation & Sales
	G-BAHJ	PA-24 Comanche 250	K. Cooper
	G-BAHL	Robin DR.400/160	J. B. McVeighty
	G-BAHP	Volmer VJ.22 Sportsman	Seaplane Group
	G-BAHS	PA-28R Cherokee Arrow 200-II	A. R. N. Morris
	G-BAHX	Cessna 182P	M. D. J. Moore
	G-BAIG	PA-34-200-2 Seneca	Mid-Anglia School of Flying
	G-BAIH	PA-28R Cherokee Arrow 200-II	M. G. West
	G-BAIK	Cessna F.150L	M. Sollitt
	G-BAIS	Cessna F.177RG	Cardinal Syndicate
	G-BAIW	Cessna F.172M	W. J. Greenfield
	G-BAIZ	Slingsby T.61A Falke	Falke Syndicate
	G-BAJA	Cessna F.177RG	D. W. Ward
	G-BAJB	Cessna F.177RG	J. D. Loveridge
	G-BAJC	Evans VP-1	S. J. Greer
	G-BAJE	Cessna 177	Dynamic Aviation BV
	G-BAJN	AA-5 Traveler	P. J. Stead
	G-BAJO	AA-5 Traveler	Montgomery Aviation Ltd

Reg.	Type	Owner or Operator	Notes
G-BAJR	PA-28 Cherokee 180	Spectrum Bravo Flying Group	
G-BAJZ	Robin DR.400/125	Rochester Aviation Ltd	
G-BAKH	PA-28 Cherokee 140	FlyBPL.com	
G-BAKJ	PA-30 Twin Comanche 160B	G. D. Colover	
G-BAKM	Robin DR.400/140	D. V. Pieri	
G-BAKN	SNCAN Stampe SV.4C	M. Holloway	
G-BAKR	Jodel D.117	R. W. Brown	
G-BAKV	PA-18 Super Cub 150	W. J. Murray	
G-BAKW	Beagle B.121 Pup 2	Cunning Stunts Flying Group	
G-BALD	Cameron O-84 balloon	C. A. Gould	
G-BALF	Robin DR.400/140	G. & D. A. Wasey	
G-BALG	Robin DR.400/180	S. G. Jones	
G-BALH	Robin DR.400/140B	G-BALH Flying Group	
G-BALJ	Robin DR.400/180	D. A. Batt & D. de Lacey-Rowe	
G-BALN	Cessna T.310Q	O'Brien Properties Ltd	
G-BALS	Tipsy Nipper T.66 Srs.3	N. C. Spooner	
G-BAMB	Slingsby T.61C Falke	H. J. Bradley	
G-BAMC	Cessna F.150L	K. Evans	
G-BAML	Bell 206B Jet Ranger II ★	Aero Venture	
G-BAMR	PA-16 Clipper	G-BAMR Flying Group	
G-BAMS	Robin DR.400/160	G-BAMS Ltd	
G-BAMT	CEA DR400/160	S. G. Jones	
G-BAMU	Robin DR.400/160	The Alternative Flying Group	
G-BAMV	Robin DR.400/180	K. Jones & E. A. Anderson	
G-BAMY	PA-28R Cherokee Arrow 200-II	C. B. Clark	
G-BANA	Robin DR.221	G. T. Pryor	
G-BANB	Robin DR.400/180	M. Ingvardsen	
G-BANC	Gardan GY-201 Minicab	C. R. Shipley	
G-BANU	Wassmer Jodel D.120	C. H. Kilner	
G-BANV	Phoenix Currie Wot	K. Knight	
G-BANW	CP.1330 Super Emeraude	P. S. Milner	
G-BANX	Cessna F.172M	Oakfleet 2000 Ltd	
G-BAOJ	MS.880B Rallye Club	R. E. Jones	
G-BAOM	MS.880B Rallye Club	P. J. D. Feehan	
G-BAOP	Cessna FRA.150L	R. D. Forster	
G-BAOS	Cessna F.172M	R. B. McLain	
G-BAOU	AA-5 Traveler	R. C. Mark	
G-BAPB	DHC.1 Chipmunk 22	R. C. P. Brookhouse	
G-BAPI	Cessna FRA.150L	Marketing Management Services International Ltd	
G-BAPJ	Cessna FRA.150L	M. D. Page	
G-BAPL	PA-23 Turbo Aztec 250E	Donington Aviation Ltd	
G-BAPP	Evans VP-1 Series 2	J. Lynden	
G-BAPR	Jodel D.11	J. F. M. Bartlett	
G-BAPS	Campbell Cougar ★	IHM/Weston-super-Mare	
G-BAPV	Robin DR.400/160	J. D. & M. Millne	
G-BAPW	PA-28R Cherokee Arrow 180	A.G. Bourne & M. W. Freeman	
G-BAPX	Robin DR.400/160	G-BAPX Group	
G-BAPY	Robin HR.100/210	G-BAPY Group	
G-BARC	Cessna FR.172J	Severn Valley Aviation Group	
G-BARF	Jodel D.112 Club	R. N. Jones	
G-BARH	Beech C.23 Sundowner	G. Moorby & J. Hinchcliffe	
G-BARN	Taylor JT.2 Titch	R. G. W. Newton	
G-BARP	Bell 206B JetRanger 2	Helispares Ltd	
G-BARS	DHC.1 Chipmunk 22 (1377)	J. Beattie & R. M. Scarre	
G-BARZ	Scheibe SF.28A Tandem Falke	K. Kiely	
G-BASH	AA-5 Traveler	BASH Flying Group	
G-BASJ	PA-28-180 Cherokee	Bristol Aero Club	
G-BASL	PA-28-140 Cherokee	P. N. Clynes	
G-BASM	PA-34-200 Seneca II	M. Gipps	
G-BASN	Beech C.23 Sundowner	S. R. Ford	
G-BASO	Lake LA-4 Amphibian	Uulster Seaplane Association Ltd	
G-BASP	Beagle B.121 Pup 1	B. J. Coutts	
G-BATC	MBB Bö.105D	South Georgia Heritage Trust	
G-BATJ	Jodel D.119	Clipgate TJ Group	
G-BATV	PA-28 Cherokee 180D	J. N. Rudsdale	
G-BATW	PA-28 Cherokee 140	C. D. Sainsbury	
G-BAUC	PA-25 Pawnee 235	Southdown Gliding Club Ltd	
G-BAUH	Jodel D.112	G. A. & D. Shepherd	
G-BAVB	Cessna F.172M	C. D. London	
G-BAVH	DHC.1 Chipmunk 22	Portsmouth Naval Gliding Club	
G-BAVL	PA-23 Aztec 250E	S. P. & A. V. Chillott	
G-BAVO	Boeing Stearman N2S (26)	R. C. McCarthy	
G-BAVR	AA-5 Traveler	A. J. McNeal	

G-BAWG – G-BBKL

BRITISH CIVIL REGISTRATIONS

Notes	Reg.	Type	Owner or Operator
	G-BAWG	PA-28R Cherokee Arrow 200-II	Solent Air Ltd
	G-BAWK	PA-28 Cherokee 140	J. Stanley
	G-BAXE	Hughes 269A	Reethorpe Engineering Ltd
	G-BAXK	Thunder Ax7-77 balloon ★	A. R. Snook
	G-BAXS	Bell 47G-5	C. R. Johnson
	G-BAXU	Cessna F.150L	M. W. Sheppardson
	G-BAXV	Cessna F.150L	CBM Associates Consulting Ltd
	G-BAXY	Cessna F.172M	Eaglesoar Ltd
	G-BAXZ	PA-28 Cherokee 140	G-BAXZ (87) Syndicate
	G-BAYL	SNCAN Nord 1101 Norecrin ★	(stored)/Chirk
	G-BAYO	Cessna 150L	J. A. & D. T. A. Rees
	G-BAYP	Cessna 150L	Yankee Papa Flying Group
	G-BAYR	Robin HR.100/210	P. D. Harries
	G-BAZC	Robin DR.400/160	S. G. Jones
	G-BAZM	Jodel D.11	A. F. Simpson
	G-BAZS	Cessna F.150L	L. W. Scattergood
	G-BAZT	Cessna F.172M	Aviation South West Ltd
	G-BBAW	Robin HR.100/210	F. A. Purvis
	G-BBAX	Robin DR.400/140	G. J. Bissex & P. H. Garbutt
	G-BBAY	Robin DR.400/140	J. C. Stubbs
	G-BBBB	Taylor JT.1 Monoplane	M. C. Arnold
	G-BBBC	Cessna F.150L	W. J. Greenfield
	G-BBBI	AA-5 Traveler	Go Baby Aviation Group
	G-BBBN	PA-28 Cherokee 180	Estuary Aviation Ltd
	G-BBBW	FRED Srs 2	M. Palfreman
	G-BBBY	PA-28 Cherokee 140	W. R. & R. Davies
	G-BBCH	Robin DR.400/2+2	The Cotswold Aero Club Ltd
	G-BBCI	Cessna 150H	A. M. & F. Alam
	G-BBCN	Robin HR.100/210	J. C. King
	G-BBCS	Robin DR.400/140	B. N. Stevens
	G-BBCY	Luton LA-4A Minor	A. W. McBlain
	G-BBCZ	AA-5 Traveler	Mercantile Developments Ltd
	G-BBDC	PA-28-140 Cherokee	E. Ford
	G-BBDE	PA-28R Cherokee Arrow 200-II	R. L. Coleman, P. Knott & Istec Services Ltd
	G-BBDG	BAC-Aérospatiale Concorde 100 ★	Brooklands Museum
	G-BBDH	Cessna F.172M	J. D. Woodward
	G-BBDL	AA-5 Traveler	Just Plane Trading Ltd
	G-BBDM	AA-5 Traveler	Jackeroo Aviation Group
	G-BBDO	PA-23 Turbo Aztec 250E	J. W. Anstee
	G-BBDP	Robin DR.400/160	Robin Lance Aviation Associates Ltd
	G-BBDT	Cessna 150H	Delta Tango Group
	G-BBDV	SIPA S.903	Eatonair Group
	G-BBEA	Luton LA-4 Minor	D. S. Evans
	G-BBEB	PA-28R Cherokee Arrow 200-II	March Flying Group
	G-BBEC	PA-28 Cherokee 180	P. & M. Corrigan
	G-BBEN	Bellanca 7GCBC Citabria	C. A. G. Schofield
	G-BBFD	PA-28R Cherokee Arrow 200-II	C. H. Rose & M. J. Green
	G-BBFL	Gardan GY-201 Minicab	R. Smith
	G-BBFV	PA-32 Cherokee Six 260	G-BBFV Syndicate
	G-BBGC	MS.893E Rallye 180GT	P. M. Nolan
	G-BBGI	Fuji FA.200-160	A and P West
	G-BBHF	PA-23 Aztec 250E	G. J. Williams
	G-BBHJ	Piper J-3C-65 Cub	Wellcross Flying Group
	G-BBHK	Noorduyn AT-16 Harvard IIB (FH153)	M. Kubrak
	G-BBHY	PA-28 Cherokee 180	Air Operations Ltd
	G-BBIF	PA-23 Aztec 250E	Marshall of Cambridge Aerospace Ltd
	G-BBIH	Enstrom F-28A-UK	Friebe France Aeronautique SARL
	G-BBII	Fiat G-46-3B (4-97/MM52801)	C. Coltri
	G-BBIL	PA-28 Cherokee 140	Saxondale Group
	G-BBIO	Robin HR.100/210	R. P. Caley
	G-BBIX	PA-28 Cherokee 140	Sterling Aviation Ltd
	G-BBJI	Isaacs Spitfire (RN218)	S. Vince
	G-BBJU	Robin DR.400/140	J. C. Lister
	G-BBJV	Cessna F.177RG	P. R. Powell
	G-BBJX	Cessna F.150L	L. W. Scattergood
	G-BBJY	Cessna F.172M	D. G. Wright
	G-BBJZ	Cessna F.172M	L. P. Burrow
	G-BBKA	Cessna F.150L	W. M. Wilson
	G-BBKB	Cessna F.150L	Justgold Ltd
	G-BBKG	Cessna FR.172J	R. Wright
	G-BBKI	Cessna F.172M	C. W. & S. A. Burman
	G-BBKL	CP.301A Emeraude	Piel G-BBKL

38

Reg.	Type	Owner or Operator	Notes
G-BBKX	PA-28 Cherokee 180	DRA Flying Club Ltd	
G-BBKY	Cessna F.150L	F. W. Astbury	
G-BBKZ	Cessna 172M	KZ Flying Group	
G-BBLH	Piper J-3C-65 Cub (31145:G-26)	Shipping & Airlines Ltd	
G-BBLS	AA-5 Traveler	A. Grant	
G-BBLU	PA-34-200 Seneca II	R. H. R. Rue	
G-BBMB	Robin DR.400/180	Regent Flying Group	
G-BBMH	EAA. Sports Biplane Model P.1	G-BBMH Flying Group	
G-BBMJ	PA-23 Aztec 250E	Nationwide Caravan Rental Services Ltd	
G-BBMN	DHC.1 Chipmunk 22	R. Steiner	
G-BBMO	DHC.1 Chipmunk 22 (WK514)	Mike Oscar Group	
G-BBMR	DHC.1 Chipmunk 22 (WB763:14)	P. J. Wood	
G-BBMT	DHC.1 Chipmunk 22	MT Group	
G-BBMV	DHC.1 Chipmunk 22 (WG348)	Spitfire Display Ltd	
G-BBMW	DHC.1 Chipmunk 22 (WK628)	G. Fielder & A. Wilson	
G-BBMZ	DHC.1 Chipmunk 22	G-BBMZ Chipmunk Syndicate	
G-BBNA	DHC.1 Chipmunk 22 (Lycoming) ★	Coventry Gliding Club Ltd	
G-BBNC	DHC.1 Chipmunk T.10 (WP790) ★	De Havilland Heritage Museum/London Colney	
G-BBND	DHC.1 Chipmunk 22 (WD286)	Bernoulli Syndicate	
G-BBNH	PA-34-200 Seneca II	M. G. D. Baverstock & ptnrs	
G-BBNI	PA-34-200 Seneca II	D. H. G. Penney	
G-BBNJ	Cessna F.150L	D. Dean & J. Pell	
G-BBNT	PA-31-350 Navajo Chieftain	Atlantic Bridge Aviation Ltd	
G-BBNZ	Cessna F.172M	J. H. Sandham Aviation	
G-BBOA	Cessna F.172M	J. D & A. M. Black	
G-BBOH	Pitts S-1S Special	Venom Jet Promotions Ltd	
G-BBOL	PA-18 Super Cub 150	N. Moore	
G-BBOO	Thunder Ax6-56 balloon	K. Meehan Tigerjack	
G-BBOR	Bell 206B JetRanger 2	M. J. Easey	
G-BBPP	PA-28 Cherokee 180	Big Red Kite Ltd (G-WACP)	
G-BBPS	Jodel D.117	A. Appleby	
G-BBRA	PA-23 Aztec 250D	P. A. R. Marin	
G-BBRB	DH.82A Tiger Moth (DF198)	R. Barham	
G-BBRC	Fuji FA.200-180	BBRC Ltd	
G-BBRI	Bell 47G-5A	Alan Mann Aviation Group Ltd	
G-BBRN	Procter Kittiwake 1 (XW784/VL)	H. M. Price	
G-BBRZ	AA-5 Traveler	B. McIntyre	
G-BBSA	AA-5 Traveler	Usworth 84 Flying Associates Ltd	
G-BBSS	DHC.1A Chipmunk 22	Coventry Gliding Club Ltd	
G-BBSW	Pietenpol Air Camper	J. K. S. Wills	
G-BBTB	Cessna FRA.150L	Solent School of Flying	
G-BBTG	Cessna F.172M	Jetstream Aero	
G-BBTH	Cessna F.172M	Tayside Aviation Ltd	
G-BBTJ	PA-23 Aztec 250E	J. A. & R. H. Cooper	
G-BBTK	Cessna FRA.150L	Cleveland Flying School Ltd	
G-BBTY	Beech C23 Sundowner	G-BBTY Group	
G-BBUJ	Cessna 421B	Aero VIP Companhia de Transportes & Servicios Aereos SA/Portugal	
G-BBUT	Western O-65 balloon	R. G. Turnbull	
G-BBUU	Piper J-3C-65 Cub	C. Stokes	
G-BBVF	SA Twin Pioneer Srs 3 ★	Museum of Flight/East Fortune	
G-BBVO	Isaacs Fury II (S1579)	W. Hinchcliffe	
G-BBXB	Cessna FRA.150L	D. C. Somerville	
G-BBXW	PA-28-151 Cherokee Warrior	Bristol Aero Club	
G-BBXY	Bellanca 7GCBC Citabria	R. R. L. Windus	
G-BBXZ	Evans VP-1	R. W. Burrows	
G-BBYB	PA-18 Super Cub 95	A. L. Walker	
G-BBYH	Cessna 182P	Ramco (UK) Ltd	
G-BBYM	HP.137 Jetstream 200 ★	Aerospace Museum/Cosford (G-AYWR)	
G-BBYP	PA-28 Cherokee 140	B. C. Costin	
G-BBYS	Cessna 182P	G-BBYS Group	
G-BBYU	Cameron O-56 balloon	British Balloon Museum	
G-BBZF	PA-28-140 Cherokee	D. Franzan	
G-BBZH	PA-28R Cherokee Arrow 200-II	G. Higgins, C. Harte and I. O'Brien	
G-BBZN	Fuji FA.200-180	D. Kynaston & ptnrs	
G-BBZV	PA-28R Cherokee Arrow 200-II	P. B. Mellor	
G-BCAH	DHC.1 Chipmunk 22 (WG316)	Century Aviation Ltd	
G-BCAP	Cameron O-56 balloon ★	Balloon Preservation Group/Lancing	
G-BCAR	Thunder Ax7-77 balloon ★	British Balloon Museum/Newbury	
G-BCAZ	PA-12 Super Cruiser	A. D. Williams	
G-BCBG	PA-23 Aztec 250E	M. J. L. Batt	
G-BCBH	Fairchild 24R-46A Argus III	Dreamticket Promotions Ltd	

Notes	Reg.	Type	Owner or Operator
	G-BCBJ	PA-25 Pawnee 235	Deeside Gliding Club (Aberdeenshire) Ltd
	G-BCBL	Fairchild 24R-46A Argus III (HB751)	F. J. Cox
	G-BCBR	AJEP/Wittman W.8 Tailwind	D. P. Jones
	G-BCBX	Cessna F.150L	P. Lodge & J. G. McVey
	G-BCBZ	Cessna 337C	J. Haden
	G-BCCC	Cessna F.150L	D. J. Parkinson
	G-BCCE	PA-23 Aztec 250E	Golf Charlie Echo Ltd
	G-BCCF	PA-28 Cherokee 180	Charlie Foxtrot Aviation
	G-BCCK	AA-5 Traveler	Prospect Air Ltd
	G-BCCR	CP.301A Emeraude (modified)	I. Taberer
	G-BCCX	DHC.1 Chipmunk 22 (Lycoming)	The Royal Air Force Gliding and Soaring Association
	G-BCCY	Robin HR.200/100	M. E. Hicks
	G-BCDK	Partenavia P.68B	Mach 014 SAS Di Albertario Michele and Co/Italy
	G-BCDL	Cameron O-42 balloon	D. P. & Mrs B. O. Turner Chums
	G-BCDN	F.27 Friendship Mk 200 ★	Instructional airframe/Norwich
	G-BCDY	Cessna FRA.150L	R. L. Nunn & T. R. Edwards
	G-BCEB	Sikorsky S-61N Mk II	Veritair Ltd
	G-BCEE	AA-5 Traveler	P. J. Marchant
	G-BCEF	AA-5 Traveler	G-BCEF Group
	G-BCEN	BN-2A-26 Islander	Reconnaissance Ventures Ltd
	G-BCEP	AA-5 Traveler	A. A. Kind & P. Ragan
	G-BCER	Gardan GY-201 Minicab	D. Beaumont
	G-BCEU	Cameron O-42 balloon	P. Glydon
	G-BCEY	DHC.1 Chipmunk 22 (WG465)	Gopher Flying Group
	G-BCFO	PA-18-150 Super Cub	D. J. Ashley
	G-BCFR	Cessna FRA.150L	Foxtrot Romeo Group
	G-BCFW	SAAB 91D Safir	D. R. Williams
	G-BCFY	Luton LA-4A Minor	M. P. Wiseman
	G-BCGB	Bensen B.8	A. Melody
	G-BCGC	DHC.1 Chipmunk 22 (WP903)	Henlow Chipmunk Group
	G-BCGH	SNCAN NC.854S	Nord Flying Group
	G-BCGI	PA-28 Cherokee 140	D. H. G. Penny
	G-BCGJ	PA-28 Cherokee 140	Demero Ltd & Transcourt Ltd
	G-BCGM	Jodel D.120	S. M. Kenyon-Roberts
	G-BCGN	PA-28 Cherokee 140	C. F. Hessey
	G-BCGS	PA-28R Cherokee Arrow 200	Arrow Aviation Group
	G-BCGW	Jodel D.11	G. H. Chittenden
	G-BCHL	DHC.1 Chipmunk 22A (WP788)	Shropshire Soaring Ltd
	G-BCHP	CP.1310-C3 Super Emeraude	G. Hughes & A. G. Just (G-JOSI)
	G-BCHT	Schleicher ASK.16	Dunstable K16 Group
	G-BCID	PA-34-200 Seneca II	Shenley Farms (Aviation) Ltd
	G-BCIH	DHC.1 Chipmunk 22 (WD363)	P. J. Richie
	G-BCIJ	AA-5 Traveler	Arrow Association
	G-BCIR	PA-28-151 Warrior	R. W. Harris
	G-BCJM	PA-28 Cherokee 140	APB Leasing Ltd
	G-BCJN	PA-28 Cherokee 140	Bristol and Wessex Aeroplane Club Ltd
	G-BCJO	PA-28R Cherokee Arrow 200	R. Ross
	G-BCJP	PA-28 Cherokee 140	J. Wilson
	G-BCKN	DHC.1A Chipmunk 22 (Lycoming)	The Royal Air Force Gliding and Soaring Association
	G-BCKS	Fuji FA.200-180AO	G. J. Ward
	G-BCKT	Fuji FA.200-180	A. G. Dobson
	G-BCKU	Cessna FRA.150L	Forge Consulting Ltd
	G-BCKV	Cessna FRA.150L	M. Bonsall
	G-BCLI	AA-5 Traveler	BCLI Group
	G-BCLL	PA-28 Cherokee 180	S. C. Hardman
	G-BCLS	Cessna 170B	M. J. Whiteman-Haywood
	G-BCLT	MS.894A Rallye Minerva 220	K. M. Bowen
	G-BCLU	Jodel D.117	G-BCLU Group
	G-BCLW	AA-1B Trainer	M. A. Soakell
	G-BCMD	PA-18 Super Cub 95	P. Stephenson
	G-BCMJ	Squarecraft Cavalier SA.102-5	N. F. Andrews
	G-BCMT	Isaacs Fury II	R.W. Burrows
	G-BCNC	Gardan GY-201 Minicab	J. R. Wraight
	G-BCNP	Cameron O-77 balloon	P. Spellward
	G-BCNX	Piper J-3C-65 Cub (540)	K. J. Lord
	G-BCNZ	Fuji FA.200-160	Y. A. Soojeri
	G-BCOB	Piper J-3C-65 Cub (329405:A-23)	C. Marklew-Brown
	G-BCOI	DHC.1 Chipmunk 22 (WP970:12)	M. J. Diggins
	G-BCOM	Piper J-3C-65 Cub	Dougal Flying Group
	G-BCOO	DHC.1 Chipmunk 22	T. G. Fielding & M. S. Morton

Reg.	Type	Owner or Operator	Notes
G-BCOR	SOCATA Rallye 100ST	T. J. Horsley	
G-BCOU	DHC.1 Chipmunk 22 (WK522)	Loweth Flying Group	
G-BCOY	DHC.1 Chipmunk 22	Coventry Gliding Club Ltd	
G-BCPD	Gardan GY-201 Minicab	P. R. Cozens	
G-BCPG	PA-28R Cherokee Arrow 200-II	Roses Flying Group	
G-BCPH	Piper J-3C-65 Cub (329934:B-72)	G. Earl	
G-BCPJ	Piper J-3C-65 Cub	J. W. Widdows	
G-BCPK	Cessna F.172M	D. C. C. Handley	
G-BCPN	AA-5 Traveler	G-BCPN Group	
G-BCPU	DHC.1 Chipmunk 22	P. Waller	
G-BCRB	Cessna F.172M	Wingstask 1995Ltd	
G-BCRE	Cameron O-77 balloon ★	Balloon Preservation Group/Lancing	
G-BCRL	PA-28-151 Warrior	BCRL Ltd	
G-BCRR	AA-5B Tiger	S. Waite	
G-BCRX	DHC.1 Chipmunk 22 (WD292)	P. J. Tuplin & M. I. Robinson	
G-BCSA	DHC.1 Chipmunk 22 (Lycoming)	The Royal Air Force Gliding and Soaring Association	
G-BCSL	DHC.1 Chipmunk 22	Chipmunk Flyers Ltd	
G-BCSX	Thunder Ax7-77 balloon	C. Wolstenholm	
G-BCTF	PA-28-151 Warrior	The St. George Flight Training Ltd	
G-BCTI	Schleicher ASK 16	Tango India Syndicate	
G-BCTK	Cessna FR.172J	M. G. E. Morton	
G-BCTT	Evans VP-1	E. R. G. Ludlow	
G-BCUB	Piper J-3C-65 Cub	A. L. Brown	
G-BCUF	Cessna F.172M	Howell Plant Hire & Construction	
G-BCUH	Cessna F.150M	M. G. Montgomerie	
G-BCUJ	Cessna F.150M	Western Airways Ltd	
G-BCUL	SOCATA Rallye 100ST	C. A. Ussher & Fountain Estates Ltd	
G-BCUO	SA Bulldog Srs 120/122	Cranfield University	
G-BCUS	SA Bulldog Srs 120/122	Falcon Group	
G-BCUV	SA Bulldog Srs 120/122 (XX704)	Flew LLP	
G-BCUW	Cessna F.177RG	S. J. Westley	
G-BCUY	Cessna FRA.150M	J. C. Carpenter	
G-BCVB	PA-17 Vagabond	A. T. Nowak	
G-BCVC	SOCATA Rallye 100ST	W. Haddow	
G-BCVE	Evans VP-2	D. Masterson & D. B. Winstanley	
G-BCVF	Practavia Pilot Sprite	D. G. Hammersley	
G-BCVG	Cessna FRA.150L	G-BCVG Flying Group	
G-BCVH	Cessna FRA.150L	C. Quist	
G-BCVJ	Cessna F.172M	Rothland Ltd	
G-BCVY	PA-34-200T Seneca II	Oxford Aviation Academy (Oxford) Ltd	
G-BCWB	Cessna 182P	M. F. Oliver & A. J. Mew	
G-BCWH	Practavia Pilot Sprite	P. F. D. Waltham	
G-BCWK	Alpavia Fournier RF-3	T. J. Hartwell	
G-BCXB	SOCATA Rallye 100ST	The Rallye Group	
G-BCXE	Robin DR.400/2+2	Weald Air Services Ltd	
G-BCXJ	Piper L-4J Cub (480752:E-39)	W. Readman	
G-BCXN	DHC.1 Chipmunk 22 (WP800)	G. M. Turner	
G-BCYH	DAW Privateer Mk. 3	G-BCYH Group	
G-BCYK	Avro CF.100 Mk 4 Canuck (18393) ★	Imperial War Museum/Duxford	
G-BCYM	DHC.1 Chipmunk 22 (WK577)	G-BCYM Group	
G-BCYR	Cessna F.172M	G. Fox	
G-BCZM	Cessna F.172M	Cornwall Flying Club Ltd	
G-BDAD	Taylor JT.1 Monoplane	C. S. Whitwell	
G-BDAG	Taylor JT.1 Monoplane	N. R. Osborne	
G-BDAH	Evans VP-1	G. H. J. Geurts	
G-BDAI	Cessna FRA.150M	B. K. & W. G. Ranger	
G-BDAK	Rockwell Commander 112	M. C. Wilson	
G-BDAO	SIPA S.91	S. B. Churchill	
G-BDAP	AJEP Tailwind	D. G. Kelly	
G-BDAR	Evans VP-1	R. F. Powell	
G-BDAY	Thunder Ax5-42S1 balloon	T. M. Donnelly Meconium	
G-BDBF	FRED Srs 2	G. E. & R. E. Collins	
G-BDBH	Bellanca 7GCBC Citabria	C. J. Gray	
G-BDBI	Cameron O-77 balloon	C. Jones	
G-BDBS	Short SD3-30 ★	Ulster Aviation Society	
G-BDBU	Cessna F.150M	S. Collins	
G-BDBV	Jodel D.11A	Seething Jodel Group	
G-BDBZ	Westland WS-55 Whirlwind (XJ398) ★	Aeroventure/Doncaster	
G-BDCD	Piper J-3C-85 Cub (480133:B-44)	Cubby Cub Group	
G-BDCI	CP.301A Emeraude	D. L. Sentance	
G-BDDF	Jodel D.120	J. V. Thompson	

Notes	Reg.	Type	Owner or Operator
	G-BDDG	Jodel D.112	J. Pool & D. G. Palmer
	G-BDDS	PA-25 Pawnee 235	Vale of Neath Gliding Club
	G-BDDX	Whittaker MW2B Excalibur ★	Cornwall Aero Park/Helston
	G-BDDZ	CP.301A Emeraude	E. C. Mort
	G-BDEC	SOCATA Rallye 100ST	J. Fingleton
	G-BDEH	Jodel D.120A	N. J. Cronin
	G-BDEI	Jodel D.9 Bébé	The Noddy Group
	G-BDEU	DHC.1 Chipmunk 22 (WP808)	Skylark Aviation Ltd
	G-BDEX	Cessna FRA.150M	A. P. F. Tucker
	G-BDEY	Piper J-3C-65 Cub	A. V. Williams
	G-BDEZ	Piper J-3C-65 Cub	M. Housley
	G-BDFB	Currie Wot	J. Jennings
	G-BDFH	Auster AOP.9 (XR240)	R. B. Webber
	G-BDFR	Fuji FA.200-160	M. S. Bird
	G-BDFU	Dragonfly MPA Mk 1 ★	Museum of Flight/East Fortune
	G-BDFY	AA-5 Traveler	Grumman Group
	G-BDGB	Gardan GY-20 Minicab	T. W. Slater
	G-BDGH	Thunder Ax7-77 balloon	R. J. Mitchener & P. F. Smart
	G-BDGM	PA-28-151 Cherokee Warrior	J. Tonge
	G-BDHK	Piper J-3C-65 Cub (329417)	Knight Flying Group
	G-BDIE	Rockwell Commander 112	J. McAleer & R. J. Adams
	G-BDIG	Cessna 182P	A. J. Macdonald
	G-BDIH	Jodel D.117	N. D. H. Stokes
	G-BDIX	DH.106 Comet 4C ★	Museum of Flight/East Fortune
	G-BDJD	Jodel D.112	J. E. Preston
	G-BDJG	Luton LA-4A Minor	Very Slow Flying Club
	G-BDJP	Piper J-3C-90 Cub	S. T. Gilbert
	G-BDJR	SNCAN Nord NC.858	R. F. M. Marson
	G-BDKC	Cessna A185F	Lude & Invergarry Farm Partnership
	G-BDKD	Enstrom F-28A	P. J. Price
	G-BDKH	CP.301A Emeraude	T. A. S. Rayner
	G-BDKJ	K & S SA.102.5 Cavalier	D. A. Garner
	G-BDKM	SIPA 903	S. W. Markham
	G-BDKW	Rockwell Commander 112A	N. J. Taaffe
	G-BDLO	AA-5A Cheetah	S. & J. Dolan
	G-BDLT	Rockwell Commander 112	D. L. Churchward
	G-BDLY	K & S SA.102.5 Cavalier	P. R. Stevens
	G-BDMS	Piper J-3C-65 Cub (FR886)	A. T. H. Martin
	G-BDMW	Jodel DR.100A	Mike Whisky Group
	G-BDNC	Taylor JT.1 Monoplane	D. W. Mathie
	G-BDNG	Taylor JT.1 Monoplane	R. B. McComish
	G-BDNT	Jodel D.92 Bébé	R. J. Stobo
	G-BDNU	Cessna F.172M	J. & K. G. McVicar
	G-BDNW	AA-1B Trainer	N. A. Baxter
	G-BDNX	AA-1B Trainer	A. & N. Clark
	G-BDOD	Cessna F.150M	OD Group
	G-BDOE	Cessna FR.172J	A. W. Todd
	G-BDOG	SA Bulldog Srs 200	D. C. Bonsall
	G-BDOL	Piper J-3C-65 Cub	L. R. Balthazor
	G-BDPA	PA-28-151 Warrior	RAF Leuchars Flying Group
	G-BDPJ	PA-25 Pawnee 235B	Swift Aerobatic Display Team
	G-BDRD	Cessna FRA.150M	Aircraft Engineers Ltd
	G-BDRF	Taylor JT.1 Monoplane	D. J. Couzens
	G-BDRG	Taylor JT.2 Titch	D. R. Gray
	G-BDRJ	DHC.1 Chipmunk 22 (WP857)	WP857 Trust
	G-BDRK	Cameron O-65 balloon	R. J. Mitchener & P. F. Smart
	G-BDSB	PA-28-181 Archer II	Testair Ltd
	G-BDSF	Cameron O-56 balloon	J. H. Greensides
	G-BDSH	PA-28 Cherokee 140 (modified)	The Wright Brothers Flying Group
	G-BDSK	Cameron O-65 balloon	Southern Balloon Group Carousel II
	G-BDSM	Slingsby T.31B Cadet III	F. C. J. Wevers/Netherlands
	G-BDTB	Evans VP-1	P. W. Boyes
	G-BDTL	Evans VP-1 series 2	P. S. Gilmour
	G-BDTO	BN-2A Mk III-2 Trislander	Aurigny Air Services Ltd (G-RBSI/G-OTSB)
	G-BDTU	Omega III gas balloon	R. G. Turnbull
	G-BDTV	Mooney M.20F	S. Redfearn
	G-BDTX	Cessna F.150M	F. W. Ellis
	G-BDUI	Cameron V-56 balloon	D. J. W. Johnson
	G-BDUL	Evans VP-1 Srs.2	J. C. Lindsay
	G-BDUM	Cessna F.150M	P. B. Millington
	G-BDUN	PA-34-200T Seneca II	R. Paris
	G-BDUO	Cessna F.150M	D. W. Locke
	G-BDUY	Robin DR.400/140B	J. G. Anderson

Reg.	Type	Owner or Operator	Notes
G-BDUZ	Cameron V-56 balloon	Zebedee Balloon Service	
G-BDVA	PA-17 Vagabond	I. M. Callier	
G-BDVB	PA-15 (PA-17) Vagabond	B. P. Gardner	
G-BDVC	PA-17 Vagabond	A. R. Caveen	
G-BDWE	Flaglor Scooter	P. King	
G-BDWH	SOCATA Rallye 150ST	M. A. Jones	
G-BDWJ	SE-5A (replica) (F8010:Z)	D. W. Linney	
G-BDWM	Mustang scale replica (FB226)	D. C. Bonsall	
G-BDWO	Howes Ax6 balloon	R. B. & C. Howes	
G-BDWP	PA-32R-300 Cherokee Lance	A. Belcastro & I. Bardelli/Italy	
G-BDWX	Jodel D.120A	R. P. Rochester	
G-BDWY	PA-28-140 Cherokee E	N. Grantham	
G-BDXX	SNCAN NC.858S	K. M. Davis	
G-BDYG	P.56 Provost T.1 (WV493) ★	Museum of Flight/East Fortune	
G-BDZA	Scheibe SF.25E Super Falke	Hereward Flying Group	
G-BDZC	Cessna F.150M	A. M. Lynn	
G-BDZD	Cessna F.172M	R. J. A. Durie	
G-BDZG	Slingsby T.59H Kestrel	R. E. Gretton	
G-BEAB	Jodel DR.1051	R. C. Hibberd	
G-BEAC	PA-28 Cherokee 140	R. Murray & A. Bagley-Murray	
G-BEAD	WG.13 Lynx ★	Instructional airframe/Middle Wallop	
G-BEAG	PA-34-200T Seneca II	Oxford Aviation Academy (Oxford) Ltd	
G-BEAH	Auster J/2 Arrow	Bedwell Hey Flying Group	
G-BEBC	Westland WS-55 Whirlwind 3 (XP355) ★	Norwich Aviation Museum	
G-BEBG	WSK-PZL SDZ-45A Ogar	The Ogar Syndicate	
G-BEBN	Cessna 177B	P. A. Gray	
G-BEBR	GY-201 Minicab	A. R. Hawes	
G-BEBS	Andreasson BA-4B	N. J. W. Reid	
G-BEBU	Rockwell Commander 112A	I. Hunt	
G-BEBZ	PA-28-151 Warrior	Airways Flight Training (Exeter) Ltd	
G-BECA	SOCATA Rallye 100ST	N. G. Ogborne	
G-BECB	SOCATA Rallye 100ST	D. H. Tonkin	
G-BECK	Cameron V-56 balloon	N. H. & A. M. Ponsford	
G-BECN	Piper J-3C-65 Cub (480480:E-44)	CN Cub Group	
G-BECT	CASA 1.131E Jungmann 2000 (A-57)	Alpha 57 Group	
G-BECW	CASA 1.131E Jungmann 2000 (A-10)	C. M. Rampton	
G-BECZ	CAARP CAP-10B	C. M. Thompson	
G-BEDB	Nord 1203 Norecrin ★	B. F. G. Lister (stored)/Chirk	
G-BEDD	Jodel D.117A	A. Boast	
G-BEDF	Boeing B-17G-105-VE (124485:DF-A)	B-17 Preservation Ltd	
G-BEDG	Rockwell Commander 112	G-BEDG Group	
G-BEDJ	Piper J-3C-65 Cub (44-80594)	R. Earl	
G-BEDP	BN-2A Mk.III-2 Trislander	Blue Island Air	
G-BEDV	V.668 Varsity T.1 (WJ945) ★	Duxford Aviation Society	
G-BEEE	Thunder Ax6-56A balloon ★	British Balloon Museum/Newbury	
G-BEEH	Cameron V-56 balloon	Sade Balloons Ltd	
G-BEEI	Cameron N-77 balloon	A. P. Griffiths	
G-BEER	Isaacs Fury II (K2075)	R. S. C. Andrews	
G-BEFA	PA-28-151 Warrior	K. T. Langstone	
G-BEFF	PA-28 Cherokee 140F	E. Merkado	
G-BEGG	Scheibe SF.25E Super Falke	G-BEGG Motorfalke	
G-BEHH	PA-32R Cherokee Lance 300	K. Swallow	
G-BEHU	PA-34-200T Seneca II	Pirin Aeronautical Ltd	
G-BEHV	Cessna F.172N	Edinburgh Air Centre Ltd	
G-BEIF	Cameron O-65 balloon	C. Vening	
G-BEIG	Cessna F.150M	R. D. Forster & M. S. B. Thorp	
G-BEII	PA-25 Pawnee 235D	Burn Gliding Club Ltd	
G-BEIL	SOCATA Rallye 150T	The Rallye Flying Group	
G-BEIP	PA-28-181 Archer II	S. Pope	
G-BEIS	Evans VP-1	D. L. Haines	
G-BEJK	Cameron S-31 balloon	Rango Balloon and Kite Company	
G-BEJV	PA-34-200T Seneca II	Oxford Aviation Academy (Oxford) Ltd	
G-BEKL	Bede BD-4E-150	F. E.Tofield	
G-BEKM	Evans VP-1	G. J. McDill	
G-BEKN	Cessna FRA.150M	T. J. Lynn	
G-BEKO	Cessna F.182Q	G. J. & F. J. Leese	
G-BELT	Cessna F.150J	A. Kumar (G-AWUV)	
G-BEMB	Cessna F.172M	Stocklaunch Ltd	
G-BEMM	Slingsby T.31B Motor Cadet III	E. and P. McEvoy	
G-BEMW	PA-28-181 Archer II	Touch & Go Ltd	
G-BEMY	Cessna FRA.150M	J. R. Power	
G-BEND	Cameron V-56 balloon	Dante Balloon Group	

Notes	Reg.	Type	Owner or Operator
	G-BENJ	Rockwell Commander 112B	BENJ Flying Group
	G-BEOD	Cessna 180H	I. Addy
	G-BEOE	Cessna FRA.150M	W. J. Henderson
	G-BEOH	PA-28R-201T Turbo Arrow III	Gloucestershire Flying Club
	G-BEOI	PA-18 Super Cub 150	Southdown Gliding Club Ltd
	G-BEOK	Cessna F.150M	KPOW Ltd
	G-BEOL	Short SC.7 Skyvan 3 variant 100	Invicta Aviation Ltd
	G-BEOX	Lockheed 414 Hudson IV (A16-199) ★	RAF Museum/Hendon
	G-BEOY	Cessna FRA.150L	J. N. Ponsford
	G-BEOZ	A.W.650 Argosy 101 ★	Aeropark/East Midlands
	G-BEPF	SNCAN Stampe SV.4A	C. C. Rollings & F. J. Hodson
	G-BEPV	Fokker S.11-1 Instructor (174)	S. W. & M. Isbister & C. Tyers
	G-BEPY	Rockwell Commander 112B	T. L. Rippon
	G-BERA	SOCATA Rallye 150ST	A. C. Stamp
	G-BERC	SOCATA Rallye 150ST	Severn Valley Aero Group
	G-BERI	Rockwell Commander 114	K. B. Harper
	G-BERN	Saffrey S-330 balloon	B. Martin
	G-BERT	Cameron V-56 balloon	Southern Balloon Group Bert
	G-BERY	AA-1B Trainer	R. H. J. Levi
	G-BETD	Robin HR.200/100	C. L. Wilsher
	G-BETE	Rollason B.2A Beta	T. M. Jones
	G-BETF	Cameron 'Champion' SS balloon ★	British Balloon Museum/Newbury
	G-BETL	PA-25 Pawnee 235D	Cambridge University Gliding Trust Ltd
	G-BETM	PA-25 Pawnee 235D	Yorkshire Gliding Club (Pty) Ltd
	G-BEUA	PA-18 Super Cub 150	London Gliding Club (Pty) Ltd
	G-BEUD	Robin HR.100/285R	E. A. & L. M. C. Payton
	G-BEUI	Piper J-3C-65 Cub	M. C. Jordan
	G-BEUP	Robin DR.400/180	Samuels LLP
	G-BEUU	PA-18 Super Cub 95	F. Sharples
	G-BEUX	Cessna F.172N	Multiflight Ltd
	G-BEUY	Cameron N-31 balloon	J. J. Daly
	G-BEVB	SOCATA Rallye 150ST	M. Smullen
	G-BEVC	SOCATA Rallye 150ST	Wolds Flyers Syndicate
	G-BEVG	PA-34-200T-2 Seneca	Direct Aviation Management Ltd
	G-BEVO	Sportavia-Pützer RF-5	M. Hill
	G-BEVP	Evans VP-2	G. Moscrop & R. C. Crowley
	G-BEVS	Taylor JT.1 Monoplane	D. Hunter
	G-BEVT	BN-2A Mk III-2 Trislander	Aurigny Air Services Ltd
	G-BEVW	SOCATA Rallye 150ST	S. W. Brown
	G-BEWN	DH.82A Tiger Moth	H. D. Labouchere
	G-BEWO	Zlin Z.326 Trener Master	P. A. Colman
	G-BEWR	Cessna F.172N	P. Lodge & J. G. McVey
	G-BEWX	PA-28R-201 Arrow III	Three Greens Arrow Group
	G-BEWY	Bell 206B JetRanger 3	Polo Aviation Ltd (G-CULL)
	G-BEXN	AA-1C Lynx	XN Group
	G-BEXW	PA-28-181 Cherokee	J. O'Keeffe
	G-BEYA	Enstrom 280C	P. George
	G-BEYB	Fairey Flycatcher (replica) (S1287) ★	F.A.A. Museum/Yeovilton
	G-BEYF	HPR.7 Herald 401 ★	Jet Heritage Museum/Bournemouth
	G-BEYL	PA-28 Cherokee 180	Yankee Lima Group
	G-BEYT	PA-28 Cherokee 140	J. N. Plange
	G-BEYV	Cessna T.210M	P. Mason & R. Turnell
	G-BEYW	Taylor JT.1 Monoplane	R. A. Abrahams
	G-BEYZ	Jodel DR.1051/M1	M. L. Balding
	G-BEZC	AA-5 Traveler	C. M. O'Connell
	G-BEZE	Rutan Vari-Eze	S. K. Cockburn
	G-BEZF	AA-5 Traveler	The G-BEZF Flying Group
	G-BEZG	AA-5 Traveler	M. D. R. Harling
	G-BEZH	AA-5 Traveler	Zulu Hotel Group
	G-BEZI	AA-5 Traveler	C. J. & L. Campbell
	G-BEZK	Cessna F.172H	S. Jones
	G-BEZL	PA-31-310 Turbo Navajo C	2 Excel Aviation Ltd
	G-BEZO	Cessna F.172M	Staverton Flying School @ Skypark Ltd
	G-BEZP	PA-32 Cherokee Six 300D	T. P. McCormack & J. K. Zealley
	G-BEZR	Cessna F.172M	J. P. Birnie
	G-BEZV	Cessna F.172M	Insch Flying Group
	G-BEZY	Rutan Vari-Eze	I. J. Pountney
	G-BEZZ	Jodel D.112	G-BEZZ Jodel Group
	G-BFAF	Aeronca 7BCM (7797)	D. C. W. Harper
	G-BFAI	Rockwell Commander 114	P. Ellingford & K. Eves
	G-BFAK	GEMS MS.892A Rallye Commodore 150	J. M. Hedges
	G-BFAP	SIAI-Marchetti S.205-20R	A. O. Broin
	G-BFAS	Evans VP-1	A. I. Sutherland

Reg.	Type	Owner or Operator	Notes
G-BFAW	DHC.1 Chipmunk 22	M. L. J. Goff	
G-BFAX	DHC.1 Chipmunk 22 (WG422)	M. F. Humphries	
G-BFBA	Jodel DR.100A	A. F. Vizoso	
G-BFBB	PA-23 Aztec 250E	D. Byrne	
G-BFBE	Robin HR.200/100	A. C. Pearson	
G-BFBM	Saffery S.330 balloon	B. Martin	
G-BFBR	PA-28-161 Warrior II	Phoenix Aviation	
G-BFBU	Partenavia P.68B	Reconnaissance Ventures Ltd	
G-BFBY	Piper J-3C-65 Cub	M. Shaw	
G-BFCT	Cessna Tu.206F	D. I. Schellingerhout	
G-BFDC	DHC.1 Chipmunk 22 (WG475)	N. F. O'Neill	
G-BFDE	Sopwith Tabloid (replica) (168) ★	RAF Museum/Hendon	
G-BFDF	SOCATA Rallye 235E	M. A. Wratten	
G-BFDI	PA-28-181 Archer II	Truman Aviation Ltd	
G-BFDK	PA-28-161 Warrior II	S. T. Gilbert	
G-BFDL	Piper J-3C-65 Cub (454537:J-04)	T. Holtbrook & B. A. Nicholson	
G-BFDO	PA-28R-201T Turbo Arrow III	J. Blackburn & J. Driver	
G-BFEB	Jodel 150	Jodel EB Group	
G-BFEF	Agusta-Bell 47G-3B1	I. F. Vaughan	
G-BFEH	Jodel D.117A	M. D. Mold	
G-BFEK	Cessna F.152	Staverton Flying School @ Skypark Ltd	
G-BFEV	PA-25 Pawnee 235	Trent Valley Aerotowing Club Ltd	
G-BFFE	Cessna F.152-II	A. J. Hastings	
G-BFFJ	Sikorsky S-61N Mk II	Veritair Ltd *Tresco*	
G-BFFP	PA-18 Super Cub 150 (modified)	East Sussex Gliding Club Ltd	
G-BFFT	Cameron V-56 balloon	R. I. M. Kerr & D. C. Boxall	
G-BFFW	Cessna F.152	Stapleford Flying Club Ltd	
G-BFGD	Cessna F.172N-II	Wannabe Flyers	
G-BFGG	Cessna FRA.150M	J. M. Machin	
G-BFGH	Cessna F.337G	S. Findlay	
G-BFGK	Jodel D.117	B. F. J. Hope	
G-BFGL	Cessna FA.152	E-Pane Ltd	
G-BFGS	MS.893E Rallye 180GT	Chiltern Flyers Ltd	
G-BFGX	Cessna FRA.150M	Aircraft Engineers Ltd	
G-BFGZ	Cessna FRA.150M	C. M. Barnes	
G-BFHH	DH.82A Tiger Moth	P. Harrison & M. J. Gambrell	
G-BFHI	Piper J-3C-65 Cub	N. Glass & A. J. Richardson	
G-BFHP	Champion 7GCAA Citabria	Citabriation Group	
G-BFHR	Jodel DR.220/2+2	J. E. Sweetman	
G-BFHU	Cessna F.152-II	M. Bonsall	
G-BFIB	PA-31 Turbo Navajo	2 Excel Aviation Ltd	
G-BFID	Taylor JT.2 Titch Mk III	M. J. Wood	
G-BFIE	Cessna FRA.150M	J. P. A. Freeman	
G-BFIG	Cessna FR.172K XPII	M. Taylor	
G-BFIN	AA-5A Cheetah	Aircraft Engineers Ltd	
G-BFIP	Wallbro Monoplane 1909 (replica) ★	Norfolk & Suffolk Aviation Museum/Flixton	
G-BFIT	Thunder Ax6-56Z balloon	J. A. G. Tyson	
G-BFIU	Cessna FR.172K XP	The G-BFIU Flying Group	
G-BFIV	Cessna F.177RG	C. Fisher	
G-BFIX	Thunder Ax7-77A balloon	R. Owen	
G-BFIY	Cessna F.150M	R. J. Scott	
G-BFJR	Cessna F.337G	Teal Aviation	
G-BFJZ	Robin DR.400/140B	Weald Air Services Ltd	
G-BFKB	Cessna F.172N	Shropshire Flying Group	
G-BFKF	Cessna FA.152	Aerolease Ltd	
G-BFKL	Cameron N-56 balloon	Merrythought Toys Ltd *Merrythought*	
G-BFLU	Cessna F.152	Swiftair Maintenance Ltd	
G-BFLX	AA-5A Cheetah	A. M. Verdon	
G-BFLZ	Beech 95-A55 Baron	R. Tang	
G-BFMF	Cassutt Racer IIIM	T. D. Gardner	
G-BFMG	PA-28-161 Warrior II	J. G. Fricker & N. T. Oakman	
G-BFMH	Cessna 177B	Aerofoil Aviation Ltd	
G-BFMK	Cessna FA.152	The Leicestershire Aero Club Ltd	
G-BFMR	PA-20 Pacer 125	J. Knight	
G-BFMX	Cessna F.172N	M. Knowles	
G-BFNG	Jodel D.112	NG Group	
G-BFNI	PA-28-161 Warrior II	Lion Services	
G-BFNK	PA-28-161 Warrior II	White Waltham Airfield Ltd	
G-BFNM	Globe GC-1B Swift	M. J. Butler	
G-BFOE	Cessna F.152	Redhill Air Services Ltd	
G-BFOF	Cessna F.152	ACS Engineering Ltd	
G-BFOG	Cessna 150M	B. F. Spafford	
G-BFOJ	AA-1 Yankee	D. D. Pharoah	

Notes	Reg.	Type	Owner or Operator
	G-BFOP	Jodel D.120	R. J. Wesley & R. Lloyd
	G-BFOU	Taylor JT.1 Monoplane	G. Bee
	G-BFOV	Cessna F.172N	D. J. Walker
	G-BFPA	Scheibe SF.25B Falke	Tay Forth Falke Syndicate
	G-BFPH	Cessna F.172K	Linc-Air Flying Group
	G-BFPO	Rockwell Commander 112B	Doerr International Ltd
	G-BFPR	PA-25 Pawnee 235D	The Windrushers Gliding Club Ltd
	G-BFPS	PA-25 Pawnee 235D	Kent Gliding Club Ltd
	G-BFPZ	Cessna F.177RG Cardinal	O. C. Baars
	G-BFRI	Sikorsky S-61	British International
	G-BFRR	Cessna FRA.150M	Romeo Romeo Flying Group
	G-BFRS	Cessna F.172N	Aerocomm Ltd
	G-BFRV	Cessna FA.152	Cristal Air Ltd
	G-BFRY	PA-25 Pawnee 260	Yorkshire Gliding Club (Pty) Ltd
	G-BFSA	Cessna F.182Q	Colledge Redfern LLP
	G-BFSC	PA-25 Pawnee 235D	Essex Gliding Club Ltd
	G-BFSD	PA-25 Pawnee 235D	Deeside Gliding Club (Aberdeenshire) Ltd
	G-BFSR	Cessna F.150J	W. Ali
	G-BFSS	Cessna FR.172G	Albedale Farms Ltd
	G-BFSY	PA-28-181 Archer II	Downland Aviation
	G-BFSZ	PA-28-161 Warrior II	R. J. Whyham (G-KBPI)
	G-BFTC	PA-28R-201T Turbo Arrow III	Top Cat Flying Group
	G-BFTF	AA-5B Tiger	F. C. Burrow Ltd
	G-BFTG	AA-5B Tiger	D. Hepburn & G. R. Montgomery
	G-BFTH	Cessna F.172N	T. W. Oakley
	G-BFTX	Cessna F.172N	Tri Society
	G-BFUB	PA-32RT-300 Lance II	Jolida Holdings Ltd
	G-BFUD	Scheibe SF.25E Super Falke	SF25E Syndicate
	G-BFUZ	Cameron V-77 balloon	Servowarm Balloon Syndicate
	G-BFVG	PA-28-181 Archer II	H. A. Schlosser
	G-BFVH	DH.2 (replica) (5964)	S. W. Turley
	G-BFVS	AA-5B Tiger	G-BFVS Flying Group
	G-BFVU	Cessna 150L	Aviation South West Ltd
	G-BFWB	PA-28-161 Warrior II	Mid-Anglia School of Flying
	G-BFWD	Currie Wot (C3009)	D. Silsbury & B. Proctor
	G-BFXF	Andreasson BA.4B	P. N. Birch
	G-BFXG	D.31 Turbulent	XG Group
	G-BFXK	PA-28 Cherokee 140	G-BFXK Owners Ltd
	G-BFXL	Albatros D.5a replica (D5397/17) ★	F.A.A. Museum/Yeovilton
	G-BFXR	Jodel D.112	R. G. Marshall
	G-BFXS	Rockwell Commander 114	Romeo Whiskey Ltd
	G-BFXW	AA-5B Tiger	J. G. Bellerby
	G-BFXX	AA-5B Tiger	W. R. Gibson
	G-BFYA	MBB Bö.105DB	Alan Mann Aviation Group Ltd
	G-BFYC	PA-32RT-300 Lance II	P. Chaumeron
	G-BFYI	Westland-Bell 47G-3B1	K. P. Mayes
	G-BFYK	Cameron V-77 balloon	L. E. Jones
	G-BFYL	Evans VP-2	F. C. Handy
	G-BFYM	PA-28-161 Warrior II	E. T. Hawkins
	G-BFYO	SPAD XIII (replica) (4513:1) ★	American Air Museum/Duxford
	G-BFYW	Slingsby T.65A Vega	S. A. Whitaker
	G-BFZB	Piper J-3C-85 Cub (480723:E5-J)	M. S. Pettit
	G-BFZD	Cessna FR.182RG	R. B. Lewis & Co
	G-BFZH	PA-28R Cherokee Arrow 200	C. S. & C. S. Soojeri
	G-BFZM	Rockwell Commander 112TC	J. A. Hart & R. J. Lamplough
	G-BFZO	AA-5A Cheetah	J. W. Cross
	G-BFZU	Cessna FA.152	BJ Aviation Ltd
	G-BFZV	Cessna F.172M	The Army Flying Association
	G-BGAA	Cessna 152 II	PJC Leasing Ltd
	G-BGAB	Cessna F.152 II	TG Aviation Ltd
	G-BGAE	Cessna F.152 II	Aerolease Ltd
	G-BGAF	Cessna FA.152	G-BGAF Group
	G-BGAG	Cessna F.172N	S. J. Green
	G-BGAJ	Cessna F.182Q II	B. Blumberg
	G-BGAX	PA-28 Cherokee 140	G-BGAX Group
	G-BGAZ	Cameron V-77 balloon	C. J. Madigan & D. H. McGibbon
	G-BGBA	Robin R.2100A	Cotswold Aviation Services Ltd
	G-BGBE	Jodel DR.1050	J. A. & B. Mawby
	G-BGBF	Druine D.31 Turbulent	T. A. Stambach
	G-BGBG	PA-28-181 Archer II	Harlow Printing Ltd
	G-BGBI	Cessna F.150L	BI Flying Group
	G-BGBK	PA-38-112 Tomahawk	Truman Aviation Ltd

Reg.	Type	Owner or Operator	Notes
G-BGBN	PA-38-112 Tomahawk	Bonus Aviation Ltd	
G-BGBR	Cessna F.172N	A. S. Bamrah	
G-BGBV	Slingsby T65A Vega	Vega Syndicate BGA2800	
G-BGBW	PA-38-112 Tomahawk	Truman Aviation Ltd	
G-BGBZ	Rockwell Commander 114	G. W. Dimmer	
G-BGCB	Slingsby T.65A Vega	T. E. J. Dutton & V. A. Watt	
G-BGCM	AA-5A Cheetah	G. & S. A. Jones	
G-BGCO	PA-44-180 Seminole	BAE Systems (Operations) Ltd	
G-BGCU	Slingsby T.65A Vega	K. Challinor	
G-BGCY	Taylor JT.1 Monoplane	A. T. Lane	
G-BGEH	Monnett Sonerai II	C. I. Selvey-Willars	
G-BGEI	Baby Great Lakes	M. T. Taylor	
G-BGES	Phoenix Currie Super Wot	N. M. Bloom	
G-BGFC	Evans VP-2	S. W. C. Hollins	
G-BGFF	FRED Srs 2	I Pearson & P. C. Appleton	
G-BGFI	AA-5A Cheetah	D. Chowanietz & A. Necker	
G-BGFJ	Jodel D.9 Bébé	O. G. Jones	
G-BGFT	PA-34-200T Seneca II	Oxford Aviation Academy (Oxford) Ltd	
G-BGFX	Cessna F.152	Redhill Air Services Ltd	
G-BGGA	Bellanca 7GCBC Citabria	L. A. King	
G-BGGB	Bellanca 7GCBC Citabria	Citabria Syndicate	
G-BGGC	Bellanca 7GCBC Citabria	G-BGGC RPA Memorial Group	
G-BGGD	Bellanca 8GCBC Scout	B. Walker & Co (Dursley) Ltd	
G-BGGE	PA-38-112 Tomahawk	Truman Aviation Ltd	
G-BGGI	PA-38-112 Tomahawk	Truman Aviation Ltd	
G-BGGL	PA-38-112 Tomahawk	Bonus Aircraft Ltd	
G-BGGM	PA-38-112 Tomahawk	Bonus Aircraft Ltd	
G-BGGO	Cessna F.152	East Midlands Flying School Ltd	
G-BGGP	Cessna F.152	East Midlands Flying School Ltd	
G-BGGU	Wallis WA-116/RR	K. H. Wallis	
G-BGGW	Wallis WA-112	K. H. Wallis	
G-BGHF	Westland WG.30 ★	IHM/Weston-super-Mare	
G-BGHI	Cessna F.152	V. R. McCready	
G-BGHJ	Cessna F.172N	Air Plane Ltd	
G-BGHM	Robin R.1180T	P. Price	
G-BGHP	Beech 76 Duchess	Magneta Ltd	
G-BGHS	Cameron N-31 balloon	G. Gray	
G-BGHT	Falconar F-12	C. R. Coates	
G-BGHU	NA T-6G Texan (115042:TA-042)	C. E. Bellhouse	
G-BGHY	Taylor JT.1 Monoplane	G. W. Hancox	
G-BGHZ	FRED Srs 2	A. J. Perry	
G-BGIB	Cessna 152 II	Redhill Air Services Ltd	
G-BGIG	PA-38-112 Tomahawk	Air Claire Ltd	
G-BGIU	Cessna F.172H	A. G. Arthur	
G-BGIY	Cessna F.172N	ACS Aviation Ltd	
G-BGKO	Gardan GY-20 Minicab	K. D. PEARCE	
G-BGKS	PA-28-161 Warrior II	Tayside Aviation Ltd	
G-BGKT	Auster AOP.9 (XN441)	Kilo Tango Group	
G-BGKU	PA-28R-201 Arrow III	Aerolease Ltd	
G-BGKV	PA-28R-201 Arrow III	R. Haverson & A. K. Lake	
G-BGKY	PA-38-112 Tomahawk	APB Leasing Ltd	
G-BGKZ	Auster J/5F Aiglet Trainer	R. B. Webber	
G-BGLA	PA-38-112 Tomahawk	J. T. Mountain	
G-BGLB	Bede BD-5B ★	Science Museum/Wroughton	
G-BGLF	Evans VP-1 Srs 2	B. A. Schlussler	
G-BGLG	Cessna 152	L. W. Scattergood	
G-BGLK	Monnett Sonerai 2L	J. Bradley	
G-BGLO	Cessna F.172N	J. R. Isabel	
G-BGLZ	Stits SA-3A Playboy	A. J. Collins	
G-BGME	SIPA 903	M. Emery (G-BCML)	
G-BGMJ	Gardan GY-201 Minicab	G-BGMJ Group	
G-BGMP	Cessna F.172G	B. M. O'Brien	
G-BGMR	Gardan GY-20 Minicab	P. A. Hall	
G-BGMS	Taylor JT.2 Titch	M. A. J. Spice	
G-BGMT	SOCATA Rallye 235E	C. G. Wheeler	
G-BGMV	Scheibe SF.25B Falke	I. P. Manley	
G-BGND	Cessna F.172N	A. J. M. Freeman	
G-BGNT	Cessna F.152	Aerolease Ltd	
G-BGNV	GA-7 Cougar	G. J. Bissex & D. D. Saint	
G-BGOD	Colt 77A balloon	C. Allen & M. D. Steuer	
G-BGOG	PA-28-161 Warrior II	W. D. Moore & F. J. Morris	
G-BGOL	PA-28R-201T Turbo Arrow III	R. G. Jackson	
G-BGON	GA-7 Cougar	Plane Talking Ltd	

Notes	Reg.	Type	Owner or Operator
	G-BGOR	AT-6D Harvard III (14863)	P. Meyrick
	G-BGPB	CCF T-6J Texan (1747)	1959 Ltd
	G-BGPD	Piper J-3C-65 Cub (479744:M-49)	P. R. Whiteman
	G-BGPH	AA-5B Tiger	Shipping & Airlines Ltd
	G-BGPI	Plumb BGP-1	B. G. Plumb
	G-BGPJ	PA-28-161 Warrior II	W. Lancs Warrior Co Ltd
	G-BGPL	PA-28-161 Warrior II	Demero Ltd & Transcourt Ltd
	G-BGPM	Evans VP-2	The Old Fokkers Flying Group
	G-BGPN	PA-18 Super Cub 150	A. R. Darke
	G-BGRE	Beech A200 Super King Air	Martin-Baker (Engineering) Ltd
	G-BGRI	Jodel DR.1051	R. G. Hallam
	G-BGRM	PA-38-112 Tomahawk	C. R. Salway
	G-BGRO	Cessna F.172M	Cammo Aviation
	G-BGRR	PA-38-112 Tomahawk	Hinton Pilot Flight Training Ltd
	G-BGRT	Steen Skybolt	O. Meier
	G-BGRX	PA-38-112 Tomahawk	Bonus Aviation Ltd
	G-BGSA	Morane MS.892E-150	D. C. Tonkin
	G-BGSH	PA-38-112 Tomahawk	Hatfield Ltd
	G-BGSJ	Piper J-3C-65 Cub	A. J. Higgins
	G-BGSV	Cessna F.172N	Southwell Air Services Ltd
	G-BGSW	Beech F33 Debonair	J. J. Noakes
	G-BGSY	GA-7 Cougar	N. D. Anderson
	G-BGTC	Auster AOP.9 (XP282)	Terranne Auster Group
	G-BGTI	Piper J-3C-65 Cub	A. P. Broad
	G-BGUB	PA-32 Cherokee Six 300E	D. P. & E. A. Morris
	G-BGVB	Robin DR.315	P. J. Leggo
	G-BGVE	CP.1310-C3 Super Emeraude	R. Whitwell
	G-BGVH	Beech 76 Duchess	Velco Marketing
	G-BGVK	PA-28-161 Warrior II	Aviation South West Ltd
	G-BGVN	PA-28RT-201 Arrow IV	John Wailing Ltd
	G-BGVS	Cessna F.172M	Orkney Flying Club
	G-BGVV	AA-5A Cheetah	W. A. Davidson
	G-BGVY	AA-5B Tiger	R. J. C. Neal-Smith
	G-BGVZ	PA-28-181 Archer II	M. & W. Walsh
	G-BGWC	Robin DR.400/180	M. A. Newman
	G-BGWM	PA-28-181 Archer II	Thames Valley Flying Club Ltd
	G-BGWN	PA-38-112 Tomahawk	J. R. Davison
	G-BGWO	Jodel D.112	G-BGWO Group
	G-BGWZ	Eclipse Super Eagle ★	F.A.A. Museum/Yeovilton
	G-BGXA	Piper J-3C-65 Cub (329471:F-44)	P. King
	G-BGXC	SOCATA TB10 Tobago	M. H. & L. J. Cundey
	G-BGXD	SOCATA TB10 Tobago	D. F. P. Finan
	G-BGXO	PA-38-112 Tomahawk	Goodwood Terrena Ltd
	G-BGXR	Robin HR.200/100	J. R. Cross
	G-BGXS	PA-28-236 Dakota	G-BGXS Group
	G-BGXT	SOCATA TB10 Tobago	J. L. Alexander
	G-BGYH	PA-28-161 Warrior II	Paper Space Ltd
	G-BGYN	PA-18 Super Cub 150	B. J. Dunford
	G-BGZF	PA-38-112 Tomahawk	APB Leasing Ltd
	G-BHAA	Cessna 152 II	Herefordshire Aero Club Ltd
	G-BHAD	Cessna A.152	T. W. Gilbert
	G-BHAI	Cessna F.152	ACS Aviation Ltd
	G-BHAJ	Robin DR.400/160	Rowantask Ltd
	G-BHAR	Westland-Bell 47G-3B1	T. J. Wright
	G-BHAV	Cessna F.152	T. M. & M. L. Jones
	G-BHAX	Enstrom F-28C-UK-2	PVS (Barnsley) Ltd
	G-BHAY	PA-28RT-201 Arrow IV	Alpha Yankee Ltd
	G-BHBA	Campbell Cricket	S. N. McGovern
	G-BHBE	Westland-Bell 47G-3B1 (Soloy)	T. R. Smith (Agricultural Machinery) Ltd
	G-BHBG	PA-32R Cherokee Lance 300	E. Schiewe
	G-BHBT	Marquart MA.5 Charger	Bravo Tango Group
	G-BHBZ	Partenavia P.68B	Reconnaissance Ventures
	G-BHCC	Cessna 172M	D. Wood-Jenkins
	G-BHCE	Jodel D.112	C. E. & M. G. Cookson
	G-BHCM	Cessna F.172H	J. Dominic
	G-BHCP	Cessna F.152	Eastern Air Executive Ltd
	G-BHCZ	PA-38-112 Tomahawk	J. E. Abbott
	G-BHDD	V.668 Varsity T.1 (WL626:P) ★	Aeropark/East Midlands
	G-BHDE	SOCATA TB10 Tobago	Alpha-Alpha Ltd
	G-BHDK	Boeing B-29A-BN (461748:Y) ★	Imperial War Museum/Duxford
	G-BHDM	Cessna F.152 II	Big Red Kite Ltd
	G-BHDP	Cessna F.182Q II	Zone Travel Ltd

48

Reg.	Type	Owner or Operator	Notes
G-BHDS	Cessna F.152 II	Redmosaic Formacao de Technicos de Aeronaves Unipessoal	
G-BHDV	Cameron V-77 balloon	P. Glydon	
G-BHDX	Cessna F.172N	GDX Ltd	
G-BHDZ	Cessna F.172N	Abbey Security Services Ltd	
G-BHEC	Cessna F.152 II	Stapleford Flying Club Ltd	
G-BHED	Cessna FA.152	TG Aviation Ltd	
G-BHEG	Jodel 150	D. M. Griffiths	
G-BHEK	CP.1315-C3 Super Emeraude	D. B. Winstanley	
G-BHEL	Jodel D.117	D. W. & S. J. McAllister	
G-BHEM	Bensen B.8M	G. C. Kerr	
G-BHEN	Cessna FA.152	Leicestershire Aero Club Ltd	
G-BHEU	Thunder Ax7-65 balloon	J. A. W. Dyer	
G-BHEV	PA-28R Cherokee Arrow 200	7-Up Group	
G-BHEX	Colt 56A balloon	A. S. Dear & ptnrs	
G-BHFC	Cessna F.152	JH Sandham Aviation	
G-BHFE	PA-44-180 Seminole	Transport Command Ltd	
G-BHFG	SNCAN Stampe SV.4C	A. D. R. Northeast & S. A. Cook	
G-BHFH	PA-34-200T Seneca II	Oxford Aviation Academy (Oxford) Ltd	
G-BHFI	Cessna F.152	BAe (Warton) Flying Club	
G-BHFJ	PA-28RT-201T Turbo Arrow IV	S. A. Cook & D. R. Northeast	
G-BHFK	PA-28-151 Warrior	G-BHFK Warrior Group	
G-BHGC	PA-18 Super Cub 150	Vectis Gliding Club Ltd	
G-BHGF	Cameron V-56 balloon	P. Smallward	
G-BHGJ	Jodel D.120	Q. M. B. Oswell	
G-BHGO	PA-32 Cherokee Six 260	A. V. Harmer	
G-BHGY	PA-28R Cherokee Arrow 200	Truman Aviation Ltd	
G-BHHE	Jodel DR.1051/M1	P. Bridges & P. C. Matthews	
G-BHHG	Cessna F.152 II	TG Aviation Ltd	
G-BHHH	Thunder Ax7-65 balloon	J. M. J. Roberts	
G-BHHK	Cameron N-77 balloon ★	British Balloon Museum	
G-BHHN	Cameron V-77 balloon	Itchen Valley Balloon Group	
G-BHIB	Cessna F.182Q	The G-BHIB Flying Group	
G-BHII	Cameron V-77 balloon	R. V. Brown	
G-BHIJ	Eiri PIK-20E-1 (898)	P. M. Yeoman	
G-BHIN	Cessna F.152	Target Aviation Ltd	
G-BHIR	PA-28R Cherokee Arrow 200	Factorcore Ltd	
G-BHIS	Thunder Ax7-65 balloon	Hedgehoppers Balloon Group	
G-BHIY	Cessna F.150K	G. J. Ball	
G-BHJF	SOCATA TB10 Tobago	Tyas Aviation Ltd	
G-BHJI	Mooney M.20J	Otomed APS/Denmark	
G-BHJK	Maule M5-235C Lunar Rocket	M. K. H. Bell	
G-BHJN	Fournier RF-4D	RF-4 Group	
G-BHJO	PA-28-161 Warrior II	Brackla Flying Group	
G-BHJS	Partenavia P.68B	Flew LLP	
G-BHJU	Robin DR.400/2+2	Ageless Aeronautics	
G-BHKR	Colt 12A balloon ★	British Balloon Museum/Newbury	
G-BHKT	Jodel D.112	G. Dawes	
G-BHLE	Robin DR.400/180	A. V. Harmer	
G-BHLH	Robin DR.400/180	G-BHLH Group	
G-BHLJ	Saffery-Rigg S.200 balloon	I. A. Rigg	
G-BHLT	DH.82A Tiger Moth	Skymax (Aviation) Ltd	
G-BHLU	Fournier RF-3	G. Sabatino	
G-BHLW	Cessna 120	L. W. Scattergood	
G-BHLX	AA-5B Tiger	M. D. McPherson	
G-BHMA	SIPA 903	H. J. Taggart	
G-BHMG	Cessna FA.152	R. J. Williamson	
G-BHMJ	Avenger T.200-2112 balloon	R. Light *Lord Anthony 1*	
G-BHMK	Avenger T.200-2112 balloon	P. Kinder *Lord Anthony 2*	
G-BHMT	Evans VP-1	R. T. Callow	
G-BHMY	F.27 Friendship Mk.200 ★	Norwich Aviation Museum	
G-BHNA	Cessna F.152 II	Eastern Air Executive Ltd	
G-BHNC	Cameron O-65 balloon	D. & C. Bareford	
G-BHNK	Jodel D.120A	K. R. Daly	
G-BHNL	Jodel D.112	November Lima Group	
G-BHNO	PA-28-181 Archer II	B. J. Richardson	
G-BHNP	Eiri PIK-20E-1	D. A. Sutton	
G-BHNV	Westlan-Bell 47G-3B1	S. W. Hutchinson	
G-BHNX	Jodel D.117	M. J. A. Trudgill	
G-BHOA	Robin DR.400/160	T. L. Trott	
G-BHOL	Jodel DR.1050	S. J. Pearson	
G-BHOM	PA-18 Super Cub 95	Oscar Mike Flying Group	
G-BHOR	PA-28-161 Warrior II	Oscar Romeo Flying Group	

Notes	Reg.	Type	Owner or Operator
	G-BHOT	Cameron V-65 balloon	Dante Balloon Group
	G-BHOZ	SOCATA TB9 Tampico	G-BHOZ Flying Group
	G-BHPK	Piper J-3C-65 Cub (238410:A-44)	L-4 Group
	G-BHPL	CASA 1.131E Jungmann 1000 (E3B-350:05-97) ★	A. Burroughes
	G-BHPS	Jodel D.120A	T. J. Price
	G-BHPZ	Cessna 172N	O'Brien Properties Ltd
	G-BHRC	PA-28-161 Warrior II	Sherwood Flying Club Ltd
	G-BHRH	Cessna FA.150K	Merlin Flying Club Ltd
	G-BHRO	Rockwell Commander 112	R. A. Blackwell
	G-BHRR	CP.301A Emeraude	T. W. Offen
	G-BHRW	Jodel DR.221	Dauphin Flying Club
	G-BHSB	Cessna 172N	J. W. Cope & M. P. Wimsey
	G-BHSD	Scheibe SF.25E Super Falke	Upwood Motorglider Group
	G-BHSE	Rockwell Commander 114	604 Sqdn Flying Group Ltd
	G-BHSN	Cameron N-56 balloon	I. Bentley
	G-BHSS	Pitts S-1S Special	N. Leis
	G-BHSY	Jodel DR.1050	T. R. Allebone
	G-BHTA	PA-28-236 Dakota	Dakota Ltd
	G-BHTC	Jodel DR.1050/M1	G. Clark
	G-BHTG	Thunder Ax6-56 Bolt balloon	The British Balloon Museum & Library Ltd
	G-BHUB	Douglas C-47A (315509:W7-S) ★	Imperial War Museum/Duxford
	G-BHUE	Jodel DR.1050	M. J. Harris
	G-BHUG	Cessna 172N	L. Marriott, R. Wainwright & B. Wharton
	G-BHUI	Cessna 152	South Warwickshire School of Flying Ltd
	G-BHUJ	Cessna 172N	Uniform Juliet Group
	G-BHUM	DH.82A Tiger Moth	S. G. Towers
	G-BHUU	PA-25 Pawnee 235	Booker Gliding Club Ltd
	G-BHVF	Jodel 150A	Groupe Ariel
	G-BHVP	Cessna 182Q	G. S. Chapman
	G-BHVR	Cessna 172N	Victor Romeo Group
	G-BHVV	Piper J-3C-65 Cub	A. V. Williams
	G-BHWA	Cessna F.152	Lincoln Enterprises Ltd
	G-BHWB	Cessna F.152	Lincoln Enterprises Ltd
	G-BHWH	Weedhopper JC-24A	G. A. Clephane
	G-BHWK	MS.880B Rallye Club	D. F. Cumberlidge
	G-BHWY	PA-28R Cherokee Arrow 200-II	Kilo Foxtrot Flying Group
	G-BHWZ	PA-28-181 Archer II	M. A. Abbott
	G-BHXA	SA Bulldog Srs 120/1210	Air Plan Flight Equipment Ltd
	G-BHXD	Jodel D.120	D. A. Garner
	G-BHXK	PA-28 Cherokee 140	S. A. Finlay
	G-BHXS	Jodel D.120	Plymouth Jodel Group
	G-BHXY	Piper J-3C-65 Cub (44-79609:44-S)	F. W. Rogers
	G-BHYA	Cessna R.182RG II	J-P. Jarier
	G-BHYC	Cessna 172RG II	IB Aeroplanes Ltd
	G-BHYD	Cessna R.172K XP II	Sylmar Aviation Services Ltd
	G-BHYG	PA-34-200T Seneca II	Oxford Aviation Academy (Oxford) Ltd
	G-BHYI	SNCAN Stampe SV.4A	D. Hicklin
	G-BHYP	Cessna F.172M	Avior Ltd
	G-BHYR	Cessna F.172M	G-BHYR Group
	G-BHYV	Evans VP-1	I. P. Manley
	G-BHYX	Cessna 152 II	Stapleford Flying Club Ltd
	G-BHZE	PA-28-181 Archer II	Zegruppe Ltd
	G-BHZH	Cessna F.152	Fly NQY Pilot Training
	G-BHZK	AA-5B Tiger	ZK Group
	G-BHZO	AA-5A Cheetah	PG Air
	G-BHZR	SA Bulldog Srs 120/1210	White Knuckle Air Ltd
	G-BHZT	SA Bulldog Srs 120/1210	D. M. Curties
	G-BHZU	Piper J-3C-65 Cub	J. K. Tomkinson
	G-BHZV	Jodel D.120A	G-BHZV Group
	G-BIAC	SOCATA Rallye 235E	G-BIAC Flying Group
	G-BIAH	Jodel D.112	P. A. Gange
	G-BIAI	WMB.2 Windtracker balloon	I. Chadwick
	G-BIAP	PA-16 Clipper	G-BIAP Flying Group
	G-BIAR	Rigg Skyliner II balloon	I. A. Rigg
	G-BIAU	Sopwith Pup (replica) (N6452) ★	F.A.A. Museum/Yeovilton
	G-BIAX	Taylor JT.2 Titch	D. M. Bland
	G-BIAY	AA-5 Traveler	P. Moderate
	G-BIBA	SOCATA TB9 Tampico	TB Aviation Ltd
	G-BIBN	Cessna FA.150K	B. V. Mayo
	G-BIBO	Cameron V-65 balloon	D. M. Hoddinott
	G-BIBS	Cameron P-20 balloon	Cameron Balloons Ltd

Reg.	Type	Owner or Operator	Notes
G-BIBT	AA-5B Tiger	Horizon Aviation Ltd	
G-BIBW	Cessna F.172N	Shields Estates Ltd	
G-BIBX	WMB.2 Windtracker balloon	I. A. Rigg	
G-BICD	Auster 5	T. R. Parsons	
G-BICE	NA AT-6C Harvard IIA (41-33275:CE)	C. M. L. Edwards	
G-BICG	Cessna F.152 II	Falcon Flying Services	
G-BICM	Colt 56A balloon	Avon Advertiser Balloon Club	
G-BICP	Robin DR.360	B. McVeighty	
G-BICR	Jodel D.120A	Beehive Flying Group	
G-BICS	Robin R.2100A	Chiltern Flying Group	
G-BICU	Cameron V-56 balloon	Black Pearl Balloons	
G-BICW	PA-28-161 Warrior II	Charlie Whisky Flying Group	
G-BICX	Maule M5-235C Lunar Rocket	I. S. McLeod & J. L. Yourell	
G-BIDD	Evans VP-1	J. Hodgkinson	
G-BIDG	Jodel 150A	D. R. Gray	
G-BIDH	Cessna 152 II	Hull Aero Club Ltd (G-DONA)	
G-BIDI	PA-28R-201 Arrow III	T. A. N. Brierley & A. Lidster	
G-BIDJ	PA-18A Super Cub 150	S. M. Hart	
G-BIDK	PA-18 Super Cub 150	Mapesbury Capital Partners Ltd	
G-BIDO	CP.301A Emeraude	A. R. Plumb	
G-BIDV	Colt 14A balloon ★	British Balloon Museum/Newbury	
G-BIDW	Sopwith 1½ Strutter (replica) (A8226) ★	RAF Museum/Hendon	
G-BIDX	Jodel D.112	P. Turton	
G-BIEJ	Sikorsky S-76A	Bristow Helicopters Ltd	
G-BIEN	Jodel D.120A	H. J. Morton/France	
G-BIEO	Jodel D.112	Clipgate Flyers	
G-BIES	Maule M5-235C Lunar Rocket	William Proctor Farms	
G-BIET	Cameron O-77 balloon	G. M. Westley	
G-BIEY	PA-28-151 Warrior	M. J. Isaac	
G-BIFA	Cessna 310R II	J. S. Lee	
G-BIFB	PA-28 Cherokee 150C	P. Coombs	
G-BIFO	Evans VP-1	D. C. Unwin	
G-BIFP	Colt 56A balloon	J. W. Adkins	
G-BIFY	Cessna F.150L	Hope Aviation Ltd	
G-BIGJ	Cessna F.172M	Cirrus Aviation Ltd	
G-BIGK	Taylorcraft BC-12D	N. P. St. J. Ramsay	
G-BIGL	Cameron O-65 balloon	P. L. Mossman	
G-BIGR	Avenger T.200-2112 balloon	R. Light	
G-BIGX	Bensen B.8M	W. C. Turner	
G-BIHD	Robin DR.400/160	G. I. J. Thomson & R. A. Hawkins	
G-BIHF	SE-5A (replica) (F943)	C. J. Zeal	
G-BIHI	Cessna 172M	E-Plane Ltd	
G-BIHO	DHC.6 Twin Otter 310	Isles of Scilly Skybus Ltd	
G-BIHT	PA-17 Vagabond	B. Carter	
G-BIHU	Saffrey S.200 balloon	B. L. King	
G-BIHX	Bensen B.8M	P. P. Willmott	
G-BIIA	Fournier RF-3	C. J. Riley	
G-BIIB	Cessna F.172M	Civil Service Flying Club (Biggin Hill) Ltd	
G-BIID	PA-18 Super Cub 95	D. A. Lacey	
G-BIIE	Cessna F.172P	S. J. Perkins	
G-BIIK	MS.883 Rallye 115	N. J. Garbett	
G-BIIT	PA-28-161 Warrior II	Tayside Aviation Ltd	
G-BIIV	PA-28-181 Archer II	J. Thuret/France	
G-BIIZ	Great Lakes 2T-1A Sport Trainer	Circa 42 Ltd	
G-BIJB	PA-18 Super Cub 150	James Aero Ltd	
G-BIJD	Bölkow Bö.208C Junior	Sikh Sydicate	
G-BIJE	Piper J-3C-65 Cub	R. L. Hayward & A. G. Scott	
G-BIJS	Luton LA-4A Minor	I. J. Smith	
G-BIJU	CP-301A Emeraude	Eastern Taildraggers Flying Group (G-BHTX)	
G-BIJV	Cessna F.152 II	Falcon Flying Services	
G-BIJW	Cessna F.152 II	Falcon Flying Services	
G-BIJX	Cessna F.152 II	Falcon Flying Services	
G-BIKC	Boeing 757-236F	DHL Air Ltd	
G-BIKE	PA-28R Cherokee Arrow 200	R. Taylor	
G-BIKF	Boeing 757-236F	DHL Air Ltd	
G-BIKG	Boeing 757-236F	DHL Air Ltd	
G-BIKI	Boeing 757-236F	DHL Air Ltd	
G-BIKJ	Boeing 757-236F	DHL Air Ltd	
G-BIKK	Boeing 757-236F	DHL Air Ltd	
G-BIKM	Boeing 757-236F	DHL Air Ltd	
G-BIKN	Boeing 757-236F	DHL Air Ltd	
G-BIKO	Boeing 757-236F	DHL Air Ltd	
G-BIKP	Boeing 757-236F	DHL Air Ltd	

Notes	Reg.	Type	Owner or Operator
	G-BIKS	Boeing 757-236F	DHL Air Ltd
	G-BIKU	Boeing 757-236F	DHL Air Ltd
	G-BIKV	Boeing 757-236F	DHL Air Ltd
	G-BIKZ	Boeing 757-236F	DHL Air Ltd
	G-BILB	WMB.2 Windtracker balloon	B. L. King
	G-BILE	Scruggs BL.2B balloon	P. D. Ridout
	G-BILG	Scruggs BL.2B balloon	P. D. Ridout
	G-BILH	Slingsby T.65C Vega	R. F. Barber
	G-BILI	Piper J-3C-65 Cub (454467:J-44)	G-BILI Flying Group
	G-BILL	PA-25 Pawnee 235	Pawnee Aviation
	G-BILR	Cessna 152 II	APB Leasing Ltd
	G-BILS	Cessna 152 II	Mona Flying Club
	G-BILU	Cessna 172RG	Full Sutton Flying Centre Ltd
	G-BILZ	Taylor JT.1 Monoplane	A. Petherbridge
	G-BIMK	Tiger T.200 Srs 1 balloon	M. K. Baron
	G-BIMM	PA-18 Super Cub 150	Spectrum Leisure Ltd
	G-BIMN	Steen Skybolt	R. J. Thomas
	G-BIMT	Cessna FA.152	Staverton Flying School @ Skypark Ltd
	G-BIMU	Sikorsky S-61N	Bristow Helicopters Ltd
	G-BIMX	Rutan Vari-Eze	D. G. Crow
	G-BIMZ	Beech 76 Duchess	R. P. Smith
	G-BINL	Scruggs BL.2B balloon	P. D. Ridout
	G-BINM	Scruggs BL.2B balloon	P. D. Ridout
	G-BINR	Unicorn UE.1A balloon	Unicorn Group
	G-BINS	Unicorn UE.2A balloon	Unicorn Group
	G-BINT	Unicorn UE.1A balloon	D. E. Bint
	G-BINX	Scruggs BL.2B balloon	P. D. Ridout
	G-BINY	Oriental balloon	J. L. Morton
	G-BIOA	Hughes 369D	AH Helicopter Services Ltd
	G-BIOB	Cessna F.172P	Network Mapping Ltd
	G-BIOC	Cessna F.150L	W. H. Milner
	G-BIOI	Jodel DR.1051/M	A. A. Alderdice
	G-BIOJ	Rockwell Commander 112TCA	A. T. Dalby
	G-BIOK	Cessna F.152	A. D. H. Macdonald
	G-BIOM	Cessna F.152	J. B. P. E. Fernandes
	G-BIOU	Jodel D.117A	M. R. Routh
	G-BIOW	Slingsby T.67A	A. B. Slinger
	G-BIPA	AA-5B Tiger	Tri-Star Developments Ltd
	G-BIPH	Scruggs BL.2B balloon	C. M. Dewsnap
	G-BIPI	Everett gyroplane	C. A. Reeves
	G-BIPN	Fournier RF-3	G-BIPN Group
	G-BIPT	Jodel D.112	C. R. Davies
	G-BIPV	AA-5B Tiger	Echo Echo Ltd
	G-BIPW	Avenger T.200-2112 balloon	B. L. King
	G-BIRD	Pitts S-1D Special	N. E. Smith
	G-BIRE	Colt 56 Bottle SS balloon	D. J. Stagg
	G-BIRH	PA-18 Super Cub 135 (R-163)	Banbury Gliding Club Ltd
	G-BIRI	CASA 1.131E Jungmann 1000	D. Watt
	G-BIRL	Avenger T.200-2112 balloon	R. Light
	G-BIRP	Arena Mk 17 Skyship balloon	A. S. Viel
	G-BIRT	Robin R.1180TD	W. D'A. Hall
	G-BIRW	MS.505 Criquet (F+IS) ★	Museum of Flight/East Fortune
	G-BISG	FRED Srs 3	T. Littlefair
	G-BISH	Cameron V-65 balloon	P. J. Bish
	G-BISL	Scruggs BL.2B balloon	P. D. Ridout
	G-BISM	Scruggs BL.2B balloon	P. D. Ridout
	G-BISS	Scruggs BL.2C balloon	P. D. Ridout
	G-BIST	Scruggs BL.2C balloon	P. D. Ridout
	G-BISX	Colt 56A balloon	C. D. Steel
	G-BISZ	Sikorsky S-76A	Bristow Helicopters Ltd
	G-BITA	PA-18 Super Cub 150	Intrepid Aviation Co
	G-BITE	SOCATA TB10 Tobago	M. A. Smith
	G-BITF	Cessna F.152 II	G-BITF Owners Group
	G-BITH	Cessna F.152 II	J. R. Hyde (G-TFSA)
	G-BITK	FRED Srs 2	I. Pearson
	G-BITM	Cessna F.172P	Dreamtrade Ltd
	G-BITO	Jodel D.112D	A. Dunbar
	G-BITY	FD.31T balloon	A. J. Bell
	G-BIUM	Cessna F.152	Eastern Air Executive Ltd
	G-BIUP	SNCAN NC.854S	J. Greenaway & T. D. Cooper
	G-BIUY	PA-28-181 Archer II	J. S. Devlin & Z. Islam
	G-BIVA	Robin R.2112	D. M. Croucher
	G-BIVB	Jodel D.112	N. M. Harwood

Reg.	Type	Owner or Operator	Notes
G-BIVF	CP.301C-3 Emeraude	T. C. Darters	
G-BIVK	Bensen B.8M	M. J. Atyeo	
G-BIWB	Scruggs RS.5000 balloon	P. D. Ridout	
G-BIWC	Scruggs RS.5000 balloon	P. D. Ridout	
G-BIWF	Warren balloon	P. D. Ridout	
G-BIWG	Zelenski Mk 2 balloon	P. D. Ridout	
G-BIWJ	Unicorn UE.1A balloon	B. L. King	
G-BIWN	Jodel D.112	C. R. Coates & P. K. Morley	
G-BIWR	Mooney M.20F	M. Broady	
G-BIWU	Cameron V-65 balloon	W. Rousell & J. Tyrrell	
G-BIWW	AA-5 Traveler	Dix-Sept Aviation Ltd	
G-BIWY	Westland WG.30 ★	Instructional airframe/Yeovil	
G-BIXA	SOCATA TB9 Tampico	W. Maxwell	
G-BIXB	SOCATA TB9 Tampico	B. G. Adams	
G-BIXH	Cessna F.152	Northumbria Flying School Ltd	
G-BIXL	P-51D Mustang (472216:HO-M)	R. Lamplough	
G-BIXN	Boeing Stearman A75N1 (FJ777)	V. S. E. Norman	
G-BIXW	Colt 56B balloon	N. A. P. Bates	
G-BIXX	Pearson Srs 2 balloon	D. Pearson	
G-BIXZ	Grob G-109	Hinton Pilot Flight Training Ltd	
G-BIYI	Cameron V-65 balloon	Sarnia Balloon Group	
G-BIYJ	PA-18 Super Cub 95	S. Russell	
G-BIYK	Isaacs Fury II	S. M. Roberts	
G-BIYP	PA-20 Pacer 125	N. S. Jean	
G-BIYR	PA-18 Super Cub 150 (R-151)	Delta Foxtrot Flying Group	
G-BIYU	Fokker S.11.1 Instructor (E-15)	Fokker Syndicate	
G-BIYW	Jodel D.112	A. Appleby	
G-BIYX	PA-28 Cherokee 140	W. B. Bateson	
G-BIYY	PA-18 Super Cub 95	A. E. & W. J. Taylor	
G-BIZE	SOCATA TB9 Tampico	B. Higgins	
G-BIZF	Cessna F.172P	R. S. Bentley	
G-BIZG	Cessna F.152	M. A. Judge	
G-BIZI	Robin DR.400/120	Headcorn Flying School Ltd	
G-BIZK	Nord 3202 (78)	A. I. Milne	
G-BIZM	Nord 3202	Global Aviation Ltd	
G-BIZO	PA-28R Cherokee Arrow 200	Lemas Air	
G-BIZR	SOCATA TB9 Tampico	P. Marie (G-BSEC)	
G-BIZV	PA-18 Super Cub 95 (18-2001)	J. P. Nugent	
G-BIZW	Champion 7GCBC Citabria	G. Read & Sons	
G-BIZY	Jodel D.112	Wayland Tunley & Associates	
G-BJAD	FRED Srs 2 ★	Newark (Nottinghamshire & Lincolnshire) Air Museum	
G-BJAE	Lavadoux Starck AS.80 ★	D. J. & S. A. E. Phillips/Coventry	
G-BJAF	Piper J-3C-65 Cub	P. J. Cottle	
G-BJAG	PA-28-181 Archer II	C. R. Chubb	
G-BJAJ	AA-5B Tiger	Draycott Tiger Club	
G-BJAL	CASA 1.131E Jungmann 1000	G-BJAL Group	
G-BJAO	Bensen B.8M	A. P. Lay	
G-BJAP	DH.82A Tiger Moth (K2587)	K. Knight	
G-BJAS	Rango NA.9 balloon	A. Lindsay	
G-BJAV	Gardan GY-80 Horizon 160	W. R.Maloney	
G-BJAY	Piper J-3C-65 Cub	D. W. Finlay	
G-BJBK	PA-18 Super Cub 95	M. S. Bird	
G-BJBM	Monnett Sonerai I	I. Pearson	
G-BJBO	Jodel DR.250/160	Wiltshire Flying Group	
G-BJBW	PA-28-161 Warrior II	152 Group	
G-BJCA	PA-28-161 Warrior II	U. Kleinheyer	
G-BJCF	CP.1310-C3 Super Emeraude	K. M. Hodson & C. G. H. Gurney	
G-BJCI	PA-18 Super Cub 150 (modified)	The Borders (Milfield) Gliding Club Ltd	
G-BJCW	PA-32R-301 Saratoga SP	Golf Charlie Whisky Ltd	
G-BJDE	Cessna F.172M	J. K. P. Amor	
G-BJDF	MS.880B Rallye 100T	C. J. dos Santos Prado	
G-BJDJ	HS.125 Srs 700B	TAG Farnborough Engineering Ltd (G-RCDI)	
G-BJDK	European E.14 balloon	Aeroprint Tours	
G-BJDW	Cessna F.172M	J. Rae	
G-BJEE	BN-2T Turbine Islander	Cormack (Aircraft Services) Ltd	
G-BJEF	BN-2B-26 Islander	Cormack (Aircraft Services) Ltd	
G-BJEI	PA-18 Super Cub 95	H. J. Cox	
G-BJEJ	BN-2T Turbine Islander	Islander Aircraft Ltd	
G-BJEL	SNCAN NC.854	C. A. James	
G-BJEV	Aeronca 11AC Chief (897)	R. F. Willcox	
G-BJEX	Bölkow Bö.208C Junior	G. D. H. Crawford	

Notes	Reg.	Type	Owner or Operator
	G-BJFC	European E.8 balloon	P. D. Ridout
	G-BJFE	PA-18 Super Cub 95	P. H. Wilmot-Allistone
	G-BJFM	Jodel D.120	J. V. George
	G-BJGM	Unicorn UE.1A balloon	D. Eaves & P. D. Ridout
	G-BJGX	Sikorsky S-76A	Bristow Helicopters Ltd
	G-BJGY	Cessna F.172P	K. & S. Martin
	G-BJHB	Mooney M.20J	Zitair Flying Club Ltd
	G-BJHK	EAA Acro Sport	M. R. Holden
	G-BJHV	Voisin Replica ★	Brooklands Museum of Aviation/Weybridge
	G-BJIA	Allport balloon	D. J. Allport
	G-BJIC	Dodo 1A balloon	P. D. Ridout
	G-BJID	Osprey 1B balloon	P. D. Ridout
	G-BJIG	Slingsby T.67A	A. D. Hodgkinson
	G-BJIV	PA-18 Super Cub 180	Yorkshire Gliding Club (Pty) Ltd
	G-BJKF	SOCATA TB9 Tampico	G-BJKF Group
	G-BJKW	Wills Aera II	J. K. S. Wills
	G-BJLC	Monnett Sonerai IIL	P. O. Yeo
	G-BJLX	Cremer balloon	P. W. May
	G-BJLY	Cremer balloon	P. Cannon
	G-BJML	Cessna 120	R. A. Smith
	G-BJMR	Cessna 310R	J. H. Sandham Aviation
	G-BJMW	Thunder Ax8-105 balloon	G. M. Westley
	G-BJMX	Jarre JR.3 balloon	P. D. Ridout
	G-BJMZ	European EA.8A balloon	P. D. Ridout
	G-BJNA	Arena Mk 117P balloon	P. D. Ridout
	G-BJND	Osprey Mk 1E balloon	A. Billington & D. Whitmore
	G-BJNG	Slingsby T.67AM	D. F. Hodgkinson
	G-BJNN	PA-38-112 Tomahawk	Carlisle Flight Training Ltd
	G-BJNY	Aeronca 11CC Super Chief	P. I. & D. M. Morgans
	G-BJNZ	PA-23 Aztec 250F	J. A. D. Richardson (G-FANZ)
	G-BJOB	Jodel D.140C	T. W. M. Beck & M. J. Smith
	G-BJOE	Jodel D.120A	H. Davies
	G-BJOT	Jodel D.117	R. A. Kilbride
	G-BJOV	Cessna F.150K	G-BJOV Flying Group
	G-BJPI	Bede BD-5G	M. D. McQueen
	G-BJRA	Osprey Mk 4B balloon	E. Osborn
	G-BJRG	Osprey Mk 4B balloon	A. E. de Gruchy
	G-BJRH	Rango NA.36 balloon	N. H. Ponsford
	G-BJRP	Cremer balloon	M. D. Williams
	G-BJRR	Cremer balloon	M. D. Williams
	G-BJRV	Cremer balloon	M. D. Williams
	G-BJSS	Allport balloon	D. J. Allport
	G-BJST	CCF T-6J Harvard IV (KF729)	M. F. Cuming, J. G. Fricker & N. T. Oakman
	G-BJSV	PA-28-161 Warrior II	Airways Flight Training (Exeter) Ltd
	G-BJSW	Thunder Ax7-65 balloon	J. Edwards
	G-BJSZ	Piper J-3C-65 Cub	K. Gilbert
	G-BJTB	Cessna A.150M	Cirrus Aviation Ltd
	G-BJTP	PA-18 Super Cub 95 (115302:TP)	P. J. Myers
	G-BJTY	Osprey Mk 4B balloon	A. E. de Gruchy
	G-BJUB	BVS Special 01 balloon	P. G. Wild
	G-BJUD	Robin DR.400/180R	Lasham Gliding Society Ltd
	G-BJUR	PA-38-112 Tomahawk	Truman Aviation Ltd
	G-BJUS	PA-38-112 Tomahawk	J. D. Williams
	G-BJUV	Cameron V-20 balloon	P. Spellward
	G-BJVC	Evans VP-2	S. J. Greer & S. E. Clarke
	G-BJVH	Cessna F.182Q	R. J. de Courcy Cuming
	G-BJVJ	Cessna F.152	Henlow Flying Club
	G-BJVK	Grob G-109	B. Kimberley
	G-BJVM	Cessna 172N	R. D. & M. S. B. Forster
	G-BJVS	CP.1310-C3 Super Emeraude	M. J. Hall
	G-BJVT	Cessna F.152	Northumbria Flying School Ltd
	G-BJVU	Thunder Ax6-56 Bolt balloon	N. R. Beckwith
	G-BJWH	Cessna F.152 II	J. D. Baines
	G-BJWI	Cessna F.172P	Flew LLP
	G-BJWT	Wittman W.10 Tailwind	Tailwind Group
	G-BJWV	Colt 17A balloon	D. T. Meyes
	G-BJWW	Cessna F.172N	Air Charter & Travel Ltd
	G-BJWX	PA-18 Super Cub 95	R. A. G. Lucas
	G-BJWY	S-55 Whirlwind HAR.21(WV198) ★	Solway Aviation Museum/Carlisle
	G-BJWZ	PA-18 Super Cub 95	G-BJWZ Syndicate
	G-BJXB	Slingsby T.67A	D. Pegley
	G-BJXK	Fournier RF-5	RF5 Syndicate
	G-BJXP	Colt 56B balloon	H. J. Anderson

Reg.	Type	Owner or Operator	Notes
G-BJXR	Auster AOP.9 (XR267)	I. Churm & J. Hanson	
G-BJXX	PA-23 Aztec 250E	V. Bojovic	
G-BJXZ	Cessna 172N	T. M. Jones	
G-BJYD	Cessna F.152 II	N. J. James	
G-BJYF	Colt 56A balloon	A. J. Moore	
G-BJYK	Jodel D.120A	M. R. Baker	
G-BJZB	Evans VP-2	R. B. McComish	
G-BJZF	DH.82A Tiger Moth	M. I. Lodge	
G-BJZN	Slingsby T.67A	ZN Group	
G-BJZR	Colt 42A balloon	Selfish Balloon Group	
G-BKAE	Jodel D.120	J. K. Davies	
G-BKAF	FRED Srs 2	N. Glass	
G-BKAM	Slingsby T.67M Firefly160	R. C. B. Brookhouse	
G-BKAO	Jodel D.112	H. Haigh	
G-BKAS	PA-38-112 Tomahawk	Hinton Pilot Flight Training Ltd	
G-BKAY	Rockwell Commander 114	D. L. Bunning	
G-BKAZ	Cessna 152	L. W. Scattergood	
G-BKBD	Thunder Ax3 balloon	P. Donkin	
G-BKBF	MS.894A Rallye Minerva 220	K. A. Hale, L. C. Clark & P. Mickleborough	
G-BKBN	SOCATA TB10 Tobago	P. M. Clayton & D. Turner	
G-BKBP	Bellanca 7GCBC Scout	M. G. & J. R. Jefferies	
G-BKBS	Bensen B8MV	L. Harrison	
G-BKBV	SOCATA TB10 Tobago	T. C. H. Wright	
G-BKBW	SOCATA TB10 Tobago	Merlin Aviation	
G-BKCC	PA-28 Cherokee 180	DR Flying Club Ltd	
G-BKCE	Cessna F.172P II	The Leicestershire Aero Club Ltd	
G-BKCI	Brügger MB.2 Colibri	M. R. Walters	
G-BKCN	Currie Wot	N. A. A. Podmore	
G-BKCV	EAA Acro Sport II	R. J. Bower	
G-BKCW	Jodel D.120	Dundee Flying Group (G-BMYF)	
G-BKCX	Mudry/CAARP CAP-10B	G. P. Gorvett	
G-BKCZ	Jodel D.120A	I. K. Ratcliffe	
G-BKDC	Monnett Sonerai II	K. J. Towell	
G-BKDH	Robin DR.400/120	Marine & Aviation Ltd	
G-BKDJ	Robin DR.400/120	S. Pritchard & I. C. Colwell	
G-BKDK	Thunder Ax7-77Z balloon	A. J. Byrne	
G-BKDP	FRED Srs 3	M. Whittaker	
G-BKDR	Pitts S-1S Special	L. E. Richardson	
G-BKDT	SE-5A (replica) (F943) ★	Yorkshire Air Museum/Elvington	
G-BKDX	Jodel DR.1050	D. G. T. & R. J. Ward	
G-BKEP	Cessna F.172M	R. M. Dalley	
G-BKER	SE-5A (replica) (F5447:N)	N. K. Geddes	
G-BKET	PA-18 Super Cub 95	H. M. MacKenzie	
G-BKEV	Cessna F.172M	Derby Arrows	
G-BKEW	Bell 206B JetRanger 3	N. R. Foster	
G-BKEY	FRED Srs 3	G. S. Taylor	
G-BKFC	Cessna F.152 II	C. Walton Ltd	
G-BKFG	Thunder Ax3 Maxi Sky Chariot balloon	S. G. Whatley	
G-BKFI	Evans VP-1	A. S. Watts	
G-BKFK	Isaacs Fury II	P. T. Catanach	
G-BKFL	Aerosport Scamp	J. Sherwood	
G-BKFM	QAC Quickie 1	G. E. Meakin	
G-BKFR	CP.301C Emeraude	Devonshire Flying Group	
G-BKFW	P.56 Provost T.1 (XF597)	Sylmar Aviation & Services Ltd	
G-BKGA	MS.892E Rallye 150GT	C. J. Spradbery	
G-BKGB	Jodel D.120	B. A. Ridgway	
G-BKGC	Maule M.6-235	The Vale of the White Horse Gliding Centre Ltd	
G-BKGD	Westland WG.30 Srs.100 ★	IHM/Weston-super-Mare	
G-BKGL	Beech D.18S (1164:64)	A. T. J. Darrah	
G-BKGM	Beech D.18S (HB275)	Skyblue Aero Services Ltd & L. S. Williams	
G-BKGR	Cameron O-65 balloon	K. Kidner & L. E. More	
G-BKGW	Cessna F.152-II	Leicestershire Aero Club Ltd	
G-BKHG	Piper J-3C-65 Cub (479766:D-63)	H. C. Cox	
G-BKHW	Stoddard-Hamilton Glasair IIRG	P. J. Mansfield	
G-BKHY	Taylor JT.1 Monoplane	B. C. J. O'Neill	
G-BKHZ	Cessna F.172P	L. R. Leader	
G-BKIB	SOCATA TB9 Tampico	G. A. Vickers	
G-BKIC	Cameron V-77 balloon	C. A. Butler	
G-BKIF	Fournier RF-6B	Tiger Airways	
G-BKII	Cessna F.172M	Sealand Aerial Photography Ltd	
G-BKIJ	Cessna F.172M	Cirrus Aviation Ltd	
G-BKIK	Cameron DG-19 airship ★	Balloon Preservation Group/Lancing	

Notes	Reg.	Type	Owner or Operator
	G-BKIR	Jodel D.117	R. Shaw & D. M. Hardaker
	G-BKIS	SOCATA TB10 Tobago	Wessex Flyers
	G-BKIT	SOCATA TB9 Tampico	Cavendish Aviation UK Ltd
	G-BKIU	Colt 17A Cloudhopper balloon	S. R. J. Pooley
	G-BKIY	Thunder Ax3 balloon ★	Balloon Preservation Group/Lancing
	G-BKIZ	Cameron V-31 balloon	A. P. S. Cox
	G-BKJB	PA-18 Super Cub 135	W. S. Stanley
	G-BKJF	MS.880B Rallye 100T	R. Neeson
	G-BKJS	Jodel D.120A	B. F. Baldock & T. J. Nicholson
	G-BKJW	PA-23 Aztec 250E	Alan Williams Entertainments Ltd
	G-BKKN	Cessna 182R	R A. Marven
	G-BKKO	Cessna 182R	E. L. King & D. S. Lightbown
	G-BKKZ	Pitts S-1D Special	P. G. Gabriele
	G-BKLO	Cessna F.172M	Stapleford Flying Club Ltd
	G-BKMA	Mooney M.20J Srs 201	Foxtrot Whisky Aviation
	G-BKMB	Mooney M.20J Srs 201	G-BKMB Flying Group
	G-BKMG	Handley Page O/400 (replica)	The Paralyser Group
	G-BKMT	PA-32R-301 Saratoga SP	P. Ashworth
	G-BKNO	Monnett Sonerai IIL	S. Hardy
	G-BKNP	Cameron V-77 balloon	P. Lesser/Sweden
	G-BKNZ	CP.301A Emeraude	J. A. Thomas
	G-BKOA	SOCATA MS.893E Rallye 180GT	M. Jarrett
	G-BKOB	Z.326 Trener Master	A. L. Rae
	G-BKOK	BN-2B-26 Islander	Cormack (Aircraft Services) Ltd
	G-BKOT	Wassmer Wa.81 Piranha	B. N. Rolfe
	G-BKOU	P.84 Jet Provost T.3 (XN637)	G-BKOU/2 Ltd
	G-BKPA	Hoffmann H-36 Dimona	J. D. Hanton & R. Matthews
	G-BKPB	Aerosport Scamp	B. R. Thompson
	G-BKPC	Cessna A.185F	P. D. Cavanagh & R. J. Illidge
	G-BKPD	Viking Dragonfly	E. P. Browne & G. J. Sargent
	G-BKPE	Jodel DR.250/160	M. Hales
	G-BKPS	AA-5B Tiger	A. E. T. Clarke
	G-BKPX	Jodel D.120A	D. M. Garrett & C. A. Jones
	G-BKPY	SAAB 91B/2 Safir (56321:U-AB) ★	Newark Air Museum
	G-BKPZ	Pitts S-1T Special	D. A. Slater
	G-BKRA	NA T-6G Texan (51-15227)	First Air Ltd
	G-BKRF	PA-18 Super Cub 95	R. Horner
	G-BKRH	Brügger MB.2 Colibri	M. R. Benwell
	G-BKRK	SNCAN Stampe SV.4C	Strathgadie Stampe Group
	G-BKRL	Chichester-Miles Leopard ★	Bournemouth Aviation Museum
	G-BKRN	Beechcraft D.18S (43-35943)	A. A. Marshall & P. L. Turland
	G-BKRZ	Dragon G-77 balloon	J. R. Barber
	G-BKSC	Saro Skeeter AOP.12 (XN351) ★	R. A. L. Falconer
	G-BKSD	Colt 56A balloon	R. L. Wright
	G-BKSE	QAC Quickie Q.1	M. D. Burns
	G-BKST	Rutan Vari-Eze	R. Towle
	G-BKSX	SNCAN Stampe SV.4C	C. A. Bailey & J. A. Carr
	G-BKTA	PA-18 Super Cub 95	M. J. Dyson
	G-BKTH	CCF Hawker Sea Hurricane IB (Z7015)	The Shuttleworth Collection
	G-BKTM	PZL SZD-45A Ogar	Hinton Ogar Group
	G-BKTV	Cessna F.152	ACS Aviation Ltd
	G-BKTZ	Slingsby T.67M Firefly	P. R. Elvidge (G-SFTV)
	G-BKUE	SOCATA TB9 Tampico	Fife TB9ers
	G-BKUI	D.31 Turbulent	E. Shouler
	G-BKUR	CP.301A Emeraude	T. Harvey
	G-BKVA	SOCATA Rallye 180T	Norfolk Gliding Club Ltd
	G-BKVC	SOCATA TB9 Tampico	J. P. Gough
	G-BKVF	FRED Srs 3	G. E. & R. E. Collins
	G-BKVG	Scheibe SF.25E Super Falke	G-BKVG Ltd
	G-BKVK	Auster AOP.9 (WZ662)	J. K. Houlgrave
	G-BKVL	Robin DR.400/160	Tatenhill Aviation Ltd
	G-BKVM	PA-18 Super Cub 150 (115684)	D. G. Caffrey
	G-BKVO	Pietenpol Air Camper	M. C. Hayes
	G-BKVP	Pitts S-1D Special	S. A. Smith
	G-BKVW	Airtour 56 balloon	L. D. & H. Vaughan
	G-BKWD	Taylor JT.2 Titch	J. F. Sully
	G-BKWR	Cameron V-65 balloon	Window on the World Ltd
	G-BKWY	Cessna F.152	Northumbria Flying School Ltd
	G-BKXA	Robin R.2100	M. Wilson
	G-BKXD	SA.365N Dauphin 2	CHC Scotia Ltd
	G-BKXF	PA-28R Cherokee Arrow 200	G. Booth
	G-BKXM	Colt 17A balloon	R. G. Turnbull
	G-BKXN	ICA-Brasov IS-28M2/80HP	R. J. S. Charnley

Reg.	Type	Owner or Operator	Notes
G-BKXO	Rutan LongEz	M. G. Parsons	
G-BKXP	Auster AOP.6	B. J. Ellis	
G-BKXR	D.31A Turbulent	G. C. Bridges	
G-BKZE	AS.332L Super Puma	CHC Scotia Ltd	
G-BKZF	Cameron V-56 balloon	C. F. Sanger-Davies	
G-BKZI	Bell 206B JetRanger 2	Bucklefields Business Devlopments Ltd	
G-BKZT	FRED Srs 2	U. Chakravorty	
G-BKZV	Bede BD-4A	T. S. Smith	
G-BLAC	Cessna FA.152	W. Ali	
G-BLAF	Stolp SA.900 V-Star	P. K. Dale	
G-BLAH	Thunder Ax7-77-1 balloon	T. M. Donnelly	
G-BLAI	Monnett Sonerai 2L	T. Simpon	
G-BLAM	Jodel DR.360	D. J. Durell	
G-BLAT	Jodel 150	G-BLAT Flying Group	
G-BLCC	Thunder Ax7-77Z balloon	W. J. Treacy & P. Murphy/Ireland	
G-BLCH	Colt 65D balloon	S. Charlish	
G-BLCI	EAA Acro Sport	M. R. Holden	
G-BLCM	SOCATA TB9 Tampico	B. Smith	
G-BLCT	Jodel DR.220 2+2	F. N. P. Maurin	
G-BLCU	Scheibe SF.25B Falke	Charlie Uniform Syndicate	
G-BLCV	Hoffmann H-36 Dimona	R. & M. Weaver	
G-BLCW	Evans VP-1	K. Lewis	
G-BLDB	Taylor JT.1 Monoplane	J. P. J. Hefford	
G-BLDD	WAG-Aero CUBy AcroTrainer	M. P. Wiseman	
G-BLDG	PA-25 Pawnee 260C	Ouse Gliding Club Ltd	
G-BLDK	Robinson R22	Flight Academy (Gyrocopters) Ltd	
G-BLDN	Rand-Robinson KR-2	P. R. Diffey	
G-BLDV	BN-2B-26 Islander	Loganair Ltd	
G-BLES	Stolp SA.750 Acroduster Too	C. J. Kingswood	
G-BLFI	PA-28-181 Archer II	Aerospares 2000 Ltd	
G-BLFZ	PA-31-310 Turbo Navajo C	London Executive Aviation Ltd	
G-BLGH	Robin DR.300/180R	Booker Gliding Club Ltd	
G-BLGS	SOCATA Rallye 180T	A. Waters	
G-BLGV	Bell 206B JetRanger 3	Patriot Flight Taining Ltd	
G-BLHH	Jodel DR.315	S. J. Luck	
G-BLHJ	Cessna F.172P	J. H. Sandham Aviation	
G-BLHM	PA-18 Super Cub 95	A. G. Edwards	
G-BLHN	Robin HR.100/285	K. A. & L. M. C. Payton	
G-BLHR	GA-7 Cougar	W. B. Orde-Powlett	
G-BLHS	Bellanca 7ECA Citabria	A. J. Wilkins	
G-BLHW	Varga 2150A Kachina	Wilburton Flying Group	
G-BLID	DH.112 Venom FB.50 (J-1605) ★	P. G. Vallance Ltd	
G-BLIK	Wallis WA-116/F/S	K. H. Wallis	
G-BLIT	Thorp T-18 CW	A. P. Tyrwhitt-Drake	
G-BLIW	P.56 Provost T.51 (177)	A. D. M. & K. B. Edie	
G-BLIX	Saro Skeeter Mk 12 (XL809)	K. M. Scholes	
G-BLIY	MS.892A Rallye Commodore	A. J. Brasher	
G-BLJM	Beech 95-B55 Baron	A. Nitsche/Germany	
G-BLJO	Cessna F.152	J. S. Develin & Z. Islam	
G-BLKA	DH.112 Venom FB.54 (WR410:N) ★	De Havilland Heritage Museum/London Colney	
G-BLKM	Jodel DR.1051	Kilo Mike Group	
G-BLKY	Beech 95-58 Baron	R. A. Perrot	
G-BLLA	Bensen B.8M	K. T. Donaghey	
G-BLLB	Bensen B.8M	D. H. Moss	
G-BLLD	Cameron O-77 balloon	G. Birchall	
G-BLLH	Jodel DR.220A 2+2	J. & J. K. Houlgrave	
G-BLLN	PA-18 Super Cub 95	N. M. Zullo	
G-BLLO	PA-18 Super Cub 95	D. G. Margetts	
G-BLLP	Slingsby T.67B	Air Navigation and Trading Co Ltd	
G-BLLR	Slingsby T.67B	R. L. Brinklow	
G-BLLS	Slingsby T.67B	D. McKendrick	
G-BLLW	Colt 56B balloon	G. Fordyce & ptnrs	
G-BLLZ	Rutan LongEz	R. S. Stoddart-Stones	
G-BLMA	Zlin 326 Trener Master	G. P. Northcott	
G-BLMC	Avro 698 Vulcan B.2A ★	Aeropark/East Midlands	
G-BLME	Robinson R22HP	Heli Air Ltd	
G-BLMG	Grob G.109B	Mike Golf Syndicate	
G-BLMI	PA-18-95 Super Cub	T. F. F. Van Erck	
G-BLMN	Rutan LongEz	XTR Design Ltd	
G-BLMP	PA-17 Vagabond	D. & M. Shrimpton.	
G-BLMR	PA-18 Super Cub 150	M. Vickers	
G-BLMT	PA-18 Super Cub 135	I. S. Runnalls	

Notes	Reg.	Type	Owner or Operator
	G-BLMW	T.66 Nipper 3	S. L. Millar
	G-BLMZ	Colt 105A balloon	M. D. Dickinson
	G-BLNO	FRED Srs 3	L. W. Smith
	G-BLOR	PA-30 Twin Comanche 160	R. L. C. Appleton
	G-BLOS	Cessna 185A (also flown with floats)	D. C. Minshaw
	G-BLOT	Colt Ax6-56B balloon	H. J. Anderson
	G-BLPA	Piper J-3C-65 Cub	A. C. Frost
	G-BLPB	Turner TSW Hot Two Wot	Papa Bravo Group
	G-BLPE	PA-18 Super Cub 95	A. A. Haig-Thomas
	G-BLPF	Cessna FR.172G	S. Culpin
	G-BLPG	Auster J/1N Alpha (16693:693)	Annic Marketing (G-AZIH)
	G-BLPH	Cessna FRA.150L	J. D. Baines
	G-BLPI	Slingsby T.67B	RAF Wyton Flying Group Ltd
	G-BLPP	Cameron V-77 balloon	G. B. Davies
	G-BLRA	BAe 146-100	BAE Systems (Corporate Air Teavel) Ltd
	G-BLRC	PA-18 Super Cub 135	Supercub Group
	G-BLRF	Slingsby T.67C	R. C. Nicholls
	G-BLRL	CP.301C-1 Emeraude	A. M. Smith
	G-BLRM	Glaser-Dirks DG.400	J. A. & W. S. Y. Stephen
	G-BLSD	DH.112 Venom FB.54 (J-1758) ★	R. Lamplough/North Weald
	G-BLSX	Cameron O-105 balloon	B. J. Petteford
	G-BLTA	Thunder Ax7-77A	K. A. Schlussler
	G-BLTC	D.31A Turbulent	S. J. Butler
	G-BLTK	Rockwell Commander 112TC	Commander TC Group
	G-BLTM	Robin HR.200/100	Barton Robin Group
	G-BLTN	Thunder Ax7-65 balloon	V. Michel
	G-BLTR	Scheibe SF.25B Falke	V. Mallon/Germany
	G-BLTS	Rutan LongEz	R. W. Cutler
	G-BLTV	Slingsby T.67B	R. L. Brinklow
	G-BLTW	Slingsby T.67B	Cheshire Air Training Services Ltd
	G-BLTY	Westland WG.30 Srs 160	D. Brem-Wilson
	G-BLUI	Thunder Ax7-65 balloon	S. Johnson
	G-BLUV	Grob G.109B	109 Flying Group
	G-BLUX	Slingsby T.67M Firefly 200	R. L. Brinklow
	G-BLUZ	DH.82B Queen Bee (LF858)	The Bee Keepers Group
	G-BLVB	Airtour AH-56 balloon	J. J. Daly
	G-BLVI	Slingsby T.67M Firefly Mk II	M. Power
	G-BLVK	CAARP CAP-10B	E. K. Coventry
	G-BLVL	PA-28-161 Warrior II	TG Aviation Ltd
	G-BLVS	Cessna 150M	D. H. G. Penney
	G-BLVW	Cessna F.172H	R. Holloway
	G-BLWD	PA-34-200T Seneca 2	Bencray Ltd
	G-BLWF	Robin HR.100/210	M. D. Parker
	G-BLWH	Fournier RF-6B-100	F. J. Hodson & C. C. Rollings
	G-BLWM	Bristol M.1C (replica) (C4994) ★	RAF Museum/Hendon
	G-BLWP	PA-38-112 Tomahawk	APB Leasing Ltd
	G-BLWT	Evans VP-1	N. Clark
	G-BLWY	Robin R.2160D	Charlie Yankee Ltd
	G-BLXA	SOCATA TB20 Trinidad	Trinidad Flyers Ltd
	G-BLXG	Colt 21A balloon	A. Walker
	G-BLXH	Fournier RF-3	R. H. W. A. Westerhuis
	G-BLXI	CP.1310-C3 Super Emeraude	R. Howard
	G-BLXO	Jodel 150	P. R. Powell
	G-BLYD	SOCATA TB20 Trinidad	Yankee Delta Corporation Ltd
	G-BLYP	Robin 3000/120	Weald Air Services
	G-BLYT	Airtour AH-77 balloon	I. J. Taylor & R. C. Kincaid
	G-BLZA	Scheibe SF.25B Falke	Zulu Alpha Syndicate
	G-BLZH	Cessna F.152 II	P. D'Costa
	G-BLZJ	Aerospatiale AS.332L Super Puma	Bristow Helicopters Ltd (G-PUMJ)
	G-BLZP	Cessna F.152	East Midlands Flying School Ltd
	G-BMAD	Cameron V-77 balloon	M. A. Stelling
	G-BMAO	Taylor JT.1 Monoplane	S. J. Alston
	G-BMAX	FRED Srs 2	D. A. Arkley
	G-BMAY	PA-18 Super Cub 135	R. W. Davies
	G-BMBB	Cessna F.150L	E. T. Hawkins
	G-BMBJ	Schempp-Hirth Janus CM	BJ Flying Group
	G-BMBZ	Scheibe SF.25E Super Falke	K. E. Ballington
	G-BMCC	Thunder Ax7-77 balloon	A. K. & C. M. Russell
	G-BMCD	Cameron V-65 balloon	R. Lillyman
	G-BMCG	Grob G.109B	D. K. R. Draper
	G-BMCI	Cessna F.172H	A. B. Davis
	G-BMCN	Cessna F.152	Cristal Air Ltd

Reg.	Type	Owner or Operator	Notes
G-BMCS	PA-22 Tri-Pacer 135	T. A. Hodges	
G-BMCV	Cessna F.152	Leicestershire Aero Club Ltd	
G-BMCX	AS.332L Super Puma	Bristow Southeast Asia Ltd	
G-BMDB	SE-5A (replica) (F235:B)	D. Biggs	
G-BMDE	Pietenpol AirCamper	P. B. Childs	
G-BMDJ	Price Ax7-77S balloon	R. A. Benham	
G-BMDK	PA-34-220T Seneca III	Air Medical Fleet Ltd	
G-BMDP	Partenavia P.64B Oscar 200	S. T. G. Lloyd	
G-BMDS	Jodel D.120	J. V. Thompson	
G-BMEA	PA-18 Super Cub 95	M. J. Butler	
G-BMEH	Jodel 150 Special Super Mascaret	R. J. & C. J. Lewis	
G-BMET	Taylor JT.1 Monoplane	M. K. A. Blyth	
G-BMEU	Isaacs Fury II	I. G. Harrison	
G-BMEX	Cessna A.150K	R. J. Grantham & D. Boatswain	
G-BMFD	PA-23 Aztec 250F	Giles Aviation Ltd (G-BGYY)	
G-BMFG	Dornier Do.27A-4	M. P. Wood	
G-BMFI	PZL SZD-45A Ogar	S. L. Morrey	
G-BMFP	PA-28-161 Warrior II	Bravo-Mike-Fox-Papa Group	
G-BMFU	Cameron N-90 balloon	J. J. Rudoni	
G-BMFY	Grob G.109B	P. J. Shearer	
G-BMGB	PA-28R Cherokee Arrow 200	Malmesbury Specialist Cars	
G-BMGC	Fairey Swordfish Mk II (W5856)	F.A.A. Museum/Yeovilton	
G-BMGG	Cessna 152 II	Falcon Flying Services	
G-BMGR	Grob G.109B	G-BMGR Group	
G-BMHA	Rutan LongEz	S. F. Elvins	
G-BMHC	Cessna U.206F	H. and R. Morley	
G-BMHL	Wittman W.8 Tailwind	H. J. Bennet	
G-BMHS	Cessna F.172M	Tango X-Ray Flying Group	
G-BMHT	PA-28RT-201T Turbo Arrow	G-BMHT Flying Group	
G-BMID	Jodel D.120	G-BMID Flying Group	
G-BMIG	Cessna 172N	BMIG Group	
G-BMIM	Rutan LongEz	R. M. Smith	
G-BMIO	Stoddard-Hamilton Glasair RG	P. Bint & L. McMahon	
G-BMIP	Jodel D.112	F. J. E. Brownsill	
G-BMIR	Westland Wasp HAS.1 (XT788) ★	Park Aviation Supply/Charlwood	
G-BMIS	Monnett Sonerai II	S. R. Edwards	
G-BMIV	PA-28R-201T Turbo Arrow III	Firmbeam Ltd	
G-BMIW	PA-28-181 Archer II	Oldbus Ltd	
G-BMIX	SOCATA TB20 Trinidad	Aviation Surrey Ltd	
G-BMIY	Oldfield Baby Great Lakes	J. B. Scott (G-NOME)	
G-BMIZ	Robinson R22 Beta	Heli Air Ltd	
G-BMJA	PA-32R-301 Saratoga SP	H. Merkado	
G-BMJB	Cessna 152	Endrick Aviation LLP	
G-BMJC	Cessna 152 II	T. Brogden	
G-BMJD	Cessna 152 II	Donair Flying Club Ltd	
G-BMJL	Rockwell Commander 114	D. J. & S. M. Hawkins	
G-BMJN	Cameron O-65 balloon	P. M. Traviss	
G-BMJO	PA-34-220T Seneca III	Fastnet Jet Alliance Ltd	
G-BMJR	Cessna T.337H	John Roberts Services Ltd (G-NOVA)	
G-BMJX	Wallis WA-116X	K. H. Wallis	
G-BMJY	Yakovlev C18M (07)	W. A. E. Moore	
G-BMKB	PA-18 Super Cub 135	Cubair Flight Training Ltd	
G-BMKC	Piper J-3C-65 Cub (329854:R-44)	J. Hirst	
G-BMKD	Beech C90A King Air	ATC (Lasham) Ltd	
G-BMKF	Jodel DR.221	S. T. & L. A. Gilbert	
G-BMKG	PA-38-112 Tomahawk II	ACS Aviation Ltd	
G-BMKJ	Cameron V-77 balloon	R. C. Thursby	
G-BMKK	PA-28R-200 Cherokee Arrow II	P. M. Murray	
G-BMKP	Cameron V-77 balloon	R. Bayly	
G-BMKR	PA-28-161 Warrior II	Field Flying Group (G-BGKR)	
G-BMKY	Cameron O-65 balloon	A. R. Rich	
G-BMLJ	Cameron N-77 balloon	C. J. Dunkley	
G-BMLK	Grob G.109B	Brams Syndicate	
G-BMLL	Grob G.109B	G-BMLL Flying Group	
G-BMLM	Beech 95-58 Baron	Atlantic Bridge Aviation Ltd	
G-BMLS	PA-28R-201 Arrow III	R. M. Shorter	
G-BMLT	Pietenpol Air Camper	W. E. R. Jenkins	
G-BMLW	Cameron O-77 balloon	M. L. & L. P. Willoughby	
G-BMLX	Cessna F.150L	J. P. A. Freeman	
G-BMMF	FRED Srs 2	R. C. Thomas	
G-BMMI	Pazmany PL.4A	P. I. Morgans	
G-BMMK	Cessna 182P	G. G. Weston	
G-BMMM	Cessna 152 II	Falcon Flying Services Ltd	

Notes	Reg.	Type	Owner or Operator
	G-BMGG	Grob G.109B	G-BMMP Ltd
	G-BMMV	ICA-Brasov IS-28M2A	C. D. King
	G-BMMW	Thunder Ax7-77 balloon	P. A. George
	G-BMNL	PA-28R Cherokee Arrow 200	Pearson Associates
	G-BMNV	SNCAN Stampe SV.4D	M. Moreau, J. de Naeyer & M. Nys
	G-BMOE	PA-28R Cherokee Arrow 200	Piper Leasing Ltd
	G-BMOF	Cessna U206G	Wild Geese Skydiving Centre
	G-BMOG	Thunder Ax7-77 balloon	R. M. Boswell
	G-BMOH	Cameron N-77 balloon	P. J. Marshall & M. A. Clarke
	G-BMOI	Partenavia P.68B	Ravenair Aircraft Ltd
	G-BMAD	ARV Super 2	R. E. Griffiths
	G-BMOL	PA-23 Aztec 250D	LDL Enterprises (G-BBSR)
	G-BMOT	Bensen B.8M	M. Fontolan
	G-BMPC	PA-28-181 Archer II	C. J. & R. J. Barnes
	G-BMPD	Cameron V-65 balloon	R. P. E. Phillips
	G-BMPL	Optica Industries OA.7 Optica	J. K. Edgley
	G-BMPP	Cameron N-77 balloon	The Sarnia Balloon Group
	G-BMPR	PA-28R-201 Arrow III	T. J. Brammer & D. T. Colley
	G-BMPS	Strojnik S-2A	G. J. Green
	G-BMPY	DH.82A Tiger Moth	N. M. Eisenstein
	G-BMRA	Boeing 757-236F	DHL Air Ltd
	G-BMRB	Boeing 757-236F	DHL Air Ltd
	G-BMRC	Boeing 757-236F	DHL Air Ltd
	G-BMRD	Boeing 757-236F	DHL Air Ltd
	G-BMRE	Boeing 757-236F	DHL Air Ltd
	G-BMRF	Boeing 757-236F	DHL Air Ltd
	G-BMRH	Boeing 757-236F	DHL Air Ltd
	G-BMRJ	Boeing 757-236F	DHL Air Ltd
	G-BMSB	VS.509 Spitfire IX (MJ627:9G-P)	M. S. Bayliss (G-ASOZ)
	G-BMSC	Evans VP-2	R. S. Acreman
	G-BMSD	PA-28-181 Archer II	H. Merkado
	G-BMSE	Valentin Taifun 17E	D. O'Donnell
	G-BMSF	PA-38-112 Tomahawk	D. A. Whitmore
	G-BMSG	SAAB 32A Lansen ★	J. E. Wilkie/Cranfield
	G-BMSL	FRED Srs 3	T. C. Darters
	G-BMTA	Cessna 152 II	ACS Aviation Ltd
	G-BMTB	Cessna 152 II	Sky Leisure Aviation (Charters) Ltd
	G-BMTC	AS.355F1 Twin Squirrel	Cambridge & Essex Air Support Unit (G-SASU/ G-BSSM/G-BKUK/G-EPOL)
	G-BMTJ	Cessna 152 II	The Pilot Centre Ltd
	G-BMTO	PA-38-112 Tomahawk	A. Sanja
	G-BMTU	Pitts S-1E Special	N. A. A. Pogmore
	G-BMTX	Cameron V-77 balloon	J. A. Langley
	G-BMUD	Cessna 182P	M. E. Taylor
	G-BMUG	Rutan LongEz	A. G. Sayers
	G-BMUJ	Colt Drachenfisch balloon	Virgin Airship & Balloon Co Ltd
	G-BMUO	Cessna A.152	Sky Leisure Aviation (Charters) Ltd
	G-BMUT	PA-34-200T Seneca II	G-DAD Air Ltd
	G-BMUU	Thunder Ax7-77 balloon	A. R. Hill
	G-BMUZ	PA-28-161 Warrior II	Northumbria Flying School Ltd
	G-BMVA	Scheibe SF.25B Falke	Kent Gliding Club Ltd
	G-BMVB	Cessna F.152	W. Ali
	G-BMVG	QAC Quickie Q.1	N. Ciattoni
	G-BMVL	PA-38-112 Tomahawk	D. R. C. Bell
	G-BMVM	PA-38-112 Tomahawk	Brimpton Flying Group
	G-BMVT	Thunder Ax7-77A balloon	M. L. & L. P. Willoughby
	G-BMVU	Monnett Moni	Stacey Aviation Ltd
	G-BMWF	ARV Super 2	G. E. Collard
	G-BMWR	Rockwell Commander 112	M. & J. Edwards
	G-BMWU	Cameron N-42 balloon ★	I. Chadwick
	G-BMWV	Putzer Elster B	Whiskey Victor Group
	G-BMXA	Cessna 152 II	ACS Aviation Ltd
	G-BMXB	Cessna 152 II	C. I. J. Young
	G-BMXC	Cessna 152 II	MK Aero Support Ltd
	G-BMYC	SOCATA TB10 Tobago	J. C. Woolard
	G-BMYG	Cessna FA.152	Greer Aviation Ltd
	G-BMYI	AA-5 Traveler	W. C. & S. C. Westran
	G-BMYU	Jodel D.120	A. J. L. Gordon
	G-BMZF	WSK-Mielec LiM-2 (MiG-15bis) (01420) ★	F.A.A. Museum/Yeovilton
	G-BMZN	Everett gyroplane	T. A. Holmes
	G-BMZS	Everett gyroplane	L. W. Cload
	G-BMZW	Bensen B.8MR	P. D. Widdicombe

Reg.	Type	Owner or Operator	Notes
G-BNAI	Wolf W-II Boredom Fighter (146-11083)	C. M. Bunn	
G-BNAJ	Cessna 152 II	Galair Ltd	
G-BNAN	Cameron V-65 balloon	Rango Balloon and Kite Company	
G-BNAW	Cameron V-65 balloon	A. Walker	
G-BNBW	Thunder Ax7-77 balloon	I. S. & S. W. Watthews	
G-BNBY	Beech 95-B55A Baron	J. Butler/France (G-AXXR)	
G-BNCB	Cameron V-77 balloon	C. W. Brown	
G-BNCM	Cameron N-77 balloon	C. A. Stone	
G-BNCO	PA-38-112 Tomahawk	D. K. Walker	
G-BNCR	PA-28-161 Warrior II	Booker Aircraft Leasing Ltd	
G-BNCS	Cessna 180	C. Elwell Transport Ltd	
G-BNCX	Hawker Hunter T.7 (XL621) ★	Brooklands Museum of Aviation/Weybridge	
G-BNCZ	Rutan LongEz	D. G. Foreman	
G-BNDE	PA-38-112 Tomahawk	B. R. Nurthen	
G-BNDG	Wallis WA-201/R Srs1	K. H. Wallis	
G-BNDN	Cameron V-77 balloon	A. Hornshaw	
G-BNDP	Brügger MB.2 Colibri	A. C. Barber	
G-BNDR	SOCATA TB10 Tobago	Monavion.fr	
G-BNDT	Brügger MB.2 Colibri	D. W. Rees	
G-BNDV	Cameron N-77 balloon	R. E. Jones	
G-BNEE	PA-28R-201 Arrow III	Britannic Management Aviation	
G-BNEL	PA-28-161 Warrior II	S. C. Westran	
G-BNEN	PA-34-200T Seneca II	CE Ventures Ltd	
G-BNEO	Cameron V-77 balloon	J. G. O'Connell	
G-BNEV	Viking Dragonfly	N. W. Eyre	
G-BNFG	Cameron O-77 balloon	Capital Balloon Club Ltd	
G-BNFN	Cameron N-105 balloon	P. Glydon	
G-BNFO	Cameron V-77 balloon	M. B. Young	
G-BNFP	Cameron O-84 balloon	M. Clarke	
G-BNFR	Cessna 152 II	A. Jahanfar	
G-BNFS	Cessna 152 II	S. J. Green	
G-BNFV	Robin DR.400/120	J. P. A. Freeman	
G-BNGE	Auster AOP.6 (TW536)	K. A. Hale	
G-BNGJ	Cameron N-77 balloon	S. W. K. Smeeton	
G-BNGN	Cameron N-77 balloon	N. Dykes	
G-BNGO	Thunder Ax7-77 balloon	J. S. Finlan	
G-BNGT	PA-28-181 Archer II	Edinburgh Flying Club Ltd	
G-BNGV	ARV Super 2	N. A. Onions & L. J. Russell	
G-BNGW	ARV Super 2	Southern Gas Turbines Ltd	
G-BNGY	ARV Super 2	J. & P. Morris (G-BMWL)	
G-BNHB	ARV Super 2	C. J. Challener	
G-BNHG	PA-38-112 Tomahawk II	Highland Aviation Training Ltd	
G-BNHJ	Cessna 152 II	The Pilot Centre Ltd	
G-BNHK	Cessna 152 II	Wayfarers Flying Group	
G-BNHL	Colt beer glass SS balloon	J. A. Viner	
G-BNHN	Colt Ariel Bottle SS balloon ★	British Balloon Museum	
G-BNHT	Fournier RF-3	G-BNHT Group	
G-BNID	Cessna 152 II	MK Aero Support Ltd	
G-BNII	Cameron N-90 balloon	Topless Balloon Group	
G-BNIK	Robin HR.200/120	G-BNIK Group	
G-BNIM	PA-38-112 Tomahawk	Air Claire Ltd	
G-BNIN	Cameron V-77 balloon	Cloud Nine Balloon Group	
G-BNIO	Luscombe 8A Silvaire	India Oscar Group	
G-BNIP	Luscombe 8A Silvaire	M. J. Diggins	
G-BNIU	Cameron O-77 balloon	Terre d'Envoi Blois Montgolfiere/France	
G-BNIV	Cessna 152 II	Cristal Air Ltd	
G-BNIW	Boeing Stearman PT-17	R. C. Goold	
G-BNJB	Cessna 152 II	Aerolease Ltd	
G-BNJC	Cessna 152 II	Stapleford Flying Club Ltd	
G-BNJH	Cessna 152 II	ACS Aviation Ltd	
G-BNJL	Bensen B.8MR	S. Ram	
G-BNJT	PA-28-161 Warrior II	Hawarden Flying Group	
G-BNJX	Cameron N-90 balloon	Mars UK Ltd	
G-BNKC	Cessna 152 II	Herefordshire Aero Club Ltd	
G-BNKD	Cessna 172N	P. J. Craig & A. D. Evans	
G-BNKE	Cessna 172N	Kilo Echo Flying Group	
G-BNKH	PA-38-112 Tomahawk	S. J. Miles	
G-BNKI	Cessna 152 II	RAF Halton Aeroplane Club Ltd	
G-BNKP	Cessna 152 II	Spectrum Leisure Ltd	
G-BNKR	Cessna 152 II	The Amphibious Flying Club Ltd	
G-BNKS	Cessna 152 II	APB Leasing Ltd	
G-BNKT	Cameron O-77 balloon	A. A. Brown	
G-BNKV	Cessna 152 II	Cristal Air Ltd	

Notes	Reg.	Type	Owner or Operator
	G-BNLA	Boeing 747-436	British Airways
	G-BNLD	Boeing 747-436	British Airways
	G-BNLE	Boeing 747-436	British Airways
	G-BNLF	Boeing 747-436	British Airways
	G-BNLG	Boeing 747-436	British Airways
	G-BNLH	Boeing 747-436	British Airways
	G-BNLI	Boeing 747-436	British Airways
	G-BNLJ	Boeing 747-436	British Airways
	G-BNLK	Boeing 747-436	British Airways
	G-BNLL	Boeing 747-436	British Airways
	G-BNLM	Boeing 747-436	British Airways
	G-BNLN	Boeing 747-436	British Airways
	G-BNLO	Boeing 747-436	British Airways
	G-BNLP	Boeing 747-436	British Airways
	G-BNLR	Boeing 747-436	British Airways
	G-BNLS	Boeing 747-436	British Airways
	G-BNLT	Boeing 747-436	British Airways
	G-BNLU	Boeing 747-436	British Airways
	G-BNLV	Boeing 747-436	British Airways
	G-BNLW	Boeing 747-436	British Airways
	G-BNLX	Boeing 747-436	British Airways
	G-BNLY	Boeing 747-436	British Airways
	G-BNLZ	Boeing 747-436	British Airways
	G-BNMB	PA-28-151 Warrior	Azure Flying Club Ltd
	G-BNMD	Cessna 152 II	T. M. Jones
	G-BNME	Cessna 152 II	M. Bonsall
	G-BNMF	Cessna 152 II	Redhill Air Services Ltd
	G-BNMH	Pietenpol Air Camper	N. M. Hitchman
	G-BNMI	Colt Flying Fantasy SS balloon	Air 2 Air Ltd
	G-BNML	Rand-Robinson KR-2	P. J. Brookman
	G-BNMO	Cessna TR.182RG	T. W. Gale & S. R. Whitling
	G-BNMX	Thunder Ax7-77 balloon	S. A. D. Beard
	G-BNNA	Stolp SA.300 Starduster Too	Banana Group
	G-BNNE	Cameron N-77 balloon	R. D. Allen, L. P. Hooper & M. J. Streat
	G-BNNO	PA-28-161 Warrior II	I. A. Anderson
	G-BNNT	PA-28-151 Warrior	S. T. Gilbert & D. J. Kirkwood
	G-BNNU	PA-38-112 Tomahawk	Lomac Aviators Ltd
	G-BNNX	PA-28R-201T Turbo Arrow III	Bristol Flying Centre Ltd
	G-BNNY	PA-28-161 Warrior II	Falcon Flying Services
	G-BNNZ	PA-28-161 Warrior II	R. West
	G-BNOB	Wittman W.8 Tailwind	D. G. Hammersley
	G-BNOF	PA-28-161 Warrior II	Tayside Aviation Ltd
	G-BNOH	PA-28-161 Warrior II	Sherburn Aero Club Ltd
	G-BNOJ	PA-28-161 Warrior II	BAE Systems (Warton) Flying Club Ltd
	G-BNOM	PA-28-161 Warrior II	J. H. Sandham Aviation
	G-BNON	PA-28-161 Warrior II	Tayside Aviation Ltd
	G-BNOP	PA-28-161 Warrior II	BAE Systems (Warton) Flying Club Ltd
	G-BNPE	Cameron N-77 balloon	R. N. Simpkins
	G-BNPF	Slingsby T.31M	S. Luck & ptnrs
	G-BNPH	P.66 Pembroke C.1 (WV740)	M. A. Stott
	G-BNPM	PA-38-112 Tomahawk	Papa Mike Aviation
	G-BNPO	PA-28-181 Archer II	NPAS Ltd
	G-BNPV	Bowers Fly-Baby 1B	J. G. Day
	G-BNPY	Cessna 152 II	G. Tennant
	G-BNRA	SOCATA TB10 Tobago	Double D Airgroup
	G-BNRG	PA-28-161 Warrior II	Glenn Aviation Ltd
	G-BNRL	Cessna 152 II	Bulldog Aviation Ltd
	G-BNRP	PA-28-181 Archer II	PA-28 Warrior Ltd
	G-BNRR	Cessna 172P	Wentworth Productions
	G-BNRX	PA-34-200T Seneca II	Truman Aviation Ltd
	G-BNRY	Cessna 182Q	K. F. & S. J. Farey
	G-BNSG	PA-28R-201 Arrow III	The Leicestershire Aero Club Ltd
	G-BNSI	Cessna 152 II	Sky Leisure Aviation (Charters) Ltd
	G-BNSL	PA-38-112 Tomahawk II	Lomac Aviators Ltd
	G-BNSM	Cessna 152 II	Cornwall Flying Club Ltd
	G-BNSN	Cessna 152 II	The Pilot Centre Ltd
	G-BNSO	Slingsby T.67M Firefly Mk II	R. M. Rennoldson
	G-BNSP	Slingsby T.67M Firefly Mk II	N. J. Heard
	G-BNSR	Slingsby T.67M Firefly Mk II	Slingsby SR Group
	G-BNST	Cessna 172N	CSG Bodyshop
	G-BNSU	Cessna 152 II	Channel Aviation Ltd
	G-BNSV	Cessna 152 II	Channel Aviation Ltd
	G-BNSY	PA-28-161 Warrior II	R. A. Brown

Reg.	Type	Owner or Operator	Notes
G-BNSZ	PA-28-161 Warrior II	H. Merkado	
G-BNTC	PA-28RT-201T Turbo Arrow IV	M. Iqbal	
G-BNTD	PA-28-161 Warrior II	S. Ramsden	
G-BNTP	Cessna 172N	Westnet Ltd	
G-BNTZ	Cameron N-77 balloon	Balloon Team	
G-BNUL	Cessna 152 II	Big Red Kite Ltd	
G-BNUN	Beech 95-58PA Baron	SMB Aviation Ltd	
G-BNUO	Beech 76 Duchess	Pace Projects Ltd and Professional Flight Simulation Ltd	
G-BNUT	Cessna 152 Turbo	Stapleford Flying Club Ltd	
G-BNUX	Hoffmann H-36 Dimona	Buckminster Dimona Syndicate	
G-BNUY	PA-38-112 Tomahawk II	D. C. Storey	
G-BNVB	AA-5A Cheetah	Pelican Project Management Ltd	
G-BNVE	PA-28-181 Archer II	Take Flight Aviation Ltd	
G-BNVT	PA-28R-201T Turbo Arrow III	Victor Tango Group	
G-BNWA	Boeing 767-336ER	British Airways	
G-BNWB	Boeing 767-336ER	British Airways	
G-BNWC	Boeing 767-336ER	British Airways	
G-BNWD	Boeing 767-336ER	British Airways	
G-BNWH	Boeing 767-336ER	British Airways	
G-BNWI	Boeing 767-336ER	British Airways	
G-BNWM	Boeing 767-336ER	British Airways	
G-BNWN	Boeing 767-336ER	British Airways	
G-BNWO	Boeing 767-336ER	British Airways	
G-BNWR	Boeing 767-336ER	British Airways	
G-BNWS	Boeing 767-336ER	British Airways	
G-BNWT	Boeing 767-336ER	British Airways	
G-BNWU	Boeing 767-336ER	British Airways	
G-BNWV	Boeing 767-336ER	British Airways	
G-BNWW	Boeing 767-336ER	British Airways	
G-BNWX	Boeing 767-336ER	British Airways	
G-BNWY	Boeing 767-336ER	British Airways	
G-BNWZ	Boeing 767-336ER	British Airways	
G-BNXE	PA-28-161 Warrior II	M. S. Brown	
G-BNXK	Nott-Cameron ULD-3 balloon	J. R. P. Nott (G-BLJN)	
G-BNXL	Glaser-Dirks DG.400	M. Lee	
G-BNXM	PA-18 Super Cub 95	C. J. Gowthorpe	
G-BNXU	PA-28-161 Warrior II	Friendly Warrior Group	
G-BNXV	PA-38-112 Tomahawk	W. B. Bateson	
G-BNXX	SOCATA TB20 Trinidad	J. C. Taylor	
G-BNXZ	Thunder Ax7-77 balloon	Hale Hot Air Balloon Group	
G-BNYD	Bell 206B JetRanger 3	Aerospeed Ltd	
G-BNYK	PA-38-112 Tomahawk	Lomac Aviators Ltd	
G-BNYL	Cessna 152 II	V. J. Freeman	
G-BNYM	Cessna 172N	Kestrel Syndicate	
G-BNYO	Beech 76 Duchess	Multiflight Ltd	
G-BNYP	PA-28-181 Archer II	R. D. Cooper	
G-BNYZ	SNCAN Stampe SV.4E	Bianchi Film Aviation Services Ltd	
G-BNZB	PA-28-161 Warrior II	Falcon Flying Services Ltd	
G-BNZC	DHC.1 Chipmunk 22 (18671:671)	The Shuttleworth Collection	
G-BNZK	Thunder Ax7-77 balloon	T. D. Marsden	
G-BNZL	Rotorway Scorpion 133	J. R. Wraight	
G-BNZM	Cessna T.210N	A. J. M. Freeman	
G-BNZN	Cameron N-56 balloon	H. B. Pilo/Sweden	
G-BNZO	Rotorway Executive	J. S. David	
G-BNZV	PA-25 Pawnee 235	Aeroklub Alpski Letalski Center Lesce/Slovenia	
G-BNZZ	PA-28-161 Warrior II	Providence Aviation Ltd	
G-BOAA	BAC-Aérospatiale Concorde 102 ★	Museum Of Flight East Fortune (G-N94AA)	
G-BOAB	BAC-Aérospatiale Concorde 102 ★	Preserved at Heathrow (G-N94AB)	
G-BOAC	BAC-Aérospatiale Concorde 102 ★	Displayed in viewing area Manchester International (G-N81AC)	
G-BOAF	BAC-Aérospatiale Concorde 102 ★	Bristol Aero Collection/Filton (G-N94AF)	
G-BOAH	PA-28-161 Warrior II	Aircraft Engineers Ltd	
G-BOAI	Cessna 152 II	Aviation Spirit Ltd	
G-BOAL	Cameron V-65 balloon	N. H. & A. M. Ponsford	
G-BOAU	Cameron V-77 balloon	G. T. Barstow	
G-BOBA	PA-28R-201 Arrow III	Bravo Aviation Ltd	
G-BOBR	Cameron N-77 balloon	Trigger Concepts Ltd	
G-BOBT	Stolp SA.300 Starduster Too	G-BOBT Group	
G-BOBV	Cessna F.150M	M. Buxton	
G-BOBY	Monnett Sonerai II	R. G. Hallam	
G-BOCG	PA-34-200T Seneca II	Oxford Aviation Academy (Oxford) Ltd	

Notes	Reg.	Type	Owner or Operator
	G-BOCI	Cessna 140A	Charlie India Aviators
	G-BOCK	Sopwith Triplane (replica) (N6290)	The Shuttleworth Collection
	G-BOCL	Slingsby T.67C	Richard Brinklow Aviation Ltd
	G-BOCM	Slingsby T.67C	Richard Brinklow Aviation Ltd
	G-BOCN	Robinson R22 Beta	Northmore Aviation Ltd
	G-BODB	PA-28-161 Warrior II	Sherburn Aero Club Ltd
	G-BODD	PA-28-161 Warrior II	L. W. Scattergood
	G-BODE	PA-28-161 Warrior II	Sherburn Aero Club Ltd
	G-BODI	Glasair III Model SH-3R	A. P. Durston
	G-BODO	Cessna 152	Enstone Sales and Services Ltd
	G-BODP	PA-38-112 Tomahawk	Flintshire Flying School Ltd
	G-BODR	PA-28-161 Warrior II	Booker Aircraft Leasing Ltd
	G-BODS	PA-38-112 Tomahawk	Coulson Flying Services Ltd
	G-BODT	Jodel D.18	L. D. McPhillips
	G-BODU	Scheibe SF.25C Falke	Hertfordshire County Scout Council
	G-BODY	Cessna 310R	Reconnaissance Ventures Ltd
	G-BODZ	Robinson R22 Beta	Langley Aviation Ltd
	G-BOEE	PA-28-181 Archer II	J. C. & G. M. Brinkley
	G-BOEH	Jodel DR.340	Piper Flyers Group
	G-BOEK	Cameron V-77 balloon	R. I. M. Kerr & ptnrs
	G-BOEM	Pitts S-2A	M. Murphy
	G-BOEN	Cessna 172M	G-BOEN Flying Group
	G-BOER	PA-28-161 Warrior II	B. Boult
	G-BOET	PA-28RT-201 Arrow IV	B. C. Chambers (G-IBEC)
	G-BOFC	Beech 76 Duchess	Magenta Ltd
	G-BOFF	Cameron N-77 balloon	R. S. McKibbin
	G-BOFL	Cessna 152 II	GEM Integrated Solutions Ltd
	G-BOFM	Cessna 152 II	GEM Integrated Solutions Ltd
	G-BOFW	Cessna A.150M	D. F. Donovan
	G-BOFY	PA-28 Cherokee 140	R. A. Brown
	G-BOFZ	PA-28-161 Warrior II	Northumbria Flying School Ltd
	G-BOGI	Robin DR.400/180	A. L. M. Shepherd
	G-BOGK	ARV Super 2	M. K. Field
	G-BOGM	PA-28RT-201T Turbo Arrow IV	G. Marsango
	G-BOGO	PA-32R-301 Saratoga SP	Diff Air KFT
	G-BOGY	Cameron V-77 balloon	A. Reimann & P. Spellward
	G-BOHA	PA-28-161 Warrior II	Phoenix Aviation
	G-BOHD	Colt 77A balloon	D. B. Court
	G-BOHH	Cessna 172N	ASL Aviation
	G-BOHI	Cessna 152 II	Cirrus Aviation Ltd
	G-BOHJ	Cessna 152 II	Airlaunch
	G-BOHM	PA-28 Cherokee 180	B. F. Keogh & R. A. Scott
	G-BOHO	PA-28-161 Warrior II	Egressus Flying Group
	G-BOHR	PA-28-151 Warrior	R. M. E. Garforth
	G-BOHT	PA-38-112 Tomahawk	St. George Flight Training Ltd
	G-BOHV	Wittman W.8 Tailwind	D. H. Greenwood
	G-BOHW	Van's RV-4	A. Mercy
	G-BOIB	Wittman W.10 Tailwind	C. R. Nash
	G-BOIC	PA-28R-201T Turbo Arrow III	M. J. Pearson
	G-BOID	Bellanca 7ECA Citabria	D. Mallinson
	G-BOIG	PA-28-161 Warrior II	D. Vallence-Pell
	G-BOIK	Air Command 503 Commander	F. G. Shepherd
	G-BOIL	Cessna 172N	Upperstack Ltd
	G-BOIO	Cessna 152	Sandham Aviation
	G-BOIR	Cessna 152	APB Leasing Ltd
	G-BOIT	SOCATA TB10 Tobago	G-BOIT Flying Group
	G-BOIV	Cessna 150M	India Victor Group
	G-BOIX	Cessna 172N	JR Flying Ltd
	G-BOIY	Cessna 172N	L. W. Scattergood
	G-BOIZ	PA-34-200T Seneca II	S. F. Tebby & Son
	G-BOJB	Cameron V-77 balloon	I. M. & S. D. Warner
	G-BOJI	PA-28RT-201 Arrow IV	Arrow Two Group
	G-BOJK	PA-34-220T Seneca III	Omega Sky Taxi Ltd (G-BRUF)
	G-BOJM	PA-28-181 Archer II	R. P. Emms
	G-BOJS	Cessna 172P	Paul's Planes Ltd
	G-BOJW	PA-28-161 Warrior II	J. R. Pearce
	G-BOJZ	PA-28-161 Warrior II	Falcon Flying Services
	G-BOKA	PA-28-201T Turbo Dakota	CBG Aviation Ltd
	G-BOKB	PA-28-161 Warrior II	Apollo Aviation Advisory Ltd
	G-BOKH	Whittaker MW7	I. Pearson
	G-BOKW	Bolkow Bo.208C Junior	L. S. Johnson
	G-BOKX	PA-28-161 Warrior II	Shenley Farms (Aviation) Ltd
	G-BOKY	Cessna 152 II	D. F. F. & J. E. Poore

Reg.	Type	Owner or Operator	Notes
G-BOLB	Taylorcraft BC-12-65	C. E. Tudor	
G-BOLC	Fournier RF-6B-100	J. D. Cohen	
G-BOLD	PA-38-112 Tomahawk	G-BOLD Group	
G-BOLE	PA-38-112 Tomahawk	Double S Group	
G-BOLG	Bellanca 7KCAB Citabria	B. R. Pearson	
G-BOLI	Cessna 172P	Boli Flying Club	
G-BOLL	Lake LA-4 Skimmer	M. C. Holmes	
G-BOLN	Colt 21A balloon	G. Everett	
G-BOLO	Bell 206B JetRanger	Hargreaves Leasing Ltd	
G-BOLP	Colt 21A balloon	Spirit Balloons Ltd	
G-BOLR	Colt 21A balloon	C. J. Sanger-Davies	
G-BOLS	FRED Srs 2	I. F. Vaughan	
G-BOLT	Rockwell Commander 114	I. R. Harnett	
G-BOLU	Robin R.3000/120	Grosvenor Aircraft Ltd	
G-BOLV	Cessna 152 II	Synergy Aircraft Leasing Ltd	
G-BOLW	Cessna 152 II	G-BOLW Flying Group	
G-BOLY	Cessna 172N	I. R. Chaplin	
G-BOMB	Cassutt Racer IIIM	D. Hart	
G-BOMN	Cessna 150F	P. A. Chamberlaine	
G-BOMO	PA-38-112 Tomahawk II	APB Leasing Ltd	
G-BOMP	PA-28-181 Archer II	H. Merkado	
G-BOMS	Cessna 172N	Penchant Ltd	
G-BOMU	PA-28-181 Archer II	J. Sawyer	
G-BOMY	PA-28-161 Warrior II	BOMY Group	
G-BOMZ	PA-38-112 Tomahawk	G-BOMZ Aviation	
G-BONC	PA-28RT-201 Arrow IV	G-BONC Holdings Group	
G-BONG	Enstrom F-28A-UK	Chobham Helicopters Ltd	
G-BONP	CFM Streak Shadow	G. J. Chater	
G-BONR	Cessna 172N	D. I. Craikl	
G-BONS	Cessna 172N	BONS Group	
G-BONT	Slingsby T.67M Mk II	Etico	
G-BONU	Slingsby T.67B	R. L. Brinklow	
G-BONW	Cessna 152 II	Lincoln Aero Club Ltd	
G-BONY	Denney Kitfox Model 1	R. Dunn & P. F. Hill	
G-BONZ	Beech V35B Bonanza	P. M. Coulten	
G-BOOB	Cameron N-65 balloon	P. J. Hooper	
G-BOOC	PA-18 Super Cub 150	S. A. C. Whitcombe	
G-BOOD	Slingsby T.31M Motor Tutor	P. K. Jenkins	
G-BOOE	GA-7 Cougar	R. J. Moller	
G-BOOF	PA-28-181 Archer II	H. Merkado	
G-BOOG	PA-28RT-201T Turbo Arrow IV	Simair Ltd	
G-BOOH	Jodel D.112	J. G. Bright	
G-BOOI	Cessna 152	Stapleford Flying Club Ltd	
G-BOOL	Cessna 172N	Wicklow Wings	
G-BOOW	Aerosport Scamp	D. A. Weldon/Ireland	
G-BOOX	Rutan LongEz	I. R. Wilde	
G-BOOZ	Cameron N-77 balloon	J. E. F. Kettley	
G-BOPA	PA-28-181 Archer II	Flyco Ltd	
G-BOPC	PA-28-161 Warrior II	Aeros Ltd	
G-BOPD	Bede BD-4	S. T. Dauncey	
G-BOPH	Cessna TR.182RG	J. M. Mitchell	
G-BOPO	Brooklands OA.7 Optica	J. K. Edgley	
G-BOPR	Brooklands OA.7 Optica	Aeroelvira Ltd	
G-BOPT	Grob G.115	LAC Flying School	
G-BOPU	Grob G.115	LAC Flying School	
G-BORB	Cameron V-77 balloon	M. H. Wolff	
G-BORD	Thunder Ax7-77 balloon	Western Region British Balloon and Airship Club Ltd	
G-BORE	Colt 77A balloon	J. D. & C. J. Medcalf	
G-BORG	Campbell Cricket	R. L. Gilmore	
G-BORK	PA-28-161 Warrior II	The Warrior Group (G-IIIC)	
G-BORL	PA-28-161 Warrior II	Westair Flying School Ltd	
G-BORM	HS.748 Srs 2B ★	Airport Fire Service/Exeter	
G-BORN	Cameron N-77 balloon	I. Chadwick	
G-BORS	PA-28-181 Archer II	Aircraft Grouping Ltd	
G-BORW	Cessna 172P	Briter Aviation Ltd	
G-BORY	Cessna 150L	D. H. G. Penney	
G-BOSB	Thunder Ax7-77 balloon	G. Bann	
G-BOSD	PA-34-200T Seneca II	Bristol Flying Centre Ltd	
G-BOSE	PA-28-181 Archer II	G-BOSE Group	
G-BOSJ	Nord 3400 (124)	A. I. Milne	
G-BOSM	Jodel DR.253B	A. G. Stevens	
G-BOSN	AS.355F1 Twin Squirrel	Helicopter Services	

Notes	Reg.	Type	Owner or Operator
	G-BOSO	Cessna A.152	J. S. Develin & Z. Islam
	G-BOTD	Cameron O-105 balloon	J. Taylor
	G-BOTF	PA-28-151 Warrior	G-BOTF Group
	G-BOTG	Cessna 152 II	Donington Aviation Ltd
	G-BOTH	Cessna 182Q	P. E. Gethin
	G-BOTI	PA-28-151 Warrior	Falcon Flying Services
	G-BOTK	Cameron O-105 balloon	N. Woodham
	G-BOTN	PA-28-161 Warrior II	Apollo Aviation Advisory
	G-BOTO	Bellanca 7ECA Citabria	G-BOTO Group
	G-BOTP	Cessna 150J	R. F. Finnis & C. P. Williams
	G-BOTU	Piper J-3C-65 Cub	T. L. Giles
	G-BOTV	PA-32RT-300 Lance II	Robin Lance Aviation Association Ltd
	G-BOTW	Cameron V-77 balloon	M. R. Jeynes
	G-BOUE	Cessna 172N	P. Gray & G. N. R. Bradley
	G-BOUF	Cessna 172N	B. P. & M. I. Sneap
	G-BOUJ	Cessna 150M	The UJ Flying Group
	G-BOUK	PA-34-200T Seneca II	C. J. & R. J. Barnes
	G-BOUL	PA-34-200T Seneca II	Oxford Aviation Academy (Oxford) Ltd
	G-BOUM	PA-34-200T Seneca II	Oxford Aviation Academy (Oxford) Ltd
	G-BOUN	Rand-Robinson KR-2	P. J. Brookman
	G-BOUT	Colomban MC.12 Cri-Cri	C. K. Farley
	G-BOUV	Bensen B.8MR	L. R. Phillips
	G-BOUZ	Cessna 150G	Atlantic Bridge Aviation Ltd
	G-BOVB	PA-15 Vagabond	J. R. Kimberley
	G-BOVK	PA-28-161 Warrior II	Multiflight Ltd
	G-BOVU	Stoddard-Hamilton Glasair III	B. R. Chaplin
	G-BOVX	Hughes 269C	Arrow Aviation Services Ltd
	G-BOWB	Cameron V-77 balloon	R. A. Benham
	G-BOWE	PA-34-200T Seneca II	Oxford Aviation Academy (Oxford) Ltd
	G-BOWM	Cameron V-56 balloon	R. S. Breakwell
	G-BOWN	PA-12 Super Cruiser	T. L. Giles
	G-BOWO	Cessna R.182	D. A. H. Morris (G-BOTR)
	G-BOWP	Jodel D.120A	J. M. Pearson
	G-BOWV	Cameron V-65 balloon	R. A. Harris
	G-BOWY	PA-28RT-201T Turbo Arrow IV	J. S. Develin & Z. Islam
	G-BOXA	PA-28-161 Warrior II	Channel Islands Aero Club (Jersey) Ltd
	G-BOXC	PA-28-161 Warrior II	Bravo Aviation Ltd
	G-BOXG	Cameron O-77 balloon	Associazione Sportiva Dilettantistica Billy Farm- Cico Farm
	G-BOXH	Pitts S-1S Special	G. R. Cotterell
	G-BOXJ	Piper J-3C-65 Cub (479897)	A. Bendkowski
	G-BOXR	GA-7 Cougar	Plane Talking Ltd
	G-BOXT	Hughes 269C	Goldenfly Ltd
	G-BOXV	Pitts S-1S Special	C. Waddington
	G-BOXW	Cassutt Racer Srs IIIM	D. I. Johnson
	G-BOYB	Cessna A.152	Modi Aviation Ltd
	G-BOYC	Robinson R22 Beta	Yorkshire Helicopters
	G-BOYF	Sikorsky S-76B	Darley Stud Management Co Ltd
	G-BOYH	PA-28-151 Warrior	R. Nightingale
	G-BOYI	PA-28-161 Warrior II	G-BOYI Group
	G-BOYL	Cessna 152 II	Redhill Air Services Ltd
	G-BOYM	Cameron O-84 balloon	M. P. Ryan
	G-BOYO	Cameron V-20 balloon	J. L. Hilditch & T. Ward
	G-BOYP	Cessna 172N	I. D. & D. Brierley
	G-BOYV	PA-28R-201T Turbo Arrow III	N. Halsall
	G-BOYX	Robinson R22 Beta	R. Towle
	G-BOZI	PA-28-161 Warrior II	Aerolease Ltd
	G-BOZN	Cameron N-77 balloon	Calarel Developments Ltd
	G-BOZO	AA-5B Tiger	J. Willis
	G-BOZR	Cessna 152 II	GEM Integrated Solutions Ltd
	G-BOZS	Pitts S-1C Special	S. D. Blakey
	G-BOZV	CEA DR.340 Major	C. J. Turner & S. D. Kent
	G-BOZW	Bensen B.8M	M. E. Wills
	G-BOZY	Cameron RTW-120 balloon	Magical Adventures Ltd
	G-BOZZ	AA-5B Tiger	Dolphin Property (Management) Ltd
	G-BPAA	Acro Advanced	B. O. & F. A. Smith
	G-BPAB	Cessna 150M	M. T. Farmer
	G-BPAF	PA-28-161 Warrior II	S. T. & T. W. Gilbert
	G-BPAJ	DH.82A Tiger Moth	P. A. Jackson (G-AOIX)
	G-BPAL	DHC.1 Chipmunk 22 (WG350)	K. F. & P. Tomsett (G-BCYE)
	G-BPAW	Cessna 150M	G-BPAW Group
	G-BPAY	PA-28-181 Archer II	H. Merkado

Reg.	Type	Owner or Operator	Notes
G-BPBJ	Cessna 152 II	W. Shaw & P. G. Haines	
G-BPBK	Cessna 152 II	Swiftair Maintenance Ltd	
G-BPBM	PA-28-161 Warrior II	Redhill Air Services Ltd	
G-BPBO	PA-28RT-201T Turbo Arrow IV	S. R. Eagle	
G-BPBP	Brügger MB.2 Colibri	D. A. Preston	
G-BPBW	Cameron O-105 balloon	T. J. Wilkinson	
G-BPCA	BN-2B-26 Islander	Loganair Ltd (G-BLNX)	
G-BPCE	Piper J-3C-65 Cub	B. M. O'Brien	
G-BPCI	Cessna R.172K	N. A. Bairstol	
G-BPCK	PA-28-161 Warrior II	Compton Abbas Airfield Ltd	
G-BPCL	SA Bulldog Srs 120/128 (HKG-6)	Isohigh Ltd	
G-BPCR	Mooney M.20K	T. & R. Harris	
G-BPCX	PA-28-236 Dakota	Blue Yonder Aviation Ltd	
G-BPDE	Colt 56A balloon	J. E. Weidema/Netherlands	
G-BPDJ	Chris Tena Mini Coupe	J. J. Morrissey	
G-BPDM	CASA 1.131E Jungmann 2000(781-32)	J. D. Haslam	
G-BPDT	PA-28-161 Warrior II	Channel Islands Aero Club (Jersey) Ltd	
G-BPDV	Pitts S-1S Special	G-BPDV Syndicate	
G-BPEM	Cessna 150K	D. Wright	
G-BPEO	Cessna 152 II	Global Skies Ltd	
G-BPES	PA-38-112 Tomahawk II	Sherwood Flying Club Ltd	
G-BPEZ	Colt 77A balloon	J. W. Adkins	
G-BPFC	Mooney M.20C	It's Plane Crazy Ltd	
G-BPFD	Jodel D.112	M. & S. Mills	
G-BPFH	PA-28-161 Warrior II	M. H. Kleiser	
G-BPFI	PA-28-181 Archer II	F. Teagle	
G-BPFL	Davis DA-2	P. E. Barker	
G-BPFM	Aeronca 7AC Champion	D. Boyce	
G-BPFZ	Cessna 152 II	Devon and Somerset Flight Training Ltd	
G-BPGC	Air Command 532 Elite	A. G. W. Davis	
G-BPGD	Cameron V-65 balloon	Gone With The Wind Ltd	
G-BPGE	Cessna U.206C	Scottish Parachute Club	
G-BPGH	EAA Acro Sport II	R. Clark & A. C. May	
G-BPGK	Aeronca 7AC Champion	D. A. Crompton & G. C. Holmes	
G-BPGT	Colt AS-80 Mk II airship	P. Porati/Italy	
G-BPGU	PA-28-181 Archer II	G. Underwood	
G-BPGZ	Cessna 150G	J. B. Scott	
G-BPHG	Robin DR.400/180	B. Brenton	
G-BPHH	Cameron V-77 balloon	C. D. Aindow	
G-BPHI	PA-38-112 Tomahawk	J. S. Devlin & Z. Islam	
G-BPHJ	Cameron V-77 balloon	C. W. Brown	
G-BPHK	Whittaker MW7	J. S. Shufflebottom	
G-BPHL	PA-28-161 Warrior II	J. D. Swales	
G-BPHO	Taylorcraft BC-12	B. J. Swanton	
G-BPHP	Taylorcraft BC-12-65	Bluebird Group	
G-BPHR	DH.82A Tiger Moth (A17-48)	N. Parry	
G-BPHU	Thunder Ax7-77 balloon	R. P. Waite	
G-BPHX	Cessna 140	M. J. Medland	
G-BPHZ	MS.505 Criquet (DM+BK)	Aero Vintage Ltd	
G-BPIF	Bensen-Parsons 2-place gyroplane	B. J. L. P. & W. J. A. L. de Saar	
G-BPII	Denney Kitfox	T. P. Lowe	
G-BPIK	PA-38-112 Tomahawk	Carlisle Flight Training Ltd	
G-BPIP	Slingsby T.31 Motor Cadet III	V. K. Meers	
G-BPIR	Scheibe SF.25E Super Falke	A. P. Askwith	
G-BPIT	Robinson R22 Beta	NA Air Ltd	
G-BPIU	PA-28-161 Warrior II	Golf India Uniform Group	
G-BPIV	B.149 Bolingbroke Mk IVT (R3821)	Blenheim (Duxford) Ltd	
G-BPIZ	AA-5B Tiger	D. A. Horsley	
G-BPJG	PA-18 Super Cub 150	M. W. Stein	
G-BPJK	Colt 77A balloon	P. Lavelle	
G-BPJP	PA-28-161 Cadet	Aviation Rentals	
G-BPJS	PA-28-161 Cadet	Redhill Air Services Ltd	
G-BPJU	PA-28-161 Cadet	Aviation Rentals	
G-BPJW	Cessna A.150K	G. Duck	
G-BPJZ	Cameron O-160 balloon	M. L. Gabb	
G-BPKF	Grob G.115	Swiftair Maintenance Ltd	
G-BPKK	Denney Kitfox Mk 1	C. P. Moss	
G-BPKM	PA-28-161 Warrior II	Brooke Park Ltd	
G-BPKR	PA-28-151 Warrior	Best Fly KFT	
G-BPKT	Piper J.5A Cub Cruiser	A. J. Greenslade	
G-BPLH	Jodel DR.1051	C. K. Farley	
G-BPLM	AIA Stampe SV.4C	C. J. Jessonl	
G-BPLR	BN-2B-20 Islander	Hebridean Air Services Ltd	

Notes	Reg.	Type	Owner or Operator
	G-BPLV	Cameron V-77 balloon	V. Grenier/France
	G-BPLZ	Hughes 369HS	M. A. & R. J. Fawcett
	G-BPMB	Maule M5-235C Lunar Rocket	Maule Flying group
	G-BPME	Cessna 152 II	Hinde Holdings Ltd
	G-BPMF	PA-28-151 Warrior	Mike Foxtrot Group
	G-BPML	Cessna 172M	N. A. Bilton
	G-BPMM	Champion 7ECA Citabria	H. J. Taggart
	G-BPMU	Nord 3202B	E. C. Murgatroyd (G-BIZJ)
	G-BPMW	QAC Quickie Q.2	P. M. Wright (G-OICI/G-OGKN)
	G-BPMX	ARV Super 2	R. A. Collins
	G-BPNI	Robinson R22 Beta	Patriot Flight Training Ltd
	G-BPNO	Zlin Z.326 Trener Master	J. A. S. Bailey & S. T. Logan
	G-BPOA	Gloster Meteor T.7 (WF877) ★	39 Restoration Group
	G-BPOB	Sopwith Camel F.1 (replica) (B2458:R)	Flying Aces Movie Aircraft Collection
	G-BPOM	PA-28-161 Warrior II	POM Flying Group
	G-BPOS	Cessna 150M	S. G. Lewis
	G-BPOT	PA-28-181 Archer II	P. S. Simpson
	G-BPOU	Luscombe 8A Silvaire	J. L. Grayer
	G-BPPA	Cameron O-65 balloon	Rix Petroleum Ltd
	G-BPPE	PA-38-112 Tomahawk	First Air Ltd
	G-BPPF	PA-38-112 Tomahawk	Bristol Strut Flying Group
	G-BPPJ	Cameron A-180 balloon	D. J. Farrar
	G-BPPK	PA-28-151 Warrior	Praxys Ltd
	G-BPPO	Luscombe 8A Silvaire	P. Dyer
	G-BPPP	Cameron V-77 balloon	Sarnia Balloon Group
	G-BPPZ	Taylorcraft BC-12D	G. C. Smith
	G-BPRA	Aeronca 11AC Chief	C. S. Tolchard
	G-BPRC	Cameron 77 Elephant SS balloon	A. Schneider/Germany
	G-BPRD	Pitts S-1C Special	Parrot Aerobatic Group
	G-BPRI	AS.355F1 Twin Squirrel	MW Helicopters Ltd (G-TVPA)
	G-BPRJ	AS.355F1 Twin Squirrel	PLM Dollar Group Ltd
	G-BPRL	AS.355F1 Twin Squirrel	MW Helicopters Ltd
	G-BPRM	Cessna F.172L	BJ Aviation Ltd (G-AZKG)
	G-BPRX	Aeronca 11AC Chief	J. E. S. Turner
	G-BPRY	PA-28-161 Warrior II	White Wings Aviation Ltd
	G-BPSH	Cameron V-77 balloon	P. G. Hossack
	G-BPSJ	Thunder Ax6-56 balloon	V. Hyland
	G-BPSL	Cessna 177	K. S. Herbert
	G-BPSO	Cameron N-90 balloon	J. Oberprieler/Germany
	G-BPSR	Cameron V-77 balloon	K. J. A. Maxwell
	G-BPSS	Cameron A-120 balloon	Anglian Countryside Balloons Ltd
	G-BPTA	Stinson 108-2	M. L. Ryan
	G-BPTD	Cameron V-77 balloon	J. Lippett
	G-BPTE	PA-28-181 Archer II	J. S. Develin & Z. Islam
	G-BPTG	Rockwell Commander 112TC	B. Ogunyemi
	G-BPTI	SOCATA TB20 Trinidad	N. Davis
	G-BPTL	Cessna 172N	D. A. Gathercole
	G-BPTS	CASA 1.131E Jungmann 1000 (E3B-153:781-75)	E. P. Parkin
	G-BPTU	Cessna 152	A. M. Alam
	G-BPTV	Bensen B.8	C. Munro
	G-BPTZ	Robinson R22 Beta	Kuki Helicopter Sales Ltd and S. J. Nicholls
	G-BPUA	EAA Sport Biplane	E. J. & M. P. Hill
	G-BPUB	Cameron V-31 balloon	M. T. Evans
	G-BPUF	Thunder Ax6-56Z balloon	R. C. & M. A. Trimble (G-BHRL)
	G-BPUL	PA-18 Super Cub 150	C. D. Duthy-James & B. M. Reed
	G-BPUM	Cessna R.182RG	R. C. Chapman
	G-BPUP	Whittaker MW7	J. H. Beard
	G-BPUR	Piper J-3L-65 Cub ★	Hawker Restorations Ltd
	G-BPUU	Cessna 140	D. R. Speight
	G-BPUW	Colt 90A balloon	S. Sonnenberg/Germany
	G-BPVA	Cessna 172F	South Lancashire Flyers Group
	G-BPVE	Bleriot IX (replica) (1) ★	Bianchi Aviation Film Services Ltd/Booker
	G-BPVH	Cub Aircraft J-3C-65 Prospector	D. E. Cooper-Maguire
	G-BPVI	PA-32-301 Saratoga SP	M. T. Coppen
	G-BPVK	Varga 2150A Kachina	D. W. Parfrey
	G-BPVM	Cameron V-77 balloon	J. Dyer
	G-BPVN	PA-32R-301T Turbo Saratoga SP	R. Weston
	G-BPVO	Cassutt Racer IIIM	K. P. Rusling
	G-BPVW	CASA 1.131E Jungmann 2000	C. & J-W. Labeij/Netherlands
	G-BPVZ	Luscombe 8E Silvaire	S. M. Thomas & A. P. Wilkie
	G-BPWB	Sikorsky S-61N	Bristow Helicopters Ltd/HM Coastguard
	G-BPWC	Cameron V-77 balloon	R. F. Davey

Reg.	Type	Owner or Operator	Notes
G-BPWE	PA-28-161 Warrior II	RPR Associates Ltd	
G-BPWG	Cessna 150M	GB Pilots Wilsford Group	
G-BPWI	Bell 206B JetRanger 3	Warren Aviation	
G-BPWK	Sportavia Fournier RF-5B	G-BPWK Flying Group	
G-BPWL	PA-25 Pawnee 235	M. H. Sims	
G-BPWM	Cessna 150L	P. D. Button	
G-BPWN	Cessna 150L	A. J. & N. J. Bissex	
G-BPWP	Rutan LongEz (modified)	D. A. Field	
G-BPWR	Cessna R.172K	J. A. & D. T. A. Rees	
G-BPWS	Cessna 172P	Chartstone Ltd	
G-BPXA	PA-28-181 Archer II	Cherokee Flying Group	
G-BPXE	Enstrom 280C Shark	A. Healy	
G-BPXG	Colt 45A balloon	Zebedee Balloon Service Ltd	
G-BPXJ	PA-28RT-201T Turbo Arrow IV	J. & M. Holubecki-France	
G-BPXX	PA-34-200T Seneca II	Yorkshire Aviation Ltd	
G-BPXY	Aeronca 11AC Chief	P. L. Turner	
G-BPYJ	Wittman W.8 Tailwind	J. P. & Y. Mills	
G-BPYL	Hughes 369D	Morcorp (BVI) Ltd	
G-BPYN	Piper J-3C-65 Cub	The Aquila Group	
G-BPYR	PA-31-310 Turbo Navajo	Excel Aviation Ltd	
G-BPYS	Cameron O-77 balloon	D. J. Goldsmith	
G-BPYT	Cameron V-77 balloon	M. H. Redman	
G-BPYY	Cameron A-180 balloon	G. D. Fitzpatrick	
G-BPZA	Luscombe 8A Silvaire	M. J. Wright	
G-BPZB	Cessna 120	Cessna 120 Group	
G-BPZC	Luscombe 8A Silvaire	C. C. & J. M. Lovell	
G-BPZD	SNCAN NC.858S	Zula Delta Syndicate	
G-BPZE	Luscombe 8E Silvaire	M. A. Watts	
G-BPZM	PA-28RT-201 Arrow IV	Airways Flight Training (Exeter) Ltd (G-ROYW/ G-CRTI)	
G-BPZP	Robin DR.400/180R	S. G. Jones	
G-BPZY	Pitts S-1C Special	J. S. Mitchell	
G-BPZZ	Thunder Ax8-105 balloon	Capricorn Balloons Ltd	
G-BRAA	Pitts S-1C Special	R. J. Hodder	
G-BRAK	Cessna 172N	Falcon Flying Services Ltd	
G-BRAM	Mikoyan MiG-21PF (503) ★	FAST Museum/Farnborough	
G-BRAR	Aeronca 7AC Champion	R. B. Armitage	
G-BRBA	PA-28-161 Warrior II	B. Willis	
G-BRBC	NA T-6G Texan	A. P. Murphy	
G-BRBD	PA-28-151 Warrior	G. Bowen	
G-BRBE	PA-28-161 Warrior II	KN Singles and Twins Aviation	
G-BRBG	PA-28 Cherokee 180	P. M. Carter	
G-BRBH	Cessna 150H	J. Maffia & H. Merkado	
G-BRBI	Cessna 172N	Skyhawk Flying Group	
G-BRBJ	Cessna 172M	N. Foster	
G-BRBK	Robin DR.400/180	R. Kemp	
G-BRBL	Robin DR.400/180	Upavon Chipmunk Group	
G-BRBM	Robin DR.400/180	R. W. Davies	
G-BRBN	Pitts S-1S Special	G-BRBN Flying Group	
G-BRBO	Cameron V-77 balloon	M. B. Murby	
G-BRBP	Cessna 152	The Pilot Centre Ltd	
G-BRBV	Piper J-4A Cub Coupe	P. Clarke	
G-BRBW	PA-28 Cherokee 140	Air Navigation and Trading Co Ltd	
G-BRBX	PA-28-181 Archer II	Trent 199 Flying Group	
G-BRCA	Jodel D.112	R. C. Jordan	
G-BRCE	Pitts S-1C Special	M. P. & S. T. Barnard	
G-BRCJ	Cameron H-20 balloon	P. A. Sweatman	
G-BRCM	Cessna 172L	S. G. E. Plessis & D. C. C. Handley	
G-BRCO	Cameron H-20 balloon	P. Lawman	
G-BRCT	Denney Kitfox Mk 2	M. L. Roberts	
G-BRCV	Aeronca 7AC Champion	P. I. and D. M. Morgans	
G-BRCW	Aeronca 11AC Chief	R. B. Griffin	
G-BRDD	Avions Mudry CAP-10B	T. A. Smith	
G-BRDF	PA-28-161 Warrior II	White Waltham Airfield Ltd	
G-BRDG	PA-28-161 Warrior II	Falcon Flying Services	
G-BRDJ	Luscombe 8A Silvaire	The Luscombe Group	
G-BRDM	PA-28-161 Warrior II	White Waltham Airfield Ltd	
G-BRDO	Cessna 177B	Cardinal Aviation	
G-BRDT	Cameron DP-70 airship	Balloon Promotion SAS	
G-BRDV	Viking Wood Products Spitfire Prototype replica (K5054) ★	Solent Sky, Southampton	
G-BRDW	PA-24 Comanche 180	I. P. Gibson	

Notes	Reg.	Type	Owner or Operator
	G-BREA	Bensen B.8MR	D. J. Martin
	G-BREB	Piper J-3C-65 Cub	J. R. Wraight
	G-BREH	Cameron V-65 balloon	S. E. & V. D. Hurst
	G-BREL	Cameron O-77 balloon	R. A. Patey
	G-BREP	PA-28RT-201 Arrow IV	Westbeach Aviation Ltd
	G-BRER	Aeronca 7AC Champion	R. N. R. Bellamy
	G-BREU	Montgomerie-Bensen B.8MR	J. S. Firth
	G-BREX	Cameron O-84 balloon	W. S. Calvert
	G-BREY	Taylorcraft BC-12D	BREY Group
	G-BREZ	Cessna 172M	L. A. Mills
	G-BRFB	Rutan LongEz	A. R. Oliver
	G-BRFC	Percival P.57 Sea Prince T.Mk.1 (WP321)	M. A. Stott
	G-BRFF	Colt 90A balloon	Amber Valley Aviation
	G-BRFI	Aeronca 7DC Champion	A. C. Lines
	G-BRFJ	Aeronca 11AC Chief	J. M. Mooney
	G-BRFL	PA-38-112 Tomahawk	A. D. Pocock
	G-BRFM	PA-28-161 Warrior II	British Disabled Flying Association
	G-BRFO	Cameron V-77 balloon	Hedge Hoppers Balloon Group
	G-BRFW	Montgomerie-Bensen B.8 2-seat	A. J. Barker
	G-BRFX	Pazmany PL.4A	D. E. Hills
	G-BRGD	Cameron O-84 balloon	R. G. Russell
	G-BRGE	Cameron N-90 balloon	Oakfield Farm Products Ltd
	G-BRGF	Luscombe 8E Silvaire	Luscombe Flying Group
	G-BRGI	PA-28 Cherokee 180	R. A. Buckfield
	G-BRGT	PA-32 Cherokee Six 260	D. A. Hitchcock
	G-BRGW	Gardan GY-201 Minicab	R. G. White
	G-BRHA	PA-32RT-300 Lance II	Lance G-BRHA Group
	G-BRHO	PA-34-200 Seneca	Andrews Professional Colour Laboratories Ltd
	G-BRHP	Aeronca O-58B Grasshopper (31923)	R. B. McComish & C. J. Willis
	G-BRHR	PA-38-112 Tomahawk	D. C. Hanss
	G-BRHX	Luscombe 8E Silvaire	J. Lakin
	G-BRHY	Luscombe 8E Silvaire	R. A. Keech
	G-BRIE	Cameron N-77 balloon	S. F. Redman
	G-BRIH	Taylorcraft BC-12D	M. J. Medland
	G-BRIJ	Taylorcraft F-19	M. W, Olliver
	G-BRIK	T.66 Nipper 3	Clipgate Nipper Group
	G-BRIL	Piper J-5A Cub Cruiser	D. J. Bone
	G-BRIO	Turner Super T-40A	S. Bidwell
	G-BRIV	SOCATA TB9 Tampico Club	S. J. Taft
	G-BRIY	Taylorcraft DF-65 (42-58678:IY)	S. R. Potts
	G-BRJA	Luscombe 8A Silvaire	A. D. Keen
	G-BRJC	Cessna 120	C. R. White
	G-BRJK	Luscombe 8A Silvaire	C. J. L. Peat & M. Richardson
	G-BRJL	PA-15 Vagabond	A. R. Williams
	G-BRJN	Pitts S-1C Special	W. Chapel
	G-BRJT	Cessna 150H	Juliet Tango Group
	G-BRJV	PA-28-161 Cadet	Northumbria Flying School Ltd
	G-BRJX	Rand-Robinson KR-2	J. R. Bell
	G-BRJY	Rand-Robinson KR-2	R. E. Taylor
	G-BRKC	Auster J/1 Autocrat	J. W. Conlon
	G-BRKH	PA-28-236 Dakota	T. A. White
	G-BRKR	Cessna 182R	A. R. D. Brooker
	G-BRKW	Cameron V-77 balloon	T. J. Parker
	G-BRKY	Viking Dragonfly Mk II	G. D. Price
	G-BRLB	Air Command 532 Elite	F. G. Shepherd
	G-BRLF	Campbell Cricket (replica)	J. L. G. McLane
	G-BRLG	PA-28RT-201T Turbo Arrow IV	P. Lodge & J. G. McVey
	G-BRLI	Piper J-5A Cub Cruiser	D. J. M. Eardley
	G-BRLL	Cameron A-105 balloon	P. A. Sweatman
	G-BRLO	PA-38-112 Tomahawk	St. George Flight Training Ltd
	G-BRLP	PA-38-112 Tomahawk	Highland Aviation Training Ltd
	G-BRLR	Cessna 150G	Blue Skys Aviation (NE) Ltd
	G-BRLS	Thunder Ax7-77 balloon	E. C. Meek
	G-BRMA	WS-51 Dragonfly HR.5 (WG719) ★	IHM/Weston-super-Mare
	G-BRMB	B.192 Belvedere HC.1	IHM/Weston-super-Mare
	G-BRME	PA-28-181 Archer II	Blue Sky Investments Ltd
	G-BRML	PA-38-112 Tomahawk	J. S. Willcocks
	G-BRMT	Cameron V-31 balloon	B. Reed
	G-BRMU	Cameron V-77 balloon	K. J. & G. R. Ibbotson
	G-BRMV	Cameron O-77 balloon	P. D. Griffiths
	G-BRNC	Cessna 150M	Penny Hydraulics Ltd
	G-BRND	Cessna 152 II	T. M. & M. L. Jones

Reg.	Type	Owner or Operator	Notes
G-BRNE	Cessna 152 II	Redhill Air Services Ltd	
G-BRNK	Cessna 152 II	D. C. & M. Bonsall	
G-BRNN	Cessna 152 II	Eastern Air Executive Ltd	
G-BRNT	Robin DR.400/180	C. E. Ponsford & ptnrs	
G-BRNU	Robin DR.400/180	November Uniform Travel Syndicate Ltd	
G-BRNV	PA-28-181 Archer II	N. S. Lyndhurst	
G-BRNW	Cameron V-77 balloon	N. Robertson & G. Smith	
G-BRNX	PA-22 Tri-Pacer 150	S. N. Askey	
G-BROE	Cameron N-65 balloon	A. I. Attwood	
G-BROG	Cameron V-65 balloon	R. Kunert	
G-BROI	CFM Streak Shadow Srs SA	R. C. Ford	
G-BROJ	Colt 31A balloon	N. J. Langley	
G-BROO	Luscombe 8E Silvaire	P. R. Bush	
G-BROR	Piper J-3C-65 Cub	White Hart Flying Group	
G-BROX	Robinson R22 Beta	J. G. Burgess	
G-BROY	Cameron V-77 balloon	C. B. McDougall	
G-BROZ	PA-18 Super Cub 150	P. G. Kynsey	
G-BRPE	Cessna 120	W. B. Bateson	
G-BRPF	Cessna 120	G. A. Robson	
G-BRPG	Cessna 120	I. C. Lomax	
G-BRPH	Cessna 120	J. A. Cook & C. J. Richardson	
G-BRPK	PA-28 Cherokee 140	G-BRPK Group	
G-BRPL	PA-28-140 Cherokee	FlyBPL.com	
G-BRPM	T.66 Nipper 3	J. H. H. Turner	
G-BRPP	Brookland Hornet (modified)	B. J. L. P. & W. J. A. L. de Saar	
G-BRPR	Aeronca O-58B Grasshopper (31952)	A. F. Kutz	
G-BRPS	Cessna 177B	E. Janssen & A. Lietaert	
G-BRPT	Rans S.10 Sakota	M. D. Moaby	
G-BRPV	Cessna 152	Eastern Air Executive Ltd	
G-BRPX	Taylorcraft BC-12D	G-BRPX Group	
G-BRPY	PA-15 Vagabond	J. & V. Hobday	
G-BRPZ	Luscombe 8A Silvaire	C. A. Flint	
G-BRRA	VS.361 Spitfire LF.IX	P. M. Andrews	
G-BRRB	Luscombe 8E Silvaire	J. Nicholls	
G-BRRF	Cameron O-77 balloon	K. P. & G. J. Storey	
G-BRRK	Cessna 182Q	Werewolf Aviation Ltd	
G-BRRR	Cameron V-77 balloon	K. P. & G. J. Storey	
G-BRRU	Colt 90A balloon	Reach For The Sky Ltd	
G-BRRY	Robinson R22 Beta	Alan Mann Aviation Group Ltd	
G-BRSA	Cameron N-56 balloon	J. F. Till	
G-BRSD	Cameron V-77 balloon	M. E. Granger	
G-BRSE	PA-28-161 Warrior II	Falcon Flying Services Ltd	
G-BRSF	VS.361 Spitfire HF.9c (RR232)	M. B. Phillips	
G-BRSL	Cameron N-56 balloon	S. Budd	
G-BRSP	Air Command 532 Elite	G. M. Hobman	
G-BRSW	Luscombe 8A Silvaire	Bloody Mary Aviation	
G-BRSX	PA-15 Vagabond	M. R. Holden	
G-BRSY	Hatz CB-1	Eaglescott Hatz Biplane Group	
G-BRTD	Cessna 152 II	152 Group	
G-BRTJ	Cessna 150F	A. G. Arthur	
G-BRTL	Hughes 369E	Road Tech Computer Systems Ltd	
G-BRTP	Cessna 152 II	R. Lee	
G-BRTT	Schweizer 269C	Fairthorpe Ltd	
G-BRTV	Cameron O-77 balloon	S. D. Wrighton	
G-BRTW	Glaser-Dirks DG.400	I. J. Carruthers	
G-BRTX	PA-28-151 Warrior	Brinkley (Meppershall) Ltd	
G-BRUB	PA-28-161 Warrior II	Flytrek Ltd	
G-BRUD	PA-28-181 Archer II	FlyBPL.com	
G-BRUG	Luscombe 8E Silvaire	N. W. Barratt	
G-BRUJ	Boeing Stearman A.75N1 (6136:205)	F. D. Milne	
G-BRUM	Cessna A.152	A. J. Gomes	
G-BRUN	Cessna 120	A. R. M. Eagle, J. A. Longworth & J. Peake (G-BRDH)	
G-BRUO	Taylor JT.1 Monoplane	S. T. S. Bygrave	
G-BRUV	Cameron V-77 balloon	T. W. & R. F. Benbrook	
G-BRUX	PA-44-180 Seminole	M. Ali	
G-BRVB	Stolp SA.300 Starduster Too	J. K. Cook	
G-BRVE	Beech D.17S	Patina Ltd	
G-BRVF	Colt 77A balloon	J. Adkins	
G-BRVG	NA SNJ-7 Texan (27)	D. Gilmour/Intrepid Aviation Co	
G-BRVH	Smyth Model S Sidewinder	B. D. Deleponte	
G-BRVI	Robinson R22 Beta	York Helicopters	
G-BRVJ	Slingsby T.31 Motor Cadet III	B. Outhwaite	

Notes	Reg.	Type	Owner or Operator
	G-BRVL	Pitts S-1C Special	M. F. Pocock
	G-BRVN	Thunder Ax7-77 balloon	D. L. Beckwith
	G-BRVO	AS.350B Ecureuil	Rotorhire LLP
	G-BRVZ	Jodel D.117	L. Holland
	G-BRWA	Aeronca 7AC Champion	J. R. Edwards
	G-BRWB	NA T-6G Texan (526)	R. Clifford
	G-BRWD	Robinson R22 Beta	Time Line International Ltd
	G-BRWP	CFM Streak Shadow	R. Biffin
	G-BRWR	Aeronca 11AC Chief	A. W. Crutcher
	G-BRWT	Scheibe SF.25C Falke	Booker Gliding Club Ltd
	G-BRWU	Luton LA-4A Minor	R. B. Webber
	G-BRWV	Brügger MB.2 Colibri	M. P. Wakem
	G-BRWX	Cessna 172P	R. A. Brown & A. C. Dove
	G-BRXA	Cameron O-120 balloon	R. J. Mansfield
	G-BRXD	PA-28-181 Archer II	R. C. G. Lywood
	G-BRXE	Taylorcraft BC-12D	B. T. Morgan & W. J. Durrad
	G-BRXF	Aeronca 11AC Chief	Aeronca Flying Group
	G-BRXG	Aeronca 7AC Champion	X-Ray Golf Flying Group
	G-BRXH	Cessna 120	BRXH Group
	G-BRXL	Aeronca 11AC Chief (42-78044)	P. L. Green
	G-BRXN	Montgomerie-Bensen B.8MR	C. M. Frerk
	G-BRXP	SNCAN Stampe SV.4C (modified)	T. Brown
	G-BRXS	Howard Special T Minus	F. A. Bakir
	G-BRXU	Aerospatiale AS.332L Super Puma	Bristow Helicopters Ltd
	G-BRXV	Robinson R22 Beta	Patriot Flight Taining Ltd
	G-BRXW	PA-24 Comanche 260	Oak Group
	G-BRXY	Pietenpol Air Camper	P. S. Ganczakowski
	G-BRZA	Cameron O-77 balloon	S. Nother
	G-BRZB	Cameron A-105 balloon	Headland Services Ltd
	G-BRZD	Hapi Cygnet SF-2A	C. I. Coghill
	G-BRZG	Enstrom F-28A	Duxburys Ltd
	G-BRZK	Stinson 108-2	Stinson Syndicate
	G-BRZL	Pitts S-1D Special	T. R. G. Barnby
	G-BRZS	Cessna 172P	YP Flying Group
	G-BRZW	Rans S.10 Sakota	D. L. Davies
	G-BRZX	Pitts S-1S Special	Zulu Xray Group
	G-BRZZ	Streak Shadow	A. J. Thomas
	G-BSAI	Stoddard-Hamilton Glasair III	K. J. & P. J. Whitehead
	G-BSAJ	CASA 1.131E Jungmann 2000	P. G. Kynsey
	G-BSAK	Colt 21A balloon	M. D. Mitchell
	G-BSAS	Cameron V-65 balloon	P. Donkin
	G-BSAV	Thunder Ax7-77 balloon	I. G. & C. A. Lloyd
	G-BSAW	PA-28-161 Warrior II	Compton Abbas Airfield Ltd
	G-BSAZ	Denney Kitfox Mk 2	A. J. Lloyd
	G-BSBA	PA-28-161 Warrior II	Falcon Flying Services Ltd
	G-BSBG	CCF Harvard IV (20310:310)	A. P. St. John
	G-BSBI	Cameron O-77 balloon	D. M. Billing
	G-BSBM	Cameron N-77 balloon	K. F. Lowry
	G-BSBR	Cameron V-77 balloon	R. P. Wade
	G-BSBT	Piper J-3C-65 Cub	A. R. Elliott
	G-BSBV	Rans S.10 Sakota	S. Bain
	G-BSBW	Bell 206B JetRanger 3	Castle Air Ltd
	G-BSCC	Colt 105A balloon	A. F. Selby
	G-BSCE	Robinson R22 Beta	Carpets Direct (GB) Ltd
	G-BSCG	Denney Kitfox Mk 2	A. Levitt
	G-BSCH	Denney Kitfox Mk 2	G. R. Moore
	G-BSCI	Colt 77A balloon	S. C. Kinsey
	G-BSCK	Cameron H-24 balloon	J. D. Shapland
	G-BSCM	Denney Kitfox Mk 2	H. D. Colliver (G-MSCM)
	G-BSCN	SOCATA TB20 Trinidad	B. W. Dye
	G-BSCO	Thunder Ax7-77 balloon	F. J. Whalley
	G-BSCP	Cessna 152 II	Moray Flying Club (1990) Ltd
	G-BSCS	PA-28-181 Archer II	Wingtask 1995 Ltd
	G-BSCV	PA-28-161 Warrior II	Southwood Flying Group
	G-BSCW	Taylorcraft BC-65	G. Johnson
	G-BSCX	Thunder Ax8-105 balloon	S. Charlish
	G-BSCY	PA-28-151 Warrior	Take Flight Aviation Ltd
	G-BSCZ	Cessna 152 II	The RAF Halton Aeroplane Club Ltd
	G-BSDA	Taylorcraft BC-12D	N. D. Dykes
	G-BSDD	Denney Kitfox Mk 2	D. C. Crawley
	G-BSDH	Robin DR.400/180	R. L. Brucciani
	G-BSDJ	Piper J-4E Cub Coupe	Ballyboughal J4 Flying Group

Reg.	Type	Owner or Operator	Notes
G-BSDK	Piper J-5A Cub Cruiser	J. E. Mead	
G-BSDL	SOCATA TB10 Tobago	Delta Lima Flying Group	
G-BSDN	PA-34-200T Seneca II	S. J. Green	
G-BSDO	Cessna 152 II	J. Vickers	
G-BSDP	Cessna 152 II	Paul's Planes Ltd	
G-BSDS	Boeing Stearman E75 (118)	L. W. Scattergood	
G-BSDW	Cessna 182P	Parker Diving Ltd	
G-BSDX	Cameron V-77 balloon	G. P. & S. J. Allen	
G-BSDZ	Enstrom 280FX	Rotormotive Ltd	
G-BSED	PA-22 Tri-Pacer 160 (modified)	M. D. N. Fisher	
G-BSEE	Rans S.9	R. P. Hothersall	
G-BSEF	PA-28 Cherokee 180	I. D. Wakeling	
G-BSEJ	Cessna 150M	C. L. Day	
G-BSEL	Slingsby T.61G Super Falke	D. G. Holley	
G-BSER	PA-28 Cherokee 160	Yorkair Ltd	
G-BSEU	PA-28-181 Archer II	K. R. Taylor	
G-BSEV	Cameron O-77 balloon	P. B. Kenington	
G-BSEX	Cameron A-180 balloon	Heart of England Balloons	
G-BSEY	Beech A36 Bonanza	P. Malam-Wilson	
G-BSFA	Aero Designs Pulsar	P. F. Lorriman	
G-BSFD	Piper J-3C-65 Cub	P. E. S. Latham	
G-BSFE	PA-38-112 Tomahawk II	ACS Aviation Ltd	
G-BSFF	Robin DR.400/180R	Lasham Gliding Society Ltd	
G-BSFP	Cessna 152T	The Pilot Centre Ltd	
G-BSFR	Cessna 152 II	Galair Ltd	
G-BSFV	Woods Woody Pusher	P. A. Gasson	
G-BSFW	PA-15 Vagabond	J. R. Kimberley	
G-BSFX	Denney Kitfox Mk 2	F. Colman	
G-BSGB	Gaertner Ax4 Skyranger balloon	B. Gaertner	
G-BSGD	PA-28 Cherokee 180	R. J. Cleverley	
G-BSGF	Robinson R22 Beta	L. B. Clark	
G-BSGG	Denney Kitfox Mk 2	C. G. Richardson	
G-BSGH	Airtour AH-56B balloon	A. R. Hardwick	
G-BSGJ	Monnett Sonerai II	J. L. Loweth	
G-BSGL	PA-28-161 Warrior II	Keywest Air Charter Ltd	
G-BSGP	Cameron N-65 balloon	R. Leslie	
G-BSGS	Rans S.10 Sakota	M. R. Parr	
G-BSGT	Cessna T.210N	E. A. T. Brenninkmeyer	
G-BSHA	PA-34-200T Seneca II	Justgold Ltd	
G-BSHC	Colt 69A balloon	Magical Adventures Ltd	
G-BSHD	Colt 69A balloon	F. W. Ewer	
G-BSHH	Luscombe 8E Silvaire	S. L. Lewis	
G-BSHK	Denney Kitfox Mk 2	D. Doyle & C. Aherne	
G-BSHO	Cameron V-77 balloon	D. J. Duckworth & J. C. Stewart	
G-BSHP	PA-28-161 Warrior II	Aviation Rentals	
G-BSHR	Cessna F.172N	Deep Cleavage Ltd (G-BFGE)	
G-BSHY	EAA Acro Sport I	R. J. Hodder	
G-BSIC	Cameron V-77 balloon	T. R. Tillson	
G-BSIF	Denney Kitfox Mk 2	S. M. Dougan	
G-BSIG	Colt 21A Cloudhopper balloon	C. J. Dunkley	
G-BSII	PA-34-200T Seneca II	R. L. Burt	
G-BSIJ	Cameron V-77 balloon	G. B. Davies	
G-BSIM	PA-28-181 Archer II	Falcon Flying Services Ltd	
G-BSIO	Cameron 80 Shed SS balloon	R. E. Jones	
G-BSIU	Colt 90A balloon	S. Travaglia/Italy	
G-BSIY	Schleicher ASK.14	P. W. Andrews	
G-BSIZ	PA-28-181 Archer II	P. J. Gerrard & M. J. Cunliffe	
G-BSJU	Cessna 150M	A. C. Williamson	
G-BSJX	PA-28-161 Warrior II	MK Aero Support Ltd	
G-BSJZ	Cessna 150J	M. H. Campbell	
G-BSKA	Cessna 150M	R. J. Cushing	
G-BSKG	Maule MX-7-180	A. J. Lewis	
G-BSKW	PA-28-181 Archer II	R. J. Whyham	
G-BSLA	Robin DR.400/180	A. B. McCoig	
G-BSLH	CASA 1.131E Jungmann 2000	M. A. Warden	
G-BSLK	PA-28-161 Warrior II	R. A. Rose	
G-BSLM	PA-28 Cherokee 160	B. K. & W. G. Ranger	
G-BSLT	PA-28-161 Warrior II	L. W. Scattergood	
G-BSLU	PA-28 Cherokee 140	W. E. Lewis	
G-BSLV	Enstrom 280FX	B. M. B Roumier	
G-BSLW	Bellanca 7ECA Citabria	J. S. Flavell	
G-BSLX	WAR Focke-Wulf Fw 190 (replica) (4+)	Fw 190 Gruppe	
G-BSMD	Nord 1101 Noralpha (+14)	J. W. Hardie	

Notes	Reg.	Type	Owner or Operator
	G-BSME	Bölkow Bö.208C1 Junior	D. J. Hampson
	G-BSMG	Montgomerie-Bensen B.8M	A. C. Timperley
	G-BSMK	Cameron O-84 balloon	G-BSMK Shareholders
	G-BSMM	Colt 31A balloon	D. V. Fowler
	G-BSMN	CFM Streak Shadow	P. J. Porter
	G-BSMT	Rans S-10 Sakota	T. D. Wood
	G-BSMU	Rans S.6 Coyote II	A. Wright (G-MWJE)
	G-BSMV	PA-17 Vagabond (modified)	A. Cheriton
	G-BSNE	Luscombe 8E Silvaire	C. B. Buscombe, R. Goldsworthy & G. Vitta
	G-BSNF	Piper J-3C-65 Cub	D. A. Hammant
	G-BSNG	Cessna 172N	A. J. & P. C. MacDonald
	G-BSNJ	Cameron N-90 balloon	D. P. H. Smith/France
	G-BSNT	Luscombe 8A Silvaire	Luscombe Quartet
	G-BSNU	Colt 105A balloon	Gone Ballooning
	G-BSNX	PA-28-181 Archer II	Redhill Air Services Ltd
	G-BSOE	Luscombe 8A Silvaire	R. G. Downhill
	G-BSOF	Colt 25A balloon	J. M. Bailey
	G-BSOG	Cessna 172M	C. Shackleton
	G-BSOJ	Thunder Ax7-77 balloon	R. J. S. Jones
	G-BSOK	PA-28-161 Warrior II	A. Oxenham
	G-BSOM	Glaser-Dirks DG.400	G-BSOM Group
	G-BSON	Green S.25 balloon	J. J. Green
	G-BSOO	Cessna 172F	The Oscar Oscar Group
	G-BSOR	CFM Streak Shadow Srs SA	A. Parr
	G-BSOU	PA-38-112 Tomahawk II	D. J. Campbell
	G-BSOX	Luscombe 8AE Silvaire	P. S Lanary
	G-BSOZ	PA-28-161 Warrior II	Highland Asset Management Ltd
	G-BSPA	QAC Quickie Q.2	G. V. McKirdy & B. K. Glover
	G-BSPC	Jodel D.140C	B. E. Cotton
	G-BSPE	Cessna F.172P	T. W. Williamson
	G-BSPG	PA-34-200T Seneca II	Andrews Professional Colour Laboratories Ltd
	G-BSPK	Cessna 195A	A. G. & D. L. Bompas
	G-BSPL	CFM Streak Shadow Srs SA	G. L. Turner
	G-BSPN	PA-28R-201T Turbo Arrow III	Wendex Vehicle Rental Ltd
	G-BSPS	BN-2B-20 Islander	G. Cormack
	G-BSRD	Cameron N-105 balloon	A. Ockelmann
	G-BSRH	Pitts S-1C Special	C. D. Swift
	G-BSRI	Lancair 235	G. Lewis
	G-BSRK	ARV Super 2	D. Nieman
	G-BSRL	Campbell Cricket Mk.4 gyroplane	M. Brudnicki
	G-BSRP	Rotorway Executive	R. J. Baker
	G-BSRR	Cessna 182Q	C. M. Moore
	G-BSRT	Denney Kitfox Mk 2	M. J. Freeman
	G-BSRX	CFM Streak Shadow	C. M. Webb
	G-BSSA	Luscombe 8E Silvaire	Luscombe Flying Group
	G-BSSB	Cessna 150L	D. T. A. Rees
	G-BSSC	PA-28-161 Warrior II	Sky Blue Flight Training
	G-BSSF	Denney Kitfox Mk 2	F. W. Astbury
	G-BSSI	Rans S.6 Coyote II	J. Currell (G-MWJA)
	G-BSSK	QAC Quickie Q.2	R. Greatrex
	G-BSSP	Robin DR.400/180R	Soaring (Oxford) Ltd
	G-BSST	BAC-Sud Concorde 002 ★	F.A.A. Museum/Yeovilton
	G-BSSV	CFM Streak Shadow	R. W. Payne
	G-BSSW	PA-28-161 Warrior II	Hinton Pilot Flight Training Ltd
	G-BSSY	Polikarpov Po-2	Richard Shuttleworth Trustees
	G-BSTC	Aeronca 11AC Chief	J. Armstrong & D. Lamb
	G-BSTE	AS.355F2 Twin Squirrel	Oscar Mayer Ltd
	G-BSTH	PA-25 Pawnee 235	Scottish Gliding Union Ltd
	G-BSTI	Piper J-3C-65 Cub	J. A. Scott
	G-BSTK	Thunder Ax8-90 balloon	M. Williams
	G-BSTL	Rand-Robinson KR-2	C. S. Hales & N. Brauns
	G-BSTM	Cessna 172L	G-BSTM Group
	G-BSTO	Cessna 152 II	Fly NQY Pilot Training
	G-BSTP	Cessna 152 II	LAC Aircraft Ltd
	G-BSTR	AA-5 Traveler	B. D. Jones
	G-BSTT	Rans S.6 Coyote II	D. G. Palmer
	G-BSTX	Luscombe 8A Silvaire	C. Chambers
	G-BSTY	Thunder Ax8-90 balloon	R. O. Leslie
	G-BSTZ	PA-28 Cherokee 140	Air Navigation & Trading Co Ltd
	G-BSUA	Rans S.6 Coyote II	A. J. Todd
	G-BSUB	Colt 77A balloon	F. W. Ewer
	G-BSUD	Luscombe 8A Silvaire	I. G. Harrison
	G-BSUF	PA-32RT-300 Lance II	P. Muller

Reg.	Type	Owner or Operator	Notes
G-BSUK	Colt 77A balloon	A. J. Moore	
G-BSUO	Scheibe SF.25C Falke	Portmoak Falke Syndicate	
G-BSUU	Colt 180A balloon	British School of Ballooning	
G-BSUV	Cameron O-77 balloon	J. F. Trehern	
G-BSUW	PA-34-200T Seneca II	NPD Direct Ltd	
G-BSUX	Carlson Sparrow II	D. Harker	
G-BSUZ	Denney Kitfox Mk 3	G. C. Long	
G-BSVB	PA-28-181 Archer II	K. A. Boost	
G-BSVE	Binder CP.301S Smaragd	Smaragd Flying Group	
G-BSVG	PA-28-161 Warrior II	Booker Aircraft Leasing Ltd	
G-BSVH	Piper J-3C-65 Cub	C. R. & K. A. Maher	
G-BSVI	PA-16 Clipper	Clipper Aviation	
G-BSVK	Denney Kitfox Mk 2	C. Cox	
G-BSVM	PA-28-161 Warrior II	EFG Flying Services	
G-BSVN	Thorp T-18	D. Prentice	
G-BSVP	PA-23-250 Aztec F	S. G. Spier	
G-BSVR	Schweizer 269C	M. K. E. Askham	
G-BSVS	Robin DR.400/100	D. McK. Chalmers	
G-BSWB	Rans S.10 Sakota	F. A. Hewitt	
G-BSWC	Boeing Stearman E75 (112)	Richard Thwaites Aviation Ltd	
G-BSWF	PA-16 Clipper	Durham Clipper Group	
G-BSWG	PA-17 Vagabond	P. E. J. Sturgeon	
G-BSWH	Cessna 152 II	Airspeed Aviation Ltd	
G-BSWI	Rans S.10 Sakota	J. M. Mooney	
G-BSWL	Slingsby T.61F Venture T.2	G-BSWL Group	
G-BSWM	Slingsby T.61F Venture T.2	Venture Gliding Group	
G-BSWR	BN-2T-26 Turbine Islander	Police Service of Northern Ireland	
G-BSWV	Cameron N-77 balloon	S. Charlish	
G-BSWX	Cameron V-90 balloon	B. J. Burrows	
G-BSWY	Cameron N-77 balloon	Nottingham Hot Air Balloon Club	
G-BSXA	PA-28-161 Warrior II	Falcon Flying Services	
G-BSXB	PA-28-161 Warrior II	S. R. Mendes	
G-BSXC	PA-28-161 Warrior II	N. Ibrahim	
G-BSXD	Soko P-2 Kraguj (30146)	S. M. Johnston	
G-BSXI	Mooney M.20E	D. H. G. Penney	
G-BSXM	Cameron V-77 balloon	C. A. Oxby	
G-BSXS	PA-28-181 Archer II	A. Klamke	
G-BSXT	Piper J-5A Cub Cruiser	R. G. Trute	
G-BSYA	Jodel D.18	K. Wright	
G-BSYF	Luscombe 8A Silvaire	M. Goldsworthy-Higgs & N. J. Taaffe	
G-BSYG	PA-12 Super Cruiser	Fat Cub Group	
G-BSYH	Luscombe 8A Silvaire	N. R. Osborne	
G-BSYJ	Cameron N-77 balloon	Chubb Fire Ltd	
G-BSYO	Piper J-3C-90 Cub	C. R. Reynolds & J. D. Fuller (G-BSMJ/G-BRHE)	
G-BSYU	Robin DR.400/180	P. D. Smoothy	
G-BSYV	Cessna 150M	E-Plane Ltd	
G-BSYW	Cessna 150M	Cada Vliegtuilgen BV/Netherlands	
G-BSYY	PA-28-161 Warrior II	British Disabled Flying Association	
G-BSYZ	PA-28-161 Warrior II	Yankee Zulu Group	
G-BSZB	Stolp SA.300 Starduster Too	D. T. Gethin	
G-BSZC	Beech C-45H (51-11701A:AF258)	Weston Ltd	
G-BSZD	Robin DR.400/180	Alfa Flight	
G-BSZF	Jodel DR.250/160	J. B. Randle	
G-BSZG	Stolp SA.100 Starduster	D. F. Chapman	
G-BSZH	Thunder Ax7-77 balloon	T. J. Wilkinson	
G-BSZI	Cessna 152 II	Eglinton Flying Club Ltd	
G-BSZJ	PA-28-181 Archer II	M. L. A. Pudney & R. D. Fuller	
G-BSZM	Montgomerie-Bensen B.8MR	A. McCredie	
G-BSZO	Cessna 152	A. Jahsanfar	
G-BSZT	PA-28-161 Warrior II	Golf Charlie Echo Ltd	
G-BSZV	Cessna 150F	C. A. Davis	
G-BSZW	Cessna 152	S. T. & T. W. Gilbert	
G-BTAG	Cameron O-77 balloon	R. A. Shapland	
G-BTAK	EAA Acrosport II	J. Mann	
G-BTAL	Cessna F.152 II	Hertfordshire Aero Club Ltd	
G-BTAM	PA-28-181 Archer II	Tri-Star Farms Ltd	
G-BTAW	PA-28-161 Warrior II	Piper Flying Group	
G-BTAZ	Evans VP-2 ★	Norwich Aviation Museum	
G-BTBA	Robinson R22 Beta	Patriot Flight Training Ltd	
G-BTBB	Thunder Ax8-105 S2 balloon	G. J. Boulden	
G-BTBC	PA-28-161 Warrior II	Best Fly KFT	
G-BTBG	Denney Kitfox Mk 2	G. N. Lawder	

Notes	Reg.	Type	Owner or Operator
	G-BTBH	Ryan ST3KR (854)	R. C. Piper
	G-BTBJ	Cessna 190	R. H. Reeves
	G-BTBL	Montgomerie-Bensen B.8MR	AES Radionic Surveillance Systems
	G-BTBU	PA-18 Super Cub 150	Betty Bu Syndicate
	G-BTBV	Cessna 140	M. J. Medland
	G-BTBW	Cessna 120	M. J. Willies
	G-BTBY	PA-17 Vagabond	F. M. Ward
	G-BTCB	Air Command 582 Sport	G. Scurrah
	G-BTCC	Grumman F6F-3 Hellcat (40467:19)	Patina Ltd
	G-BTCD	P-51D-25-NA Mustang (413704:87-H)	Pelham Ltd
	G-BTCE	Cessna 152	S. T. Gilbert
	G-BTCH	Luscombe 8E Silvaire	G-BTCH Flying Group
	G-BTCI	PA-17 Vagabond	T. R. Whittome
	G-BTCM	Cameron N-90 balloon	G. Everett (G-BMPW)
	G-BTCS	Colt 90A balloon	Branded Sky Ltd
	G-BTCZ	Cameron Chateau 84 balloon	Balleroy Developpement SAS
	G-BTDA	Slingsby T.61G Falke	G-BTDA Group
	G-BTDC	Denney Kitfox Mk 2	M. A. Potter
	G-BTDD	CFM Streak Shadow	S. H. Merrony
	G-BTDE	Cessna C-165 Airmaster	R. H. Screen
	G-BTDI	Robinson R22	S. Klinge
	G-BTDN	Denney Kitfox Mk 2	M. G. Rummey
	G-BTDR	Aero Designs Pulsar	R. A. Blackwell
	G-BTDS	Colt 77A balloon	C. P. Witter Ltd
	G-BTDT	CASA 1.131E Jungmann 2000	T. A. Reed
	G-BTDV	PA-28-161 Warrior II	Falcon Flying Services Ltd
	G-BTDW	Cessna 152 II	J. H. Sandham Aviation
	G-BTDZ	CASA 1.131E Jungmann 2000	R. J. & M. Pickin
	G-BTEE	Cameron O-120 balloon	Floating Sensations
	G-BTEL	CFM Streak Shadow	J. E. Eatwell
	G-BTES	Cessna 150H	C. Burt-Brown & G. G. Saint
	G-BTET	Piper J-3C-65 Cub	City of Oxford Flying Group
	G-BTEU	SA.365N-2 Dauphin	Multiflight Ltd
	G-BTEW	Cessna 120	J. H. Milne & T. H. Bishop
	G-BTFA	Denney Kitfox Mk 2	K. R. Peek
	G-BTFC	Cessna F.152 II	Aircraft Engineers Ltd
	G-BTFE	Bensen-Parsons 2-seat gyroplane	D. C. Ellis
	G-BTFG	Boeing Stearman A75N1 (441)	TG Aviation Ltd
	G-BTFJ	PA-15 Vagabond	B. McCready
	G-BTFK	Taylorcraft BC-12D	A. O'Rourke
	G-BTFL	Aeronca 11AC Chief	BTFL Group
	G-BTFM	Cameron O-105 balloon	Edinburgh University Hot Air Balloon Club
	G-BTFO	PA-28-161 Warrior II	Flyfar Ltd
	G-BTFP	PA-38-112 Tomahawk	St.George Flight Training Ltd
	G-BTFT	Beech 58 Baron	Fastwing Air Charter Ltd
	G-BTFU	Cameron N-90 balloon	J. J. Rudoni & A. C. K. Rawson
	G-BTFV	Whittaker MW7	S. J. Luck
	G-BTFX	Bell 206B JetRanger	Amcay Ltd
	G-BTGD	Rand-Robinson KR-2 (modified)	B M. Neary
	G-BTGH	Cessna 152 II	S. J. Green
	G-BTGI	Rearwin 175 Skyranger	J. M. Fforde
	G-BTGJ	Smith DSA-1 Miniplane	G. J. Knowles
	G-BTGL	Light Aero Avid Flyer	J. S. Clair-Quentin
	G-BTGM	Aeronca 7AC Champion	A. J. McLuskie
	G-BTGO	PA-28 Cherokee 140	Demero Ltd & Transcourt Ltd
	G-BTGR	Cessna 152 II	A. J. Gomes
	G-BTGS	Stolp SA.300 Starduster Too	G. N. Elliott & ptnrs (G-AYMA)
	G-BTGT	CFM Streak Shadow	I. Heunis (G-MWPY)
	G-BTGW	Cessna 152 II	Stapleford Flying Club Ltd
	G-BTGX	Cessna 152 II	Stapleford Flying Club Ltd
	G-BTGY	PA-28-161 Warrior II	Stapleford Flying Club Ltd
	G-BTGZ	PA-28-181 Archer II	Nick Deyong Ltd
	G-BTHE	Cessna 150L	J. E. Preston
	G-BTHF	Cameron V-90 balloon	N. J. & S. J. Langley
	G-BTHK	Thunder Ax7-77 balloon	M. S.Trend
	G-BTHM	Thunder Ax8-105 balloon	Montgolfieres Club de L'Orme/France
	G-BTHP	Thorp T.211	M. Gardner
	G-BTHX	Colt 105A balloon	PSH Skypower Ltd
	G-BTHY	Bell 206B JetRanger 3	Suffolk Helicopters Ltd
	G-BTID	PA-28-161 Warrior II	Aviation South West Ltd
	G-BTIE	SOCATA TB10 Tobago	Aviation Spirit Ltd
	G-BTIF	Denney Kitfox Mk 3	D. S. Lally
	G-BTIG	Montgomerie-Bensen B.8MR	G. H. Leeming

Reg.	Type	Owner or Operator	Notes
G-BTII	AA-5B Tiger	R. Clarke	
G-BTIJ	Luscombe 8E Silvaire	S. J. Hornsby	
G-BTIL	PA-38-112 Tomahawk	B. J. Pearson	
G-BTIM	PA-28-161 Cadet	White Waltham Airfield Ltd	
G-BTIR	Denney Kitfox Mk 2	R. B. Wilson	
G-BTIV	PA-28-161 Warrior II	Warrior Group	
G-BTJA	Luscombe 8E Silvaire	S. R. Jones	
G-BTJB	Luscombe 8E Silvaire	M. Loxton	
G-BTJC	Luscombe 8F Silvaire	M. Colson	
G-BTJD	Thunder Ax8-90 S2 balloon	P. Richardson	
G-BTJF	Thunder Ax10-180 balloon	Airborne Adventures Ltd	
G-BTJH	Cameron O-77 balloon	M. Saveri	
G-BTJL	PA-38-112 Tomahawk	J. S. Devlin & Z. Islam	
G-BTJO	Thunder Ax9-140 balloon	G. P. Lane	
G-BTJS	Montgomerie-Bensen B.8MR	T. A. Holmes	
G-BTJU	Cameron V-90 balloon	Flambe Balloons Ltd	
G-BTJX	Rans S.10 Sakota	P. C. Avery	
G-BTKA	Piper J-5A Cub Cruiser	M. J. Walker	
G-BTKB	Renegade Spirit 912	P. J. Calvert	
G-BTKD	Denney Kitfox Mk 4	R. A. Hills	
G-BTKL	MBB Bö.105DB-4	Veritair Ltd	
G-BTKP	CFM Streak Shadow	I. M. Moxon	
G-BTKT	PA-28-161 Warrior II	Biggin Hill Flying Club Ltd	
G-BTKV	PA-22 Tri-Pacer 160	R. A. Moore	
G-BTKX	PA-28-181 Archer II	D. J. Perkins	
G-BTLB	Wassmer Wa.52 Europa	The G-BTLB Group	
G-BTLG	PA-28R Cherokee Arrow 200	P. J. Moore	
G-BTLL	Pilatus P.3-03	R. E. Dagless	
G-BTLM	PA-22 Tri-Pacer 160	F & H (Aircraft)	
G-BTLP	AA-1C Lynx	Partlease Ltd	
G-BTMA	Cessna 172N	East of England Flying Group Ltd	
G-BTMK	Cessna R.172K XPII	K. E. Halford	
G-BTMO	Colt 69A balloon	Thunder & Colt	
G-BTMP	Campbell Cricket	P. W. McLaughlin	
G-BTMR	Cessna 172M	Linley Aviation Ltd	
G-BTMT	Denney Kitfox Mk 1	L. G. Horne	
G-BTMV	Everett Srs 2 gyroplane	L. Armes	
G-BTMW	Zenair CH.701 STOL	K. Kerr	
G-BTNA	Robinson R22 Beta	Attitude Arobatics Ltd	
G-BTNC	AS.365N-2 Dauphin 2	Multiflight Ltd	
G-BTNE	PA-28-161 Warrior II	Fly Welle Ltd	
G-BTNH	PA-28-161 Warrior II	Falcon Flying Services Ltd (G-DENH)	
G-BTNO	Aeronca 7AC Champion	J. M. Farquhar	
G-BTNR	Denney Kitfox Mk 3	High Notions Flying Group	
G-BTNT	PA-28-151 Warrior	Azure Flying Club Ltd	
G-BTNV	PA-28-161 Warrior II	G. M. Bauer & A. W. Davies	
G-BTNW	Rans S.6-ESA Coyote II	R. C. Holmes	
G-BTOC	Robinson R22 Beta	Swift Helicopter Services Ltd	
G-BTOG	DH.82A Tiger Moth	TOG Group	
G-BTOL	Denney Kitfox Mk 3	P. J. Gibbs	
G-BTON	PA-28 Cherokee 140	Group G-BTON	
G-BTOO	Pitts S-1C Special	T. L. Davis	
G-BTOP	Cameron V-77 balloon	J. J. Winter	
G-BTOT	PA-15 Vagabond	J. E. D. Rogerson	
G-BTOU	Cameron O-120 balloon	J. J. Daly	
G-BTOW	SOCATA Rallye 180GT	M. Jarrett	
G-BTOZ	Thunder Ax9-120 S2 balloon	H. G. Davies	
G-BTPA	BAe ATP	Atlantic Airlines Ltd	
G-BTPC	BAe ATP	Atlantic Airlines Ltd	
G-BTPE	BAe ATP	Atlantic Airlines Ltd	
G-BTPF	BAe ATP	Atlantic Airlines Ltd	
G-BTPG	BAe ATP	Atlantic Airlines Ltd	
G-BTPH	BAe ATP	Atlantic Airlines Ltd	
G-BTPJ	BAe ATP	Deutsche Leasing Sverige AB	
G-BTPL	BAe ATP	European Turboprop Management AB	
G-BTPT	Cameron N-77 balloon	H. J. Andrews	
G-BTPV	Colt 90A balloon	Balloon Preservation Group	
G-BTPX	Thunder Ax8-90 BALLOON	B. J. Ross	
G-BTRC	Light Aero Avid Speedwing	Grangecote Ltd	
G-BTRF	Aero Designs Pulsar	P. F. Crosby & C. Smith	
G-BTRG	Aeronca 65C Super Chief	A. Welburn	
G-BTRI	Aeronca 11CC Super Chief	P. A. Wensak	
G-BTRK	PA-28-161 Warrior II	Stapleford Flying Club Ltd	

Notes	Reg.	Type	Owner or Operator
	G-BTRL	Cameron N-105 balloon	J. Lippett
	G-BTRO	Thunder Ax8-90 balloon	Capital Balloon Club Ltd
	G-BTRR	Thunder Ax7-77 balloon	P. J. Wentworth
	G-BTRS	PA-28-161 Warrior II	Airwise Flying Group
	G-BTRT	PA-28R Cherokee Arrow 200-II	Romeo Tango Group
	G-BTRU	Robin DR.400/180	R. H. Mackay
	G-BTRW	Slingsby T.61F Venture T.2	RW Group
	G-BTRY	PA-28-161 Warrior II	Oxford Aviation Academy (Oxford) Ltd
	G-BTRZ	Jodel D.18	A. P. Aspinall
	G-BTSJ	PA-28-161 Warrior II	Fly NQY Pilot Training
	G-BTSN	Cessna 150G	M. L. F. Langrick
	G-BTSP	Piper J-3C-65 Cub	A. Corcoran
	G-BTSR	Aeronca 11AC Chief	J. M. Miller
	G-BTSV	Denney Kitfox Mk 3	R. J. Folwell
	G-BTSW	Colt AS-80 Mk II airship	Gefa-Flug GmbH/Germany
	G-BTSX	Thunder Ax7-77 balloon	C. Moris-Gallimore/Portugal
	G-BTSY	EE Lightning F.6 (XR724) ★	Lightning Association
	G-BTSZ	Cessna 177A	Henlow Aviation Ltd
	G-BTTD	Montgomerie-Bensen B.8MR	A. J. P. Herculson
	G-BTTL	Cameron V-90 balloon	A. J. Baird
	G-BTTO	BAe ATP	Atlantic Airlines Ltd (G-OEDE)
	G-BTTR	Aerotek Pitts S-2A Special	Yellowbird Adventures
	G-BTTW	Thunder Ax7-77 balloon	J. Kenny
	G-BTTY	Denney Kitfox Mk 2	B. J. Clews
	G-BTTZ	Slingsby T.61F Venture T.2	G-BTTZ Group
	G-BTUA	Slingsby T.61F Venture T.2	Shenington Gliding Club
	G-BTUB	Yakovlev C.11	G. G. L. James
	G-BTUC	EMB-312 Tucano ★	Ulster Aviation Heritage
	G-BTUG	SOCATA Rallye 180T	Herefordshire Gliding Club Ltd
	G-BTUH	Cameron N-65 balloon	J. S. Russon
	G-BTUK	Aerotek Pitts S-2A Special	S. H. Elkington
	G-BTUL	Aerotek Pitts S-2A Special	J. M. Adams
	G-BTUM	Piper J-3C-65 Cub	G-BTUM Syndicate
	G-BTUR	PA-18 Super Cub 95 (modified)	M. C. Curtis
	G-BTUS	Whittaker MW7	C. T. Bailey
	G-BTUW	PA-28-151 Warrior	T. S. Kemp
	G-BTUZ	American General AG-5B Tiger	R. V. Grocott
	G-BTVA	Thunder Ax7-77 balloon	C. M. Waters
	G-BTVC	Denney Kitfox Mk 2	M. J. Downes
	G-BTVE	Hawker Demon I (K8203)	Demon Displays Ltd
	G-BTVV	Cessna FA.337G	C. Keane
	G-BTVW	Cessna 152 II	TGD Leasing Ltd
	G-BTVX	Cessna 152 II	The Flight Centre 2010 Ltd
	G-BTWB	Denney Kitfox Mk 3	J. & O. Houlihan (G-BTTM)
	G-BTWC	Slingsby T.61F Venture T.2	The Royal Air Force Gliding and Soaring Association
	G-BTWD	Slingsby T.61F Venture T.2	York Gliding Centre
	G-BTWE	Slingsby T.61F Venture T.2	Aston Down G-BTWE Syndicate
	G-BTWF	DHC.1 Chipmunk 22 (WK549)	G-BTWF Group
	G-BTWI	EAA Acro Sport I	J. O'Connell
	G-BTWJ	Cameron V-77 balloon	C. Gingell & M. Holden-Wadsworth
	G-BTWL	WAG-Aero Acro Sport Trainer	J. P. M. & P. White
	G-BTWX	SOCATA TB9 Tampico	T. I. Murtough
	G-BTWY	Aero Designs Pulsar	R. Bishop
	G-BTWZ	Rans S.10 Sakota	J. T. Phipps
	G-BTXD	Rans S.6-ESA Coyote II	A. I. Sutherland
	G-BTXF	Cameron V-90 balloon	G. Thompson
	G-BTXI	Noorduyn AT-16 Harvard IIB (FE695)	Patina Ltd
	G-BTXK	Thunder Ax7-65 balloon	A. F. Selby
	G-BTXM	Colt 21A Cloudhopper balloon	H. J. Andrews
	G-BTXT	Maule MXT-7-180 Star Rocket	B. de Greef & N. Lasnier
	G-BTXX	Bellanca 8KCAB Decathlon	Tatenhill Aviation Ltd
	G-BTXZ	Zenair CH.250	G-BTXZ Group
	G-BTYC	Cessna 150L	Polestar Aviation Ltd
	G-BTYH	Pottier P.80S	R. G. Marshall
	G-BTYI	PA-28-181 Archer II	Godiva Imaging Ltd
	G-BTYT	Cessna 152 II	Cristal Air Ltd
	G-BTYX	Cessna 140	R. F. Richards
	G-BTZA	Beech F33A Bonanza	G-BTZA Group
	G-BTZB	Yakovlev Yak-50 (10 yellow)	D. H. Boardman
	G-BTZD	Yakovlev Yak-1 (1342)	Historic Aircraft Collection Ltd
	G-BTZE	LET Yakovlev C.11	M. V. Rijkse
	G-BTZO	SOCATA TB20 Trinidad	J. F. Busby

Reg.	Type	Owner or Operator	Notes
G-BTZP	SOCATA TB9 Tampico	M. W. Orr	
G-BTZS	Colt 77A balloon	P. T. R. Ollivere	
G-BTZV	Cameron V-77 balloon	D. J. & H. M. Brown	
G-BTZX	Piper J-3C-65 Cub	ZX Cub Group	
G-BTZY	Colt 56A balloon	K. J. & M. E. Gregory	
G-BTZZ	CFM Streak Shadow	D. R. Stennett	
G-BUAB	Aeronca 11AC Chief	J. Reed	
G-BUAF	Cameron N-77 balloon	Zebedee Balloon Service Ltd	
G-BUAG	Jodel D.18	A. L. Silcox	
G-BUAI	Everett Srs 3 gyroplane	D. Stevenson	
G-BUAJ	Cameron N-90 balloon	High Road Balloons	
G-BUAM	Cameron V-77 balloon	N. Florence	
G-BUAT	Thunder Ax9-120 balloon	S. W. K. Smeeton	
G-BUAV	Cameron O-105 balloon	D. & T. Dorrell	
G-BUAX	Rans S.10 Sakota	P. D. J. Brown	
G-BUBL	Thunder Ax8-105 balloon ★	British Balloon Museum/Newbury	
G-BUBN	BN-2B-26 Islander	Isles of Scilly Skybus Ltd	
G-BUBS	Lindstrand LBL-77B balloon	B. J. Bower	
G-BUBT	Stoddard Hamilton Glasair IIS RG	D. Bonucchi	
G-BUBU	PA-34-220T Seneca III	Brinor (Holdings) Ltd	
G-BUBW	Robinson R22 Beta	HQ Aviation Ltd	
G-BUBY	Thunder Ax8-105 S2 balloon	T. M. Donnelly	
G-BUCA	Cessna A.150K	BUCA Group	
G-BUCC	CASA 1.131E Jungmann 2000 (BU+CC)	P. L. Gaze (G-BUEM)	
G-BUCG	Schleicher ASW.20L (modified)	W. B. Andrews	
G-BUCH	Stinson V-77 Reliant	Gullwing Trading Ltd	
G-BUCI	Auster AOP.9 (XP242)	Historic Aircraft Flight Reserve Collectio	
G-BUCK	CASA 1.131E Jungmann 1000 (BU+CK)	Jungmann Flying Group	
G-BUCM	Hawker Sea Fury FB.11	Patina Ltd	
G-BUCO	Pietenpol Air Camper	A. James	
G-BUCT	Cessna 150L	Linking Partners BV/Nrtherlands	
G-BUDA	Slingsby T.61F Venture T.2	G-BUDA Syndicate	
G-BUDC	Slingsby T.61F Venture T.2 (ZA652)	G. Jones	
G-BUDE	PA-22 Tri-Pacer 135 (tailwheel)	P. Robinson	
G-BUDI	Aero Designs Pulsar	R. W. L. Oliver	
G-BUDK	Thunder Ax7-77 balloon	W. Evans	
G-BUDL	Auster 3 (NX534)	K. B. Owen	
G-BUDN	Cameron 90 Shoe SS balloon	Magical Adventures Ltd	
G-BUDO	PZL-110 Koliber 150	A. S. Vine	
G-BUDR	Denney Kitfox Mk 3	H. D. Colliver	
G-BUDS	Rand-Robinson KR-2	D. W. Munday	
G-BUDT	Slingsby T.61F Venture T.2	G-BUDT Group	
G-BUDU	Cameron V-77 balloon	T. M. G. Amery	
G-BUDW	Brügger MB.2 Colibri	S. P. Barrett (G-GODS)	
G-BUEC	Van's RV-6	A. H. Harper	
G-BUED	Slingsby T.61F Venture T.2	617 VGS Group	
G-BUEF	Cessna 152 II	Channel Aviation	
G-BUEG	Cessna 152 II	Aviation South West Ltd	
G-BUEI	Thunder Ax8-105 balloon	K. P. Barnes	
G-BUEK	Slingsby T.61F Venture T.2	G-BUEK Group	
G-BUEN	VPM M-14 Scout	C. R. Gordon	
G-BUEP	Maule MX-7-180	N. J. B. Bennett	
G-BUEW	Rans S-6 Coyote II	C. Cheeseman (G-MWYE)	
G-BUFG	Slingsby T.61F Venture T.2	K. E. Ballington	
G-BUFH	PA-28-161 Warrior II	Solent School of Flying	
G-BUFR	Slingsby T.61F Venture T.2	East Sussex Gliding Club Ltd	
G-BUFY	PA-28-161 Warrior II	Bickertons Aerodromes Ltd	
G-BUGE	Bellanca 7GCAA Cltabria	V. Vaughan & N. O'Brien	
G-BUGG	Cessna 150F	C. P. J. Taylor & D. M. Forshaw	
G-BUGI	Evans VP-2	D. P. Busby & A. Temple	
G-BUGJ	Robin DR.400/180	W. E. R. Jenkins	
G-BUGL	Slingsby T.61F Venture T.2	VMG Group	
G-BUGP	Cameron V-77 balloon	R. Churcher	
G-BUGS	Cameron V-77 balloon	S. J. Dymond	
G-BUGT	Slingsby T.61F Venture T.2	Bambi Aircraft Group	
G-BUGV	Slingsby T.61F Venture T.2	Oxfordshire Sportflying Ltd	
G-BUGW	Slingsby T.61F Venture T.2	Holdcroft Aviatioin Services Ltd & Transcourt Ltd	
G-BUGY	Cameron V-90 balloon	Dante Balloon Group	
G-BUGZ	Slingsby T.61F Venture T.2	Dishforth Flying Group	
G-BUHA	Slingsby T.61F Venture T.2 (ZA634:C)	Saltby Flying Group	

Notes	Reg.	Type	Owner or Operator
	G-BUHM	Cameron V-77 balloon	L. A. Watts
	G-BUHO	Cessna 140	W. B. Bateson
	G-BUHR	Slingsby T.61F Venture T.2	The Northumbria Gliding Club Ltd
	G-BUHS	Stoddard-Hamilton Glasair SH TD-1	T. F. Horrocks
	G-BUHU	Cameron N-105 balloon	Unipart Balloon Club
	G-BUHZ	Cessna 120	The Cessna 120 Group
	G-BUIF	PA-28-161 Warrior II	Northumbria Flying School Ltd
	G-BUIG	Campbell Cricket (replica)	J. A. English
	G-BUIH	Slingsby T.61F Venture T.2	Falcon Gliding Group
	G-BUIJ	PA-28-161 Warrior II	OPS Aero Support Services
	G-BUIK	PA-28-161 Warrior II	Falcon Flying Services
	G-BUIL	CFM Streak Shadow	A. A. Castleton
	G-BUIN	Thunder Ax7-77 balloon	P. C. Johnson
	G-BUIP	Denney Kitfox Mk 2	Avcomm Developments Ltd
	G-BUIR	Light Aero Avid Speedwing Mk 4	S. J. Handley
	G-BUIZ	Cameron N-90 balloon	Balloon Preservation Flying Group
	G-BUJA	Slingsby T.61F Venture T.2	The Royal Air Force Gliding and Soaring Association
	G-BUJB	Slingsby T.61F Venture T.2	Falke Syndicate
	G-BUJE	Cessna 177B	FG93 Group
	G-BUJH	Colt 77B balloon	B. Fisher
	G-BUJI	Slingsby T.61F Venture T.2	Solent Venture Syndicate Ltd
	G-BUJJ	Avid Speedwing	T. M. Buick
	G-BUJK	Montgomerie-Bensen B.8MR	P. C. W. Raine
	G-BUJM	Cessna 120	Cessna 120 Flying Group
	G-BUJN	Cessna 172N	Warwickshire Aviation Ltd
	G-BUJO	PA-28-161 Warrior II	Falcon Flying Services
	G-BUJP	PA-28-161 Warrior II	Phoenix Aviation
	G-BUJV	Light Aero Avid Speedwing Mk 4	C. Thomas
	G-BUJW	Thunder Ax8-90 S2 balloon	G. J. Grimes
	G-BUJX	Slingsby T.61F Venture T.2	The Burn Gliding Club Ltd
	G-BUJZ	Rotorway Executive 90 (modified)	M. P. Swoboda
	G-BUKB	Rans S.10 Sakota	M. K. Blatch
	G-BUKF	Denney Kitfox Mk 4	Kilo Foxtrot Group
	G-BUKH	D.31 Turbulent	J. G. Wilkins
	G-BUKI	Thunder Ax7-77 balloon	Virgin Balloon Flights
	G-BUKK	Bücker Bü 133C Jungmeister (U-80)	E. J. F. McEntee
	G-BUKO	Cessna 120	K. Handley
	G-BUKP	Denney Kitfox Mk 2	RNAV Europe Ltd
	G-BUKR	MS.880B Rallye Club 100T	G-BUKR Flying Group
	G-BUKU	Luscombe 8E Silvaire	Silvaire Flying Group
	G-BUKY	CCF Harvard 4M (52-8543)	N. T. Oakman
	G-BUKZ	Evans VP-2	P. R. Farnell
	G-BULB	Thunder Ax7-77 balloon	G. B. Davies
	G-BULC	Light Aero Avid Flyer Mk 4	C. Nice
	G-BULF	Colt 77A balloon	P. Goss & T. C. Davies
	G-BULG	Van's RV-4	V. D. Long
	G-BULH	Cessna 172N Skyhawk II	FlyBPL.com
	G-BULJ	CFM Streak Shadow	C. C. Brown
	G-BULL	SA Bulldog Srs 120/128 (HKG-5)	N. V. Sills
	G-BULN	Colt 210A balloon	H. G. Davies
	G-BULO	Luscombe 8A Silvaire	B. W. Foulds
	G-BULT	Campbell Cricket	A. T. Pocklington
	G-BULY	Light Aero Avid Flyer	S. J. Perkins
	G-BULZ	Denney Kitfox Mk 2	T. G. F. Trenchard
	G-BUMP	PA-28-181 Archer II	S. F. Payne & D. J. Lennan
	G-BUNB	Slingsby T.61F Venture T.2	The Royal Air Force Gliding and Soaring Association
	G-BUNC	PZL-104 Wilga 35	R. F. Goodman
	G-BUND	PA-28RT-201T Turbo Arrow IV	E. Culot
	G-BUNG	Cameron N-77 balloon	A. Kaye
	G-BUNO	Lancair 320	J. Softley
	G-BUOA	Whittaker MW6-S Fatboy Flyer	H. N. Graham
	G-BUOB	CFM Streak Shadow	J. M. Hunter
	G-BUOD	SE-5A (replica) (B595:W)	M. D. Waldron/Belgium
	G-BUOE	Cameron V-90 balloon	A. Derbyshire
	G-BUOF	D.62B Condor	R. P. Loxton
	G-BUOI	PA-20-135 Pacer	Foley Farm Flying Group
	G-BUOK	Rans S.6-ESA Coyote II	J. R. S. Heaton
	G-BUOL	Denney Kitfox Mk 3	O. P. Sparrow
	G-BUON	Light Aero Avid Aerobat	I. A. J. Lappin
	G-BUOR	CASA 1.131E Jungmann 2000	M. I. M. S. Voest/Netherlands
	G-BUOS	VS.394 Spitfire FR.XVIII	Spitfire Ltd

Reg.	Type	Owner or Operator	Notes
G-BUOW	Aero Designs Pulsar XP	T. J. Hartwell	
G-BUPA	Rutan LongEz	N. G. Henry	
G-BUPB	Stolp SA.300 Starduster Too	J. R. Edwards & J. W. Widdows	
G-BUPC	Rollason Beta B.2	C. A. Rolph	
G-BUPF	Bensen B.8R	P. W. Hewitt-Dean	
G-BUPI	Cameron V-77 balloon	S. M. Sherwin (G-BOUC)	
G-BUPM	VPM M-16 Tandem Trainer	A. Kitson	
G-BUPP	Cameron V-42 balloon	C. L. Schoeman	
G-BUPR	Jodel D.18	R. W. Burrows	
G-BUPU	Thunder Ax7-77 balloon	R. C. Barkworth & D. G. Maguire/USA	
G-BUPV	Great Lakes 2T-1A	R. J. Fray	
G-BUPW	Denney Kitfox Mk 3	S. G. Metcalfe	
G-BURD	Cessna F.172N	Tayside Aviation Ltd	
G-BURE	Jodel D.9	N. P. St.J. Ramsay	
G-BURG	Colt 77A balloon	P. A. & M. Still	
G-BURH	Cessna 150E	C. A. Davis	
G-BURI	Enstrom F-28C	D. W. C. Holmes	
G-BURJ	HS.748 Srs.2A	Clewer Aviation Ltd	
G-BURL	Colt 105A balloon	J. E. Rose	
G-BURN	Cameron O-120 balloon	G. Gray	
G-BURP	Rotorway Executive 90	N. K. Newman	
G-BURR	Auster AOP.9	Annic Aviation	
G-BURS	Sikorsky S-76A	Premiair Aviation Services Ltd (G-OHTL)	
G-BURT	PA-28-161 Warrior II	Paul's Planes Ltd	
G-BURZ	Hawker Nimrod II (K3661:362)	Historic Aircraft Collection Ltd	
G-BUSH	Airbus A.320-211	SASOF TR-44 Aviation Ireland Ltd	
G-BUSI	Airbus A.320-211	SASOF TR-44 Aviation Ireland Ltd	
G-BUSN	Rotorway Executive 90	J. A. McGinley	
G-BUSR	Aero Designs Pulsar	S. S. Bateman & R. A. Watts	
G-BUSS	Cameron 90 Bus SS balloon	Magical Adventures Ltd	
G-BUSV	Colt 105A balloon	M. N. J. Kirby	
G-BUSW	Rockwell Commander 114	J. Vicoll	
G-BUTB	CFM Streak Shadow	H. O. Maclean	
G-BUTD	Van's RV-6	B. S. Carpenter	
G-BUTE	Anderson EA-1 Kingfisher	T. Crawford (G-BRCK)	
G-BUTF	Aeronca 11AC Chief	Fox Flying Group	
G-BUTG	Zenair CH.601HD	A. J. Thomas	
G-BUTH	CEA DR.220 2+2	Phoenix Flying Group	
G-BUTJ	Cameron O-77 balloon	D. Hoddinott	
G-BUTK	Murphy Rebel	A. J. Gibson	
G-BUTM	Rans S.6-116 Coyote II	J. D. Sinclair-Day	
G-BUTT	Cessna FA150K	Ag-Raum GmbH/Germany (G-AXSJ)	
G-BUTX	CASA 1.133C Jungmeister (ES.1-4)	Bucker Flying Group	
G-BUTY	Brügger MB.2 Colibri	R. M. Lawday	
G-BUTZ	PA-28 Cherokee 180C	M. H. Canning (G-DARL)	
G-BUUA	Slingsby T.67M Firefly Mk II	M. Geroschus	
G-BUUB	Slingsby T.67M Firefly Mk II	The Leicestershire Aero Club Ltd	
G-BUUC	Slingsby T.67M Firefly Mk II	Swiftair Maintenance Ltd	
G-BUUE	Slingsby T.67M Firefly Mk II	J. R. Bratty	
G-BUUF	Slingsby T.67M Firefly Mk II	Tiger Airways	
G-BUUI	Slingsby T.67M Firefly Mk II	Bustard Flying Club Ltd	
G-BUUJ	Slingsby T.67M Firefly Mk II	Durham Tees Flight Training Ltd	
G-BUUK	Slingsby T.67M Firefly Mk II	Avalanche Aviation Ltd	
G-BUUM	PA-28RT-201 Arrow IV	CCHM Aviation Ltd	
G-BUUP	BAe ATP	Atlantic Airlines Ltd	
G-BUUR	BAe ATP	Atlantic Airlines Ltd	
G-BUUU	Cameron Bottle SS balloon ★	British Balloon Museum/Newbury	
G-BUUX	PA-28 Cherokee 180D	Aero Group 78	
G-BUVA	PA-22-135 Tri-Pacer	Oaksey VA Group	
G-BUVE	Colt 77B balloon	G. D. Philpot	
G-BUVL	Fisher Super Koala	A. D. Malcolm	
G-BUVM	CEA DR.250/160	G-BUVM Group	
G-BUVN	CASA 1.131E Jungmann 2000(BI-005)	W. Van Egmond/Netherlands	
G-BUVO	Cessna F.182P	Romeo Mike Flying Group (G-WTFA)	
G-BUVR	Christen A.1 Husky	A. E. Poulson	
G-BUVT	Colt 77A balloon	N. A. Carr	
G-BUVW	Cameron N-90 balloon	P. Spellward	
G-BUVX	CFM Streak Shadow	T. J. Shaw	
G-BUWE	SE-5A (replica) (C9533:M)	Airpark Flight Centre Ltd	
G-BUWF	Cameron N-105 balloon	R. E. Jones	
G-BUWH	Parsons 2-seat gyroplane	R. V. Brunskill	
G-BUWI	Lindstrand LBL-77A balloon	Capital Balloon Club Ltd	
G-BUWJ	Pitts S-1C Special	M. A. Sims	

Notes	Reg.	Type	Owner or Operator
	G-BUWK	Rans S.6-116 Coyote II	R. Warriner
	G-BUWL	Piper J-4A	M. L. Ryan
	G-BUWR	CFM Streak Shadow	T. Harvey
	G-BUWS	Denney Kitfox Mk 2	J. E. Brewis
	G-BUWT	Rand-Robinson KR-2	G. Bailey-Woods
	G-BUWU	Cameron V-77 balloon	T. R. Dews
	G-BUXA	Colt 210A balloon	Balloon School International Ltd
	G-BUXC	CFM Streak Shadow	N. R. Beale
	G-BUXD	Maule MXT-7-160	I. D. McClelland
	G-BUXI	Steen Skybolt	BUXI Group
	G-BUXK	Pietenpol Air Camper	B. M. D. Nelson
	G-BUXL	Taylor JT.1 Monoplane	P. J. Hebdon
	G-BUXN	Beech C23 Sundowner	Private Pilots Syndicate
	G-BUXS	MBB Bö.105DBS/4	Bond Air Services (G-PASA/G-BGWP)
	G-BUXW	Thunder Ax8-90 S2 balloon	N. T. Parry
	G-BUXX	PA-17 Vagabond	R. H. Hunt
	G-BUXY	PA-25 Pawnee 235	Bath, Wilts & North Dorset Gliding Club Ltd
	G-BUYB	Aero Designs Pulsar	P. Robichaud
	G-BUYC	Cameron 80 Concept balloon	R. P. Cross
	G-BUYD	Thunder Ax8-90 balloon	S. McGuigan
	G-BUYF	Falcon XP	M. J. Hadland
	G-BUYK	Denney Kitfox Mk 4	M. S. Shelton
	G-BUYL	RAF 2000GT gyroplane	M. H. J. Goldring
	G-BUYO	Colt 77A balloon	S. F. Burden/Netherlands
	G-BUYS	Robin DR.400/180	G-BUYS Flying Group
	G-BUYU	Bowers Fly-Baby 1A	R. Metcalfe
	G-BUYY	PA-28 Cherokee 180	G-BUYY Group
	G-BUZA	Denney Kitfox Mk 3	A. O'Brien/Ireland
	G-BUZB	Aero Designs Pulsar XP	S. M. Macintyre
	G-BUZC	Everett Srs 3A gyroplane	M. P. L'Hermette
	G-BUZE	Avid Speed Wing	F. Sayyah
	G-BUZG	Zenair CH.601HD	R. M. Ballard
	G-BUZH	Aero Designs Star-Lite SL-1	C. A. McDowall
	G-BUZK	Cameron V-77 balloon	Zebedee Balloon Service Ltd
	G-BUZM	Light Aero Avid Flyer Mk 3	R. McLuckie & O. G. Jones
	G-BUZO	Pietenpol Air Camper	D. A. Jones
	G-BUZR	Lindstrand LBL-77A balloon	Lindstrand Technologies Ltd
	G-BUZT	Kolb Twinstar Mk 3	J. A. G. Robb
	G-BUZZ	Agusta-Bell 206B JetRanger 2	Rivermead Aviation Ltd
	G-BVAB	Zenair CH.601HDS	B. N. Rides
	G-BVAC	Zenair CH.601HD	J. A. Tyndall & S. Wisedale
	G-BVAF	Piper J-3C-65 Cub	G-BVAF Group
	G-BVAH	Denney Kitfox Mk.3	S. Allinson
	G-BVAI	PZL-110 Koliber 150	B. G. Ell
	G-BVAM	Evans VP-1	Breighton VP-1 Group
	G-BVAO	Colt 25A balloon	M. E. Dworski
	G-BVAW	Staaken Z-1 Flitzer (D-692)	L. R. Williams
	G-BVAY	Rutan Vari-Eze	D. A. Young
	G-BVAZ	Montgomerie-Bensen B.8MR	N. Steele
	G-BVBF	PA-28-151 Warrior	R. K. Spence
	G-BVBK	Colt Flying Coffe Jar SS balloon	M. E. White
	G-BVBR	Light Aero Avid Speedwing	J. M. Baldwin & O. Kotova
	G-BVBS	Cameron N-77 balloon	Heart of England Balloons
	G-BVCA	Cameron N-105 balloon	Kent Ballooning
	G-BVCG	Van's RV-6	A. W. Shellis & I. C. Smit
	G-BVCL	Rans S.6-116 Coyote II	A. M. Colman
	G-BVCN	Colt 56A balloon	G. A. & I. Chadwick & S. Richards
	G-BVCO	FRED Srs 2	I. W. Bremner
	G-BVCP	Piper CP.1 Metisse	B. M. Diggins
	G-BVCS	Aeronca 7BCM Champion	A. C. Lines
	G-BVCT	Denney Kitfox Mk 4	A. F. Reid
	G-BVCY	Cameron H-24 balloon	A. C. K. Rawson & J. J. Rudoni
	G-BVDB	Thunder Ax7-77 balloon	S. J. Hollingsworth & M. K. Bellamy (G-ORDY)
	G-BVDC	Van's RV-3	B. S. Carpenter
	G-BVDF	Cameron Doll 105 SS balloon	A. Kaye & K-H Gruenauer
	G-BVDH	PA-28RT-201 Arrow IV	J. Germanos
	G-BVDI	Van's RV-4	J. G. Gorman & H. Tallini
	G-BVDJ	Campbell Cricket (replica)	S. Jennings
	G-BVDM	Cameron 60 Concept balloon	M. P. Young
	G-BVDO	Lindstrand LBL-105A balloon	K. Graham
	G-BVDP	Sequoia F.8L Falco	N. M. Turner
	G-BVDR	Cameron O-77 balloon	N. J. Logue

Reg.	Type	Owner or Operator	Notes
G-BVDS	Lindstrand LBL-69A balloon	Lindstrand Hot-Air Balloons Ltd	
G-BVDT	CFM Streak Shadow	L. P. Harper	
G-BVDW	Thunder Ax8-90 balloon	S. C. Vora	
G-BVDX	Cameron V-90 balloon	R. K. Scott	
G-BVDY	Cameron 60 Concept balloon	P. Baker/Ireland	
G-BVDZ	Taylorcraft BC-12D	N. Rushen	
G-BVEA	Mosler Motors N.3 Pup	G-BVEA Group (G-MWEA)	
G-BVEH	Jodel D.112	M. L. Copland	
G-BVEL	Evans VP-1 Srs.2	M. J. & S. J. Quinn	
G-BVEN	Cameron 80 Concept balloon	R. M. Powell	
G-BVEP	Luscombe 8A Master	B. H. Austen	
G-BVER	DHC.2 Beaver 1 (XV268)	Seaflite Ltd (G-BTDM)	
G-BVEV	PA-34-200 Seneca	G-BVEV Flying Group	
G-BVEW	Lindstrand LBL-150A balloon	S. J. Colin	
G-BVEY	Denney Kitfox Mk 4-1200	J. H. H. Turner	
G-BVEZ	P.84 Jet Provost T.3A (XM479)	Newcastle Jet Provost Co Ltd	
G-BVFA	Rans S.10 Sakota	D. S. Wilkinson	
G-BVFB	Cameron N-31 balloon	P. Lawman	
G-BVFF	Cameron V-77 balloon	R. J. Kerr & G. P. Allen	
G-BVFM	Rans S.6-116 Coyote II	F. B. C. de Beer	
G-BVFO	Light Aero Avid Speedwing	T. G. Solomon	
G-BVFR	CFM Streak Shadow	J. H. Pope	
G-BVFS	Slingsby T.31M	S. R. Williams	
G-BVFU	Cameron 105 Sphere SS balloon	Stichting Phoenix/Netherlands	
G-BVFZ	Maule M5-180C Lunar Rocket	R. C. Robinson	
G-BVGA	Bell 206B JetRanger3	Findon Air Services	
G-BVGB	Thunder Ax8-105 S2 balloon	E. K. Read	
G-BVGE	WS-55 Whirlwind HAR.10 (XJ729)	J. F. Kelly/Ireland	
G-BVGF	Shaw Europa	T. C. Hyde	
G-BVGH	Hawker Hunter T.7 (XL573)	M. Stott	
G-BVGI	Pereira Osprey II	D. Westoby	
G-BVGJ	Cameron C-80 balloon	J. M. J. & V. F. Roberts	
G-BVGK	Lindstrand LBL Newspaper SS balloon	H. Holmqvist	
G-BVGO	Denney Kitfox Mk 4-1200	P. Madden	
G-BVGP	Bücker Bü 133 Jungmeister (U-95)	M. V. Rijkse	
G-BVGT	Auster J/1 (modified)	K. D. & C. S. Rhodes	
G-BVGW	Luscombe 8A Silvaire	J. Smith	
G-BVGX	Thunder Ax8-90 S2 balloon	G-BVGX Group/New Zealand	
G-BVGY	Luscombe 8E Silvaire	Torquil Aviation Ltd	
G-BVGZ	Fokker Dr.1 (replica) (450/17) ★	R. A. Fleming	
G-BVHC	Grob G.115D-2 Heron	Tayside Aviation Ltd	
G-BVHD	Grob G.115D-2 Heron	Tayside Aviation Ltd	
G-BVHE	Grob G.115D-2 Heron	Tayside Aviation Ltd	
G-BVHF	Grob G.115D-2 Heron	Tayside Aviation Ltd	
G-BVHG	Grob G.115D-2 Heron	Tayside Aviation Ltd	
G-BVHI	Rans S.10 Sakota	J. D. Amos	
G-BVHJ	Cameron A-180 balloon	S. J. Boxall	
G-BVHK	Cameron V-77 balloon	A. R. Rich	
G-BVHL	Nicollier HN.700 Menestrel II	W. Dobinson & D. Hawkins	
G-BVHM	PA-38-112 Tomahawk	Hinton Pilot Flight Training Ltd (G-DCAN)	
G-BVHO	Cameron V-90 balloon	N. W. B. Bews	
G-BVHR	Cameron V-90 balloon	G. P. Walton	
G-BVHS	Murphy Rebel	S. T. Raby	
G-BVHV	Cameron N-105 balloon	Kent Ballooning	
G-BVIA	Rand-Robinson KR-2	K. Atkinson	
G-BVIE	PA-18 Super Cub 95 (modified)	J. C. Best (G-CLIK/G-BLMB)	
G-BVIF	Montgomerie-Bensen B.8MR	R. M. & D. Mann	
G-BVIK	Maule MXT-7-180 Star Rocket	Graveley Flying Group	
G-BVIL	Maule MXT-7-180 Star Rocket	K. & S. C. Knight	
G-BVIS	Brügger MB.2 Colibri	B. H. Shaw	
G-BVIV	Light Aero Avid Speedwing	S. Styles	
G-BVIW	PA-18-Super Cub 150	I. H. Logan	
G-BVIZ	Shaw Europa	The Europa Group	
G-BVJF	Montgomerie-Bensen B.8MR	D. M. F. Harvey	
G-BVJG	Cyclone AX3/K	J. Gilroy (G-MYOP)	
G-BVJK	Glaser-Dirks DG.800A	J. S. Forster	
G-BVJN	Shaw Europa	JN Europa Group	
G-BVJT	Cessna F.406	Nor Leasing	
G-BVJU	Evans VP-1	BVJU Flying Club & Associates	
G-BVJX	Marquart MA.5 Charger	A. E. Cox	
G-BVKB	Boeing 737-59D	bmi Baby (stored)	
G-BVKF	Shaw Europa	T. R. Sinclair	
G-BVKG	Colt Flying Hot Dog SS balloon	Longbreak Ltd/USA	

Notes	Reg.	Type	Owner or Operator
	G-BVKK	Slingsby T.61F Venture T.2	Buckminster Gliding Club Ltd
	G-BVKL	Cameron A-180 balloon	Dragon Balloon Co Ltd
	G-BVKM	Rutan Vari-Eze	J. P. G. Lindquist/Switzerland
	G-BVKU	Slingsby T.61F Venture T.2	G-BVKU Syndicate
	G-BVLA	Lancair 320	Eaglescott Lancair Group
	G-BVLD	Campbell Cricket (replica)	C. Berry
	G-BVLF	CFM Starstreak Shadow SS-D	J. C. Pratelli
	G-BVLG	AS.355F1 Twin Squirrel	PLM Dollar Group PLC
	G-BVLH	Shaw Europa	D. Barraclough
	G-BVLL	Lindstrand LBL-210A balloon	Airborne Balloon Flights Ltd
	G-BVLN	Aero Designs Pulsar XP	D. A. Campbell
	G-BVLP	PA-38-112 Tomahawk	J. Hornby
	G-BVLR	Van's RV-4	RV4 Group
	G-BVLT	Bellanca 7GCBC Citabria	Slade Associates
	G-BVLU	D.31 Turbulent	C. D. Bancroft
	G-BVLV	Shaw Europa	Euro 39 Group
	G-BVLX	Slingsby T.61F Venture T.2	The Royal Air Force Gliding and Soaring Association
	G-BVMA	Beech 200 Super King Air	Dragonfly Aviation Services Ltd (G-VPLC)
	G-BVME	AS.365N2 Dauphin 2	CHC Scotia Ltd
	G-BVMH	WAG-Aero Sport Trainer (39624:D-39)	J. Mathews
	G-BVMJ	Cameron 95 Eagle SS balloon	R. D. Sargeant
	G-BVMM	Robin HR.200/100	Gloster Aero Group
	G-BVMN	Ken Brock KB-2 gyroplane	G-BVMN Group
	G-BVMR	Cameron V-90 balloon	I. R. Comley
	G-BVMU	Yakovlev Yak-52 (09 yellow)	Ascendances SPRL/Belgium
	G-BVNG	DH.60G-III Moth Major	P. & G. Groves
	G-BVNI	Taylor JT-2 Titch	G. de Halle
	G-BVNS	PA-28-181 Archer II	Scottish Airways Flyers (Prestwick) Ltd
	G-BVNU	FLS Aerospace Sprint Club	M. D. R. Elmes
	G-BVNY	Rans S.7 Courier	S. Hazleden
	G-BVOC	Cameron V-90 balloon	H. W. R. Stewart
	G-BVOH	Campbell Cricket (replica)	A. Kitson
	G-BVOI	Rans S.6-116 Coyote II	M. J. Whiteman-Haywood
	G-BVOK	Yakovlev Yak-52 (55 grey)	Trans Holdings Ltd
	G-BVOP	Cameron N-90 balloon	October Gold Ballooning Ltd
	G-BVOR	CFM Streak Shadow	J. M. Chandler
	G-BVOS	Shaw Europa	Durham Europa Group
	G-BVOW	Shaw Europa	H. P. Brooks
	G-BVOY	Rotorway Executive 90	C. H. Drake
	G-BVOZ	Colt 56A balloon	British School of Ballooning
	G-BVPA	Thunder Ax8-105 S2 balloon	Firefly Balloon Promotions
	G-BVPD	CASA 1.131E Jungmann 2000	D. Bruton
	G-BVPM	Evans VP-2 Coupé	P. Marigold
	G-BVPN	Piper J-3C-65 Cub	C. Sarcelet (G-TAFY)
	G-BVPS	Jodel D.112	BAT Group
	G-BVPV	Lindstrand LBL-77B balloon	P. G. Hill
	G-BVPW	Rans S.6-116 Coyote II	T. B. Woolley
	G-BVPX	Bensen B.8 (modified) Tyro Gyro	A. W. Harvey
	G-BVPY	CFM Streak Shadow	A. J. Grant
	G-BVRA	Shaw Europa	N. E. Stokes
	G-BVRH	Taylorcraft BL.65	M. J. Kirk
	G-BVRJ	Avro RJ-70	QinetiQ Ltd
	G-BVRL	Lindstrand LBL-21A balloon	T. J. Orchard & M. E. Banks
	G-BVRU	Lindstrand LBL-105A balloon	C & R Jemmett
	G-BVRV	Van's RV-4	A. Troughton
	G-BVRZ	PA-18 Super Cub 95	R. W. Davison
	G-BVSB	TEAM mini-MAX	D. G. Palmer
	G-BVSD	SE.3130 Alouette II (V-54)	M. J. Cuttell
	G-BVSF	Aero Designs Pulsar	R. J. & J. A. Freestone
	G-BVSN	Light Aero Avid Speedwing	R. C. Bowley
	G-BVSP	P.84 Jet Provost T.3A (XM370)	H. G. Hodges & Son Ltd
	G-BVSS	Jodel D.150	A. L. Breckell
	G-BVST	Jodel D.150	A. Shipp/Breighton
	G-BVSX	TEAM mini-MAX 91	J. A. Clark
	G-BVSZ	Pitts S-1E (S) Special	H. J. Morton
	G-BVTA	Tri-R Kis	A. F. Prosser
	G-BVTC	P.84 Jet Provost T.5A (XW333)	Global Aviation Ltd
	G-BVTD	CFM Streak Shadow	M. Walton
	G-BVTL	Colt 31A balloon	A. Lindsay
	G-BVTM	Cessna F.152 II	RAF Halton Aeroplane Club (G-WACS)
	G-BVTN	Cameron N-90 balloon	P. Zulehner/Austria
	G-BVTV	Rotorway Executive 90	D. W. J. Lee

Reg.	Type	Owner or Operator	Notes
G-BVTW	Aero Designs Pulsar	R. J. Panther	
G-BVTX	DHC.1 Chipmunk 22A (WP809)	TX Flying Group	
G-BVUA	Cameron O-105 balloon	Wickers World Ltd	
G-BVUC	Colt 56A balloon	J. F. Till	
G-BVUG	Betts TB.1 (Stampe SV.4C)	H. F. Fekete (G-BEUS)	
G-BVUH	Thunder Ax6-65B balloon	K. B. Chapple	
G-BVUI	Lindstrand LBL-25A balloon	J. W. Hole	
G-BVUK	Cameron V-77 balloon	H. G. Griffiths & W. A. Steel	
G-BVUM	Rans S.6-116 Coyote II	M. A. Abbott	
G-BVUN	Van's RV-4	D. J. Harvey	
G-BVUT	Evans VP-1 Srs. 2	M. J. Barnett	
G-BVUU	Cameron C-80 balloon	T. M. C. McCoy	
G-BVUV	Shaw Europa	R. J. Mills	
G-BVUZ	Cessna 120	T. K. Duffy	
G-BVVB	Carlson Sparrow II	L. M. McCullen	
G-BVVE	Jodel D.112	M. Balls	
G-BVVG	Nanchang CJ-6A (68)	Nanchang CJ6A Group	
G-BVVH	Shaw Europa	T. G. Hoult	
G-BVVI	Hawker Audax I (K5600)	Aero Vintage Ltd	
G-BVVK	DHC.6 Twin Otter 310	Loganair Ltd/Flybe	
G-BVVL	EAA Acro Sport II	G-BVVL Syndicate	
G-BVVM	Zenair CH.601HD	D. Macdonald	
G-BVVN	Brügger MB.2 Colibri	N. F. Andrews	
G-BVVP	Shaw Europa	I. Mansfield	
G-BVVR	Stits SA-3A Playboy	R. B. Armitage	
G-BVVS	Van's RV-4	E. G. & N. S. C. English	
G-BVVU	Lindstrand LBL Four SS balloon	Magical Adventures Ltd/USA	
G-BVVW	Yakovlev Yak-52	M. Blackman	
G-BVVZ	Corby CJ-1 Starlet	P. V. Flack	
G-BVWB	Thunder Ax8-90 S2 balloon	M. A. Stelling & K. C. Tanner	
G-BVWC	EE Canberra B.6 (WK163)	Classic Aviation Projects Ltd	
G-BVWD	Avro RJ85	Trident Aviation Leasing Services (Jersey) Ltd	
G-BVWI	Cameron light bulb SS balloon	Mobberley Balloon Collection	
G-BVWM	Shaw Europa	A. Head	
G-BVWW	Lindstrand LBL-90A balloon	J. D. A. Shields	
G-BVWY	Porterfield CP.65	R. L. Earl & B. Morris	
G-BVWZ	PA-32-301 Saratoga	The Saratoga (WZ) Group	
G-BVXA	Cameron N-105 balloon	R. E. Jones	
G-BVXC	EE Canberra B.6 (WT333) ★	Classic Aviation Projects Ltd/Bruntingthorpe	
G-BVXD	Cameron O-84 balloon	Hedge Hoppers Balloon Group	
G-BVXE	Steen Skybolt	J. Buglass (G-LISA)	
G-BVXJ	CASA 1.133 Jungmeister	C. Butler & G. G. Ferriman	
G-BVXK	Yakovlev Yak-52 (26 grey)	Yak UK Ltd	
G-BVXM	AS.350B Ecureuil	The Berkeley Leisure Group Ltd	
G-BVXR	DH.104 Devon C.2 (XA880)	M. Whale & M. W. A. Lunn	
G-BVYF	PA-31-350 Navajo Chieftain	J. A. Rees & D. T. Rees (G-SAVE)	
G-BVYG	CEA DR.300/180	Ulster Gliding Club Ltd	
G-BVYK	TEAM mini-MAX	A. G. Ward	
G-BVYM	CEA DR.300/180	London Gliding Club (Pty) Ltd	
G-BVYO	Robin R.2160	D. J. S. McClean	
G-BVYP	PA-25 Pawnee 235B	Bidford Airfield Ltd	
G-BVYU	Cameron A-140 balloon	S. Charlish	
G-BVYX	Light Aero Avid Speedwing Mk 4	J. E. Lipman	
G-BVYY	Pietenpol Air Camper	Pietenpol G-BVYY Group	
G-BVYZ	Stemme S.10V	L. Gubbay	
G-BVZD	Tri-R Kis Cruiser	J. M. Angiolini & G. Melling	
G-BVZE	Boeing 737-59D	bmi Baby (stored)	
G-BVZJ	Rand-Robinson KR-2	G. M. Rundle	
G-BVZN	Cameron C-80 balloon	S. J. Clarke	
G-BVZO	Rans S.6-116 Coyote II	P. J. Brion	
G-BVZR	Zenair CH.601HD	R. A. Perkins	
G-BVZT	Lindstrand LBL-90A balloon	J. Edwards	
G-BVZV	Rans S.6-116 Coyote II	A. H. & F. A. Macaskill	
G-BVZX	Cameron H-34 balloon	R. H. Etherington	
G-BVZZ	DHC.1 Chipmunk 22 (WP795)	Portsmouth Naval Gliding Club	
G-BWAB	Jodel D.14	D. Braim	
G-BWAC	Waco YKS-7	D. N. Peters	
G-BWAD	RAF 2000GT gyroplane	A. Melody	
G-BWAF	Hawker Hunter F.6A (XG160:U) ★	Bournemouth Aviation Museum/Bournemouth	
G-BWAG	Cameron O-120 balloon	P. M. Skinner	
G-BWAH	Montgomerie-Bensen B.8MR	J. B. Allan	
G-BWAI	CFM Streak Shadow	C. M. James	

Notes	Reg.	Type	Owner or Operator
	G-BWAJ	Cameron V-77 balloon	T. J. Wilkinson
	G-BWAN	Cameron N-77 balloon	I. Chadwick
	G-BWAO	Cameron C-80 balloon	M. D. Freeston & S. Mitchell
	G-BWAP	FRED Srs 3	G. A. Shepherd
	G-BWAR	Denney Kitfox Mk 3	I. Wightman
	G-BWAT	Pietenpol Air Camper	P. W. Aitchison
	G-BWAU	Cameron V-90 balloon	K. M. & A. M. F. Hall
	G-BWAV	Schweizer 269C	Helihire
	G-BWAW	Lindstrand LBL-77A balloon	D. Bareford
	G-BWBI	Taylorcraft F-22A	R. T. G. Preston
	G-BWBT	Lindstrand LBL-90A balloon	British Telecommunications PLC
	G-BWBY	Schleicher ASH-26E	P. M. Wells
	G-BWBZ	ARV-1 Super 2	M. P. Holdstock
	G-BWCA	CFM Streak Shadow	I. C. Pearson
	G-BWCK	Everett Srs 2 gyroplane	B. F. Pearson
	G-BWCS	P.84 Jet Provost T.5 (XW293:Z)	J. H. Ashcroft
	G-BWCT	Tipsy T.66 Nipper 1	J. S. Hemmings & C. R. Steer
	G-BWCV	Shaw Europa	G. C. McKirdy
	G-BWCY	Murphy Rebel	S. Burrow
	G-BWDB	ATR-72-202	Aurigny Air Services Ltd
	G-BWDH	Cameron N-105 balloon	M. A. Scholes
	G-BWDM	Lindstrand LBL-120A balloon	A. N. F. Pertwee
	G-BWDP	Shaw Europa	S. Attubato
	G-BWDS	P.84 Jet Provost T.3A (XM424)	Aviation Heritage Ltd
	G-BWDT	PA-34-220T Seneca III	H. R. Chambers (G-BKHS)
	G-BWDX	Shaw Europa	J. Robson
	G-BWDZ	Sky 105-24 balloon	M. T. Wiltshire
	G-BWEA	Lindstrand LBL-120A balloon	S. R. Seager
	G-BWEB	P.84 Jet Provost T.5A (XW422:3)	J. Miller
	G-BWEE	Cameron V-42 balloon	A. J. Davey/Germany
	G-BWEF	SNCAN Stampe SV.4C	Acebell G-BWEF Syndicate (G-BOVL)
	G-BWEG	Shaw Europa	R. J. Marsh
	G-BWEM	VS.358 Seafire L.IIIC (RX168)	Mark One Partners LLC
	G-BWEN	Macair Merlin GT	D. A. Hill
	G-BWEU	Cessna F.152 II	Eastern Air Executive Ltd
	G-BWEW	Cameron N-105 balloon	Unipart Balloon Club
	G-BWEY	Bensen B.8	F. G. Shepherd
	G-BWEZ	Piper J-3C-65 Cub (436021)	J. G. McTaggart
	G-BWFG	Robin HR.200/120B	Air Atlantique Ltd
	G-BWFH	Shaw Europa	G. C. Grant
	G-BWFJ	Evans VP-1	G. Robson
	G-BWFK	Lindstrand LBL-77A balloon	Balloon Preservation Flying Group
	G-BWFM	Yakovlev Yak-50	Fox Mike Group
	G-BWFN	Hapi Cygnet SF-2A	G-BWFN Group
	G-BWFO	Colomban MC.15 Cri-Cri	K. D. & C. S. Rhodes
	G-BWFT	Hawker Hunter T.8M (XL602)	G. I. Begg
	G-BWFX	Shaw Europa	A. D. Stewart
	G-BWFZ	Murphy Rebel	D. K. Shead (G-SAVS)
	G-BWGA	Lindstrand LBL-105A balloon	R. Thompson
	G-BWGF	P.84 Jet Provost T.5A (XW325)	Viper Jet Provost Group Ltd
	G-BWGJ	Chilton DW.1A	T. J. Harrison
	G-BWGL	Hawker Hunter T.8C (XJ615)	Stichting Hawker Hunter Foundation/Netherlands
	G-BWGO	Slingsby T.67M Firefly 200	R. Gray
	G-BWGS	BAC.145 Jet Provost T.5A (XW310)	M. P. Grimshaw
	G-BWGU	Cessna 150F	Goodair Leasing Ltd
	G-BWGY	HOAC Katana DV.20	JL Flying Ltd
	G-BWHA	Hawker Hurricane IIB (Z5252)	Historic Flying Ltd
	G-BWHD	Lindstrand LBL-31A balloon	M. R. Noyce & R. P. E. Phillips
	G-BWHI	DHC.1 Chipmunk 22A (WK624)	N. E. M. Clare
	G-BWHK	Rans S.6-116 Coyote II	S. J. Wakeling
	G-BWHM	Sky 140-24 balloon	C. J. S. Limon
	G-BWHP	CASA 1.131E Jungmann (S4+A07)	J. F. Hopkins
	G-BWHR	Tipsy Nipper T.66 Srs 1	L. R. Marnef
	G-BWHS	RAF 2000 gyroplane	B. J. Payne
	G-BWHU	Westland Scout AH.1 (XR595)	N. J. F. Boston
	G-BWIA	Rans S.10 Sakota	A. C. G. T. da Costa, J. A. F. Monteiro & R. M. M. Moura
	G-BWIB	SA Bulldog Srs 120/122 (XX514)	B. I. Robertson/USA
	G-BWID	D.31 Turbulent	N. Huxtable
	G-BWII	Cessna 150G	J. D. G. Hicks (G-BSKB)
	G-BWIJ	Shaw Europa	R. Lloyd
	G-BWIK	DH.82A Tiger Moth (NL985)	P. J. Lawton
	G-BWIL	Rans S-10	S. H. Leahy

Reg.	Type	Owner or Operator	Notes
G-BWIP	Cameron N-90 balloon	K. C. Tanner	
G-BWIR	Dornier 328-100	Suckling Airways (Cambridge) Ltd	
G-BWIV	Shaw Europa	T. G. Ledbury	
G-BWIW	Sky 180-24 balloon	T. M. Donnelly	
G-BWIX	Sky 120-24 balloon	J. M. Percival	
G-BWIZ	QAC Quickie Tri-Q 200	M. C. Davies	
G-BWJB	Thunder Ax8-105 balloon	Justerini & Brooks Ltd	
G-BWJG	Mooney M.20J	S. Nahum	
G-BWJH	Shaw Europa	I. R. Willis	
G-BWJM	Bristol M.1C (replica) (C4918)	The Shuttleworth Collection	
G-BWJY	DHC.1 Chipmunk 22 (WG469)	K. J. Thompson	
G-BWKF	Cameron N-105 balloon	M. Buono/Italy	
G-BWKK	Auster A.O.P.9 (XP279)	C. A. Davis & D. R. White	
G-BWKT	Stephens Akro Laser	P. D. Begley	
G-BWKU	Cameron A-250 balloon	British School of Ballooning	
G-BWKV	Cameron V-77 balloon	A. P. Wallace	
G-BWKW	Thunder Ax8-90 balloon	Gone With The Wind Ltd	
G-BWKZ	Lindstrand LBL-77A balloon	J. H. Dobson	
G-BWLD	Cameron O-120 balloon	D. Pedri & ptnrs/Italy	
G-BWLF	Cessna 404	Reconnaisance Ventures Ltd (G-BNXS)	
G-BWLJ	Taylorcraft DCO-65 (42-35870/129)	B. J. Robe	
G-BWLL	Murphy Rebel	F. W. Parker	
G-BWLM	Sky 65-24 balloon	W. J. Brogan	
G-BWLY	Rotorway Executive 90	P. W. & I. P. Bewley	
G-BWMB	Jodel D.119	C. Hughes	
G-BWMC	Cessna 182P	Iscavia Ltd	
G-BWMF	Gloster Meteor T.7 (WA591)	Aviation Heritage Ltd	
G-BWMH	Lindstrand LBL-77B balloon	A. P. Jay	
G-BWMI	PA-28RT-201T Turbo Arrow IV	O. Cowley & R. Pascoe	
G-BWMJ	Nieuport 17/2B (replica) (N1977:8)	R. Gauld-Galliers & M. R. Lancombe	
G-BWMK	DH.82A Tiger Moth (T8191)	K. F. Crumplin	
G-BWMN	Rans S.7 Courier	P. J. Tyler	
G-BWMO	Oldfield Baby Lakes	D. Maddocks (G-CIII)	
G-BWMS	DH.82A Tiger Moth	Stichting Vroege Vogels/Netherlands	
G-BWMU	Cameron 105 Monster Truck SS balloon	Magical Adventures Ltd/Canada	
G-BWMV	Colt AS-105 Mk II airship	D. Stuber/Germany	
G-BWMX	DHC.1 Chipmunk 22 (WG407:67)	407th Flying Group	
G-BWMY	Cameron Bradford & Bingley SS balloon	Magical Adventures Ltd/USA	
G-BWNB	Cessna 152 II	South Warwickshire School of Flying	
G-BWNC	Cessna 152 II	South Warwickshire School of Flying	
G-BWND	Cessna 152 II	South Warwickshire School of Flying Ltd & G. Davies	
G-BWNI	PA-24 Comanche 180	W. A. Stewart	
G-BWNJ	Hughes 269C	L. R. Fenwick	
G-BWNK	D,H,C,1 Chipmunk 22 (WD390)	WD390 Group	
G-BWNM	PA-28R Cherokee Arrow 180	M. & R. C. Ramnial	
G-BWNO	Cameron O-90 balloon	T. Knight	
G-BWNP	Cameron 90 Club SS balloon	H. Cusden & J. Edwards	
G-BWNS	Cameron O-90 balloon	I. C. Steward	
G-BWNT	DHC.1 Chipmunk 22 (WP901)	P. G. D. Bell & A. Stafford	
G-BWNU	PA-38-112 Tomahawk	Kemble Aero Club Ltd	
G-BWNY	Aeromot AMT-200 Super Ximango	Powell-Brett Associates Ltd	
G-BWNZ	Agusta A109C	Anglo Beef Processors Ltd	
G-BWOB	Luscombe 8F Silvaire	P. R. Bush	
G-BWOF	P.84 Jet Provost T.5	Techair London Ltd	
G-BWOH	PA-28-161 Cadet	Redhill Air Services Ltd	
G-BWOI	PA-28-161 Cadet	Aviation Rentals	
G-BWOJ	PA-28-161 Cadet	Aviation Rentals	
G-BWOK	Lindstrand LBL-105G balloon	Lindstrand Hot Air Balloons Ltd	
G-BWOR	PA-18 Super Cub 135	C. D. Baird	
G-BWOV	Enstrom F-28A	P. A. Goss	
G-BWOW	Cameron N-105 balloon	Skybus Ballooning	
G-BWOY	Sky 31-24 balloon	C. Wolstenholme	
G-BWOZ	CFM Streak Shadow SA	J. A. Lord	
G-BWPC	Cameron V-77 balloon	H. Vaughan	
G-BWPE	Murphy Renegade Spirit UK	J. Hatswell/France	
G-BWPF	Sky 120-24 balloon	J. Francis	
G-BWPH	PA-28-181 Archer II	H. Merkado	
G-BWPJ	Steen Skybolt	D. Houghton	
G-BWPP	Sky 105-24 balloon	The Sarnia Balloon Group	
G-BWPS	CFM Streak Shadow SA	P. J. Mogg	
G-BWPT	Cameron N-90 balloon	G.Everett	
G-BWPZ	Cameron N-105 balloon	D. M. Moffat	

Notes	Reg.	Type	Owner or Operator
	G-BWRA	Sopwith LC-1T Triplane (replica) (N500)	J. G. Brander (G-PENY)
	G-BWRC	Light Aero Avid Speedwing	C. G. Thompson
	G-BWRO	Shaw Europa	G-BWRO Europa Group
	G-BWRR	Cessna 182Q	A. & R. Reid
	G-BWRS	SNCAN Stampe SV.4C	G. P. J. M. Valvekens/Belgium
	G-BWRT	Cameron 60 Concept balloon	Zebedee Balloon Service Ltd
	G-BWRZ	Lindstrand LBL-105A balloon	N. Dykes
	G-BWSB	Lindstrand LBL-105A balloon	R. Calvert-Fisher
	G-BWSC	PA-38-112 Tomahawk II	The Hawstead Flying Group
	G-BWSD	Campbell Cricket	R. F. G. Moyle
	G-BWSG	P.84 Jet Provost T.5 (XW324/K)	J. Bell
	G-BWSH	P.84 Jet Provost T.3A (XN498)	Global Aviation Ltd
	G-BWSI	K & S SA.102.5 Cavalier	B. W. Shaw
	G-BWSJ	Denney Kitfox Mk 3	J. M. Miller
	G-BWSL	Sky 77-24 balloon	D. Baggley
	G-BWSN	Denney Kitfox Mk 3	M. J. Laundy
	G-BWSU	Cameron N-105 balloon	A. M. Marten
	G-BWSV	Yakovlev Yak-52	M. W. Fitch
	G-BWTB	Lindstrand LBL-105A balloon	Servatruc Ltd
	G-BWTC	Zlin Z.242L	S. W. Turley
	G-BWTD	Zlin Z.242L	Oxford Aviation Academy (Oxford) Ltd
	G-BWTE	Cameron O-140 balloon	Cameron Flights Southern Ltd
	G-BWTG	DHC.1 Chipmunk 22 (WB671:910)	R. G. T. de Man/Netherlands
	G-BWTH	Robinson R22 Beta	Helicopter Services
	G-BWTJ	Cameron V-77 balloon	A. J. Montgomery
	G-BWTK	RAF 2000 GTX-SE gyroplane	M. Love
	G-BWTN	Lindstrand LBL-90A balloon	J. A. Lomas
	G-BWTO	DHC.1 Chipmunk 22 (WP984)	Skycraft Services Ltd
	G-BWTW	Mooney M.20C	T. J. Berry
	G-BWUA	Campbell Cricket	N. J. Orchard
	G-BWUE	Hispano HA.1112M1L	Historic Flying Ltd (G-AWHK)
	G-BWUH	PA-28-181 Archer III	A. Davis
	G-BWUJ	Rotorway Executive 162F	Southern Helicopters Ltd
	G-BWUK	Sky 160-24 balloon	Cameron Flights Southern Ltd
	G-BWUL	Noorduyn AT-16 Harvard IIB	G-BWUL Flying Group
	G-BWUN	DHC.1 Chipmunk 22 (WD310)	T. Henderson
	G-BWUP	Shaw Europa	V. Goddard
	G-BWUS	Sky 65-24 balloon	N. A. P. Bates
	G-BWUT	DHC.1 Chipmunk 22 (WZ879)	Herbert Aviation Ltd
	G-BWUU	Cameron N-90 balloon	Bailey Balloons Ltd
	G-BWUV	DHC.1 Chipmunk 22A (WK640)	A. C. Darby
	G-BWUZ	Campbell Cricket (replica)	K. A. Touhey
	G-BWVB	Pietenpol Air Camper	E. B. Toulson
	G-BWVC	Jodel D.18	R. W. J. Cripps
	G-BWVF	Pietenpol Air Camper	N. Clark
	G-BWVI	Stern ST.80	I. Pearson
	G-BWVM	Colt AA-1050 balloon	B. B. Baxter Ltd
	G-BWVN	Whittaker MW7	S. T. G. Ingram
	G-BWVR	Yakovlev Yak-52 (52 yellow)	I. Parkinson
	G-BWVS	Shaw Europa	D. R. Bishop
	G-BWVT	DHA.82A Tiger Moth	R. Jewitt
	G-BWVU	Cameron O-90 balloon	J. Atkinson
	G-BWVY	DHC.1 Chipmunk 22 (WP896)	N. Gardner
	G-BWVZ	DHC.1 Chipmunk 22A (WK590)	D. Campion/Belgium
	G-BWWA	Ultravia Pelican Club GS	J. S. Aplin
	G-BWWB	Shaw Europa	P. Levi
	G-BWWC	DH.104 Dove 7 (XM223)	Air Atlantique Ltd
	G-BWWE	Lindstrand LBL-90A balloon	B. J. Newman
	G-BWWF	Cessna 185A	T. N. Bartlett & S. M. C. Harvey
	G-BWWG	SOCATA Rallye 235E	J. J. Frew
	G-BWWJ	Hughes 269C	R. J. Scott (G-BMYZ)
	G-BWWK	Hawker Nimrod I (S1581)	Patina Ltd
	G-BWWL	Colt Flying Egg SS balloon	Magical Adventures Ltd/USA
	G-BWWN	Isaacs Fury II (K8303:D)	J. S. Marten-Hale
	G-BWWT	Dornier 328-100	Suckling Airways (Cambridge) Ltd/Flybe
	G-BWWU	PA-22 Tri-Pacer 150	K. M. Bowen
	G-BWWW	BAe Jetstream 3102	British Aerospace PLC
	G-BWWX	Yakovlev Yak-50	D. P. McCoy/Ireland
	G-BWWY	Lindstrand LBL-105A balloon	M. J. Smith
	G-BWXA	Slingsby T.67M Firefly 260	Swift Aircraft Ltd
	G-BWXB	Slingsby T.67M Firefly 260	Swift Aircraft Ltd
	G-BWXC	Slingsby T.67M Firefly 260	Swift Aircraft Ltd
	G-BWXD	Slingsby T.67M Firefly 260	Swift Aircraft Ltd

Reg.	Type	Owner or Operator	Notes
G-BWXE	Slingsby T.67M Firefly 260	Swift Aircraft Ltd	
G-BWXF	Slingsby T.67M Firefly 260	Swift Aircraft Ltd	
G-BWXG	Slingsby T.67M Firefly 260	Swift Aircraft Ltd	
G-BWXH	Slingsby T.67M Firefly 260	Swift Aircraft Ltd	
G-BWXI	Slingsby T.67M Firefly 260	Swift Aircraft Ltd	
G-BWXJ	Slingsby T.67M Firefly 260	Swift Aircraft Ltd	
G-BWXK	Slingsby T.67M Firefly 260	Swift Aircraft Ltd	
G-BWXL	Slingsby T.67M Firefly 260	Airspeed BVBA/Belgium	
G-BWXM	Slingsby T.67M Firefly 260	Skelleftea Aeroclub AB/Sweden	
G-BWXN	Slingsby T.67M Firefly 260	Swift Aircraft Ltd	
G-BWXP	Slingsby T.67M Firefly 260	D. S. McGregor	
G-BWXR	Slingsby T.67M Firefly 260	Swift Aircraft Ltd	
G-BWXS	Slingsby T.67M Firefly 260	Swift Aircraft Ltd	
G-BWXT	Slingsby T.67M Firefly 260	Cranfield University	
G-BWXU	Slingsby T.67M Firefly 260	Swift Aircraft Ltd	
G-BWXV	Slingsby T.67M Firefly 260	TC Trading & Consulting SPRL/BVBA	
G-BWXX	Slingsby T.67M Firefly 260	Swift Aircraft Ltd	
G-BWXY	Slingsby T.67M Firefly 260	Swift Aircraft Ltd	
G-BWXZ	Slingsby T.67M Firefly 260	Swift Aircraft Ltd	
G-BWYB	PA-28 Cherokee 160	A. J. Peters	
G-BWYD	Shaw Europa	F. H. Mycroft	
G-BWYI	Denney Kitfox Mk3	D. R. Piercy	
G-BWYK	Yakovlev Yak-50	Foley Farm Flying Group	
G-BWYN	Cameron O-77 balloon	W. H. Morgan (G-ODER)	
G-BWYO	Sequoia F.8L Falco	M. C. R. Sims	
G-BWYR	Rans S.6-116 Coyote II	D. A. Lord	
G-BWYU	Sky 120-24 balloon	Aerosauras Balloons Ltd	
G-BWZA	Shaw Europa	T. G. Cowlishaw	
G-BWZG	Robin R.2160	Sherburn Aero Club Ltd	
G-BWZJ	Cameron A-250 balloon	Balloon Club of Great Britain	
G-BWZU	Lindstrand LBL-90B balloon	K. D. Pierce	
G-BWZY	Hughes 269A	Reeve Newfields Ltd (G-FSDT)	
G-BXAB	PA-28-161 Warrior II	TG Aviation Ltd (G-BTGK)	
G-BXAC	RAF 2000 GTX-SE gyroplane	J. A. Robinson	
G-BXAF	Pitts S-1D Special	N. J. Watson	
G-BXAJ	Lindstrand LBL-14A balloon	Oscair Project AB/Sweden	
G-BXAK	Yakovlev Yak-52 (44 black)	J. Calverley	
G-BXAN	Scheibe SF-25C Falke	C. Falke Syndicate	
G-BXAO	Avtech Jabiru SK	P. J. Thompson	
G-BXAU	Pitts S-1 Special	L. Westnage	
G-BXAX	Cameron N-77 balloon ★	Balloon Preservation Group	
G-BXAY	Bell 206B JetRanger 3	Viewdart Ltd	
G-BXBA	Cameron A-210 balloon	Reach For The Sky Ltd	
G-BXBB	PA-20 Pacer 150	M. E. R. Coghlan	
G-BXBK	Avions Mudry CAP-10B	S. Skipworth	
G-BXBL	Lindstrand LBL-240A balloon	Firefly Balloon Promotions	
G-BXBM	Cameron O-105 balloon	Bristol University Hot Air Ballooning Society	
G-BXBU	Avions Mudry CAP-10B	J. F. Cosgrave & H. R. Pearson	
G-BXBZ	PZL-104 Wilga 80	J. H. Sandham Aviation	
G-BXCA	Hapi Cygnet SF-2A	J. D. C. Henslow	
G-BXCC	PA-28-201T Turbo Dakota	Greer Aviation Ltd	
G-BXCD	TEAM mini-MAX 91A	A. Maltby	
G-BXCG	Jodel DR.250/160	CG Group	
G-BXCJ	Campbell Cricket (replica)	A. G. Peel	
G-BXCN	Sky 105-24 balloon	Nottingham Hot-Air Balloon Club	
G-BXCO	Colt 120A balloon	J. R. Lawson	
G-BXCP	DHC.1 Chipmunk 22 (WP859)	M. P. O'Connor	
G-BXCT	DHC.1 Chipmunk 22 (WB697)	Wickenby Aviation	
G-BXCU	Rans S.6-116 Coyote II	S. C. Ord	
G-BXCV	DHC.1 Chipmunk 22 (WP929)	Ardmore Aviation Services Ltd/Hong Kong	
G-BXCW	Denney Kitfox Mk 3	M. J. Blanchard	
G-BXDA	DHC.1 Chipmunk 22 (WP860)	D. C. Mowat	
G-BXDB	Cessna U.206F	D. A. Howard (G-BMNZ)	
G-BXDE	RAF 2000GTX-SE gyroplane	B. Jones	
G-BXDF	Beech 95-B55 Baron	Equity Air CharterChesh-Air Ltd	
G-BXDG	DHC.1 Chipmunk 22 (WK630)	Felthorpe Flying Group	
G-BXDH	DHC.1 Chipmunk 22 (WD331)	Royal Aircraft Establishment Aero Club Ltd	
G-BXDI	DHC.1 Chipmunk 22 (WD373)	Sunrise Global Aviation Ltd	
G-BXDN	DHC.1 Chipmunk 22 (WK609)	W. D. Lowe, G. James & L. A. Edwards	
G-BXDO	Rutan Cozy	J. Foreman	
G-BXDP	DHC.1 Chupmunk 22 (WK642)	Gipsy Captains	
G-BXDR	Lindstrand LBL-77A balloon	A. J. & A. R. Brown	

Notes	Reg.	Type	Owner or Operator
	G-BXDS	Bell 206B JetRanger III	Aerospeed Limited (G-TAMF/G-OVBJ)
	G-BXDU	Aero Designs Pulsar	M. P. Board
	G-BXDV	Sky 105-24 balloon	N. A. Carr
	G-BXDY	Shaw Europa	S. Attubato & D. G. Watts
	G-BXDZ	Lindstrand LBL-105A balloon	D. J. & A. D. Sutcliffe
	G-BXEC	DHC.1 Chipmunk 22 (WK633)	D. S. Hunt
	G-BXEJ	VPM M-16 Tandem Trainer	AES Radionic Surveillance Systems
	G-BXEN	Cameron N-105 balloon	E. Ghio/Italy
	G-BXES	P.66 Pembroke C.1 (XL954)	Air Atlantique Ltd
	G-BXEX	PA-28-181 Archer II	R. Mayle
	G-BXEZ	Cessna 182P	Forhawk Ltd
	G-BXFB	Pitts S-1 Special	J. F. Dowe
	G-BXFC	Jodel D.18	B. S. Godbold
	G-BXFE	Avions Mudry CAP-10B	Avion Aerobatic Ltd
	G-BXFG	Shaw Europa	A. Rawicz-Szczerbo
	G-BXFI	Hawker Hunter T.7 (WV372)	Canfield Hunter Ltd
	G-BXFK	CFM Streak Shadow	A. G. Sindrey
	G-BXFN	Colt 77A balloon	Charter Ballooning Ltd
	G-BXGA	AS.350B2 Ecureuil	PLM Dollar Group Ltd
	G-BXGD	Sky 90-24 balloon	Servo & Electronic Sales Ltd
	G-BXGG	Shaw Europa	D. J. Joyce
	G-BXGH	Diamond Katana DA20-A1	M. Dorrian
	G-BXGL	DHC.1 Chipmunk 22	Booker Aircraft Leasing Ltd
	G-BXGM	DHC.1 Chipmunk 22 (WP928:D)	Chipmunk G-BXGM Group
	G-BXGO	DHC.1 Chipmunk 22 (WB654:U)	Trees Group
	G-BXGP	DHC.1 Chipmunk 22 (WZ882)	Eaglescott Chipmunk Group
	G-BXGS	RAF 2000 gyroplane	D. W. Howell
	G-BXGT	I.I.I. Sky Arrow 650T	J. S. C. Goodale
	G-BXGV	Cessna 172R	Skyhawk Group
	G-BXGX	DHC.1 Chipmunk 22 (WK586:V)	The Real Flying Co.Ltd
	G-BXGY	Cameron V-65 balloon	Dante Balloon Group
	G-BXGZ	Stemme S.10V	G. S. Craven & A. J. Garner
	G-BXHA	DHC.1 Chipmunk 22 (WP925)	H. M. & S. Roberts
	G-BXHE	Lindstrand LBL-105A balloon	L. H. Ellis
	G-BXHF	DHC.1 Chipmunk 22 (WP930:J)	Hotel Fox Syndicate
	G-BXHH	AA-5A Cheetah	A. W. Daffin
	G-BXHJ	Hapi Cygnet SF-2A	I. J. Smith
	G-BXHL	Sky 77-24 balloon	Zebedee Balloon Service Ltd
	G-BXHO	Lindstrand Telewest Sphere SS balloon	Magical Adventures Ltd
	G-BXHR	Stemme S.10V	J. H. Rutherford
	G-BXHT	Bushby-Long Midget Mustang	K. Manley
	G-BXHU	Campbell Cricket Mk 6	P. J. Began
	G-BXHY	Shaw Europa	Jupiter Flying Group
	G-BXIA	DHC.1 Chipmunk 22 (WB615)	Dales Aviation
	G-BXIC	Cameron A-275 balloon	Aerosaurus Balloons LLP
	G-BXIE	Colt 77B balloon	I. R. Warrington
	G-BXIF	PA-28-161 Warrior II	Piper Flight Ltd
	G-BXIG	Zenair CH.701 STOL	A. J. Perry
	G-BXIH	Sky 200-24 balloon	Kent Ballooning
	G-BXII	Shaw Europa	D. A. McFadyean
	G-BXIJ	Shaw Europa	R. James
	G-BXIM	DHC.1 Chipmunk 22 (WK512)	A. B. Ashcroft & P. R. Joshua
	G-BXIO	Jodel DR.1050M	R. S. Palmer
	G-BXIT	Zebedee V-31 balloon	Zebedee Balloon Service Ltd
	G-BXIX	VPM M-16 Tandem Trainer	P. P. Willmott
	G-BXIY	Blake Bluetit (BAPC37)	M. J. Aubrey
	G-BXIZ	Lindstrand LBL-31A balloon	J. S. Russon
	G-BXJB	Yakovlev Yak-52	Yak Display Group
	G-BXJC	Cameron A-210 balloon	British School of Ballooning
	G-BXJD	PA-28 Cherokee 180C	M. G. A. Hussein
	G-BXJG	Lindstrand LBL-105B balloon	C. E. Wood
	G-BXJH	Cameron N-42 balloon	D. M. Hoddinott
	G-BXJJ	PA-28-161 Cadet	White Waltham Airfield Ltd
	G-BXJM	Cessna 152	ACS Aviation Ltd
	G-BXJO	Cameron O-90 balloon	Dragon Balloon Co Ltd
	G-BXJP	Cameron C-80 balloon	A. Sarrasin
	G-BXJS	Schempp-Hirth Janus CM	Janus Syndicate
	G-BXJT	Sky 90-24 balloon	J. G. O'Connell
	G-BXJY	Van's RV-6	J. P. Kynaston
	G-BXJZ	Cameron C-60 balloon	J. M. Stables
	G-BXKF	Hawker Hunter T.7 (XL577/V)	R. F. Harvey
	G-BXKL	Bell 206B JetRanger 3	Swattons Aviation Ltd
	G-BXKM	RAF 2000 GTX-SE gyroplane	A. H. Goddard

Reg.	Type	Owner or Operator	Notes
G-BXKO	Sky 65-24 balloon	Ecole de Pilotage Franche-Comte Montgolfieres/France	
G-BXKU	Colt AS-120 Mk II airship	D. C. Chipping/Portugal	
G-BXKW	Slingsby T.67M Firefly 200	J-F Jansen & A. Huygens	
G-BXKX	Auster V	J. A. Clark	
G-BXLF	Lindstrand LBL-90A balloon	W. Rousell & J. Tyrrell	
G-BXLG	Cameron C-80 balloon	S. M. Anthony	
G-BXLK	Shaw Europa	R. G. Fairall	
G-BXLN	Fournier RF-4D	P. W. Cooper & M. R. Fox	
G-BXLO	P.84 Jet Provost T.4 (XR673/L)	Century Aviation Ltd	
G-BXLP	Sky 90-24 balloon	D. Bedford & J. Edwards	
G-BXLS	PZL-110 Koliber 160A	D. C. Bayes	
G-BXLT	SOCATA TB200 Tobago XL	C., G. & J. Fisher & D. Fitton	
G-BXLW	Enstrom F.28F	Rhoburt Ltd	
G-BXLY	PA-28-151 Warrior	Multiflight Ltd (G-WATZ)	
G-BXMF	Cassutt Racer IIIM	P. R. Fabish	
G-BXMG	RAF 2000 GTX gyroplane	J. S. Wright	
G-BXMM	Cameron A-180 balloon	High Road Balloons	
G-BXMV	Scheibe SF.25C Falke 1700	K. E. Ballington	
G-BXMX	Currie Wot	M. R. Coreth	
G-BXMY	Hughes 269C	R. J. Scott	
G-BXNA	Light Aero Avid Flyer	A. P. Daines	
G-BXNC	Shaw Europa	J. K. Cantwell	
G-BXNN	DHC.1 Chipmunk 22 (WP983:B)	E. N. Skinner	
G-BXNS	Bell 206B JetRanger 3	Sterling Helicopters Ltd	
G-BXNT	Bell 206B JetRanger 3	Sterling Helicopters Ltd	
G-BXOA	Robinson R22 Beta	MG Group Ltd	
G-BXOC	Evans VP-2	M. P. Wiseman	
G-BXOF	Diamond Katana DA20-A1	Aircraft Engineers Ltd	
G-BXOI	Cessna 172R	E. J. Watts	
G-BXOJ	PA-28-161 Warrior III	Tayside Aviation Ltd	
G-BXOM	Isaacs Spitfire	S. Vince	
G-BXON	Auster AOP.9	C. J. & D. J. Baker	
G-BXOT	Cameron C-70 balloon	Dante Balloon Group	
G-BXOU	CEA DR.360	J. A. Lofthouse	
G-BXOX	AA-5A Cheetah	R. L. Carter & P. J. Large	
G-BXOY	QAC Quickie Q.235	C. C. Clapham	
G-BXOZ	PA-28-181 Archer II	Spritetone Ltd	
G-BXPC	Diamond Katana DA20-A1	Cubair Flight Training Ltd	
G-BXPD	Diamond Katana DA20-A1	Cubair Flight Training Ltd	
G-BXPI	Van's RV-4	B. M. Diggins	
G-BXPK	Cameron A-250 balloon	Alba Ballooning Ltd	
G-BXPM	Beech 58 Baron	Foyle Flyers Ltd	
G-BXPP	Sky 90-24 balloon	S. J. Farrant	
G-BXPR	Colt 110 Can SS balloon	P. O. Wagner/Germany	
G-BXPT	Ultramagic H-77 balloon	G. D. O. Bartram/Andorra	
G-BXRA	Avions Mudry CAP-10B	J. W. Scott	
G-BXRB	Avions Mudry CAP-10B	T. T. Duhig	
G-BXRC	Avions Mudry CAP-10B	Group Alpha	
G-BXRF	CP.1310-C3 Super Emeraude	D. T. Gethin	
G-BXRM	Cameron A-210 balloon	Cameron Flights Southern Ltd	
G-BXRO	Cessna U.206G	M. Penny	
G-BXRP	Schweizer 269C	AH Helicopter Services Ltd	
G-BXRR	Westland Scout AH.1	M. Soor	
G-BXRS	Westland Scout AH.1 (XW613)	B-N Group Ltd	
G-BXRT	Robin DR.400-180	T. P. Usborne	
G-BXRV	Van's RV-4	Cleeve Flying Grouip	
G-BXRY	Bell 206B JetRanger	Corbett Holdings Ltd	
G-BXRZ	Rans S.6-116 Coyote II	M. P. Hallam	
G-BXSC	Cameron C-80 balloon	N. A. Apsey	
G-BXSD	Cessna 172R	R. Paston	
G-BXSE	Cessna 172R	MK Aero Support Ltd	
G-BXSG	Robinson R22 Beta II	Rivermead Aviation Ltd	
G-BXSH	Glaser-Dirks DG.800B	R. O'Conor	
G-BXSI	Avtech Jabiru SK	P. F. Gandy	
G-BXSP	Grob G.109B	Deeside Grob Group	
G-BXSR	Cessna F172N	N. C. K. G. Copeman	
G-BXST	PA-25 Pawnee 235C	The Northumbria Gliding Club Ltd	
G-BXSU	TEAM mini-MAX 91A	I. A. Coates (G-MYGL)	
G-BXSV	SNCAN Stampe SV.4C	P. A. Greenhalgh	
G-BXSX	Cameron V-77 balloon	D. R. Medcalf	
G-BXSY	Robinson R22 Beta II	N. M. G. Pearson	
G-BXTB	Cessna 152	Durham Tees Flight Training Ltd	

Notes	Reg.	Type	Owner or Operator
	G-BXTD	Shaw Europa	P. R. Anderson
	G-BXTF	Cameron N-105 balloon	Flying Pictures Ltd
	G-BXTG	Cameron N-42 balloon	P. M. Watkins & S. M. M. Carden
	G-BXTH	Westland Gazelle HT.1 (XW866)	Armstrong Aviation Ltd
	G-BXTI	Pitts S-1S Special	Fly Hire Ltd
	G-BXTJ	Cameron N-77 balloon	Chubb Fire Ltd Chubb
	G-BXTO	Hindustan HAL-6 Pushpak	P. Q. Benn
	G-BXTS	Diamond Katana DA20-A1	I. M. Armitage & D. J. Short
	G-BXTT	AA-5B Tiger	J. Ducray
	G-BXTV	Bug Mk.4 helicopter	B. R. Cope
	G-BXTW	PA-28-181 Archer III	Davison Plant Hire
	G-BXTY	PA-28-161 Cadet	Flew LLP
	G-BXTZ	PA-28-161 Cadet	Flew LLP
	G-BXUA	Campbell Cricket Mk.5	A. W. Harvey
	G-BXUC	Robinson R22 Beta	Rivermead Aviation Ltd/Switzerland
	G-BXUF	Agusta-Bell 206B JetRanger 3	SJ Contracting Services Ltd
	G-BXUG	Lindstrand Baby Bel SS balloon	K-H. Gruenauer/Germany
	G-BXUH	Lindstrand LBL-31A balloon	K. Gruenauer
	G-BXUI	Glaser-Dirks DG.800B	J. Le Coyte
	G-BXUM	Shaw Europa	D. Bosomworth
	G-BXUO	Lindstrand LBL-105A balloon	Lindstrand Technologies Ltd
	G-BXUS	Sky 65-24 balloon	PSH Skypower Ltd
	G-BXUU	Cameron V-65 balloon	M. D. Freeston & S. Mitchell
	G-BXUW	Cameron Colt 90A balloon	V. Beardall
	G-BXUX	Brandli Cherry BX-2	M. F. Fountain
	G-BXUY	Cessna 310Q	G. A. Vickers
	G-BXVA	SOCATA TB200 Tobago XL	M. Goehen
	G-BXVB	Cessna 152 II	PJC (Leasing) Ltd
	G-BXVD	CFM Streak Shadow SA	I. J. C. Burman
	G-BXVG	Sky 77-24 balloon	M. Wolf
	G-BXVK	Robin HR.200/120B	Modi Aviation Ltd
	G-BXVM	Van's RV-6A	J. C. Lomax
	G-BXVO	Van's RV-6A	P. J. Hynes & M. E. Holden
	G-BXVP	Sky 31-24 balloon	T. Dudman
	G-BXVR	Sky 90-24 balloon	P. Hegarty
	G-BXVS	Brügger MB.2 Colibri	G. T. Snoddon
	G-BXVT	Cameron O-77 balloon	R. P. Wade
	G-BXVU	PA-28-161 Warrior II	Jet Connections Ltd
	G-BXVV	Cameron V-90 balloon	Adeilad Cladding
	G-BXVX	Rutan Cozy	G. E. Murray
	G-BXVY	Cessna 152	Stapleford Flying Club Ltd
	G-BXWA	Beech 76 Duchess	Aviation South West Ltd
	G-BXWB	Robin HR.100/200B	W. A. Brunwin
	G-BXWG	Sky 120-24 balloon	M. E. White
	G-BXWH	Denney Kitfox Mk.4-1200	M. G. Porter
	G-BXWK	Rans S.6-ESA Coyote II	P. B. Davey
	G-BXWL	Sky 90-24 balloon	D. J. Baggley
	G-BXWO	PA-28-181 Archer II	J. S. Develin & Z. Islam
	G-BXWP	PA-32 Cherokee Six 300	R. J. Sharpe
	G-BXWR	CFM Streak Shadow	M. A. Hayward (G-MZMI)
	G-BXWT	Van's RV-6	R. C. Owen
	G-BXWU	FLS Aerospace Sprint 160	Aeroelvia Ltd
	G-BXWV	FLS Aerospace Sprint 160	Aeroelvia Ltd
	G-BXWX	Sky 25-16 balloon	C. O'Neill & G. Davis
	G-BXXG	Cameron N-105 balloon	R. N. Simpkins
	G-BXXH	Hatz CB-1	R. D. Shingler
	G-BXXI	Grob G.109B	M. N. Martin
	G-BXXJ	Colt Flying Yacht SS balloon	Magical Adventures Ltd/USA
	G-BXXK	Cessna FR.172N	P. Porter
	G-BXXL	Cameron N-105 balloon	Flying Pictures Ltd
	G-BXXN	Robinson R22 Beta	Helicopter Services
	G-BXXO	Lindstrand LBL-90B balloon	G. P. Walton
	G-BXXP	Sky 77-24 balloon	T. R. Wood
	G-BXXS	Sky 105-24 balloon	Flying Pictures Ltd
	G-BXXT	Beech 76 Duchess	Pridenote Ltd
	G-BXXU	Colt 31A balloon	Sade Balloons Ltd
	G-BXXW	Enstrom F-28F	D. A. Marks (G-SCOX)
	G-BXYE	CP.301-C1 Emeraude	D. T. Gethin
	G-BXYF	Colt AS-105 GD airship	LN Flying Ltd
	G-BXYI	Cameron H-34 balloon	S. P. Harrowing
	G-BXYJ	Jodel DR.1050	G-BXYJ Group
	G-BXYM	PA-28 Cherokee 235	Redfly Aviation Ltd
	G-BXYO	PA-28RT-201 Arrow IV	S. Viner

Reg.	Type	Owner or Operator	Notes
G-BXYP	PA-28RT-201 Arrow IV	G. I. Cooper	
G-BXYT	PA-28RT-201 Arrow IV	Falcon Flying Services Ltd	
G-BXZA	PA-38-112 Tomahawk	Aviatlantic	
G-BXZB	Nanchang CJ-6A (2632019)	R. Davy & J. L. Swallow	
G-BXZF	Lindstrand LBL-90A balloon	B. T. Harris	
G-BXZI	Lindstrand LBL-90A balloon	J. A. Viner	
G-BXZK	MDH MD-900 Explorer	Dorset Police Air Support Unit	
G-BXZO	Pietenpol Air Camper	P. J. Cooke	
G-BXZU	Micro Aviation Bantam B.22-S	M. E. Whapham & R. W. Hollamby	
G-BXZV	CFM Streak Shadow	M. D. O'Brien	
G-BXZY	CFM Streak Shadow Srs DD	G. T. Webster	
G-BYAT	Boeing 757-204ER	Thomson Airways Ltd	
G-BYAV	Taylor JT.1 Monoplane	D. M. Lockley	
G-BYAW	Boeing 757-204ER	Thomson Airways Ltd	
G-BYAX	Boeing 757-204ER	Thomson Airways Ltd	
G-BYAY	Boeing 757-204ER	Thomson Airways Ltd	
G-BYAZ	CFM Streak Shadow	A. G. Wright	
G-BYBC	Agusta-Bell 206B JetRanger 2	Sky Charter UK Ltd (G-BTWW)	
G-BYBD	Cessna F.172H	D. G. Bell & J. Cartmell (G-OBHX/G-AWMU)	
G-BYBE	Jodel D.120A	J. M. Alexander	
G-BYBF	Robin R.2160i	D. J. R. Lloyd-Evans	
G-BYBH	PA-34-200T Seneca II	Goldspear (UK) Ltd	
G-BYBI	Bell 206B JetRanger 3	Castle Air Ltd	
G-BYBJ	Medway Hybred 44XLR	M. Gardner	
G-BYBK	Murphy Rebel	J. R. Howard	
G-BYBL	Gardan GY-80 Horizon 160D	M. J. Sutton	
G-BYBM	Avtech Jabiru SK	P. J. Hatton	
G-BYBN	Cameron N-77 balloon	M. G. Howard	
G-BYBO	Medway Hybred 44XLR Eclipser	C. Hershaw	
G-BYBP	Cessna A.185F	G. M. S. Scott	
G-BYBR	Rans S.6-116 Coyote II	S. & A. F. Williams	
G-BYBS	Sky 80-16 balloon	B. K. Rippon	
G-BYBU	Renegade Spirit UK	R. L. Williams	
G-BYBV	Mainair Rapier	M. W. Robson	
G-BYBX	Slingsby T.67M Firefly 260	Slingsby Advanced Composites Ltd	
G-BYBY	Thorp T.18C Tiger	P. G. Mair	
G-BYBZ	Jabiru SK	D. Licheri	
G-BYCA	PA-28 Cherokee 140D	R. Steptoe	
G-BYCD	Cessna 140 (modified)	G. P. James	
G-BYCF	Robinson R22 Beta II	Aero Maintenance Ltd	
G-BYCJ	CFM Shadow Srs DD	P. I. Hodgson	
G-BYCM	Rans S.6-ES Coyote II	E. W. McMullan	
G-BYCN	Rans S.6-ES Coyote II	T. J. Croskery	
G-BYCP	Beech B200 Super King Air	London Executive Aviation Ltd	
G-BYCS	Jodel DR.1051	CS Group	
G-BYCT	Aero L-29A Delfin	M. P. Grimshaw & M. C. Hall	
G-BYCV	Meridian Maverick 430	A. Vaughan	
G-BYCW	Mainair Blade 912	P. C. Watson	
G-BYCX	Westland Wasp HAS.1	C. J. Marsden	
G-BYCY	I.I.I. Sky Arrow 650T	K. A. Daniels	
G-BYCZ	Avtech Jabiru SK	T. Herbert	
G-BYDB	Grob G.115B	J. B. Baker	
G-BYDE	VS.361 Spitfire LF. IX (PT879)	P. A. Teichman	
G-BYDF	Sikorsky S-76A	Brecqhou Development Ltd	
G-BYDG	Beech C24R Sierra	Professional Flight Simulation Ltd	
G-BYDJ	Colt 120A balloon	D. K. Hempleman-Adams	
G-BYDK	SNCAN Stampe SV.4C	Bianchi Aviation Film Services Ltd	
G-BYDL	Hawker Hurricane IIB (Z5207)	P. J. Lawton	
G-BYDT	Cameron N-90 balloon	R. M. Stanley	
G-BYDV	Van's RV-6	B. F. Hill	
G-BYDY	Beech 58 Baron	Pilot Services Flying Group Ltd	
G-BYDZ	Pegasus Quantum 15-912	A. Mundy	
G-BYEA	Cessna 172P	M. Gates	
G-BYEC	Glaser-Dirks DG.800B	The 23 Syndicate	
G-BYEE	Mooney M.20K	Double Echo Flying Group	
G-BYEH	CEA Jodel DR.250	S. T. Scully	
G-BYEJ	Scheibe SF-28A Tandem Falke	D. Shrimpton	
G-BYEK	Stoddard Hamilton Glastar	M. W. Meynell	
G-BYEL	Van's RV-6	D. Millar	
G-BYEM	Cessna R.182 RG	Bickertons Aerodromes Ltd	
G-BYEO	Zenair CH.601HDS	J. R. Clarke	
G-BYER	Cameron C-80 balloon	J. M. Langley	

Notes	Reg.	Type	Owner or Operator
	G-BYES	Cessna 172P	Surrey Aviation Ltd
	G-BYEW	Pegasus Quantum 15-912	W. B. J. Davis
	G-BYEY	Lindstrand LBL-21 Silver Dream balloon	Oscair Project Ltd/Sweden
	G-BYFA	Cessna F.152 II	Redhill Air Services Ltd (G-WACA)
	G-BYFC	Avtech Jabiru SK	M. Flint
	G-BYFF	Pegasus Quantum 15-912	Kemble Flying Club
	G-BYFI	CFM Starstreak Shadow SA	J. A. Cook
	G-BYFJ	Cameron N-105 balloon	R. J. Mercer
	G-BYFK	Cameron Printer 105 SS balloon	Mobberley Balloon Collection
	G-BYFL	Diamond HK.36 TTS	Seahawk Gliding Club
	G-BYFM	Jodel DR.1050M-1 (replica)	A. J. Roxburgh
	G-BYFR	PA-32R-301 Saratoga II HP	Buckleton Ltd
	G-BYFT	Pietenpol Air Camper	G. Everett
	G-BYFV	TEAM mini-MAX 91	W. E. Gillham
	G-BYFX	Colt 77A balloon	Wye Valley Aviation Ltd
	G-BYFY	Avions Mudry CAP-10B	R. N. Crosland
	G-BYGA	Boeing 747-436	British Airways
	G-BYGB	Boeing 747-436	British Airways
	G-BYGC	Boeing 747-436	British Airways
	G-BYGD	Boeing 747-436	British Airways
	G-BYGE	Boeing 747-436	British Airways
	G-BYGF	Boeing 747-436	British Airways
	G-BYGG	Boeing 747-436	British Airways
	G-BYHC	Cameron Z-90 balloon	S. M. Sherwin
	G-BYHE	Robinson R22 Beta	Helicopter Services Ltd
	G-BYHG	Dornier 328-100	Suckling Airways (Cambridge) Ltd
	G-BYHH	PA-28-161 Warrior III	Stapleford Flying Club Ltd
	G-BYHI	PA-28-161 Warrior II	T. W. & W. S. Gilbert
	G-BYHJ	PA-28R-201 Arrow	Flew LLP
	G-BYHK	PA-28-181 Archer III	T-Air Services
	G-BYHL	DHC.1 Chipmunk 22 (WG308)	M. R. & I. D. Higgins
	G-BYHO	Mainair Blade 912	T. Porter & D. Whiteley
	G-BYHP	CEA DR.253B	HP Flying Group
	G-BYHR	Pegasus Quantum 15-912	I. D. Chantler
	G-BYHS	Mainair Blade 912	Telzor Group
	G-BYHT	Robin DR.400/180R	Deeside Robin Group
	G-BYHU	Cameron N-105 balloon	ABC Flights Ltd
	G-BYHV	Raj Hamsa X'Air 582	M. G. Adams
	G-BYHY	Cameron V-77 balloon	P. Spellward
	G-BYIA	Avtech Jabiru SK	M. D. Doyle
	G-BYIB	Rans S.6-ES Coyote II	W. Anderson
	G-BYID	Rans S.6-ES Coyote II	R. M. Watson
	G-BYIE	Robinson R22 Beta II	G. R. S. Harrison
	G-BYII	TEAM mini-MAX	G. Wilkinson
	G-BYIJ	CASA 1.131E Jungmann 2000	R. N. Crosland
	G-BYIK	Shaw Europa	P. M. Davis
	G-BYIL	Cameron N-105 balloon	N. W. N. Townshend
	G-BYIM	Avtech Jabiru UL	A. & J. McVey
	G-BYIN	RAF 2000 gyroplane	J. R. Legge
	G-BYIO	Colt 105A balloon	N. Charbonnier/Italy
	G-BYIP	Aerotek Pitts S-2A Special	D. P. Heather-Hayes
	G-BYIR	Aerotek Pitts S-1S Special	S. Kramer
	G-BYIS	Pegasus Quantum 15-912	D. J. Ramsden
	G-BYIU	Cameron V-90 balloon	H. Micketeit/Germany
	G-BYIV	Cameron PM-80 balloon	A. Schneider/Germany
	G-BYIW	Cameron PM-80 balloon	Team Ballooning/Germany
	G-BYIX	Cameron PM-80 balloon	A. Schneider/Germany
	G-BYIY	Lindstrand LBL-105B balloon	J. H. Dobson
	G-BYJA	RAF 2000 GTX-SE	C. R. W. Lyne
	G-BYJB	Mainair Blade 912	P. C. Terry
	G-BYJC	Cameron N-90 balloon	A. G. Merry
	G-BYJD	Avtech Jabiru UL	M. W. Knights
	G-BYJE	TEAM Mini-MAX 91	T. A. Willcox
	G-BYJF	Thorpe T.211	AD Aviation Ltd
	G-BYJG	Lindstrand LBL-77A balloon	Lindstrand Hot-Air Balloons Ltd
	G-BYJH	Grob G.109B	A. J. Buchanan
	G-BYJI	Shaw Europa	M. Gibson (G-ODTI)
	G-BYJK	Pegasus Quantum 15-912	K. D. Smith
	G-BYJL	Aero Designs Pulsar	F. A. H. Ashmead
	G-BYJM	Cyclone AX2000	R. W. Kraike
	G-BYJN	Lindstrand LBL-105A balloon	B. Meeson
	G-BYJO	Rans S.6-ES Coyote II	D. J. Warren
	G-BYJP	Aerotek Pitts S-1S Special	Eaglescott Pitts Group

Reg.	Type	Owner or Operator	Notes
G-BYJR	Lindstrand LBL-77B balloon	B. M. Reed	
G-BYJS	SOCATA TB20 Trinidad	A. P. Bedford	
G-BYJT	Zenair CH.601HD	J. D. T. Tannock	
G-BYJW	Cameron Sphere 105 balloon	Balleroy Developpement SAS	
G-BYJX	Cameron C-70 balloon	B. Perona	
G-BYKA	Lindstrand LBL-69A balloon	B. Meeson	
G-BYKB	Rockwell Commander 114	Hayling Island Safety Consultancy Ltd	
G-BYKC	Mainair Blade 912	G. W. Cameron & C. S. Harrison	
G-BYKD	Mainair Blade 912	D. C. Boyle	
G-BYKF	Enstrom F-28F	S. C. Severeyns & G. T. Williams	
G-BYKG	Pietenpol Air Camper	K. B. Hodge	
G-BYKI	Cameron N-105 balloon	J. A. Leahy/Ireland	
G-BYKJ	Westland Scout AH.1	Austen Associates	
G-BYKK	Robinson R44	Dragonfly Aviation	
G-BYKL	PA-28-181 Archer II	Transport Command Ltd	
G-BYKP	PA-28R-201T Turbo Arrow IV	D. W. Knox & D. L. Grimes	
G-BYKT	Pegasus Quantum 15-912	N. J. Howarth	
G-BYKU	BFC Challenger II	K. W. Seedhouse	
G-BYKW	Lindstrand LBL-77B balloon	K. Allemand/France	
G-BYKX	Cameron N-90 balloon	G. Davis	
G-BYLB	D. H. 82A Tiger Moth	P. A. Layzell	
G-BYLC	Pegasus Quantum 15-912	A. Cordes	
G-BYLD	Pietenpol Air Camper	S. Bryan	
G-BYLI	Nova Vertex 22 hang glider	M. Hay	
G-BYLJ	Letov LK-2M Sluka	W. J. McCarroll	
G-BYLL	Sequoia F.8L Falco	N. J. Langrick	
G-BYLO	T.66 Nipper Srs 1	M. J. A. Trudgill	
G-BYLP	Rand-Robinson KR-2	C. S. Hales	
G-BYLS	Bede BD-4	P. J. Greenrod	
G-BYLT	Raj Hamsa X'Air 582	T. W. Phipps	
G-BYLV	Thunder Ax8-105 S2 balloon	kb Voli Di Chiozzi Bartolomeo EC SAS/Italy	
G-BYLW	Lindstrand LBL-77A balloon	Associazione Gran Premio Italiano	
G-BYLX	Lindstrand LBL-105A balloon	Italiana Aeronavi/Italy	
G-BYLY	Cameron V-77 balloon (1)	R. Bayly/Italy (G-ULIA)	
G-BYLZ	Rutan Cozy	W. S. Allen	
G-BYMB	Diamond Katana DA20-C1	S. Staniulis & A. Zakaras	
G-BYMD	PA-38-112 Tomahawk II	M. A. Petrie	
G-BYMF	Pegasus Quantum 15-912	G. R. Stockdale	
G-BYMG	Cameron A-210 balloon	Cloud Nine Balloon Co	
G-BYMH	Cessna 152	PJC (Leasing) Ltd	
G-BYMI	Pegasus Quantum 15	N. C. Grayson	
G-BYMJ	Cessna 152	PJC (Leasing) Ltd	
G-BYMK	Dornier 328-100	Suckling Airways (Cambridge) Ltd	
G-BYMN	Rans S.6-ESA Coyote II	R. J. P. Herivel	
G-BYMO	Campbell Cricket	C. N. Enmarch	
G-BYMP	Campbell Cricket Mk 1	J. J. Fitzgerald	
G-BYMR	Raj Hamsa X'Air R100(3)	W. Drury	
G-BYMU	Rans S.6-ES Coyote II	I. R. Russell	
G-BYMV	Rans S.6-ES Coyote II	R. M. Moulton	
G-BYMW	Boland 52-12 balloon	C. Jones	
G-BYMX	Cameron A-105 balloon	H. Reis/Germany	
G-BYMY	Cameron N-90 balloon	A. Cakss	
G-BYNA	Cessna F.172H	D. M. White (G-AWTH)	
G-BYND	Pegasus Quantum 15	W. J. Upton	
G-BYNE	Pilatus PC-6/B2-H4 Turbo Porter	D. M. Penny	
G-BYNF	NA-64 Yale I (3349)	R. S. Van Dijk	
G-BYNI	Rotorway Exec 90	M. Bunn	
G-BYNK	Robin HR.200/160	Penguin Flight Group	
G-BYNM	Mainair Blade 912	J. P. Hanlon & A. C. McAllister	
G-BYNN	Cameron V-90 balloon	Cloud Nine Balloon Group	
G-BYNP	Rans S.6-ES Coyote II	R. J. Lines	
G-BYNS	Avtech Jabiru SK	D. K. Lawry	
G-BYNU	Cameron Thunder Ax7-77 balloon	J. A. W. Dyer	
G-BYNW	Cameron H-34 balloon	I. M. Ashpole	
G-BYNX	Cameron RX-105 balloon	Cameron Balloons Ltd	
G-BYNY	Beech 76 Duchess	Magenta Ltd	
G-BYOB	Slingsby T.67M Firefly 260	Stapleford Flying Club Ltd	
G-BYOD	Slingsby T.67C	D. I. Stanbridge	
G-BYOG	Pegasus Quantum 15-912	M. D. Hinge	
G-BYOH	Raj Hamsa X'Air 582 (1)	J. Owen	
G-BYOI	Sky 80-16 balloon	D. J. Tofton	
G-BYOJ	Raj Hamsa X'Air 582 (1)	S. E. J. M. McDonald	
G-BYOK	Cameron V-90 balloon	D. S. Wilson	

Notes	Reg.	Type	Owner or Operator
	G-BYOM	Sikorsky S-76C (modified)	Starspeed Ltd (G-IJCB)
	G-BYON	Mainair Blade	R. Campbell-Moore
	G-BYOO	CFM Streak Shadow	G. R. Eastwood
	G-BYOR	Raj Hamsa X'Air 582(7)	R. Dilkes
	G-BYOT	Rans S.6-ES Coyote II	G. Shaw
	G-BYOU	Rans S.6-ES Coyote II	P. G. Bright & G. Thompson
	G-BYOV	Pegasus Quantum 15-912	M. Howland
	G-BYOW	Mainair Blade	M. Taylor & T. Smith
	G-BYOX	Cameron Z-90 balloon	D. R. Rawlings
	G-BYOZ	Mainair Rapier	A. G. Lomas
	G-BYPB	Pegasus Quantum 15-912	Cleaprop Microlight School Ltd
	G-BYPD	Cameron A-105 balloon	Headland Hotel Ltd
	G-BYPE	Gardan GY-80 Horizon 160D	P. B. Hodgson
	G-BYPF	Thruster T.600N	M. A. Beadman
	G-BYPG	Thruster T.600N	M. A. Roxburgh
	G-BYPH	Thruster T.600N	D. M. Canham
	G-BYPJ	Pegasus Quantum 15-912	M. Watson
	G-BYPL	Pegasus Quantum 15-912	IP. Lister
	G-BYPM	Shaw Europa XS	G. F. Stratton
	G-BYPN	MS.880B Rallye Club	R. Edwards and D. & S. A. Bell
	G-BYPO	Raj Hamsa X'Air 582 (1)	D. W. Willis
	G-BYPR	Zenair CH.601HD Zodiac	R. Line
	G-BYPT	Rans S.6-ES Coyote II	G. P. & P. T. Willcox
	G-BYPU	PA-32R-301 Saratoga SP	AM Blatch Electrical Contractors Ltd
	G-BYPW	Raj Hamsa X'Air 583 (3)	K. J. Kimpton
	G-BYPY	Ryan ST3KR (001)	T. Curtis-Taylor
	G-BYPZ	Rans S.6-116 Super 6	R. A. Blackbourne
	G-BYRC	Westland WS-58 Wessex HC.2 (XT671)	D. Brem-Wilson
	G-BYRG	Rans S.6-ES Coyote II	S. J. Macmillan
	G-BYRJ	Pegasus Quantum 15-912	R. W. Taplin
	G-BYRK	Cameron V-42 balloon	R. Kunert
	G-BYRO	Mainair Blade	P. W. F. Coleman
	G-BYRR	Mainair Blade 912	G. R. Sharples
	G-BYRU	Pegasus Quantum 15-912	L. M. Westwood
	G-BYRV	Raj Hamsa X'Air 582 (1)	A. D. Russell
	G-BYRX	Westland Scout AH.1 (XT634)	Edwalton Aviation Ltd
	G-BYRY	Slingsby T.67M Firefly 200	PI Air Services SPRL/Belgium
	G-BYSA	Shaw Europa XS	R. L. Hitchcock
	G-BYSE	Agusta-Bell 206B JetRanger 2	C. I. Motors Ltd (G-BFND)
	G-BYSF	Avtech Jabiru UL	P. F. Morgan
	G-BYSG	Robin HR.200/120B	Modi Aviation Ltd
	G-BYSI	WSK-PZL Koliber 160A	J. & D. F. Evans
	G-BYSJ	DHC.1 Chipmunk 22 (WB569:R)	C. H. Green
	G-BYSK	Cameron A-275 balloon	Balloon School (International) Ltd
	G-BYSM	Cameron A-210 balloon	Balloon School (International) Ltd
	G-BYSN	Rans S.6-ES Coyote II	M. Salisbury
	G-BYSP	PA-28-181 Archer II	Take Flight Aviation Ltd
	G-BYSS	Medway Rebel SS	K. A. Sutton
	G-BYSV	Cameron N-120 balloon	S. Simmington
	G-BYSX	Pegasus Quantum 15-912	P. Simpson
	G-BYSY	Raj Hamsa X'Air 582 (1)	T. N. & Y. M. Farley
	G-BYTB	SOCATA TB20 Trinidad	Watchman Aircraft Ltd
	G-BYTC	Pegasus Quantum 15-912	Microlight Flight Lessons
	G-BYTI	PA-24 Comanche 250	M. Carruthers & G. Auchterlonie
	G-BYTJ	Cameron C-80 balloon	A. J. Gregory
	G-BYTK	Avtech Jabiru UL	G. R. Phillips
	G-BYTL	Mainair Blade 912	D. A. Meek & T.J. Burrow
	G-BYTM	Dyn' Aero MCR-01	I. Lang & E. J. Clarke
	G-BYTN	DH.82A Tiger Moth (N6720:VX)	R. Merewood & J. W. Freckington
	G-BYTR	Raj Hamsa X'Air 582 (1)	B. Wyatt
	G-BYTS	Montgomerie-Bensen B.8MR gyroplane	C. Seaman
	G-BYTU	Mainair Blade 912	G-BYTES
	G-BYTV	Avtech Jabiru UK	M. G. Speers
	G-BYTW	Cameron O-90 balloon	Sade Balloons Ltd
	G-BYTZ	Raj Hamsa X'Air 582 (1)	R. Armstrong
	G-BYUA	Grob G.115E Tutor	Babcock Aerospace Ltd
	G-BYUB	Grob G.115E Tutor	Babcock Aerospace Ltd
	G-BYUC	Grob G.115E Tutor	Babcock Aerospace Ltd
	G-BYUD	Grob G.115E Tutor	Babcock Aerospace Ltd
	G-BYUE	Grob G.115E Tutor	Babcock Aerospace Ltd
	G-BYUF	Grob G.115E Tutor	Babcock Aerospace Ltd
	G-BYUG	Grob G.115E Tutor	Babcock Aerospace Ltd
	G-BYUH	Grob G.115E Tutor	Babcock Aerospace Ltd

Reg.	Type	Owner or Operator	Notes
G-BYUI	Grob G.115E Tutor	Babcock Aerospace Ltd	
G-BYUJ	Grob G.115E Tutor	Babcock Aerospace Ltd	
G-BYUK	Grob G.115E Tutor	Babcock Aerospace Ltd	
G-BYUL	Grob G.115E Tutor	Babcock Aerospace Ltd	
G-BYUM	Grob G.115E Tutor	Babcock Aerospace Ltd	
G-BYUN	Grob G.115E Tutor	Babcock Aerospace Ltd	
G-BYUO	Grob G.115E Tutor	Babcock Aerospace Ltd	
G-BYUP	Grob G.115E Tutor	Babcock Aerospace Ltd	
G-BYUR	Grob G.115E Tutor	Babcock Aerospace Ltd	
G-BYUS	Grob G.115E Tutor	Babcock Aerospace Ltd	
G-BYUU	Grob G.115E Tutor	Babcock Aerospace Ltd	
G-BYUV	Grob G.115E Tutor	Babcock Aerospace Ltd	
G-BYUW	Grob G.115E Tutor	Babcock Aerospace Ltd	
G-BYUX	Grob G.115E Tutor	Babcock Aerospace Ltd	
G-BYUY	Grob.G.115E Tutor	Babcock Aerospace Ltd	
G-BYUZ	Grob G.115E Tutor	Babcock Aerospace Ltd	
G-BYVA	Grob G.115E Tutor	Babcock Aerospace Ltd	
G-BYVB	Grob G.115E Tutor	Babcock Aerospace Ltd	
G-BYVC	Grob G.115E Tutor	Babcock Aerospace Ltd	
G-BYVD	Grob G.115E Tutor	Babcock Aerospace Ltd	
G-BYVE	Grob G.115E Tutor	Babcock Aerospace Ltd	
G-BYVF	Grob G.115E Tutor	Babcock Aerospace Ltd	
G-BYVG	Grob G.115E Tutor	Babcock Aerospace Ltd	
G-BYVH	Grob G.115E Tutor	Babcock Aerospace Ltd	
G-BYVI	Grob G.115E Tutor	Babcock Aerospace Ltd	
G-BYVJ	Grob G.115E Tutor	Babcock Aerospace Ltd	
G-BYVK	Grob G.115E Tutor	Babcock Aerospace Ltd	
G-BYVL	Grob G.115E Tutor	Babcock Aerospace Ltd	
G-BYVM	Grob G.115E Tutor	Babcock Aerospace Ltd	
G-BYVO	Grob G.115E Tutor	Babcock Aerospace Ltd	
G-BYVP	Grob G.115E Tutor	Babcock Aerospace Ltd	
G-BYVR	Grob G.115E Tutor	Babcock Aerospace Ltd	
G-BYVS	Grob G.115E Tutor	Babcock Aerospace Ltd	
G-BYVT	Grob G.115E Tutor	Babcock Aerospace Ltd	
G-BYVU	Grob G.115E Tutor	Babcock Aerospace Ltd	
G-BYVV	Grob G.115E Tutor	Babcock Aerospace Ltd	
G-BYVW	Grob G.115E Tutor	Babcock Aerospace Ltd	
G-BYVX	Grob G.115E Tutor	Babcock Aerospace Ltd	
G-BYVY	Grob G.115E Tutor	Babcock Aerospace Ltd	
G-BYVZ	Grob G.115E Tutor	Babcock Aerospace Ltd	
G-BYWA	Grob G.115E Tutor	Babcock Aerospace Ltd	
G-BYWB	Grob G.115E Tutor	Babcock Aerospace Ltd	
G-BYWC	Grob G.115E Tutor	Babcock Aerospace Ltd	
G-BYWD	Grob G.115E Tutor	Babcock Aerospace Ltd	
G-BYWE	Grob G.115E Tutor	Babcock Aerospace Ltd	
G-BYWF	Grob G.115E Tutor	Babcock Aerospace Ltd	
G-BYWG	Grob G.115E Tutor	Babcock Aerospace Ltd	
G-BYWH	Grob G.115E Tutor	Babcock Aerospace Ltd	
G-BYWI	Grob G.115E Tutor	Babcock Aerospace Ltd	
G-BYWJ	Grob G.115E Tutor	Babcock Aerospace Ltd	
G-BYWK	Grob G.115E Tutor	Babcock Aerospace Ltd	
G-BYWL	Grob G.115E Tutor	Babcock Aerospace Ltd	
G-BYWM	Grob G.115E Tutor	Babcock Aerospace Ltd	
G-BYWN	Grob G.115E Tutor	Babcock Aerospace Ltd	
G-BYWO	Grob G.115E Tutor	Babcock Aerospace Ltd	
G-BYWP	Grob G.115E Tutor	Babcock Aerospace Ltd	
G-BYWR	Grob G.115E Tutor	Babcock Aerospace Ltd	
G-BYWS	Grob G.115E Tutor	Babcock Aerospace Ltd	
G-BYWT	Grob G-115E Tutor	Babcock Aerospace Ltd	
G-BYWU	Grob G.115E Tutor	Babcock Aerospace Ltd	
G-BYWV	Grob G.115E Tutor	Babcock Aerospace Ltd	
G-BYWW	Grob G.115E Tutor	Babcock Aerospace Ltd	
G-BYWX	Grob G.115E Tutor	Babcock Aerospace Ltd	
G-BYWY	Grob G.115E Tutor	Babcock Aerospace Ltd	
G-BYWZ	Grob G.115E Tutor	Babcock Aerospace Ltd	
G-BYXA	Grob G.115E Tutor	Babcock Aerospace Ltd	
G-BYXB	Grob G.115E Tutor	Babcock Aerospace Ltd	
G-BYXC	Grob G.115E Tutor	Babcock Aerospace Ltd	
G-BYXD	Grob G.115E Tutor	Babcock Aerospace Ltd	
G-BYXE	Grob G.115E Tutor	Babcock Aerospace Ltd	
G-BYXF	Grob G.115E Tutor	Babcock Aerospace Ltd	
G-BYXG	Grob G.115E Tutor	Babcock Aerospace Ltd	
G-BYXH	Grob G.115E Tutor	Babcock Aerospace Ltd	

Notes	Reg.	Type	Owner or Operator
	G-BYXI	Grob G.115E Tutor	Babcock Aerospace Ltd
	G-BYXJ	Grob G.115E Tutor	Babcock Aerospace Ltd
	G-BYXK	Grob G.115E Tutor	Babcock Aerospace Ltd
	G-BYXL	Grob G.115E Tutor	Babcock Aerospace Ltd
	G-BYXM	Grob G.115E Tutor	Babcock Aerospace Ltd
	G-BYXN	Grob G.115E Tutor	Babcock Aerospace Ltd
	G-BYXO	Grob G.115E Tutor	Babcock Aerospace Ltd
	G-BYXP	Grob G.115E Tutor	Babcock Aerospace Ltd
	G-BYXS	Grob G.115E Tutor	Babcock Aerospace Ltd
	G-BYXT	Grob G.115E Tutor	Babcock Aerospace Ltd
	G-BYXW	Medway Eclipser	G. A. Hazell
	G-BYXX	Grob G.115E Tutor	Babcock Aerospace Ltd
	G-BYXY	Grob G.115E Tutor	Babcock Aerospace Ltd
	G-BYXZ	Grob G.115E Tutor	Babcock Aerospace Ltd
	G-BYYA	Grob G.115E Tutor	Babcock Aerospace Ltd
	G-BYYB	Grob G.115E Tutor	Babcock Aerospace Ltd
	G-BYYC	Hapi Cygnet SF-2A	G. H. Smith
	G-BYYE	Lindstrand LBL-77A balloon	Virgin Balloon Flights
	G-BYYG	Slingsby T.67C	The Pathfinder Flying Club Ltd
	G-BYYL	Avtech Jabiru UL 450	M. J. Hillier & W. J. Lee
	G-BYYM	Raj Hamsa X'Air 582 (1)	S. M. S. Smith
	G-BYYN	Pegasus Quantum 15-912	R. J. Bullock
	G-BYYO	PA-28R -201 Arrow III	Stapleford Flying Club Ltd
	G-BYYP	Pegasus Quantum 15	D. A. Linsey-Bloom
	G-BYYR	Raj Hamsa X'Air 582 (4)	T. D. Bawden
	G-BYYT	Avtech Jabiru UL 450	A. C. Cale and A. J. Young.
	G-BYYX	TEAM mini-MAX 91	P. S. Lewinton
	G-BYYY	Pegasus Quantum 15-912	Clearprop Microlight School Ltd
	G-BYYZ	Staaken Z-21A Flitzer	T. White
	G-BYZA	AS.355F2 Twin Squirrel	MMAir Ltd
	G-BYZB	Mainair Blade	A. M. Thornley
	G-BYZF	Raj Hamsa X'Air 582 (1)	R. P. Davies
	G-BYZG	Cameron A-275 balloon	Cameron Flights Southern Ltd
	G-BYZL	Cameron GP-65 balloon	P. Thibo
	G-BYZO	Rans S.6-ES Coyote II	Golf Zulu Oscar Group
	G-BYZP	Robinson R22 Beta	T. I. McGlone
	G-BYZR	I.I.I. Sky Arrow 650TC	G-BYZR Flying Group
	G-BYZS	Avtech Jabiru UL-450	D. P. Pearson
	G-BYZT	Nova Vertex 26	M. Hay
	G-BYZU	Pegasus Quantum 15	N. I. Clifton
	G-BYZV	Sky 90-24 balloon	P. Farmer
	G-BYZW	Raj Hamsa X'Air 582 (2)	J. Magill
	G-BYZX	Cameron R-90 balloon	D. K. Hempleman-Adams
	G-BYZY	Pietenpol Aircamper	D. M. Hanchett
	G-BZAE	Cessna 152	APB Leasing Ltd
	G-BZAI	Pegasus Quantum 15	S. I. Close
	G-BZAK	Raj Hamsa X'Air 582 (1)	G. L. Daniels
	G-BZAL	Mainair Blade 912	J. Potts
	G-BZAM	Europa	K. N. Cobb
	G-BZAP	Avtech Jabiru UL-450	I. J. Grindley & D. R. Griffiths
	G-BZAR	Denney Kitfox 4-1200 Speedster	N. J. France (G-LEZJ)
	G-BZAS	Isaacs Fury II (K5673)	N. C. Stone
	G-BZAT	Avro RJ100	Asian Express Airline Ltd/Tajikistan
	G-BZAX	Avro RJ100	Asian Express Airline Ltd/Tajikistan
	G-BZAZ	Avro RJ100	Triangle Regional Aircraft Leasing Ltd
	G-BZBC	Rans S.6-ES Coyote II	A. J. Baldwin
	G-BZBE	Cameron A-210 balloon	Cameron Flights Southern Ltd
	G-BZBF	Cessna 172M	L. W. Scattergood
	G-BZBH	Thunder Ax6-65 balloon	P. J. Hebdon & A. C. Fraser
	G-BZBI	Cameron V-77 balloon	C. & A. I. Gibson
	G-BZBJ	Lindstrand LBL-77A balloon	P. T. R. Ollivere
	G-BZBL	Lindstrand LBL-120A balloon	East Coast Balloons Ltd
	G-BZBO	Stoddard-Hamilton Glasair III	M. B. Hamlett/France
	G-BZBP	Raj Hamsa X'Air 582 (1)	J. L. B. Roy
	G-BZBR	Pegasus Quantum 15-912	P. D. Neilson
	G-BZBS	PA-28-161 Warrior III	Aviation Rentals
	G-BZBT	Cameron H-34 Hopper balloon	D. G. Such
	G-BZBU	Robinson R22	I. C. Macdonald
	G-BZBW	Rotorway Executive 162F	Southern Helicopters Ltd
	G-BZBX	Rans S.6-ES Coyote II	P. J. Taylor
	G-BZBZ	Jodel D.9	P. A. Gasson
	G-BZDA	PA-28-161 Warrior III	White Waltham Airfield Ltd

Reg.	Type	Owner or Operator	Notes
G-BZDC	Mainair Blade	E. J. Wells & P. J. Smith	
G-BZDD	Mainair Blade 912	J. C. & R. D. P. Cadle	
G-BZDE	Lindstrand LBL-210A balloon	Toucan Travel Ltd	
G-BZDF	CFM Streak Shadow SA	W. M. Moylan	
G-BZDH	PA-28R Cherokee Arrow 200-II	G-BZDH Ltd	
G-BZDJ	Cameron Z-105 balloon	BWS Security Systems Ltd	
G-BZDK	X'Air 582(2)	G. W. Perry	
G-BZDM	Stoddard-Hamilton Glastar	F. G. Miskelly	
G-BZDN	Cameron N-105 balloon	I. R. Warrington & P. A. Foot	
G-BZDP	SA Bulldog Srs 120/121 (XX551:E)	R. M. Raikes	
G-BZDR	Tri-R Kis	J. M. & J. A. Jackson	
G-BZDS	Pegasus Quantum 15-912	K. C. Yeates	
G-BZDT	Maule MXT-7-180	Strongcrete Ltd	
G-BZDV	Westland Gazelle HT.2	D. A. Gregory	
G-BZEA	Cessna A.152	Sky Leisure Aviation (Charters) Ltd	
G-BZEB	Cessna 152	Sky Leisure Aviation (Charters) Ltd	
G-BZEC	Cessna 152	Sky Leisure Aviation (Charters) Ltd	
G-BZED	Pegasus Quantum 15-912	D. Crozier	
G-BZEE	Agusta-Bell 206B JetRanger 2	Rocket Aviation Ltd	
G-BZEG	Mainair Blade	R. P. Cookson	
G-BZEJ	Raj Hamsa X'Air 582 (7)	H-Flight X'Air Flying Group	
G-BZEL	Mainair Blade 912	T. McCormack	
G-BZEN	Avtech Jabiru UL-450	N. W. Cawley	
G-BZEP	SA Bulldog Srs 120/121 (XX561:7)	A. J. Amato	
G-BZER	Raj Hamsa X'Air R100 (1)	N. P. Lloyd & H. Lloyd-Jones	
G-BZES	Rotorway Executive 90	Southern Helicopters Ltd (G-LUFF)	
G-BZEU	Raj Hamsa X'Air 582 (2)	R. Marrs	
G-BZEW	Rans S.6-ES Coyote II	M. J. Wooldridge	
G-BZEY	Cameron N-90 balloon	Northants Auto Parts and Service Ltd	
G-BZEZ	CFM Streak Shadow	G. J. Pearce	
G-BZFA	Avro 146 RJ70	Trident Turboprop (Dublin) Ltd	
G-BZFB	Robin R.2112A	J. T. Britcher	
G-BZFC	Pegasus Quantum 15-912	G. Addison	
G-BZFD	Cameron N-90 balloon	C. D. & E. Gingell	
G-BZFG	Sky 105 balloon	Virgin Airship & Balloon Co Ltd	
G-BZFH	Pegasus Quantum 15-912	D. W. Adams	
G-BZFI	Avtech Jabiru UL	Group Family	
G-BZFN	SA Bulldog Srs 120/121 (XX667:16)	Risk Logical Ltd	
G-BZFP	DHC.6 Twin Otter 310	Loganair Ltd/Flybe.com	
G-BZFR	Extra EA.300/L	T. C. Beadle	
G-BZFS	Mainair Blade 912	N. R. Stockton	
G-BZFT	Murphy Rebel	R. Dixon	
G-BZFU	Lindstrand LBL HS-110 HA Airship	Lindstrand Hot Air Balloons Ltd	
G-BZFV	Zenair CH.601UL	M. E. Caton	
G-BZGA	DHC.1 Chipmunk 22 (WK585)	The Real Flying Co Ltd	
G-BZGB	DHC.1 Chipmunk 22 (WZ872:E)	G. Briggs	
G-BZGF	Rans S.6-ES Coyote II	C. A. Purvis & D. F. Castle	
G-BZGH	Cessna F.172N	Wicklow Wings	
G-BZGJ	Thunder Ax10-180 S2 balloon	Merlin Balloons	
G-BZGK	NA OV-10B Bronco (99+32)	Aircraft Restoration Co Ltd	
G-BZGL	NA OV-10B Bronco (99+26)	Aircraft Restoration Co Ltd	
G-BZGM	Mainair Blade 912	D. Avery	
G-BZGO	Robinson R44	Flight Academy (Gyrocopters) Ltd	
G-BZGR	Rans S.6-ES Coyote II	J. M. Benton	
G-BZGS	Mainair Blade 912	M. J. Holmes	
G-BZGT	Avtech Jabiru UL-450	P. J. Swain	
G-BZGV	Lindstrand LBL-77A balloon	J. H. Dryden	
G-BZGW	Mainair Blade	M. Liptrot	
G-BZGX	Raj Hamsa X'Air 582 (6)	P. J. Gleeson	
G-BZGY	Dyn'Aéro CR.100	B. Appleby	
G-BZGZ	Pegasus Quantum 15-912	D. W. Beech	
G-BZHA	Boeing 767-336ER	British Airways	
G-BZHB	Boeing 767-336ER	British Airways	
G-BZHC	Boeing 767-336ER	British Airways	
G-BZHE	Cessna 152	International Artists Sports Management Ltd	
G-BZHF	Cessna 152	Modi Aviation Ltd	
G-BZHG	Tecnam P92 Echo	R. W. F. Boarder	
G-BZHJ	Raj Hamsa X'Air 582 (7)	S. Hardy	
G-BZHL	Noorduyn AT-16 Harvard IIB	R. H. Cooper & S. Swallow	
G-BZHN	Pegasus Quantum 15-912	A. M. Sirant	
G-BZHO	Pegasus Quantum 15	T. H. Beales	
G-BZHR	Avtech Jabiru UL-450	G. W. Rowbotham & W. Turner	
G-BZHT	PA-18A Super Cub 150	Lakes Gliding Club	

Notes	Reg.	Type	Owner or Operator
	G-BZHU	Wag-Aero Sport Trainer	Teddy Boys Flying Group
	G-BZHV	PA-28-181 Archer III	R. M. & T. A. Limb
	G-BZHX	Thunder Ax11-250 S2 balloon	Wizard Balloons Ltd
	G-BZHY	Mainair Blade 912	M. Morris
	G-BZIA	Raj Hamsa X'Air 700 (1)	J. L. Pritchett
	G-BZIC	Lindstrand LBL Sun SS balloon	Ballongaventyr 1 Sakne AB/Sweden
	G-BZID	Montgomerie-Bensen B.8MR	A. Gault
	G-BZIG	Thruster T.600N	K. M. Jones
	G-BZIH	Lindstrand LBL-31A balloon	H. & L. D. Vaughan
	G-BZII	Extra EA.300/1	Innovative Converged Devices Ltd
	G-BZIJ	Robin DR.400/500	Rob Airways Ltd
	G-BZIK	Cameron A-250 balloon	Breckland Balloons Ltd
	G-BZIL	Colt 120A balloon	Champagne Flights
	G-BZIM	Pegasus Quantum 15-912	S. Jelley
	G-BZIO	PA-28-161 Warrior III	White Waltham Airfield Ltd
	G-BZIP	Montgomerie-Bensen B.8MR	C. D. Prebble
	G-BZIS	Raj Hamsa X'Air 582 (2)	T. Welch
	G-BZIT	Beech 95-B55 Baron	Propellorhead Aviation Ltd
	G-BZIV	Avtech Jabiru UL	V. R. Leggott
	G-BZIW	Pegasus Quantum 15-912	J. M. Hodgson
	G-BZIX	Cameron N-90 balloon	M. Stefanini & P. Marmugi/Italy
	G-BZIY	Raj Hamsa X'Air 582 (2)	A. L. A. Gill
	G-BZIZ	Ultramagic H-31 balloon	G. D. O. Bartram
	G-BZJC	Thruster T.600N	M. H. Moulai
	G-BZJD	Thruster T.600T	C. C. Belcher
	G-BZJG	Cameron A-400 balloon	Cameron Balloons Ltd
	G-BZJH	Cameron Z-90 balloon	Balloon SpA
	G-BZJI	Nova X-Large 37 paraplane	M. Hay
	G-BZJJ	Robinson R22 Beta	E. Sorvillo/Italy
	G-BZJM	VPM M-16 Tandem Trainer	D. Wood
	G-BZJN	Mainair Blade 912	L. Campbell & M. A. Haughey
	G-BZJO	Pegasus Quantum 15	W. C. Bryan
	G-BZJP	Zenair CH.701UL	B. J. Fallows
	G-BZJR	Montgomerie-Bensen B.8MR	C. R. Gordon (G-IPFM)
	G-BZJV	CASA 1-131E Jungmann 1000	R. A. Cumming
	G-BZJW	Cessna 150F	P. Ligertwood
	G-BZJZ	Pegasus Quantum 15	S. Baker
	G-BZKC	Raj Hamsa X'Air 582 (11)	J. E. Evans
	G-BZKD	Stolp Starduster Too	P. & C. Edmunds
	G-BZKE	Lindstrand LBL-77B balloon	H. Cresswell
	G-BZKF	Rans S.6-ES Coyote II	A. W. Lowrie
	G-BZKL	PA-28R-201 Arrow III	M. A. & M. H. Cromati
	G-BZKO	Rans S.6-ES Coyote II	G. Millar
	G-BZKU	Cameron Z-105 balloon	N. A. Fishlock
	G-BZKV	Cameron Sky 90-24 balloon	Omega Selction Services Ltd
	G-BZKW	Ultramagic M-27 balloon	T. G. Church
	G-BZLC	WSK-PZL Koliber 160A	G. F. Smith
	G-BZLE	Rans S.6-ES Coyote II	B. M. Davis
	G-BZLF	CFM Shadow Srs CD	D. W. Stacey
	G-BZLG	Robin HR.200/120B	Flew LLP
	G-BZLH	PA-28-161 Warrior II	Aviation Rentals
	G-BZLK	Slingsby T.31M Motor Tutor	G. Smith
	G-BZLL	Pegasus Quantum 15-912	R. Torrie
	G-BZLP	Robinson R44	Polar Helicopters Ltd
	G-BZLS	Cameron Sky 77-24 balloon	D. W. Young
	G-BZLU	Lindstrand LBL-90A balloon	A. E. Lusty
	G-BZLV	Avtech Jabiru UL-450	G. Dalton
	G-BZLX	Pegasus Quantum 15-912	D. McCabe & M. Harris
	G-BZLY	Grob G.109B	R. W. Hegmann
	G-BZLZ	Pegasus Quantum 15-912	A. S. Martin
	G-BZMB	PA-28R-201 Arrow III	Thurrock Arrow Group
	G-BZMC	Avtech Jabiru UL	D. Maddison
	G-BZMD	SA Bulldog Srs 120/121 (XX554)	Mad Dog Flying Group
	G-BZME	SA Bulldog Srs 120/121 (XX698:9)	S. J. Whitworth
	G-BZMF	Rutan LongEz	Go-Ez Group
	G-BZMG	Robinson R44	G. Martinelli/Italy
	G-BZMH	SA Bulldog Srs 120/121 (XX692:A)	M. E. J. Hingley
	G-BZMJ	Rans S.6-ES Coyote II	R. J. G. Clark
	G-BZML	SA Bulldog Srs 120/121 (XX693:07)	I. D. Anderson
	G-BZMM	Robin DR.400/180R	N. A. C. Norman
	G-BZMO	Robinson R22 Beta	Polar Helicopters Ltd
	G-BZMR	Raj Hamsa X'Air 582 (2)	M. Grime
	G-BZMS	Mainair Blade	T. R. Villa

Reg.	Type	Owner or Operator	Notes
G-BZMT	PA-28-161 Warrior III	White Waltham Airfield Ltd	
G-BZMW	Pegasus Quantum 15-912	A. W. Micklem	
G-BZMY	SPP Yakovlev Yak C-11	Russian Radials Ltd	
G-BZMZ	CFM Streak Shadow	J. F. F. Fouche	
G-BZNC	Pegasus Quantum 15-912	D. E. Wall	
G-BZND	Sopwith Pup (replica) (N5199)	M. A. Goddard	
G-BZNE	Beech B300 Super King Air	Skyhopper LLP	
G-BZNF	Colt 120A balloon	N. Charbonnier/Italy	
G-BZNH	Rans S.6-ES Coyote II	S. R. A. Brierley	
G-BZNJ	Rans S.6-ES Coyote II	R. A. McKee	
G-BZNK	Morane Saulnier MS.315-D2 (354)	R. H. Cooper & S. Swallow	
G-BZNM	Pegasus Quantum 15	J. T. Davies	
G-BZNN	Beech 76 Duchess	Flew LLP	
G-BZNP	Thruster T.600N	J. D. Gibbons	
G-BZNS	Mainair Blade	A. G. Laycock	
G-BZNT	Aero L-29 Delfin	S. M. Norman	
G-BZNU	Cameron A-300 balloon	Balloon School (International) Ltd	
G-BZNV	Lindstrand LBL-31A balloon	G. R. Down	
G-BZNW	Isaacs Fury II (K2048)	S. M. Johnston	
G-BZNX	SOCATA MS.880B Rallye Club	Air & Ground Aviation Ltd	
G-BZNY	Shaw Europa XS	W. J. Harrison	
G-BZOB	Slepcev Storch (6G-ED)	P. J. Clegg	
G-BZOE	Pegasus Quantum 15	G. Rokita	
G-BZOF	Montgomerie-Bensen B.8MR gyroplane	S. J. M. Ledingham	
G-BZOG	Dornier 328-100	Suckling Airways (Cambridge) Ltd	
G-BZOI	Nicollier HN.700 Menestrel II	S. J. McCollum	
G-BZOL	Robin R.3000/140	S. D. Baker	
G-BZON	SA Bulldog Srs 120/121 (XX528:D)	D. J. Critchley	
G-BZOO	Pegasus Quantum 15-912	A. J. Maxfield	
G-BZOR	Robinson R44	CN Joinery and Building Services Ltd	
G-BZOR	TEAM mini-MAX 91	T. P. V. Sheppard	
G-BZOU	Pegasus Quantum 15-912	M. A. Bradford	
G-BZOV	Pegasus Quantum 15-912	D. Turner	
G-BZOW	Whittaker MW7	G. W. Peacock	
G-BZOX	Cameron Colt 90B balloon	D. J. Head	
G-BZOY	Beech 76 Duchess	Aviation Rentals	
G-BZOZ	Van's RV-6	M. & S. Sheppard	
G-BZPA	Mainair Blade 912S	J. McGoldrick	
G-BZPD	Cameron V-65 balloon	P. Spellward	
G-BZPF	Scheibe SF-24B Motorspatz	D. & M. Shrimpton	
G-BZPG	Beech C24R Sierra 200	Wycombe Air Centre Ltd	
G-BZPH	Van's RV-4	G-BZPH RV-4 Group	
G-BZPI	SOCATA TB20 Trinidad	K. M. Brennan	
G-BZPJ	Beech 76 Duchess	K. O'Connor	
G-BZPK	Cameron C-80 balloon	D. L. Homer	
G-BZPN	Mainair Blade 912S	G. R. Barker	
G-BZPR	Ultramagic N-210 balloon	Cameron Flights Southern Ltd	
G-BZPS	SA Bulldog Srs 120/121 (XX658:07)	A. J. Robinson & M. J. Miller	
G-BZPT	Ultramagic N-210 balloon	South Downs Ballooning Ltd	
G-BZPV	Lindstrand LBL-90B balloon	D. P. Hopkins	
G-BZPW	Cameron V-77 balloon	J. Vonka	
G-BZPX	Ultramagic S-105 balloon	Scotair Balloons	
G-BZPY	Ultramagic H-31 balloon	Scotair Balloons	
G-BZPZ	Mainair Blade	D. & M. Bailey	
G-BZRA	Rans S.6-ES Coyote II	M. Allen	
G-BZRB	Mainair Blade	K. J. Barnard	
G-BZRJ	Pegasus Quantum 15-912	G-BZRJ Group	
G-BZRO	PA-30 Twin Comanche C	Gloucester Comanche Group	
G-BZRP	Pegasus Quantum 15-912	T. P. Williams	
G-BZRR	Pegasus Quantum 15-912	R. Carlin	
G-BZRS	Eurocopter EC 135T2	Bond Air Services Ltd	
G-BZRT	Beech 76 Duchess	Aviation Rentals	
G-BZRV	Van's RV-6	N. M. Hitchman	
G-BZRW	Mainair Blade 912S	G. J. E. Alcorn	
G-BZRY	Rans S.6-ES Coyote II	A. G. Smith	
G-BZRZ	Thunder Ax11-250 S2 balloon	A. C. K. Rawson & J. J. Rudoni	
G-BZSB	Pitts S-1S Special	A. D. Ingold	
G-BZSC	Sopwith Camel F.1 (replica)	The Shuttleworth Collection	
G-BZSE	Hawker Hunter T.8B (WV322:Y)	Canfield Hunter Ltd	
G-BZSG	Pegasus Quantum 15-912	S. Andrews	
G-BZSH	Ultramagic H-77 balloon	P. M. G. Vale	
G-BZSI	Pegasus Quantum 15	D. G. Cull	
G-BZSM	Pegasus Quantum 15	C. A. Brock	

Notes	Reg.	Type	Owner or Operator
	G-BZSO	Ultramagic M-77C balloon	C. C. Duppa-Miller
	G-BZSP	Stemme S.10	A. Flewelling & L. Bleaken
	G-BZSS	Pegasus Quantum 15-912	T. R. Marsh
	G-BZST	Jabiru SPL-450	D. J and L. Rhys
	G-BZSX	Pegasus Quantum 15-912	J. P. Neilan
	G-BZSY	SNCAN Stampe SV.4A	G. J. N. Valvekens/Belgium
	G-BZSZ	Avtech Jabiru UL-450	T. J. Heaton
	G-BZTA	Robinson R44	Jarretts Motors Ltd
	G-BZTC	TEAM mini-MAX 91	G. G. Clayton
	G-BZTD	Thruster T.600T 450 JAB	B. O. McCartan
	G-BZTF	Yakovlev Yak-52	KY Flying Group
	G-BZTH	Shaw Europa	T. J. Houlihan
	G-BZTJ	CASA Bü 133C Jungmeister	R. A. Seeley
	G-BZTK	Cameron V-90 balloon	E. Appollodorus
	G-BZTM	Mainair Blade	P. A. Houston
	G-BZTN	Europa XS	R. S. Gent
	G-BZTR	Mainair Blade	K. Thomas
	G-BZTS	Cameron 90 Bertie Bassett SS balloon	Trebor Bassett Ltd
	G-BZTT	Cameron A-275 balloon	Cameron Flights Southern Ltd
	G-BZTU	Mainair Blade 912	C. T. Halliday
	G-BZTV	Mainair Blade 912S	R. D. McManus
	G-BZTW	Hunt Wing Avon 582 (1)	T. S. Walker
	G-BZTX	Mainair Blade 912	K. A. Ingham
	G-BZTY	Avtech Jabiru UL	R. P. Lewis
	G-BZUB	Mainair Blade	J. Campbell
	G-BZUC	Pegasus Quantum 15-912	G. Breen/Portugal
	G-BZUD	Lindstrand LBL-105A balloon	A. Nimmo
	G-BZUE	Pegasus Quantum 15-912	P. O'Rourke
	G-BZUF	Mainair Rapier	B. Craig
	G-BZUG	RL.7A XP Sherwood Ranger	J. G. Boxall
	G-BZUH	Rans S.6-ES Coyote II	B. E. Toulson
	G-BZUI	Pegasus Quantum 15-912	A. P. Slade
	G-BZUK	Lindstrand LBL-31A balloon	G. R. J. Luckett/USA
	G-BZUL	Avtech Jabiru UL	J. G. Campbell
	G-BZUO	Cameron A-340HL balloon	Cameron Flights Southern Ltd
	G-BZUP	Raj Hamsa X'Air Jabiru(3)	M. T. Sheelan
	G-BZUU	Cameron C-90 balloon	D. C. Ball
	G-BZUV	Cameron H-24 balloon	J. N. Race
	G-BZUX	Pegasus Quantum 15	C. Gorvett
	G-BZUY	Van's RV-6	T. W. Wielkopolski
	G-BZUZ	Hunt Avon-Blade R.100 (1)	C. F. Janes
	G-BZVA	Zenair CH.701UL	M. W. Taylor
	G-BZVB	Cessna FR.172H	Victor Bravo Group (G-BLMX)
	G-BZVE	Cameron N-133 balloon	A. Bellini
	G-BZVI	Nova Vertex 24 hang glider	M. Hay
	G-BZVJ	Pegasus Quantum 15	R. Blackhall
	G-BZVK	Raj Hamsa X'Air 582 (2)	M. Donnelly
	G-BZVM	Rans S.6-ES Coyote II	D. P. Sudworth
	G-BZVN	Van's RV-6	Syndicate RV6 G-BZVN
	G-BZVR	Raj Hamsa X'Air 582 (4)	R. F. E. Berry
	G-BZVT	I.I.I. Sky Arrow 650T	D. J. Goldsmith
	G-BZVU	Cameron Z-105 balloon	Ballooning Network Ltd
	G-BZVV	Pegasus Quantum 15-912	S. Runcie
	G-BZVW	Ilyushin IL-2 Stormovik	S. Swallow & R. H. Cooper
	G-BZVX	Ilyushin IL-2 Stormovik	S. Swallow & R. H. Cooper
	G-BZWB	Mainair Blade 912	K. Roberts
	G-BZWC	Raj Hamsa X'Air Falcon 912 (1)	G. Hayes
	G-BZWG	PA-28 Cherokee 140	H. Merkado
	G-BZWH	Cessna 152	ACS Engineering Ltd
	G-BZWJ	CFM Streak Shadow	T. A. Morgan
	G-BZWK	Avtech Jabiru SK	G. M. Bolger
	G-BZWM	Pegasus XL-Q	D. T. Evans
	G-BZWN	Van's RV-8	A. J. Symms & R. D. Harper
	G-BZWR	Mainair Rapier	M. A. Steele
	G-BZWS	Pegasus Quantum 15-912	G-BZWS Syndicate
	G-BZWT	Technam P.92-EM Echo	R. F. Cooper
	G-BZWU	Pegasus Quantum 15-912	C. A. Reynolds
	G-BZWV	Steen Skybolt	D. E. Blaxland
	G-BZWX	Whittaker MW5D Sorcerer	J. Bate
	G-BZWZ	Van's RV-6	A. P. Mardlin
	G-BZXA	Raj Hamsa X'Air V2 (1)	J. Bulpin
	G-BZXB	Van's RV-6	B. J. King-Smith & D. J. Akerman
	G-BZXC	SA Bulldog Srs 120/121 (XX612:A, 03)★	Carnegie College

Reg.	Type	Owner or Operator	Notes
G-BZXI	Nova Philou 26 hang glider	M. Hay	
G-BZXK	Robin HR.200/120B	Flew LLP	
G-BZXM	Mainair Blade 912	B. Birtle	
G-BZXN	Avtech Jabiru UL-450	D. A. Hall	
G-BZXO	Cameron Z-105 balloon	D. K. Jones & K. D. Thomas	
G-BZXP	Kiss 400-582 (1)	A. Fairbrother	
G-BZXR	Cameron N-90 balloon	F. R. Battersby	
G-BZXS	SA Bulldog Srs 120/121 (XX631:W)	K. J. Thompson	
G-BZXT	Mainair Blade 912	M. C. Wright	
G-BZXV	Pegasus Quantum 15-912	P. I. Oliver	
G-BZXW	VPM M-16 Tandem Trainer	P. J. Troy-Davies (G-NANA)	
G-BZXX	Pegasus Quantum 15-912	D. J. Johnston & D. Ostle	
G-BZXY	Robinson R44	Helicopter Services Ltd	
G-BZXZ	SA Bulldog Srs 120/121 (XX629:V)	R. Bray	
G-BZYA	Rans S.6-ES Coyote II	M. R. Osbourn	
G-BZYD	Westland Gazelle AH.1 (XZ239)	Aerocars Ltd	
G-BZYG	Glaser-Dirks DG.500MB	R. C. Bromwich	
G-BZYI	Nova Phocus 123 hang glider	M. Hay	
G-BZYK	Avtech Jabiru UL	Cloudbase Aviation G-BZYK	
G-BZYM	Raj Hamsa X'Air 700 (1A)	R. R. Celentano	
G-BZYN	Pegasus Quantum 15-912	J. Cannon	
G-BZYR	Cameron N-31 balloon	C. J. Sanger-Davies	
G-BZYS	Micro Aviation Bantam B.22-S	D. L. Howell	
G-BZYT	Interavia 80TA	J. King	
G-BZYU	Whittaker MW6 Merlin	K. J. Cole	
G-BZYV	Snowbird Mk.V 582 (1)	M. A. Oakley	
G-BZYX	Raj Hamsa X'Air 700 (1A)	A. M. Sutton	
G-BZYY	Cameron N-90 balloon	M. E. Mason	
G-BZZD	Cessna F.172M	R. H. M. Richardson-Bunbury (G-BDPF)	
G-CAHA	PA-34-200T Seneca II	TGD Leasing Ltd	
G-CALL	PA-23 Aztec 250F	J. D. Moon	
G-CAMM	Hawker Cygnet (replica)	Richard Shuttleworth Trustees	
G-CAMP	Cameron N-105 balloon	Hong Kong Balloon & Airship Club	
G-CAMR	BFC Challenger II	P. R. A. Walker	
G-CAPI	Mudry/CAARP CAP-10B	PI Group (G-BEXR)	
G-CAPX	Avions Mudry CAP-10B	H. J. Pessall	
G-CARS†	Pitts S-2A Special (replica)★	Toyota Ltd	
G-CBAB	SA Bulldog Srs 120/121 (XX543:F)	J. N. R. Davidson, L. C. T. George & P. J. R. Hill	
G-CBAD	Mainair Blade 912	J. Stocking	
G-CBAF	Lancair 320	L. H. & M. van Cleeff	
G-CBAK	Robinson R44	CEL Electrical Logistics Ltd	
G-CBAL	PA-28-161 Warrior II	Azure Flying Club Ltd	
G-CBAN	SA Bulldog Srs 120/121 (XX668:1)	C. Hilliker	
G-CBAP	Zenair CH.601UL	A. G. Marsh	
G-CBAR	Stoddard-Hamilton Glastar	C. M. Barnes	
G-CBAS	Rans S.6-ES Coyote II	S. Stockill	
G-CBAT	Cameron Z-90 balloon	British Telecommunications PLC	
G-CBAU	Rand-Robinson KR-2	C. B. Copsey	
G-CBAV	Raj Hamsa X'Air V.2 (1)	D. W. Stamp & G. J. Lampitt	
G-CBAW	Cameron A-300 balloon	D. K. Hempleman-Adams	
G-CBAX	Tecnam P92-EA Echo	L. Collier	
G-CBAZ	Rans S.6-ES Coyote II	E. S. Wills	
G-CBBB	Pegasus Quantum 15-912	F. A. Dimmock	
G-CBBC	SA Bulldog Srs 120/121 (XX515:4)	Bulldog Support Ltd	
G-CBBF	Beech 76 Duchess	Flew LLP	
G-CBBG	Mainair Blade	G-CBBG Flying Group	
G-CBBH	Raj Hamsa X'Air 582 (11)	S. P. Macdonald	
G-CBBK	Robinson R22	R. J. Everett	
G-CBBL	SA Bulldog Srs 120/121 (XX550:Z)	A. Cunningham	
G-CBBM	Savannah VG Jabiru (1)	C. E. Passmore	
G-CBBN	Pegasus Quantum 15-912	G-CBBN Flying Group	
G-CBBO	Whittaker MW5D Sorcerer	P. J. Gripton	
G-CBBP	Pegasus Quantum 15-912	C. E. Thompson	
G-CBBS	SA Bulldog Srs 120/121 (XX694:E)	Newcastle Aerobatic Academy Ltd	
G-CBBT	SA Bulldog Srs 120/121 (XX695:3)	Newcastle Bulldog Group Ltd	
G-CBBW	SA Bulldog Srs 120/121 (XX619:T)	S. E. Robbottom-Scott	
G-CBCB	SA Bulldog Srs 120/121 (XX537:C)	M. W. Minary The General Aviation Trading Co Ltd	
G-CBCD	Pegasus Quantum 15	I. A. Lumley	
G-CBCF	Pegasus Quantum 15-912	P. A. Bromley	
G-CBCH	Zenair CH.701UL	L. G. Millen	
G-CBCI	Raj Hamsa X'Air 582 (2)	C. P. Lincoln	

Notes	Reg.	Type	Owner or Operator
	G-CBCK	Tipsy T.66 Nipper Srs 3	N. M. Bloom (G-TEDZ)
	G-CBCL	Stoddard-Hamilton Glastar	M. I. Weaver
	G-CBCM	Raj Hamsa X'Air 700 (1A)	M. Ellis
	G-CBCP	Van's RV-6A	G-CBCP Group
	G-CBCR	SA Bulldog Srs 120/121 (XX702:P)	D. Wells
	G-CBCX	Pegasus Quantum 15	D. W. Allen
	G-CBCY	Beech C24R Sierra Super	Wycombe Air Centre Ltd
	G-CBCZ	CFM Streak Shadow SLA	J. O'Malley-Kane
	G-CBDC	Thruster T.600N 450-JAB	P. M. Yeoman
	G-CBDD	Mainair Blade	G. Hird
	G-CBDG	Zenair CH.601HD	R. E. Lasnier
	G-CBDH	Flight Design CT2K	K. Tuck
	G-CBDI	Denney Kitfox Mk.2	J. G. D. Barbour
	G-CBDJ	Flight Design CT2K	P. J. Walker
	G-CBDK	SA Bulldog Srs 120/121 (XX611:7)	J. N. Randle
	G-CBDL	Mainair Blade	M. D. Howe
	G-CBDM	Tecnam P92-EM Echo	J. J. Cozens
	G-CBDN	Mainair Blade	T. Peckham
	G-CBDP	Mainair Blade 912	R. J. Roberts
	G-CBDS	SA Bulldog Srs 120/121 (XX707:4)	J. R. Parry
	G-CBDU	Quad City Challenger II	E. J. Brooks
	G-CBDV	Raj Hamsa X'Air 582	Delta Victor Group
	G-CBDX	Pegasus Quantum 15	P. Sinkler
	G-CBDZ	Pegasus Quantum 15-912	D. G. Fisher
	G-CBEB	Kiss 400-582 (1)	M. Harris
	G-CBEC	Cameron Z-105 balloon	A. L. Ballarino/Italy
	G-CBED	Cameron Z-90 balloon	John Aimo Balloons SAS/Italy
	G-CBEE	PA-28R Cherokee Arrow 200	IHC Ltd
	G-CBEF	SA Bulldog Srs 120/121 (XX621:H)	A. L. Butcher & F. W. Sandwell
	G-CBEH	SA Bulldog Srs 120/121 (XX521:H)	J. E. Lewis
	G-CBEI	PA-22 Colt 108	D. Sharp
	G-CBEJ	Colt 120A balloon	The Cotswold Balloon Co. Ltd
	G-CBEK	SA Bulldog Srs 120/121 (XX700:17)	B. P. Robinson
	G-CBEM	Mainair Blade	K. W. Bodley
	G-CBEN	Pegasus Quantum 15-912	A. T. Cook
	G-CBES	Shaw Europa XS	M. R. Hexley
	G-CBEU	Pegasus Quantum 15-912	S. D. Cox
	G-CBEV	Pegasus Quantum 15-912	A. S. R. Czajka
	G-CBEW	Flight Design CT2K	Shy Talk Group
	G-CBEX	Flight Design CT2K	A. G. Quinn
	G-CBEY	Cameron C-80 balloon	D. V. Fowler
	G-CBEZ	Robin DR.400/180	K. V. Field
	G-CBFA	Diamond DA40 Star	Lyrastar Ltd
	G-CBFE	Raj Hamsa X'Air V.2 (1)	T. D. Wolstenholme
	G-CBFF	Cameron O-120 balloon	T. M. C. McCoy
	G-CBFH	Thunder Ax8-105 S2 balloon	D. V. Fowler & A. N. F. Pertwee
	G-CBFJ	Robinson R44	F. Klinge
	G-CBFK	Murphy Rebel	P. J. Gibbs
	G-CBFM	SOCATA TB21 Trinidad	Exec Flight Ltd
	G-CBFN	Robin DR.100/200B	Foxtrot November Group
	G-CBFO	Cessna 172S	P. Gray
	G-CBFP	SA Bulldog Srs 120/121 (XX636:Y)	R. Nisbet & A. R. Dix
	G-CBFU	SA Bulldog Srs 120/121 (XX628:9)	J. R. & S. J. Huggins
	G-CBFW	Bensen B.8	A. J. Thomas
	G-CBFX	Rans S.6-ES Coyote II	D. R. Burridge
	G-CBFY	Cameron Z-250 balloon	M. L. Gabb
	G-CBGB	Zenair CH.601UL	J. F. Woodham
	G-CBGC	SOCATA TB10 Tobago	Tobago Aviation Ltd
	G-CBGD	Zenair CH.701UL	I. S. Walsh
	G-CBGE	Tecnam P92-EM Echo	J. P. Spiteri
	G-CBGG	Pegasus Quantum 15	T. E. Davies
	G-CBGH	Teverson Bisport	M. J. Larroucau
	G-CBGJ	Aeroprakt A.22 Foxbat	M. McCall
	G-CBGL	MH.1521M Broussard	MAXB Group
	G-CBGO	Murphy Maverick 430	C. R. Ellis & E. A. Wrathall
	G-CBGP	Ikarus C.42 FB UK	C. F. Welby
	G-CBGR	Avtech Jabiru UL-450	R. G. Kirkland
	G-CBGS	Cyclone AX2000	JAT Group
	G-CBGU	Thruster T.600N 450-JAB	B. R. Cardosi
	G-CBGV	Thruster T.600N 450	R. J. Humphries
	G-CBGW	Thruster T.600N 450-JAB	A. R. Pluck
	G-CBGX	SA Bulldog Srs 120/121 (XX622:B)	Henfield Lodge Ltd
	G-CBGZ	Westland Gazelle HT.2 (ZB646:59/CU)	D. Weatherhead Ltd

Reg.	Type	Owner or Operator	Notes
G-CBHA	SOCATA TB10 Tobago	Oscar Romeo Aviation Ltd	
G-CBHB	Raj Hamsa X'Air 582 (5)	F. G. Shepherd	
G-CBHC	RAF 2000 GTX-SE gyroplane	A. J. Thomas	
G-CBHG	Mainair Blade 912S	B. S. Hope	
G-CBHI	Shaw Europa XS	Active Aviation Ltd	
G-CBHJ	Mainair Blade 912	B. C. Jones	
G-CBHK	Pegasus Quantum 15 (HKS)	B. Dossett	
G-CBHM	Mainair Blade 912	F. J. Thorne	
G-CBHN	Pegasus Quantum 15-912	G. G. Cook	
G-CBHO	Gloster Gladiator II (N5719)	Retro Track & Air (UK) Ltd	
G-CBHP	Corby CJ-1 Starlet	D. H. Barker	
G-CBHR	Lazer Z200	A. Windel	
G-CBHT	Dassault Falcon 900EX	GE Capital Equipment Finance Ltd (G-GPWH)	
G-CBHU	RL.5A Sherwood Ranger	G-CBHU Group	
G-CBHW	Cameron Z-105 balloon	Bristol Chamber of Commerce, Industry & Shipping	
G-CBHX	Cameron V-77 balloon	N. A. Apsey	
G-CBHY	Pegasus Quantum 15-912	A. Hope	
G-CBHZ	RAF 2000 GTX-SE gyroplane	M. P. Donnelly	
G-CBIB	Flight Design CT2K	T. R. Villa	
G-CBIC	Raj Hamsa X'Air V2 (2)	J. T. Blackburn & D. R. Sutton	
G-CBID	SA Bulldog Srs 120/121(XX549:6)	Red Dog Group/Bulldog Group	
G-CBIE	Flight Design CT2K	B. M. Jones & S. R. McKiernan	
G-CBIF	Avtech Jabiru SPL-450	S. N. J. Huxtable	
G-CBIH	Cameron Z-31 balloon	Gone With The Wind Ltd	
G-CBIJ	Ikarus C.42 FB UK Cyclone	J. A. Smith	
G-CBIL	Cessna 182K	E. Bannister (G-BFZZ)	
G-CBIM	Lindstrand LBL-90A balloon	R. K. Parsons	
G-CBIN	TEAM mini-MAX 91	A. R. Mikolaczyk	
G-CBIP	Thruster T.600N 450-JAB	D. R. Seabrook	
G-CBIR	Thruster T.600N 450-JAB	E. G. White	
G-CBIS	Raj Hamsa X'Air 582 (2)	P. T. W. T. Derges	
G-CBIT	RAF 2000 GTX-SE gyroplane	Terrafirma Services Ltd	
G-CBIU	Cameron 95 Flame SS balloon	PSH Skypower Ltd	
G-CBIV	Skyranger 912 (1)	J. N. Whelan	
G-CBIX	Zenair CH.601UL	R. A. & B. M. Roberts	
G-CBIY	Aerotechnik EV-97 Eurostar	S. J. Smith	
G-CBIZ	Pegasus Quantum 15-912	B. Cook	
G-CBJD	Stoddard-Hamilton Glastar	K. F. Farey	
G-CBJE	RAF 2000 GTX-SE gyroplane	V. G. Freke	
G-CBJG	DHC.1 Chipmunk 20 (1373)	C. J. Rees	
G-CBJH	Aeroprakt A.22 Foxbat	H. Smith	
G-CBJJ	SA Bulldog Srs 120/121 (XX525)	T. Marnix & H. Van Snick	
G-CBJL	Kiss 400-582 (1)	R. E. Morris	
G-CBJM	Avtech Jabiru SP-470	G. R. T. Elliott	
G-CBJO	Pegasus Quantum 15-912	R. H. Lowndes	
G-CBJP	Zenair CH.601UL	R. E. Peirse	
G-CBJR	Aerotechnik EV-97A Eurostar	Madley Flying Group	
G-CBJS	Cameron C-60 balloon	N. Ivison	
G-CBJT	Mainair Blade	P. T. Flanagan	
G-CBJV	Rotorway Executive 162F	P. W. Vaughan	
G-CBJW	Ikarus C.42 Cyclone FB UK	G. D. Jones	
G-CBJX	Raj Hamsa X'Air Falcon J22	N. & E. Hart	
G-CBJZ	Westland Gazelle HT.3	K. G. Theurer/Germany	
G-CBKA	Westland Gazelle HT.3 (XZ937:Y)	J. Windmill	
G-CBKB	Bücker Bü 181C Bestmann	W. R. & G. D. Snadden	
G-CBKD	Westland Gazelle HT.2	Flying Scout Ltd	
G-CBKE	Kiss 400-582 (1)	T. H. Parr	
G-CBKF	Easy Raider J2.2 (1)	B. S. Carpenter	
G-CBKG	Thruster T.600N 450 JAB	Silver Shadow Group	
G-CBKI	Cameron Z-90 balloon	S. Askey	
G-CBKJ	Cameron Z-90 balloon	Invista (UK) Holdings Ltd	
G-CBKK	Ultramagic S-130 balloon	Hayrick Ltd	
G-CBKL	Raj Hamsa X'Air Jabiru(2)	Caithness X-Air Group	
G-CBKM	Mainair Blade 912	R. Arkle	
G-CBKN	Mainair Blade 912	D. S. Clews	
G-CBKO	Mainair Blade 912S	S. J. Taft	
G-CBKR	PA-28-161 Warrior III	Yeovil Auto Tuning	
G-CBKS	Kiss 400-582 (1)	S. Kilpin	
G-CBKU	Ikarus C.42 Cyclone FB UK	C. Blackburn	
G-CBKW	Pegasus Quantum 15-912	W. G. Coulter	
G-CBKY	Avtech Jabiru SP-470	P. R. Sistern	
G-CBLA	Aero Designs Pulsar XP	J. P. Kynaston	

Notes	Reg.	Type	Owner or Operator
	G-CBLB	Technam P.92-EM Echo	R. Lewis-Evans
	G-CBLD	Mainair Blade 912S	N. E. King
	G-CBLE	Robin R.2120U	Flew LLP
	G-CBLF	Raj Hamsa X'Air 582 (11)	B. J. Harper & P. J. Soukup
	G-CBLK	Hawker Hind	Aero Vintage Ltd
	G-CBLL	Pegasus Quantum 15-912	G. J. McNally
	G-CBLM	Mainair Blade 912	A. S. Saunders
	G-CBLN	Cameron Z-31 balloon	P. M. Oggioni
	G-CBLO	Lindstrand LBL-42A balloon	R. J. Clements
	G-CBLP	Raj Hamsa X'Air Falcon	A. C. Parsons
	G-CBLS	Fiat CR.42	Fighter Collection Ltd
	G-CBLT	Mainair Blade 912	B. J. Bader
	G-CBLU	Cameron C-90 balloon	A. G. Martin
	G-CBLW	Raj Hamsa X'Air Falcon 582(3)	R. G. Halliwell
	G-CBLX	Kiss 400-582 (1)	A. Campbell
	G-CBLY	Grob G.109B	G-CBLY Syndicate
	G-CBLZ	Rutan LongEz	S. K. Cockburn
	G-CBMA	Raj Hamsa X'Air 582 (10)	O. C. Rash
	G-CBMB	Cyclone Ax2000	T. H. Chadwick
	G-CBMC	Cameron Z-105 balloon	B. R. Whatley
	G-CBMD	IDA Bacau Yakovlev Yak-52 (10 yellow)	R. J. Hunter
	G-CBME	Cessna F.172M	Skytrax Aviation Ltd
	G-CBMI	Yakovlev Yak-52	I. A. Harding
	G-CBMK	Cameron Z-120 balloon	G. Davies
	G-CBML	DHC.6 Twin Otter 310	Isles of Scilly Skybus Ltd
	G-CBMM	Mainair Blade 912	W. L. Millar
	G-CBMO	PA-28 Cherokee 180	T. Rawlings
	G-CBMP	Cessna R.182	Orman (Carrolls Farm) Ltd
	G-CBMR	Medway Eclipser	D. S. Blofeld
	G-CBMT	Robin DR.400/180	A. C. Williamson
	G-CBMU	Whittaker MW6-S Fat Boy Flyer	A. M. Witt
	G-CBMV	Pegasus Quantum 15	G. Poulett
	G-CBMW	Zenair CH.701 UL	Forge consulting Ltd
	G-CBMX	Kiss 400-582 (1)	C. D. Gates & J. A. Slocombe
	G-CBMZ	Aerotechnik EV-97 Eurostar	J. C. O'Donnell
	G-CBNA	Flight Design CT2K	J. R. Fyfe
	G-CBNB	Eurocopter EC 120B	Arenberg Consultadoria E Servicos LDA/Madeira
	G-CBNC	Mainair Blade 912	K. L. Smith
	G-CBNF	Rans S.7 Courier	M. Henderson
	G-CBNG	Robin R.2112	R. K. Galbally & E. W. Russell
	G-CBNI	Lindstrand LBL-180A balloon	K. W. Scott
	G-CBNJ	Raj Hamsa X'Air 912 (1)	N. C. Marciano
	G-CBNL	Dyn'Aéro MCR-01 Club	D. H. Wilson
	G-CBNO	CFM Streak Shadow	D. J. Goldsmith
	G-CBNT	Pegasus Quantum 15-912	B. H. Goldsmith
	G-CBNV	Rans S.6-ES Coyote II	J. D. Henderson
	G-CBNW	Cameron N-105 balloon	Bailey Balloons
	G-CBNX	Mongomerie-Bensen B.8MR	A. C. S. M. Hart
	G-CBNZ	TEAM hi-MAX 1700R	A. P. S. John
	G-CBOA	Auster B.8 Agricola Srs 1	C. J. Baker
	G-CBOC	Raj Hamsa X'Air 582 (5)	A. J. McAleer
	G-CBOE	Hawker Hurricane IIB	P. J. Tuplin & P. W. Portelli
	G-CBOF	Shaw Europa XS	I. W. Ligertwood
	G-CBOG	Mainair Blade 912S	OG Group
	G-CBOK	Rans S.6-ES Coyote II	I. Johnson
	G-CBOM	Mainair Blade 912	G. Suckling
	G-CBOO	Mainair Blade 912S	Oscar Oscar Group
	G-CBOP	Avtech Jabiru UL-450	D. W. Batchelor
	G-CBOR	Cessna F.172N	Vetsonic LLP
	G-CBOS	Rans S.6-ES Coyote II	J. T. Athulathmudali
	G-CBOW	Cameron Z-120 balloon	Turner Balloons Ltd
	G-CBOY	Pegasus Quantum 15-912	Charlie Boy Syndicate
	G-CBOZ	IDA Bacau Yakovlev Yak-52	T. M. Boxall
	G-CBPC	Sportavia-Putzer RF-5B Sperber	Lee RF-5B Group
	G-CBPD	Ikarus C.42 Cyclone FB UK	Waxwing Group
	G-CBPE	SOCATA TB10 Tobago	A. F. Welch
	G-CBPI	PA-28R-201 Arrow III	M. J. Richardson
	G-CBPL	TEAM mini-MAX 93	P. R. G. Morley
	G-CBPM	Yakovlev Yak-50 (50 black)	P. W. Ansell
	G-CBPR	Avtech Jabiru UL-450	D. G. Bennett
	G-CBPR	Avtech Jabiru UL-450	S. I. Laurence
	G-CBPU	Raj Hamsa X'Air R100(3)	R. Power
	G-CBPV	Zenair CH.601UL	R. D. Barnard

Reg.	Type	Owner or Operator	Notes
G-CBPW	Lindstrand LBL-105A balloon	A. C. Elson	
G-CBRB	Ultramagic S-105 balloon	I. S. Bridge	
G-CBRC	Jodel D.18	B. W. Shaw	
G-CBRD	Jodel D.18	J. D. Haslam	
G-CBRE	Mainair Blade 912	J. Jones	
G-CBRG	Cessna 560XL Citation Excel	Queensway Aviation Ltd	
G-CBRJ	Mainair Blade 912S	R. W. Janion	
G-CBRK	Ultramagic M-77 balloon	R. T. Revel	
G-CBRM	Mainair Blade	M. H. Levy	
G-CBRO	Robinson R44	R. D. Jordan	
G-CBRR	Aerotechnik EV-97A Eurostar	T. O. Powley	
G-CBRT	Murphy Elite	T. W. Baylie	
G-CBRV	Cameron C-90 balloon	C. J. Teall	
G-CBRW	Aerostar Yakovlev Yak-52 (50 grey)	Max-Alpha Aviation GmbH/Germany	
G-CBRX	Zenair CH.601UL Zodiac	C. J. Meadows	
G-CBRZ	Kiss 400-582(1)	J. J. Ryan/Ireland	
G-CBSF	Westland Gazelle HT.2	Falcon Aviation Ltd	
G-CBSH	Westland Gazelle HT.3 (XX406:P)	Alltask Ltd	
G-CBSI	Westland Gazelle HT.3 (XZ934:U)	P. S. Unwin	
G-CBSK	Westland Gazelle HT.3 (ZB627:A)	Falcon Flying Group	
G-CBSL	IDA Bacau Yakovlev Yak-52 (67 red)	N. & A. D. Barton	
G-CBSO	PA-28-181 Archer II	Archer One Ltd	
G-CBSP	Pegasus Quantum 15-912	W. Lofts	
G-CBSR	Yakovlev Yak-52	Grovinvest Srl	
G-CBSS	IDA Bacau Yakovlev Yak-52	E. J. F. Verhellen/Belgium	
G-CBSU	Avtech Jabiru UL	K. R. Crawley	
G-CBSV	Montgomerie-Bensen B.8MR	J. A. McGill	
G-CBSZ	Mainair Blade 912S	P. J. Nolan	
G-CBTB	I.I.I. Sky Arrow 650TS	J. S. Hudson	
G-CBTD	Pegasus Quantum 15-912	D. Baillie	
G-CBTE	Mainair Blade 912|S	K. J. Miles	
G-CBTG	Ikarus C42 FB UK Cyclone	G-CBTG Flying Group	
G-CBTK	Raj Hamsa X'Air 582 (5)	M. Shaw	
G-CBTL	Monnett Moni	P. N. Stacey	
G-CBTM	Mainair Blade	D. A. A. Hewitt	
G-CBTN	PA-31 Navajo C	Durban Aviation Services Ltd	
G-CBTO	Rans S.6-ES Coyote II	D. Wakefield	
G-CBTR	Lindstrand LBL-120A balloon	R. H. Etherington	
G-CBTS	Gloster Gamecock (replica)	Retro Track & Air (UK) Ltd	
G-CBTT	PA-28-181 Archer II	Citicourt Aviation Ltd (G-BFMM)	
G-CBTW	Mainair Blade 912	K. J. Austwick	
G-CBTX	Denney Kitfox Mk.2	G. I. Doake	
G-CBUA	Extra EA.230	S. Pedersen	
G-CBUC	Raj Hamsa X'Air 582 (5)	R. S. Noremberg	
G-CBUD	Pegasus Quantum 15-912	G. N. S. Farrant	
G-CBUE	Ultramagic N-250 balloon	Elinore French Ltd	
G-CBUF	Flight Design CT2K	N. A. Thomas	
G-CBUG	Technam P.92-EM Echo	J. J. Bodnarec	
G-CBUI	Westland Wasp HA.1 (XT420:606)	The Helicopter Squadron Ltd	
G-CBUJ	Raj Hamsa X'Air 582 (10)	M. A. Curtis	
G-CBUK	Van's RV-6A	P. G. Greenslade	
G-CBUN	Barker Charade	D. R. Wilkinson & T. Coldwell	
G-CBUO	Cameron O-90 balloon	W. J. Treacy & P. M. Smith	
G-CBUP	VPM M-16 Tandem Trainer	J. S. Firth	
G-CBUR	Zenair CH.601UL	R. Simpson	
G-CBUS	Pegasus Quantum 15	J. Liddiard	
G-CBUU	Pegasus Quantum 15-912	D. & P. Allman	
G-CBUW	Cameron Z-133 balloon	Balloon School (International) Ltd	
G-CBUX	Cyclone AX2000	S. N. Pryor	
G-CBUY	Rans S.6-ES Coyote II	I. L. Johnson	
G-CBUZ	Pegasus Quantum 15	D. G. Seymour	
G-CBVA	Thruster T.600N 450	D. J. Clingan	
G-CBVB	Robin R.2120U	Flew LLP	
G-CBVC	Raj Hamsa X'Air 582 (5)	G. Weir	
G-CBVD	Cameron C-60 balloon	Phoenix Balloons Ltd	
G-CBVF	Murphy Maverick	H. A. Leek	
G-CBVG	Mainair Blade 912S	A. M. Buchanan	
G-CBVH	Lindstrand LBL-120A balloon	Line Packaging & Display Ltd	
G-CBVK	Schroeder Fire Balloons G balloon	S. Travaglia	
G-CBVM	Aerotechnik EV-97 Eurostar	M. Sharpe	
G-CBVN	Pegasus Quik	C. Kearney	
G-CBVR	Skyranger 912 (2)	S. H. Lunney	
G-CBVS	Skyranger 912 (2)	S. C. Cornock	

Notes	Reg.	Type	Owner or Operator
	G-CBVT	Yakovlev Yak-52	M. A. G. Lopez
	G-CBVU	PA-28R Cherokee Arrow 200-II	S. Crowley
	G-CBVV	Cameron N-120 balloon	John Aimo Balloons SAS/Italy
	G-CBVX	Cessna 182P	P. & A. de Weerdt
	G-CBVY	Ikarus C.42 Cyclone FB UK	H. T. Beattie
	G-CBVZ	Flight Design CT2K	A. N. D. Arthur
	G-CBWA	Flight Design CT2K	Sun Fun Luxury Travel
	G-CBWB	PA-34-200T Seneca II	Gama Engineering Ltd
	G-CBWD	PA-28-161 Warrior III	J. Wright
	G-CBWE	Aerotechnik EV-97 Eurostar	J. & C. W. Hood
	G-CBWG	Aerotechnik EV-97 Eurostar	C. Long & M. P. & T. Middleton
	G-CBWI	Thruster T. 600N 450	P. L. Jarvis
	G-CBWJ	Thruster T. 600N 450	Voliamo Group
	G-CBWK	Ultramagic H-77 balloon	H. C. Peel
	G-CBWN	Campbell Cricket Mk.6	P. J. Croft
	G-CBWO	Rotorway Executive 162F	N. T. Oakman
	G-CBWP	Shaw Europa	T. W. Greaves
	G-CBWS	Whittaker MW6 Merlin	W. Turner
	G-CBWU	Rotorway Executive 162F	F. A. Cavaciuti
	G-CBWV	Falconar F-12A Cruiser	A. Ackland
	G-CBWW	Skyranger 912 (2)	N. S. Wellsl
	G-CBWY	Raj Hamsa X'Air 582 (6)	J. C. Rose
	G-CBWZ	Robinson R22 Beta	Sundial Aviation Ltd
	G-CBXA	Raj Hamsa X'Air 582 (5)	G-CBXA Flying Group
	G-CBXB	Lindstrand LBL-150A balloon	M. A. Webb
	G-CBXC	Ikarus C.42 Cyclone FB UK	J. A. Robinson
	G-CBXE	Easy Raider J2.2 (3)	A. K. Day
	G-CBXF	Easy Raider J2.2 (2)	M. R. Grunwell
	G-CBXG	Thruster T.600N 450	Newtownards Microlight Group
	G-CBXJ	Cessna 172S	Steptoe and Sons Properties Ltd
	G-CBXK	Robinson R22 Mariner	Kington Building Supplies Ltd
	G-CBXM	Mainair Blade	B. A. Coombe
	G-CBXN	Robinson R22 Beta II	N. M. G. Pearson
	G-CBXR	Raj Hamsa X-Air Falcon 582 (1)	A. R. Rhodes
	G-CBXS	Skyranger J2.2 (1)	C. J. Erith
	G-CBXU	TEAM mini-MAX 91A	C. D. Hatcher
	G-CBXW	Shaw Europa XS	R. G. Fairall
	G-CBXZ	Rans S.6-ES Coyote II	D. Tole
	G-CBYB	Rotorway Executive 162F	Clark Contracting
	G-CBYC	Cameron Z-275 balloon	Virgin Balloon Flights
	G-CBYD	Rans S.6-ES Coyote II	R. Burland
	G-CBYE	Pegasus Quik	C. E. Morris
	G-CBYF	Mainair Blade	J. Ayre
	G-CBYH	Aeroprakt A.22 Foxbat	G. C. Moore
	G-CBYI	Pegasus Quantum 15-503	The G-BCYI Group
	G-CBYJ	Steen Skybolt	The Skybolt Group
	G-CBYM	Mainair Blade	S. Webb
	G-CBYN	Shaw Europa XS	G. M. Tagg
	G-CBYO	Pegasus Quik	G-CBYO Syndicate
	G-CBYP	Whittaker MW6-S Fat Boy Flyer	R. J. Grainger
	G-CBYS	Lindstrand LBL-21 balloon France	B. M. Reed/France
	G-CBYT	Thruster T.600N 450	T. G. V. Oyston
	G-CBYU	PA-28-161 Warrior II	Stapleford Flying Club Ltd
	G-CBYV	Pegasus Quantum 15-912	G-CBYV Syndicate
	G-CBYW	Hatz CB-1	T. A. Hinton
	G-CBYY	Robinson R44	AMS Aviation Ltd
	G-CBYZ	Tecnam P92-EM Echo-Super	B. Weaver
	G-CBZA	Mainair Blade	M. Lowe
	G-CBZB	Mainair Blade	P. H. Evans
	G-CBZD	Mainair Blade	G. F. Jones
	G-CBZE	Robinson R44	Alps (Scotland) Ltd
	G-CBZF	Robinson R22 Beta	Fly Executive Ltd
	G-CBZG	Rans S.6-ES Coyote II	W. Chang
	G-CBZH	Pegasus Quik	B. D. Searle
	G-CBZJ	Lindstrand LBL-25A balloon	Pegasus Ballooning
	G-CBZK	Robin DR.400/180	R. A. Fleming
	G-CBZL	Westland Gazelle HT.3	Armstrong Aviation Ltd
	G-CBZM	Avtech Jabiru SPL-450	M. E. Ledward
	G-CBZN	Rans S.6-ES Coyote II	R. G. Morris
	G-CBZP	Hawker Fury I (K5674)	Historic Aircraft Collection
	G-CBZR	PA-28R-201 Arrow III	D. J. Medcraft
	G-CBZS	Aurora	J. Lynden
	G-CBZT	Pegasus Quik	A. P. Portsmouth

Reg.	Type	Owner or Operator	Notes
G-CBZU	Lindstrand LBL-180A balloon	Adventure Balloons Ltd	
G-CBZW	Zenair CH.701UL	T. M. Siles	
G-CBZX	Dyn' Aero MCR-01 ULC	A. C. N. Freeman & M. P. Wilson	
G-CBZZ	Cameron Z-275 balloon	A. C. K. Rawson & J. J. Rudoni	
G-CCAB	Mainair Blade	A. J. Morris	
G-CCAC	Aerotech EV-97 Eurostar	D. C. Lugg	
G-CCAD	Mainair Pegasus Quik	L. A. Hosegood & M. J. Mawle	
G-CCAE	Avtech Jabiru UL-450	D. Logan	
G-CCAF	Skyranger 912 (1)	D. W. & M. L. Squire	
G-CCAG	Mainair Blade 912	A. Robinson	
G-CCAK	Zenair CN.601HD	A. Kimmond	
G-CCAL	Technam P.92-EA Echo	M. Rudd	
G-CCAP	Robinson R22 Beta II	D. Baker, M. Healer & H. Price	
G-CCAR	Cameron N-77 balloon	D. P. Turner	
G-CCAS	Pegasus Quik	Caunton Alpha Syndicate	
G-CCAT	AA-55A Cheetah	A. Ohringer (G-OAJH/G-KILT/G-BJFA)	
G-CCAV	PA-28-181 Archer II	Archer II Ltd	
G-CCAW	Mainair Blade 912	A. D. Carr	
G-CCAY	Cameron Z-42 balloon	P. Stern	
G-CCAZ	Mainair Pegasus Quik	J. P. Floyd	
G-CCBA	Skyranger R.100	Fourstrokes Group	
G-CCBB	Cameron N-90 balloon	S. C. A. & L. D. Craze	
G-CCBC	Thruster T.600N 450	E. J. Girling & J. A. E. Bowen	
G-CCBF	Maule M.5-235C	C. G. Sims (G-NHVH)	
G-CCBG	Skyranger V.2 + (1)	P. R. Mailer & F. Stannard	
G-CCBH	PA-28 Cherokee 236	J. R. Hunt & M. Kenny	
G-CCBI	X'Air R100 (2)	O. Sanda	
G-CCBJ	Skyranger 912 (2)	C. S. Robinson	
G-CCBK	Aerotechnik EV-97 Eurostar	B. S. Waycott	
G-CCBL	Agusta-Bell 206B JetRanger 3	Formula Karting Ltd	
G-CCBM	Aerotechnik EV-97 Eurostar	W. Graves	
G-CCBN	Scale Replica SE-5a (80105/19)	V. C. Lockwood	
G-CCBR	Jodel D.120	A. Dunne & M. Munnelly	
G-CCBT	Cameron Z-90 balloon	I. J. Sharpe	
G-CCBV	Cameron Z-225 balloon	New Spirit Baloons ASBL, Luxembourg	
G-CCBW	Sherwood Ranger	A. L. Virgoe	
G-CCBX	Raj Hamsa X'Air 133 (2)	R. G. Cheshire	
G-CCBY	Avtech Jabiru UL-450	D. M. Goodman	
G-CCBZ	Aero Designs Pulsar	J. M. Keane	
G-CCCA	VS.509 Spitfire Tr.IX	Historic Flying Ltd (G-BHRH/G-TRIX)	
G-CCCB	Thruster T.600N 450	G-CCCB Flying Group	
G-CCCD	Mainair Pegasus Quantum 15	R. N. Gamble	
G-CCCE	Aeroprakt A.22 Foxbat	P. Sykes	
G-CCCF	Thruster T.600N 450	P. R. Norman	
G-CCCG	Mainair Pegasus Quik	D. Seiler	
G-CCCH	Thruster T600N 450	G. Scullion	
G-CCCI	Medway Eclipse R	C. Dunford	
G-CCCJ	Nicollier HN.700 Menestrel II	G. A. Rodmell	
G-CCCK	Skyranger 912 (2)	P. L. Braniff	
G-CCCM	Skyranger 912 (2)	Connel Gliding Group	
G-CCCN	Robin R.3000/160	DR Flyers 2	
G-CCCO	Aerotechnik EV-97A Eurostar	D. R. G. Whitelaw	
G-CCCR	Best Off Sky Ranger 912(2)	E. Foster & J. H. Peet	
G-CCCU	Thruster T.600N 450	A. F. Cashin	
G-CCCV	Raj Hamsa X'Air Falcon 133 (1)	G. J. Boyer	
G-CCCW	Pereira Osprey 2	D. J. Southward	
G-CCCY	Skyranger 912 (2)	A. Watson	
G-CCDB	Mainair Pegasus Quik	A. Pritchard	
G-CCDD	Mainair Pegasus Quik	M. P. Hadden & M. H. Rollins	
G-CCDF	Mainair Pegasus Quik	R. P. McGann	
G-CCDG	Skyranger 912 (1)	Freebird Group	
G-CCDH	Skyranger 912 (2)	M. L. Willmington	
G-CCDJ	Raj Hamsa X'Air Falcon 582 (2)	P. White	
G-CCDK	Pegasus Quantum 15-912	G. Charman	
G-CCDL	Raj Hamsa X'Air Falcon 582 (2)	G. M. Brown	
G-CCDM	Mainair Blade	P. R. G. Morley	
G-CCDO	Mainair Pegasus Quik	S. T. Welsh	
G-CCDP	Raj Hamsa X'Air R.100 (3)	F. J. McGuigan	
G-CCDR	Raj Hamsa X'Air Falcon Jabiru	F. Overall	
G-CCDS	Nicollier HN.700 Menestrel II	B. W. Gowland	
G-CCDU	Tecnam P92-EM Echo	D. R. Baker	
G-CCDV	Thruster T.600N 450	G. C. Hobson	

Notes	Reg.	Type	Owner or Operator
	G-CCDW	Skyranger 582 (1)	Debts R Us Family Group
	G-CCDX	Aerotechnik EV-97 Eurostar	J. M. Swash
	G-CCDY	Skyranger 912 (2)	N. H. Copperthwaite
	G-CCDZ	Pegasus Quantum 15-912	K. D. Baldwin
	G-CCEA	Mainair Pegasus Quik	G. D. Ritchie
	G-CCEB	Thruster T.600N 450	Thruster Air Services Ltd
	G-CCED	Zenair CH.601UL	R. P. Reynolds
	G-CCEE	PA-15 Vagabond	I. M. Callier (G-VAGA)
	G-CCEF	Shaw Europa	C. P. Garner
	G-CCEH	Skyranger 912 (2)	ZC Owners
	G-CCEJ	Aerotechnik EV-97 Eurostar	N. A. Quintin
	G-CCEK	Kiss 400-582 (1)	R. C. Hinkins & M. Thurlbourn
	G-CCEL	Avtech Jabiru UL	S. K. Armstrong
	G-CCEM	Aerotechnik EV-97 Eurostar	Oxenhope Flying Group
	G-CCEN	Cameron Z-120 balloon	R. Hunt
	G-CCEO	Thunder Ax10-180 S2 balloon	P. Heitzeneder/Austria
	G-CCEP	Raj Hamsa X'Air Falcon Jabiru	F. J. Csuka
	G-CCES	Raj Hamsa X'Air 3203(1)	G. V. McCloskey
	G-CCET	Nova Vertex 28 hang glider	M. Hay
	G-CCEU	RAF 2000 GTX-SE gyroplane	N. G. Dovaston
	G-CCEW	Mainair Pegasus Quik	N. F. Mackenzie
	G-CCEY	Raj Hamsa X'582 (11)	P. F. F. Spedding
	G-CCEZ	Easy Raider J2.2	P. J Clegg
	G-CCFA	Kiss 400-582 (1)	A. E. Barron
	G-CCFB	Mainair Pegasus Quik	P. Bailey
	G-CCFC	Robinson R44 II	H. J. Walters
	G-CCFD	BFC Challenger II	W. Oswald
	G-CCFE	Tipsy Nipper T.66 Srs 2	R. A. Weller
	G-CCFG	Dyn'Aéro MCR-01 Club	P. H. Milward
	G-CCFI	PA-32 Cherokee Six 260	McManus Truck & Trailer Spares Ltd
	G-CCFJ	Kolb Twinstar Mk.3	D. Travers
	G-CCFK	Shaw Europa	C. R. Knapton
	G-CCFL	Mainair Pegasus Quik	P. G. Mallon
	G-CCFO	Pitts S-1S Special	R. J. Anderson
	G-CCFS	Diamond DA40D Star	R. H. Butterfield
	G-CCFT	Mainair Pegasus Quantum 15-912	D. A. Bannister
	G-CCFU	Diamond DA40D Star	Jetstream Aviation Academy/Greece
	G-CCFV	Lindstrand LBL-77A balloon	Alton Aviation Ltd
	G-CCFW	WAR Focke-Wulf Fw.190	D. B. Conway
	G-CCFX	EAA Acrosport 2	C. D. Ward
	G-CCFY	Rotorway Executive 162F	Southern Helicopters Ltd
	G-CCFZ	Ikarus C.42 FB UK	B. W. Drake
	G-CCGB	TEAM mini-MAX	A. D, Pentland
	G-CCGC	Mainair Pegasus Quik	R. W. Street
	G-CCGE	Robinson R22 Beta	Patriot Aviation Ltd
	G-CCGF	Robinson R22 Beta	Multiflight Ltd
	G-CCGG	Jabiru Aircraft Jabiru J400	S. C. E Twiss
	G-CCGH	Supermarine Aircraft Spitfire Mk.26 (AB196)	Cokebusters Ltd
	G-CCGK	Mainair Blade	C. M. Babiy & M. Hurn
	G-CCGM	Kiss 450-582 (1)	M. Nazm
	G-CCGO	Medway AV8R	D. A. Coupland
	G-CCGP	Bristol Type 200	R. L. Holman
	G-CCGR	Raj Hamsa X'Air 133 (1)	A. Greenwell
	G-CCGS	Dornier 328-100	Suckling Airways (Cambridge) Ltd
	G-CCGT	Cameron Z-425 balloon	A. A. Brown
	G-CCGU	Van's RV-9A	B. J. Main & ptnrs
	G-CCGW	Shaw Europa	D. Buckley
	G-CCGY	Cameron Z-105 balloon	Cameron Balloons Ltd
	G-CCGZ	Cameron Z-250 balloon	Cameron Flights Southern Ltd
	G-CCHA	Diamond DA40D Star	Diamond Hire UK Ltd
	G-CCHD	Diamond DA40D Star	Flying Time Ltd
	G-CCHH	Pegasus Quik	C. A. Green
	G-CCHI	Mainair Pegasus Quik	M. R. Starling
	G-CCHL	PA-28-181 Archer iii	Archer Three Ltd
	G-CCHM	Kiss 450	M. J. Jessup
	G-CCHN	Corby CJ.1 Starlet	N. S. Dell
	G-CCHO	Mainair Pegasus Quik	M. Allan
	G-CCHP	Cameron Z-31 balloon	M. H. Redman
	G-CCHR	Easy Raider 583 (1)	M. P. Wiseman
	G-CCHS	Raj Hamsa X'Air 582	N. H. Gokul
	G-CCHT	Cessna 152	J. S. Devlin & Z. Islam
	G-CCHV	Mainair Rapier	K. L. Smith

Reg.	Type	Owner or Operator	Notes
G-CCHW	Cameron Z-77 balloon	A. Murphy	
G-CCHX	Scheibe SF.25C Falke	Lasham Gliding Society Ltd	
G-CCID	Jabiru Aircraft Jabiru J400	G-CCID Syndicate	
G-CCIF	Mainair Blade	S. P. Moores	
G-CCIG	Aero Designs Pulsar	P. Maguire	
G-CCIH	Mainair Pegasus Quantum 15	T. Smith	
G-CCII	ICP Savannah Jabiru (3)	D. Chaloner	
G-CCIJ	PA-28R Cherokee Arrow 180	S. A. Hughes	
G-CCIK	Skyranger 912 (2)	M. D. Kirby	
G-CCIO	Skyranger 912 (2)	B. Berry	
G-CCIR	Van's RV-8	N. W. Charles	
G-CCIS	Scheibe SF.28A Tandem Falke	The Tandem-Falke Syndicate	
G-CCIT	Zenair CH.701UL	J. A. R. Hughes	
G-CCIU	Cameron N-105 balloon	W. W. Leitlein	
G-CCIV	Mainair Pegasus Quik	G. H. Ousby	
G-CCIW	Raj Hamsa X'Air 582 (2)	N. Watts	
G-CCIY	Skyranger 912 (2)	L. F. Tanner	
G-CCIZ	PZL-110 Koliber 160A	J. P. Nugent	
G-CCJA	Skyranger 912 (2)	C. Day	
G-CCJB	Zenair CH.701 STOL	E. G. Brown	
G-CCJD	Mainair Pegasus Quantum 15	P. Clark	
G-CCJF	Cameron C-90 balloon	Balloon School International Ltd	
G-CCJH	Lindstrand LBL-90A balloon	J. R. Hoare	
G-CCJI	Van's RV-6	A. Jenkins	
G-CCJJ	Medway Pirana	P. K. Bennett	
G-CCJK	Aerostar Yakovlev Yak-52	G-CCJK Group	
G-CCJL	Super Marine Aircraft Spitfire XXVI	M. W. Hanley & P. M. Whitaker	
G-CCJM	Mainair Pegasus Quik	S. R. Smyth	
G-CCJN	Rans S.6ES Coyote II	D. L. Frankland, J. M. Kirtley & T. W. Stewart	
G-CCJO	ICP-740 Savannah Jabiru 4	R. & I. Fletcher	
G-CCJT	Skyranger 912 (2)	Juliet Tango Group	
G-CCJU	ICP MXP-740 Savannah Jabiru (4)	A. R. & M. A. Baxter	
G-CCJV	Aeroprakt A.22 Foxbat	Foxbat UK015 Syndicate	
G-CCJW	Skyranger 912 (2)	J. R. Walter	
G-CCJX	Shaw Europa XS	J. S. Baranski	
G-CCJY	Cameron Z-42 balloon	D. J. Griffin	
G-CCKF	Skyranger 912 (2)	D. McCabe & M. Harris	
G-CCKG	Skyranger 912 (2)	C. E. Penny	
G-CCKH	Diamond DA40D Star	Flying Time Ltd	
G-CCKI	Diamond DA40D Star	S. C. Horwood	
G-CCKJ	Raj Hamsa X'Air 133 (3)	G. A. Davidson	
G-CCKL	Aerotechnik EV-97A Eurostar	G-CCKL Group	
G-CCKM	Mainair Pegasus Quik	W. T. Milburn & P. A. Kershaw	
G-CCKN	Nicollier HN.700 Menestrel II	C. R. Partington	
G-CCKO	Mainair Pegasus Quik	I. A. Macadam	
G-CCKP	Robin DR.400/120	Duxford Flying Group	
G-CCKR	Pietenpol Air Camper	C. R. Thompson	
G-CCKT	Hapi Cygnet SF-2	P. W. Abraham	
G-CCKW	PA-18 Super Cub 135	P. A. Layzell (G-GDAM)	
G-CCKX	Lindstrand LBL-210A balloon	Alba Ballooning Ltd	
G-CCKY	Lindstrand LBL-240A balloon	Cameron Flights Southern Ltd	
G-CCKZ	Customcraft A-25 balloon	M. J. Axtell	
G-CCLF	Best Off Skyranger 912 (2)	J. Bannister & N. J. Sutherland	
G-CCLG	Lindstrand LBL-105A balloon	M. A. Derbyshire	
G-CCLH	Rans S.6-ES Coyote II	K. R. Browne	
G-CCLM	Mainair Pegasus Quik	D. J. Shippen & C. C. Colclough	
G-CCLO	Ultramagic H-77 balloon-	J. P. Moore	
G-CCLP	ICP MXP-740 Savannah	C. J. Powell & A. H. Watkins	
G-CCLR	Schleicher Ash 26E	M. T. Burton & A. Darby	
G-CCLS	Comco Ikarus C.42 FB UK	B. D. Wykes	
G-CCLU	Best Off Skyranger 912	C. M. Babiy	
G-CCLW	Diamond DA40D Star	Shacklewell Diamond Group	
G-CCLX	Mainair Pegasus Quik	J. W. Edwards	
G-CCMC	Jabiru Aircraft Jabiru UL 450	K. J. Simpson	
G-CCMD	Mainair Pegasus Quik	J. T. McCormack	
G-CCME	Mainair Pegasus Quik	Caunton Graphites Syndicate	
G-CCMH	M.2H Hawk Major	J. A. Pothecary	
G-CCMI	SA Bulldog Srs 120/121 (XX513:10)	H. R. M. Tyrrell (G-KKKK)	
G-CCMJ	Easy Raider J2.2 (1)	G. F. Clews	
G-CCMK	Raj Hamsa X'Air Falcon	G. J. Digby	
G-CCML	Mainair Pegasus Quik	D. Renton	
G-CCMM	Dyn'Aéro MCR-01 ULC Banbi	J. D. Harris	
G-CCMN	Cameron C-90 balloon	A.E. Austin	

Notes	Reg.	Type	Owner or Operator
	G-CCMO	Aerotechnik EV-97 Eurostar	G. Hardman
	G-CCMP	Aerotechnik EV-97A Eurostar	E. K. McAlinden
	G-CCMR	Robinson R22 Beta	G. F. Smith
	G-CCMS	Mainair Pegasus Quik	Barton Charlie Charlie Group
	G-CCMT	Thruster T.600N 450	G. L. Logan
	G-CCMU	Rotorway Executive 162F	D. J. Fravigar & J. Smith
	G-CCMW	CFM Shadow Srs.DD	M. Wilkinson
	G-CCMX	Skyranger 912 (2)	K. J. Cole
	G-CCMZ	Best Off Skyranger 912 (2)	D. D. Appleford
	G-CCNA	Jodel DR.100A (Replica)	R. Everitt
	G-CCNC	Cameron Z-275 balloon	J. D. & K. Griffiths
	G-CCND	Van's RV-9A	K. S. Woodard
	G-CCNE	Mainair Pegasus Quantum 15	G. D. Barker
	G-CCNF	Raj Hamsa X'Air 582 Falcon 133	R. E. Williams
	G-CCNG	Flight Design CT2K	S. C. Reeve
	G-CCNH	Rans S.6ES Coyote II	J. E. Howard
	G-CCNJ	Skyranger 912 (2)	J. D. Buchanan
	G-CCNL	Raj Hamsa X'Air Falcon 133(1)	S. E. Vallance
	G-CCNM	Mainair Pegasus Quik	J. G. McMinn
	G.CCNN	Cameron Z-90 balloon	J. H. Turner
	G-CCNP	Flight Design CT2K	M. J. Hawkins
	G-CCNR	Skyranger 912 (2)	K. Washbourne
	G-CCNS	Skyranger 912 (2)	J. A Warters
	G-CCNT	Ikarus C.42 FB80	November Tango Group
	G-CCNU	Skyranger J2.2 (2)	P. D. Priestley
	G-CCNW	Mainair Pegasus Quantum Lite	J. Childs
	G-CCNX	CAB CAP-10B	Arc Input Ltd
	G-CCNY	Robinson R44	J. & S. J. Strange
	G-CCNZ	Raj Hamsa X'Air 133 (1)	A. Tucker
	G-CCOB	Aero C.104 Jungmann	C. W. Tomkins
	G-CCOC	Mainair Pegasus Quantum 15	A. J. Owen
	G-CCOF	Rans S.6-ESA Coyote II	A. J. Wright & M. Govan
	G-CCOG	Mainair Pegasus Quik	A. O. Sutherland
	G-CCOK	Mainair Pegasus Quik	A. R. Walker
	G-CCOM	Westland Lysander IIIA (V9312)	Propshop Ltd
	G-CCOP	Ultramagic M-105 balloon	M. E. J. Whitewood
	G-CCOR	Sequoia F.8L Falco	D. J. Thoma
	G-CCOS	Cameron Z-350 balloon	Wickers World Ltd
	G-CCOT	Cameron Z-105 balloon	Airborne Adventures Ltd
	G-CCOU	Mainair Pegasus Quik	D. E. J. McVicker
	G-CCOV	Shaw Europa XS	B. C. Barton
	G-CCOW	Mainair Pegasus Quik	J. R. Houston
	G-CCOY	NA AT-6D Harvard II	Classic Flying Machine Collection Ltd
	G-CCOZ	Monnett Sonerai II	W. H. Cole
	G-CCPA	Kiss 400-582(1)	C.P. Astridge
	G-CCPC	Mainair Pegasus Quik	P. M. Coppola
	G-CCPD	Campbell Cricket Mk.4	T. H. Geake
	G-CCPE	Steen Skybolt	C. Moore
	G-CCPF	Skyranger 912 (2)	A. R. Tomlinson
	G-CCPG	Mainair Pegasus Quik	A.W. Lowrie
	G-CCPH	EV-97 TeamEurostar UK	A. H. Woolley
	G-CCPJ	EV-97 TeamEurostar UK	J. S. Webb
	G-CCPK	Murphy Rebel	B. A. W. Bridgewater
	G-CCPL	Skyranger 912 (2)	G-CCPL Group
	G-CCPM	Mainair Blade 912	P. S. Davies
	G-CCPN	Dyn'Aéro MCR-01 Club	M. Sibson
	G-CCPO	Cameron N-77 balloon	A. M. Daniels (G-MITS)
	G-CCPP	Cameron 70 Concept balloon	Sarnia Balloon Group
	G-CCPS	Ikarus C.42 FB100 VLA	H. Cullens
	G-CCPT	Cameron Z-90 balloon	Charter Ballooning Ltd
	G-CCPV	Jabiru J400	J. R. Lawrence & M. J. Worrall
	G-CCPW	BAe Jetstream 3102	Linksair Ltd
	G-CCPY	Hughes 369D	Alpha Properties (London) Ltd
	G-CCPZ	Cameron Z-225 balloon	Cameron Flights Southern Ltd
	G-CCRA	Glaser-Dirks DG-800B	R. Fischer
	G-CCRB	Kolb Twinstar Mk.3 (modified)	M. Daly
	G-CCRC	Cessna Tu.206G	D. M. Penny
	G-CCRF	Mainair Pegasus Quantum 15	N. F. Taylor
	G-CCRG	Ultramagic M-77 balloon	Wickers World Ltd
	G-CCRH	Cameron Z-315 balloon	B. J. Palfreyman
	G-CCRI	Raj Hamsa X'Air 582 (5)	R. W. Wallace
	G-CCRJ	Shaw Europa	J. F. Cliff
	G-CCRK	Luscombe 8A Silvaire	J. R. Kimberley

Reg.	Type	Owner or Operator	Notes
G-CCRN	Thruster T.600N 450	R. A. Wright	
G-CCRP	Thruster T.600N 450	M. M. Lane (G-ULLY)	
G-CCRR	Skyranger 912 (1)	M. Cheetham	
G-CCRS	Lindstrand LBL-210A balloon	Aerosaurus Ballooning Ltd	
G-CCRT	Mainair Pegasus Quantum 15	N. Mitchell	
G-CCRV	Skyranger 912 (2)	R. O'Malley-White	
G-CCRW	Mainair Pegasus Quik	S. O. Hutchinson	
G-CCRX	Jabiru UL-450	M. Everest	
G-CCSD	Mainair Pegasus Quik	S. J. M. Morling	
G-CCSF	Mainair Pegasus Quik	D. G. Barnes & A. Sorah	
G-CCSG	Cameron Z-275 balloon	Wickers World Ltd	
G-CCSH	Mainair Pegasus Quik	N. C. Milnes	
G-CCSI	Cameron Z-42 balloon	IKEA Ltd	
G-CCSJ	Cameron A-275 balloon	Cameron Flights Southern Ltd	
G-CCSL	Mainair Pegasus Quik	A. J. Harper	
G-CCSN	Cessna U.206G	K. Brady	
G-CCSO	Raj Hamsa X'Air Falcon	D. J. Brightman	
G-CCSP	Cameron N-77 balloon	Ballongforeningen Oscair I Goteberg/Sweden	
G-CCSR	Aerotechnik EV-97A Eurostar	Sierra Romeo Flying Group	
G-CCSS	Lindstrand LBL-90A balloon	British Telecom	
G-CCST	PA-32R-301 Saratoga	G. R. Balls	
G-CCSU	IDA Bacau Yakovlev Yak-52	S. Ullrich/Germany	
G-CCSV	ICP MXP-740 Savannah Jabiru (1)	R. D. Wood	
G-CCSW	Nott PA balloon	J. R. P.Nott	
G-CCSX	Skyranger 912	T. Jackson	
G-CCSY	Mainair Pegasus Quik	I. K. Macleod	
G-CCTA	Zenair CH.601UL Zodiac	G. E. Reynolds	
G-CCTC	Mainair Pegasus Quik	D. R. Purslow	
G-CCTD	Mainair Pegasus Quik	R. N. S. Taylor	
G-CCTE	Dyn'Aéro MCR-01 Banbi	B. J. Mills & N. J. Milnes	
G-CCTF	Aerotek Pitts S-2A Special	Stampe and Pitts Flying Group	
G-CCTG	Van's RV-3B	A. Donald	
G-CCTH	Aerotechnik EV-97 TeamEurostar UK	M. W. Fitch	
G-CCTI	Aerotechnik EV-97 Teameurostar	Flylight Airsports Ltd	
G-CCTL	Robinson R44 II	B. Daly	
G-CCTM	Mainair Blade	J. N. Hanso	
G-CCTO	Aerotechnik EV-97 Eurostar	A. J. Bolton	
G-CCTP	Aerotechnik EV-97 Eurostar	P. E. Rose	
G-CCTR	Skyranger 912	G. Lampit & D. W. Stamp	
G-CCTS	Cameron Z-120 balloon	F. R. Hart	
G-CCTT	Cessna 172S	ACS Engineering Ltd	
G-CCTU	Mainair Pegasus Quik	J. J. C. Parrish & I. D. Smart	
G-CCTV	Rans S.6ESA Coyote II	G. & S. Simons	
G-CCTW	Cessna 152	R. J. Dempsey	
G-CCTX	Rans S.8ES Coyote II	T. Osbourne	
G-CCTZ	Mainair Pegasus Quik 912S	S. Baker	
G-CCUA	Mainair Pegasus Quik	J. Finer	
G-CCUB	Piper J-3C-65 Cub	G. Cormack	
G-CCUE	Ultramagic T-180 balloon	Cameron Flights Southern Ltd	
G-CCUF	Skyranger 912(2)	R. E. Parker	
G-CCUH	RAF 2000 GTX-SE gyroplane	J. H. Haverhals	
G-CCUI	Dyn'Aéro MCR-01 Banbi	J. T. Morgan	
G-CCUK	Agusta A109-II	Eastern Atlantic Helicopters Ltd	
G-CCUL	Shaw Europa XS	Europa 6	
G-CCUO	Hughes 369D	Claremont Air Services	
G-CCUR	Mainair Pegasus Quantum 15-912	D. W. Power & D. James	
G-CCUT	Aerotechnik EV-97 Eurostar	Doctor and the Medics	
G-CCUY	Shaw Europa	N. Evans	
G-CCUZ	Thruster T.600N 450	Fly 365 Ltd	
G-CCVA	Aerotechnik EV-97 Eurostar	K. J. Scott	
G-CCVF	Lindstrand LBL-105 balloon	Alan Patterson Design	
G-CCVH	Curtiss H-75A-1 (82:8)	The Fighter Collection	
G-CCVI	Zenair CH.701 SP	The 701 Group	
G-CCVJ	Raj Hamsa X'Air Falcon 133	I. S. Doig	
G-CCVK	Aerotechnik EV-97 TeamEurostar UK	J. Holditch	
G-CCVL	Zenair CH.601XL Zodiac	A. Y-T. Leung & G. Constantine	
G-CCVM	Van's RV-7A	J. G. Small	
G-CCVN	Jabiru SP-470	Teesside Aviators Group	
G-CCVP	Beech 58	Richard Nash Cars Ltd	
G-CCVR	Skyranger 912(2)	M. J. Batchelor	
G-CCVS	Van's RV-6A	J. Edgeworth (G-CCVC)	
G-CCVT	Zenair CH.601UL Zodiac	P. Millar	
G-CCVU	Robinson R22 Beta II	J. H. P. S. Sargent	

Notes	Reg.	Type	Owner or Operator
	G-CCVW	Nicollier HN.700 Menestrel II	B. F. Enock
	G-CCVX	Mainair Tri Flyer 330	J. A. Shufflebotham
	G-CCVZ	Cameron O-120 balloon	T. M. C. McCoy
	G-CCWC	Skyranger 912	W. Goldsmith
	G-CCWE	Lindstrand LBL-330A balloon	Adventure Balloons Ltd
	G-CCWF	Raj Hamsa X'Air 133	F. Loughran
	G-CCWH	Dyn'Aéro MCR-01 Bambi	B. J. Mills & N. J. Mines
	G-CCWJ	Robinson R44 II	Saxon Logistics Ltd
	G-CCWL	Mainair Blade	M. E. Rushworth
	G-CCWM	Robin DR.400/180	D. M. Scorer
	G-CCWO	Mainair Pegasus Quantum 15-912	R. Fitzgerald
	G-CCWP	Aerotechnik EV-97 TeamEurostar UK	Sky Blue Flight Training
	G-CCWR	Mainair Pegasus Quik	A. Harding
	G-CCWU	Skyranger 912	W. J. Byrd
	G-CCWV	Mainair Pegasus Quik	C. Buttery
	G-CCWW	Mainair Pegasus Quantum 15-912	I. W. Barlow
	G-CCWZ	Raj Hamsa X'Air Falcon 133	H. L. Mickleborough
	G-CCXA	Boeing Stearman A75N-1 Kaydet (669)	Skymax (Aviation) Ltd
	G-CCXB	Boeing Stearman B75N1	C. D. Walker
	G-CCXC	Avion Mudry CAP-10B	Skymax (Aviation) Ltd
	G-CCXD	Lindstrand LBL-105B balloon	Silver Ghost Balloon Club
	G-CCXE	Cameron Z-120 balloon	M. R. Andreas
	G-CCXF	Cameron Z-90 balloon	R. G. March & T. J. Maycock
	G-CCXG	SE-5A (replica) (C5430)	C. Morris
	G-CCXH	Skyranger J2.2	M. J. O'Connor
	G-CCXK	Pitts S-1S Special	P. G. Bond
	G-CCXM	Skyranger 912(1)	C. J. Finnigan
	G-CCXN	Skyranger 912(1)	S. E. Garner & G. P. Martin
	G-CCXO	Corgy CJ-1 Starlet	S. C. Ord
	G-CCXP	ICP Savannah Jabiru	B. J. Harper
	G-CCXR	Mainair Pegasus Blade	P. L. Owen
	G-CCXS	Montgomerie-Bensen B.8MR	A. Morgan
	G-CCXT	Mainair Pegasus Quik	C. Turner
	G-CCXU	Diamond DA40D Star	R. J. & L. Hole
	G-CCXV	Thruster T.600N 450	T. Collins
	G-CCXW	Thruster T.600N 450	G-CCXW Syndicate
	G-CCXX	AG-5B Tiger	P. D. Lock
	G-CCXZ	Mainair Pegasus Quik	K. J. Sene
	G-CCYB	Escapade 912(1)	B. E. & S. M. Renehan
	G-CCYC	Robinson R44 II	Derg Developments Ltd/Ireland
	G-CCYE	Mainair Pegasus Quik	J. Lane
	G-CCYG	Robinson R44	Moorland Windows
	G-CCYI	Cameron O-105 balloon	Media Balloons Ltd
	G-CCYJ	Mainair Pegasus Quik	YJ Syndicate
	G-CCYL	MainairPegasus Quantum 15	A. M. Goulden
	G-CCYM	Skyranger 912	I. Pilton
	G-CCYO	Christen Eagle II	P. C. Woolley
	G-CCYP	Colt 56A balloon	Magical Adventures Ltd
	G-CCYR	Ikarus C.42 FB80	Airbourne Aviation Ltd
	G-CCYS	Cessna F.182Q	S. Dyson
	G-CCYU	Ultramagic S-90 balloon	A. R. Craze
	G-CCYX	Bell 412	RCR Aviation Ltd
	G-CCYY	PA-28-161 Warrior II	Flightcontrol Ltd
	G-CCYZ	Dornier EKW C3605	CW Tomkins Ltd
	G-CCZA	SOCATA MS.894A Rallye Minerva 220	R. N. Aylett
	G-CCZB	Mainair Pegasus Quantum 15	A. Johnson
	G-CCZD	Van's RV-7	D. Powell
	G-CCZI	Cameron A-275 balloon	Balloon School (International) Ltd
	G-CCZJ	Raj Hamsa X' Air Falcon 582	P. A. Lindford
	G-CCZK	Zenair CH.601 UL Zodiac	R. J. Hopkins & J. Lonergan
	G-CCZL	Ikarus C-42 FB80	Shadow Aviation Ltd
	G-CCZM	Skyranger 912S	D. Woodward
	G-CCZN	Rans S.6-ES Coyote II	R. D. Proctor
	G-CCZO	Mainair Pegasus Quik	P. G. Penhaligan
	G-CCZR	Medway Raven Eclipse R	K. A. Sutton
	G-CCZS	Raj Hamsa X'Air Falcon 582	A. T. Kilpatrick
	G-CCZT	Van's RV-9A	Zulu Tango Flying Group
	G-CCZV	PA-28-151 Warrior	P. D. P. Deal
	G-CCZW	Mainair Pegasus Blade	A. F. & M. S. Foster
	G-CCZX	Robin DR.400/180	M. Conrad
	G-CCZY	Van's RV-9A	V. Nash
	G-CCZZ	Aerotechnik EV-97 Eurostar	B. M Starck & J. P. Aitken
	G-CDAA	Mainair Pegasus Quantum 15-912	I. A. Macadam

Reg.	Type	Owner or Operator	Notes
G-CDAB	Glasair Super IISRG	W. L. Hitchins	
G-GDAC	Aerotechnik EV-97 TeamEurostar	Nene Valley Microlights Ltd	
G-CDAD	Lindstrand LBL-25A balloon	G. J. Madelin	
G-CDAE	Van's RV-6A	K. J. Fleming	
G-CDAG	Mainair Blade	K. I. Making	
G-CDAI	Robin DR.400/140B	D. Hardy & J. Sambrook	
G-CDAK	Zenair CH.601 UK Zodiac	W. K. Evans	
G-CDAL	Zenair CH.601UL Zodiac	R. J. Howell	
G-CDAO	Mainair Pegasus Quantum 15 -912	J. C. Duncan	
G-CDAP	Aerotechnik EV-97 TeamEurostar UK	Mainair Microlight School Ltd	
G-CDAR	Mainair Pegasus Quik	A. R. Pitcher	
G-CDAT	ICP MXP-740 Savannah Jabiru	G. M. Railson	
G-CDAX	Mainair Pegasus Quik	L. Hurman	
G-CDAY	Skyranger 912	G-CDAY Group	
G-CDAZ	Aerotechnik EV-97 Eurostar	M. C. J. Ludlow	
G-CDBA	Skyranger 912(S)	P. J. Brennan	
G-CDBB	Mainair Pegasus Quik	G. Hall	
G-CDBD	Jabiru J400	I. D. Rutherford	
G-CDBE	Montgomerie-Bensen B.8M	P. Harwood	
G-CDBG	Robinson R22 Beta	Jepar Rotorcraft	
G-CDBJ	Yakovlev Yak-3	C. E. Bellhouse	
G-CDBK	Rotorway Executive 162F	N. K. Foreman	
G-CDBM	Robin DR.400/180	C. M. Simmonds	
G-CDBO	Skyranger 912	G-CDBO Flying Group	
G-CDBR	Stolp SA.300 Starduster Too	R. J. Warren	
G-CDBS	MBB Bö.105DBS-4	Bond Air Services Ltd	
G-CDBU	Ikarus C.42 FB100	S. E. Meehan	
G-CDBV	Skyranger 912S	K. Hall	
G-CDBX	Shaw Europa XS	R. Marston	
G-CDBY	Dyn'Aero MCR-01 ULC	A. Thornton	
G-CDBZ	Thruster T.600N 450	BZ Flying Group	
G-CDCB	Robinson R44 II	L. Paarsch	
G-CDCC	Aerotechnik EV-97A Eurostar	R. E. & & N. G. Nicholson	
G-CDCD	Van's RVF-9A	RV9ers	
G-CDCE	Avions Mudry CAP-10B	The Tiger Club (1990) Ltd	
G-CDCF	Mainair Pegasus Quik	T. J. Gayton-Polley	
G-CDCG	Ikarus C.42 FB UK	N. E. Ashton & R. H. J. Jenkins	
G-CDCH	Skyranger 912(2)	K. Kormi	
G-CDCI	Pegasus Quik	R. J. Allarton	
G-CDCK	Mainair Pegasus Quik	R. Solomons	
G-CDCM	Ikarus C.42 FB UK	S. T. Allen	
G-CDCO	Ikarus C.42 FB UK	G. S. Gee-Carter & K. A. O'Neill	
G-CDCP	Avtech Jabiru J400	M. W. T. Wilson	
G-CDCR	Savannah Jabiru(1)	T. Davidson	
G-CDCS	PA-12 Super Cruiser	D. Todorovic	
G-CDCT	Aerotechnik EV-97 TeamEurostar UK	G. R. Nicholson	
G-CDCU	Mainair Pegasus Blade	W. S. Clare	
G-CDCV	Robinson R44 II	3GR Comm Ltd	
G-CDCW	Escapade 912 (1)	P. Nicholls	
G-CDDA	SOCATA TB20 Trinidad	Oxford Aviation Academy (Oxford) Ltd	
G-CDDB	Grob/Schempp-Hirth CS-11	K. D. Barber/France	
G-CDDF	Mainair Pegasus Quantum 15-912	B. C. Blackburn & J. L. Dalgetty	
G-CDDG	PA-26-161 Warrior II	Smart People Don't Buy Ltd	
G-CDDH	Raj Hamsa X'Air Falcon	G. Loosley	
G-CDDI	Thruster T.600N 450	R. Nayak	
G-CDDK	Cessna 172M	M. H. & P. R. Kavern	
G-CDDL	Cameron Z-350 balloon	Balloon School (International) Ltd	
G-CDDM	Lindstrand LBL 90A balloon	A. M. Holly	
G-CDDN	Lindstrand LBL 90A balloon	Flying Enterprises	
G-CDDO	Raj Hamsa X'Air 133(2)	S. Bain	
G-CDDP	Lazer Z.230	D. E. H. Nichols	
G-CDDR	Skyranger 582(1)	M. Jones	
G-CDDS	Zenair CH.601HD	S. Foreman	
G-CDDT	SOCATA TB20 Trinidad	Oxford Aviation Academy (Oxford) Ltd	
G-CDDU	Skyranger 912(2)	J. S. G. Down & R. Newton	
G-CDDV	Cameron Z-250 balloon	Alba Ballooning Ltd	
G-CDDW	Aeroprakt A.22 Foxbat	M. Raflewski	
G-CDDX	Thruster T.600N 450	B. S. P. Finch	
G-CDDY	Van's RV-8	The AV8ors	
G-CDEA	SAAB 2000	Air Kilroe Ltd	
G-CDEB	SAAB 2000	Eastern Airways	
G-CDEF	PA-28-161 Cadet	Western Air (Thruxton) Ltd	
G-CDEH	ICP MXP-740 Savannah	P. E. Terrell	

Notes	Reg.	Type	Owner or Operator
	G-CDEM	Raj Hamsa X' Air 133	R. J. Froud
	G-CDEN	Mainair Pegasus Quantum 15 912	J. D. J. Spragg
	G-CDEO	PA-28 Cherokee 180	VVB Engineering Services Ltd
	G-CDEP	Aerotechnik EV-97 TeamEurostar	Echo Papa Group
	G-CDER	PA-28-161 Warrior II	Archer Five Ltd
	G-CDET	Culver LCA Cadet	J. Gregson
	G-CDEU	Lindstrand LBL-90B balloon	N. Florence & P. J. Marshall
	G-CDEV	Escapade 912 (1)	M. B. Devenport
	G-CDEW	Pegasus Quik	K. M. Sullivan
	G-CDEX	Shaw Europa	K. Martindale
	G-CDEZ	Robinson R44 II	Heli Air Ltd
	G-CDFA	Kolb Twinstar Mk3 Extra	S. Soar & W. A. Douthwaite
	G-CDFD	Scheibe SF.25C Falke	The Royal Air Force Gliding and Soaring Association
	G-CDFG	Mainair Pegasus Quik	D. Gabbott
	G-CDFI	Colt 31A balloon	A. M. Holly
	G-CDFJ	Skyranger 912	L. A. Hosegood
	G-CDFK	Jabiru UL-450	J. A. Ellis
	G-CDFL	Zenair CH.601UL	Caunton Zodiac Group
	G-CDFM	Raj Hamsa X'Air 582 (5)	W. A. Keel-Stocker
	G-CDFN	Thunder Ax7-77 balloon	E. Rullo/Italy
	G-CDFO	Pegasus Quik	The Foxtrot Oscars
	G-CDFP	Skyranger 912 (1)	J. M. Gammidge
	G-CDFR	Mainair Pegasus Quantum 15	A. Jopp
	G-CDFU	Rans S.6-ES Coyote II	J. A. & M. K. Ashmore
	G-CDFY	Beech B.200 Super King Air	BAE Systems Marine Ltd
	G-CDGA	Taylor JT.1 Monoplane	R. M. Larimore
	G-CDGB	Rans S.6-116 Coyote	S. Penoyre
	G-CDGC	Pegasus Quik	A. T. K. Crozier
	G-CDGD	Pegasus Quik	I. D. & V. A. Milne
	G-CDGE	Edge XT912-IIIB	M. R. Leyshon
	G-CDGF	Ultramagic S-105 balloon	D. & K. Bareford
	G-CDGG	Dyn'Aéro MCR-01 Club	N. Rollins
	G-CDGH	Rans S.6-ES Coyote	G-CDGH Group
	G-CDGI	Thruster T600N 450	R. North
	G-CDGN	Cameron C-90 balloon	M. C. Gibbons
	G-CDGO	Pegasus Quik	J. C. Townsend
	G-CDGP	Zenair CH 601XL	B. & P. J. Chandler
	G-CDGR	Zenair CH 701UL	I. A. R. Sim
	G-CDGS	AG-5B Tiger	M. R. O'B. Thompson
	G-CDGT	Montgomerie-Parsons Two Place g/p	J. B. Allan
	G-CDGU	VS.300 Spitfire I (X4276)	Peter Monk Ltd
	G-CDGW	PA-28-181 Archer III	Rutland Flying Group
	G-CDGX	Pegasus Quantum 15-912	S. R. Green
	G-CDGY	VS.349 Spitfire Mk VC	Aero Vintage Ltd
	G-CDHA	Skyranger 912S(1)	A. T. Cameron
	G-CDHC	Slingsby T67C	N. J. Morgan
	G-CDHE	Skyranger 912(2)	R. G. Jeffrey
	G-CDHF	PA-30 Twin Comanche B	Reid International (Guernsey) Ltd
	G-CDHG	Mainair Pegasus Quik	T. W. Pelan
	G-CDHH	Robinson R44 II	Abwood Homes/Ireland
	G-CDHJ	Lindstrand LBL-90B balloon	Lindstrand Hot Air Balloons Ltd
	G-CDHM	Pegasus Quantum 15	M. R. Smith
	G-CDHN	Lindstrand LBL-317A balloon	Aerosaurus Balloons Ltd
	G-CDHO	Raj Hamsa X'Air 133 (1)	G. P. Masters
	G-CDHR	Ikarus C.42 FB80	Airbourne Aviation Ltd
	G-CDHU	Skyranger 912 (2)	G-CDHU Group
	G-CDHX	Aeroprakt A.22 Foxbat	N. E. Stokes
	G-CDHY	Cameron Z-90 balloon	D. M. Roberts
	G-CDHZ	Nicollier HN.700 Menestrel II	G. E. Whittaker
	G-CDIA	Thruster T.600N 450	T. Davidson
	G-CDIB	Cameron Z-350Z balloon	Ballooning Network Ltd
	G-CDIF	Mudry CAP-10B	J. D. Gordon
	G-CDIG	Aerotechnik EV-97 Eurostar	P. D. Brisco & J. Young
	G-CDIH	Cameron Z-275 balloon	Bailey Balloons Ltd
	G-CDIJ	Skyranger 912 (2)	D. Anders & M. Cunningham
	G-CDIL	Pegasus Quantum 15-912	G. J. Prisk
	G-CDIO	Cameron Z-90 balloon	Slowfly Montgolfiere SNC/Italy
	G-CDIP	Skyranger 912S(1)	A. Ryan
	G-CDIR	Mainair Pegasus Quantum 15-912	W. Traynor-Keen
	G-CDIS	Cessna 150F	S. P. Fox
	G-CDIT	Cameron Z-105 balloon	Bailey Balloons Ltd
	G-CDIU	Skyranger 912S(1)	Darley Moor Flyers Club

Reg.	Type	Owner or Operator	Notes
G-CDIX	Ikarus C.42 FB.100	T. G. Greenhill & J. G. Spinks	
G-CDIY	Aerotechnik EV-97A Eurostar	R. E. Woolsey	
G-CDIZ	Escapade 912(3)	E. G. Bishop & E. N. Dunn	
G-CDJB	Van's RV-4	J. Mann	
G-CDJD	ICP MXP-740 Savannah Jabiru (4)	D. W. Mullin	
G-CDJE	Thruster T.600N 450	C. H. Ford	
G-CDJF	Flight Design CT2K	P. A. James	
G-CDJG	Zenair 601UL Zodiac	D. Garcia	
G-CDJI	Ultramagic M-120 balloon	The Ballooning Business Ltd	
G-CDJJ	IAV Yakovlev Yak-52	J. J. Miles	
G-CDJK	Ikarus C.42 FB 80	Cornish Aviation Ltd	
G-CDJL	Avtech Jabiru J400	J. Gardiner	
G-CDJM	Zenair CH.601XL	P. G. Hayward	
G-CDJN	RAF 2000 GTX-SE gyroplane	D. J. North	
G-CDJO	DH.82A Tiger Moth	D. Dal Bon	
G-CDJP	Skyranger 912(2)	I. A. Cunningham	
G-CDJR	Aerotechnik EV-97 TeamEurostar	K. C. Lye & M. D. White	
G-CDJU	CASA 1.131E Jungmann Srs.1000	P. Gaskell	
G-CDJV	Beech A.36 Bonanza	Atlantic Bridge Aviation Ltd/Lydd	
G-CDJX	Cameron N-56 balloon	Cameron Balloons Ltd	
G-CDJY	Cameron C-80 balloon	British Airways PLC	
G-CDKA	SAAB 2000	Eastern Airways	
G-CDKB	SAAB 2000	Eastern Airways	
G-CDKE	Rans S6-ES Coyote II	J. E. Holloway	
G-CDKF	Escapade 912 (1)	K. R. Butcher	
G-CDKH	Skyranger 912S (1)	C. Lenaghan	
G-CDKI	Skyranger 912S (1)	J. M. Hucker	
G-CDKJ	Silence Twister	A. H. R. Stansfield	
G-CDKK	Mainair Pegasus Quik	P. M. Knight	
G-CDKL	Escapade 912 (2)	M. A. Hodgson & D. Maidment	
G-CDKM	Pegasus Quik	P. Lister	
G-CDKN	ICP MXP-740 Savannah Jabiru (4)	T. Wicks	
G-CDKO	ICP MXP-740 Savannah Jabiru (4)	C. Jones & B. Hunter	
G-CDKP	Avtech Jabiru UL-D Calypso	Rochester Microlights Ltd	
G-CDKX	Skyranger J.2 .2 (1)	E. Lewis	
G-CDKY	Robinson R44	Specialist Technical Solutions Ltd	
G-CDKZ	Thunder Ax10-160 S2 balloon	Cameron Flights Southern Ltd	
G-CDLA	Mainair Pegasus Quik	C. R. Stevens	
G-CDLB	Cameron Z-120 balloon	J. A. Hibberd and Tchemma Products	
G-CDLC	CASA 1.131E Jungmann 2000	R. D. Loder	
G-CDLD	Mainair Pegasus Quik 912S	W. Williams	
G-CDLG	Skyranger 912 (2)	M. R. Foreman	
G-CDLI	Airco DH.9 (E8894)	Aero Vintage Ltd	
G-CDLJ	Mainair Pegasus Quik	J. S. James & R. S. Keyser	
G-CDLK	Skyranger 912S	L. E. Cowling	
G-CDLL	Dyn'Aéro MCR-01 ULC	R. F. Connell	
G-CDLR	ICP MXP / 740 Savannah Jabiru (4)	A. J. Burton & P. Read	
G-CDLS	Jabiru Aircrraft Jabiru J400	Kestrel Group	
G-CDLT	Raytheon Hawker 800XP	Gama Aviation Ltd	
G-CDLW	Zenair ZH.601UL Zodiac	W. A. Stphen	
G-CDLY	Cirrus SR20	Partside Aviation Ltd	
G-CDLZ	Mainair Pegasus Quantum 15-912	C. M. Jeffrey & J. L. Dalgetty	
G-CDMA	PA-28-151 Warrior	A. Cabre	
G-CDMC	Cameron Z-105 balloon	First Flight	
G-CDMD	Robin DR.400/500	P. R. Liddle	
G-CDME	Van's RV-7	M. W. Elliott	
G-CDMF	Van's RV-9A	J. R. Bowden	
G-CDMG	Robinson R22 Beta	Heli Aitch Be Ltd	
G-CDMH	Cessna P.210N	J. G. Hinley	
G-CDMJ	Mainair Pegasus Quik	M. J. R. Dean	
G-CDMK	Montgomerie-Bensen B8MR	P. Rentell	
G-CDML	Mainair Pegasus Quik	P. O'Rourke	
G-CDMM	Cessna 172P Skyhawk	Cristal Air Ltd	
G-CDMN	Van's RV-9	G. J. Smith	
G-CDMO	Cameron S Can-100 balloon	A. Schneider/Germany	
G-CDMP	Best Off Skyranger 912(1)	J. A. Charlton	
G-CDMS	Ikarus C,42 FB 80	Airbourne Aviation Ltd	
G-CDMT	Zenair CH.601XL Zodiac	B. A. Ritchie	
G-CDMU	Mainair Pegasus Quik	T. M. Bolton & S. D. Jones	
G-CDMV	Best Off Skyranger 912S(1)	D. O'Keeffe & K. E. Rutter	
G-CDMX	PA-28-161 Warrior II	S. Collins	
G-CDMY	PA-28-161 Warrior II	J. S. Develin & Z. Islam	
G-CDMZ	Mainair Pegasus Quik	R. Solomons	

Notes	Reg.	Type	Owner or Operator
	G-CDNA	Grob G.109A	Army Gliding Association
	G-CDND	GA-7 Cougar	C. J. Chaplin
	G-CDNE	Best Off Skyranger 912S(1)	G-CDNE Syndicate
	G-CDNF	Aero Design Pulsar 3	D. Ringer
	G-CDNG	Aerotechnik EV-97 TeamEurostar UK	G-CDNG Syndicate
	G-CDNH	Mainair Pegasus Quik	C. D. Andrews
	G-CDNI	Aerotechnik EV-97 TeamEurostar UK	G-CDNI Group
	G-CDNJ	Colomban MC-15 Cri Cri	Cri Cri Group
	G-CDNM	Aerotechnik EV-97 TeamEurostar UK	H. C. Lowther
	G-CDNO	Westland Gazelle AH.1 (XX432)	CJ Helicopters
	G-CDNP	Aerotechnik EV-97 TeamEurostar UK	Eaglescott Eurostar Group
	G-CDNR	Ikarus C.42 FB1000	G. P. Burns
	G-CDNS	Westland Gazelle AH.1 (XZ321)	Falcon Aviation Ltd
	G-CDNT	Zenair CH.601XL Zodiac	W. McCormack
	G-CDNW	Ikarus C.42 FB UK	W. Gabbott
	G-CDNY	Jabiru SP-470	G. Lucey
	G-CDNZ	Ultramagic M-120 balloon	R. H. Etherington/Italy
	G-CDOA	EV-97 TeamEurostar UK	A. Costello & J. Cunliffe
	G-CDOB	Cameron C-90 balloon	G. D. & S. M. Philpot
	G-CDOC	Mainair Quik GT450	D. M. Broom
	G-CDOE	Avro 146 RJ70	Trident Turboprop (Dublin) Ltd
	G-CDOF	Avro 146 RJ70	Trident Turboprop (Dublin) Ltd
	G-CDOG	Lindstrand LBL-Dog SS balloon	ABC Flights Ltd
	G-CDOJ	Schweizer 269C-1	Alan Mann Aviation Group Ltd
	G-CDOK	Ikarus C.42 FB 100	M Aviation Ltd
	G-CDOM	Mainair Pegasus Quik	G-CDOM Flying Group
	G-CDON	PA-28-161 Warrior II	G-CDON Group
	G-CDOO	Mainair Pegasus Quantum 15-912	O. C. Harding
	G-CDOP	Mainair Pegasus Quik	H. A. Duthie & R. C. Tadman
	G-CDOR	Mainair Blade	J. D. Otter
	G-CDOT	Ikarus C.42 FB 100	A. C. Anderson
	G-CDOV	Skyranger 912(2)	B. Richardson
	G-CDOY	Robin DR.400/180R	Lasham Gliding Society Ltd
	G-CDOZ	EV-97 TeamEurostar UK	J. P. McCall
	G-CDPA	Alpi Pioneer 300	N. D. White
	G-CDPB	Skyranger 982(1)	N. S. Bishop
	G-CDPD	Mainair Pegasus Quik	M. D. Vearncombe
	G-CDPE	Skyranger 912(2)	D. Workman
	G-CDPG	Crofton Auster J1-A	P. & T. Groves
	G-CDPH	Tiger Cub RL5A LW Sherwood Ranger ST	K. F. Crumplin
	G-CDPI	Zenair CH.601UL Zodiac	Leicestershire Police
	G-CDPJ	Van's RV-8	P. Johnson
	G-CDPL	EV-97 TeamEurostar UK	C. I. D. H Garrison
	G-CDPN	Ultramagic S-105	D. J. MacInnes
	G-CDPP	Ikarus C42 FB UK	H. M. Owen
	G-CDPS	Raj Hamsa X'Air 133	J. D. Macnamara
	G-CDPV	PA-34-200T Seneca II	Globebrow Ltd
	G-CDPW	Mainair Pegasus Quantum 15-912	T. P. R. Wright
	G-CDPY	Shaw Europa	A. Burrill
	G-CDPZ	Flight Design CT2K	M. E. Henwick
	G-CDRC	Cessna 182Q Skylane	R. S. Hill and Sons
	G-CDRD	AirBorne XT912-B Edge/Streak III-B	Fly NI Ltd
	G-CDRF	Cameron Z-90 balloon	Chalmers Ballong Corps
	G-CDRG	Mainair Pegasus Quik	R. J. Gabriel
	G-CDRH	Thruster T.600N	Carlisle Thruster Group
	G-CDRI	Cameron O-105 balloon	Snapdragon Balloon Group
	G-CDRJ	Tanarg/Ixess 15 912S(1)	M. Delves-Yates
	G-CDRN	Cameron Z-225 balloon	Balloon School (International) Ltd
	G-CDRO	Ikarus C42 F880	Airbourne Aviation Ltd
	G-CDRP	Ikarus C42 FB80	D. S. Parker
	G-CDRR	Mainair Pegasus Quantum 15-912	W. O. Fogden
	G-CDRS	Rotorway Executive 162F	R. C. Swann
	G-CDRT	Mainair Pegasus Quik	R. Tetlow
	G-CDRU	CASA 1.131E Jungmann 2000	P. Cunniff
	G-CDRV	Van's RV-9A	R. J. Woodford
	G-CDRW	Mainair Pegasus Quik	G. L. Fearon
	G-CDRX	Cameron Z-225 balloon	Balloon School (International) Ltd
	G-CDRY	Ikarus C42 FB100 VLA	R. J. Mitchell
	G-CDRZ	Balóny Kubícek BB22 balloon	Club Amatori Del Volo In Montgolfiera
	G-CDSA	Mainair Pegasus Quik	G-CDSA Group
	G-CDSB	Alpi Pioneer 200	T. A. & P. M. Pugh
	G-CDSC	Scheibe SF.25C Rotax-Falke	Devon & Somerset Motorglider Group

Reg.	Type	Owner or Operator	Notes
G-CDSD	Alpi Pioneer 300	J. A. Ball	
G-CDSF	Diamond DA40D Star	Flying Time Ltd	
G-CDSH	ICP MXP-740 Savannah Jabiru(5)	T. N. Huggins-Haig	
G-CDSK	Reality Escapade Jabiru(3)	R. H. Sear	
G-CDSM	P & M Aviation Quik GT450	S. L. Cogger	
G-CDSN	Raj Hamsa X'Air Jabiru(3)	S. P. Heard	
G-CDSS	Mainair Pegasus Quik	P. A. Bass	
G-CDST	Ultramagic N-250 balloon	Cameron Flights Southern Ltd	
G-CDSW	Ikarus C.42 FB UK	R. W. Skelton & J. Toner	
G-CDSX	EE Canberra T.Mk.4 (VN799)	Aviation Heritage Ltd	
G-CDSY	Robinson R44	D. Romagnoli	
G-CDTA	EV-97 TeamEurostar UK	R. D. Stein	
G-CDTB	Mainair Pegasus Quantum 15-912	D. W. Corbett	
G-CDTD	Eurocopter AS350B2 Ecureuil	TEC Aircraft Leasing GmbH & Co KG	
G-CDTG	Diamond DA42 Twin Star	Aviation Rentals	
G-CDTH	Schempp-Hirth Nimbus 4DM	M. A. V. Gatehouse	
G-CDTI	Messerschmitt Bf.109E (4034)	Rare Aero Ltd	
G-CDTJ	Escapade Jabiru(1)	R. N. R. Bellamy	
G-CDTL	Avtech Jabiru J-400	M. I. Sistern	
G-CDTO	P & M Quik GT450	A. R. Watt	
G-CDTP	Skyranger 912S (1)	P. M. Whitaker	
G-CDTR	P & M Quik GT450	M. G. Freeman	
G-CDTT	Savannah Jabiru(4)	M. J. Day	
G-CDTU	EV-97 TeamEurostar UK	G-CDTU Group	
G-CDTV	Tecnam P2002 EA Sierra	S. A. Noble	
G-CDTX	Cessna F.152	J. S. Develin & Z. Islam	
G-CDTY	Savannah Jabiru (5)	H. Cooke & B. Robertson	
G-CDTZ	Aeroprakt A.22 Foxbat	P. C. Piggott & M. E. Hughes	
G-CDUE	Robinson R44	P. L. Hynds	
G-CDUH	P & M Quik GT450	A. P. & P. R. Santus	
G-CDUJ	Lindstrand LBL 31A balloon	J. M. Frazer	
G-CDUK	Ikarus C.42 FB UK	D. M. Lane	
G-CDUL	Skyranger 912S (2)	T. W. Thiele & C. D. Hogbourne	
G-CDUS	Skyranger 912S (1)	G. Devlin & J. Northage	
G-CDUT	Jabiru J400	T. W. & A. Pullin.	
G-CDUU	P & M Quik GT450	Caunton Charlie Delta Group	
G-CDUV	Savannah Jabiru(5)	D. M. Blackman	
G-CDUW	Aeronca C3	N. K. Geddes	
G-CDUX	PA-32 Cherokee Six 300	D. J. Mason	
G-CDUY	Thunder & Colt 77A balloon	G. Birchall	
G-CDVA	Skyranger 912 (2)	S. J. Dovey	
G-CDVB	Agusta A.109E Power	Agusta Westland Ltd	
G-CDVD	Aerotechnik EV-97A Eurostar	P. Ritchie	
G-CDVF	Rans S.6-ES Coyote II	B. J. Mould	
G-CDVG	Pegasus Quik	C. M. Lewis	
G-CDVH	Pegasus Quantum 15	M. J. Hyde	
G-CDVI	Ikarus C42 FB80	Airbourne Aviation Ltd	
G-CDVJ	Montgomerie-Bensen B8MR	D. J. Martin	
G-CDVK	Savannah Jabiru (5)	M. Peters	
G-CDVL	Alpi Pioneer 300	J. D. Clabon	
G-CDVN	P & M Quik GT450	P. Warrener	
G-CDVO	P & M Quik	D. Sykes	
G-CDVR	P & M Quik GT450	Flying Group G-CDVR	
G-CDVS	Europa XS	J. F. Lawn	
G-CDVT	Van's RV-6	P. J. Wood	
G-CDVU	Aerotechnik EV-97 TeamEurostar	W. D. Kyle & T. J. Dowling	
G-CDVV	SA Bulldog Srs. 120/121 (XX626:02, W)	W. H. M. Mott	
G-CDVX	TP-47G-10-GU Thunderbolt (42-25068)	Patina Ltd	
G-CDVZ	P & M Quik GT450	S. M. Green & M. D. Peacock	
G-CDWB	Skyranger 912(2)	V. J. Morris	
G-CDWD	Cameron Z-105 balloon	Bristol University Ballooning Society	
G-CDWE	Nord NC.856 Norvigie	R. H. & J. A. Cooper	
G-CDWG	Dyn'Aéro MCR-01 Club	S. E. Gribble	
G-CDWH	Curtiss P-40B (41-13297/284)	The Fighter Collection	
G-CDWI	Ikarus C42 FB80	The Scottish Flying Club	
G-CDWJ	Flight Design CTSW	G. P. Rood	
G-CDWK	Robinson R44	B. Morgan	
G-CDWL	Raj Hamsa X'Air 582 (5)	The CDWL Flying Group	
G-CDWM	Skyranger 912S (1)	R. W. Marshall	
G-CDWN	Ultramagic N-210 balloon	S. R. Seager	
G-CDWO	P & M Quik GT450	G. W. Carwardine	
G-CDWP	P & M Quik GT450	R. W. Thornborough	
G-CDWR	P & M Quik GT450	G-CDWR Group	

Notes	Reg.	Type	Owner or Operator
	G-CDWS	P & M Quik GT450	H. N. Barrott
	G-CDWT	Flight Design CTSW	R. Scammell
	G-CDWU	Zenair CH.601UL Zodiac	A. D. Worrall
	G-CDWW	P & M Quik GT450	J. H. Bradbury
	G-CDWX	Lindstrand LBL 77A balloon	LSB Public Relations Ltd
	G-CDWZ	P & M Quik GT450	B. J. Holloway
	G-CDXA	Robinson R44 Raven	Northumbria Helicopters Ltd
	G-CDXD	Medway SLA100 Executive	A. J. Baker & G. Withers
	G-CDXF	Lindstrand LBL 31A balloon	R. S. Mohr
	G-CDXG	P & M Pegasus Quantum 15-912	A. P. Fox
	G-CDXH	Avro RJ100	Trident Jet Leasing (Ireland) Ltd
	G-CDXI	Cessna 182P	B. G. McBeath
	G-CDXJ	Jabiru J400	J. C. Collingwood
	G-CDXK	Diamond DA42 Twin Star	A. M. Healy
	G-CDXL	Flight Design CTSW	A. K. Paterson
	G-CDXN	P & M Quik GT450	Microflight Aviation Ltd
	G-CDXP	Aerotechnik EV-97 Eurostar	R. J. Crockett
	G-CDXR	Replica Fokker DR.1	J. G. Day
	G-CDXS	Aerotechnik EV-97 Eurostar	J. C. Rose
	G-CDXT	Van's RV-9	T. M. Storey
	G-CDXU	Chilton DW.1A	M. Gibbs
	G-CDXW	Cameron Orange 120 SS balloon	You've Been Tangoed
	G-CDXX	Robinson R44 Raven II	Nedroc Aviation Services Ltd
	G-CDXY	Skystar Kitfox Mk.7	D. E. Steade
	G-CDYB	Rans S.6-ES Coyote II	D. E. Rubery
	G-CDYD	Ikarus C42 FB80	C42 Group
	G-CDYI	BAe Jetstream 4100	Eastern Airways
	G-CDYJ	Best Off Skyranger 912(1)	N. A. Thomas
	G-CDYL	Lindstrand LBL-77A balloon	J. H. Dobson
	G-CDYM	Murphy Maverick 430	M. R. Cann
	G-CDYO	Ikarus C42 FB80	A. R. Hughes
	G-CDYP	Aerotechnik EV-97 TeamEurostar UK	R. V. Buxton & R. Cranborne
	G-CDYR	Bell 206L-3 LongRanger III	Yorkshire Helicopters
	G-CDYT	Ikarus C42 FB80	J. W. D. Blythe
	G-CDYU	Zenair CH.701UL	A. Gannon
	G-CDYX	Lindstrand LBL-77B balloon	H. M. Savage
	G-CDYY	Alpi Pioneer 300	B. Williams
	G-CDYZ	Van's RV-7	Holden Group Ltd
	G-CDZA	Alpi Pioneer 300	J. F. Dowe
	G-CDZB	Zenair CH.601UL Zodiac	L. J. Dutch
	G-CDZD	Van's RV-9A	D. King
	G-CDZG	Ikarus C42-FB80	Mainair Microlight School Ltd
	G-CDZO	Lindstrand LBL-60X balloon	R. D. Parry
	G-CDZR	Nicollier HN.700 Menestrel II	G-CDZR Flying Group
	G-CDZS	Kolb Twinstar Mk.3 Extra	P. W. Heywood
	G-CDZT	Beech B200 Super King Air	BAE Systems Ltd
	G-CDZU	ICP MXP-740 Savannah Jabiru (5)	P. J. Cheney
	G-CDZW	Cameron N-105 balloon	Backetorp Byggconsult AB
	G-CDZY	Medway SLA 80 Executive	Medway Microlights
	G-CDZZ	Rotorsport UK MT-03	H. E. Simons
	G-CEAE	Boeing 737-229	European Skybus Ltd
	G-CEAH	Boeing 737-229	European Aviation Ltd
	G-CEAK	Ikarus C42 FB80	Barton Heritage Flying Group
	G-CEAM	Aerotechnik EV-97 TeamEurostar UK	Flylight Airsports Ltd
	G-CEAN	Ikarus C42 FB80	T. Penn & C. P. Roche
	G-CEAO	Jurca MJ.5 Sirocco	P. S. Watts
	G-CEAR	Alpi Pioneer 300	A. Parker
	G-CEAT	Zenair CH.601HDS Zodiac	T. B. Smith
	G-CEAU	Robinson R44	Mullahead Property Co Ltd
	G-CEAV	Ultramagic M-105 balloon	G. Everett
	G-CEAX	Ultramagic S-130 balloon	Anglian Countryside Balloons Ltd
	G-CEAY	Ultramagic H-42 balloon	J. D. A. Shields
	G-CEBA	Zenair CH.601XL Zodiac	P. G. Morris
	G-CEBC	ICP MXP-740 Savannah Jabiru (5)	E. W. Chapman
	G-CEBE	Schweizer 269C-1	Millburn World Travel Services Ltd
	G-CEBF	Aerotechnik EV-97A Eurostar	M. Lang
	G-CEBG	Balóny Kubicek BB26 balloon	P. M. Smith
	G-CEBH	Tanarg 912S/Bionix 15	D. A. Chamberlain
	G-CEBI	Kolb Twinstar Mk.3	R. W. Livingstone
	G-CEBK	PA-31-350 Navajo Chieftain	De Jong Management BV
	G-CEBL	Balóny Kubicek BB20GP balloon	Associazione Sportiva Aerostatica Lombada/Italy
	G-CEBM	P & M Quik GT450	S. P. Jones

Reg.	Type	Owner or Operator	Notes
G-CEBN	Avro RJ100	Trident Jet Leasing (Ireland) Ltd	
G-CEBO	Ultramagic M-65C balloon	M. J. Woodcock	
G-CEBP	EV-97 TeamEurostar UK	T. R. Southall	
G-CEBT	P & M Quik GT450	A. J. Riddell	
G-CEBW	P-51D Mustang	Dental Insurance Solutions Ltd	
G-CEBZ	Zenair CH.601UL Zodiac	I. M. Ross & A Watt	
G-CECA	P & M Quik GT450	A. Weatherall	
G-CECC	Ikarus C42 FB80	G-CECC Group	
G-CECD	Cameron C-90 balloon	S. P. Harrowing	
G-CECE	Jabiru UL-D	ST Aviation Ltd	
G-CECF	Just/Reality Escapade Jabiru (3)	M. M. Hamer	
G-CECG	Jabiru UL-D	S. M. Spencer	
G-CECH	Jodel D.150	W. R. Prescott	
G-CECI	Pilatus PC-6/B2-H4 Turbo Porter	D. M. Penny	
G-CECJ	Aeromot AMT-200S Super Ximango	C. J. & S. C. Partridge	
G-CECK	ICP MXP-740 Savannah Jabiru (5)	E. McClure	
G-CECL	Ikarus C42 FB80	C. Lee	
G-CECO	Hughes 269C	H. Larcombe	
G-CECP	Best Off Skyranger 912(2)	A. Asslanian	
G-CECS	Lindstrand LBL-105A balloon	R. P. Ashford	
G-CECU	Boeing 767-222	UK International Airlines Ltd	
G-CECV	Van's RV-7	D. M. Stevens	
G-CECX	Robinson R44	Dolphin Property (Management) Ltd	
G-CECY	EV-97 Eurostar	M. R. M. Welch	
G-CECZ	Zenair CH.601XL Zodiac	Bluebird Aviation	
G-CEDB	Just/Reality Escapade Jabiru (4)	R. F. Morton	
G-CEDC	Ikarus C42 FB100	P. D. Ashley	
G-CEDE	Flight Design CTSW	F. Williams & J. A. R. Hartley	
G-CEDF	Cameron N-105 balloon	Bailey Balloons Ltd	
G-CEDG	Robinson R44	P. J. Barnes	
G-CEDI	Best Off Skyranger 912(2)	L. Call & G. Finney	
G-CEDJ	Aero Designs Pulsar XP	P. F. Lorriman	
G-CEDK	Cessna 750 Citation X	The Duke of Westminster	
G-CEDL	TEAM Minimax 91	A. J. Weir	
G-CEDN	Pegasus Quik	R. G. Beecham	
G-CEDO	Raj Hamsa X'Air Falcon 133(2)	OCTN Trust	
G-CEDR	Ikarus C42 FB80	Newtownards Microlight Group	
G-CEDT	Tanarg/Ixess 15 912S(1)	N. S. Brayn	
G-CEDV	Evektor EV-97 TeamEurostar UK	Airbourne Aviation Ltd	
G-CEDW	TEAM Minimax 91	J. K. Buckingham	
G-CEDX	Evektor EV-97 TeamEurostar UK	C. P. Davis	
G-CEDZ	Best Off Skyranger 912(2)	J. E. Walendowski & I. Bell	
G-CEEB	Cameron C-80 balloon	Cameron Balloons Ltd	
G-CEEC	Raj Hamsa X'Air Hawk	P. J. Callis & B. G. King	
G-CEED	ICP MXP-740 Savannah Jabiru(5)	A. C. Thompson	
G-CEEE	Robinson R44	C. R. Caswell	
G-CEEG	Alpi Pioneer 300	D. McCormack	
G-CEEI	P & M Quik GT450	G. L. Hall	
G-CEEJ	Rans S-7S Courier	J. M. Lister	
G-CEEK	Cameron Z-105 balloon	PSH Skypower Ltd	
G-CEEL	Ultramagic S-90 balloon	San Paolo Company SRL	
G-CEEM	P & M Quik GT450	D. P. Sayer	
G-CEEN	PA-28-161 Cadet	White Waltham Airfield Ltd	
G-CEEO	Flight Design CTSW	E. McCallum	
G-CEEP	Van's RV-9A	M. P. Comley, N. Horseman & K. Rose	
G-CEER	ELA 07R	F. G. Shepherd	
G-CEES	Cameron C-90 balloon	P. C. May	
G-CEEU	PA-28-161 Cadet	White Waltham Airfield Ltd	
G-CEEV	PA-28-161 Warrior III	Plane Talking Ltd	
G-CEEW	Ikarus C42 FB100	D. McCartan	
G-CEEX	ICP MXP-740 Savannah Jabiru(5)	G. M. Teasdale	
G-CEEY	PA-28-161 Warrior III	ASG Leasing Ltd	
G-CEEZ	PA-28-161 Warrior III	Plane Talking Ltd	
G-CEFA	Ikarus C42 FB100 VLA	J. Morrisroe	
G-CEFB	Ultramagic H-31 balloon	J. L. Guy	
G-CEFC	Super Marine Spitfire 26	D. R. Bishop	
G-CEFJ	Sonex	R. W. Chatterton	
G-CEFK	Evektor EV-97 TeamEurostar UK	P. Morgan	
G-CEFM	Cessna 152	Cristal Air Ltd	
G-CEFP	Jabiru J430	G. Hammond	
G-CEFS	Cameron C-100 balloon	Gone With The Wind Ltd	
G-CEFT	Whittaker MW5-D Sorcerer	W. Bruce	
G-CEFV	Cessna 182T Skylane	G. H. Smith and Son	

Notes	Reg.	Type	Owner or Operator
	G-CEFY	ICP MXP-740 Savannah Jabiru(4)	B. Hartley
	G-CEFZ	Evektor EV-97 TeamEurostar UK	Robo Flying Group
	G-CEGE	Fairchild SA.226TC Metro II	BCA Charters Ltd
	G-CEGG	Lindstrand LBL-25A Cloudhopper balloon	C. G. Dobson
	G-CEGH	Van's RV-9A	M. E. Creasey
	G-CEGI	Van's RV-8	D. R. Fraser & R. Tye
	G-CEGJ	P & M Quik GT450	Flylight Airsports Ltd
	G-CEGK	ICP MXP-740 Savannah VG Jabiru(1)	S. Woolmington
	G-CEGL	Ikarus C42 FB100	M. A. McLoughlin
	G-CEGO	Evektor EV-97A Eurostar	N. J. Keeling, R. F. McLachlan & J. A. Charlton
	G-CEGP	Beech 200 Super King Air	Cega Air Ambulance UK Ltd (G-BXMA)
	G-CEGR	Beech 200 Super King Air	Henfield Lodge Ltd
	G-CEGS	PA-28-161 Warrior II	White Waltham Airfield Ltd
	G-CEGT	P & M Quik GT450	J. Plenderleith
	G-CEGU	PA-28-151 Warrior	Aviation Rentals
	G-CEGV	P & M Quik GT450	Flexwing Ruffians Group
	G-CEGW	P & M Quik GT450	P. Barrow
	G-CEGZ	Ikarus C42 FB80	C42 Swift Instruction Group
	G-CEHC	P & M Quik GT450	G-CEHC Syndicate
	G-CEHD	Best Off Skyranger 912(2)	A. W. Martin
	G-CEHE	Medway SLA 100 Executive	R. P. Stoner
	G-CEHG	Ikarus C42 FB100	C. J. Hayward & C. Walters
	G-CEHI	P & M Quik GT450	A. Costello
	G-CEHL	EV-97 TeamEurostar UK	Poet Pilot (UK) Ltd
	G-CEHM	Rotorsport UK MT-03	K. B. Laskowski
	G-CEHN	Rotorsport UK MT-03	P. A. Harwood
	G-CEHR	Auster AOP.9	J. Cooke & R. B. Webber
	G-CEHS	CAP.10B	M. D. Wynne
	G-CEHT	Rand KR-2	P. P. Geoghegan
	G-CEHV	Ikarus C42 FB80	Mainair Microlight School Ltd
	G-CEHW	P & M Quik GT450	G-CEHW Group
	G-CEHX	Lindstrand LBL-9A balloon	P. Baker
	G-CEHZ	Edge XT912-B/Streak III-B	J. Horan
	G-CEIA	Rotorsport UK MT-03	M. P Chetwynd-Talbot
	G-CEIB	Yakovlev Yak-18A	R. A. Fleming
	G-CEID	Van's RV-7	A. Moyce
	G-CEIE	Flight Design CTSW	D. K. Ross
	G-CEIG	Van's RV-7	W. K. Wilkie
	G-CEIH	Avro RJ100	Trident Jet Leasing (Ireland) Ltd
	G-CEII	Medway SLA80 Executive	F. J. Clarehugh
	G-CEIK	Ultramagic M-90 ballon	M. R. W. Steyaert
	G-CEIL	Bassett Escapade 912(2)	D. E. Bassett
	G-CEIS	Jodel DR.1050	G. R. Richardson
	G-CEIT	Van's RV-7	S. S. Gould
	G-CEIV	Tanarg/Ixess 15 912S(2)	W. R. Cross
	G-CEIW	Europa	R. Scanlan
	G-CEIX	Alpi Pioneer 300	R. S. C. Andrews
	G-CEIY	Ultramagic M-120 balloon	A. Cesarano/Italy
	G-CEIZ	PA-28-161 Warrior II	IZ Aviation
	G-CEJA	Cameron V-77 balloon	G. Gray (G-BTOF)
	G-CEJC	Cameron N-77 balloon	D. J. Stagg
	G-CEJD	PA-28-161 Warrior III	Western Air (Thruxton) Ltd
	G-CEJE	Wittman W.10 Tailwind	R. A. Povall
	G-CEJF	PA-28-161 Cadet	Aviation Rentals
	G-CEJG	Ultramagic M-56 balloon	Dragon Balloon Co.Ltd
	G-CEJI	Lindstrand LBL-105A balloon	Richard Nash Cars Ltd
	G-CEJJ	P & M Quik GT450	Juliet Juliet Group
	G-CEJK	Lindstrand LBL-260A balloon	Cameron Flights Southen Ltd
	G-CEJL	Ultramagic H-31 balloon	Robert Wiseman Dairies PLC
	G-CEJN	Mooney M.20F	G. R. Wakeley
	G-CEJV	PA-28-161 Cadet	Aviation Rentals
	G-CEJW	Ikarus C42 FB80	M. I. Deeley
	G-CEJX	P & M Quik GT450	P. Stewart & A. J. Huntly
	G-CEJY	Aerospool Dynamic WT9 UK	R. G. Bennett
	G-CEJZ	Cameron C-90 balloon	M. J. Woodcock
	G-CEKA	Robinson R-44 II	N. J. Whittingham
	G-CEKC	Medway SLA100 Executive	B. W. Webb
	G-CEKD	Flight Design CTSW	M. K. Arora
	G-CEKE	Robin DR400/180	M. F. Cuming
	G-CEKG	P & M Quik GT450	G-CEKG Flying Group
	G-CEKI	Cessna 172P	N. Houghton
	G-CEKJ	Evektor EV-97A Eurostar	C. W. J. Vershoyle-Greene
	G-CEKK	Best Off Sky Ranger Swift 912S(1)	M. S. Schofield & B. W. G. Stanbridge

Reg.	Type	Owner or Operator	Notes
G-CEKO	Robin DR400/100	R. J. Hopkins	
G-CEKS	Cameron Z-105 balloon	Phoenix Balloons Ltd	
G-CEKT	Flight Design CTSW	Charlie Tango Group	
G-CEKV	Europa	K. Atkinson	
G-CEKW	Jabiru J430	J430 Syndicate	
G-CELA	Boeing 737-377	Jet 2	
G-CELB	Boeing 737-377	Jet 2	
G-CELC	Boeing 737-377	Jet 2 (G-OBMA)	
G-CELD	Boeing 737-377	Jet 2 (G-OBMB)	
G-CELE	Boeing 737-377	Jet 2 (G-MONN)	
G-CELF	Boeing 737-377	Jet 2	
G-CELG	Boeing 737-377	Jet 2	
G-CELH	Boeing 737-330	Jet 2	
G-CELI	Boeing 737-330	Jet 2	
G-CELJ	Boeing 737-330	Jet 2	
G-CELK	Boeing 737-330	Jet 2	
G-CELM	Cameron C-80 balloon	L. Greaves	
G-CELO	Boeing 737-33AQC	Jet 2	
G-CELP	Boeing 737-330QC	Jet 2	
G-CELR	Boeing 737-330QC	Jet 2	
G-CELS	Boeing 737-377	Jet 2	
G-CELU	Boeing 737-377	Jet 2	
G-CELV	Boeing 737-377	Jet 2	
G-CELW	Boeing 737-377	Jet 2	
G-CELX	Boeing 737-377	Jet 2	
G-CELY	Boeing 737-377	Jet 2	
G-CELZ	Boeing 737-377	Jet 2	
G-CEMA	Alpi Pioneer 200	D. M. Bracken	
G-CEMB	P & M Quik GT450	D. W. Logue	
G-CEMC	Robinson R44 Raven II	Heliart Ltd	
G-CEME	Evektor EV-97 Eurostar	F. W. McCann	
G-CEMF	Cameron C-80 balloon	Linear Communications Consultants Ltd	
G-CEMG	Ultramagic M-105 balloon	Comunicazione In Volo SRL/Italy	
G-CEMI	Europa XS	B. D. A. Morris	
G-CEMK	Boeing 767-222	UK International Airlines Ltd	
G-CEML	P & M Pegasus Quik	S. Cooke	
G-CEMM	P & M Quik GT450	M. A. Rhodes	
G-CEMO	P & M Quik GT450	L. E. Craig	
G-CEMR	Mainair Blade 912	A. D. Cameron	
G-CEMS	MDH MD900 Explorer	Yorkshire Air Ambulance Ltd.	
G-CEMT	P & M Quik GT450	W. Barden & S. E. Robinson	
G-CEMU	Cameron C-80 balloon	J. G. O'Connell	
G-CEMV	Lindstrand LBL-105A balloon	R. G. Turnbull	
G-CEMW	Lindstrand LBL Bananas balloon	Top Banana Balloon Team (G-OCAW)	
G-CEMX	P & M Pegasus Quik	S. J. Meehan	
G-CEMY	Alpi Pioneer 300	J. C. A. Garland & P. F. Salter	
G-CEMZ	Pegasus Quik	D. Jessop	
G-CENA	Dyn'Aero MCR-01 ULC Banbi	I. N. Drury & D. Goodman	
G-CENB	Evektor EV-97 TeamEurostar UK	K. J. Gay	
G-CEND	Evektor EV-97 TeamEurostar UK	Flylight Airsports Ltd	
G-CENE	Flight Design CTSW	The CT Flying Group	
G-CENG	SkyRanger 912(2)	R. A. Knight	
G-CENH	Tecnam P2002-EA Sierra	M. W. Taylor	
G-CENI	Supermarine Spitfire Mk.26	R. Ellingworth & A. G. Thomas	
G-CENJ	Medway SLA 951	M. Ingleton	
G-CENK	Schempp-Hirth Nimbus 4DT	R. A. Christie	
G-CENL	P & M Quik GT450	P. Von Sydow & S. Baker	
G-CENM	Evektor EV-97 Eurostar	N. D. Meer	
G-CENN	Cameron C-60 balloon	Stonebee Ltd	
G-CENO	Aerospool Dynamic WT9 UK	R. O. Lewthwaite	
G-CENP	Ace Magic Laser	A. G. Curtis	
G-CENR	ELA 07S	M. S. Gough	
G-CENS	SkyRanger Swift 912S(1)	M. & N. D. Stannard	
G-CENV	P & M Quik GT450	RAF Microlight Flying Association	
G-CENW	Evektor EV-97A Eurostar	Southside Flyers	
G-CENX	Lindstrand LBL-360A	Wickers World Ltd	
G-CENZ	Aeros Discus/Alize	J. D. Buchanan	
G-CEOB	Pitts S-1 Special	N. J. Radford	
G-CEOC	Tecnam P2002-EA Sierra	M. A. Lomas	
G-CEOF	PA-28R-201 Arrow	J. H. Sandham Aviation	
G-CEOG	PA-28R-201 Arrow	A. J. Gardiner	
G-CEOH	Raj Hamsa X'Air Falcon ULP(1)	J. C. Miles	
G-CEOI	Cameron C-60 balloon	M. E. White	

Notes	Reg.	Type	Owner or Operator
	G-CEOJ	Eurocopter EC 155B	Starspeed Ltd
	G-CEOL	Flylight Lightfly-Discus	A. Bill
	G-CEOM	Jabiru UL-450	J. R. Caylow
	G-CEON	Raj Hamsa X'Air Hawk	K. S. Campbell
	G-CEOO	P & M Quik GT450	S. Moran
	G-CEOP	Aeroprakt A22-L Foxbat	J. G. Miller
	G-CEOS	Cameron C-90 balloon	British School of Ballooning
	G-CEOT	Dudek ReAction Sport/Bailey Quattro 175	J. Kelly
	G-CEOU	Lindstrand LBL-31A balloon	Lindstrand Hot Air Balloons Ltd
	G-CEOV	Lindstrand LBL-120A balloon	Lindstrand Hot Air Balloons Ltd
	G-CEOW	Europa XS	R. W. Wood
	G-CEOX	Rotorsport UK MT-03	A. J. Saunders
	G-CEOY	Schweizer 269C-1	Helitrex Aviation Services
	G-CEOZ	Paramania Action GT26/PAP Chariot Z	A. M. Shepherd
	G-CEPL	Super Marine Spitfire Mk.26 (P9398)	S. R. Marsh
	G-CEPM	Jabiru J430	T. R. Sinclair
	G-CEPN	Kolb Firefly	I. Brewster
	G-CEPP	P & M Quik GT450	W. M. Studley
	G-CEPR	Cameron Z-90 balloon	Sport Promotion SRL/Italy
	G-CEPS	TL2000UK Sting Carbon	C. E. & R. P. Reeves
	G-CEPU	Cameron Z-77 balloon	Liquigas SPA
	G-CEPV	Cameron Z-77 balloon	Liquigas SPA
	G-CEPW	Alpi Pioneer 300	N. K. Spedding
	G-CEPX	Cessna 152	Cristal Air Ltd
	G-CEPY	Ikarus C42 FB80	L. Lay
	G-CEPZ	DR.107 One Design	CEPZ Flying Group
	G-CERB	SkyRanger Swift 912S(1)	J. J. Littler
	G-CERC	Cameron Z-350 balloon	Ballooning Network Ltd
	G-CERD	D.H.C.1 Chipmunk 22	A. C. Darby
	G-CERE	Evektor EV-97 TeamEurostar UK	Airbourne Aviation Ltd
	G-CERF	Rotorsport UK MT-03	P. J. Robinson
	G-CERH	Cameron C-90 balloon	A. Walker
	G-CERI	Shaw Europa XS	S. J. M. Shepherd
	G-CERK	Van's RV-9A	P. E. Brown
	G-CERL	Ultramagic M-77 balloon	A. M. Holly
	G-CERN	P & M Quik GT450	P. M. Jackson
	G-CERO	Agusta A109C	Castle Air Ltd (G-OBEK/G-CDDJ)
	G-CERP	P & M Quik GT450	G. R. Cassie, A. J. L. Coulson, D. A. Howe & S. O. Kennedy
	G-CERT	Mooney M.20K	J. A. Nisbet
	G-CERV	P & M Quik GT450	East Fortune Flyers
	G-CERW	P & M Pegasus Quik	D. J. Cornelius
	G-CERX	Hawker 850XP	Hangar 8 Management Ltd
	G-CERY	SAAB 2000	Eastern Airways
	G-CERZ	SAAB 2000	Eastern Airways
	G-CESA	Replica Jodel DR.1050	T. J. Bates
	G-CESD	SkyRanger Swift 912S(1)	S. E. Dancaster
	G-CESH	Cameron Z-90 balloon	M. Rowlands
	G-CESI	Aeroprakt A22-L Foxbat	D. N. L. Howell
	G-CESJ	Raj Hamsa X'Air Hawk	J. Bolton & R. Shewan
	G-CESM	TL2000UK Sting Carbon	E. Stephenson
	G-CESR	P & M Quik GT450	G. Kerr
	G-CEST	Robinson R44	Scotia Helicopters Ltd
	G-CESU	Robinson R22 Beta	M. Boni
	G-CESV	EV-97 TeamEurostar UK	N. Jones
	G-CESW	Flight Design CTSW	J. Whiting
	G-CESZ	CZAW Sportcruiser	S. Eccles
	G-CETB	Robin DR.400/180	QR Flying Club
	G-CETD	PA-28-161 Warrior III	Plane Talking Ltd
	G-CETE	PA-28-161 Warrior III	Plane Talking Ltd
	G-CETF	Flight Design CTSW	I. Epton
	G-CETK	Cameron Z-145 balloon	R. H. Etherington
	G-CETL	P & M Quik GT450	J. I. Greenshields
	G-CETM	P & M Quik GT450	I. Burnside
	G-CETN	Hummel Bird	A. A. Haseldine
	G-CETO	Best Off Sky Ranger Swift 912S(1)	S. C. Stoodley
	G-CETP	Van's RV-9A	D. Boxall & S. Hill
	G-CETR	Ikarus C42 FB100	A. E. Lacy-Hulbert
	G-CETS	Van's RV-7	TS Group
	G-CETT	Evektor EV-97 TeamEurostar UK	Tango Tango Group
	G-CETU	Best Off Sky Ranger Swift 912S(1)	A. Raithby & N. McCusker
	G-CETV	Best Off Sky Ranger Swift 912S(1)	C. J. Johnson

Reg.	Type	Owner or Operator	Notes
G-CETX	Alpi Pioneer 300	J. M. P. Ree	
G-CETY	Rans S-6-ES Coyote II	J. North	
G-CETZ	Ikarus C42 FB100	Airways Airsports Ltd	
G-CEUE	BN-2B-20 Islander	Britten-Norman Aircraft Ltd	
G-CEUF	P & M Quik GT450	G. T. Snoddon	
G-CEUH	P & M Quik GT450	G. J. McNally	
G-CEUJ	SkyRanger Swift 912S(1)	J. P. Batty & J. R. C. Brightman	
G-CEUL	Ultramagic M-105 balloon	R. A. Vale	
G-CEUM	Ultramagic M-120 balloon	Bridges Van Hire Ltd	
G-CEUN	Orlican Discus CS	The Royal Air Force Gliding and Soaring Association	
G-CEUR	Schempp-Hirth Ventus 2cT	G. Coppin	
G-CEUT	Hoffman H-36 Dimona II	A. L. D. Munro & M. Tolson	
G-CEUU	Robinson R44 II	A. Stafford-Jones	
G-CEUV	Cameron C-90 balloon	I. Parsons	
G-CEUW	Zenair CH.601XL Zodiac	J. S. Griffiths	
G-CEUZ	P & M Quik GT450	B. S. Smy	
G-CEVA	Ikarus C42 FB80	The Scottish Flying Group	
G-CEVB	P & M Quik GT450	A. Cuthill	
G-CEVC	Van's RV-4	P. A. Brook	
G-CEVD	Rolladen-Schneider LS3	Victor Delta Syndicate	
G-CEVE	Centrair 101A	T. P. Newham	
G-CEVF	BAe.146-200	Triangle Regional Aircraft Leasing Ltd	
G-CEVG	P & M Pegasus Quik	Bartn Quik Group	
G-CEVH	Cameron V-65 balloon	J. A. Atkinson	
G-CEVJ	Alpi Pioneer 200	B. W. Bartlett	
G-CEVK	Schleicher Ka 6CR	K6 Syndicate	
G-CEVL	Fairchild M-62A Cornell	UK Cornell Group	
G-CEVM	Tecnam P2002-EA Sierra	R. C. Mincik	
G-CEVN	Rolladen-Schneider LS7	N. Gaunt & B. C. Toon	
G-CEVO	Grob G.109B	T.J. Wilkinson	
G-CEVP	P & M Quik GT450	P. J. Lowe	
G-CEVS	EV-97 TeamEurostar UK	Hotel Victor Flying Group	
G-CEVT	Dudek Reaction 27/Bailey Quattro 175	J. Kelly	
G-CEVU	Savannah VG Jabiru(4)	I. C. May	
G-CEVV	Rolladen-Schneider LS3	LS3 307 Syndicate	
G-CEVW	P & M Quik GT450	R. W. Sutherland	
G-CEVX	Aeriane Swift Light PAS	J. S. Firth	
G-CEVY	Rotorsport UK MT-03	P. Robinson	
G-CEVZ	Centrair ASW-20FL	B. Watkins	
G-CEWC	Schleicher ASK-21	London Gliding Club Proprietary Ltd	
G-CEWD	P & M Quik GT450	J. Murphy	
G-CEWE	Schempp-Hirth Nimbus 2	T. Clark	
G-CEWF	Jacobs V35 Airchair balloon	G. F. & I. Chadwick & M. G. Roberts	
G-CEWG	Aerola Alatus-M	Flylight Airsports Ltd	
G-CEWH	P & M Quik GT450	B. W. Hunter	
G-CEWI	Schleicher ASW-19B	S. R. Edwards	
G-CEWK	Cessna 172S	S. Howe	
G-CEWL	Alpi Pioneer 200	G-CEWL Ltd	
G-CEWM	DHC.6 Twin Otter 300	Isles of Scilly Skybus Ltd	
G-CEWN	Diamond DA-42 Twin Star	Airedale Mechanical and Electrical Ltd	
G-CEWO	Schleicher Ka 6CR	DQS Group	
G-CEWP	Grob G.102 Astir CS	G-CEWP Flying Group	
G-CEWR	Aeroprakt A22-L Foxbat	C. S. Bourne & G. P. Wiley	
G-CEWS	Zenair CH.701SP	D. L. Aspinall & G. E. MacCuish	
G-CEWT	Flight Design CTSW	A and R. W. Osborne	
G-CEWU	Ultramagic H-77 balloon	P. C. Waterhouse	
G-CEWW	Grob G.102 Astir CS	G. J. Walker	
G-CEWX	Cameron Z-350 balloon	Original Bristol FM Ltd	
G-CEWY	Quicksilver GT500	R. J. Scott	
G-CEWZ	Schempp-Hirth Discus bT	J. F. Goudie	
G-CEXL	Ikarus C42 FB80	Syndicate C42-1	
G-CEXM	Best Off Sky Ranger Swift 912S(1)	A. F. Batchelor	
G-CEXN	Cameron A-120 balloon	Dragon Balloon Company Ltd	
G-CEXO	PA-28-161 Warrior III	Durham Tees Flight Training Ltd	
G-CEXP	HPR.7 Herald 209 ★	Towing and rescue trainer/Gatwick	
G-CEXX	Rotorsport UK MT-03	D. B. Roberts	
G-CEYC	DG Flugzeugbau DG-505 Elan Orion	Scottish Gliding Union Ltd	
G-CEYD	Cameron N-31 balloon	Black Pearl Balloons (G-LLYD)	
G-CEYE	PA-32R-300 Cherokee Lance	G. R. & S. W. Case	
G-CEYF	Eurocopter EC135 T1	Starspeed Ltd (G-HARP)	
G-CEYG	Cessna 152	S. J. & T. Powell and A. H. Haynes	
G-CEYH	Cessna 152	Cornwall Flying Club Ltd	

Notes	Reg.	Type	Owner or Operator
	G-CEYK	Europa XS	A. B. Milne
	G-CEYL	Bombardier BD-700-1A10 Global Express	Aravco Ltd
	G-CEYM	Van's RV-6	R. B. Skinner
	G-CEYN	Grob G.109B	G-CEYN Flying Group
	G-CEYO	Aerospatiale AS.350B2 Ecureuil	FB Heliservices Ltd
	G-CEYP	North Wing Design Stratus/ATF	J. S. James
	G-CEYR	Rotorsport UK MT-03	N. Wright
	G-CEYU	SA.365N1 Dauphin 2	Multiflight Ltd
	G-CEYX	Rotorsport UK MT-03	N. Creveul
	G-CEYY	EV-97 TeamEurostar UK	N. J. James
	G-CEYZ	Sikorsky S-76C	Bristow Helicopters Ltd
	G-CEZA	Ikarus C42 FB80	P. Harper & P. J. Morton
	G-CEZB	Savannah VG Jabiru(1)	J. Finch
	G-CEZD	EV-97 TeamEurostar	G. P. Jones
	G-CEZE	Best Off Sky Ranger Swift 912S	G-CEZE Group
	G-CEZF	EV-97 TeamEurostar UK	D. J. Dick
	G-CEZH	Aerochute Dual	G. Stokes
	G-CEZI	PA-28-161 Cadet	Chalrey Ltd
	G-CEZK	Stolp S.750 Acroduster Too	R. I. M. Hague
	G-CEZL	PA-28-161 Cadet	Chalrey Ltd
	G-CEZM	Cessna 152	Cristal Air Ltd
	G-CEZN	Pacific Airwave Pulse 2/Skycycle	G. W. Cameron
	G-CEZO	PA-28-161 Cadet	Chalrey Ltd
	G-CEZR	Diamond DA.40D Star	Flying Time Ltd
	G-CEZS	Zenair CH.601HDS Zodiac	R. Wyness
	G-CEZT	P & M Aviation Quik GT450	B. C. Blackburn
	G-CEZU	CFM Streak Shadow SA	D. E. Foster
	G-CEZV	Zenair CH.601HDS Zodiac	H. R. Carey
	G-CEZW	Jodel D.150 Mascaret	N. J. Kilford
	G-CEZX	P & M Aviation Quik GT450	N. J. Braund
	G-CEZZ	Flight Design CTSW	J. A. Lynch
	G-CFAG	Rotorsport UK MT-03	M. D. Cole
	G-CFAJ	DG-300 Elan	S. Marriott
	G-CFAK	Rotorsport UK MT-03	R. M. Savage
	G-CFAM	Schempp-Hirth Nimbus 3/24.5	Nimbus III Syndicate J15
	G-CFAO	Rolladen-Schneider LS4	V. R. Roberts
	G-CFAP	Interplane ZJ-Viera	Flylight Airsports Ltd
	G-CFAR	Rotorsport UK MT-03	P. M. Twose
	G-CFAS	Escapade Jabiru(3)	C. G. N. Boyd
	G-CFAT	P & M Aviation Quik GT450	T. G. Jackson
	G-CFAU	Cameron Z-105 balloon	High On Adventure Balloons Ltd
	G-CFAV	Ikarus C42 FB80	P. E. Scopes
	G-CFAW	Lindstrand LBL-35A Cloudhopper balloon	A. Walker
	G-CFAX	Ikarus C42 FB80	R. E. Parker & B. Cook
	G-CFAY	Sky 120-24 balloon	G. B. Lescott
	G-CFBA	Schleicher ASW-20BL	C. R. Little
	G-CFBB	Schempp-Hirth Standard Cirrus	L. Dale
	G-CFBC	Schleicher ASW-15B	CFBC Group
	G-CFBE	Ikarus C42 FB80	C. A. Hasell
	G-CFBF	Lindstrand LBL 203T gas balloon	S and D Leisure (Europe) Ltd
	G-CFBH	Glaser-Dirks DG-100G Elan	IBM Gliding Club
	G-CFBJ	Rotorsport UK MT-03	C-More Flying Ltd
	G-CFBK	BAC 167 Strikemaster Mk.80A (1125)	Everett Aerospace
	G-CFBL	Best Off Sky Ranger Swift 912S(1)	D. Hemmings
	G-CFBM	P & M Quantum 15-912	G-CFBM Flying Group
	G-CFBN	Glasflugel Mosquito B	S. R. & J. Nash
	G-CFBO	Reality Escapade Jabiru(3)	J. F. Thornton
	G-CFBS	Best Off Sky Ranger Swift 912S(1)	A. J. Tyler
	G-CFBT	Schempp-Hirth Ventus bT	488 (Gransden) Group
	G-CFBV	Schleicher ASK-21	London Gliding Club Proprietary Ltd
	G-CFBW	DG-100G Elan	G-CFBW Syndicate
	G-CFBX	Beech C90GTI King Air	J. M. Lynch
	G-CFBY	Best Off Sky Ranger Swift 912S(1)	J. A. Armin
	G-CFBZ	Schleicher Ka 6CR	R. H. W. Martyn
	G-CFCA	Schempp-Hirth Discus b	M. R. Hayden
	G-CFCB	Centrair 101	T. J. Berriman & M. Phillimore
	G-CFCC	Cameron Z-275 balloon	Ballooning Network Ltd
	G-CFCD	SkyRanger Swift 912S(1)	D. & L. Payn
	G-CFCE	Raj Hamsa X'Air Hawk	B. M. Tibenham
	G-CFCF	Aerochute Dual	C. J. Kendal & S. G. Smith

Reg.	Type	Owner or Operator	Notes
G-CFCH	Campbell Cricket Mk.4	E. J. Barton	
G-CFCI	Cessna F.172N	J. Blacklock	
G-CFCJ	Grob G.102 Astir CS	A. J. C. Beaumont & P. Hardwick	
G-CFCK	Best Off Sky Ranger 912S(1)	C. M. Sperring	
G-CFCL	Rotorsport UK MT-03	M. D. Reece	
G-CFCM	Robinson R44	A. J. Brough	
G-CFCN	Schempp-Hirth Standard Cirrus	P. C. Bunniss	
G-CFCP	Rolladen-Schneider LS6-a	R. E. Robertson	
G-CFCR	Schleicher Ka-6E	R. F. Whittaker	
G-CFCS	Schempp-Hirth Nimbus 2C	J. Luck & P. Dolling	
G-CFCT	EV-97 TeamEurostar UK	Sutton Eurostar Group	
G-CFCU	Lindstrand LBL-203T gas balloon	Lindstrand Aeroplatforms Ltd	
G-CFCV	Schleicher ASW-20	M. J. Davis	
G-CFCW	Rotorsport UK MT-03	C. M. Jones	
G-CFCX	Rans S-6-ES Coyote II	D. & S. Morrison	
G-CFCY	Best Off Sky Ranger Swift 912S(1)	M. E. & T. E. Simpson	
G-CFCZ	P & M Quik GT450	P. K. Dale	
G-CFDA	Schleicher ASW-15	N. B. Coggins	
G-CFDC	P & M Aviation Quik GT450	P. R. Davies	
G-CFDE	Schempp-Hirth Ventus bT	P. Clay	
G-CFDF	Ultramagic S-90 balloon	Edinburgh University Hot Air Balloon Club	
G-CFDG	Schleicher Ka 6CR	Delta-Golf Group	
G-CFDI	Van's RV-6	M. D. Challoner	
G-CFDJ	EV-97 TeamEurostar UK	J. D. J. Spragg & M. Jones	
G-CFDK	Rans S-6-ES Coyote II	Conair Sports Ltd	
G-CFDL	P & M QuikR	P and M Aviation Ltd	
G-CFDM	Schempp-Hirth Discus b	J. L. & T. G. M. Whiting	
G-CFDN	Best Off Sky Ranger Swift 912S(1)	A. C. Richards	
G-CFDO	Flight Design CTSW	D. I. Waller	
G-CFDP	Flight Design CTSW	N. Fielding	
G-CFDS	TL2000UK Sting Carbon	TL Sting G-CFDS Group	
G-CFDT	Aerola Alatus-M	I White	
G-CFDU	BB03 Trya/BB103	J. M. Macleod	
G-CFDV	Sikorsky S-76C	Bristow Helicopters Ltd	
G-CFDX	PZL-Bielsko SZD-48-1 Jantar Standard 2	A. Phillips	
G-CFDY	P &M Quik GT450	C. N. Thornton	
G-CFDZ	Flight Design Exxtacy/Alize	N. C. O. Watney	
G-CFEA	Cameron C-90 balloon	A. M. Holly	
G-CFEB	Cameron C-80 balloon	A. M. Holly	
G-CFED	Van's RV-9	E. W. Taylor	
G-CFEE	Evektor EV-97 Eurostar	G.CFEE Flying Group	
G-CFEF	Grob G.102 Astir CS	Oxford University Gliding Club	
G-CFEG	Schempp-Hirth Ventus b/16.6	P. Ottomaniello	
G-CFEH	Centrair 101 Pegase	Booker Gliding Club Ltd	
G-CFEJ	Schempp-Hirth Discus b	Lima Charlie Syndicate	
G-CFEK	Cameron Z-105 balloon	R. M. Penny (Plant Hire and Demolition) Ltd	
G-CFEL	EV-97 Eurostar	S. R. Green	
G-CFEI	RAF 2000 GTX-SE	A. M. Wells	
G-CFEM	P & M Aviation Quik GT450	A. M. King	
G-CFEN	PZL-Bielsko SZD-50-3 Puchacz	The Northumbria Gliding Club Ltd	
G-CFEO	EV-97 Eurostar	J. B. Binks	
G-CFER	Schempp-Hirth Discus b	S. R. Westlake	
G-CFES	Schempp-Hirth Discus b	P. W. Berridge	
G-CFET	Van's RV-7	J. Astor	
G-CFEV	P & M Pegasus Quik	W. T. Davis	
G-CFEX	P & M Quik GT450	H. Wilson	
G-CFEY	Aerola Alatus-M	M. S. Hayman	
G-CFEZ	CZAW Sportcruiser	J. F. Barber & J. R. Large	
G-CFFA	Ultramagic M-90 balloon	Proxim SPA/Italy	
G-CFFB	Grob G.102 Astir CS	M. H. Simms	
G-CFFC	Centrair 101A	P. Lazenby	
G-CFFE	EV-97 TeamEurostar UK	M. Lawton	
G-CFFF	Pitts S-1S Special	P. J. Roy	
G-CFFG	Aerochute Dual	R. J. Watkin	
G-CFFH	Aeros Discus 15T Dragonfly	D. Wilson	
G-CFFJ	Flight Design CTSW	R. Germany	
G-CFFL	Lindstrand LBL-317A balloon	Aerosarus Balloons Ltd	
G-CFFN	P & M Quik GT450	Kent County Scout Council	
G-CFFO	P & M Quik GT450	D. E. McGauley & J. R. North	
G-CFFS	Centrair 101A	W. Murray	
G-CFFT	Schempp-Hirth Discus b	P. R. Wilson	
G-CFFU	Glaser-Dirks DG-101G Elan	FFU Group	
G-CFFV	PZL-Bielsko SZD-51-1 Junior	Herefordshire Gliding Club Ltd	

Notes	Reg.	Type	Owner or Operator
	G-CFFX	Schempp-Hirth Discus b	P. J. Richards
	G-CFFY	PZL-Bielsko SZD-51-1 Junior	Scottish Gliding Union Ltd
	G-CFGA	VS Spitfire VIII	The Pembrokeshire Spitfire Aeroplane Company Ltd
	G-CFGB	Cessna 680 Citation Sovereign	Keepflying LLP
	G-CFGC	Demoiselle	R. B. Hewing
	G-CFGD	P & M Quik GT450	D. J. Revell
	G-CFGE	Stinson 108-1 Voyager	M. J. Medland
	G-CFGF	Schempp-Hirth Nimbus 3T	R. E. Cross
	G-CFGG	Rotorsport UK MT-03	C. M. Jones
	G-CFGH	Jabiru J160	D. F. Sargant & D. J. Royce
	G-CFGI	VS.358 Seafire Mk.II (MB293)	Mark One Partners LLC
	G-CFGJ	VS.300 Spitfire I (N3200)	Mark One Partners LLC
	G-CFGK	Grob G.102 Astir CS	P. Allingham
	G-CFGM	Ikarus C42	R. S. O'Carroll
	G-CFGN	VS.300 Spitfire IA	Mark One Partners LLC
	G-CFGO	Best Off Sky Ranger Swift 912S	R. G. Hearsey & C. Lamb
	G-CFGP	Schleicher ASW-19	A. E. Prime
	G-CFGR	Schleicher ASK-13	Portsmouth Naval Gliding Centre
	G-CFGT	P & M Aviation Quik GT450	G. I. Taylor
	G-CFGU	Schempp-Hirth Standard Cirrus	D. Higginbottom
	G-CFGV	P & M Quik GT450	R. Bennett
	G-CFGX	EV-97 TeamEurostar UK	Golf XRay Group
	G-CFGY	Rotorsport UK MT-03	G. J. Slater & N. D. Leak
	G-CFGW	Centrair 101A	L. P. Smith
	G-CFGZ	Flight Design CTSW	B. Gorvett
	G-CFHB	Micro Aviation B.22J Bantam	P. Rayson
	G-CFHC	Micro Aviation B.22J Bantam	B. J. Syson
	G-CFHD	Schleicher ASW-20 BL	196 Syndicate
	G-CFHF	PZL-Bielsko SZD-51-1	Black Mountains Gliding Club
	G-CFHG	Schempp-Hirth Mini Nimbus C	R. W. & M. P. Weaver
	G-CFHI	Van's RV-9	J. R. Dawe
	G-CFHJ	Centrair 101A Pegase	Booker Gliding Club Ltd
	G-CFHK	Aeroprakt A22-L Foxbat	R. Bellew
	G-CFHL	Rolladen-Schneider LS4	I. P. Hicks
	G-CFHM	Schleicher ASK-13	Lasham Gliding Society Ltd
	G-CFHN	Schleicher K 8B	The Nene Valley Gliding Club Ltd
	G-CFHO	Grob G.103 Twin Astir II	The Surrey Hills Gliding Club Ltd
	G-CFHP	Ikarus C42 FB80	Airbourne Aviation Ltd
	G-CFHR	Schempp-Hirth Discus b	M. Fursedon, J. Jervis & T. Turner
	G-CFHS	Tchemma T01/77 balloon	D. J. Farrar
	G-CFHU	Robinson R22 Beta	Cameron and Brown Partnership
	G-CFHW	Grob G.102 Astir CS	P. Haliday
	G-CFHX	Schroeder Fire Balloons G22/24 balloon	T. J. Ellenrieder
	G-CFHY	Fokker Dr.1 Triplane replica	P. G. Bond
	G-CFHZ	Schleicher Ka 6CR	G. D. Leatherland
	G-CFIA	Best Off Sky Ranger Swift 912S(1)	D. I. Hall
	G-CFIC	Jodel DR.1050/M1	J. H. & P. I. Kempton
	G-CFID	Tanarg/Ixess 15 912S	D. Smith
	G-CFIE	Rotorsport UK MT-03	A. McCredie
	G-CFIF	Christen Eagle II	CFG Flying Group
	G-CFIG	P & M Aviation Quik GT450	J. Whitfield
	G-CFIH	Piel CP.1320	I. W. L. Aikman
	G-CFII	DH.82A Tiger Moth	Motair LLP
	G-CFIJ	Christen Eagle II	U. Wendt
	G-CFIK	Lindstrand LBL-60X balloon	L. Sambrook
	G-CFIL	P & M Aviation Quik GT450	S. N. Catchpole
	G-CFIM	P & M Aviation Quik GT450	A. Szczepanek
	G-CFIO	Cessna 172S	Skytrek Air Services
	G-CFIS	Jabiru UL-D	O. Matthews
	G-CFIT	Ikarus C42 FB100	G-CFIT Group
	G-CFIU	CZAW Sportcruiser	G. Everett & D. Smith
	G-CFIW	Balony Kubicek BB20XR balloon	H. C. J. Williams
	G-CFIY	Ikarus C42 FB100	D. M. Robbins
	G-CFIZ	Best Off Sky Ranger 912(2)	J. A. Hartshorne
	G-CFJB	Rotorsport UK MT-03	N. J. Hargreaves
	G-CFJF	Schempp-Hirth SHK-1	J. F. Mills
	G-CFJG	Best Off Sky Ranger Swift 912S(1)	C. M. Gray
	G-CFJH	Grob G.102 Astir CS77	P. Hardman
	G-CFJI	Ultramagic M-105 balloon	Comunicazione in Volo Srl/Italy
	G-CFJJ	Best Off Sky Ranger Swift 912S(1)	J. J. Ewing
	G-CFJK	Centrair 101A	D. Lewis
	G-CFJL	Raj Hamsa X'Air Hawk	G. L. Craig

Reg.	Type	Owner or Operator	Notes
G-CFJM	Rolladen-Schneider LS4-a	K. Woods & S. Hill	
G-CFJN	Diamond DA.40D Star	Atlantic Flight Training Ltd	
G-CFJO	Diamond DA.40D Star	Atlantic Flight Training Ltd	
G-CFJP	Cameron N-56 balloon	V. J. M. L de Gail	
G-CFJR	Glaser-Dirks DG-300 Club Elan	W. Palmer & H. Smith	
G-CFJS	Glaser-Dirks DG-300 Club Elan	K. L. Goldsmith	
G-CFJU	Raj Hamsa X'Air Hawk	R. J. Minns & H. M. Wooldridge	
G-CFJV	Schleicher ASW-15	R. Abercrombie	
G-CFJW	Schleicher K7	K7 Group	
G-CFJX	DG-300 Elan	Crown Service Gliding Club	
G-CFJZ	Schempp-Hirth SHK-1	B. C. Irwin & R. H. Hanna	
G-CFKA	Rotorsport MT-03	Yorkshire Gyro Syndicate	
G-CFKB	CZAW Sportcruiser	KB Flying Group	
G-CFKD	Raj Hamsa X'Air Falcon Jabiru(2)	A. M. Fawthrop	
G-CFKE	Raj Hamsa X'Air Hawk	S. Rance	
G-CFKF	Cameron Z-210 balloon	First Flight	
G-CFKG	Rolladen-Schneider LS4-a	FKG Group	
G-CFKH	Zenair CH.601XL Zodiac	M. A. Baker	
G-CFKJ	P & M Aviation Quik GT450	B. Geary	
G-CFKK	Flylight Dragonfly	C. G. Langham	
G-CFKL	Schleicher ASW-20 BL	J. Ley	
G-CFKM	Schempp-Hirth Discus b	Lasham Gliding Society Ltd	
G-CFKN	Lindstrand GA22 Mk.II airship	Lindstrand Technologies Ltd	
G-CFKO	P & M Aviation Quik GT450	D. W. C. Beer	
G-CFKP	Performance Designs Barnstormer/ Voyager	M. R. M. Harrall	
G-CFKR	P & M Aviation Pegasus Quik	R. D. Ballard	
G-CFKS	Flight Design CTSW	D. J. M. Williams	
G-CFKT	Schleicher K 8B	FKT Group	
G-CFKU	P & M Aviation Quik GT450	C. A. Hasell	
G-CFKV	Savannah VG Jabiru(1)	D. Thorpe & K. N. Rigley	
G-CFKW	Alpi Pioneer 200	A. A. Mortimer	
G-CFKX	Cameron Z-160 balloon	Virgin Balloon Flights	
G-CFKY	Schleicher Ka 6CR	J. A. Timmis	
G-CFKZ	Europa XS	N. P. Davis	
G-CFLA	P & M Aviation Quik GT450	P. H. Woodward	
G-CFLC	Glaser-Dirks DG-300 Club Elan	J. L.Hey	
G-CFLD	Ikarus C42 FB80	L. McWilliams	
G-CFLE	Schempp-Hirth Discus b	D. A. Humphreys & S. J. A. McCracken	
G-CFLF	Rolladen-Schneider LS4-a	D. Lamb	
G-CFLG	CZAW Sportcruiser	D. A. Buttress	
G-CFLH	Schleicher K8B	The South Wales Gliding Club Ltd	
G-CFLI	Europa Aviation Europa	A. & E. Bennett	
G-CFLK	Cameron C-90 balloon	J. R. Rivers-Scott	
G-CFLL	EV-97 Eurostar	D. R. Lewis	
G-CFLM	P & M Pegasus Quik	The JAG Flyers	
G-CFLN	Best Off Sky Ranger Swift 912S(1)	D. Bletcher	
G-CFLO	Rotorsport UK MT-03	R. G. Mulford	
G-CFLP	D.31 Turbulent	Eaglescott Turbulent Group	
G-CFLR	P & M Aviation Quik GT450	N. J. Lister	
G-CFLS	Schleicher Ka 6CR	University College London Union	
G-CFLU	SAAB 2000	Eastern Airways	
G-CFLV	SAAB 2000	Eastern Airways	
G-CFLW	Schempp-Hirth Standard Cirrus 75	J. Pack	
G-CFLX	DG-300 Club Elan	R. Emms	
G-CFLZ	Scheibe SF-27A Zugvogel V	SF Group	
G-CFMA	BB03 Trya/BB103	D. Sykes	
G-CFMB	P & M Aviation Quik GT450	Countermine Technologies PLC	
G-CFMC	Van's RV-9A	G-CFMC Flying Group	
G-CFMD	P & M Aviation Quik GT450	Wilson G. Jamieson Ltd	
G-CFME	SOCATA TB10 Tobago	G. M. Paeckmeyer & B. B. Singh	
G-CFMH	Schleicher ASK-13	Lasham Gliding Society Ltd	
G-CFMI	Best Off Sky Ranger 912(1)	P. Shelton	
G-CFMM	Cessna 172S	Cristal Air Ltd	
G-CFMN	Schempp-Hirth Ventus cT	FMN Glider Syndicate	
G-CFMO	Schempp-Hirth Discus b	P. D. Bagnall	
G-CFMP	Europa XS	M. P. Gamble	
G-CFMR	Ultramagic V-14 balloon	M. W. A. Shemilt	
G-CFMS	Schleicher ASW-15	Loughborough Students Union Gliding Club	
G-CFMT	Schempp-Hirth Standard Cirrus	J. M. Brooke	
G-CFMU	Schempp-Hirth Standard Cirrus	P. S. Carder	
G-CFMV	Aerola Alatus-M	P. J. Wood	
G-CFMW	Scheibe SF-25C	The Windrushers Gliding Club Ltd	

Notes	Reg.	Type	Owner or Operator
	G-CFMX	PA-28-161 Warrior II	Stapleford Flying Club Ltd
	G-CFMY	Rolladen-Schneider LS7	G-CFMY Group
	G-CFNB	Cameron TR-70 balloon	Balslooning Team BVBA/Belgium
	G-CFNC	Flylight Dragonfly	W. G. Minns
	G-CFND	Schleicher Ka 6E	C. Scutt
	G-CFNE	PZL-Bielsko SZD-38A Jantar 1	T. Robson, J. Murray & I. Gordon
	G-CFNF	Robinson R44 II	S. G. Dykes
	G-CFNG	Schleicher ASW-24	P. H. Pickett
	G-CFNH	Schleicher ASW-19	S. N. & P. E. S. Longland
	G-CFNI	Airborne Edge XT912-B/Streak III-B	Fly NI Ltd
	G-CFNK	Slingsby T.65A Vega	I. P. Goldstraw
	G-CFNL	Schempp-Hirth Discus b	A. S. Ramsay & P. P. Musto
	G-CFNM	Centrair 101B Pegase	D. T. Hartley
	G-CFNO	Best Off Sky Ranger Swift 912S(1)	P. R. Hanman
	G-CFNP	Schleicher Ka 6CR	P. Pollard-Wilkins
	G-CFNR	Schempp-Hirth Discus b	J. I. H. Mitcheson
	G-CFNS	Glaser-Dirks DG-300 Club Elan	P. E. Williams, K. F. Byrne & J. M. Price
	G-CFNT	Glaser-Dirks DG-600	G-CFNT Group
	G-CFNU	Rolladen Schneider LS4-a	R. J. Simpson
	G-CFNV	CZAW Sportcruiser	N. D. McAllister & M. Owen
	G-CFNW	EV-97 TeamEurostar UK	The Scottish Aero Club Ltd
	G-CFNX	Tanarg/Ixess 13 912S(1)	Flylight Airsports Ltd
	G-CFNY	Flylight Dragonfly	M. J. Jessop
	G-CFNZ	Airborne Edge XT912-B/Streak III-B	P. Walton
	G-CFOB	Schleicher ASW-15B	G. J. Chisholm
	G-CFOC	Glaser-Dirks DG200/17	DG202 Flying Syndicate
	G-CFOF	Scheibe SF-27A Zugvogel V	S. Maddex
	G-CFOG	Ikarus C42 FB UK	P. D. Coppin
	G-CFOI	Cessna 172N	P. Fearon
	G-CFOJ	Eurocopter EC.155 B1	Starspeed Ltd
	G-CFOM	Scheibe SF27A	K. A. Ford & R. D. Noon
	G-CFON	Wittman W8 Tailwind	C. F. O'Neill
	G-CFOO	P & M Aviation Quik R	Microavionics
	G-CFOP	Cameron Hopping Bag 120 SS balloon	J. Ravibalan
	G-CFOR	Schleicher K 8B	Dorset Gliding Club Ltd
	G-CFOS	Flylight Dragonfly	P. S. Bendall
	G-CFOT	PZL-Bielsko SZD-48-3 Jantar Standard 3	T. Greenwood
	G-CFOU	Schleicher K7	Vectis Gliding Club Ltd
	G-CFOV	CZAW Sportcruiser	J. G. Murphy
	G-CFOW	Best Off Sky Ranger Swift 912S(1)	Oscar Whiskey Syndicate
	G-CFOX	Marganski MDM-1	Fox Syndicate
	G-CFOY	Schempp-Hirth Discus b	B. W. Mills, J. W. Slater & R. F. Dowty
	G-CFOZ	Rolladen-Schneider LS1-f	L51 Group
	G-CFPA	CZAW Sportcruiser	T. W. Lorimer
	G-CFPB	Schleicher ASW-15B	G-CFPB Syndicate
	G-CFPD	Rolladen-Schneider LS7	LS7 Group
	G-CFPE	Schempp-Hirth Ventus cT	R. Palmer
	G-CFPF	Scheibe L-Spatz 55	N. C. Stone
	G-CFPG	AMS-Flight Carat A	A. Collinson
	G-CFPH	Centrair ASW-20F	A. L. D. Munro & J. R. King
	G-CFPI	P & M Aviation Quik GT450	G-CFPI Group
	G-CFPJ	CZAW Sportcruiser	S. R. Winter
	G-CFPL	Schempp-Hirth Ventus c	R. V. Barrett
	G-CFPM	PZL-Bielsko SZD-51-1 Junior	Kent Gliding Club Ltd
	G-CFPN	Schleicher ASW-20	M. Rayner
	G-CFPP	Schempp-Hirth Nimbus 2B	R. Jones & R. Murfitt
	G-CFPR	P & M Aviation Quik R	A. G. N. Coulon
	G-CFPS	Sky 25-16 balloon	G. B. Lescott
	G-CFPT	Schleicher ASW-20	L. Hornsey and L. Weeks Syndicate
	G-CFPW	Glaser-Dirks DG-600	P. B. Gray
	G-CFRC	Schempp-Hirth Nimbus 2B	Tim and Martin Nimbus 2B Group
	G-CFRE	Schleicher Ka 6E	K6-FRE Syndicate
	G-CFRF	Lindstrand LBL-31A	RAF Halton Hot Air Balloon Club
	G-CFRH	Schleicher ASW-20CL	J. N. Wilton
	G-CFRI	Ultramagic N-355 balloon	Kent Ballooning
	G-CFRJ	Schempp-Hirth Standard Cirrus	J. Francis & P. Gould
	G-CFRK	Schleicher ASW-15B	P. R. Boet
	G-CFRL	Grob G.102 Astir CS	The South Wales Gliding Club Ltd
	G-CFRM	SkyRanger Swift 912S(1)	R. K. & T. A. Willcox
	G-CFRN	Rotorsport UK MTO Sport	P. E. Scopes
	G-CFRP	Centrair 101A Pegase	Goalrace Ltd
	G-CFRR	Centrair 101A	G-CFRR Syndicate
	G-CFRS	Scheibe Zugvogel IIIB	G-CFRS Flying Group

Reg.	Type	Owner or Operator	Notes
G-CFRT	EV-97 TeamEurostar UK	G. J. Slater & N. D. Leak	
G-CFRV	Centrair 101A	P. J. Britten	
G-CFRW	Schleicher ASW-20L	R. M. Green	
G-CFRX	Centrair 101A	S. Woolrich	
G-CFRY	Zenair CH 601UL	C. K. Fry	
G-CFRZ	Schempp-Hirth Standard Cirrus	S. G. Lapworth	
G-CFSB	Tecnam P2002-RG Sierra	W. J. Gale and Son	
G-CFSD	Schleicher ASK-13	Portsmouth Naval Gliding Centre	
G-CFSE	Cameron H-340HL balloon	Balloon School (International) Ltd	
G-CFSF	P & M Aviation QuikR	C. J. Gordon	
G-CFSG	Van's RV-9	R. A. L. Hubbard	
G-CFSH	Grob G.102 Astir CS Jeans	Buckminster Gliding Club Ltd	
G-CFSI	Aerola Alatus-M	T. J. Birkbeck	
G-CFSJ	Jabiru J160	D. P. Bird	
G-CFSK	Dyn'Aero MCR-01 VLA Sportster	S. Collins	
G-CFSL	Kubicek BB-26Z balloon	M. R. Jeynes	
G-CFSM	Cessna 172Q	Zentelligence Ltd	
G-CFSO	Flylight Dragonfly/Aeros Discus 15T	J. G. McMinn	
G-CFSR	DG-300 Elan	A. P. Montague	
G-CFSS	Schleicher Ka 6E	FSS Syndicate	
G-CFST	Schleicher ASH-25E	D. Tucker & K. H. Lloyd	
G-CFSW	Skyranger Swift 912S(1)	S. B. & L. S. Williams	
G-CFSX	Savannah VG Jabiru(1)	J. P. Swadling	
G-CFTA	Ace Magic Laser	P and M Aviation Ltd	
G-CFTB	Schleicher Ka 6CR	D. J. Baldwin	
G-CFTC	PZL-Bielsko SZD-51-1 Junior	Seahawk Gliding Club	
G-CFTD	Schleicher ASW-15B	G-CFTD Flying Group	
G-CFTF	Roe 1 Triplane Replica	E. A. Verdon-Roe	
G-CFTG	P & M Aviation Quik R	A. V. Cosser	
G-CFTH	PZL-Bielsko SZD-50-3 Puchacz	Buckminster Gliding Club Ltd	
G-CFTI	Evektor EV-97A Eurostar	R. J. Dance	
G-CFTJ	Aerotechnik EV-97A Eurostar	C. B. Flood	
G-CFTK	Grob G.102 Astir CS Jeans	Ulster Gliding Club Ltd	
G-CFTL	Schleicher ASW-20CL	J. S. & S. V. Shaw	
G-CFTM	Cameron C-80 balloon	P. A. Meecham	
G-CFTN	Schleicher K 8B	Mendip Gliding Club Ltd	
G-CFTO	Ikarus C42 FB80	Fly Hire Ltd	
G-CFTP	Schleicher ASW-20CL	D. J. Pengilley	
G-CFTR	Grob G.102 Astir CS77	The University of Nottingham Students Union	
G-CFTS	Glaser-Dirks DG-300 Club Elan	FTS Syndicate	
G-CFTT	Van's RV-7	R. I. & D. J. Blain	
C-CFTU	Flylight Dragonfly	R. J. Cook	
G-CFTV	Rolladen-Schneider LS7-WL	D. Hilton	
G-CFTW	Schempp-Hirth Discus b	230 Syndicate	
G-CFTX	Jabiru J160	R. K. Creasey	
G-CFTY	Rolladen-Schneider LS7-WL	J. A. Thomson & A. Burgess	
G-CFTZ	Evektor EV-97 Eurostar	G. G. Bevis	
G-CFUA	Van's RV-9A	I. M. Macleod	
G-CFUB	Schleicher Ka 6CR	C. Boyd	
G-CFUD	Skyranger Swift 912S(1)	G-CFUD Group	
G-CFUE	Alpi Pioneer 300 Hawk	A. Dayani	
G-CFUF	Ultramagic N-300 balloon	Merlin Balloons	
G-CFUG	Grob G.109B	Portsmouth Naval Gliding Centre	
G-CFUH	Schempp-Hirth Ventus c	C. G. T. Huck	
G-CFUI	Hunt Wing/Avon 503(4)	R. F. G. Moyle	
G-CFUJ	Glaser-Dirks DG-300 Elan	Foxtrot Uniform Juliet Group	
G-CFUL	Schempp-Hirth Discus b	Discus 803 Syndicate	
G-CFUN	Schleicher ASW-20CL	D. C. W. Sanders	
G-CFUP	Schempp-Hirth Discus b	Lasham Gliding Society Ltd	
G-CFUR	Schempp-Hirth Ventus cT	A. P. Carpenter	
G-CFUS	PZL-Bielsko SZD-51-1 Junior	Scottish Gliding Union Ltd	
G-CFUT	Glaser-Dirks DG-300 Club Elan	M. J. Barnett	
G-CFUU	DG-300 Club Elan	S. K. Ruffell	
G-CFUV	Rolladen-Schneider LS7-WL	E. Alston	
G-CFUW	Rotorsport UK MTO Sport	D. A. Robertson	
G-CFUX	Cameron C-80 balloon	A. M. Holly	
G-CFUY	PZL-Bielsko SZD-50-3 Puchacz	The Bath, Wilts and North Dorset Gliding Club	
G-CFUZ	CZAW Sportcruiser	M. W. Bush	
G-CFVA	P & M Quik GT450	Countermine Technologies PLC	
G-CFVC	Schleicher ASK-13	Mendip Gliding Club Ltd	
G-CFVE	Schempp-Hirth Nimbus 2	L. Mitchell	
G-CFVF	Kiss 400-582(1)	J. D. Pinkney	
G-CFVG	Rotorsport UK MTO Sport	K. J. Whitehead	

Notes	Reg.	Type	Owner or Operator
	G-CFVH	Rolladen-Schneider LS7	C. C. & J. C. Marshall
	G-CFVI	Evektor EV-97 TeamEurostar	Nene Valley Microlights Ltd
	G-CFVJ	Cvjetkovic CA-65 Skyfly	D. Hunter
	G-CFVK	Skyranger HKS(1)	Flylight Airsports Ltd
	G-CFVL	Scheibe Zugvogel IIIB	The G-CFVL Flying Group
	G-CFVM	Centrair 101A Pegase	S. H. North
	G-CFVN	Centrair 101A Pegase	G-CFVN Group
	G-CFVP	Centrair 101A Pegase	Foxtrot Victor Papa Group
	G-CFVR	Europa XS	K. A. O'Neill
	G-CFVT	Schempp-Hirth Nimbus 2	I. Dunkley
	G-CFVU	Schleicher ASK-13	The Vale of the White Horse Gliding Centre Ltd
	G-CFVV	Centrair 101A Pegase	Cambridge Gliding Club Ltd
	G-CFVW	Schempp-Hirth Ventus bT	A. D. Johnson
	G-CFVX	Cameron C-80 balloon	A. M. Holly
	G-CFVY	Cameron A-120 balloon	Rocket Media (UK) Ltd
	G-CFVZ	Schleicher Ka 6E	N. R. Bowers
	G-CFWA	Schleicher Ka 6CR	C. C. Walley
	G-CFWB	Schleicher ASK-13	Cotswold Gliding Club
	G-CFWC	Grob G.103C Twin III Acro	The South Wales Gliding Club Ltd
	G-CFWD	Rotorsport UK MTO Sport	Gower Gyronautics
	G-CFWE	PZL-Bielsko SZD-50-3 Puchacz	Deeside Gliding Club (Aberdeenshire) Ltd
	G-CFWF	Rolladen-Schneider LS7	G. B. Hibberd
	G-CFWH	Scheibe SF27A	A. S. Carter
	G-CFWI	Kubicek BB-22Z balloon	V. Gounon
	G-CFWJ	P & M Quik GT450	H. C. Jones
	G-CFWK	Schempp-Hirth Nimbus-3DT	29 Syndicate
	G-CFWL	Schleicher K8B	A. S. Burton
	G-CFWM	Glaser-Dirks DG-300 Club Elan	FWM Group
	G-CFWN	P & M Quik GT450	G-CFWN Group
	G-CFWO	Murphy Maverick 430	S. P. Rice
	G-CFWP	Schleicher ASW-19B	980 Syndicate
	G-CFWR	Best Off Sky Ranger 912(2)	J. Mills & A. M. Wood
	G-CFWS	Schleicher ASW-20C	662 Syndicate
	G-CFWT	PZL-Bielsko SZD-50-3 Puchacz	Coventry Gliding Club Ltd
	G-CFWU	Rolladen-Schneider LS7-WL	Whiskey Uniform Group
	G-CFWV	Van's RV-7	S. J. Carr & D. K. Sington
	G-CFWW	Schleicher ASH-25E	G-CFWW Syndicate
	G-CFWY	Centrair 101A Pegase	S. Foster
	G-CFWZ	Schleicher ASW-19B	Whiskey Zulu Gliding Group
	G-CFXA	Grob G.104 Speed Astir IIB	A. V. Jupp & D. C. White
	G-CFXB	Schleicher K 8B	R. Sansom
	G-CFXC	Schleicher Ka 6E	A. K. Bailey & G. Pook
	G-CFXD	Centrair 101A Pegase	D. G. England & R. Banks
	G-CFXF	Magni M-16C Tandem Trainer	M. W. King
	G-CFXG	Flylight Dragonfly	N. L. Stammers
	G-CFXH	Schleicher K 7	P. Fabian
	G-CFXI	Lindstrand LBL Box balloon	A. M. Holly
	G-CFXJ	Schleicher ASW-24	A. & G. S. J. Bambrook
	G-CFXK	Flylight Dragonfly	P. J. Clegg
	G-CFXL	Lindstrand LBL-90A balloon	A. M. Holly
	G-CFXM	Schempp-Hirth Discus bT	G. R. E. Bottomley
	G-CFXN	CZAW Sportcruiser	R. Underwood & J. D. Boyce
	G-CFXO	PZL-Bielsko SZD-50-3 Puchacz	Coventry Gliding Club Ltd
	G-CFXP	Lindstrand LBL-105A balloon	Shaun Bradley Project Services Ltd
	G-CFXR	Lindstrand LBL-105A balloon	Lindstrand Hot Air Balloons Ltd
	G-CFXS	Schleicher Ka 6E	B. C. F. Wade & R. B. Woodhouse
	G-CFXT	Naval Aircraft Factory N3N-3	R. H. & J. A. Cooper
	G-CFXU	Schleicher Ka-6E	FXU Syndicate
	G-CFXW	Schleicher K8B	The South Wales Gliding Club Ltd
	G-CFXX	P & M Quik R	M. C. Shortman
	G-CFXY	Schleicher ASW-15B	E. L. Youle
	G-CFXZ	P & M Quik R	P. C. Bishop
	G-CFYA	PZL-Bielsko SZD-50-3 Puchacz	Cairngorm Gliding Club
	G-CFYB	Rolladen-Schneider LS7	A. T. Macdonald & V. P. Haley
	G-CFYC	Schempp-Hirth Ventus b	G. Smith
	G-CFYD	Aeroprakt A22-L Foxbat	A. P. Fenn
	G-CFYE	Scheibe Zugvogel IIIB	R. Staines
	G-CFYF	Schleicher ASK-21	London Gliding Club Proprietary Ltd
	G-CFYG	Glasflugel Club Libelle 205	FYG Syndicate
	G-CFYH	Rolladen-Schneider LS4-a	G. W. & C. A. Craig
	G-CFYI	Grob G.102 Astir CS	A. C. Arthurs & P. T. Raisbeck
	G-CFYJ	Schempp-Hirth Standard Cirrus	FYJ Syndicate
	G-CFYK	Rolladen-Schneider LS7-WL	R. R. Ward

Reg.	Type	Owner or Operator	Notes
G-CFYL	PZL-Bielsko SZD-50-3 Puchacz	Deeside Gliding Club (Aberdeenshire) Ltd	
G-CFYM	Schempp-Hirth Discus bT	B. F. Laverick-Smith	
G-CFYN	Schempp-Hirth Discus b	N. White & P. R. Foulger	
G-CFYO	P & M Quik R	M. H. Bond	
G-CFYP	FBM & W Silex M/Flyke/Monster	A. J. R. Carver	
G-CFYR	LET L-23 Super Blanik	G-CFYR Group	
G-CFYS	Dynamic WT9 UK	E. M. Middleton	
G-CFYT	Beech 58 Baron	Construcciones Navales Palacio SL/Spain	
G-CFYU	Glaser-Dirks DG-100 Elan	I. M. & C. Shepherd	
G-CFYV	Schleicher ASK-21	The Bristol Gliding Club Proprietary Ltd	
G-CFYW	Rolladen-Schneider LS7	C. Bessant	
G-CFYX	Schempp-Hirth Discus b	Discus FYX Group	
G-CFYY	Schleicher ASK-13	Lasham Gliding Society Ltd	
G-CFYZ	Schleicher ASH-25	171 Syndicate	
G-CFZA	PZL-Bielsko SZD-51-1	Booker Gliding Club Ltd	
G-CFZB	Glasflugel H201B Standard Libelle	J. C. Meyer	
G-CFZD	Jabiru J430	C. J. Judd & A. Macknish	
G-CFZF	PZL-Bielsko SZD-51-1 Junior	Devon and Somerset Gliding Club Ltd	
G-CFZH	Schempp-Hirth Ventus c	FZH Group	
G-CFZI	Savannah Jabiru (5)	J. T., A. L. & O. D. Lewis	
G-CFZJ	VS.388 Seafire F.46	C. T. Charleston	
G-CFZK	Schempp-Hirth Standard Cirrus	S. Lucas & R. Burgoyne	
G-CFZL	Schleicher ASW-20 CL	A. L. & R. M. Housden	
G-CFZM	Avro RJ85	Triangle Regional Aircraft Leasing Ltd	
G-CFZO	Schempp-Hirth Nimbus 3	954 Syndicate	
G-CFZP	PZL-Bielsko SZD-51-1 Junior	Portsmouth Naval Gliding Centre	
G-CFZR	Schleicher Ka 6CR	J. Vickers	
G-CFZS	Cameron A-140 balloon	Eastern Safaris Europe Ltd	
G-CFZT	Ace Magic Laser	P. L. Wilkinson	
G-CFZV	Rolladen-Schneider LS7	W. M. Davies	
G-CFZW	Glaser-Dirks DG-300 Club Elan	D. O'Flanagan & G. Stilgoe	
G-CFZX	Rotorsport UK MTO Sport	Gyro-I Ltd	
G-CFZZ	LET L-33 Solo	The Andreas L33 Group	
G-CGAA	Flylight Dragonfly	G. Adkins	
G-CGAB	AB Sportine LAK-12 Lietuva	W. T. Emery	
G-CGAC	P & M Quik GT450	A. Gillett	
G-CGAD	Rolladen-Schneider LS3	P. B. Turner	
G-CGAF	Schleicher ASK-21	Lasham Gliding Society Ltd	
G-CGAG	Scleicher ASK-21	Stratford on Avon Gliding Club Ltd	
G-CGAH	Schempp-Hirth Standard Cirrus	J. W. Williams	
G-CGAI	Raj Hamsa X'Air Hawk	P. J. Kilshaw	
G-CGAJ	Alpi Pioneer 400	C. Rusalen	
G-CGAK	Acrosport II	P. D. Sibbons	
G-CGAL	P & M Quik R	R. A. Keene	
G-CGAM	Schleicher ASK-21	Oxford University Gliding Club	
G-CGAN	Glasflugel H301 Libelle	S. & C. A. Noujaim	
G-CGAO	DHC.1 Chipmunk 22	P. Jeffery	
G-CGAP	Schempp-Hirth Ventus bT	J. R. Greenwell	
G-CGAR	Rolladen-Schneider LS6-c	A. Warbrick	
G-CGAS	Schempp-Hirth Ventus cT	G. M. J. Monaghan	
G-CGAT	Grob G.102 Astir CS	N. J. Hooper & S. J. Chapman	
G-CGAU	Glasflugel H201B Standard Libelle	G-CGAU Group	
G-CGAV	Scheibe SF-27A Zugvogel V	GAV Syndicate	
G-CGAW	Beech 200 Super King Air	Aerodynamics Ltd	
G-CGAX	PZL-Bielsko SZD-55-1 Promyk	I. D. Macro & P. Gold	
G-CGAZ	P & M Aviation Quik R	E. J. Douglas	
G-CGBA	Schleicher ASK-13	The Burn Gliding Club Ltd	
G-CGBB	Schleicher ASK-21	University of Edinburgh Sports Union	
G-CGBC	Balony Kubicek BB26Z balloon	N. Charbonnier	
G-CGBD	PZL-Bielsko SZD-50-3	The Northumbria Gliding Club Ltd	
G-CGBF	Schleicher ASK-21	London Gliding Club Pty Ltd	
G-CGBG	Rolladen-Schneider LS6-18w	C. Villa	
G-CGBH	Raj Hamsa X'Air Hawk	S. E. McEwen	
G-CGBI	VS.349 Spitfire LF.VB	D. Luck	
G-CGBJ	Grob G.102 Astir CS	Banbury Gliding Club Ltd	
G-CGBK	Grob G.102 Astir CS	Yorkshire Gliding Club (Pty) Ltd	
G-CGBL	Rolladen-Schneider LS7-WL	P. A. Roche	
G-CGBM	Flight Design CTSW	R. J. D. Mellor	
G-CGBN	Schleicher ASK-21	Essex and Suffolk Gliding Club Ltd	
G-CGBO	Rolladen-Schneider LS6	G-CGBO Syndicate	
G-CGBR	Rolladen-Schneider LS6-c	V. L. Brown	
G-CGBS	Glaser-Dirks DG-300 Club Elan	A. Gillanders & M. C. Chalmers	

Notes	Reg.	Type	Owner or Operator
	G-CGBU	Centrair 101A Pegase	D. J. Arblaster & R. M. Rowland
	G-CGBV	Schleicher ASK-21	Wolds Gliding Club Ltd
	G-CGBX	Schleicher ASW-22	D. A. Ashby
	G-CGBY	Rolladen-Schneider LS7	I. Ashdown
	G-CGBZ	Glaser-Dirks DG-500 Elan Trainer	Needwood Forest Gliding Club Ltd
	G-CGCA	Schleicher ASW-19B	Deeside Gliding Club (Aberdeenshire) Ltd
	G-CGCC	PZL-Bielsko SZD-51-1 Junior	Coventry Gliding Club Ltd
	G-CGCD	Schempp-Hirth Standard Cirrus	Cirrus Syndicate
	G-CGCE	Magni M16C Tandem Trainer	A. J. A. Fowler
	G-CGCF	Schleicher ASK-23	Needwood Forest Gliding Club Ltd
	G-CGCH	CZAW Sportcruiser	C. Harrison
	G-CGCK	PZL-Bielsko SZD-50-3 Puchacz	Kent Gliding Club Ltd (G-BTJV)
	G-CGCL	Grob G.102 Astir CS	J. A. Williams
	G-CGCM	Rolladen-Schneider LS6-c	G. R. Glazebrook
	G-CGCN	MCR-01 Club	D. J. Smith
	G-CGCO	Schempp-Hirth Cirrus VTC	T. W. Slater
	G-CGCP	Schleicher Ka-6CR	D. & B. Clarke
	G-CGCR	Schleicher ASW-15B	ASW15B 748 Group
	G-CGCS	Glasflugel Club Libelle 205	D. G. Coats
	G-CGCT	Schempp-Hirth Discus b	P. J. Brown
	G-CGCU	PZL-Bielsko SZD-50-3 Puchacz	Buckminster Gliding Club Ltd
	G-CGCV	Raj Hamsa X'Air Hawk	W. J. Whyte
	G-CGCW	Skyranger Swift 912(1)	C. M. Wilkes
	G-CGCX	Schleicher ASW-15	C. D. Bingham
	G-BGCY	Centrair 101A Pegase	GCY Group
	G-CGDA	Rolladen-Schneider LS3-17	A. R. Fish
	G-CGDB	Schleicher K 8B	The Welland Gliding Club Ltd
	G-CGDC	Rotorsport UK MTO Sport	R. E. Derham & T. R. Kingsley
	G-CGDD	Bolkow Phoebus C	G. C. Kench
	G-CGDE	Schleicher Ka 6CR	K6 Syndicate
	G-CGDF	Schleicher Ka 6BR	H. Marshall & D. Pask
	G-CGDG	Cameron C-80 balloon	Atlantic Balooning BVBA/Belgium
	G-CGDH	Europa XS	Lincolnshire Aviation Ltd
	G-CGDI	EV-97A Eurostar	D. Street
	G-CGDJ	PA-28-161 Warrior II	C. G. D. Jones (G-ETDA)
	G-CGDK	Schleicher K 8B	Vale of Neath Gliding Club
	G-CGDL	P & M Quik R	S. J. Bunce
	G-CGDM	Sonex Sonex	D. Scott
	G-CGDN	Rolladen-Schneider LS3-17	S. J. Pepler
	G-CGDO	Grob G.102 Astir CS	P. Lowe & R. Bostock
	G-CGDR	Schempp-Hirth Discus CS	J. H. C. Friend
	G-CGDS	Schleicher ASW-15B	B. Birk & P. A. Crouch
	G-CGDT	Schleicher ASW-24	Tango 54 Syndicate
	G-CGDV	CSA Sportcruiser	Delta Victor Group
	G-CGDW	CSA Sportcruiser	Onega Ltd
	G-CGDX	Orlican Discus CS	Coventry Gliding Club Ltd
	G-CGDY	Schleicher ASW-15B	Cloud Nine Syndicate
	G-CGDZ	Schleicher ASW-24	J. M. Norman
	G-CGEA	Schleicher Ka 6CR	C. M. Alton & P. R. E. Welby-Everard
	G-CGEB	Grob G.102 Astir CS77	T. R. Dews
	G-CGEC	Flight Design CTLS	S. Munday
	G-CGEE	Glasflugel H201B Standard Libelle	C. Metcalfe & J. Kelsey
	G-CGEF	La Mouette Hytrike Srs A	A. Lucchesi & G. Thevenot
	G-CGEG	Schleicher K 8B	Darlton Gliding Club Ltd
	G-CGEH	Schleicher ASW-15B	P. Nayeri
	G-CGEI	Cessna 550 Citation Bravo	S. W. Bond
	G-CGEJ	Alpi Pioneer 200-M	P. S. & N. Bewley
	G-CGEL	PZL-Bielsko SZD-50-3	The Northumbria Gliding Club Ltd
	G-CGEM	Schleicher Ka 6CR	GEM Syndicate
	G-CGEN	RAF 2000	D. E. Worley
	G-CGEO	CSA Sportcruiser	The Jester Flying Group
	G-CGEP	Schempp-Hirth Standard Cirrus	D. J. Bundock
	G-CGER	Cameron Z-105 balloon	CV Fly Communication SRL/Italy
	G-CGEU	Flylight Dragonfly	D. Newbrook
	G-CGEV	Heliopolis Gomhouria Mk.6	A. Brier
	G-CGEW	Rotorsport UK MTO Sport	G. W. Libby & C. W. Rose
	G-CGEX	P & M Quik GT450	D. L. Clark
	G-CGEY	Julian CD Dingbat	G. Carr
	G-CGEZ	Raj Hamsa X'Air Hawk	M. Howes & B. J. Ellis
	G-CGFB	BB03 Trya/BB103	B. J. Fallows
	G-CGFG	Cessna 152	Cristal Air Ltd
	G-CGFH	Cessna T182T Turbo Skylane	H. Riffkin
	G-CGFI	MS.885 Super Rallye	AC Civil Engineering Ltd

Reg.	Type	Owner or Operator	Notes
G-CGFJ	Cessna 172M	T. I. Murtough	
G-CGFK	Ace Magic Laser	C. J. Boseley	
G-CGFN	Cameron C-60 balloon	R. S. Mohr	
G-CGFO	Ultramagic H-42 balloon	J. A. W. Dyer	
G-CGFP	Pietenpol Aircamper	D. Hetherington	
G-CGFR	Lindstrand LBL HS-120 Airship	Lindstrand Hot Air Balloons Ltd	
G-CGFS	Nanchang CJ-6A	L. C. Myall	
G-CGFU	Schempp-Hirth Mini-Nimbus C	Mini Nimbus Syndicate	
G-CGFY	Lindstrand LBL-105A balloon	G. J. Grimes	
G-CGFZ	Thruster T.600N 450	K. J. Crompton	
G-CGGD	Eurocopter AS365N2 Dauphin 2	Multiflight Ltd	
G-CGGE	Cameron Z-275 balloon	Wickers World Ltd	
G-CGGF	Robinson R44 II	Sky Helicopteros SL	
G-CGGG	Robinson R44	K. Hayes (G-SJDI)	
G-CGGH	Sky 220-24 balloon	Zebedee Balloon Service Ltd	
G-CGGJ	Schweizer 269C-1	Patriot Aviation Ltd	
G-CGGK	Westland Wasp HAS Mk.1	The Real Aeroplane Co.Ltd	
G-CGGL	Rotorsport UK MTOSport	A. D. Lysser	
G-CGGM	EV-97 TeamEurostar UK	GM Group	
G-CGGN	Dassault Falcon 7X	TAG Aviation (UK) Ltd	
G-CGGO	Robin DR.400-180 Regent	AWE Holdings Ltd	
G-CGGP	Autogyro MTOSport	N. Cowley	
G-CGGS	Robinson R44 II	Oakfield Investments Ltd	
G-CGGT	P & M Quik GT450	M. Earp	
G-CGGV	Rotorsport UK MTO Sport	S. Morris	
G-CGGW	Rotorsport UK MTO Sport	P. Adams	
G-CGGX	TEAM Minimax 91	P. D. Parry	
G-CGGY	UltraMagic N-425 balloon	Anglian Countryside Balloons Ltd	
G-CGGZ	UltraMagic S-90 balloon	P. Lawman	
G-CGHA	P & M Quik R	K. M. Hughes	
G-CGHB	NAMC CJ-6A	M. J. Harvey	
G-CGHC	Pioneer 300 Hawk	M. Bettaglio	
G-CGHD	Cessna 172S	Steptoe & Son Properties Ltd	
G-CGHE	Flight Design CTSW	P & M Aviation Ltd	
G-CGHG	P & M Quik GT450	J. & K. D. McAlpine	
G-CGHH	P & M Quik R	C. Pyle & N. Richardson	
G-CGHJ	Staaken Z-21A Flitzer	D. J. Ashley	
G-CGHK	Alpi Pioneer 300 Hawk	D. J. Ashley	
G-CGHL	Rotorsport UK MTOSport	C. S. Mackenzie	
G-CGHM	PA-28 Cherokee 140	North Wales Air Academy Ltd	
G-CGHN	Aeros Discus/Alize	R. Simpson & N. Sutton	
G-CGHO	P & M Quik R	N. Creveau	
G-CGHR	Magic Laser	N. P. Power	
G-CGHS	DG Flugzeugbau DG-808C	M. A. V. Gatehouse	
G-CGHT	Dyn'Aero MCR-01 Banbi	J. F. McAulay (G-POOP)	
G-CGHU	Hawker Hunter T.Mk.8C	Hawker Hunter Aviation Ltd	
G-CGHV	Raj Hamsa X'Air Hawk	G. A. J. Salter	
G-CGHW	Czech Sport Aircraft Sportcruiser	Sport Cruiser 290 Group	
G-CGHZ	P & M Quik R	J. Rockey	
G-CGIA	Paramania Action/Bailey Quattro 175	A. E. C. Phillips	
G-CGIB	Magic Cyclone	S. J. Oxnard	
G-CGIC	Rotorsport MTO Sport	J. Harmon & K. Snell	
G-CGID	PA-31-350 Navajo Chieftain	T. Michaels	
G-CGIE	Flylight Dragonfly	Flylight Airsports Ltd	
G-CGIF	Flylight Dragonfly	G. Nicholas	
G-CGIG	Lindstrand LBL-90A balloon	Cameron Flights Southern Ltd	
G-CGIH	Cameron C-90 balloon	W. Bracken	
G-CGIJ	Agusta Westland AW139	HM Coastguard	
G-CGIK	Isaacs Spitfire	A. J. Harpley	
G-CGIL	CZAW Sportcruiser	G-CGIL Group	
G-CGIM	Ace Aviation Magic Laser	C. Royle	
G-CGIN	Paramania Action GT/Bailey Quattro 175	A. E. C. Phillips	
G-CGIO	Medway SLA100 Executive	K. J. Draper	
G-CGIP	CZAW Sportcruiser	R. Vincent	
G-CGIR	Remos GX	L. R. Marks & J. A. Pereira	
G-CGIS	Cameron Parachutist 110 SS balloon	K. Gruenauer (G-RIPS)	
G-CGIU	AX1 balloon	M. W. A. Shemilt	
G-CGIV	Kolb Firefly	W. A. Emmerson	
G-CGIW	Sikorsky S-76C-2	Bristow Helicopters (International) Ltd	
G-CGIX	Rotorsport UK MTO Sport	J. K. Houldcroft	
G-CGIY	Piper J3C-65	R. C. Cummings	
G-CGIZ	Flight Design CTSW	J. Hilton	
G-CGJB	Schempp-Hirth Duo Discus T	G. J. Basey	

Notes	Reg.	Type	Owner or Operator
	G-CGJC	Rotorsport UK MTO Sport	J. C. Collingwood
	G-CGJD	Rotorsport UK Calidus	C. Collins
	G-CGJE	VS.361 Spitfire IX	Historic Flight Ltd
	G-CGJF	Fokker E.111 Replica	I. Brewster
	G-CGJH	P & M Quik GT450	B. Montila
	G-CGJI	Best Off Skyranger 912S(1)	Flylight Airsports Ltd
	G-CGJJ	P & M Quik R	A. J. Hubbard
	G-CGJL	CZAW Sportcruiser	G-CGJL Flying Group
	G-CGJM	Skyranger Swift 912S(1)	J. P. Metcalfe
	G-CGJN	Van's RV-7	E. K. Coventry
	G-CGJO	P & M Quik R	D. E. Lord
	G-CGJP	Van's RV-10	K. D. Taylor
	G-CGJS	CZAW Sportcruiser	J. M. Tiley
	G-CGJT	CZAW Sportcruiser	D. F. Toller
	G-CGJV	Lindstrand LBL Motorbike SS balloon	Lindstrand Hot Air Balloons Ltd
	G-CGJW	RAF 2000 GTX-SE	J. J. Wollen
	G-CGJX	SA.341B Gazelle AH Mk.1	B. W. Stuart
	G-CGJY	SA.341D Gazelle HT Mk.3	P. J. Whitaker
	G-CGJZ	SA.341D Gazelle HT Mk.3	A. W. J. Stuart
	G-CGKA	Grob G115E Tutor	Babcock Aerospace Ltd
	G-CGKB	Grob G115E Tutor	Babcock Aerospace Ltd
	G-CGKC	Grob G115E Tutor	Babcock Aerospace Ltd
	G-CGKD	Grob G115E Tutor	Babcock Aerospace Ltd
	G-CGKE	Grob G115E Tutor	Babcock Aerospace Ltd
	G-CGKF	Grob G115E Tutor	Babcock Aerospace Ltd
	G-CGKG	Grob G115E Tutor	Babcock Aerospace Ltd
	G-CGKH	Grob G115E Tutor	Babcock Aerospace Ltd
	G-CGKI	Grob G115E Tutor	Babcock Aerospace Ltd
	G-CGKJ	Grob G115E Tutor	Babcock Aerospace Ltd
	G-CGKK	Grob G115E Tutor	Babcock Aerospace Ltd
	G-CGKL	Grob G115E Tutor	Babcock Aerospace Ltd
	G-CGKM	Grob G115E Tutor	Babcock Aerospace Ltd
	G-CGKN	Grob G115E Tutor	Babcock Aerospace Ltd
	G-CGKO	Grob G115E Tutor	Babcock Aerospace Ltd
	G-CGKP	Grob G115E Tutor	Babcock Aerospace Ltd
	G-CGKR	Grob G115E Tutor	Babcock Aerospace Ltd
	G-CGKS	Grob G115E Tutor	Babcock Aerospace Ltd
	G-CGKT	Grob G115E Tutor	Babcock Aerospace Ltd
	G-CGKU	Grob G115E Tutor	Babcock Aerospace Ltd
	G-CGKV	Grob G115E Tutor	Babcock Aerospace Ltd
	G-CGKW	Grob G115E Tutor	Babcock Aerospace Ltd
	G-CGKX	Grob G115E Tutor	Babcock Aerospace Ltd
	G-CGKY	Cessna 182T	T. A. E. Dobell
	G-CGKZ	Best Off Sky Ranger Swift 912S(1)	A. Worthington
	G-CGLB	Airdrome Dream Classic	S. J. Ball
	G-CGLC	Czech Sport Aircraft Sportcruiser	P. Taylor
	G-CGLE	Flylight Dragonfly	B. Skelding
	G-CGLF	Magni M-16C Tandem Trainer	J. S. Walton
	G-CGLG	P & M Quik GT450	P. H. Evans
	G-CGLI	Alpi Pioneer 200M	B. A. Lyford
	G-CGLJ	TL 2000UK Sting Carbon	L. A. James
	G-CGLK	Magni M-16C Tandem Trainer	R. M. Savage
	G-CGLL	Rotorsport UK MTO Sport	P. J. Troy-Davies
	G-CGLM	Rotorsport UK MTO Sport	J. Owen
	G-CGLN	Jabiru J430	J. R. Frohnsdorff & C. H. K. Hood
	G-CGLO	P & M Quik R	A. P. Watkins
	G-CGLP	CZAW Sportcruiser	P. S. Tanner
	G-CGLR	Czech Sport Aircraft Sportcruiser	G-CGLR Group
	G-CGLT	Czech Sport Aircraft Sportcruiser	P. J. V. Dibble
	G-CGLW	P & M Pegasus Quik	S. Dixon
	G-CGLY	Rotorsport UK Calidus	R. J. Steel
	G-CGLZ	TL 2000UK Sting Carbon	T. Booth
	G-CGMA	Ace Magic Laser	J. N. Hanson
	G-CGMB	Embraer EMB-135ER	Eastern Airways
	G-CGMC	Embraer EMB-135ER	Eastern Airways
	G-CGMD	Rotorsport UK Calidus	D.W. Leeming
	G-CGME	Ellipse Fuji/Pulma 2000	I. M. Vass
	G-CGMF	Cessna 560XL Citation XLS	Multiflight Charter Services LLP
	G-CGMG	Van's RV-9	D. J. Bone
	G-CGMH	Jodel D150A Mascaret	G. S. Jackson
	G-CGMI	P & M Quik GT450	W. G. Reynolds
	G-CGMJ	P & M Quik R	C. D. Waldron
	G-CGMK	Best Off Sky Ranger 582(1)	G. J. Burley

Reg.	Type	Owner or Operator	Notes
G-CGML	TL 2000UK Sting Carbon	G. T. Leedham	
G-CGMM	CZAW Sportcruiser	TAF and Co	
G-CGMN	Best Off Sky Ranger Swift 912S	T. C. Butterworth	
G-CGMO	Ace Magic Laser	G. J. Latham	
G-CGMP	CZAW Sportcruiser	M. Payne	
G-CGMR	Colt Bibendum-110 balloon	Mobberley Balloon Collection (G-GRIP)	
G-CGMS	Sutton/Aquilair KID 1	K. A. Sutton	
G-CGMU	Sikorsky S-92A	HM Coastguard	
G-CGMV	Roko Aero NG 4HD	Eshott NG4 Group	
G-CGMW	Alpi Pioneer 200M	M. S. McCrudden	
G-CGMX	Cameron TR-70 balloon	Cameron Balloons Ltd	
G-CGMZ	P & M Quik R	M. W. Houghton	
G-CGNA	Cameron Super FMG-100 balloon	Cameron Balloons Ltd	
G-CGNC	Rotorsport UK MTO Sport	Comedy South West Ltd	
G-CGND	Robinson R44 II	Ajax Machinery	
G-CGNE	Robinson R44 II	Heli Air Ltd	
G-CGNG	CZAW Sportcruiser	T. Dounias	
G-CGNH	Escapade Jabiru(1)	A. H. Paul	
G-CGNI	Ikarus C42 FB80	A. G. Cummings	
G-CGNJ	Cameron Z-105 balloon	Loughborough Students Union Hot Air Balloon Club	
G-CGNK	P & M Quik GT450	G. W. Hillidge	
G-CGNL	Cameron Z-90 balloon	A. M. Holly	
G-CGNM	Magni M-16C Tandem Trainer	Evolo Ltd	
G-CGNN	Montgomerie-Bensen B.8MR	P. M. Ryder	
G-CGNO	P & M Quik GT450	Airways Airsports Ltd	
G-CGNP	Embraer EMB-500 Phenom 100	Flairjet Ltd	
G-CGNR	Van's RV-6	N. Rawlinson	
G-CGNS	Sky 65-24 balloon	R. L. Bovell	
G-CGNU	Avro RJ100	Asian Express Airline Ltd	
G-CGNV	Reality Escapade	M. J. Whatley	
G-CGNW	Scheibe SF-25C Falke	The Royal Air Force Gliding and Soaring Association	
G-CGNX	Rotorsport UK MTO Sport	L. McCallum	
G-CGNY	Cessna 340A	P. W. J. Sharpe-Brash	
G-CGNZ	Europa XS	C. D. Meek	
G-CGOA	Cessna 550 Citation II	Xclusive Jet Charter Ltd (G-JMDW)	
G-CGOB	P & M Quik R	P & M Aviation Ltd	
G-CGOC	Sikorsky S-92A	HM Coastguard	
G-CGOD	Cameron N-77 balloon	G. P. Lane	
G-CGOG	Evektor EV-97A Eurostar	J. S. Holden	
G-CGOH	Cameron C-80 balloon	Spirit Balloons Ltd	
G-CGOI	Stewart S-51 Mustang (413926 E2-S)	K. E. Armstrong	
G-CGOJ	Jodel D.11	J. A. Macleod	
G-CGOK	Ace Magic Cyclone	V. Grayson	
G-CGOL	Jabiru J430	J. V. Sanders	
G-CGOM	Flight Design MC	P and M Aviation Ltd	
G-CGOO	Sorrell SNS-8 Hyperlight	W. F. Hayward	
G-CGOP	Sikorsky S-76C	Bristow Helicopters Ltd	
G-CGOR	Jodel D.18	R. D. Cook	
G-CGOS	PA-28-161 Warrior III	S. H. B. Smith	
G-CGOT	Rotorsport UK Calidus	P. Slater	
G-CGOU	Sikorsky S-76C	Bristow Helicopters Ltd	
G-CGOV	Raj Hamsa X'Air Falcon 582(2)	N. D. Brown	
G-CGOW	Cameron Z-77 balloon	J. F. Till	
G-CGOX	Raj Hamsa X'Air Hawk	Oscar Xray Group	
G-CGOZ	Cameron GB-1000 free gas balloon	Cameron Balloons Ltd	
G-CGPA	Ace Magic Cyclone	A. Williams	
G-CGPB	Magni M-24C	D. Beevers	
G-CGPC	P & M Pegasus Quik	A. C. Barnes & D. W. Watson	
G-CGPD	Ultramagic S-90 balloon	S. J. Farrant	
G-CGPE	P & M Quik GT450	E. H. Gatehouse	
G-CGPF	Flylight Dragonfly	K. T. Vinning	
G-CGPG	Rotosport UK MTO Sport	H. A. Batchelor	
G-CGPH	Ultramagic S-50 balloon	The Packhouse Ltd	
G-CGPI	Eurocopter EC135 T2+	Bond Air Services Ltd (G-TAGG)	
G-CGPJ	Robin DR.400-140	W. H. Cole & P. Dass	
G-CGPK	Rotorsport UK MT-03	Ellis Flying Group (G-RIFS)	
G-CGPL	Sonex Sonex	P. C. Askew	
G-CGPN	SOCATA MS.880B Rallye Club	J. Fingleton	
G-CGPO	TL2000UK Sting Carbon	G. A. Squires	
G-CGPR	Czech Sport Aircraft Pipersport	J. T. Langford	
G-CGPS	EV-97 Eurostar SL	P. R. Jenson & R. A. Morris	

Notes	Reg.	Type	Owner or Operator
	G-CGPV	Cameron C-80 balloon	D. G. Such & M. Tomlin
	G-CGPW	Raj Hamsa X'Air Hawk	C. Parkinson
	G-CGPX	Zenair CH.601XL Zodiac	A. James
	G-CGPY	Boeing A75L 300 Stearman	M. P. Dentith
	G-CGPZ	Rans S-4 Coyote	C. Saunders
	G-CGRB	Flight Design CTLS	I. R. Jones
	G-CGRC	P & M Quik R	R. J. Cook
	G-CGRD	Cirrus SR22	Craigaird Property Trading Ltd
	G-CGRE	Cessna F.172H	Parachuting Aircraft Ltd
	G-CGRF	Lindstrand LBL-140A balloon	Lindstrand Hot Air Balloons Ltd
	G-CGRJ	Carnet Paramotor	M. Carnet
	G-CGRL	Robinson R44	A. Williamson
	G-CGRM	VS.329 Spitfire Mk.IIA	J. C. Radford
	G-CGRN	Pazmany PL-4A	G. Hudson
	G-CGRO	Robin DR.400/140B	Exeter Aviation Ltd
	G-CGRP	Pitts P12	R. F. Warner
	G-CGRR	P & M Quik	A. W. Buchan
	G-CGRS	P & M Quik	J. Crosby
	G-CGRU	Sikorsky S-76C	Bristow Helicopters Ltd
	G-CGRV	DG Flugzeugbau DG-1000M	BR Aviation Ltd
	G-CGRW	P & M Quik	W. B. Russell
	G-CGRX	Cessna F.172N	Iscavia Ltd
	G-CGRY	Magni M-24C	K. Herbert
	G-CGRZ	Magni M-24C	J. M. Foster
	G-CGSA	Flylight Dragonfly	G. Sykes
	G-CGSB	Cessna 525A Citationjet CJ2	Sol Aviation Companhia de Aviaco Lda/Portugal
	G-CGSC	Quad City Challenger II	L. Gregory
	G-CGSD	Magni M-16C	The Gyrocopter Company UK Ltd
	G-CGSE	Embraer EMB-135BJ Legacy 650	GE Capital Corporation (Leasing) Ltd
	G-CGSG	Cessna 421C	J. R. Shannon
	G-CGSH	Evektor EV-97 TeamEurostar UK	D. B. Medland
	G-CGSI	Zenair CH.601HDS Zodiac	E. McHugh
	G-CGSJ	Bombardier BD700-1A10 Global Express	Abbeville Holdings Ltd
	G-CGSO	P & M Quik GT450	Light Vending Ltd
	G-CGSP	Cessna 152	C. M. de CamposCosta Cabral
	G-CGSU	Cassutt Racer IIIM	D. J. Howell
	G-CGSW	Flylight Motorfloater	M. P. Wimsey
	G-CGSX	Aeroprakt A22-L Foxbat	P. J. Trimble
	G-CGSY	Stemme S6-RT	D. B. Smith
	G-CGSZ	Schempp-Hirth Ventus 2CM	D. B. Smith
	G-CGTA	Taylorcraft BC-12-65	D. P. Busby
	G-CGTB	Taylorcraft BC-12D	D. P. & D. S. Busby
	G-CGTC	BN-2T-4S Islander	Britten-Norman Aircraft Ltd
	G-CGTD	EV-97 TeamEurostar UK	R. J. Butler
	G-CGTE	Cherry BX-2	D.Roberts
	G-CGTF	AutoGyro MT-03	N. R. Osborne
	G-CGTG	Skyranger 912S(1)	B. A. McMahon
	G-CGTK	Magni M-24C	S. Brogden
	G-CGTL	Alpi Pioneer 300	M. S. Ashby
	G-CGTM	Cessna 172S	Skytrek Air Services
	G-CGTR	Best Off Sky Ranger Nynja 912S(1)	M. Jenvey
	G-CGTS	Cameron A-140 balloon	A. A. Brown
	G-CGTT	EV-97 Eurostar SL	D. L. Walker
	G-CGTU	P & M Quik GT450	I. G. R. Christie
	G-CGTV	MXP-740 Savannah VG Jabiru(1)	B. L. Cook & P. Etherington
	G-CGTW	Flylight MotorFloater	S. J. Varden
	G-CGTX	CASA 1-131E Jungmann Srs 2000	G. Hunter & T. A. S. Rayner
	G-CGTY	Cameron Z-250 balloon	The Cotswold Balloon Co.Ltd
	G-CGTZ	Reality Escapade Kid	E. O. Otun
	G-CGUD	Lindstrand LBL-77A balloon	I. J. Sharpe
	G-CGUE	Aroprakt A-22-L Foxbat	A. T. Hayward
	G-CGUG	P & M Quik R	J. D. Lawrance
	G-CGUI	Clutton FRED Srs.II	I. Pearson
	G-CGUK	VS.300 Spitfire 1A (X4650)	Comanche Warbirds Ltd
	G-CGUL	Gulfstream V-SP	Gama Aviation Ltd
	G-CGUN	Alpha R2160	Quo Vadis UK Ltd
	G-CGUO	DH.83C Fox Moth	R. I. Souch
	G-CGUP	P & M Quik GT450	D. J. Allen
	G-CGUR	P & M QuikR	S. D. Couch
	G-CGUS	Embraer ERJ-145MP	ECC Leasing Co.Ltd
	G-CGUT	Balloon Works Firefly 9B-15	J. N. Uhrmann
	G-CGUU	Sky Ranger Nynja 912S(1)	J. A. Hunt
	G-CGUV	Balloon Works Firefly 9B-15	J. N. Uhrmann

Reg.	Type	Owner or Operator	Notes
G-CGUW	Tecnam P2002-EA Sierra	D. J. Burton	
G-CGUY	Rotorsport UK Calidus	R. F. Harrison	
G-CGUZ	Cessna 525A CitationJet CJ2	Gama Aviation Ltd	
G-CGVA	Aeroprakt A-22-L Foxbat	T. R. C. Griffin	
G-CGVC	PA-28-181 Archer III	Western Air (Thruxton) Ltd	
G-CGVD	Van's RV-12	RV12 Flying Group	
G-CGVE	Raj Hamsa X'Air Hawk	P. Millership	
G-CGVG	Flight Design CTSW	J. T. James	
G-CGVH	Flylight Motorfloater	P. F. Mayes	
G-CGVI	Tanarg/Bionix 15 912S(1)	Flylight Airsports Ltd	
G-CGVJ	Europa XS	D. Glowa	
G-CGVK	Autogyro UK Calidus	B & H Mouldings Ltd	
G-CGVM	Lindstrand LBL-35A Cloudhopper balloon	Airship and Balloon Co.Ltd	
G-CGVO	Alpi Pioneer 400	F. A. Cavaciuti	
G-CGVP	EV-97 Eurstar	G. R. Pritchard	
G-CGVR	Flight Design CTLS	P & M Aviation Ltd	
G-CGVS	Raj Hamsa X'Air Hawk	J. Anderson	
G-CGVT	EV-97 TeamEurostar UK	Mainair Microlight School Ltd	
G-CGVU	Avro RJ85	Trident Turboprop (Dublin) Ltd	
G-CGVV	Cameron Z-90 Balloon	Cameron Balloons Ltd	
G-CGVX	Europa	M. P. Sambrook	
G-CGVY	Cameron Z-77 balloon	M. P. Hill	
G-CGVZ	Zenair CH.601XL Zodiac	K. A. Dilks	
G-CGWA	Ikarus C42 FB80 Bravo	M. A. Bull	
G-CGWB	Agusta AW139	CHC Scotia Ltd/HM Coastguard	
G-CGWC	Ultramagic H-31 balloon	G. Everett	
G-CGWD	Robinson R-44	J. M. Henderson	
G-CGWE	EV-97A Eurostar	W. S. Long	
G-CGWF	Van's RV-7	M. S. Hill	
G-CGWG	Van's RV-7	G. Waters	
G-CGWH	CZAW Sportcruiser	P. J. F. Spedding	
G-CGWI	Supermarine Aircraft Spitfire Mk.26	Bertha Property LLP	
G-CGWK	Ikarus C42 FB80	GS Aviation (Europe) Ltd	
G-CGWL	Sky Ranger Nynja 912S(1)	Exodus Airsports Ltd	
G-CGWM	Dragonfly Lite	P. A. Gardner	
G-CGWN	Dragonfly Lite	P. M. Finlay	
G-CGWO	Tecnam P2002-JF Sierra	Shropshire Aero Club Ltd	
G-CGWP	Aeroprakt A22-L Foxbat	P. K. Goff	
G-CGWR	Nord NC.856A Norvigie	R. B. McLain	
G-CGWS	Raj Hamsa X'Air Hawk	J. A. T. Wheatley	
G-CGWT	Best Off Sky Ranger Swift 912(1)	N. A. & P. A. Allwood	
G-CGWU	UltraMagic S-90 balloon	K. Graham	
G-CGWV	Embraer EMB-145MP	Eastern Airways	
G-CGWX	Cameron C-90 balloon	J. D. A. Shields	
G-CGWZ	P & M QuikR	N. D. Leak	
G-CGXB	Glasair Super IIS RG	P. J. Brion	
G-CGXC	Flylight Dragonfly	W. Lofts	
G-CGXE	P & M Quik GT450	A, G. Hughes	
G-CGXF	North Wing Stratus/Skycycle	G. W. Cameron	
G-CGXG	Yakovlev Yak-3M	Chameleon Technologies Ltd	
G-CGXI	Ikarus C42 FB80	G. V. Aggett	
G-CGXJ	Schweizer 269C-1	Milford Aviation	
G-CGXL	Robin DR.400/180	SPH Groundworks Ltd (G-GLKE)	
G-CGXN	American Legend Cub	Beaver (UK) Ltd	
G-CGXO	Lindstrand LBL-105A balloon	Aerosaurus Balloons Ltd	
G-CGXP	Grob G.109B	Gransden Grob XP	
G-CGXR	Van's RV-9A	Solway Flyers 2010 Ltd	
G-CGXS	Avro RJ-85	Trident Aviation Leasing Services (Jersey) Ltd (G-JAYV)	
G-CGXT	Kowacs Midgie	J. P. Kovacs	
G-CGXV	P & M Quik R	D. W. Allen	
G-CGXW	Grob G.109B	I. B. Kennedy	
G-CGXX	ICP MXP-740 Savannah HKS(1)	P. Hayward	
G-CGXY	Flylight Dragonfly	A. I. Lea	
G-CGXZ	AutoGyro MTO Sport	G-CGXZ Flying Group	
G-CGYA	Stoddard-Hamilton Glasair III	Aerocars Ltd	
G-CGYB	EV-97 TeamEurostar UK	J. Waite	
G-CGYC	Aeropro Eurofox 912(S)	D. C. Fairbrass	
G-CGYD	Fairey Firefly TT.1	Propshop Ltd	
G-CGYE	Schroeder Fire Balloons G balloon	M. Cutraro	
G-CGYF	Gloster Gamecock II	Retro Track & Air (UK) Ltd	
G-CGYG	Aeropro Eurofox 912(S)	Highland Gliding Club Ltd	
G-CGYH	Magni M-24C	J. L. Ward	

Notes	Reg.	Type	Owner or Operator
	G-CGYI	Van's RV-12	R. A. Smith
	G-CGYJ	VS.361 Spitfire HF.IX	K. M. Perkins
	G-CGYM	AT-16 Harvard IIB	Reflight Airworks Ltd
	G-CGYO	Van's RV-6A	F. D. Cowan
	G-CGYP	Best Off Sky Ranger 912(2)	Yankee Papa Group
	G-CGYR	Avro RJ-85	Trident Turboprop (Dublin) Ltd
	G-CGYS	Avro RJ-85	Trident Aviation Leasing Services (Jersey) Ltd
	G-CGYT	Flylight Dragonfly	G-CGYT Syndicate
	G-CGYU	Avro RJ-85	Trident Turboprop (Dublin) Ltd
	G-CGYV	Avro RJ-85	Trident Turboprop (Dublin) Ltd
	G-CGYW	Sikorsky S-92A	Bristow Helicopters Ltd
	G-CGYY	MXP-740 Savannah VG Jabiru(1)	Carlisle Skyrangers
	G-CGYZ	P & M Quik GT450	M. Florence
	G-CGZA	Kolb Twinstar Mk.3 Xtra	A. Wilson
	G-CGZB	Avro RJ-85	Trident Aviation Leasing Services (Jersey) Ltd
	G-CGZD	Eurocopter EC135 P2	Bond Air Services Ltd
	G-CGZE	Rotorsport UK MTO Sport	The Gyrocopter Company UK Ltd
	G-CGZF	EV-97 TeamEurostar UK	24/7 Rescue and Recovery (Membury) Ltd
	G-CGZG	AutoGyro MTO Sport	D. C. Dewey
	G-CGZI	SOCATA TB-21 Trinidad TC	K. B. Hallam
	G-CGZJ	ITV Dakota XL	C. J. Lines
	G-CGZL	Flylight Motor Floater Fox 16T	Flylight Airsports Ltd
	G-CGZM	AutoGyro MTO Sport	A. K. & J. A. Hughes
	G-CGZN	Dudek Synthesis 31/Nirvana Carbon	M. J. Parker
	G-CGZO	Avro RJ-85	Trident Aviation Leasing Services (Jersey) Ltd
	G-CGZP	Curtiss P-40F Kittyhawk (41-19841 X-17)	The Fighter Collection
	G-CGZR	Cameron Z-350 balloon	Ballooning Network Ltd
	G-CGZT	Aeroprakt A22-L Foxbat	R. J. Davey
	G-CGZU	VS.361 Spitfire F.IXc	M. A. Bennett
	G-CGZV	Europa XS	R. W. Collings
	G-CGZW	Scheibe SF-25C Falke	Glidesport UK Ltd
	G-CGZY	EV-97 TeamEurostar UK	Exodus Airsports Ltd
	G-CGZZ	Kubicek BB22E balloon	A. M. Holly
	G-CHAB	Schleicher Ka 6CR	W. J. Hunter
	G-CHAC	PZL-Bielsko SZD-50-3 Puchacz	Peterborough and Spalding Gliding Club Ltd
	G-CHAD	Aeroprakt A.22 Foxbat	DJB Foxbat
	G-CHAE	Glasflugel H205 Club Libelle	J. C. Cavill & R. S. Hanslip
	G-CHAF	PZL-Bielsko SZD-50-3 Puchacz	Seahawk Gliding Club
	G-CHAG	Guimbal Cabri G2	European Helicopter Importers Ltd
	G-CHAH	Shaw Europa	T. Higgins
	G-CHAI	Bombardier CL.601-3R	Hangar 8 Management Ltd (G-FBFI)
	G-CHAJ	Cirrus SR22	S. R. Kay
	G-CHAK	Boeing 737-505	European Aviation Ltd
	G-CHAM	Cameron 90 Pot SS balloon	Pendle Balloon Company
	G-CHAN	Robinson R22 Beta	Aztec Aviators Ltd
	G-CHAO	Rolladen-Schneider LS6-b	A. R. J. Hughes
	G-CHAP	Robinson R44	Brierley Lifting Tackle Co Ltd
	G-CHAR	Grob G.109B	The Royal Air Force Gliding and Soaring Association
	G-CHAS	PA-28-181 Archer II	G-CHAS Flying Group
	G-CHAU	Cameron C-80 balloon	G. G. Cannon & P. Haworth
	G-CHAW	Replica Fokker EIII	S. W. C. Duckworth
	G-CHAX	Schempp-Hirth Standard Cirrus	C. Keating & R. Jarvis
	G-CHAY	Rolladen-Schneider LS7	N. J. Leaton
	G-CHBA	Rolladen-Schneider LS7	LS7 729 Group
	G-CHBB	Schleicher ASW-24	London Gliding Club Propietary Ltd
	G-CHBC	Rolladen-Schneider LS6-c	A. Crowden
	G-CHBD	Glaser-Dirks DG-200	Bravo Delta Group
	G-CHBE	Glaser-Dirks DG-300 Club Elan	DG 356 Group
	G-CHBF	Schempp-Hirth Nimbus 2C	J. A. Clark
	G-CHBG	Schleicher ASW-24	Imperial College of Science, Technology and Medicine
	G-CHBH	Grob G.103C Twin III Acro	Imperial College of Science, Technology and Medicine
	G-CHBJ	Westland Gazelle AH.Mk.1	MW Helicopters Ltd
	G-CHBK	Grob G.103 Twin Astir II	S. Naylor
	G-CHBL	Grob G.102 Astir CS77	C. Morris
	G-CHBM	Grob G.102 Astir CS77	P. W. Brown
	G-CHBN	Westland Gazelle AH Mk.1	MW Helicopters Ltd
	G-CHBO	Schleicher Ka 6CR	C. J. Sturdy
	G-CHBP	Glaser-Dirks DG-500	A. Taverna
	G-CHBR	Westland Gazelle AH Mk.1	MW Helicopters Ltd

Reg.	Type	Owner or Operator	Notes
G-CHBS	PZL-Bielsko SZD-41A Jantar Standard 1	P. J. Chaisty & D. Hendry	
G-CHBT	Grob G.102 Astir CS Jeans	Astir Syndicate	
G-CHBU	Centrair ASW-20F	M. Staljan, S. Brogger & C. Behrendt	
G-CHBV	Schempp-Hirth Nimbus 2B	G. J. Evison, J. Lynas & R. Strarup	
G-CHBW	Jurca Spitfire	T. A. Major	
G-CHBX	Lindstrand LBL-77A balloon	Lindstrand Hot Air Balloons Ltd	
G-CHBY	Agusta AW.139	Bristow Helicopters Ltd	
G-CHBZ	TL2000UK Sting Carbon	C. R. Ashley	
G-CHCF	AS.332L-2 Super Puma	CHC Scotia Ltd	
G-CHCG	AS.332L-2 Super Puma	CHC Scotia Ltd	
G-CHCH	AS.332L-2 Super Puma	CHC Scotia Ltd	
G-CHCI	AS.332L-2 Super Puma	CHC Scotia Ltd	
G-CHCJ	EC.225LP Super Puma	CHC Scotia Ltd	
G-CHCK	Sikorsky S-92A	CHC Scotia Ltd	
G-CHCL	EC.225LP Super Puma	CHC Scotia Ltd	
G-CHCM	EC.225LP Super Puma	CHC Scotia Ltd	
G-CHCN	EC.225LP Super Puma	CHC Scotia Ltd	
G-CHCO	AS.365N2 Dauphin 2	CHC Scotia Ltd	
G-CHCP	Agusta AB.139	CHC Scotia Ltd	
G-CHCR	AS.365N2 Dauphin 2	British International Helicopter Services Ltd	
G-CHCS	Sikorsky S-92A	CHC Scotia Ltd	
G-CHCT	Agusta AB.139	CHC Scotia Ltd	
G-CHCU	AS.332L2 Super Puma II	CHC Scotia Ltd	
G-CHCX	EC.225LP Super Puma	CHC Scotia Ltd	
G-CHCY	AS.332L2 Super Puma	CHC Scotia Ltd	
G-CHCZ	Sikorsky S-92A	CHC Scotia Ltd	
G-CHDA	Pilatus B4-PC11AF	HDA Syndicate	
G-CHDB	PZL-Bielsko SZD-51-1 Junior	Stratford on Avon Gliding Club Ltd	
G-CHDD	Centrair 101B Pegase 90	591 Glider Syndicate	
G-CHDE	Pilatus B4-PC11AF	A. A. Jenkins	
G-CHDH	Lindstrand LBL-77A balloon	Spirit Balloons Ltd	
G-CHDJ	Schleicher ASW-20CL	G. E. G. Lambert & L. M. M. Sebreights	
G-CHDK	Magni M-16C Tandem Trainer	Gyromania Ltd	
G-CHDL	Schleicher ASW-20	137 Syndicate	
G-CHDM	P & M QuikR	A. Sheveleu	
G-CHDN	Schleicher K 8B	Upward Bound Trust	
G-CHDP	PZL-Bielsko SZD-50-3 Puchacz	Heron Gliding Club	
G-CHDR	DG-300 Elan	R. Robins	
G-CHDS	Rans S-6-ES Coyote II	M. Bradley	
G-CHDT	Avro RJ-85	Trident Aviation Leasing Services (Ireland) Ltd	
G-CHDU	PZL-Bielsko SZD-51-1 Junior	Cambridge Gliding Club Ltd	
G-CHDV	Schleicher ASW-19B	ASW Aviation	
G-CHDW	Pilatus B4-PC11AF	D. Poll	
G-CHDX	Rolladen-Schneider LS7-WL	D. Holborn & R. T. Halliburton	
G-CHDY	Schleicher K 8B	V. Mallon	
G-CHDZ	Cameron O-120 balloon	R. J. Mansfield	
G-CHEB	Shaw Europa	I. C. Smit & P. Whittingham	
G-CHEC	PZL-Bielsko SZD-55-1	D. Pye	
G-CHED	Flylight Dragonfly	J. D. Ellis	
G-CHEE	Schempp-Hirth Discus b	A. Henderson	
G-CHEF	Glaser-Dirks DG-500 Elan Trainer	Yorkshire Gliding Club (Proprietary) Ltd	
G-CHEG	AB Sportine Aviacija LAK-12	Z. Kmita, R. Hannigan & S. Grant	
G-CHEH	Rolladen-Schneider LS7-WL	P. Candler	
G-CHEI	Cameron Z-275 balloon	Airborne Balloon Flights Ltd	
G-CHEJ	Schleicher ASW-15B	A. F. F. Webb	
G-CHEK	PZL-Bielsko SZD-51-1	Cambridge Gliding Club Ltd	
G-CHEL	Colt 77B balloon	Chelsea Financial Services PLC	
G-CHEM	PA-34-200T Seneca II	London Executive Aviation Ltd	
G-CHEN	Schempp-Hirth Discus b	G-CHEN Group	
G-CHEO	Schleicher ASW-20	The Eleven Group	
G-CHEP	PZL-Bielsko SZD-50-3 Puchacz	Peterborough and Spalding Gliding Club Ltd	
G-CHER	PA-38-112 Tomahawk II	Carlisle Flight Training Ltd	
G-CHEU	Lindstrand LTL-203T tethered gas balloon	Portmany Park S	
G-CHEW	Rolladen-Schneider LS6-c18	D. N. Tew	
G-CHEX	Aero Designs Pulsar	D. R. Piercey	
G-CHEY	PA-31T2 Cheyenne IIXL	Provident Partners Ltd	
G-CHFA	Schempp-Hirth Ventus b/16.6	A. K. Lincoln	
G-CHFB	Schleicher Ka-6CR	P. J. Galloway	
G-CHFC	P & M Quik GTR	A. Niarchos	
G-CHFD	Agusta AW.109SP	Flight Charter Services Pty Ltd	
G-CHFE	Avro RJ-85	Trident Aviation Leasing Services (Ireland) Ltd	

Notes	Reg.	Type	Owner or Operator
	G-CHFF	Schempp-Hirth Standard Cirrus	Foxtrot 2 Group
	G-CHFG	Van's RV-6	RV Flying Group
	G-CHFH	PZL-Bielsko SZD-50-3	Trent Valley Aerotowing Club Ltd
	G-CHFI	Ibis Magic GS700 LSA	Nilsoft Ltd
	G-CHFK	PA-32-360 Cherokee Six	British Disabled Flying Association
	G-CHFL	Scheibe SF-25C Falke	Glidesport UK Ltd
	G-CHFM	Cameron Z-120 balloon	David Hathaway Transport Ltd
	G-CHFN	Aerodyne Jumbe L/Trike Buggy	D. Newton
	G-CHFO	P & M Quik GTR	G. J. Slater
	G-CHFP	Hawker Sea Fury T.Mk.20 (WG655)	N. Grey
	G-CHFR	Avro RJ-85	Trident Turboprop (Dublin) Ltd
	G-CHFS	Replica Fokker E.111	J. G. Day
	G-CHFT	Tanarg Bionix 15 912S(1)	N. C. Stubbs
	G-CHFU	P & M Quik GTR	W. K. C. Davies
	G-CHFV	Schempp-Hirth Ventus B/16.6	A. Cliffe & B. Pearson
	G-CHFW	Schleicher K 8B	Oxford Gliding Co.Ltd
	G-CHFX	Schempp-Hirth Nimbus 4T	B. Flewett & A. I. Perley
	G-CHFZ	Best Off Sky Ranger Nynja 912S(1)	G-CHFZ Group
	G-CHGA	P & M Quik GTR	P & M Aviation Ltd
	G-CHGB	Grob G.102 Astir CS	G. Jaques, P. Hollamby & G. Clark
	G-CHGD	Lindstrand LBL-69X balloon	P. Burrows
	G-CHGE	EV-97 TeamEurostar UK	I. C. Tandy
	G-CHGF	Schleicher ASW-15B	HGF Flying Group
	G-CHGG	Schempp-Hirth Standard Cirrus	HGG Flying Group
	G-CHGI	Beech A.36 Bonanza	Atlantic Bridge Aviation Ltd
	G-CHGJ	Flylight MotorFloater Fox 16T	A. Brooks
	G-CHGK	Schempp-Hirth Discus bT	P. W. Berridge
	G-CHGL	Bell 206B JetRanger II	Vantage Aviation Ltd (G-BPNG/G-ORTC)
	G-CHGM	Groppo Trail	D. Cassidy
	G-CHGN	Ace Aviation Easy Riser Spirit	Airways Airsports Ltd
	G-CHGO	AB Sportine Aviacija LAK-12	P. Raymond & J-M Peuffier
	G-CHGP	Rolladen-Schneider LS6-c	D. J. Miller
	G-CHGR	AB Sportline Aviacija LAK-12	M. R. Garwood
	G-CHGS	Schempp-Hirth Discus b	G-CHGS Syndicate
	G-CHGT	FFA Diamant 16.5	T. E. Lynch
	G-CHGU	Ace Aviation Easy Riser Touch	Airways Airsports Ltd
	G-CHGV	Glaser-Dirks DG500/22 Elan	Hotel Golf Victor Syndicate
	G-CHGW	Centrair ASW-20F	S. C. Moss
	G-CHGX	AB Sportine LAK-12 Lietuva	M. Jenks
	G-CHGY	Schleicher ASW-27-18	G-CHGY Flying Group
	G-CHGZ	Schempp-Hirth Discus bT	G-CHGZ Syndicate
	G-CHHA	Avro RJ-85	Trident Turboprop (Dublin) Ltd
	G-CHHB	Aeroprakt A22-LS Foxbat	R. Stalker
	G-CHHC	Cameron A-300 balloon	Wickers World Ltd
	G-CHHD	Sherwood Ranger XP	M. Taylor
	G-CHHF	Sikorsky S-92A	Bristow Helicopters Ltd
	G-CHHG	Dudek Synthesis	R. W. Houldsworth
	G-CHHH	Rolladen-Schneider LS6-c	P. H. Rackham
	G-CHHI	Van's RV-7	M. G. Jefferies
	G-CHHJ	Aeropro Eurofox 912	K. J. Watt
	G-CHHK	Schleicher ASW-19B	M. Walker
	G-CHHL	Cameron C-80 balloon	H. G. Griffiths & W. A. Steel
	G-CHHM	AB Sportline LAK-12 Lietuva	D. Martin
	G-CHHN	Schempp-Hirth Ventus b/16.6	N. A. C. Norman & R. K. Forrest
	G-CHHO	Schempp-Hirth Discus bT	97Z Syndicate
	G-CHHP	Schempp-Hirth Discus b	F. R. Knowles
	G-CHHR	PZL-Bielsko SZD-55-1 Promyk	R. T. & G. Starling
	G-CHHS	Schleicher ASW-20	P.J. Rocks & D. Britt
	G-CHHT	Rolladen-Schneider LS6-c	F. Roles
	G-CHHU	Rolladen-Schneider LS6-c	J. M. Hall & P. Shuttleworth
	G-CHHV	Junqua Ibis RJ.03	J. J. R. Joubert
	G-CHHW	AB Sportine LAK-12	A. J. Dibdin
	G-CHHX	Wassmer WA.26P Squale	M. H. Gagg
	G-CHHY	Ace Magic Laser	S. W. Walker
	G-CHHZ	Schempp-Hirth Cirrus	B. J. Dawson & S. E. Richardson
	G-CHIA	North American SNJ-5 Texan	The Warplane Flying Company Ltd
	G-CHIB	Lindstrand LBL-77A balloon	Lindstrand Hot Air Balloons Ltd
	G-CHID	Eurofox 912	J. W. Taylor
	G-CHIE	Dudek Nucleon 34/Flymecc Mini Trike	J. M. Keen
	G-CHIF	Ozone Power Speedster/Bailey Quattro	T. A. Dobbins
	G-CHIG	Grob G.109B	Southdown Gliding Club Ltd
	G-CHIH	Aeropro Eurofox 912(S)	Banbury Gliding Club Ltd

Reg.	Type	Owner or Operator	Notes
G-CHII	CASA 1-131 Jungmann	J. A. Sykes	
G-CHIJ	Ikarus C42 FB80	G. E. Cole	
G-CHIK	Cessna F.152	Stapleford Flying Club Ltd (G-BHAZ)	
G-CHIM	Ultramagic H-31 balloon	G. Everett	
G-CHIN	Avro RJ-85	Trident Turboprop (Dublin) Ltd	
G-CHIO	Cameron Z-120 balloon	Cameron Balloons Ltd	
G-CHIP	PA-28-181 Archer II	J. A. Divis	
G-CHIR	Van's RV-7	F. Sharples	
G-CHIS	Robinson R22 Beta	Staffordshire Helicopters Training Ltd	
G-CHIT	AutoGyro MTO Sport	N. G. H. Staunton	
G-CHIV	P & M Quik R	G. H. Sharwood-Smith	
G-CHIW	Raj Hamsa X'Air Hawk	M. D. Boley	
G-CHIX	Robin DR.400/500	P. A. & R. Stephens	
G-CHIY	Flylight MotorFloater	W. Seal	
G-CHIZ	Flylight Dragonfly	J. Paterson	
G-CHJB	Flylight Dragonfly	Celtic Solutions Ltd	
G-CHJC	Rolladen-Schneider LS6-c	F. J. Davies	
G-CHJD	Schleicher Ka 6E	A. G. Linfield	
G-CHJE	Schleicher K 8B	M. P. Webb	
G-CHJF	Rolladen-Schneider LS6-c	J. L. Bridge	
G-CHJG	Evektor EV-97 TeamEurostar UK	S. Hoyle	
G-CHJH	Schempp-Hirth Discus bT	Hotel Juliet Hotel Group	
G-CHJI	Embraer ERL170-100LR	ECC Leasing Co.Ltd	
G-CHJK	Cessna T.206H Turbo Stationair	G. G. Weston	
G-CHJL	Schempp-Hirth Discus bT	Discus JL Group	
G-CHJM	Cameron C-80 balloon	C. L. Smith	
G-CHJN	Schempp-Hirth Standard Cirrus	P. M. Hardingham	
G-CHJO	Bushby-Long Midget Mustang M-1	R. J. Hodder	
G-CHJP	Schleicher Ka-6CR	D. M. Cornelius	
G-CHJR	Glasflugel H201B Standard Libelle	B. O. Marcham & B. Magnani	
G-CHJS	Schleicher ASW-27-18E	J. D. Spencer	
G-CHJT	Centrair ASW-20F	R. J. Pirie & M. S. R. Broadway	
G-CHJV	Grob G.102 Astir CS	Cotswold Gliding Club	
G-CHJW	P & M Quik GTR	A. C. Rowlands	
G-CHJX	Rolladen-Schneider LS6-c	M. R. Haynes & P. Robinson	
G-CHJY	Schempp-Hirth Standard Cirrus	R. S. Rose	
G-CHJZ	Luscombe 8E Silvaire Deluxe	P. Durdey	
G-CHKA	Orlican Discus CS	R. W. & M. P. Weaver	
G-CHKB	Grob G.102 Astir CS77	G-CHKB Group	
G-CHKC	Schempp-Hirth Standard Cirrus	A. Taylor	
G-CHKD	Schempp-Hirth Standard Cirrus	R. Jeffcoate	
G-CHKE	Embraer EMB-505 Phenom 300	Flairjet Ltd	
G-CHKF	Grob G.109B	T. R. Dews	
G-CHKG	Best Off Skyranger Nynja 912S(1)	S. Worthington	
G-CHKH	Schleicher ASW-28	D. Bradley	
G-CHKI	Sikorsky S-92A	Bristow Helicopters Ltd	
G-CHKK	Schleicher K8B	R. E. Johnston	
G-CHKL	Cameron 120 Kookaburra SS balloon	Eagle Ltd/Australia	
G-CHKM	Grob G.102 Astir CS Jeans	Essex and Suffolk Gliding Club Ltd	
G-CHKN	Kiss 400-582(1)	P. J. Higgins	
G-CHKO	Best Off Skyranger Swift 912S(1)	S. D. J. Harvey	
G-CHKP	Avro RJ85	Trident Turboprop (Dublin) Ltd	
G-CHKR	Jastreb Standard Cirrus G/81	N. A. White	
G-CHKS	Jastreb Standard Cirrus G/81	G. G. Butler	
G-CHKU	Schempp-Hirth Standard Cirrus	T. J. Wheeler & T. M. O'Sullivan	
G-CHKV	Scheibe Zugvogel IIIA	Dartmoor Gliding Society Ltd	
G-CHKW	Robinson R44	Fin Air Trade SAS	
G-CHKX	Rolladen-Schneider LS4-B	J. McMackin	
G-CHKY	Schempp-Hirth Discus b	C. V. Hill & O. J. Anderson	
G-CHKZ	CARMAM JP 15-36AR Aiglon	T. A. & A. J. Hollings	
G-CHLB	Rolladen-Schneider LS4-b	E. G. Leach & K. F. Rogers	
G-CHLC	Pilatus B4-PC11AF	E. Lockhart	
G-CHLD	AutoGyro MTO Sport	A. D. Lysser	
G-CHLE	Cameron A-160 balloon	Virgin Baloon Flights	
G-CHLH	Schleicher K 8B	Shenington Gliding Club	
G-CHLI	Cosmik Aviation Superchaser	Cosmik Aviation Ltd	
G-CHLK	Glasflugel H.301 Libelle	G. L. J. Barrett	
G-CHLL	Lindstrand LBL-90A balloon	P. J. Hollingsworth	
G-CHLM	Schleicher ASW-19B	R. A. Colbeck	
G-CHLN	Schempp-Hirth Discus CS	Portsmouth Naval Gliding Centre	
G-CHLO	Grob G.109B	F. Waller	
G-CHLP	Schleicher ASK-21	Southdown Gliding Club Ltd	

Notes	Reg.	Type	Owner or Operator
	G-CHLR	Embraer EMB-135BJ Legacy	ECC Leasing Co.Ltd
	G-CHLS	Schempp-Hirth Discus b	R. A. Lennard
	G-CHLU	Westland WA.341G Gazelle AH.Mk.1	Kemet Global Ltd
	G-CHLV	Schleicher ASW-19B	P. J. Belcher & R. I. Brickwood
	G-CHLW	Westland WA.341G Gazelle AH.Mk.1	Kemet Global Ltd
	G-CHLX	Schleicher ASH-25	A. di Stasi
	G-CHLY	Schempp-Hirth Discus CS	S. J. Pearce
	G-CHLZ	Best Off Skyranger 582(1)	S. K. Ridge
	G-CHMA	PZL-Bielsko SZD-51-1 Junior	The Welland Gliding Club Ltd
	G-CHMB	Glaser-Dirks DG-300 Elan	A. D. & P. Langlands
	G-CHMC	Ozone Power Speedster/Bailey Quattro	D. J. Piper
	G-CHMD	DG Flugzeugbau LS8-T	G-CHMD Flying Group
	G-CHME	Glaser-Dirks DG-300 Elan	D. J. Baldwin & J. Stiles
	G-CHMF	Westland WA.341G Gazelle AH.Mk.1	Kemet Global Ltd
	G-CHMG	ICA IS-28B2	A. Sutton, R. Maksymowicz & A. J. Palfreyman
	G-CHMH	Schleicher K8B	Shenington Gliding Club
	G-CHMI	Lindstrand LBL-105A balloon	J. A. Lawton
	G-CHMJ	Sikorsky S-92A	Bristow Helicopters Ltd
	G-CHMK	Rolladen-Schneider LS6-18W	R. C. Hodge
	G-CHML	Schempp-Hirth Discus CS	I. D. Bateman
	G-CHMM	Glasflugel 304B	Delta 19 Group
	G-CHMN	Raj Hamsa X'Air Falcon D(2)	J. Anderson & D. Thrower
	G-CHMO	Orlican Discus CS	S. Barter
	G-CHMP	Bellanca 7ACA Champ	I. J. Langley
	G-CHMR	Embraer EMB-145MP	Eastern Airways
	G-CHMS	Glaser-Dirks DG-100	A. Phillips
	G-CHMT	Glasflugel Mosquito B	J. Taberham
	G-CHMU	CARMAM JP-15/36AR Aiglon	G-CHMU Group
	G-CHMV	Schleicher ASK-13	The Windrushers Gliding Club Ltd
	G-CHMW	Evektor EV-97 Eurostar SL	N. R. Beale
	G-CHMX	Rolladen-Schneider LS4-a	K. P. Nakhla & L Couval
	G-CHMY	Schempp-Hirth Standard Cirrus	HMY Syndicate
	G-CHMZ	Fedorov ME7 Mechta	R. Andrews
	G-CHNA	Glaser-Dirks DG-500/20 Elan	G-CHNA Group
	G-CHNB	Scheibe SF-28A	S. E. Abbott
	G-CHNC	Schleicher ASK-19B	T. J. Highton
	G-CHND	Ultramagic H-65	N. Dykes
	G-CHNE	Schempp-Hirth Nimbus 2B	P. J. Uden
	G-CHNF	Schempp-Hirth Duo Discus	Booker Gliding Club Ltd
	G-CHNH	Schempp-Hirth Nimbus 2C	C. J. Pollard
	G-CHNI	Magni M-24C	A. R. Waitson
	G-CHNJ	Eurocopter AS.365N3 Dauphin II	FB Heliservices Ltd
	G-CHNK	PZL-Bielsko SZD-51-1 Junior	Booker Gliding Club Ltd
	G-CHNM	Standard Cirrus G/81	Bicester Cirrus Crew
	G-CHNO	Cameron C-60 balloon	J. F. Till
	G-CHNP	Dragon Chaser	Flylight Airsports Ltd
	G-CHNR	P & M Quik GTR	S. J. Sheppard
	G-CHNT	Schleicher ASW-15	S. J. Lintott & I. Dawkins
	G-CHNU	Schempp-Hirth Nimbus 4DT	D. E. Findon
	G-CHNV	Rolladen-Schneider LS4-b	S. K. Armstrong & P. H. Dixon
	G-CHNW	Schempp-Hirth Duo Discus	G-CHNW Group
	G-CHNY	Centrair 101A Pegase	M. O. Breen
	G-CHNZ	Centrair 101A Pegase	R. H. Partington
	G-CHOA	Bell 206B-3 JetRanger III	Haverholme Farm Partnership
	G-CHOB	Boeing 737-883	FGL Aircraft Ireland Ltd
	G-CHOD	Schleicher ASW-20	S. E. Archer-Jones & A. Duerden
	G-CHOE	Robin DR400/140B	Exavia Ltd
	G-CHOF	CARMAM M100S	M. A. Farrelly
	G-CHOG	AB Sportine LAK-12	J. M. Pursey
	G-CHOH	Boeing 737-883	FGL Aircraft Ireland Ltd
	G-CHOI	White Monoplane 1912 Canard Pusher	J. Aubert
	G-CHOO	Ikarus C42 FB80	GS Aviation (Europe) Ltd
	G-CHOP	Westland-Bell 47G-3B1	Leamington Hobby Centre Ltd
	G-CHOR	Schempp-Hirth Discus b	The Windrushers Gliding Club Ltd
	G-CHOT	Grob G.102 Astir CS77	Southdown Gliding Club Ltd
	G-CHOX	Shaw Europa XS	Chocs Away Ltd
	G-CHOY	Schempp-Hirth Mini Nimbus C	A. H. Sparrow
	G-CHOZ	Rolladen-Schneider LS6-18W	R. E. Scott
	G-CHPA	Robinson R22 Beta	Rivermead Aviation Ltd/Switzerland
	G-CHPB	Avro RJ-85	Trident Turboprop (Dublin) Ltd
	G-CHPC	Schleicher ASW-20 CL	B. L. Liddard & P. J. Williams
	G-CHPD	Rolladen-Schneider LS6-c18	C. J. & K. A. Teagle

Reg.	Type	Owner or Operator	Notes
G-CHPE	Schleicher ASK-13	Dumfries and District Gliding Club	
G-CHPF	Lindstrand LBL-500A balloon	Lindstrand Hot Air Balloons Ltd	
G-CHPG	Cirrus SR-20	S. G. Jones	
G-CHPH	Schempp-Hirth Discus CS	I. N & S. G. Hunt	
G-CHPI	DHC.1 Chipmunk Mk.22	G-CHPI Group	
G-CHPK	Van's RV-8	Viscount A. C. Andover (G-JILS)	
G-CHPL	Rolladen-Schneider LS4-b	Southdown Gliding Club Ltd	
G-CHPO	Schleicher Ka-6CR	N. Robinson	
G-CHPR	Robinson R22 Beta	C. Gozzi	
G-CHPT	Federov ME7 Mechta	Midland Gliding Club Ltd	
G-CHPV	Schleicher ASK-21	Scottish Gliding Union Ltd	
G-CHPW	Schleicher ASK-21	Scottish Gliding Union Ltd	
G-CHPX	Schempp-Hirth Discus CS	G-CHRS Group	
G-CHPY	DHC.1 Chipmunk 22 (WB652:V)	Devonair Executive Business Travel Ltd	
G-CHRC	Glaser-Dirks DG500/20 Elan	DG500-390 Syndicate	
G-CHRD	Flylight Dragonlite	I. A. Barclay	
G-CHRG	PZL-Bielsko SZD-51-1 Junior	Scottish Gliding Union Ltd	
G-CHRH	Schempp-Hirth Discus 2cT	C. Hyett	
G-CHRJ	Schleicher K 8B	Shenington Gliding Club	
G-CHRK	Centrair 101 Pegase	P. T. Bushill & M. Morris	
G-CHRL	Schempp-Hirth Standard Cirrus	D. J. Allen	
G-CHRM	Ikarus C42 FB80 Bravo	D. R. Stevens	
G-CHRN	Schleicher ASK-18	Stratford on Avon Gliding Club Ltd	
G-CHRS	Schempp-Hirth Discus CS	M. Santopinto	
G-CHRV	Van's RV-7	R. E. Tyers	
G-CHRW	Schempp-Hirth Duo Discus	802 Syndicate	
G-CHRX	Schempp-Hirth Discus a	D. S. Lodge	
G-CHRY	Medway EclipseR	S. D. McLaughlin	
G-CHSB	Glaser-Dirks DG-303 Elan	C. M. Hawkes & J. Weddell	
G-CHSD	Schempp-Hirth Discus b	G-CHSD Group	
G-CHSE	Grob G.102 Astir CS77	G. J. Armes	
G-CHSG	Scheibe SF27A	HSG Syndicate	
G-CHSH	Scheibe Zugvogel IIIB	R. D. Newton	
G-CHSK	Schleicher ASW-20CL	A. J. Watson & C. C. Ramshorn	
G-CHSM	Schleicher ASK-13	Stratford on Avon Gliding Club Ltd	
G-CHSN	Schleicher Ka-6CR	Needwood Forest Gliding Club Ltd	
G-CHSO	Schempp-Hirth Discus b	Midland Gliding Club Ltd	
G-CHSU	Eurocopter EC 135T1	Eurocopter UK Ltd	
G-CHSX	Scheibe SF-27A	Essex & Suffolk Gliding Club Ltd	
G-CHSZ	Rolladen-Schneider LS8-a	I. G. Garden	
G-CHTA	AA-5A Cheetah	C. A. Johnson & K. T. Pierce (G-BFRC)	
G-CHTB	Schempp-Hirth Janus	Janus G-CHTB Syndicate	
G-CHTC	Schleicher ASW-15B	G-CHTC Group	
G-CHTD	Grob G.102 Astir CS	S. Waldie	
G-CHTE	Grob G.102 Astir CS77	HTE Group	
G-CHTF	AB Sportline LAK-12	M. Tolson	
G-CHTM	Rolladen-Schneider LS8-18	M. J. Chapman	
G-CHTR	Grob G.102 Astir CS	I. P. & D. M. Wright	
G-CHTS	Rolladen-Schneider LS8-18	P. T. Cunnison	
G-CHTN	Schleicher ASW-22	R. C. Hodge	
G-CHTO	Rans S-7S	J. D. Llewellyn	
G-CHTU	Schempp-Hirth Cirrus	Open Cirrus Group	
G-CHTV	Schleicher ASK-21	Cambridge Gliding Club Ltd	
G-CHUA	Schleicher ASW-19B	G. D. Vaughan	
G-CHUD	Schleicher ASK-13	London Gliding Club Propietary Ltd	
G-CHUE	Schleicher ASW-27	M. J. Smith	
G-CHUF	Schleicher ASK-13	The Welland Gliding Club Ltd	
G-CHUG	Shaw Europa	C. M. Washington	
G-CHUH	Schempp-Hirth Janus	Janus D31 Syndicate	
G-CHUJ	Centrair ASW-20F	P. D. Ruskin	
G-CHUK	Cameron O-77 balloon	R. P. E. Phillips	
G-CHUL	Schempp-Hirth Cirrus	Cirrus CHUL Group	
G-CHUN	Grob G.102 Astir CS Jeans	Staffordshire Gliding Club Ltd	
G-CHUO	Federov ME7 Mechta	J. D. A. Cooper & W. H. Ollis	
G-CHUR	Schempp-Hirth Cirrus	M. Rossiter & A. G. Thomas	
G-CHUS	Scheibe SF27A Zugvogel V	SF27 HUS Syndicate	
G-CHUT	Centrair ASW-20F	S. R. Phelps	
G-CHUU	Schleicher ASK-13	Upward Bound Trust	
G-CHUY	Schempp-Hirth Ventus cT	M. A. & M. N. Challans	
G-CHUZ	Schempp-Hirth Discus bT	P. A. Gelsthorpe	
G-CHVA	Agusta A.109E Power	Sloane Helicopters Ltd	
G-CHVF	Rolladen-Schneider LS8-18	J. Haigh	

Notes	Reg.	Type	Owner or Operator
	G-CHVG	Schleicher ASK-21	Rattlesden Gliding Club Ltd
	G-CHVH	Pilatus B4-PC11AF	London Gliding Club Proprietary Ltd
	G-CHVK	Grob G.102 Astir CS	P. G. Goulding
	G-CHVL	Rolladen-Schneider LS8-18	Cumulus Gliding Syndicate
	G-CHVM	Glaser-Dirks DG-300	Glider Syndicate 303
	G-CHVN	Bombardier CL600-2B16 Challenger	Hangar 8 AOC Ltd
	G-CHVO	Schleicher ASK-13	R. Brown
	G-CHVP	Schleicher ASW-20	P. J. Williams
	G-CHVR	Schempp-Hirth Discus b	Yorkshire Gliding Club (Proprietary) Ltd
	G-CHVT	Schempp-Hirth Ventus 2b	Victor Tango Group
	G-CHVU	Rolladen-Schneider LS8-a	European Soaring Club
	G-CHVV	Rolladen-Schneider LS4-b	A. J. Bardgett
	G-CHUW	Rolladen-Schneider LS8-18	S8 Group
	G-CHVX	Centrair ASW-20F	Banbury Gliding Club Ltd
	G-CHVW	Scleicher ASK-13	Rattlesden Gliding Club Ltd
	G-CHVZ	Schempp-Hirth Standard Cirrus	ABC Soaring
	G-CHWA	Schempp-Hirth Ventus 2c	C. Garton
	G-CHWB	Schempp-Hirth Duo Discus	Lasham Gliding Society Ltd
	G-CHWC	Glasflugel Standard Libelle 201B	Whiskey Charlie Group
	G-CHWD	Schempp-Hirth Standard Cirrus	M. R. Hoskins
	G-CHWF	Jastreb Standard Cirrus G/81	M. D. Langford & M. C. Mann
	G-CHWG	Glasflugel Standard Libelle 201B	M. Kalweit
	G-CHWH	Schempp-Hirth Ventus cT	M. J. Philpott
	G-CHWL	Rolladen-Schneider LS8-a	W. M. Coffee
	G-CHWP	Glaser-Dirks DG-100G Elan	K. H. Bates
	G-CHWS	Rolladen-Schneider LS8-18	G. E. & H. B. Chalmers
	G-CHWT	Schleicher K 8B	Shenington Gliding Club
	G-CHWW	Grob G.103A Twin II Acro	Crown Service Gliding Club
	G-CHWY	Schempp-Hirth Standard Cirrus	D. D. Copeland
	G-CHXA	Scheibe Zugvogel IIIB	G-CHXA Group
	G-CHXB	Grob G.102 Astir CS77	T. S. Miller
	G-CHXD	Schleicher ASW-27	J. Quartermaine & M. Jerman
	G-CHXE	Schleicher ASW-19B	M. J. Hargreaves
	G-CHXF	Cameron A-140 balloon	Gone With The Wind Ltd
	G-CHXH	Schempp-Hirth Discus b	Deesside Gliding Club (Aberdeenshire) Ltd
	G-CHXJ	Schleicher ASK-13	Cotswold Gliding Club
	G-CHXM	Grob G.102 Astir CS	University of Bristol Students Union
	G-CHXO	Schleicher ASH-25	The Eleven Group
	G-CHXP	Schleicher ASK-13	The Vale of the White Horse Gliding Centre Ltd
	G-CHXR	Schempp-Hirth Ventus cT	560 Group
	G-CHXT	Rolladen-Schneider LS-4a	H. Hingley
	G-CHXU	Schleicher ASW-19B	UCLU
	G-CHXV	Schleicher ASK-13	Aquila Gliding Club Ltd
	G-CHXW	Rolladen-Schneider LS8-18	W. Aspland
	G-CHXX	Schempp-Hirth Standard Cirrus	A. Coatsworth & R. M. Wootten
	G-CHXZ	Rolladen-Schneider LS4	G-CHXZ Group
	G-CHYA	Rolladen-Schneider LS6c-18	Y. Melou
	G-CHYD	Schleicher ASW-24	E. S. Adlard
	G-CHYE	DG-505 Elan Orion	The Bristol Gliding Club Proprietary Ltd
	G-CHYF	Rolladen-Schneider LS8-18	R. E. Francis
	G-CHYH	Rolladen-Schneider LS3-17	B. Silke
	G-CHYJ	Schleicher ASK-21	Highland Gliding Club Ltd
	G-CHYK	Centrair ASW-20FL	Kilo Twenty Group
	G-CHYP	PZL-Bielsko SZD-50-3 Puchacz	Rattlesden Gliding Club Ltd
	G-CHYR	Schleicher ASW-27	A. J. Manwaring & A. R. Hutchings
	G-CHYS	Schleicher ASK-21	Army Gliding Association
	G-CHYT	Schleicher ASK-21	Army Gliding Association
	G-CHYU	Schempp-Hirth Discus CS	Army Gliding Association
	G-CHYX	Schleicher K 8B	Oxford University Gliding Club
	G-CHYY	Schempp-Hirth Nimbus 3DT	G-CHYY Syndicate
	G-CHZB	PZL-Swidnik PW-5 Smyk	The Burn Gliding Club Ltd
	G-CHZD	Schleicher ASW-15B	C. P. Ellison & S. Barber
	G-CHZE	Schempp-Hirth Discus CS	HZE Glider Syndicate
	G-CHZG	Rolladen-Schneider LS8-18	M. J. & T. J. Webb
	G-CHZH	Schleicher Ka 6CR	C. Hankinson
	G-CHZJ	Schempp-Hirth Standard Cirrus	P. Mucha
	G-CHZM	Rolladen-Schneider LS4-a	J. M. Bevan
	G-CHZO	Schleicher ASW-27	A. A. Gilmore
	G-CHZR	Schleicher ASK-21	K21 HZR Group
	G-CHZU	Schempp-Hirth Standard Cirrus	S. A. W. Becker
	G-CHZV	Schempp-Hirth Standard Cirrus	S. M. Sheard
	G-CHZX	Schleicher K 8B	S. M. Chapman & S. Potter

Reg.	Type	Owner or Operator	Notes
G-CHZY	Rolladen-Schneider LS4-a	N. P. Wedi	
G-CHZZ	Schleicher ASW-20L	LD Syndicate	
G-CIAN	Unicorn Ax6 balloon	G. A. & I. Chadwick	
G-CIAO	I.I.I. Sky Arrow 1450-L	G. Arscott	
G-CIAS	BN-2B-21 Islander	Channel Island Air Search Ltd (G-BKJM)	
G-CIBO	Cessna 180K	CIBO Ops Ltd	
G-CIDD	Bellanca 7ECA Citabria	M. J. Medland	
G-CIEL	Cessna 560XL Citation Excel	Enerway Ltd	
G-CIGY	Westland-Bell 47G-3B1	M. L. Romeling (G-BGXP)	
G-CIRI	Cirrus SR20	Cirrus Flyers Group	
G-CIRU	Cirrus SR20	Cirrent BV/Netherlands	
G-CITR	Cameron Z-105 balloon	A. Kaye	
G-CITY	PA-31-350 Navajo Chieftain	Blue Sky Investments Ltd	
G-CIVA	Boeing 747-436	British Airways	
G-CIVB	Boeing 747-436	British Airways	
G-CIVC	Boeing 747-436	British Airways	
G-CIVD	Boeing 747-436	British Airways	
G-CIVE	Boeing 747-436	British Airways	
G-CIVF	Boeing 747-436	British Airways	
G-CIVG	Boeing 747-436	British Airways	
G-CIVH	Boeing 747-436	British Airways	
G-CIVI	Boeing 747-436	British Airways	
G-CIVJ	Boeing 747-436	British Airways	
G-CIVK	Boeing 747-436	British Airways	
G-CIVL	Boeing 747-436	British Airways	
G-CIVM	Boeing 747-436	British Airways	
G-CIVN	Boeing 747-436	British Airways	
G-CIVO	Boeing 747-436	British Airways	
G-CIVP	Boeing 747-436	British Airways	
G-CIVR	Boeing 747-436	British Airways	
G-CIVS	Boeing 747-436	British Airways	
G-CIVT	Boeing 747-436	British Airways	
G-CIVU	Boeing 747-436	British Airways	
G-CIVV	Boeing 747-436	British Airways	
G-CIVW	Boeing 747-436	British Airways	
G-CIVX	Boeing 747-436	British Airways	
G-CIVY	Boeing 747-436	British Airways	
G-CIVZ	Boeing 747-436	British Airways	
G-CIXB	Grob G.109B	G-CIXB Syndicate	
G-CIZZ	Beech 58 Baron	Bonanza Flying Club Ltd	
G-CJAI	P & M Quik GT450	J. C. Kitchen	
G-CJAL	Schleicher Ka 6E	JAL Syndicate	
G-CJAO	Schempp-Hirth Discus b	O. Kahn	
G-CJAP	Ikarus C42 FB80	J. A. Paley	
G-CJAR	Schempp-Hirth Discus bT	S. P. Withey	
G-CJAS	Glasflugel Standard Libelle 201B	M. J. Collett	
G-CJAT	Schleicher K8B	Wolds Gliding Club Ltd	
G-CJAV	Schleicher ASK-21	Wolds Gliding Club Ltd	
G-CJAW	Glaser-Dirks DG-200/17	P. D. Harvey	
G-CJAX	Schleicher ASK-21	Wolds Gliding Club Ltd	
G-CJAY	Mainair Pegasus Quik GT450	J. C. Kitchen	
G-CJAZ	Grob G.102 Astir CS Jeans	The Bath, Wilts and North Dorset Gliding Club	
G-CJBB	Rolladen-Schneider LS8-a	H. A. Brunt	
G-CJBC	PA-28 Cherokee 180	J. B. Cave	
G-CJBH	Eiriavion PIK-20D	537 Syndicate	
G-CJBJ	Schempp-Hirth Standard Cirrus	S. T. Dutton	
G-CJBK	Schleicher ASW-19B	D. Caielli, P. Deane & G. Nixon	
G-CJBM	Schleicher ASK-21	The Burn Gliding Club Ltd	
G-CJBO	Rolladen-Schneider LS8-18	L7 Syndicate	
G-CJBR	Schempp-Hirth Discus b	G-CJBR Group	
G-CJBT	Schleicher ASW-19B	G. Dennis	
G-CJBW	Schempp-Hirth Discus bT	G-CJBW Syndicate	
G-CJBX	Rolladen-Schneider LS4-a	P. W. Lee	
G-CJBY	AB Sportine LAK-12	P. G. Steggles & N. Clarke	
G-CJBZ	Grob G.102 Astir CS	The Royal Air Force Gliding Association	
G-CJCA	Schleicher ASW-15B	S. Briggs	
G-CJCD	Schleicher ASW-24	M. D. Evershed	
G-CJCF	Grob G.102 Astir CS77	The Northumbria Gliding Club Ltd	
G-CJCG	PZL-Swidnik PW-5 Smyk	M. Evans & T. J Wallace	
G-CJCJ	Schempp-Hirth Standard Cirrus	G-CJCJ Syndicate	
G-CJCK	Schempp-Hirth Discus bT	P. J. Tiller & T. Wright	

Notes	Reg.	Type	Owner or Operator
	G-CJCM	Schleicher ASW-27	J. R. Klunder & K. E. Singer
	G-CJCN	Schempp-Hirth Standard Cirrus 75	F. J. Bradley
	G-CJCT	Schempp-Hirth Nimbus 4T	D. S. Innes
	G-CJCU	Schempp-Hirth Standard Cirrus B	R. A. Davenport
	G-CJCW	Grob G.102 Astir CS77	G. E. Iles & N. G. Smith
	G-CJCX	Schempp-Hirth Discus bT	C. W. M. Claxton
	G-CJCY	Rolladen-Schneider LS8-18	R. Visona & R. Zaccour
	G-CJCZ	Schleicher Ka 6CR	N. Barnes
	G-CJDB	Cessna 525 Citationjet	Breed Aircraft Ltd
	G-CJDC	Schleicher ASW-27	T. A. Sage
	G-CJDD	Glaser-Dirks DG-200/17	M. Bond
	G-CJDE	Rolladen-Schneider LS8-18	B. Kerby & M. Davies
	G-CJDF	Schleicher ASH-25E	522 Syndicate
	G-CJDG	Rolladen-Schneider LS6-b	R. H. & A. Moss
	G-CJDJ	Rolladen-Schneider LS3	J. C. Burdett
	G-CJDK	Rolladen-Schneider LS8-18	B. Bredenbeck
	G-CJDM	Schleicher ASW-15B	C. J. H. Donnelly
	G-CJDN	Cameron C-90 balloon	N. Ivison
	G-CJDP	Glaser-Dirks DG-200/17	The Owners of JDP
	G-CJDR	Schleicher ASW-15	M. J. Waters
	G-CJDS	Schempp-Hirth Standard Cirrus 75	P. Nicholls
	G-CJDT	Rolladen-Schneider LS8-a	J. N. & L. Rebbeck
	G-CJDV	DG Flugzeugbau DG-300 Elan Acro	J. M. Gilbey & B. D. Michael
	G-CJDX	Wassmer WA-28	R. Hutchinson
	G-CJDY	Rolladen-Schneider LS8-18	P. O. R. Paterson
	G-CJEA	Rolladen-Schneider LS8-18	P. Morgan
	G-CJEB	Schleicher ASW-24	P. C. Scholz
	G-CJEC	PZL-Bielsko SZD-50-3 Puchasz	Cambridge Gliding Club Ltd
	G-CJED	Schempp-Hirth Nimbus 3/24.5	J. Edyvean
	G-CJEE	Schleicher ASW-20L	B. Pridgeon
	G-CJEH	Glasflugel Mosquito B	M. J. Vickery
	G-CJEL	Schleicher ASW-24	S. M. Chapman
	G-CJEM	Schempp-Hirth Duo Discus	Duo Discus 572 Flying Group
	G-CJEP	Rolladen-Schneider LS4-b	C. F. Carter & N. Backes
	G-CJER	Schempp-Hirth Standard Cirrus 75	Cirrus Group
	G-CJEU	Glasflugel Standard Libelle	D. B. Johns
	G-CJEV	Schempp-Hirth Standard Cirrus	R. P. Hypher & E. M. Morris
	G-CJEW	Schleicher Ka 6CR	CJEW Syndicate
	G-CJEX	Schempp-Hirth Ventus 2a	D. S. Watt
	G-CJEZ	Glaser-Dirks DG-100	R. Kehr
	G-CJFA	Schempp-Hirth Standard Cirrus	P. M. Sheahan
	G-CJFC	Schempp-Hirth Discus CS	The Royal Air Force Gliding and Soaring Association
	G-CJFE	Schempp-Hirth Janus CE	A. Cordonnier
	G-CJFH	Schempp-Hirth Duo Discus	The Royal Air Force Gliding and Soaring Association
	G-CJFJ	Schleicher ASW-20CL	R. J. Stirk
	G-CJFK	Schleicher ASW-20L	J. M. Herman
	G-CJFM	Schleicher ASK-13	Darlton Gliding Club Ltd
	G-CJFR	Schempp-Hirth Ventus cT	L. Rayment, D. Ryall & D. W. Smith
	G-CJFT	Schleicher K-8B	The Surrey Hills Gliding Club Ltd
	G-CJFU	Schleicher ASW-19B	M. T. Stanley
	G-CJFX	Rolladen-Schneider LS8-a	P. E. Baker
	G-CJFZ	Fedorov ME7 Mechta	R. J. Colbourne
	G-CJGB	Schleicher K 8B	Edensoaring Ltd
	G-CJGD	Scleicher K 8B	R. E. Pettifer & C. A. McLay
	G-CJGE	Schleicher ASK-21	M. R. Wall
	G-CJGF	Schempp-Hirth Ventus c	R. D. Slater
	G-CJGG	P & M Quik GT450	J. M. Pearce
	G-CJGH	Schempp-Hirth Nimbus 2C	G-CJGH Syndicate
	G-CJGJ	Schleicher ASK-21	Midland Gliding Club Ltd
	G-CJGK	Eiri PIL-200	The Four Aces
	G-CJGL	Schempp-Hirth Discus CS	The Royal Air Force Gliding and Soaring Association
	G-CJGM	Schempp-Hirth Discus CS	The Royal Air Force Gliding and Soaring Association
	G-CJGN	Schempp-Hirth Standard Cirrus	P. A. Shuttleworth
	G-CJGR	Schempp-Hirth Discus bT	S. P. Wareham & G. W. Kemp
	G-CJGS	Rolladen-Schneider LS8-18	T. Stupnik
	G-CJGU	Schempp-Hirth Mini-Nimbus B	N. D. Ashton
	G-CJGW	Schleicher ASK-13	Darlton Gliding Club Ltd
	G-CJGX	Schleicher K 8B	Andreas K8 Group

Reg.	Type	Owner or Operator	Notes
G-CJGY	Schempp-Hirth Standard Cirrus	P. J. Shout	
G-CJGZ	Glasflugel Standard Libelle 201B	A. & D. M. Cornish	
G-CJHD	Schleicher Ka 6E	The Royal Air Force Gliding and Soaring Association	
G-CJHE	Astir CS77	Aero Club de Portugal	
G-CJHG	Grob G.102 Astir CS	P. L. E. Zelazowski	
G-CJHJ	Glasflugel Standard Libelle 201B	N. P. Marriott	
G-CJHK	Schleicher K8B	Stratford on Avon Gliding Club Ltd	
G-CJHL	Schleicher Ka 6E	J. R. Gilbert	
G-CJHM	Schempp-Hirth Discus b	J. C. Thwaites	
G-CJHN	Grob G.102 Astir CS Jeans	J. C. Hurne	
G-CJHO	Schleicher ASK-18	RAF Gliding and Soaring Association	
G-CJHP	Flight Design CTSW	S. J. Reader	
G-CJHR	Centrair SNC34C Alliance	The Borders (Milfield) Gliding Club Ltd	
G-CJHS	Schleicher ASW-19B	JHS Syndicate	
G-CJHU	Rolladen-Schneider LS8-18	C. F. Jordan	
G-CJHW	Glaser-Dirks DG-200	A. W. Thornhill & S. Webster	
G-CJHX	Bolkow Phoebus C	J. Hewitt	
G-CJHY	Rolladen-Schneider LS8-18	L. E. N. Tanner & N. Wall	
G-CJHZ	Schleicher ASW-20	T. J. Stanley	
G-CJJB	Rolladen-Schneider LS4	M. Tomlinson	
G-CJJD	Schempp-Hirth Discus bT	C. E. Turner & D. Wilson	
G-CJJE	Schempp-Hirth Discus a	A. Soffici	
G-CJJF	Schleicher ASW-27	A. R. Armstrong	
G-CJJH	DG Flugzeugbau DG-800S	J. S. Weston	
G-CJJJ	Schempp-Hirth Standard Cirrus	R. McLuckie	
G-CJJK	Rolladen-Schneider LS8-18	A. D. Roch	
G-CJJL	Schleicher ASW-19B	G-CJJL Group	
G-CJJP	Schempp-Hirth Duo Discus	N. Clements	
G-CJJT	Schleicher ASW-27	Portsmouth Naval Gliding Centre	
G-CJJU	Rolladen-Schneider LS8-a	A. J. French & M. N. Marshall	
G-CJJX	Schleicher ASW-15B	STJ Syndicate	
G-CJJZ	Schempp-Hirth Discus bT	S. J. C. Parker	
G-CJKA	Schleicher ASK-21	East Sussex Gliding Club Ltd	
G-CJKB	PZL-Swidnik PW-5 Smyk	N. Dickenson	
G-CJKD	Rolladen-Schneider LS8-18	D. G. Glover & A. Cockerell	
G-CJKE	PZL-Swidnik PW-5 Smyk	The Burn Gliding Club Ltd	
G-CJKF	Glaser-Dirks DG-200	D. O. Sandells & R. K. Stafford	
G-CJKG	Schleicher ASK-18	The Royal Air Force Gliding and Soaring Association	
G-CJKJ	Schleicher ASK-21	The Royal Air Force Gliding and Soaring Association	
G-CJKK	Schleicher ASK-21	Army Gliding Association	
G-CJKM	Glaser-Dirks DG200/17	G. F. Coles & E. W. Russell	
G-CJKN	Rolladen-Schneider LS8-18	G. C. Lewis	
G-CJKO	Schleicher ASK-21	The Royal Air Force Gliding and Soaring Association	
G-CJKP	Rolladen-Schneider LS4-b	D. M. Hope	
G-CJKS	Schleicher ASW-19B	R. J. P. Lancaster	
G-CJKT	Schleicher ASK-13	The Royal Air Force Gliding and Soaring Association	
G-CJKU	Schleicher ASK-18	Derbyshire & Lancashire Gliding Club Ltd	
G-CJKV	Grob G.103A Twin II Acro	The Welland Gliding Club Ltd	
G-CJKW	Grob G.102 Astir CS77	The Bath, Wilts and North Dorset Gliding Club Ltd	
G-CJKY	Schempp-Hirth Ventus cT	G. V. Matthews & M. P. Osborn	
G-CJKZ	Schleicher ASK-21	The Royal Air Force Gliding and Soaring Association	
G-CJLA	Schempp-Hirth Ventus 2cT	S. G. Jones	
G-CJLC	Schempp-Hirth Discus CS	The Royal Air Force Gliding and Soaring Association	
G-CJLF	Schleicher ASK-13	Army Gliding Association	
G-CJLG	PZL-Bielsko SZD-51-1 Junior	Army Gliding Association	
G-CJLH	Rolladen-Schneider LS4	JLH Syndicate	
G-CJLJ	Rolladen-Schneider LS4-b	Army Gliding Association	
G-CJLK	Rolladen-Schneider LS7	D. N. Munro & J. P. W. Roche-Kelly	
G-CJLL	Robinson R44 II	AT and P Rentals Ltd	
G-CJLN	Rolladen-Schneider LS8-18	The Royal Air Force Gliding and Soaring Association	
G-CJLO	Schleicher ASK-13	Bowland Forest Gliding Club Ltd	
G-CJLP	Schempp-Hirth Discus CS	The Royal Air Force Gliding and Soaring Association	

Notes	Reg.	Type	Owner or Operator
	G-CJLR	Grob G.102 Astir CS	The Royal Air Force Gliding and Soaring Association
	G-CJLS	Schleicher K-8B	E. Ustenler
	G-CJLV	Schleicher Ka 6E	J. M. & J. C. Cooper
	G-CJLW	Schempp-Hirth Discus CS	The Royal Air Force Gliding and Soaring Association
	G-CJLY	Schleicher ASW-27	L. M. Astle & P. C. Piggott
	G-CJLZ	Grob G.103A Twin II Acro	21 Syndicate
	G-CJMA	Schleicher ASK-18	The Royal Air Force Gliding and Soaring Association
	G-CJMD	Embraer RJ135BJ	Corporate Jet Management Ltd
	G-CJMG	PZL-Bielsko SZD-51-1 Junior	Kent Gliding Club Ltd
	G-CJMJ	Schleicher ASK-13	The Royal Air Force Gliding and Soaring Association
	G-CJMK	Schleicher ASK-18	The Royal Air Force Gliding and Soaring Association
	G-CJML	Grob G.102 Astir CS77	The Royal Air Force Gliding and Soaring Association
	G-CJMN	Schempp-Hirth Nimbus 2	R. A. Holroyd
	G-CJMO	Rolladen-Schneider LS8-18	D. J. Langrick
	G-CJMP	Schleicher ASK-13	East Sussex Gliding Club Ltd
	G-CJMS	Schleicher ASK-21	The Royal Air Force Gliding and Soaring Association
	G-CJMT	Rolladen-Schneider LS8-18	D. P. & K. M. Draper
	G-CJMU	Rolladen-Schneider LS8-18	302 Flying Group
	G-CJMV	Schempp-Hirth Nimbus-2C	G. Tucker & K. R. Walton
	G-CJMW	Schleicher ASK-13	The Royal Air Force Gliding and Soaring Association
	G-CJMX	Schleicher ASK-13	Shalbourne Soaring Society Ltd
	G-CJMY	PZL-Bielsko SZD-51-1 Junior	Highland Gliding Club Ltd
	G-CJMZ	Schleicher ASK-13	The Royal Air Force Gliding and Soaring Association
	G-CJNA	Grob G.102 Astir CS Jeans	Shenington Gliding Club
	G-CJNB	Rolladen-Schneider LS8-18	Tatenhill Aviation Ltd
	G-CJNE	Schempp-Hirth Discus 2a	R. Priest
	G-CJNF	Schempp-Hirth Discus 2a	J. N. Rebbeck
	G-CJNG	Glasflugel Standard Libelle 201B	C. A. Willson
	G-CJNJ	Rolladen-Schneider LS8-18	A. B. Laws
	G-CJNK	Rolladen-Schneider LS8-18	Army Gliding Association
	G-CJNN	Schleicher K 8B	Buckminster Gliding Club Ltd
	G-CJNO	Glaser-Dirks DG-300 Elan	Yankee Kilo Group
	G-CJNP	Rolladen-Schneider LS6-b	E. & P. S. Fink
	G-CJNR	Glasflugel Mosquito B	S. L. Barnes & C. R. North
	G-CJNT	Schleicher ASW-19B	M. D. Borrowdale
	G-CJNZ	Glaser-Dirks DG-100	T. Tordoff & R. Jones
	G-CJOA	Schempp-Hirth Discus b	The Royal Air Force Gliding and Soaring Association
	G-CJOB	Schleicher K 8B	JQB Syndicate
	G-CJOC	Schempp-Hirth Discus bT	287 Syndicate
	G-CJOD	Rolladen-Schneider LS8-18	The Royal Air Force Gliding and Soaring Association
	G-CJOE	Schempp-Hirth Standard Cirrus	D. I. Bolsdon & P. T. Johnson
	G-CJOG	Grob G.103A Twin II Acro	Acro Syundicate
	G-CJOJ	Schleicher K 8B	P. W. Burgess
	G-CJON	Grob G.102 Astir CS77	The Royal Air Force Gliding and Soaring Association
	G-CJOO	Schempp-Hirth Duo Discus	185 Syndicate
	G-CJOP	Centrair 101A Pegase	P. A. Woodcock
	G-CJOR	Schempp-Hirth Ventus 2cT	A. M. George & N. A. Maclean
	G-CJOS	Schempp-Hirth Standard Cirrus	G-CJOS Group
	G-CJOU	AB Sportline Aviacija LAK-17A	B. Dorozko
	G-CJOV	Schleicher ASW-27	J. W. White
	G-CJOW	Schempp-Hirth Cirrus VTC	North Wales Gliding Club Ltd
	G-CJOX	Schleicher ASK-21	Southdown Gliding Club Ltd
	G-CJOZ	Schleicher K 8B	Derbyshire and Lancashire Gliding Club Ltd
	G-CJPA	Schempp-Hirth Duo Discus	Coventry Gliding Club Ltd
	G-CJPC	Schleicher ASK-13	Shalbourne Soaring Society Ltd
	G-CJPJ	Grob G.104 Speed Astir IIB	R. J. L. Maisonpierre
	G-CJPL	Rolladen-Schneider LS8-18	I. A. Reekie
	G-CJPM	Grob G.102 Astir CS Jeans	G-CJPM Syndicate
	G-CJPO	Schleicher ASK-18	The Royal Air Force Gliding and Soaring Association

Reg.	Type	Owner or Operator	Notes
G-CJPP	Schempp-Hirth Discus b	Scottish Gliding Union Ltd	
G-CJPR	Rolladen-Schneider LS8-18	D. M. Byass & J. A. McCoshim	
G-CJPT	Schleicher ASW-27	R. C. Willis-Fleming	
G-CJPV	Schleicher ASK-13	Cyprus Gliding Group/Cyprus	
G-CJPW	Glaser-Dirks DG-200	A. Brownbridge & A. Kitchen	
G-CJPX	Schleicher ASW-15	R. Hayden & P. Daly	
G-CJPY	Schleicher ASK-13	The Royal Air Force Gliding and Soaring Association	
G-CJPZ	Schleicher ASK-18	The Royal Air Force Gliding and Soaring Association	
G-CJRA	Rolladen-Schneider LS8-18	J. Williams	
G-CJRB	Schleicher ASW-19B	J. W. Baxter	
G-CJRC	Glaser-Dirks DG-300 Elan	P. J. Sillett	
G-CJRD	Grob G.102 Astir CS	A. J. Hadwin & S. J. Kape	
G-CJRE	Scleicher ASW-15	R. A. Starling	
G-CJRF	PZL-Bielsko SZD-50-3 Puchacz	Wolds Gliding Club Ltd	
G-CJRG	Schempp-Hirth Standard Cirrus	N. J. Laux	
G-CJRH	Schleicher ASW-27	C. Jackson & P. C. Jarvis	
G-CJRJ	PZL-Bielsko SZD-50-3 Puchacz	Derbyshire & Lancashire Gliding Club Ltd	
G-CJRL	Glaser-Dirks DG-100G Elan	P. Lazenby	
G-CJRM	Grob G.102 Astir CS	M. P. Webb	
G-CJRN	Glaser-Dirks DG-200/17	T. G. Roberts	
G-CJRR	Schempp-Hirth Discus bT	N. A. Hays	
G-CJRT	Schempp-Hirth Standard Cirrus	JRT Syndicate	
G-CJRU	Schleicher ASW-24	S. A. Kerby	
G-CJRV	Schleicher ASW-19B	M. Roome & R. Taylor	
G-CJRX	Schleicher ASK-13	The Royal Air Force Gliding and Soaring Association	
G-CJSA	Nanchang NAMC CJ-6A	Bogaerts Aviation BVBA	
G-CJSC	Schempp-Hirth Nimbus-3DT	S. G. Jones	
G-CJSD	Grob G.102 Astir CS	The Royal Air Force Gliding and Soaring Association	
G-CJSE	Schempp-Hirth Discus b	Imperial College of Science, Technology and Medicine	
G-CJSG	Schleicher Ka 6E	A. J. Emck	
G-CJSH	Grob G.102 Club Astir IIIB	Lasham Gliding Society Ltd	
G-CJSJ	Rolladen-Schneider LS7-WL	S. P. Woolcock	
G-CJSK	Grob G.102 Astir CS	Sierra Kilo Group	
G-CJSL	Schempp-Hirth Ventus cT	D. Latimer	
G-CJSN	Schleicher K 8B	Cotswold Gliding Club	
G-CJSS	Schleicher ASW-27	G. K. & S. R. Drury	
G-CJST	Rolladen-Schneider LS1-c	W. A. Bowness & E. Richar	
G-CJSU	Rolladen-Schneider LS8-18	J. G. Bell	
G-CJSV	Schleicher ASK-13	The Royal Air Force Gliding and Soaring Association	
G-CJSW	Rolladen-Schneider LS4-a	C. Benoit	
G-CJSX	AMS-Flight DG-500	Oxford Gliding Company Ltd	
G-CJSZ	Schleicher ASK-18	C. Weston	
G-CJTB	Schleicher ASW-24	V17 Syndicate	
G-CJTH	Schleicher ASW-24	R. J. & J. E. Lodge	
G-CJTJ	Schempp-Hirth Mini-Nimbus B	R. A. Bowker	
G-CJTK	DG Flugzeugbau DG-300 Elan Acro	A. Jorgensen	
G-CJTL	Rolladen-Schneider LS8-18	J. M. & R. S. Hood	
G-CJTM	Rolladen-Schneider LS8-18	A. D. Holmes	
G-CJTN	Glaser-Dirks DG-300 Elan	A. D. Noble & P. W. Schartau	
G-CJTO	Glasflugel H303A Mosquito	Tango Oscar Group	
G-CJTP	Schleicher ASW-20L	C. A. Sheldon	
G-CJTR	Rolladen-Schneider LS7-WL	D53 Syndicate	
G-CJTS	Schempp-Hirth Cirrus VTC	G-CJTS Cirrus Group	
G-CJTU	Schempp-Hirth Duo Discus T	JTU Syndicate	
G-CJTW	Glasflugel Mosquito B	S. Urry	
G-CJTY	Rolladen-Schneider LS8-a	BBC (London) Club	
G-CJUB	Schempp-Hirth Discus CS	Coventry Gliding Club Ltd	
G-CJUD	Denney Kitfox Mk 3	D. Joy	
G-CJUF	Schempp-Hirth Ventus 2cT	M. H. B. Pope	
G-CJUJ	Schleicher ASW-27	P. A. Ivens	
G-CJUK	Grob G.102 Astir CS	P. Freer & S. J. Calvert	
G-CJUM	Schempp-Hirth Duo Discus T	2 UP Group	
G-CJUN	Schleicher ASW-19B	M. P. S. Roberts	
G-CJUP	Schempp-Hirth Discus 2b	The Discuss 2 Uniform Papa Group	
G-CJUR	Valentin Mistral C	M. J. W. Harris	
G-CJUS	Grob G.102 Astir CS	East Sussex Gliding Club Ltd	

Notes	Reg.	Type	Owner or Operator
	G-CJUU	Schempp-Hirth Standard Cirrus	H. R. Fraser
	G-CJUV	Schempp-Hirth Discus b	Lasham Gliding Society Ltd
	G-CJUX	Aviastroitel AC-4C	R. J. Walton
	G-CJUZ	Schleicher ASW-19B	K. W. Clarke
	G-CJVA	Schempp-Hirth Ventus 2cT	M. S. Armstrong
	G-CJVB	Schempp-Hirth Discus bT	C. J. Edwards
	G-CJVC	PZL-Bielsko SZD-51-1 Junior	York Gliding Centre Ltd
	G-CJVE	Eiriavion PIK-20D	S. R. Wilkinson
	G-CJVF	Schempp-Hirth Discus CS	J. Hodgson
	G-CJVG	Schempp-Hirth Discus bT	S. J. Bryan & P. J. Bramley
	G-CJVJ	AB Sportine LAK-17A	J. A. Sutton
	G-CJVL	DG-300 Elan	A. T. Vidion & A. Griffiths
	G-CJVM	Schleicher ASW-27	G. K. Payne
	G-CJVP	Glaser-Dirks DG-200	M. S. Howey & S. Leadbeater
	G-CJVS	Schleicher ASW-28	Zulu Glasstek Ltd
	G-CJVU	Standard Cirrus CS-11-75L	Cirrus 75 Syndicate
	G-CJVV	Schempp-Hirth Janus C	J50 Syndicate
	G-CJVW	Schleicher ASW-15	Victor Whiskey Group
	G-CJVX	Schempp-Hirth Discus CS	G-CJVX Syndicate
	G-CJVZ	Schleicher ASK-21	Yorkshire Gliding Club (Proprietary) Ltd
	G-CJWA	Schleicher ASW-28	P. R. Porter & M. J. Taylor
	G-CJWB	Schleicher ASK-13	East Sussex Gliding Club Ltd
	G-CJWD	Schleicher ASK-21	London Gliding Club Proprietary Ltd
	G-CJWF	Schleicher ASW-27	B. A. Fairston & A. Stotter
	G-CJWG	Schempp-Hirth Nimbus 3	880 Group
	G-CJWJ	Schleicher ASK-13	The Royal Air Force Gliding and Soaring Association
	G-CJWK	Schempp-Hirth Discus bT	722 Syndicate
	G-CJWM	Grob G.103 Twin Astir II	Norfolk Gliding Club Ltd
	G-CJWP	Bolkow Phoebus B1	A. Fidler
	G-CJWR	Grob G.102 Astir CS	Cairngorn Gliding Club
	G-CJWT	Glaser-Dirks DG-200	K. R. Nash
	G-CJWU	Schempp-Hirth Ventus bT	B. C. P. & C. Crook
	G-CJWX	Schempp-Hirth Ventus 2cT	M. M. A. Lipperheide & S. G. Olender
	G-CJXA	Schempp-Hirth Nimbus 3	Y44 Syndicate
	G-CJXB	Centrair 201B Marianne	Marianne Syndicate
	G-CJXC	Wassmer WA28	A. P. Montague
	G-CJXG	Eiriavion PIK-20D	W5 Group
	G-CJXL	Schempp-Hirth Discus CS	J. Hall & M. J. Hasluck
	G-CJXM	Schleicher ASK-13	The Windrushers Gliding Club
	G-CJXN	Centrair 201B	R. D. Trussell
	G-CJXP	Glaser-Dirks DG-100	N. L. Morris
	G-CJXR	Schempp-Hirth Discus b	Cambridge Gliding Club Ltd
	G-CJXT	Schleicher ASW-24B	P. McAuley
	G-CJXW	Schempp-Hirth Duo Discus T	R. A. Beatty
	G-CJXX	Pilatus B4-PC11AF	N. H. Buckenham
	G-CJXY	Neukom Elfe S4A	J. Hunt
	G-CJYC	Grob G.102 Astir CS	R. A. Christie
	G-CJYD	Schleicher ASW-27	J. E. Gatfield
	G-CJYE	Schleicher ASK-13	North Wales Gliding Club Ltd
	G-CJYF	Schempp Hirth Discus CS	W. J. Winthrop
	G-CJYL	AB Sportine Aviacija LAK-12	A. Camerotto
	G-CJYO	Glaser-Dirks DG-100G Elan	A. M. Booth
	G-CJYP	Grob G.102 Club Astir II	Astir Syndicate BGA4891
	G-CJYR	Schempp-Hirth Duo Discus T	CJYR Flying Group
	G-CJYS	Schempp-Hirth Mini Nimbus C	A. Jenkins
	G-CJYU	Schempp-Hirth Ventus 2cT	The Royal Air Force Gliding and Soaring Association
	G-CJYV	Schleicher K8B	Club Agrupacion de Pilotos del Sureste/Spain
	G-CJYW	Schleicher K8B	Club Agrupacion de Pilotos del Sureste/Spain
	G-CJYX	Rolladen-Schneider LS3-17	D. Meyer-Beeck & V. G. Diaz
	G-CJZB	DG-500 Elan Orion	Bicester JZB Syndicate
	G-CJZE	Schleicher ASK-13	Needwood Forest Gliding Club Ltd
	G-CJZG	Schempp-Hirth Discus bT	I. K. G. Mitchell
	G-CJZH	Schleicher ASW-20 CL	C. P. Gibson & A. Hunt
	G-CJZK	DG-505 Elan Orion	Devon and Somerset Gliding Club Ltd
	G-CJZL	Schempp-Hirth Mini Nimbus B	P. A. Dunthorne
	G-CJZM	Schempp-Hirth Ventus 2a	S. Crabb
	G-CJZN	Schleicher ASW-28	P. J. Coward
	G-CJZY	Grob G.102 Standard Astir III	Lasham Gliding Society Ltd
	G-CJZZ	Rolladen-Schneider LS7	Birkett Air Services Ltd

Reg.	Type	Owner or Operator	Notes
G-CKAC	Glaser-Dirks DG-200	M. G. Stringer	
G-CKAE	Centrair 101A Pegase	Rattlesden Gliding Club Ltd	
G-CKAK	Schleicher ASW-28	S. J. Kelman	
G-CKAL	Schleicher ASW-28	D. A. Smith	
G-CKAM	Glasflugel Club Libelle 205	P. A. Cronk & R. C. Tallowin	
G-CKAN	PZL-Bielsko SZD-50-3 Puchacz	The Bath Wilts and North Dorset Gliding Club Ltd	
G-CKAP	Schempp-Hirth Discus CS	KAP Syndicate	
G-CKAR	Schempp-Hirth Duo Discus T	977 Syndicate	
G-CKAS	Schempp-Hirth Ventus 2cT	KAS Club	
G-CKAU	DG Flugzeugbau DG-303 Elan Acro	G. Earle	
G-CKAX	AMS-Flight DG-500 Elan Orion	York Gliding Centre Ltd	
G-CKAY	Grob G.102 Astir CS	D. Ryder & P. Carrington	
G-CKBA	Centrair 101A Pegase	KBA Pegase 101A Syndicate	
G-CKBC	Rolladen-Schneider LS6-c	A. W. Lyth	
G-CKBD	Grob G.102 Astir CS	R. A. Morriss	
G-CKBF	AMS-Flight DG-303 Elan	A. L. Garfield	
G-CKBG	Schempp-Hirth Ventus 2cT	71 Syndicate	
G-CKBH	Rolladen-Schneider LS6	F. C. Ballard & P. Walker	
G-CKBK	Schempp-Hirth Ventus 2cT	D. Rhys-Jones	
G-CKBL	Grob G.102 Astir CS	Norfolk Gliding Club Ltd	
G-CKBM	Schleicher ASW-28	C. S. & M. E. Newland-Smith	
G-CKBN	PZL-Bielsko SZD-55-1 Promyk	N. D. Pearson	
G-CKBT	Schempp-Hirth Standard Cirrus	P. R. Johnson	
G-CKBU	Schleicher ASW-28	G. C. Metcalfe	
G-CKBV	Schleicher ASW-28	P. Whipp	
G-CKBX	Schleicher ASW-27	M. Wright & T. J. Davies	
G-CKCB	Rolladen-Schneider LS4-a	The Bristol Gliding Club Proprietary Ltd	
G-CKCD	Schempp-Hirth Ventus 2cT	R. S. Jobar & S. G. Jones	
G-CKCE	Schempp-Hirth Ventus 2cT	M. W. Cater & J. P. Walker	
G-CKCH	Schempp-Hirth Ventus 2cT	J. J. Pridal & L. R. Marks	
G-CKCJ	Schleicher ASW-28	S. L. Withall	
G-CKCK	Enstrom 280FX	Rhoburt Ltd	
G-CKCM	Glasflugel Standard Libelle 201B	G. A. Cox	
G-CKCN	Schleicher ASW-27	W. J. Head	
G-CKCP	Grob G.102 Astir CS	Norfolk Gliding Club Ltd	
G-CKCR	AB Sportine Aviacija LAK-17A	M. Kessler/Italy	
G-CKCT	Schleicher ASK-21	Kent Gliding Club Aircraft Ltd	
G-CKCV	Schempp-Hirth Duo Discus T	WE4 Group	
G-CKCY	Schleicher ASW-20	J. Sugden	
G-CKCZ	Schleicher ASK-21	Booker Gliding Club Ltd	
G-CKDA	Schempp-Hirth Ventus 2B	D. J. Eade	
G-CKDB	Schleicher Ka 6CR	Banbury Gliding Club Ltd	
G-CKDC	Centrair ASW-20F	M. Staljan, S. Brogger & C. Behrendt	
G-CKDF	Schleicher ASK-21	Portsmouth Naval Gliding Centre	
G-CKDK	Rolladen-Schneider LS4-a	M. C. & P. A. Ridger	
G-CKDN	Schleicher ASW-27B	J. S. McCullagh	
G-CKDO	Schempp-Hirth Ventus 2cT	M. W. Edwards	
G-CKDP	Schleicher ASK-21	Kent Gliding Club Aircraft Ltd	
G-CKDR	PZL-Bielsko SZD-48-3 Jantar Standard 3	G. Hyrkowski	
G-CKDS	Schleicher ASW-27	A. W. Gillett & G. D. Morris	
G-CKDU	Glaser-Dirks DG-200/17	P. G. Noonan	
G-CKDV	Schempp-Hirth Ventus B/16.6	M. A. Codd	
G-CKDW	Schleicher ASW-27	C. Colton	
G-CKDX	Glaser-Dirks DG-200	Delta X Ray Group	
G-CKDY	Glaser-Dirks DG-100	503 Group	
G-CKDZ	Schempp-Hirth Standard Cirrus 75	Charlie 75	
G-CKEA	Schempp-Hirth Cirrus 18	C. M. Reed	
G-CKEB	Schempp-Hirth Standard Cirrus	A. J. Mugleston	
G-CKED	Schleicher ASW-27B	A. & R. Maskell	
G-CKEE	Grob G.102 Astir CS	Essex and Suffolk Gliding Club Ltd	
G-CKEJ	Schleicher ASK-21	London Gliding Club Proprietary Ltd	
G-CKEK	Schleicher ASK-21	Devon and Somerset Gliding Club Ltd	
G-CKEP	Rolladen-Schneider LS6-b	G-CKEP Group	
G-CKER	Schleicher ASW-19B	W. A. Bowness & E. Richards	
G-CKES	Schempp-Hirth Cirrus 18	D. Judd & N. Hawley	
G-CKET	Rolladen-Schneider LS8-8	M. B. Jefferyes & J. C. Taylor	
G-CKEV	Schempp-Hirth Duo Discus	The Royal Air Force Gliding and Soaring Association	
G-CKEY	PA-28-161 Warrior II	Warwickshire Aviation Ltd	
G-CKEZ	DG Flugzeugbau LS8	D. A. Jesty	
G-CKFA	Schempp-Hirth Standard Cirrus 75	G. C. Bell	
G-CKFB	Schempp-Hirth Discus-2T	P. L. & P. A. G. Holland	

Notes	Reg.	Type	Owner or Operator
	G-CKFC	Schempp-Hirth Ventus 2cT	P. Lecci
	G-CKFD	Schleicher ASW-27B	W. T. Craig
	G-CKFE	Eiriavion PIK-20D	O. Houlihan
	G-CKFG	Grob G.103A Twin II Acro	The Surrey Hills Gliding Club Ltd
	G-CKFH	Schempp-Hirth Mini Nimbus	G-CKFH Flying Group
	G-CKFJ	Schleicher ASK-13	York Gliding Centre Ltd
	G-CKFK	Schempp-Hirth Standard Cirrus 75	P. R. Wilkinson
	G-CKFL	Rolladen-Schneider LS4	D. O'Brien & D. R. Taylor
	G-CKFN	DG Flugzeugbau DG1000	Yorkshire Gliding Club (Proprietary) Ltd
	G-CKFP	Schempp-Hirth Ventus 2cxT	C. R. Sutton
	G-CKFR	Schleicher ASK-13	Club Acrupacion de Pilotos del Sureste/Spain
	G-CKFT	Schempp-Hirth Duo Discus T	Duo Discus Syndicate
	G-CKFV	DG Flugzeugbau LS8-t	G. A. Rowden & K. I. Arkley
	G-CKFY	Schleicher ASK.21	Cambridge Gliding Club
	G-CKGA	Schempp-Hirth Ventus 2cxT	D. R. Campbell
	G-CKGC	Schempp-Hirth Ventus 2cxT	C. P. A. Jeffery
	G-CKGD	Schempp-Hirth Ventus 2cxT	C. Morris
	G-CKGF	Schempp-Hirth Duo Discus T	Duo 233 Group
	G-CKGH	Grob G.102 Club Astir II	I. M. Gavan
	G-CKGK	Schleicher ASK-21	The Royal Air Force Gliding & Soaring Association
	G-CKGL	Schempp-Hirth Ventus 2cT	Kilo Golf Lima Syndicate
	G-CKGM	Centrair 101A Pegase	S. France
	G-CKGU	Schleicher ASW-19B	ASW 19 KGU Group
	G-CKGV	Schleicher ASW-20	A. H. Reynolds
	G-CKGX	Schleicher ASK-21	Coventry Gliding Club Ltd
	G-CKGY	Scheibe Bergfalke IV	B. R. Pearson
	G-CKHA	PZL SZD-51-1 Junior	Devon & Somerset Gliding Club Ltd
	G-CKHB	Rolladen-Schneider LS3	C. J. Cole
	G-CKHC	DG Flugzeugbau DG.505	G-CKHC Group
	G-CKHD	Schleicher ASW-27B	N. D Tillett
	G-CKHE	AB Sportine Aviacija LAK-17AT	N. J. Gough & A. J. Garrity
	G-CKHG	Schleicher ASW-27B	R. A. F. King
	G-CKHH	Schleicher ASK-13	Lincolnshire Gliding Club Ltd
	G-CKHK	Schempp-Hirth Duo Discus T	Duo Discus Syndicate
	G-CKHM	Centrair 101A Pegase 90	J. Randall & J. A. Tipler
	G-CKHN	PZL SZD-51-1 Junior	The Nene Valley Gliding Club Ltd
	G-CKHR	PZL-Bielsko SZD-51-1 Junior	Wolds Gliding Club Ltd
	G-CKHS	Rolladen-Schneider LS7-WL	M. Lawson & D. Wallis
	G-CKHV	Glaser-Dirks DG-100	G-CKHV Trust
	G-CKHW	PZL SZD-50-3 Puchacz	Derbyshire and Lancashire Gliding Club Ltd
	G-CKJB	Schempp-Hirth Ventus bT	J. R. Matthews & J. R. Rayner
	G-CKJC	Schempp-Hirth Nimbus 3T	A. C. Wright
	G-CKJD	Schempp-Hirth Cirrus 75-VTC	P. J. P. Vanden Boer
	G-CKJE	DG Flugzeugbau LS8-18	M. D. Wells
	G-CKJF	Schempp-Hirth Standard Cirrus	L. A. Lawes
	G-CKJG	Schempp-Hirth Cirrus VTC	S. J. Wright
	G-CKJH	Glaser-Dirks DG.300 Elan	Yorkshire Gliding Club
	G-CKJJ	DG Flugzeugbau DG-500 Elan Orion	Ulster Gliding Club Ltd
	G-CKJL	Scleicher ASK-13	Lincolnshire Gliding Club Ltd
	G-CKJM	Schempp-Hirth Ventus cT	G-CKJM Group
	G-CKJN	Schleicher ASW-20	R. Logan
	G-CKJP	Schleicher ASK-21	The Royal Air Force Gliding and Soaring Association
	G-CKJS	Schleicher ASW-28-18E	G-CKJS Syndicate
	G-CKJV	Schleicher ASW-28-18E	A. C. Price
	G-CKJZ	Schempp-Hirth Discus bT	G-CKJZ Group
	G-CKKB	Centrair 101A Pegase	D. M. Rushton
	G-CKKC	DG Flugzeugbau DG-300 Elan Acro	Charlie Kilo Kilo Charlie Syndicate
	G-CKKE	Schempp-Hirth Duo Discus T	The Foxtrot Group
	G-CKKF	Schempp-Hirth Ventus 2cT	A. R. MacGregor
	G-CKKH	Schleicher ASW-27	P. L. Hurd
	G-CKKK	AB Sportine Aviacija LAK-17A	C. J. Nicolas
	G-CKKP	Schleicher ASK-21	Bowland Forest Gliding Club Ltd
	G-CKKR	Schleicher ASK-13	The Windrushers Gliding Club Ltd
	G-CKKV	DG Flugzeugbau DG-1000S	Lasham Gliding Society Ltd
	G-CKKX	Rolladen-Schneider LS4-A	B. W. Svenson
	G-CKKY	Schempp-Hirth Duo Discus T	P. D. Duffin
	G-CKLA	Schleicher ASK-13	Booker Gliding Club Ltd
	G-CKLC	Glasflugel H206 Hornet	L. P. Woodage
	G-CKLD	Schempp-Hirth Discus 2cT	J. P. Galloway
	G-CKLF	Schempp-Hirth Janus	Kilo Lima Foxtrot
	G-CKLG	Rolladen-Schneider LS4	P. M. Scheiwiller

Reg.	Type	Owner or Operator	Notes
G-CKLN	Rolladen-Schneider LS4-A	Army Gliding Association	
G-CKLP	Scleicher ASW-28-18	J. T. Birch	
G-CKLR	Pezetel SZD-55-1	Zulu Five Gliding Group (G-CKLM)	
G-CKLS	Rolladen-Schneider LS4	Wolds Gliding Club Ltd	
G-CKLT	Schempp-Hirth Nimbus 3/24.5	G. N. Thomas	
G-CKLV	Schempp-Hirth Discus 2cT	S. Baker	
G-CKLW	Schleicher ASK-21	Yorkshire Gliding Club	
G-CKLY	DG Flugzeugbau DG-1000T	G-CKLY Group	
G-CKMA	DG Flugzeugbau LS8-T	W. J. Morecraft	
G-CKMB	AB Sportline Aviacija LAK-19T	D. J. McKenzie	
G-CKMD	Schempp-Hirth Standard Cirrus	S. A. Crabb	
G-CKME	DG Flugzeugbau LS8-T	S. M. Smith	
G-CKMF	Centrair 101A Pegase	D. L. M. Jamin	
G-CKMG	Glaser-Dirks DG-101G Elan	R. A. Johnson	
G-CKMI	Schleicher K8C	V. Mallon	
G-CKMJ	Schleicher Ka 6CR	V. Mallon	
G-CKML	Schempp-Hirth Duo Discus T	G-CKML Group	
G-CKMM	Schleicher ASW-28-18E	R. G. Munro	
G-CKMO	Rolladen-Schneider LS7-WL	G. E. M. Turpin	
G-CKMP	AB Sportine Aviacija LAK-17A	J. L. McIver	
G-CKMT	Grob G103C	Essex & Suffolk Gliding Club Ltd	
G-CKMV	Rolladen-Schneider LS3-17	S. Procter & M. P. Woolmer	
G-CKMW	Schleicher ASK-21	The Royal Air Force Gliding & Soaring Association	
G-CKMZ	Schleicher ASW-28-18	J. R. Martindale	
G-CKNB	Schempp-Hirth Standard Cirrus	A. Booker	
G-CKNC	Caproni Calif A21S	J. J. & M. E. Pritchard	
G-CKND	DG Flugzeugbau DG-1000T	KND Group	
G-CKNE	Schempp-Hirth Standard Cirrus 75-VTC	G. D. E. Macdonald	
G-CKNF	DG Flugzeugbau DG-1000T	Six November Fox	
G-CKNG	Schleicher ASW-28-18E	M. P. Brockinhton	
G-CKNK	Glaser-Dirks DG.500	Cotswold Gliding Club	
G-CKNL	Schleicher ASK-21	Buckminster Gliding Club Ltd	
G-CKNM	Scleicher ASK-18	I. L. Pattingale	
G-CKNO	Schempp-Hirth Ventus 2cxT	C. McEwen	
G-CKNR	Schempp-Hirth Ventus 2cxT	R. J. Nicholls	
G-CKNS	Rolladen-Schneider LS4-A	I. R. Willows	
G-CKNV	Schleicher ASW-28-18E	D. G. Brain	
G-CKOD	Schempp-Hirth Discus BT	A. L. Harris & M. W. Talbot	
G-CKOE	Schleicher ASW-27-18	R. C. Bromwich	
G-CKOH	DG Flugzeugbau DG-1000T	Oscar Hotel Group	
G-CKOI	AB Sportine Aviacija LAK-17AT	C. G. Corbett	
G-CKOK	Schempp-Hirth Discus 2cT	B. D. Scougall	
G-CKOL	Schempp-Hirth Duo Discus T	Oscar Lima Syndicate	
G-CKOM	Schleicher ASW-27-18	L. M. P. Wells	
G-CKON	Schleicher ASW-27-18E	J. P. Gorringe	
G-CKOO	Schleicher ASW-27-18E	A. Darlington, J. P. Lewis & C. T. P. Williams	
G-CKOR	Glaser-Dirks DG-300 Elan	J. A. Sparrow	
G-CKOT	Schleicher ASK-21	Ulster Gliding Club Ltd	
G-CKOU	AB Sportine Aviacija LAK-19T	PAC LAK Syndicate	
G-CKOW	DG-505 Elan Orion	Southdown Gliding Club Ltd	
G-CKOX	AMS-Flight DG-505 Elan Orion	Seahawk Gliding Club	
G-CKOY	Schleicher ASW-27-18E	G-CKOY Group	
G-CKOZ	Schleicher ASW-27-18E	E. W. Johnston	
G-CKPA	AB Sportline Aviacija LAK-19T	O. R. Momege	
G-CKPE	Schempp-Hirth Duo Discus	Portsmouth Naval Gliding Centre	
G-CKPG	Schempp-Hirth Discus 2cT	G. Knight & P. Rowden	
G-CKPJ	Neukom S-4D Elfe	S. Szladowski	
G-CKPK	Schempp-Hirth Ventus 2cxT	I. C. Lees	
G-CKPM	DG Flugzeugbau LS8-T	8T Soaring	
G-CKPN	PZL-Bielsko SZD-51-1 Junior	Rattlesden Gliding Club Ltd	
G-CKPO	Schempp-Hirth Duo Discus xT	KPO Syndicate	
G-CKPP	Schleicher ASK-21	The Gliding Centre	
G-CKPU	Schleicher ASW-27-18E	A. J. Kellerman	
G-CKPV	Schempp-Hirth HS.7 Mini-Nimbus B	D. K. McCarthy	
G-CKPX	ZS Jezow PW-6U	J. C. Gibson	
G-CKPY	Schempp-Hirth Duo Discus xT	Duo-Discus Syndicate	
G-CKPZ	Schleicher ASW-20	T. Davies	
G-CKRB	Schleicher ASK-13	Derbyshire and Lancashire Gliding Club Ltd	
G-CKRC	Schleicher ASW-28-18E	M. Woodcock	
G-CKRD	Schleicher ASW-27-18E	R. F. Thirkell	
G-CKRF	DG-300 Elan	G. A. King	

Notes	Reg.	Type	Owner or Operator
	G-CKRH	Grob G.103 Twin Astir II	Staffordshire Gliding Club Ltd
	G-CKRI	Schleicher ASK-21	Kent Gliding Club Aircraft Ltd
	G-CKRJ	Schleicher ASW-27-18E	J. J. Marshall
	G-CKRN	Grob G.102 Astir CS	Yorkshire Gliding Club (Proprietary) Ltd
	G-CKRO	Schempp-Hirth Duo Discus T	Duo Discus Syndicate KRO
	G-CKRR	Schleicher ASW-15B	C. D. Ellis
	G-CKRS	FFA Diamant 16.5	G-CKRS Syndicate
	G-CKRU	ZS Jezow PW-6U	Cotswold Gliding Club
	G-CKRV	Schleicher ASW-27-18E	Z. Marczynski
	G-CKRW	Schleicher ASK-21	The Royal Air Force Gliding and Soaring Association
	G-CKRX	Jezow PW-6U	Cotswold Gliding Club
	G-CKSC	Czech Sport Aircraft Sportcruiser	Czechmate Syndicate
	G-CKSD	Rolladen-Schneider LS8-a	S. E. Coles
	G-CKSK	Pilatus B4-PC11	K. Steinmair
	G-CKSL	Schleicher ASW-15B	Sierra Lima Group
	G-CKSM	Schempp-Hirth Duo Discus T	J. H. May & S. P. Ball
	G-CKSX	Schleicher ASW-27-18E	M. C. Foreman
	G-CKSY	Rolladen-Schneider LS-7-WL	C. M. Lewis
	G-CKTB	Schempp-Hirth Ventus 2cT	M. H. Player
	G-CKTC	Schleicher Ka 6CR	Tango Charlie Group
	G-CKZT	PA-28-235 Cherokee Pathfinder	U. Chakravorty
	G-CLAC	PA-28-161 Warrior II	G-CLAC Group
	G-CLAR	EC.225LP Super Puma	CHC Scotia Ltd
	G-CLAV	Shaw Europa	G. Laverty
	G-CLAY	Bell 206B JetRanger 3	Claygate Distribution Ltd (G-DENN)
	G-CLDS	Rotorsport UK Calidus	Rotorsport UK Ltd
	G-CLEA	PA-28-161 Warrior II	Freedom Aviation Ltd
	G-CLEE	Rans S.6-ES Coyote II	P. S. Chapman
	G-CLEG	Flight Design CTSW	C. A. S. Powell
	G-CLEM	Bölkow Bö.208A2 Junior	G-CLEM Group (G-ASWE)
	G-CLEO	Zenair CH.601HD	K. M. Bowen
	G-CLES	Scheicher ASW-27-18E	A. P. Brown & N. D. Tillett
	G-CLEU	Glaser-Dirks DG-200	S. F. Tape
	G-CLFB	Rolladen-Schneider LS4-A	B. Harker
	G-CLFC	Mainair Blade	G. N. Cliffe & G. Marshall
	G-CLFH	Schleicher ASW-20C	T. Fordwich-Gorefly & P. Armstrong
	G-CLFX	Schempp-Hirth Duo Discus T	A. L. Baillie
	G-CLFZ	Schleicher ASW-18E	C. F. Cownden & J. P. Davies
	G-CLGC	Schempp-Hirth Duo Discus	London Gliding Club Proprietary Ltd
	G-CLGL	Schempp-Hirth Ventus 2c	M. J. Collett and A. Hegner
	G-CLGR	Glasflugel Club Libelle 205	A. A. Gillon
	G-CLGT	Rolladen-Schneider LS4	C. B. & N. M. Hill
	G-CLGU	Schleicher ASW-27-18	T. J. Scott
	G-CLGW	Centrair 101A Pegase	M. White
	G-CLGZ	Schempp-Hirth Duo Discus T	D. R. Irving
	G-CLHF	Scheibe Bergfalke IV	Andreas Gliding Club Ltd
	G-CLHG	Schempp-Hirth Discus b	S. J. Edinborough
	G-CLIC	Cameron A-105 balloon	R. S. Mohr
	G-CLIF	Ikarus C42 FB UK	C. Sims
	G-CLIN	Ikarus C42 FB100	G. C. Linley
	G-CLJE	Schleicher ASH-25M	G. F. Mann
	G-CLJK	PZL-Bielsko SZD-51-1 Junior	Coventry Gliding Club Ltd
	G-CLJZ	Schleicher ASH-31Mi	J. C. Thompson
	G-CLKF	Schempp-Hirth Cirrus VTC	E. C. Wright
	G-CLKG	Schempp-Hirth Janus CM	Lakes Janus Group
	G-CLOE	Sky 90-24 balloon	J. Skinner
	G-CLOS	PA-34-200 Seneca II	R. A. Doherty
	G-CLOW	Beech 200 Super King Air	Clowes (Estates) Ltd
	G-CLRK	Sky 77-24 balloon	William Clark & Son (Parkgate) Ltd
	G-CLUE	PA-34-200T Seneca II	P. Pigg
	G-CLUX	Cessna F.172N	J. & K. Aviation
	G-CLWN	Cameron Clown SS balloon	Magical Adventures Ltd (G-UBBE)
	G-CMAS	Embraer EMB-135BJ Legacy	Execujet (UK) Ltd
	G-CMBR	Cessna 172S	C. M. B. Reid
	G-CMBS	MDH MD-900 Explorer	West Yorkshire Police Authority
	G-CMED	SOCATA TB9 Tampico	D. Primorac
	G-CMEW	Aerospool Dynamic WT9 UK	Yeoman Light Aircraft Co.Ltd
	G-CMGC	PA-25 Pawnee 235	G. G. L. James (G-BFEX)
	G-CMOR	Skyranger 912(2)	M. C. McCart

Reg.	Type	Owner or Operator	Notes
G-CMOS	Cessna T.303 Crusader	C. J. Moss	
G-CMPC	Titan T-51 Mustang	J. A. Carey	
G-CMSN	Robinson R22 Beta	Kuki Helicopter Sales Ltd (G-MGEE//G-RUMP)	
G-CMWK	Grob G.102 Astir CS	S. J. Saunders	
G-CMXX	Robinson R44 II	Northern Excavators Ltd	
G-CNAB	Avtech Jabiru UL	E. M. Christoffersen	
G-CNCN	Rockwell Commander 112CA	G. R. Frost	
G-CNHB	Van's RV-7	M. E. Wood	
G-CNUK	Dassault Falcon 7X	TAG Aviation (UK) Ltd	
G-COAI	Cranfield A.1	Cranfield University (G-BCIT)	
G-COBI	Beech 300 Super King Air	Cobham Flight Inspection Ltd	
G-COBM	Beech 300 Super King Air	Cobham Flight Inspection Ltd	
G-COBO	ATR-72-212A	Aurigny Air Services Ltd	
G-COBS	Diamond DA.42 M-NG	Cobham Flight Inspection Ltd	
G-COCO	Cessna F.172M	P. C. Sheard & R. C. Larder	
G-CODY	Kolb Twinstar Mk.3 Extra	J. W. Codd	
G-COIN	Bell 206B JetRanger 2	J. P. Niehorster	
G-COLA	Beech F33C Bonanza	Airport Direction Ltd (G-BUAZ)	
G-COLH	PA-28 Cherokee 140	Full Sutton Flying Centre Ltd (G-AVRT)	
G-COLI	Rotorsport UK MT-03	C. Gilholm	
G-COLR	Colt 69A balloon ★	British School of Ballooning/Lancing	
G-COLS	Van's RV-7A	C. Terry	
G-COLY	Aeropro Eurofox 912(S)	C. J. Norman	
G-COMB	PA-30 Twin Comanche 160B	Just Plane Trading Ltd (G-AVBL)	
G-COML	Eurocopter EC120B	Combilift	
G-COMP	Cameron N-90 balloon	Computacenter Ltd	
G-CONA	Flight Design CTLS	S. Connah (G-CGED)	
G-CONB	Robin DR.400/180	M. D. Souster (G-BUPX)	
G-CONC	Cameron N-90 balloon	A. A. Brown	
G-CONL	SOCATA TB10 Tobago	J. M. Huntington	
G-CONN	Eurocopter EC.120B Colibri	M. J. Connors (G-BZMK)	
G-CONR	Champion 7GCBC Scout	Aerofoyle Group	
G-CONV	Convair CV-440-54 ★	Reynard Nursery/Carluke	
G-CONY	BAe Jetstream 3101	Linksair Ltd	
G-COOK	Cameron N-77 balloon	IAZ (International) Ltd	
G-COOT	Taylor Coot A	P. M. Napp	
G-COPS	Piper J-3C-65 Cub	R. W. Sproat	
G-CORA	Shaw Europa XS	A. P. Gardner (G-ILUM)	
G-CORB	SOCATA TB20 Trinidad	Corvid Aviation Ltd	
G-CORD	Slingsby T.66 Nipper 3	A. V. Lamprell (G-AVTB)	
G-CORL	AS.350B3 Ecureuil	Abbeyflight Ltd	
G-CORW	PA-28-180 Cherokee C	R. P. Osborne & C. A. Wilson (G-AVRY)	
G-COSF	PA-28-161 Warrior II	PA-28 Warrior Ltd	
G-COSY	Lindstrand LBL-56A balloon	M. H. Read & J. E. Wetters	
G-COTH	MD-900 Explorer	Police Aviation Services Ltd	
G-COTT	Cameron 60 Cottage SS balloon	Dragon Balloon Co Ltd	
G-COUZ	X'Air 582(2)	D. J. Couzens	
G-COVA	PA-26-161 Warrior III	Coventry (Civil) Aviation Ltd (G-CDCL)	
G-COVB	PA-28-161 Warrior III	Coventry (Civil) Aviation Ltd	
G-COVE	Avtech Jabiru UL	A. A. Rowson	
G-COVZ	Cessna F.150M	R. A. Doherty (G-BCRT)	
G-COWN	P & M Quik GTR	B. J. Partridge & J. A. Valentine	
G-COXS	Aeroprakt A.22 Foxbat	S. Cox	
G-COZI	Rutan Cozy III	R. Machin	
G-CPAO	Eurocopter EC.135P2+	Cheshire Police Authority	
G-CPAS	Eurocopter EC.135P2+	Cleveland Police Authority	
G-CPCD	CEA DR.221	P. J. Taylor	
G-CPDA	DH.106 Comet 4C (XS235) ★	C. Walton Ltd/Bruntingthorpe	
G-CPDW	Avions Mudry CAP.10B	Hilfa Ltd	
G-CPEU	Boeing 757-236	Thomson Airways Ltd	
G-CPEV	Boeing 757-236	Thomson Airways Ltd	
G-CPFC	Cessna F.152 II	Falcon Flying Services Ltd	
G-CPFM	PA-28-161 Warrior II	M. O'Rourke (G-BNNS)	
G-CPII	Avions Mudry CAP-231	A. D. Hoy	
G-CPMK	DHC.1 Chipmunk 22 (WZ847)	P. A. Walley	
G-CPMS	SOCATA TB20 Trinidad	Charlotte Park Management Services Ltd	
G-CPOL	AS.355F1 Twin Squirrel	MW Helicopters Ltd	
G-CPPM	North American Harvard II	S. D. Wilch	
G-CPRR	Cessna 680 Citation Sovereign	Bookajet Aircraft Management Ltd	

Notes	Reg.	Type	Owner or Operator
	G-CPSH	Eurocopter EC 135T1	West Yorkshire Police Authority
	G-CPSS	Cessna 208B Grand Caravan	Army Parachute Association
	G-CPTM	PA-28-151 Warrior	T. J. & C. Mackay (G-BTOE)
	G-CPTR	Rotorsport UK Calidus	A. Marshall (G-CGLH)
	G-CPXC	Avions Mudry CAP-10C	Medcentres Property Portfolio Ltd
	G-CRAB	Skyranger 912 (1)	J. O. Williams
	G-CRAR	CZAW Sportcruiser	J. S. Kinsey
	G-CRBV	Balóny Kubí ek BB26 balloon	Charter Ballooning Ltd
	G-CRDY	Agusta-Bell 206A JetRanger	Jac-Heli SARL (G-WHAZ)
	G-CRES	Denney Kitfox Mk 3	J. McGoldrick
	G-CREY	SeaRey Amphibian	A. F. Reid & P. J. Gallagher
	G-CRIC	Colomban MC.15 Cri-Cri	R. S. Stoddart-Stones
	G-CRIK	Colomban MC.15 Cri-Cri	C. R. Harrison
	G-CRIL	Rockwell Commander 112B	Rockwell Aviation Group
	G-CRIS	Taylor JT.1 Monoplane	C. R. Steer
	G-CRJW	Schleicher ASW-27-18	R. J. Welford
	G-CRLA	Cirrus SR20	Aero Club Heidelberg EV/Germany
	G-CROB	Shaw Europa XS T-G	R. G. Hallam
	G-CROL	Maule MXT-7-180	J. R. Pratt
	G-CROP	Cameron Z-105 balloon	PSH Skypower Ltd
	G-CROW	Robinson R44	Longmoore Ltd
	G-CROY	Shaw Europa	M. T. Austin
	G-CRSR	Czech Sport Aircraft Sportcruiser	G-CRSR Flying Group
	G-CRST	Agusta A.109E Power	Castle Air Ltd (G-WRBI)
	G-CRUI	CZAW Sportcruiser	J. Massey
	G-CRUM	Westland Scout AH.1 (XV137)	G-CRUM Group
	G-CRUZ	Cessna T.303	Bank Farm Ltd
	G-CRWZ	CZAW Sportcruiser	P. B. Lowry
	G-CRZA	CZAW Sportcruiser	A. J. Radford
	G-CSAM	Van's RV-9A	B. G. Murray
	G-CSAV	Thruster T.600N 450	D. J. N. Brown
	G-CSAW	CZAW Sportcruiser	B. C. Fitzgerald-O'Connor
	G-CSBD	PA-28-236 Dakota	I. J. Harper (G-CSBO)
	G-CSBM	Cessna F.150M	M. Howells
	G-CSCS	Cessna F.172N	C.Sullivan
	G-CSDJ	Avtech Jabiru UL	M. Smith
	G-CSDR	Corvus CA22	Crusader Syndicate
	G-CSFC	Cessna 150L	Foxtrot Charlie Flying Group
	G-CSFD	Ultramagic M-90 balloon	L. A. Watts
	G-CSFT	PA-23 Aztec 250D ★	Aces High Ltd (G-AYKU)
	G-CSGT	PA-28-161 Warrior II	C. P. Awdry (G-BPHB)
	G-CSIX	PA-32 Cherokee Six 300	A. J. Hodge
	G-CSKW	Van's RV-7	G-CSKW Group (G-CDJW)
	G-CSMK	Aerotechnik EV-97 Eurostar	R. Frey
	G-CSPR	Van's RV-6A	P. J. Pengilly
	G-CSTL	Bell 206B-3 JetRanger III	Castle Air Ltd (G-HIER/G-BRFD)
	G-CSUE	ICP MXP-740 Savannah Jabiru (5)	J. R. Stratton
	G-CSVS	Boeing 757-236	European Air Transport Leipzig GmbH (G-IEAC)
	G-CSZM	Zenair CH.601XL Zodiac	C. Budd
	G-CTAG	Rolladen-Schneider LS8-18	C. D. R. Tagg
	G-CTAM	Cirrus SR22	M. R. Munn
	G-CTAV	Aerotechnik EV-97 Eurostar	P. Simpson
	G-CTCC	Diamond DA42 Twin Star	CTC Aviation Group PLC (G-OCCZ)
	G-CTCD	Diamond DA42 Twin Star	CTC Aviation Group PLC
	G-CTCE	Diamond DA42 Twin Star	CTC Aviation Group PLC
	G-CTCF	Diamond DA42 Twin Star	CTC Aviation Group PLC
	G-CTCG	Diamond DA42 Twin Star	I. Annenskiy
	G-CTCH	Diamond DA42 Twin Star	CTC Aviation Group PLC
	G-CTCL	SOCATA TB10 Tobago	Gift Aviation Club (G-BSIV)
	G-CTDH	Flight Design CT2K	A. D. Thelwall
	G-CTDW	Flight Design CTSW	S. L. Morris
	G-CTED	Van's RV-7A	E. W. Lyon
	G-CTEL	Cameron N-90 balloon	M. R. Noyce
	G-CTFL	Robinson R44	T. G. Tunnelling Ltd (G-CLOT)
	G-CTIO	SOCATA TB20 Trinidad	I. R. Hunt
	G-CTIX	VS.509 Spitfire T.IX (PT462)	A. A. Hodgson
	G-CTKL	Noorduyn AT-16 Harvard IIB (54137)	M. R. Simpson
	G-CTLS	Flight Design CTLS	D. J. Haygreen
	G-CTNG	Cirrus SR20	K. S. Mitchell & J. Crackett

Reg.	Type	Owner or Operator	Notes
G-CTOY	Denney Kitfox Mk 3	J. I. V. Hill	
G-CTPW	Bell 206B JetRanger 3	Aviation Rentals	
G-CTRL	Robinson R22 Beta	Central Helicopters Ltd	
G-CTUG	PA-25 Pawnee 235	The Borders (Milfield) Gliding Club Ltd	
G-CTWO	Schempp-Hirth Standard Cirrus	R. J. Griffin	
G-CTZO	SOCATA TB20 Trinidad GT	G-CTZO Group	
G-CUBA	PA-32R-301T Turbo Saratoge	M. Atlass	
G-CUBB	PA-18 Super Cub 180	Bidford Gliding Ltd	
G-CUBE	Skyranger 912 (2)	A. I. Medler	
G-CUBI	PA-18 Super Cub 125	G. T. Fisher	
G-CUBJ	PA-18 Super Cub 150 (18-5395:CDG)	A. L. Grisay	
G-CUBN	PA-18 Super Cub 150	N. J. R. Minchin	
G-CUBP	PA-18 Super Cub 150	D. W. Berger	
G-CUBS	Piper J-3C-65 Cub	S. M. Rolfe (G-BHPT)	
G-CUBW	WAG-Aero Acro Trainer	B. G. Plumb & ptnrs	
G-CUBY	Piper J-3C-65 Cub	C. A. Bloom (G-BTZW)	
G-CUCP	Cessna P337H Pressurized Skymaster	G. G. L. James	
G-CUCU	Colt 180A balloon	S. R. Seage	
G-CUDY	Enstrom 480B	D'Arcy Holdings Ltd (G-REAN)	
G-CUGC	Schleicher ASW-19B	Cambridge University Gliding Club (G-CKEX)	
G-CUIK	QAC Quickie Q.200	C. S. Rayner	
G-CUMU	Schempp-Hirth Discus b	C. E. Fernando	
G-CUPP	Pitts S-2A	Avmarine Ltd	
G-CURV	Avid Speedwing	K. S. Kelso	
G-CUTE	Dyn'Aéro MCR-01	E. G. Shimmin	
G-CUTH	P & M Quik R	A. R. & S. Cuthbertson	
G-CVAL	Ikarus C42 FB100	G. W. F. Morton	
G-CVBF	Cameron A-210 balloon	Virgin Balloon Flights Ltd	
G-CVII	Dan Rihn DR.107 One Design	One Design Group	
G-CVIX	DH.110 Sea Vixen D.3 (XP924)	Drilling Systems Ltd	
G-CVMI	PA-18 Super Cub 150	D. Heslop & T. P. Spurge	
G-CVST	Jodel D.140E	D. Runnalls & R. Sheridan	
G-CVXN	Cessna F.406 Caravan	Caledonian Airborne Systems Ltd (G-SFPA)	
G-CVZT	Schempp-Hirth Ventus 2cT	C. D. Sterritt & M. W. Conboy	
G-CWAG	Sequoia F. 8L Falco	D. R. Austin	
G-CWAL	Raj Hamsa X'Air 133	L. R. Morris	
G-CWAY	Ikarus C42 FB100	M. Conway	
G-CWBM	Phoenix Currie Wot	G-CWBM Group (G-BTVP)	
G-CWEB	P & M Quik GT450	M & K. A. Forsyth	
G-CWFA	PA-38-112 Tomahawk	T. Mikschaitis (G-BTGC)	
G-CWFC	PA-38-112 Tomahawk ★	Cardiff-Wales Flying Club Ltd (G-BRTA)	
G-CWFS	Tecnam P2002-JF Sierra	VLA Management Ltd	
G-CWIC	Mainair Pegasus Quik	G-CWIC Group	
G-CWIS	Diamond DA.20 Star	R. A. Eve	
G-CWLC	Schleicher ASH-25	G-CWLC Group	
G-CWMC	P & M Quik GT450	A. R. Hughes	
G-CWMT	Dyn'Aéro MCR-01 Bambi	J. Jones	
G-CWOW	Balony Kubicek BB45Z balloon	Skybus Ballooning	
G-CWTD	Aeroprakt A22 Foxbat	E. Fogarty	
G-CWVY	Mainair Pegasus Quik	G-CWVY Group	
G-CXCX	Cameron N-90 balloon	Cathay Pacific Airways (London) Ltd	
G-CXDZ	Cassutt Speed Two	J. A. H. Chadwick	
G-CXIP	Thruster T.600N	India Papa Syndicate	
G-CXLS	Cessna 560 XL Citation XLS	Aviation Beauport Ltd (G-PKRG)	
G-CXSM	Cessna 172R	S. Eustathiou (G-BXSM)	
G-CYGI	HAPI Cygnet SF-2A	B. Brown	
G-CYLL	Sequoia F.8L Falco	N. J. Langrick & A. J. Newall	
G-CYLS	Cessna T.303	R. Berridge (G-BKXI)	
G-CYMA	GA-7 Cougar	Cyma Petroleum (UK) Ltd (G-BKOM)	
G-CYPM	Cirrus SR22	R. M. Steeves	
G-CYRA	Kolb Twinstar Mk. 3 (Modified)	S. J. Fox (G-MYRA)	
G-CYRL	Cessna 182T	D. R. Rayne	
G-CYRS	Bell 206L Long Ranger	HJS Helicopters Ltd	
G-CZAC	Zenair CH.601XL	K. W. Eskins	
G-CZAG	Sky 90-24 balloon	S. Paszkowicz	
G-CZAW	CZAW Sportcruiser	Sprite Aviation Services Ltd	

Notes	Reg.	Type	Owner or Operator
	G-CZCZ	Avions Mudry CAP-10B	M. Farmer
	G-CZMI	Skyranger 912 (2)	L. M. Bassett
	G-CZNE	BN-2B-20 Islander	Skyhopper LLP (G-BWZF)
	G-CZOS	Cirrus SR20	H. G. Dilloway
	G-CZSC	CZAW Sportcruiser	F. J. Wadia
	G-DAAN	Eurocopter EC 135P2+	Eurocopter UK Ltd
	G-DAAT	Eurocopter EC 135T2	Bond Air Services Ltd
	G-DAAZ	PA-28RT-201T Turbo Arrow IV	Calais Ltd
	G-DABS	Robinson R22 Beta II	Helicom Ltd
	G-DACA	P.57 Sea Prince T.1 (WF118) ★	P. G. Vallance Ltd/Charlwood
	G-DACE	Corben Baby Ace D	G. N. Holland (G-BTSB)
	G-DACF	Cessna 152 II	T. M. & M. L. Jones (G-BURY)
	G-DADA	Rotorsport UK MT-03	J. C. Hilton-Johnson
	G-DADG	PA-18-150 Super Cub	F. J. Cox
	G-DADJ	Glaser-Dirks DG-200	M. Roberts
	G-DADZ	CZAW Sportcruiser	Meon Flying Group
	G-DAGF	EAA Acrosport II	D. A. G. Fraser
	G-DAGJ	Zenair CH.601HD Zodiac	D. A. G. Johnson
	G-DAGS	Cessna 525A Citationjet CJ2	Air Charter Scotland Ltd
	G-DAIR	Luscombe 8A Silvaire	D. F. Soul (G-BURK)
	G-DAIV	Ultramagic H-77 balloon	D. Harrison-Morris
	G-DAJB	Boeing 757-2T7	Monarch Airlines Ltd
	G-DAJC	Boeing 757-31K	Thomas Cook Airlines Ltd
	G-DAKK	Douglas C-47A	General Technics Ltd
	G-DAKM	Diamond DA40D Star	K. MacDonald
	G-DAKO	PA-28-236 Dakota	Methods Consulting Ltd
	G-DAME	Vans RV-7	H. Manners
	G-DAMY	Shaw Europa	U. A. Schliessler & R. J. Kelly
	G-DANA	Jodel DR.200 (replica)	Cheshire Eagles (G-DAST)
	G-DAND	SOCATA TB10 Tobago	S. Gledden & L. Hopwood-Robinson
	G-DANY	Avtech Jabiru UL	D. A. Crosbie
	G-DAPH	Cessna 180K	T. W. Harris
	G-DASA	Dassault Falcon 50	Bramptonia Ltd (G-ITIH)
	G-DASH	Rockwell Commander 112	D. & M. Nelson (G-BDAJ)
	G-DASS	Ikarus C.42 FB100	D. D. J. Rossdale
	G-DATG	Cessna F.182P	Oxford Aeroplane Co Ltd
	G-DAVB	Aerosport Scamp	D. R. Burns
	G-DAVD	Cessna FR.172K	D. M. Driver & S. Copeland
	G-DAVE	Jodel D.112	I. D. Worthington
	G-DAVG	Robinson R44 II	AG Aviation Ltd (G-WOWW)
	G-DAVM	Akrotech Europe CAP.10B	D. Moorman
	G-DAVS	AB Sportine Aviacija LAK-17AT	G-DAVS Syndicate
	G-DAVZ	Cessna 182T Skylane	D. J. Lawrence
	G-DAWG	SA Bulldog Srs 120/121 (XX522)	S. J. Wood
	G-DAWZ	Glasflugel 304 CZ	B. Vikstrom
	G-DAYI	Europa	A. F. Day
	G-DAYS	Europa	D. A. Gittins
	G-DAYZ	Pietenpol Air Camper	D. W. Melville
	G-DAZZ	Van's RV-8	Wishanger RV8
	G-DBCA	Airbus A.319-131	British Airways plc
	G-DBCB	Airbus A.319-131	British Airways plc
	G-DBCC	Airbus A.319-131	British Airways plc
	G-DBCD	Airbus A.319-131	British Airways plc
	G-DBCE	Airbus A.319-131	British Airways plc
	G-DBCF	Airbus A.319-131	British Airways plc
	G-DBCG	Airbus A.319-131	British Airways plc
	G-DBCH	Airbus A.319-131	British Airways plc
	G-DBCI	Airbus A.319-131	British Airways plc
	G-DBCJ	Airbus A.319-131	British Airways plc
	G-DBCK	Airbus A.319-131	British Airways plc
	G-DBDB	VPM M-16 Tandem Trainer	D. R. Bolsover (G-IROW)
	G-DBIN	Medway SLA 80 Executive	S. P. Hoskins
	G-DBJD	PZL-Bielsko SZD-9BIS Bocian 1D	Bertie the Bocian Glider Syndicate
	G-DBKL	VS.379 Spitfire F.Mk.XIV	P. M. Andrews
	G-DBLA	Boeing 767-35EER	Thomson Airways Ltd
	G-DBND	Schleicher Ka 6CR	A. H. Hall
	G-DBNH	Schleicher Ka 6CR	The Bath, Wilts and North Dorset Gliding Club Ltd
	G-DBNP	Slingsby T.50 Skylark 4	D. H. Smith
	G-DBOD	Cessna 172S	Goodwood Road Racing Co Ltd
	G-DBOL	Schleicher Ka 6CR	A. C. Thorne
	G-DBRT	Slingsby T.51 Dart	C. W. Logue

Reg.	Type	Owner or Operator	Notes
G-DBRU	Slingsby T.51 Dart	P. S. Whitehead	
G-DBRY	Slingsby T.51 Dart	D. J. Knights	
G-DBSA	Slingsby T.51 Dart	G. Burton	
G-DBSL	Slingsby T.51 Dart	G-DBSL Group	
G-DBSR	Kubicek BB26Z balloon	G. J. Bell	
G-DBTF	Schleicher Ka 6CR	T. Fletcher	
G-DBTJ	Schleicher Ka 6CR	I. G. Robinson	
G-BDTM	Schleicher Ka 6CR	The Nene Valley Gliding Club Ltd	
G-DBUZ	Schleicher Ka 6CR	J. J. Hartwell	
G-DBVB	Schleicher K7	Dartmoor Gliding Society Ltd	
G-DBVH	Slingsby T.51 Dart 17R	P. G. Addy	
G-DBVR	Schleicher Ka 6CR	J. R. Ross & J. M. Brooke	
G-DBVX	Schleicher Ka 6CR	R. Lynch	
G-DBVY	LET L-13 Blanik	Victor Yankee Group	
G-DBVZ	Schleicher Ka 6CR	G-DBVZ Group	
G-DBWC	Schleicher Ka 6CR	Stratford on Avon Gliding Club Ltd	
G-DBWJ	Slingsby T.51 Dart 17R	M. F. Defendi	
G-DBWM	Slingsby T.51 Dart 17R	P. L. Poole	
G-DBWO	Slingsby T.51 Dart	G. Winch	
G-DBWP	Slingsby T-51 Dart 17R	R. Johnson	
G-DBWS	Slingsby T.51 Dart 17R	R. D. Broome	
G-DBXE	Slingsby T.51 Dart	Group G-DBXE	
G-DBXG	Slingsby T.51 Dart 17R	J. M. Whelan	
G-DBXT	Schleicher Ka 6CR	C. I. Knowles	
G-DBYC	Slingsby T.51 Dart 17R	R. L. Horsnell & N. A. Jaffray	
G-DBYG	Slingsby T.51 Dart 17R	W. T. Emery	
G-DBYL	Schleicher Ka 6CR	Channel Gliding Club Ltd	
G-DBYM	Schleicher Ka 6CR	K. S. Smith	
G-DBYU	Schleicher Ka-6CR	G. B. Sutton	
G-DBYX	Schleicher Ka-6E	J. R. Dent	
G-DBZF	Slingsby T.51 Dart 17R	S. Rhenius & D. Charles	
G-DBZJ	Slingsby T.51 Dart 17R	K. Richards	
G-DBZX	Schleicher Ka 6CR	T. S. Marlow	
G-DCAE	Schleicher Ka 6E	J. R. & P. R. Larner	
G-DCAG	Schleicher Ka 6E	715 Syndicate	
G-DCAM	Eurocopter AS.355NP Ecureuil 2	Cameron Charters LLP	
G-DCAO	Schempp-Hirth SHK-1	M. G. Entwisle & A. K. Bartlett	
G-DCAS	Schleicher Ka 6E	R. F. Tindall	
G-DCAZ	Slingsby T-51 Dart 17R	D. A. Bullock & Man L. C.	
G-DCBA	Slingsby T.51 Dart 17R	K. T. Kreis	
G-DCBI	Schweizer 269C-1	N. Colclough	
G-DCBM	Schleicher Ka 6CR	R. J. Shepherd	
G-DCBW	Schleicher ASK-13	Stratford on Avon Gliding Club Ltd	
G-DCBY	Schleicher Ka 6CR	R. G. Appleboom	
G-DCCA	Schleicher Ka 6E	R. K. Forrest	
G-DCCB	Schempp-Hirth SHK-1	CCB Syndicate	
G-DCCD	Schleicher Ka 6E	Charlie Charlie Delta Group	
G-DCCE	Schleicher ASK-13	Oxford Gliding Co.Ltd	
G-DCCF	Schleicher ASK-13	Norfolk Gliding Club Ltd	
G-DCCG	Schleicher Ka 6E	R. J. Playle	
G-DCCL	Schleicher Ka 6E	G-DCCL Group	
G-DCCM	Schleicher ASK-13	The Burn Gliding Club Ltd	
G-DCCP	Schleicher ASK-13	Lima 99 Syndicate	
G-DCCR	Schleicher Ka 6E	A. Shaw	
G-DCCT	Schleicher ASK-13	Stratford on Avon Gliding Club Ltd	
G-DCCU	Schleicher Ka 6E	J. L. Hasker	
G-DCCV	Schleicher Ka 6E	C. H. Page	
G-DCCW	Schleicher ASK-13	Needwood Forest Gliding Club Ltd	
G-DCCX	Schleicher ASK-13	Trent Valley Gliding Club Ltd	
G-DCCY	Schleicher ASK-13	Devon and Somerset Gliding Club Ltd	
G-DCCZ	Schleicher ASK-13	The Windrushers Gliding Club Ltd	
G-DCDA	Schleicher Ka 6E	D. Close, A. Smith & J. Tonkin	
G-DCDC	Lange E1 Antares	J. D. Williams	
G-DCDF	Schleicher Ka 6E	CDF Syndicate	
G-DCDG	FFA Diamant 18	J. Cashin & D. McCarty	
G-DCDH	Schempp-Hirth Cirrus	DCDH Syndicate	
G-DCDO	Ikarus C42 FB80	C42 Dodo Syndicate	
G-DCDW	Diamant 18	D. R. Chapman	
G-DCDZ	Schleicher Ka 6E	J. R. J. Minns	
G-DCEB	PZL-Bielsko SZD-9BIS Bocian 1E	The Bath, Wilts and North Dorset Gliding Club Ltd	

Notes	Reg.	Type	Owner or Operator
	G-DCEC	Schempp-Hirth Cirrus	Cirrus 18 Group
	G-DCEM	Schleicher Ka 6E	E. W. Black
	G-DCEN	PZL-Bielsko SZD-30 Pirat	D. P. Aherne
	G-DCEO	Schleicher Ka 6E	C. L. Lagden & J. C. Green
	G-DCEW	Schleicher Ka 6E	J. W. Richardson and Partners Group
	G-DCEX	Schleicher ASK-13	R. B. Walker
	G-DCFA	Schleicher ASK-13	Booker Gliding Club Ltd
	G-DCFE	Schleicher ASK-13	Loughborough Students Union Gliding Club
	G-DCFF	Schleicher K 8B	Derbyshire and Lancashire Gliding Club Ltd
	G-DCFG	Schleicher ASK-13	The Nene Valley Gliding Club Ltd
	G-DCFK	Schempp-Hirth Cirrus	P. D. Whitters
	G-DCFL	Schleicher Ka 6E	M. B. Pridal
	G-DCFS	Glasflugel Standard Libelle 201B	P. J. Flack
	G-DCFW	Glasflugel Standard Libelle 201B	D. J. Edwardes & T. J. Price
	G-DCFX	Glasflugel Standard Libelle 201B	K. D. Fishenden
	G-DCFY	Glasflugel Standard Libelle 201B	C. W. Stevens
	G-DCGB	Schleicher Ka 6E	P. M. Turner & S. C. Male
	G-DCGD	Schleicher Ka 6E	Charlie Golf Delta Group
	G-DCGE	Schleicher Ka 6E	C. V. Hill & P. C. Hazlehurst
	G-DCGH	Schleicher K 8B	K7 (1971) Syndicate
	G-DCGM	FFA Diamant 18	J. G. Batch
	G-DCGO	Schleicher ASK-13	Oxford Gliding Company Ltd
	G-DCGY	Schempp-Hirth Cirrus	M. P. Gadd & G. Nevisky
	G-DCHB	Schleicher Ka 6E	D. L. Jones
	G-DCHJ	Bolkow Phoebus C	D. C. Austin
	G-DCHL	PZL-Bielsko SZD-30	A. P. P. Scorer & A. Stocks
	G-DCHT	Schleicher ASW-15	P. G. Roberts & J. M. Verrill
	G-DCHU	Schleicher K 8B	Highland Gliding Club K8 Syndicate
	G-DCHW	Schleicher ASK-13	Dorset Gliding Club Ltd
	G-DCHZ	Schleicher Ka 6E	B. L. Cooper
	G-DCJB	Bolkow Phoebus C	R. Idle
	G-DCJF	Schleicher K-8B	G. Smith
	G-DCJJ	Bolkow Phoebus C	P. N. Maddocks
	G-DCJK	Schempp-Hirth SHK-1	R. H. Short
	G-DCJM	Schleicher K-8B	Midland Gliding Club Ltd
	G-DCJN	Schempp-Hirth SHK-1	R. J. Makin
	G-DCJR	Schempp-Hirth Cirrus	J. C. K. Brown
	G-DCJY	Schleicher Ka 6CR	CJY Syndicate
	G-DCKD	PZL-Bielsko SZD-30	Dartmoor Gliding Society Ltd
	G-DCKK	Cessna F.172N	KK Group
	G-DCKL	Schleicher Ka 6E	BGA1603 Owners Syndicate
	G-DCKN	PZL-Bielsko SZD-9bis Bocian 1E	Dartmoor Gliding Society Ltd
	G-DCKP	Schleicher ASW-15	ASW 15-BGA1606 Partnership
	G-DCKR	Schleicher ASK-13	Midland Gliding Club Ltd
	G-DCKV	Schleicher ASK-13	Black Mountains Gliding Club
	G-DCKY	Glasflugel Standard Libelle 201B	G. Herbert
	G-DCKZ	Schempp-Hirth Standard Cirrus	G. I. Bustin
	G-DCLA	Schempp-Hirth Standard Cirrus	S. A. Lees
	G-DCLM	Glasflugel Standard Libelle 201B	C. J. Heide & R. Smith
	G-DCLO	Schempp-Hirth Cirrus	Bravo Delta Group
	G-DCLP	Glasflugel Standard Libelle 201B	D. Heaton
	G-DCLT	Schleicher K7	A. H. Watkins
	G-DCLV	Glasflugel Standard Libelle 201B	K. Vanderputten
	G-DCLZ	Schleicher Ka 6E	G-DCLZ Flying Group
	G-DCMF	PZL-Bielsko SZD-32A Foka 5	B. T. Green
	G-DCMG	Schleicher K7	B. Czerwinski, M. Norbert, M. Oleksiewicz & K. Pindral
	G-DCMI	Mainair Pegasus Quik	T. F. Fitzsimons
	G-DCMK	Schleicher ASK-13	The South Wales Gliding Club Ltd
	G-DCMN	Schleicher K 8B	The Bristol Gliding Club Proprietary Ltd
	G-DCMO	Glasflugel Standard Libelle 201B	M. E. Wolff & L. C. Wood
	G-DCMR	Glasflugel Standard Libelle 201B	G-DCMR Group
	G-DCMS	Glasflugel Standard Libelle 201B	Libelle 602 Syndicate
	G-DCMV	Glasflugel Standard Libelle 201B	M. Izdorczak
	G-DCMW	Glasflugel Standard Libelle 201B	T. Rose
	G-DCNC	Schempp-Hirth Standard Cirrus	Cirrus 273 Syndicate
	G-DCND	PZL-Bielsko SZD-9bis Bocian 1E	Angus Gliding Club Ltd
	G-DCNE	Glasflugel Standard Libelle 201B	25 Syndicate
	G-DCNG	Glasflugel Standard Libelle 201B	M. C. J. Gardner
	G-DCNJ	Glasflugel Standard Libelle 201B	R. Thornley
	G-DCNM	PZL-Bielsko SZD-9bis Bocian 1E	Bocian Syndicate
	G-DCNP	Glasflugel Standard Libelle 201B	I. G. Carrick & D. J. Miles

Reg.	Type	Owner or Operator	Notes
G-DCNS	Slingsby T.59A Kestrel	J. R. Greenwell	
G-DCNW	Slingsby T.59F Kestrel	S. R. Watson	
G-DCNX	Slingsby T.59F Kestrel	M. Boxall	
G-DCOJ	Slingsby T.59A Kestrel	T. W. Treadaway	
G-DCOR	Schempp-Hirth Standard Cirrus	H. R. Ford	
G-DCOY	Schempp-Hirth Standard Cirrus	A. D. Walsh & M. R. Latham	
G-DCPA	MBB BK.117C-1C	Veritair Aviation Ltd (G-LFBA)	
G-DCPB	Eurocopter MBB-BK 117C-2	Devon & Cornwall Constabulary	
G-DCPD	Schleicher ASW-17	A. J. Hewitt	
G-DCPG	Schleicher K7	A. L. Maitland & D. N. Mackay	
G-DCPJ	Schleicher KA6E	G-DCPJ Group	
G-DCPM	Glasflugel Standard Libelle 201B	N. Godson & P. E. Jessop	
G-DCPU	Schempp-Hirth Standard Cirrus	P. J. Ketelaar	
G-DCPV	PZL-Bielsko SZD-30 Pirat	CPV Group	
G-DCRB	Glasflugel Standard Libelle 201B	A. I. Mawer	
G-DCRH	Schempp-Hirth Standard Cirrus	P. E. Thelwall	
G-DCRN	Schempp-Hirth Standard Cirrus	J. Craig & L. Runhaar	
G-DCRO	Glasflugel Standard Libelle 201B	G-DCRO Group	
G-DCRS	Glasflugel standard Libelle 201B	J. R. Hiley & M. W. Fisher	
G-DCRT	Schleicher ASK-13	Bowland Forest Gliding Club Ltd	
G-DCRV	Glasflugel Standard Libelle 201B	G. G. Dale	
G-DCRW	Glasflugel Standard Libelle 201B	C. J. Davison	
G-DCSB	Slingsby T.59F Kestrel	W. Fischer	
G-DCSD	Slingsby T.59D Kestrel	L. P. Davidson	
G-DCSE	Robinson R44	Heli Air Ltd	
G-DCSF	Slingsby T.59F Kestrel 19	R. Birch & S. Glassett	
G-DCSG	Robinson R44	Voute Sales Ltd (G-TRYG)	
G-DCSI	Robinson R44 II	Enable International Ltd (G-TGDL)	
G-DCSJ	Glasflugel Standard Libelle 201B	P. J. Gill	
G-DCSK	Slingsby T.59D Kestrel	Kestrel CSK Group	
G-DCSN	Pilatus B4-PC11AF	J. S. Firth	
G-DCSP	Pilatus B4-PC11	G-DCSP Group	
G-DCSR	Glasflugel Standard Libelle 201B	Glasgow and West of Scotland Gliding Club	
G-DCTB	Schempp-Hirth Standard Cirrus	I. M. Young & S. McCurdy	
G-DCTE	Schleicher ASW-17	C. A. & S. C. Noujaim	
G-DCTJ	Slingsby T.59D Kestrel	R. M. Theil	
G-DCTL	Slingsby T.59D Kestrel	E. S. E. Hibbard	
G-DCTM	Slingsby T.59D Kestrel	C. Roney	
G-DCTO	Slingsby T.59D Kestrel	K. A. Moules	
G-DCTP	Slingsby T.59D Kestrel	D. C. Austin	
G-DCTR	Slingsby T.59D Kestrel	M. W. Hands	
G-DCTT	Schempp-Hirth Standard Cirrus	E. Sparrow	
G-DCTU	Glasflugel Standard Libelle 201B	F. K. Hutchinson & P. M. Davies	
G-DCTV	PZL-Bielsko SZD-30	Black Mountains Gliding Club	
G-DCTX	PZL-Bielsko SZD-30	Dave King, John Cooper, Ben Fantham Group	
G-DCUB	Pilatus B4-PC11	Staffordshire Gliding Club Ltd	
G-DCUC	Pilatus B4-PC11	G. M. Cumner	
G-DCUD	Yorkshire Sailplanes YS53 Sovereign	T. J. Wilkinson	
G-DCUJ	Glasflugel Standard Libelle 201B	T. G. B. Hobbis	
G-DCUO	Pilatus B4-PC11	Cotswold Gliding Club	
G-DCUS	Schempp-Hirth Cirrus VTC	R. C. Graham	
G-DCUT	Pilatus B4 PC11AF	A. L. Walker	
G-DCVE	Schempp-Hirth Cirrus VTC	H. Whybrow	
G-DCVG	Pilatus B4-PC11AF	M. Kempf	
G-DCVK	Pilatus B4-PC11AF	J. P. Marriott	
G-DCVL	Glasflugel Standard Libelle 201B	J. Williams	
G-DCVP	PZL-Bielsko SZD-9bis Bocian 1E	Portmoak CVP Group	
G-DCVR	PZL-Bielsko SZD-30 Pirat	M. T. Pitorak	
G-DCVS	PZL-Bielsko SZD-36A	I. A. Burgin	
G-DCVV	Pilatus B4-PC11AF	Syndicate CVV	
G-DCVW	Slingsby T.59D Kestrel	J. J. Green	
G-DCVY	Slingsby T.59D Kestrel	N. Dickenson	
G-DCWA	Slingsby T.59D Kestrel	D. J. Jeffries	
G-DCWB	Slingsby T.59D Kestrel	Kestrel 677 Syndicate	
G-DCWD	Slingsby T.59D Kestrel	Deeside Kestrel Group	
G-DCWE	Glasflugel Standard Libelle 201B	T. W. J. Stoker	
G-DCWF	Slingsby T.59D Kestrel	P. F. Nicholson	
G-DCWG	Glasflugel Standard Libelle 201B	Libelle 322 Group	
G-DCWH	Schleicher ASK-13	York Gliding Centre Ltd	
G-DCWJ	Schleicher K7	Angus Gliding Club K7 Syndicate	
G-DCWR	Schempp-Hirth Cirrus VTC	CWR Group	
G-DCWS	Schempp-Hirth Cirrus VTC	Cirrus G-DCWS Syndicate	

Notes	Reg.	Type	Owner or Operator
	G-DCWT	Glasflugel Standard Libelle 201B	B. J. Darton
	G-DCWX	Glasflugel Standard Libelle	C. A. Weyman
	G-DCWY	Glasflugel Standard Libelle 201B	S. J. Taylor
	G-DCWZ	Glasflugel Standard Libelle 201B	C. Maul
	G-DCXI	Slingsby T.61F Venture T.2	611 Vintage Flight (G-BUDB)
	G-DCXK	Glasflugel Standard Libelle 201B	J. M. Whelan
	G-DCXM	Slingsby T.59D Kestrel	R. P. Beck & T. Potter
	G-DCXV	Yorkshire Sailplanes YS-53 Sovereign	T53 Syndicate
	G-DCYA	Pilatus B4 PC-11	B4-072 Group
	G-DCYD	PZL-Bielsko SZD-30 Pirat	G-DCYD First Group
	G-DCYG	Glasflugel H201B Standard Libelle	R. Barsby & A. C. S. Lintott
	G-DCYM	Schempp-Hirth Standard Cirrus	K. M. Fisher
	G-DCYO	Schempp-Hirth Standard Cirrus	G. M. Maguire, P. Summers & M. Layton
	G-DCYP	Schempp-Hirth Standard Cirrus	A. F. Scott
	G-DCYT	Schempp-Hirth Standard Cirrus	R. Robertson
	G-DCYZ	Schleicher K 8B	Oxford Gliding Co.Ltd
	G-DCZD	Pilatus B4 PC-11AF	T. Dale
	G-DCZE	PZL-Bielsko SZD-30	L. A. Bean
	G-DCZG	PZL-Bielsko SZD-30	J. T. Pajdak
	G-DCZJ	PZL-Bielsko SZD-30	B. L. C. Gordon
	G-DCZN	Schleicher ASW-15B	G-DCZN Group
	G-DCZR	Slingsby T.59D Kestrel	R. P. Brisbourne
	G-DCZU	Slingsby T.59D Kestrel	M. P. Edwards
	G-DCZZ	Slingsby T.59D Kestrel	C. J. Lowrie
	G-DDAC	PZL-Bielsko SZD-36A	R. J. A. Colenso
	G-DDAJ	Shempp-Hirth Nimbus 2	North Devon Gliding Club Nimbus Group
	G-DDAK	Schleicher K-7	Vale of Neath Gliding Club
	G-DDAN	PZL-Bielsko SZD-30	J. M. A. Shannon
	G-DDAP	SZL-Bielsko SZD-30	Delta Alpha Papa Group
	G-DDAS	Schempp-Hirth Standard Cirrus	G. Goodenough
	G-DDAU	PZL-Bielsko SZD-30	Buckminster Gliding Club Ltd
	G-DDAV	Robinson R44 II	Wilpot Ltd
	G-DDAW	Schleicher Ka 6CR	R. G. Charlesson
	G-DDAY	PA-28R-201T Turbo Arrow III	G-DDAY Group (G-BPDO)
	G-DDBB	Slingsby T.51 Dart 17R	S. Foster
	G-DDBC	Pilatus B4-PC11	J. H. France & G. R. Harris
	G-DDBD	Shaw Europa XS	B. Davies
	G-DDBG	ICA IS-29D	P. S. Whitehead
	G-DDBK	Slingsby T.59D Kestrel	523 Syndicate
	G-DDBN	Slingsby T.59D Kestrel	I. B. Kennedy
	G-DDBP	Glasflugel Club Libelle 205	J. P. Beach
	G-DDBS	Slingsby T.59D Kestrel	M. Bond
	G-DDBV	PZL-Bielsko SZD-30	L. Clarke
	G-DDCA	PZL-Bielsko SZD-36A Cobra 15	J. Young & J. R. Aylesbury
	G-DDCC	Glasflugel Standard Libelle 201B	G-DDCC Syndicate
	G-DDCW	Schleicher Ka 6CR	B. W. Rendall
	G-DDDA	Schempp-Hirth Standard Cirrus	A. J. Davis
	G-DDDB	Schleicher ASK-13	Shenington Gliding Club
	G-DDDE	PZL-Bielsko SZD-38A Jantar 1	Jantar One Syndicate
	G-DDDJ	Learjet 45	RCS Trading Corporation Ltd
	G-DDDL	Schleicher K8B	G-DDDL Group
	G-DDDM	Schempp-Hirth Cirrus	DDM Syndicate
	G-DDDR	Schempp-Hirth Standard Cirrus	J. D. Ewence
	G-DDDY	P & M Quik GT450	J. W. Dodson
	G-DDEA	Slingsby T.59D Kestrel	A. Pickles
	G-DDEB	Slingsby T.59D Kestrel	J. L. Smoker
	G-DDEG	ICA IS-28B2	P. S. Whitehead
	G-DDEO	Glasflugel H205 Club Libelle	N. J. Mitchell
	G-DDEP	Schleicher Ka-6CR	M. D. Brooks
	G-DDEV	Schleicher Ka-6CR	DEV Group
	G-DDEW	ICA-Brasov IS-29D	G. V. Prater
	G-DDEX	LET-13 Blanik	Blanik DEX Group
	G-DDFC	Schempp-Hirth Standard Cirrus	C. E. & I. Helme
	G-DDFE	Molino PIK-20B	M. A. Roff-Jarrett
	G-DDFK	Molino PIK-20B	B. H. & M. J. Fairclough
	G-DDFL	PZL-Bielsko SZD-38A Jantar 1	G-DDFL Group
	G-DDFN	Glaser-Dirks DG-100	K. Smith
	G-DDFR	Grob G.102 Astir CS	The Windrushers Gliding Club Ltd
	G-DDGA	Schleicher K-8B	The Welland Gliding Club Ltd
	G-DDGE	Schempp-Hirth Standard Cirrus	A. S. Cobbett
	G-DDGG	Schleicher Ka 6E	N. F. Holmes & F. D. Platt

Reg.	Type	Owner or Operator	Notes
G-DDGH	PZL-Bielsko SZD-30 Pirat	M. Ling	
G-DDGJ	Champion 8KCAB	Western Air (Thruxton) Ltd	
G-DDGK	Schleicher Ka 6CR	R. G. Olsen	
G-DDGV	Breguet 905S Fauvette	J. N. Lee	
G-DDGX	Schempp-Hirth Standard Cirrus 75	USKGC Group	
G-DDGY	Schempp-Hirth Nimbus 2B	Nimbus 195 Group	
G-DDHA	Schleicher K 8B	Shalborne Soaring Society Ltd	
G-DDHC	PZL-Bielsko SZD-41A	P. J. Kelly	
G-DDHE	Slingsby T.53B	Aviation Preservation Society of Scotland	
G-DDHG	Schleicher Ka 6CR	Angus Gliding Club Ltd	
G-DDHH	Eiriavion PIK-20B	D. M. Steed	
G-DDHJ	Glaser-Dirks DG-100	G. E. McLaughlin	
G-DDHK	Glaser-Dirks DG-100	B. J. & C. M. Griffin	
G-DDHL	Glaser-Dirks DG-100	DHL Syndicate	
G-DDHT	Schleicher Ka 6E	S. Foster	
G-DDHW	Schempp-Hirth Nimbus 2	M. J. Carruthers & D. Thompson	
G-DDHX	Schempp-Hirth Standard Cirrus B	J. Franke	
G-DDHZ	PZL-Bielsko SZD-30	Peterborough and Spalding Gliding Club	
G-DDIG	Rockwell Commander 114	Daedalus Flying Group (G-CCDT)	
G-DDJB	Schleicher K-8B	Portsmouth Naval Gliding Centre	
G-DDJD	Grob G.102 Astir CS	P. E. Gascoigne	
G-DDJF	Schempp-Hirth Duo Discus T	R. J. H. Fack	
G-DDJK	Schleicher ASK-18	Booker Gliding Club Ltd	
G-DDJN	Eiriavion PIK-20B	M. Ireland & S. Lambourne	
G-DDJR	Schleicher Ka 6CR	Syndicate K6	
G-DDJX	Grob G.102 Astir CS	Trent Valley Gliding Club Ltd	
G-DDKC	Schleicher K 8B	Yorkshire Gliding Club (Proprietary) Ltd	
G-DDKD	Glasflugel Hornet	Hornet Syndicate	
G-DDKE	Schleicher ASK-13	The South Wales Gliding Club Ltd	
G-DDKG	Schleicher Ka 6CR	C. B. Woolf	
G-DDKL	Schempp-Hirth Nimbus 2	G. J. Croll	
G-DDKM	Glasflugel Hornet	R. S. Lee	
G-DDKN	Schleicher Ka 6CR	A. Ciccone	
G-DDKR	Grob G.102 Astir CS	Oxford Gliding Co.Ltd	
G-DDKS	Grob G.102 Astir CS	Oxford Gliding Co.Ltd	
G-DDKT	Eiriavion PIK-20B	F. P. Wilson	
G-DDKU	Grob G.102 Astir CS	Delta Kilo Uniform Syndicate	
G-DDKV	Grob G.102 Astir CS	T. J. Ireson	
G-DDKW	Grob G.102 Astir CS	M. A. Sandwith	
G-DDKX	Grob G.102 Astir CS	L. R. Bennett	
G-DDLA	Pilatus B4 PC-11	P. R. Seddon	
G-DDLB	Schleicher ASK-18	The Vale of the White Horse Gliding Centre Ltd	
G-DDLC	Schleicher ASK-13	Lasham Gliding Society Ltd	
G-DDLE	Schleicher Ka 6E	P. J. Abbott & J. Banks	
G-DDLG	Schempp-Hirth Standard Cirrus 75	S. Naylor	
G-DDLH	Grob G.102 Astir CS77	M. D. & M. E. Saunders	
G-DDLJ	Eiriavion PIK-20B	M. S. Parkes	
G-DDLM	Grob G.102 Astir CS	P. W. McEnery	
G-DDLP	Schleicher Ka 6CR	J. R. Crosse	
G-DDLS	Schleicher K 8B	North Devon Gliding Club	
G-DDLT	ICA IS-28B2	P. S. Whitehead	
G-DDLY	Eiriavion PIK-20D	M. Conrad	
G-DDMB	Schleicher K 8B	Crown Service Gliding Club	
G-DDMD	Glaser-Dirks DG-100	K. G. Guest	
G-DDMG	Schleicher K 8B	Dorset Gliding Club Ltd	
G-DDMH	Grob G.102 Astir CS	C. K. Lewis	
G-DDMK	Schempp-Hirth SHK-1	D. Breeze	
G-DDML	Schleicher K-7	Dumfries and District Gliding Club	
G-DDMM	Schempp-Hirth Nimbus 2	T. Linee	
G-DDMN	Glasflugel Mosquito	DMN Group	
G-DDMO	Schleicher Ka 6E	S. D. Hawkin	
G-DDMP	Grob G.102 Astir CS	Kingswood Syndicate	
G-DDMR	Grob G.102 Astir CS	Mendip Gliding Club Ltd	
G-DDMS	Glasflugel Standard Libelle 201B	G-DDMS Group	
G-DDMU	Eiriavion PIK-20D	J. Mjels	
G-DDMV	NA T-6G Texan (493209)	C. Dabin	
G-DDMX	Schleicher ASK-13	Dartmoor Gliding Society Ltd	
G-DDNC	Grob G.102 Astir CS	W. J. Veitch	
G-DDND	Pilatus B4-PC11AF	DND Group	
G-DDNE	Grob G.102 Astir CS77	621 Astir Syndicate	
G-DDNG	Schempp-Hirth Nimbus 2	Nimbus 265 Syndicate	
G-DDNK	Grob G.102 Astir CS	G-DDNK Group	

Notes	Reg.	Type	Owner or Operator
	G-DDNT	PZL-Bielsko SZD-30	R. K. Lashly
	G-DDNU	PZL-Bielsko SZD-42-1 Jantar 2	C. D. Rowland & D. Chalmers-Brown
	G-DDNV	Schleicher ASK-13	Channel Gliding Club Ltd
	G-DDNW	Schleicher Ks 6CR	K. Marchant & C. Styles
	G-DDNX	Schleicher Ka 6CR	Black Mountains Gliding Club
	G-DDNZ	Schleicher K 8B	Southampton University Gliding Club
	G-DDOA	Schleicher ASK-13	Essex and Suffolk Gliding Club Ltd
	G-DDOB	Grob G.102 Astir CS77	C. E. Hutson
	G-DDOC	Schleicher Ka 6CR	W. St. G. V. Stoney
	G-DDOE	Grob G.102 Astir CS77	Heron Gliding Club
	G-DDOF	Schleicher Ka 6CR	A. J. Watson
	G-DDOG	SA Bulldog Srs 120/121 (XX524:04)	Deltaero Ltd
	G-DDOK	Schleicher Ka 6E	R. S. Hawley & S. Y. Duxbury
	G-DDOR	Grob G.102 Astir CS77	V. A. Watt
	G-DDOU	Eiriavion PIK-20D	J. M. A. Shannon
	G-DDOX	Schleicher K-7	The Nene Valley Gliding Club Ltd
	G-DDPA	Schleicher ASK-18	J. P. Kirby
	G-DDPH	Schempp-Hirth Mini-Nimbus B	J. W. Murdoch
	G-DDPK	Glasflugel H303A Mosquito	G. Lawley
	G-DDPL	Eiriavion PIK-20D	437 Syndicate
	G-DDPO	Grob G.102 Astrir CS77	Dorset Gliding Club Ltd
	G-DDPY	Grob G.102 Astir CS77	C. A. Bailey
	G-DDRA	Schleicher Ka 6CR	K6CR Group Shobdon
	G-DDRB	Glaser-Dirks DG-100	DRB Syndicate
	G-DDRD	Schleicher Ka 6CR	Essex and Suffolk Gliding Club Ltd
	G-DDRE	Schleicher Ka 6CR	I. D. King
	G-DDRJ	Schleicher ASK-13	Lasham Gliding Society Ltd
	G-DDRL	Scheibe SF26A	T. A. Lipinski
	G-DDRM	Schleicher K 7	K7 DRM Syndicate
	G-DDRN	Glasflugel H303A Mosquito	A. & V. R. Roberts
	G-DDRO	Grob G.103 Twin Astir	Astir 258 Syndicate
	G-DDRP	Pilatus B4-PC11	DRP Syndicate
	G-DDRT	Eiriavion PIK-20D	PIK 688 Syndicate
	G-DDRV	Schleicher K 8B	DRV Syndicate
	G-DDRW	Grob G.102 Astir CS	I. W. & J. R. King
	G-DDRY	Schleicher Ka 6CR	M. K. Bradford
	G-DDRZ	Schleicher K-8B	East Sussex Gliding Club Ltd
	G-DDSB	Schleicher Ka-6E	G. B. Griffiths
	G-DDSF	Schleicher K-8B	University of Edinburgh Sports Union
	G-DDSG	Schleicher Ka 6CR	P. S. Whitehead
	G-DDSH	Grob G.102 Astir CS77	Astir 648 Syndicate
	G-DDSJ	Grob G.103 Twin Astir II	Herefordshire Gliding Club Ltd
	G-DDSL	Grob G.103 Twin Astir	DSL Group
	G-DDSP	Schempp-Hirth Mini Nimbus B	270 Syndicate
	G-DDST	Schleicher ASW-20L	C. J. Davison
	G-DDSU	Grob G.102 Astir CS77	Bowland Forest Gliding Club Ltd
	G-DDSV	Pilatus B4-PC11AF	G. M. Drinkell & S. J. Brenton
	G-DDSX	Schleicher ASW-19B	T. Johns, J. F. L. Scaife & J. F. Stoneman
	G-DDSY	Schleicher Ka-6CR	G. Jones & P. J. Shuff
	G-DDTA	Glaser-Dirks DG-200	G. A. Nash
	G-DDTC	Schempp-Hirth Janus B	Darlton Gliding Club Ltd
	G-DDTE	Schleicher ASW-19B	G. R. Purcell
	G-DDTG	Schempp-Hirth SHK-1	A. P. Benbow
	G-DDTK	Glasflugel Mosquito B	P. France
	G-DDTM	Glaser-Dirks DG-200	R. S. Skinner
	G-DDTN	Schleicher K 8B	C. G. & G. N. Thomas
	G-DDTP	Schleicher ASW-20	T. S. & S. M. Hills
	G-DDTS	CARMAM M-100S	I. A. Macadam
	G-DDTU	Schempp-Hirth Nimbus 2B	Nimbus Syndicate
	G-DDTV	Glasflugel Mosquito B	S. R. Evans
	G-DDTW	PZL-Bielsko SZD-30 Pirat	NDGC Pirat Syndicate
	G-DDTX	Glasflugel Mosquito B	P. T. S. Nash
	G-DDTY	Glasflugel H303 Mosquito B	W. H. L. Bullimore
	G-DDUB	Glasflugel H303 Mosquito B	M. W. Cartney
	G-DDUE	Schleicher ASK-13	Army Gliding Association
	G-DDUF	Schleicher K 8B	M. Staljan
	G-DDUH	Scheibe L-Spatz 55	R. J. Aylesbury & J. Young
	G-DDUK	Schleicher K-8B	The Bristol Gliding Club Propietary Ltd
	G-DDUL	Grob G.102 Astir CS77	W. I. H. Hall
	G-DDUR	Schleicher Ka 6CR	B. N. Bromley & M. Witthread
	G-DDUS	Schleicher Ka 6E	W. Ellis
	G-DDUT	Schleicher ASW-20	M. E. Doig & E. T. J. Murphy

Reg.	Type	Owner or Operator	Notes
G-DDUY	Glaser-Dirks DG-100	R. L. & K. P. McLean	
G-DDVB	Schleicher ASK-13	Essex and Suffolk Gliding Club Ltd	
G-DDVC	Schleicher ASK-13	Staffordshire Gliding Club Ltd	
G-DDVG	Schleicher Ka-6CR	G-DDVG Banana Group	
G-DDVH	Schleicher Ka 6E	M. A. K. Cropper	
G-DDVK	PZL-Bielsko SZD-48 Jantar Standard 2	D. S. Sigournay	
G-DDVL	Schleicher ASW-19	A. C. M. Phillips & P. K. Newman	
G-DDVM	Glasflugel H205 Club Libelle	M. A. Field	
G-DDVN	Eiriavion PIL-20D-78	T. P. Bassett & A. D. Butler	
G-DDVP	Schleicher ASW-19	VP Syndicate	
G-DDVS	Schempp-Hirth Standard Cirrus	J. C. & T. J. Milner	
G-DDVV	Schleicher ASW-20L	A. M. Hooper	
G-DDVX	Schleicher ASK-13	Shenington Gliding Club	
G-DDVY	Schempp-Hirth Cirrus	M. G. Ashton & G. Martin	
G-DDVZ	Glasflugel H303 Mosquito B	B. H. Shaw & R. Spreckley	
G-DDWB	Glasflugel H303 Mosquito B	D. T. Edwards	
G-DDWC	Schleicher Ka 6E	D. E. Jones	
G-DDWG	Schleicher K-8B	Dartmoor Gliding Society Ltd	
G-DDWJ	Glaser-Dirks DG-200	A. P. Kamp & P. R. Desmond	
G-DDWL	Glasflugel Mosquito B	H. A. Stanford	
G-DDWN	Schleicher K7 Rhonadler	L. R. & J. E. Merritt	
G-DDWP	Glasflugel Mosquito B	I. H. Murdoch	
G-DDWR	Glasflugel Mosquito B	C. D. Lovell	
G-DDWS	Eiriavion PIK-20D	D. G. Slocombe	
G-DDWT	Slingsby T.65C Vega	A. P. Grimley	
G-DDWU	Grob G.102 Astir CS	G-DDWU Syndicate	
G-DDWW	Slingsby T.65A Vega	D. M. Thomas	
G-DDWZ	Schleicher ASW-19B	P. Woodcock	
G-DDXA	Glasflugel H303 Mosquito B	G-DDXA Group	
G-DDXB	Schleicher ASW-20	81 Syndicate	
G-DDXD	Slingsby T.65A Vega	G-DDXD Flying Group	
G-DDXE	Slingsby T.65A Vega	H. K. Rattray	
G-DDXF	Slingsby T.65A Vega	B. A. Walker	
G-DDXG	Slingsby T.65A Vega	DXG Group	
G-DDXH	Schleicher Ka 6E	D. E. Findon	
G-DDXJ	Grob G.102 Astir CS77	M. T. Stickland	
G-DDXK	Centrair ASW-20F	E. & A. Townsend	
G-DDXL	Schempp-Hirth Standard Cirrus	C. J. Button	
G-DDXN	Glaser-Dirks DG-200	J. A. Johnston	
G-DDXT	Schempp-Hirth Mini-Nimbus C	S. E. Evans	
G-DDXW	Glasflugel Mosquito B	I. W. Myles & J. E. Shaw	
G-DDXX	Schleicher ASW-19B	Cotswold Gliding Club	
G-DDYC	Schleicher Ka 6CR	F. J. Bradley	
G-DDYE	Schleicher ASW-20L	P. J. L. Howell	
G-DDYF	Grob G.102 Astir CS77	York Gliding Centre Ltd	
G-DDYH	Glaser-Dirks DG-200	P. Johnson	
G-DDYJ	Schleicher Ka 6CR	Upward Bound Trust	
G-DDYL	CARMAM JP 15-36AR	P. A. Pickering	
G-DDYR	Schleicher K7	University of the West of England Gliding Club	
G-DDYU	Schempp-Hirth Nimbus -2C	C. B. Shepperd	
G-DDYX	Schleicher ASW-20	M. D. Wright	
G-DDZA	Slingsby T.65A Vega	K-H. Kuntze	
G-DDZB	Slingsby T.65A Vega	A. A. Black	
G-DDZF	Schempp-Hirth Standard Cirrus	G-DDZF Group	
G-DDZG	Schleicher ASW-19B	M. P. Theo	
G-DDZJ	Grob G.102 Astir CS Jeans	Mendip Astir Syndicate	
G-DDZM	Slingsby T.65A Vega	A. Mattano	
G-DDZN	Slingsby T.65A Vega	D. A. White	
G-DDZP	Slingsby T.65A Vega	M. T. Crews	
G-DDZR	IS-28B2	The Furness Gliding Club Proprietary Ltd	
G-DDZT	Eiriavion PIK-20D	PIK-20D 106 Group	
G-DDZU	Grob G.102 Astir CS	P. Clarke	
G-DDZV	Scheibe SF-27A	N. Newham	
G-DDZW	Schleicher Ka 6CR	S. W. Naylor	
G-DDZY	Schleicher ASW-19B	M. C. Fairman	
G-DEAE	Schleicher ASW-20L	R. Burghall	
G-DEAF	Grob G.102 Astir CS77	The Borders (Milfield) Gliding Club Ltd	
G-DEAG	Slingsby T.65A Vega	G-DEAG Group	
G-DEAH	Schleicher Ka 6E	M. Lodge	
G-DEAJ	Schempp-Hirth Nimbus 2	R. M. Crockett	
G-DEAK	Glasflugel H303 Mosquito B	T. A. L. Barnes	

Notes	Reg.	Type	Owner or Operator
	G-DEAM	Schempp-Hirth Nimbus 2B	Alpha Mike Syndicate
	G-DEAN	Solar Wings Pegasus XL-Q	Y. G. Richardson (G-MVJV)
	G-DEAR	Eiriavion PIK-20D	G-DEAR Group
	G-DEAT	Eiriavion PIK-20D	A. Spencer & D. Bieniasz
	G-DEAU	Schleicher K7	The Welland Gliding Club Ltd
	G-DEAV	Schempp-Hirth Mini-Nimbus C	G. D. H. Crawford
	G-DEAW	Grob G.102 Astir CS77	EAW Group
	G-DEBR	Shaw Europa	P. Curley
	G-DEBT	Pioneer 300	N. J. T. Tonks
	G-DEBX	Schleicher ASW-20	S. M. Economou & R. M Harris
	G-DECC	Schleicher Ka 6CR	Redwing
	G-DECF	Schleicher Ka 6CR	ECF Group
	G-DECJ	Slingsby T.65A Vega	J. E. B. Hart
	G-DECL	Slingsby T.65A Vega	J. M. Sherman
	G-DECM	Slingsby T.65A Vega	F. Wilson
	G-DECO	Dyn'Aéro MCR-01 Club	G-DECO Flying Group
	G-DECP	Rolladen-Schneider LS3-17	M. H. Ewer & K. Fear
	G-DECR	P & M Quik R	D. V. Lawrence
	G-DECS	Glasflugel H303 Mosquito B	S. Briggs & G. Richardson
	G-DECW	Schleicher ASK-21	Norfolk Gliding Club Ltd
	G-DECZ	Schleicher ASK-21	Booker Gliding Club Ltd
	G-DEDG	Schleicher Ka 6CR	S. J. Wood
	G-DEDH	Glasflugel H303 Mosquito B	B. L. Liddiard
	G-DEDJ	Glasflugel H303 Mosquito B	D. Martin & R. Bollow
	G-DEDK	Schleicher K7 Rhonadler	North Wales Gliding Club Ltd
	G-DEDM	Glaser-Dirks DG-200	A. H. G. St.Pierre
	G-DEDN	Glaser-Dirks DG-100G	DG 280 Syndicate
	G-DEDU	Schleicher ASK-13	Channel Gliding Club Ltd
	G-DEDX	Slingsby T.65D Vega	G. Kirkham
	G-DEDY	Slingsby T.65D Vega	T. McKinley
	G-DEDZ	Slingsby T.65C Vega	R. C. R. Copley
	G-DEEA	Slingsby T.65C Vega	Borders Sports Vega Syndicate (337)
	G-DEEC	Schleicher ASW-20L	D. Beams
	G-DEED	Schleicher K-8B	The Windrushers Gliding Club Ltd
	G-DEEF	Rolladen-Schneider LS3-17	Echo Echo Foxtrot Group
	G-DEEG	Slingsby T.65C Vega	Vega Syndicate
	G-DEEO	Schleicher ASW-19	K. Kiely
	G-DEEJ	Schleicher ASW-20L	G-DEEJ Group
	G-DEEK	Schempp-Hirth Nimbus 2C	R. Cassidy & W. P. Stephen
	G-DEEM	Schleicher K-8	The South Wales Gliding Club Ltd
	G-DEEN	Schempp-Hirth Standard Cirrus 75	G-DEEN Flying Group
	G-DEEO	Grob G.102 Club Astir II	G-DEEO Group
	G-DEEP	Wassmer WA.26P Squale	B. J. Key & A. S. Jones
	G-DEES	Rolladen-Schneider LS3-17	J. B. Illidge
	G-DEEW	Schleicher Ka 6CR	S. M. Dodds
	G-DEEX	Rolladen-Schneider LS3-17	The LS3 Flyers
	G-DEEZ	Denney Kitfox Mk.3	J. D. & D. Cheesman
	G-DEFA	Schleicher ASW-20L	Eight Eighties Syndicate
	G-DEFB	Schempp-Hirth Nimbus 2C	N. Revell
	G-DEFE	Centrair ASW-20F	W. A. Horne & D. A. Mackenzie
	G-DEFF	Schempp-Hirth Nimbus 2C	J. W. L. Clarke and P. J. D. Smith
	G-DEFN	Scheibe L-Spatz 55	P. L. E. Duguay
	G-DEFS	Rolladen-Schneider LS3	P. R. Thomas
	G-DEFT	Flight Design CTSW	G-DEFT Group
	G-DEFV	Schleicher ASW-20	A. R. McKillen
	G-DEFW	Slingsby T.65C Sport Vega	Darlton Gliding Club Ltd
	G-DEFZ	Rolladen-Schneider LS3-a	EFZ Syndicate
	G-DEGE	Rolladen-Schneider LS3-a	EGE Glider Syndicate
	G-DEGF	Slingsby T.65D Vega	Shalbourne Soaring Society Ltd
	G-DEGH	Slingsby T.65C Vega	K. Dykes, M. J. Davies & R. A. Starling
	G-DEGJ	Slingsby T.65C Vega	Cotswold Vega Syndicate
	G-DEGK	Schempp-Hirth Standard Cirrus	G. Deane
	G-DEGN	Grob G.103 Twin Astir II	Staffordshire Gliding Club Ltd
	G-DEGP	Schleicher ASW-20L	S. Pozerskis
	G-DEGS	Schempp-Hirth Nimbus 2CS	R. C. Nichols
	G-DEGT	Slingsby T.65D Vega	Vega Syndicate EGT
	G-DEGW	Schempp-Hirth Mini-Nimbus C	I. F. Barnes and Partners
	G-DEGX	Slingsby T.65C Vega	Haddenham Vega Syndicate
	G-DEGZ	Schleicher ASK-21	Black Mountains Gliding Club
	G-DEHC	Eichelsdorfer SB-5B	J. A. Castle
	G-DEHG	Slingsby T.65C Vega	Vega Syndicate
	G-DEHH	Schempp-Hirth Ventus a	J. A. White

BRITISH CIVIL REGISTRATIONS

G-DEHK– G-DEON

Reg.	Type	Owner or Operator	Notes
G-DEHK	Rolladen-Schneider LS4	S. Eyles	
G-DEHM	Schleicher Ka 6E	J. B. Symonds	
G-DEHO	Schleicher ASK-21	Lasham Gliding Society Ltd	
G-DEHP	Schempp-Hirth Nimbus 2C	D. J. King	
G-DEHT	Schempp-Hirth Nimbus 2C	Nimbus 2C Syndicate	
G-DEHU	Glasflugel 304	F. Townsend	
G-DEHV	Schleicher ASW-20L	M. A. & B. A. Roberts	
G-DEHY	Slingsby T.65D Vega	Vega Syndicate	
G-DEHZ	Schleicher ASW-20L	D. Crimmins	
G-DEIA	Cessna 560XL Citation XLS	Jaymax Jersey Ltd	
G-DEJA	ICA IS-28B2	M. H. Simms	
G-DEJB	Slingsby T.65C Vega	D. Tait & I. G. Walker	
G-DEJC	Slingsby T.65C Vega	I. Powis	
G-DEJD	Slingsby T.65D Vega	R. L. & K. P. McLean	
G-DEJE	Slingsby T.65C Vega	Crown Service Gliding Club	
G-DEJF	Schleicher K 8B	Cotswold Gliding Club	
G-DEJH	Eichelsdorfer SB-5E	S. E. Richardson & B. J. Dawson	
G-DEJR	Schleicher ASW-19B	J. C. M. Docherty	
G-DEJY	PZL-Bielsko SZD-9bis Bocian 1D	G-DEJY Group	
G-DEJZ	Scheibe SF26A	J. M. Collin	
G-DEKA	Cameron Z-90 balloon	P. G. Bogliaccino	
G-DEKC	Schleicher Ka 6E	S. L. Benn	
G-DEKF	Grob G.102 Club Astir III	The Bristol Gliding Club Proprietary Ltd	
G-DEKG	Schleicher ASK-21	Army Gliding Association	
G-DEKJ	Schempp-Hirth Ventus b	I. J. Metcalfe	
G-DEKS	Scheibe SF27A Zugvogel V	J. C. Johnson	
G-DEKT	Wassmer WA.30	D. C. Reynolds	
G-DEKU	Schleicher ASW-20L	A. J. Gillson	
G-DEKV	Rolladen-Schneider LS4	S. L. Helstrip	
G-DEKW	Schempp-Hirth Nimbus 2B	V. Luscombe-Mahoney	
G-DELA	Schleicher ASW-19B	S. G. Jones	
G-DELB	Robinson R-22 Beta ★	Aero Venture	
G-DELD	Slingsby T65C Vega	ELD Syndicate	
G-DELF	Aero L-29A Delfin	G. P. Williams	
G-DELG	Schempp-Hirth Ventus b/16.6	A. G. Machin	
G-DELN	Grob G.102 Astir CS Jeans	Bowland Forest Gliding Club Ltd	
G-DELO	Slingsby T.65D Vega	I. Sim	
G-DELR	Schempp-Hirth Ventus b	I. D. Smith	
G-DELU	Schleicher ASW-20L	V. Derrick	
G-DELZ	Schleicher ASW-20L	D. A. Fogden	
G-DEME	Glaser-Dirks DG-200/17	E. D. Casagrande	
G-DEMF	Rolladen-Schneider LS4	R. N. Johnston & M. C. Oggelsby	
G-DEMG	Rolladen-Schneider LS4	R. C. Bowsfield	
G-DEMH	Cessna F.172M (modified)	M. Hammond (G-BFLO)	
G-DEMJ	Slingsby T65C Sport Vega	Vega G-DEMJ Syndicate	
G-DEMM	AS.350B2 Ecureuil	Three Counties Helicopter Co.Ltd	
G-DEMN	Slingsby T.65D Vega	C. D. Sword	
G-DEMP	Slingsby T.65C Vega	The Surrey Hills Gliding Club Ltd	
G-DEMR	Slingsby T.65C Vega	J. Wozny	
G-DEMT	Rolladen-Schneider LS4	M. R. Fox	
G-DEMU	Glaser-Dirks DG-202/17	A. Butterfield & N. Swinton	
G-DEMZ	Slingsby T65A Vega	Vega Syndicate (G-BGCA)	
G-DENB	Cessna F.150G	C. R. Haden (G-ATZZ)	
G-DENC	Cessna F.150G	G-DENC Cessna Group (G-AVAP)	
G-DEND	Cessna F.150M	R. N. Tate (G-WAFC/G-BDFI)	
G-DENE	PA-28 Cherokee 140	Hinton Pilot Flight Training Ltd (G-ATOS)	
G-DENI	PA-32 Cherokee Six 300	A. Bendkowski (G-BAIA)	
G-DENJ	Schempp-Hirth Ventus b/16.6	S. Boyden	
G-DENO	Glasflugel Standard Libelle 201B	D. M. Bland	
G-DENS	Binder CP.301S Smaragd	Garston Smaragd Group	
G-DENU	Glaser-Dirks DG-100G	435 Syndicate	
G-DENV	Schleicher ASW-20L	R. D. Hone	
G-DENX	PZL-Bielsko SZD-48 Jantar Standard 2	J. M. Hire	
G-DEOA	Rolladen-Schneider LS4	A. A. Jenkins & R. L. Smith	
G-DEOB	PZL-Bielsko SZD-30	R. M. Golding	
G-DEOD	Grob G.102 Astir CS77	D. S. Fenton	
G-DEOE	Schleicher ASK-13	Essex Gliding Club Ltd	
G-DEOF	Schleicher ASK-13	Essex Gliding Club Ltd	
G-DEOJ	Centrair ASW-20FL	J. E. Gatfield	
G-DEOK	Centrair 101A Pegase	J. V. D. Hoek & J. Hunt	
G-DEOM	Carman M100S	S. W. Hutchinson	
G-DEON	Schempp-Hirth Nimbus 3	117 Syndicate	

169

Notes	Reg.	Type	Owner or Operator
	G-DEOT	Grob G.103A Twin II Acro	R. Tyrrell
	G-DEOU	Pilatus B4-PC11	D. J. Blackman
	G-DEOV	Schempp-Hirth Janus C	Burn Gliding Club Ltd
	G-DEOW	Schempp-Hirth Janus C	383 Syndicate
	G-DEOX	Carmam M-200 Foehn	B. S. Goodspeed
	G-DEOZ	Schleicher K 8B	Cotswold Gliding Club
	G-DEPD	Schleicher ASK-21	EPD Glider Syndicate
	G-DEPE	Schleicher ASW-19B	P. A. Goulding
	G-DEPF	Centrair ASW-20FL	323 Syndicate
	G-DEPG	CARMAM M100S	J. D. Owen
	G-DEPP	Schleicher ASK-13	Mendip Gliding Club Ltd
	G-DEPS	Schleicher ASW-20L	C. Beveridge
	G-DEPT	Schleicher K-8B	C. S. Warren
	G-DEPU	Glaser-Dirks DG-101G Elan	J. F. Rogers
	G-DEPX	Schempp-Hirth Ventus b/16.6	M. E. S. Thomas
	G-DERA	Centrair ASW-20FL	R. J. Lockett
	G-DERH	Schleicher ASK-21	The Burn Gliding Club Ltd
	G-DERJ	Schleicher ASK-21	The Royal Air Force Gliding and Soaring Association
	G-DERR	Schleicher ASW-19B	D. Clarke
	G-DERS	Schleicher ASW-19B	V. J. R. Day & J. Hubberstey
	G-DERV	Cameron Truck SS balloon	J. M. Percival
	G-DERX	Centrair 101A Pegase	A. Delaney & J. Innes
	G-DESB	Schleicher ASK-21	The Old Boys
	G-DESC	Rolladen-Schneider LS4	J. Crawford & J. M. Staley
	G-DESH	Centrair 101A	J. E. Moore
	G-DESJ	Schleicher K8B	Bowland Forest Gliding Club Ltd
	G-DESO	Glaser-Dirks DG-300 Elan	G. R. P. Brown
	G-DESU	Schleicher ASK-21	Banbury Gliding Club Ltd
	G-DETA	Schleicher ASK-21	P. Hawkins
	G-DETD	Schleicher K8B	Cotswold Gliding Club
	G-DETG	Rolladen-Schneider LS4	K. J. Woods
	G-DETJ	Centrair 101A	S. C. Phillips
	G-DETK	PZL-Bielsko SZD-48 Jantar Standard 2	I. W. Paterson
	G-DETM	Centrair 101A	D. Bowden
	G-DETV	Rolladen-Schneider LS4	P. Fabian
	G-DETY	Rolladen-Schneider LS4	D. T. Staff
	G-DETZ	Schleicher ASW-20CL	The 20 Syndicate
	G-DEUC	Schleicher ASK-13	The Bristol Gliding Club Proprietary Ltd
	G-DEUD	Schleicher ASW-20C	R. Tietema
	G-DEUF	PZL-Bielsko SZD-50-3	Puchacz Group
	G-DEUH	Rolladen-Schneider LS4	F. J. Parkinson
	G-DEUJ	Schempp-Hirth Ventus b/16.6	S. C. Renfrew
	G-DEUK	Centrair ASW-20FL	P. A. Clark
	G-DEUS	Schempp-Hirth Ventus b/16.6	R. J. Whitaker
	G-DEUV	PZL-Bielsko SZD-42-2 Jantar 2B	G. V. McKirdy
	G-DEUX	AS.355F Ecureuil 2	Elmridge Ltd
	G-DEUY	Schleicher ASW-20BL	ASW20BL-G-DUEY Group
	G-DEVF	Schempp-Hirth Nimbus 3T	A. G. Leach
	G-DEVH	Schleicher Ka 10	C. W. & K. T. Matten
	G-DEVJ	Schleicher ASK-13	Lasham Gliding Society Ltd
	G-DEVK	Grob G.102 Astir CS	Peterborough and Spalding Gliding Club Ltd
	G-DEVL	Eurocopter EC 120B	Saxon Logistics Ltd
	G-DEVM	Centrair 101A	Seahawk Gliding Club
	G-DEVO	Centrair 101A	G-DEVO Pegase Glider
	G-DEVP	Schleicher ASK-13	Lasham Gliding Society Ltd
	G-DEVS	PA-28 Cherokee 180	180 Group/Blackbushe (G-BGVJ)
	G-DEVV	Schleicher ASK-23	Midland Gliding Club Ltd
	G-DEVW	Schleicher ASK-23	London Gliding Club Proprietary Ltd
	G-DEVX	Schleicher ASK-23	London Gliding Club Proprietary Ltd
	G-DEVY	Schleicher ASK-23	London Gliding Club Proprietary Ltd
	G-DEWE	P & M Flight Design CTSW	Comunica Industries International Ltd
	G-DEWG	Grob G.103A Twin II Acro	J. P. Ryan
	G-DEWI	Rotorsport UK MTO Sport	D. V. Nockels
	G-DEWP	Grob G.103A Twin II Acro	Cambridge Gliding Club Ltd
	G-DEWR	Grob G.103A Twin II Acro	The Bristol Gliding Club Proprietary Ltd
	G-DEWY	Alpi Pioneer 300	W. D. Dewey (G-SRAW)
	G-DEWZ	Grob G.103A Twin II Acro	T. R. Dews
	G-DEXA	Grob G.103A Twin II Acro	Trent Valley Aerotowing Club Ltd
	G-DEXP	ARV Super 2	R. W. Clarke
	G-DEXT	Robinson R44 II	Berkley Properties Ltd

Reg.	Type	Owner or Operator	Notes
G-DFAF	Schleicher ASW-20L	A. S. Miller	
G-DFAR	Glasflugel H205 Club Libelle	Alpha Romeo Syndicate	
G-DFAT	Schleicher ASK-13	Dorset Gliding Club Ltd	
G-DFAV	ICA IS-32A	Ibis 32 Syndicate	
G-DFAW	Schempp-Hirth Ventus b/16.6	P. R. Stafford-Allen	
G-DFBD	Schleicher ASW-15B	D. A. Wilson	
G-DFBE	Rolladen-Schneider LS6	J. B. Van Woerden	
G-DFBJ	Schleicher K 8B	Bidford Gliding & Flying Club Ltd	
G-DFBM	Schempp-Hirth Nimbus 3/24.5	D. Gardiner	
G-DFBO	Schleicher ASW-20BL	454 Syndicate	
G-DFBR	Grob G.102 Astir CS77	773 Syndicate	
G-DFBY	Schempp-Hirth Discus b	D. Latimer	
G-DFCD	Centrair 101A	G. J. Bass	
G-DFCK	Schempp-Hirth Ventus b	S. A. Adlard	
G-DFCL	Schleicher K 8B	Bidford Gliding Ltd	
G-DFCM	Glaser-Dirks DG-300	A. Davis & I. D. Roberts	
G-DFCW	Schleicher ASK-13	Lasham Gliding Society Ltd	
G-DFCY	Schleicher ASW-15	M. R. Shaw	
G-DFDF	Grob G.102 Astir CS	The Bristol Gliding Club Proprietary Ltd	
G-DFDW	Glaser-Dirks DG-300	C. M. Hadley	
G-DFEB	Grob G.102 Club Astir III	Lasham Gliding Society Ltd	
G-DFEO	Schleicher ASK-13	Lasham Gliding Society Ltd	
G-DFEX	Grob G.102 Astir CS77	J. Taylor	
G-DFFP	Schleicher ASW-19B	Foxtrot Papa Group	
G-DFGJ	Schleicher Ka 6CR	K6 Syndicate	
G-DFGT	Glaser-Dirks DG-300 Elan	T. J. Gray	
G-DFHS	Schempp-Hirth Ventus cT	154 Group	
G-DFHY	Scheibe SF-27A	J. M. Pursey	
G-DFJJ	Schempp-Hirth Ventus cT	S. G. Jones	
G-DFJO	Schempp-Hirth Ventus cT	FJO Syndicate	
G-DFKH	Schleicher Ka 6CR	I. A. Megarry	
G-DFKI	Westland Gazelle HT.2	Bourne Park Aviation Group (G-BZOT)	
G-DFKX	Schleicher Ka 6CR	J. E. Herring	
G-DFMG	Schempp-Hirth Discus b	M. T. Davis & J. Melvin	
G-DFOG	Rolladen-Schneider LS7	J. J. Shaw	
G-DFOX	AS.355F1 Twin Squirrel	Potter Aviation Ltd (G-NAAS/G-BPRG/G-NWPA)	
G-DFRA	Rolladen-Schneider LS6-b	79 Syndicate	
G-DFSA	Grob G.102 Astir CS	Astir 498 Syndicate	
G-DFTJ	PZL-Bielsko SZD-48-1 Jantar Standard 2	P. Nock	
G-DFUN	Van's RV-6	G-DFUN Flying Group	
G-DFWJ	Rolladen-Schneider LS7-WL	G-DFWJ Group	
G-DFXR	Sportine Aviacija LAK-12	Hinton Pilot Flight Training Ltd	
G-DGAL	Ikarus C42 FB80 Bravo	D. & P. A. Gall	
G-DGAW	Schleicher Ka 6CR	H. C. Yorke & D. Searle	
G-DGBE	Schleicher Ka-6CR-P	L. Ferguson-Dalling	
G-DGCL	Glaser-Dirks DG.800B	C. J. Lowrie	
G-DGDJ	Rolladen-Schneider LS4-a	450 Syndicate	
G-DGFD	Robinson R44 II	FD Aviarion Ltd (G-CGNF)	
G-DGFY	Flylight Dragonfly	M. R. Sands	
G-DGHI	Dyn'Aéro MCR-01 Club	D. G. Hall	
G-DGIK	DG Flugzeugbau DG.1000S	R. P. Davis	
G-DGIO	Glaser-Dirks DG-100G Elan	DG1 Group	
G-DGIV	Glaser-Dirks DG.800B	S. M. Tilling & J. Vella-Grech	
G-DGKB	Centrair ASW-20F	G. K. Bain	
G-DGMT	III Sky Arrow 650 T	A. Powell	
G-DGOD	Robinson R22 Beta	Startrade GmbH/Germany	
G-DGPS	Diamond DA-42 Twin Star	Flight Calibration Services Ltd	
G-DGRA	DG Flugzeugbau DG-808C	R. Arkle	
G-DGSC	CZAW Sportcruiser	D. J. Gunn	
G-DGSM	Glaser-Dirks DG-400-17	T. E. Snoddy & L. J. McKelvie	
G-DHAA	Glasflugel H201B Standard Libelle	D. J. Jones & R. N. Turner	
G-DHAD	Glasflugel H201B Standard Libelle	R. Hines	
G-DHAH	Aeronca 7BCM Champion	Alpha Hotel Group (G-JTYE)	
G-DHAL	Schleicher ASK-13	The Windrushers Gliding Club Ltd	
G-DHAP	Schleicher Ka 6E	M.Fursedon & T. Turner	
G-DHAT	Glaser-Dirks DG-200/17	G-DHAT Group	
G-DHCA	Grob G.103 Twin Astir	A. C. Jordan	
G-DHCC	DHC.1 Chipmunk 22 (WG321:G)	Eureka Aviation BVBA/Belgium	
G-DHCE	Schleicher ASW-19B	G-DHCE Syndicate	
G-DHCF	PZL-Bielsko SZD-50-3	Shalbourne Soaring Society Ltd	

Notes	Reg.	Type	Owner or Operator
	G-DHCJ	Grob G.103A Twin II Acro	Peterborough and Spalding Gliding Club Ltd
	G-DHCL	Schempp-Hirth Discus b	C. E. Broom & L. Chicot
	G-DHCO	Glasflugel Standard Libelle 201B	M. J. Birch
	G-DHCR	PZL-Bielsko SZD-51-1	East Sussex Gliding Club Ltd
	G-DHCU	DG-300 Club Elan	R. B. Hankey & M. S. Smith
	G-DHCV	Schleicher ASW-19B	J. E. G. Savage
	G-DHCW	PZL-Bielsko SZD-51-1	Deeside Gliding Club (Aberdeenshire) Ltd
	G-DHCX	Schleicher ASK-21	Devon and Somerset Gliding Club Ltd
	G-DHCZ	DHC.2 Beaver 1	Propshop Ltd (G-BUCJ)
	G-DHDH	Glaser-Dirks DG-200	J. T. Newbery
	G-DHDV	DH.104 Dove 8 (VP981)	Air Atlantique Ltd
	G-DHEB	Schleicher Ka 6CR	J. Burrow
	G-DHEM	Schempp-Hirth Discus CS	473 Syndicate
	G-DHER	Schleicher ASW-19B	R. R. Bryan
	G-DHES	Centrair 101A	C. J. Cole & D. R. Bennett
	G-DHET	Rolladen-Schneider LS6-c18	M. P. Brooks
	G-DHEV	Schempp-Hirth Cirrus	HEV Group
	G-DHGL	Schempp-Hirth Discus b	R. G. Corbin & S. E. Buckley
	G-DHGS	Robinson R22 Beta	Fly Executive Ltd
	G-DHGY	SZD-24C Foka	A. B. Clarke & G. J. Furniss
	G-DHJH	Airbus A.321-211	Thomas Cook Airlines Ltd
	G-DHJZ	Airbus A.320-214	Thomas Cook Airlines Ltd
	G-DHKL	Schempp-Hirth Discus bT	M. A. Thorne
	G-DHLE	Boeing 767-3JHF	DHL Air Ltd
	G-DHLF	Boeing 767-3JHF	DHL Air Ltd
	G-DHLG	Boeing 767-3JHF	DHL Air Ltd
	G-DHLH	Boeing 767-3JHF	DHL Air Ltd
	G-DHLK	Boeing 767-3HJF	DHL Air Ltd
	G-DHMP	Schempp-Hirth Discus b	HMP Discus Syndicate
	G-DHNX	Rolladen-Schneider LS4-b	M. B. Margetson
	G-DHOC	Scheibe Bergfalke II-55	R. Karch
	G-DHOK	Schleicher ASW-20CL	S. D. Minson
	G-DHOP	Van's RV-9A	A. S. Orme
	G-DHOX	Schleicher ASW-15B	P. Ridgill & A. Griffiths
	G-DHPA	Issoire E-78 Silene	P. Woodcock
	G-DHPM	OGMA DHC.1 Chipmunk 20 (1365)	P. Meyrick
	G-DHPR	Schempp-Hirth Discus b	G. J. Bowser
	G-DHRG	Airbus A.320-214	Thomas Cook Airlines Ltd
	G-DHRR	Schleicher ASK-21	Lakes Gliding Club
	G-DHSJ	Schempp-Hirth Discus b	D. Byrne
	G-DHSL	Schempp-Hirth Ventus 2c	H. G. Woodsend
	G-DHSR	AB Sportine LAK-12 Lietuva	G. Forster
	G-DHSS	DH.112 Venom FB.50 (WR360:K)	Aviation and Computer Consultancy Ltd
	G-DHTG	Grob G.102 Astir CS	Trent Valley Gliding Club Ltd
	G-DHTT	DH.112 Venom FB.50 (WR421)	Aviation and Computer Consultancy Ltd (G-BMOC)
	G-DHUB	PZL-Bielsko SZD-48-3	C. J. M. Chatburn
	G-DHUK	Schleicher Ka 6CR	Essex Gliding Club Ltd
	G-DHUU	DH.112 Venom FB.50 (WR410)	Aviation and Computer Consultancy Ltd (G-BMOD)
	G-DHVM	DH.112 Venom FB.50 (WR470)	Air Atlantique Ltd/Coventry (G-GONE)
	G-DHYL	Schempp-Hirth Ventus 2a	M. J. Cook
	G-DHZF	DH.82A Tiger Moth (N9192)	C. A.Parker & M. R. Johnson (G-BSTJ)
	G-DIAT	PA-28 Cherokee 140	Hinton Pilot Flight Training Ltd (G-BCGK)
	G-DICK	Thunder Ax6-56Z balloon	R. D. Sargeant
	G-DIDG	Van's RV-7	E. T. & D. K. Steele
	G-DIDY	Thruster T600T 450	D. R. Sims
	G-DIGG	Robinson R44 II	Thames Materials Ltd
	G-DIGI	PA-32 Cherokee Six 300	D. Stokes
	G-DIGS	Hughes 369HE	Mackinnon Construction Ltd (G-DIZZ)
	G-DIKY	Murphy Rebel	Stoke Golding Flyers
	G-DIME	Rockwell Commander 114	H. B. Richardson
	G-DINA	AA-5B Tiger	Portway Aviation Ltd
	G-DINO	Pegasus Quantum 15	F. Strath (G-MGMT)
	G-DIPI	Cameron 80 Tub SS balloon	C. G. Dobson
	G-DIPM	PA-46-350P Malibu Mirage	MAS Mix Ltd
	G-DIRK	Glaser-Dirks DG.400	D. J. Blackman
	G-DISA	SA Bulldog Srs 120/125	I. W. Whiting
	G-DISK	PA-24 Comanche 250	Brock Paints Ltd (G-APZG)
	G-DISO	Jodel 150	P. F. Craven
	G-DIWY	PA-32 Cherokee Six 300	IFS Chemicals Ltd

Reg.	Type	Owner or Operator	Notes
G-DIXY	PA-28-181 Archer III	Modern Air (UK) Ltd	
G-DIZI	Escapade	J. A. & J. M. Iszard	
G-DIZO	Jodel D.120A	D. Aldersea (G-EMKM)	
G-DIZY	PA-28R-201T Turbo Arrow III	Dizy Aviation Ltd	
G-DJAA	Schempp-Hirth Janus B	Bidford Gliding & Flying Club Ltd	
G-DJAB	Glaser-Dirks DG-300 Elan	I. G. Johnston	
G-DJAC	Schempp-Hirth Duo Discus	G-DJAC Group	
G-DJAD	Schleicher ASK-21	The Borders (Milfield) Gliding Club Ltd	
G-DJAE	Cessna 500 Citation	R. C. Lyne (G-JEAN)	
G-DJAH	Schempp-Hirth Discus b	K. Neave & C. F. M. Smith	
G-DJAN	Schempp-Hirth Discus b	N. F. Perren	
G-DJAY	Avtech Jabiru UL-450	G. S. Stokes	
G-DJBC	Ikarus C42 FB100	D. Meegan	
G-DJCR	Varga 2150A Kachina	D. J. C. Robertson (G-BLWG)	
G-DJET	Diamond DA42 Twin Star	Diamond Executive Aviation Ltd	
G-DJGG	Schleicher ASW-15B	A. A. Cole	
G-DJHP	Valentin Mistral C	P. B. Higgs	
G-DJJA	PA-28-181 Archer II	Interactive Aviation Ltd	
G-DJLL	Schleicher ASK-13	Bidford Gliding & Flying Club Ltd	
G-DJMC	Schleicher ASK-21	The Royal Air Force Gliding and Soaring Association	
G-DJMD	Schempp-Hirth Discus b	G-DJMD Flying Group	
G-DJMM	Cessna 172S	J. Browne & M. Manston	
G-DJNC	ICA-Brasov IS-28B2	Delta Juliet November Group	
G-DJNH	Denney Kitfox Mk 3	N. S. Lomax	
G-DJST	Ixess 912(1)	K. Buckley	
G-DJVY	Scintex CP.1315-C3 Super Emeraude	A. P. Goodwin	
G-DJWS	Schleicher ASW-15B	B. Pridgeon	
G-DKBA	DKBA AT 0301-0 balloon	I. Chadwick	
G-DKDP	Grob G.109	Grob 4	
G-DKEM	Bell 407	True Course Helicopter Ltd	
G-DKEN	Rolladen-Schneider LS4-a	K. L. Sangster and B. Lytollis	
G-DKEY	PA-28-161 Warrior II	PA-28 Warrior Ltd	
G-DKFU	Schempp-Hirth Ventus 2cxT	W. F. Payton (G-CKFU)	
G-DKGF	Viking Dragonfly ★	(stored)/Enstone	
G-DKNY	Robinson R44 II	Williamair Ltd	
G-DKTA	PA-28-236 Dakota	G. Beattie & C. J. T. Kitchen	
G-DLAA	Cessna 208 Caravan 1 ✓	Aerodynamics Ltd	
G-DLAB	Beech 99	Aerodynamics Ltd	
G-DLAC	Cessna 208B Grand Caravan	Credit Cooperatif-Coopamat & Natixis Lease	
G-DLAK	Cessna 208 Caravan 1	Aerodynamics Ltd	
G-DLAL	Beech E90 King Air	Aerodynamics Ltd	
G-DLCB	Shaw Europa	K. Richards	
G-DLDL	Robinson R22 Beta	Cambridge Aviation Ltd	
G-DLEE	SOCATA TB9 Tampico Club	D. A. Lee (G-BPGX)	
G-DLFN	Aero L-29 Delfin	J. A. Southern	
G-DLOM	SOCATA TB20 Trinidad	J. N. A. Adderley	
G-DLTC	Hawker 900XP	Hangar 8 Management Ltd	
G-DLTR	PA-28 Cherokee 180E	R. A. Brown (G-AYAV)	
G-DMAC	Avtech Jabiru SP-430	C. J. Pratt	
G-DMAH	SOCATA TB20 Trinidad	William Cook Aviation Ltd	
G-DMBO	Van's RV-7	C. J. Goodwin	
G-DMCA	Douglas DC-10-30 ★	Forward fuselage/Manchester Airport Viewing Park	
G-DMCI	Ikarus C42 FB100	D. McCartan	
G-DMCS	PA-28R Cherokee Arrow 200-II	Arrow Associates (G-CPAC)	
G-DMCT	Flight Design CT2K	A. M. Sirant	
G-DMCW	Magni M-24C	B. A. Carnegie (G-CGVF)	
G-DMND	Diamond DA42 Twin Star	MC Air Ltd	
G-DMON	Xtremeair XA-42 Sbach 342	P. F. Brice & R. M. Hockey	
G-DMPP	Diamond DA42 Twin Star	Diamond Executive Aviation Ltd	
G-DMRS	Robinson R44 II	Nottinghamshire Helicopters (2004) Ltd	
G-DMSS	Westland Gazelle HT.3 (XW858:C)	G. Wood	
G-DMWW	CFM Shadow Srs DD	G-DMWW Flying Group	
G-DNBH	Raj Hamsa X'Air Hawk	D. N. B. Hearn	
G-DNGA	Balóny Kubíček BB.20	G. J. Bell	
G-DNGR	Colt 31A balloon	G. J. Bell	

Notes	Reg.	Type	Owner or Operator
	G-DKNY	Ikarus C42 FB80	D. N. K. & M. A. Symon
	G-DNOP	PA-46-350P Malibu Mirage	Campbell Aviation Ltd
	G-DOBS	Van's RV-8	R. G. Dobney
	G-DOCA	Boeing 737-436	British Airways
	G-DOCB	Boeing 737-436	British Airways
	G-DOCE	Boeing 737-436	British Airways
	G-DOCF	Boeing 737-436	British Airways
	G-DOCG	Boeing 737-436	British Airways
	G-DOCH	Boeing 737-436	British Airways
	G-DOCL	Boeing 737-436	British Airways
	G-DOCN	Boeing 737-436	British Airways
	G-DOCO	Boeing 737-436	British Airways
	G-DOCS	Boeing 737-436	British Airways
	G-DOCT	Boeing 737-436	British Airways
	G-DOCU	Boeing 737-436	British Airways
	G-DOCV	Boeing 737-436	British Airways
	G-DOCW	Boeing 737-436	British Airways
	G-DOCX	Boeing 737-436	British Airways
	G-DOCY	Boeing 737-436	British Airways (G-BVBY)
	G-DOCZ	Boeing 737-436	British Airways (G-BVBZ)
	G-DODB	Robinson R22 Beta	Heliyorks Ltd
	G-DODD	Cessna F.172P-II	K. Watts
	G-DODG	Aerotechnik EV-97A Eurostar	K. G. Vaughan
	G-DOEA	AA-5A Cheetah	Fairway Flying Services (G-RJMI)
	G-DOFY	Bell 206B JetRanger 3	Castle Air Ltd
	G-DOGE	SA Bulldog Srs 100/101	Mid America (UK) Ltd (G-AZHX)
	G-DOGG	SA Bulldog Srs 120/121 (XX638)	P. Sengupta
	G-DOGI	Robinson R22 Beta	Southern Heliservices Ltd (G-BVGS)
	G-DOGZ	Horizon 1	M. J. Nolan
	G-DOIG	CZAW Sportcruiser	J. H. Doyle
	G-DOIN	Skyranger 912(S)1	A. G. Borer
	G-DOIT	AS.350B1 Ecureuil	FB Heliservices Ltd
	G-DOLF	AS.365N3 Dauphin II	Profred Partners LLP
	G-DOLI	Cirrus SR20	Furness Asset Management Ltd
	G-DOLY	Cessna T.303	KW Aviation Ltd (G-BJZK)
	G-DOME	PA-28-161 Warrior III	Target Aviation Ltd
	G-DOMS	Aerotechnik EV-97A Eurostar	R. K. & C. A. Stewart
	G-DONI	AA-5B Tiger	W. P. Moritz (G-BLLT)
	G-DONS	PA-28RT-201T Turbo Arrow IV	C. E. Griffiths
	G-DONT	Xenair CH.601XL Zodiac	K. Dickson
	G-DOOM	Cameron Z-105 balloon	Test Flight
	G-DORM	Robinson R44 II	Aero-Heli Ltd
	G-DORN	EKW C-3605	R. G. Gray
	G-DORS	Eurocopter EC 135T2+	Premier Fund Leasing
	G-DORY	Cameron Z-315 balloon	P. Baker
	G-DOSA	Diamond DA42 Twin Star	DO Systems Ltd
	G-DOSB	Diamond DA42 Twin Star	DO Systems Ltd
	G-DOSC	Diamond DA42 Twin Star	DO Systems Ltd
	G-DOTT	CFM Streak Shadow	R. J. Bell
	G-DOTW	Savannah VG Jabiru(1)	I. S. Wright
	G-DOTY	Van's RV-7	H. A. Daines
	G-DOVE	Cessna 182Q	G. Wills
	G-DOVE†	D. H. 104 Devon C.2 ★	E. Surrey College/Gatton Point, Redhill (G-KOOL)
	G-DOVS	Robinson R44 II	D. B. Hamilton
	G-DOWN	Colt 31A balloon	M. Williams
	G-DOZI	Ikarus C.42 FB100	D. A. Izod
	G-DOZZ	Best Off Sky Ranger Swift 912S(1)	J. P. Doswell
	G-DPEP	Aero AT-3 R100	Limerick Flying Club (Coonagh) Ltd
	G-DPJR	Sikorsky S-76B	Blackbird Logistics Ltd (G-JCBA)
	G-DPPF	Augusta A.109E Power	Dyfed-Powys Police Authority
	G-DPYE	Robin DR400/500	C. R. J. Walker
	G-DRAM	Cessna FR.172F (floatplane)	H. R. Mitchell
	G-DRAT	Slingsby T.51 Dart 17R	W. R. Longstaff
	G-DRAW	Colt 77A balloon	A. G. Odell
	G-DRCS	Schleicher ASH-25E	C. R. Smithers
	G-DREG	Superchaser	N. R. Beale
	G-DREI	Fokker DR.1 Triplane Replica	P. M. Brueggemann
	G-DREX	Cameron Saturn-110 balloon	M. A. Trimble
	G-DRFC	ATR-42-300	Blue Islands Ltd

Reg.	Type	Owner or Operator	Notes
G-DRGC	P & M Quik GT450	D. R. G. Cornwell	
G-DRGS	Cessna 182S	Walter Scott & Partners Ltd	
G-DRIV	Robinson R44 II	MFH Helicopters Ltd	
G-DRMM	Shaw Europa	T. J. Harrison	
G-DROL	Robinson R44 II	M. R. Lord (G-OPDG)	
G-DROP	Cessna U.206C	K. Brady (G-UKNO/G-BAMN)	
G-DRPK	Reality Escapade	P. A. Kirkham	
G-DRRT	Slingsby T.51 Dart 17R	1516 Dart Syndicate (G-DBXH)	
G-DRSV	CEA DR.315 (modified)	R. S. Voice	
G-DRYS	Cameron N-90 balloon	C. A. Butter	
G-DRZF	CEA DR.360	P. K. Kaufeler	
G-DSFT	PA-28R Cherokee Arrow 200-II	J. Jones (G-LFSE/G-BAXT)	
G-DSGC	PA-25 Pawnee 235C	Devon & Somerset Gliding Club Ltd	
G-DSID	PA-34-220T Seneca III	I. S. Gillbe	
G-DSKI	Aerotechnik EV-97 Eurostar	G-DSKI Group	
G-DSKY	Diamond DA.42 Twin Star	Diamond Executive Aviation Ltd (G-CDSZ)	
G-DSLL	Pegasus Quantum 15-912	R. G. Jeffery	
G-DSMA	P & M Aviation Quik R	IP Rights Ltd	
G-DSPK	Cameron Z-140	Bailey Balloons Ltd	
G-DSPL	Diamond DA40 Star	Dynamic Signal Processing Ltd (G-GBOS)	
G-DSPY	Diamond D42M Twin Star	Diamond Executive Aviation Ltd	
G-DSPZ	Robinson R44 II	Focal Point Communications Ltd	
G-DSVN	Rolladen-Schneider LS8-18	A. R. Paul	
G-DTAR	P & M Aviation Quik GT450	D. Tarvit	
G-DTCP	PA-32R-300 Cherokee Lance	R. S. Cook (G-TEEM)	
G-DTFF	Cessna T.182T Turbo Skylane	Ridgway Aviation Ltd	
G-DTFL	PA-46-500TP Malibu Meridian	Tyrone Fabrication Ltd	
G-DTOY	Ikarus C.42.FB100	C. W. Laske	
G-DTSM	EV-97 TeamEurostar UK	J. R. Stothart	
G-DTUG	Wag-Aero Super Sport	D. A. Bullock	
G-DTWO	Schempp-Hirth Discus 2A	O. M. McCormack	
G-DUBI	Lindstrans LBL-120A balloon	A. Nimmo	
G-DUDE	Van's RV-8	W. M. Hodgkins	
G-DUDI	Rotorsport UK MTO Sport	Cloud 9 Gyro Flight Ltd	
G-DUDZ	Robin DR.400/180	D. H. Pattison (G-BXNK)	
G-DUFF	Rand Robinson KR-2	J. I. B. Duff	
G-DUGE	Ikarus C42 FB UK	D. Stevenson	
G-DUGI	Lindstrand LBL-90A balloon	R. P. Waite	
G-DUKY	Robinson R44	English Braids Ltd	
G-DUMP	Customcraft A-25 balloon	P. C. Bailey	
G-DUNK	Cessna F172M Skyhawk	Devon and Somerset Flight Training Ltd	
G-DUNS	Lindstrand LBL-90A balloon	A. Murphy	
G-DUOT	Schempp-Hirth Duo Discus T	G-DUOT Soaring Group	
G-DURO	Shaw Europa	W. R. C. Williams-Wynne	
G-DURX	Thunder 77A balloon	R. C. and M. A. Trimble	
G-DUSK	DH.115 Vampire T.11 (XE856) ★	Bournemouth Aviation Museum	
G-DUST	Stolp SA.300 Starduster Too	N. M. Robinson	
G-DUVL	Cessna F.172N	G-DUVL Flying Group	
G-DVAA	Eurocopter EC135 T2+	Devon Air Ambulance Trading Co.Ltd	
G-DVBF	Lindstrand LBL-210A balloon	Virgin Balloon Flights	
G-DVMI	Van's RV-7	G-DVMI Group	
G-DVON	DH.104 Devon C.2 (VP955)	C. L. Thatcher	
G-DWCE	Robinson R44 II	Jim Davies Civil Engineering Ltd	
G-DWEM	Eurocopter EC135 T2	Bond Air Services Ltd (G-SSXX/G-SSSX)	
G-DWIA	Chilton D.W.1A	D. Elliott	
G-DWIB	Chilton D.W.1B (replica)	J. Jennings	
G-DWJM	Cessna 550 Citation II	TL Aviation Instrad LLP (G-BJIR)	
G-DWMS	Avtech Jabiru UL-450	B. J. Weighell	
G-DWPH	Ultramagic M-77 balloon	Ultramagic SA/Spain	
G-DXLT	Schempp-Hirth Duo Discus xLT	G-DXLT Group	
G-DYCE	Robinson R44 II	Moorland Windows	
G-DYKE	Dyke JD.2 Delta	M. S. Bird	
G-DYMC	Aerospool Dynamic WT9 UK	S. Hoyle	
G-DYNA	Dynamic WT9 UK	Yeoman Light Aircraft Co.Ltd	
G-DYNM	Aerospool Dynamic WT9 UK	November Mike Group	

Notes	Reg.	Type	Owner or Operator
	G-DZDZ	Rolladen-Schneider LS4	I. MacArthur
	G-DZKY	Diamond DA.40D Star	Dusky Aviation Ltd (G-CEZP)
	G-DZZY	Champion 8KCAB	Paul's Planes Ltd
	G-EAGA	Sopwith Dove (replica)	A. Wood
	G-EAOU†	Vickers Vimy (replica)(NX71MY)	Greenco (UK) Ltd
	G-EASD	Avro 504L	G. M. New
	G-EASQ†	Bristol Babe (replica) (BAPC87) ★	Bristol Aero Collection (stored)/Kemble
	G-EAVX	Sopwith Pup (B1807)	K. A. M. Baker
	G-EBED†	Vickers 60 Viking (replica) (BAPC114)★	Brooklands Museum of Aviation/Weybridge
	G-EBHX	DH.53 Humming Bird	The Shuttleworth Collection
	G-EBIA	RAF SE-5A (F904)	The Shuttleworth Collection
	G-EBIB	RAF SE-5A ★	Science Museum/South Kensington
	G-EBIC	RAF SE-5A (F938) ★	RAF Museum/Hendon
	G-EBIR	DH.51	The Shuttleworth Collection
	G-EBJE	Avro 504K (E449) ★	RAF Museum/Hendon
	G-EBJG	Parnall Pixie IIIH	Midland Aircraft Preservation Society
	G-EBJI	Hawker Cygnet (replica)	C. J. Essex
	G-EBJO	ANEC IIH	The Shuttleworth Collection
	G-EBKY	Sopwith Pup (9917)	The Shuttleworth Collection
	G-EBLV	DH.60 Cirrus Moth	British Aerospace PLC
	G-EBMB	Hawker Cygnet I ★	RAF Museum/Cosford
	G-EBNV	English Electric Wren	The Shuttleworth Collection
	G-EBQP	DH.53 Humming Bird (J7326) ★	P. L. Kirk & T. G. Pankhurst
	G-EBWD	DH.60X Hermes Moth	The Shuttleworth Collection
	G-EBZM	Avro 594 Avian IIIA ★	Manchester Museum of Science & Industry
	G-EBZN	DH.60X Moth	J. Hodgkinson (G-UAAP)
	G-ECAC	Alpha R21620U	Bulldog Aviation Ltd
	G-ECAD	Cessna FA.152	Bulldog Aviation Ltd (G-JEET/G-BHMF)
	G-ECAE	Royal Aircraft Factory SE.5A	H. A. D. Monro
	G-ECAF	Robin HR.200-120B	Bulldog Aviation Ltd (G-BZET)
	G-ECAK	Cessna F.172M	Bulldog Aviation Ltd (G-BENK)
	G-ECAM	EAA Acrosport II	C. England
	G-ECAN	DH.84 Dragon	Norman Aircraft Trust
	G-ECBH	Cessna F.150K	ECBH Flying Group
	G-ECBI	Schweizer 269C-1	Iris Aviation Ltd
	G-ECDB	Schleicher Ka 6E	C. W. R. Neve
	G-ECDS	DH.82A Tiger Moth	N. C. Wilson
	G-ECDX	DH.71 Tiger Moth (replica)	M. D. Souch
	G-ECEA	Schempp-Hirth Cirrus	CEA Group
	G-ECGC	Cessna F.172N	S. Din
	G-ECGO	Bölkow Bö.208C1 Junior	P. Norman
	G-ECHB	Dassault Falcon 900DX	TAG Aviation (UK) Ltd
	G-ECJM	PA-28R-201T Turbo Arrow III	Regishire Ltd (G-FESL/G-BNRN)
	G-ECKB	Escapade 912(2)	C. M. & C. P. Bradford
	G-ECLW	Glasflugel Standard Libelle 201B	R. G. Parker
	G-ECMC	Robinson R22 Beta	Bulldog Aviation Ltd (G-LSWL)
	G-ECMK	PA-18-150 Super Cub	Just Plane Trading Ltd
	G-ECOA	DHC.8-402 Dash Eight	Flybe.com
	G-ECOB	DHC.8-402 Dash Eight	Flybe.com
	G-ECOC	DHC.8-402 Dash Eight	Flybe.com
	G-ECOD	DHC.8-402 Dash Eight	Flybe.com
	G-ECOE	DHC.8-402 Dash Eight	Flybe.com
	G-ECOF	DHC.8-402 Dash Eight	Flybe.com
	G-ECOG	DHC.8-402 Dash Eight	Flybe.com
	G-ECOH	DHC.8-402 Dash Eight	Flybe.com
	G-ECOI	DHC.8-402 Dash Eight	Flybe.com
	G-ECOJ	DHC.8-402 Dash Eight	Flybe.com
	G-ECOK	DHC.8-402 Dash Eight	Flybe.com
	G-ECOL	Schempp-Hirth Nimbus 2	M. Upex & L. I. Rigby
	G-ECOM	DHC.8-402 Dash Eight	Flybe.com
	G-ECON	Cessna 172M	Aviation Rentals (G-JONE)
	G-ECOO	DHC.8-402 Dash Eight	Flybe.com
	G-ECOP	DHC.8-402 Dash Eight	Flybe.com
	G-ECOR	DHC.8-402 Dash Eight	Flybe.com
	G-ECOT	DHC.8-402 Dash Eight	Flybe.com
	G-ECOX	Grega GN.1 Air Camper	H. C. Cox
	G-ECPA	Glasflugel H201B Standard Libelle	M. J. Witton
	G-ECSW	Pilatus B4-PC11AF	B. L. Cooper
	G-ECTF	Comper CLA.7 Swift Replica	P. R. Cozens

Reg.	Type	Owner or Operator	Notes
G-ECUB	PA-18 Super Cub 150	G-ECUB Flying Group (G-CBFI)	
G-ECUK	Eurocopter AS.350B3 Ecureuil	Loxwood Holdings Ltd	
G-ECVB	Pietenpol Air Camper	G. Edwards	
G-ECVZ	Staaken Z-1S Flitzer	V. D. Long	
G-ECXL	PZL-Bielsko SZD-30 Pirat	Charlie X-Ray Lima Group	
G-EDAV	SA Bulldog Srs 120/121 (XX534:B)	Edwalton Aviation Ltd	
G-EDAY	BAe Jetstream 3101	Skylease Sweden AB	
G-EDBD	PZL-Bielsko SZD-30 Pirat	S. P. Burgess	
G-EDCJ	Cessna 525 CitationJet	Jetphase Ltd	
G-EDCL	Cessna 525 CitationJet	Air Charter Scotland (Holdings) Ltd	
G-EDCM	Cessna 525 CitationJet	Air Charter Scotland (Holdings) Ltd	
G-EDDD	Schempp-Hirth Nimbus 2	C. A. Mansfield (G-BKPM)	
G-EDDS	CZAW Sportcruiser	E. H. Bishop	
G-EDDV	PZL-Bielsko SZD-38A Jantar 1	S. R. Bruce	
G-EDEE	Comco Ikarus C.42 FB100	C. L. & D. Godfrey	
G-EDEL	PA-32-300 Cherokee Six D	I. Blamire	
G-EDEN	SOCATA TB10 Tobago	Group Eden	
G-EDEO	Beech B.24R Sierra 200	G-EDEO Group	
G-EDFS	Pietenpol Air Camper	J. V. Comfort	
G-EDGA	PA-28-161 Warrior II	The RAF Halton Aeroplane Club Ltd	
G-EDGE	Jodel 150	A. D. Edge	
G-EDGI	PA-28-161 Warrior II	Medcentres Property Portfolio Ltd	
G-EDGJ	Zivko Edge 360	D. G. Jenkins	
G-EDGY	Flight Test Edge 540	C. R. A. Scrope	
G-EDLY	Airborne Edge 912/Streak IIIB	M. & P. L. Eardley	
G-EDMC	Pegasus Quantum 15-912	D. Allan & J. Hunter	
G-EDNA	PA-38-112 Tomahawk	P. J. Montgomery	
G-EDRE	Lindstrand LBL 90A balloon	Edren Homes Ltd	
G-EDRV	Van's RV-6A	G-EDRV Flying Group	
G-EDTO	Cessna FR.172F	N. G. Hopkinson	
G-EDVK	RH78 Tiger Light	M. Peters (G-MZGT)	
G-EDVL	PA-28R Cherokee Arrow 200-II	J. S. Devlin & Z. Islam (G-BXIN)	
G-EDYO	PA-32-260 Cherokee Six	R. Bursey & A. D. Paton	
G-EEAD	Slingsby T.65A Vega	D. S. Smith	
G-EEBA	Slingsby T.65A Vega	J. A. Cowie & K. Robertson	
G-EEBD	Scheibe Bergfalke IV	F. A. P. M. Otten	
G-EEBF	Schempp-Hirth Mini Nimbus C	M. Pingel	
G-EEBK	Schempp-Hirth Mini Nimbus C	G. S. Bell	
G-EEBL	Schleicher ASK-13	Derbyshire and Lancashire Gliding Club Ltd	
G-EEBN	Centrair ASW-20FL	S. MacArthur & R. Carlisle	
G-EEBR	Glaser-Dirks DG200/17	N. J. L. Busvine	
G-EEBS	Scheibe Zugvogel IIIA	J. A. Stockford	
G-EEBZ	Schleicher ASK-13	Booker Gliding Club Ltd	
G-EECC	Aerospool Dynamic WT9 UK	C. V. Ellingworth	
G-EECK	Slingsby T65A Vega	The ECK Syndicate	
G-EECO	Lindstrand LBL-25A balloon	A. Jay	
G-EEDE	Centrair ASW-20F	G. M. Cumner	
G-EEEK	Extra EA.300/200	A. R. Willis	
G-EEER	Schempp-Hirth Mini Nimbus C	D. J. Uren	
G-EEEZ	Champion 8KCAB	Les Wallen Manufacturing Ltd	
G-EEFA	Cameron Z-90 balloon	A. Murphy	
G-EEFK	Centrair ASW-20FL	A. P. Balkwill & G. B. Monslow	
G-EEFT	Schempp-Hirth Nimbus 2B	S. A. Adlard	
G-EEGL	Christen Eagle II	M. P. Swoboda & S. L. Nicholson	
G-EEGU	PA-28-161 Warrior II	Premier Flight Training Ltd	
G-EEJE	PA-31 Navajo B	Geeje Ltd	
G-EEKA	Glaser-Dirks DG-202/17	M. J. R. Lindsay & P. Hayward	
G-EEKS	Pegasus Quantum 15-912	D. Subhani (G-BYIZ)	
G-EEKY	PA-28 Cherokee 140B	Cherokee Aviation Ltd	
G-EELS	Cessna 208B Caravan 1	Glass Eels Ltd	
G-EELT	Rolladen-Schneider LS4	ELT Syndicate	
G-EELY	Schleicher Ka 6CR	K6 ELY Syndicate	
G-EENA	PA-32R-301 Saratoga SP	Gamit Ltd	
G-EENE	Rolladen-Schneider LS4	R. A. Hine	
G-EENI	Shaw Europa	M. P. Grimshaw	
G-EENK	Schleicher ASK-21	Essex Gliding Club Ltd	
G-EENN	Schempp-Hirth Nimbus 3	M. W. Dickson	
G-EENT	Glasflugel 304	M. Hastings & P. D. Morrison	
G-EENW	Schleicher ASW-20L	G-EENW Group	
G-EENZ	Schleicher ASW-19B	O. L. Pugh	

Notes	Reg.	Type	Owner or Operator
	G-EEPJ	Pitts S-1S Special	P. Westerby-Jones
	G-EERH	Ruschmeyer R.90-230RG	D. Sadler
	G-EERV	Van's RV-6	M. Crunden & C. B. Stirling
	G-EERY	Robinson R22	EGB (Helicopters) Ltd
	G-EESA	Shaw Europa	C. Deith (G-HIIL)
	G-EESY	Rolladen-Schneider LS4	G. S. Morley
	G-EETG	Cessna 172Q Cutlass	Tango Golf Flying Group
	G-EETH	Schleicher K.8B	Bowland Forest Gliding Club Ltd
	G-EEUP	SNCAN Stampe SV.4C	A. M. Wajih
	G-EEVL	Grob G.102 Astir CS77	G. D. E. Macdonald
	G-EEWS	Cessna T.210N	A. N. Macdonald & S. M. Jack
	G-EEWZ	Mainair Pegasus Quik	A. J. Roche
	G-EEYE	Mainair Blade 912	B. J. Egerton
	G-EEZO	DG Flugzeugbau DG-808C	G-ZO Syndicate
	G-EEZR	Robinson R44	Geezer Aviation LLP
	G-EEZS	Cessna 182P	D. A. G. Johnson
	G-EEZZ	Zenair CH.601XL Zodiac	K. W. Allan
	G-EFAM	Cessna 182S Skylane	G-EFAM Flying Group
	G-EFAT	Robinson R44 II	U. Momberg
	G-EFBP	Cessna FR.172K	B. & R. J. Howard
	G-EFCG	Aeropro Eurofox 912(S)	C. A. White
	G-EFCM	PA-28-180 Cherokee D	ATC Trading Ltd
	G-EFGH	Robinson R22 Beta	Ryvoan Aviation Ltd
	G-EFJD	MBB Bo.209 Monsun	E. J. Smith
	G-EFLT	Glasflugel Standard Libelle 201B	P. A. Tietema
	G-EFLY	Centrair ASW-20FL	I. D. & J. H. Atherton
	G-EFOF	Robinson R22 Beta	NT Burton Aviation
	G-EFOX	Eurofox 912(2)	A. R. Grist
	G-EFRP	Bower Fly Baby 1A	R. A. Phillips (G-BFRD)
	G-EFSF	Cessna FR.172K	A. Vaughan
	G-EFSM	Slingsby T.67M Firefly 260	A. J. Macdonald (G-BPLK)
	G-EFTE	Bölkow Bö.207	B. Morris & R. L. Earl
	G-EFTF	AS.350B Ecureuil	T French & Son (G-CWIZ/G-DJEM/G-ZBAC/
			G-SEBI/G-BMCU)
	G-EFUN	Bishop & Castelli E-Go	A. W. Bishop & G. Castelli
	G-EFVS	Wassmer WA.52 Europa	D. F. Hurn
	G-EGAG	SOCATA TB20 Trinidad	D. & E. Booth
	G-EGAL	Christen Eagle II	Eagle Partners
	G-EGBS	Van's RV-9A	Shobdon RV-9A Group
	G-EGEG	Cessna 172R	C. D. Lever
	G-EGEL	Christen Eagle II	G-EGEL Flying Group
	G-EGGI	Ikarus C.42FB UK	A. G. & G. J. Higgins
	G-EGGS	Robin DR.400/180	G-EGGS Syndicate
	G-EGGZ	Best Off Sky Ranger Swift 912S(1)	J. C. Sheardown
	G-EGHH	Hawker Hunter F.58 (J-4083)	Heritage Aviation Developments Ltd
	G-EGIA	UltraMagic M-65C balloon	Balloon Promotion SAS/Italy
	G-EGIL	Christen Eagle II	Smoke On Go Ltd
	G-EGJA	SOCATA TB20 Trinidad	Sinthesis SA
	G-EGKE	SOCATA Rallye 180TS	Suffolk Soaring Tug Group
	G-EGLE	Christen Eagle II	D. Thorpe
	G-EGLG	PA-31 Turbo Navajo C	H. Merkado (G-OATC/G-OJPW/G-BGCC)
	G-EGLL	PA-28-161 Warrior II	Booker Aircraft Leasing Ltd (G-BLEJ)
	G-EGLS	PA-28-181 Archer III	O. Sylvester
	G-EGLT	Cessna 310R	Reconnaissance Ventures Ltd (G-BHTV)
	G-EGPG	PA-18-135 Super Cub	G. Cormack (G-BWUC)
	G-EGRV	Van's RV-8	B. M. Gwynnett (G-PHMG)
	G-EGSJ	Jabiru J400	Seething Jabiru Group (G-MGRK)
	G-EGTB	PA-28-161 Warrior II	Aviation Advice & Consulting Ltd (G-BPWA)
	G-EGTC	Robinson R44	MFH Helicopters Ltd (G-CCNK)
	G-EGTR	PA-28-161 Cadet	Aviation Rentals (G-BRSI)
	G-EGUR	Jodel D.140B	S. H. Williams
	G-EGVA	PA-28R-200 Cherokee Arrow	M. Williams
	G-EGVO	Dassault Falcon 900EX	TAG Aviation (UK) Ltd
	G-EGWN	American Champion 7ECA	The Royal Air Force Halton Aeroplane Club Ltd
	G-EHAA	MDH MD.900 Explorer	Police Aviation Services Ltd (G-GNAA)
	G-EHAV	Glasflugel Standard Libelle 201B	A. Liran & M. Truelove
	G-EHBJ	CASA 1.131E Jungmann 2000	E. P. Howard
	G-EHCB	Schempp-Hirth Nimbus 3DT	G-EHCB Group
	G-EHCC	PZL-Bielsko SZD-50-3 Puchacz	Heron Gliding Club

Reg.	Type	Owner or Operator	Notes
G-EHCZ	Schleicher K8B	The Surrey Hills Gliding Club Ltd	
G-EHDS	CASA 1.131E Jungmann 2000	C. W. N. & A. A. M. Huke (G-DUDS)	
G-EHGF	PA-28-181 Archer II	G. P. Robinson	
G-EHGW	Cessna 550 Citation Bravo	Eurojet Aviation Ltd (G-FCDB)	
G-EHIC	Jodel D.140B	G-EHIC Group	
G-EHLX	PA-28-181 Archer II	ASG Leasing Ltd	
G-EHMF	Isaacs Fury II	M. W. Bodger	
G-EHMJ	Beech S35 Bonanza	A. J. Daley	
G-EHMM	Robin DR.400/180R	Booker Gliding Club Ltd	
G-EHMS	MD Helicopters MD-900	London's Air Ambulance Ltd	
G-EHTT	Schleicher ASW-20CL	HTT Syndicate	
G-EHUP	Aérospatiale SA.341G Gazelle 1	MW Helicopters Ltd	
G-EHXP	Rockwell Commander 112A	A. L. Stewart	
G-EIBM	Robinson R22 Beta	HJS Helicopters Ltd (G-BUCL)	
G-EICK	Cessna 172S	Centenary Flying Group	
G-EIGG	BAe Jetstream 3102	Linksair Ltd	
G-EIKY	Shaw Europa	J. D. Milbank	
G-EINI	Europa XS	K. J. Burns (G-KDCC)	
G-EIRE	Cessna T.182T	J. Byrne	
G-EISG	Beech A36 Bonanza	R. J. & B. Howard	
G-EISO	SOCATA MS.892A Rallye Commodore 150	EISO Group	
G-EITE	Luscombe 8F Silvaire	S. R. H. Martin	
G-EIWT	Cessna FR.182RG	J. R. Pybus	
G-EIZO	Eurocopter EC 120B	R. M. Bailey	
G-EJAC	Mudry CAP.232	G. C. J. Cooper, P. Varinot & E. Vazeille (G-OGBR)	
G-EJAE	GlaserDirks DG-200	D. L. P. H. Waller	
G-EJAR	Airbus A.319-111	EasyJet Airline Co Ltd	
G-EJBI	Bolkow Bo.207	J. O'Donnell & J. L. Bone	
G-EJEL	Cessna 550 Citation II	Futura Trading SAS	
G-EJGO	Z.226HE Trener	S. K. T. & C. M. Neofytou	
G-EJHH	Schempp-Hirth Standard Cirrus	D. M. Cornelius	
G-EJIM	Schempp-Hirth Discus 2cT	J. Lynchehaun	
G-EJJB	Airbus A.319-111	EasyJet Airline Co Ltd	
G-EJOC	AS.350B Ecureuil	Air and Ground Aviation Ltd (G-GEDS/ G-HMAN/G-SKIM/G-BIVP)	
G-EJRC	Robinson R44 II	Perry Farming Co.	
G-EJRS	PA-28-161 Cadet	Carlisle Flight Traing Ltd	
G-EJTC	Robinson R44	N. Parkhouse	
G-EJWI	Flight Design CTLS	E. Wright	
G-EKEY	Schleicher ASW-20 CL	K. W. Payne	
G-EKIM	Alpi Pioneer 300	M. Langmead	
G-EKIR	PA-28-262 Cadet	Aeros Leasing Ltd	
G-EKKL	PA-28-161 Warrior II	Apollo Aviation Advisory Ltd	
G-EKOS	Cessna FR.182 RG	S. Charlton	
G-ELAM	PA-30 Twin Comanche160B	Hangar 39 Ltd (G-BAWU/G-BAWV)	
G-ELDR	PA-32 Cherokee Six 260	Demero Ltd	
G-ELEE	Cameron Z-105 balloon	M. A. Stelling	
G-ELEN	Robin DR.400/180	Foster ELEN Group	
G-ELIS	PA-34-200T Seneca II	Global Aviation SA (G-BOPV)	
G-ELIZ	Denney Kitfox Mk 2	A. J. Ellis	
G-ELKA	Christen Eagle II	J. T. Matthews	
G-ELKS	Avid Speedwing Mk 4	J. C. Thompson	
G-ELLA	PA-32R-301 Saratoga IIHP	C. C. W. Hart	
G-ELLE	Cameron N-90 balloon	D. J. Stagg	
G-ELLI	Bell 206B JetRanger 3	Italian Clothes Ltd	
G-ELMH	NA AT-6D Harvard III (42-84555:EP-H)	M. Hammond	
G-ELSE	Diamond DA42 Twin Star	R. Swann	
G-ELSI	Tanarg/Ixess 15 912S(1)	D. Daniel	
G-ELUE	PA-28-161 Warrior II	Freedom Aviation Ltd	
G-ELUN	Robin DR.400/180R	Cotswold DR.400 Syndicate	
G-ELUT	PA-28R Cherokee Arrow 200-II	Green Arrow Europe Ltd	
G-ELWK	Van's RV-12	J. Devlin	
G-ELZN	PA-28-161 Warrior II	ZN Flying Group	
G-ELZY	PA-28-161 Warrior II	Redhill Air Services Ltd	
G-EMAA	Eurocopter EC 135T2	Bond Air Services Ltd	

G-EMAC – G-EOMK

Notes	Reg.	Type	Owner or Operator
	G-EMAC	Robinson R22 Beta	Unique Helicopters (NI) Ltd (G-CBDB)
	G-EMAX	PA-31-350 Navajo Chieftain	Atlantic Bridge Aviation Ltd
	G-EMBC	Embraer RJ145EP	ECC Leasing Co.Ltd
	G-EMBH	Embraer RJ145EU	Aircraft Solutions ERJ-145 LLC
	G-EMBI	Embraer RJ145EP	bmi regional
	G-EMBJ	Embraer RJ145EP	bmi regional
	G-EMBM	Embraer RJ145EU	Aircraft Solutions Lux II SARL
	G-EMBN	Embraer RJ145EP	bmi regional
	G-EMBO	Embraer RJ145EP	Aircraft Solutions ERJ-145LLC
	G-EMBP	Embraer RJ145EU	Eastern Airways (Europe) Ltd
	G-EMCA	Commander Aircraft 114B	S. Roberts
	G-EMDM	Diamond DA40-P9 Star	D. J. Munson
	G-EMHC	Agusta A109E Power	NT Burton Aviation
	G-EMHK	MBB Bö.209 Monsun 150FV	T. A. Crone (G-BLRD)
	G-EMID	Eurocopter EC 135P2	East Midlands Air Support Unit
	G-EMIN	Shaw Europa	S. A. Lamb
	G-EMJA	CASA 1.131E Jungmann 2000	C. R. Maher
	G-EMLE	Aerotechnik EV-97 Eurostar	A. R. White
	G-EMLS	Cessna T210L Turbo Centurion	I. K. F. Simcock
	G-EMLY	Pegasus Quantum 15	S. J. Reid
	G-EMMM	Diamond DA40 Star	A. J. Leigh
	G-EMMS	PA-38-112 Tomahawk	Ravenair Aircraft Ltd/Liverpool
	G-EMMY	Rutan Vari-Eze	M. J. Tooze
	G-EMOL	Schweizer 269C-1	Bournemouth Helicopters Ltd
	G-EMSA	Czech Sport Aircraft Sportcruiser	A. C. & M. A. Naylor
	G-EMSI	Shaw Europa	P. W. L. Thomas
	G-EMSY	DH.82A Tiger Moth	G-EMSY Group (G-ASPZ)
	G-ENBD	Lindstrand LBL-120A balloon	A. Nimmo
	G-ENBW	Robin DR.400-180R	Bicester Robin Crew
	G-ENCE	Partenavia P.68B	Bicton Aviation (G-OROY/G-BFSU)
	G-ENEA	Cessna 182P	Air Ads Ltd
	G-ENEE	CFM Streak Shadow SA	A. L. & S. Roberts
	G-ENES	Bell 206B JetRanger III	Celtic Energy Ltd
	G-ENGO	Steen Skybolt	R. G. Fulton
	G-ENGR	Head AX8-105 balloon	Royal Engineers Balloon Club
	G-ENHP	Enstrom 480B	H. J. Pelham
	G-ENIA	Staaken Z-21 Flitzer	A. F. Wankowski
	G-ENID	Reality Escapade	Q. Irving
	G-ENIE	Tipsy T.66 Nipper 3	R. J. Ripley
	G-ENII	Cessna F.172M	J. Howley
	G-ENIO	Pitts S-2C Special	Advanced Flying (London) Ltd
	G-ENNA	PA-28-161 Warrior II	Falcon Flying Serices Ltd (G-ESFT)
	G-ENNI	Robin R.3000/180	I. F. Doubtfire
	G-ENNK	Cessna 172S	Pooler-LMT Ltd
	G-ENNY	Cameron V-77 balloon	J. H. Dobson
	G-ENOA	Cessna F.172F	M. K. Acors (G-ASZW)
	G-ENRE	Avtech Jabiru UL	P. R. Turton
	G-ENRI	Lindstrand LBL-105A balloon	P. G. Hall
	G-ENST	CZAW Sportcruiser	Enstone Flyers
	G-ENTL	P & M Quik R	A. Kurt-Elli
	G-ENTS	Van's RV-9A	L. G. Johnson
	G-ENTT	Cessna F.152 II	C. & A. R. Hyett (G-BHHI)
	G-ENTW	Cessna F.152 II	Firecrest Aviation Ltd, C. Oates & C. Castledine (G-BFLK)
	G-ENVO	MBB Bo.105CBS-4	F. C. Owen
	G-ENVR	Dornier 228-201	National Environment Research Council
	G-ENVY	Mainair Blade 912	P. J. Lomax & J. A. Robinson
	G-ENXA	Falcon 900EX	Enex Aviation Ltd
	G-ENZO	Cameron Z-105 balloon	Garelli VI SPA
	G-EOFS	Shaw Europa	A. Fletcher & G. Plenderleith
	G-EOFW	Pegasus Quantum 15-912	G-EOFW Microlight Group
	G-EOGE	Gefa-Flug AS105GD airship (hot air)	George Brazil Airship Ltd
	G-EOHL	Cessna 182L	G. P. James
	G-EOID	Aeroprakt A22-L Foxbat	M. D. Northwood
	G-EOIN	Zenair CH.701UL	T. R. Sinclair
	G-EOJB	Robinson R44 II	G. J. Braithwaite (G-EDES)
	G-EOLD	PA-28-161 Warrior II	M. A. Ward
	G-EOLX	Cessna 172N	Westward Airways (Lands End) Ltd
	G-EOMA	Airbus A.330-243	Monarch Airlines Ltd
	G-EOMK	Robin DR400/180	MK Group

Reg.	Type	Owner or Operator	Notes
G-EOPH	Cameron C-90 balloon	A. J. Cherrett	
G-EORG	PA-38-112 Tomahawk	Control Developments (UK) Ltd	
G-EORJ	Shaw Europa	P. E. George	
G-EPAR	Robinson R22 Beta II	Jepar Rotorcraft	
G-EPDI	Cameron N-77 balloon	R. Moss	
G-EPGI	Cessna 560 Citation XLS	GEPGI Aviation Ltd	
G-EPIC	Jabiru UL-450	T. Chadwick	
G-EPOC	Jabiru UL-450	S. Cope	
G-EPOX	Aero Designs Pulsar XP	D. R. Stansfield	
G-EPSN	Ultramagic M-105 balloon	G. Everett	
G-EPTR	PA-28R Cherokee Arrow 200-II	ACS Aviation Ltd	
G-ERCO	Ercoupe 415D	A. R. & M. V. Tapp	
G-ERDA	Staaken Z-21A Flitzer	J. Cresswell	
G-ERDS	DH.82A Tiger Moth	W. A. Gerdes	
G-ERFS	PA-28-161 Warrior II	Medcentres Property Portfolio Ltd	
G-ERIC	Rockwell Commander 112TC	G. M. & J. M. Grunwell	
G-ERIE	Raytheon Beech 400A	Platinum Executive Aviation Ltd	
G-ERIK	Cameron N-77 balloon	T. M. Donnelly	
G-ERIW	Staaken Z-21 Flitzer	R. I. Wasey	
G-ERJA	Embraer RJ145EP	Falak Fin Nine Ltd	
G-ERJC	Embraer RJ145EP	Falak Fin Ten Ltd	
G-ERMO	ARV Super 2	S. Vince (G-BMWK)	
G-ERNI	PA-28-181 Archer II	J. Gardener & N. F. P. Hopwood (G-OSSY)	
G-EROB	Europa XS	R. J. Bull (G-RBJW)	
G-EROL	Westland SA.341G Gazelle 1	MW Helicopters Ltd (G-NONA/G-FDAV/G-RIFA/ G-ORGE/G-BBHU)	
G-EROM	Robinson R22 Beta	EBG (Helicopters) Ltd	
G-EROS	Cameron H-34 balloon	Evening Standard Co Ltd	
G-ERRY	AA-5B Tiger	The GERRY Group (G-BFMJ)	
G-ERTE	Skyranger 912S (1)	A. P. Trumper	
G-ERTI	Staaken Z-21A Flitzer	A. M. Wyndham	
G-ERYR	P & M Aviation Quik GT450	R. D. Ellis	
G-ESCA	Escapade Jabiru (1)	G. W. E. & R. H. May	
G-ESCC	Escapade 912	G. & S. Simons	
G-ESCI	MD900 Explorer	Police Aviation Services Ltd	
G-ESCP	Escapade 912(1)	M. J. Bromley	
G-ESET	Eurocopter EC.130B4 Ecureuil	Cyclix LLP	
G-ESEX	Eurocopter EC 135T2	West Yorkshire Police Authority	
G-ESGA	Reality Escapade	I. Bamford	
G-ESKA	Escapade 912	J. A. Harris	
G-ESME	Cessna R.182 II (15211)	G. C. Cherrington (G-BNOX)	
G-ESSL	Cessna 182R Skylane II	Euro Seaplane Services Ltd	
G-ESTA	Cessna 550 Citation II	Executive Aviation Services Ltd (G-GAUL)	
G-ESTR	Van's RV-6	S. D. Glover	
G-ESUS	Rotorway Executive 162F	Southern Helicopters Ltd	
G-ETAT	Cessna 172S Skyhawk	Fredair Ltd	
G-ETBY	PA-32 Cherokee Six 260	G-ETBY Group (G-AWCY)	
G-ETDC	Cessna 172P	The Moray Flying Club	
G-ETFF	Robinson R44	Ridgway Aviation (G-HSLJ)	
G-ETHY	Cessna 208	N. A. Moore	
G-ETIM	Eurocopter EC 120B	Tenterfield (Holdings) Ltd	
G-ETIN	Robinson R22 Beta	HQ Aviation Ltd	
G-ETIV	Robin DR.400/180	L. A. Seers	
G-ETME	Nord 1002 Pingouin (KG+EM)	108 Flying Group	
G-ETNT	Robinson R44	Irwin Plant Hire	
G-ETOJ	AutoGyro Calidus	N. W. Thomas	
G-ETOU	Agusta A.109S Grand	P. J. Ogden	
G-ETUG	Aeropro Eurofox 912(S)	R. M. Cornwell	
G-ETUS	Bell 206B-2 JetRanger II	D & G Cars Ltd (G-JBHH/G-SCOO/G-CORC/ G-CJHI/G-BBFB)	
G-ETVS	Alpi Pioneer 300 Hawk	V. Serazzi	
G-EUAB	Europa XS	A. D. Stephens	
G-EUAN	Jabiru UL-D	M. Wade & M. Lusted	
G-EUDO	Agusta AW.139	CHC Scotia Ltd	
G-EUFO	Rolladen-Schneider LS7-WL	J. R. Bane & M. G. Woollard	
G-EUJG	Avro 594 Avian IIIA	R. I. & D. E. Souch	
G-EUKS	Westland Widgeon III	R. I. Souch	

Notes	Reg.	Type	Owner or Operator
	G-EUNA	Airbus A.318-112	British Airways
	G-EUNB	Airbus A.318-112	British Airways
	G-EUNG	Europa NG	D. I. Stanbridge
	G-EUNI	Beech B200 Super King Air	Universita Telematica E-Campus (G-TAGH)
	G-EUOA	Airbus A.319-131	British Airways
	G-EUOB	Airbus A.319-131	British Airways
	G-EUOC	Airbus A.319-131	British Airways
	G-EUOD	Airbus A.319-131	British Airways
	G-EUOE	Airbus A.319-131	British Airways
	G-EUOF	Airbus A.319-131	British Airways
	G-EUOG	Airbus A.319-131	British Airways
	G-EUOH	Airbus A.319-131	British Airways
	G-EUOI	Airbus A.319-131	British Airways
	G-EUOJ	Airbus A.319-131	British Airways
	G-EUOK	Airbus A.319-131	British Airways
	G-EUOL	Airbus A.319-131	British Airways
	G-EUPA	Airbus A.319-131	British Airways
	G-EUPB	Airbus A.319-131	British Airways
	G-EUPC	Airbus A.319-131	British Airways
	G-EUPD	Airbus A.319-131	British Airways
	G-EUPE	Airbus A.319-131	British Airways
	G-EUPF	Airbus A.319-131	British Airways
	G-EUPG	Airbus A.319-131	British Airways
	G-EUPH	Airbus A.319-131	British Airways
	G-EUPJ	Airbus A.319-131	British Airways
	G-EUPK	Airbus A.319-131	British Airways
	G-EUPL	Airbus A.319-131	British Airways
	G-EUPM	Airbus A.319-131	British Airways
	G-EUPN	Airbus A.319-131	British Airways
	G-EUPO	Airbus A.319-131	British Airways
	G-EUPP	Airbus A.319-131	British Airways
	G-EUPR	Airbus A.319-131	British Airways
	G-EUPS	Airbus A.319-131	British Airways
	G-EUPT	Airbus A.319-131	British Airways
	G-EUPU	Airbus A.319-131	British Airways
	G-EUPV	Airbus A.319-131	British Airways
	G-EUPW	Airbus A.319-131	British Airways
	G-EUPX	Airbus A.319-131	British Airways
	G-EUPY	Airbus A.319-131	British Airways
	G-EUPZ	Airbus A.319-131	British Airways
	G-EUSO	Robin DR.400/140 Major	Weald Air Services Ltd
	G-EUUA	Airbus A.320-232	British Airways
	G-EUUB	Airbus A.320-232	British Airways
	G-EUUC	Airbus A.320-232	British Airways
	G-EUUD	Airbus A.320-232	British Airways
	G-EUUE	Airbus A.320-232	British Airways
	G-EUUF	Airbus A.320-232	British Airways
	G-EUUG	Airbus A.320-232	British Airways
	G-EUUH	Airbus A.320-232	British Airways
	G-EUUI	Airbus A.320-232	British Airways
	G-EUUJ	Airbus A.320-232	British Airways
	G-EUUK	Airbus A.320-232	British Airways
	G-EUUL	Airbus A.320-232	British Airways
	G-EUUM	Airbus A.320-232	British Airways
	G-EUUN	Airbus A.320-232	British Airways
	G-EUUO	Airbus A.320-232	British Airways
	G-EUUP	Airbus A.320-232	British Airways
	G-EUUR	Airbus A.320-232	British Airways
	G-EUUS	Airbus A.320-232	British Airways
	G-EUUT	Airbus A.320-232	British Airways
	G-EUUU	Airbus A.320-232	British Airways
	G-EUUV	Airbus A.320-232	British Airways
	G-EUUW	Airbus A.320-232	British Airways
	G-EUUX	Airbus A.320-232	British Airways
	G-EUUY	Airbus A.320-232	British Airways
	G-EUUZ	Airbus A.320-232	British Airways
	G-EUXC	Airbus A.321-231	British Airways
	G-EUXD	Airbus A.321-231	British Airways
	G-EUXE	Airbus A.321-231	British Airways
	G-EUXF	Airbus A.321-231	British Airways
	G-EUXG	Airbus A.321-231	British Airways
	G-EUXH	Airbus A.321-231	British Airways

Reg.	Type	Owner or Operator	Notes
G-EUXI	Airbus A.321-231	British Airways	
G-EUXJ	Airbus A.321-231	British Airways	
G-EUXK	Airbus A.321-231	British Airways	
G-EUXL	Airbus A.321-231	British Airways	
G-EUXM	Airbus A.321-231	British Airways	
G-EUYA	Airbus A.320-232	British Airways	
G-EUYB	Airbus A.320-232	British Airways	
G-EUYC	Airbus A.320-232	British Airways	
G-EUYD	Airbus A.320-232	British Airways	
G-EUYE	Airbus A.320-232	British Airways	
G-EUYF	Airbus A.320-232	British Airways	
G-EUYG	Airbus A.320-232	British Airways	
G-EUYH	Airbus A.320-232	British Airways	
G-EUYI	Airbus A.320-232	British Airways	
G-EUYJ	Airbus A.320-232	British Airways	
G-EUYK	Airbus A.320-232	British Airways	
G-EUYL	Airbus A.320-232	British Airways	
G-EUYM	Airbus A.320-232	British Airways	
G-EUYN	Airbus A.320-232	British Airways	
G-EVAJ	Best Off Skyranger 912S(1)	A. B. Gridley	
G-EVBF	Cameron Z-350 balloon	Virgin Balloon Flights	
G-EVET	Cameron 80 Concept balloon	L. O. & H. Vaughan	
G-EVEY	Thruster T.600N 450-JAB	The G-EVEY Flying Group	
G-EVIE	PA-28-181 Warrior II	Tayside Aviation Ltd (G-ZULU)	
G-EVIG	Evektor EV-97 TeamEurostar UK	A. S. Mitchell	
G-EVII	Schempp-Hirth Ventus 2cT	Ventus G-EVII Syndicate	
G-EVIL	Xtremeair XA-41	Unlimited Aerobatics Ltd	
G-EVIP	Agusta A.109E Power Elite	Castle Air Ltd (G-JJJL/G-CEJS)	
G-EVLE	Rearwin 8125 Cloudster	M. C. Hiscock (G-BVLK)	
G-EVPH	Aerotechnik EV-97 Eurostar	A. H. Woolley	
G-EVPI	Evans VP-1 Srs 2	C. P. Martyr	
G-EVRD	Beech 390 Premier 1	Commercial Aviation Charters Ltd	
G-EVRO	Aerotechnik EV-97 Eurostar	Newtownards Microlight Group	
G-EVSL	Aerotechnik EV-97 Eurostar SL	M. Vouros	
G-EVSW	Evektor EV-97 Sportstar	Cosmik Aviation Ltd	
G-EVTO	PA-28-161 Warrior II	Redhill Air Services Ltd	
G-EWAD	Robinson R44 II	Excel Law Ltd	
G-EWAN	Prostar PT-2C	C. G. Shaw	
G-EWBC	Avtec Jabiru SK	E. W. B. Comber	
G-EWEN	Aeropro Eurofox 912(S)	M. H. Talbot	
G-EWES	Pioneer 300	D. A. Ions	
G-EWEW	AB Sportine Aviacija LAK-19T	J. B. Strzebrakowski	
G-EWIZ	Pitts S-2E Special	R. S. Goodwin	
G-EWME	PA-28 Cherokee 235	C. J. Mewis & E. S. Ewen	
G-EWZZ	CZAW Sportcruiser	G. Fraser	
G-EXAM	PA-28RT-201T Turbo Arrow IV	RR. S. Urquhart & A. Cameron	
G-EXEC	PA-34-200 Seneca	Sky Air Travel Ltd	
G-EXES	Shaw Europa XS	D. Barraclough	
G-EXEX	Cessna 404	Reconnaissance Ventures Ltd	
G-EXGC	Extra EA.300/200	P. J. Bull	
G-EXHL	Cameron C-70 balloon	R. K. Gyselynck	
G-EXII	Extra EA.300	A. D. Hoy	
G-EXIL	Extra EA.300/S	C. W. Burkett & S. French	
G-EXIT	MS.893E Rallye 180GT	G-EXIT Group	
G-EXLL	Zenair CH.601	J. L. Adams	
G-EXLT	Extra EA.300/LT	J. W. Marshall	
G-EXPL	Champion 7GCBC Citabria	P. Koehmann	
G-EXTR	Extra EA.260	S. J. Carver	
G-EXXL	Zenair CH.601XL Zodiac	B. McFadden	
G-EYAK	Yakovlev Yak-50 (50 yellow)	P. N. A. Whitehead	
G-EYAS	Denney Kitfox Mk 2	R. E. Hughes	
G-EYCO	Robin DR.400/180	M. J. Hanlon	
G-EYNL	MBB Bö.105DBS/5	Alan Mann Aviation Group Ltd	
G-EYOR	Van's RV-6	S. I. Fraser	
G-EYRE	Bell 206L-1 LongRanger	European Aviation and Technical Services Ltd	
G-EYUP	Cessna 560XL Citation XLS	Harrock Aviation Ltd	
G-EZAA	Airbus A.319-111	easyJet Airline Co Ltd	

Notes	Reg.	Type	Owner or Operator
	G-EZAB	Airbus A.319-111	easyJet Airline Co Ltd
	G-EZAC	Airbus A.319-111	easyJet Airline Co Ltd
	G-EZAD	Airbus A.319-111	easyJet Airline Co Ltd
	G-EZAF	Airbus A.319-111	easyJet Airline Co Ltd
	G-EZAG	Airbus A.319-111	easyJet Airline Co Ltd
	G-EZAI	Airbus A.319-111	easyJet Airline Co Ltd
	G-EZAJ	Airbus A.319-111	easyJet Airline Co Ltd
	G-EZAK	Airbus A.319-111	easyJet Airline Co Ltd
	G-EZAL	Airbus A.319-111	easyJet Airline Co Ltd
	G-EZAM	Airbus A.319-111	easyJet Airline Co Ltd (G-CCKA)
	G-EZAN	Airbus A.319-111	easyJet Airline Co Ltd
	G-EZAO	Airbus A.319-111	easyJet Airline Co Ltd
	G-EZAP	Airbus A.319-111	easyJet Airline Co Ltd
	G-EZAR	Pegasus Quik	D. McCormack
	G-EZAS	Airbus A.319-111	easyJet Airline Co Ltd
	G-EZAT	Airbus A.319-111	easyJet Airline Co Ltd
	G-EZAU	Airbus A.319-111	easyJet Airline Co Ltd
	G-EZAV	Airbus A.319-111	easyJet Airline Co Ltd
	G-EZAW	Airbus A.319-111	easyJet Airline Co Ltd
	G-EZAX	Airbus A.319-111	easyJet Airline Co Ltd
	G-EZAY	Airbus A.319-111	easyJet Airline Co Ltd
	G-EZAZ	Airbus A.319-111	easyJet Airline Co Ltd
	G-EZBA	Airbus A.319-111	easyJet Airline Co Ltd
	G-EZBB	Airbus A.319-111	easyJet Airline Co Ltd
	G-EZBC	Airbus A.319-111	easyJet Airline Co Ltd
	G-EZBD	Airbus A.319-111	easyJet Airline Co Ltd
	G-EZBE	Airbus A.319-111	easyJet Airline Co Ltd
	G-EZBF	Airbus A.319-111	easyJet Airline Co Ltd
	G-EZBG	Airbus A.319-111	easyJet Airline Co Ltd
	G-EZBH	Airbus A.319-111	easyJet Airline Co Ltd
	G-EZBI	Airbus A.319-111	easyJet Airline Co Ltd
	G-EZBJ	Airbus A.319-111	easyJet Airline Co Ltd
	G-EZBK	Airbus A.319-111	easyJet Airline Co Ltd
	G-EZBL	Airbus A.319-111	easyJet Airline Co Ltd
	G-EZBM	Airbus A.319-111	easyJet Airline Co Ltd
	G-EZBN	Airbus A.319-111	easyJet Airline Co Ltd
	G-EZBO	Airbus A.319-111	easyJet Airline Co Ltd
	G-EZBR	Airbus A.319-111	easyJet Airline Co Ltd
	G-EZBT	Airbus A.319-111	easyJet Airline Co Ltd
	G-EZBU	Airbus A.319-111	easyJet Airline Co.Ltd
	G-EZBV	Airbus A.319-111	easyJet Airline Co.Ltd
	G-EZBW	Airbus A.319-111	easyJet Airline.Co.Ltd
	G-EZBX	Airbus A.319-111	easyJet Airline Co.Ltd
	G-EZBY	Airbus A.319-111	easyJet Airline Co.Ltd
	G-EZBZ	Airbus A.319-111	easyJet Airline Co.Ltd
	G-EZDA	Airbus A.319-111	easyJet Airline Co.Ltd
	G-EZDB	Airbus A.319-111	easyJet Airline Co.Ltd
	G-EZDC	Airbus A.319-111	easyJet Airline Co Ltd (G-CCKB)
	G-EZDD	Airbus A.319-111	easyJet Airline Co.Ltd
	G-EZDE	Airbus A.319-111	easyJet Airline Co.Ltd
	G-EZDF	Airbus A.319-111	easyJet Airline Co.Ltd
	G-EZDG	Rutan Vari-Eze	S. E. Upfield (G-EZOS)
	G-EZDH	Airbus A.319-111	easyJet Airline Co.Ltd
	G-EZDI	Airbus A.319-111	easyJet Airline Co.Ltd
	G-EZDJ	Airbus A.319-111	easyJet Airline Co.Ltd
	G-EZDK	Airbus A.319-111	easyJet Airline Co.Ltd
	G-EZDL	Airbus A.319-111	easyJet Airline Co.Ltd
	G-EZDM	Airbus A.319-111	easyJet Airline Co.Ltd
	G-EZDN	Airbus A.319-111	easyJet Airline Co.Ltd
	G-EZDO	Airbus A.319-111	easyJet Airline Co.Ltd
	G-EZDP	Airbus A.319-111	easyJet Airline Co.Ltd
	G-EZDR	Airbus A.319-111	easyJet Airline Co.Ltd
	G-EZDS	Airbus A.319-111	easyJet Airline Co.Ltd
	G-EZDT	Airbus A.319-111	easyJet Airline Co.Ltd
	G-EZDU	Airbus A.319-111	easyJet Airline Co.Ltd
	G-EZDV	Airbus A.319-111	easyJet Airline Co.Ltd
	G-EZDW	Airbus A.319-111	easyJet Airline Co Ltd
	G-EZDX	Airbus A.319-111	easyJet Airline Co.Ltd
	G-EZDY	Airbus A.319-111	easyJet Airline Co.Ltd
	G-EZDZ	Airbus A.319-111	easyJet Airline Co.Ltd
	G-EZEB	Airbus A.319-111	easyJet Airline Co Ltd
	G-EZED	Airbus A.319-111	easyJet Airline Co Ltd

Reg.	Type	Owner or Operator	Notes
G-EZEG	Airbus A.319-111	easyJet Airline Co Ltd	
G-EZEL	Westland SA.341G Gazelle 1	W. R. Pitcher (G-BAZL)	
G-EZES	Airbus A.319-111	easyJet Airline Co Ltd	
G-EZET	Airbus A.319-111	easyJet Airline Co Ltd	
G-EZEV	Airbus A.319-111	easyJet Airline Co Ltd	
G-EZEW	Airbus A.319-111	easyJet Airline Co Ltd	
G-EZEZ	Airbus A.319-111	easyJet Airline Co Ltd	
G-EZFA	Airbus A.319-111	easyJet Airline Co Ltd	
G-EZFB	Airbus A.319-111	easyJet Airline Co.Ltd	
G-EZFC	Airbus A.319-111	easyJet Airline Co.Ltd	
G-EZFD	Airbus A.319-111	easyJet Airline Co.Ltd	
G-EZFE	Airbus A.319-111	easyJet Airline Co.Ltd	
G-EZFF	Airbus A.319-111	easyJet Airline Co.Ltd	
G-EZFG	Airbus A.319-111	easyJet Airline Co.Ltd	
G-EZFH	Airbus A.319-111	easyJet Airline Co.Ltd	
G-EZFI	Airbus A.319-111	easyJet Airline Co.Ltd	
G-EZFJ	Airbus A.319-111	easyJet Airline Co.Ltd	
G-EZFK	Airbus A.319-111	easyJet Airline Co.Ltd	
G-EZFL	Airbus A.319-111	easyJet Airline Co.Ltd	
G-EZFM	Airbus A.319-111	easyJet Airline Co.Ltd	
G-EZFN	Airbus A.319-111	easyJet Airline Co.Ltd	
G-EZFO	Airbus A.319-111	easyJet Airline Co.Ltd	
G-EZFP	Airbus A.319-111	easyJet Airline Co.Ltd	
G-EZFR	Airbus A.319-111	easyJet Airline Co.Ltd	
G-EZFS	Airbus A.319-111	easyJet Airline Co.Ltd	
G-EZFT	Airbus A.319-111	easyJet Airline Co.Ltd	
G-EZFU	Airbus A.319-111	easyJet Airline Co.Ltd	
G-EZFV	Airbus A.319-111	easyJet Airline Co.Ltd	
G-EZFW	Airbus A.319-111	easyJet Airline Co.Ltd	
G-EZFX	Airbus A.319-111	easyJet Airline Co.Ltd	
G-EZFY	Airbus A.319-111	easyJet Airline Co.Ltd	
G-EZFZ	Airbus A.319-111	easyJet Airline Co.Ltd	
G-EZGA	Airbus A.319-111	easyJet Airline Co.Ltd	
G-EZGB	Airbus A.319-111	easyJet Airline Co.Ltd	
G-EZGC	Airbus A.319-111	easyJet Airline Co.Ltd	
G-EZGD	Airbus A.319-111	easyJet Airline Co.Ltd	
G-EZGE	Airbus A.319-111	easyJet Airline Co.Ltd	
G-EZGF	Airbus A.319-111	easyJet Airline Co.Ltd	
G-EZGG	Airbus A.319-111	easyJet Airline Co.Ltd	
G-EZGH	Airbus A.319-111	easyJet Airline Co.Ltd	
G-EZGI	Airbus A.319-111	easyJet Airline Co.Ltd	
G-EZGJ	Airbus A.319-111	easyJet Airline Co.Ltd	
G-EZGK	Airbus A.319-111	easyJet Airline Co.Ltd	
G-EZGL	Airbus A.319-111	easyJet Airline Co.Ltd	
G-EZGM	Airbus A.319-111	easyJet Airline Co.Ltd	
G-EZGN	Airbus A.319-111	easyJet Airline Co.Ltd	
G-EZGP	Airbus A.319-111	easyJet Airline Co.Ltd	
G-EZIC	Airbus A.319-111	easyJet Airline Co Ltd	
G-EZIH	Airbus A.319-111	easyJet Airline Co Ltd	
G-EZII	Airbus A.319-111	easyJet Airline Co Ltd	
G-EZIJ	Airbus A.319-111	easyJet Airline Co Ltd	
G-EZIK	Airbus A.319-111	easyJet Airline Co Ltd	
G-EZIL	Airbus A.319-111	easyJet Airline Co Ltd	
G-EZIM	Airbus A.319-111	easyJet Airline Co Ltd	
G-EZIN	Airbus A.319-111	easyJet Airline Co Ltd	
G-EZIO	Airbus A.319-111	easyJet Airline Co Ltd	
G-EZIP	Airbus A.319-111	easyJet Airline Co Ltd	
G-EZIR	Airbus A.319-111	easyJet Airline Co Ltd	
G-EZIS	Airbus A.319-111	easyJet Airline Co Ltd	
G-EZIT	Airbus A.319-111	easyJet Airline Co Ltd	
G-EZIV	Airbus A.319-111	easyJet Airline Co Ltd	
G-EZIW	Airbus A.319-111	easyJet Airline Co Ltd	
G-EZIX	Airbus A.319-111	easyJet Airline Co Ltd	
G-EZIY	Airbus A.319-111	easyJet Airline Co Ltd	
G-EZIZ	Airbus A.319-111	easyJet Airline Co Ltd	
G-EZMH	Airbus A.319-111	easyJet Airline Co Ltd (G-CCKD)	
G-EZMS	Airbus A.319-111	easyJet Airline Co Ltd	
G-EZNC	Airbus A.319-111	easyJet Airline Co Ltd (G-CCKC)	
G-EZPG	Airbus A.319-111	easyJet Airline Co Ltd	
G-EZSM	Airbus A.319-111	easyJet Airline Co Ltd (G-CCKE)	
G-EZTA	Airbus A.320-214	easyJet Airline Co.Ltd	
G-EZTB	Airbus A.320-214	easyJet Airline Co.Ltd	

Notes	Reg.	Type	Owner or Operator
	G-EZTC	Airbus A.320-214	easyJet Airline Co.Ltd
	G-EZTD	Airbus A.320-214	easyJet Airline Co.Ltd
	G-EZTE	Airbus A.320-214	easyJet Airline Co.Ltd
	G-EZTF	Airbus A.320-214	easyJet Airline Co.Ltd
	G-EZTG	Airbus A.320-214	easyJet Airline Co.Ltd
	G-EZTH	Airbus A.320-214	easyJet Airline Co.Ltd
	G-EZTI	Airbus A.320-214	easyJet Airline Co.Ltd
	G-EZTJ	Airbus A.320-214	easyJet Airline Co.Ltd
	G-EZTK	Airbus A.320-214	easyJet Airline Co.Ltd
	G-EZTL	Airbus A.320-214	easyJet Airline Co.Ltd
	G-EZTM	Airbus A.320-214	easyJet Airline Co.Ltd
	G-EZTR	Airbus A.320-214	easyJet Airline Co.Ltd
	G-EZTT	Airbus A.320-214	easyJet Airline Co.Ltd
	G-EZTV	Airbus A.320-214	easyJet Airline Co.Ltd
	G-EZTX	Airbus A.320-214	easyJet Airline Co.Ltd
	G-EZTY	Airbus A.320-214	easyJet Airline Co.Ltd
	G-EZTZ	Airbus A.320-214	easyJet Airline Co.Ltd
	G-EZUA	Airbus A.320-214	easyJet Airline Co.Ltd
	G-EZUB	Zenair CH.601HD Zodiac	R. A. C. Stephens
	G-EZUC	Airbus A.320-214	easyJet Airline Co.Ltd
	G-EZUD	Airbus A.320-214	easyJet Airline Co.Ltd
	G-EZUF	Airbus A.320-214	easyJet Airline Co.Ltd
	G-EZUG	Airbus A.320-214	easyJet Airline Co.Ltd
	G-EZUH	Airbus A.320-214	easyJet Airline Co.Ltd
	G-EZUI	Airbus A.320-214	easyJet Airline Co.Ltd
	G-EZUJ	Airbus A.320-214	easyJet Airline Co.Ltd
	G-EZUK	Airbus A.320-214	easyJet Airline Co.Ltd
	G-EZUL	Airbus A.320-214	easyJet Airline Co.Ltd
	G-EZUM	Airbus A.320-214	easyJet Airline Co.Ltd
	G-EZUN	Airbus A.320-214	easyJet Airline Co.Ltd
	G-EZUO	Airbus A.320-214	easyJet Airline Co.Ltd
	G-EZUP	Airbus A.320-214	easyJet Airline Co.Ltd
	G-EZUR	Airbus A.320-214	easyJet Airline Co.Ltd
	G-EZUS	Airbus A.320-214	easyJet Airline Co.Ltd
	G-EZUT	Airbus A.320-214	easyJet Airline Co.Ltd
	G-EZUU	Airbus A.320-214	easyJet Airline Co.Ltd
	G-EZUV	Airbus A.320-214	easyJet Airline Co.Ltd
	G-EZUW	Airbus A.320-214	easyJet Airline Co.Ltd
	G-EZUX	Airbus A.320-214	easyJet Airline Co.Ltd
	G-EZUY	Airbus A.320-214	easyJet Airline Co.Ltd
	G-EZUZ	Airbus A.320-214	easyJet Airline Co.Ltd
	G-EZVS	Colt 77B balloon	A. J. Lovell
	G-EZWA	Airbus A.320-214	easyJet Airline Co.Ltd
	G-EZWB	Airbus A.320-214	easyJet Airline Co.Ltd
	G-EZWC	Airbus A.320-214	easyJet Airline Co.Ltd
	G-EZWD	Airbus A.320-214	easyJet Airline Co.Ltd
	G-EZWE	Airbus A.320-214	easyJet Airline Co.Ltd
	G-EZWF	Airbus A.320-214	easyJet Airline Co.Ltd
	G-EZWG	Airbus A.320-214	easyJet Airline Co.Ltd
	G-EZXO	Colt 56A balloon	I. Lilja
	G-EZZA	Shaw Europa XS	J. C. R. Davey
	G-EZZE	CZAW Sportcruiser	G. Verity
	G-EZZL	Westland Gazelle HT.3	Regal Group UK (G-CBKC)
	G-EZZY	Evektor EV-97 Eurostar	D. P. Creedy
	G-FACE	Cessna 172S	Oxford Aviation Services Ltd
	G-FADF	PA-18-150 Super Cub	A. J. Neale
	G-FAIR	SOCATA TB10 Tobago	Fairwings Ltd
	G-FAJC	Alpi Pioneer 300 Hawk	M. Clare
	G-FAJM	Robinson R44 II	Ryvoan Aviation Ltd
	G-FALC	Aeromere F.8L Falco	D. M. Burbridge (G-AROT)
	G-FAME	Starstreak Shadow SA-II	S. R. Whitehead
	G-FAMH	Zenair CH.701	F. Omaraie-Hamdanie
	G-FANC	Fairchild 24R-46 Argus III	A. T. Fines
	G-FANL	Cessna FR.172K XP-II	J. A. Rees
	G-FARE	Robinson R44 II	Toriamos Ltd/Ireland
	G-FARL	Pitts S-1E Special	T. I. Williams
	G-FARO	Aero Designs Star-Lite SL.1	S. C. Goozee
	G-FARR	Jodel 150	G. H. Farr
	G-FARY	QAC Quickie Tri-Q	A. Bloomfield and A. Underwood
	G-FASH	Hughes 369D	The Packshot Company Ltd (G-ERIS/G-PJMD/ G-BMJV)

Reg.	Type	Owner or Operator	Notes
G-FATB	Rockwell Commander 114B	James D. Pearce & Co	
G-FATE	Falco F8L	G-FATE Flying Group	
G-FAVC	DH.80A Puss Moth	Liddell Aircraft Ltd	
G-FAVS	PA-32-300 Cherokee Six	Cool Flourish Ltd (G-BKEK)	
G-FBAT	Aeroprakt A.22 Foxbat	J. Jordan	
G-FBEA	Embraer ERJ190-200LR	Flybe.com	
G-FBEB	Embraer ERJ190-200LR	Flybe.com	
G-FBEC	Embraer ERJ190-200LR	Flybe.com	
G-FBED	Embraer ERJ190-200LR	Flybe.com	
G-FBEE	Embraer ERJ190-200LR	Flybe.com	
G-FBEF	Embraer ERJ190-200LR	Flybe.com	
G-FBEG	Embraer ERJ190-200LR	Flybe.com	
G-FBEH	Embraer ERJ190-200LR	Flybe.com	
G-FBEI	Embraer ERJ190-200LR	Flybe.com	
G-FBEJ	Embraer ERJ190-200LR	Flybe.com	
G-FBEK	Embraer ERJ190-200LR	Flybe.com	
G-FBEL	Embraer ERJ190-200LR	Flybe.com	
G-FBEM	Embraer ERJ190-200LR	Flybe.com	
G-FBEN	Embraer ERJ190-200LR	Flybe.com	
G-FBII	Ikarus C.42 FB100	F. Beeson	
G-FBJA	Embraer ERJ170-200STD	Flybe.com	
G-FBJB	Embraer ERJ170-200STD	Flybe.com	
G-FBJC	Embraer ERJ170-200STD	Flybe.com	
G-FBJD	Embraer ERJ170-200STD	Flybe.com	
G-FBJE	Embraer ERJ170-200STD	Flybe.com	
G-FBJF	Embraer ERJ170-200STD	Flybe.com	
G-FBJG	Embraer ERJ170-200STD	Flybe.com	
G-FBJH	Embraer ERJ170-200STD	Flybe.com	
G-FBJI	Embraer ERJ170-200STD	Flybe.com	
G-FBJL	Dassault Falcon 2000	TAG Aviation (UK) Ltd	
G-FBKB	Cessna 510 Citation Mustang	Blink Ltd	
G-FBKC	Cessna 510 Citation Mustang	Blink Ltd	
G-FBKD	Cessna 510 Citation Mustang	Blink Ltd	
G-FBLK	Cessna 510 Citation Mustang	Blink Ltd	
G-FBOY	Skystar Kitfox Mk 7	A. Bray	
G-FBPL	PA-34-200 Seneca	Purple Horse Sales and Hire Ltd (G-BBXK)	
G-FBRN	PA-28-181 Archer II	Herefordshire Aero Club Ltd	
G-FBSS	Aeroprakt A22-LS Foxbat	A. K. & L. Lynn	
G-FBTT	Aeroprakt A22-L Foxbat	T. D. Reid	
G-FBWH	PA-28R Cherokee Arrow 180	F. A. Short	
G-FCAV	Schleicher ASK-13	M. F. Cuming	
G-FCBI	Schweizer 269C-1	Lift West Ltd	
G-FCCC	Schleicher ASK-13	Shenington Gliding Club	
G-FCED	PA-31T2 Cheyenne IIXL	Provident Partners Ltd	
G-FCKD	Eurocopter EC 120B	Red Dragon Management LLP	
G-FCLA	Boeing 757-28A	Thomas Cook Airlines Ltd	
G-FCLB	Boeing 757-28A	Thomas Cook Airlines Ltd	
G-FCLD	Boeing 757-25F	Thomas Cook Airlines Ltd	
G-FCLE	Boeing 757-28A	Thomas Cook Airlines Ltd	
G-FCLF	Boeing 757-28A	Thomas Cook Airlines Ltd	
G-FCLH	Boeing 757-28A	Thomas Cook Airlines Ltd	
G-FCLI	Boeing 757-28A	Thomas Cook Airlines Ltd	
G-FCLJ	Boeing 757-2Y0	Thomas Cook Airlines Ltd	
G-FCLK	Boeing 757-2Y0	Thomas Cook Airlines Ltd	
G-FCOM	Slingsby T.59F Kestrel	P. A. C. Wheatcroft & A. G. Truman	
G-FCSL	PA-32-350 Navajo Chieftain	Culross Aerospace Ltd (G-CLAN)	
G-FCSP	Robin DR.400/180	S. Eustace	
G-FCUK	Pitts S-1C Special	H. C. Luck	
G-FCUM	Robinson R44 II	The Grange Country Club Ltd	
G-FDDY	Schleicher Ka 6CR	M. D. Brooks	
G-FDPS	Aviat Pitts S-2C Special	Flights and Dreams Ltd	
G-FDZA	Boeing 737-8K5	Thomson Airways Ltd	
G-FDZB	Boeing 737-8K5	Thomson Airways Ltd	
G-FDZD	Boeing 737-8K5	Thomson Airways Ltd	
G-FDZE	Boeing 737-8K5	Thomson Airways Ltd	
G-FDZF	Boeing 737-8K5	Thomson Airways Ltd	
G-FDZG	Boeing 737-8K5	Thomson Airways Ltd	
G-FDZJ	Boeing 737-8K5	Thomson Airways Ltd	
G-FDZR	Boeing 737-8K5	Thomson Airways Ltd	

Notes	Reg.	Type	Owner or Operator
	G-FDZS	Boeing 737-8K5	Thomson Airways Ltd
	G-FDZT	Boeing 737-8K5	Thomson Airways Ltd
	G-FDZU	Boeing 737-8K5	Thomson Airways Ltd
	G-FDZW	Boeing 737-8K5	Thomson Airways Ltd
	G-FDZX	Boeing 737-8K5	Thomson Airways Ltd
	G-FDZY	Boeing 737-8K5	Thomson Airways Ltd
	G-FDZZ	Boeing 737-8K5	Thomson Airways Ltd
	G-FEAB	PA-28-181 Archer III	Feabrex Ltd
	G-FEBB	Grob G.104 Speed Astir IIB	M. Ogbe
	G-FEBJ	Schleicher ASW-19B	A. P. Hatton
	G-FECO	Grob G.102 Astir CS77	C. Peterson
	G-FEEF	Jodel DR.220-2 + 2	A. C. Walker
	G-FEET	Mainair Pegasus Quik	M. P. Duckett
	G-FELC	Cirrus SR22	F. Rossello
	G-FELD	Rotorsport UK MTO Sport	S. Pearce
	G-FELL	Shaw Europa	M. C. Costin & J. A. Inglis
	G-FELM	PA-28-180 Cherokee C	F. P. M. Vaille
	G-FELT	Cameron N-77 balloon	Allan Industries Ltd
	G-FELX	CZAW Sportcruiser	T. F. Smith
	G-FERN	Mainair Blade 912	M. H. Moulai
	G-FERV	Rolladen-Schneider LS4	R. J. J. Bennett
	G-FESS	Pegasus Quantum 15-912	P. M. Fessi (G-CBBZ)
	G-FEVS	PZL-Bielsko SZD-50-3 Puchacz	The Borders (Milfield) Gliding Club Ltd
	G-FEWG	Fuji FA.200-160	Caseright Ltd (G-BBNV)
	G-FEZZ	Bell 206B JetRanger II	R. J. Myram
	G-FFAB	Cameron N-105 balloon	B. J. Hammond
	G-FFAF	Cessna F.150L	R. Henderson
	G-FFBG	Cessna F.182Q	W. G. E. James
	G-FFEN	Cessna F.150M	B. Emerson & J. Tuckwell
	G-FFFT	Lindstrand LBL-31A balloon	W. Rousell & J. Tyrrell
	G-FFIT	Pegasus Quik	R. G. G. Pinder
	G-FFOX	Hawker Hunter T.7B (WV318:D)	Core Jets Ltd
	G-FFRA	Dassault Falcon 20DC	FR Aviation Ltd
	G-FFRI	AS.355F1 Twin Squirrel	Sterling Helicopters Ltd (G-GLOW/G-PAPA/ G-CNET/G-MCAH)
	G-FFTI	SOCATA TB20 Trinidad	R. Lenk
	G-FFUN	Pegasus Quantum 15	J. R. F. Hollingshead
	G-FFWD	Cessna 310R	T. S. Courtman (G-TVKE/G-EURO)
	G-FGAZ	Schleicher Ka 6E	C. M. Billings, B. A. & M. A. Roberts
	G-FGID	Vought FG-1D Corsair (KD345:130-A)	Patina Ltd
	G-FGSI	Montgomerie-Bensen B8MR	F. G. Shepherd
	G-FHAS	Scheibe SF.25E Super Falke	D. C. Mason
	G-FIAT	PA-28 Cherokee 140	Demero Ltd & Transcourt Ltd (G-BBYW)
	G-FIBS	AS.350BA Ecureuil	G. Mazza/Italy
	G-FICS	Flight Design CTSW	A. Lovat & J. I. Spring
	G-FIDL	Thruster T.600N 450	T. A. Colman (G-CBIO)
	G-FIFA	Cessna 404 Titan	RVL Aviation Ltd (G-TVIP/G-KIWI/G-BHNI)
	G-FIFE	Cessna FA.152	The Moray Flying Club (1990) (G-BFYN)
	G-FIFI	SOCATA TB20 Trinidad	F. A. Saker (G-BMWS)
	G-FIFT	Ikarus C.42 FB 100	A. R. Jones
	G-FIFY	Colomban MC-30 Luciole	
	G-FIGA	Cessna 152	Merseyflight Ltd
	G-FIGB	Cessna 152	A. J. Gomes
	G-FIGP	Boeing 737-2E7	European Skybus Ltd (G-BMDF)
	G-FIII	Extra EA.300/L	J. S. Allison (G-RGEE)
	G-FIJJ	Cessna F.177RG	D. R. Vale (G-AZFP)
	G-FIJV	Lockheed L.188CF Electra	Atlantic Airlines Ltd
	G-FILE	PA-34-200T Seneca	Bristol Flying Centre Ltd
	G-FINA	Cessna F.150L	A. G. Freeman (G-BIFT)
	G-FIND	Cessna F.406	Reconnaissance Ventures Ltd
	G-FINT	Piper L-4B Grasshopper	G. & H. M. Picarella
	G-FINZ	I.I.I Sky Arrow 650T	W. N. Blair-Hickman
	G-FIRM	Cessna 550 Citation Bravo	The Cambridge Aero Club Ltd
	G-FIRZ	Murphy Renegade Spirit UK	S. Koutsoukos
	G-FITY	Europa XS	D. C. A. Moore & M. Fielder
	G-FIXX	Van's RV-7	Hambilton Engineering Ltd
	G-FIZU	Lockheed L.188CF Electra	Atlantic Airlines Ltd

Reg.	Type	Owner or Operator	Notes
G-FIZY	Shaw Europa XS	J. S. Davis (G-DDSC)	
G-FIZZ	PA-28-161 Warrior II	G-FIZZ Group	
G-FJET	Cessna 550 Citation II	London Executive Aviation Ltd (G-DCFR/ G-WYLX/G-JETD)	
G-FJMS	Partenavia P.68B	J. B. Randle (G-SVHA)	
G-FJTH	Aeroprakt A.22 Foxbat	B. Gurling	
G-FKNH	PA-15 Vagabond	M. J. Mothershaw	
G-FKOS	PA-28-181 Archer II	M. K. Johnson	
G-FLAG	Colt 77A balloon	B. A. Williams	
G-FLAV	PA-28-161 Warrior II	The Crew Flying Group	
G-FLBA	DHC.8-402 Dash Eight	Flybe.com	
G-FLBB	DHC.8-402 Dash Eight	Flybe.com	
G-FLBC	DHC.8-402 Dash Eight	Flybe.com	
G-FLBD	DHC.8-402 Dash Eight	Flybe.com	
G-FLBE	DHC.8-402 Dash Eight	Flybe.com	
G-FLBK	Cessna 510 Citation Mustang	Blink Ltd	
G-FLCA	Fleet Model 80 Canuck	E. C. Taylor	
G-FLCT	Hallam Fleche	R. G. Hallam	
G-FLDG	Skyranger 912	A. J. Gay	
G-FLEA	SOCATA TB10 Tobago	P. Mather	
G-FLEE	ZJ-Viera	P. C. Piggott	
G-FLEX	Mainair Pegasus Quik	L. A. Read	
G-FLGT	Lindstrand LBL-105A balloon	Ballongaventyr I. Skane AB/Sweden	
G-FLIK	Pitts S-1S Special	R. P. Millinship	
G-FLIP	Cessna FA.152	Cristal Air Ltd (G-BOES)	
G-FLIS	Magni M.16C	M. L. L. Temple	
G-FLIT	Rotorway Executive 162F	R. S. Snell	
G-FLIZ	Staaken Z-21 Flitzer	M. J. Clark	
G-FLKE	Scheibe SF.25C Falke	The Royal Air Force Gliding & Soaring Association	
G-FLKS	Scheibe SF.25C Falke	London Gliding Club Propietary Ltd	
G-FLKY	Cessna 172S	M. E. Falkingham	
G-FLOR	Shaw Europa	A. F. C. van Eldik	
G-FLOW	Cessna 172N	P. H. Archard	
G-FLOX	Shaw Europa	DPT Group	
G-FLPI	Rockwell Commander 112	J. P. Thorpe	
G-FLTC	BAe 146-300	E3205 Trading Ltd (G-JEBH/G-BVTO/G-NJID)	
G-FLUZ	Rolladen-Schneider LS8-18	D. M. King	
G-FLYA	Mooney M.20J	B. Willis	
G-FLYB	Ikarus C.42 FB100	G-FLYB Group	
G-FLYC	Ikarus C.42 FB100	Solent Flight Ltd	
G-FLYF	Mainair Blade 912	D. G. Adley	
G-FLYG	Slingsby T.67C	G. Laden	
G-FLYI	PA-34-200 Seneca II	Falcon Flying Services Ltd (G-BHVO)	
G-FLYM	Ikarus C42 FB100	R. S. O'Carroll	
G-FLYP	Beagle B.206 Srs 2	Key Publishing Ltd (G-AVHO)	
G-FLYT	Shaw Europa	K. F. & R. Richardson	
G-FLYW	Beech B.200 Super King Air	J. A. Rees (G-LIVY/G-PSTR)	
G-FLYX	Robinson R44 II	R. D. Hagger	
G-FLYY	BAC.167 Strikemaster 80A	G-FLYY Strikemaster Ltd	
G-FLZA	Staaken Z-21A Flitzer	R. Pybus	
G-FLZR	Staaken Z-21 Flitzer	I. V. Staines	
G-FMAM	PA-28-151 Warrior (modified)	Airtime Aviation Holdings Ltd (G-BBXV)	
G-FMBS	Inverted US 12	W. P. Wright	
G-FMGG	Maule M5-235C Lunar Rocket	S. Bierbaum (G-RAGG)	
G-FMKA	Diamond HK.36TC Super Dimona	G. P. Davis	
G-FMSG	Cessna FA.150K	G. Owen/Gamston (G-POTS/G-AYUY)	
G-FNAV	PA-31-350 Navajo Chieftain	Flight Calibration Services Ltd (G-BFFR)	
G-FNEY	Cessna F.177RG	F. Ney	
G-FNLD	Cessna 172N	Papa Hotel Flying Group	
G-FOFO	Robinson R44 II	Kuki Helicopter Sales Ltd	
G-FOGG	Cameron N-90 balloon	J. P. E. Money-Kyrle	
G-FOGI	Shaw Europa XS	B. Fogg	
G-FOKK	Fokker DR1 (replica)	P. D. & S. E. Ford	
G-FOKR	Fokker E.III Replica	Eshott Eindecker Group	
G-FOLD	Light Aero Avid Speedwing	B. W. & G. Evans	

Notes	Reg.	Type	Owner or Operator
	G-FOLI	Robinson R22 Beta II	G. M. Duckworth
	G-FOLY	Aerotek Pitts S-2A Modified	C. T. Charleston
	G-FOPP	Lancair 320	Airsport (UK) Ltd
	G-FORA	Schempp-Hirth Ventus cT	G. Bailey & J. D. Sorrell
	G-FORC	SNCAN Stampe SV.4C	C. C. Rollings & F. J. Hodson
	G-FORD	SNCAN Stampe SV.4C	P. H. Meeson
	G-FORM	Learjet 45	Broomco 3598 Ltd
	G-FORZ	Pitts S-1S Special	N. W. Parkinson
	G-FOSY	MS.880B Rallye Club	A. G. Foster (G-AXAK)
	G-FOWL	Colt 90A balloon	M. R. Stokoe
	G-FOWS	Cameron N-105 balloon	Ezmerelda Balloon Syndicate
	G-FOXA	PA-28-161 Cadet	Leicestershire Aero Club Ltd
	G-FOXB	Aeroprakt A.22 Foxbat	G. D. McCullough
	G-FOXC	Denney Kitfox Mk 3	T. Willford
	G-FOXD	Denney Kitfox Mk 2	P. P. Trangmar
	G-FOXE	Denney Kitfox Mk 2	K. M. Pinkar
	G-FOXF	Denney Kitfox Mk 4	M. S. Goodwin
	G-FOXG	Denney Kitfox Mk 2	J. U. McKercher
	G-FOXI	Denney Kitfox	I. M. Walton
	G-FOXL	Zenair CH.601XL Zodiac	R. W. Taylor
	G-FOXM	Bell 206B JetRanger 2	Tyringham Charter & Group Services (G-STAK/G-BNIS)
	G-FOXS	Denney Kitfox Mk 2	S. P. Watkins & C. C. Rea
	G-FOXX	Denney Kitfox	A. W. Hodder
	G-FOXZ	Denney Kitfox	S. C. Goozee
	G-FOZY	Van's RV-7	M. G. Forrest (G-COPZ)
	G-FOZZ	Beech A36 Bonanza	Go To Air Ltd
	G-FPIG	PA-28-151 Warrior	G. F. Strain (G-BSSR)
	G-FPLD	Beech 200 Super King Air	Cobham Flight Inspection Ltd
	G-FPLE	Beech 200 Super King Air	Cobham Flight Inspection Ltd
	G-FPSA	PA-28-161 Warrior II	Interactive Dynamics Ltd (G-RSFT/G-WARI)
	G-FRAD	Dassault Falcon 20E	Cobham Leasing Ltd (G-BCYF)
	G-FRAF	Dassault Falcon 20E	FR Aviation Ltd
	G-FRAG	PA-32 Cherokee Six 300E	T. A. Houghton
	G-FRAH	Dassault Falcon 20DC	FR Aviation Ltd
	G-FRAI	Dassault Falcon 20E	FR Aviation Ltd
	G-FRAJ	Dassault Falcon 20E	FR Aviation Ltd
	G-FRAK	Dassault Falcon 20DC	FR Aviation Ltd
	G-FRAL	Dassault Falcon 20DC	FR Aviation Ltd
	G-FRAN	Piper J-3C-90 Cub(480321:H-44)	Essex L-4 Group (G-BIXY)
	G-FRAO	Dassault Falcon 20DC	FR Aviation Ltd
	G-FRAP	Dassault Falcon 20DC	FR Aviation Ltd
	G-FRAR	Dassault Falcon 20DC	FR Aviation Ltd
	G-FRAS	Dassault Falcon 20C	FR Aviation Ltd
	G-FRAT	Dassault Falcon 20C	FR Aviation Ltd
	G-FRAU	Dassault Falcon 20C	FR Aviation Ltd
	G-FRAW	Dassault Falcon 20ECM	FR Aviation Ltd
	G-FRAY	Cassutt IIIM (modified)	C. I. Fray
	G-FRCE	Folland Gnat T.Mk.1	Red Gnat Ltd
	G-FRDY	Dynamic WT9 UK	Peter Dodd Consultants
	G-FRGN	PA-28-236 Dakota	P. J. Vacher
	G-FRGT	P & M Quik GT450	G-FRGT Group
	G-FRIK	P & M Quik GT450	G-FRIK Group
	G-FRIL	Lindstrand LBL-105A balloon	S. Travaglia
	G-FRJB	Britten Sheriff SA-1 ★	Aeropark
	G-FRNK	Skyranger 912(2)	D. L. Foxley & G. Lace
	G-FROM	Ikarus C.42 FB100	G-FROM Group
	G-FRSX	VS.388 Seafire F.46 (LA564)	Seafire Displays Ltd
	G-FRYI	Beech 200 Super King Air	London Executive Aviation Ltd (G-OAVX/ G-IBCA/G-BMCA)
	G-FRYL	Beech 390 Premier 1	Hawk Air Ltd
	G-FRZN	Agusta A109S Grand	Iceland Foods Ltd
	G-FSEU	Beech 200 Super King Air	Fly Wales
	G-FSHA	Denney Kitfox Mk 2	P. P. Trangmar
	G-FSZY	TB-10 Tobago	P. J. Bentley
	G-FTAX	Cessna 421C	Gold Air International Ltd (G-BFFM)
	G-FTIL	Robin DR.400/180R	RAF Wyton Flying Club Ltd
	G-FTIN	Robin DR.400/100	YP Flying Group

Reg.	Type	Owner or Operator	Notes
G-FTSE	BN-2A Mk.III-2 Trislander	Aurigny Air Services Ltd (G-BEPI)	
G-FUEL	Robin DR.400/180	R. Darch	
G-FUFU	Agusta A.109 Grand	Air Harrods Ltd	
G-FUKM	Westland Gazelle AH.1 (ZA730)	Falcon Aviation Ltd	
G-FULL	PA-28R Cherokee Arrow 200-II	Stapleford Flying Club Ltd (G-HWAY/G-JULI)	
G-FULM	Sikorsky S-76C	Air Harrods Ltd	
G-FUND	Thunder Ax7-65Z balloon	G. B. Davies	
G-FUNK	Yakovlev Yak-50	Redstar Aero Services Ltd	
G-FUNN	Plumb BGP-1	P. E. Barker	
G-FURI	Isaacs Fury II	S. M. Johnston	
G-FURZ	Best Off Sky Ranger Nynja 912S(1)	S. R. Swift	
G-FUSE	Cameron N-105 balloon	S. A. Lacey	
G-FUUN	Silence SA.180 Twister	A. W. McKee	
G-FUZZ	PA-18 Super Cub 95 (51-15319)	G. W. Cline	
G-FVEE	Monnett Sonerai 1	J. S. Baldwin	
G-FVEL	Cameron Z-90 balloon	Fort Vale Engineering Ltd	
G-FWAY	Lindstrand LBL-90A balloon	H. W. R. Stewart	
G-FWJR	Ultramagic M-56 balloon	Harding and Sons Ltd	
G-FWKS	Tanarg/Ixess 15 912S(1)	M. A. Coffin (G-SYUT)	
G-FWPW	PA-28-236 Dakota	P. A. & F. C. Winters	
G-FXBT	Aeroprakt A.22 Foxbat	R. H. Jago	
G-FXII	VS.366 Spitfire F.XII (EN224)	Air Leasing Ltd	
G-FYAN	Williams Westwind MLB	M. D. Williams	
G-FYAO	Williams Westwind MLB	M. D. Williams	
G-FYAU	Williams Westwind Mk 2 MLB	M. D. Williams	
G-FYAV	Osprey Mk 4E2 MLB	C. D. Egan & C. Stiles	
G-FYBX	Portswood Mk XVI MLB	I. Chadwick	
G-FYCL	Osprey Mk 4G MLB	P. J. Rogers	
G-FYCV	Osprey Mk 4D MLB	M. Thomson	
G-FYDF	Osprey Mk 4DV	K. A. Jones	
G-FYDI	Williams Westwind Two MLB	M. D. Williams	
G-FYDN	European 8C MLB	P. D. Ridout	
G-FYDO	Osprey Mk 4D MLB	N. L. Scallan	
G-FYDP	Williams Westwind Three MLB	M. D. Williams	
G-FYDS	Osprey Mk 4D MLB	N. L. Scallan	
G-FYEK	Unicorn UE.1C MLB	D. & D. Eaves	
G-FYEO	Eagle Mk 1 MLB	M. E. Scallan	
G-FYEV	Osprey Mk 1C MLB	M. E. Scallan	
G-FYEZ	Firefly Mk 1 MLB	M. E. & N. L. Scallan	
G-FYFI	European E.84DS MLB	M. Stelling	
G-FYFJ	Williams Westland 2 MLB	M. D. Williams	
G-FYFN	Osprey Saturn 2 MLB	J. & M. Woods	
G-FYFW	Rango NA-55 MLB	Rango Balloon and Kite Company	
G-FYFY	Rango NA-55RC MLB	Rango Balloon and Kite Company	
G-FYGC	Rango NA-42B MLB	L. J. Wardle	
G-FYGJ	Airspeed 300 MLB	N. Wells	
G-FYGM	Saffrey/Smith Princess MLB	A. Smith	
G-FZZA	General Avia F22-A	APB Leasing Ltd	
G-FZZI	Cameron H-34 balloon	Magical Adventures Ltd	
G-GABI	Lindstrand LBL-35A Cloudhopper balloon	R. D. Sargeant	
G-GABS	Cameron TR-70 balloon	N. M. Gabriel	
G-GABY	Bombardier BD-700-1A10 Global Express	Bookajet Ltd	
G-GACA	P.57 Sea Prince T.1 (WP308:572CU) ★	P. G. Vallance Ltd/Charlwood	
G-GACB	Robinson R44 II	A. C. Barker	
G-GAEA	Aquila AT01	Stamp Aviation Ltd	
G-GAEB	Aquila AT01	Stamp Aviation Ltd	
G-GAFA	PA-34-200T Seneca II	Oxford Aviation Academy (Oxford) Ltd	
G-GAFT	PA-44-180 Seminole	Bravo Aviation Ltd	
G-GAII	Hawker Hunter GA.11 (XE685)	Hawker Hunter Aviation Ltd	
G-GAJB	AA-5B Tiger	G-GAJB Group (G-BHZN)	
G-GALA	PA-28 Cherokee 180E	FlyBPL.com	
G-GALB	PA-28-161 Warrior II	LB Aviation Ltd	
G-GALL	PA-38-112 Tomahawk	J. T. Mountain (G-BTEV)	
G-GAMA	Beech 58 Baron	Gama Aviation Ltd (G-WWIZ/G-BBSD)	
G-GAME	Cessna T.303	J. & R. K. Hyatt	

Notes	Reg.	Type	Owner or Operator
	G-GAND	Agusta-Bell 206B Jet Ranger	The Henderson Group (G-AWMK)
	G-GANE	Sequoia F.8L Falco	S. J. Gane
	G-GAOH	Robin DR.400 / 2 +2.	S. D. Baker & M. Stott
	G-GAOM	Robin DR.400 / 2+2	P. M. & P. A. Chapman
	G-GARI	Ace Aviation Touch/Buzz	G. B. Shaw
	G-GASP	PA-28-181 Archer II	G-GASP Flying Group
	G-GASS	Thunder Ax7-77 balloon	Servowarm Balloon Syndicate
	G-GAST	Van's RV-8	G. M. R. Abrey
	G-GATE	Robinson R44 II	J. W. Gate
	G-GATT	Robinson R44 II	B. W. Faulkner
	G-GAVH	P & M Quik	J. M. Mooney
	G-GAWA	Cessna 140	C140 Group (G-BRSM)
	G-GAZA	Aérospatiale SA.341G Gazelle 1	The Auster Aircraft Co Ltd (G-RALE/G-SFTG)
	G-GAZN	P & M Quik GT450	C. Hughes
	G-GAZO	Ace Magic Cyclone	G. J. Pearce
	G-GAZZ	Aérospatiale SA.341G Gazelle 1	Cheqair Ltd
	G-GBAO	Robin R1180TD	J. Toulorge
	G-GBBB	Schleicher ASH-25	ASH25 BB Glider Syndicate
	G-GBBT	Ultramagic M-90 balloon	British Telecommunications PLC
	G-GBCC	Ikarus C42 FB100	I. R. Westrope
	G-GBEE	Mainair Pegasus Quik	M. G. Evans
	G-GBET	Ikarus C42 FB UK	Olympic Flying Club (G-BDBMK/G-MROY)
	G-GBFF	Cessna F.172N	Aviation Rentals
	G-GBFR	Cessna F.177RG	Airspeed Aviation Ltd
	G-GBGA	Scheibe SF.25C Falke	The Royal Air Force Gliding and Soaring Association
	G-GBGB	Ultramagic M.105 balloon	Universal Car Services Ltd
	G-GBGF	Cameron Dragon SS balloon	Magical Adventures Ltd (G-BUVH)
	G-GBHI	SOCATA TB10 Tobago	J. Watt
	G-GBJP	Mainair Pegasus Quantum 15	M. P. Chew
	G-GBLP	Cessna F.172M	Aviate Scotland Ltd (G-GWEN)
	G-GBMR	Beech B200 Super King Air	M and R Aviation LLP
	G-GBOB	Alpi Pioneer 300 Hawk	R. E. Burgess
	G-GBPP	Rolladen-Schneider LS6-c18	G. J. Lyons & R. Sinden
	G-GBRB	PA-28 Cherokee 180C	Bravo Romeo Group
	G-GBRU	Bell 206B JetRanger 3	R. A. Fleming Ltd (G-CDGV)
	G-GBRV	Van's RV-9A	G. Carter & K. L. Chorley (G-THMB)
	G-GBSL	Beech 76 Duchess	M. H. Cundsy (G-BGVG)
	G-GBTA	Boeing 737-436	British Airways (G-BVHA)
	G-GBTB	Boeing 737-436	British Airways (G-BVHB)
	G-GBTL	Cessna 172S	Bohana Technology Ltd
	G-GBUE	Robin DR.400/120A	J. A. Kane (G-BPXD)
	G-GBUN	Cessna 182T	G. M. Bunn
	G-GBVX	Robin DR400/120A	The Leuchars Flying Company
	G-GBXF	Robin HR200/120	B. A. Mills
	G-GBXS	Europa XS	Europa Group
	G-GCAC	Europa XS T-G	J. L. Gunn
	G-GCAT	PA-28 Cherokee 140B	Group Cat (G-BFRH)
	G-GCCL	Beech 76 Duchess	Aerolease Ltd
	G-GCDA	Cirrus SR20	Aircraft Grouping Ltd
	G-GCDB	Cirrus SR20	Aircraft Grouping Ltd
	G-GCDC	Cirrus SR20	Stamp Aviation Ltd
	G-GCDD	Cirrus SR20	Stamp Aviation Ltd
	G-GCEA	Pegasus Quik	S. F. Beardsell
	G-GCFM	Diamond DA.40D Star	VifoGmbhsrl/Germany
	G-GCIY	Robin DR.400-140B	M. S. Lonsdale
	G-GCJA	Rolladen-Schneider LS8-18	N. T. Mallender
	G-GCKI	Mooney M.20K	B. Barr
	G-GCMM	Agusta A109E	Hadleigh Partners
	G-GCMW	Grob G.102 Astir CS	M. S. F. Wood
	G-GCUF	Robin DR400/160	Exeter Aviation Ltd
	G-GCYC	Cessna F.182Q	A. G. Dodd
	G-GDAV	Robinson R44 II	G. H. Weston
	G-GDEF	Robin DR.400/120	J. M. Shackleton
	G-GDER	Robin R.1180TD	Berkshire Aviation Services Ltd
	G-GDEZ	BAe 125 Srs.100B	Frewton Ltd
	G-GDFB	Boeing 737-33A	Jet 2
	G-GDFC	Boeing 737-8K2	Jet 2
	G-GDFD	Boeing 737-8K5	Jet 2
	G-GDFE	Boeing 737-3Q8	Jet 2

Reg.	Type	Owner or Operator	Notes
G-GDFF	Boeing 737-85P	Jet 2	
G-GDFG	Boeing 737-36Q	Jet 2	
G-GDFH	Boeing 737-3Y5	Jet 2	
G-GDFJ	Boeing 737-804	Jet 2 (G-CDZI)	
G-GDFK	Boeing 737-36N	Jet 2 (G-STRE/G-XBHX)	
G-GDFL	Boeing 737-36N	Jet 2	
G-GDJF	Robinson R44 II	Berkley Properties Ltd (G-DEXT)	
G-GDKR	Robin DR400/140B	L. J. Milbank	
G-GDMW	Beech 76 Duchess	Flew LLP	
G-GDOG	PA-28R Cherokee Arrow 200-II	The Mutley Crew Group (G-BDXW)	
G-GDSG	Agusta A109E Power	Pendley Farm	
G-GDRV	Van's RV-6	J. R. S. Heaton & R. Feather	
G-GDTL	Airbus A.320-231	MyTravel Airways	
G-GDTU	Avions Mudry CAP-10B	D. C. Cooper & A. L. Farr	
G-GECO	Hughes 369HS	N. Duggan (G-ATVEE/G-GCXK)	
G-GEEP	Robin R.1180TD	The Aiglon Flying Group	
G-GEHL	Cessna 172S	Ebryl Ltd	
G-GEHP	PA-28RT-201 Arrow IV	Aeros Leasing Ltd	
G-GEKO	Parmania Revolution/Kobra Kilo (modified)	D. J. Eldridge	
G-GEMM	Cirrus SR20	Schmolke Grosskuechensysteme GmbH	
G-GEMS	Thunder Ax8-90 Srs 2 balloon	Kraft Bauprojekt GmbH/Germany	
G-GEMX	P&M Quik GT450	A. R. Oliver	
G-GEOF	Pereira Osprey 2	G. Crossley	
G-GEOS	Diamond HK.36 TTC-ECO Super Dimona	University Court (School of Geosciences) of the University of Edinburgh	
G-GERS	Robinson R44 II	M. Virdee	
G-GERT	Van's RV-7	Barnstormers	
G-GERY	Stoddard-Hamilton Glastar	S. G. Brown	
G-GEZZ	Bell 206B JetRanger II	Rivermead Aviation Ltd	
G-GFAA	Slingsby T.67A	Slingsby Flying Group (G-BJXA)	
G-GFCA	PA-28-161 Cadet	Aeros Leasing Ltd	
G-GFCB	PA-28-161 Cadet	A. J. Warren	
G-GFDA	Diamond DA.42 Twin Star	Saltaire Motor Co.Ltd (G-CEFX)	
G-GFEA	Cessna 172S	Allan Jefferies (G-CEDY)	
G-GFEY	PA-34-200T Seneca II	The G-GFEY Owners Group	
G-GFFE	Boeing 737-528	Pineapple Ltd	
G-GFIA	Cessna 152	Aircraft Grouping Ltd	
G-GFIB	Cessna F.152	Flight Academy Barton Ltd (G-BPIO)	
G-GFID	Cessna 152 II	P. J. Montgomery (G-BORJ)	
G-GFIE	Cessna 152	Aircraft Grouping Ltd (G-CEUS)	
G-GFIG	Cessna 152	Westbeach Aviation Ltd (G-BNOZ)	
G-GFKY	Zenair CH.250	R. G. Kelsall	
G-GFLY	Cessna F.150L	Hangar 1 Ltd	
G-GFNO	Robin ATL	B. F. Walker	
G-GFOX	Aeroprakt A.22 Foxbat	G. F. Elvis	
G-GFRA	PA-28RT-201T Turbo Arrow IV	NSP Ltd (G-LROY/G-BNTS)	
G-GFRO	Robin ATL	B. F. Walker	
G-GFSA	Cessna 172R Skyhawk	Aircraft Grouping Ltd	
G-GFTA	PA-28-161 Warrior III	One Zero Three Ltd	
G-GFTB	PA-28-161 Warrior III	One Zero Three Ltd	
G-GGDV	Schleicher Ka 6E	H. J. Fox	
G-GGGG	Thunder Ax7-77A balloon	T. A. Gilmour	
G-GGHZ	Robin ATL	Modesto's Bakeries Ltd	
G-GGJK	Robin DR.400/140B	Headcorn Jodelers	
G-GGLE	PA-22 Colt 108 (tailwheel)	J. Guillemot & B. L. Morgan	
G-GGOW	Colt 77A balloon	R. Foster	
G-GGRR	SA Bulldog Srs 120/121 (XX614:V)	C. G. Sims (G-CBAM)	
G-GGTT	Agusta-Bell 47G-4A	P. R. Smith	
G-GGWW	Beech 76 Duchess	Avto Engineering Holding Group (G-BGRG)	
G-GHEE	Aerotechnik EV-97 Eurostar	C. J. Ball	
G-GHER	AS.355N Ecureuil II	Gallagher Air LLP	
G-GHKX	PA-28-161 Warrior II	Aviation Rentals	
G-GHOP	Cameron Z-77 balloon	Lakeside Lodge Golf Centre	
G-GHOW	Cessna F.182Q	Oscar Whiskey Flying Group	
G-GHRW	PA-28RT-201 Arrow IV	P. Cowley (G-ONAB/G-BHAK)	
G-GHZJ	SOCATA TB9 Tampico	P. K. Hayward	

Notes	Reg.	Type	Owner or Operator
	G-GIBB	Robinson R44 II	Tingdene Aviation Ltd
	G-GIBP	Moravan Zlin Z.526 Trener Master	D. G. Cowden
	G-GIDY	Shaw Europa XS	Gidy Group
	G-GIGA	Vulcanair P68C	Apem Aviation Ltd
	G-GIGI	MS.893A Rallye Commodore	D. J. Moore (G-AYVX)
	G-GIGZ	Van's RV-8	The Giggzy Group
	G-GILI	Robinson R44	Twylight Management Ltd
	G-GIPC	PA-32R-301 Saratoga SP	S. Empson
	G-GIRY	AG-5B Tiger	Romeo Yankee Flying Group
	G-GIST	Luscombe 8E Silvaire	J. B. Brown (G-AKUH)
	G-GIVE	Cameron A-300 balloon	Cameron Flights Southern Ltd
	G-GIWT	Shaw Europa XS	A. Twigg
	G-GJCD	Robinson R22 Beta	J. C. Lane
	G-GJMB	Bombardier CL-600-2B19 Challenger 850	Corporate Jet Management Ltd (G-CJMB)
	G-GKAT	Enstrom 280C	D. G. Allsop & A. J. Clark
	G-GKEV	Alpi Pioneer 300	A. P. Sellars
	G-GKFC	RL-5A LW Sherwood Ranger	P. A. Durrans (G-MYZI)
	G-GKKI	Avions Mudry CAP 231EX	L. Love
	G-GKRC	Cessna 180K	S. J. Beaty
	G-GKUE	SOCATA TB-9 Tampico Club	E. Pavanello & D. Peverley
	G-GLAD	Gloster G.37 Gladiator II (N5903:H)	Patina Ltd
	G-GLAK	AB Sportine LAK-12	C. Roney
	G-GLAW	Cameron N-90 balloon	R. A. Vale
	G-GLBX	Bombardier BD700-1A10 Global Express	Finesse Executive Ltd
	G-GLED	Cessna 150M	Firecrest Aviation Ltd and H. Vara
	G-GLHI	Skyranger 912	S. F. Winter
	G-GLIB	Robinson R44	G. P. Glibbery
	G-GLID	Schleicher ASW-28-18E	S. Bovin and Compagnie Belge d'Assurances Aviation
	G-GLII	Great Lakes 2T-1A-2	T. J. Richardson
	G-GLOC	Extra EA.300/200	The Cambridge Aero Club Ltd
	G-GLST	Great Lakes Sport Trainer	D. A. Graham
	G-GLTT	PA-31-350 Navajo Chieftain	Blue Sky Investments Ltd
	G-GLUC	Van's RV-6	P. Shoesmith & J. M. Whitham
	G-GLUE	Cameron N-65 balloon	L. J. M. Muir & G. D. Hallett
	G-GMAA	Learjet 45	Gama Aviation Ltd
	G-GMAB	BAe 125 Srs 1000A	Gama Aviation Ltd (G-BUWX)
	G-GMAC	Gulfstream G-IVSP	Gama Aviation Ltd
	G-GMAX	SNCAN Stampe SV.4C	G. H. Stinnes (G-BXNW)
	G-GMCM	AS.350B3 Ecureuil	T. J. Morris Ltd
	G-GMED	PA-42-720 Cheyenne IIA	Air Medical Fleet Ltd
	G-GMIB	Robin DR400/500	St. David's Farm & Equine Practice
	G-GMKD	Robin HR200/120B	J. Owens
	G-GMKE	Robin HR200/120B	Pilot Flying Group
	G-GMPB	BN-2T-4S Defender 4000	Greater Manchester Police Authority (G-BWPU)
	G-GMPX	MDH MD-900 Explorer	Greater Manchester Police Authority
	G-GMSI	SOCATA TB9 Tampico	M. L. Rhodes
	G-GNJW	Ikarus C.42	N. C. Pearse
	G-GNRV	Van's RV-9A	N. K. Beavins
	G-GNTB	SAAB SF.340A	Loganair Ltd
	G-GNTF	SAAB SF.340A	Loganair Ltd
	G-GOAC	PA-34-200T Seneca II	Oxford Aviation Academy (Oxford) Ltd
	G-GOAL	Lindstrand LBL-105A balloon	I. Chadwick
	G-GOBD	PA-32R-301 Saratoga IIHP	F. & M. Garventa (G-OARW)
	G-GOBT	Colt 77A balloon	British Telecom PLC
	G-GOCX	Cameron N-90 balloon	R. D. Parry/Hong Kong
	G-GOER	Bushby-Long Midget Mustang	J. M. Keane
	G-GOES	Robinson R44-II	Fordville Ltd
	G-GOFF	Extra EA.300/LC	George J. Goff Ltd
	G-GOGB	Lindstrand LBL ,90A	J. Dyer (G-CDFX)
	G-GOGW	Cameron N-90 balloon	S. E. Carroll
	G-GOHI	Cessna 208 Caravan 1 amphibian	S. Ulrich
	G-GOLF	SOCATA TB10 Tobago	B. Lee
	G-GOOF	Flylight Dragonfly	P. C. Bailey
	G-GORE	CFM Streak Shadow	M. S. Clinton
	G-GORV	Van's RV-8	G-GORV Group

Reg.	Type	Owner or Operator	Notes
G-GOSL	Robin DR.400/180	R. M. Gosling (G-BSDG)	
G-GOSS	Jodel DR.221	Avon Flying Group	
G-GOTC	GA-7 Cougar	Western Air (Thruxton) Ltd and Bucklefield Business Developments Ltd	
G-GOTH	PA-28-161 Warrior III	Stamp Aviation Ltd	
G-GOUL	Agusta-Bell 206B Jet Ranger III	Castle Air Ltd (G-ONTV)	
G-GOUP	Robinson R22 Beta	M. A. Bennett (G-DIRE)	
G-GOWF	Eurocopter EC.135 T2+	Bond Air Services Ltd	
G-GPAG	Van's RV-6	P. A. Green	
G-GPAT	Beech 76 Duchess	Folada Aero & Technical Services Ltd	
G-GPEG	Sky 90-24 balloon	N. T. Parry	
G-GPMW	PA-28RT-201T Turbo Arrow IV	Calverton Flying Group Ltd	
G-GPPN	Cameron TR-70 balloon	Backetorp Byggconsult AB	
G-GPSF	Jabiru J430	P. S. Furlow	
G-GREY	PA-46-350P Malibu Mirage	S. T. Day & S. C. Askham	
G-GRIN	Van's RV-6	Burel Air Ltd	
G-GRIZ	PA-18-135 Super Cub (modified)	P. N. Elkington (G-BSHV)	
G-GRMN	Aerospool Dynamic WT9 UK	R. M. North	
G-GRND	Agusta A109S	Galegrove 2 LBG	
G-GROE	Grob G.115A	H. Merkado	
G-GROL	Maule MXT-7-180	D. C. Croll & ptnrs	
G-GROW	Cameron N-77 balloon	Derbyshire Building Society	
G-GRPA	Ikarus C.42 FB100	R. Wood	
G-GGRH	Robinson R44	Heli Air Ltd	
G-GRRR	SA Bulldog Srs 120/122	Horizons Europe Ltd (G-BXGU)	
G-GRSR	Schempp-Hirth Discus bT	SR Group	
G-GRVE	Van's RV-6	G-GRVE Group	
G-GRVY	Van's RV-8	P. H. Yarrow	
G-GRWL	Lilliput Type 4 balloon	A. E. & D. E. Thomas	
G-GRWW	Robinson R44 II	G. R. Williams (G-HEEL)	
G-GRYN	Rotorsport UK Calidus	K. Hedger	
G-GRYZ	Beech F33A Bonanza	J. Kawadri & M. Kaveh	
G-GRZD	Gulfstream V-SP	TAG Aviation (UK) Ltd	
G-GRZZ	Robinson R44 II	Graegill Aviation Ltd	
G-GSAL	Fokker E.III Reolica	Grass Strip Aviation Ltd	
G-GSCV	Ikarus C42 FB UK	Jabeuqe Ltd	
G-GSMT	Rotorsport UK MTOSport	C. D. Jackson	
G-GSPG	Hughes 369HS	S. Giddings Aviation	
G-GSPY	Robinson R44 II	Percy Wood Leisure Ltd	
G-GSRV	Robin DR.400/500	R. G. Fairall	
G-GSSD	Boeing 747-87UF	Global Supply Systems Ltd/British Airways Cargo	
G-GSSE	Boeing 747-87UF	Global Supply Systems Ltd/British Airways Cargo	
G-GSSF	Boeing 747-87UF	Global Supply Systems Ltd/British Airways Cargo	
G-GSSO	Gulfstream GV-SP	TAG Aviation (UK) Ltd	
G-GSST	Grob G.102 Astir CS77	770 Group	
G-GSYJ	Diamond DA42 Twin Star	Crosby Aviation (Jersey) Ltd	
G-GSYL	PA-28RT-201T Turbo Arrow IV	S. J. Sylvester (G-DAAH)	
G-GSYS	PA-34-220T Seneca V	SYS (Scaffolding Contractors) Ltd	
G-GTAX	PA-31-350 Navajo Chieftain	Hadagain Investments Ltd (G-OIAS)	
G-GTEE	P & M Quik GT450	M. McLaughlin	
G-GTFC	P & M Quik	A. J. Fell	
G-GTGT	P & M Quik GT.450	W. G. Minns	
G-GTHM	PA-38-112 Tomahawk	R. J. Grainger	
G-GTJD	P & M Quik GT450	P. Craigie	
G-GTJM	Eurocopter EC 120B Colibri	D. Robson	
G-GTOM	Alpi Pioneer 300	S. C. Oliphant	
G-GTRR	P & M Quik GTR	Fly Hire Ltd	
G-GTSO	P & M Quik GT450	C. Bayliss	
G-GTTP	P & M Quik GT450	S. Turnbull	
G-GTVM	Beech 58 Baron	Baron Flying Club Ltd	
G-GTWO	Schleicher ASW-15	J. M. G. Carlton & R. Jackson	
G-GUCK	Beech C23 Sundowner 180	J. T. Francis (G-BPYG)	
G-GULP	I.I.I. Sky Arrow 650T	S. Marriott	
G-GULZ	Christen Eagle II	T. N. Jinks	
G-GUMS	Cessna 182P	L. W. Scattergood (G-CBMN)	
G-GUNS	Cameron V-77 balloon	V. Grenier	
G-GUNZ	Van's RV-8	Bibielle UK Ltd	

Notes	Reg.	Type	Owner or Operator
	G-GURN	PA-31 Navajo C	Batair Ltd (G-BHGA)
	G-GURU	PA-28-161 Warrior II	P. J. Wiseman
	G-GUSS	PA-28-151 Warrior	The Sierra Flying Group (G-BJRY)
	G-GVPI	Evans VP-1 srs.2	G. Martin
	G-GWIZ	Colt Clown SS balloon	Magical Adventures Ltd
	G-GWYN	Cessna F.172M	Magic Carpet Flying Co
	G-GYAK	Yakovlev Yak-50	M. W. Levy & M. V. Rijske
	G-GYAT	Gardan GY-80 Horizon 180	Rochester GYAT Flying Group Club
	G-GYAV	Cessna 172N	Southport & Merseyside Aero Club (1979) Ltd
	G-GYRO	Campbell Cricket	J. W. Pavitt
	G-GYTO	PA-28-161 Warrior III	Smart People Don't Buy Ltd
	G-GZDO	Cessna 172N	Cambridge Hall Aviation
	G-GZIP	Rolladen-Schneider LS8-18	D. S. S. Haughton
	G-GZRP	PA-42-720 Cheyenne IIIA	Air Medical Fleet Ltd
	G-HAAH	Schempp-Hirth Ventus 2cT	The V66 Syndicate
	G-HAAT	MDH MD.900 Explorer	Police Aviation Services Ltd (G-GMPS)
	G-HABI	Best Off SkyRanger 912S(1)	J. Habicht
	G-HABS	Cessna 172S	Apem Aviation Ltd (G-RGAP)
	G-HABT	Supermarine Aircraft Spitfire Mk.26	Smart People UK Ltd
	G-HACE	Van's RV-6A	D. C. McElroy
	G-HACK	PA-18 Super Cub 150	Intrepid Aviation Co
	G-HACS	Tecnam P2002-JF	The RAF Halton Aeroplane Club Ltd
	G-HADD	P & M Quik R	T. J. Barker
	G-HAEF	EV-97 TeamEurostar UK	RAF Microlight Flying Association
	G-HAFG	Cessna 340A	Pavilion Aviation Ltd
	G-HAFT	Diamond DA42 Twin Star	Atlantic Flight Training Ltd
	G-HAGL	Robinson R44 II	Devon Helicopters Ltd
	G-HAIB	Aviat A-1B Husky	H. Brockmueller
	G-HAIG	Rutan LongEz	C. Docherty
	G-HAIR	Robin DR.400/180	S. P. Copson
	G-HAJJ	Glaser-Dirks DG.400	W. G. Upton & J. G. Kosak
	G-HALC	PA-28R Cherokee Arrow 200	Halcyon Aviation Ltd
	G-HALJ	Cessna 140	Hangar 1 Ltd
	G-HALL	PA-22 Tri-Pacer 160	F. P. Hall (G-ARAH)
	G-HALT	Mainair Pegasus Quik	J. McGrath
	G-HAMI	Fuji FA.200-180	K. G. Cameron & M. P. Antoniak & P. Fairlie (G-OISF/G-BAPT)
	G-HAMM	Yakovlev Yak-50	Propeller Studios Ltd
	G-HAMP	Bellanca 7ACA Champ	R. J. Grimstead
	G-HAMR	PA-28-161 Warrior II	Electric Scribe 2000 Ltd
	G-HAMS	Pegasus Quik	D. R. Morton
	G-HANA	Westland WS-58 Wessex HC.2	R. A. Fidler
	G-HANG	Diamond DA42 Twin Star	Atlantic Flight Training Ltd
	G-HANS	Robin DR.400 2+2	J. S. Russell
	G-HANY	Agusta-Bell 206B JetRanger 3	Beech Holdings Ltd (G-ESAL/G-BHXW/G-JEKP)
	G-HAPE	Pietenpol Aircamper	J. P. Chape
	G-HAPI	Lindstrand LBL-105A balloon	Adventure Balloons Ltd
	G-HAPY	DHC.1 Chipmunk 22A (WP803)	Astrojet Ltd
	G-HARD	Dyn'Aéro MCR-01 ULC	N. A. Burnet
	G-HARE	Cameron N-77 balloon	D. H. Sheryn & C. A. Buck
	G-HARI	Raj Hamsa X'Air V2 (2)	J. Blackburn
	G-HARK	Canadair CL.600-2B16	Corbridge Ltd
	G-HARN	PA-28-181 Archer II	K. Saxton (G-DENK/G-BXRJ)
	G-HARR	Robinson R22 Beta	Unique Helicopters Ltd
	G-HART	Cessna 152 (tailwheel)	Air Atlantique Ltd (G-BPBF)
	G-HARY	Alon A-2 Aircoupe	M. B. Willis (G-ATWP)
	G-HATF	Thorp T-18CW	A. T. Fraser
	G-HATZ	Hatz CB-1	S. P. Rollason
	G-HAUL	Westland WG.30 Srs 300 ★	IHM/Weston-super-Mare
	G-HAUT	Schempp-Hirth Mini Nimbus C	530 Syndicate
	G-HAVI	Eurocopter EC.130B4	J. & J. Havakin
	G-HAYY	Czech Sport Aircraft Sportcruiser	B. R. W. Hay
	G-HAZE	Thunder Ax8-90 balloon	T. G. Church
	G-HBBC	DH.104 Dove 8	Roger Gawn 2007 Family Trust (G-ALFM)
	G-HBBH	Ikarus C42 FB100	Golf Bravo Hotel Group
	G-HBEK	Agusta A109C	HPM Investments Ltd (G-RNLD/G-DATE)

Reg.	Type	Owner or Operator	Notes
G-HBJT	Eurocopter EC.155B1	Starspeed Ltd	
G-HBMW	Robinson R22	Durham Flying Syndicate (G-BOFA)	
G-HBOB	Eurocopter EC135 T2+	Bond Air Services Ltd/Thames Valley Air Ambulance	
G-HBOS	Scheibe SF-25C Rotax-Falke	Coventry Gliding Club Ltd	
G-HBRO	Eurocopter AS.355NP Ecureuil 2	Henry Brothers (Magherafelt) Ltd	
G-HBUG	Cameron N-90 balloon	Black Horse Ballooning Club (G-BRCN)	
G-HCAC	Schleicher Ka 6E	Ka 6E 994 Group	
G-HCCL	Beech B200GT Super King Air	J. M. Lynch	
G-HCFC	Agusta A.109E Power	Castle Air Ltd	
G-HCGD	Learjet 45	TAG Aviation (UK) Ltd	
G-HCPD	Cameron C-80 balloon	H. Crawley& P. Dopson	
G-HCSA	Cessna 525A CJ2	Bookajet Aircraft Management Ltd	
G-HDAE	DHC.1 Chipmunk 22	Airborne Classics Ltd	
G-HDEF	Robinson R44 II	Arena Aviation Ltd (G-LOCO/G-TEMM)	
G-HDEW	PA-32R-301 Saratoga SP	A. H. Biddulph & P. R. Ellis	
G-HDIX	Enstrom 280FX	Clovetree Ltd	
G-HDTV	Agusta A109A-II	Castle Air Ltd (G-BXWD)	
G-HEAD	Colt Flying Head SS balloon	Ikeair	
G-HEAN	AS.355NP Ecureuil 2	Brookview Developments Ltd	
G-HEBB	Schleicher ASW-27-18E	E. Y. Heinonen	
G-HEBI	BN-2B-26 Islander	Hebridean Air Services Ltd (G-BSPT)	
G-HEBO	BN-2B-20 Islander	Hebridean Air Services Ltd (G-BUBK)	
G-HEBS	BN-2B-26 Islander	Hebridean Air Services Ltd (G-BUBJ)	
G-HEBZ	BN-2A-26 Islander	Cormack (Aircraft Services) Ltd (G-BELF)	
G-HECB	Fuji FA.200-160	H. E. W. E. Bailey (G-BBZO)	
G-HEHE	Eurocopter EC.120B Colibri	HE Group Ltd	
G-HEKK	RAF 2000 GTX-SE gyroplane	C. J. Watkinson (G-BXEB)	
G-HEKL	Percival Mew Gull Replica	D. Beale	
G-HELA	SOCATA TB10 Tobago	PMF Group	
G-HELE	Bell 206B JetRanger 3	B. E. E. Smith (G-OJFR)	
G-HELN	Piper PA-18-95 Super Cub	Helen Group	
G-HELV	DH.115 Vampire T.55 (XJ771)	Aviation Heritage Ltd	
G-HEMN	Eurocopter EC135 T2+	Bond Air Services Ltd	
G-HEMZ	Agusta A109S Grand	Sloane Helicopters Ltd	
G-HENT	SOCATA Rallye 110ST	F. Monds	
G-HENY	Cameron V-77 balloon	R. S. D'Alton	
G-HEOI	Eurocopter EC135 P2+	Staffordshire & West Mercia Police Authorities	
G-HERC	Cessna 172S	Cambridge Aero Club Ltd	
G-HERD	Lindstrand LBL-77B balloon	S. W. Herd	
G-HERT	BAE Herti	BAe Systems (Operations) Ltd	
G-HEWI	Piper J-3C-90 Cub	Denham Grasshopper Group (G-BLEN)	
G-HEWS	Hughes 369D ★	Spares' use	
G-HEXE	Colt 17A balloon	A. Dunnington	
G-HEYY	Cameron 72 Bear SS balloon	Magical Adventures Ltd	
G-HFBM	Curtiss Robin C-2	D. M. Forshaw	
G-HFCA	Cessna A.150L	T. H. Scott	
G-HFCB	Cessna F.150L	P. R. Mortimer	
G-HFCL	Cessna F.152	MK Aero Support Ltd (G-BGLR)	
G-HFCT	Cessna F.152	Stapleford Flying Club Ltd	
G-HFLY	Robinson R44 II	Helifly (UK) Ltd	
G-HFRH	DHC-1 Chipmunk 22	Sunrise Global Aviation Ltd	
G-HGAS	Cameron N-77 balloon	N. J. Tovey	
G-HGPI	SOCATA TB20 Trinidad	M. J. Jackson	
G-HGRB	Robinson R44	Hields Aviation (G-BZIN)	
G-HHAA	HS. Buccaneer S.2B (XX885)	Hawker Hunter Aviation Ltd	
G-HHAC	Hawker Hunter F.58 (J-4021)	Hawker Hunter Aviation Ltd (G-BWIU)	
G-HHDR	Cessna 182T	D. R. & H. Howell	
G-HHII	Hawker Hurricane 2B (BE505: XP-L)	Hangar 11 Collection (G-HRLO)	
G-HHPM	Cameron Z-105 balloon	J. Armstrong	
G-HIBM	Cameron N-145 balloon	Alba Ballooning Ltd	
G-HICU	Schleicher ASW-27-18E	G. Smith & N. Hoare	
G-HIEL	Robinson R22 Beta	Crown Helicopters Ltd	
G-HIJK	Cessna 421C	DO Systems Ltd (G-OSAL)	
G-HIJN	Ikarus C.42 FB80	R. W. Thornborough	

Notes	Reg.	Type	Owner or Operator
	G-HILI	Van's RV-3B	A. G. & E. A. Hill
	G-HILO	Rockwell Commander 114	J. G. Gleeson & J. J. Toomey
	G-HILS	Cessna F.172H	LS Flying Group (G-AWCH)
	G-HILT	SOCATA TB10 Tobago	S. Harrison
	G-HILY	Zenair CH.600 Zodiac	K. V. Hill & D. Woolliscroft (G-BRII)
	G-HILZ	Van's RV-8	A. G. & E. A. Hill
	G-HIMM	Cameron Z-105 balloon	C. M. D. Haynes
	G-HIND	Maule MT-7-235	M. A. Ashmole
	G-HINZ	Avtec Jabiru SK	P. J. Jackson
	G-HIPO	Robinson R22 Beta	SI Plan Electronics (Research) Ltd (G-BTGB)
	G-HIRE	GA-7 Cougar	London Aerial Tours Ltd (G-BGSZ)
	G-HITM	Raj Hamsa X'Air 582 (1)	S. E. Bettley
	G-HITT	Hawker Hurricane 1	H. Taylor
	G-HIUP	Cameron A-250 balloon	J. D. & K. Griffiths
	G-HIVA	Cessna 337A	G. J. Banfield (G-BAES)
	G-HIVE	Cessna F.150M	M. P. Lynn (G-BCXT)
	G-HIYA	Best Off Skyranger 912(2)	R. D. & C. M. Parkinson
	G-HIZZ	Robinson R22 II	Flyfare (G-CNDY/G-BXEW)
	G-HJSM	Schempp-Hirth Nimbus 4DM	G. Paul (G-ROAM)
	G-HJSS	AIA Stampe SV.4C (modified)	H. J. Smith (G-AZNF)
	G-HKAA	Schempp-Hirth Duo Discus T	A. Aveling
	G-HKCF	Enstrom 280C-UK	HKC Helicopter Services (G-MHCF/G-GSML/ G-BNNV)
	G-HKHM	Hughes 369B	Heli Air Ltd
	G-HLCF	Starstreak Shadow SA-II	F. E. Tofield
	G-HLEE	Best Off Sky Ranger J2.2(1)	P. G. Hill
	G-HLEL	American Blimp Corp. A-60+ airship	Van Wanger Airships Europe Ltd
	G-HLOB	Cessna 172S	Goodwood Road Racing Co.Ltd
	G-HMBJ	Rockwell Commander 114B	D. W. R. Best
	G-HMCA	EV-97 TeamEurostar UK	RAF Microlight Flying Association
	G-HMCB	Skyranger Swift 912S(1)	R. W. Goddin
	G-HMCD	Ikarus C42 FB80	RAF Microlight Flying Association
	G-HMCE	Ikarus C42 FB80	RAF Microlight Flying Association
	G-HMDX	MDH MD-900 Explorer	Police Aviation Services Ltd
	G-HMED	PA-28-161 Warrior III	Eglinton Flying Club Ltd
	G-HMEI	Dassault Falcon 900	Executive Jet Group Ltd
	G-HMHM	Rotorsport UK MTO Sport	S. D. Evans
	G-HMJB	PA-34-220T Seneca III	W. B. Bateson
	G-HMKA	Gefa-Flug AS105GD	Llego Papa/UK LLC Ltd
	G-HMPS	CZAW Sportcruiser	H. & P. Shedden
	G-HMPT	Agusta-Bell 206B JetRanger 2	Yorkshire Helicopters
	G-HNGE	Ikarus C42 FB100	Compton Abbas Airfield Ltd
	G-HNTR	Hawker Hunter T.7 (XL571:V) ★	Yorkshire Air Museum/Elvington
	G-HOBO	Denney Kitfox Mk 4	J. P. Donovan
	G-HOCA	Robinson R44 II	Heli Air Ltd
	G-HOCK	PA-28 Cherokee 180	G-HOCK Flying Club (G-AVSH)
	G-HOFF	P & M Aviation Quik GT450	L. Mazurek
	G-HOFM	Cameron N-56 balloon	Magical Adventures Ltd
	G-HOGS	Cameron 90 Pig SS balloon	Magical Adventures Ltd
	G-HOJO	Schempp-Hirth Discus 2a	S. G. Jones
	G-HOLA	PA-28-201T Turbo Dakota	J. Prescott (G-BNYB)
	G-HOLD	Robinson R44 II	Mignini and Petrini Spa/Italy
	G-HOLE	P & M Quik GT450	C. J. R. Hardman (G-CEBD)
	G-HOLI	Ultramagic M-77 balloon	G. Everett
	G-HOLM	Eurocopter EC.120B Colibri	Oxford Air Services Ltd
	G-HOLY	ST.10 Diplomate	M. K. Barsham
	G-HONG	Slingsby T.67M Firefly 200	Jewel Aviation and Technology Ltd
	G-HONI	Robinson R22 Beta	Patriot Aviation Ltd (G-SEGO)
	G-HONK	Cameron O-105 balloon	M. A. Green
	G-HONY	Lilliput Type 1 Srs A balloon	A. E. & D. E. Thomas
	G-HOOD	SOCATA TB20 Trinidad GT	M. J. Hoodless
	G-HOPA	Lindstrand LBL-35A balloon	S. F. Burden/Netherlands
	G-HOPE	Beech F33A Bonanza	Hope Aviation Ltd
	G-HOPR	Lindstrand LBL-25A balloon	K. C. Tanner
	G-HOPY	Van's RV-6A	R. C. Hopkinson
	G-HORK	Pioneer 300 Hawk	R. Y. Kendal

BRITISH CIVIL REGISTRATIONS

G-HOSS – G-HURN

Reg.	Type	Owner or Operator	Notes
G-HOSS	Beech F33A	T. D. Broadhurst	
G-HOTA	EV-97 TeamEurostar UK	W. Chang	
G-HOTB	Eurocopter EC155 B1	Noirmont (EC155) Ltd (G-CEXZ)	
G-HOTM	Cameron C-80 balloon	M. N. Macleod	
G-HOTR	P & M Quik GTR	M. E. Fowler	
G-HOTZ	Colt 77B balloon	C. J. & S. M. Davies	
G-HOUS	Colt 31A balloon ★	The British Balloon Museum and Library	
G-HOWE	Thunder Ax7-77 balloon	C. Suggitt	
G-HOWI	Cessna F.182Q	H. Poulson	
G-HOWL	RAF 2000 GTX-SE gyroplane	C. J. Watkinson	
G-HOXN	Van's RV-9	XRay November Flying Club	
G-HPAD	Bell 206B JetRanger 2	Helipad Ltd (G-CITZ/G-BRTB)	
G-HPEN	Ultramagic M-120 balloon	G. Holtam	
G-HPJT	HpH Glasflugel 304S	JT Group	
G-HPOL	MDH MD-902 Explorer	Humberside Police Authority	
G-HPPY	Learjet 40	European Skyjets Ltd	
G-HPSF	Rockwell Commander 114B	R. W. Scandrett	
G-HPSL	Rockwell Commander 114B	M. B. Endean	
G-HPUX	Hawker Hunter T.7 (XL587)	Hawker Hunter Aviation Ltd	
G-HPWA	Van's RV-8	M. de Ferranti	
G-HRAF	Schleicher ASK-13	Upward Bound Trust (G-DETS)	
G-HRBS	Robinson R22 Beta	Fly Executive Ltd	
G-HRCC	Robin HR200/100	P. R and J. S. Johnson	
G-HRHE	Robinson R22 Beta	J. Porter (G-BTWP)	
G-HRIO	Robin HR.100/120	R. Mullender	
G-HRLI	Hawker Hurricane 1 (V7497)	Hawker Restorations Ltd	
G-HRLK	SAAB 91D/2 Safir	Sylmar Aviation & Services Ltd (G-BRZY)	
G-HRLM	Brügger MB.2 Colibri	N. M. Booth	
G-HRND	Cessna 182T	H. B. Gregorian	
G-HROI	Rockwell Commander RC.112	Intereuropean Aviation Ltd	
G-HRPN	Robinson R44 II	M. Lazzari	
G-HRVD	CCF Harvard IV	HRVD Group (G-BSBC)	
G-HRVS	Van's RV-8	D. J. Harvey	
G-HRYZ	PA-28-180 Cherokee Archer	Gama Engineering Ltd (G-WACR/G-BCZF)	
G-HSAR	Agusta A.109E Power	Caste Air Ltd	
G-HSBC	Lindstrand LBL-69X balloon	A. Nimmo	
G-HSEB	Pegasus Quantum 15-912	D. Gwyther (G-BYNO)	
G-HSKE	Aviat A-18 Husky	R. B. Armitage & S. L. Davis	
G-HSKI	Aviat A-1B	C. J. R. Flint	
G-HSOO	Hughes 369HE	A. Shade Greener (F1) Ltd (G-BFYJ)	
G-HSTH	Lindstrand LBL. HS-110 balloon	Lindstrand Hot Air Balloons Ltd	
G-HSXP	Raytheon Hawker 850XP	Fowey Services Ltd	
G-HTAX	PA-31-350 Navajo Chieftain	Hadagain Investments Ltd	
G-HTBT	Rotorsport UK Calidus	T. J. Troy-Davies	
G-HTEL	Robinson R44	Henley Aviation Ltd	
G-HTFU	Gippsland GA8-TC 320 Airvan	Skydive London Ltd	
G-HTML	P & M Aviation Quik R	A. P. Whitmarsh	
G-HTRL	PA-34-220T Seneca III	Air Medical Fleet Ltd (G-BXXY)	
G-HTWE	Rans S6-116	H. C. C. Coleridge	
G-HUBB	Partenavia P.68B	Ravenair Aircraft Ltd	
G-HUBY	Embraer EMB-135BJ Legacy	London Executive Aviation Ltd	
G-HUCH	Cameron 80 Carrots SS balloon	Magical Adventures Ltd (G-BYPS)	
G-HUES	Hughes 369HS	D. G. Beecroft & A. Gilligan (G-GASC/ G-WELD/G-FROG)	
G-HUEW	Shaw Europa XS	C. R. Wright	
G-HUEY	Bell UH-1H	MX Jets Ltd	
G-HUFF	Cessna 182P	Highfine Ltd	
G-HUKA	MDH Hughes 369E	B. P. Stein (G-OSOO)	
G-HULK	Skyranger 912(2)	L. C. Stockman	
G-HULL	Cessna F.150M	Hull Aero Club Ltd	
G-HUMH	Van's RV-9A	H. A. Daines	
G-HUND	Aviat A-1B Husky	U Ladurner	
G-HUNI	Bellanca 7GCBC Scout	R. G. Munro	
G-HUPW	Hawker Hurricane 1 (R4118:UP-W)	Minmere Farm Partnership	
G-HURI	CCF Hawker Hurricane XIIA (Z5140/HA-C)	Historic Aircraft Collection Ltd	
G-HURN	Robinson R22 Beta	CMT Aviation Partnership	

199

Notes	Reg.	Type	Owner or Operator
	G-HUSK	Aviat A-1B	G. D. Ettlmayr
	G-HUTE	Aerochute Dual	W. A. Kimberlin
	G-HUTT	Denney Kitfox Mk.2	H. D. Colliver
	G-HUTY	Van's RV-7	S. A. Hutt
	G-HVAN	RL-5A LW Sherwood Ranger ST	P. S. Taylor
	G-HVBF	Lindstrand LBL-210A balloon	Virgin Balloon Flights
	G-HVER	Robinson R44 II	Equation Associates Ltd
	G-HVRD	PA-31-350 Navajo Chieftain	N. Singh (G-BEZU)
	G-HVRZ	Eurocopter EC 120B	EDM Helicopters Ltd
	G-HWAA	Eurocopter EC 135T2	Bond Air Services Ltd
	G-HXTD	Robin DR.400/180	P. Malone
	G-HYLL	Robinson R44	Holbeck GHYLL Country House Hotel Ltd (G-KLAS)
	G-HYLT	PA-32R-301 Saratoga SP	T. G. Gordon
	G-HYST	Enstrom 280FX Shark	M. Jop
	G-IACA	Sikorsky S-92A	Bristow Helicopters Ltd
	G-IACB	Sikorsky S-92A	Bristow Helicopters Ltd
	G-IACC	Sikorsky S-92A	Bristow Helicopters Ltd
	G-IACD	Sikorsky S-92A	Bristow Helicopters Ltd
	G-IACE	Sikorsky S-92A	Bristow Helicopters Ltd
	G-IACF	Sikorsky S-92A	Bristow Helicopters Ltd
	G-IAJJ	Robinson R44 II	O'Connor Utilities Ltd
	G-IAJS	Ikarus C.42 FB UK	A. J. Slater
	G-IANB	Glaser-Dirks DG-800B	I. S. Bullous
	G-IANC	SOCATA TB10 Tobago	P. D. Seed (G-BIAK)
	G-IANH	SOCATA TB10 Tobago	R. J. Wright
	G-IANI	Shaw Europa XS T-G	I. F. Rickard & I. A. Watson
	G-IANJ	Cessna F.150K	J. A. & D. T. A. Rees (G-AXVW)
	G-IANN	Kolb Twinstar Mk 3	I. Newman
	G-IANW	AS.350B3 Ecureuil	Milford Aviation Services Ltd
	G-IANZ	P & M Quik GT450	Forward Agronomy Ltd
	G-IARC	Stoddard-Hamilton Glastar	A. A. Craig
	G-IASA	Beech B.200 Super King Air	IAS Medical Ltd
	G-IASM	Beech B.200 Super King Air	MIAW LLP (G-OEAS)
	G-IBAZ	Ikarus C.42 FB100	B. R. Underwood
	G-IBBC	Cameron 105 Sphere SS balloon	Balloon Preservation Group
	G-IBBS	Shaw Europa	R. H. Gibbs
	G-IBCF	Cameron Z-105 balloon	Cash 4 Cars
	G-IBED	Robinson R22A	Brian Seedle Helicopters Blackpool (G-BMHN)
	G-IBFC	BFC Challenger II	K. J. Underwood
	G-IBFF	Beech A23-24 Musketeer Super	J. Lankfer (G-AXCJ)
	G-IBFP	VPM .M.16 Tandem Trainer	B. F. Pearson
	G-IBFW	PA-28R-201 Arrow III	Archer Four Ltd
	G-IBHH	Hughes 269C	Alpha Properties (London) Ltd (G-BSCD)
	G-IBIG	Bell 206B JetRanger 3	Big Heli-Charter Ltd (G-BORV)
	G-IBII	Pitts S-2A Special	Aerobatic Displays Ltd (G-XATS)
	G-IBLP	P & M Quik GT450	B. L. Prime
	G-IBME	SA.342J Gazelle	Gazelle Management Services LLP
	G-IBMS	Robinson R44	Beoley Mill Software Ltd
	G-IBNH	Westland Gazelle HT Mk.2 (XW853)	Buckland Newton Hire Ltd (G-SWWM)
	G-IBSY	VS.349 Spitfire Mk.VC	Fairfax Spitfires LLP (G-VMIJ)
	G-IBUZ	CZAW Sportcruiser	G. L. Fearon
	G-IBZA	Cessna 550 Citation II	International Flight Referral BVBA/Belgium (G-OTIS)
	G-ICAS	Pitts S-2B Special	J. C. Smith
	G-ICBM	Stoddard-Hamilton Glasair III Turbine	G. V. Walters & D. N. Brown
	G-ICDM	Jabiru UL-450	D. J. R. Wenham (G-CEKM)
	G-ICES	Thunder Ax6-56 balloon ★	British Balloon Museum & Library Ltd
	G-ICKY	Lindstrand LBL-77A balloon	P. & S. J. Donkin
	G-ICMT	Evektor EV-97 Eurostar	R. Haslam
	G-ICOI	Lindstrand LBL-105A balloon	F. Schroeder/Germany
	G-ICOM	Cessna F.172M	C. G. Elesmore (G-BFXI)
	G-ICON	Rutan LongEz	S. J. & M. A. Carradice
	G-ICRS	Ikarus C.42 FB UK Cyclone	Ikarus Flying Group Ltd
	G-ICSG	AS.355F1 Twin Squirrel	RCR Aviation Ltd (G-PAMI/G-BUSA)

Reg.	Type	Owner or Operator	Notes
G-ICWT	Pegasus Quantum 15-912	M. E. Rees	
G-IDAY	Skyfox CA-25N Gazelle	G. G. Johnstone	
G-IDEB	AS.355F1 Ecureuil 2	MW Helicopters Ltd (G-ORMA/G-SITE/G-BPHC)	
G-IDER	Orlican Discus CS	A. J. Preston & D. B. Keith	
G-IDII	Dan Rihn DR.107 One Design	C. Darlow	
G-IDOL	Evektor EV-97 Eurostar	J. L. Almey	
G-IDRO	Bombardier BD700-1A10 Global Express	Corporate Jet Management Ltd	
G-IDUP	Enstrom 280C Shark	Antique Buildings Ltd (G-BRZF)	
G-IDWR	Hughes 369HS	Copley Electrical Contractors (G-AXEJ)	
G-IEEF	Raj Hamsa X'Air Hawk	P. J. Sheehy	
G-IEIO	PA-34-200T Seneca II	Sky Zone Servicos Aereos Lda	
G-IEJH	Jodel 150A	A. Turner & D. Worth (G-BPAM)	
G-IENN	Cirrus SR20	Renneta Ltd (G-TSGE)	
G-IFAB	Cessna F.182Q	Bristol & West Aeroplane Club Ltd	
G-IFBP	AS.350B2 Ecureuil	Frank Bird Aviation	
G-IFFR	PA-32 Cherokee Six 300	Brendair (G-BWVO)	
G-IFFY	Flylight Dragonfly	R. D. Leigh	
G-IFIF	Cameron TR-60 balloon	M. G. Howard	
G-IFIT	PA-31-350 Navajo Chieftain	Dart Group PLC (G-NABI/G-MARG)	
G-IFLE	Aerotechnik EV-97 TeamEurostar UK	M. R. Smith	
G-IFLI	AA-5A Cheetah	C. M. Petherbridge	
G-IFLP	PA-34-200T Seneca II	ACS Aviation Ltd	
G-IFRH	Agusta A109C	Helicopter Services Ltd	
G-IFTE	HS.125 Srs 700B	Albion Aviation Management Ltd (G-BVFI)	
G-IFTF	BAe 125 Srs 800B	Albion Aviation Management Ltd (G-RCEJ/ G-GEIL)	
G-IFWD	Schempp-Hirth Ventus cT	J. C. Ferguson & C. J. Hamilton	
G-IGEL	Cameron N-90 balloon	Computacenter Ltd	
G-IGGL	SOCATA TB10 Tobago	G-IGGL Flying Group (G-BYDC)	
G-IGHH	Enstrom 480	Raw Sports Ltd	
G-IGHT	Van's RV-8	E. A. Yates	
G-IGIA	AS.350B3 Ecureuil	Faloria Ltd	
G-IGIE	SIAI Marchetti SF.260	Flew LLP	
G-IGII	Shaw Europa	C. D. Peacock	
G-IGLE	Cameron V-90 balloon	G-IGLE Group	
G-IGLI	Schempp-Hirth Duo Discus T	C. Fox	
G-IGLL	AutoGyro MTO Sport	I. M. Donnellan	
G-IGLY	P & M Aviation Quik GT450	K. G. Grayson & R. D. Leigh	
G-IGLZ	Champion 8KCAB	Woodgate Aviation (IOM) Ltd	
G-IGPW	Eurocopter EC 120B	PDQ Rotor Ltd (G-CBRI)	
G-IGTE	SIAI Marchetti F.260	D. Fletcher & J. J. Watts	
G-IGWT	Bombardier CL600-2B19	Skywings Ltd	
G-IGZZ	Robinson R44 II	Rivermead Aviation Ltd	
G-IHOP	Cameron Z-31 balloon	N. W. Roberts	
G-IHOT	Aerotechnik EV-97 Eurostar UK	Exodos Airsports Ltd	
G-IIAC	Aeronca 11AC Chief	Fox Flying Group (G-BTPY)	
G-IIAI	Mudry CAP.232	J. Bennett	
G-IIAN	Aero Designs Pulsar	I. G. Harrison	
G-IICC	Van's RV-4	R. H. Clifton (G-MARX)	
G-IICT	Schempp-Hirth Ventus 2Ct	P. McLean	
G-IICX	Schempp-Hirth Ventus 2cxT	S. G. Jones	
G-IIDC	Midget Mustang	D. Cooke (G-IIMT/G-BDGA)	
G-IIDI	Extra EA.300/L	Power Aerobatics Ltd (G-XTRS)	
G-IIDR	Ikarus C42 FB100	D. M. Richards	
G-IIDY	Aerotek Pitts S-2B Special	The S-2B Group (G-BPVP)	
G-IIEX	Extra EA.300/L	S. G. Jones	
G-IIFM	Edge 360	F. L. McGee	
G-IIFX	Marganski MDM-1	Swift Aerobatic Display Team	
G-IIGI	Van's RV-4	T. D. R. Hardy	
G-IIHI	Extra 300/SC	YAK UK Ltd	
G-IIID	Dan Rihn DR.107 One Design	D. A. Kean	
G-IIIE	Aerotek Pitts S-2B Special	Dianagomesdasilva Aerobatics	
G-IIIG	Boeing Stearman A75N1	Stearman G-IIIG Group /Belgium (G-BSDR)	
G-IIII	Aerotek Pitts S-2B Special	Aerospace Optics Ltd	
G-IIIK	Extra EA.300/SC	Extra 300SC LLP	

Notes	Reg.	Type	Owner or Operator
	G-IIIL	Pitts S-1T Special	Empyreal Airways Ltd
	G-IIIM	Stolp SA.100 Starduster	H. Mackintosh
	G-IIIO	Schempp-Hirth Ventus 2CM	S. J. Clark
	G-IIIP	Pitts S-1D Special	R. S. Grace (G-BLAG)
	G-IIIR	Pitts S-1S Special	R. O. Rogers
	G-IIIT	Aerotek Pitts S-2A Special	Aerobatic Displays Ltd
	G-IIIX	Pitts Super Stinker 11-260	S. D. Barnard & A. N. R. Houghton
	G-IIIX	Pitts S-1S Special	D. S. T. Eggleton (G-LBAT/G-UCCI/G-BIYN)
	G-IIIZ	Sukhoi Su-26M	P. M. M. Bonhommy
	G-IIJC	Midget Mustang	Iconic Aviation Ltd (G-CEKU)
	G-IIMI	Extra EA.300/L	Firebird Aerobatics Ltd
	G-IINI	Van's RV-9A	Parachuting Aircraft Ltd
	G-IIOO	Schleicher ASW-27-18E	M. Clarke
	G-IIPB	DR.107 One Design	P. D. Baisden
	G-IIPT	Robinson R22 Beta	W. M. Gray (G-FUSI)
	G-IIPZ	Mudry CAP.232	S. P. R. Madle & J. Murfitt
	G-IIRG	Stoddard-Hamilton Glasair IIS RG	A. C. Lang
	G-IIRI	Xtreme Air Sbach 300	One Sky Aviation LLP
	G-IIRP	Mudry CAP.232	R. J. Pickin
	G-IIRV	Van's RV-7	D. S. Watson
	G-IIRW	Van's RV-8	R. Winward
	G-IITC	Mudry CAP.232	T. W. Cassells
	G-IIXF	Van's RV-7	C. A. & S. Noujaim
	G-IIXI	Extra EA.300/L	B. Nielsen
	G-IIXX	Parsons 2-seat gyroplane	J. M. Montgomerie
	G-IIYK	Yakovlev Yak-50	D. A. Hammant
	G-IIZI	Extra EA.300	Power Aerobatics Ltd
	G-IJAC	Light Aero Avid Speedwing Mk 4	I. J. A. Charlton
	G-IJAG	Cessna 182T Skylane	AG Group
	G-IJBB	Enstrom 480	R. P. Bateman (G-LIVA/G-PBTT)
	G-IJMC	Magni M-16 Tandem Trainer	R. F. G. Moyle (G-POSA/G-BVJM)
	G-IJOE	PA-28RT-201T Turbo Arrow IV	J. H. Bailey
	G-IKAH	Slingsby T.51 Dart 17R	K. A. Hale
	G-IKAP	Cessna T.303	T. M. Beresford
	G-IKBP	PA-28-161 Warrior II	F. J. Page
	G-IKEA	Cameron 120 Ikea SS balloon	IKEA Ltd
	G-IKES	Stoddard-Hamilton GlaStar	M. Stow
	G-IKEV	Jabiru UL-450	D. I. Taylor
	G-IKON	Van's RV-4	S. Sampson
	G-IKOS	Cessna 550 Citation Bravo	Medox Enterprises Ltd
	G-IKRK	Shaw Europa	K. R. Kesterton
	G-IKRS	Ikarus C.42 FK UK Cyclone	K. J. Warburton
	G-IKUS	Ikarus C.42 FB UK Cyclone	C. I. Law
	G-ILBO	Rolladen-Schneider LS3-A	J. P. Gilbert
	G-ILBT	Cessna 182T	G. E. Gilbert
	G-ILDA	VS.361 Spitfire HF.IX (SM520 : KJ-1)	Spitfire Display Ltd (G-BXHZ)
	G-ILEE	Colt 56A balloon	G. I. Lindsay
	G-ILES	Cameron O-90 balloon	G. N. Lantos
	G-ILIB	PZL-Bielsko SZD-36A	D. Poll
	G-ILLE	Boeing Stearman A75L3 (379)	M. Minkler
	G-ILLG	Robinson R44 II	C. B. Ellis
	G-ILLY	PA-28-181 Archer II	R. A. & G. M. Spiers
	G-ILPD	SIAI Marchetti F.260C	M. Mignini/Italy
	G-ILRS	Ikarus C.42 FB UK Cyclone	J. J. Oliver
	G-ILSE	Corby CJ-1 Starlet	S. Stride
	G-ILTS	PA-32 Cherokee Six 300	P. G. Teasdale & Foremans Aviation Ltd (G-CVOK)
	G-ILUA	Alpha R2160I	A. R. Haynes
	G-ILYA	Agusta-Bell 206B Jet Ranger II	Elmdawn Ltd (G-MHMH/G-HOLZ/G-CDBT)
	G-IMAB	Europa XS	T. J. Price
	G-IMAC	Canadair CL-600-2A12 Challenger	Gama Aviation Ltd
	G-IMAD	Cessna 172P	Leus Aviation Ltd
	G-IMAG	Colt 77A balloon ★	Balloon Preservation Group
	G-IMBI	QAC Quickie 1	J. D. King (G-BWIT)
	G-IMBL	Bell 407	Northern Flights Ltd
	G-IMBY	Pietenpol AirCamper	C. Brockis
	G-IMCD	Van's RV-7	I. G. McDowell
	G-IMEA	Beech 200 Super King Air	2 Excel Aviation Ltd (G-OWAX)

Reg.	Type	Owner or Operator	Notes
G-IMEC	PA-31 Navajo C	Planeco Ltd (G-BFOM)	
G-IMEL	Rotary Air Force RAF 2000 GTX-SE	N. A. Smith	
G-IMHK	P & M Quik R	J. Waite	
G-IMME	Zenair CH.701 STOL	M. Spearman	
G-IMMI	Escapade Kid	J. Pearce	
G-IMMY	Robinson R44	Tony Cain Leisure Services	
G-IMNY	Escapade 912	D. S. Bremner	
G-IMOK	Hoffmann HK-36R Super Dimona	A. L. Garfield	
G-IMPS	Skyranger Nynja 912S	B. J. Killick	
G-IMPX	Rockwell Commander 112B	Impatex Computer Systems Ltd	
G-IMPY	Light Aero Avid Flyer C	T. R. C. Griffin	
G-IMUP	Tanarg/Ixess 15 912S (1)	A. Wakeham	
G-INCA	Glaser-Dirks DG.400	K. D. Hook	
G-INCE	Skyranger 912(2)	N.P. Sleigh	
G-INDC	Cessna T.303	J-Ross Developments Ltd	
G-INDI	Pitts S-2C Special	L. Coesens	
G-INDX	Robinson R44	Kinetic Computers Ltd	
G-INDY	Robinson R44	Lincoln Aviation	
G-INGA	Thunder Ax8-84 balloon	M. L. J. Ritchie	
G-INGS	American Champion 8KCAB	Scotflight Ltd	
G-INII	Pitts S-1 Special	C. Davidson (G-BTEF)	
G-INJA	Ikarus C42 FB UK	C. E. Walls	
G-INNI	Jodel D.112	Clipgate Group	
G-INNY	SE-5A (replica) (F5459:Y)	M. J. Speakman	
G-INSR	Cameron N-90 balloon	P. J. Waller	
G-INTS	Van's RV-4	N. J. F. Campbell	
G-INTV	AS.355F2 Ecureuil 2	Arena Aviation Ltd (G-JETU)	
G-IOCO	Beech 58 Baron	Anchor Shipping Agents SRL/Italy	
G-IOFR	Lindstrand LBL-105A balloon	RAF Halton Hot Air Balloon Club	
G-IOIA	I.I.I. Sky Arrow 650T	P.J. Lynch, P.G. Ward, N.J.C. Ray	
G-IOMI	Cameron Z-105 balloon	Elgas SRL/Italy	
G-IONX	Dassault Falcon 7X	TAG Aviation (UK) Ltd	
G-IOOI	Robin DR.400/160	N. B. Mason	
G-IOOP	Christen Eagle II	A. P. S. Maynard	
G-IOOZ	Agusta A109S Grand	Hundred Percent Aviation Ltd	
G-IOPT	Cessna 182P	Indy Oscar Group	
G-IORG	Robinson R22 Beta	Staffordshire Helicopters Training Ltd	
G-IORV	Van's RV-10	A. F. S. & B. L. Caldecourt	
G-IOSI	Jodel DR.1051	D. C. & M. Brooks	
G-IOSL	Van's RV-9	S. Leach (G-CFIX)	
G-IOSO	Jodel DR.1050	A. E. Jackson	
G-IOWE	Shaw Europa XS	P. G. Leonard	
G-IPAD	Cessna F.172M	D. G. Smith (G-BCCD)	
G-IPAT	Jabiru SP	H. Adams	
G-IPAX	Cessna 560XL Citation Excel	Pacific Aviation Ltd	
G-IPEP	Beech 95-B55 Baron	P. E. T. Price (G-FABM)	
G-IPJF	Robinson R44 II	Specialist Group International Ltd (G-RGNT/ G-DMCG)	
G-IPKA	Alpi Pioneer 300	M. E. Hughes	
G-IPOD	Europa XS	J. Wighton (G-CEBV)	
G-IPSI	Grob G.109B	D. G. Margetts (G-BMLO)	
G-IPUP	Beagle B.121 Pup 2	Swift Flying Group	
G-IRAF	RAF 2000 GTX-SE gyroplane	A. W. Buckey & J. M. Kent	
G-IRAL	Thruster T600N 450	J. Giraldez	
G-IRAP	Bombardier BD-700-1A10 Global Express	TAG Aviation (UK) Ltd (G-CJME)	
G-IRAR	Van's RV-9	J. Maplethorpe	
G-IRED	Ikarus C42 FB100	Red-Air UK	
G-IREN	SOCATA TB-20 Trinidad GT	Chios Aeroclub	
G-IRGJ	Champion 7ECA Citabria Aurora	T. A. Mann	
G-IRIS	AA-5B Tiger	C. Nichol (G-BIXU)	
G-IRJX	Avro RJX-100 ★	Manchester Heritage Museum ✓	
G-IRKB	PA-28R-201 Arrow III	M. Ruter	
G-IRLE	Schempp-Hirth Ventus cT	D. J. Scholey	
G-IRLI	P & M Quik GTR	A. S. Markey	
G-IRLY	Colt 90A balloon	C. E. R. Smart	
G-IRLZ	Lindstrand LBL-60X balloon	A. M. Holly	
G-IROE	Flight Design CTSW	S. Roe	

Notes	Reg.	Type	Owner or Operator
	G-IRON	Shaw Europa XS	T. M. Clark
	G-IROS	Rotorsport UK Calidus	JB Aviation Ltd
	G-IRPC	Cessna 182Q	A. T. Jeans (G-BSKM)
	G-IRPW	Europa XS	R. P. Wheelwright
	G-IRSH	Embraer EMB-135RJ	Legemb Ltd
	G-IRTM	DG Flugzeugbau DG-1000M	ATSI Ltd
	G-IRYC	Schweizer 269-1	Virage Helicopter Acadewmy LLP
	G-ISAR	Cessna 421C	Rescue Global Management Services Ltd (G-BHKJ)
	G-ISAX	PA-28-181 Archer III	Spectrum Flying Group
	G-ISBD	Alpi Pioneer 300 Hawk	B. Davies
	G-ISCD	Czech Sport Aircraft Sportcruiser	P. W. Shepherd
	G-ISDB	PA-28-161 Warrior II	Action Air Services Ltd (G-BWET)
	G-ISDN	Boeing Stearman A75N1	D. R. L. Jones
	G-ISEH	Cessna 182R	S. J. Nash (G-BIWS)
	G-ISEL	Best Off Skyranger 912 (2)	P. A. Robertson
	G-ISEW	P & M Quik GT450	S. P. McVeigh
	G-ISFC	PA-31-310 Turbo Navajo B	T. M. Latiff (G-BNEF)
	G-ISHA	PA-28-161 Warrior III	LAC Flying School
	G-ISHK	Cessna 172S	Matchpage Ltd
	G-ISLB	BAe Jetstream 3201	Blue Islands Ltd
	G-ISLC	BAe Jetstream 3202	Blue Islands Ltd
	G-ISLD	BAe Jetstream 3202	Blue Islands Ltd
	G-ISLF	Aerospatiale ATR-42-500	Blue Islands Ltd
	G-ISMA	Van's RV-7	S. Marriott (G-STAF)
	G-ISMO	Robinson R22 Beta	Moy Motorsport Ltd
	G-ISMS	Sorrell SNS-7 Hyperbipe	D. G. Curran (G-HIPE)
	G-ISON	AirBike UK Elite	AirBike UK Ltd
	G-ISPH	Bell 206B JetRanger 2	Blades Aviation (UK) LLP (G-OPJM)
	G-ISSV	Eurocopter EC 155B1	Bristow Helicopters Ltd
	G-ISSY	Eurocopter EC 120B	D. R. Williams (G-CBCG)
	G-ISZA	Aerotek Pitts S-2A Special	F. L. McGee (G-HISS/G-BLVU)
	G-ITAF	SIAI-Marchetti SF.260AM	N. A. Whatling
	G-ITAR	Magni M-16C Tandem Trainer	B. Lesslie
	G-ITAV	Eurocopter EC225LP Super Puma	CHC Scotia Ltd
	G-ITBT	Alpi Pioneer 300 Hawk	F. Paolini
	G-ITII	Aerotech Pitts S-2A Special	P. J. Kirkpatrick
	G-ITIM	Dassault Falcon 7X	TAG Aviation (UK) Ltd
	G-ITOI	Cameron N-90 balloon	Flying Pictures Ltd
	G-ITPH	Robinson R44 II	Helicopter Services Europe Ltd
	G-ITVM	Lindstrand LBL-105A balloon	Elmer Balloon Team
	G-ITWB	DHC.1 Chipmunk 22	I. T. Whitaker-Bethe
	G-IUAN	Cessna 525 CitationJet	R. F. Celada SPA/Italy
	G-IUII	Aerostar Yakovlev Yak-52	A. L. Grisay
	G-IUMB	Schleicher ASW-20L	M. S. Szymkowicz
	G-IVAC	Airtour AH-77B balloon	T. D. Gibbs
	G-IVAL	CAB CAP-10B	I. Valentine
	G-IVAN	Shaw TwinEze	A. M. Aldridge
	G-IVAR	Yakovlev Yak-50	A. H. Soper
	G-IVEN	Robinson R44 II	OKR Group/Ireland
	G-IVER	Shaw Europa XS	I. Phillips
	G-IVES	Shaw Europa	M. W. Olliver (G-JOST)
	G-IVET	Shaw Europa	K. J. Fraser
	G-IVII	Vqn's RV-7	M. A. N. Newall
	G-IVIV	Robinson R44	D. Brown
	G-IVJM	Agusta A109E Power	Air Harrods Ltd (G-MOMO)
	G-IVOR	Aeronca 11AC Chief	South Western Aeronca Group
	G-IWIN	Raj Hamsa X'Air Hawk	H. R. Bethune
	G-IWIZ	Flylight Dragonfly	S. Wilson
	G-IWON	Cameron V-90 balloon	D. P. P. Jenkinson (G-BTCV)
	G-IWRB	Agusta A109A-II	Maison Air Ltd (G-VIPT)
	G-IXII	Christen Eagle II	Eagle Flying Group (G-BPZI)
	G-IXXI	Schleicher ASW-27-18E	G. P. Stingemore
	G-IYRO	RAF2000 GTX-SE	R. Boese (G-BXDD)
	G-IZIP	Learjet 45	Gama Aviation Ltd (G-OLDW)
	G-IZIT	Rans S.6-116 Coyote II	D. J. Flower

Reg.	Type	Owner or Operator	Notes
G-IZZI	Cessna T.182T	D. J. & E-S Lucey	
G-IZZS	Cessna 172S	Air Claire Ltd	
G-IZZZ	Champion 8KCAB	Phoenix Flyers Ltd	
G-JAAB	Avtech Jabiru UL	R. Holt	
G-JABB	Avtech Jabiru UL	R. J. Sutherland	
G-JABE	Jabiru Aircraft Jabiru UL-D	H. M. Manning and P. M. Jones	
G-JABI	Jabiru Aircraft Jabiru J400	Anvilles Flying Group	
G-JABJ	Jabiru Aircraft Jabiru J400	L. B. W. & F. H. Hancock	
G-JABS	Avtech Jabiru UL-450	Jabiru Flying Group	
G-JABU	Jabiru J430	S. D. Miller	
G-JABY	Avtech Jabiru UL-450	F. Patterson & B. J. Robe	
G-JABZ	Avtech Jabiru UL-450	J. T. Grant	
G-JACA	PA-28-161 Warrior II	The Pilot Centre Ltd	
G-JACB	PA-28-181 Archer III	P. R. Coe (G-PNNI)	
G-JACH	PA-28-181 Archer III	Alderney Flight Training Ltd (G-IDPH)	
G-JACI	Bell 206L-4 LongRanger IV	Morgan Airborne LLP	
G-JACK	Cessna 421C	JCT 600 Ltd	
G-JACO	Avtech Jabiru UL	C. D. Matthews/Ireland	
G-JACS	PA-28-181 Archer III	Modern Air (UK) Ltd	
G-JADJ	PA-28-181 Archer III	ACS Aviation Ltd	
G-JADW	Ikarus C42 FB80	J. W. & D. A. Wilding	
G-JAEE	Van's RV-6A	J. A. E. Edser	
G-JAES	Bell 206B JetRanger 3	Helicom Ltd (G-STOX/G-BNIR)	
G-JAFT	Diamond DA.42 Twin Star	Atlantic Flight Training Ltd	
G-JAGS	Cessna FRA.150L	RAF Marham Flying Club (G-BAUY)	
G-JAGY	Europa XS	J. S. Chaggar	
G-JAIR	Mainair Blade	G. Spittlehouse	
G-JAJA	Robinson R44 II	J. D. Richardson	
G-JAJB	AA-5A Cheetah	Active Aviation Ltd	
G-JAJK	PA-31-350 Navajo Chieftain	Blue Sky Investments Ltd (G-OLDB/G-DIXI)	
G-JAJP	Avtech Jabiru UL	J. Anderson	
G-JAKF	Robinson R44 Raven II	J. G. Froggatt	
G-JAKI	Mooney M.20R	J. M. Moss & D. M. Abrahamson	
G-JAKS	PA-28 Cherokee 160	K. Harper (G-ARVS)	
G-JAMA	Schweizer 269C-1	R. J. Scott	
G-JAME	Zenair CH 601UL	A. Batters (G-CDFZ)	
G-JAMP	PA-28-151 Warrior	Lapwing Flying Group Ltd (G-BRJU)	
G-JAMY	Shaw Europa XS	J. P. Sharp	
G-JAMZ	P & M QuikR	S. Cuthbertson	
G-JANA	PA-28-181 Archer II	S. Hoo-Hing	
G-JANB	Colt Flying Bottle SS balloon	Justerini & Brooks Ltd	
G-JANI	Robinson R44	JT Helicopters Ltd	
G-JANN	PA-34-220T Seneca III	D. J. Whitcombe	
G-JANS	Cessna FR.172J	S. F. Scott	
G-JANT	PA-28-181 Archer II	Janair Aviation Ltd	
G-JAOC	Best Off Sky Ranger Swift 912S(1)	M. J. Stolworthy & K. G. Winter	
G-JAPK	Grob G.130A Twin II Acro	Cairngorm Gliding Club	
G-JARM	Robinson R44	J. Armstrong	
G-JASE	PA-28-161 Warrior II	Mid-Anglia School of Flying	
G-JASS	Beech B200 Super King Air	Platinum Executive Aviation LLP	
G-JAVO	PA-28-161 Warrior II	Victor Oscar Ltd (G-BSXW)	
G-JAWC	Pegasus Quantum 15-912	M. J. Robbins	
G-JAWZ	Pitts S-1S Special	A. R. Harding	
G-JAXS	Avtech Jabiru UL	J. P. Pullin	
G-JAYI	Auster J/1 Autocrat	Aviation Heritage Ltd	
G-JAYS	Skyranger 912S(1)	R. A. Green	
G-JAYZ	CZAW Sportcruiser	J. Williams	
G-JBAS	Neico Lancair 200	A. Slater	
G-JBBZ	AS.350B3 Ecureuil	BZ Air Ltd	
G-JBDB	Agusta-Bell 206B JetRanger	Dicksons Van World Ltd (G-OOPS/G-BNRD)	
G-JBDH	Robin DR.400/180	W. A. Clark	
G-JBEN	Mainair Blade 912	G. J. Bentley	
G-JBII	Robinson R22 Beta	Alan Mann Aviation Group Ltd (G-BXLA)	
G-JBIS	Cessna 550 Citation II	247 Jet Ltd	
G-JBIZ	Cessna 550 Citation II	247 Jet Ltd	
G-JBKA	Robinson R44	J. G. Harrison	
G-JBLZ	Cessna 550 Citation Bravo	247 Jet Ltd	
G-JBRE	Rotorsport UK MT-03	J. B. R. Elliot	
G-JBRG	Agusta A109A II	Jetworx Ltd (G-TMUR/G-CEPO)	
G-JBRN	Cessna 182S	Williams Industrial Services Ltd (G-RITZ)	

Notes	Reg.	Type	Owner or Operator
	G-JBRS	Van's RV-8	C. Jobling
	G-JBSP	Avtech Jabiru SP-470	C. R. James
	G-JBTR	Van's RV-8	R. A. Ellis
	G-JBUL	Best Off Skyranger 912(2)	J. Bulpin (G-CDJC)
	G-JBUZ	Robin DR400/180R Remorqueur	D. A. Saywell
	G-JCAP	Robinson R22 Beta	Just Plane Trading Ltd
	G-JCAS	PA-28-181 Archer II	Charlie Alpha Ltd
	G-JCBB	Gulfstream V-SP	J. C. Bamford Excavators Ltd
	G-JCBJ	Sikorsky S-76C	J. C. Bamford Excavators Ltd
	G-JCBX	Dassault Falcon 900EX	J. C. Bamford Excavators Ltd
	G-JCJC	Colt Flying Jeans SS balloon	Magical Adventures Ltd
	G-JCKT	Stemme S.10VT	J. C. Taylor
	G-JCMW	Rand KR-2	S. H. Leahy
	G-JCOP	Eurocopter AS.350B3 Ecureuil	Optimum Ltd
	G-JCUB	PA-18 Super Cub 135	Vintage Aircraft Flying Group
	G-JCWM	Robinson R44 II	M. L. J. Goff
	G-JCWS	Reality Escapade 912(2)	J. C. W. Seward
	G-JDBC	PA-34-200T Seneca II	JD Aviation Ltd (G-BDEF)
	G-JDEE	SOCATA TB20 Trinidad	JDEE Group
	G-JDEL	Jodel 150	K. F. & R. Richardson (G-JDLI)
	G-JDPB	PA-28R-201T Turbo Arrow III	BC Arrow Ltd (G-DNCS)
	G-JDRD	Alpi Pioneer 300	R. J. Doughton
	G-JEAF	Fokker F.27 Friendship Mk.500	Executive Jet Support Ltd
	G-JEAJ	BAe 146-200	Trident Aviation Leasing Services (Jersey) Ltd (G-OLCA)
	G-JEBS	Cessna 172S	Patriot Aviation Ltd
	G-JECE	DHC.8-402 Dash Eight	Flybe.com
	G-JECF	DHC.8-402 Dash Eight	Flybe.com
	G-JECG	DHC.8-402 Dash Eight	Flybe.com
	G-JECH	DHC.8-402 Dash Eight	Flybe.com
	G-JECI	DHC.8-402 Dash Eight	Flybe.com
	G-JECJ	DHC.8-402 Dash Eight	Flybe.com
	G-JECK	DHC.8-402 Dash Eight	Flybe.com
	G-JECL	DHC.8-402 Dash Eight	Flybe.com
	G-JECM	DHC.8-402 Dash Eight	Flybe.com
	G-JECN	DHC.8-402 Dash Eight	Flybe.com
	G-JECO	DHC.8-402 Dash Eight	Flybe.com
	G-JECP	DHC.8-402 Dash Eight	Flybe.com
	G-JECR	DHC.8-402 Dash Eight	Flybe.com
	G-JECX	DHC.8-402 Dash Eight	Flybe.com
	G-JECY	DHC.8-402 Dash Eight	Flybe.com
	G-JECZ	DHC.8-402 Dash Eight	Flybe.com
	G-JEDH	Robin DR.400/180	J. B. Hoolahan
	G-JEDI	DHC.8-402 Dash Eight	Amra Leasing Ltd
	G-JEDK	DHC.8-402 Dash Eight	Amra Leasing Ltd
	G-JEDM	DHC.8-402 Dash Eight	Flybe.com
	G-JEDN	DHC.8-402 Dash Eight	Flybe.com
	G-JEDO	DHC.8-402 Dash Eight	Flybe.com
	G-JEDP	DHC.8-402 Dash Eight	Flybe.com
	G-JEDR	DHC.8-402 Dash Eight	Flybe com
	G-JEDS	Andreasson BA-4B	S. B. Jedburgh (G-BEBT)
	G-JEDT	DHC.8-402 Dash Eight	Flybe com
	G-JEDU	DHC.8-402 Dash Eight	Flybe com
	G-JEDV	DHC.8-402 Dash Eight	Flybe.com
	G-JEDW	DHC.8-402 Dash Eight	Flybe.com
	G-JEEP	Evektor EV-97 Eurostar	G-JEEP Group (G-CBNK)
	G-JEFA	Robinson R44	Simlot Ltd
	G-JEJE	RAF 2000 GTX-SE gyroplane	A. F. Smallacombe
	G-JEJH	Jodel DR.1050 Ambassadeur	Bredon Hill Flying Group
	G-JEMA	BAe ATP	PTB (Emerald) Pty Ltd
	G-JEMC	BAe ATP	PTB (Emerald) Pty Ltd
	G-JEMI	Lindstrand LBL-90A balloon	J. A. Lawton
	G-JEMM	Jodel DR.1050	D. W. Garbe
	G-JENA	Mooney M.20K	Jena Air Force
	G-JENI	Cessna R.182	R. A. Bentley
	G-JENK	Ikarus C42 FB80	P. J. Oakey
	G-JERO	Shaw Europa XS	P. Jenkinson and N. Robshaw
	G-JESE	AS.355F2 Ecureuil 2	Arena Aviation Ltd (G-EMHH/G-BYKH)
	G-JESI	AS.350B Ecureuil	Staske Construction Ltd (G-JOSS/G-WILX/ G-RAHM/G-UNIC/G-COLN/G-BHIV)

Reg.	Type	Owner or Operator	Notes
G-JESS	PA-28R-201T Turbo Arrow III	R. E. Trawicki (G-REIS)	
G-JETA	Cessna 550 Citation II	Icon Two Ltd (G-RDBS)	
G-JETC	Cessna 550 Citation II	Interceptor Aviation Ltd (G-JCFR)	
G-JETH	Hawker Sea Hawk FGA.6 (XE489) ★	P. G. Vallance Ltd/Charlwood	
G-JETM	Gloster Meteor T.7 (VZ638) ★	P. G. Vallance Ltd/Charlwood	
G-JETO	Cessna 550 Citation II	Air Charter Scotland Ltd (G-RVHT)	
G-JETX	Bell 206B JetRanger 3	Morgan Airborne LLP	
G-JETZ	Hughes 369E	GJP Helicopters Ltd	
G-JEWL	Van's RV-7	H. A. & J. S. Jewell	
G-JEZA	Agusta AW.139	CHC Scotia Ltd	
G-JEZZ	Skyranger 912S(1)	N. J. Brownlow & P. W. Day	
G-JFAN	P & M Quik R	J. F. A. Nicol	
G-JFDI	Dynamic WT9 UK	M. S. Gregory	
G-JFER	Rockwell Commander 114B	P. S. Jones (G-HPSE)	
G-JFLO	Aerospool Dynamic WT9 UK	J. Flood	
G-JFLY	Schleicher ASW-24	Cambridge Gliding Club Ltd	
G-JFMK	Zenair CH.701SP	J. D. Pearson	
G-JFRV	Van's RV-7A	J. H. Fisher	
G-JFWI	Cessna F.172N	Staryear Ltd	
G-JGBI	Bell 206L-4 LongRanger	Dorbcrest Homes Ltd	
G-JGCA	VS.361 Spitfire LF.IXe (TE517)	P. M. Andrews (G-CCIX/G-BIXP)	
G-JGMN	CASA 1.131E Jungmann 2000	P. D. Scandrett	
G-JGSI	Pegasus Quantum 15-912	A. Fern	
G-JHAA	Csameron Z-90 balloon	C. L. Thompson	
G-JHAC	Cessna FRA.150L	J. H. A. Clarke (G-BACM)	
G-JHDD	Czech Sport Aircraft Sportcruiser	D. Draper & J. W. Hagley	
G-JHEW	Robinson R22 Beta	Heli Air Ltd	
G-JHKP	Shaw Europa XS	J. D. Heykoop	
G-JHNY	Cameron A.210 balloon	Floarting Sensations Ltd	
G-JHPC	Cessna 182T	J. R. Turner	
G-JHYS	Shaw Europa	G-JHYS Group	
G-JIBO	BAe Jetstream 3102	Blue Islands Ltd (G-OJSA/G-BTYG)	
G-JIFI	Schempp-Hirth Duo Discus T	620 Syndicate	
G-JIII	Stolp SA.300 Starduster Too	VTIO Co	
G-JIIL	Pitts S-2A Special	A. G. Griffiths	
G-JILY	Robinson R44	R. R. Orr	
G-JIMB	Beagle B.121 Pup 1	K. D. H. Gray & P. G. Fowler (G-AWWF)	
G-JIMC	Van's RV-7	J. Chapman	
G-JIMH	Cessna F.152 II	D. J. Howell (G-SHAH)	
G-JIMM	Shaw Europa XS	J. Riley	
G-JIMP	Messerschmitt Bf 109G-2	G. B. E. Pearce	
G-JIMZ	Van's RV-4	J.W.Hale	
G-JINI	Cameron V-77 balloon	I. R. Warrington	
G-JINX	Silence SA.180 Twister	P. M. Wells	
G-JIVE	MDH Hughes 369E	Sleekform Ltd (G-DRAR)	
G-JJAB	Jabiru J400	K. Ingebrigtsen	
G-JJAN	PA-28-181 Archer II	J. S. Develin & Z. Islam	
G-JJEN	PA-28-181 Archer III	K. M. R. Jenkins	
G-JJFB	Eurocopter EC.120B Colibri	J. G. Rhoden	
G-JJIL	Extra EA.300/L	Link Goals SP ZOO	
G-JJSI	BAe 125 Srs 800B	Gama Leasing Ltd (G-OMGG)	
G-JJWL	Robinson R44	Willbeth Ltd	
G-JKAY	Robinson R44	Jamiroquai Ltd	
G-JKEL	Van's RV-7	J. D. Kelsall (G-LNNE)	
G-JKKK	Cessna 172S	P. Eaton	
G-JKMH	Diamond DA42 Twin Star	ADR Aviation	
G-JKMJ	Diamond DA42 Twin Star	Medox Enterprises Ltd	
G-JKRV	Schempp-Hirth Arcus T	G-JKRV Syndicate	
G-JLAT	Aerotechnik EV-97 Eurostar	J. Latimer	
G-JLCA	PA-34-200T Seneca II	Tayside Aviation Ltd (G-BOKE)	
G-JLEE	Agusta-Bell 206B JetRanger 3	J. S. Lee (G-JOKE/G-CSKY/G-TALY)	
G-JLHS	Beech A36 Bonanza	I. G. Meredith	
G-JLIN	PA-28-161 Cadet	JH Sandham Aviation	
G-JLLT	Aerotechnik EV-97 Eurostar	J. Latimer	
G-JLRW	Beech 76 Duchess	Airways Flight Training	

Notes	Reg.	Type	Owner or Operator
	G-JMAA	Boeing 757-3CQ	Thomas Cook Airlines Ltd
	G-JMAB	Boeing 757-3CQ	Thomas Cook Airlines Ltd
	G-JMAC	BAe Jetstream 4100 ★	Jetstream Club, Liverpool Marriott Hotel South, Speke (G-JAMD/G-JXLI)
	G-JMAL	Jabiru UL-D	A. D. Sutton
	G-JMCD	Boeing 757-25F	Thomas Cook Airlines Ltd
	G-JMCE	Boeing 757-25F	Thomas Cook Airlines Ltd ✓
	G-JMCG	Boeing 757-2G5	Thomas Cook Airlines Ltd
	G-JMCL	Boeing 737-322	Atlantic Airlines Ltd
	G-JMCM	Boeing 737-3YO	Atlantic Airlines Ltd
	G-JMDI	Schweizer 269C	D. A. Sempers (G-FLAT)
	G-JMED	Learjet 35A	Air Medical Fleet Ltd, Argyll Ltd & Provident Partners Ltd
	G-JMJR	Cameron Z-90	J. M. Reck/France
	G-JMKE	Cessna 172S	115CR (146) Ltd
	G-JMKM	AutoGyro MTO Sport	K. O. Maurer
	G-JMMY	PA-28R-200 Cherokee Arrow B	JMMY Ltd (G-GYMM/G-AYWW)
	G-JMON	Agusta A109A-II	Elmridge Ltd (G-RFDS/G-BOLA)
	G-JMOS	PA-34-220T Seneca V	Moss Aviation LLP
	G-JMRV	Van's RV-7	J. W. Marshall
	G-JMTS	Robin DR.400/180	G-JMTS Group
	G-JNAS	AA-5A Cheetah	C. J. Williams
	G-JNET	Robinson R22 Beta	R. L. Hartshorn
	G-JNMA	VS.379 Spitfire FR.Mk.XIVe	P. M. Andrews
	G-JNNB	Colt 90A balloon	N. A. P. Godfrey
	G-JNSC	Schempp-Hirth Janus CT	D. S. Bramwell
	G-JNUS	Schempp-Hirth Janus C	N. A. Peatfield
	G-JOAL	Beech B200 Super King Air	South Coast Air Charter LLP
	G-JOBA	P & M Quik GT450	B. Hall
	G-JOBS	Cessna T182T	Tech Travel Ltd (G-BZVF)
	G-JODL	Jodel D.1050/M	D. Silsbury
	G-JOED	Lindstrand LBL-77A balloon	G. R. Down
	G-JOEY	BN-2A Mk III-2 Trislander	Aurigny Air Services (G-BDGG)
	G-JOHA	Cirrus SR20	N. Harris
	G-JOID	Cirrus SR20	I. F. Doubtfire
	G-JOJO	Cameron A-210 balloon	A. C. Rawson & J. J. Rudoni
	G-JOKR	Extra EA.300/L	C. Jefferies
	G-JOLY	Cessna 120	B. V. Meade
	G-JONB	Robinson R22 Beta	J. Bignall
	G-JONG	Rotorway Executive 162F	J. V. George
	G-JONL	CZAW Sportcruiser	J. R. Linford
	G-JONM	PA-28-181 Archer III	J. H. Massey
	G-JONO	Colt 77A balloon★	British Balloon Museum and Library
	G-JONT	Cirrus SR22	J. A. Green
	G-JONX	Aeropro Eurofox 912(1)	A. J. South
	G-JONY	Cyclone AX2000 HKS	K. R. Matheson
	G-JONZ	Cessna 172P	Truman Aviation Ltd
	G-JONT	Cirrus SR22	J. A. Green
	G-JOOL	Mainair Blade 912	P. C. Collins
	G-JORD	Robinson R44 II	Overby Ltd
	G-JOTA	Beech B.90 King Air	Jota Aircraft Leasing Ltd (G-OJRO)
	G-JOTB	Beech C.90 King Air	Jota Aircraft Leasing Ltd
	G-JOYT	PA-28-181 Archer II	John K. Cathcart Ltd (G-BOVO)
	G-JOYZ	PA-28-181 Archer III	S. Wilson
	G-JPAL	AS.355N Twin Squirrel	JPM Ltd
	G-JPAT	Robin HR.200/100	L. Girardier
	G-JPBA	Van's RV-6	S. B. Austin
	G-JPEG	BN-2A-20 Islander	Apem Aviation Ltd (G-BEDW)
	G-JPIP	Schempp-Hirth Discus bT	S. Cervantes
	G-JPJR	Robinson R44 II	Longstop Investments Ltd
	G-JPMA	Avtech Jabiru UL	Jabiru Aviation Merseyside
	G-JPOT	PA-32R-301 Saratoga SP	P.J.Wolstencroft (G-BIYM)
	G-JPRO	P.84 Jet Provost T.5A (XW433)	Air Atlantique Ltd
	G-JPTV	P.84 Jet Provost T.5A (XW354)	Century Aviation Ltd
	G-JPVA	P.84 Jet Provost T.5A (XW289)	H. Cooke (G-BVXT)
	G-JPWM	Skyranger 912 (2)	R. S. Waters & M. Pittock
	G-JRED	Robinson R44	J. Reddington Ltd
	G-JREE	Maule MX-7-180	C. R. P. Briand

Reg.	Type	Owner or Operator	Notes
G-JRME	Jodel D.140E	J. E. & L. L. Rex	
G-JRSL	Agusta A109E Power	Perment Ltd	
G-JRVB	Van's RV-8	J. W. Salter	
G-JSAK	Robinson R22 Beta II	Tukair Aircraft Charter	
G-JSAT	BN-2T Turbine Islander	MV Capital Ltd (G-BVFK)	
G-JSCA	PA-28RT-201 Arrow IV	I. P. Haddon (G-ICSA)	
G-JSEY	Bollonbau Worner NL-STU/1000	M. Leblanc	
G-JSON	Cameron N-105 balloon	Up and Away Ballooning Ltd	
G-JSPL	Avtech Jabiru SPL-450	A. E. Stowe	
G-JSRV	Van's RV-6	J. Stringer	
G-JSSD	HP.137 Jetstream 3001 ★	Museum of Flight/East Fortune	
G-JTBX	Bell 206B Jet Ranger III	J. Tobias (G-EWAW/G-DORB)	
G-JTEM	Van's RV-7	J. C. Bacon	
G-JTHU	Agusta AW.109SP	Jetheli Ltd	
G-JTJT	Robinson R44	Skyrunner Aviation Ltd	
G-JTNC	Cessna 500 Citation	Eurojet Aviation Ltd (G-OEJA/G-BWFL)	
G-JTPC	Aeromot AMT-200 Super Ximango	G. J. & J. T. Potter	
G-JTSA	Robinson R44 II	S. Novotny	
G-JUDD	Avtech Jabiru UL-450H	G. S. Elder	
G-JUDE	Robin DR.400/180	Bravo India Flying Group Ltd	
G-JUDY	AA-5A Cheetah	Gray Hooper Holt LLP	
G-JUGE	Aerotechnik EV-97 TeamEurostar UK	L. J. Appleby	
G-JUGS	Autogyro MTOSport	S. J. M. Hornsby	
G-JUIN	Cessna T.303 Crusader	F. Kratky	
G-JULE	P & M Quik GT450	G. Almond	
G-JULL	Stemme S.10VT	J. P. C. Fuchs	
G-JULU	Cameron V-90 balloon	J. M. Searle	
G-JULZ	Shaw Europa	J. S. Firth	
G-JUNG	CASA 1.131E Jungmann 1000 (E3B-143)	A. Burroughes	
G-JURG	Rockwell Commander 114A	Wright Aviation Dunchurch Ltd	
G-JUST	Beech F33A Bonanza	L. J. Macpherson	
G-JVBF	Lindstrand LBL-210A balloon	Virgin Balloon Flights	
G-JVBP	Aerotechnik EV-97 Team Eurostar UK	B. J. Partridge & J. A. Valentine	
G-JVJK	Alpi Pioneer 300 Hawk	F. M. Magnat	
G-JWBI	Agusta-Bell 206B JetRanger 2	J. W. Bonser (G-RODS/G-NOEL/G-BCWN)	
G-JWCM	SA Bulldog Srs 120/1210	Goon Aviation Ltd	
G-JWDB	Ikarus C.42 FB80	A. R. Hughes	
G-JWDS	Cessna F.150G	G. Sayer (G-AVNB)	
G-JWEB	Robinson R44	P. T. Birdsall	
G-JWIV	Jodel DR.1051	C. M. Fitton	
G-JWJW	CASA 1-131E Jungmann Srs.2000	J. W. & J. T. Whicher	
G-JWNW	Magni M-16C Tandem Trainer	A. G. Jones	
G-JWXS	Shaw Europa XS T-G	J. Wishart	
G-JXTA	BAe Jetstream 3103	Jetstream Executive Travel Ltd	
G-JXTC	BAe Jetstream 3108★	University of Glamorgan instructional airframe (G-LOGT/G-BSFH)	
G-JYAK	Yakovlev Yak-50 (93 white outline)	J. W. Stow	
G-JYRO	Rotorsport UK MT-03	A. Richards	
G-KAAT	MDH MD-902 Explorer	Police Aviation Services Ltd (G-PASS)	
G-KAEW	Fairey Gannet AEW Mk.3	M. Stott	
G-KAFT	Diamond DA40D Star	Atlantic Flight Training Ltd	
G-KAIR	PA-28-181 Archer II	Blue Sky Investments Ltd	
G-KALS	Bombardier BD-100-1A10	Concolor Ltd	
G-KAMP	PA-18 Super Cub 135	G. Cormack	
G-KAMY	AT-6D Harvard III	Orion Enterprises Ltd	
G-KANE	Aerospatiale SA.341G Gazelle 1	MW Helicopters Ltd (G-GAZI)	
G-KANZ	Westland Wasp HAS.1	T. J. Manna	
G-KAOM	Scheibe SF.25C Falke	Falke G-KAOM Syndicate	
G-KAOS	Van's RV-7	J. L. Miles	
G-KAPW	P.56 Provost T.1 (XF603)	The Shuttleworth Collection	
G-KARA	Brügger MB.2 Colibri	C. L. Hill (G-BMUI)	
G-KARI	Fuji FA.200-160	C. P. Rowley	
G-KARK	Dyn'Aéro MCR-01 Club	R. Bailes-Brown	

Notes	Reg.	Type	Owner or Operator
	G-KARN	Rotorway Executive 90	I. R. Brown (G-VART/G-BSUR)
	G-KART	PA-28-161 Warrior II	N. Clark
	G-KASW	Rotorsport UK Calidus	K. C. Wigley
	G-KASX	VS.384 Seafire Mk.XVII (SX336)	T. J. Manna (G-BRMG)
	G-KATE	Westland WG.30 Srs 100 ★	(stored)/Yeovil
	G-KATI	Rans S.7 Courier	T. S. D. Lyle
	G-KATT	Cessna 152 II	Skytaxi KFT (G-BMTK)
	G-KATZ	Flight Design CT2K	A. N. D. Arthur
	G-KAWA	Denney Kitfox Mk 2	L. E. Donaldson
	G-KAXF	Hawker Hunter F.6A (N-294)	Stichting Dutch Hawker Hunter Foundation/Netherlands
	G-KAXT	Westland Wasp HAS.1 (XT787)	T. E. Martin
	G-KAYH	Extra EA.300/L	R. C. Howe/Netherlands
	G-KAYI	Cameron Z-90 balloon	Snow Business International Ltd
	G-KAZA	Sikorsky S-76C	Bristow Helicopters Ltd
	G-KAZB	Sikorsky S-76C	Bristow Helicopters Ltd
	G-KAZI	Mainair Pegasus Quantum 15-912	Fairlight Engineering Ltd
	G-KBOJ	Autogyro MTOSport	K. M. G. Barnett
	G-KBOX	Flight Design CTSW	C. R. Mason
	G-KBWP	Schempp-Hirth Arcus T	B. F. & P. Walker
	G-KCHG	Schempp-Hirth Ventus Ct	Ventus KJW Syndicate
	G-KCIG	Sportavia RF-5B	Deeside Fournier Group
	G-KCIN	PA-28-161 Cadet	S. J. Green (G-CDOX)
	G-KCWJ	Schempp-Hirth Duo Discus T	G-KCWJ Group
	G-KDEY	Scheibe SF.25E Super Falke	Falke Syndicate
	G-KDIX	Jodel D.9 Bébé	J. A. Sykes
	G-KDMA	Cessna 560 Citation V	Gamston Aviation Ltd
	G-KDOG	SA Bulldog Srs 120/121 (XX624:E)	M. van den Broeck
	G-KEAM	Schleicher ASH 26E	I. W. Paterson
	G-KEDK	Discus BT	G. N. Fraser
	G-KEEF	Commander Aircraft 112A	K. D. Pearse
	G-KEEN	Stolp SA.300 Starduster Too	Sharp Aerobatics Ltd/Netherlands
	G-KEES	PA-28 Cherokee 180	C. N. Ellerbrook
	G-KEJY	Aerotechnik EV-97 TeamEurostar UK	Kemble Eurostar 1
	G-KELI	Robinson R44 Raven II	KN Network Services Ltd
	G-KELL	Van's RV-6	K. A Keigher/Ireland
	G-KELS	Van's RV-7	F. W. Hardiman
	G-KELV	Diamond DA42 Twin Star	K. K. Freeman (G-CTCH)
	G-KELX	Van's RV-6	A. L. Burton (G-HAMY)
	G-KELZ	Van's RV-8	B. F. Hill (G-DJRV)
	G-KEMC	Grob G.109	Norfolk Gliding Club Ltd
	G-KEMI	PA-28-181 Archer III	Modern Air (UK) Ltd
	G-KENB	Air Command 503 Commander	K. Brogden
	G-KENG	Rotorsport UK MT-03	K. A. Graham
	G-KENI	Rotorway Executive	P. A. Taylor
	G-KENM	Luscombe 8EF Silvaire	M. G. Waters
	G-KENW	Robin DR400/500	K. J. White
	G-KENZ	Rutan Vari-Eze	K. M. McConnel I (G-BNUI)
	G-KEPE	Schempp-Hirth Nimbus 3DT	G-KEPE Group
	G-KEPP	Rans S.6-ES Coyote II	R. G. Johnston
	G-KESS	Glaser-Dirks DG-400	M. T. Collins & T. Flude
	G-KEST	Steen Skybolt	G-KEST Syndicate
	G-KESY	Slingsby T.59D Kestrel	A. J. Whiteman & P. J. R. Hogarth
	G-KETH	Agusta-Bell 206B JetRanger 2	DAC Leasing Ltd
	G-KEVB	PA-28-181 Archer III	Palmair Ltd
	G-KEVG	Rotorsport UK MT-03	K. J. Robinson & R. N. Bodley
	G-KEVI	Jabiru J400	P. Horth & P. G. Macintosh
	G-KEVK	Flight Design CTSW	K. Kirby
	G-KEVL	Rotorway Executive 162F	K. D. Longhurst (G-CBIK)
	G-KEVZ	P & M Quik R	K. Mallin
	G-KEWT	Ultramagic M.90 balloon	R. F. Penney
	G-KEYS	PA-23 Aztec 250F	Giles Aviation Ltd
	G-KEYY	Cameron N-77 balloon	B. N. Trowbridge (G-BORZ)
	G-KFAN	Scheibe SF.25B Falke	R. G. & J. A. Boyes
	G-KFLY	Flight Design CTSW	P. J. Gulliford (G-LFLY)
	G-KFOX	Denney Kitfox	I. R. Lawrence & R. Hampshire
	G-KFZI	KFZ-1 Tigerfalck	L. R. Williams

Reg.	Type	Owner or Operator	Notes
G-KGAO	Scheibe SF.25C Falke 1700	Falke 2000 Group	
G-KGAW	Scheibe SF-25C	D. M. Hook	
G-KHCC	Schempp-Hirth Ventus Bt	J. L. G. McLane	
G-KHCG	AS.355F2 Ecureuil II	London Helicopter Centres Ltd (G-SDAY/ G-SYPA/G-BPRE)	
G-KHEA	Scheibe SF-25B Falke	M. Housley	
G-KHEH	Grob G.109B	N. A. Tziros	
G-KHOP	Zenair CH.601HDS Zodiac	K. Hopkins	
G-KHRE	MS.893E Rallye 150SV	Kingsmuir Group	
G-KICK	Pegasus Quantum 15-912	G. van der Gaag	
G-KIDD	Jabiru J430	R. L. Lidd (G-CEBB)	
G-KIEV	DKBA AT 0300-0 balloon	The Volga Balloon Team	
G-KIGR	Schleicher ASH-25E	G-KIGR ASH Syndicate	
G-KIII	Extra EA.300/L	Extra 200 Ltd	
G-KIMA	Zenair CH.601XL Zodiac	L. D. Johnston	
G-KIMB	Robin DR.340/140	R. M. Kimbell	
G-KIMH	Rotorsport UK MTO Sport	P. B. Harrison	
G-KIMK	Partenavia P.68B	M. Konstantinovic (G-BCPO)	
G-KIMM	Shaw Europa XS	P. A. D. Clarke	
G-KIMY	Robin DR.400/140B	S. G. Jones	
G-KIRB	Europa XS	P. Handford (G-OIZI)	
G-KIRC	Pietenpol Air Camper	M. Kirk (G-BSVZ)	
G-KISS	Rand-Robinson KR-2	E. A. Rooney	
G-KITH	Alpi Pioneer 300	K. G. Atkinson	
G-KITI	Pitts S-2E Special	B. R. Cornes	
G-KITS	Shaw Europa	J. R. Evernden	
G-KITT	Curtiss P-40M Kittyhawk (42-10855)	P.A. Teichman	
G-KITY	Denney Kitfox Mk 2	Kitfox KFM Group	
G-KIZZ	Kiss 450-582	D. L. Price	
G-KJBS	CSA Sportcruiser	S. M. Lowe	
G-KKAM	Schleicher ASW-22BLE	D. P. Taylor	
G-KKAZ	Airbus A.320-214	Thomas Cook Airlines Ltd	
G-KKER	Avtech Jabiru SPL-450	M. A. Coffin	
G-KKEV	DHC.8-402 Dash Eight	Flybe.com	
G-KLAW	Christen Eagle II	R. S. Goodwin & B. Lovering	
G-KLNB	Beech 300 Super King Air	Saxonair Charter Ltd	
G-KLNE	Hawker 900XP	Saxonair Charter Ltd	
G-KLNJ	Robinson R44 II	Saxonair Charter Ltd	
G-KLNK	Eurocopter EC135 P2+	Saxonair Charter Ltd (G-VGMB)	
G-KLNP	Eurocopter EC120B Colibri	Saxonair Charter Ltd	
G-KLNR	Hawker 400A	Saxonair Charter Ltd	
G-KLNW	Cessna 510 Citation Mustang	Saxonair Charter Ltd	
G-KLOE	Raytheon Hawker 800XP	Gama Aviation Ltd (G-OJWB)	
G-KLYE	Best Off Sky Ranger Swift 912S(1)	J. F. Murphy	
G-KMBB	Scheibe SF-25D Falke	Hinton Pilot Flight Training Ltd	
G-KMFW	Glaser-Dirks DG-800B	F. Pilkington & S. S. M. Turner	
G-KMKM	AutoGyro MTO Sport	O. & T. Brooking	
G-KMRV	Van-s RV-9A	G. K. Mutch	
G-KNCG	PA-32-301FT 6X	MJC Aviation Ltd	
G-KNEE	Ultramagic M-77C balloon	M. A.Green	
G-KNEK	Grob G.109B	Syndicate 109	
G-KNIB	Robinson R22 Beta II	C. G. Knibb	
G-KNIX	Cameron Z-315 balloon	Cameron Flights Southern Ltd	
G-KNOW	PA-32 Cherokee Six 300	Allsite Services & Logistics Ltd	
G-KNYA	PA-32R-301T Saratoga II TC	C. Sharp	
G-KNYT	Robinson R44	Aircol	
G-KOBH	Schempp-Hirth Discus bT	C. F. M. Smith & K. Neave	
G-KOCO	Cirrus SR22	R. Fitzgerald	
G-KODA	Cameron O-77 balloon	K. Stamurs	
G-KOFM	Glaser-Dirks DG.600/18M	A. Mossman	
G-KOKL	Hoffmann H-36 Dimona	Dimona Group	
G-KOLB	Kolb Twinstar Mk 3A	M. P. Wiseman	
G-KOLI	WSK PZL-110 Koliber 150	J. R. Powell	
G-KONG	Slingsby T.67M Firefly 200	R. C. Morton	

Notes	Reg.	Type	Owner or Operator
	G-KORE	Sportavia SFS31 Milan	J. R. Edyvean
	G-KOTA	PA-28-236 Dakota	M. D. Rush
	G-KOYY	Schempp-Hirth Nimbus 4T	R. Kalin
	G-KPEI	Cessna 560XL Citation	Queensway Aviation Ltd
	G-KPLG	Schempp-Hirth Ventus 2cM	M. F. Lassan & A. C. Broadbridge
	G-KPTN	Dassault Falcon 50	TAG Aviation (UK) Ltd
	G-KRES	Stoddard-Hamilton Glasair IIS RG	A. D. Murray
	G-KRIB	Robinson R44 II	Cribarth Helicopters
	G-KRII	Rand-Robinson KR-2	M. R. Cleveley
	G-KRMA	Cessna 425 Corsair	Speedstar Holdings Ltd
	G-KRNW	Eurocopter EC 135T2	Bond Air Services Ltd
	G-KRUZ	CZAW Sportcruiser	A. W. Shellis & P. Whittingham
	G-KSFR	Bombardier BD-100-1A10 Challenger	The Lily Partnership LLP
	G-KSHI	Beech A36 Bonanza	Hangar 11 Collection
	G-KSIR	Stoddard-Hamilton Glasair IIS RG	K. M. Bowen
	G-KSIX	Schleicher Ka 6E	C. D. Sterritt
	G-KSKS	Cameron N-105 balloon	Kiss the Sky Ballooning
	G-KSKY	Sky 77-24 balloon	J. W. Dale
	G-KSSA	MDH MD-900 Explorer	Police Aviation Services Ltd
	G-KSSH	MDH MD-900 Explorer	Police Aviation Services Ltd (G-WMID)
	G-KSVB	PA-24 Comanche 260	Knockin Flying Club Ltd
	G-KTEE	Cameron V-77 balloon	A. Ruitenburg
	G-KTIA	Hawker 900XP	TAG Aviation (UK) Ltd
	G-KTKT	Sky 260-24 balloon	Adventure Balloons Ltd
	G-KTTY	Denney Kitfox Model 3	S. D. Morris (G-LESJ)
	G-KTWO	Cessna 182T	S. J. G. Mole
	G-KUGG	Schleicher ASW-27-18E	R. E. D. Bailey
	G-KUIK	Mainair Pegasus Quik	P. Nugent
	G-KUIP	CZAW Sportcruiser	A. J. Kuipers
	G-KUKI	Robinson R22 Beta	HJS Helicopters Ltd
	G-KULA	Best Off Skyranger 912ULS	G. S. Cridland
	G-KUPP	Flight Design CTSW	S. J. Peet
	G-KURK	J-3C-65 Cub	M. J. Kirk
	G-KUTI	Flight Design CTSW	D. F. & S. M. Kenny
	G-KUTU	Quickie Q.2	R. Nash & J. Parkinson
	G-KUUI	J-3C-65 Cub	V. S. E. Norman
	G-KVBF	Cameron A-340HL balloon	Virgin Balloon Flights
	G-KVIP	Beech 200 Super King Air	Capital Air Charter Ltd
	G-KWAK	Scheibe SF.25C	Mendip Gliding Club Ltd
	G-KWIC	Mainair Pegasus Quik	Microlight Flight Lessons
	G-KWKI	QAC Quickie Q.200	R. Greatrex
	G-KWKR	P and M Aviation QuikR	L. G. White
	G-KXXI	Schleicher ASK-21	C. G. Bell
	G-KYLE	Thruster T600N 450	MKS Syndicate
	G-KYTE	Piper PA-28-161 Warrior II	G. Whitlow (G-BRRN)
	G-LABS	Shaw Europa	C. T. H. Pattinson
	G-LACA	PA-28-161 Warrior II	J. H. Mitchell
	G-LACB	PA-28-161 Warrior II	LAC Flying School
	G-LACC	Cameron C-90 balloon	Directorate Army Aviation
	G-LACD	PA-28-181 Archer III	Target Aviation Ltd (G-BYBG)
	G-LACI	Cessna 172S Skyhawk	D. C. & J. Taylor
	G-LACR	Denney Kitfox	C. M. Rose
	G-LADD	Enstrom 480	Foscombe Transport LLP
	G-LADS	Rockwell Commander 114	D. F. Soul
	G-LADZ	Enstrom 480	Falcon Helicopters Ltd
	G-LAFF	Cameron TR-84 Srs.2 balloon	Balloonists Supporting Barretstown
	G-LAFT	Diamond DA40D Star	Atlantic Flight Training Ltd
	G-LAGR	Cameron N-90 balloon	J. R. Clifton
	G-LAID	Robinson R44 II	SARL Tolla Ciel
	G-LAIN	Robinson R22 Beta	Patriot Aviation Ltd
	G-LAIR	Stoddard-Hamilton Glasair IIS FT	A. I.O'Broin & S. T. Raby
	G-LAKE	Lake LA-250 Renegade	Lake Aviation Ltd

Reg.	Type	Owner or Operator	Notes
G-LAKI	Jodel DR.1050	G. Cameron (G-JWBB)	
G-LALE	Embraer EMB-135BJ Legacy	London Executive Avition Ltd	
G-LAMM	Shaw Europa	S. A. Lamb	
G-LAMP	Cameron 110 Lampbulb SS balloon	S. A. Lacey	
G-LAMS	Cessna F.152 II	APB Leasing Ltd	
G-LANC	Avro 683 Lancaster X (KB889) ★	Imperial War Museum/Duxford	
G-LAND	Robinson R22 Beta	Heli Air Ltd	
G-LANE	Cessna F.172N	·A. Holmes	
G-LANS	Cessna 182T	AK Enterprises Ltd	
G-LAOL	PA-28RT-201 Arrow IV	Arrow Flying Group	
G-LARA	Robin DR.400/180	K. D. & C. A. Brackwell	
G-LARE	PA-39 Twin Comanche 160 C/R	Glareways (Neasden) Ltd	
G-LARK	Helton Lark 95	N. Huxtable & K Keen	
G-LARR	AS.350B3 Squirrel	Larsen Manufacturing Ltd	
G-LASN	Skyranger J2.2(1)	A. J. Coote	
G-LASR	Stoddard-Hamilton Glasair II	G. Lewis	
G-LASS	Rutan Vari-Eze	J. Mellor	
G-LASU	Eurocopter EC 135T2	Lancashire Constabulary Air Support Unit	
G-LATE	Falcon 2000EX	Hangar 8 Management Ltd	
G-LAVE	Cessna 172R	M. L. Roland (G-BYEV)	
G-LAWX	Sikorsky S-92A	Air Harrods Ltd	
G-LAZL	PA-28-161 Warrior II	Highland Aviation Training Ltd	
G-LAZR	Cameron O-77 balloon	Wickers World Ltd	
G-LAZZ	Stoddard-Hamilton Glastar	A. N. Evans	
G-LBAC	Evektor EV-97 TeamEurostar UK	G. Burder & A. Cox	
G-LBAL	Agusta AW139	Haughey Air Ltd	
G-LBDC	Bell 206B JetRanger III	Fresh Direct Travel Ltd	
G-LBMM	PA-28-161 Warrior II	M. A. Jones	
G-LBRC	PA-28RT-201 Arrow IV	D. J. V. Morgan	
G-LBUK	Lindstrand LBL-77A balloon	Morrison Design Ltd	
G-LBUZ	Aerotechnick EV-97A Eurostar	D. P. Tassart	
G-LCDH	Bombardier CL600-2B16 Challenger	TAG Aviation (UK) Ltd	
G-LCGL	Comper CLA.7 Swift (replica)	R. A. Fleming	
G-LCKY	Flight Design CTSW	G. D. Honey	
G-LCLE	Colomban MC-30 Luciole	J. A. Harris	
G-LCMW	TL 2000UK Sting Carbon	M. J. White & L. Chadwick	
G-LCOC	BN-2A Mk III Trislander	Blue Island Air	
G-LCOK	Colt 69A balloon	Hot-Air Balloon Co Ltd (G-BLWI)	
G-LCPL	AS.365N-2 Dauphin 2	Charterstyle Ltd	
G-LCUB	PA-18 Super Cub 95	The Tiger Club 1990 Ltd (G-AYPR)	
G-LCYD	Embraer ERJ170-100STD	BA Cityflyer Ltd	
G-LCYE	Embraer ERJ170-100STD	BA Cityflyer Ltd	
G-LCYF	Embraer ERJ170-100STD	BA Cityflyer Ltd	
G-LCYG	Embraer ERJ170-100STD	BA Cityflyer Ltd	
G-LCYH	Embraer ERJ170-100STD	BA Cityflyer Ltd	
G-LCYI	Embraer ERJ170-100STD	BA Cityflyer Ltd	
G-LCYJ	Embraer ERJ190-100SR	BA Cityflyer Ltd	
G-LCYK	Embraer ERJ190-100SR	BA Cityflyer Ltd	
G-LCYL	Embraer ERJ190-100SR	BA Cityflyer Ltd	
G-LCYM	Embraer ERJ190-100SR	BA Cityflyer Ltd	
G-LCYN	Embraer ERJ190-100SR	BA Cityflyer Ltd	
G-LCYO	Embraer ERJ190-100SR	BA Cityflyer Ltd	
G-LCYP	Embraer ERJ190-100SR	BA Cityflyer Ltd	
G-LCYR	Embraer ERJ190-100SR	BA Cityflyer Ltd	
G-LDAH	Skyranger 912 (2)	P. D. Brookes & L. Dickinson	
G-LDER	Schleicher ASW-22	P. Shrosbree & D. Starer	
G-LDFM	Cessna 560XL Citation Excel	Granard Ltd	
G-LDVO	Europa Aviation Europa XS	D. J. Park	
G-LDWS	Jodel D.150	M. Howells (G-BKSS)	
G-LDYS	Colt 56A balloon	M. J. Myddelton	
G-LEAA	Cessna 510 Citation Mustang	London Executive Aviation Ltd	
G-LEAB	Cessna 510 Citation Mustang	London Executive Aviation Ltd	
G-LEAC	Cessna 510 Citation Mustang	London Executive Aviation Ltd	
G-LEAF	Cessna F.406	Reconnaisance Ventures Ltd	
G-LEAH	Alpi Pioneer 300	A. Bortolan	
G-LEAI	Cessna 510	London Executive Aviation Ltd	
G-LEAM	PA-28-236 Dakota	G-LEAM Group (G-BHLS)	
G-LEAS	Sky 90-24 balloon	C. I. Humphrey	

Notes	Reg.	Type	Owner or Operator
	G-LEAU	Cameron N-31 balloon	P. L. Mossman
	G-LEAX	Cessna 560XL Citation XLS	London Executive Aviation Ltd
	G-LEAZ	Bombardier BD700-1A10 Challenger 300	London Executive Aviation Ltd
	G-LEBE	Shaw Europa	J. E. Fallis
	G-LECA	AS.355F1 Twin Squirrel	HFS (Aviation) Ltd (G-BNBK)
	G-LEDE	Zenair CH.601UL Zodiac	P. Boyle
	G-LEDR	Westland Gazelle HT.2	R. D. Leader (G-CBSB)
	G-LEED	Denney Kitfox Mk 2	M. G. Rummey
	G-LEEE	Avtech Jabiru UL-450	J. P. Mimnagh
	G-LEEH	Ultramagic M-90 balloon	Sport Promotion SRL/Italy
	G-LEEJ	Hughes 369HS	S. J. Halliwell
	G-LEEK	Reality Escapade	G-LEEK Phoenix Flying Group
	G-LEEN	Aero Designs Pulsar XP	R. B. Hemsworth (G-BZMP/G-DESI)
	G-LEES	Glaser-Dirks DG.400 (800)	Active Aviation Ltd
	G-LEEZ	Bell 206L-1 LongRanger 2	Pennine Helicopters Ltd (G-BPCT)
	G-LEGC	Embraer EMB-135BJ Legacy	Delos Engineering Corporation
	G-LEGG	Cessna F.182Q	W. A. L. Mitchell (G-GOOS)
	G-LEGO	Cameron O-77 balloon	P. M. Traviss
	G-LEGY	Flight Design CTLS	P. J. Clegg
	G-LELE	Lindstrand LBL-31A balloon	D. S. Wilson
	G-LEMI	Van's RV-8	The Lord Rotherwick
	G-LEMM	Ultramagic Z-90 balloon	M. Maranoni/Italy
	G-LENF	Mainair Blade 912S	G. D. Fuller
	G-LENI	AS.355F1 Twin Squirrel	Grid Defence Systems Ltd (G-ZFDB/G-BLEV)
	G-LENN	Cameron V-56 balloon	D. J. Groombridge
	G-LENS	Thunder Ax7-77Z balloon	R. S. Breakwell
	G-LENX	Cessna 172N	November XRay Ltd
	G-LEOD	Pietenpol Aircamper	I. D. McCleod
	G-LEOS	Robin DR.400/120	R. J. O. Walker
	G-LESH	BB Microlight BB03 Trya/Alien	L. R. Hodgson
	G-LESZ	Denney Kitfox Mk 5	G. M. Park
	G-LETS	Vans RV-7	M. O'Hearne
	G-LEVI	Aeronca 7AC Champion	G-LEVI Group
	G-LEVO	Robinson R44 II	Leavesley Aviation Ltd
	G-LEXX	Van's RV-8	S. Emery
	G-LEXY	Van's RV-8	AGH Software Solutions Ltd
	G-LEZE	Rutan LongEz	Bill Allen's Autos Ltd
	G-LFES	AB Sportine LAK-17B FES	P. C. Piggott
	G-LFIX	VS.509 Spitfire T.IX (ML407)	C. S. Grace
	G-LFOR	Piper J3C-65 Cub	A. Hoskins & J. C. Gowdy
	G-LFPT	Cessna 510 Citation Mustang	General Asset-Finance Capital I BV/Netherlands
	G-LFSA	PA-38-112 Tomahawk	Liverpool Flying School Ltd (G-BSFC)
	G-LFSB	PA-38-112 Tomahawk	J. D. Burford
	G-LFSC	PA-28 Cherokee 140	P. G. Smith (G-BGTR)
	G-LFSG	PA-28 Cherokee 180E	Liverpool Flying School Ltd (G-AYAA)
	G-LFSH	PA-38-112 Tomahawk	Liverpool Flying School Ltd (G-BOZM)
	G-LFSI	PA-28 Cherokee 140	Flying Group G-LFSI (G-AYKV)
	G-LFSJ	PA-28-161 Warrior II	FlyBPL.com
	G-LFSM	PA-38-112 Tomahawk	Liverpool Flying School Ltd (G-BWNR)
	G-LFSN	PA-38-112 Tomahawk	Liverpool Flying School Ltd (G-BNYV)
	G-LFSR	PA-28RT-201 Arrow IV	Liverpool Flying School Ltd (G-JANO)
	G-LFVB	VS.349 Spitfire LF.Vb (EP120)	Patina Ltd
	G-LGAR	Learjet 60	TAG Aviation (UK) Ltd
	G-LGCA	Robin DR.400/180R	London Gliding Club Proprietary Ltd
	G-LGCB	Robin DR.400/180R	London Gliding Club Proprietary Ltd
	G-LGCC	Robin DR 400/180R	London Gliding Club Proprietary Ltd (G-BNXI)
	G-LGEZ	Rutan Long-EZ	P. C. Elliott
	G-LGKD	Gulfstream 550	TAG Aviation (UK) Ltd
	G-LGLG	Cameron Z-210 balloon	Flying Circus SRL/Spain
	G-LGNA	SAAB SF.340B	Loganair Ltd/Flybe.com
	G-LGNB	SAAB SF.340B	Loganair Ltd/Flybe.com
	G-LGNC	SAAB SF.340B	Loganair Ltd/Flybe.com
	G-LGND	SAAB SF.340B	Loganair Ltd/Flybe.com (G-GNTH)
	G-LGNE	SAAB SF.340B	Loganair Ltd/Flybe.com (G-GNTI)
	G-LGNF	SAAB SF.340B	Loganair Ltd/Flybe.com (G-GNTJ)
	G-LGNG	SAAB SF.340B	Loganair Ltd/Flybe.com
	G-LGNH	SAAB SF.340B	Loganair Ltd/Flybe.com
	G-LGNI	SAAB SF.340B	Loganair Ltd/Flybe.com
	G-LGNJ	SAAB SF.340B	Loganair Ltd/Flybe.com
	G-LGNK	SAAB SF.340B	Loganair Ltd/Flybe.com

Reg.	Type	Owner or Operator	Notes
G-LGNL	SAAB SF.340B	Loganair Ltd/Flybe.com	
G-LGNM	SAAB SF.340B	Loganair Ltd/Flybe.com	
G-LGNN	SAAB SF.340B	Loganair Ltd/Flybe.com	
G-LGOC	Aero AT-3 R100	London Transport Flying Club Ltd	
G-LHCA	Robinson R22 Beta	London Helicopter Centres Ltd	
G-LHCB	Robinson R22 Beta	London Helicopter Centres Ltd (G-SIVX)	
G-LHCD	Robinson R22 Beta	London Helicopter Centres Ltd (G-CDED)	
G-LHCI	Bell 47G-5	Heli-Highland Ltd (G-SOLH/G-AZMB)	
G-LHEL	AS.355F2 Twin Squirrel	Beechview Aviation Ltd	
G-LHER	Czech Sport Aircraft Piper Sport	M. P. Lhermette	
G-LHMS	Eurocopter EC 120B Colibri	Hadley Helicopters Ltd	
G-LHXL	Robinson R44	Lloyd Helicopters Europe Ltd	
G-LIBB	Cameron V-77 balloon	R. J. Mercer	
G-LIBI	Glasflugel Standard Libelle 201B	G. Spreckley	
G-LIBL	Glasflugel Standard Libelle 201B	P. A. Tietema	
G-LIBS	Hughes 369HS	R. J. H. Strong	
G-LIBY	Glasflugel Standard Libelle 201B	R. P. Hardcastle	
G-LICK	Cessna 172N II	Sky Back Ltd (G-BNTR)	
G-LIDA	Hoffmann H36 Dimona	Bidford Airfield Ltd	
G-LIDE	PA-31-350 Navajo Chieftain	Blue Sky Investments Ltd	
G-LIDL	Cameron A-300 balloon	Cameron Flights Southern Ltd	
G-LIDY	Schleicher ASW-27B	T. Stuart	
G-LIGA	Kubicek BB-S/Fish balloon	I. Charbonnier	
G-LIKE	Europa	N. G. Henry (G-CHAV)	
G-LILY	Bell 206B JetRanger 3	T. S. Brown (G-NTBI)	
G-LIMO	Bell 206L-1 LongRanger	Heliplayer Ltd	
G-LIMP	Cameron C-80 balloon	T. & B. Chamberlain	
G-LINE	AS.355N Twin Squirrel	National Grid Electricity Transmission PLC	
G-LINN	Shaw Europa XS	T. Pond	
G-LINS	Robinson R22 Beta	Rotorum (G-DMCD/G-OOLI)	
G-LIOA	Lockheed 10A ElectraH (NC5171N) ★	Science Museum/South Kensington	
G-LION	PA-18 Super Cub 135 (R-167)	JG Jones Haulage Ltd	
G-LIOT	Cameron O-77 balloon	N. D. Eliot	
G-LIPE	Robinson R22 Beta	Auriga Ltd (G-BTXJ)	
G-LIPS	Cameron 90 Lips SS balloon	Reach For The Sky Ltd (G-BZBV)	
G-LISS	AutoGyro UK Calidus	J. M. & M. J. Newman	
G-LITE	Rockwell Commander 112A	B. G. Rhodes	
G-LITS	P & M Quik R	A. Dixon	
G-LITZ	Pitts S-1E Special	H. J. Morton	
G-LIVH	Piper J-3C-65 Cub (330238:A-24)	U. E. Allman	
G-LIVS	Schleicher ASH-26E	P. O. Sturley	
G-LIZI	PA-28 Cherokee 160	G-LIZI Group (G-ARRP)	
G-LIZY	Westland Lysander III (V9673) ★	G. A. Warner/Duxford	
G-LIZZ	PA-E23 Aztec 250E	I. Kazi & T. J. Nathan (G-BBWM)	
G-LJCC	Murphy Rebel	P. H. Hyde	
G-LKTB	PA-28-181 Archer III	L. D. Charles & J. J. Kennedy	
G-LLCH	Cessna 172S	K. Neilson (G-PLBI)	
G-LLEW	Aeromot AMT-200S Super Ximango	Echo Whiskey Ximango Syndicate	
G-LLIZ	Robinson R44 II	W. R. Harford	
G-LLLL	Rolladen-Schneider LS8-18	P. C. Fritche	
G-LLMW	Diamond DA42 Twin Star	Ming W. L.	
G-LLOY	Alpi Pioneer 300	A. R. Lloyd	
G-LMAO	Cessna F.172N	Skyview R Us Ltd	
G-LMBO	Robinson R44	Thurston Helicopters Ltd	
G-LMCB	Raj Hamsa X'Air Hawk	B. N. Thresher	
G-LMLV	Dyn'Aéro MCR-01	G-LMLV Flying Group	
G-LNAA	MDH MD-900 Explorer	Police Aviation Services Ltd	
G-LNCT	MDH MD-900 Explorer	Police Aviation Services Ltd	
G-LNDS	Robinson R44	MC Air Ltd	
G-LNIG	Flylight Dragonfly	N. R. Henry	
G-LNKS	BAe Jetstream 3102	Linksair Ltd (G-JURA)	
G-LOAD	Dan Rihn DR.107 One Design	M. J. Clark	
G-LOAM	Flylight MotorFloater	M. F. Cowlishaw	
G-LOAN	Cameron N-77 balloon	P. Lawman	
G-LOBO	Cameron O-120 balloon	Solo Aerostatics	

Notes	Reg.	Type	Owner or Operator
	G-LOCH	Piper J-3C-65 Cub	M. C. & M. R. Greenland
	G-LOFB	Lockheed L.188CF Electra	Atlantic Airlines Ltd
	G-LOFC	Lockheed L.188CF Electra	Atlantic Airlines Ltd
	G-LOFE	Lockheed L.188CF Electra	Atlantic Airlines Ltd
	G-LOFM	Maule MX-7-180A	Air Atlantique Ltd
	G-LOFT	Cessna 500 Citation I	Fox Tango (Jersey) Ltd
	G-LOIS	Avtech Jabiru UL	B. O Harvey
	G-LOKI	Ultramagic M-77C balloon	L. J. M. Muir & G. D. Hallett
	G-LOLA	Beech A36 Bonanza	K. Payne
	G-LOLL	Cameron V-77 balloon	R. K. McCulloch
	G-LONE	Bell 206L-1 LongRanger	Central Helicopters Ltd
	G-LOOC	Cessna 172S	Goodwood Road Racing Co.Ltd
	G-LOON	Cameron C-60 balloon	Atlantic Ballooning BVBA/Belgium
	G-LOOP	Pitts S-1C Special	D. Shutter
	G-LORC	PA-28-161 Cadet	Sherburn Aero Club Ltd
	G-LORD	PA-34-200T Seneca II	H. E. Held-Ruf
	G-LORN	Avions Mudry CAP-10B	D. G. R. & P. M. Wansbrough
	G-LORR	PA-28-181 Archer III	Shropshire Aero Club Ltd
	G-LORT	Light Aero Avid Speedwing 4	L. M. Thomas
	G-LORY	Thunder Ax4-31Z balloon	A. J. Moore
	G-LOSI	Cameron Z-105 balloon	Aeropubblicita Vicenza SRL/Italy
	G-LOSM	Gloster Meteor NF.11 (WM167)	Aviation Heritage Ltd
	G-LOST	Denney Kitfox Mk 3	J. H. S. Booth
	G-LOSY	Aerotechnik EV-97 Eurostar	C. D. Reeves
	G-LOTA	Robinson R44	Rahtol Ltd
	G-LOTI	Bleriot XI (replica) ★	Brooklands Museum Trust Ltd
	G-LOWS	Sky 77-24 balloon	A. J. Byrne & D. J. Bellinger
	G-LOWZ	P & M Quik GT450	P. R. Biggs
	G-LOYA	Cessna FR.172J	Just Plane Trading Ltd (G-BLVT)
	G-LOYD	Aérospatiale SA.341G Gazelle 1	S. Athgerton (G-SFTC)
	G-LOYN	Robinson R44 II	C. J. Siva-Jothy
	G-LPAD	Lindstrand LBL-105A balloon	Line Packaging & Display Ltd
	G-LPIN	P & M Aviation Quik R	Arnold Gilpin Associates Ltd
	G-LREE	Grob G.109B	G-LREE Group
	G-LRGE	Lindstrand LBL-330A balloon	Adventure Balloons Ltd
	G-LSAA	Boeing 757-236	Jet 2 (G-BNSF)
	G-LSAB	Boeing 757-27B	Jet 2 (G-OAHF)
	G-LSAC	Boeing 757-23A	Jet 2
	G-LSAD	Boeing 757-236	Jet 2 (G-OOOS/G-BRJD)
	G-LSAE	Boeing 757-27B	Jet 2
	G-LSAG	Boeing 757-21B	Jet 2
	G-LSAH	Boeing 757-21B	Jet 2
	G-LSAI	Boeing 757-21B	Jet 2
	G-LSAJ	Boeing 757-236	Jet 2 (G-CDUP/G-OOOT/G-BRJJ)
	G-LSAK	Boeing 757-23N	Jet 2
	G-LSAN	Boeing 757-2K2	Jet 2
	G-LSCM	Cessna 172S	G. A. Luscombe
	G-LSCP	Rolladen-Schneider LS6-18W	L. G. Blows & M. F. Collins
	G-LSED	Rolladen-Schneider LS6-c	McKnight/Baker Syndicate
	G-LSFB	Rolladen-Schneider LS7-WL	P. Thomson
	G-LSFI	AA-5A Cheetah	J. Ibbotson (G-BGSK)
	G-LSFR	Rolladen-Schneider LS4	A. Mulder
	G-LSFT	PA-28-161 Warrior II	Biggin Hill Flying Club Ltd (G-BXTX)
	G-LSGB	Rolladen-Schneider LS6-b	T. J. Brenton
	G-LSGM	Rolladen-Schneider LS3-17	M. R. W. Crook
	G-LSHI	Colt 77A balloon	J. H. Dobson
	G-LSIF	Rolladen-Schneider LS1-f	R. C. Godden
	G-LSIV	Rolladen-Schneider LS4	264 Syndicate
	G-LSIX	Rolladen-Schneider LS6-18W	D. P. Masson & A. V. W. Nunn
	G-LSJE	Escapade Jabiru(1)	L. S. J. Webb
	G-LSKV	Rolladen-Schneider LS8-18	J. R. W. Luxton & S. C. Williams
	G-LSKY	Mainair Pegasus Quik	G. R. Hall & P. R. Brooker
	G-LSLS	Rolladen-Schneider LS4	288 Syndicate
	G-LSMB	Dassault Falcon 2000EX	Aviation Beauport Ltd
	G-LSPH	Van's RV-8	R. S. Partridge-Hicks
	G-LSTR	Stoddard-Hamilton Glastar	A. Vaughan
	G-LSVI	Rolladen-Schneider LS6-c18	R. Hanks

Reg.	Type	Owner or Operator	Notes
G-LTFB	PA-28 Cherokee 140	Polishing Consulting Ltd (G-AVLU)	
G-LTFC	PA-28 Cherokee 140B	N. M. G. Pearson (G-AXTI)	
G-LTRF	Sportavia Fournier RF-7	D. Radewald (G-EHAP)	
G-LTSB	Cameron LTSB-90 balloon	ABC Flights Ltd	
G-LTSK	Bombardier CL600-2B16 Challenger	TAG Aviation (UK) Ltd	
G-LTWA	Robinson R44	L. T. W. Alderman	
G-LUBB	Cessna 525 Citationjet	Hangar 8 Management Ltd	
G-LUBE	Cameron N-77 balloon	A. C. K. Rawson	
G-LUBY	Jabiru J430	K. Luby	
G-LUCK	Cessna F.150M	MK Consulting Engineers Ltd	
G-LUCL	Colomban MC-30 Luciole	R. C. Teverson	
G-LUDM	Van's RV-8	D. F. Sargant	
G-LUED	Aero Designs Pulsar	J. C. Anderson	
G-LUEK	Cessna 182T	B. F. Lueken	
G-LUEY	Rans S-7S Courier	S. Garfield	
G-LUKA	Beech G.58 Baron	J. N. Bentley Ltd	
G-LUKE	Rutan LongEz	R. A. Pearson	
G-LULA	Cameron C-90 balloon	S. D. Davis	
G-LULU	Grob G.109	A. P. Bowden	
G-LULV	Diamond DA-42 Twin Star	Deltabond Ltd	
G-LUNE	Mainair Pegasus Quik	D. Muir	
G-LUNG	Rotorsport UK MT-03	P. Krysiak	
G-LUNY	Pitts S-1S Special	G-LUNY Group	
G-LUON	Schleicher ASW-27-18E	P. C. Naegeli	
G-LUPY	Marganski Swift S-1	P. R. J. Conran	
G-LUSC	Luscombe 8E Silvaire	M. Fowler	
G-LUSH	PA-28-151 Warrior	S. S. Bamrah	
G-LUSI	Luscombe 8F Silvaire	P. H. Isherwood	
G-LUSK	Luscombe 8F Silvaire	M. A. Lamprell & P. J. Laycock (G-BRGG)	
G-LUST	Luscombe 8E Silvaire	C. J. Watson	
G-LUXE	BAe 146-301	BAE Systems (Operations) Ltd (G-SSSH)	
G-LUXY	Cessna 551 Citation IISP	Longhan Ltd	
G-LVCY	Colomban MC-30 Luciole	C. Wright	
G-LVDC	Bell 206L Long Ranger III	Freshair UK Ltd (G-OFST/G-BXIB)	
G-LVES	Cessna 182S	R. W. & A. M. Glaves (G-ELIE)	
G-LVPL	Edge XT912 B/Streak III/B	C. D. Connor	
G-LWDC	Canadair CL600-2A12 Challenger	African Petroleum Ltd	
G-LWLW	Diamond DA.40D Star	M. P. Wilkinson (G-CCLV)	
G-LWNG	Aero Designs Pulsar	A. B. Wood (G-OMKF)	
G-LXUS	Alpi Pioneer 300	A. & J. Oswald	
G-LYDA	Hoffmann H-36 Dimona	G-LYDA Flying Group	
G-LYDF	PA-31-350 Navajo Chieftain	Atlantic Bridge Aviation Ltd	
G-LYFA	IDABacau Yakovlev Yak-52	Fox Alpha Group	
G-LYNC	Robinson R22 Beta II	Subacoustech Ltd	
G-LYND	PA-25 Pawnee 235	York Gliding Centre Ltd (G-ASFX/G-BSFZ)	
G-LYNI	Aerotechnik EV-97 Eurostar	M. W. Holmes & A. C. Thomson	
G-LYNK	CFM Shadow Srs DD	B. A. Richards	
G-LYNX	Westland WG.13 Lynx (ZB500)	IHM/Weston-super-Mare	
G-LYPG	Avtech Jabiru UL	A. J. Geary	
G-LYPH	Rolladen-Schneider LS8-18-st	S. & S. Barter	
G-LYSA	Schleicher ASW-20L	L. A. Humphries	
G-LYTE	Thunder Ax7-77 balloon	G. M. Bulme	
G-LZED	AutoGyro MTO Sport	L. Zivanovic	
G-LZII	Laser Z200	K. G. Begley	
G-LZZY	PA-28RT-201T Turbo Arrow IV	A. C. Gradidge (G-BMHZ)	
G-MAAM	CFM Shadow Srs.C	S. J. Halliwell (G-MTCA)	
G-MAAN	Shaw Europa XS	P. S. Mann	
G-MABE	Cessna F.150L	I. D. McClelland (G-BLJP)	
G-MABL	Quik GTR	S. J. Reid	
G-MACA	Robinson R22 Beta	Jepar Rotorcraft	
G-MACE	Hughes 369E	West Country Helicopters Ltd	
G-MACH	SIAI-Marchetti SF.260	Cheyne Motors Ltd	
G-MACK	PA-28R Cherokee Arrow 200-II	M. D. Hinge	
G-MACN	Cirrus SR22	J. D. M. Tickell	

Notes	Reg.	Type	Owner or Operator
	G-MACO	Bombardier CL600-2B16 Challenger	Perfect Aviation UK Ltd (G-MACP/G-CGFF/ G-OCSF)
	G-MACU	Robinson R44 II	HQ Aviation Ltd (G-SEFI)
	G-MADV	P & M Quik GT450	D. A. Valentine
	G-MAFA	Cessna F.406	Directflight Ltd (G-DFLT)
	G-MAFB	Cessna F.406	Directflight Ltd
	G-MAFE	Dornier 228-202K	FR Aviation Ltd (G-OALF/G-MLDO)
	G-MAFF	BN-2T Turbine Islander	FR Aviation Ltd (G-BJEO)
	G-MAFI	Dornier 228-202K	FR Aviation Ltd
	G-MAFT	Diamond DA.40 Star	Atlantic Flight Training Ltd
	G-MAGC	Cameron Grand Illusion SS balloon	Magical Adventures Ltd
	G-MAGG	Pitts S-1SE Special	O. T. Elmer
	G-MAGK	Schleicher ASW-20L	A. G. K. Mackenzie
	G-MAGL	Sky 77-24 balloon	RCM SRL/Luxembourg
	G-MAGN	Magni M-24C	Net2Net IPS Ltd
	G-MAGZ	Robin DR.400/500	T. J. Thomas
	G-MAIE	PA-32RT-301T Turbo Saratoga II TC	Sub Marine Services Ltd
	G-MAIN	Mainair Blade 912	G. L. Logan & R. Wells
	G-MAIR	PA-34-200T Seneca II	Ravenair Aircraft Ltd
	G-MAJA	BAe Jetstream 4102	Eastern Airways
	G-MAJB	BAe Jetstream 4102	Eastern Airways (G-BVKT)
	G-MAJC	BAe Jetstream 4102	Eastern Airways (G-LOGJ)
	G-MAJD	BAe Jetstream 4102	Eastern Airways (G-WAWR)
	G-MAJE	BAe Jetstream 4102	Eastern Airways (G-LOGK)
	G-MAJF	BAe Jetstream 4102	Eastern Airways (G-WAWL)
	G-MAJG	BAe Jetstream 4102	Eastern Airways (G-LOGL)
	G-MAJH	BAe Jetstream 4102	Eastern Airways (G-WAYR)
	G-MAJI	BAe Jetstream 4102	Eastern Airways (G-WAND)
	G-MAJJ	BAe Jetstream 4102	Eastern Airways (G-WAFT)
	G-MAJK	BAe Jetstream 4102	Eastern Airways
	G-MAJL	BAe Jetstream 4102	Eastern Airways
	G-MAJR	DHC.1 Chipmunk 22 (WP805)	C. Adams
	G-MAJS	Airbus A.300B4-605R	Monarch Airlines Ltd
	G-MAJU	BAe Jetstream 4100	Eastern Airways
	G-MAJW	BAe Jetstream 4100	Eastern Airways
	G-MAJY	BAe Jetstream 4100	Eastern Airways
	G-MAJZ	BAe Jetstream 4100	Eastern Airways
	G-MAKE	Rotorsport UK Calidus	P. M. Ford
	G-MAKI	Robinson R44	Hoe Leasing Ltd
	G-MAKK	Aeroprakt A22-L Foxbat	M. A. McKillop
	G-MAKS	Cirrus SR22	C. S. Mullan
	G-MALA	PA-28-181 Archer II	M. & D. Aviation (G-BIIU)
	G-MALC	AA-5 Traveler	B. P. Hogan (G-BCPM)
	G-MALS	Mooney M.20K-231	P. Mouterde
	G-MALT	Colt Flying Hop SS balloon	P. J. Stapley
	G-MANC	BAe ATP	European Turboprop Management AB (G-LOGF)
	G-MANH	BAe ATP	Atlantic Airlines Ltd (G-LOGC/G-OLCC)
	G-MANN	Aérospatiale SA.341G Gazelle 1	MW Helicopters Ltd
	G-MANO	BAe ATP	Atlantic Airlines Ltd (G-UIET)
	G-MANW	Tri-R Kis	M. T. Manwaring
	G-MANX	FRED Srs 2	S. Styles
	G-MANZ	Robinson R44 II	Steve Hill Ltd
	G-MAOL	Agusta AW109SP Grand New	Mash Aviation Ltd
	G-MAPP	Cessna 402B	Reconnaisance Ventures Ltd
	G-MAPR	Beech A36 Bonanza	M. J. B. Cozens
	G-MARA	Airbus A.321-231	Monarch Airlines Ltd
	G-MARE	Schweizer 269C	The Earl of Caledon
	G-MARF	Robinson R44 II	Time Line International Ltd (G-OSJL)
	G-MARO	Skyranger J2.2 (2)	J. F. Northey
	G-MARZ	Thruster T.600N 450	S. W. Plume
	G-MASC	Jodel 150A	K. F. & R. Richardson
	G-MASF	PA-28-181 Archer II	Mid-Anglia School of Flying
	G-MASH	Westland-Bell 47G-4A	Kinetic Avionics Ltd (G-AXKU)
	G-MASI	P & M Quik GT450	D. M. Merritt-Holman
	G-MASS	Cessna 152 II	MK Aero Support Ltd (G-BSHN)
	G-MATE	Moravan Zlin Z.50LX	S. A. W. Becker
	G-MATS	Colt GA-42 airship	P. A. Lindstrand
	G-MATT	Robin R.2160	Flew LLP (G-BKRC)
	G-MATY	Robinson R22 Beta	MT Aviation
	G-MATZ	PA-28 Cherokee 140	Midland Air Training School (G-BASI)
	G-MAUK	Colt 77A balloon	B. Meeson
	G-MAUS	Shaw Europa XS	A. P. Ringrose

Reg.	Type	Owner or Operator	Notes
G-MAVI	Robinson R22 Beta	Northumbria Helicopters Ltd	
G-MAVV	Aero AT-3 R100	Medcentres Property Portfolio Ltd	
G-MAXG	Pitts S-1S Special	MAXG Group	
G-MAXI	PA-34-200T Seneca II	Draycott Seneca Syndicate Ltd	
G-MAXP	Raytheon Hawker 800XP	Xclusive Jet Charter Ltd (G-CGHY)	
G-MAXS	Mainair Pegasus Quik 912S	W. J. Walker	
G-MAXV	Van's RV-4	R. S. Partridge-Hicks	
G-MAYB	Robinson R44	Highmark Aviation Ltd	
G-MAYE	Bell 407	M. Maye	
G-MAZA	Rotorsport UK MT-03	N. Crownshaw & M. Manson	
G-MAZY†	DH.82A Tiger Moth ★	Newark Air Museum	
G-MBAA	Hiway Skytrike Mk 2	M. J. Aubrey	
G-MBAB	Hovey Whing-Ding II	M. J. Aubrey	
G-MBAD	Weedhopper JC-24A	M. Stott	
G-MBAF	R. J. Swift 3	C. G. Wrzesien	
G-MBAW	Pterodactyl Ptraveller	J. C. K. Scardifield	
G-MBBB	Skycraft Scout 2	A. J. & B. Chalkley	
G-MBBJ	Hiway Demon	M. J. Aubrey	
G-MBBM	Eipper Quicksilver MX	J. Brown	
G-MBCJ	Mainair Sports Tri-Flyer	R. A. Smith	
G-MBCK	Eipper Quicksilver MX	P. Rowbotham	
G-MBCL	Sky-Trike/Typhoon	P. J. Callis	
G-MBCX	Airwave Nimrod 165	M. Maylor	
G-MBDG	Eurowing Goldwing	A. J. Glynn	
G-MBDL	AES Lone Ranger ★	North East Aircraft Museum	
G-MBDM	Southdown Sigma Trike	A. R. Prentice	
G-MBET	MEA Mistral Trainer	B. H. Stephens	
G-MBGF	Twamley Trike	T. B. Woolley	
G-MBHE	American Aerolights Eagle	R. J. Osborne	
G-MBHK	Flexiform Skytrike	K. T. Vinning	
G-MBHZ	Pterodactyl Ptraveller	J. C. K. Scardifield	
G-MBIA	Flexiform Sealander Skytrike	I. P. Cook	
G-MBIT	Hiway Demon Skytrike	K. S. Hodgson	
G-MBIZ	Mainair Tri-Flyer	D. M. A. Templeman/E. F. C. Clapham/ S. P. Slade/W. B. S. Dobie	
G-MBJF	Hiway Skytrike Mk II	C. H. Bestwick	
G-MBJK	American Aerolights Eagle	B. W. Olley	
G-MBJL	Airwave Nimrod	A. G. Lowe	
G-MBJM	Striplin Lone Ranger	C. K. Brown	
G-MBKY	American Aerolight Eagle	M. J. Aubrey	
G-MBKZ	Hiway Skytrike	S. I. Harding	
G-MBLU	Southdown Lightning L.195	C. R. Franklin	
G-MBMG	Rotec Rally 2B	J. R. Pyper	
G-MBOF	Pakes Jackdaw	L. G. Pakes	
G-MBOH	Microlight Engineering Mistral	N. A. Bell	
G-MBPB	Pterodactyl Ptraveller	N. A. Bell	
G-MBPJ	Moto-Delta	J. B. Jackson	
G-MBPX	Eurowing Goldwing	A. R. Channon	
G-MBRB	Electraflyer Eagle 1	R. C. Bott	
G-MBRD	American Aerolights Eagle	R. J. Osborne	
G-MBRH	Ultraflight Mirage Mk II	R. W. F. Boarder	
G-MBSJ	American Aerolights Eagle 215B	T. J. Gayton-Polley	
G-MBSX	Ultraflight Mirage II	C. J. Draper	
G-MBTH	Whittaker MW4	M. W. J. Whittaker	
G-MBTJ	Solar Wings Microlight	H. A. Comber	
G-MBTW	Raven Vector 600	W. A. Fuller	
G-MBUZ	Wheeler Scout Mk II	A. C. Thorne	
G-MBYM	Eipper Quicksilver MX	M. P. Harper & L. L. Perry	
G-MBZO	Tri-Pacer 330	A. N. Burrows	
G-MBZV	American Aerolights Eagle	M. J. Aubrey	
G-MCAB	Gardan GY-201 Minicab	P. G. Hooper	
G-MCAI	Robinson R44 II	M. C. Allen	
G-MCAN	Agusta A109S Grand	Cannon Air LLP	
G-MCAP	Cameron C-80 balloon	L. D. Pickup	
G-MCCF	Thruster T.600N	C. C. F. Fuller	
G-MCCY	IDA Bacau Yakolev Yak-52	D. P. McCoy/Ireland	
G-MCDB	VS.361 Spitfire LF.IX	M. Collenette	
G-MCEL	Pegasus Quantum 15-912	F. Hodgson	
G-MCJL	Pegasus Quantum 15-912	Lincoln Enterprises Ltd	
G-MCLY	Cessna 172P	McAully Flying Group Ltd	

Notes	Reg.	Type	Owner or Operator
	G-MCMC	SOCATA TBM-700	SogestaoAdministraca Gerencia SA
	G-MCMS	Aero Designs Pulsar	R. J. Bost
	G-MCOW	Lindstrand LBL-77A balloon	S. & S. Villiers
	G-MCOX	Fuji FA.200-180AO	W. Surrey Engineering (Shepperton) Ltd
	G-MCPI	Bell 206B JetRanger 3	Castle Air Charters Ltd (G-ONTB)
	G-MCPR	PA-32-301T Turbo Saratoga	M. C. Plomer-Roberts (G-MOLL)
	G-MCRO	Dyn'Aero MCR-01	G. Hawkins
	G-MCUB	Escapade	W. H. Bliss
	G-MCXV	Colomban MC.15 Cri-Cri	P. C. Appleton
	G-MDAC	PA-28-181 Archer II	S. A. Nicklen
	G-MDAY	Cessna 170B	M. Day
	G-MDBA	Dassault Falcon 2000	Execujet (UK) Ltd
	G-MDBC	Pegasus Quantum 15-912	J. H. Bradbury
	G-MDBD	Airbus A.330-243	Thomas Cook Airlines Ltd
	G-MDDT	Robinson R44 II	M. D. Tracey
	G-MDGE	Robinson R22 Beta	C. J. Siva-Jothy (G-OGOG/G-TILL)
	G-MDJE	Cessna 208 Caravan 1 (amphibian)	Aerodynamics Ltd
	G-MDJN	Beech 95-B55 Baron	WAFO Schnecken und Zylinder GmbH (G-SUZI/G-BAXR)
	G-MDKD	Robinson R22 Beta	Heli Air Ltd
	G-MDPI	Agusta A109A-II	Langfast Ltd (G-PERI/G-EXEK/G-SLNE/ G-EEVS/G-OTSL)
	G-MEDF	Airbus A.321-231	British Airways PLC
	G-MEDG	Airbus A.321-231	British Airways PLC
	G-MEDH	Airbus A.320-232	British Airways PLC
	G-MEDJ	Airbus A.321-232	British Airways PLC
	G-MEDK	Airbus A.320-232	British Airways PLC
	G-MEDL	Airbus A.321-231	British Airways PLC
	G-MEDM	Airbus A.321-231	British Airways PLC
	G-MEDN	Airbus A.321-231	British Airways PLC
	G-MEDU	Airbus A.321-231	British Airways PLC
	G-MEDX	Agusta A109E Power	Sloane Helicopters Ltd
	G-MEEE	Schleicher ASW-20L	T. E. Macfadyen
	G-MEET	Learjet 40	Nazca Aviation Ltd
	G-MEGA	PA-28R-201T Turbo Arrow III	H. de Vries
	G-MEGG	Shaw Europa XS	M. E. Mavers
	G-MEGN	Beech B200 Super King Air	Dragonfly Aviation Services Ltd
	G-MEGS	Cessna 172S	The Cambridge Aero Club Ltd
	G-MELL	CZAW Sportcruiser	G. A. & J. A. Mellins
	G-MELS	PA-28-181 Archer III	P. J. Sowood
	G-MELT	Cessna F.172H	Falcon Aviation Ltd (G-AWTI)
	G-MEME	PA-28R-201 Arrow III	Henry J. Clare Ltd
	G-MENU	Robinson R44 II	Eagles in Flight Ltd
	G-MEOW	CFM Streak Shadow	G. J. Moor
	G-MEPU	Rotorsport UK MT-03	M. C. Elliott
	G-MERC	Colt 56A balloon	A. F. & C. D. Selby
	G-MERE	Lindstrand LBL-77A balloon	R. D. Baker
	G-MERF	Grob G.115A	G-MERF Group
	G-MERL	PA-28RT-201 Arrow IV	W. T. Jenkins
	G-MESH	CZAW Sportcruiser	M. E. S. Heaton
	G-METH	Cameron C-90 balloon	A. & D. Methley
	G-MEUP	Cameron A-120 balloon	J. M. Woodhouse
	G-MFAC	Cessna F.172H	Cezzy Flying Group (G-AVGZ)
	G-MFEF	Cessna FR.172J	M. & E. N. Ford
	G-MFHI	Shaw Europa	Hi Fliers
	G-MFLA	Robin HR200/120B	Multiflight Ltd (G-HHUK)
	G-MFLB	Robin HR200/120B	Multiflight Ltd (G-BXOR)
	G-MFLC	Robin HR200/120B	Multiflight Ltd (G-BXGW)
	G-MFLD	Robin HR200/120B	Multiflight Ltd (G-BXDT)
	G-MFLE	Robin HR200/120B	Multiflight Ltd (G-BYLH)
	G-MFLI	Cameron V-90 balloon	J. M. Percival
	G-MFLJ	P & M Quik GT450	M. F. Jakeman
	G-MFLM	Cessna F.152 II	Multiflight Ltd (G-BFFC)
	G-MFLY	Mainair Rapier	J. J. Tierney
	G-MFMF	Bell 206B JetRanger 3	Lomas Helicopters (G-BJNJ)
	G-MFMM	Scheibe SF.25C Falke	J. E. Selman
	G-MFOX	Aeropro Eurofox 912	R. M. Cornwell
	G-MGAG	Aviasud Mistral 532GB	S. B. Love

Reg.	Type	Owner or Operator	Notes
G-MGAN	Robinson R44	FlyBPL.com	
G-MGCA	Jabiru Aircraft Jabiru UL	K. D. Pearce	
G-MGCB	Pegasus XL-Q	M. G. Gomez	
G-MGCK	Whittaker MW6-S FT	A. Chidlow & M. W. J. Whittaker	
G-MGDL	Pegasus Quantum 15	M. J. Buchanan	
G-MGEC	Rans S.6-ESD-XL Coyote II	M. Lowe & D. Williams	
G-MGEF	Pegasus Quantum 15	G. D. Castell	
G-MGFC	Aeropro Eurofox 912(1)	M. G. F. Cawson	
G-MGFK	Pegasus Quantum 15	F. A. A. Kay	
G-MGGG	Pegasus Quantum 15	R. A. Beauchamp	
G-MGGT	CFM Streak Shadow SAM	D. R. Stansfield	
G-MGGV	Pegasus Quantum 15-912	K. Loder	
G-MGIC	Ace Magic Cyclone	K. A. Armstrong	
G-MGMM	PA-18 Super Cub 150	Alice's Flying Group	
G-MGNE	Embraer EMB-505 Phenom 300	Flairjet Ltd	
G-MGOD	Medway Raven	A. Wherrett/N. R. Andrew/D. J. Millward	
G-MGOO	Renegade Spirit UK Ltd	J. Aley	
G-MGPA	Ikarus C42 FB100	S. Ashley	
G-MGPD	Pegasus XL-R	H. T. Mounfield	
G-MGPH	CFM Streak Shadow	V. C. Readhead (G-RSPH)	
G-MGPX	Kolb Twinstar Mk.3 Extra	S. P. Garton	
G-MGRH	Quad City Challenger II	A. Hepburn	
G-MGTG	Pegasus Quantum 15	R. B. Milton (G-MZIO)	
G-MGTR	Hunt Wing	A. C. Ryall	
G-MGTV	Thruster T.600N 450	R. Bingham	
G-MGTW	CFM Shadow Srs DD	G. T. Webster	
G-MGUN	Cyclone AX2000	M. A. Boffin	
G-MGUY	CFM Shadow Srs BD	Shadow Flight Centre Ltd	
G-MGWH	Thruster T300	J. J. Hill	
G-MGWI	Robinson R44	Ed Murray and Sons Ltd (G-BZEF)	
G-MHAR	PA-42-720 Cheyenne IIIA	BAE Systems (Operations) Ltd	
G-MHCE	Enstrom F-28A	C. Roumet (G-BBHD)	
G-MHCM	Enstrom 280FX	Kingswood Bank LLP (G-IBWF/G-ZZWW/G-BSIE)	
G-MHGS	Stoddard-Hamilton Glastar	M. Henderson	
G-MHIS	Cessna 550 Citation Bravo	Mail Handling International Ltd (G-IDAB)	
G-MHJK	Diamond DA42 Twin Star	Plane Talking Ltd	
G-MHMR	Pegasus Quantum 15-912	Hadair	
G-MHRV	Van's RV-6A	M. R. Harris	
G-MICE	Cessna 510 Citation Mustang	Fteron Ltd	
G-MICG	Gefa-Flug AS105GD hot air airship	Avio San Michele SRL/Italy	
G-MICH	Robinson R22 Beta	Tiger Helicopters Ltd (G-BNKY)	
G-MICI	Cessna 182S	Steve Parrish Racing (G-WARF)	
G-MICK	Cessna F.172N	Branscombe Airfield Ltd	
G-MICM	Lindstrand LTL203T Tethered gas balloon	Avio San Michelle SRA/Italy	
G-MICY	Everett Srs 1 gyroplane	D. M. Hughes	
G-MIDD	PA-28 Cherokee 140	Midland Air Training School (G-BBDD)	
G-MIDG	Midget Mustang	C. E. Bellhouse	
G-MIDO	Airbus A.320-232	British Airways PLC	
G-MIDS	Airbus A.320-232	British Airways PLC	
G-MIDT	Airbus A.320-232	British Airways PLC	
G-MIDX	Airbus A.320-232	British Airways PLC	
G-MIDY	Airbus A.320-232	British Airways PLC	
G-MIFF	Robin DR.400/180	G. E. Snushall	
G-MIGG	WSK-Mielec LiM-5 (1211) ★	D. Miles (G-BWUF)	
G-MIII	Extra EA.300/L	Angels High Ltd	
G-MIKE	Brookland Hornet	M. H. J. Goldring	
G-MIKI	Rans S.6-ESA Coyote II	S. P. Slade	
G-MILA	Cessna F.172N	P. J. Miller	
G-MILD	Scheibe SF.25C Falke	P. G. Marks	
G-MILE	Cameron N-77 balloon	Miles Air Ltd	
G-MILF	Harmon Rocket II	E. Stinton	
G-MILN	Cessna 182Q	G-MILN Group	
G-MIME	Shaw Europa	P. Lewis & N. G. Ley	
G-MIND	Cessna 404	Reconnaissance Ventures Ltd	
G-MINN	Lindstrand LBL-90A balloon	S. M. & D. Johnson (G-SKKC/G-OHUB)	
G-MINS	Nicollier HN.700 Menestrel II	R. Fenion	
G-MINT	Pitts S-1S Special	T. R. G. Barnby	
G-MIOO	M.100 Student ★	Museum of Berkshire Aviation/Woodley (G-APLK)	

Notes	Reg.	Type	Owner or Operator
	G-MIRA	Jabiru SP-340	C. P. L. Helson/Belgium (G-LUMA)
	G-MIRM	Stinson HW-75 Voyager	M. Howells (G-BMSA/G-BCUM)
	G-MIRN	Remos GX	M. Kurkic
	G-MISH	Cessna 182R	Graham Churchill Plant Ltd (G-RFAB/G-BIXT)
	G-MISJ	CZAW Sportcruiser	M. T. Dawson
	G-MISK	Robinson R44	C. A. Rosenberg (G-BYCE)
	G-MISS	Taylor JT.2 Titch	D. Beale
	G-MITE	Raj Hamsa X'Air Falcon	K. McKay
	G-MITZ	Cameron N-77 balloon	Colt Car Co Ltd
	G-MJAD	Eipper Quicksilver MX	J. McCullough
	G-MJAE	American Aerolights Eagle	T. B. Woolley
	G-MJAJ	Eurowing Goldwing	M. J. Aubrey
	G-MJAM	Eipper Quicksilver MX	J. C. Larkin
	G-MJAN	Hiway Skytrike	G. M. Sutcliffe
	G-MJBK	Swallow B	M. A. Newbould
	G-MJBL	American Aerolights Eagle	B. W. Olley
	G-MJCU	Tarjani	J. K. Ewing
	G-MJDE	Huntair Pathfinder	P. Rayson
	G-MJDJ	Hiway Skytrike Demon	A. J. Cowan
	G-MJEO	American Aerolights Eagle	A. M. Shaw
	G-MJER	Flexiform Striker	D. S. Simpson
	G-MJFM	Huntair Pathfinder	M. J. Aubrey
	G-MJFX	Skyhook TR-1	M. R. Dean
	G-MJFZ	Hiway Demon/Tri-flyer	A. W. Lowrie
	G-MJHC	Ultrasports Tripacer 330	G. J. Simoni
	G-MJHR	Southdown Lightning	B. R. Barnes
	G-MJHV	Hiway Demon 250	A. G. Griffiths
	G-MJIA	Flexiform Striker	D. G. Ellis
	G-MJIR	Eipper Quicksilver MX	H. Feeney
	G-MJJA	Huntair Pathfinder	J. M. Watkins & R. D. Bateman
	G-MJJK	Eipper Quicksilver MXII	J. McCullough
	G-MJKB	Striplin Skyranger	A. P. Booth
	G-MJKO	Goldmarque 250 Skytrike	M. J. Barry
	G-MJKP	Super Scorpion/Sky-Trike ★	Aero Venture
	G-MJKX	Ultralight Skyrider Phantom	L. R. Graham
	G-MJMN	Mainair Tri-Flyer 330/Flexiform Striker	A. Bishop
	G-MJMR	Solar Wings Typhoon	J. C. S. Jones
	G-MJOC	Huntair Pathfinder	A. J. Glynn
	G-MJOE	Eurowing Goldwing	R. J. Osborne
	G-MJPE	Hiway Demon Skytrike	T. G. Elmhirst
	G-MJPV	Eipper Quicksilver MX	F. W. Ellis
	G-MJRL	Eurowing Goldwing	M. Daniels
	G-MJSF	Skyrider Airsports Phantom	B. J. Towers
	G-MJSL	Dragon 200	M. J. Aubrey
	G-MJSO	Hiway Skytrike	D. C. Read
	G-MJSP	Romain Tiger Cub 440	A. R. Sunley
	G-MJST	Pterodactyl Ptraveller	B. W. Olley
	G-MJSY	Eurowing Goldwing	A. J. Rex
	G-MJSZ	DH Wasp	J. J. Hill
	G-MJTM	Aerostructure Pipistrelle 2B	A. M. Sirant
	G-MJTX	Skyrider Airsports Phantom	P. D. Coppin
	G-MJTY	Huntair Pathfinder Mk.1	A. S. Macdonald
	G-MJTZ	Skyrider Airsports Phantom	B. J. Towers
	G-MJUR	Skyrider Aviation Phantom	M. J. Whiteman-Haywood
	G-MJUW	MBA Tiger Cub 440	D. G. Palmer
	G-MJUX	Skyrider Airsports Phantom	T. J. Searle
	G-MJVF	CFM Shadow	J. A. Cook
	G-MJVN	Ultrasports Puma 440	R. McGookin
	G-MJVP	Eipper Quicksilver MX II	G. J. Ward
	G-MJVU	Eipper Quicksilver MX II	F. J. Griffith
	G-MJVY	Dragon Srs 150	J. C. Craddock
	G-MJWB	Eurowing Goldwing	D. G. Palmer
	G-MJWF	Tiger Cub 440	R. A. & T. Maycock
	G-MJWK	Huntair Pathfinder	V. Tabacek
	G-MJYV	Mainair Triflyer 2 Seat	H. L. Phillips
	G-MJYW	Wasp Gryphon III	P. D. Lawrence
	G-MJYX	Mainair Tri-Flyer/Hiway Demon	K. G. Grayson & R. D. Leigh
	G-MJZK	Southdown Puma Sprint 440	R. J. Osborne
	G-MJZX	Hummer TX	M. J. Aubrey
	G-MKAA	Boeing 747-2S4F	Transatlantic Aviation Ltd

Reg.	Type	Owner or Operator	Notes
G-MKAK	Colt 77A balloon	A. C. Ritchie	
G-MKAS	PA-28 Cherokee 140	3G's Flying Group (G-BKVR)	
G-MKBA	Boeing 747-2B5F	Belfairs (UK) Ltd	
G-MKCA	Boeing 747-2B5B	Transatlantic Aviation Ltd	
G-MKDA	Boeing 747-2B5F	Transatlantic Aviation Ltd	
G-MKEA	Boeing 747-249F	Belfairs (UK) Ltd	
G-MKER	P & M QuikR	M. C. Kerr	
G-MKEV	EV-96 Eurostar	K. Laud	
G-MKGA	Boeing 747-2R7F	Transatlantic Aviation Ltd	
G-MKIA	VS.300 Spitfire Mk.1A (P9374)	Mark One Partners LLC	
G-MKKA	Boeing 747-219B	European Aviation Ltd	
G-MKVB	VS.349 Spitfire LF.VB (BM597)	Historic Aircraft Collection	
G-MKXI	VS.365 Spitfire PR.XI (PL624:R)	P. A. Teichman	
G-MLAL	Jabiru J400	J. M. Pipping	
G-MLAS	Cessna 182E ★	Parachute jump trainer/St. Merryn	
G-MLAW	P & M Quik GT450	S. M. Redding	
G-MLHI	Maule MX-7-180 Star Rocket	Maulehigh (G-BTMJ)	
G-MLJL	Airbus A.330-243	Thomas Cook Airlines Ltd	
G-MLKE	P & M Aviation Quik R	G. Oliver	
G-MLLE	CEA DR.200A-B	A. D. Evans	
G-MLLI	PA-32RT-300 Lance II	Evans Aircraft Ltd (G-JUPP/G-BNJF)	
G-MLWI	Thunder Ax7-77 balloon	M. L. & L. P. Willoughby	
G-MLXP	Europa XS	M. Davies	
G-MLZZ	Best Off Sky Ranger Swift 912S(1)	T. Couston	
G-MMAC	Dragon Srs.200	J. F. Ashton & J. P. Kirwan	
G-MMAG	MBA Tiger Cub 440	M. J. Aubrey	
G-MMAR	Mainair Gemini/Southdown Puma Sprint	B. A. Fawkes	
G-MMBE	MBA Tiger Cub 440	A. Gannon	
G-MMBL	Southdown Puma	B. J. Farrell	
G-MMBU	Eipper Quicksilver MX II	D. A. Norwood	
G-MMCV	Solar Wings Typhoon III	G. Addison	
G-MMDN	Flexiform Striker	M. G. Griffiths	
G-MMDP	Southdown Sprint X	M. Bryan	
G-MMEK	Medway Hybred 44XL	M. G. J. Bridges	
G-MMFE	Flexiform Striker	W. Camm	
G-MMFV	Flexiform Striker	R. A. Walton	
G-MMGF	MBA Tiger Cub 440	S. R. Davis	
G-MMGL	MBA Tiger Cub 440	H. E. Dunning	
G-MMGS	Solar Wings Panther XL	G. C. Read	
G-MMGT	Solar Wings Typhoon	H. Cook	
G-MMGV	Whittaker MW5 Sorcerer	M. W. J. Whittaker & G. N. Haffey	
G-MMHE	Gemini Sprint	N. L. Zaman	
G-MMHL	Hiway Super Scorpion	E. J. Blyth	
G-MMHN	MBA Tiger Cub 440	M. J. Aubrey	
G-MMHS	SMD Viper	C. J. Meadows	
G-MMIE	MBA Tiger Cub 440	B. M. Olliver	
G-MMIZ	Lightning MkII	D. Coging	
G-MMJD	Southdown Puma Sprint	M. P. Robertshaw	
G-MMJF	Ultrasports Panther Dual 440	I. A. Macadam	
G-MMJV	MBA Tiger Cub 440	D. G. Palmer	
G-MMKA	Ultrasports Panther Dual	R. S. Wood	
G-MMKM	Flexiform Dual Striker	S. W. Hutchinson	
G-MMKP	MBA Tiger Cub 440	J. W. Beaty	
G-MMKR	Southdown Lightning DS	C. R. Madden	
G-MMKX	Skyrider Phantom 330	G. J. Lampitt	
G-MMLE	Eurowing Goldwing SP	M. J. Aubrey	
G-MMMG	Eipper Quicksilver MXL	J. G. Campbell	
G-MMMH	Hadland Willow	M. J. Hadland	
G-MMML	Dragon 150	M. J. Aubrey	
G-MMMN	Ultrasports Panther Dual 440	C. Downton	
G-MMNB	Eipper Quicksilver MX	M. J. Lindop	
G-MMNC	Eipper Quicksilver MX	W. S. Toulmin	
G-MMNH	Dragon 150	T. J. Barlow	
G-MMNN	Buzzard	E. W. Sherry	
G-MMOB	Southdown Sprint	D. Woolcock	
G-MMOK	Solar Wings Panther XL	R. F. & A. J. Foster	
G-MMPH	Southdown Puma Sprint	J. Siddle	
G-MMPL	Flexiform Dual Striker	P. D. Lawrence	
G-MMPO	Mainair Gemini/Flash	M.A Feber	
G-MMPZ	Teman Mono-Fly	H. Smith	

Notes	Reg.	Type	Owner or Operator
	G-MMRH	Highway Skytrike	A. M. Sirant
	G-MMRL	Solar Wings Panther XL	R. J. Hood
	G-MMRN	Southdown Puma Sprint	D. C. Read
	G-MMRP	Mainair Gemini	J. C. S. Jones
	G-MMRW	Flexiform Dual Striker	M. D. Hinge
	G-MMSA	Ultrasports Panther XL	T. W. Thiele & G. Savage
	G-MMSG	Solar Wings Panther XL-S	R. W. McKee
	G-MMSH	Solar Wings Panther XL	I. J. Drake
	G-MMSP	Mainair Gemini/Flash	J. Whiteford
	G-MMTD	Mainair Tri-Flyer 330	W. E. Teare
	G-MMTL	Mainair Gemini	K. Birkett
	G-MMTR	Ultrasports Panther	P. M. Kelsey
	G-MMTY	Fisher FP.202U	M. A. Welch
	G-MMUA	Southdown Puma Sprint	M. R. Crowhurst
	G-MMUO	Mainair Gemini/Flash	D. R. Howells & B. D. Bastin
	G-MMUV	Southdown Puma Sprint	D. C. Read
	G-MMUW	Mainair Gemini/Flash	J. C. K. Scardifield
	G-MMUX	Gemini Sprint	A. S. Gillespie
	G-MMVA	Southdown Puma Sprint	C. E. Tomkins
	G-MMVH	Southdown Raven	G. W. & K. M. Carwardine
	G-MMVI	Southdown Puma Sprint	G. R. Williams
	G-MMVS	Skyhook Pixie	B. W. Olley
	G-MMWG	Greenslade Mono-Trike	G-MMWG Group
	G-MMWS	Mainair Tri-Flyer	P. H. Risdale
	G-MMWX	Southdown Puma Sprint	G. A. Webb
	G-MMXL	Mainair Gemini Flash	G. W. Warner
	G-MMXO	Southdown Puma Sprint	D. J. Tasker
	G-MMXU	Mainair Gemini/Flash	T. J. Franklin
	G-MMXV	Mainair Gemini/Flash	M. A. Boffin
	G-MMYL	Cyclone 70	A. W. Nancarrow
	G-MMZA	Mainair Gemini/Flash	G. T. Johnston
	G-MMZD	Mainair Gemini/Flash	S. McDonnell
	G-MMZK	Mainair Gemini/Flash	G. Jones & B. Lee
	G-MMZV	Mainair Gemini/Flash	N. M. Toulson
	G-MMZW	Southdown Puma Sprint	M. G. Ashbee
	G-MNAE	Mainair Gemini/Flash	G. C. luddington
	G-MNAI	Ultrasports Panther XL-S	R. G. Cameron
	G-MNAZ	Solar Wings Pegasus XL-R	R. W. houldsworth
	G-MNBA	Solar Wings Pegasus XL-R	L. Hughes
	G-MNBB	Solar Wings Pegasus XL-R	D. A. Blackston
	G-MNBC	Solar Wings Pegasus XL-R	R. T. Parry
	G-MNBI	Solar Wings Panther XL-S	M. O'Connell
	G-MNBM	Southdown Puma Sprint	C. Hall-Gardiner
	G-MNBN	Mainair Gemini/Flash	I. Bond
	G-MNBP	Mainair Gemini/Flash	B. J. James
	G-MNBS	Mainair Gemini/Flash	P. A. Comins
	G-MNBT	Mainair Gemini/Flash	R. R. A. Dean
	G-MNCA	Hiway Demon 175	M. A. Sirant
	G-MNCF	Mainair Gemini/Flash	C. F. Janes
	G-MNCG	Mainair Gemini/Flash	T. Lynch
	G-MNCM	CFM Shadow Srs B	K. G. D. Macrae
	G-MNCO	Eipper Quicksilver MXII	S. Lawton
	G-MNCP	Southdown Puma Sprint	D. A. Payne
	G-MNCS	Skyrider Airsports Phantom	K. J. Underwood
	G-MNCU	Medway Hybred 44XL	J. E. Evans
	G-MNCV	Medway Hybred 44XL	M. J. Turland
	G-MNDD	Mainair Scorcher Solo	L. Hurman
	G-MNDE	Medway Half Pint	Delta Echo Half Pint Group
	G-MNDM	Mainair Gemini/Flash	J. C. Birkbeck
	G-MNDU	Midland Sirocco 377GB	M. A. Collins
	G-MNDY	Southdown Puma Sprint	A. M. Coupland
	G-MNEG	Mainair Gemini/Flash	A. Sexton/Ireland
	G-MNEH	Mainair Gemini/Flash	I. Rawson
	G-MNER	CFM Shadow Srs B	F. C. Claydon
	G-MNET	Mainair Gemini/Flash	I. P. Stubbins
	G-MNEY	Mainair Gemini/Flash	D. A. Spiers
	G-MNFB	Southdown Puma Sprint	C. Lawrence
	G-MNFF	Mainair Gemini/Flash	C. H. Spencer & R. P. Cook
	G-MNFG	Southdown Puma Sprint	M. Ingleton
	G-MNFL	AMF Chevvron	S. S. M. Turner
	G-MNFM	Mainair Gemini/Flash	P. M. Fidell

Reg.	Type	Owner or Operator	Notes
G-MNFN	Mainair Gemini/Flash	J. R. Martin	
G-MNFP	Mainair Gemini/Flash	S. E. Walsh	
G-MNGD	Solar Wings Typhoon/Tri-Pacer	I. White	
G-MNGG	Solar Wings Pegasus XL-R	I. D. Mallinson	
G-MNGK	Mainair Gemini/Flash	G. P. Warnes	
G-MNGM	Mainair Gemini/Flash	R. J. Webb	
G-MNGW	Mainair Gemini/Flash	F. R. Stephens	
G-MNHD	Solar Wings Pegasus XL-R	J. R. Hackett	
G-MNHE	Solar Wings Pegasus XL-R	A. Daujotis	
G-MNHH	Solar Wings Panther XL-S	F. J. Williams	
G-MNHI	Solar Wings Pegasus XL-R	R. W. Matthews	
G-MNHJ	Solar Wings Pegasus XL-R	C. Council	
G-MNHK	Solar Wings Pegasus XL-R	G. J. Eaton	
G-MNHL	Solar Wings Pegasus XL-R	The Microlight School (Lichfield) Ltd	
G-MNHM	Solar Wings Pegasus XL-R	P. A. Howell	
G-MNHN	Solar Wings Pegasus XL-R	M. Devlin	
G-MNHR	Solar Wings Pegasus XL-R	B. D. Jackson	
G-MNHZ	Mainair Gemini/Flash	I. O. S. Ross	
G-MNIA	Mainair Gemini/Flash	A. E. Dix	
G-MNID	Mainair Gemini/Flash	M. I. Potts	
G-MNIG	Mainair Gemini/Flash	A. B. Woods	
G-MNIH	Mainair Gemini/Flash	N. H. S. Insall	
G-MNII	Mainair Gemini/Flash	R. F. Finnis	
G-MNIK	Pegasus Photon	M. Belemet	
G-MNIM	Maxair Hummer	K. Wood	
G-MNIW	Airwave Nimrod/Tri-Flyer	C. Murphy	
G-MNIZ	Mainair Gemini/Flash	A. G. Power	
G-MNJB	Southdown Raven	W. Flood	
G-MNJD	Southdown Puma Sprint	S. D. Smith	
G-MNJJ	Solar Wings Pegasus Flash	P. A. Shelley	
G-MNJL	Solar Wings Pegasus Flash	S. D. Thomas	
G-MNJN	Solar Wings Pegasus Flash	P. Ayres	
G-MNJR	Solar Wings Pegasus Flash	M. G. Ashbee	
G-MNJS	Southdown Puma Sprint	E. A. Frost	
G-MNJX	Medway Hybred 44XL	H. A. Stewart	
G-MNKB	Solar Wings Pegasus Photon	M. E. Gilbert	
G-MNKC	Solar Wings Pegasus Photon	K. B. Woods	
G-MNKD	Solar Wings Pegasus Photon	A. M. Sirant	
G-MNKE	Solar Wings Pegasus Photon	H. C. Lowther	
G-MNKG	Solar Wings Pegasus Photon	S. N. Robson	
G-MNKK	Solar Wings Pegasus Photon	M. E. Gilbert	
G-MNKM	MBA Tiger Cub 440	A. R. Sunley	
G-MNKN	Skycraft Scout Mk.3-3R	M. A. Aubrey	
G-MNKO	Solar Wings Pegasus Flash	T. A. Goundry	
G-MNKP	Solar Wings Pegasus Flash	I. N. Miller	
G-MNKU	Southdown Puma Sprint	S. P. O'Hannrachain	
G-MNKW	Solar Wings Pegasus Flash	G. J. Eaton	
G-MNKX	Solar Wings Pegasus Flash	T. A. Newton	
G-MNKZ	Southdown Raven	D. M. Pecheur	
G-MNLI	Mainair Gemini/Flash	S. A. V. Smith	
G-MNLT	Southdown Raven	J. L. Stachini	
G-MNMC	Mainair Gemini Sprint	J. C. Peat	
G-MNMG	Mainair Gemini/Flash	N. A. M. Beyer-Kay	
G-MNMK	Solar Wings Pegasus XL-R	A. F. Smallacombe	
G-MNMM	Aerotech MW5 Sorcerer	S. F. N. Warnell	
G-MNMU	Southdown Raven	M. J. Curley	
G-MNMV	Mainair Gemini/Flash	S. Staig	
G-MNMW	Aerotech MW6 Merlin	E. F. Clapham	
G-MNMY	Cyclone 70	N. R. Beale	
G-MNNA	Southdown Raven	D. & G. D. Palfrey	
G-MNNF	Mainair Gemini/Flash	W. J. Gunn	
G-MNNG	Solar Wings Photon	K. B. Woods	
G-MNNL	Mainair Gemini/Flash II	C. L. Rumney	
G-MNNM	Mainair Scorcher Solo	L. L. Perry & S. R. Leeper	
G-MNNO	Southdown Raven	M. J. Robbins	
G-MNNS	Eurowing Goldwing	B. K. Harrison & F. W. McCann	
G-MNNY	Solar Wings Pegasus Flash	C. W. Payne	
G-MNPC	Mainair Gemini/Flash	M. S. McGimpsey	
G-MNPY	Mainair Scorcher Solo	E. Rawlinson	
G-MNPZ	Mainair Scorcher Solo	S. Stevens	
G-MNRD	Ultraflight Lazair IIIE	Sywell Lazair Group	
G-MNRE	Mainair Scorcher Solo	A. P. Pearce	

Notes	Reg.	Type	Owner or Operator
	G-MNRI	Hornet Dual Trainer	R. H. Goll
	G-MNRM	Hornet Dual Trainer	I. C. Cannan
	G-MNRS	Southdown Raven	M. C. Newman
	G-MNRT	Midland Ultralights Sirocco	R. F. Hinton
	G-MNRX	Mainair Gemini/Flash II	R. Downham
	G-MNRZ	Mainair Scorcher Solo	A. Costello
	G-MNSJ	Mainair Gemini/Flash	P. Cooney
	G-MNSL	Southdown Raven X	P. B. Robinson
	G-MNSY	Southdown Raven X	L. A. Hosegood
	G-MNTD	Aerial Arts Chaser 110SX	B. Richardson
	G-MNTE	Southdown Raven X	E. Foster
	G-MNTK	CFM Shadow Srs B	M. J. Bromley
	G-MNTP	CFM Shadow Srs B	E. G. White
	G-MNTV	Mainair Gemini/Flash II	A.M. Sirant
	G-MNUF	Mainair Gemini/Flash II	K. Jones
	G-MNUI	Skyhook Cutlass Dual	M. Holling
	G-MNUR	Mainair Gemini/Flash II	J. S. Hawkins
	G-MNUX	Solar Wings Pegasus XL-R	M. Devlin
	G-MNVB	Solar Wings Pegasus XL-R	M. Cairns
	G-MNVE	Solar Wings Pegasus XL-R	M. P. Aris
	G-MNVG	Solar Wings Pegasus Flash II	D. J. Ward
	G-MNVI	CFM Shadow Srs B	D. R. C. Pugh
	G-MNVJ	CFM Shadow Srs CD	G. Mudd
	G-MNVK	CFM Shadow Srs B	A. K. Atwell
	G-MNVO	Hovey Whing-Ding II	C. Wilson
	G-MNVT	Mainair Gemini/Flash II	ACB Hydraulics
	G-MNVV	Mainair Gemini/Flash II	T. Wilbor
	G-MNVW	Mainair Gemini/Flash II	J. C. Munro-Hunt
	G-MNVZ	Solar Wings Pegasus Photon	J. J. Russ
	G-MNWG	Southdown Raven X	D. Murray
	G-MNWI	Mainair Gemini/Flash II	I. E. Chapman
	G-MNWL	Aerial Arts 130SX	E. H. Snook
	G-MNWO	Mainair Gemini/Flash II	P. Burgess
	G-MNWY	CFM Shadow Srs C	R. R. L. & S. R. Potts
	G-MNXE	Southdown Raven X	A. E. Silvey
	G-MNXF	Southdown Raven X	D. E. Gwenin
	G-MNXG	Southdown Raven X	E. M. & M. A. Williams
	G-MNXO	Medway Hybred 44XLR	R. P. Taylor
	G-MNXU	Mainair Gemini/Flash II	J. M. Hucker
	G-MNXX	CFM Shadow Srs BD	M. Nazm
	G-MNXZ	Whittaker MW5 Sorcerer	A. J. Glynn
	G-MNYA	Solar Wings Pegasus Flash II	C. Trollope
	G-MNYC	Solar Wings Pegasus XL-R	J. S. Hawkins
	G-MNYD	Aerial Arts 110SX Chaser	B. Richardson
	G-MNYE	Aerial Arts 110SX Chaser	R. J. Ripley
	G-MNYF	Aerial Arts 110SX Chaser	R. W. Twamley
	G-MNYM	Southdown Raven X	R. L. Davis
	G-MNYP	Southdown Raven X	A. G. Davies
	G-MNYU	Pegasus XL-R	G. L. Turner
	G-MNYW	Solar Wings Pegasus XL-R	M. P. Waldock
	G-MNYX	Solar Wings Pegasus XL-R	P. F. Mayes
	G-MNZB	Mainair Gemini/Flash II	P. A. Ryder
	G-MNZC	Mainair Gemini/Flash II	C. J. Whittaker
	G-MNZD	Mainair Gemini/Flash II	N. D. Carter
	G-MNZJ	CFM Shadow Srs BD	E. W. Laidlaw
	G-MNZK	Solar Wings Pegasus XL-R	P. J. Appleby
	G-MNZP	CFM Shadow Srs B	J. G. Wakeford
	G-MNZS	Aerial Arts 130SX	N. R. Beale
	G-MNZU	Eurowing Goldwing	P. D. Coppin & P. R. Millen
	G-MNZW	Southdown Raven X	T. A. Willcox
	G-MNZZ	CFM Shadow Srs B	Shadow Aviation Ltd
	G-MOAC	Beech F33A Bonanza	R. M. Camrass
	G-MOAN	Aeromot AMT-200S Super Ximango	A. E. Mayhew
	G-MODE	Eurocopter EC 120B	Cardy Construction Ltd
	G-MOFB	Cameron O-120 balloon	D. M. Moffat
	G-MOFZ	Cameron O-90 balloon	D. M. Moffat
	G-MOGI	AA-5A Cheetah	Octopus GmbH/Germany (G-BFMU)
	G-MOGS	CZAW Sportcruiser	J. M. Oliver
	G-MOGY	Robinson R22 Beta	Northumbria Helicopters Ltd
	G-MOKE	Cameron V-77 balloon	G-MOKE ASBC/Luxembourg
	G-MOLA	Evektor EV-97 TeamEurostar UK	J. Bate

Reg.	Type	Owner or Operator	Notes
G-MOMA	Thruster T.600N 450	Compton Abbas Microlight Group (G-CCIB)	
G-MONI	Monnett Moni	P. N. Stacey	
G-MONJ	Boeing 757-2T7	Monarch Airlines Ltd	
G-MONK	Boeing 757-2T7	Monarch Airlines Ltd	
G-MONS	Airbus A.300-605R	Monarch Airlines Ltd	
G-MONX	Airbus A.320-212	Monarch Airlines Ltd	
G-MOOR	SOCATA TB10 Tobago	P. D. Kirkham (G-MILK)	
G-MOOS	P.56 Provost T.1 (XF690)	H. Cooke (G-BGKA)	
G-MOOV	CZAW Sportcruiser	G-MOOV Syndicate	
G-MOPS	Best Off Sky Ranger Swift 912S	P. Stretton	
G-MOSA	Morane Saulnier MS317	A. C. Whitehead	
G-MOSJ	Beech C.90GTi King Air	Moss Aviation LLP	
G-MOSS	Beech D55 Baron	D. J. da Costa Marques (G-AWAD)	
G-MOSY	Cameron O-84 balloon	P. L. Mossman	
G-MOTA	Bell 206B JetRanger 3	J. W. Sandle	
G-MOTH	DH.82A Tiger Moth (K2567)	P. T. Szluha	
G-MOTI	Robin DR.400/500	Tango India Flying Group	
G-MOTO	PA-24 Comanche 180	S. M. R. Hickman (G-EDHE/G-ASFH)	
G-MOTW	Meyers OTW-145	J. K. Padden	
G-MOUL	Maule M6-235	M. Klinge	
G-MOUR	HS. Gnat T.1 (XR991)	Heritage Aircraft Ltd	
G-MOUT	Cessna 182T	C. Mountain	
G-MOVI	PA-32R-301 Saratoga SP	G-BOON Ltd (G-MARI)	
G-MOWG	Aeroprakt A22-L Foxbat	J. Smith	
G-MOZI	Glasflugel Mosquito	J. Christensen & P. Smith	
G-MOZZ	Avions Mudry CAP-10B	N. Skipworth	
G-MPAA	PA-28-181 Archer III	Shropshire Aero Club Ltd	
G-MPAC	Ultravia Pelican PL	J. H. Leigh t/a The Clipgate Flying Grp	
G-MPAT	EV-97 TeamEurostar UK	P. J. Dale	
G-MPBH	Cessna FA.152	The Moray Flying Club (1996) Ltd (G-FLIC/ G-BILV)	
G-MPCD	Airbus A.320-212	Monarch Airlines Ltd	
G-MPHY	Ikarus C42 FB100	P. Murphy	
G-MPIT	CFM Shadow Srs DD	P. Cicconetti (G-MZOM)	
G-MPLA	Cessna 182T	Oxford Aviation Academy (Oxford) Ltd	
G-MPLB	Cessna 182T	Oxford Aviation Academy (Oxford) Ltd	
G-MPLC	Cessna 182T	Oxford Aviation Academy (Oxford) Ltd	
G-MPLD	Cessna 182T	Oxford Aviation Academy (Oxford) Ltd	
G-MPMP	Bombardier CL600-2B16 Challenger	TAG Aviation (UK) Ltd (G-JMMP)	
G-MPRL	Cessna 210M	Mike Stapleton & Co.Ltd	
G-MPSA	Eurocopter MBB BK-117C-2	The Mayor's Office for Policing & Crime	
G-MPSB	Eurocopter MBB BK-117C-2	The Mayor's Office for Policing & Crime	
G-MPSC	Eurocopter MBB BK-117C-2	The Mayor's Office for Policing & Crime	
G-MPSP	Bombardier CL600-2B16 Challenger	Bluejets Ltd (G-MPCW/G-JMMD)	
G-MPWI	Robin HR.100/210	P. G. Clarkson & S. King	
G-MRAJ	Hughes 369E	A. Jardine	
G-MRAM	Mignet HM.1000 Balerit	R. A. Marven	
G-MRAP	Bombardier BD100-1A10 Challenger 300	Ability Air Charter LLP	
G-MRDC	Robinson R44 II	E. M. Montefusco	
G-MRDS	CZAW Sportcruiser	P. Wood	
G-MRED	Christavia Mk 1	The Barton Group	
G-MRJJ	Mainair Pegasus Quik	J.H. Sparks	
G-MRJK	Airbus A.320-214	Monarch Airlines Ltd	
G-MRJP	Silence Twister	M. D. Carruthers	
G-MRKS	Robinson R44	TJD Trade Ltd (G-RAYC)	
G-MRKT	Lindstrand LBL-90A balloon	Marketplace Public Relations (London) Ltd	
G-MRLL	NA P-51D Mustang (413521:5Q-B)	M. Hammond	
G-MRLN	Sky 240-24 balloon	Merlin Balloons	
G-MRLS	AutoGyro Calidus	M. R. Love	
G-MRME	Gefa-Flug AS 105 GD airship	Airship Over Atlanta Ltd	
G-MRMJ	Eurocopter AS.365N3 Dauphin 2	Whirligig Ltd	
G-MROC	Pegasus Quantum 15-912	P. Hill & M. A. Metzler	
G-MROD	Van's RV-7A	K. R. Emery	
G-MRPH	Murphy Rebel	P. & B. S. Metson	
G-MRPT	Cessna 172S	Kuki Helicopter Sales Ltd (G-UFCC)	
G-MRRR	Hughes 369E	J. Paxton	
G-MRRY	Robinson R44 II	F. V. Neefs	
G-MRSN	Robinson R22 Beta	Yorkshire Helicopters Ltd	
G-MRSS	Ikarus C42 FB80	Purple Aviation Ltd	

Notes	Reg.	Type	Owner or Operator
	G-MRST	PA-28 RT-201 Arrow IV	Calverton Flying Group Ltd
	G-MRTN	SOCATA TB10 Tobago	G. C. Jarvis (G-BHET)
	G-MRTY	Cameron N-77 balloon	R. A. Vale & ptnrs
	G-MRVK	Czech Sport Aircraft Pipersport	M. Farrugia
	G-MRVL	Van's RV-7	L. W. Taylor
	G-MRVN	PZL-Bielsko SZD-50-3	The Bath, Wilts and North Dorset Gliding Club Ltd
	G-MSAL	MS.733 Alcyon (143)	M. Isbister t/a Alcyon Flying Group
	G-MSFC	PA-38-112 Tomahawk	Sherwood Flying Club Ltd
	G-MSFT	PA-28-161 Warrior II	Western Air (Thruxton) Ltd (G-MUMS)
	G-MSIX	Glaser-Dirks DG.800B	G-MSIX Group
	G-MSKY	Ikarus C.42 FB100 VLA	P. M. Yeoman & J. S. Mason
	G-MSON	Cameron Z-90 balloon	Regional Property Services Ltd
	G-MSOO	Revolution Mini 500 helicopter	R. H. Ryan
	G-MSPT	Eurocopter EC 135T2	M Sport Ltd
	G-MSPY	Pegasus Quantum 15-912	B. E. Wagenhauser
	G-MSTG	NA P-51D Mustang (414419:LH-F)	M. Hammond
	G-MSTR	Cameron 110 Monster SS Balloon	Monster Syndicate (G-OJOB)
	G-MTAB	Mainair Gemini/Flash II	L. Clarkson
	G-MTAC	Mainair Gemini/Flash II	R. Massey
	G-MTAF	Mainair Gemini/Flash II	A. G. Lister
	G-MTAG	Mainair Gemini/Flash II	M. J. Cowie & J. P. Hardy
	G-MTAH	Mainair Gemini/Flash II	A. J. Rowe
	G-MTAI	Solar Wings Pegasus XL-R	S. T. Elkington
	G-MTAP	Southdown Raven X	M. C. Newman
	G-MTAS	Whittaker MW5 Sorcerer	R. J. Scott
	G-MTAV	Solar Wings Pegasus XL-R	S. Fairweather
	G-MTAW	Solar Wings Pegasus XL-R	M. G. Ralph
	G-MTAX	Solar Wings Pegasus XL-R	L. J. Tonkinson
	G-MTAY	Solar Wings Pegasus XL-R	S. A. McLatchie
	G-MTAZ	Solar Wings Pegasus XL-R	M. O'Connell
	G-MTBB	Southdown Raven X	A. Miller
	G-MTBD	Mainair Gemini/Flash II	J. G. Jones
	G-MTBE	CFM Shadow Srs BD	S. K. Brown
	G-MTBH	Mainair Gemini/Flash II	P. & T. Sludds
	G-MTBJ	Mainair Gemini/Flash II	P. J. & R. M. Perry
	G-MTBL	Solar Wings Pegasus XL-R	R. N. Whiting
	G-MTBN	Southdown Raven X	A. J. & S. E. Crosby-Jones
	G-MTBO	Southdown Raven X	J. Liversuch
	G-MTBP	Aerotech MW5 Sorcerer	L. J. Greenhough
	G-MTBR	Aerotech MW5 Sorcerer	R. Poulter
	G-MTBS	Aerotech MW5 Sorcerer	D. J. Pike
	G-MTCK	SW Pegasus Flash	A. M. Chilingirov
	G-MTCM	Southdown Raven X	J. C. Rose
	G-MTCP	Aerial Arts Chaser 110SX	B. Richardson
	G-MTCU	Mainair Gemini/Flash II	T. J. Philip
	G-MTDD	Aerial Arts Chaser 110SX	B. Richardson
	G-MTDE	American Aerolights 110SX	J. T. Meager
	G-MTDF	Mainair Gemini/Flash II	P. G. Barnes
	G-MTDK	Aerotech MW-5B Sorcerer	C. C. Wright
	G-MTDO	Eipper Quicksilver MXII	D. L. Ham
	G-MTDR	Mainair Gemini/Flash II	D. J. Morriss
	G-MTDU	CFM Shadow Srs BD	A. Harris
	G-MTDW	Mainair Gemini/Flash II	S. R. Leeper
	G-MTDY	Mainair Gemini/Flash II	S. Penoyre
	G-MTEB	Solar Wings Pegasus XL-R	D. P. Gawlowski
	G-MTEC	Solar Wings Pegasus XL-R	R. W. Glover
	G-MTEE	Solar Wings Pegasus XL-R	The Microlight School (Lichfield) Ltd
	G-MTEK	Mainair Gemini/Flash II	G. M. Wrigley & M. O'Hearne
	G-MTER	Solar Wings Pegasus XL-R	G. Carr
	G-MTES	Solar Wings Pegasus XL-R	N. P. Read
	G-MTET	Solar Wings Pegasus XL-R	K. Gilsenan
	G-MTEU	Solar Wings Pegasus XL-R	T. E. Thomas
	G-MTEY	Mainair Gemini/Flash II	A. Wells
	G-MTFA	Pegasus XL-R	S. Hindle
	G-MTFB	Solar Wings Pegasus XL-R	K. P. Smith
	G-MTFC	Medway Hybred 44XLR	J. K. Masters
	G-MTFG	AMF Chevvron 232	J. Batchelor
	G-MTFM	Solar Wings Pegasus XL-R	P. R. G. Morley
	G-MTFN	Aerotech MW5 Sorcerer	S. M. King
	G-MTFT	Solar Wings Pegasus XL-R	S. J. Ward

Reg.	Type	Owner or Operator	Notes
G-MTFU	CFM Shadow Srs CD	G. J. Jones & D. C. Lees	
G-MTGA	Mainair Gemini/Flash	I. White	
G-MTGB	Thruster TST Mk 1	M. J. Aubrey	
G-MTGC	Thruster TST Mk 1	G. M. Cruise-Smith	
G-MTGD	Thruster TST Mk 1	B. A. Janaway	
G-MTGF	Thruster TST Mk 1	B. Swindon	
G-MTGL	Solar Wings Pegasus XL-R	R. & P. J. Openshaw	
G-MTGM	Solar Wings Pegasus XL-R	I. J. Steele	
G-MTGO	Mainair Gemini/Flash	J. Ouru	
G-MTGR	Thruster TST Mk 1	M. R. Grunwell	
G-MTGS	Thruster TST Mk 1	R. J. Nelson	
G-MTGV	CFM Shadow Srs BD	V. R. Riley	
G-MTGW	CFM Shadow Srs BD	N. Hart	
G-MTHH	Solar Wings Pegasus XL-R	J. Palmer	
G-MTHJ	Solar Wings Pegasus XL-R	M. R. Harrison	
G-MTHN	Solar Wings Pegasus XL-R	M. T. Seal	
G-MTHT	CFM Shadow Srs BD	A. P. Jones	
G-MTHV	CFM Shadow Srs BD	P. G. Kavanagh	
G-MTIA	Mainair Gemini/Flash IIA	G. W. Jennings	
G-MTIB	Mainair Gemini/Flash IIA	M. D. Maclagan	
G-MTIE	Solar Wings Pegasus XL-R	P. Wibberley	
G-MTIH	Solar Wings Pegasus XL-R	R. D. Layton	
G-MTIJ	Solar Wings Pegasus XL-R	M. J. F. Gilbody	
G-MTIK	Southdown Raven X	G. A. Oldershaw	
G-MTIL	Mainair Gemini/Flash IIA	M. Ward	
G-MTIM	Mainair Gemini/Flash IIA	T. M. Swan	
G-MTIO	Solar Wings Pegasus XL-R	A. R. Wade	
G-MTIR	Solar Wings Pegasus XL-R	P. Jolley	
G-MTIS	Solar Wings Pegasus XL-R	Upottery Aerotow Club	
G-MTIW	Solar Wings Pegasus XL-R	G. S. Francis	
G-MTIX	Solar Wings Pegasus XL-R	S. Pickering	
G-MTIZ	Solar Wings Pegasus XL-R	S. L. Blount	
G-MTJB	Mainair Gemini/Flash IIA	B. Skidmore	
G-MTJC	Mainair Gemini/Flash IIA	T. A. Dockrell	
G-MTJE	Mainair Gemini/Flash IIA	S. R. Eskins	
G-MTJG	Medway Hybred 44XLR	M. A. Trodden	
G-MTJH	SW Pegasus Flash	C. G. Ludgate	
G-MTJL	Mainair Gemini/Flash IIA	P. Marriner	
G-MTJT	Mainair Gemini/Flash IIA	D. F. Greatbanks	
G-MTJV	Mainair Gemini/Flash IIA	R. W. Hocking	
G-MTJX	Hornet Dual Trainer/Raven	J. P. Kirwan	
G-MTKA	Thruster TST Mk 1	M. J. Coles & S. R. Williams	
G-MTKB	Thruster TST Mk 1	M. Hanna	
G-MTKD	Thruster TST Mk 1	E. Spain/Ireland	
G-MTKG	Solar Wings Pegasus XL-R	S. J. Halliwell	
G-MTKH	Solar Wings Pegasus XL-R	B. P. Hoare	
G-MTKI	Solar Wings Pegasus XL-R	M. Wady	
G-MTKR	CFM Shadow Srs BD	D. P. Eichhorn	
G-MTKW	Mainair Gemini/Flash IIA	J. H. McIvor	
G-MTKZ	Mainair Gemini/Flash IIA	G-MTKZ Syndicate	
G-MTLB	Mainair Gemini/Flash IIA	M. J. Jones	
G-MTLC	Mainair Gemini/Flash IIA	R. J. Alston	
G-MTLG	Solar Wings Pegasus XL-R	G. J. Simoni	
G-MTLL	Mainair Gemini/Flash IIA	M. S. Lawrence	
G-MTLM	Thruster TST Mk 1	R.J. Nelson	
G-MTLN	Thruster TST Mk 1	P. W. Taylor	
G-MTLT	Solar Wings Pegasus XL-R	K. M. Mayling	
G-MTLV	Solar Wings Pegasus XL-R	P. Cave	
G-MTLX	Medway Hybred 44XLR	D. A. Coupland	
G-MTLY	Solar Wings Pegasus XL-R	I. Johnston	
G-MTLZ	Whittaker MW5 Sorcerer	J. O'Keeffe	
G-MTMA	Mainair Gemini/Flash IIA	G-MTMA Flying Group	
G-MTMC	Mainair Gemini/Flash IIA	Rovogate Ltd	
G-MTMF	Solar Wings Pegasus XL-R	H. T. M. Smith	
G-MTMG	Solar Wings Pegasus XL-R	C. W. & P. E. F. Suckling	
G-MTML	Mainair Gemini/Flash IIA	J. F. Ashton	
G-MTMR	Hornet Dual Trainer/Raven	D. J. Smith	
G-MTMT	Mainair Gemini/Flash IIA	C. Pickvance	
G-MTMV	Mainair Gemini/Flash IIA	G. J. Small	
G-MTMW	Mainair Gemini/Flash IIA	F. Lees	
G-MTMX	CFM Shadow Srs BD	D. R. White	
G-MTNC	Mainair Gemini/Flash IIA	M. G. Titmus & M. E. Cook	

Notes	Reg.	Type	Owner or Operator
	G-MTND	Medway Hybred 44XLR	Butty Boys Flying Group
	G-MTNE	Medway Hybred 44XLR	A. G. Rodenburg
	G-MTNF	Medway Hybred 44XLR	P. A. Bedford
	G-MTNG	Mainair Gemini/Flash IIA	A. N. Bellis
	G-MTNI	Mainair Gemini/Flash IIA	F. J. Clarehugh
	G-MTNJ	Mainair Gemini/Flash IIA	S. M. Cook
	G-MTNL	Mainair Gemini/Flash IIA	R. A. Matthews
	G-MTNM	Mainair Gemini/Flash IIA	P. M. Cary
	G-MTNO	Solar Wings Pegasus XL-Q	P. J. Knibb & G. J. Rowe
	G-MTNP	Solar Wings Pegasus XL-Q	L. A. Washer
	G-MTNR	Thruster TST Mk 1	A. M. Sirant
	G-MTNT	Thruster TST Mk 1	M. McKenzie
	G-MTNU	Thruster TST Mk 1	T. H. Brearley
	G-MTNV	Thruster TST Mk 1	J. B. Russell
	G-MTOA	Solar Wings Pegasus XL-R	R. A. Bird
	G-MTOH	Solar Wings Pegasus XL-R	H. Cook
	G-MTON	Solar Wings Pegasus XL-R	D. J. Willett
	G-MTOY	Solar Wings Pegasus XL-R	G-MTOY Group
	G-MTOZ	Solar Wings Pegasus XL-R	C. P. Davies
	G-MTPB	Mainair Gemini/Flash IIA	C. P. Whitwell
	G-MTPE	Solar Wings Pegasus XL-R	J. Bassett
	G-MTPF	Solar Wings Pegasus XL-R	P. M. Watts & A. S. Mitchel
	G-MTPH	Solar Wings Pegasus XL-R	G. Barker & L. Blight
	G-MTPI	Solar Wings Pegasus XL-R	R. J. Bullock
	G-MTPJ	Solar Wings Pegasus XL-R	D. Lockwood
	G-MTPL	Solar Wings Pegasus XL-R	C. J. Jones
	G-MTPM	Solar Wings Pegasus XL-R	D. K. Seal
	G-MTPR	Solar Wings Pegasus XL-R	T. Kenny
	G-MTPU	Thruster TST Mk 1	N. Hay
	G-MTPW	Thruster TST Mk 1	K. Hawthorne
	G-MTPX	Thruster TST Mk 1	T. Snook
	G-MTPY	Thruster TST Mk 1	H. N. Baumgartner
	G-MTRA	Mainair Gemini/Flash IIA	A. Davis
	G-MTRC	Midlands Ultralights Sirocco 377G	D. Thorpe
	G-MTRM	Solar Wings Pegasus XL-R	M. Morris
	G-MTRO	Solar Wings Pegasus XL-R	D. Rowland
	G-MTRS	Solar Wings Pegasus XL-R	J. J. R. Tickle
	G-MTRX	Whittaker MW5 Sorceror	W. Turner
	G-MTRZ	Mainair Gemini/Flash IIA	D. S. Lally
	G-MTSC	Mainair Gemini/Flash IIA	J. Kilpatrick
	G-MTSH	Thruster TST Mk 1	R. R. Orr
	G-MTSJ	Thruster TST Mk 1	S. R. Cockram
	G-MTSK	Thruster TST Mk 1	J. S. Pyke
	G-MTSM	Thruster TST Mk 1	R. J. Webb
	G-MTSS	Solar Wings Pegasus XL-R	V. Marchant
	G-MTSZ	Solar Wings Pegasus XL-R	D. L. Pickover
	G-MTTA	Solar Wings Pegasus XL-R	J. P. Anderson
	G-MTTE	Solar Wings Pegasus XL-R	C. F. Barnard
	G-MTTF	Aerotech MW6 Merlin	P. Cotton
	G-MTTI	Mainair Gemini/Flash IIA	R. J. Drake
	G-MTTM	Mainair Gemini/Flash IIA	M. Anderson
	G-MTTN	Ultralight Flight Phantom	F. P. Welsh
	G-MTTP	Mainair Gemini/Flash IIA	A. Ormson
	G-MTTU	Solar Wings Pegasus XL-R	A. Friend
	G-MTTW	Mainair Gemini/Flash IIA	G-MTTW Trustee Group
	G-MTTY	Solar Wings Pegasus XL-Q	N. A. Perry
	G-MTTZ	Solar Wings Pegasus XL-Q	G. D. Hall
	G-MTUA	Solar Wings Pegasus XL-R	Fly Hire Ltd
	G-MTUC	Thruster TST Mk 1	S. T. G. Ingram
	G-MTUD	Thruster TST Mk 1	S. Cooper & J. Parker
	G-MTUI	Solar Wings Pegasus XL-R	J. Pool
	G-MTUK	Solar Wings Pegasus XL-R	G. McLaughlin
	G-MTUN	Solar Wings Pegasus XL-Q	M. J. O'Connor
	G-MTUP	Solar Wings Pegasus XL-Q	B. P. Vinall
	G-MTUR	Solar Wings Pegasus XL-Q	G. Ball
	G-MTUS	Solar Wings Pegasus XL-Q	G. Nicol
	G-MTUT	Solar Wings Pegasus XL-Q	R. E. Bull
	G-MTUV	Mainair Gemini/Flash IIA	D. Baker & S. Taylor
	G-MTUY	Solar Wings Pegasus XL-Q	H. C. Lowther
	G-MTVH	Mainair Gemini/Flash IIA	P. H. Statham
	G-MTVI	Mainair Gemini/Flash IIA	R. A. McDowell
	G-MTVJ	Mainair Gemini/Flash IIA	P. J. Ensinger

Reg.	Type	Owner or Operator	Notes
G-MTVP	Thruster TST Mk 1	J. M. Evans	
G-MTVR	Thruster TST Mk 1	D. R. Lucas	
G-MTVT	Thruster TST Mk.1	W. H. J. Knowles	
G-MTVV	Thruster TST Mk 1	J. H. Askew	
G-MTVX	Solar Wings Pegasus XL-Q	D. A. Foster	
G-MTWG	Mainair Gemini/Flash IIA	N. Mackenzie & P. S. Bunting	
G-MTWH	CFM Shadow Srs BD	I. W. Hogg	
G-MTWK	CFM Shadow Srs BD	J. P. Batty & J. R. C. Brightman	
G-MTWR	Mainair Gemini/Flash IIA	J. B. Hodson	
G-MTWS	Mainair Gemini/Flash IIA	M. P. Duncan & C. R. Stewart	
G-MTWX	Mainair Gemini/Flash IIA	J. Donley	
G-MTWY	Thruster TST Mk 1	J. F. Gardner	
G-MTWZ	Thruster TST Mk 1	M. J. Aubrey	
G-MTXA	Thruster TST Mk 1	B. Dennis	
G-MTXB	Thruster TST Mk 1	J. J. Hill	
G-MTXC	Thruster TST Mk.1	W. Macleod	
G-MTXD	Thruster TST Mk 1	G. A. Diggins	
G-MTXJ	Solar Wings Pegasus XL-Q	E. W. Laidlaw	
G-MTXK	Solar Wings Pegasus XL-Q	D. R. G. Whitelaw	
G-MTXL	Noble Hardman Snowbird Mk IV	P. J. Collins	
G-MTXM	Mainair Gemini/Flash IIA	H. J. Vinning	
G-MTXO	Whittaker MW6	T. L. Dean	
G-MTXR	CFM Shadow Srs BD	S. A. O'Neill	
G-MTXU	Snowbird Mk.IV	M. A. Oakley	
G-MTXZ	Mainair Gemini/Flash IIA	J. S. Hawkins	
G-MTYC	Solar Wings Pegasus XL-Q	C. I. D. H. Garrison	
G-MTYD	Solar Wings Pegasus XL-Q	R. S. Colebrook	
G-MTYF	Solar Wings Pegasus XL-Q	D. J. Hineson	
G-MTYH	Solar Wings Pegasus XL-Q	R. J. Turner	
G-MTYI	Solar Wings Pegasus XL-Q	D. Ewing	
G-MTYL	Solar Wings Pegasus XL-Q	M. P. Bawden	
G-MTYR	Solar Wings Pegasus XL-Q	D. T. Evans	
G-MTYS	Solar Wings Pegasus XL-Q	R. G. Wall	
G-MTYV	Southdown Raven X	S. R. Jones	
G-MTYW	Raven X	R. Solomons	
G-MTYY	Solar Wings Pegasus XL-R	L. A. Hosegood	
G-MTZA	Thruster TST Mk 1	J. F. Gallagher	
G-MTZB	Thruster TST Mk 1	J. E. Davies	
G-MTZC	Thruster TST Mk 1	B. McCann	
G-MTZE	Thruster TST Mk 1	B. S. P. Finch	
G-MTZF	Thruster TST Mk 1	J. M. English	
G-MTZG	Mainair Gemini/Flash IIA	A. P. Fenn	
G-MTZH	Mainair Gemini/Flash IIA	D. C. Hughes	
G-MTZL	Mainair Gemini/Flash IIA	N. S. Brayn	
G-MTZM	Mainair Gemini/Flash IIA	W. Anderson	
G-MTZO	Mainair Gemini/Flash IIA	R. C. Hinds	
G-MTZR	Solar Wings Pegasus XL-Q	P. J. Hatchett	
G-MTZW	Mainair Gemini/Flash IIA	M. Kalausis	
G-MTZX	Mainair Gemini/Flash IIA	R. G. Cuckow	
G-MTZY	Mainair Gemini/Flash IIA	K. M. Gough & R. Dunn	
G-MTZZ	Mainair Gemini/Flash IIA	G. J. Cadden	
G-MUCK	Lindstrand LBL 77A	C. J. Wootton	
G-MUDD	Hughes 369E	Derwen Plant Co.Ltd	
G-MUDI	PA-18-150 Super Cub	R. S. Grace (G-BCFO)	
G-MUDY	PA-18-150 Super Cub	C. S. Grace (G-OTUG)	
G-MUIR	Cameron V-65 balloon	L. C. M. Muir	
G-MUKY	Van's RV-8	I. E. K. Mackay	
G-MULT	Beech 76 Duchess	Folada Aero & Technical Services Ltd	
G-MUMM	Colt 180A balloon	D. K. Hempleman-Davis	
G-MUMY	Vans RV-4	S. D. Howes	
G-MUNI	Mooney M.20J	P. R. Williams	
G-MUPP	Lindstrand LBL-90A balloon	J. A. Viner	
G-MURG	Van's RV-6	Cadmium Lake Ltd	
G-MUSH	Robinson R44 II	Heli Air Ltd/Wellesbourne	
G-MUSO	Rutan LongEz	N. M. Robbins	
G-MUTT	CZAW Sportcruiser	W. Gillam	
G-MUTZ	Avtech Jabiru J430	N. C. Dean	
G-MUZY	Titan T-51 Mustang	D. Stephens	
G-MVAC	CFM Shadow Srs BD	R. G. Place	
G-MVAH	Thruster TST Mk 1	M. W. H. Henton	

Notes	Reg.	Type	Owner or Operator
	G-MVAI	Thruster TST Mk 1	G. E. Norton
	G-MVAJ	Thruster TST Mk 1	D. Watson
	G-MVAM	CFM Shadow Srs BD	C. P. Barber
	G-MVAN	CFM Shadow Srs BD	R. W. Frost
	G-MVAO	Mainair Gemini/Flash IIA	S. W. Grainger
	G-MVAP	Mainair Gemini/Flash IIA	B. D. Pettit
	G-MVAR	Solar Wings Pegasus XL-R	A. J. Thomas
	G-MVAV	Solar Wings Pegasus XL-R	D. J. Utting
	G-MVAW	Solar Wings Pegasus XL-Q	A. A. Annaev
	G-MVAX	Solar Wings Pegasus XL-Q	N. M. Cuthbertson
	G-MVAY	Solar Wings Pegasus XL-Q	V. O. Morris
	G-MVBC	Aerial Arts Tri-Flyer 130SX	D. Beer
	G-MVBF	Mainair Gemini/Flash IIA	P. H. Norman
	G-MVBJ	Solar Wings Pegasus XL-R	M. Sims
	G-MVBK	Mainair Gemini/Flash IIA	B. R. McLoughlin
	G-MVBL	Mainair Gemini/Flash IIA	S. T. Cain
	G-MVBN	Mainair Gemini/Flash IIA	N. C. Stone
	G-MVBO	Mainair Gemini/Flash IIA	J. A. Brown
	G-MVBP	Thruster TST Mk 1	G-MVBP Group
	G-MVBT	Thruster TST Mk 1	TST Group Flying
	G-MVBZ	Solar Wings Pegasus XL-R	A. G. Butler
	G-MVCA	Solar Wings Pegasus XL-R	R. Walker
	G-MVCC	CFM Shadow Srs BD	Shadow Group
	G-MVCD	Medway Hybred 44XLR	V. W. Beynon
	G-MVCF	Mainair Gemini/Flash IIA	M. W. Luke
	G-MVCL	Solar Wings Pegasus XL-Q	T. E. Robinson
	G-MVCM	Solar Wings Pegasus XL-Q	P. J. Croney
	G-MVCR	Solar Wings Pegasus XL-Q	P. Hoeft
	G-MVCS	Solar Wings Pegasus XL-Q	J. J. Sparrow
	G-MVCT	Solar Wings Pegasus XL-Q	G. S. Lampitt
	G-MVCV	Solar Wings Pegasus XL-Q	G. Stewart
	G-MVCW	CFM Shadow Srs BD	D. A. Coupland
	G-MVCY	Mainair Gemini/Flash IIA	A. M. Smith
	G-MVCZ	Mainair Gemini/Flash IIA	P. J. Devine
	G-MVDA	Mainair Gemini/Flash IIA	C. Tweedley
	G-MVDE	Thruster TST Mk 1	G. L. Roberts
	G-MVDF	Thruster TST Mk 1	G-MVDF Syndicate
	G-MVDH	Thruster TST Mk 1	T. W. Davis
	G-MVDJ	Medway Hybred 44XLR	W. D. Hutchins
	G-MVDK	Aerial Arts Chaser S	S. Adams
	G-MVDL	Aerial Arts Chaser S	N. P. Lloyd
	G-MVDP	Aerial Arts Chaser S	R. G. Mason
	G-MVDT	Mainair Gemini/Flash IIA	D. C. Stephens
	G-MVDV	Solar Wings Pegasus XL-R	K. Mudra
	G-MVDY	Solar Wings Pegasus XL-R	C. G. Murphy
	G-MVDZ	Solar Wings Pegasus XL-R	A. K. Pickering
	G-MVEG	Solar Wings Pegasus XL-R	A. M. Shaw
	G-MVEH	Mainair Gemini/Flash IIA	R. A. Needham
	G-MVEI	CFM Shadow Srs BD	I. G. Ferguson
	G-MVEL	Mainair Gemini/Flash IIA	M. R. Starling
	G-MVEN	CFM Shadow Srs BD	B. D. Ronaghan
	G-MVES	Mainair Gemini/Flash IIA	J. Helm
	G-MVET	Mainair Gemini/Flash IIA	N. J. Case & D. P. Turner
	G-MVEV	Mainair Gemini/Flash IIA	K. Davies
	G-MVFA	Solar Wings Pegasus XL-Q	D. J. Bromley
	G-MVFB	Solar Wings Pegasus XL-Q	M. O. Bloy
	G-MVFC	Solar Wings Pegasus XL-Q	J. K. Ewing
	G-MVFD	Solar Wings Pegasus XL-Q	C. D. Humphries
	G-MVFE	Solar Wings Pegasus XL-Q	S. J. Weeks
	G-MVFF	Solar Wings Pegasus XL-Q	A. Makepiece
	G-MVFH	CFM Shadow Srs BD	M. D. Goad
	G-MVFJ	Thruster TST Mk 1	B. E. Reneham
	G-MVFL	Thruster TST Mk 1	E. J. Wallington
	G-MVFM	Thruster TST Mk 1	G. J. Boyer
	G-MVFO	Thruster TST Mk 1	M. D. Harris
	G-MVFT	Solar Wings Pegasus XL-R	J. Bohea
	G-MVFX	Thruster TST Mk 1	A. M. Dalgetty
	G-MVFZ	Solar Wings Pegasus XL-R	R. K. Johnson
	G-MVGA	Aerial Arts Chaser S	N. R. Beale
	G-MVGC	AMF Chevvron 2-32	W. Fletcher
	G-MVGD	AMF Chevvron 2-32	T. R. James
	G-MVGF	Aerial Arts Chaser S	P. J. Higgins

Reg.	Type	Owner or Operator	Notes
G-MVGG	Aerial Arts Chaser S	J. A. Horn	
G-MVGH	Aerial Arts Chaser S	J. A. Horn	
G-MVGI	Aerial Arts Chaser S	J. E. Orbell	
G-MVGK	Aerial Arts Chaser S	D. J. Smith	
G-MVGM	Mainair Gemini/Flash IIA	J. K. Clayton	
G-MVGN	Solar Wings Pegasus XL-R	M. J. Smith	
G-MVGO	Solar Wings Pegasus XL-R	J. B. Peacock	
G-MVGP	Solar Wings Pegasus XL-R	J. P. Cox	
G-MVGY	Medway Hybred 44XL	M. Vines	
G-MVGZ	Ultraflight Lazair IIIE	D. M. Broom	
G-MVHD	CFM Shadow Srs BD	F. McManus	
G-MVHE	Mainair Gemini/Flash IIA	R. J. Lear	
G-MVHG	Mainair Gemini/Flash II	C. A. J. Elder	
G-MVHH	Mainair Gemini/Flash IIA	A. M. Lynch	
G-MVHI	Thruster TST Mk 1	G. L. Roberts	
G-MVHJ	Thruster TST Mk 1	F. Omaraie-Hamdanie	
G-MVHK	Thruster TST Mk 1	D. J. Gordon	
G-MVHL	Thruster TST Mk 1	G. Jones	
G-MVHP	Solar Wings Pegasus XL-Q	J. B. Gasson	
G-MVHR	Solar Wings Pegasus XL-Q	J. M. Hucker	
G-MVHS	Solar Wings Pegasus XL-Q	A. P. Clarke	
G-MVIB	Mainair Gemini/Flash IIA	LSA Systems	
G-MVIE	Aerial Arts Chaser S	T. M. Stiles	
G-MVIF	Medway Raven X	A. C. Hing	
G-MVIG	CFM Shadow Srs BD	M. J. Green	
G-MVIH	Mainair Gemini/Flash IIA	T. M. Gilesnan	
G-MVIL	Noble Hardman Snowbird Mk IV	S. J. Reid	
G-MVIN	Noble Hardman Snowbird Mk.IV	C. P. Dawes	
G-MVIO	Noble Hardman Snowbird Mk.IV	C. R. Taylor	
G-MVIP	AMF Chevvron 232	M. S. Westman	
G-MVIR	Thruster TST Mk 1	T. D. B. Gardner	
G-MVIU	Thruster TST Mk 1	Anglesey Thrusters Syndicate	
G-MVIV	Thruster TST Mk 1	G. Rainey	
G-MVIX	Mainair Gemini/Flash IIA	S. G. A. Milburn	
G-MVJC	Mainair Gemini/Flash IIA	B. Temple	
G-MVJD	Solar Wings Pegasus XL-R	P. E. Woodhead	
G-MVJE	Mainair Gemini FlashIIA	M. D. Payne	
G-MVJF	Aerial Arts Chaser S	V. S. Rudham	
G-MVJG	Aerial Arts Chaser S	T. H. Scott	
G-MVJJ	Aerial Arts Chaser S	C. W. Potts	
G-MVJK	Aerial Arts Chaser S	S. P. Maher	
G-MVJN	Solar Wings Pegasus XL-Q	J. B. Allan	
G-MVJP	Solar Wings Pegasus XL-Q	S. H. Bakowski	
G-MVJR	Solar Wings Pegasus XL-Q	A. D. Jackson	
G-MVJU	Solar Wings Pegasus XL-Q	J. C. Sutton	
G-MVKB	Medway Hybred 44XLR	J. Newby	
G-MVKC	Mainair Gemini/Flash IIA	M. Faulkner	
G-MVKH	Solar Wings Pegasus XL-R	K. M. Elson	
G-MVKJ	Solar Wings Pegasus XL-R	G. V. Warner	
G-MVKK	Solar Wings Pegasus XL-R	G. P. Burns	
G-MVKL	Solar Wings Pegasus XL-R	J. Powell-Tuck	
G-MVKN	Solar Wings Pegasus XL-Q	N. N. James	
G-MVKO	Solar Wings Pegasus XL-Q	A. R. Hughes	
G-MVKP	Solar Wings Pegasus XL-Q	J. Williams	
G-MVKS	Solar Wings Pegasus XL-Q	K. S. Wright	
G-MVKT	Solar Wings Pegasus XL-Q	P. Roberts	
G-MVKU	Solar Wings Pegasus XL-Q	I. K. Priestley	
G-MVKV	Solar Wings Pegasus XL-Q	D. R. Stansfield	
G-MVKW	Solar Wings Pegasus XL-Q	A. T. Scott	
G-MVKZ	Aerial Arts Chaser S	K. P. Smith	
G-MVLA	Aerial Arts Chaser S	K. R. Emery	
G-MVLB	Aerial Arts Chaser S	R. P. Wilkinson	
G-MVLC	Aerial Arts Chaser S	B. R. Barnes	
G-MVLD	Aerial Arts Chaser S	J. D. Doran	
G-MVLE	Aerial Arts Chaser S	R. G. hooker	
G-MVLJ	CFM Shadow Srs B	R. S. Cochrane	
G-MVLS	Aerial Arts Chaser S	R. J. Turner	
G-MVLT	Aerial Arts Chaser S	P. H. Newson	
G-MVLX	Solar Wings Pegasus XL-Q	J. F. Smith	
G-MVLY	Solar Wings Pegasus XL-Q	I. B. Osborn	
G-MVMA	Solar Wings Pegasus XL-Q	G. C. Winter-Goodwin	
G-MVMC	Solar Wings Pegasus XL-Q	I. W. Barlow	

Notes	Reg.	Type	Owner or Operator
	G-MVMG	Thruster TST Mk 1	A. D. McCaldin
	G-MVMI	Thruster TST Mk 1	P. A. D. Chubb
	G-MVMK	Medway Hybred 44XLR	D. J. Lewis
	G-MVML	Aerial Arts Chaser S	G. C. Luddington
	G-MVMM	Aerial Arts Chaser S	D. Margereson
	G-MVMR	Mainair Gemini/Flash IIA	P. W. Ramage
	G-MVMT	Mainair Gemini/Flash IIA	R. F. Sanders
	G-MVMW	Mainair Gemini/Flash IIA	G. Jones
	G-MVMX	Mainair Gemini/Flash IIA	E. A. Dygutowicz
	G-MVNA	Powerchute Raider	J. McGoldrick
	G-MVNC	Powerchute Raider	S. T. P. Askew
	G-MVNE	Powerchute Raider	A. E. Askew
	G-MVNK	Powerchute Raider	A. E. Askew
	G-MVNL	Powerchute Raider	E. C. Rhodes
	G-MVNM	Gemini/Flash IIA	C. D. Phillips
	G-MVNP	Aerotech MW5 (K) Sorcerer	A. M. Edwards
	G-MVNR	Aerotech MW5 (K) Sorcerer	E. I. Rowlands-Jones
	G-MVNS	Aerotech MW5 (K) Sorcerer	A. M. Sirant
	G-MVNW	Mainair Gemini/Flash IIA	D. Furey & D. W. Robinson
	G-MVNX	Mainair Gemini/Flash IIA	A. R. Lynn
	G-MVNY	Mainair Gemini/Flash IIA	M. K. Buckland
	G-MVNZ	Mainair Gemini/Flash IIA	Microlight Flight Lessons
	G-MVOB	Mainair Gemini/Flash IIA	E. Cave & P. Norton
	G-MVOD	Aerial Arts Chaser 110SX	N. R. Beale
	G-MVOF	Mainair Gemini/Flash IIA	J. H. Brooks
	G-MVOJ	Noble Hardman Snowbird Mk IV	C. D. Beetham
	G-MVON	Mainair Gemini/Flash IIA	D. S. Lally
	G-MVOO	AMF Chevvron 2-32	M. K. Field
	G-MVOP	Aerial Arts Chaser S	D. Thorpe
	G-MVOR	Mainair Gemini/Flash IIA	P. T. & R. M. Jenkins
	G-MVOT	Thruster TST Mk 1	Galaxy Microlights
	G-MVOV	Thruster TST Mk 1	G-MVOV Group
	G-MVPA	Mainair Gemini/Flash IIA	J. E. Milburn
	G-MVPB	Mainair Gemini/Flash IIA	G. A. Harper
	G-MVPC	Mainair Gemini/Flash IIA	W. O. Flannery
	G-MVPD	Mainair Gemini/Flash IIA	P. Thelwel
	G-MVPF	Medway Hybred 44XLR	G. H. Crick
	G-MVPH	Whittaker MW6 Merlin	A. K. Mascord
	G-MVPI	Mainair Gemini/Flash IIA	R. Guild
	G-MVPK	CFM Shadow Srs B	P. Sarfas
	G-MVPM	Whittaker MW6 Merlin	K. W. Curry
	G-MVPN	Whittaker MW6 Merlin	A. M. Field
	G-MVPR	Solar Wings Pegasus XL-Q	C. R. Grainger
	G-MVPS	Solar Wings Pegasus XL-Q	R. J. Hood
	G-MVPW	Solar Wings Pegasus XL-R	C. A. Mitchell
	G-MVPX	Solar Wings Pegasus XL-Q	N. Ionita
	G-MVPY	Solar Wings Pegasus XL-Q	G. H. Dawson
	G-MVRA	Mainair Gemini/Flash IIA	F. Flood
	G-MVRB	Mainair Gemini/Flash	G. Callaghan
	G-MVRD	Mainair Gemini/Flash IIA	A. R. Helm
	G-MVRG	Aerial Arts Chaser S	F. S. Ogden
	G-MVRH	Solar Wings Pegasus XL-Q	K. Farr
	G-MVRI	Solar Wings Pegasus XL-Q	P. Martin
	G-MVRM	Mainair Gemini/Flash IIA	R. A. Gardiner
	G-MVRO	CFM Shadow Srs CD	K. H. Creed
	G-MVRP	CFM Shadow Srs BD	P. K. Jenkins
	G-MVRR	CFM Shadow Srs BD	S. P. Christian
	G-MVRS	CFM Shadow Srs BD ★	Aero Venture
	G-MVRT	CFM Shadow Srs BD	P. J. Houtman
	G-MVRW	Solar Wings Pegasus XL-Q	F. Gardner & C. A. Hamps
	G-MVRZ	Medway Hybred 44XLR	I. Oswald
	G-MVSE	Solar Wings Pegasus XL-Q	L. B. Richardson
	G-MVSG	Aerial Arts Chaser S	M. Roberts
	G-MVSI	Medway Hybred 44XLR	C. T. H. Tenison
	G-MVSJ	Aviasud Mistral 532	D. W. Curtis
	G-MVSM	Midland Ultralights Sirocco	C. G. Benham
	G-MVSO	Mainair Gemini/Flash IIA	A. B. Shayes
	G-MVSP	Mainair Gemini/Flash IIA	D. R. Buchanan
	G-MVST	Mainair Gemini/Flash IIA	M. D. Harper
	G-MVSW	Solar Wings Pegasus XL-Q	K. Perratt
	G-MVSX	Solar Wings Pegasus XL-Q	A. R. Law
	G-MVTA	Solar Wings Pegasus XL-Q	K. Gigney

Reg.	Type	Owner or Operator	Notes
G-MVTD	Whittaker MW6 Merlin	G. R. Reynolds	
G-MVTF	Aerial Arts Chaser S 447	S. R. McKiernan	
G-MVTI	Solar Wings Pegasus XL-Q	P. J. Taylor	
G-MVTJ	Solar Wings Pegasus XL-Q	M. P. & R. A. Wells	
G-MVTL	Aerial Arts Chaser S	N. D. Meer	
G-MVTM	Aerial Arts Chaser S	G. L. Davies	
G-MVUA	Mainair Gemini/Flash IIA	E. W. Hughes	
G-MVUB	Thruster T.300	A. K. Grayson	
G-MVUC	Medway Hybred 44XLR	B. Pounder	
G-MVUF	Solar Wings Pegasus XL-Q	G. P. Blakemore	
G-MVUG	Solar Wings Pegasus XL-Q	J. M. N. Oud	
G-MVUI	Solar Wings Pegasus XL-Q	J. K. Edgecombe & P. E. Hadley	
G-MVUJ	Solar Wings Pegasus XL-Q	J. H. Cooper	
G-MVUO	AMF Chevvron 2-32	W. D. M. Turtle	
G-MVUP	Aviasud Mistral 532GB	S. S. Perry	
G-MVUR	Hornet RS-ZA	G. R. Puffett	
G-MVUS	Aerial Arts Chaser S	H. Poyzer	
G-MVUU	Hornet ZA	K. W. Warn	
G-MVVI	Medway Hybred 44XLR	C. J. Turner	
G-MVVK	Solar Wings Pegasus XL-R	A. J. Weir	
G-MVVO	Solar Wings Pegasus XL-Q	A. L. Scarlett	
G-MVVP	Solar Wings Pegasus XL-Q	I. Pite	
G-MVVT	CFM Shadow Srs BD	W. F. Hayward	
G-MVVV	AMF Chevvron 2-32	J. S. Firth	
G-MVVZ	Powerchute Raider	A. E. Askew	
G-MVWJ	Powerchute Raider	N. J. Doubek	
G-MVWN	Thruster T.300	R. D. Leigh	
G-MVWR	Thruster T.300	G. Rainey	
G-MVWS	Thruster T.300	R. J. Hunphries	
G-MVWW	Aviasud Mistral	Golf Whisky Whisky Group	
G-MVWZ	Aviasud Mistral	C. Buckley	
G-MVXA	Brewster I MW6	J. C. Gates	
G-MVXB	Mainair Gemini/Flash IIA	P. A. Henderson	
G-MVXC	Mainair Gemini/Flash IIA	A. Worthington	
G-MVXJ	Medway Hybred 44XLR	P. J. Wilks	
G-MVXN	Aviasud Mistral	P. W. Cade	
G-MVXP	Aerial Arts Chaser S	P. Blackbourn & S. T. Hayes	
G-MVXR	Mainair Gemini/Flash IIA	D. M. Bayne	
G-MVXV	Aviasud Mistral	D. L. Chalk & G. S. Jefferies	
G-MVXX	AMF Chevvron 232	T. R. James	
G-MVYC	Solar Wings Pegasus XL-Q	P. E. L. Street	
G-MVYD	Solar Wings Pegasus XL-Q	B. Birtle	
G-MVYE	Thruster TST Mk 1	M. J. Aubrey	
G-MVYI	Hornet R-ZA	K. W. Warn	
G-MVYN	Hornet RS-ZA	E. C. Rhodes	
G-MVYR	Medway Hybred 44XLR	K. J. Clarke	
G-MVYS	Mainair Gemini/Flash IIA	P. D. Finch	
G-MVYT	Noble Hardman Snowbird Mk IV	M. A. Oakley	
G-MVYV	Noble Hardman Snowbird Mk IV	D. W. Hayden	
G-MVYW	Noble Hardman Snowbird Mk IV	T. J. Harrison	
G-MVYX	Noble Hardman Snowbird Mk IV	R. McBlain	
G-MVYY	Aerial Arts Chaser S508	R. G. Mason	
G-MVYZ	CFM Shadow Srs BD	T. G. Solomon	
G-MVZA	Thruster T.300	M. A. McLoughlin	
G-MVZC	Thruster T.300	S. Dougan	
G-MVZD	Thruster T.300	G-MVZD Syndicate	
G-MVZE	Thruster T.300	T. L. Davis	
G-MVZI	Thruster T.300	R. R. R. Whittern	
G-MVZJ	Solar Wings Pegasus XL-Q	G. P. Burns	
G-MVZK	Quad City Challenger II	A. Clift	
G-MVZL	Solar Wings Pegasus XL-Q	P. R. Dobson	
G-MVZM	Aerial Arts Chaser S	R. Cotterell	
G-MVZO	Medway Hybred 44XLR	S. J. Taft	
G-MVZP	Murphy Renegade Spirit UK	The North American Syndicate	
G-MVZS	Mainair Gemini/Flash IIA	R. L. Beese	
G-MVZT	Solar Wings Pegasus XL-Q	C. J. Meadows	
G-MVZU	Solar Wings Pegasus XL-Q	M. G. McMurray	
G-MVZV	Solar Wings Pegasus XL-Q	K. D. Masters	
G-MVZX	Renegade Spirit UK	G. Holmes	
G-MVZZ	AMF Chevvron 232	W. A. L. Mitchell	
G-MWAB	Mainair Gemini/Flash IIA	J. E. Buckley	
G-MWAC	Solar Wings Pegasus XL-Q	H. Lloyd-Hughes	

Notes	Reg.	Type	Owner or Operator
	G-MWAD	Solar Wings Pegasus XL-Q	J. K.Evans
	G-MWAE	CFM Shadow Srs BD	M. D. Brown
	G-MWAF	Solar Wings Pegasus XL-R	R. Horner
	G-MWAN	Thruster T.300	E. J. Girling
	G-MWAP	Thruster T.300	The Wanda Flying Group
	G-MWAT	Solar Wings Pegasus XL-Q	D. G. Seymour
	G-MWAV	Solar Wings Pegasus XL-R	T. Woodward
	G-MWAW	Whittaker MW6 Merlin	P. Hunnisett
	G-MWBI	Medway Hybred 44XLR	G. E. Coates
	G-MWBJ	Medway Sprint	C. C. Strong
	G-MWBK	Solar Wings Pegasus XL-Q	A. W. Jarvis
	G-MWBL	Solar Wings Pegasus XL-R	J. C. Ring
	G-MWBS	Hornet RS-ZA	P. D. Jaques
	G-MWBW	Hornet RS-ZA	C. G. Bentley
	G-MWBY	Hornet RS-ZA	IP Rights Ltd
	G-MWCB	Solar Wings Pegasus XL-Q	R. J. Lockyer
	G-MWCC	Solar Wings Pegasus XL-R	I. K. Priestley
	G-MWCE	Mainair Gemini/Flash IIA	B. A. Tooze
	G-MWCF	Solar Wings Pegasus XL-R	S. P. Tkaczyk
	G-MWCG	Microflight Spectrum	C. Ricketts
	G-MWCH	Rans S.6 Coyote	G-MWCH Group
	G-MWCK	Powerchute Kestrel	A. E. Askew
	G-MWCL	Powerchute Kestrel	R. W. Twamley
	G-MWCM	Powerchute Kestrel	J. R. Hewitt
	G-MWCN	Powerchute Kestrel	A. E. Askew
	G-MWCO	Powerchute Kestrel	J. R. E. Gladstone
	G-MWCP	Powerchute Kestrel	R. S. McFadyen
	G-MWCS	Powerchute Kestrel	S. T. P. Askew
	G-MWCY	Medway Hybred 44XLR	J. K. Masters
	G-MWDB	CFM Shadow Srs BD	M. D. Meade
	G-MWDC	Solar Wings Pegasus XL-R	R. Littler
	G-MWDE	Hornet RS-ZA	H. G. Reid
	G-MWDI	Hornet RS-ZA	R. J. Perrin
	G-MWDK	Solar Wings Pegasus XL-R	T. Wicks
	G-MWDL	Solar Wings Pegasus XL-R	D. J. Windsor
	G-MWDN	CFM Shadow Srs BD	N. R. Henry
	G-MWDS	Thruster T.300	A. W. Nancarrow
	G-MWDZ	Eipper Quicksilver MXL II	S. Cooper & J. Parker
	G-MWEG	Solar Wings Pegasus XL-Q	S. P. Michlig
	G-MWEH	Solar Wings Pegasus XL-Q	K. A. Davidson
	G-MWEK	Whittaker MW5 Sorcerer	D. W. & M. L. Squire
	G-MWEL	Mainair Gemini/Flash IIA	E. St John-Foti
	G-MWEN	CFM Shadow Srs BD	C. Dawn
	G-MWEO	Whittaker MW5 Sorcerer	J. Morton
	G-MWEP	Rans S.4 Coyote	E. J. Wallington
	G-MWER	Solar Wings Pegasus XL-Q	J. A. O'Neill
	G-MWES	Rans S.4 Coyote	A. P. Love
	G-MWEZ	CFM Shadow Srs CD	G-MWEZ Group
	G-MWFC	TEAM mini-MAX (G-BTXC)	P. C. C. H. Crossley
	G-MWFD	TEAM mini-MAX	J. T. Blackburn
	G-MWFF	Rans S.4 Coyote	P. J. Greenrod
	G-MWFG	Powerchute Kestrel	R. I. Simpson
	G-MWFL	Powerchute Kestrel	M. A. Stevenson
	G-MWFT	MBA Tiger Cub 440	J. R. Ravenhill
	G-MWFU	Quad City Challenger II UK	C. J. Whittaker
	G-MWFV	Quad City Challenger II UK	M. Liptrot
	G-MWFW	Rans S.4 Coyote	M. P. Hallam
	G-MWFX	Quad City Challenger II UK	I. M. Walton
	G-MWFY	Quad City Challenger II UK	C. C. B. Soden
	G-MWFZ	Quad City Challenger II UK	A. Slade
	G-MWGA	Rans S.5 Coyote	P. C. Burns
	G-MWGI	Whittaker MW5 (K) Sorcerer	J. R. Surbey
	G-MWGJ	Whittaker MW5 (K) Sorcerer	I. Pearson
	G-MWGK	Whittaker MW5 (K) Sorcerer	R. J. Cook
	G-MWGL	Solar Wings Pegasus XL-Q	F. McGlynn
	G-MWGN	Rans S.4 Coyote II	V. Hallam
	G-MWGR	Solar Wings Pegasus XL-Q	M. Jady
	G-MWGU	Powerchute Kestrel	M. Pandolfino
	G-MWGZ	Powerchute Kestrel	J. L. Lynch
	G-MWHC	Solar Wings Pegasus XL-Q	P. J. Lowery
	G-MWHF	Solar Wings Pegasus XL-Q	N. J. Troke
	G-MWHG	Solar Wings Pegasus XL-Q	I. A. Lumley

Reg.	Type	Owner or Operator	Notes
G-MWHH	TEAM mini-MAX	I. D. Worthington	
G-MWHI	Mainair Gemini/Flash	P. Harwood	
G-MWHL	Solar Wings Pegasus XL-Q	S. J. Reader	
G-MWHO	Mainair Gemini/Flash IIA	C. Campion-Sheen	
G-MWHP	Rans S.6-ESD Coyote	J. F. Bickerstaffe	
G-MWHR	Mainair Gemini/Flash IIA	B. Brazier	
G-MWHT	Solar Wings Pegasus Quasar	C. G. Jarvis	
G-MWHX	Solar Wings Pegasus XL-Q	N. P. Kelly	
G-MWIA	Mainair Gemini/Flash IIA	G. J. Green	
G-MWIB	Aviasud Mistral	J. Broome	
G-MWIE	Solar Wings Pegasus XL-Q	X. S. Norman	
G-MWIF	Rans S.6-ESD Coyote II	K. Kelly	
G-MWIG	Mainair Gemini/Flash IIA	A. P. Purbrick	
G-MWIM	Solar Wings Pegasus Quasar	M. C. Keeley	
G-MWIO	Rans S.4 Coyote	K. T. Short	
G-MWIP	Whittaker MW6 Merlin	B. J. Merret & D. Beer	
G-MWIS	Solar Wings Pegasus XL-Q	P. G. Strangward	
G-MWIU	Pegasus Quasar TC	W. Hepburn	
G-MWIW	Solar Wings Pegasus Quasar	W. R. Furness	
G-MWIX	Solar Wings Pegasus Quasar	G. Hawes	
G-MWIZ	CFM Shadow Srs BD	T. P. Ryan	
G-MWJF	CFM Shadow Srs BD	S. N. White	
G-MWJH	Solar Wings Pegasus Quasar	L. A. Hosegood	
G-MWJI	Solar Wings Pegasus Quasar	L. Luscombe	
G-MWJJ	Solar Wings Pegasus Quasar	G. F. Campbell & I. A. Gilroy	
G-MWJK	Solar Wings Pegasus Quasar	M. Richardson	
G-MWJN	Solar Wings Pegasus XL-Q	J. C. Corrall	
G-MWJP	Medway Hybred 44XLR	C. D. Simmons	
G-MWJR	Medway Hybred 44XLR	T. G. Almond	
G-MWJT	Solar Wings Pegasus Quasar	D. L. Mitchell	
G-MWKE	Hornet R-ZA	D. R. Stapleton	
G-MWKO	Solar Wings Pegasus XL-Q	P. M. Golden	
G-MWKX	Microflight Spectrum	C. R. Ions	
G-MWKY	Solar Wings Pegasus XL-Q	D. R. Williams	
G-MWKZ	Solar Wings Pegasus XL-Q	G. K. Wilderspin	
G-MWLB	Medway Hybred 44XLR	G. P. D. Coan	
G-MWLD	CFM Shadow Srs BD	J. J. Hansen	
G-MWLE	Solar Wings Pegasus XL-R	D. Stevenson	
G-MWLG	Solar Wings Pegasus XL-R	C. Cohen	
G-MWLJ	Solar Wings Pegasus Quasar	P 7 M Aviation Ltd	
G-MWLK	Solar Wings Pegasus Quasar	D. J. Shippen	
G-MWLL	Solar Wings Pegasus XL-Q	A. J. Bacon	
G-MWLM	Solar Wings Pegasus XL-Q	M. C. Wright	
G-MWLN	Whittaker MW6-S Fatboy Flyer	S. J. Field	
G-MWLO	Whittaker MW6 Merlin	G-MWLO Flying Group	
G-MWLP	Mainair Gemini/Flash IIA	C. E. J. Moultrie	
G-MWLS	Medway Hybred 44XLR	M. A. Oliver	
G-MWLU	Solar Wings Pegasus XL-R	T. P. G. Ward	
G-MWLW	TEAM mini-MAX	E. J. Oteng	
G-MWLX	Mainair Gemini/Flash IIA	J. K. Kerr, B. O. Lyell & P. A. Smith	
G-MWLZ	Rans S.4 Coyote	B. O. McCartan	
G-MWMB	Powerchute Kestrel	E. C. Rhodes	
G-MWMC	Powerchute Kestrel	Talgarreg Flying Club	
G-MWMD	Powerchute Kestrel	D. J. Jackson	
G-MWMF	Powerchute Kestrel	P. J. Blundell	
G-MWMG	Powerchute Kestrel	M. D. Walton	
G-MWMH	Powerchute Kestrel	E. W. Potts	
G-MWMI	SolarWings Pegasus Quasar	R. G. Wyatt	
G-MWML	SolarWings Pegasus Quasar	S. C. Key	
G-MWMM	Mainair Gemini/Flash IIA	N. H. Taylor	
G-MWMN	Solar Wings Pegasus XL-Q	P. A. Arnold & N. A. Rathbone	
G-MWMO	Solar Wings Pegasus XL-Q	D. S. F. McNair	
G-MWMV	Solar Wings Pegasus XL-R	M. Nutting	
G-MWMW	Renegade Spirit UK	P. Wise	
G-MWMX	Mainair Gemini/Flash IIA	P. G. Hughes/Ireland	
G-MWMY	Mainair Gemini/Flash IIA	A. D. Bales	
G-MWNB	Solar Wings Pegasus XL-Q	P. F. J. Rogers	
G-MWND	Tiger Cub Developments RL.5A	D. A. Pike	
G-MWNE	Mainair Gemini/Flash IIA	D. Matthews	
G-MWNF	Renegade Spirit UK	R. Haslam	
G-MWNG	Solar Wings Pegasus XL-Q	H. C. TRhomson	
G-MWNK	Solar Wings Pegasus Quasar	G. S. Lynn	

Notes	Reg.	Type	Owner or Operator
	G-MWNL	Solar Wings Pegasus Quasar	N. H. S. Install
	G-MWNO	AMF Chevvron 232	I. K. Hogg
	G-MWNP	AMF Chevvron 232	M. K. Field
	G-MWNR	Renegade Spirit UK	RJR Flying Group
	G-MWNS	Mainair Gemini/Flash IIA	J. G. Hilliard
	G-MWNT	Mainair Gemini/Flash IIA	November Tango Group
	G-MWNU	Mainair Gemini/Flash IIA	C. C. Muir
	G-MWNX	Powerchute Kestrel	J. H. Greenroyd
	G-MWOC	Powerchute Kestrel	D. M. F. Harvey
	G-MWOD	Powerchute Kestrel	T. Morgan
	G-MWOE	Powerchute Raider	S. T. P. Askew
	G-MWOH	Solar Wings Pegasus XL-R	J. D. Buchanan
	G-MWOI	Solar Wings Pegasus XL-R	B. T. Geoghegan
	G-MWOJ	Mainair Gemini/Flash IIA	C. J. Pryce
	G-MWOO	Renegade Spirit UK	R. C. Wood
	G-MWOR	Solar Wings Pegasus XL-Q	S. E. Smith
	G-MWOV	Whittaker MW6 Merlin	S. Jeffs
	G-MWOY	Solar Wings Pegasus XL-Q	S. P. Griffin
	G-MWPB	Mainair Gemini/Flash IIA	J. Fenton
	G-MWPC	Mainair Gemini/Flash IIA	S. J. Ware
	G-MWPD	Mainair Gemini/Flash IIA	M. R. Picksley
	G-MWPE	Solar Wings Pegasus XL-Q	E. C. R. Hudson
	G-MWPF	Mainair Gemini/Flash IIA	G. P. Taggart
	G-MWPG	Microflight Spectrum	D. Brunton
	G-MWPH	Microflight Spectrum	A. Whittaker
	G-MWPN	CFM Shadow Srs CD	W. R. H. Thomas
	G-MWPO	Mainair Gemini/Flash IIA	W. Anderson
	G-MWPP	CFM Streak Shadow	A. J. Price
	G-MWPR	Whittaker MW6 Merlin	S. F. N. Warnell
	G-MWPS	Renegade Spirit UK	M. D. Stewart
	G-MWPW	AMF Chevvron 2-32C	M. S. Westman
	G-MWPX	Solar Wings Pegasus XL-R	R. J. Wheeler
	G-MWPZ	Renegade Spirit UK	J. Ievers
	G-MWRC	Mainair Gemini/Flash IIA	T. Karczewski
	G-MWRD	Mainair Gemini/Flash IIA	D. Morton
	G-MWRE	Mainair Gemini/Flash IIA	J. Davies
	G-MWRF	Mainair Gemini/Flash IIA	N. Hay
	G-MWRH	Mainair Gemini/Flash IIA	D. Ben-Lamri
	G-MWRJ	Mainair Gemini/Flash IIA	J. M. Breaks
	G-MWRL	CFM Shadow Srs.CD	I. W. Hogg
	G-MWRN	Solar Wings Pegasus XL-R	Malvern Aerotow Club
	G-MWRR	Mainair Gemini/Flash IIA	J. Clark t/a G-MWRR Group
	G-MWRS	Ultravia Super Pelican	T. B. Woolley
	G-MWRT	Solar Wings Pegasus XL-R	G. L. Gunnell
	G-MWRU	Solar Wings Pegasus XL-R	M. Corcoran
	G-MWRY	CFM Shadow Srs CD	A. T. Armstrong
	G-MWSA	TEAM mini-MAX	G. J. Jones
	G-MWSB	Mainair Gemini/Flash IIA	P. J. Bosworth
	G-MWSC	Rans S.6-ESD Coyote II	I. Fernihough
	G-MWSD	Solar Wings Pegasus XL-Q	A. M. Harley
	G-MWSF	Solar Wings Pegasus XL-R	J. J. Freeman
	G-MWSI	Solar Wings Pegasus Quasar TC	K. C. Noakes
	G-MWSJ	Solar Wings Pegasus XL-Q	R. J. Collison
	G-MWSK	Solar Wings Pegasus XL-Q	J. Doogan
	G-MWSL	Mainair Gemini/Flash IIA	C. W. Frost
	G-MWSM	Mainair Gemini/Flash IIA	R. M. Wall
	G-MWSO	Solar Wings Pegasus XL-R	M. A. Clayton
	G-MWSP	Solar Wings Pegasus XL-R	S. I. Hatherall
	G-MWST	Medway Hybred 44XLR	A. Ferguson
	G-MWSU	Medway Hybred 44XLR	T. De Landro
	G-MWSW	Whittaker MW6 Merlin	S. F. N. Warnell
	G-MWSX	Whittaker MW5 Sorcerer	P. J. Hellyer
	G-MWSY	Whittaker MW5 Sorcerer	J. E. Holloway
	G-MWSZ	CFM Shadow Srs CD	M. W. W. Clotworthy
	G-MWTC	Solar Wings Pegasus XL-Q	M. M. Chittenden
	G-MWTI	Solar Wings Pegasus XL-Q	O. G. Johns
	G-MWTJ	CFM Shadow Srs CD	Shadow Tango Juliet Group
	G-MWTL	Solar Wings Pegasus XL-R	B. Lindsay
	G-MWTN	CFM Shadow Srs CD	M. J. Broom
	G-MWTO	Mainair Gemini/Flash IIA	E. Beckett
	G-MWTP	CFM Shadow Srs CD	R. E. M. Gibson-Bevan
	G-MWTR	Mainair Gemini/Flash IIA	C. Montlake

Reg.	Type	Owner or Operator	Notes
G-MWTT	Rans S.6-ESD Coyote II	L. E. Duffin	
G-MWTZ	Mainair Gemini/Flash IIA	C. W. R. Felce	
G-MWUA	CFM Shadow Srs CD	Cloudbase Aviation	
G-MWUB	Solar Wings Pegasus XL-R	T. R. L. Bayley	
G-MWUD	Solar Wings Pegasus XL-R	A. J. Weir	
G-MWUI	AMF Chevvron 2-32C	S. Wilson	
G-MWUK	Rans S.6-ESD Coyote II	G. K. Hoult	
G-MWUL	Rans S.6-ESD Coyote II	D. M. Bayne	
G-MWUN	Rans S.6-ESD Coyote II	J. Parke	
G-MWUO	Solar Wings Pegasus XL-Q	A. P. Slade	
G-MWUR	Solar Wings Pegasus XL-R	Nottingham Aerotow Club	
G-MWUS	Solar Wings Pegasus XL-R	H. R. Loxton	
G-MWUU	Solar Wings Pegasus XL-R	B. R. Underwood	
G-MWUV	Solar Wings Pegasus XL-R	C. D. Baines	
G-MWUW	Solar Wings Pegasus XL-R	Ultraflight Microlights Ltd	
G-MWUX	Solar Wings Pegasus XL-Q	B. D. Attwell	
G-MWUZ	Solar Wings Pegasus XL-Q	S. R. Nanson	
G-MWVA	Solar Wings Pegasus XL-Q	D. P. Henderson	
G-MWVE	Solar Wings Pegasus XL-R	W. A. Keel-Stocker	
G-MWVF	Solar Wings Pegasus XL-R	J. B. Wright	
G-MWVG	CFM Shadow Srs CD	Shadow Aviation Ltd	
G-MWVH	CFM Shadow Srs CD	M. McKenzie	
G-MWVL	Rans S.6-ESD Coyote II	J. C. Gates	
G-MWVM	Solar Wings Pegasus Quasar II	A. A. Edmonds	
G-MWVN	Mainair Gemini/Flash IIA	J. McCafferty	
G-MWVO	Mainair Gemini/Flash IIA	I. B. Plested	
G-MWVP	Renegade Spirit UK	P. D. Mickleburgh	
G-MWVT	Mainair Gemini/Flash IIA	R. M. Wigman	
G-MWVY	Mainair Gemini/Flash IIA	B. Plunkett	
G-MWVZ	Mainair Gemini/Flash IIA	R. W. Twamley	
G-MWWB	Mainair Gemini/Flash IIA	W. P. Seward	
G-MWWC	Mainair Gemini/Flash IIA	D. & A. Margereson	
G-MWWD	Renegade Spirit	R. A. Arrowsmith	
G-MWWH	Solar Wings Pegasus XL-Q	R. G. Wall	
G-MWWI	Mainair Gemini/Flash IIA	M. A. S. Nesbitt	
G-MWWK	Mainair Gemini/Flash IIA	S. D. Puddle	
G-MWWN	Mainair Gemini/Flash IIA	R. Whitby	
G-MWWR	Microflight Spectrum	T. H. Evans	
G-MWWS	Thruster T.300	J. Parker	
G-MWWV	Solar Wings Pegasus XL-Q	R. W. Livingstone	
G-MWWZ	Cyclone Chaser S	P. K. Dale	
G-MWXF	Mainair Mercury	D. McAuley	
G-MWXH	Solar Wings Pegasus Quasar IITC	R. P. Wilkinson	
G-MWXJ	Mainair Mercury	P. J. Taylor	
G-MWXK	Mainair Mercury	M. P. Wilkinson	
G-MWXP	Solar Wings Pegasus XL-Q	A. P. Attfield	
G-MWXV	Mainair Gemini/Flash IIA	T. A. Daniel	
G-MWXW	Cyclone Chaser S	I. D. Edwards	
G-MWXX	Cyclone Chaser S 447	P. I. Frost	
G-MWXY	Cyclone Chaser S 447	D. Curtis	
G-MWXZ	Cyclone Chaser S 508	D. L. Hadley	
G-MWYA	Mainair Gemini/Flash IIA	R. F. Hunt	
G-MWYC	Solar Wings Pegasus XL-Q	R. M. Jarvis	
G-MWYD	CFM Shadow Srs C	F. E. Greenfield	
G-MWYE	Rans S.6-ESD Coyote II	G. A. M. Moffat	
G-MWYG	Mainair Gemini/Flash IIA	S. P. McVeigh	
G-MWYI	Solar Wings Pegasus Quasar II	T. S. Chadfield	
G-MWYJ	Solar Wings Pegasus Quasar II	A. Clarke & L. B. Hughes	
G-MWYL	Mainair Gemini/Flash IIA	A. J. Hinks	
G-MWYM	Cyclone Chaser S 1000	C. J. Meadows	
G-MWYS	CGS Hawk 1 Arrow	Civilair	
G-MWYT	Mainair Gemini/Flash IIA	J. R. Kendall	
G-MWYU	Solar Wings Pegasus XL-Q	L. A. Dotchin	
G-MWYV	Mainair Gemini/Flash IIA	R. Bricknell	
G-MWYY	Mainair Gemini/Flash IIA	R. D. Allard	
G-MWYZ	Solar Wings Pegasus XL-Q	D. P. Graham	
G-MWZA	Mainair Mercury	A. J. Malham	
G-MWZB	AMF Microlight Chevvron 2-32C	E. Ratcliffe	
G-MWZD	Solar Wings Pegasus Quasar IITC	N. W. Mallen	
G-MWZF	Solar Wings Pegasus Quasar IITC	R. G. T. Corney	
G-MWZI	Solar Wings Pegasus XL-R	K. J. Slater	
G-MWZJ	Solar Wings Pegasus XL-R	P. Kitchen	

Notes	Reg.	Type	Owner or Operator
	G-MWZL	Mainair Gemini/Flash IIA	D. Renton
	G-MWZM	TEAM mini-MAX 91	I. D. Worthington
	G-MWZO	Solar Wings Pegasus Quasar IITC	A. Robinson
	G-MWZP	Solar Wings Pegasus Quasar IITC	C. Garton
	G-MWZR	Solar Wings Pegasus Quasar IITC	R. Veart
	G-MWZS	Solar Wings Pegasus Quasar IITC	G. Bennett
	G-MWZU	Solar Wings Pegasus XL-R	A. D. Winebloom
	G-MWZV	Solar Wings Pegasus XL-R	D. J. Newby
	G-MWZY	Solar Wings Pegasus XL-R	Darley Moor Airsports Club Ltd
	G-MWZZ	Solar Wings Pegasus XL-R	The Microlight School (Lichfield) Ltd
	G-MXII	Pitts Model 12	P. T. Borchert
	G-MXMX	PA-46R-350T Malibu Matrix	Feabrex Ltd
	G-MXPH	BAC.167 Strikemaster Mk 84 (311)	R. S. Partridge-Hicks (G-SARK)
	G-MXVI	VS.361 Spitfire LF.XVIe (TE184:D)	S. R. Stead
	G-MYAB	Solar Wings Pegasus XL-R	A. N. F. Stewart
	G-MYAC	Solar Wings Pegasus XL-Q	M. E. Gilman
	G-MYAE	Solar Wings Pegasus XL-Q	C. R. Bunce
	G-MYAF	Solar Wings Pegasus XL-Q	K. H. Almond
	G-MYAG	Quad City Challenger II	I. Ciziks
	G-MYAH	Whittaker MW5 Sorcerer	I. D. Worthington
	G-MYAI	Mainair Mercury	J. Ellerton
	G-MYAJ	Rans S.6-ESD Coyote II	J. Beattie
	G-MYAN	Whittaker MW5 (K) Sorcerer	A. F. Reid
	G-MYAO	Mainair Gemini/Flash IIA	R. A. Chapman
	G-MYAR	Thruster T.300	G. Hawkins
	G-MYAS	Mainair Gemini/Flash IIA	J. R. Davis
	G-MYAT	TEAM mini-MAX	M. W. Hands
	G-MYAZ	Renegade Spirit UK	R. Smith
	G-MYBA	Rans S.6-ESD Coyote II	A. M. Hughes
	G-MYBB	Maxair Drifter	M. Ingleton
	G-MYBC	CFM Shadow Srs CD	P. C. H. Clarke
	G-MYBE	Solar Wings Pegasus Quasar IITC	G. Bullock & A. Turner
	G-MYBF	Solar Wings Pegasus XL-Q	K. H. Pead
	G-MYBI	Rans S.6-ESD Coyote II	D. Wilkinson
	G-MYBJ	Mainair Gemini/Flash IIA	G. C. Bowers
	G-MYBM	TEAM mini-MAX	B. Hunter
	G-MYBN	Hiway Demon 175	B. R. Lamming
	G-MYBR	Solar Wings Pegasus XL-Q	M. J. Larbey & G. T. Hunt
	G-MYBT	Solar Wings Pegasus Quasar IITC	G. A. Rainbow-Ockwell
	G-MYBU	Cyclone Chaser S 447	R. L. Arscott
	G-MYBV	Solar Wings Pegasus XL-Q	L. R. Hodgson
	G-MYBW	Solar Wings Pegasus XL-Q	J. S. Chapman
	G-MYCA	Whittaker MW6 Merlin	R. A. L-V. Harris
	G-MYCB	Cyclone Chaser S 447	P. Sykes
	G-MYCE	Solar Wings Pegasus Quasar IITC	S. W. Barker
	G-MYCJ	Mainair Mercury	C. A. McLean
	G-MYCK	Mainair Gemini/Flash IIA	T. Kelly
	G-MYCL	Mainair Mercury	P. B. Cole
	G-MYCM	CFM Shadow Srs CD	C. I. Chegwen
	G-MYCN	Mainair Mercury	P. Lowham
	G-MYCO	Renegade Spirit UK	T. P. Williams
	G-MYCP	Whittaker MW6 Merlin	W. Turner
	G-MYCR	Mainair Gemini/Flash IIA	A. P. King
	G-MYCS	Mainair Gemini/Flash IIA	M. Parkinson
	G-MYCT	TEAM Mini-MAX 91	R. Smith
	G-MYCX	Powerchute Kestrel	S. J. Pugh-Jones
	G-MYDA	Powerchute Kestrel	K. J. Greatrix
	G-MYDC	Mainair Mercury	K. M. C. Littlefair
	G-MYDD	CFM Shadow Srs CD	C. H. Gem/Spain
	G-MYDE	CFM Shadow Srs CD	D. N. L. Howell
	G-MYDF	TEAM mini-MAX	J. G. Bright
	G-MYDJ	Solar Wings Pegasus XL-R	Cambridgeshire Aerotow Club
	G-MYDK	Rans S.6-ESD Coyote II	J. W. Caush & W. Doyle
	G-MYDN	Quad City Challenger II	T. C. Hooks
	G-MYDP	Kolb Twinstar Mk 3	Norberts Flying Group
	G-MYDR	Thruster Tn.300	H. G. Soper
	G-MYDT	Thruster T.300	J. B. Grotrian
	G-MYDU	Thruster T.300	S. Collins
	G-MYDV	Mainair Gemini /Flash IIA	S. J. Mazilis
	G-MYDX	Rans S.6-ESD Coyote II	J. R. Tomlin

Reg.	Type	Owner or Operator	Notes
G-MYDZ	Mignet HM.1000 Balerit	D. S. Simpson	
G-MYEA	Solar Wings Pegasus XL-Q	A. M. Taylor	
G-MYED	Solar Wings Pegasus XL-R	G-MYED Group	
G-MYEH	Solar Wings Pegasus XL-R	J. Spuffard	
G-MYEI	Cyclone Chaser S447	D. J. Hyatt	
G-MYEJ	Cyclone Chaser S447	A. W. Lowrie	
G-MYEK	Solar Wings Pegasus Quasar IITC	The Microlight School (Lichfield) Ltd	
G-MYEM	Solar Wings Pegasus Quasar IITC	D. J. Moore	
G-MYEN	Solar Wings Pegasus Quasar IITC	T. J. Feeney	
G-MYEO	Solar Wings Pegasus Quasar IITC	A. K. Robinson	
G-MYER	Cyclone AX3/503	T. F. Horrocks	
G-MYES	Rans S.6-ESD Coyote II	S. J. Mathison	
G-MYET	Whittaker MW6 Merlin	G. Campbell	
G-MYEX	Powerchute Kestrel	R. J. Watkin	
G-MYFA	Powerchute Kestrel	M. Phillips	
G-MYFH	Quad City Challenger II	C. Lockwood	
G-MYFK	Solar Wings Pegasus Quasar IITC	M. A. Azeem & P. T. M. Kroef	
G-MYFL	Solar Wings Pegasus Quasar IITC	C. C. Wright	
G-MYFO	Cyclone Airsports Chaser S	J. K. Evans	
G-MYFP	Mainair Gemini/Flash IIA	A. Brier & M. P. Lomax	
G-MYFR	Mainair Gemini/Flash IIA	J. R. Hairsine	
G-MYFT	Mainair Scorcher	M. R. Kirby	
G-MYFU	Mainair Gemini/Flash IIA	J. Payne	
G-MYFV	Cyclone AX3/503	J. K. Sargent	
G-MYFW	Cyclone AX3/503	Microlight School (Lichfield) Ltd	
G-MYGD	Cyclone AX3/503	G. M. R. Keenan	
G-MYGF	TEAM mini-MAX	R. D. Barnard	
G-MYGK	Cyclone Chaser S 508	P. C. Collins	
G-MYGM	Quad City Challenger II	G. J. Williams & J. White	
G-MYGN	AMF Chevvron 2-32C	P. J. Huston	
G-MYGO	CFM ShadowSrs CD	Thorley Motors Ltd	
G-MYGP	Rans S.6-ESD Coyote II	R. H. Y. Farrer	
G-MYGR	Rans S.6-ESD Coyote II	W. Scott	
G-MYGT	Solar Wings Pegasus XL-R	Condors Aerotow Syndicate	
G-MYGU	Solar Wings Pegasus XL-R	J. A. Sims	
G-MYGV	Solar Wings Pegasus XL-R	J. A. Crofts & G. M. Birkett	
G-MYGZ	Mainair Gemini/Flash IIA	G. J. Molloy	
G-MYHG	Cyclone AX/503	N. P. Thomson & C. Alsop	
G-MYHH	Cyclone AX/503	D. J. Harber	
G-MYHI	Rans S.6-ESD Coyote II	I. J. Steele	
G-MYHJ	Cyclone AX3/503	B. J. Palfreyman	
G-MYHK	Rans S.6-ESD Coyote II	M. R. Williamson	
G-MYHL	Mainair Gemini/Flash IIA	M. Coates & H. B. Blackwell	
G-MYHM	Cyclone AX3/503	G-MYHM Group	
G-MYHN	Mainair Gemini/Flash IIA	H. J. Timms	
G-MYHP	Rans S.6-ESD Coyote II	K. E. Gair & D. M. Smith	
G-MYHR	Cyclone AX3/503	C. W. Williams	
G-MYIA	Quad City Challenger II	I. Pearson	
G-MYIF	CFM Shadow Srs CD	P. J. Edwards	
G-MYIH	Mainair Gemini/Flash IIA	A. N. Huddart	
G-MYII	TEAM mini-MAX	G. H. Crick	
G-MYIK	Kolb Twinstar Mk 3	B. A. Janaway	
G-MYIL	Cyclone Chaser S 508	R. A. Rawes	
G-MYIN	Solar Wings Pegasus Quasar IITC	W. P. Hughes	
G-MYIP	CFM Shadow Srs CD	T. Bailey	
G-MYIR	Rans S.6-ESD Coyote II	P. D. Smalley	
G-MYIS	Rans S.6-ESD Coyote II	I. S. Everett & M. Stott	
G-MYIT	Cyclone Chaser S 508	R. Barringer	
G-MYIV	Mainair Gemini/Flash IIA	P. Norton & T. Williams	
G-MYIX	Quad City Challenger II	M. Alaman	
G-MYIY	Mainair Gemini/Flash IIA	D. Jackson	
G-MYIZ	TEAM mini-MAX 2	J. C. Longmore	
G-MYJC	Mainair Gemini/Flash IIA	M. N. Irven	
G-MYJD	Rans S.6-ESD Coyote II	A. A. Ross	
G-MYJF	Thruster T.300	P. F. McConville	
G-MYJG	Thruster T.300	J. W. Rice	
G-MYJJ	Solar Wings Pegasus Quasar IITC	T. A. Willcox	
G-MYJK	Solar Wings Pegasus Quasar IITC	The Microlight School (Lichfield) Ltd	
G-MYJM	Mainair Gemini/Flash IIA	J. G. Treanor	
G-MYJO	Cyclone Chaser S 508	A. W. Rawlings	
G-MYJS	Solar Wings Pegasus Quasar IITC	J. P. Rooms	
G-MYJT	Solar Wings Pegasus Quasar IITC	S. Ferguson	

Notes	Reg.	Type	Owner or Operator
	G-MYJU	Solar Wings Pegasus Quasar IITC	D. Al-Bassam
	G-MYJZ	Whittaker MW5D Sorcerer	M. A. Summers
	G-MYKA	Cyclone AX3/503	T. Whittall
	G-MYKB	Kolb Twinstar Mk 3	T. Antell
	G-MYKE	CFM Shadow Srs BD	MKH Engineering
	G-MYKF	Cyclone AX3/503	M. A. Collins
	G-MYKG	Mainair Gemini/Flash IIA	B. D. Walker
	G-MYKH	Mainair Gemini/Flash IIA	A. W. Leadley
	G-MYKJ	TEAM mini-MAX	T. de Breffe Gardner
	G-MYKO	Whittaker MW6-S Fat Boy Flyer	J. A. Weston
	G-MYKR	Solar Wings Pegasus Quasar IITC	C. Stallard
	G-MYKS	Solar Wings Pegasus Quasar IITC	D. J. Oskis
	G-MYKV	Mainair Gemini/Flash IIA	P. J. Gulliver
	G-MYKX	Mainair Mercury	D. T. McAfee
	G-MYKZ	TEAM mini-MAX	R. Targonski
	G-MYLB	TEAM mini-MAX	J. G. Burns
	G-MYLC	Solar Wings Pegasus Quantum 15	C. McKay
	G-MYLD	Rans S.6-ESD Coyote II	E. Kaplan
	G-MYLE	Solar Wings Pegasus Quantum 15	Quantum Quartet
	G-MYLF	Rans S.6-ESD Coyote II	A. J. Spencer
	G-MYLG	Mainair Gemini/Flash IIA	N. J. Axworthy
	G-MYLH	Solar Wings Pegasus Quantum 15	G. Carr
	G-MYLI	Solar Wings Pegasus Quantum 15	A. M. Keyte
	G-MYLK	Solar Wings Pegasus Quantum 15	G-MYLK Group
	G-MYLL	Solar Wings Pegasus Quantum 15	M. P. Bawden
	G-MYLM	Solar Wings Pegasus Quasar IITC	M. W. Scott
	G-MYLN	Kolb Twinstar Mk 3	J. F. Joyes
	G-MYLO	Rans S.6-ESD Coyote II	P. Bowers
	G-MYLP	Kolb Twinstar Mk 3	R. Thompson (G-BVCR)
	G-MYLR	Mainair Gemini/Flash IIA	A. L. Lyall
	G-MYLS	Mainair Mercury	W. K. C. Davies
	G-MYLT	Mainair Blade	T. D. Hall
	G-MYLV	CFM Shadow Srs CD	Aviation for Paraplegics and Tetraplegics Trust
	G-MYLW	Rans S.6-ESD Coyote II	A. D. Dias
	G-MYLX	Medway Raven	K. Hayley
	G-MYMB	Solar Wings Pegasus Quantum 15	D. B. Jones
	G-MYMC	Solar Wings Pegasus Quantum 15	I. A. Macadam
	G-MYMH	Rans S.6-ESD Coyote II	P. V. Stevens
	G-MYMI	Kolb Twinstar Mk.3	F. J. Brown
	G-MYMJ	Medway Raven	N. Brigginshaw
	G-MYMK	Mainair Gemini/Flash IIA	A. Britton
	G-MYML	Mainair Mercury	D. J. Dalley
	G-MYMM	Ultraflight Fun 18S	N. P. Power
	G-MYMN	Whittaker MW6 Merlin	K. J. Cole
	G-MYMP	Rans S.6-ESD Coyote II	R. L. Flowerday (G-CHAZ)
	G-MYMR	Rans S.6-ESD Coyote II	J. Minogue
	G-MYMS	Rans S.6-ESD Coyote II	P. G. Briscoe
	G-MYMV	Mainair Gemini/Flash IIA	A. J. Evans
	G-MYMW	Cyclone AX3/503	L. J. Perring
	G-MYMX	Solar Wings Pegasus Quantum 15	I. A. Thomson
	G-MYMZ	Cyclone AX3/503	Microlight School (Lichfield) Ltd
	G-MYNB	Solar Wings Pegasus Quantum 15	J. A. Gregorig
	G-MYND	Mainair Gemini/Flash IIA	S. Wild
	G-MYNE	Rans S.6-ESD Coyote II	J. L. Smoker
	G-MYNF	Mainair Mercury	C. I. Hemingway
	G-MYNH	Rans S.6-ESD Coyote II	E. F. & V. M. Clapham
	G-MYNI	TEAM mini-MAX	I. Pearson
	G-MYNK	Solar Wings Pegasus Quantum 15	L. Hughes
	G-MYNL	Solar Wings Pegasus Quantum 15	S. J. Whalley
	G-MYNN	Solar Wings Pegasus Quantum 15	V. Loy
	G-MYNO	Solar Wings Pegasus Quantum 15	P. A. C. R. Stephens
	G-MYNP	Solar Wings Pegasus Quantum 15	K. A. Davidson
	G-MYNR	Solar Wings Pegasus Quantum 15	C. A. Reynolds
	G-MYNS	Solar Wings Pegasus Quantum 15	F. J. McVey
	G-MYNT	Solar Wings Pegasus Quantum 15	C. D. Arnold
	G-MYNV	Solar Wings Pegasus Quantum 15	J. Goldsmith-Ryan
	G-MYNX	CFM Streak Shadow SA	S. P. Fletcher
	G-MYNY	Kolb Twinstar Mk 3	I. F. Hill
	G-MYNZ	Solar Wings Pegasus Quantum 15	P. W. Rogers
	G-MYOA	Rans S6-ESD Coyote II	N. S. M. Day
	G-MYOG	Kolb Twinstar Mk 3	T. A. Womersley
	G-MYOH	CFM Shadow Srs CD	D. R. Sutton

Reg.	Type	Owner or Operator	Notes
G-MYOL	Air Creation Fun 18S GTBIS	S. N. Bond	
G-MYON	CFM Shadow Srs CD	A. Munro	
G-MYOO	Kolb Twinstar Mk 3	P. D. Coppin	
G-MYOR	Kolb Twinstar Mk 3	R. W. Hocking	
G-MYOS	CFM Shadow Srs CD	C. A. & E. J. Bowles	
G-MYOT	Rans S.6-ESD Coyote II	D. E. Wilson	
G-MYOU	Solar Wings Pegasus Quantum 15	D. J. Tasker	
G-MYOV	Mainair Mercury	P. Newton	
G-MYOX	Mainair Mercury	K. Driver	
G-MYOZ	Quad City Challenger II UK	A. R. Thomson	
G-MYPA	Rans S.6-ESD Coyote II	M. A. Azeem	
G-MYPC	Kolb Twinstar Mk 3	S. J. Ball	
G-MYPE	Mainair Gemini/Flash IIA	C. A. Carstairs	
G-MYPG	Solar Wings Pegasus XL-Q	V. Ashwell	
G-MYPH	Solar Wings Pegasus Quantum 15	I. E. Chapman	
G-MYPI	Solar Wings Pegasus Quantum 15	P. L. Jarvis	
G-MYPJ	Rans S.6-ESD Coyote II	K. A. Eden	
G-MYPL	CFM Shadow Srs CD	G. I. Madden	
G-MYPN	Solar Wings Pegasus Quantum 15	P. J. S. Albon	
G-MYPP	Whittaker MW6-S Fat Boy Flyer	G. Everett & D. Smith	
G-MYPR	Cyclone AX3/503	K. D. Parnell	
G-MYPS	Whittaker MW6 Merlin	I. S. Bishop	
G-MYPT	CFM Shadow Srs CD	R. Gray	
G-MYPV	Mainair Mercury	B. Donnan	
G-MYPW	Mainair Gemini/Flash IIA	T. C. Edwards	
G-MYPX	Solar Wings Pegasus Quantum 15	C. Cleveland & M. M. P. Evans	
G-MYPY	Solar Wings Pegasus Quantum 15	C. Cheasman	
G-MYPZ	Quad City Challenger II	E. G. Astin	
G-MYRC	Mainair Blade	M. P. Sanderson	
G-MYRD	Mainair Blade	D. R. Slater	
G-MYRE	Cyclone Chaser S	S. W. Barker	
G-MYRF	Solar Wings Pegasus Quantum 15	P. D. Gregory	
G-MYRG	TEAM mini-MAX	J. Jones	
G-MYRH	Quad City Challenger II	G. Cousins	
G-MYRK	Renegade Spirit UK	D. J. Newton	
G-MYRL	TEAM mini-MAX	J. N. Hanson	
G-MYRN	Solar Wings Pegasus Quantum 15	I. L. Waghorn	
G-MYRP	Letov LK-2M Sluka	R. M. C. Hunter	
G-MYRS	Solar Wings Pegasus Quantum 15	I. G. Poutney	
G-MYRT	Solar Wings Pegasus Quantum 15	Poet Pilot (UK) Ltd	
G-MYRU	Cyclone AX3/503	W. A. Emmerson	
G-MYRV	Cyclone AX3/503	M. Gardiner	
G-MYRW	Mainair Mercury	G. C. Hobson	
G-MYRY	Solar Wings Pegasus Quantum 15	N. J. Lindsay	
G-MYRZ	Solar Wings Pegasus Quantum 15	R. E. Forbes	
G-MYSA	Cyclone Chaser S 508	S. D. J. Harvey	
G-MYSB	Solar Wings Pegasus Quantum 15	H. G. Reid	
G-MYSC	Solar Wings Pegasus Quantum 15	K. R. White	
G-MYSD	BFC Challlenger II	C. W. Udale	
G-MYSG	Mainair Mercury	P. A. Parry	
G-MYSI	HM14/93	A. R. D. Seaman	
G-MYSJ	Mainair Gemini/Flash IIA	A. Warnock	
G-MYSK	Team Minimax 91	T. D. Wolstenholme	
G-MYSL	Aviasud Mistral	J. E. Midder	
G-MYSM	CFM Shadow Srs CD	L. W. Stevens	
G-MYSO	Cyclone AX3/50	R. Bowden	
G-MYSP	Rans S.6-ESD Coyote II	A. J. Alexander, K. G. Diamond & D. V. Marjason	
G-MYSR	Solar Wings Pegasus Quatum 15	W. G. Craig	
G-MYSU	Rans S.6-ESD Coyote II	C. N. Nairn	
G-MYSV	Aerial Arts Chaser	G. S. Highley	
G-MYSW	Solar Wings Pegasus Quantum 1	I. A. Macadam	
G-MYSX	Solar Wings Pegasus Quantum 1	L. E. Lesurf	
G-MYSY	Solar Wings Pegasus Quantum 15	B. D. S. Vere	
G-MYSZ	Mainair Mercury	W. Fletcher & R. J. Coppin	
G-MYTB	Mainair Mercur	P. J. Higgins	
G-MYTD	Mainair Blade	B. E. Warburton & D. B. Meades	
G-MYTE	Rans S.6-ESD Coyote II	R. A. Currinn	
G-MYTH	CFM Shadow Srs CD	S. G. Smith	
G-MYTI	Solar Wings Pegasus Quantum 15	K. M. Gaffney	
G-MYTJ	Solar Wings Pegasus Quantum 15	L. Blight	
G-MYTK	Mainair Mercury	D. A. Holroyd	
G-MYTL	Mainair Blade	I. T. Callagham & J. W. Coventry	

Notes	Reg.	Type	Owner or Operator
	G-MYTN	Solar Wings Pegasus Quantum 15	M. Humphries
	G-MYTO	Quad City Challenger II	A. Studley
	G-MYTP	Arrowflight Hawk II	R. J. Turner
	G-MYTT	Quad City Challenger II	D. M. Lockley
	G-MYTU	Mainair Blade	A. Worthington
	G-MYTY	CFM Streak Shadow Srs M	D. A. Daniel
	G-MYUA	Air Creation Fun 18S GTBIS	J. Leden
	G-MYUC	Mainair Blade	A. D. Clayton
	G-MYUD	Mainair Mercury	P. W. Margetson
	G-MYUF	Renegade Spirit	F. Overall
	G-MYUH	Solar Wings Pegasus XL-Q	K. S. Daniels
	G-MYUI	Cyclone AX3/503	T. Crocombe
	G-MYUL	Quad City Challenger II UK	N. V. & B. M. R. Van Cleve
	G-MYUN	Mainair Blade	G. A. Barratt
	G-MYUO	Solar Wings Pegasus Quantum 15	E. J. Hughes
	G-MYUP	Letov LK-2M Sluka	J. C. Dawson
	G-MYUS	CFM Shadow Srs CD	Aviation for Paraplegics and Tetraplegics Trust
	G-MYUU	Pegasus Quantum 15	J. L. Parker
	G-MYUV	Pegasus Quantum 15	Group Uniform Victor
	G-MYUW	Mainair Mercury	G. C. Hobson
	G-MYUZ	Rans S.6-ESD Coyote II	R. J. Field
	G-MYVA	Kolb Twinstar Mk 3	E. Bayliss
	G-MYVB	Mainair Blade	P. Mountain
	G-MYVC	Pegasus Quantum 15	D. P. Clarke
	G-MYVE	Mainair Blade	K. B. Richards
	G-MYVG	Letov LK-2M Sluka	S. P. Halford
	G-MYVH	Mainair Mercury	R. H. de C. Ribeiro
	G-MYVI	Air Creation Fun 18S GTBIS	Flylight Airsports Ltd
	G-MYVJ	Pegasus Quantum 15	A. I. McPherson & P. W. Davidson
	G-MYVK	Pegasus Quantum 15	O. C. Rash
	G-MYVL	Mainair Mercury	P. J. Judge
	G-MYVM	Pegasus Quantum 15	G. J. Gibson
	G-MYVN	Cyclone AX3/503	F. Watt
	G-MYVO	Mainair Blade	S. S. Raines
	G-MYVP	Rans S.6-ESD Coyote II	K. J. Legg
	G-MYVR	Pegasus Quantum 15	J. M. Webster
	G-MYVV	Medway Hybred 44XLR	S. Perity
	G-MYVY	Mainair Blade	G. Heeks
	G-MYVZ	Mainair Blade	R. Llewellyn
	G-MYWC	Hunt Wing	M. A. Coffin
	G-MYWE	Thruster T.600	W. A. Stephenson
	G-MYWG	Pegasus Quantum 15	S. L. Greene
	G-MYWH	Hunt Wing/Experience	G. N. Hatchett
	G-MYWJ	Pegasus Quantum 15	L. M. Sams & I. Clarkson
	G-MYWK	Pegasus Quantum 15	M. Garvey
	G-MYWL	Pegasus Quantum 15	S. J. Prouse
	G-MYWM	CFM Shadow Srs CD	N. McKinley
	G-MYWN	Cyclone Chaser S 508	R. A. Rawes
	G-MYWO	Pegasus Quantum 15	S. Newlands
	G-MYWP	Kolb Twinstar Mk 3	P. R. Day
	G-MYWR	Pegasus Quantum 15	R. Horton
	G-MYWS	Cyclone Chaser S 447	M. H. Broadbent
	G-MYWT	Pegasus Quantum 15	P. B. J. Eveleigh
	G-MYWU	Pegasus Quantum 15	J. R. Buttle
	G-MYWV	Rans S.4C Coyote	P. G. Anthony & D. A. Crouchman
	G-MYWW	Pegasus Quantum 15	C. W. Bailie
	G-MYWY	Pegasus Quantum 15	A. S. R. Czajka
	G-MYXA	TEAM mini-MAX 91	D. C. Marsh
	G-MYXB	Rans S.6-ESD Coyote II	K. Gerrard
	G-MYXC	Quad City Challenger II	M. Alaman
	G-MYXD	Pegasus Quasar IITC	A. Cochrane
	G-MYXE	Pegasus Quantum 15	J. F. Bolton
	G-MYXF	Air Creation Fun GT503	D. J. N. Brown
	G-MYXH	Cyclone AX3/503	M. Alaman
	G-MYXI	Aries 1	H. Cook
	G-MYXJ	Mainair Blade	S. N. Robson
	G-MYXK	Quad City Challenger II	P. J. Collins
	G-MYXL	Mignet HM.1000 Baleri	R. W. Hollamby
	G-MYXM	Mainair Blade	S. C. Hodgson
	G-MYXN	Mainair Blade	P. K. Dale
	G-MYXO	Letov LK-2M Sluka	I. A. Macadam
	G-MYXP	Rans S.6-ESD Coyote II	R. S. Amor

Reg.	Type	Owner or Operator	Notes
G-MYXS	Kolb Twinstar Mk 3	B. B. Boniface	
G-MYXT	Pegasus Quantum 15	G. Cousins	
G-MYXU	Thruster T.300	D. W. Wilson	
G-MYXV	Quad City Challenger II	T. S. Savage	
G-MYXW	Pegasus Quantum 15	J. Uttley	
G-MYXX	Pegasus Quantum 15	G. Fish	
G-MYXY	CFM Shadow Srs CD	S. P. Hatherall	
G-MYXZ	Pegasus Quantum 15	A. K. Hole	
G-MYYA	Mainair Blade	K. J. Watt	
G-MYYB	Pegasus Quantum 15	A. L. Johnson & D. S. Ross	
G-MYYC	Pegasus Quantum 15	S. B. Cooper	
G-MYYD	Cyclone Chaser S 447	E. Kelly	
G-MYYF	Quad City Challenger II	J. G. & J. A. Smith	
G-MYYH	Mainair Blade	D. J. Dodd	
G-MYYI	Pegasus Quantum 15	C. M. Day	
G-MYYJ	Hunt Wing	R. M. Jarvis	
G-MYYK	Pegasus Quantum 15	J. D. Philp	
G-MYYL	Cyclone AX3/503	R. Ferguson	
G-MYYP	AMF Chevvron 2-45CS	J. Cook	
G-MYYR	TEAM mini-MAX 91	L. S. Bailey	
G-MYYS	TEAM mini-MAX	J. Pulford	
G-MYYV	Rans S.6-ESD Coyote IIXL	J. Rochead	
G-MYYW	Mainair Blade	M. D. Kirby	
G-MYYX	Pegasus Quantum 15	B. J. Chapman	
G-MYYY	Mainair Blade	E. D. Lockie	
G-MYYZ	Medway Raven X	J. W. Leaper	
G-MYZB	Pegasus Quantum 15	M. A. Lovatt	
G-MYZC	Cyclone AX3/503	P. E. Owen	
G-MYZE	TEAM mini-MAX	J. Broome	
G-MYZF	Cyclone AX3/503	Microflight (Ireland) Ltd	
G-MYZG	Cyclone AX3/503	I. A. Holden	
G-MYZH	Chargus Titan 38	T. J. Gayton-Polley	
G-MYZJ	Pegasus Quantum 15	G. Graham	
G-MYZK	Pegasus Quantum 15	G. G. Wilson	
G-MYZL	Pegasus Quantum 15	A. N. Grant	
G-MYZM	Pegasus Quantum 15	J. V. Clewer	
G-MYZP	CFM Shadow Srs DD	A. C. Holmes	
G-MYZR	Rans S.6-ESD Coyote II	Rans Clan	
G-MYZV	Rans S.6-ESD Coyote II	B. W. Savory	
G-MYZY	Pegasus Quantum 15	C. Chapman	
G-MZAA	Mainair Blade	A. G. Butler	
G-MZAB	Mainair Blade	D. C. Nixon	
G-MZAC	Quad City Challenger II	T. R. Gregory	
G-MZAE	Mainair Blade	D. J. Guild	
G-MZAF	Mainair Blade	P. F. Mayes	
G-MZAG	Mainair Blade	M. J. P. Sanderson	
G-MZAH	Rans S.6-ESD Coyote II	R. Warriner	
G-MZAJ	Mainair Blade	M. P. Daley	
G-MZAK	Mainair Mercury	I. Rawson	
G-MZAM	Mainair Blade	G-MZAM Syndicate	
G-MZAN	Pegasus Quantum 15	P. M. Leahy	
G-MZAP	Mainair Blade	K. D. Adams	
G-MZAR	Mainair Blade	P. Bowden	
G-MZAS	Mainair Blade	T. Carter	
G-MZAT	Mainair Blade	M. J. Moulton	
G-MZAU	Mainair Blade	A. F. Glover	
G-MZAV	Mainair Blade	C. R. Buckle	
G-MZAW	Pegasus Quantum 15	C. A. Mackenzie	
G-MZAZ	Mainair Blade	P. J. Pickering	
G-MZBB	Pegasus Quantum 15	T. Campbell	
G-MZBC	Pegasus Quantum 15	B. M. Quinn	
G-MZBD	Rans S-6-ESD-XL Coyote II	J. P. & M. P. Tilzey	
G-MZBF	Letov LK-2M Sluka	V. Simpson	
G-MZBG	Hodder MW6-A	E. I. Rowlands-Jons & M. W. Kilvert	
G-MZBH	Rans S.6-ESD Coyote II	D. Sutherland	
G-MZBK	Letov LK-2M Sluka	R. M. C. Hunter	
G-MZBL	Mainair Blade	C. J. Rubery	
G-MZBN	CFM Shadow Srs B	W. J. Buskell	
G-MZBO	Pegasus Quantum 15	K. C. Beattie	
G-MZBS	CFM Shadow Srs D	S. K. Ryan	
G-MZBT	Pegasus Quantum 15	A. C. Barlow	

Notes	Reg.	Type	Owner or Operator
	G-MZBU	Rans S.6-ESD Coyote II	R. S. Marriott
	G-MZBV	Rans S.6-ESD Coyote II	R. I. Cannan & C. N. Carine
	G-MZBW	Quad City Challenger II UK	R. M. C. Hunter
	G-MZBY	Pegasus Quantum 15	I. J. Rawlinson
	G-MZBZ	Quad City Challenger II UK	T. R. Gregory
	G-MZCA	Rans S.6-ESD Coyote II	W. Scott
	G-MZCB	Cyclone Chaser S 447	R. W. Keene
	G-MZCC	Mainair Blade 912	K. S. Rissmann
	G-MZCD	Mainair Blade	T. Drury & S. P. Maxwell
	G-MZCE	Mainair Blade	I. C. Hindle
	G-MZCF	Mainair Blade	C. Hannanby
	G-MZCH	Whittaker MW6-S Fatboy Flyer	J. A. Weston
	G-MZCI	Pegasus Quantum 15	P. H. Risdale
	G-MZCJ	Pegasus Quantum 15	C. R. Madden
	G-MZCK	AMF Chevvron 2-32C	M. Daly
	G-MZCM	Pegasus Quantum 15	J. E. Bullock
	G-MZCN	Mainair Blade	P. Mulvey
	G-MZCR	Pegasus Quantum 15	J. E. P. Stubberfield
	G-MZCS	TEAM mini-MAX	J. Aley
	G-MZCT	CFM Shadow Srs CD	W. G. Gill
	G-MZCU	Mainair Blade	C. E. Pearce
	G-MZCV	Pegasus Quantum 15	I. Davidson
	G-MZCW	Pegasus Quantum 15	K. L. Baldwin
	G-MZCY	Pegasus Quantum 15	G. Murphy
	G-MZDA	Rans S.6-ESD Coyote IIXL	R. Plummer
	G-MZDB	Pegasus Quantum 15	Scottish Aerotow Club
	G-MZDC	Pegasus Quantum 15	M. T. Jones
	G-MZDD	Pegasus Quantum 15	A. J. Todd
	G-MZDE	Pegasus Quantum 15	R. G. Hedley
	G-MZDF	Mainair Blade	M. Liptrot
	G-MZDG	Rans S.6-ESD Coyote IIXL	S. E. H. Newington
	G-MZDH	Pegasus Quantum 15	A. T. Willis
	G-MZDJ	Medway Raven X	R. Bryan & S. Digby
	G-MZDK	Mainair Blade	P. Combellack
	G-MZDL	Whittaker MW6-S Fatboy Flyer	N. Hogarth
	G-MZDM	Rans S.6-ESD Coyote II	M. E. Nicholas
	G-MZDN	Pegasus Quantum 15	P. G. Ford
	G-MZDP	AMF Chevvron 2-32	J. Pool
	G-MZDS	Cyclone AX3/503	S. F. N. Warnell
	G-MZDT	Mainair Blade	G. A. Davidson & I. Lee
	G-MZDU	Pegasus Quantum 15	G. Breen/Portugal
	G-MZDV	Pegasus Quantum 15	S. A. Mallett
	G-MZDX	Letov LK-2M Sluka	J. L. Barker
	G-MZDY	Pegasus Quantum 15	M. J. King
	G-MZDZ	Hunt Wing	E. W. Laidlaw
	G-MZEA	BFC Challenger II	G. S. Cridland
	G-MZEB	Mainair Blade	R. A. Campbell
	G-MZEC	Pegasus Quantum 15	A. B. Godber
	G-MZED	Mainair Blade	G. G. Wilson
	G-MZEE	Pegasus Quantum 15	J. L. Brogan
	G-MZEG	Mainair Blade	R. Jacques
	G-MZEH	Pegasus Quantum 15	P. S. Hall
	G-MZEJ	Mainair Blade	P. G. Thomas
	G-MZEK	Mainair Mercury	G. Crane
	G-MZEL	Cyclone Airsports AX3/503	L. M. Jackson & R. I. Simpson
	G-MZEM	Pegasus Quantum 15	L. H. Black
	G-MZEN	Rans S.6-ESD Coyote II	P. R. Hutty
	G-MZEO	Rans S.6-ESD Coyote IIXL	R. W. Lenthall
	G-MZEP	Mainair Rapier	A. G. Bird
	G-MZER	Cyclone AX2000	N. I. Garland
	G-MZES	Letov LK-2N Sluka	J. L. Self
	G-MZEU	Rans S.6-ESD Coyote IIXL	N. Grugan
	G-MZEV	Mainair Rapier	W. T. Gardner
	G-MZEW	Mainair Blade	T. D. Holder
	G-MZEX	Pegasus Quantum 15	J. P. Quinlan
	G-MZEY	Micro Bantam B.22	P. J. Glover
	G-MZEZ	Pegasus Quantum 15	M. J. Ing
	G-MZFA	Cyclone AX2000	G. S. Highley
	G-MZFB	Mainair Blade	A. J. Plant
	G-MZFC	Letov LK-2M Sluka	F. Overall
	G-MZFD	Mainair Rapier	C. J. Kew
	G-MZFE	Hunt Wing	G. J. Latham

Reg.	Type	Owner or Operator	Notes
G-MZFF	Hunt Wing	B. J. Adamson	
G-MZFG	Pegasus Quantum 15	A. M. Prentice	
G-MZFH	AMF Chevvron 2-32C	A. Greenwell	
G-MZFL	Rans S.6-ESD Coyote IIXL	H. Adams	
G-MZFM	Pegasus Quantum 15	M. McLaughlin	
G-MZFN	Rans S.6.ESD Coyote IIXL	C. J. & W. R. Wallbank	
G-MZFO	Thruster T.600N	S. J. P. Stevenson	
G-MZFS	Mainair Blade	P. L. E. Zelazowski	
G-MZFT	Pegasus Quantum 15	C. Childs	
G-MZFU	Thruster T.600N	J. R. Wilkinson	
G-MZFX	Cyclone AX2000	Avon Aerotow Group	
G-MZFY	Rans S.6-ESD Coyote IIXL	L. G. Tserkezos	
G-MZFZ	Mainair Blade	D. J. Bateman	
G-MZGA	Cyclone AX2000	K. G. Grayson & R. D. Leigh	
G-MZGB	Cyclone AX2000	P. Hegarty	
G-MZGC	Cyclone AX2000	C. E. Walls	
G-MZGD	Rans S.5 Coyote II	P. J. Greenrod	
G-MZGF	Letov LK-2M Sluka	G. Lombardi	
G-MZGG	Pegasus Quantum 15	P. J. Hopkins	
G-MZGH	Hunt Wing/Avon 462	J. H. Cole	
G-MZGI	Mainair Blade 912	H. M. Roberts	
G-MZGJ	Kolb Twinstar Mk 1	L. G. G. Faulkner	
G-MZGK	Pegasus Quantum 15	C. D. Cross & S. H. Moss	
G-MZGL	Mainair Rapier	D. Thrower	
G-MZGM	Cyclone AX2000	A. F. Smallacombe	
G-MZGN	Pegasus Quantum 15	B. J. Youngs	
G-MZGO	Pegasus Quantum 15	S. F. G. Allen	
G-MZGP	Cyclone AX2000	Buchan Light Aeroplane Club	
G-MZGR	TEAM mini-MAX	K. G. Seeley	
G-MZGS	CFM Shadow Srs BD	C. S. Nagy	
G-MZGU	Arrowflight Hawk II (UK)	J. N. Holden	
G-MZGV	Pegasus Quantum 15	B. A. & D. K. Janaway	
G-MZGW	Mainair Blade	R. Almond	
G-MZGX	Thruster T.600N	K. J. Underwood	
G-MZGY	Thruster T.600N 450	I. A. Macadam	
G-MZHA	Thruster T.600N	P. Stark	
G-MZHB	Mainair Blade	D. W. Curtis	
G-MZHD	Thruster T.600N	B. E. Foster	
G-MZHF	Thruster T.600N	L. Swift	
G-MZHG	Whittaker MW6-T Merlin	D. R. Thompson	
G-MZHI	Pegasus Quantum 15	F. R. Macdonald	
G-MZHJ	Mainair Rapier	G. Standish & R. Jones	
G-MZHK	Pegasus Quantum 15	R. Hussain	
G-MZHM	Team Himax 1700R	M. H. McKeown	
G-MZHN	Pegasus Quantum 15	F. W. Ferichs	
G-MZHO	Quad City Challenger II	J. Pavelin	
G-MZHP	Pegasus Quantum 15	W. J. Flood	
G-MZHR	Cyclone AX2000	D. K. Wedge	
G-MZHS	Thruster T.600T	J. R. Davis	
G-MZHT	Whittaker MW6 Merlin	G. J. Chadwick	
G-MZHV	Thruster T.600T	H. G. Denton	
G-MZHW	Thruster T.600N	H. & G. Willingham	
G-MZHY	Thruster T.600N	J. P. & R. E. Jones	
G-MZIB	Pegasus Quantum 15	S. Murphy	
G-MZID	Whittaker MW6 Merlin	C. P. F. Sheppard	
G-MZIE	Pegasus Quantum 15	Flylight Airsports Ltd	
G-MZIF	Pegasus Quantum 15	D. Parsons	
G-MZIH	Mainair Blade	N. J. Waller	
G-MZIJ	Pegasus Quantum 15	D. L. Wright	
G-MZIK	Pegasus Quantum 15	C. M. Wilkinson	
G-MZIL	Mainair Rapier	A. J. Owen & J. C. Price	
G-MZIM	Mainair Rapier	M. J. McKegney	
G-MZIR	Mainair Blade	S. Connor	
G-MZIS	Mainair Blade	M. K. Richings	
G-MZIT	Mainair Blade 912	P. M. Horn	
G-MZIU	Pegasus Quantum 15-912	A. P. Douglas-Dixon	
G-MZIV	Cyclone AX2000	C. J. Tomlin	
G-MZIW	Mainair Blade	S. R. Pickering	
G-MZIX	Mignet HM.1000 Balerit	P. E. H. Scott	
G-MZIY	Rans S.6 Coyote II	G. Munro	
G-MZIZ	Renegade Spirit UK (G-MWGP)	B. L. R. J. Keeping	
G-MZJA	Mainair Blade	P. L. Dowd	

Notes	Reg.	Type	Owner or Operator
	G-MZJD	Mainair Blade	M. Howard
	G-MZJE	Mainair Rapier	G. Ramsay & G. Shand
	G-MZJF	Cyclone AX2000	D. J. Lewis & V. E. Booth
	G-MZJG	Pegasus Quantum 15	K. M. C. Compton
	G-MZJH	Pegasus Quantum 15	P. Copping
	G-MZJJ	Murphy Maverick	M. F. Farrer
	G-MZJK	Mainair Blade	P. G. Angus
	G-MZJL	Cyclone AX2000	M. H. Owen
	G-MZJM	Rans S.6-ESD Coyote IIXL	K. A. Hastie
	G-MZJO	Pegasus Quantum 15	D. J. Cook
	G-MZJP	Whittaker MW6-S Fatboy Flyer	R. C. Funnell & D. J. Burton
	G-MZJR	Cyclone AX2000	N. A. Martin
	G-MZJT	Pegasus Quantum 15	N. Hammerton
	G-MZJV	Mainair Blade 912	M. A. Roberts
	G-MZJW	Pegasus Quantum 15	M. J. J. Clutterbuck
	G-MZJX	Mainair Blade	N. Cowell & D. Nicholls
	G-MZJY	Pegasus Quantum 15	M. F. Turff
	G-MZJZ	Mainair Blade	I. J. Richardson
	G-MZKA	Pegasus Quantum 15	S. P. Tkaczyk
	G-MZKC	Cyclone AX2000	D. J. Pike
	G-MZKD	Pegasus Quantum 15	T. M. Frost
	G-MZKE	Rans S.6-ESD Coyote IIXL	P. A. Flaherty
	G-MZKF	Pegasus Quantum 15	J. W. Sandars
	G-MZKG	Mainair Blade	N. S. Rigby
	G-MZKH	CFM Shadow Srs DD	S. P. H. Calvert
	G-MZKI	Mainair Rapier	D. L. Aspinall
	G-MZKJ	Mainair Blade	The G-MZKJ Group
	G-MZKL	Pegasus Quantum 15	G. Williams
	G-MZKN	Mainair Rapier	J. McAloney
	G-MZKR	Thruster T.600N	R. J. Arnett
	G-MZKS	Thruster T.600N	P. J. Hepburn
	G-MZKT	Thruster T.600N	Great Thornes Flying Group
	G-MZKU	Thruster T.600N	A. S. Day
	G-MZKV	Mainair Blade 912	J. D. Harriman
	G-MZKW	Quad City Challenger II	K. W. Warn
	G-MZKY	Pegasus Quantum 15	P. S. Constable
	G-MZKZ	Mainair Blade	R. P. Wolstenholme
	G-MZLA	Pegasus Quantum 15	A. J. Harris
	G-MZLC	Mainair Blade 912	S. Turnbull
	G-MZLD	Pegasus Quantum 15	D. Hamilton
	G-MZLE	Maverick (G-BXSZ)	J. S. Hill
	G-MZLF	Pegasus Quantum 15	S. Seymour
	G-MZLG	Rans S.6-ESD Coyote IIXL	F. Y. Allery
	G-MZLI	Mignet HM.1000 Balerit	A. G. Barr
	G-MZLJ	Pegasus Quantum 15	R. M. Williams
	G-MZLL	Rans S.6-ESD Coyote II	J. A. Willats & G. W. Champion
	G-MZLM	Cyclone AX2000	P. E. Hadley
	G-MZLN	Pegasus Quantum 15	P. A. Greening
	G-MZLP	CFM Shadow Srs D	D. J. Gordon
	G-MZLR	Solar Wings Pegasus XL-Q	B. Lorraine
	G-MZLT	Pegasus Quantum 15	P. E. Woodhead
	G-MZLV	Pegasus Quantum 15	A. Armsby
	G-MZLW	Pegasus Quantum 15	R. W. R. Crevel & D. P. Hampson
	G-MZLX	Micro Aviation B.22S Bantam	V. J. Vaughan
	G-MZLY	Letov LK-2M Sluka	W. McCarthy
	G-MZLZ	Mainair Blade	W. Biddulph
	G-MZMA	Solar Wings Pegasus Quasar IITC	M. L. Pardoe
	G-MZMC	Pegasus Quantum 15	J. J. Baker
	G-MZMD	Mainair Blade 912	S. George
	G-MZME	Medway Eclipser	P. A. Wenham
	G-MZMF	Pegasus Quantum 15	A. J. Tranter
	G-MZMG	Pegasus Quantum 15	A. G. Kemp
	G-MZMH	Pegasus Quantum 15	M. Hurtubise
	G-MZMJ	Mainair Blade	D. Wilson
	G-MZMK	Chevvron 2-32C	I. C. Lewis
	G-MZML	Mainair Blade 912	T. C. Edwards
	G-MZMM	Mainair Blade 912	J. Lynch
	G-MZMN	Pegasus Quantum 912	R. H. Cheesley
	G-MZMO	TEAM mini-MAX 91	R. E. Main
	G-MZMP	Mainair Blade	A. M. Beale
	G-MZMT	Pegasus Quantum 15	J. A. Davies
	G-MZMU	Rans S.6-ESD Coyote II	P. F. Berry & T. D. Wood

Reg.	Type	Owner or Operator	Notes
G-MZMV	Mainair Blade	P. B. Smith	
G-MZMW	Mignet HM.1000 Balerit	M. E. Whapham	
G-MZMX	Cyclone AX2000	L. A. Lacy	
G-MZMY	Mainair Blade	C. J. Millership	
G-MZMZ	Mainair Blade	W. A. Stacey	
G-MZNA	Quad City Challenger II UK	S. Hennessy	
G-MZNB	Pegasus Quantum 15	F. Gorse	
G-MZNC	Mainair Blade 912	A. J. Harrison	
G-MZND	Mainair Rapier	D. W. Stamp	
G-MZNG	Pegasus Quantum 15	The Scottish Flying Club	
G-MZNH	CFM Shadow Srs DD	P. A. James	
G-MZNJ	Mainair Blade	R. A. Hardy	
G-MZNM	TEAM mini-MAX	S. M. Williams	
G-MZNN	TEAM mini-MAX	P. J. Bishop	
G-MZNO	Mainair Blade	I. M. & V. M. Vass	
G-MZNR	Pegasus Quantum 15	E. S. Wills	
G-MZNS	Pegasus Quantum 15	S. Uzochukwu	
G-MZNT	Pegasus Quantum 15-912	N. W. Barnett	
G-MZNU	Mainair Rapier	B. Johnson	
G-MZNV	Rans S.6-ESD Coyote II	A. P. Thomas	
G-MZNX	Thruster T.600N	B. Rogan	
G-MZNY	Thruster T.600N	G. Price	
G-MZNZ	Letov LK-2M Sluka	B. F. Crick	
G-MZOC	Mainair Blade	A. S. Davies	
G-MZOD	Pegasus Quantum 15	M. C. Robinson	
G-MZOE	Cyclone AX2000	G-MZOE Flying Group	
G-MZOF	Mainair Blade	R. M. Ellis	
G-MZOG	Pegasus Quantum 15-912	D. Smith	
G-MZOH	Whittaker MW5D Sorcerer	I. Pearson	
G-MZOI	Letov LK-2M Sluka	E. Bentley	
G-MZOJ	Pegasus Quantum 15	G. P. Church	
G-MZOK	Whittaker MW6 Merlin	G-MZOK Syndicate	
G-MZOP	Mainair Blade 912	K. M. Thorogood	
G-MZOS	Pegasus Quantum 15-912	J. R. Moore	
G-MZOV	Pegasus Quantum 15	Pegasus XL Group	
G-MZOW	Pegasus Quantum 15-912	G. P. Burns	
G-MZOX	Letov LK-2M Sluka	D. L. Hadley	
G-MZOY	TEAM Mini-MAX 91	P. R. & S. E. Whitehouse	
G-MZOZ	Rans S.6-ESD Coyote IIXL	S. G. & D. C. Emmons	
G-MZPH	Mainair Blade	J. D. Hoyland	
G-MZPJ	TEAM mini-MAX	K. R. Emery	
G-MZPW	Pegasus Quasar IITC	N. S. Payne	
G-MZRC	Pegasus Quantum 15	M. Hopkins	
G-MZRM	Pegasus Quantum 15	R. Milwain	
G-MZRS	CFM Shadow Srs CD	R. Barton	
G-MZTS	Aerial Arts Chaser S	D. G. Ellis (G-MVDM)	
G-MZUB	Rans S.6-ESD Coyote IIXL	R. E. Main	
G-MZZT	Kolb Twinstar Mk 3	D. E. Martin	
G-MZZY	Mainair Blade 912	A. Mucznik	
G-NAAA	MBB Bö.105DBS/4	Heli Invest BV/Netherlands (G-BUTN/G-AZTI)	
G-NAAL	Bombardier CL600-2B16 Challenger	Hangar 8 AOC Malta Ltd	
G-NACA	Norman NAC-2 Freelance 180	A. R. Norman	
G-NACI	Norman NAC-1 Srs 100	L. J. Martin (G-AXFB)	
G-NACL	Norman NAC-6 Fieldmaster	EPA Aircraft Co Ltd (G-BNEG)	
G-NACO	Norman NAC-6 Fieldmaster	EPA Aircraft Co Ltd	
G-NACP	Norman NAC-6 Fieldmaster	EPA Aircraft Co Ltd	
G-NADO	Titan Tornado SS	Euro Aviation LLP	
G-NADS	TEAM mini-MAX 91	R. L. Williams	
G-NADZ	Van's RV-4	R. A. Pritchard (G-BROP)	
G-NAGG	Rotorsport UK MT-03	C. A. Clements	
G-NANI	Robinson R44 II	MOS Gmbh	
G-NANO	Avid Speed Wing	T. M. C. Handley	
G-NAPO	Pegasus Quantum 15-912	J. M. Brigham	
G-NAPP	Van's RV-7	R. C. Meek	
G-NARG	Tanarg/Ixess 15 912S (1)	K. Kirby	
G-NARO	Cassutt Racer	C. Ball & R. Supply (G-BTXR)	
G-NARR	Stolp SA300 Starduster Too	G. J. D. Thomson	
G-NATT	Rockwell Commander 114A	Northgleam Ltd	
G-NATY	HS. Gnat T.1 (XR537) ★	Drilling Systems Ltd	
G-NBDD	Robin DR.400/180	B. & S. E. Chambers	

Notes	Reg.	Type	Owner or Operator
	G-NBEL	AS.355F1 Ecureuil 2	Latitude Aviation Ltd (G-SKYW/G-TBIS/G-TALI)
	G-NBSI	Cameron N-77 balloon	Nottingham Hot-Air Balloon Club
	G-NCCC	Bombardier CL600-2B16	TAG Aviation (UK) Ltd
	G-NCFC	PA-38-112 Tomahawk II	A. M. Heynen
	G-NCUB	Piper J-3C-65 Cub	R. J. Willies (G-BGXV)
	G-NDAA	MBB Bö.105DBS-4	Bond Air Services Ltd (G-WMAA/G-PASB/ G-BDMC)
	G-NDAD	Medway SLA100 Executive	K. Angel
	G-NDOL	Europa	S. Longstaff
	G-NDOT	Thruster T.600N	P. C. Bailey
	G-NDPA	Ikarus C42 FB UK	P. A. Pilkington
	G-NEAL	PA-32-260 Cherokee Six	I. Parkinson (G-BFPY)
	G-NEAT	Europa	P. F. D. Foden
	G-NEAU	Eurocopter EC 135T2	Northumbria Police Authority
	G-NEDS	Skyranger Nynja 912S(1)	H. Van Allen
	G-NEEL	Rotorway Executive 90	I. C. Bedford
	G-NEIL	Thunder Ax3 balloon	R. M. Powell
	G-NELI	PA-28R Cherokee Arrow 180	MK Aero Support Ltd
	G-NEMO	Raj Hamsa X'Air Jabiru (4)	G. F. Allen
	G-NEON	PA-32 Cherokee Six 300B	P. J. P. Coutney
	G-NEPB	Cameron N-77 balloon	The Post Office
	G-NESA	Shaw Europa XS	A. M. Kay
	G-NESE	Tecnam P2002-JF	N. & S. Easton
	G-NESH	Robinson R44 II	M. Tancock
	G-NEST	Christen Eagle II	P. J. Nonat
	G-NESV	Eurocopter EC 135T1	Eurocopter UK Ltd
	G-NESW	PA-34-220T Seneca III	G. C. U. Guida
	G-NESY	PA-18 Super Cub 95	V. Featherstone
	G-NETR	AS.355F1 Twin Squirrel	PLM Dollar Group Ltd (G-JARV/G-OGHL)
	G-NETT	Cessna 172S	Aero-Club Rhein-Nahe EV
	G-NETY	PA-18 Super Cub 150	N. B. Mason
	G-NEWT	Beech 35 Bonanza	J. S. Allison (G-APVW)
	G-NEWZ	Bell 206B JetRanger 3	Guay Tulliemet Aviation Ltd
	G-NFLA	BAe Jetstream 3102	Cranfield University (G-BRGN/G-BLHC)
	G-NFLC	HP.137 Jetstream 1H (G-AXUI) ★	Instructional airframe/Perth
	G-NFLY	Tecnam P2002-EA Sierra	C. N. Hodgson
	G-NFNF	Robin DR.400/180	M. Child, W. Cobb & J. Archer
	G-NFON	Van's RV-8	N. F. O'Neill
	G-NGLS	Aerospool Dynamic WT9 UK	The Nigels Ltd
	G-NHAA	AS.365N-2 Dauphin 2	The Great North Air Ambulance Service (G-MLTY)
	G-NHAB	AS.365N-2 Dauphin 2	The Great North Air Ambulance Service (G-DAUF)
	G-NHAC	AS.365N-2 Dauphin 2	The Great North Air Ambulance Service
	G-NHRH	PA-28 Cherokee 140	C. J. Milsom
	G-NHRJ	Shaw Europa XS	D. A. Lowe
	G-NICC	Aerotechnik EV-97 Team Eurostar UK	Pickup and Son Ltd
	G-NICI	Robinson R44	David Fishwick Vehicles Sales Ltd
	G-NICK	PA-18 Super Cub	M. W. Zipfell
	G-NICS	Best Off Sky Ranger Swift 912S(1)	I. A. Forrest & C. K. Richardson
	G-NIDG	Aerotechnik EV-97 Eurostar	Skydrive Ltd
	G-NIEN	Van's RV-9A	NIEN Group
	G-NIFE	SNCAN Stampe SV.4A (156)	Tiger Airways
	G-NIGC	Avtech Jabiru UL-450	W. D. Brereton
	G-NIGE	Luscombe 8E Silvaire	Garden Party Ltd (G-BSHG)
	G-NIGL	Shaw Europa	N. M. Graham
	G-NIGS	Thunder Ax7-65 balloon	S. D. Annett
	G-NIKE	PA-28-181 Archer II	Key Properties Ltd
	G-NIKK	Diamond Katana DA20-C1	Cubair Flight Training Ltd
	G-NIKO	Airbus A.321-211	Thomas Cook Airlines Ltd
	G-NIKS	Aeropro Eurofox 912(1)	N. G. Heywood
	G-NIKX	Robinson R-44 II	P. R. Holloway
	G-NIMA	Balóny Kubíček BB30Z balloon	C. Williamson
	G-NIMB	Schempp-Hirth Nimbus 2C	M. J. Slade
	G-NIME	Cessna T.206H Turbo Stationair	Whitby Seafoods Ltd
	G-NINA	PA-28-161 Warrior II	A. P. Gorrod (G-BEUC)
	G-NINC	PA-28-180 Cherokee	Flintshire Flying School Ltd
	G-NIND	PA-28-180 Cherokee	Aquarelle Investments Ltd

Reg.	Type	Owner or Operator	Notes
G-NINE	Murphy Renegade 912	R. C. McCarthy	
G-NIOG	Robinson R44 II	Helicopter Sharing Ltd	
G-NIOS	PA-32R-301 Saratoga SP	Plant Aviation	
G-NIPA	Slingsby T.66 Nipper 3	R. J. O. Walker (G-AWDD)	
G-NIPP	Slingsby T.66 Nipper 3	R. J. Porter (G-AVKJ)	
G-NIPR	Slingsby T.66 Nipper 3	P. A. Gibbs (G-AVXC)	
G-NIPS	Tipsy T.66 Nipper 2	B. W. Faulkner	
G-NIPY	Hughes 369HS	Jet Aviation (Northwest) Ltd	
G-NISA	Robinson R44 II	G. P. Jones (G-HTMT)	
G-NISH	Van's RV-8	N. H. F. Hampton & S. R. Whitling	
G-NITA	PA-28 Cherokee 180	T. Clifford (G-AVVG)	
G-NIVA	Eurocopter EC 155B1	Lanthwaite Aviation Ltd	
G-NIVT	Schempp-Hirth Nimbus 4T	G-NIVT Gliding Group	
G-NJBA	Rotorway Executive 162F	British Waterproofing Ltd	
G-NJET	Schempp-Hirth Ventus cT	V. S. Bettle	
G-NJPW	P & M Quik GT450	N. J. P. West	
G-NJSH	Robinson R22 Beta	ATN Farms	
G-NJSP	Jabiru J430	N. J. S. Pitman	
G-NJTC	Aeroprakt A22-L Foxbat	B. Jackson & T. F. Casey	
G-NLCH	Lindstrand LBL-35A balloon	S. A. Lacey	
G-NLEE	Cessna 182Q	C. G. D. Jones (G-TLTD)	
G-NLMB	Zenair CH.601UL Zodiac	N. Lamb	
G-NLPA	Hawker 750	Hangar 8 Management Ltd	
G-NLYB	Cameron N-105 balloon	P. H. E. Van Overwalle/Belgium	
G-NMAK	Airbus A.319-115	Twinjet Aircraft Sales Ltd	
G-NMBG	Jabiru J400	P. R. Hendry-Smith & H. I. Smith	
G-NMCL	Eurofox 912(S)	N. R. McLeod	
G-NMID	Eurocopter EC 135T2	Derbyshire Constabulary	
G-NMOS	Cameron C-80 balloon	C. J. Thomas & M. C. East	
G-NMRV	Van's RV-6	R. Taggart	
G-NNAC	PA-18 Super Cub 135	PAW Flying Services Ltd	
G-NNON	Mainair Blade	D. R. Kennedy	
G-NOAH	Airbus A.319-115CJ	Acropolis Aviation Ltd	
G-NOCK	Cessna FR.182RG II	M. K. Aves (G-BGTK)	
G-NODE	AA-5B Tiger	Ultranomad Sro	
G-NOIL	BN-2A-26 Islander	Aerospace Resources Ltd (G-BJWO/G-BAXC)	
G-NOMO	Cameron O-31 balloon	Balloon Promotion SAS/Italy	
G-NOMZ	Balony Kubicek BB-S Gnome SS balloon	A. M. Holly	
G-NONE	Dyn'Aéro MCR-01 ULC	M. A. Collins	
G-NONI	AA-5 Traveler	November India Group (G-BBDA)	
G-NOOR	Commander 114B	As-Al Ltd	
G-NORA	Ikarus C.42 FB UK	N. A. Rathbone	
G-NORB	Saturne S110K hang glider	R. N. Pearce	
G-NORD	SNCAN NC.854	A. D. Pearce	
G-NORK	Bell 206B-3 JetRanger III	R. S. Forsyth	
G-NOSE	Cessna 402B	Reconnaissance Ventures Ltd (G-MPCU)	
G-NOTE	PA-28-181 Archer III	J. Beach	
G-NOTS	Skyranger 912S(1)	D. J. Vickery	
G-NOTT	Nott ULD-2 balloon	J. R. P. Nott	
G-NOUS	Cessna 172S	Flyglass Ltd	
G-NOWW	Mainair Blade 912	R. S. Sanby	
G-NOXY	Robinson R44	S. A. Knox (G-VALV)	
G-NPKJ	Van's RV-6	M. R. Turner	
G-NPPL	Comco Ikarus C.42 FB.100	Papa Lima Group	
G-NREG	Bombardier CL600-2B16 Challenger	Skymiddleeast UK Ltd	
G-NRIA	Beech 23 Musketeer	Respondmatte Flugeliclub	
G-NRMA	Dan Rihn DR.107 One Design	A. W. Brown	
G-NROY	PA-32RT-300 Lance II	B. Nedjati-Gilani (G-LYNN/G-BGNY)	
G-NRRA	SIAI-Marchetti SF.260 ★	G. Boot	
G-NSBB	Ikarus C.42 FB-100 VLA	M. Pratt	
G-NSEW	Robinson R44	G-NSEW Ltd	
G-NSKB	Aeroprakt A22-L Foxbat	N. F. Smith	
G-NSOF	Robin HR.200/120B	Modi Aviation Ltd	
G-NSTG	Cessna F.150F	Westair Flying Services Ltd (G-ATNI)	

Notes	Reg.	Type	Owner or Operator
	G-NTVE	Beagle A-61 Terrier 3	R. E. Dagless (G-ASIE)
	G-NTWK	AS.355F2 Twin Squirrel	PLM Dollar Group (G-FTWO/G-OJOR/G-BMUS)
	G-NUDE	Robinson R44	The Last Great Journey Ltd (G-NSYT)
	G-NUFC	Best Off Skyranger 912S(1)	C. R. Rosby
	G-NUGC	Grob G.103A Twin II Acro	The University of Nottingham Students Union
	G-NUKA	PA-28-181 Archer II	N. Ibrahim
	G-NULA	Flight Design CT2K	L. I. Bailey
	G-NUNI	Lindstrand LBL-77A balloon	The University of Nottingham
	G-NUTA	Christen Eagle II	Blue Eagle Group
	G-NUTT	Mainair Pegasus Quik	NUTT Syndicate
	G-NVBF	Lindstrand LBL-210A balloon	Virgin Balloon Flights
	G-NWAA	Eurocopter EC 135T2	Bond Air Services Ltd
	G-NWFA	Cessna 150M	North Weald Flying Group Ltd (G-CFBD)
	G-NWFC	Cessna 172P	North Weald Flying Group Ltd
	G-NWFG	Cessna 172P	North Weald Flying Group Ltd
	G-NWFS	Cessna 172P	North Weald Flying Group Ltd (G-TYMS)
	G-NWOI	Eurocopter EC135 P2+	North Wales Police Authority
	G-NWPR	Cameron N-77 balloon	D. B. Court
	G-NWPS	Eurocopter EC 135T1	Santander Asset Finance PLC
	G-NXOE	Cessna 172S	Goodwood Road Racing Co.Ltd
	G-NXUS	Nexus Mustang	G. W. Miller
	G-NYKS	Cessna 182T	N. B. Le-Grys
	G-NYMB	Schempp-Hirth Nimbus 3	Nimbus Syndicate
	G-NYMF	PA-25 Pawnee 235D	Bristol Gliding Club Pty Ltd
	G-NYNA	Van's RV-9A	B. Greathead & S. Hiscox
	G-NYNE	Schleicher ASW-27-18E	R. C. W. Ellis
	G-NZGL	Cameron O-105 balloon	R. A. Vale & ptnrs
	G-NZSS	Boeing Stearman N2S-5 (343251:27)	R. W. Davies
	G-OAAA	PA-28-161 Warrior II	Red Hill Air Services Ltd
	G-OAAF	BAe ATP	Atlantic Airlines Ltd (G-JEMB)
	G-OABB	Jodel D.150	K. Manley
	G-OABC	Colt 69A balloon	P. A. C. Stuart-Kregor
	G-OABO	Enstrom F-28A	C. R. Taylor (G-BAIB)
	G-OABR	AG-5B Tiger	A. J. Neale
	G-OACA	PA-44-180 Seminole	H. Merkado (G-GSFT)
	G-OACE	Valentin Taifun 17E	I. F. Wells
	G-OACF	Robin DR.400/180	A. C. Fletcher
	G-OACI	MS.893E Rallye 180GT	Full Sutton Flying Centre Ltd
	G-OADY	Beech 76 Duchess	Multiflight Ltd
	G-OAER	Lindstrand LBL-105A balloon	M. P. Rowley
	G-OAFF	Cessna 208 Caravan 1	Army Parachute Association
	G-OAFR	Cameron Z-105 balloon	PSH Skypower Ltd
	G-OAGI	FLS Aerospace Sprint 160	Black Art Composites Ltd (G-FLSI)
	G-OAGL	Bell 206B JetRanger 3	AGL Helicopters (G-CORN/G-BHTR)
	G-OAHC	Beech F33C Bonanza	Cirrus Aviation Ltd (G-BTTF)
	G-OAJB	Cyclone AX2000	A. J. Allan (G-MZFJ)
	G-OAJC	Robinson R44	Adare International Transport Ltd
	G-OAJL	Ikarus C.42 FB100	G. D. M. McCullogh
	G-OAJS	PA-39 Twin Comanche 160 C/R	S. Vansteenkiste (G-BCIO)
	G-OAKI	BAe Jetstream 3102	AIS Airlines BV/Netherlands
	G-OALD	SOCATA TB20 Trinidad	Gold Aviation
	G-OALH	Tecnam P92-EA Echo	K. D. Pearce
	G-OAMF	Pegasus Quantum 15-912	G. A. Viquerat
	G-OAMI	Bell 206B JetRanger 2	Leamington Hobby Centre Ltd (G-BAUN)
	G-OAML	Cameron AML-105 balloon	Stratton Motor Co (Norfolk) Ltd
	G-OAMP	Cessna F.177RG	J-F. Pitot (G-AYPF)
	G-OANI	PA-28-161 Warrior II	J. F. Mitchell
	G-OANN	Zenair CH.601HD	Zodiac Group Mona
	G-OAPE	Cessna T.303	C. Twiston-Davies & P. L. Drew
	G-OAPR	Brantly B.2B	Helicopter International Magazine
	G-OAPW	Glaser-Dirks DG.400	P. L. Poole
	G-OARA	PA-28R-201 Arrow III	Obmit Ltd
	G-OARC	PA-28RT-201 Arrow IV	Plane Talking Ltd (G-BMVE)
	G-OARI	PA-28R-201 Arrow III	Flew LLP
	G-OARO	PA-28R-201 Arrow III	Booker Aircraft Leasing Ltd

Reg.	Type	Owner or Operator	Notes
G-OARS	Cessna 172S	Whitespace Work Software Ltd	
G-OART	PA-23 Aztec 250D	Prescribing Services Ltd (G-AXKD)	
G-OARU	PA-28R-201 Arrow III	S. J. Green	
G-OARV	ARV Super 2	I. F. Davidson	
G-OASH	Robinson R22 Beta	J. C. Lane	
G-OASJ	Thruster T.600N 450	A. E. Turner	
G-OASP	AS.355F2 Twin Squirrel	Helicopter Services Ltd	
G-OASW	Schleicher ASW-27	M. P. W. Mee	
G-OATE	Mainair Pegasus Quantum 15-912	S. J. Goate	
G-OATV	Cameron V-77 balloon	A. W. & E. P. Braund-Smith	
G-OATZ	Van's RV-12	J. Jones & J. W. Armstrong	
G-OAVA	Robinson R22 Beta	Phoenix Helicopter Academy Ltd	
G-OAWL	Agusta AW.139	Profred Partners LLP	
G-OAWS	Colt 77A balloon	P. Lawman	
G-OBAB	Lindstrand LBL-35A Cloudhopper balloon	B. A. Bower	
G-OBAK	PA-28R-201T Turbo Arrow III	G-OBAK Group Aviation	
G-OBAL	Mooney M.20J	G-OBAL Group	
G-OBAN	Jodel D.140B	S. R. Cameron (G-ATSU)	
G-OBAP	Zenair CH.701SP	J. M. Gale & A. D. Janaway	
G-OBAX	Thruster T.600N 450-JAB	G. B. Denton	
G-OBAZ	Best Off Skyranger 912(2)	B. J. Marsh	
G-OBBO	Cessna 182S	A. E. Kedros	
G-OBDA	Diamond Katana DA20-A1	Oscar Papa Ltd	
G-OBDN	PA-28-161 Warrior II	R. M. Bennett	
G-OBEE	Boeing Stearman A75N-1 (3397:174)	P. G. Smith	
G-OBEI	SOCATA TB200 Tobago XL	K. Stoter	
G-OBEN	Cessna 152 II	Globibussola Lda (G-NALI/G-BHVM)	
G-OBET	Sky 77-24 balloon	P. M. Watkins & S. M. Carden	
G-OBFE	Sky 120-24 balloon	J. Sonnabend	
G-OBFS	PA-28-161 Warrior III	Claris Aviation Ltd	
G-OBIB	Colt 120A balloon	M. B. Vennard	
G-OBIL	Robinson R22 Beta	Helicopter Services Ltd	
G-OBIO	Robinson R22 Beta	Burbage Farms Ltd	
G-OBJB	Lindstrand LBL-90A balloon	B. J. Bower	
G-OBJH	Colt 77A balloon	Hayrick Ltd	
G-OBJM	Taylor JT.1 Monoplane	C. D. Davidson	
G-OBJP	Pegasus Quantum 15-912	S. J. Baker	
G-OBJT	Shaw Europa	B. J. Tarmar (G-MUZO)	
G-OBLC	Beech 76 Duchess	Pridenote Ltd	
G-OBLU	Cameron H-34 balloon	John Aimo Balloons SAS/Italy	
G-OBMI	Mainair Blade	S. R. Kirkham & D. F. Reeves	
G-OBMP	Boeing 737-3Q8	bmi Baby (stored)	
G-OBMS	Cessna F.172N	Mike Sierra Group	
G-OBNA	PA-34-220T Seneca V	Palmair Ltd	
G-OBNC	BN-2B-20 Islander	Britten-Norman Aircraft Ltd	
G-OBOF	Remos GX	D. Hawkins	
G-OBPP	Schleicher ASG-29E	M. H. Patel	
G-OBRA	Cameron Z-315 balloon	Cameron Flights Southern Ltd	
G-OBRO	Alpi Pioneer 200M	A. Brown	
G-OBRY	Cameron N-180 balloon	A. C. K. Rawson & J. J. Rudoni	
G-OBSM	Robinson R44 Raven	Patriot Aviation Ltd (G-CDSE)	
G-OBSR	Partenavia P68	Ravenair Aircraft Ltd	
G-OBTS	Cameron C-90 balloon	D. G. Such	
G-OBUP	DG Flugzeugbau DG-808C	R. A. Roberts	
G-OBUU	Replica Comper CLA Swift	J. A. Pothecary & R. H. Hunt	
G-OBUY	Colt 69A balloon	Balloon Preservation Flying Group	
G-OBUZ	Van's RV-6	A. F. Hall	
G-OBWP	BAe ATP	European Turboprop Management AB (G-BTPO)	
G-OBYD	Boeing 767-304ER	Thomsonfly Ltd	
G-OBYF	Boeing 767-304ER	Thomsonfly Ltd	
G-OBYG	Boeing 767-3Q8ER	Thomsonfly Ltd	
G-OBYH	Boeing 767-304ER	Thomsonfly Ltd	
G-OBYT	Agusta-Bell 206A JetRanger	R. J. Everett (G-BNRC)	
G-OBZR	Aerostyle Breezer LSA	D. Curtin & S. Greenall	
G-OCAC	Robin R-2112	The Cotswold Aero Club Ltd (G-EWHT)	
G-OCAD	Sequoia F.8L Falco	D. R. Vale	
G-OCAM	AA-5A Cheetah	R. E. Dagless (G-BLHO)	
G-OCBI	Schweizer 269C-1	Alpha Properties (London) Ltd	
G-OCBT	IDA Bacau Yakovlev Yak-52	Cambridge Business Travel	
G-OCCD	Diamond DA40D Star	Flying Pictures Ltd	

Notes	Reg.	Type	Owner or Operator
	G-OCCF	Diamond DA40D Star	Aviation Rentals
	G-OCCG	Diamond DA40D Star	Aviation Maintenance Ltd
	G-OCCH	Diamond DA40D Star	Innovative Aviation (Leeds) Ltd
	G-OCCK	Diamond DA40D Star	Westbeach Aviation Ltd
	G-OCCL	Diamond DA40D Star	Westbeach Aviation Ltd
	G-OCCN	Diamond DA40D Star	Aviation Rentals
	G-OCCO	Diamond DA40D Star	Plane Talking Ltd
	G-OCCP	Diamond DA40D Star	Plane Talking Ltd
	G-OCCR	Diamond DA40D Star	P. Plaisted
	G-OCCS	Diamond DA40D Star	Plane Talking Ltd
	G-OCCT	Diamond DA40D Star	Plane Talking Ltd
	G-OCCU	Diamond DA40D Star	Chalrey Ltd
	G-OCCX	Diamond DA42 Twin Star	Westbeach Aviation Ltd
	G-OCDC	Best Off Sky Ranger Nynja 912S(1)	C. D. Church
	G-OCDP	Flight Design CTSW	M. A. Beadman
	G-OCDW	Jabiru UL	G. Bennett
	G-OCEG	Beech B.200 Super King Air	Cega Aviation Ambulance UK Ltd.
	G-OCFC	Robin R.2160	Cornwall Flying Club Ltd
	G-OCFD	Bell 206B JetRanger 3	Rushmere Helicopters LLP (G-WGAL/G-OICS)
	G-OCFM	PA-34-200 Seneca II	Stapleford Flying Club Ltd (G-ELBC/G-BANS)
	G-OCFT	Bombasrdier CL600-2B16 Challenger	Hangar 8 Management Ltd
	G-OCGC	Robin DR.400-180R	Cambridge Gliding Club Ltd
	G-OCHM	Robinson R44	Westleigh Developments Ltd
	G-OCJZ	Cessna 525A Citationjet CJ2	Go West Ltd
	G-OCLC	Aviat A-1B Husky	R. F. Pooler
	G-OCLH	Avro RJ-85	Trident Aviation Leasing Services (Jersey) Ltd
	G-OCMM	Agusta A109A II	Castle Air Ltd (G-BXCB/G-ISEB/G-IADT/G-HBCA)
	G-OCMS	EV-97 TeamEurostar UK	C. M. Saysell
	G-OCMT	EV-97 TeamEurostar UK	P. Crowhurst
	G-OCOD	Bombardier CL600-2B16 Challenger	Hangar 8 Management Ltd
	G-OCOK	American Champion 8KCAB Super Decathlon	J. D. May
	G-OCON	Robinson R44	P. Kelly
	G-OCOV	Robinson R22 Beta	Heli Air Ltd
	G-OCPC	Cessna FA.152	E. & M. O'Toole
	G-OCRI	Colomban MC.15 Cri-Cri	M. J. J. Dunning
	G-OCRL	Europa	R. J. Lewis (G-OBEV)
	G-OCRZ	CZAW Sportcruiser	P. Marsden
	G-OCST	Agusta-Bell 206B JetRanger 3	Lift West Ltd (G-BMKM)
	G-OCTI	PA-32 Cherokee Six 260	D. G. Williams (G-BGZX)
	G-OCTS	Cameron Z-90 balloon	Collett Transport Services Ltd
	G-OCTU	PA-28-161 Cadet	Glenn Aviation Ltd
	G-OCUB	Piper J-3C-90 Cub	Zebedee Flying Group
	G-OCZA	CZAW Sportcruiser	S. M. Dawson
	G-ODAC	Cessna F.152 II	T. M. Jones (G-BITG)
	G-ODAD	Colt 77A balloon	J. H. Dobson
	G-ODAF	Lindstrand LBL-105A balloon	T. J. Horne
	G-ODAK	PA-28-236 Dakota	Booker Aircraft Leasing Ltd
	G-ODAY	Cameron N-56 balloon	British Balloon Museum & Library
	G-ODAZ	Robinson R44 II	S. L. Walton
	G-ODBN	Lindstrand LBL Flowers SS balloon	Magical Adventures Ltd
	G-ODCC	Bell 206L-3 Long Ranger III	DCC Aviation
	G-ODCH	Schleicher ASW-20L	P. J. Stratten
	G-ODCR	Robinson R44 II	D. Lynn
	G-ODDS	Aerotek Pitts S-2A	A. C. Cassidy
	G-ODDY	Lindstrand LBL-105A balloon	P. & T. Huckle
	G-ODDZ	Schempp-Hirth Duo Discus T	P. A. King
	G-ODEB	Cameron A-250 balloon	A. Derbyshire
	G-ODEE	Van's RV-6	D. Cook
	G-ODEL	Falconar F-11-3	G. F. Brummell
	G-ODGS	Avtech Jabiru UL-450	S. R. Eskins
	G-ODHB	Robinson R44	A. J. Mossop
	G-ODHL	Cameron N-77 balloon	DHL International (UK) Ltd
	G-ODIN	Avions Mudry CAP-10B	CAP Ten
	G-ODJD	Raj Hamsa X'Air 582 (7)	S. Richens
	G-ODJF	Lindstrand LBL-90B balloon	Helena Dos Santos SA/Portugal
	G-ODJG	Shaw Europa	K. R. Challis & C. S. S. Andersson
	G-ODJH	Mooney M.20C	R. M. Schweitzer/Netherlands (G-BMLH)
	G-ODOC	Robinson R44	A. Bristow
	G-ODOG	PA-28R Cherokee Arrow 200-II	M. Brancart (G-BAAR)
	G-ODPJ	VPM M-16 Tandem Trainer	K. J. Robinson & S. Palmer (G-BVWX)

Reg.	Type	Owner or Operator	Notes
G-ODRD	PA-32R-301T Saratoga II	Interceptor Properties Ltd	
G-ODSK	Boeing 737-37Q	bmi Baby (stored)	
G-ODTW	Shaw Europa	D. T. Walters	
G-ODUD	PA-28-181 Archer II	S. Barlow, R. N. Ingle & R. J. Murray (G-IBBO)	
G-ODUO	Schempp-Hirth Duo Discus	3D Syndicate	
G-ODUR	Raytheon Hawker 900XP	Hangar 8 Ltd	
G-ODVB	CFM Shadow Srs DD	L. J. E. Moss	
G-ODXB	Lindstrand LBL-120A balloon	A. Nimmo	
G-OEAC	Mooney M.20J	S. Lovatt	
G-OEAT	Robinson R22 Beta	C. Y. O. Seeds Ltd (G-RACH)	
G-OEBC	Ultramagic N-300 balloon	European Balloon Display Co.Ltd	
G-OECM	Commander 114B	ECM (Vehicle Delivery Service) Ltd	
G-OECO	Flylight Dragonfly	P. A. & M. W. Aston	
G-OEDB	PA-38-112 Tomahawk	M. A. Petrie (G-BGGJ)	
G-OEDP	Cameron N-77 balloon	M. J. Betts	
G-OEGG	Cameron Egg-65 SS balloon	Mobberley Balloon Collection	
G-OEGL	Christen Eagle II	The Eagle Flight Syndicate	
G-OEKS	Ikarus C42 FB80	J. D. Smith	
G-OELD	Pegasus Quantum 15-912	R. P. Butler	
G-OELZ	Wassmer WA.52 Europa	G-OELZ Group	
G-OEMT	MBB BK-117 C-1	Sterling Helicopters Ltd	
G-OERR	Lindstrand LBL-60A balloon	P. C. Gooch	
G-OERS	Cessna 172N	E. R. Stevens (G-SSRS)	
G-OESY	Easy Raider J2.2 (1)	J. Gray	
G-OETI	Bell 206B JetRanger 3	T. A. Wells (G-RMIE/G-BPIE)	
G-OETV	PA-31-350 Navajo Chieftain	Hinde Holdings Ltd	
G-OEVA	PA-32-260 Cherokee Six	M. G. Cookson & G. A. Thornton (G-FLJA/G-AVTJ)	
G-OEWD	Raytheon 390 Premier 1	Bookajet Aircraft Management Ltd	
G-OEZI	Easy Raider J2.2(2)	C. D. Pidler	
G-OEZY	Shaw Europa	A. W. Wakefield	
G-OFAA	Cameron Z-105 balloon	R. A. Schwab	
G-OFAL	Ozone Roadster/Bailey Quattro	Malcolm Roberts Heating, Plumbing and Electrical Ltd	
G-OFAS	Robinson R22 Beta	Alan Mann Aviation Group Ltd	
G-OFBU	Ikarus C.42 FB UK	Old Sarum C42 Group	
G-OFCM	Cessna F.172L	Sirius Aviation Ltd (G-AZUN)	
G-OFDT	Mainair Pegasus Quik	J. Smith	
G-OFER	PA-18 Super Cub 150	White Watham Airfield Ltd	
G-OFFA	Pietenpol Air Camper	OFFA Group	
G-OFEO	Extra EA.300/L	2 Excel Aviation Ltd	
G-OFGC	Aeroprakt A22-L Foxbat	J. M. Fearn	
G-OFIT	SOCATA TB10 Tobago	GFI Aviation Group (G-BRIU)	
G-OFIX	Grob G.109B	T. R. Dews	
G-OFJC	Eiriavion PIK-20E	G. Bailey, J. D. Sorrell & D. Thomas	
G-OFLI	Colt 105A balloon	Virgin Airship & Balloon Co Ltd	
G-OFLT	EMB-110P1 Bandeirante ★	Rescue trainer/Aveley, Essex (G-MOBL/G-BGCS)	
G-OFLY	Cessna 210M	A. P. Mothew	
G-OFMC	Avro RJ100	Trident Jet (Dublin) Ltd (G-CDUI)	
G-OFOA	BAe 146-100	Formula One Administration Ltd (G-BKMN/G-ODAN)	
G-OFOM	BAe 146-100	Formula One Management Ltd (G-BSLP/G-BRLM)	
G-OFOX	Denney Kitfox	P. R. Skeels	
G-OFRB	Everett gyroplane	T. N. Holcroft-Smith	
G-OFRY	Cessna 152	Devon and Somerset Flight Training Ltd	
G-OFSP	CZAW Sportcruiser	F. S. Pullman	
G-OFTC	Agusta A109E Power	Castle Air Ltd	
G-OFTI	PA-28 Cherokee 140	G-OFTI Group	
G-OGAR	PZL SZD-45A Ogar	P. Rasmussen t/a Perranporth Ogar Flying Group	
G-OGAS	Westland WG.30 Srs 100 ★	(stored)/Yeovil (G-BKNW)	
G-OGAY	Baloney Kubicek BB-26 balloon	J. W. Soukup	
G-OGAZ	Aérospatiale SA.341G Gazelle 1	Killochries Fold (G-OCJR/G-BRGS)	
G-OGBD	Boeing 737-3L9	bmi Baby (stored)	
G-OGCA	PA-28-161 Warrior II	Cardiff-Wales Aviation Services Ltd	
G-OGEM	PA-28-181 Archer II	GEM Integrated Solutions Ltd	
G-OGEO	Aérospatiale SA.341G Gazelle 1	George Steel Contract Services (G-BXJK)	
G-OGES	Enstrom 280FX	G. E. Werkle (G-CBYL)	
G-OGET	PA-39 Twin Comanche	D. Saxton (G-AYXY)	
G-OGFS	BAe.125 Srs 800B	Aircraft Holdings Ltd (G-GRGA/G-DCTA/G-OSPG/G-ETOM/G-BVFC/G-TPHK/G-FDSL)	

Notes	Reg.	Type	Owner or Operator
	G-OGGB	Grob G.102 Astir CS	Golf Brave Group
	G-OGGM	Cirrus SR22	Morson Human Resources Ltd
	G-OGGS	Thunder Ax8-84 balloon	G. Gamble & Sons (Quorn) Ltd
	G-OGGY	Aviat A.1B	C. A. I. Hickling
	G-OGIL	Short SD3-30 Variant 100 ★	North East Aircraft Museum/Usworth (G-BITV)
	G-OGJC	Robinson R44 II	Telecom Advertising & Promotions Ltd
	G-OGJM	Cameron C-80 balloon	G. F. Madelin
	G-OGJP	Commander 114B	M. J. Church
	G-OGJS	Puffer Cozy	G. J. Stamper
	G-OGKB	Sequoia Falco F8L	G. K. Brothwood
	G-OGLY	Cameron Z-105 balloon	H. M. Ogston
	G-OGOD	P & M Quik GT450	C. M. Theakstone
	G-OGOS	Everett gyroplane	N. A. Seymour
	G-OGSA	Avtech Jabiru SPL-450	G-OGSA Group
	G-OGSK	Embraer EMB-135BJ Legacy	TAG Aviation (UK) Ltd
	G-OGTR	P & M Quik GTR	A. S. R. Czajka& P. L. Jarvis
	G-OGTS	Air Command 532 Elite	GTS Engineering (Coventry) Ltd
	G-OHAC	Cessna F.182Q	Maguirelzatt LLP
	G-OHAL	Pietenpol Air Camper	UK Pietenpol Club Flying Group
	G-OHAM	Robinson R44 II	Hamsters Wheel Productions Ltd (G-GBEN/ G-CDJZ)
	G-OHAV	ATG Ltd HAV-3	Hybrid Air Vehicles Ltd
	G-OHCP	AS.355F1 Twin Squirrel	Staske Construction Ltd (G-BTVS/G-STVE/ G-TOFF/G-BKJX)
	G-OHDC	Colt Film Cassette SS balloon ★	Balloon Preservation Group
	G-OHGA	Hughes O-6A (69-16011)	MSS Holdings (UK) Ltd
	G-OHGC	Scheibe SF.25C Falke	Heron Gliding Club
	G-OHIG	EMB-110P1 Bandeirante ★	Air Salvage International/Alton (G-OPPP)
	G-OHIO	Dyn'Aero MCR-01	J. M. Keane
	G-OHIY	Van's RV-10	M. A. Hutton
	G-OHJE	Alpi Pioneer 300 Hawk	H. J. Edwards
	G-OHJV	Robinson R44	HJV Ltd
	G-OHKS	Pegasus Quantum 15-912	S. J. Farr
	G-OHLI	Robinson R44 II	NCS Partnership
	G-OHMS	AS.355F1 Twin Squirrel	HFS (Aviation) Ltd
	G-OHNO	Yakovlev Yak-55	J. Fesl
	G-OHOV	Rotorway Executive 162F	M. G. Bird
	G-OHPC	Cessna 208 Caravan 1	S. Ulrich
	G-OHPH	HpH Glasflugel 304MS	G-OHPH Group
	G-OHVR	Robinson R44 II	Transparent Film Products Ltd
	G-OHWV	Raj Hamsa X'Air 582(6)	P. B. Readings
	G-OHYE	Thruster T.600N 450	A. P. W. O'Brien (G-CCRO)
	G-OIBM	Rockwell Commander 114	H. A. Barrs (G-BLVZ)
	G-OIBO	PA-28 Cherokee 180	Azure Flying Club Ltd (G-AVAZ)
	G-OIFM	Cameron 90 Dude SS balloon	Magical Adventures Ltd
	G-OIHC	PA-32R-301 Saratoga IIHP	N. J. Lipczynski (G-PUSK)
	G-OIIO	Robinson R22 Beta	Whizzard Helicopters (G-ULAB)
	G-OIMC	Cessna 152 II	East Midlands Flying School Ltd
	G-OINN	UltraMagic H-31 balloon	G. Everett
	G-OIOB	Mudry CAP.10B	J. Ceotto
	G-OIOZ	Thunder Ax9-120 S2 balloon	R. H. Etherington
	G-OIRP	Gulfstream G200	Air Charter Scotland Ltd
	G-OISO	Cessna FRA.150L	B. A. & L. A. Mills (G-BBJW)
	G-OITV	Enstrom 280C-UK-2	C. W. Brierley Jones (G-HRVY/G-DUGY/G-BEEL)
	G-OIVN	Liberty XL-2	I. Shaw
	G-OJAB	Avtech Jabiru SK	Flying Spanners Group
	G-OJAC	Mooney M.20J	Hornet Engineering Ltd
	G-OJAG	Cessna 172S	Sunfun Luxury Coaches
	G-OJAN	Robinson R22 Beta	J. C. Lane (G-SANS/G-BUHX)
	G-OJAS	Auster J/1U Workmaster	D. S. Hunt
	G-OJAZ	Robinson R44	P. C. Twigg
	G-OJBB	Enstrom 280FX	Pendragon (Design & Build) Ltd
	G-OJBM	Cameron N-90 balloon	P. Spinlove
	G-OJBS	Cameron N-105A balloon	Up & Away Ballooning Ltd
	G-OJBW	Lindstrand LBL J & B Bottle SS balloon	N. A. P. Godfrey
	G-OJCW	PA-32RT-300 Lance II	P. G. Dobson
	G-OJDA	EAA Acrosport II	D. B. Almey
	G-OJDC	Thunder Ax7-77 balloon	A. Heginbottom
	G-OJDS	Ikarus C.42 FB 80	The Rans Group

Reg.	Type	Owner or Operator	Notes
G-OJEG	Airbus A.321-231	Monarch Airlines Ltd	
G-OJEH	PA-28-181 Archer II	P. C. & M. A. Greenaway	
G-OJEN	Cameron V-77 balloon	C. & C. Westwood	
G-OJGC	Van's RV-4	J. G. Claridge	
G-OJGT	Maule M.5-235C	Newnham Joint Flying Syndicate	
G-OJHC	Cessna 182P	Stapleford Flying Club Ltd	
G-OJHL	Shaw Europa	M. D. Burns & G. Rainey	
G-OJIL	PA-31-350 Navajo Chieftain	Redhill Aviation Ltd	
G-OJIM	PA-28R-201T Turbo Arrow III	G-OJIM Flyers Ltd	
G-OJJV	P & M Pegasus Quik	J. J. Valentine	
G-OJKM	Rans S.7 Courier	A. J. Gibney	
G-OJLD	Van's RV-7	J. L. Dixon	
G-OJLH	TEAM mini-MAX 91	J. Riley (G-MYAW)	
G-OJMB	Airbus A.330-243	Thomas Cook Airlines Ltd	
G-OJMF	Enstrom 280FX	Manchester Helicopter Centre Ltd (G-DDOD)	
G-OJMR	Airbus A.300B4-605R	Monarch Airlines Ltd	
G-OJMS	Cameron Z-90 balloon	Joinersoft Ltd	
G-OJNB	Linsdrand LBL-21A balloon	N. A. P. Godfrey	
G-OJNE	Schempp-Hirth Nimbus 3T	J. N. Ellis	
G-OJON	Taylor JT.2 Titch	Freelance Aviation Ltd	
G-OJPS	Bell 206B JetRanger 2	Milford Aviation (G-UEST/G-ROYB/G-BLWU)	
G-OJRH	Robinson R44	J. R. Holgate	
G-OJRM	Cessna T.182T	Colne Airways Ltd	
G-OJSA	BAe Jetstream 3102	Diamond Air Charter Ltd	
G-OJSF	A.23 Aztec 250F	Comed Aviation Ltd (G-SFHR/G-BHSO)	
G-OJSH	Thruster T.600N 450 JAB	G-OJSH Group	
G-OJVA	Van's RV-6	J. A. Village	
G-OJVH	Cessna F.150H	G. H. Tempest-Hay (G-AWJZ)	
G-OJVL	Van's RV-6	S. E. Tomlinson	
G-OJWB	Hawker 800XP	Langford Lane Ltd	
G-OJWS	PA-28-161 Warrior II	P. J. Ward	
G-OKAG	PA-28R Cherokee Arrow 180	Alpha-Golf Flying Group	
G-OKAY	Pitts S-1E Special	S. R. S. Evans	
G-OKBT	Colt 25A Mk II balloon	British Telecommunications PLC	
G-OKCC	Cameron N-90 balloon	D. J. Head	
G-OKCP	Lindstrand LBL Battery SS balloon	D. Bedford & J. Edwards (G-MAXX)	
G-OKED	Cessna 150L	L. J. Pluck	
G-OKEM	Mainair Pegasus Quik	W. J. Hardy	
G-OKEN	PA-28R-201T Turbo Arrow III	K. Woodcock	
G-OKER	Van's RV-7	R. M. Johnson	
G-OKEV	Shaw Europa	K. A. Kedward	
G-OKEW	UltraMagic M-65C balloon	Hampshire Balloons Ltd	
G-OKEY	Robinson R22 Beta	Alan Mann Aviation Group Ltd	
G-OKID	Reality Escapade Kid	V. H. Hallam	
G-OKIM	Best Off Sykyranger 912 (2)	K. P. Taylor	
G-OKIS	Tri-R Kis	M. R. Cleveley	
G-OKMA	Tri-R Kis	K. Miller	
G-OKPW	Tri-R Kis	P. J. Reilly	
G-OKTI	Aquila AT01	P. H. Ferdinand	
G-OKYA	Cameron V-77 balloon	R. J. Pearce	
G-OKYM	PA-28 Cherokee 140	North Wales Air Academy Ltd (G-AVLS)	
G-OLAA	Alpi Pioneer 300 Hawk	G. G. Hammond	
G-OLAU	Robinson R22 Beta	MPW Aviation Ltd	
G-OLAW	Lindstrand LBL-25A balloon	George Law Plant Ltd	
G-OLCP	AS.355N Twin Squirrel	Charterstyle Ltd (G-CLIP)	
G-OLDG	Cessna T.182T	Gold Aviation Ltd (G-CBTJ)	
G-OLDH	Aérospatiale SA.341G Gazelle 1	MW Helicopters Ltd (G-UTZY/G-BKLV)	
G-OLDM	Pegasus Quantum 15-912	J. W. Holme	
G-OLDO	Eurocopter EC.120B Colibri	Gold Aviation Ltd (G-HIGI)	
G-OLDP	Mainair Pegasus Quik	A. G. Woodward	
G-OLDT	Learjet 45	Gold Aviation Ltd	
G-OLDX	Cessna 182T	Gold Air International Ltd (G-IBZT)	
G-OLEE	Cessna F.152	Redhill Air Services Ltd	
G-OLEM	Jodel D.18	G. E. Roe (G-BSBP)	
G-OLEW	Vans RV-7A	A. Burani	
G-OLEZ	Piper J-3C-65 Cub	L. Powell (G-BSAX)	
G-OLFA	AS.350B3 Ecureuil	Heliaviation Ltd	
G-OLFB	Pegasus Quantum 15-912	J. G. & P. Callan	
G-OLFF	Cameron Z-120 balloon	A. Nimmo	
G-OLFO	Robinson R44	Crinstown Aviation Ltd	

Notes	Reg.	Type	Owner or Operator
	G-OLFT	Rockwell Commander 114	D. A. Tubby (G-WJMN)
	G-OLFZ	P & M Quik GT450	A. J. Boyd
	G-OLGA	Starstreak Shadow SA-II	N. T. O'Donnell
	G-OLHR	Cassutt Racer IIIM	P. A. Hall & A. R. Lewis (G-BNJZ)
	G-OLJT	Mainair Gemini Flash IIA	M. H. Moulai
	G-OLLI	Cameron O-31 SS balloon	The British Balloon Museum & Library Ltd
	G-OLLS	Cessna U.206H Floatplane	Loch Lomond Seaplanes Ltd
	G-OLNT	SA.365N1 Dauphin 2	LNT Aviation Ltd (G-POAV/G-BOPI)
	G-OLOW	Robinson R44	C. O. Semik
	G-OLPM	P & M Quik R	T. J. Billingham
	G-OLRT	Robinson R22 Beta	The Henderson Group
	G-OLSA	Breezer LSA	RGV Aviation Ltd
	G-OLSF	PA-28-161 Cadet	Flew LLP (G-OTYJ)
	G-OLUG	Cameron Z-120 balloon	K. H. Gruenauer
	G-OMAF	Dornier 228-200	FR Aviation Ltd
	G-OMAG	Cessna 182B	Bodmin Light Aeroplane Services Ltd
	G-OMAL	Thruster T.600N 450	M. Howland
	G-OMAO	SOCATA TB-20 Trinidad	Alpha Oscar Group (G-GDGR)
	G-OMAS	Cessna A.150M	M. A. Segar (G-BTFS)
	G-OMAT	PA-28 Cherokee 140	Midland Air Training School (G-JIMY/G-AYUG)
	G-OMBI	Cessna 525B Citationjet CJ3	Ravenheat Manufacturing Ltd
	G-OMCC	AS.350B Ecureuil	MJH Capital Ltd (G-JTCM/G-HLEN/G-LOLY)
	G-OMCH	PA-28-161 Warrior III	Chalrey Ltd
	G-OMDB	Van's V-6A	D. A. Roseblade
	G-OMDD	Thunder Ax8-90 S2 balloon	M. D. Dickinson
	G-OMDH	Hughes 369E	Stilgate Ltd
	G-OMDR	Agusta-Bell 206B JetRanger 3	Castle Air Ltd (G-HRAY/G-VANG/G-BIZA)
	G-OMEA	Cessna 560XL Citation XLS	Marshall Executive Aviation
	G-OMEL	Robinson R44	J. M. & L. Prowse (G-BVPB)
	G-OMEM	Eurocopter EC 120B	Aero Maintenance Ltd (G-BXYD)
	G-OMEN	Cameron Z-90 balloon	M. G. Howard
	G-OMER	Avtech Jabiru UL-450	G. D. Omer (G-GPAS)
	G-OMEX	Zenair CH.701 UL	S. J. Perry
	G-OMEZ	Zenair CH.601HDS	GOMEZ Group
	G-OMGH	Robinson R44 II	Universal Energy Ltd
	G-OMGR	Cameron Z-105 balloon	Omega Resource Group PLC
	G-OMHC	PA-28RT-201 Arrow IV	Fly BPL.com
	G-OMHD	EE Canberra PR.Mk.9 (XH134)	Midair SA
	G-OMHI	Mills MH-1	J. P. Mills
	G-OMHP	Avtech Jabiru UL	J. Livingstone
	G-OMIA	MS.893A Rallye Commodore 180	L. Perryman
	G-OMIK	Shaw Europa	M. J. Clews
	G-OMIW	Pegasus Quik	M. I. Woodward
	G-OMJA	PA-28-181 Archer II	R. D. Masters & S. Walker
	G-OMJT	Rutan LongEz	M. J. Timmons
	G-OMLS	Bell 206B JetRanger 2	P. A. Leverton
	G-OMMG	Robinson R22 Beta	CDS Aviation Ltd (G-BPYX)
	G-OMMM	Colt 90A balloon	A. & M. Frayling
	G-OMNI	PA-28R Cherokee Arrow 200D	Cotswold Aviation Services Ltd (G-BAWA)
	G-OMOO	Ultramagic T-150 balloon	Robert Wiseman Dairies PLC
	G-OMPW	Mainair Pegasus Quik	M. P. Wimsey
	G-OMRB	Cameron V-77 balloon	I. J. Jevons
	G-OMRC	Van's RV-10	A. W. Collett
	G-OMRH	Cessna 550 Citation Bravo	McAir Services LLP
	G-OMRP	Flight Design CTSW	M. E. Parker
	G-OMSA	Flight Design CTSW	Microlight Sport Aviation Ltd
	G-OMST	PA-28-161 Warrior III	Mid-Sussex Timber Co Ltd (G-BZUA)
	G-OMSV	Beech B.200GT King Air	JPM Ltd
	G-OMUM	Rockwell Commander 114	M. Lai & G. Syrakis
	G-OMYJ	Airbus A.321-211	Thomas Cook Airlines Ltd (G-OOAF/G-UNID/ G-UKLO)
	G-OMYT	Airbus A.330-243	Thomas Cook Airlines Ltd (G-MOJO)
	G-ONAA	North American Rockwell OV-10B Bravo	Invicta Aviation Ltd
	G-ONAF	Naval Aircraft Factory N3N-3 (4406:12)	N3N-3 Group
	G-ONAT	Grob G.102 Astir CS77	N. A. Toogood
	G-ONAV	PA-31-310 Turbo Navajo C	Panther Aviation Ltd (G-IGAR)
	G-ONCB	Lindstrand LBL-31A balloon	M. D. Freeston & S. Mitchell
	G-ONCS	Slingsby T.66 Nipper 3	Ardleigh Flying Group (G-AZBA)
	G-ONEP	Robinson R44 II	Neptune Property Developments Ltd
	G-ONES	Slingsby T.67M Firefly 200	Aquaman Aviation Ltd

Reg.	Type	Owner or Operator	Notes
G-ONET	PA-28 Cherokee 180E	Hatfield Flying Club Ltd (G-AYAU)	
G-ONEZ	Glaser-Dirks DG-200/17	One Zulu Group	
G-ONFL	Murphy Maverick 430	G. J. Johnson (G-MYUJ)	
G-ONGC	Robin DR.400/180R	Norfolk Gliding Club Ltd	
G-ONHH	Forney F-1A Aircoupe	R. D. I. Tarry (G-ARHA)	
G-ONIC	Evektor EV-97 Sportstar Max	D. M. Jack	
G-ONIG	Murphy Elite	N. S. Smith	
G-ONIX	Cameron C-80 balloon	Above All Services Ltd	
G-ONKA	Aeronca K	N. J. R. Minchin	
G-ONNE	Westland Gazelle HT.3 (XW858:C)	A. M. Parkes (G-DMSS)	
G-ONON	RAF 2000 GTX-SE gyroplane	M. P. Lhermette	
G-ONPA	PA-31-350 Navajo Chieftain	Synergy Aircraft Leasing Ltd	
G-ONSO	Pitts S-1C Special	S. H. Brun (G-BRRS)	
G-ONUN	Van's RV-6A	K. R. H. Wingate	
G-OOAN	Boeing 767-39HER	Thomson Airways Ltd (G-UKLH)	
G-OOBA	Boeing 757-26N	Thomson Airways Ltd	
G-OOBB	Boeing 757-28A	Thomson Airways Ltd	
G-OOBC	Boeing 757-28A	Thomson Airways Ltd	
G-OOBD	Boeing 757-28A	Thomson Airways Ltd	
G-OOBE	Boeing 757-28A	Thomson Airways Ltd	
G-OOBF	Boeing 757-28A	Thomson Airways Ltd	
G-OOBG	Boeing 757-236	Thomson Airways Ltd	
G-OOBH	Boeing 757-236	Thomson Airways Ltd	
G-OOBI	Boeing 757-2B7	Thomson Airways Ltd	
G-OOBJ	Boeing 757-2B7	Thomson Airways Ltd	
G-OOBK	Boeing 767-324ER	Thomsonf AirwaysLtd	
G-OOBL	Boeing 767-324ER	Thomson Airways Ltd	
G-OOBM	Boeing 767-324ER	Thomson Airways Ltd	
G-OOBN	Boeing 757-2G5	Thomson Airways Ltd	
G-OOBP	Boeing 757-2G5	Thomson Airways Ltd	
G-OOBR	Boeing 757-204	Thomson Airways Ltd (G-BYAN)	
G-OOCH	Ultramagic H-42 balloon	P. C. Gooch	
G-OODE	SNCAN Stampe SV.4C (modified)	G-OODE Flying Group (G-AZNN)	
G-OODI	Pitts S-1D Special	C. Hutson & R. S. Wood (G-BBBU)	
G-OODM	Cessna 525A Citation CJ2	Air Charter Scotland Ltd	
G-OODW	PA-28-181 Archer II	Redhill Air Services Ltd	
G-OOER	Lindstrand LBL-25A balloon	Airborne Adventures Ltd	
G-OOEX	Cirrus SR22T	Data Interchange PLC	
G-OOEY	Balony Kubicek BB-222 balloon	A. W. Holly	
G-OOFE	Thruster T.600N 450	R. P. Tribe	
G-OOFT	PA-28-161 Warrior III	Plane Talking Ltd	
G-OOGO	GA-7 Cougar	M. M. Naviede	
G-OOGS	GA-7 Cougar	P. Pigg (G-BGJW)	
G-OOGY	P & M Quik R	Cambridge Road Professional Services Ltd	
G-OOIO	AS.350B3 Ecureuil	Hovering Ltd	
G-OOJC	Bensen B.8MR	S. Henley	
G-OOJP	Commander 114B	R. J. Rother	
G-OOLE	Cessna 172M	P. S. Eccersley (G-BOSI)	
G-OOMA	PA-28-161 Warrior II	Aviation Advice and Consulting Ltd (G-BRBB)	
G-OOMF	PA-18-150 Super Cub	C. G. Bell	
G-OONA	Robinson R44 II	Malaika Developments LLP	
G-OONE	Mooney M.20J	Go One Aviation Ltd	
G-OONK	Cirrus SR22	N. P. Kingdon	
G-OONY	PA-28-161 Warrior II	D. A. Field	
G-OONZ	P & M Aviation Quik	A. P. Burch	
G-OOON	PA-34-220T Seneca III	Pelican Air Ltd	
G-OOPE	Airbus A.321-211	Thomson Airways Ltd (G-OOAE/G-UNIF)	
G-OOPH	Airbus A.321-211	PBL0781 Ltd (G-OOAH/G-UNIE)	
G-OORV	Van's RV-6	T. I. Williams	
G-OOSE	Rutan Vari-Eze	B. O. Smith & J. A. Towers	
G-OOSH	Zenair CH.601UL Zodiac	A. G. Ransom	
G-OOSY	DH.82A Tiger Moth	G. Berryman	
G-OOTC	PA-28R-201T Turbo Arrow III	D. G. & C. M. King (G-CLIV)	
G-OOTT	Eurocopter AS.350B3 Ecureuil	R. J. Green	
G-OOUK	Cirrus SR22	R. S. Tomlinson	
G-OOWS	Eurocopter AS.350B3 Ecureuil	Millburn World Travel Services Ltd	
G-OOXP	Aero Designs Pulsar XP	P. C. Avery	
G-OPAG	PA-34-200 Seneca II	A. H. Lavender (G-BNGB)	
G-OPAH	Eurocopter EC135 T2 +	VLL Ltd (G-RWLA)	
G-OPAM	Cessna F.152 II (tailwheel)	PJC Leasing Ltd (G-BFZS)	

Notes	Reg.	Type	Owner or Operator
	G-OPAT	Beech 76 Duchess	R. D. J. Axford (G-BHAO)
	G-OPAZ	Pazmany PL.2	P. M. Harrison
	G-OPCG	Cessna 182T	S. K. Pomfret
	G-OPEJ	TEAM Minimax 91A	P. E. Jackson
	G-OPEN	Bell 206B	Gazelle Aviation LLP
	G-OPEP	PA-28RT-201T Turbo Arrow IV	SAM Ltd
	G-OPET	PA-28-181 Archer II	Cambrian Flying Group Ltd
	G-OPFA	Pioneer 300	S. Eddison & R. Minett
	G-OPFR	Diamond DA.42 Twin Star	P. F. Rothwell
	G-OPFT	Cessna 172R Skyhawk	AJW Construction Ltd
	G-OPHT	Schleicher ASH-26E	J. S. Wand
	G-OPIC	Cessna FRA.150L	A. V. Harmer (G-BGNZ)
	G-OPIK	Eiri PIK-20E	G-OPIK Syndicate
	G-OPIT	CFM Streak Shadow Srs SA	I. J. Guy
	G-OPJD	PA-28RT-201T Turbo Arrow IV	J. M. McMillan
	G-OPJK	Shaw Europa	P. J. Kember
	G-OPJS	Pietenpol Air Camper	P. J. Shenton
	G-OPKF	Cameron 90 Bowler SS balloon	D. K. Fish
	G-OPLC	DH.104 Dove 8	Columba Aviation Ltd (G-BLRB)
	G-OPME	PA-23 Aztec 250D	A. A. Mattacks & R. G. Pardo (G-ODIR/G-AZGB)
	G-OPMP	Robinson R44 II	E. K. Richardson (G-HHHH)
	G-OPMT	Lindstrand LBL-105A balloon	K. R. Karlstrom
	G-OPNH	Stoddard-Hamilton Glasair IIRG	A. J. E. & A. E. Smith (G-CINY)
	G-OPPO	Groppo Trail	A. C. Hampson
	G-OPRC	Shaw Europa XS	M. J. Ashby-Arnold
	G-OPRM	Bombardier CL600-2B16 Challenger	Oryx Jet Ltd
	G-OPSF	PA-38-112 Tomahawk	P. I. Higham (G-BGZI)
	G-OPSG	Aeropro Eurofox 912(S)	P. S. Gregory
	G-OPSL	PA-32R-301 Saratoga SP	Defence Vision Systems Pte Ltd (G-IMPW)
	G-OPSS	Cirrus SR20	Clifton Aviation Ltd
	G-OPST	Cessna 182R	M. J. G. Wellings & Welmacs Ltd
	G-OPTC	PA-44-180 Seminole	M. J. Edgeworth (G-BGTF)
	G-OPTF	Robinson R44 II	D. Fahy
	G-OPTI	PA-28-161 Warrior II	A. K. Hulme
	G-OPUB	Slingsby T.67M Firefly 160	A. L. Waller (G-DLTA/G-SFTX)
	G-OPUK	PA-28-161 Warrior III	Dennis and Robinson Ltd
	G-OPUP	Beagle B.121 Pup 2	F. A. Zubiel (G-AXEU)
	G-OPUS	Avtech Jabiru SK	K. W. Whistance
	G-OPVM	Van's RV-9A	J. A. & J. C. Ferguson
	G-OPWS	Mooney M.20K	D. S. Overton
	G-OPYE	Cessna 172S	Far North Aviation
	G-OPYO	Alpi Pioneer 300 Hawk	T. J. Franklin & D. S. Simpson
	G-ORAC	Cameron 110 Van SS balloon	A. G. Kennedy
	G-ORAE	Van's RV-7	R. W. Eaton
	G-ORAF	CFM Streak Shadow	A. P. Hunn
	G-ORAM	Thruster T600N 450	D. W. Wilson
	G-ORAR	PA-28-181 Archer III	P. N. & S. M. Thornton
	G-ORAS	Clutton FRED Srs 2	A. I. Sutherland
	G-ORAU	Evektor EV-97A Eurostar	W. R. C. Williams-Wynne
	G-ORAY	Cessna F.182Q II	Unicorn Consultants Ltd (G-BHDN)
	G-ORBK	Robinson R44 II	T2 Technology Ltd (G-CCNO)
	G-ORBS	Mainair Blade	J. W. Dodson
	G-ORCA	Van's RV-4	I. A. Harding
	G-ORCC	AutoGyro Calidus	R. P. Churchill-Coleman
	G-ORCW	Schempp-Hirth Ventus 2cT	J. C. A. Garland & M. S. Hawkins
	G-ORDB	Cessna 550 Citation Bravo	Equipe Air Ltd
	G-ORDH	AS.355N Twin Squirrel	Harpin Ltd
	G-ORDM	Cessna 182T	The Cambridge Aero Club Ltd (G-KEMY)
	G-ORDS	Thruster T.600N 450	G. J. Pill
	G-ORED	BN-2T Turbine Islander	B-N Group Ltd (G-BJYW)
	G-ORGY	Cameron Z-210 balloon	Cameron Flights Southern Ltd
	G-ORIG	Glaser-Dirks DG.800A	P. Crawley
	G-ORIX	ARV K1 Super 2	T. M. Lyons (G-BUXH/G-BNVK)
	G-ORJW	Laverda F.8L Falco Srs 4	Viking BV/Netherlands
	G-ORKI	Eurocopter AS.350B3 Ecureuil	Jet Helicopters Ltd
	G-ORKY	AS.350B2 Ecureuil	PLM Dollar Group Ltd
	G-ORLA	P & M Pegasus Quik	J. Summers
	G-ORMB	Robinson R22 Beta	Scotia Helicopters Ltd
	G-ORMW	Ikarus C.42 FB100	B. J. Jenkins
	G-OROD	PA-18 Super Cub 150	B. W. Faulkner
	G-OROS	Ikarus C.42 FB80	R. I. Simpson

Reg.	Type	Owner or Operator	Notes
G-ORPC	Shaw Europa XS	P. W. Churms	
G-ORPR	Cameron O-77 balloon	S. R. Vining	
G-ORRG	Robin DR.400-180 Regent	Radley Robin Group	
G-ORTH	Beech E90 King Air	Gorthair Ltd	
G-ORUG	Thruster T.600N 450	D. J. N. Brown	
G-ORVE	Van's RV-6	R. J. F. Swain & F. M. Sperryn	
G-ORVG	Van's RV-6	RV Group	
G-ORVI	Van's RV-6	J. D. N. Cooke	
G-ORVR	Partenavia P.68B	Ravenair Aircraft Ltd (G-BFBD)	
G-ORVS	Van's RV-9	C. J. Marsh	
G-ORYX	Hawker 900XP	Oryx Jet Ltd	
G-ORZA	Diamond DA42 Twin Star	M. J. Hill (G-FCAC)	
G-OSAT	Cameron Z-105 balloon	Lotus Balloons Ltd	
G-OSAW	QAC Quickie Q.2	S. A. Wilson (G-BVYT)	
G-OSAZ	Robinson R22	Hi-Air (Redditch) Ltd (G-DERB/G-BPYH)	
G-OSCC	PA-32 Cherokee Six 300	BG & G Airlines Ltd (G-BGFD)	
G-OSCO	TEAM mini-MAX 91	V. Grayson	
G-OSCR	Robinson R44 II	Staffordshire Helicopters Training Ltd (G-MIKS)	
G-OSEA	BN-2B-26 Islander	W. T. Johnson & Sons (Huddersfield) Ltd (G-BKOL)	
G-OSEP	Mainair Blade 912	J. D. Smith	
G-OSFB	Diamond HK.36TTC Super Dimona	Oxfordshire Sportflying Ltd	
G-OSFS	Cessan F.177RG	D. G. Wright	
G-OSHK	Schempp-Hirth SHK-1	P. B. Hibbard	
G-OSHL	Robinson R22 Beta	Sloane Helicopters Ltd	
G-OSIC	Pitts S-1C Special	J. A. Dodd (G-BUAW)	
G-OSII	Cessna 172N	India India Flying Group (G-BIVY)	
G-OSIS	Pitts S-1S Special	N. J. Riddin	
G-OSIT	Pitts S-1T Special	C. J. J. Robertson	
G-OSJF	PA-23-250 Aztec F	R. Tang (G-SFHR/G-BHSO)	
G-OSJN	Shaw Europa XS	N. Landell-Mills & R. J. Tobin	
G-OSKP	Enstrom 480	C. C. Butt	
G-OSKR	Skyranger 912 (2)	K. Clark	
G-OSKY	Cessna 172M	Skyhawk Leasing Ltd	
G-OSLD	Shaw Europa XS	S. Percy & C. Davies	
G-OSLO	Schweizer 269C	A. H. Helicopter Services Ltd	
G-OSMD	Bell 206B JetRanger 2	Dial House Consultants Ltd (G-LTEK/G-BMIB)	
G-OSND	Cessna FRA.150M	Group G-OSND (G-BDOU)	
G-OSOD	P & M Quik GTR	J. R. Elcocks	
G-OSOE	HS.748 Srs 2A	PTB (Emerald) Pty Ltd (G-AYYG)	
G-OSON	P & M QuikR	R. Parr	
G-OSPD	Aerotechnik EV-97 TeamEurostar UK	I. Nicholls	
G-OSPH	Ikarus C42 FB100	SPH Groundworks Ltd	
G-OSPK	Cessna 172S	R. W. Denny	
G-OSPS	PA-18 Super Cub 95	R. C. Lough	
G-OSPY	Cirrus SR20	Cambridge Guarantee Ltd	
G-OSRL	Learjet 45	S. R. Lloyd	
G-OSSA	Cessna Tu.206B	Skydive St.Andrews Ltd	
G-OSST	Colt 77A balloon	A. A. Brown	
G-OSTC	AA-5A Cheetah	5th Generation Designs Ltd	
G-OSTL	Ikarus C.42 FB 100	G-OSTL Syndicate	
G-OSTY	Cessna F.150G	Prospects Learning Foundation Ltd (G-AVCU)	
G-OSUP	Lindstrand LBL-90A balloon	M. E. Banks	
G-OSUS	Mooney M.20K	J. B. King	
G-OSUT	Scheibe SF-25C Rotax-Falke	Yorkshire Gliding Club (Pty.) Ltd	
G-OSZA	Aerotek Pitts S-2A	Septieme Ciel	
G-OSZB	Christen Pitts S-2B Special	K. A. Fitton & A. M. Gent (G-OGEE)	
G-OSZS	Pitts S-2S Special	L. V. Nieuwenhove	
G-OTAL	ARV Super 2	J. M. Cullen (G-BNGZ)	
G-OTAM	Cessna 172M	G. V. White	
G-OTAN	PA-18 Super Cub 135 (54-2445)	A. & J. D. Owen	
G-OTAZ	Hawker 900XP	Hangar 8 Management Ltd	
G-OTCH	Streak Shadow	R. M. M. & A. G. Moura	
G-OTCV	Skyranger 912S (1)	T. C. Viner	
G-OTCZ	Schempp-Hirth Ventus 2cT	D. H. Conway t/a CZ Group	
G-OTDI	Diamond DA40D Star	P. Dormoy	
G-OTEC	Tecnam P2002 Sierra Deluxe	C. W. Thirtle	
G-OTEL	Thunder Ax8-90 balloon	J. W. Adkins	
G-OTEN	Cessna 750 Citation X	Pendley Aviation LLP	
G-OTFL	Eurocopter EC 120B	J. Henshall (G-IBRI)	

Notes	Reg.	Type	Owner or Operator
	G-OTFT	PA-38-112 Tomahawk	P. Tribble (G-BNKW)
	G-OTGA	PA-28R-201 Arrow III	TG Aviation Ltd
	G-OTHE	Enstrom 280C-UK Shark	G. E. Heritage (G-OPJT/G-BKCO)
	G-OTIB	Robin DR.400/180R	The Windrushers Gliding Club Ltd
	G-OTIG	AA-5B Tiger	L. Burke (G-PENN)
	G-OTIM	Bensen B.8MV	T. J. Deane
	G-OTIV	Aerospool Dynamic WT9 UK	D. N. E. d'Ath
	G-OTJH	Pegasus Quantum 15-912	L. R. Gartside
	G-OTJS	Robinson R44 II	Kuki Helicopter Sales Ltd
	G-OTLC	Grumman AA-5 Traveller	Total Logistics Concepts Ltd (G-BBUF)
	G-OTNA	Robinson R44 Raven II	Abel Developments Ltd
	G-OTOE	Aeronca 7AC Champion	D. Cheney (G-BRWW)
	G-OTOO	Stolp SA.300 Starduster Too	I. M. Castle
	G-OTOP	P & M Quik R	S. D. Pain
	G-OTRV	Van's RV-6	E. N. Burnett
	G-OTRY	Schleicher ASW-24	A. R. Harrison & G. Pursey
	G-OTSP	AS.355F1 Twin Squirrel	MW Helicopters Ltd (G-XPOL/G-BPRF)
	G-OTTY	Rotorsport UK Calidus	J. M. Giles
	G-OTUI	SOCATA TB20 Trinidad	D. J. Wood (G-KKDL/G-BSHU)
	G-OTUN	Aerotechnik EV-97 Eurostar	S. P. Slater
	G-OTVI	Robinson R44 II	Summit Media Ltd
	G-OTVR	PA-34-220T Seneca V	IAS Medical Ltd
	G-OTYE	Aerotechnik EV-97 Eurostar	A. B. Godber & J. Tye
	G-OTYP	PA-28 Cherokee 180	T. C. Lewis
	G-OUCH	Cameron N-105 balloon	A. C. Elson
	G-OUDA	Aeroprakt A22-L Foxbat	A. R. Cattell
	G-OUGH	Yakovlev Yak-52	I. M. Gough (G-LAOK)
	G-OUHI	Shaw Europa XS	N. M. Graham
	G-OUIK	Mainair Pegasus Quik	D. G. Baker
	G-OUMC	Lindstrand LBL-105A balloon	J. Francis
	G-OUNI	Cirrus SR20	Schonborn Park Baubetreuunh GmbH/ (G-TABI)
	G-OURO	Shaw Europa	I. M. Mackay
	G-OUVI	Cameron O-105 balloon	Bristol University Hot Air Ballooning Society
	G-OVAL	Ikarus C.42 FB100	N. G. Tomes
	G-OVBF	Cameron A-250 balloon	Virgin Balloon Flights
	G-OVBL	Lindstrand LBL-150A balloon	R. J. Henderson
	G-OVET	Cameron O-56 balloon	A. R. Hardwick & E. Fearon
	G-OVFM	Cessna 120	T. B. Parmenter
	G-OVFR	Cessna F.172N	Marine and Aviation Ltd
	G-OVIA	Lindstrand LBL-105A balloon	N. C. Lindsey
	G-OVII	Van's RV-7	T. J. Richardson
	G-OVIN	Rockwell Commander 112TC	G. Vekaria
	G-OVIV	Aerostyle Breezer LSA	P. & V. Lynch
	G-OVLA	Ikarus C.42 FB	Webb Plant Sales
	G-OVMC	Cessna F.152 II	Swiftair Maintenance Ltd
	G-OVNE	Cessna 401A H	Norwich Aviation Museum
	G-OVNR	Robinson R22 Beta	Glenntrade Ltd
	G-OVOL	Skyranger 912S(1)	A. S. Docherty
	G-OVON	PA-18-95 Super Cub	V. F. A. Stanley
	G-OWAI	Schleicher ASK-21	Scottish Gliding Union
	G-OWAL	PA-34-220T Seneca III	R. G. & W. Allison
	G-OWAN	Cessna 210D Centurion	G. Owen
	G-OWAP	PA-28-161 Cherokee Warrior II	Aviation Advice & Consulting (G-BXNH)
	G-OWAR	PA-28-161 Warrior II	Bickertons Aerodromes Ltd
	G-OWAZ	Pitts S-1C Special	P. E. S. Latham (G-BRPI)
	G-OWBA	Alpi Pioneer 300 Hawk	L. J. Tonkinson
	G-OWBR	Tipsy Nipper T.66 series 2	W. J. Y. Ronge
	G-OWEL	Colt 105A balloon	S. R. Seager
	G-OWEN	K & S Jungster	R. C. Owen
	G-OWET	Thurston TSC-1A2 Teal	A. R. Wyatt
	G-OWFS	Cessna A.152	Westair Flying Services Ltd (G-DESY/G-BNJE)
	G-OWGC	Slingsby T.61F Venture T.2	Wolds Gliding Club Ltd
	G-OWIL	Cessna 120	R. Flanagan (G-BTYW)
	G-OWLC	PA-31 Turbo Navajo	Channel Airways Ltd (G-AYFZ)
	G-OWMC	Thruster T.600N	Wilts Microlight Centre
	G-OWOW	Cessna 152 II	Plane Talking Ltd (G-BMSZ)
	G-OWRC	Cessna F.152 II	Unimat SA/France
	G-OWRT	Cessna 182G	L. Townsend (G-ASUL)
	G-OWWW	Shaw Europa	R. F. W. Holder

Reg.	Type	Owner or Operator	Notes
G-OWYE	Lindstrand LBL-240A balloon	Wye Valley Aviation Ltd	
G-OWYN	Aviamilano F.14 Nibbio	R. Nash	
G-OXBA	Cameron Z-160 balloon	J. E. Rose	
G-OXBC	Cameron A-140 balloon	J. E. Rose	
G-OXBY	Cameron N-90 balloon	C. A. Oxby	
G-OXII	Van's RV-12	J. A. King	
G-OXKB	Cameron 110 Sports Car SS balloon	D. M. Moffat	
G-OXLS	Cessna 560XL Citation XLS	Go XLS Ltd	
G-OXOM	PA-28-161 Cadet	Aviation Rentals (G-BRSG)	
G-OXPS	Falcon XPS	J. C. Greenslade (G-BUXP)	
G-OXRS	Bombardier BD700 1A10 Global Express	Profred Partners LLP	
G-OXVI	VS.361 Spitfire LF.XVIe (TD248:CR-S)	Spitfire Ltd	
G-OYAK	Yakovlev C-11 (9 white)	A. H. Soper	
G-OYES	Mainair Blade 912	B. McAdam & A. Hatton	
G-OYIO	Robin DR.400/120	Exeter Aviation Ltd	
G-OYST	Agusta-Bell 206B JetRanger 2	L. E. V. Knifton (G-JIMW/G-UNIK/G-TPPH/ G-BCYP)	
G-OYTE	Rans S.6ES Coyote II	N. D. Major	
G-OZAR	Enstrom 480	Benham Helicopters Ltd (G-BWFF)	
G-OZBB	Airbus A.320-212	Monarch Airlines Ltd	
G-OZBE	Airbus A.321-231	Monarch Airlines Ltd	
G-OZBF	Airbus A.321-231	Monarch Airlines Ltd	
G-OZBG	Airbus A.321-231	Monarch Airlines Ltd	
G-OZBH	Airbus A.321-231	Monarch Airlines Ltd	
G-OZBI	Airbus A.321-231	Monarch Airlines Ltd	
G-OZBK	Airbus A.320-214	Monarch Airlines Ltd	
G-OZBL	Airbus A.321-231	Monarch Airlines Ltd (G-MIDE)	
G-OZBM	Airbus A.321-231	Monarch Airlines Ltd (G-MIDJ)	
G-OZBN	Airbus A.321-231	Monarch Airlines Ltd (G-MIDK)	
G-OZBO	Airbus A.321-231	Monarch Airlines Ltd (G-MIDM)	
G-OZBP	Airbus A.321-231	Monarch Airlines Ltd (G-TTIB)	
G-OZBR	Airbus A.321-231	Monarch Airlines Ltd	
G-OZBS	Airbus A.321-231	Monarch Airlines Ltd (G-TTIA)	
G-OZBT	Airbus A.321-231	Monarch Airlines Ltd (G-TTIH)	
G-OZBU	Airbus A.321-231	Monarch Airlines Ltd (G-TTII)	
G-OZBW	Airbus A.320-214	Monarch Airlines Ltd (G-OOPP/G-OOAS)	
G-OZBX	Airbus A.320-214	Monarch Airlines Ltd (G-OOPU/G-OOAU)	
G-OZBY	Airbus A.320-214	Monarch Airlines Ltd (G-OOAR)	
G-OZEE	Light Aero Avid Speedwing Mk 4	G. D. Bailey	
G-OZEF	Shaw Europa XS	Z. M. Ahmad	
G-OZIE	Jabiru J400	S. A. Bowkett	
G-OZIO	Aquila AT01	Caseright Ltd	
G-OZOI	Cessna R.182	J. R. G. & F. L. G. Fleming (G-ROBK)	
G-OZOO	Cessna 172N	R. A. Brown (G-BWEI)	
G-OZOZ	Schempp-Hirth Nimbus 3DT	G-OZOZ Syndicate	
G-OZRH	BAe 146-200	Calder Ltd	
G-OZZE	Lambert Mission M108	A. & J. Oswald	
G-OZZI	Jabiru SK	A. H. Godfrey	
G-OZZO	Avions Mudry CAP.231	R. M. Buchan	
G-PACE	Robin R.1180T	M. T. Fitzpatrick & T. C. Wise	
G-PACL	Robinson R22 Beta	Whizzard Helicopters	
G-PACO	Sikorsky S-76C	Cardinal Helicopter Services	
G-PACT	PA-28-181 Archer III	A. Parsons	
G-PADE	Escapade Jabiru(3)	C. L. G. Innocent	
G-PADI	Cameron V-77 balloon	C. Chardon	
G-PAFC	Cameron C-70 balloon	D. R. Rawlings	
G-PAFF	AutoGyro MTO Sport	S. R. Paffett	
G-PAFR	Glaser-Dirks DG-300 Elan	Y. G. J-P. Clave	
G-PAIG	Grob G.109B	M. E. Baker	
G-PAIZ	PA-12 Super Cruiser	B. R. Pearson	
G-PALI	Czech Sport Aircraft Piper Sport	P. A. Langley	
G-PAMY	Robinson R44 II	Batchelor Aviation Ltd	
G-PAPE	Diamond DA42 Twin Star	Diamond Executive Aviation Ltd	
G-PARG	Pitts S-1C Special	M. Kotsageridis	
G-PARI	Cessna 172RG Cutlass	V. A. Holliday	
G-PASH	AS.355F1 Twin Squirrel	MW Helicopters Ltd	
G-PASN	Enstrom F-28F	Passion 4 Health International Ltd (G-BSHZ)	

Notes	Reg.	Type	Owner or Operator
	G-PATF	Shaw Europa	E. P. Farrell
	G-PATG	Cameron O-90 balloon	s. Neighbour & N. Symonds
	G-PATI	Cessna F.172M	Nigel Kenny Aviation Ltd (G-WACZ/G-BCUK)
	G-PATN	SOCATA TB10 Tobago	G-PATN Owners Group (G-LUAR)
	G-PATO	Zenair CH.601UL Zodiac	N. D. Townend
	G-PATP	Lindstrand LBL-77A balloon	P. Pruchnickyj
	G-PATS	Shaw Europa	G-PATS Flying Group
	G-PATX	Lindstrand LBL-90A balloon	P. C. Gooch
	G-PATZ	Shaw Europa	H. P. H. Griffin
	G-PAVL	Robin R.3000/120	MintLPG Ltd
	G-PAWL	PA-28 Cherokee 140	G-PAWL Group (G-AWEU)
	G-PAWN	PA-25 Pawnee 260C	A. P. Meredith (G-BEHS)
	G-PAWS	AA-5A Cheetah	M. J. Patrick
	G-PAWZ	Best Off Sky Ranger Swift 912S(1)	L. Moore
	G-PAXX	PA-20 Pacer 135 (modified)	I. P. Burnett
	G-PAYD	Robin DR.400/180	M. J. Bennett
	G-PAZY	Pazmany PL.4A	M. Richardson (G-BLAJ)
	G-PBAT	Czech Sport Aircraft Sportcruiser	P. M. W. Bath
	G-PBCL	Cessna 182P	Kammon BV/Netherlands
	G-PBEC	Van's RV-7	P. G. Reid
	G-PBEE	Robinson R44	Echo Echo Syndicate
	G-PBEK	Agusta A109A	Castle Air Ltd (G-BXIV)
	G-PBEL	CFM Shadow Srs DD	S. Fairweather
	G-PBIX	VS.361 Spitfire LF XVI E	Pemberton-Billing LLP (G-XVIA)
	G-PBRL	Robinson R22	Cardy Construction Ltd
	G-PBWR	Agusta A109S Grand	Helix Helicopters Ltd
	G-PBYA	Consolidated PBY-5A Catalina (433915)	Catalina Aircraft Ltd
	G-PBYY	Enstrom 280FX	S. Craske (G-BXKV)
	G-PBZN	AS.350B Ecureuil	Quarry and Mining Equipment Ltd (G-MURP)
	G-PCAT	SOCATA TB10 Tobago	S. D. Johnson (G-BHER)
	G-PCCC	Alpi Pioneer 300	R. Pidcock
	G-PCDP	Zlin Z.526F Trener Master	P. A. Colman
	G-PCMC	P & M Quik R	M. J. & P. J. Canty
	G-PCOP	Beech B200 Super King Air	Albert Batlett and Sons (Airdrie) Ltd
	G-PDAY	Augusta A109S Grand	Proquip (Group) Ltd (G-CDWY)
	G-PDGE	Eurocopter EC 120B	A. J. Wicklow
	G-PDGF	AS.350B2 Ecureuil	PLM Dollar Group Ltd (G-FROH)
	G-PDGG	Aeromere F.8L Falco Srs 3	P. D. G. Grist
	G-PDGI	AS.350B1 Ecureuil	PLM Dollar Group Ltd (G-BVJE)
	G-PDGK	SA.365N Dauphin 2	PLM Dollar Group Ltd (G-HEMS)
	G-PDGN	SA.365N Dauphin 2	PLM Dollar Group Ltd (G-TRAF/G-BLDR)
	G-PDGR	AS.350B2 Ecureuil	PLM Dollar Group Ltd (G-RICC/G-BTXA)
	G-PDGS	AS.355F2 Ecureuil 2	PLM Dollar Group Ltd
	G-PDGT	AS.355F2 Ecureuil 2	PLM Dollar Group Ltd (G-BOOV)
	G-PDHJ	Cessna T.182R	P. G. Vallance Ltd
	G-PDOC	PA-44-180 Seminole	Medicare (G-PVAF)
	G-PDOG	Cessna O-1E Bird Dog (24550)	J. D. Needham
	G-PDSI	Cessna 172N	DA Flying Group
	G-PEAR	P &M Pegasus Quik	C. D. Hayle
	G-PECK	PA-32-300 Cherokee Six D	L. M. Empson (G-ETAV/G-MCAR/G-LADA/G-AYWK)
	G-PEER	Cessna 525A Citationjet CJ2	Air Charter Scotland (Holdings) Ltd (G-SYGC/G-HGRC)
	G-PEGA	Pegasus Quantum 15-912	M. Konisti
	G-PEGE	Skyranger 912	A. N. Hughes
	G-PEGI	PA-34-200T Seneca II	ACS Aviation Ltd
	G-PEGY	Shaw Europa	A. Carter
	G-PEGZ	Centrair 101A Pegase	G-PEGZ Group
	G-PEJM	PA-28-181 Archer III	S. J. Clark
	G-PEKT	SOCATA TB20 Trinidad	H. E. Prew-Smith
	G-PENH	Ultramagic M-90 balloon	G. Holtam
	G-PEPE	Cessna 560XL Citation XLS	Fram Partners LLP
	G-PERB	Agusta AW.139	Bond Offshore Helicopters Ltd
	G-PERC	Cameron N-90 balloon	I. R. Warrington
	G-PERE	Robinson R22 Beta	R. F. McLachlan
	G-PERR	Cameron 60 Bottle SS balloon ★	British Balloon Museum/Newbury
	G-PEST	Hawker Tempest II (MW401)	Tempest Two Ltd

Reg.	Type	Owner or Operator	Notes
G-PETH	PA-24-260C Comanche	J. V. Hutchinson	
G-PETO	Hughes 369HM	P. E. Tornberg (G-HAUS/G-KBOT/G-RAMM)	
G-PETR	PA-28-140 Cherokee	A. A. Gardner (G-BCJL)	
G-PETS	Diamond DA42NG Twin Star	Diamond Executive Aviation Ltd	
G-PEYO	Gefa-Flug AS 105 GD airship	International Merchandising Promotion and Services SA	
G-PFAA	EAA Biplane Model P	T. A. Fulcher	
G-PFAF	FRED Srs 2	M. S. Perkins	
G-PFAH	Evans VP-1	J. A. Scott	
G-PFAP	Currie Wot/SE-5A (C1904:Z)	J. H. Seed	
G-PFAR	Isaacs Fury II (K2059)	M. A. Watts	
G-PFAT	Monnett Sonerai II	H. B. Carter	
G-PFAW	Evans VP-1	R. F. Shingler	
G-PFCL	Cessna 172S	C. H. S. Carpenter	
G-PFCT	Learjet 45	The Fighter Collection Ltd (G-GOMO/G-OLDF/ G-JRJR)	
G-PFFN	Beech 200 Super King Air	The Puffin Club Ltd	
G-PFSL	Cessna F.152	P. A. Simon	
G-PGAC	MCR-01	G. A. Coatesworth	
G-PGBR	Vulcanair P-68R	Caseright Ltd	
G-PGFG	Tecnam P92-EM Echo	P. G. Fitzgerald	
G-PGGY	Robinson R44	J. Henshall	
G-PGHM	Air Creation Kiss 450	D. Subhani	
G-PGSA	Thruster T.600N	B. S. Davis	
G-PGSI	Pierre Robin R2160	M. A. Spencer	
G-PHAA	Cessna F.150M	Douglas Held Aviation Ltd (G-BCPE)	
G-PHAB	Cirrus SR22	G3 Aviation Ltd (G-MACL)	
G-PHAT	Cirrus SR20	Hetherington Properties Ltd	
G-PHCJ	Vol Mediterrani VM-1 Esqual C	C. R. James	
G-PHLY	Cessna FRA150L	M. Bonsall	
G-PHNM	Embraer EMB-500 Phenom 100	YC Investments	
G-PHNX	Schempp-Hirth Duo Discus Xt	J. L. Birch & R. Maskell	
G-PHOR	Cessna FRA.150L Aerobat	M. Bonsall (G-BACC)	
G-PHOX	Aeroprakt A22-L Foxbat	J. D. Webb	
G-PHSE	Balony Kubicek BB26Z balloon	The Packhouse Ltd	
G-PHSI	Colt 90A balloon	P. H. Strickland	
G-PHTG	SOCATA TB10 Tobago	A. J. Baggarley	
G-PHUN	Cessna FRA.150L Aerobat	M. Bonsall (G-BAIN)	
G-PHVM	Van's RV-8	G. Howes & V. Millard	
G-PHXS	Shaw Europa XS	P. Handford	
G-PHYL	Denney Kitfox Mk 4	J. S. A. Evans	
G-PHYS	Jabiru SP-470	C. Mayer	
G-PHYZ	Jabiru J430	P. C. Knight	
G-PIAF	Thunder Ax7-65 balloon	L. Battersley	
G-PICX	P & M Aviation QuikR	C. J. Meadows	
G-PIEL	CP.301A Emeraude	P. R. Thorne (G-BARY)	
G-PIES	Thunder Ax7-77Z balloon	S. J. Hollingsworth & M. K. Bellamy	
G-PIET	Pietenpol Air Camper	A. R. Wyatt	
G-PIGG	Lindstrand LBL Pig SS balloon	I. Heidenreich/Germany	
G-PIGI	Aerotechnik EV-97 Eurostar	Pigs Might Fly Group	
G-PIGS	SOCATA Rallye 150ST	Boonhill Flying Group (G-BDWB)	
G-PIGY	Short SC.7 Skyvan Srs 3A Variant 100	Invicta Aviation Ltd	
G-PIII	Pitts S-1D Special	On A Roll Aerobatics Group (G-BETI)	
G-PIIT	Pitts S-2 Special	R. Reid	
G-PIKD	Eiriavion PIK-20D-78	M. C. Hayes	
G-PIKE	Robinson R22 Mariner	Sloane Helicopters Ltd	
G-PIKK	PA-28 Cherokee 140	Coventry Aviators Flying Group (G-AVLA)	
G-PILE	Rotorway Executive 90	J. B. Russell	
G-PILL	Light Aero Avid Flyer Mk 4	D. R. Meston	
G-PILY	Pilatus B4 PC-11	N. Frost & K. E. Fox	
G-PILZ	AutoGyro MT-03	G. Millward	
G-PIMM	Ultramagic M-77 balloon	G. Everett	
G-PIMP	Robinson R44	Maxim Gestioni SRL	
G-PINC	Cameron Z-90 balloon	C. W. Clarke	
G-PING	AA-5A Cheetah	J. A. Newbold	
G-PINO	AutoGyro MTO Sport	P. A. Tolman	
G-PINT	Cameron 65 Barrel SS balloon	D. K. Fish	
G-PINX	Lindstrand Pink Panther SS balloon	Magical Adventures Ltd/USA	
G-PION	Alpi Pioneer 300	P. F. J. Burton	

Notes	Reg.	Type	Owner or Operator
	G-PIPI	Mainair Pegasus Quik	N. R. Williams
	G-PIPP	PA-32R-301T Saratoga II TC	Poores Travel Consultants Ltd
	G-PIPR	PA-18 Super Cub 95	R. Forfitt & A. J. J. Sproule (G-BCDC)
	G-PIPS	Van's RV-4	P. N. Davis
	G-PIPY	Cameron 105 Pipe SS balloon	D. M. Moffat
	G-PITS	Pitts S-2AE Special	P. N. A. & S. N. Whithead
	G-PITT	Pitts S-2 Special	Mansfield Property Consultancy Ltd
	G-PITZ	Pitts S-2A Special	J. A. Coutts
	G-PIXE	Colt 31A balloon	J. F. Trehern
	G-PIXI	Pegasus Quantum 15-912	K. J. Rexter
	G-PIXL	Robinson R44 II	Flying TV Ltd
	G-PIXX	Robinson R44 II	Flying TV Ltd
	G-PIXY	Supermarine Aircraft Spitfire Mk.26 (RK855)	R. Collenette
	G-PJLO	Boeing 767-35EER	Thomson Airways Ltd
	G-PJMT	Lancair 320	V. Hatton & P. Gilroy
	G-PJPJ	Boeing 737-5H6	Celestrial Aviation Trading Ltd (G-GFFJ)
	G-PJSY	Van's RV-6	P. J. York
	G-PJTM	Cessna FR.172K II	R. & J. R. Emery (G-BFIF)
	G-PKPK	Schweizer 269C	C. H. Dobson
	G-PLAD	Kolb Twinstar Mk 3 Extra	P. J. Ladd
	G-PLAJ	BAe Jetstream 3102	Skybird SP Ltd
	G-PLAL	Eurocopter EC 135T2	Eurocopter UK Ltd
	G-PLAN	Cessna F.150L	G-PLAN Flying Group
	G-PLAR	Vans RV-9A	M. P. Board
	G-PLAY	Robin R.2112	Alpha Flying Group
	G-PLAZ	Rockwell Commander 112	I. Hunt (G-RDCI/G-BFWG)
	G-PLEE	Cessna 182Q	Peterlee Parachute Centre
	G-PLIP	Diamond DA.40D Star	C. A. & D. R. Ho
	G-PLLT	Lindstrand Box SS balloon	Lindstrand Hot Air Balloons Ltd
	G-PLMH	AS.350B2 Ecureuil	PLM Dollar Group Ltd
	G-PLMI	SA.365C-1 Dauphin	PLM Dollar Group Ltd
	G-PLOP	Magni M-24C	C. A. Ho
	G-PLOW	Hughes 269B	C. Walton Ltd (G-AVUM)
	G-PLPC	Schweizer Hughes 269C	A. R. Baker
	G-PLPL	Agusta A109E Power	Iceland Foods Ltd (G-TMWC)
	G-PLPM	Shaw Europa XS	P. L. P. Mansfield
	G-PLSA	Aero Designs Pulsar XP	J. L. A. Campbell (G-NEVS)
	G-PLSR	P & M PulsR	P and M Aviation Ltd
	G-PMAM	Cameron V-65 balloon	P. A. Meecham
	G-PMGG	Agusta-Bell 206A JetRanger	P. M. Gallagher (G-EEGO/G-PELS/G-DNCN)
	G-PMHT	SOCATA TBM850	Ewan Air
	G-PMNF	VS.361 Spitfire HF.IX (TA805:FX-M)	P. R. Monk
	G-PNEU	Colt 110 Bibendum SS balloon	P. A. Rowley
	G-PNGC	Schleicher ASK-21	Portsmouth Naval Gliding Centre
	G-PNIX	Cessna FRA.150L	Dukeries Aviation (G-BBEO)
	G-POET	Robinson R44 II	D. M. McGarrity
	G-POGO	Flight Design CT2K	L. I. Bailey
	G-POLA	Eurocopter EC 135 P2+	West Midlands Police Authority
	G-POLI	Robinson R44 II	Luxtronic Ltd
	G-POLL	Skyranger 912 (1)	D. L. Pollitt
	G-POLY	Cameron N-77 balloon	S. Church & S. Jenkins
	G-POND	Oldfield Baby Lakes	U. Reichert/Germany
	G-POOH	Piper J-3C-65 Cub	P. Robinson
	G-POOL	ARV Super 2	P. A. Dawson (G-BNHA)
	G-POPA	Beech A36 Bonanza	C. J. O'Sullivan
	G-POPE	Eiri PIK-20E-1	G-POPE Syndicate
	G-POPI	SOCATA TB10 Tobago	I. S. Hacon & C. J. Earle (G-BKEN)
	G-POPW	Cessna 182S	D. L. Price
	G-POPY	Best Off Sky Ranger Swift 912S(1)	S. G. Penk & S. J. Sant
	G-PORK	AA-5B Tiger	R. A. Lambert (G-BFHS)
	G-POSH	Colt 56A balloon	B. K. Rippon (G-BMPT)
	G-POUX	Pou du Ciel-Bifly	G. D. Priest
	G-POWC	Boeing 737-33A	Titan Airways Ltd
	G-POWD	Boeing 767-36N	Titan Airways Ltd
	G-POWF	Avro RJ100	Titan Airways Ltd (G-CFAA)
	G-POWG	Cessna 525A Citationjet CJ2	Hagondale Ltd

Reg.	Type	Owner or Operator	Notes
G-POWH	Boeing 757-256	Titan Airways Ltd	
G-POWL	Cessna 182R	B. W. Powell	
G-POZA	Escapade Jabiru ULP (1)	M. R. Jones	
G-PPBA	Embraer EMB-135BJ Legacy	TAG Aviation (UK) Ltd	
G-PPFS	Cessna FRA.150L	M. Bonsall (G-AZJY)	
G-PPIO	Cameron C-90 balloon	A. Murphy	
G-PPLG	Rotorsport UK MT-03	J. E. Butler	
G-PPLL	Van's RV-7A	A. Payne & P. Young	
G-PPLO	Fournier RF-4D	R. V. Timhede	
G-PPOD	Europa Aviation Europa XS	S. Easom	
G-PPPP	Denney Kitfox Mk 3	R. Powers	
G-PRAG	Brügger MB.2 Colibri	Colibri Flying Group	
G-PRAH	Flight Design CT2K	G. N. S. Farrant	
G-PRDH	AS.355F2 Ecureuil 2	EZ-Int Ltd	
G-PRET	Robinson R44	Heliservices	
G-PREY	Pereira Osprey II	N. S. Dalrymple (G-BEPB)	
G-PREZ	Robin DR.400/500	Regent Group	
G-PRFI	Agusta-Bell 206B Jet Ranger II	P. Fox (G-CPTS)	
G-PRII	Hawker Hunter PR.11 (XG194)	Interactive Dynamics Ltd	
G-PRIM	PA-38-112 Tomahawk	Braddock Ltd	
G-PRIV	VS.353 Spitfire PR.IV	P. R. Arnold	
G-PRKR	Canadair CL600-2B16 Challenger 604	TAG Aviation (UK) Ltd	
G-PRLY	Avtech Jabiru SK	N. C. Cowell (G-BYKY)	
G-PROJ	Robinson R44 II	Project Racing Team Ltd	
G-PROO	Hawker 4000 Horizon	TAG Aviation (UK) Ltd	
G-PROS	Van's RV-7A	A. J. & S. A. Sutcliffe	
G-PROV	P.84 Jet Provost T.52A (T.4)	Provost Group	
G-PROW	Aerotechnik EV-97A Eurostar	Nene Valley Microlights Ltd	
G-PRSI	Pegasus Quantum 15-912	G-PRSI Group	
G-PRTT	Cameron N-31 balloon	A. Kaye	
G-PRXI	VS.365 Spitfire PR.XI (PL983)	Propshop Ltd	
G-PSAX	Lindstrand LBL-77B balloon	M. V. Farrant & I. Risbridger	
G-PSFG	Robin R.21601	Mardenair Ltd (G-COVD/G-BYOF)	
G-PSGC	PA-25 Pawnee 260C (modified)	Peterborough & Spalding Gliding Club Ltd (G-BDDT)	
G-PSHK	Schempp-Hirth SHK-1	P. Gentil	
G-PSIR	Jurca MJ.77 Gnatsum (474008 'VF-R')	P. W. Carlton & D. F. P. Finan	
G-PSKY	Skyranger 912S(1)	P. W. Curnock & J. W. Wilcox	
G-PSNI	Eurocopter EC 135T2	Police Service of Northern Ireland	
G-PSNO	Eurocopter MBB BK-117C-2	Police Service of Northern Ireland	
G-PSNR	MBB-BK 117 C-2	Eurocopter UK Ltd (G-LFRS)	
G-PSON	Colt Cylinder One SS balloon	Balloon Preservation Flying Group	
G-PSRT	PA-28-151 Warrior	P. A. S. Dyke (G-BSGN)	
G-PSST	Hunter F.58A	Heritage Aviation Developments Ltd	
G-PSUE	CFM Shadow Srs CD	D. A. Crosbie (G-MYAA)	
G-PSUK	Thruster T.600N 450	Thruster Syndicate	
G-PTAG	Shaw Europa	R. C. Harrison	
G-PTAR	Best Off Skyranger 912S(1)	P. Vergette	
G-PTCA	Cessna F.172P	Shernburn Ltd	
G-PTCC	PA-28RT-201 ArrowIV	Shernburn Ltd (G-BXYS)	
G-PTDP	Bücker Bü133C Jungmeister	T. J. Reeve (G-AEZX)	
G-PTEA	PA-46-350P Malibu Mirage	P. J. Caiger	
G-PTFL	Eurocopter AS.350BA Ecureuil	Tyrone Fabrication Ltd	
G-PTOO	Bell 206L-4 LongRanger 4	P2 Air Ltd	
G-PTRE	SOCATA TB20 Trinidad	Trantshore Ltd (G-BNKU)	
G-PTRI	Cessna 182T	G-PTRI LLP	
G-PTTS	Aerotek Pitts S-2A	P. & J. Voce	
G-PTWO	Pilatus P2-05 (U-110)	R. Vojta	
G-PUDL	PA-18 Super Cub 150	C. M. Edwards	
G-PUDS	Shaw Europa	M. J. Riley	
G-PUFF	Thunder Ax7-77A balloon	Intervarsity Balloon Club	
G-PUGS	Cessna 182H	N. C. & M. F. Shaw	
G-PUKA	Jabiru Aircraft Jabiru J400	D. P. Harris	
G-PULR	Pitts S-2AE	A. Ayre	
G-PUMM	AS.332L Super Puma	CHC Scotia Ltd	
G-PUMN	AS.332L Super Puma	CHC Scotia Ltd	
G-PUMO	AS.332L-2 Super Puma	CHC Scotia Ltd	

Notes	Reg.	Type	Owner or Operator
	G-PUMS	AS.332L-2 Super Puma	CHC Scotia Ltd
	G-PUNK	Thunder Ax8-105 balloon	S. C. Kinsey
	G-PUNT	Robinson R44 II	R. D. Cameron
	G-PUPP	Beagle B.121 Pup 2	A. D. Wood (G-BASD)
	G-PUPS	Cameron Z-210 balloon	High On Adventure Balloons Ltd
	G-PUPY	Shaw Europa XS	D. A. Cameron
	G-PURE	Cameron can 70 SS balloon	Mobberley Balloon Collection
	G-PURL	PA-32R-301 Saratoga II	A. P.H. & E. Hay
	G-PURP	Lindstrand LBL-90° balloon	C. & P. Mackley
	G-PURR	AA-5A Cheetah	D. H. Green (G-BJDN)
	G-PURS	Rotorway Executive	J. E. Houseman
	G-PUSA	Gefa-Flug AS105GD Hot Air Airship	Skyking Aviation Ltd
	G-PUSI	Cessna T.303	Crusader Craft
	G-PUSS	Cameron N-77 balloon	B. D. Close
	G-PUTT	Cameron Golfball 76 SS balloon	Lakeside Lodge Golf Centre
	G-PVBF	Lindstrand LBL-260S balloon	Virgin Balloon Flights
	G-PVCV	Robin DR400/140	Bustard Flying Club Ltd
	G-PVET	DHC.1 Chipmunk 22 (WB565)	Connect Properties Ltd
	G-PVHT	Dassault Falcon 7X	TAG Aviation (UK) Ltd
	G-PVML	Robin DR400/140B	Weald Air Services Ltd
	G-PVSS	P & M Quik GT450	K. & L. Ramsay
	G-PVST	Thruster T.600N 450	V. J. Vaughan
	G-PWAD	Eurocopter EC.120B Colibri	Bapchild Motoring World (Kent) Ltd
	G-PWBE	DH.82A Tiger Moth	M. F. Newman
	G-PWIT	Bell 206L-1 LongRanger	Formal Holdings Ltd (G-DWMI)
	G-PWNS	Cessna 525 Citationjet	Hangar 8 Management Ltd
	G-PWUL	Van's RV-6	D. C. Arnold
	G-PYNE	Thruster T.600N 450	R. Dereham
	G-PYPE	Van's RV-7	R. & L. Pyper
	G-PYRO	Cameron N-65 balloon	A. C. Booth
	G-PZAS	Schleicher ASW-27-18	A. P. C. Sampson
	G-PZAZ	PA-31-350 Navajo Chieftain	Argyll Ltd (G-VTAX/G-UTAX)
	G-PZPZ	P & M Aviation Pegasus Quantum 15-912	J. Urrutia
	G-RAAA	Bombardier BD700-1A10 Global Express	TAG Aviation (UK) Ltd
	G-RAAF	VS.359 Spitfire VIII	Composite Mast Engineering and Technology Ltd
	G-RABS	Alpi Pioneer 300	J. Mullen
	G-RACA	P.57 Sea Prince T.1 (571/CU) ★	(stored)/Long Marston
	G-RACO	PA-28R Cherokee Arrow 200-II	Graco Group Ltd
	G-RACR	Ultramagic M-65C balloon	R. A. Vale
	G-RACY	Cessna 182S	N. J. Fuller
	G-RADI	PA-28-181 Archer II	I. Davidson
	G-RADR	Douglas AD-4NA Skyraider (126922:503)	Orion Enterprises Ltd (G-RAID)
	G-RADY	Bombardier CL600-2B19 Challenger 850	TAG Aviation (UK) Ltd
	G-RAEF	Schempp-Hirth SHK-1	R. A. Earnshaw-Fretwell
	G-RAEM	Rutan LongEz	G. F. H. Singleton
	G-RAES	Boeing 777-236	British Airways
	G-RAFA	Grob G.115	RAF College Flying Club Ltd
	G-RAFB	Grob G.115	RAF College Flying Club Ltd
	G-RAFC	Robin R.2112	RAF Charlie Group
	G-RAFE	Thunder Ax7-77 balloon	Giraffe Balloon Syndicate
	G-RAFG	Slingsby T.67C Firefly	G. S. Evans
	G-RAFH	Thruster T.600N 450	G-RAFH Group
	G-RAFR	Skyranger J2.2(1)	A. M. Hemmings
	G-RAFS	Thruster T.600N 450	Caunton GRAFS Syndicate
	G-RAFT	Rutan LongEz	W. S. Allen
	G-RAFV	Avid Speedwing	Fox Victor Group (G-MOTT)
	G-RAFW	Mooney M.20E	Vinola (Knitwear) Manufacturing Co Ltd (G-ATHW)
	G-RAFY	Best Off Sky Ranger Swift 912S(1)	M. A. Evans & C. R. Cawley
	G-RAFZ	RAF 2000 GTX-SE	John Pavitt (Engineers) Ltd
	G-RAGE	Wilson Cassutt IIIM	R. S. Grace (G-BEUN)
	G-RAGS	Pietenpol Air Camper	S. H. Leonard
	G-RAGT	PA-32-301FT Cherokee Six	Oxhill Aviation
	G-RAIG	SA Bulldog Srs 100/101	Power Aerobatics Ltd (G-AZMR)

Reg.	Type	Owner or Operator	Notes
G-RAIR	Schleicher ASH-25	P. T. Reading	
G-RAIX	CCF AT-16 Harvard 4 (KF584)	M. R. Paul (G-BIWX)	
G-RAJA	Raj Hamsa X'Air 582 (2)	C. Roadnight	
G-RAJJ	BAe 146-200	Cello Aviation Ltd (G-CFDH)	
G-RALA	Robinson R44 Clipper II	Rala Aviation Ltd	
G-RALF	Rotorway Executive 162F	I. C. Bedford (G-BZOM)	
G-RAMA	Cameron C-70 balloon	Poppies (UK) Ltd	
G-RAMI	Bell 206B JetRanger 3	Yorkshire Helicopters	
G-RAMP	Piper J-3C-65 Cub	J. A. Holman & T. A. Hinton	
G-RAMS	PA-32R-301 Saratoga SP	Mike Sierra LLP	
G-RAMY	Bell 206B JetRanger 2	Lincair Ltd	
G-RAPD	Hughes 369E	FS Aviation LLP	
G-RAPH	Cameron O-77 balloon	P. A. Sweatman	
G-RAPI	Lindstrand LBL-105A balloon	P. A. Foot	
G-RARB	Cessna 172N	Prior Group Holdings Ltd	
G-RARE	Thunder Ax5-42 SS balloon ★	Balloon Preservation Group	
G-RASA	Diamond DA42 Twin Star	C. D. Hill	
G-RASC	Evans VP-2	R. F. Powell	
G-RASH	Grob G.109E	G-RASH Syndicate	
G-RATC	Van's RV-4	A. F. Ratcliffe	
G-RATD	Van's RV-8	J. R. Pike	
G-RATE	AA-5A Cheetah	G-RATE Flying Group (G-BIFF)	
G-RATH	Rotorway Executive 162F	W. H. Cole	
G-RATI	Cessna F.172M	D. Daniel (G-PATI/G-WACZ/G-BCUK)	
G-RATV	PA-28RT-201T Turbo Arrow IV	Tango Victor Ltd (G-WILS)	
G-RATZ	Shaw Europa	W. Goldsmith	
G-RAVE	Southdown Raven X	M. J. Robbins (G-MNZV)	
G-RAVN	Robinson R44	Brambledown Aircraft Hire	
G-RAWB	P & M Quik GT450	R. Blatchford	
G-RAWS	Rotorway Executive 162F	R. P. Robinson	
G-RAYB	P & M Quik GT450	R. Blatchford	
G-RAYH	Zenair CH.701UL	R. Horner	
G-RAYO	Lindstrand LBL-90A balloon	R. Owen	
G-RAYS	Zenair CH.250	A. D. Lowe	
G-RAYY	Cirrus SR22	Alquiler de Veleros SL/Spain	
G-RAYZ	Tecnam P2002-EA Sierra	R. Wells	
G-RAZY	PA-28-181 Archer II	T. H. Pemberton (G-REXS)	
G-RAZZ	Maule MX-7-180	C. S. Baird	
G-RBBB	Shaw Europa	T. J. Hartwell	
G-RBCA	Agusta A109A II	G-RBCA Ltd (G-TBGL/G-VJCB/G-BOUA)	
G-RBCI	BN-2A Mk.III-2 Trislander	Aurigny Air Services Ltd (G-BDWV)	
G-RBCT	Schempp-Hirth Ventus 2Ct	M. J. Weston & J. D. Huband	
G-RBMV	Cameron O-31 balloon	P. D. Griffiths	
G-RBND	Embraer EMB-135BJ Legacy 650	Portrack Global Ltd	
G-RBNS	Embraer EMB-135BJ Legacy 650	Portrack Global Ltd	
G-RBOS	Colt AS-105 airship ★	Science Museum/Wroughton	
G-RBOW	Thunder Ax-7-65 balloon	R. S. McDonald	
G-RBSN	Ikarus C.42 FB80	P. B. & M. Robinson	
G-RCAV	Bombardier CL600-2B16 Challenger	Hangar 8 Management Ltd	
G-RCED	Rockwell Commander 114	D. J. and D. Pitman	
G-RCHL	P & M Quik GT450	R. M. Broughton	
G-RCHY	Aerotechnik EV-97 Eurostar	N. McKenzie	
G-RCKT	Harmon Rocket II	K. E. Armstrong	
G-RCMC	Murphy Renegade 912	J. Matcham	
G-RCMF	Cameron V-77 balloon	J. M. Percival	
G-RCML	Sky 77-24 balloon	R. C. M. Sarl/Luxembourg	
G-RCNB	Eurocopter EC.120B	C. B. Ellis	
G-RCOH	Cameron Cube 105 SS balloon	A. M. Holly	
G-RCOM	Bell 206L-3 LongRanger 3	G. R. S. Harrison	
G-RCRC	P & M Quik	R. M. Brown	
G-RCSR	Replica de Havilland DH.88 Comet	K. Fern	
G-RCST	Jabiru J430	G. R. Cotterell	
G-RCUB	Piper L-18C (modified)	N. F. O'Neill	
G-RCUS	Schempp-Hirth Arcus T	R. B. Witter	
G-RCWK	Cessna 182T Skylane	R. C. W. King	
G-RDAD	Reality Escapade ULP(1)	R. W. Burge	
G-RDAY	Van's RV-9	R. M. Day	
G-RDCO	Avtech Jabiru J430	J. M. Record	
G-RDFX	Aero AT-3	B. Wilson	

Notes	Reg.	Type	Owner or Operator
	G-RDHS	Shaw Europa XS	R. D. H. Spencer
	G-RDNS	Rans S.6-S Super Coyote	P. G. Cowling & J. S. Crofts
	G-RDPH	P & M Quik R	R. S. Partidge-Hicks
	G-READ	Colt 77A balloon	Intervarsity Balloon Club
	G-REAF	Jabiru J400	R. E. Afia
	G-REAH	PA-32R-301 Saratoga SP	M. Q. Tolbod & S. J. Rogers (G-CELL)
	G-REAR	Lindstrand LBL-69X balloon	A. M. Holly
	G-REAS	Van's RV-6A	T. J. Smith
	G-REBB	Murphy Rebel	M. Stow
	G-RECO	Jurca MJ-5L Sirocco	J. D. Tseliki
	G-REDC	Pegasus Quantum 15-912	S. Houghton
	G-REDE	Eurocopter AS.365N3 Dauphin 2	Bond Offshore Helicopters Ltd
	G-REDF	Eurocopter AS.365N3 Dauphin 2	Bond Offshore Helicopters Ltd
	G-REDG	Eurocopter AS.365N3 Dauphin 2	Bond Offshore Helicopters Ltd
	G-REDH	Eurocopter AS.365N3 Dauphin 2	Bond Offshore Helicopters Ltd
	G-REDJ	Eurocopter AS.332L-2 Super Puma	International Aviation Leasing Ltd
	G-REDK	Eurocopter AS.332L-2 Super Puma	International Aviation Leasing Ltd
	G-REDM	Eurocopter AS.332L-2 Super Puma	International Aviation Leasing Ltd
	G-REDN	Eurocopter AS.332L-2 Super Puma	International Aviation Leasing Ltd
	G-REDO	Eurocopter AS.332L-2 Super Puma	International Aviation Leasing Ltd
	G-REDP	Eurocopter AS.332L-2 Super Puma	International Aviation Leasing Ltd
	G-REDR	Eurocopter AS.225LP Super Puma	International Aviation Leasing Ltd
	G-REDT	Eurocopter EC.225LP Super Puma	International Aviation Leasing LLP
	G-REDV	Eurocopter EC.225LP Super Puma	Bond Offshore Helicopters Ltd
	G-REDW	Eurocopter EC.225LP Super Puma	Bond Offshore Helicopters Ltd
	G-REDX	Experimental Aviation Berkut	G. V. Waters
	G-REDY	Robinson R22 Beta	L. lampieri
	G-REDZ	Thruster T.600T 450	N. S. Dell
	G-REEC	Sequoia F.8L Falco	J. D. Tseliki
	G-REED	Mainair Blade 912S	I. C. Macbeth
	G-REEF	Mainair Blade 912S	G. Mowll
	G-REEM	AS.355F1 Twin Squirrel	Heliking Ltd (G-EMAN/G-WEKR/G-CHLA)
	G-REER	Centrair 101A Pegase	R. L. Howorth & G. C. Stinchcombe
	G-REES	Jodel D.140C	G-REES Flying Group
	G-REGC	Zenair CH.601XL Zodiac	G. P. Coutie
	G-REGE	Robinson R44	Rotorvation Helicopters
	G-REGI	Cyclone Chaser S508	G. S. Stokes (G-MYZW)
	G-REGS	Thunder Ax7-77 balloon	D. R. Rawlings
	G-REJP	Europa XS	A. Milner
	G-REKO	Pegasus Quasar IITC	J. Horan (G-MWWA)
	G-RELL	D.62B Condor	P. S. Grellier (G-OPJH/G-AVDW)
	G-REMH	Bell 206B-3 JetRanger III	Flightpath Ltd
	G-RENI	Balony Kubicek BB-30Z balloon	A. M. Holly
	G-RENO	SOCATA TB10 Tobago	V. W. Ood
	G-RESC	MBB BK.117C-1	Veritair ASviation Ltd
	G-RESG	Dyn'Aéro MCR-01 Club	R. E. S. Greenwood
	G-REST	Beech P35 Bonanza	C. R. Taylor (G-ASFJ)
	G-RETA	CASA 1.131 Jungmann 2000	Richard Shuttleworth Trustees (G-BGZC)
	G-REVE	Van's RV-6	J. D. Winder
	G-REVO	Skyranger 912(2)	H. Murray
	G-REYS	Canadair CL600-2B16 Challenger 604	TAG Aviation
	G-RFIO	Aeromot AMT-200 Super Ximango	M. D. Evans
	G-RFLY	Extra EA.300/L	H. B. Sauer
	G-RFOX	Denney Kitfox Mk 3	J. R. Chapman & G. Harrington
	G-RFSB	Sportavia RF-5B	G-RFSB Group
	G-RFUN	Robinson R44	Brooklands Developments Ltd
	G-RGSG	Raytheon Hawker 900XP	Hangar 8 Management Ltd
	G-RGTS	Schempp-Hirth Discus b	G. R. & L. R. Green
	G-RGUS	Fairchild 24A-46A Argus III (44-83184)	T. R. Coulton & J. L. Bryan
	G-RGZT	Cirrus SR20	M. Presenti
	G-RHAM	Skyranger 582(1)	I. Smart & T. Driffield
	G-RHCB	Schweizer 269C-1	Lift West Ltd
	G-RHMS	Embraer EMB-135BJ Legacy	TAG Aviation (UK) Ltd
	G-RHOS	ICP MXP-740 Savannah VG Jabiru(1)	J. C. Munro-Hunt
	G-RHYM	PA-31-310 Turbo Navajo B	2 Excel Aviation Ltd (G-BJLO)
	G-RHYS	Rotorway Executive 90	A. K. Voase
	G-RIAM	SOCATA TB10 Tobago	H. Varia

Reg.	Type	Owner or Operator	Notes
G-RIBA	P & M Quik GT450	R. J. Murphy	
G-RICK	Beech 95-B55 Baron	J. Jack (G-BAAG)	
G-RICO	AG-5B Tiger	Delta Lima Flying Group	
G-RICS	Shaw Europa	The Flying Property Doctor	
G-RIDA	Eurocopter AS.355NP Ecureuil 2	National Grid Electricity Transmission PLC	
G-RIDE	Stephens Akro	R. Mitchell	
G-RIDG	Van's RV-7	C. Heathcote	
G-RIEF	DG Flugzeugbau DG-1000T	EF Gliding Group	
G-RIET	Hoffmann H.36 Dimona	Dimona Gliding Group	
G-RIEV	Rolladen-Schneider LS8-18	R. D. Grieve	
G-RIFB	Hughes 269C	AA Consultants Ltd	
G-RIFN	Avion Mudry CAP-10B	D. E. Starkey & R. A. J. Spurrell	
G-RIFO	Schempp-Hirth Standard Cirrus 75-VTC	L. de Marchi (G-CKGT)	
G-RIFY	Christen Eagle II	C. J. Gow	
G-RIGB	Thunder Ax7-77 balloon	N. J. Bettin	
G-RIGH	PA-32R-301 Saratoga IIHP	G. M. R. Graham	
G-RIGS	PA-60 Aerostar 601P	G. G. Caravatti & P. G. Penati/Italy	
G-RIHN	Dan Rihn DR.107 One Design	P. J. Burgess	
G-RIII	Vans RV-3B	R. S. Grace & D. H. Burge	
G-RIIV	Van's RV-4	M. R. Overall	
G-RIKI	Mainair Blade 912	RIKI Group	
G-RIKS	Shaw Europa XS	R. Morris	
G-RIKY	Mainair Pegasus Quik	S. Clarke	
G-RILA	Flight Design CTSW	P. A. Mahony	
G-RILY	Monnett Sonnerai 2L	A Sharp	
G-RIMB	Lindstrand LBL-105A balloon	D. Grimshaw	
G-RIME	Lindstrand LBL-25A balloon	N. Ivison	
G-RIMM	Westland Wasp HAS.1 (XT435:430)	G. P. Hinkley	
G-RINN	Mainair Blade	P. Hind	
G-RINO	Thunder Ax7-77 balloon	D. J. Head	
G-RINS	Rans S.6-ESA Coyote II	R. W. Hocking	
G-RINT	CFM Streak Shadow	D. Grint	
G-RINZ	Van's RV-7	P. Chaplin (G-UZZL)	
G-RIPA	Partenavia P68 Observer 2	Apem Ltd	
G-RIPH	VS.384 Seafire F.XVII	Seafire Displays Ltd (G-CDTM)	
G-RISA	PA-28-180 Cherokee C	D. B. Riseborough (G-ATZK)	
G-RISE	Cameron V-77 balloon	D. L. Smith	
G-RISH	Rotorway Exeecutive 162F	C. S. Rische	
G-RISK	Hughes 369E	Wavendon Social Housing Ltd	
G-RISY	Van's RV-7	G-RISY Group	
G-RIVA	SOCATA TBM-700N	Airpark One Ltd	
G-RIVE	Jodel D.153	P. Fines	
G-RIVR	Thruster T.600N 450	Thruster Air Services Ltd	
G-RIVT	Van's RV-6	N. Reddish	
G-RIXA	J-3C-65 Cub	J. J. Rix	
G-RIXS	Shaw Europa XS	R. Iddon	
G-RIXY	Cameron Z-77 balloon	Rix Petroleum Ltd	
G-RIZE	Cameron O-90 balloon	S. F. Burden/Netherlands	
G-RIZI	Cameron N-90 balloon	R. Wiles	
G-RIZZ	PA-28-161 Warrior II	Modi Aviation Ltd	
G-RJAH	Boeing Stearman A75N1	R. J. Horne	
G-RJAM	Sequoia F.8L Falco	D. G. Drew	
G-RJCC	Cessna 172S	R. J. Chapman	
G-RJCP	Rockwell Commander 114B	Heltor Ltd	
G-RJMS	PA-28R-201 Arrow III	M. G. Hill	
G-RJRJ	Evektor EV-97A Eurostar	D. P. Myatt	
G-RJWW	Maule M5-235C Lunar Rocket	D. E. Priest (G-BRWG)	
G-RJWX	Shaw Europa XS	J. R. Jones	
G-RJXA	Embraer RJ145EP	bmi regional	
G-RJXB	Embraer RJ145EP	bmi regional	
G-RJXC	Embraer RJ145EP	bmi regional	
G-RJXD	Embraer RJ145EP	bmi regional	
G-RJXE	Embraer RJ145EP	bmi regional	
G-RJXF	Embraer RJ145EP	bmi regional	
G-RJXG	Embraer RJ145EP	bmi regional	
G-RJXH	Embraer RJ145EP	bmi regional	
G-RJXI	Embraer RJ145EP	bmi regional	
G-RJXJ	Embraer RJ135LR	bmi regional	
G-RJXK	Embraer RJ135LR	bmi regional	
G-RJXL	Embraer RJ135LR	bmi regional	
G-RJXM	Embraer RJ145MP	bmi regional	

Notes	Reg.	Type	Owner or Operator
	G-RJXP	Embraer RJ135ER	bmi regional (G-CDFS)
	G-RJXR	Embraer RJ145EP	bmi regional (G-CCYH)
	G-RKEL	Agusta-Bell 206B JetRanger 3	Nunkeeling Ltd
	G-RKKT	Cessna FR.172G	K. L. Irvine (G-AYJW)
	G-RLEF	Hawker Hurricane XII	P. J. Lawton
	G-RLMW	Tecnam P2002-EA Sierra	G. J. Slater
	G-RLON	BN-2A Mk III-2 Trislander	Aurigny Air Services Ltd (G-ITEX/G-OCTA/ G-BCXW)
	G-RLWG	Ryan ST3KR	R. A. Fleming
	G-RMAC	Shaw Europa	P. J. Lawless
	G-RMAN	Aero Designs Pulsar	M. B. Redman
	G-RMAX	Cameron C-80 balloon	J. Kenny
	G-RMCS	Cessna 182R	R. W. C. Sears
	G-RMHE	Aerospool Dynamic WT9 UK	R. M. Hughes-Ellis
	G-RMIT	Van's RV-4	J. P. Kloos
	G-RMMA	Dassault Falcon 900EX	Execujet (UK) Ltd
	G-RMMT	Europa XS	N. Schmitt
	G-RMPI	Whittaker MW5D Sorcerer	N. R. Beale
	G-RMPS	Van's RV-12	K. D. Boardman
	G-RMPY	Aerotechnik EV-97 Eurostar	N. R. Beale
	G-RMRV	Van's RV-7A	R. Morris
	G-RMTO	Rotorsport UK MTO Sport	J. R. S. Heaton
	G-RMUG	Cameron Nescafe Mug 90 SS balloon	The British Balloon Museum & Library Ltd
	G-RNAC	IDA Bacau Yakovlev Yak-52	RNAEC Group
	G-RNAS	DH.104 Sea Devon C.20 (XK896) ★	Airport Fire Service/Filton
	G-RNBW	Bell 206B JetRanger 2	Rainbow Helicopters Ltd
	G-RNCH	PA-28-181 Archer II	Carlisle Flight Training Ltd
	G-RNDD	Robin DR.400/500	Witham (Specialist Vehicles) Ltd
	G-RNER	Cessna 510 Citation Mustang	A. Shade Greener (F1) Ltd
	G-RNGO	Robinson R22 Beta II	M. Flandina
	G-RNHF	Hawker Sea Fury T.Mk.20 (VX281)	Naval Aviation Ltd (G-BCOW)
	G-RNIE	Cameron 70 Ball SS balloon	N. J. Bland
	G-RNLI	VS.236 Walrus I (W2718) ★	Walrus Aviation Ltd
	G-RNRM	Cessna A.185F	Skydive St. Andrews Ltd
	G-RNRS	SA Bulldog Srs.100/101	Power Aerobatics Ltd (G-AZIT)
	G-ROAD	Robinson R44 II	Aztec Aviators Ltd
	G-ROBD	Shaw Europa	M. P. Wiseman
	G-ROBG	P & M Quik GT450	Exodus Airsports Ltd
	G-ROBJ	Robin DR.500/200i	D. R. L. Jones
	G-ROBN	Pierre Robin R1180T	N. D. Anderson
	G-ROBT	Hawker Hurricane I (P2902:DX-X)	R. A. Roberts
	G-ROBY	Colt 17A balloon	Virgin Airship & Balloon Co Ltd
	G-ROBZ	Grob G109B	Bravo Zulu Group
	G-ROCH	Cessna T.303	R. S. Bentley
	G-ROCK	Thunder Ax7-77 balloon	M. A. Green
	G-ROCO	ACLA Sirocco	D. C. Arnold
	G-ROCR	Schweizer 269C	Hayles Aviation
	G-ROCT	Robinson R44 II	A. von Liechtenstein
	G-RODC	Steen Skybolt	D. G. Girling
	G-RODD	Cessna 310R II	R. J. Herbert Engineering Ltd (G-TEDD/G-MADI)
	G-RODG	Avtech Jabiru UL	G-RODG Group
	G-RODI	Isaacs Fury (K3731)	M. J. Bond
	G-RODJ	Ikarus C42 FB80	D. A. Perkins
	G-RODO	Shaw Europa XS	R. M. Carson (G-ROWI)
	G-RODZ	Van's RV-3A	M. J. Wood
	G-ROEI	Avro Roe 1 Replica	Brooklands Museum Trust Ltd
	G-ROEN	Cameron C-70 balloon	R. M. W. Romans
	G-ROFS	Groppo Trail	R. F. Bond
	G-ROGY	Cameron 60 Concept balloon	S. A. Laing
	G-ROKO	Roko-Aero NG-4HD	M. Coaten & D. S. Watson
	G-ROKT	Cessna FR.172E	G-ROKT Flying Club Ltd
	G-ROKY	Gruppo Trail	Skyview Systems Ltd
	G-ROLF	PA-32R-301 Saratoga SP	P. F. Larkins
	G-ROLL	Pitts S-2A Special	Aerobatic Displays Ltd
	G-ROLY	Cessna F.172N	M. Bonsall (G-BHIH)
	G-ROME	I.I.I. Sky Arrow 650TC	Sky Arrow (Kits) UK Ltd
	G-ROMP	Extra 230H	G. G. Ferriman

Reg.	Type	Owner or Operator	Notes
G-ROMW	Cyclone AX2000	K. V. Falvey	
G-RONA	Shaw Europa	C. M. Noakes	
G-RONG	PA-28R Cherokee Arrow 200-II	D. Griffiths & S. P. Rooney	
G-RONI	Cameron V-77 balloon	R. E. Simpson	
G-RONS	Robin DR.400/180	R. & K. Baker	
G-RONW	FRED Srs 2	F. J. Keitch	
G-ROOK	Cessna F.172P	Rolim Ltd	
G-ROOO	Jabiru J430	J. L. Almey (G-HJZN)	
G-ROOV	Shaw Europa XS	P. W. Hawkins & K. Siggery	
G-ROPO	Groppo Trail	R. D. P. Cadle	
G-ROPP	Groppo Trail	P. T. Price	
G-RORB	Spitfire Mk.26	Golf Romeo Bravo Club	
G-RORI	Folland Gnat T.1 (XR538)	Heritage Aircraft Ltd	
G-RORY	Piaggio FWP.149D	M. Edwards (G-TOWN)	
G-ROSI	Thunder Ax7-77 balloon	J. E. Rose	
G-ROTS	CFM Streak Shadow Srs SA	J. Edwards	
G-ROUP	Cessna F.172M	Perranporth Flying School Ltd (G-BDPH)	
G-ROUS	PA-34-200T Seneca II	Oxford Aviation Training Ltd	
G-ROVE	PA-18 Super Cub 135	S. J. Gaveston	
G-ROVY	Robinson R22 Beta	Fly Executive Ltd	
G-ROWA	Aquila AT01	Chicory Crops Ltd	
G-ROWE	Cessna F.182P	D. Rowe	
G-ROWL	AA-5B Tiger	T. A. Timms	
G-ROWR	Robinson R44	R. A. Oldworth	
G-ROWS	PA-28-151 Warrior	Air Academy	
G-ROXI	Cameron C-90 balloon	N. R. Beckwith	
G-ROYC	Avtech Jabiru UL450	M. W. Hanley	
G-ROYM	Robinson R44 II	Business Agility Ltd	
G-ROYN	Robinson R44	Napier Helicopters Ltd (G-DCON)	
G-ROZE	Magni M-24C	R. I. Simpson	
G-ROZI	Robinson R44	Rotormotive Ltd	
G-ROZZ	Ikarus C.42 FB 80	A. J. Blackwell	
G-RPAF	Europa XS	G-RPAF Group	
G-RPAX	CASA 1-133 Jungmeister	A. J. E. Smith	
G-RPCC	Europa XS	R. P. Churchill-Coleman	
G-RPEZ	Rutan LongEz	M. P. Dunlop	
G-RPPO	Groppo Trail	G. N. Smith	
G-RPRV	Van's RV-9A	M. G. Titmus	
G-RRAK	Enstrom 480B	B. Satherley (G-RIBZ)	
G-RRAT	CZAW Sportcruiser	G. Sipson	
G-RRCU	CEA DR.221B Dauphin	Merlin Flying Club Ltd	
G-RRED	PA-28-181 Archer II	J. P. Reddington	
G-RRFC	SOCATA TB20 Trinidad GT	C. A. Hawkins	
G-RRFF	VS.329 Spitfire Mk.IIB	P. Maksimczyk	
G-RRGN	VS.390 Spitfire PR.XIX (PS853)	Rolls-Royce PLC (G-MXIX)	
G-RROB	Robinson R44 II	R. S. Rai	
G-RRRZ	Van's RV-8	D. J. C. Davidson	
G-RRSR	Piper J-3C-65 Cub (480173:57-H)	R. W. Roberts	
G-RRVX	Van's RV-10	R. D. Mastersd	
G-RSAF	BAC.167 Strikemaster 80A	Viper Classics Ltd	
G-RSAM	P & M Quik GTR	S. F. Beardsell	
G-RSCU	Agusta A.109E	Sloane Helicopters Ltd	
G-RSHI	PA-34-220T Seneca V	R. S. Hill and Sons	
G-RSKR	PA-28-161 Warrior II	ACS Engineering Ltd (G-BOJY)	
G-RSKY	Skyranger 912(2)	C. G. Benham & C. H. Tregonning	
G-RSMC	Medway SLA 100 Executive	W. S. C. Toulmin	
G-RSSF	Denney Kitfox Mk 2	R. W. Somerville	
G-RSWO	Cessna 172R	G. Fischer	
G-RSWW	Robinson R22 Beta	Kington building Supplies Ltd	
G-RSXL	Cessna 560 Citation XLS	Aircraft Leasing Overseas Ltd	
G-RTBI	Thunder Ax6-56 balloon	P. J. Waller	
G-RTFM	Jabiru J400	I. A. Macphee	
G-RTHS	Rans S-6-ES Coyote II	T. Harrison-Smith	
G-RTIN	Rotorsport UK MT-03	P. McCrory	
G-RTMS	Rans S.6 ES Coyote II	C. J. Arthur	
G-RTMY	Ikarus C.42 FB 100	Mike Yankee Group	
G-RTRT	PZL-104MA Wilga 2000	E. A. M. Austin	
G-RTRV	V an's RV-9A	R. Taylor	

Notes	Reg.	Type	Owner or Operator
	G-RUBB	AA-5B Tiger	D. E. Gee
	G-RUBE	Embraer EMB-135BJ Legacy	Autumn Breeze International Ltd
	G-RUBY	PA-28RT-201T Turbo Arrow IV	Arrow Aircraft Group (G-BROU)
	G-RUCK	Bell 206B-3 JetRanger III	J. A. Ruck
	G-RUES	Robin HR.100/210	R. H. R. Rue
	G-RUFF	Mainair Blade 912	C. W. THompson
	G-RUFS	Avtech Jabiru UL	M. Bastin
	G-RUGS	Campbell Cricket Mk 4 gyroplane	J. L. G. McLane
	G-RUIA	Cessna F.172N	D. C. Parry
	G-RULE	Robinson R44 Raven II	Huckair
	G-RUMI	Noble Harman Snowbird Mk.IV	G. Crossley (G-MVOI)
	G-RUMM	Grumman F8F-2P Bearcat (121714:201B)	Patina Ltd
	G-RUMN	AA-1A Trainer	M. T. Manwaring
	G-RUMW	Grumman FM-2 Wildcat (JV579:F)	Patina Ltd
	G-RUNS	P & M Quik GT450	S. Nicol
	G-RUNT	Cassutt Racer IIIM	D. P. Lightfoot
	G-RUPS	Cameron TR-70 balloon	R. M. Stanley
	G-RUSL	Van's RV-6A	G. R. Russell
	G-RUSO	Robinson R22 Beta	R. M. Barnes-Gorell
	G-RUSS	Cessna 172N ★	Leisure Lease (stored)/Southend
	G-RUVE	Van's RV-8	J. P. Brady & D. J. Taylor
	G-RUVI	Zenair CH.601UL	P. G. Depper
	G-RUVY	Van's RV-9A	R. D. Taylor
	G-RUZZ	Robinson R44 II	Russell Harrison PLC
	G-RVAB	Van's RV-7	I. M. Belmore & A. T. Banks
	G-RVAC	Van's RV-7	A. F. S. & B. Caldecourt
	G-RVAH	Van's RV-7	H. W. Hall
	G-RVAL	Van's RV-8	R. N. York
	G-RVAN	Van's RV-6	D. Broom
	G-RVAT	Van's RV-8	T. R. Grief
	G-RVAW	Van's RV-6	C. Rawlings & R. J. Tomlinson
	G-RVBA	Van's RV-8A	D. P. Richard
	G-RVBC	Van's RV-6A	B. J. Clifford
	G-RVBF	Cameron A-340 balloon	Virgin Balloon Flights
	G-RVBI	Van's RV-8	M. A. N. Newall
	G-RVCE	Van's RV-6A	C. & M. D. Barnard
	G-RVCH	Van's RV-8A	R. J. Birt
	G-RVCL	Van's RV-6	M. A. Wyer
	G-RVDG	Van's RV-9	D. M. Gill
	G-RVDH	Van's RV-8	D. J. Harrison (G-ONER)
	G-RVDJ	Van's RV-6	J. D. Jewitt
	G-RVDP	Van's RV-4	O. Florin
	G-RVDR	Van's RV-6A	P. R. Redfern
	G-RVDX	Van's RV-4	P. J. Scullion (G-FTUO)
	G-RVEE	Van's RV-6	J. C. A. Wheeler
	G-RVEI	Van's RV-8	D. Stephens
	G-RVEM	Van's RV-7A	E. M. Farquharson & G. J. Newby (G-CBJU)
	G-RVER	Van's RV-4	R. D. E. Holah
	G-RVET	Van's RV-6	D. R. Coleman
	G-RVGA	Van's RV-6A	R. Emery
	G-RVGO	Van's RV-10	D. C. Arnold
	G-RVIA	Van's RV-6A	K. R. W. Scull & J. Watkins
	G-RVIB	Van's RV-6	P. D. Gorman
	G-RVIC	Van's RV-6A	I. T. Corse
	G-RVII	Van's RV-7	P. H. C. Hall
	G-RVIN	Van's RV-6	R. G. Jines
	G-RVIO	Van's RV-10	R. C. Hopkinson
	G-RVIS	Van's RV-8	I. V. Sharman
	G-RVIT	Van's RV-6	P. J. Shotbolt
	G-RVIV	Van's RV-4	S. B. Robson
	G-RVIW	Van's RV-9	G. S. Scott
	G-RVIX	Van's RV-9A	J. R. Holt & C. S. Simmons
	G-RVIZ	Van's RV-12	J. E. Singleton
	G-RVJM	Van's RV-6	M. D. Challoner
	G-RVJO	Van's RV-9A	J. C. Simpson
	G-RVJP	Van's RV-9A	R. M. Palmer
	G-RVJW	Van's RV-4	J. M. Williams
	G-RVLC	Van's RV-9A	L. J. Clark
	G-RVMB	Van's RV-9A	M. James & R. W. Littledale
	G-RVMT	Van's RV-6	M. J. Aldridge

Reg.	Type	Owner or Operator	Notes
G-RVMZ	Van's RV-8	A. E. Kay	
G-RVNA	PA-38-112 Tomahawk	Ravenair Aircraft Ltd (G-DFLY)	
G-RVNB	PA-38-112 Tomahawk	Ravenair Aircraft Ltd (G-SUKI/G-BPNV)	
G-RVNC	PA-38-112 Tomahawk	Ravenair Aircraft Ltd (G-BTJK)	
G-RVND	PA-38-112 Tomahawk	Ravenair Aircraft Ltd (G-BTAS)	
G-RVNE	Partenavia P.68B	Ravenair Aircraft Ltd (G-SAMJ)	
G-RVNH	Van's RV-9A	N. R. Haines	
G-RVNI	Van's RV-6A	G-RVNI Group	
G-RVNP	Partenavia P.68B	Ravenair Aircraft Ltd	
G-RVNS	Van's RV-4	B. R. Hunter (G-CBGN)	
G-RVPH	Van's RV-8	J. C. P. Herbert	
G-RVPL	Van's RV-8	B. J. Summers	
G-RVPM	Van's RV-4	D. P. Lightfoot (G-RVDS)	
G-RVPW	Van's RV-6A	P. Waldron	
G-RVRA	PA-28 Cherokee 140	Par Contractors Ltd (G-OWVA)	
G-RVRB	PA-34-200T Seneca II	Ravenair Aircraft Ltd (G-BTAJ)	
G-RVRC	PA-23 Aztec 250E	C. J. Williams (G-BNPD)	
G-RVRD	PA-23 Aztec 250E	Ravenair Aircraft Ltd (G-BRAV/G-BBCM)	
G-RVRE	Partenavia P.68B	Ravenair Aircraft Ltd	
G-RVRI	Cessna 172H Skyhawk	L. Kelly (G-CCCC)	
G-RVRJ	PA-E23 Aztec 250E	Ravenair Aircraft Ltd (G-BBGB)	
G-RVRK	PA-38-112 Tomahawk	Ravenair Aircraft Ltd (G-BGZW)	
G-RVRL	PA-38-112 Tomahawk	Ravenair Aircraft Ltd (G-BGZW/G-BGBY)	
G-RVRM	PA-38-112 Tomahawk	Ravenair Aircraft Ltd (G-BGEK)	
G-RVRN	PA-28-161 Warrior II	Ravenair Aircraft Ltd (G-BPID)	
G-RVRO	PA-38-112 Tomahawk II	Ravenair Aircraft Ltd (G-BOUD)	
G-RVRP	Van's RV-7	R. C. Parris	
G-RVRR	PA-38-112 Tomahawk	Ravenair Aircraft Ltd (G-BRHT)	
G-RVRT	PA-28-140 Cherokee C	Ravenair Aircraft Ltd (G-AYKX)	
G-RVRU	PA-38-112 Tomahawk	Ravenair Aircraft Ltd (G-NCFE/G-BKMK)	
G-RVRV	Van's RV-4	P. Jenkins	
G-RVRW	PA-23 Aztec 250E	Ravenair Aircraft Ltd (G-BAVZ)	
G-RVRX	Partenavia P.68B	Ravenair Aircraft Ltd (G-PART)	
G-RVRY	PA-38-112 Tomahawk	Ravenair Aircraft Ltd (G-BTND)	
G-RVRZ	PA-23-250 Aztec E	Ravenair Aircraft Ltd (G-NRSC/G-BSFL)	
G-RVSA	Van's RV-6A	W. H. Knott	
G-RVSD	Van's RV-9A	S. W. Damarell	
G-RVSG	Van's RV-9A	S. Gerrish	
G-RVSH	Van's RV-6A	S. J. D. Hall	
G-RVSR	Van's RV-8	R. K. & S. W. Elders	
G-RVST	Van's RV-6	J. D. Rooney (G-BXYX)	
G-RVSX	Van's RV-6	R. L. & V. A. West	
G-RVTE	Van's RV-6	E. McShane & T. Feeny	
G-RVTN	Van's RV-10	C. I. Law	
G-RVTT	Van's RV-7	A. Phillips	
G-RVTW	Van's RV-12	A. P. Watkins	
G-RVUK	Van's RV-7	P. D. G. Grist	
G-RVVI	Van's RV-6	G. G. Ferriman	
G-RVVY	Van's RV-10	P. R. Marskell	
G-RVWJ	Van's RV-9A	N. J. Williams-Jones	
G-RVXP	Van's RV-3B	A. N. Buchan	
G-RWAY	Rotorway Executive 162F	C. R. Johnson (G-URCH)	
G-RWEW	Robinson R44	Northern Heli Charters	
G-RWGS	Robinson R44 II	R. W. G. Simpson	
G-RWIA	Robinson R22 Beta	GPS Fabrications Ltd (G-BOEZ)	
G-RWIN	Rearwin 175	A. B. Bourne & N. D. Battye	
G-RWLY	Shaw Europa XS	C. R. Arcle	
G-RWMW	Zenair CH.601XL Zodiac	R. W. H. Watson (G-DROO)	
G-RWSS	Denney Kitfox Mk 2	R. W. Somerville	
G-RWWW	WS-55 Whirlwind HCC.12 (XR486)★	IHM/Weston-super-Mare	
G-RXUK	Lindstrand LBL-105A balloon	C. C. & R. K. Scott	
G-RYAL	Avtech Jabiru UL	S. A. Ivell	
G-RYDR	Rotorsport UK MT-03	A. D. McCutcheon	
G-RYNS	PA-32-301FT Cherokee Six	D. A. Earle	
G-RYPE	DG Flugzeugbau DG-1000T	DG-1000T Partners	
G-RYPH	Mainair Blade 912	I. A. Cunningham	
G-RYZZ	Robinson R44 II	Rivermead Aviation Ltd	
G-RZEE	Schleicher ASW-19B	L. Y. Smith	

Notes	Reg.	Type	Owner or Operator
	G-RZLY	Flight Design CTSW	J. D. Macnamara
	G-SAAA	Flight Design CTSW	P. J. Watson & A. J. Kolleng
	G-SABA	PA-28R-201T Turbo Arrow III	C. A. Burton (G-BFEN)
	G-SABB	Eurocopter EC 135T1	Bond Air Services Ltd
	G-SABR	NA F-86A Sabre (8178:FU-178)	Golden Apple Operations Ltd
	G-SACH	Stoddard-Hamilton Glastar	R. S. Holt
	G-SACI	PA-28-161 Warrior II	PJC (Leasing) Ltd
	G-SACM	TL2000UK Sting Carbon	M. Clare
	G-SACO	PA-28-161 Warrior II	Stapleford Flying Club Ltd
	G-SACR	PA-28-161 Cadet	Sherburn Aero Club Ltd
	G-SACS	PA-28-161 Cadet	Sherburn Aero Club Ltd
	G-SACT	PA-28-161 Cadet	Sherburn Aero Club Ltd
	G-SACX	Aero AT-3 R100	Sherburn Aero Club Ltd
	G-SACY	Aero AT-3 R100	Sherburn Aero Club Ltd
	G-SAFE	Cameron N-77 balloon	P. J. Waller
	G-SAFI	CP.1320 Super Emeraude	C. S. Carleton-Smith
	G-SAFR	SAAB 91D Safir	Sylmar Aviation & Services Ltd
	G-SAGA	Grob G.109B	G-GROB Ltd/Booker
	G-SAGE	Luscombe 8A Silvaire	C. Howell (G-AKTL)
	G-SAHI	Trago Mills SAH-1	Hotel India Group
	G-SAIG	Robinson R44 II	Torfield Aviation Ltd
	G-SAIR	Cessna 421C	Air Support Aviation Services Ltd (G-OBCA)
	G-SAJA	Schempp-Hirth Discus 2	J. G. Arnold
	G-SALA	PA-32 Cherokee Six 300E	R. M. J. Harrison & J. W. A. Portch
	G-SALE	Cameron Z-90 balloon	R. D. Baker
	G-SAMC	Ikarus C42 FB80	G. Cooper
	G-SAMG	Grob G.109B	The Royal Air Force Gliding and Soaring Association
	G-SAMY	Shaw Europa	K. R. Tallent
	G-SAMZ	Cessna 150D	Fly More Aviation Ltd (G-ASSO)
	G-SANL	Bombardier BD700-1A10 Global Express	Sanctuary Aviation LLP
	G-SAOC	Schempp-Hirth Discus 2cT	The Royal Air Force Gliding and Soaring Association
	G-SAPM	SOCATA TB20 Trinidad	G-SAPM Ltd (G-EWFN)
	G-SARA	PA-28-181 Archer II	Apollo Aviation Advisory Ltd
	G-SARB	Sikorsky S-92A	CHC Scotia Ltd (HM Coastguard)
	G-SARC	Sikorsky S-92A	CHC Scotia Ltd (HM Coastguard)
	G-SARD	Agusta Westland AW139	CHC Scotia Ltd (HM Coastguard)
	G-SARJ	P & M Quik GT450	A. R. Jones
	G-SARM	Ikarus C.42 FB80	G-SARM Group
	G-SARV	Van's RV-4	Hinton Flying Group
	G-SASA	Eurocopter EC 135T1	Bond Air Services Ltd
	G-SASB	Eurocopter EC 135T2+	Bond Air Services Ltd
	G-SASC	Beech B200C Super King Air	Gama Aviation Ltd
	G-SASD	Beech B200C Super King Air	Gama Aviation Ltd
	G-SASG	Schleicher ASW-27-18E	F. B. Jeynes
	G-SASH	MDH MD.900 Explorer	Yorkshire Air Ambulance Ltd
	G-SASI	CZAW Sportcruiser	A. S. Arundell
	G-SASK	PA-31P Pressurised Navajo	Middle East Business Club Ltd (G-BFAM)
	G-SASM	Westland Scout AH.Mk.1	C. J. Marsden
	G-SASY	Eurocopter EC.130 B4	R. J. H. Smith
	G-SATN	PA-25-260 Pawnee C	The Royal Gliding and Soaring Association
	G-SAUO	Cessna A.185F	T. G. Lloyd
	G-SAUK	Rans S6-ES	M. D. Tulloch
	G-SAVY	Savannah VG Jabiru(1)	C. S. Hollingworth & S. P. Yardley
	G-SAWI	PA-32RT-300T Turbo Lance II	Regularity Ltd
	G-SAXT	Schempp-Hirth Duo Discus Xt	The Royal Air Force Gliding and Soaring Association
	G-SAYS	RAF 2000 GTX-SE gyroplane	K. J. Whitehead
	G-SAZY	Avtech Jabiru J400	S.M. Pink
	G-SAZZ	CP.328 Super Emeraude	D. J. Long
	G-SBAE	Cessna F.172P	BAe (Warton) Flying Club
	G-SBAG	Phoenix Currie Wot	R. W. Clarke (G-BFAH)
	G-SBAP	Rans S-6 ES Coyote II	Royal Aeronautical Society
	G-SBDB	Remos GX	G-SBDB Group
	G-SBIZ	Cameron Z-90 balloon	Snow Business International Ltd
	G-SBKR	SOCATA TB10 Tobago	S. C. M. Bagley
	G-SBKS	Cessna 206H Stationair	Alard Properties Ltd
	G-SBLT	Steen Skybolt	Skybolt Group

Reg.	Type	Owner or Operator	Notes
G-SBOL	Steen Skybolt	M. P. Barley	
G-SBRK	Aero AT-3 R100	Sywell Aerodrome Ltd	
G-SBUS	BN-2A-26 Islander	Isles of Scilly Skybus Ltd (G-BMMH)	
G-SCAN	Vinten-Wallis WA-116/100	K. H. Wallis	
G-SCBI	SOCATA TB20 Trinidad	Ace Services	
G-SCCZ	CZAW Sportcruiser	J. W. Ellis	
G-SCHI	AS.350B2 Ecureuil	Patriot Aviation Ltd	
G-SCHO	Robinson R22 Beta	Blades Aviation (UK) LLP	
G-SCHZ	Eurocopter AS.355N Ecureuil II	Veritair Aviation Ltd (G-STON)	
G-SCII	Agusta A109C	Plattreid Ltd (G-JONA)	
G-SCIP	SOCATA TB20 Trinidad GT	The Studio People Ltd	
G-SCLX	FLS Aerospace Sprint 160	E. J. F. McEntee (G-PLYM)	
G-SCNN	Schempp-Hirth Standard Cirrus	G. C. Short	
G-SCOL	Gippsland GA-8 Airvan	Parachuting Aircraft Ltd	
G-SCPD	Escapade 912 (1)	R. K. W. Moss	
G-SCPI	CZAW Sportcruiser	I. M. Speight & P. R. W. Goslin	
G-SCPL	PA-28 Cherokee 140	Aeros Leasing Ltd (G-BPVL)	
G-SCRZ	CZAW Sportcruiser	P. H. Grant	
G-SCSC	CZAW Sportcruiser	G-SCSC Group	
G-SCTA	Westland Scout AH.1	G. R. Harrison	
G-SCUB	PA-18 Super Cub 135 (542447)	M. E. Needham	
G-SCUL	Rutan Cozy	K. R. W. Scull	
G-SCVF	Czech Sprt Aircraft Sportcruiser	V. Flintham	
G-SCZR	CZAW Sportcruiser	R. Manning	
G-SDAT	Flight Design CTSW	CTSW Alfa Tango Group	
G-SDCI	Bell 206B JetRanger 2	S. D. Coomes (G-GHCL/G-SHVV)	
G-SDEC	American Champion 8KCAB	D. Boag	
G-SDEV	DH. 104 Sea Devon C.20 (XK895)	Aviation Heritage Ltd	
G-SDFM	Aerotechnik EV-97 Eurostar	G-SDFM Group	
G-SDNI	VS.361 Spitfire LF.IX E	P. M. Andrews	
G-SDOB	Tecnam P2002-EA Sierra	S. P. S. Dornan	
G-SDOI	Aeroprakt A.22 Foxbat	S. A. Owen	
G-SDOZ	Tecnam P92-EA Echo Super	Cumbernauld Flyers G-SDOZ	
G-SEAI	Cessna U.206G (amphibian)	K. O'Conner	
G-SEAT	Colt 42A balloon	Virgin Balloon Flights	
G-SEBN	Skyranger 912S(1)	C. M. James	
G-SEDO	Cameron N-105 balloon	Wye Valley Aviation Ltd	
G-SEED	Piper J-3C-65 Cub	J. H. Seed	
G-SEEE	Pegasus Quik GT450	I. M. Spence	
G-SEEK	Cessna T.210N	A. Hopper	
G-SEHK	Cessna 182T	S. Holland	
G-SEJW	PA-28-161 Warrior II	Premier Flight Training Ltd	
G-SELA	Cessna 152	L. W. Scattergood (G-FLOP)	
G-SEGA	Cameron Sonic 90 SS balloon	M. E. White	
G-SELB	PA-28-161 Warrior II	L. W. Scattergood (G-LFSK)	
G-SELC	Diamond DA42 Twin Star	Stapleford Flying Club Ltd	
G-SELF	Shaw Europa	N. D. Crisp & ptnrs	
G-SELL	Robin DR.400/180	C. R. Beard Farmers Ltd	
G-SELY	Agusta-Bell 206B JetRanger 3	DSC North Ltd	
G-SEMI	PA-44-180 Seminole	J. Benfield & M. Djukic (G-DENW)	
G-SEMR	Cessna T206H Turbo Stationair	Semer LLP	
G-SENA	Rutan LongEz	G. Bennett	
G-SEND	Colt 90A balloon	Air du Vent/France	
G-SENE	PA-34-200T Seneca II	M. O'Hara	
G-SENS	Eurocopter EC.135T2+	Saville Air Services	
G-SENT	Bombardier BD700-1A10 Global Express	Royal Scot Leasing Ltd	
G-SENX	PA-34-200T Seneca II	First Air Ltd (G-DARE/G-WOTS/G-SEVL)	
G-SEPT	Cameron N-105 balloon	A. G. Merry	
G-SERE	Diamond DA42 Twin Star	Sere Ltd	
G-SERL	SOCATA TB10 Tobago	D. J. Hawes (G-LANA)	
G-SERV	Cameron N-105 balloon	PSH Skypower Ltd	
G-SESA	RAF SE.5A 75 replica	D. J. Calvert	
G-SETI	Cameron Sky 80-16 balloon	R. P. Allan	
G-SEUK	Cameron TV-80 ss balloon	Mobberley Balloon Collection	
G-SEVA	SE-5A (replica) (F141:G)	I. D. Gregory	
G-SEVE	Cessna 172N	MK Aero Support Ltd	
G-SEVN	Van's RV-7	N. Reddish	
G-SEXE	Scheibe SF.25C Falke	SF25C G-SESE Syndicate	
G-SEXX	PA-28-161 Warrior II	Weald Air Services Ltd	

Notes	Reg.	Type	Owner or Operator
	G-SEXY	AA-1 Yankee ★	Jetstream Club, Liverpool Marriott Hotel South, Speke (G-AYLM)
	G-SFAR	Ikarus C42 FB100	Hadair
	G-SFLA	Ikarus C42 FB80	Solent Flight Ltd
	G-SFLB	Ikarus C42 FB80	Solent Flight Ltd
	G-SFLY	Diamond DA40 Star	L. & N. P. L. Turner
	G-SFPB	Cessna F.406	Reims Aviation Industries SA/France
	G-SFRY	Thunder Ax7-77 balloon	M. Rowlands
	G-SFSL	Cameron Z-105 balloon	A. J. Gregory
	G-SFTZ	Slingsby T.67M Firefly 160	Western Air (Thruxton) Ltd
	G-SGEN	Ikarus C.42 FB 80	G. A. Arturi
	G-SGRP	Agusta AW.109SP Grand New	WA Developments International Ltd
	G-SGSE	PA-28-181 Archer II	U. Patel (G-BOJX)
	G-SHAA	Enstrom 280-UK	C. J. Vincent
	G-SHAF	Robinson R44 II	Tresillian Leisure Ltd
	G-SHAK	Cameron Cabin SS balloon	Magical Adventures Ltd (G-ODIS)
	G-SHAL	Bombardier CL-600-2B19	TAG Aviation (UK) Ltd
	G-SHAN	Robinson R44 II	M. Herzog
	G-SHAR	Cessna 182T Skylane	J. E. R. Gardner
	G-SHAY	PA-28R-201T Turbo Arrow III	Alpha Yankee Flying Group (G-BFDG/G-JEFS)
	G-SHBA	Cessna F.152	Paul's Planes Ltd
	G-SHED	PA-28-181 Archer II	G-SHED Flying Group (G-BRAU)
	G-SHEE	P & M Quik GT450	L. Cottle
	G-SHEZ	Mainair Pegasus Quik	R. Wells
	G-SHHH	Glaser-Dirks DG-100G	P. J. Masson
	G-SHIM	CFM Streak Shadow	K. R. Anderson
	G-SHIP	PA-23 Aztec 250F ★	Midland Air Museum/Coventry
	G-SHMI	Evektor EV-97 Team EuroStar UK	Poet Pilot (UK) Ltd
	G-SHMK	Cirrus SR22T	Avicon
	G-SHOG	Colomban MC.15 Cri-Cri	K. D. & C. S. Rhodes (G-PFAB)
	G-SHOW	MS.733 Alycon	J. Wesson
	G-SHRK	Enstrom 280C-UK	Flighthire Ltd/Belgium (G-BGMX)
	G-SHRN	Schweizer 269C-1	CSL Industrial Ltd
	G-SHRT	Robinson R44 II	Air and Ground Aviation Ltd
	G-SHSH	Shaw Europa	S. G. Hayman & J. Price
	G-SHSP	Cessna 172S	Shropshire Aero Club Ltd
	G-SHUC	Rans S-6-ESD Coyote II	T. A. England (G-MYKN)
	G-SHUF	Mainair Blade	G. Holdcroft
	G-SHUG	PA-28R-201T Turbo Arrow III	G-SHUG Ltd
	G-SHUU	Enstrom 280C-UK-2	Startrade GmbH/Germany (G-OMCP/G-KENY/ G-BJFG)
	G-SHUV	Aerosport Woody Pusher	J. R. Wraigh
	G-SHWK	Cessna 172S	Cambridge Aero Club Ltd
	G-SIAI	SIAI-Marchetti SF.260W	Air Training Services
	G-SIBK	Raytheon Beech A36 Bonanza	B. & S. J. Shaw
	G-SICA	BN-2B-20 Islander	Shetland Leasing and Property Development Ltd (G-SLAP)
	G-SICB	BN-2B-20 Islander	Shetlands Islands Council (G-NESU/G-BTVN)
	G-SIGN	PA-39 Twin Comanche 160 C/R	D. Buttle
	G-SIIE	Christen Pitts S-2B Special	J. & T. J. Bennett (G-SKYD)
	G-SIII	Extra EA.300	J. E. Probert
	G-SIIS	Pitts S-1S Special	R. P. Marks (G-RIPE)
	G-SIJJ	North American P-51D-NA Mustang (472035)	P. A. Teichman
	G-SIJW	SA Bulldog Srs 120/121 (XX630:5)	M. Miles
	G-SILS	Pietenpol Skyscout	D. Silsbury
	G-SILY	Pegasus Quantum 15	S. D. Sparrow
	G-SIMI	Cameron A-315 balloon	Balloon Safaris
	G-SIMM	Ikarus C.42 FB 100 VLA	D. Simmons
	G-SIMP	Avtech Jabiru SP	A. C. A. Hayes
	G-SIMS	Robinson R22 Beta	Heli Air Ltd
	G-SIMY	PA-32-300 Cherokee Six	I. Simpson (G-OCPF/G-BOCH)
	G-SINK	Schleicher ASH-25	G-SINK Group
	G-SIPA	SIPA 903	A. C. Leak & G. S. Dilland (G-BGBM)
	G-SIPP	Lindstrand Ibl-35a Cloudhopper balloon	N. Bourke
	G-SIRD	Robinson R44 II	Peglington Productions Ltd
	G-SIRE	Best Off Sky Ranger Swift 912S(1)	A. B. King
	G-SIRO	Dassault Falcon 900EX	Condor Aviation LLP

BRITISH CIVIL REGISTRATIONS

Reg.	Type	Owner or Operator	Notes
G-SIRS	Cessna 560XL Citation Excel	London Executive Aviation Ltd	
G-SISI	Schempp-Hirth Duo Discus	Glider Sierra India	
G-SISU	P & M Quik GT450	Executive and Business Aviation Support Ltd	
G-SITA	Pegasus Quantum 15-912	A. F. S. McDougall	
G-SIVJ	Westland Gazelle HT.2	Skytrace (UK) Ltd (G-CBSG)	
G-SIVK	MBB Bolkow Bo.105DBS-4	C. J. Siva-Jothy (G-PASX)	
G-SIVR	MDH MD.900 Explorer	C. J. Siva-Jothy	
G-SIVW	Lake LA-250 Renegade	C. J. Siva-Jothy	
G-SIXC	Douglas DC-6B★	The DC-6 Diner/Coventry	
G-SIXD	PA-32 Cherokee Six 300D	M. B. Paine & I. Gordon	
G-SIXG	AutoGyro MTO Sport	K. O. Maurer	
G-SIXT	PA-28-161 Warrior II	Booker Aircraft Leasing Ltd (G-BSSX)	
G-SIXX	Colt 77A balloon	S. Drawbridge	
G-SIXY	Van's RV-6	C. J. Hall & C. R. P. Hamlett	
G-SIZZ	Jabiru J400	K. J. Betteley	
G-SJBI	Pitts S-2C Special	S. L. Walton	
G-SJCH	BN-2T-4S Defender 4000	Hampshire Police Authority (G-BWPK)	
G-SJES	Evektor EV-97 TeamEurostar UK	Purple Aviation Ltd	
G-SJKR	Lindstrand LBL-90A balloon	S. J. Roake	
G-SJMH	Robin DR.400-140B	C. S. & J. A. Bailey	
G-SJPI	Dynamic WT9 UK	S. J. Phillips	
G-SJSS	Bombardier CL600-2B16	TAG Aviation (UK) Ltd	
G-SKAN	Cessna F.172M	M. Richardson & J. Williams (G-BFKT)	
G-SKAZ	Aero AT-3 r100	G-SKAZ Flying Group	
G-SKCI	Rutan Vari-Eze	C. Hannan	
G-SKEN	Cessna 182T	Kenward Orthopaedic Ltd	
G-SKEW	Mudry CAP-232	J. H. Askew	
G-SKIE	Steen Skybolt	K. G. G. Howe and M. J. Coles	
G-SKKY	Cessna 172S Skyhawk	J. Herbert & G. P. Turner	
G-SKNT	Pitts S-2A	First Light Aviation Ltd (G-PEAL)	
G-SKOT	Cameron V-42 balloon	S. A. Laing	
G-SKPG	Best Off Skyranger 912 (2)	T. Farncombe	
G-SKPH	Yakovlev Yak-50	R. S. Partridge-Hicks & I. C. Austin (G-BWWH)	
G-SKPP	Eurocopter EC.120B Colbri	Bournemouth Helicopters Ltd (G-MKII)	
G-SKRA	Best Off Skyranger 912S (1)	P. A. Banks	
G-SKRG	Best Off Skyranger 912 (2)	I. D. Town	
G-SKSW	Best Off Sky Ranger Swift 912S	M. D. & S. M. North	
G-SKUA	Stoddard-Hamilton Glastar	F. P. Smiddy (G-LEZZ/G-BYCR)	
G-SKYC	Slingsby T.67M Firefly	T. W. Cassells (G-BLDP)	
G-SKYE	Cessna TU.206G	RAF Sport Parachute Association	
G-SKYF	SOCATA TB10 Tobago	W. L. McNeil	
G-SKYJ	Cameron Z-315 balloon	Cameron Flights Southern Ltd	
G-SKYK	Cameron A-275 balloon	Cameron Flights Southern Ltd	
G-SKYL	Cessna 182S	Skylane Aviation Ltd	
G-SKYN	AS.355F1 Twin Squirrel	Arena Aviation Ltd (G-OGRK/G-BWZC/G-MODZ)	
G-SKYO	Slingsby T.67M-200	R. H. Evelyn	
G-SKYR	Cameron A-180 balloon	Cameron Flights Southern Ltd	
G-SKYT	I.I.I. Sky Arrow 650TC	W. M. Bell & S. J. Brooks	
G-SKYU	Cameron A-210 balloon	Cameron Flights Southern Ltd	
G-SKYV	PA-28RT-201T Turbo Arrow IV	North Yorks Properties Ltd (G-BNZG)	
G-SKYW	AS355F1	Skywalker Aviation Ltd (G-BTIS/G-TALI)	
G-SKYX	Cameron A-210 balloon	Cameron Flights Southern Ltd	
G-SKYY	Cameron A-275 balloon	Cameron Flights Southern Ltd	
G-SLAC	Cameron N-77 balloon	A. Barnes	
G-SLAK	Thruster T.600N 450	M. P. Williams (G-CBXH)	
G-SLAR	Agusta A109C	MW Helicopters Ltd (G-OWRD/G-USTC/G-LAXO)	
G-SLCE	Cameron C-80 balloon	A. M. Holly	
G-SLCT	Diamond DA42NG Twin Star	Stapleford Flying Club Ltd	
G-SLEA	Mudry/CAARP CAP-10B	M. J. M. Jenkins & N. R. Thorburn	
G-SLII	Cameron O-90 balloon	J. Edwards	
G-SLIP	Easy Raider	D. R. Squires	
G-SLMG	Diamond HK.36 TTC Super Dimona	G-SLMG Syndicate	
G-SLNM	EV-97 TeamEurostar UK	N. W. Mayes	
G-SLNT	Flight Design CTSW	K. Kirby	
G-SLNW	Robinson R22 Beta	Heli-4 Charter LLP (G-LNIC)	
G-SLYN	PA-28-161 Warrior II	Flew LLP	
G-SMAN	Airbus A.330-243	Monarch Airlines Ltd	

Notes	Reg.	Type	Owner or Operator
	G-SMAS	BAC.167 Strikemaster 80A (1104)	M. A. Petrie
	G-SMBM	Pegasus Quantum 15-912	P. A. Henretty
	G-SMDH	Shaw Europa XS	S. W. Pitt
	G-SMDJ	AS.350B2 Ecureuil	Denis Ferranti Hovernights Ltd
	G-SMIG	Cameron O-65 balloon	R. D. Parry
	G-SMIL	Lindstrand LBL-105A balloon	A. L. Wade
	G-SMLI	Groppo Trail	A. M. Wilson
	G-SMMA	Cessna F.406 Caravan II	Secretary of State for Scotland per Environmental and Rural Affairs Department
	G-SMMB	Cessna F.406 Caravan II	Secretary of State for Scotland per Environmental and Rural Affairs Department
	G-SMRS	Cessna 172F	M. R. Sarling
	G-SMRT	Lindstrand LBL-260A balloon	Cameron Flights Southern Ltd
	G-SMTH	PA-28 Cherokee 140	R. W. Harris & A. Jahanfar (G-AYJS)
	G-SMYK	PZL-Swidnik PW-5 Smyk	PW-5 Syndicate
	G-SNAL	Cessna 182T	N. S. Lyndhurst
	G-SNEV	CFM Streak Shadow SA	J. D. Reed
	G-SNIF	Cameron A-300 balloon	A. C. K. Rowson & Sudoni
	G-SNOG	Kiss 400-582 (1)	B. H. Ashman
	G-SNOP	Shaw Europa	V. F. Flett (G-DESL/G-WWWG)
	G-SNOW	Cameron V-77 balloon	I. Welsford
	G-SNOZ	Shaw Europa	P. O. Bayliss (G-DONZ)
	G-SNSA	Agusta AW139	CHC Scotia Ltd
	G-SNSB	Agusta AW139	CHC Scotia Ltd
	G-SNUZ	PA-28-161 Warrior II	Freedom Aviation Ltd
	G-SNZY	Learjet 45	European Skyjets Ltd
	G-SOAF	BAC.167 Strikemaster Mk. 82A (425)	Strikemaster Flying Club
	G-SOAR	Eiri PIK-20E	L. J. Kaye
	G-SOAY	Cessna T.303	Wrekin Construction Co Ltd
	G-SOBI	PA-28-181 Archer II	G-SOBI Flying Group
	G-SOCK	Mainair Pegasus Quik	K. R. McCartney
	G-SOCT	Yakovlev Yak-50 (AR-B)	C. R. Turton
	G-SOHO	Diamond DA40D Star	Soho Aviation Ltd
	G-SOKO	Soko P-2 Kraguj (30149)	P. C. Avery (G-BRXK)
	G-SOLA	Aero Designs Star-Lite SL.1	G. P. Thomas
	G-SONA	SOCATA TB10 Tobago	J. Freeman (G-BIBI)
	G-SONE	Cessna 525A Citationjet	CJ 525 Ltd
	G-SONX	Sonex	M. Chambers
	G-SOOA	Cessna172S	Goodwood Road Racing Co.Ltd
	G-SOOC	Hughes 369HS	R.J.H. Strong (G-BRRX)
	G-SOOS	Colt 21A balloon	P. J. Stapley
	G-SOOT	PA-28 Cherokee 180	J. A. Bridger (G-AVNM)
	G-SOPH	Skyranger 912(2)	S. Marathe
	G-SORA	Glaser-Dirks DG.500/22	C. A. Boyle, C. P. Arthur, B. Douglas & R. Jackson
	G-SOUL	Cessna 310R	Reconnaissance Ventures Ltd
	G-SOVB	Learjet 45	Murray Air Ltd (G-OLDJ)
	G-SPAM	Avid Aerobat (modified)	M. Durcan
	G-SPAO	Eurocopter EC135	Bond Air Services Ltd
	G-SPAT	Aero AT-3 R100	S2T Aero Ltd
	G-SPCZ	CZAW Sportcruiser	R. J. Robinson
	G-SPDR	DH.115 Sea Vampire T.22 (N6-766)	M. J. Cobb
	G-SPDY	Raj Hamsa X'Air Hawk	G. H. Gilmour-White
	G-SPED	Alpi Pioneer 300	C. F. Garrod
	G-SPEE	Robinson R22 Beta	Heliclub de laValle du Loing (G-BPJC)
	G-SPEL	Sky 220-24 balloon	Cameron Flights Southern Ltd
	G-SPEY	Agusta-Bell 206B JetRanger 3	Castle Air Ltd (G-BIGO)
	G-SPFX	Rutan Cozy	B. D. Tutty
	G-SPHU	Eurocopter EC 135T2+	Bond Air Services Ltd
	G-SPIN	Pitts S-2A Special	P. Avery
	G-SPIP	SNCAN Stampe SV.4C	A. G. & P. M. Solleveld (G-BTIO)
	G-SPIT	VS.379 Spitfire FR.XIV (MV268)	Patina Ltd (G-BGHB)
	G-SPJE	Robinson R44 II	Abel Alarm Co.Ltd
	G-SPMM	Best Off Sky Ranger Swift 912S(1)	L. Chesworth & M. L. Sumner
	G-SPOG	Jodel DR.1050	G-SPOG Group (G-AXVS)
	G-SPTR	Robinson R44 II	Heli Air Ltd
	G-SPUR	Cessna 550 Citation II	London Executive Aviation Ltd
	G-SPUT	Yakovlev Yak-52	N. J. Stillwell (G-BXAV)
	G-SPVK	AS.350B3 Ecureuil	Stratos Aviation LLP (G-CERU)

Reg.	Type	Owner or Operator	Notes
G-SPXX	VS.356 Spitfire F.22	P. R. Arnold	
G-SPYS	Robinson R44 II	SKB Partners LLP	
G-SRAH	Schempp-Hirth Mini-Nimbus C	P. Hawkins	
G-SRBN	Embraer EMB-500 Phenom 100	Hangar 8 Management Ltd	
G-SRDG	Dassault Falcon 7X	Triair (Bermuda) Ltd	
G-SRII	Easy Raider 503	K. Myles	
G-SROE	Westland Scout AH.1 (XP907)	Saunders-Roe Helicopter Ltd	
G-SRPH	Robinson R44	Rooney Helicopter Hire	
G-SRRA	Tecnam P2002-EA Sierra	J. Dunn	
G-SRTT	Cirrus SR22	S. A. Breslaw	
G-SRUM	Aero AT-3 R100	Medcentres Property Portfolio Ltd	
G-SRVO	Cameron N-90 balloon	Servo & Electronic Sales Ltd	
G-SRVY	Partenavia P.68 Observer 2	C Aviation Ltd	
G-SRWN	PA-28-161 Warrior II	S. Smith (G-MAND/G-BRKT)	
G-SRYY	Shaw Europa XS	I. O'Brien	
G-SRZZ	Cirrus SR22	M. P. Bowcock	
G-SSCL	MDH Hughes 369E	Shaun Stevens Contractors Ltd	
G-SSDR	Scooter	J. Attard	
G-SSIX	Rans S.6-116 Coyote II	R. I. Kelly	
G-SSKY	BN-2B-26 Islander	Isles of Scilly Skybus Ltd (G-BSWT)	
G-SSLM	Cessna 510 Citation Mustang	M. Richardson	
G-SSRD	Balony Kubicek BB17XR balloon	A. M. Holly	
G-SSSC	Sikorsky S-76C	CHC Scotia Ltd	
G-SSSD	Sikorsky S-76C	CHC Scotia Ltd	
G-SSSE	Sikorsky S-76C	CHC Scotia Ltd	
G-SSTI	Cameron N-105 balloon	A. A. Brown	
G-SSWV	Sportavia Fournier RF-5B	Fournier Flying Group	
G-STAV	Cameron O-84 balloon	Blenheim Scout Group	
G-STAY	Cessna FR.172K	J. M. Wilkins	
G-STBA	Boeing 777-336ER	British Airways	
G-STBB	Boeing 777-36NER	British Airways	
G-STBC	Boeing 777-36NER	British Airways	
G-STBD	Boeing 777-36NER	British Airways	
G-STBE	Boeing 777-36NER	British Airways	
G-STBF	Boeing 777-336ER	British Airways	
G-STBY	Flylight MotorFloater	A. G. Bramley	
G-STCH	Fiesler Fi 156A-1 Storch (GM+AI)	P. R. Holloway	
G-STDL	Phillips ST.2 Speedtwin	Speedtwin Developments Ltd (G-DPST)	
G-STEA	PA-28R Cherokee Arrow 200	D. W. Breden	
G-STEE	EV-97 Eurostar	S. G. Beeson	
G-STEM	Stemme S.10V	G-STEM Group	
G-STEN	Stemme S.10 (4)	G-STEN Syndicate	
G-STEP	Schweizer 269C	M. Johnson	
G-STEU	Rolladen-Schneider LS6-18W	F. K. Russell	
G-STEV	Jodel DR.221	S. W. Talbot	
G-STGR	Agusta 109S Grand	A. W. Jenkinson	
G-STHA	PA-31-350 Navajo Chieftain	Hinde Holdings Ltd (G-GLUG/G-BLOE/G-NITE)	
G-STIN	TL 2000UK Sting Carbon	N. A. Smith	
G-STIX	Van's RV-7	R. D. S. Jackson	
G-STME	Stemme S 10-VT	R. A. Roberts	
G-STMP	SNCAN Stampe SV.4A	A. C. Thorne	
G-STMT	Dassault Falcon 7X	TAG Aviation (UK) Ltd	
G-STNG	TL2000UK Sting Carbon	Geesting 3 Syndicate	
G-STNR	IDA Bacau Yakovlev Yak-52	S. M. Norman (G-BWOD)	
G-STNS	Agusta A109A-II	Patriot Flight Training Ltd	
G-STOD	ICP MXP-740 Savannah VG Jabiru(1)	S. B. Todd	
G-STOK	Colt 77B balloon	A. C. Booth	
G-STOO	Stolp Starduster Too	K. F. Crumplin	
G-STOP	Robinson R44 Raven II	HLQ Services Ltd/Ireland	
G-STOW	Cameron 90 Wine Box SS balloon	Flying Enterprises	
G-STPI	Cameron A-210 balloon	The Ballooning Business Ltd	
G-STPK	Lambert Mission M108	S. T. P. Kember	
G-STRG	Cyclone AX2000	Pegasus Flight Training (Cotswolds)	
G-STRK	CFM Streak Shadow SA	E. J. Hadley	
G-STRL	AS.355N Twin Squirrel	Harrier Enterprises Ltd	
G-STSN	Stinson 108-3 Voyager	M. S. Colebrook (G-BHMR)	
G-STUA	Aerotek Pitts S-2A Special (modified)	G-STUA Group	
G-STUB	Christen Pitts S-2B Special	A. F. D. Kingdon	
G-STUF	Learjet 40	Concierge Aviation Ltd	

Notes	Reg.	Type	Owner or Operator
	G-STUI	Pitts S-2AE	S. L. Goldspink
	G-STUN	TL2000UK Sting Carbon	D. Russell (G-KEVT)
	G-STUY	Robinson R44 II	Central Helicopters Ltd
	G-STVT	CZAW Sportcruiser	S. Taylor
	G-STWO	ARV Super 2	P. M. Paul
	G-STZZ	TL2000UK Sting Carbon	W. R. Field
	G-SUAU	Cameron C-90 balloon	A. Heginbottom
	G-SUCH	Cameron V-77 balloon	D. G. Such (G-BIGD)
	G-SUCK	Cameron Z-105 balloon	R. P. Wade
	G-SUCT	Robinson R22	Irwin Plant Sales
	G-SUEB	PA-28-181 Archer III	Curtis Moore Aviation Ltd
	G-SUED	Thunder Ax8-90 balloon	E. C. Lubbock & S. A. Kidd (G-PINE)
	G-SUEI	Diamond DA.42 Twin Star	Sue Air
	G-SUEL	P & M Quik GT450	J. M. Ingram
	G-SUER	Bell 206B JetRanger	Aerospeed Ltd (G-CBYX)
	G-SUET	Bell 206B JetRanger	Aerospeed Ltd (G-BLZN)
	G-SUEW	Airbus A.320-214	Thomas Cook Airlines Ltd
	G-SUEX	Agusta-Bell 206B JetRanger 2	Aerospeed Ltd (G-AYBC/G-BTWW)
	G-SUEY	Bell 206L-1 Long Ranger	Aerospeed Ltd
	G-SUEZ	Agusta-Bell 206B JetRanger 2	Aerospeed Ltd
	G-SUFK	Eurocopter EC 135P2+	West Yorkshire Police Authority
	G-SUGA	Embraer EMB-135BJ Legacy 650	Amsair Aircraft Ltd
	G-SUKY	P & M Quik R	S. J. Reid
	G-SUMX	Robinson R22 Beta	J. A. Bickerstaffe
	G-SUMZ	Robinson R44 II	Frankham Bros Ltd
	G-SUNN	Robinson R44	R. Purchase
	G-SUPA	PA-18 Super Cub 150	R. D. Masters
	G-SURG	PA-30 Twin Comanche 160B	A. R. Taylor (G-VIST/G-AVHG)
	G-SURY	Eurocopter EC 135T2	West Yorkshire Police Authority
	G-SUSE	Shaw Europa XS	P. R. Tunney
	G-SUSI	Cameron V-77 balloon	J. H. Dryden
	G-SUSX	MDH MD-902 Explorer	West Yorkshire Police Authority
	G-SUTD	Jabiru UL-D	W. J. Lister
	G-SUTN	I.I.I. Sky Arrow 650TC	D. J. Goldsmith
	G-SUZN	PA-28-161 Warrior II	St. George Flight Training Ltd
	G-SVAS	PA-18-150 Super Cub	Richard Shuttleworth Trustees
	G-SVDG	Jabiru SK	R. Tellegen
	G-SVEA	PA-28-161 Warrior II	G-SVEA Group
	G-SVEN	Centrair 101A Pegase	G7 Group
	G-SVET	Yakovlev Yak-50	Yak-50 Group
	G-SVEY	Vulcanair P-68TC Observer 2	C Aviation Ltd
	G-SVIP	Cessna 421B Golden Eagle II	R. P. Bateman
	G-SVIV	SNCAN Stampe SV.4C	J. E. Keighley
	G-SVNC	Rolladen-Schneider LS4	M. C. Jenkins
	G-SVNX	Dassault Falcon 7X	Executive Jet Charter Ltd
	G-SVPN	PA-32R-301T Turbo Saratoga	LAC Marine Ltd
	G-SWAK	Oldfield Baby Lakes	A. G. Fowles
	G-SWAT	Robinson R44 II	Unique Helicopters (NI) Ltd
	G-SWAY	PA-18-150 Super Cub	R. Lillywhite
	G-SWCT	Flight Design CTSW	J. A. Shufflebotham
	G-SWEE	Beech 95-B55 Baron	Orman (Carrolls Farm) Ltd (G-AZDK)
	G-SWEL	Hughes 369HS	M. A. Crook & A. E. Wright (G-RBUT)
	G-SWIF	VS.541 Swift F.7 (XF114) ★	Solent Sky, Southampton
	G-SWIG	Robinson R44	S. Goddard
	G-SWIP	Silence Twister	Zulu Glasstek Ltd (G-RIOT)
	G-SWLL	Aero AT-3 R100	Sywell Aerodrome Ltd
	G-SWON	Pitts S-1S Special	S. L. Goldspink
	G-SWOT	Currie Wot (C3011:S)	P. N. Davis
	G-SWSW	Schempp-Hirth Ventus bT	R. Kalin
	G-SWYM	CZAW Sportcruiser	R. W. Beal
	G-SXIX	Rans S.19	J. L. Almey
	G-SXTY	Learjet 60	TAG Aviation (UK) Ltd
	G-SYCO	Europa	P. J. Tiller
	G-SYEL	Aero AT-3 R100	Sywell Aerodrome Ltd
	G-SYFW	Focke-Wulf Fw.190 replica (2+1)	J. C. Metcalf
	G-SYGA	Beech B200 Super King Air	Synergy Aircraft Leasing Ltd (G-BPPM)
	G-SYLJ	Embraer RJ135BJ	TAG Aviation (UK) Ltd

Reg.	Type	Owner or Operator	Notes
G-SYLV	Cessna 208B Grand Caravan	WAS Aircraft Leasing Ltd	
G-SYNA	Embraer EMB-135BJ Legacy 650	Etlagh Aviation Ltd (G-VILP)	
G-SYPS	MDH MD.900 Explorer	South Yorkshire Police Authority	
G-SYWL	Aero AT-3 R100	Sywell Aerodrome Ltd	
G-TAAB	Cirrus SR22	TAA UK Ltd	
G-TAAC	Cirrus SR20	TAA UK Ltd	
G-TABB	Schempp-Hirth Ventus 2cT	G. Tabbner	
G-TABS	EMB-110P1 Bandeirante	Alan Mann Aviation Group Ltd (G-PBAC)	
G-TACK	Grob G.109B	A. P. Mayne	
G-TAFC	Maule M7-2358 Super Rocket	The Amphibious Flying Club Ltd	
G-TAFF	CASA 1.131E Jungmann 1000	R. A. Fleming (G-BFNE)	
G-TAFI	Bücker Bü 133C Jungmeister	R. P. Lamplough	
G-TAGE	Bombardier CL600-2B16 Challenger	Aviation (UK) Ltd	
G-TAGF	Dassault Falcon 900DX	TAG Aviation (UK) Ltd	
G-TAGK	Dassault Falcon 900DX	TAG Aviation (UK) Ltd	
G-TAGR	Europa	C. G. Sutton	
G-TAJF	Lindstrand LBL-77A balloon	T. A. J. Fowles	
G-TAKE	AS.355F1 Ecureuil II	Arena Aviation Ltd (G-OITN)	
G-TALA	Cessna 152 II	Tatenhill Aviation Ltd (G-BNPZ)	
G-TALB	Cessna 152 II	Tatenhill Aviation Ltd (G-BORO)	
G-TALC	Cessna 152	Tatenhill Aviation Ltd (G-BPBG)	
G-TALD	Cessna F.152	Tatenhill Aviation Ltd (G-BHRM)	
G-TALE	PA-28-181 Archer II	Tatenhill Aviation Ltd (G-BJOA)	
G-TALF	PA-24-250 Comanche	Tatenhill Aviation Ltd (G-APUZ)	
G-TALG	PA-28-151 Warrior	Tatenhill Aviation Ltd (G-BELP)	
G-TALH	PA-28-181 Archer II	Tatenhill Aviation Ltd (G-CIFR)	
G-TALJ	Grumman AA-5 Traveler	Tatenhill Aviation Ltd (G-BBUE)	
G-TALN	Rotorway A600 Talon	Southern Helicopters Ltd	
G-TAMC	Schweizer 269D	Alan Mann Aviation Group Ltd	
G-TAMD	Schweizer 269D	Elmridge Ltd	
G-TAMR	Cessna 172S	Caledonian Air Surveys Ltd	
G-TAMS	Beech A23-24 Musketeer Super	Aerograde Ltd	
G-TANA	Tanarg 912S(2)/Ixess 15	A. P. Marks	
G-TANG	Tanarg 912S(2)/Ixess 15	N. L. Stammers	
G-TANJ	Raj Hamsa X'Air 582(5)	M. M. & P. M. Stoney	
G-TANK	Cameron N-90 balloon	D. J., A. H. & A. M. Mercer	
G-TANS	SOCATA TB20 Trinidad	B. J. Ryan	
G-TANY	EAA Acrosport 2	P. J. Tanulak	
G-TAPE	PA-23 Aztec 250D	Ravenair Aircraft Ltd	
G-TAPS	PA-28RT-201T Turbo Arrow IV	P. G. Doble	
G-TARN	Pietenpol Air Camper	P. J. Heilbron	
G-TARR	P & M Quik	A. Edwards	
G-TART	PA-28-236 Dakota	N. K. G. Prescot	
G-TASH	Cessna 172N (modified)	N. Pletl	
G-TASK	Cessna 404	Reconnaissance Ventures Ltd	
G-TATO	Robinson R22	Skyrunner Aviation Ltd	
G-TATR	Replica Travelair R Type	R. A. Seeley	
G-TATS	AS.350BA Ecureuil	T. J. Hoare	
G-TATT	Gardan GY-20 Minicab	Tatt's Group	
G-TAWA	Boeing 737-8K5	Thomson Airways Ltd	
G-TAWB	Boeing 737-8K5	Thomson Airways Ltd	
G-TAWC	Boeing 737-8K5	Thomson Airways Ltd	
G-TAWD	Boeing 737-8K5	Thomson Airways Ltd	
G-TAWF	Boeing 737-8K5	Thomson Airways Ltd	
G-TAWG	Boeing 737-8K5	Thomson Airways Ltd	
G-TAWH	Boeing 737-8K5	Thomson Airways Ltd	
G-TAWI	Boeing 737-8K5	Thomson Airways Ltd	
G-TAWJ	Boeing 737-8K5	Thomson Airways Ltd	
G-TAWK	Boeing 737-8K5	Thomson Airways Ltd	
G-TAWL	Boeing 737-8K5	Thomson Airways Ltd	
G-TAYC	Gulfstream G450	TAG Aviation (UK) Ltd	
G-TAYI	Grob G.115	K. P. Widdowson & K. Hackshall (G-DODO)	
G-TAYL	Pitts S-1S Special	R. S. Taylor	
G-TAZZ	Dan Rihn DR.107 One Design	N. J. Riddin	
G-TBAE	BAe 146-200	BAE Systems (Corporate Travel Ltd) (G-HWPB/G-BSRU/G-OSKI/G-JEAR)	
G-TBAG	Murphy Renegade II	M. R. Tetley	
G-TBBC	Pegasus Quantum 15-912	J. Horn	
G-TBEA	Cessna 525A Citation CJ2	Centreline Air Charter Ltd	
G-TBGT	SOCATA TB10 Tobago GT	P. G. Sherry & A. J. Simmonds	

Notes	Reg.	Type	Owner or Operator
	G-TBHH	AS355F2 Twin Squirrel	Alpha Properties (London) Ltd (G-HOOT/ G-SCOW/G-POON/G-MCAL)
	G-TBIO	SOCATA TB10 Tobago	R. G. L. Solomon and J. S. Ritchie
	G-TBJP	Mainair Pegasus Quik	R. J. Price
	G-TBLB	P & M Quik GT450	B. L. Benson
	G-TBLY	Eurocopter EC 120B	AD Bly Aircraft Leasing Ltd
	G-TBMR	P & M Aviation Quik GT450	B. Robertson
	G-TBMW	Murphy Renegade Spirit	S. J. & M. J. Spavins (G-MYIG)
	G-TBOK	SOCATA TB10 Tobago	TB10 Ltd
	G-TBSV	SOCATA TB20 Trinidad GT	Condron Concrete Ltd
	G-TBTB	Robinson R44	H S (Holdings) Ltd (G-CDUN)
	G-TBTN	SOCATA TB10 Tobago	Airways International Ltd (G-BKIA)
	G-TBUK	AA-5A Cheetah	T. M. Buick (G-PADD/G-ESTE/G-GHNC)
	G-TBXX	SOCATA TB20 Trinidad	Aeroplane Ltd
	G-TBZO	SOCATA TB20 Trinidad	R. P. Lewis
	G-TCAC	Airbus A.320-232	Thomas Cook Airlines Ltd (G-ERAA)
	G-TCAD	Airbus A.320-214	Thomas Cook Airlines Ltd
	G-TCAL	Robinson R44 II	C. M. Gough-Cooper
	G-TCAN	Colt 69A balloon	H. C. J. Williams
	G-TCAS	Cameron Z-275 balloon	The Ballooning Business Ltd
	G-TCBB	Boeing 757-236	Thomas Cook Airlines Ltd
	G-TCBC	Boeing 757-236	Thomas Cook Airlines Ltd
	G-TCCA	Boeing 767-31K	Thomas Cook Airlines Ltd (G-SJMC)
	G-TCCB	Boeing 767-31KER	Thomas Cook Airlines Ltd (G-DIMB)
	G-TCDA	Airbus A.321-211	Thomas Cook Airlines Ltd (G-JOEE)
	G-TCEE	Hughes 369HS	Aviation Styling Ltd (G-AZVM)
	G-TCHI	VS.509 Spitfire Tr.9	M. B. Phillips
	G-TCHO	VS Spitfire Mk.IX	B. Phillips
	G-TCHZ	VS.329 Spitfire IIA	M. B. Phillips
	G-TCNM	Tecnam P92-EA Echo	F. G. Walker
	G-TCNY	Mainair Pegasus Quik	L. A. Maynard
	G-TCTC	PA-28RT-200 Arrow IV	P. Salemis
	G-TCUB	Piper J-3C-65 Cub (modified)	C. Kirk
	G-TCXA	Airbus A.330-243	Thomas Cook Airlines Ltd
	G-TDJN	North American AT-6D Harvard III	D. J. Nock
	G-TDKI	CZAW Sportcruiser	D. R. Kendall
	G-TDOG	SA Bulldog Srs 120/121 (XX538:O)	G. S. Taylor
	G-TDRA	Cessna 172S Skyhawk	TDR Aviation Ltd
	G-TDSA	Cessna F.406 Caravan II	Nor Leasing
	G-TDVB	Dyn' Aero MCR-01ULC	D. V. Brunt
	G-TDYN	Aerospool Dynamic WT9 UK	A. A. & L. J. Rice
	G-TEBZ	PA-28R-201 Arrow III	Smart People Don't Buy Ltd
	G-TECA	Tecnam P2002-JF	Aeros Holdings Ltd
	G-TECC	Aeronca 7AC Champion	N. J. Orchard-Armitage
	G-TECH	Rockwell Commander 114	A. S. Turner (G-BEDH)
	G-TECI	Tecnam P2002-JF	Polarb Air Ltd
	G-TECK	Cameron V-77 balloon	M. W. A. Shemilt
	G-TECM	Tecnam P92-EM Echo	N. G. H. Staunton
	G-TECO	Tecnam P92-EM Echo	A. N. Buchan
	G-TECS	Tecnam P2002-EA Sierra	D. A. Lawrence
	G-TECT	Tecnam P2006T	Polarb Air Ltd
	G-TEDB	Cessna F.150L	P. S. Buckland (G-AZLZ)
	G-TEDI	Best Off Skyranger J2.2(1)	J. E. McGee
	G-TEDW	Kiss 450-582 (2)	S. S. Pratt
	G-TEDY	Evans VP-1	N. K. Marston (G-BHGN)
	G-TEFC	PA-28 Cherokee 140	Foxtrot Charlie Flyers
	G-TEGS	Bell 206B JetRanger III	E. Drinkwater
	G-TEHL	CFM Streak Shadow	L. T. Flower (G-MYJE)
	G-TEKK	Tecnam P2006T	Aeros Holdings Ltd
	G-TELC	Rotorsport UK MT-03	C. M. Jones
	G-TELY	Agusta A109A-II	Castle Air Ltd
	G-TEMB	Tecnam P2000-EA Sierra	M. B. Hill
	G-TEMP	PA-28 Cherokee 180	F. Busch International Ltd (G-AYBK)
	G-TEMT	Hawker Tempest II (MW763)	Tempest Two Ltd
	G-TENG	Extra EA.300/L	D. McGinn
	G-TENT	Auster J/1N Alpha	R. Callaway-Lewis (G-AKJU)
	G-TERA	Vulcanair P68 Observer 2	APEM Aviation Ltd
	G-TERN	Shaw Europa	J. Smith
	G-TERR	Mainair Pegasus Quik	T. R. Thomas

Reg.	Type	Owner or Operator	Notes
G-TERY	PA-28-181 Archer II	J. R. Bratherton (G-BOXZ)	
G-TESI	Tecnam P2002 EA Sierra	C. C. Burgess	
G-TESR	Tecnam P2002-RG Sierra	Tecnam UK Ltd	
G-TEST	PA-34-200 Seneca	Stapleford Flying Club Ltd (G-BLCD)	
G-TEWS	PA-28-140 Cherokee	D. Barron & S. G. Brown (G-KEAN/G-AWTM)	
G-TEXN	North American T-6G Texan (3072:72)	Spitfire Display Ltd (G-BHTH)	
G-TEZZ	CZAW Sportcruiser	T. D. Baker	
G-TFIX	Mainair Pegasus Quantum 15-912	T. G. Jones	
G-TFLX	P & M Quik GT450	L. A. Wood	
G-TFLY	Air Creation Kiss 450-582 (1)	A. J. Ladell	
G-TFOG	Best Off Skyranger 912(2)	T. J. Fogg	
G-TFOX	Denney Kitfox Mk.2	T. W. Hopferwieser	
G-TFRB	Air Command 532 Elite	F. R. Blennerhassett	
G-TFUN	Valentin Taifun 17E	North West Taifun Group	
G-TFYN	PA-32RT-300 Lance II	R. C. Poolman	
G-TGER	AA-5B Tiger	D. T. Pangbourne (G-BFZP)	
G-TGGR	Eurocopter EC 120B	Messiah Corporation Ltd	
G-TGRA	Agusta A109A	Tiger Helicopters Ltd	
G-TGRD	Robinson R22 Beta II	Tiger Helicopters Ltd (G-OPTS)	
G-TGRE	Robinson R22A	Tiger Helicopters Ltd (G-SOLD)	
G-TGRS	Robinson R22 Beta	Tiger Helicopters Ltd (G-DELL)	
G-TGRZ	Bell 206B JetRanger 3	Tiger Helicopters Ltd (G-BXZX)	
G-TGTT	Robinson R44 II	Air'Opale (G-STUS)	
G-TGUN	Aero AT-3 R100	Medcentres Property Portfolio Ltd	
G-THAT	Raj Hamsa X'Air Falcon 912 (1)	E. E. Colley	
G-THEO	TEAM mini-MAX 91	G. Evans	
G-THFC	Embraer RJ135BJ Legacy	Raz Air Ltd (G-RRAZ/G-RUBN)	
G-THFW	Bell 206B-3 JetRanger III	Fly Heli Wales Ltd	
G-THIN	Cessna FR.172E	I. C. A. Ussher (G-BXYY)	
G-THLA	Robinson R22 Beta	Thurston Helicopters Ltd & J. W. F. Tuke	
G-THOM	Thunder Ax-6-56 balloon	T. H. Wilson	
G-THOC	Boeing 737-59D	TAG Aviation (Stansted) Ltd (G-BVKA)	
G-THOP	Boeing 737-3U3	Aircraft Finance Trust Ireland Ltd	
G-THOT	Avtech Jabiru SK	S. G. Holton	
G-THRE	Cessna 182S	J. P. Monjalet	
G-THRM	Schleicher ASW-27	C. G. Starkey (G-CJWC)	
G-THSL	PA-28R-201 Arrow III	D. M. Markscheffe	
G-TIAC	Tiger Cub RL5A LW Sherwood Ranger	The Light Aircraft Co.Ltd	
G-TICH	Taylor JT.2 Titch	R. Davitt	
G-TIDS	Jodel 150	M. R. Parker	
G-TIDY	Best Off Sky Ranger Nynja 912S(1)	P. Rigby	
G-TIFG	Ikarus C42 FB80	The Ikarus Flying Group	
G-TIGA	DH.82A Tiger Moth	D. E. Leatherland (G-AOEG)	
G-TIGC	AS.332L Super Puma	Bristow Helicopters Ltd (G-BJYH)	
G-TIGE	AS.332L Super Puma	Bristow Helicopters Ltd (G-BJYJ)	
G-TIGF	AS.332L Super Puma	Vector Aerospace Financial Services Ireland Ltd	
G-TIGJ	AS.332L Super Puma	Vector Aerospace Financial Services Ireland Ltd	
G-TIGS	AS.332L Super Puma	Bristow Helicopters Ltd	
G-TIGV	AS.332L Super Puma	Bristow Helicopters Ltd	
G-TIII	Aerotek Pitts S-2A Special	Treble India Group	
G-TILE	Robinson R22 Beta	Fenland Helicopters Ltd	
G-TIMB	Rutan Vari-Eze	P. G. Kavanagh (G-BKXJ)	
G-TIMC	Robinson R44	T. Clark Aviation LLP (G-CDUR)	
G-TIMH	Robinson R22	Central Helicopters Ltd	
G-TIMK	PA-28-181 Archer II	Minimal Risk Consultancy Ltd	
G-TIMM	Folland Gnat T.1 (XM693)	Heritage Aircraft Ltd	
G-TIMP	Aeronca 7BCM Champion	R. B. Valler	
G-TIMS	Falconar F-12A	T. Sheridan	
G-TIMX	Head AX8-88B balloon	T. S. Crowdy	
G-TIMY	Gardan GY-80 Horizon 160	R. G. Whyte	
G-TINA	SOCATA TB10 Tobago	A. Lister	
G-TINK	Robinson R22 Beta	Airtask Group PLC	
G-TINS	Cameron N-90 balloon	J. R. Clifton	
G-TINT	Aerotechnik EV-97 Team Eurostar UK	I. A. Cunningham	
G-TINY	Z.526F Trener Master	D. Evans	
G-TIPJ	Cameron Z-77 balloon	J. R. Lawson	
G-TIPS	Nipper T.66 Srs.3	F. V. Neefs	
G-TIVS	Rans S.6-ES Coyote II	A. P. Michell	

Notes	Reg.	Type	Owner or Operator
	G-TIVV	Aerotechnik EV-97 Team Eurostar UK	I. Shulver
	G-TJAG	PA-34-220T Seneca V	Morgan Airborne LLP
	G-TJAL	Jabiru SPL-430	D. W. Cross
	G-TJAV	Mainair Pegasus Quik	D. Allan & J. Hunter
	G-TJAY	PA-22 Tri-Pacer 135	D. Pegley
	G-TJDM	Van's RV-6A	J. D. Michie
	G-TKAY	Shaw Europa	A. M. Kay
	G-TKEV	P & M Quik R	O. P. Gall
	G-TKIS	Tri-R Kis	T. J. Bone
	G-TKNO	UltraMagic S-50 balloon	P. Dickinson
	G-TLAC	Sherwood Ranger ST	The Light Aircraft Co.Ltd
	G-TLDL	Medway SLA 100 Executive	D. T. Lucas
	G-TLET	PA-28-161 Cadet	ADR Aviation (G-GFCF/G-RHBH)
	G-TLFK	Cessna 680 Citation Sovereign	International Jetclub Ltd
	G-TLOY	Alpi Pioneer 400	A. R. Lloyd
	G-TLST	TL 2000UK Sting Carbon	I. Foster
	G-TLTL	Schempp-Hirth Discus CS	E. K. Armitage
	G-TMAN	Roadster/Adventure Funflyer Quattro	P. A. Mahony
	G-TMAX	Evektor EV-97 Sportstar Max	Cosmik Aviation Ltd
	G-TMCB	Best Off Skyranger 912 (2)	J. R. Davis
	G-TMCC	Cameron N-90 balloon	M. S. Jennings
	G-TMRB	Short SD3-60 Variant 100	HD Air Ltd (G-SSWB/G-BMLE)
	G-TNGO	Van's RV-6	R. Marsden
	G-TNJB	P & M Quik R	C. J. Shorter
	G-TNRG	Tanarg/Ixess 15 912S(2)	J. W. Mann
	G-TNTN	Thunder Ax6-56 balloon	H. M. Savage & J. F. Trehern
	G-TOAD	Jodel D.140B	J. H. Stevens & J. Whittle
	G-TOBA	SOCATA TB10 Tobago	E. Downing
	G-TOBI	Cessna F.172K	TOBI Group (G-AYVB)
	G-TODD	ICA IS-28M2A	C. I. Roberts & C. D. King
	G-TODG	Flight Design CTSW	S. J. Sykes
	G-TOFT	Colt 90A balloon	C. S. Perceval
	G-TOGO	Van's RV-6	I. R. Thomas
	G-TOHS	Cameron V-31 balloon	J. P. Moore
	G-TOLI	Robinson R44 II	Coleman Cantle Partnership
	G-TOLL	PA-28R-201 Arrow III	Arrow Aircraft Ltd
	G-TOLS	Robinson R44	K. N. Tolley (G-CBOT)
	G-TOLY	Robinson R22 Beta	Helicopter Services Ltd (G-NSHR)
	G-TOMC	NA AT-6D Harvard III	A. A. Marshall
	G-TOMJ	Flight Design CT2K	K. Brown
	G-TOMX	MCR-01 VLA Sportster	P. T. Knight
	G-TOMZ	Denney Kitfox Mk.2	S. J. Spavins
	G-TONE	Pazmany PL-4	P. I. Morgans
	G-TONN	Mainair Pegasus Quik	D. R. Richards
	G-TOOB	Schempp-Hirth Discus 2b	M. F. Evans
	G-TOOL	Thunder Ax8-105 balloon	D. V. Howard
	G-TOPB	Cameron Z-140 balloon	Anana Ltd
	G-TOPC	AS.355F1 Twin Squirrel	Kinetic Avionics Ltd
	G-TOPK	Shaw Europa XS	P. J. Kember
	G-TOPO	PA-23-250 Turbo Aztec	Blue Sky Investments Ltd (G-BGWW)
	G-TOPS	AS.355F1 Twin Squirrel	Sterling Helicopters (G-BPRH)
	G-TORC	PA-28R Cherokee Arrow 200	Haimoss Ltd
	G-TORE	P.84 Jet Provost T.3A ★	Instructional airframe/City University, Islington
	G-TORI	Zenair CH.701SP	M. J. Maddock (G-CCSK)
	G-TORK	Cameron Z-105 balloon	M. E. Dunstan-Sewell
	G-TORN	Flight Design CTSW	J. A. Moss
	G-TOSH	Robinson R22 Beta	Heli Air Ltd
	G-TOTN	Cessna 210M	Quay Financial Strategies Ltd (G-BVZM)
	G-TOTO	Cessna F.177RG	TOTO Flying Group (G-OADE/G-AZKH)
	G-TOUR	Robin R.2112	A. Carnegie
	G-TOWS	PA-25 Pawnee 260	Lasham Gliding Society Ltd
	G-TOYD	Boeing 737-33V	bmi Baby (G-EZYT) (stored)
	G-TOYF	Boeing 737-36N	bmi Baby (G-IGOO/G-SMDB) (stored)
	G-TOYG	Boeing 737-36N	bmi Baby (G-IGOJ) (stored)
	G-TOYH	Boeing 737-36N	bmi Baby (G-IGOY) (stored)
	G-TOYI	Boeing 737-3Q8	bmi Baby (stored)

Reg.	Type	Owner or Operator	Notes
G-TOYJ	Boeing 737-36M	bmi Baby (stored)	
G-TOYK	Boeing 737-33R	bmi Baby (stored)	
G-TOYL	Boeing 737-36N	bmi Baby (G-THOL/G-IGOK) (stored)	
G-TOYM	Boeing 737-36Q	bmi Baby (G-OHAJ) (stored)	
G-TOYZ	Bell 206B JetRanger 3	Potter Aviation Ltd (G-RGER)	
G-TPAL	P & M Aviation Quik GT450	R. Robertson	
G-TPSL	Cessna 182S	A. N. Purslow	
G-TPSY	Champion 8KCAB Super Decathlon	G. R. Potts (G-CEOE)	
G-TPTP	Robinson R44	A. N. Purslow	
G-TPWL	P & M Quik GT450	The G-TPWL Group	
G-TPWX	Heliopolis Gomhouria Mk.6 (TP+WX)	W. H. Greenwood	
G-TRAC	Robinson R44	C. J. Sharples	
G-TRAM	Pegasus Quantum 15-912	G-TRAM Group	
G-TRAN	Beech 76 Duchess	Multiflight Ltd (G-NIFR)	
G-TRAT	Pilatus PC-12/45	Flew LLP	
G-TRAW	Augusta A.109E	Castle Air Ltd	
G-TRAX	Cessna F.172M	Skytrax Aviation Ltd	
G-TRBO	Schleicher ASW-28-18E	A. Cluskey	
G-TRCY	Robinson R44	Sugarfree Air Ltd	
G-TREC	Cessna 421C	Sovereign Business Integration PLC (G-TLOL)	
G-TREE	Bell 206B JetRanger 3	Bush Woodlands	
G-TREK	Jodel D.18	R. H. Mole	
G-TREX	Alpi Pioneer 300	S. R. Winter	
G-TRIB	Lindstrand LBL HS-110 airship	S. L. Bell	
G-TRIC	DHC.1 Chipmunk 22 (18013:013)	C. B. Dominguez (G-AOSZ)	
G-TRIG	Cameron Z-90 balloon	Hedge Hoppers Balloon Group	
G-TRIM	Monnett Moni	E. A. Brotherton-Ratcliffe	
G-TRIN	SOCATA TB20 Trinidad	M. Hardy & M. J. Porter	
G-TRJB	Beech A36 Bonanza	G. A. J. Bowles	
G-TRNG	Agusta A109E Power	Castle Air Ltd (G-NWOY/G-JMXA)	
G-TROY	NA T-28A Fennec (51-7692)	S. G. Howell & S. Tilling	
G-TRTM	DG Flugzeugbau DG-808C	D. T. S. Walsh	
G-TRUE	MDH Hughes 369E	N. E. Bailey	
G-TRUK	Stoddard-Hamilton Glasair RG	M. P. Jackson	
G-TRUX	Colt 77A balloon	Servowarm Baloon Syndicate	
G-TRYK	Kiss 400-582 (1)	M. P. Sanderson	
G-TRYX	Enstrom 480B	Atryx Aviation LLP	
G-TSAC	Tecnam P2002-EA Sierra	A. G. Cozens	
G-TSDS	PA-32R-301 Saratoga SP	I. R. Jones (G-TRIP/G-HOSK)	
G-TSGA	PA-28R-201 Arrow III	TSG Aviation Ltd (G-ONSF/G-EMAK)	
G-TSGJ	PA-28-181 Archer II	Golf Juliet Flying Club	
G-TSHO	Ikarus C42 FB80	A. P. Shoobert	
G-TSIM	Titan T-51 Mustang	B. J. Chester-Master	
G-TSIX	AT-6C Harvard IIA (111836:JZ-6)	Century Aviation Ltd	
G-TSJF	Cessna 525B CitationJet CJ3	Lunar Jet Ltd	
G-TSKD	Raj Hamsa X'Air Jabiru J.2.2.	T. Sexton & K. B. Dupuy	
G-TSKS	EV-97 TeamEurostar UK	Purple Aviation Ltd	
G-TSKY	Beagle B.121 Pup 2	R. G. Hayes (G-AWDY)	
G-TSLC	Schweizer 269C-1	Bournemouth Helicopters Ltd	
G-TSLS	Bombardier BD700-1A11 Global 5000	Oryx Jet Ltd	
G-TSOB	Rans S.6-ES Coyote II	S. Luck	
G-TSOL	EAA Acrosport 1	J. A. Wojda (G-BPKI)	
G-TSUE	Shaw Europa	H. J. C. Maclean	
G-TSWI	Lindstrand LBL-90A balloon	R. J. Gahan	
G-TSWZ	Cameron Z-77 balloon	Group 1st Ltd	
G-TTAT	ICP MXP-740 Savannah VG Jabiru(1)	A. N. Green	
G-TTDD	Zenair CH.701 STOL	D. B. Dainton & V. D. Asque	
G-TTFG	Colt 77B balloon	T. J. & M. J. Turner (G-BUZF)	
G-TTOB	Airbus A.320-232	British Airways PLC	
G-TTOE	Airbus A.320-232	British Airways PLC	
G-TTOY	CFM Streak Shadow SA	J. Softley	
G-TTRL	Van's RV-9A	J. E. Gattrell	
G-TUBB	Avtech Jabiru UL	A. H. Bower	
G-TUCK	Van's RV-8	N. G. R. Moffat	
G-TUGG	PA-18 Super Cub 150	Ulster Gliding Club Ltd	
G-TUGI	CZAW Sportcruiser	T. J. Wilson	
G-TUGS	PA-25-235 Pawnee D	J. A. Stephen (G-BFEW)	

Notes	Reg.	Type	Owner or Operator
	G-TUGY	Robin DR.400/180	TUGY Group
	G-TUGZ	Robin DR.400/180R	Buckminster Gliding Club Ltd
	G-TUNE	Robinson R22 Beta	Heli Air Ltd (G-OJVI)
	G-TURF	Cessna F.406	Reconnaissance Ventures Ltd
	G-TUTU	Cameron O-105 balloon	A. C. K. Rawson & J. J. Rudoni
	G-TVAM	MBB Bo105DBS-4	South Georgis Heritage Trust (G-SPOL)
	G-TVBF	Lindstrand LBL-310A balloon	Virgin Balloons Flights
	G-TVCO	Gippsland GA-8 Airvan	Zyox Ltd
	G-TVHB	Eurocopter EC 135 P2+	West Yorkshire Police Authority
	G-TVHD	AS.355F2 Ecureuil 2	Arena Aviation Ltd
	G-TVII	Hawker Hunter T.7 (XX467:86)	G-TVII Group/Exeter
	G-TVIJ	CCF Harvard IV (T-6J) (28521:TA-521)	R. W. Davies (G-BSBE)
	G-TVSI	Campbell Cricket Replica	C. Smith
	G-TWAZ	Rolladen-Schneider LS7-WL	S. Derwin
	G-TWEL	PA-28-181 Archer II	International Aerospace Engineering Ltd
	G-TWEY	Colt 69A balloon	N. Bland
	G-TWIN	PA-44-180 Seminole	Transport Command Ltd
	G-TWIS	Silence Twister	C. S. & K. D. Rhodes
	G-TWIZ	Rockwell Commander 114	B. C. & P. M. Cox
	G-TWLV	Van's RV-12	G-TWLV Group
	G-TWNN	Beech 76 Duchess	Folada Aero and Technical Services Ltd
	G-TWOA	Schempp-Hirth Discus 2a	P. Krumm
	G-TWOC	Schempp-Hirth Ventus 2cT	D. Heslop
	G-TWOO	Extra EA.300/200	Skyboard Aerobatics Ltd (G-MRKI)
	G-TWOP	Cessna 525A Citationjet CJ2	Centreline Air Charter Ltd (G-ODAG)
	G-TWRL	Pitts S-1S Special	C. Dennis
	G-TWSR	Silence Twister	J. A. Hallam
	G-TWSS	Silence Twister	A. P. Hatton
	G-TWTR	Robinson R44 II	Heli Aviation Ltd
	G-TWTW	Denney Kitfox Mk.2	R. M. Bremner
	G-TXAN	AT-6D Harvard III (FX301)	P. J. Lawton (G-JUDI)
	G-TYAK	IDA Bacau Yakovlev Yak-52	S. J. Ducker
	G-TYER	Robin DR.400/500	Robin Group
	G-TYGA	AA-5B Tiger	G-TYGA Group (G-BHNZ)
	G-TYGR	Best Off Skyranger 912S (1)	M. J. Poole
	G-TYKE	Avtech Jabiru UL-450	D. R. Harper
	G-TYMO	DH.82A Tiger Moth	N. Rose
	G-TYNA	PA-28-181 Archer II	Winged Bull Aviation
	G-TYNE	SOCATA TB20 Trinidad	N. V. Price
	G-TYPH	BAe.146-200	BAE Systems (Corporate Air Travel) Ltd (G-BTVT)
	G-TYRE	Cessna F.172M	J. S. C. English
	G-TZEE	SOCATA TB10 Tobago	Zytech Ltd
	G-TZII	Thorp T.211B	M. J. Newton
	G-UACA	Skyranger R.100(2)	R. G. Hicks
	G-UAKE	NA P-51D-5-NA Mustang	P. S. Warner
	G-UANO	DHC.1 Chipmunk 22	Advanced Flight Training Ltd (G-BYYW)
	G-UANT	PA-28 Cherokee 140	Air Navigation & Trading Co Ltd
	G-UAPA	Robin DR.400/140B	Fluirdados Sociedade Aeronautica/Portugal
	G-UAPO	Ruschmeyer R.90-230RG	P. Randall
	G-UART	Moravan Zlin Z-242L	Oxford Aviation Academy (Oxford) Ltd (G-EKMN)
	G-UAVA	PA-30 Twin Comanche	Small World Aviation Ltd
	G-UCAM	PA-31-350 Navajo Chieftain	Blue Sky Investments Ltd (G-NERC/G-BBXX)
	G-UCCC	Cameron 90 Sign SS balloon	Unipart Group of Companies Ltd
	G-UCLU	Schleicher ASK-21	University College London Union
	G-UDET	Replica Fokker E.111	M. J. Clark
	G-UDGE	Thruster T.600N	G-UDGE Syndicate (G-BYPI)
	G-UDMS	PA-46R-350T Malibu Matrix	J. C. M. Critchley & S. Harding
	G-UDOG	SA Bulldog Srs 120/121 (XX518:S)	M. van den Broek
	G-UFAW	Raj Hamsa X'Air 582 (5)	P. Batchelor
	G-UFCB	Cessna 172S	The Cambridge Aero Club Ltd
	G-UFCF	Cessna 172S	Innovative Converged Devices Ltd

Reg.	Type	Owner or Operator	Notes
G-UFCG	Cessna 172S	Ulster Flying Club (1961) Ltd	
G-UFCH	Cessna 172S	Air-Unlimited Sweden AB/Sweden	
G-UFCI	Cessna 172S	Ulster Flying Club (1961) Ltd	
G-UFCL	Tecnam P2002-JF Sierra	Ulster Flying Club (1961) Ltd	
G-UFCM	Tecnam P2002-JF Sierra	Ulster Flying Club (1961) Ltd	
G-UFLY	Cessna F.150H	Westair Flying Services Ltd (G-AVVY)	
G-UFOE	Grob G.115	Swiftair Maintenance Ltd	
G-UFOX	Aeropro Eurofox 912	G-UFOX Group	
G-UHGB	Bell 205A-1	Heli-Lift Services	
G-UHIH	Bell UH-1H Iroquois (21509)	MSS Holdings Ltd	
G-UHOP	UltraMagic H-31 balloon	S. J. Roake	
G-UIKR	P & M Quik R	A. M. Sirant	
G-UILA	Aquila AT01	Aquila Sport Aeroplanes LLP	
G-UILD	Grob G.109B	K. Butterfield	
G-UILE	Lancair 320	R. J. Martin	
G-UILT	Cessna T.303	D. L. Tucker (G-EDRY)	
G-UIMB	Guimbal Cabri G2	Helitrain Ltd	
G-UINN	Stolp SA.300 Starduster Too	J. D. H. Gordon	
G-UJAB	Avtech Jabiru UL	C. A. Thomas	
G-UJGK	Avtech Jabiru UL	W. G. Upton & J. G. Kosak	
G-UKAW	Agusta A.109E	Agusta Westland Ltd	
G-UKOZ	Avtech Jabiru SK	D. J. Burnett	
G-UKPS	Cessna 208 Caravan 1	UK Parachute Services Ltd	
G-UKRB	Colt 105A balloon	Virgin Airship & Balloon Co Ltd	
G-UKUK	Head Ax8-105 balloon	P. A. George	
G-ULAS	DHC.1 Chipmunk 22 (WK517)	ULAS Flying Club Ltd/Denham	
G-ULES	AS.355F2 Twin Squirrel	Select Plant Hire Company Ltd (G-OBHL/-HARO/G-DAFT/G-BNNN)	
G-ULHI	SA Bulldog Srs.100/101	Power Aerobatics Ltd (G-OPOD/G-AZMS)	
G-ULIA	Cameron V-77 balloon	J. T. Wilkinson	
G-ULPS	Everett Srs 1 gyroplane	C. J. Watkinson (G-BMNY)	
G-ULSY	Ikarus C.42 FB 80	B. W. Rooke	
G-ULTA	Ultramagic M-65C	G. A. Board	
G-ULTR	Cameron A-105 balloon	P. Glydon	
G-UMAS	Rotorsport UK MT-03	BAE Systems (Operations) Ltd	
G-UMBO	Thunder Ax7-77A balloon	Virgin Airship & Balloon Co Ltd	
G-UMBY	Hughes 369E	HQ Aviation Ltd	
G-UMKA	Dassault Falcon 7X	Hyperion Aviation Ltd	
G-UMMI	PA-31-310 Turbo Navajo	2 Excel Aviation Ltd (G-BGSO)	
G-UMMS	EV-97 TeamEurostar UK	A. C. Lees (G-ODRY)	
G-UMMY	Best Off Skyranger J2.2(2)	A. R. Williams	
G-UMPY	Shaw Europa	GDBMK Ltd	
G-UNDD	PA-23 Aztec 250E	G. J. & D. P. Deadman (G-BATX)	
G-UNER	Lindstrand LBL-90A balloon	St. Dunstans	
G-UNES	Van's RV-6	C. A. Greatrex	
G-UNGE	Lindstrand LBL-90A balloon	Silver Ghost Balloon Club (G-BVPJ)	
G-UNGO	Pietenpol Air Camper	A. R. Wyatt	
G-UNIN	Schempp-Hirth Ventus b	U9 Syndicate	
G-UNIV	Montgomerie-Parsons 2-seat gyroplane	University of Glasgow (G-BWTP)	
G-UNIX	VPM M16 Tandem Trainer	A. P. Wilkinson	
G-UNKY	Ultramagic S-50 balloon	A. M. Holly	
G-UNNA	Jabiru UL-450WW	N. D. A. Graham	
G-UNRL	Lindstrand LBL-RR21 balloon	Alton Aviation Ltd	
G-UORO	Shaw Europa	D. Dufton	
G-UPFS	Waco UPS-7	D. N. Peters & N. R. Finlayson	
G-UPHI	Best Off Skyranger Swift 912S(1)	Flylight Airsports Ltd	
G-UPID	Bowers Fly Baby 1A	R. D. Taylor	
G-UPOI	Cameron TR-84 S1 balloon	Beatwax Ltd	
G-UPTA	Skyranger 912S (1)	S. J. Joseph	
G-UPUP	Cameron V-77 balloon	S. F. Burden/Netherlands	
G-UPUZ	Lindstrand LBL-120A balloon	C.J. Sanger-Davies	
G-UROP	Beech 95-B55 Baron	S. C. Smith	

Notes	Reg.	Type	Owner or Operator
	G-URRR	Air Command 582 Sport	L. Armes
	G-URRU	Bombardier CL600-2B16 Challenger	Executive Jet Charter Ltd
	G-URSA	Sikorsky S-76C	Premiair Aviation Services Ltd (G-URSS)
	G-URUH	Robinson R44	Heli Air Ltd
	G-USAA	Cessna F.150G	A. Naish (G-OIDW)
	G-USAR	Cessna 441 Conquest	I. Annenskiy
	G-USIL	Thunder Ax7-77 balloon	Window On The World Ltd
	G-USKY	Aviat A-1B Husky	L. W. H. Griffith
	G-USMC	Cameron Chestie 90 SS balloon	J. W. Soukup
	G-USRV	Van's RV-6	W. D. Garlick & R. J. Napp
	G-USSY	PA-28-181 Archer II	The Leicestershire Aero Club Ltd
	G-USTH	Agusta A109A-II	Stratton Motor Co.(Norfolk) Ltd
	G-USTS	Agusta A109A-II	MB Air Ltd (G-MKSF)
	G-USTY	FRED Srs 2	I. Pearson
	G-UTRA	Ultramagic M-77 balloon	Ultrait Ltd
	G-UTSI	Rand-Robinson KR-2	K. B. Gutridge
	G-UTSY	PA-28R-201 Arrow III	J. P. Quoniam
	G-UTZI	Robinson R44 II	S. K. Miles/Spain
	G-UURO	Aerotechnik EV-97 Eurostar	Romeo Oscar Syndicate
	G-UVBF	Lindstrand LBL-400A balloon	Virgin Balloon Flights
	G-UVIP	Cessna 421C	MM Air Ltd (G-BSKH)
	G-UVNR	BAC.167 Strikemaster Mk 87	P. Turek (G-BXFS)
	G-UYAD	Bombardier CL600-2B16	Coldstream SARL/Luxembourg
	G-UYFI	Eurocopter EC120B Colibri	Papa Fly Ltd
	G-UZLE	Colt 77A balloon	G. B. Davies
	G-UZUP	Aerotechnik EV-97A Eurostar	G-UZUP EV-97 Flying Group
	G-VAAC	PA-28-181 Archer III	J. N. D. de Jager (G-CCDN)
	G-VAAV	P & M Quik R	A. Voyce
	G-VAIR	Airbus A.340-313	Virgin Atlantic Airways Ltd *Maiden Tokyo*
	G-VALS	Pietenpol Air Camper	J. R. D. Bygraves
	G-VALY	SOCATA TB21 Trinidad GT Turbo	R. J. Thwaites and Westflight Aviation Ltd
	G-VALZ	Cameron N-120 balloon	J. D. & K. Griffiths
	G-VANA	Gippsland GA-8 Airvan	P. Marsden
	G-VANC	Gippsland GA-8 Airvan	Irish Skydiving Club Ltd
	G-VAND	Gippsland GA-8 Airvan	Irish Skydiving Club Ltd
	G-VANN	Van's RV-7A	D. N. & J. A. Carnegie
	G-VANS	Van's RV-4	R. J. Marshall
	G-VANX	Gippsland GA-8 Airvan	Airkix Aircraft Ltd
	G-VANZ	Van's RV-6A	S. J. Baxter
	G-VARG	Varga 2150A Kachina	J. Denton
	G-VAST	Boeing 747-41R	Virgin Atlantic Airways Ltd *Ladybird*
	G-VATL	Airbus A.340-642	Virgin Atlantic Airways Ltd *Miss Kitty,born October 2003*
	G-VBAA	Cameron A-400 balloon	Virgin Balloon Flights
	G-VBAB	Cameron A-400 balloon	Virgin Balloon Flights
	G-VBAD	Cameron A-300 balloon	Virgin Balloon Flights
	G-VBAE	Cameron A-400 balloon	Virgin Balloon Flights
	G-VBCA	Cirrus SR22	C. A. S. Atha
	G-VBFA	Ultramagic N-250 balloon	Virgin Balloon Flights
	G-VBFB	Ultramagic N-355 balloon	Virgin Balloon Flights
	G-VBFC	Ultramagic N-250 balloon	Virgin Balloon Flights
	G-VBFD	Ultramagic N-250 balloon	Virgin Balloon Flights
	G-VBFE	Ultramagic N-255 balloon	Virgin Balloon Flights
	G-VBFF	Lindstrand LBL-360A balloon	Virgin Balloon Flights
	G-VBFG	Cameron Z-350 balloon	Virgin Balloon Flights
	G-VBFH	Cameron Z-350 balloon	Virgin Balloon Flights
	G-VBFI	Cameron Z-350 balloon	Virgin Balloon Flights
	G-VBFJ	Cameron Z-350 balloon	Virgin Balloon Flights
	G-VBFK	Cameron Z-350 balloon	Virgin Balloon Flights
	G-VBFL	Cameron Z-400 balloon	Virgin Balloon Flights
	G-VBFM	Cameron Z-375 balloon	Virgin Balloon Flights
	G-VBFN	Cameron Z-375 balloon	Virgin Balloon Flights
	G-VBFO	Cameron Z-375 balloon	Virgin Balloon Flights
	G-VBFP	Ultramagic N-425 balloon	Virgin Balloon Flights

Reg.	Type	Owner or Operator	Notes
G-VBFR	Cameron Z-375 balloon	Virgin Balloon Flights	
G-VBFS	Cameron Z-375 balloon	Virgin Balloon Flights	
G-VBFT	Cameron Z-375 balloon	Virgin Balloon Flights	
G-VBFU	Cameron A-400 balloon	Virgin Balloon Flights	
G-VBFV	Cameron Z-400 balloon	Virgin Balloon Flights	
G-VBFW	Cameron Z-77 balloon	Virgin Balloon Flights	
G-VBFX	Cameron Z-400 balloon	Virgin Balloon Flights	
G-VBFY	Cameron Z-400 balloon	Virgin Balloon Flights	
G-VBFZ	Cameron A-300 balloon	Virgin Balloon Flights	
G-VBIG	Boeing 747-4Q8	Virgin Atlantic Airways Ltd *Tinkerbelle*	
G-VBLU	Airbus A.340-642	Virgin Atlantic Airways Ltd *Soul Sister*	
G-VBPM	Cirrus SR22	de Banke Aviation LLP	
G-VBUG	Airbus A.340-642	Virgin Atlantic Airways Ltd	
G-VCIO	EAA Acro Sport II	C. M. Knight	
G-VCJH	Robinson R22 Beta	Time Line International Ltd	
G-VCML	Beech 58 Baron	St. Angelo Aviation Ltd	
G-VCXT	Schempp-Hirth Ventus 2cT	R. F. Aldous/Germany	
G-VDIR	Cessna T.310R	J. Driver	
G-VDOG	Cessna 305C Bird Dog (24582)	D. K. Shead	
G-VECD	Robin R.1180T	B. Lee	
G-VECG	Robin R.2160	I. A. Anderson	
G-VECT	Cessna 560XL Citation Excel	Fly Vectra Ltd	
G-VEGA	Slingsby T.65A Vega	R. A. Rice (G-BFZN)	
G-VEIL	Airbus A.340-642	Virgin Atlantic Airways Ltd *Queen of the Skies*	
G-VEIT	Robinson R44 II	Field Marshall Helicopters Ltd	
G-VELA	SIAI-Marchetti S.205-22R	G-VELA Group	
G-VELD	Airbus A.340-313	Virgin Atlantic Airways Ltd *African Queen*	
G-VELO	Velocity 173RG	J. Bergin	
G-VENC	Schempp-Hirth Ventus 2cT	J. B. Giddins	
G-VENI	DH.112 Venom FB.50 (VV612)	Aviation and Computer Consultancy Ltd	
G-VENM	DH.112 Venom FB.50 (WK436)	Aviation Heritage Ltd (G-BLIE)	
G-VERA	Gardan GY-201 Minicab	D. K. Shipton	
G-VETA	Hawker Hunter T.Mk.7	Viper ClassicS Ltd (G-BVWN)	
G-VETS	Enstrom 280C-UK Shark	B. G. Rhodes (G-FSDC/G-BKTG)	
G-VEYE	Robinson R22	K. A. Jones (G-BPTP)	
G-VEZE	Rutan Vari-Eze	Go Eze Flying	
G-VFAB	Boeing 747-4Q8	Virgin Atlantic Airways Ltd *Lady Penelope*	
G-VFAR	Airbus A.340-313	Virgin Atlantic Airways Ltd *Diana*	
G-VFAS	PA-28R-200 Cherokee Arrow	P. Wood (G-MEAH/G-BSNM)	
G-VFDS	Van's RV-8	S. T. G. Lloyd	
G-VFIT	Airbus A.340-642	Virgin Atlantic Airways Ltd *Dancing Queen*	
G-VFIZ	Airbus A.340-642	Virgin Atlantic Airways Ltd *Bubbles*	
G-VFOX	Airbus A.340-642	Blue Aviation Ltd	
G-VGAG	Cirrus SR20 GTS	Alfred Graham Ltd	
G-VGAL	Boeing 747-443	Virgin Atlantic Airways Ltd *Jersey Girl*	
G-VGAS	Airbus A.340-542	Virgin Atlantic Airways Ltd *Varga Girl*	
G-VGBR	Airbus A.330-343	Virgin Atlantic Airways Ltd	
G-VGEM	Airbus A.330-343	Virgin Atlantic Airways Ltd	
G-VGMC	Eurocopter AS.355N Ecureuil II	Cheshire Helicopters Ltd (G-HEMH)	
G-VGMG	Eurocopter AS.350B Ecureuil II	Lomas Helicopters (G-KELY/G-WKRD/G-BUJG/G-HEAR)	
G-VGOA	Airbus A.340-642	Virgin Atlantic Airways Ltd *Indian Princess*	
G-VGVG	Savannah VG Jabiru(1)	M. A. Jones	
G-VHOT	Boeing 747-4Q8	Virgin Atlantic Airways Ltd *Tubular Belle* ✓	
G-VICC	PA-28-161 Warrior II	Freedom Aviation Ltd (G-JFHL)	
G-VICI	DH.112 Venom FB.50 (J-1573)	Aviation and Computer Consultancy Ltd	
G-VICM	Beech F33C Bonanza	Velocity Engineering Ltd	
G-VICS	Commander 114B	N. Griffin	
G-VICT	PA-31-310 Turbo Navajo	Aviation Leasing ACS (G-BBZI)	
G-VIEW	Vinten-Wallis WA-116/100	K. H. Wallis	
G-VIIA	Boeing 777-236	British Airways	
G-VIIB	Boeing 777-236	British Airways	
G-VIIC	Boeing 777-236	British Airways	
G-VIID	Boeing 777-236	British Airways	
G-VIIE	Boeing 777-236	British Airways	
G-VIIF	Boeing 777-236	British Airways	

Notes	Reg.	Type	Owner or Operator
	G-VIIG	Boeing 777-236	British Airways
	G-VIIH	Boeing 777-236	British Airways
	G-VIIJ	Boeing 777-236	British Airways
	G-VIIK	Boeing 777-236	British Airways
	G-VIIL	Boeing 777-236	British Airways
	G-VIIM	Boeing 777-236	British Airways
	G-VIIN	Boeing 777-236	British Airways
	G-VIIO	Boeing 777-236	British Airways
	G-VIIP	Boeing 777-236	British Airways
	G-VIIR	Boeing 777-236	British Airways
	G-VIIS	Boeing 777-236	British Airways
	G-VIIT	Boeing 777-236	British Airways
	G-VIIU	Boeing 777-236	British Airways
	G-VIIV	Boeing 777-236	British Airways
	G-VIIW	Boeing 777-236	British Airways
	G-VIIX	Boeing 777-236	British Airways
	G-VIIY	Boeing 777-236	British Airways
	G-VIIZ	CZAW Sportcruiser	Skyview Systems Ltd
	G-VIKE	Bellanca 1730A Viking	R. Waas
	G-VIKS	Maule MT-7-235 Super Rocket	V. Sharma
	G-VILA	Avtech Jabiru UL	G. T. Clipstone (G-BYIF)
	G-VILL	Lazer Z.200 (modified)	The G-VILL Group (G-BOYZ)
	G-VINB	Agusta AW.139	Bond Offshore Helicopters Ltd
	G-VINE	Airbus A.330-343	Virgin Atlantic Airways Ltd
	G-VIPA	Cessna 182S	Stallingborough Aviation Ltd
	G-VIPH	Agusta A109C	Cheqair Ltd(G-BVNH/G-LAXO)
	G-VIPI	BAe 125 Srs 800B	Yeates of Leicester Ltd
	G-VIPP	PA-31-350 Navajo Chieftain	Capital Air Charter Ltd
	G-VIPR	Eurocopter EC 120B Colibri	Amey Aviation LLP
	G-VIPU	PA-31-350 Navajo Chieftain	Capital Air Charter Ltd
	G-VIPV	PA-31-350 Navajo Chieftain	Capital Air Charter Ltd
	G-VIPW	PA-31-350 Navajo Chieftain	Capital Air Charter Ltd
	G-VIPX	PA-31-350 Navajo Chieftain	Capital Air Charter Ltd
	G-VIPY	PA-31-350 Navajo Chieftain	Capital Air Charter Ltd
	G-VIRR	Robin DR.400/500	R. A. Walters (G-IYCO)
	G-VIRU	Agusta A109E Power	MRY Ltd
	G-VITA	Dassault Falcon 7X	Casanova Air 7X Ltd
	G-VITE	Robin R.1180T	G-VITE Flying Group
	G-VITL	Lindstrand LBL-105A balloon	Vital Resources
	G-VIVA	Thunder Ax7-65 balloon	R. J. Mitchener
	G-VIVI	Taylor JT.2 Titch	D. G. Tucker
	G-VIVM	P.84 Jet Provost T.5	K. Lyndon-Dykes (G-BVWF)
	G-VIVO	Nicollier HN700 Menestrel II	D. G. Tucker
	G-VIVS	PA-28-151 Cherokee Warrior	S. J. Harrison & V. A. Donnelly
	G-VIXN	DH.110 Sea Vixen FAW.2 (XS587) ★	P. G. Vallance Ltd/Charlwood
	G-VIXX	Alpi Pioneer 300	B. F. Walker (G-CESE/G-CERJ)
	G-VIZA	LBL-260A balloon	A. Nimmo
	G-VIZZ	Sportavia RS.180 Sportsman	Exeter Fournier Group
	G-VJET	Avro 698 Vulcan B.2 (XL426) ★	Vulcan Restoration Trust
	G-VJMJ	Agusta-Bell 206B JetRanger II	Total Digital Solutions Ltd (G-PEAK/G-BLJE)
	G-VKGO	Embraer EMB-500 Phenom 100	M-Kick LP
	G-VKIT	Shaw Europa	T. H. Crow
	G-VKSS	Airbus A.330-343	Virgin Atlantic Airways Ltd *Mademoiselle Rouge*
	G-VKUP	Cameron Z-90 balloon	A. & H. A. Evans
	G-VLCC	Schleicher ASW-27-18E	Viscount Cobham
	G-VLCN	Avro 698 Vulcan B.2 (XH558) ★	Vulcan to the Sky Trust/Bruntingthorpe
	G-VLIP	Boeing 747-443	Virgin Atlantic Airways Ltd *Hot Lips*
	G-VLTT	Diamond DA.42 Twin Star	The Leninton Company
	G-VLUV	Airbus A.330-343	Virgin Atlantic Airways Ltd
	G-VMCG	PA-38-112 Tomahawk	P. J. Montgomery (G-BSVX)
	G-VMEG	Airbus A.340-642	Blue Aviation Ltd
	G-VMIJ	VS 349 Spitfire Mk.VC	I. D. Ward
	G-VMJM	SOCATA TB10 Tobago	S. C. Brown (G-BTOK)
	G-VMVM	Cessna Z-77 balloon	Virgin Balloon Flights
	G-VNAP	Airbus A.340-642	Virgin Atlantic Airways Ltd *Sleeping Beauty*
	G-VNOM	DH.112 Venom FB.50 (J-1632) ★	de Havilland Heritage Museum/London Colney

Reg.	Type	Owner or Operator	Notes
G-VNON	Escapade Jabiru (3)	P. A. Vernon	
G-VNTS	Schempp-Hirth Ventus bT	911 Syndicatem	
G-VNYC	Airbus A.330-343	Virgin Atlantic Airways Ltd	
G-VOAR	PA-28-181 Archer III	Solent Flight Ltd	
G-VOCE	Robinson R22	J. J. Voce (G-BSCL)	
G-VODA	Cameron N-77 balloon	H. Cusden	
G-VOGE	Airbus A.340-642	Blue Aviation Ltd	
G-VOID	PA-28RT-201 Arrow IV	Doublecube Aviation LLP	
G-VOIP	Westland SA.341G Gazelle	Q. Milne (G-HOBZ/G-CBSJ)	
G-VOLO	Alpi Pioneer 300	J. Buglass	
G-VONA	Sikorsky S-76A	Premier Aviation Holdings Ltd (G-BUXB)	
G-VONB	Sikorsky S-76B	Premier Aviation Holdings Ltd (G-POAH)	
G-VONC	Sikorsky S-76B	Premier Aviation Holdings Ltd	
G-VONE	Eurocopter AS355N Twin Squirrel	London Helicopter Centres Ltd (G-LCON)	
G-VONG	AS.355F1 Twin Squirrel	Airbourne Solutions Ltd (G-OILX/G-RMGN/ G-BMCY)	
G-VONH	AS.355F1 Twin Squirrel	London Helicopter Centres Ltd (G-BKUL/G-FFHI/ G-GWHH)	
G-VONK	AS.355F1 Squirrel	Airbourne Solutions Ltd (G-BLRI/G-NUTZ)	
G-VONS	PA-32R-301T Saratoga IITC	W. S. Stanley	
G-VOOM	Pitts S-1S Special	VOOM Syndicate	
G-VORN	Aerotechnik EV-97 Eurostar	J. Parker (G-ODAV)	
G-VPAT	Evans VP-1 Srs 2	A. P. Twort	
G-VPPL	SOCATA TB20 Trinidad	P. Murer, L. Printie & P. J. Wood (G-BPAS)	
G-VPSJ	Shaw Europa	J. D. Bean	
G-VRAY	Airbus A.330-343	Virgin Atlantic Airways Ltd	
G-VRCW	Cessna P.210N	M. Mignini/Italy	
G-VRED	Airbus A.340-642	Virgin Atlantic Airways Ltd *Scarlet Lady*	
G-VROC	Boeing 747-41R	Virgin Atlantic Airways Ltd *Mustang Sally*	
G-VROE	Avro 652A Anson T.21 (WD413)	Air Atlantique Ltd (G-BFIR)	
G-VROM	Boeing 747-443	Virgin Atlantic Airways Ltd	
G-VROS	Boeing 747-443	Virgin Atlantic Airways Ltd *English Rose*	
G-VROY	Boeing 747-443	Virgin Atlantic Airways Ltd *Pretty Woman*	
G-VRVB	Van's RV-8	R. J. Verrall (G-CETI)	
G-VSGE	Cameron O-105 balloon	G. Sbocchelli	
G-VSHY	Airbus A.340-642	Avaio Ltd	
G-VSIX	Schempp-Hirth Ventus 2cT	V6 Group	
G-VSSH	Airbus A.340-642	Virgin Atlantic Airways Ltd *Sweet Dreamer*	
G-VSTR	Stolp SA-900 V-Star	R. L. Hanreck	
G-VSUN	Airbus A.340-313	Virgin Atlantic Airways Ltd *Rainbow Lady*	
G-VSXY	Airbus A.330-343	Virgin Atlantic Airways Ltd *Beauty Queen*	
G-VTAL	Beech V35 Bonanza	M. Elsey	
G-VTCT	Schempp-Hirth Ventus-2cT	V26 Syndicate	
G-VTGE	Bell 206L LongRanger	Vantage Helicopters Ltd (G-ELIT)	
G-VTII	DH.115 Vampire T.11 (XX507:74)	Vampire Preservation Group, Bournemouth	
G-VTOL	Hawker Siddeley Harrier T.52 ★	Brooklands Museum of Aviation/Weybridge	
G-VTOP	Boeing 747-4Q8	Virgin Atlantic Airways Ltd *Virginia Plain*	
G-VTUS	Schempp-Hirth Ventus 2cT	Ventus 02 Syndicate	
G-VTWO	Schempp-Hirth Ventus 2c	F. & B. Birlison	
G-VUEA	Cessna 550 Citation II	AD Aviation Ltd (G-BWOM)	
G-VUEZ	Cessna 550 Citation II	AD Aviation Ltd	
G-VUFO	Airbus A.330-343	Virgin Atlantic Airways Ltd	
G-VULC	Avro 698 Vulcan B.2A (XM655) ★	Radarmoor Ltd/Wellesbourne	
G-VVBA	AS.355F2 Ecureuil II	Hinde Holdings Ltd (G-DBOK)	
G-VVBE	Robinson R22 Beta	Hinde Holdings Ltd (G-OTOY/G-BPEW)	
G-VVBF	Colt 315A balloon	Virgin Balloon Flights	
G-VVBK	PA-34-200T Seneca II	Ravenair Aircraft Ltd (G-BSBS/G-BDRI)	
G-VVBL	Robinson R44 II	Hinde Holdings Ltd	
G-VVBO	Bell 206L-3 LongRanger III	Hinde Holdings Ltd	
G-VVIP	Cessna 421C	Cranfield Aerospace Ltd (G-BMWB)	
G-VVPA	Bombardier CL600-2B16	TAG Aviation (UK) Ltd	
G-VVTV	Diamond DA42 Twin Star	A. D. R. Northeast	
G-VVVV	Skyranger 912 (2)	J. Thomas	
G-VVWW	Enstrom 280C Shark	P. J. Odendaal	

Notes	Reg.	Type	Owner or Operator
	G-VWAG	Airbus A.330-343	Virgin Atlantic Airways Ltd
	G-VWEB	Airbus A.340-642	Virgin Atlantic Airways Ltd *Surfer Girl*
	G-VWIN	Airbus A.340-642	Virgin Atlantic Airways Ltd *Lady Luck*
	G-VWKD	Airbus A.340-642	Virgin Atlantic Airways Ltd *Miss Behavin'*
	G-VWOW	Boeing 747-41R	Virgin Atlantic Airways Ltd *Cosmic Girl*
	G-VXLG	Boeing 747-41R	Virgin Atlantic Airways Ltd *Ruby Tuesday*
	G-VYAK	Yakovlev Yak-18T	A. I. McRobbie
	G-VYGB	Airbus A.330-243	Air Tanker Ltd
	G-VYGG	Airbus A.330-243	Air Tanker Ltd
	G-VYOU	Airbus A.340-642	Virgin Atlantic Airways Ltd *Emmeline Heaney born August 2006*
	G-VYPO	DH.115 Sea Vampire T.35 (N6-766)	N. Rose (G-SPDR)
	G-VZIM	Alpha R2160	I. M. Hollingsworth
	G-VZON	ATR-72-212A	Aurigny Air Services Ltd
	G-WAAS	MBB Bö.105DBS-4	South Georgia Heritage Trust (G-ESAM/G-BUIB/G-BDYZ)
	G-WABB	Dassault Falcon 900EX	TAG Aviation (UK) Ltd
	G-WABH	Cessna 172S Skyhawk	Blackhawk Aviation Ltd
	G-WACB	Cessna F.152 II	Booker Aircraft Leasing Ltd
	G-WACE	Cessna F.152 II	Booker Aircraft Leasing Ltd
	G-WACF	Cessna 152 II	Booker Aircraft Leasing Ltd
	G-WACG	Cessna 152 II	Booker Aircraft Leasing Ltd
	G-WACH	Cessna FA.152 II	Booker Aircraft Leasing Ltd
	G-WACI	Beech 76 Duchess	Booker Aircraft Leasing Ltd
	G-WACJ	Beech 76 Duchess	Booker Aircraft Leasing Ltd
	G-WACL	Cessna F.172N	A. G. Arthur (G-BHGG)
	G-WACO	Waco UPF-7	R. F. L. Cuypers/Belgium
	G-WACT	Cessna F.152 II	N. Clark (G-BKFT)
	G-WACU	Cessna FA.152	Booker Aircraft Leasing Ltd (G-BJZU)
	G-WACW	Cessna 172P	Technical Power & Maintenance Ltd
	G-WACY	Cessna F.172P	The Vintage Wings Aviation Co.Ltd
	G-WADI	PA-46-350P Malibu Mirage	Air Malibu AG/Liechtenstein
	G-WADS	Robinson R22 Beta	Whizzard Helicopters (G-NICO)
	G-WADZ	Lindstrand LBL-90A balloon	A. K. C., J. E. H., M. H. & Y. K. Wadsworth (G-CGVN)
	G-WAGA	Wag-Aero Wagabond	A. I. Sutherland (G-BNJA)
	G-WAGG	Robinson R22 Beta II	N. J. Wagstaff Leasing
	G-WAGN	Stinson 108-3 Voyager	S. E. H. Ellcome
	G-WAGS	Robinson R44 II	Huckair
	G-WAHL	QAC Quickie	A. A. A. Wahlberg
	G-WAIR	PA-32-301 Saratoga	Finningley Aviation
	G-WAIT	Cameron V-77 balloon	C. P. Brown
	G-WAKE	Mainair Blade 912	J. E. Rourke
	G-WAKY	Cyclone AX2000	R. Knight & R. Hinton
	G-WALI	Robinson R44 II	Casdron Enterprises Ltd
	G-WALY	Maule MX-7-180	J. R. Colthurst
	G-WALZ	Best Off Sky Ranger Nynja 912S(1)	R. J. Thomas
	G-WAMS	PA-28R-201 Arrow	Stapleford Flying Club Ltd
	G-WAPA	Robinson R44 II	Aerocorp Ltd
	G-WARA	PA-28-161 Warrior III	Aviation Rentals
	G-WARB	PA-28-161 Warrior III	OSF Ltd
	G-WARD	Taylor JT.1 Monoplane	R. P. J. Hunter
	G-WARE	PA-28-161 Warrior II	N. M. G. Pearson
	G-WARH	PA-28-161 Warrior III	KN Singles & Twins Aviation Consultants BV
	G-WARO	PA-28-161 Warrior III	T. G. D. Leasing Ltd
	G-WARP	Cessna 182F Sylane	R. D. Fowden (G-ASHB)
	G-WARR	PA-28-161 Warrior II	B. Huda
	G-WARS	PA-28-161 Warrior III	Blaneby Ltd
	G-WARU	PA-28-161 Warrior III	Smart People Don't Buy Ltd
	G-WARV	PA-28-161 Warrior III	Bickertons Aerodromes Ltd
	G-WARW	PA-28-161 Warrior III	Lomac Aviators Ltd
	G-WARX	PA-28-161 Warrior III	C. M. A. Clark
	G-WARY	PA-28-161 Warrior III	Target Aviation Ltd
	G-WARZ	PA-28-161 Warrior III	Target Aviation Ltd
	G-WASC	Eurocopter EC.135 T2+	Bond Air Services Ltd
	G-WASN	Eurocopter EC.135 T2+	Bond Air Services Ltd
	G-WASS	Eurocopter EC.135 T2+	Bond Air Services Ltd
	G-WATR	Christen A1 Husky	S. N. Gregory

Reg.	Type	Owner or Operator	Notes
G-WAVA	Robin HR.200/120B	Smart People Don't Buy Ltd	
G-WAVE	Grob G.109B	C. G. Wray	
G-WAVI	Robin HR.200/120B	T. J. Hennig (G-BZDG)	
G-WAVS	PA-28-161 Warrior III	TGD Leasing Ltd (G-WARC)	
G-WAVT	Robin R.2160i	Sokratherm GmbH Energie und Warmtechnik (G-CBLG)	
G-WAVV	Robon HR200/120B	TGD Leasing Ltd (G-GORF)	
G-WAVY	Grob G.109B	G-WAVY Group	
G-WAWW	P & M Quik GT450	G. Postans	
G-WAYS	Lindstrand LBL-105A balloon	Lindstrand Hot Air Balloons Ltd	
G-WAZP	Skyranger 912 (2)	L. V. McClune	
G-WAZZ	Pitts S-1S Special	J. P. Taylor (G-BRRP)	
G-WBEV	Cameron N-77 balloon	T. J. & M. Turner (G-PVCU)	
G-WBLY	Mainair Pegasus Quik	A. J. Lindsey	
G-WBTS	Falconar F-11	M. K. Field (G-BDPL)	
G-WBVS	Diamond DA.4D Star	G. W. Beavis	
G-WCAO	Eurocopter EC 135T2	Avon & Somerset Constabulary & Gloucestershire Constabulary	
G-WCAT	Colt Flying Mitt SS balloon	I. Chadwick	
G-WCCI	Embraer RJ135BJ Legacy	Altarello Ltd (G-REUB)	
G-WCCP	Beech B200 Super King Air	William Cook Aviation Ltd	
G-WCEI	MS.894E Rallye 220GT	R. A. L. Lucas (G-BAOC)	
G-WCKD	Eurocopter EC130 B4	Batchelor Aviation Ltd (G-CFWX)	
G-WCKM	Best Off Sky Ranger 912(1)	J. Depree & B. Janson	
G-WCRD	Aérospatiale SA.341G Gazelle	MW Helicopters Ltd	
G-WCUB	PA-18 Super Cub 150	P. A. Walley	
G-WDEB	Thunder Ax-7-77 balloon	A. Heginbottom	
G-WDGC	Rolladen-Schneider LS8-18	W. D. G. Chappel (G-CEWJ)	
G-WDKR	AS.355F1 Ecureuil 2	Cheshire Helicopters Ltd (G-NEXT/G-OMAV)	
G-WEAT	Robinson R44 II	R. F. Brook	
G-WEBI	Hughes 369E	M. Webb	
G-WEBY	Ace Magic Cyclone	B. W. Webster	
G-WEBS	American Champion 7ECA Citabria	P. J. Webb	
G-WEED	Ace Magic Laser	R. D. Leigh	
G-WEEE	Ace Magic Cyclone	K. G. Grayson & R. D. Leigh	
G-WEEK	Skyranger 912(2)	D. J. Prothero	
G-WEFR	Alpi Pioneer 200-M	Cardiff Backpacker Caerdydd Ltd	
G-WEGO	Robinson R44 II	Helimove Ltd	
G-WELY	Agusta A109E Power	Titan Airways Ltd	
G-WENA	AS.355F2 Ecureuil II	Multiflight Ltd (G-CORR/G-MUFF/G-MOBI)	
G-WEND	PA-28RT-201 Arrow IV	Tayside Aviation Ltd	
G-WERY	SOCATA TB20 Trinidad	WERY Flying Group	
G-WESX	CFM Streak Shadow	M. Catania	
G-WETI	Cameron N-31 balloon	C. A. Butter & J. J. T. Cooke	
G-WEWI	Cessna 172	T. J. Wassell (G-BSEP)	
G-WFFW	PA-28-161 Warrior II	S. Letheren & D. Jelly	
G-WFLY	Mainair Pegasus Quik	D. E. Lord	
G-WFOX	Robinson R22 Beta II	Rotorfun Aviation	
G-WGCS	PA-18 Super Cub 95	S. C. Thompson	
G-WGSC	Pilatus PC-6/B2-H4 Turbo Porter	D. M. Penny	
G-WGSI	Tanarg/Ixess 13 912S(1)	J. A. Ganderton	
G-WHAL	QAC Quickie	A. A. M. Wahiberg	
G-WHAM	AS.350B3 Ecureuil	Horizon Helicopter Hire Ltd	
G-WHAT	Colt 77A balloon	M. A. Scholes	
G-WHEE	Pegasus Quantum 15-912	Airways Airsports Ltd	
G-WHEN	Tecnam P92-EM Echo	N. Harrison	
G-WHIM	Colt 77A balloon	D. L. Morgan	
G-WHOG	CFM Streak Shadow	B. R. Cannell	
G-WHOO	Rotorway Executive 162F	J. White	
G-WHRL	Schweizer 269C	P. A. Adams & T. S. Davies	
G-WHST	AS.350B2 Ecureuil	Keltruck Ltd (G-BWYA)	
G-WHYS	ICP MXP-740 Savannah VG Jabiru(1)	D. J. Whysall	
G-WIBB	Jodel D.18	C. J. Bragg	
G-WIBS	CASA 1-131E Jungmann 2000	C. Willoughby	

Notes	Reg.	Type	Owner or Operator
	G-WICH	Clutton FRED Srs II	L. A. Tomlinson
	G-WIFE	Cessna R.182 RG II	Wife 182 Group (G-BGVT)
	G-WIFI	Cameron Z-90 balloon	M. E. White
	G-WIGY	Pitts S-1S Special	R. E. Welch (G-ITTI)
	G-WIII	Schempp-Hirth Ventus bT	I. G. Carrick
	G-WIIZ	Augusta-Bell 206B JetRanger 2	Tiger Helicopters Ltd (G-DBHH/G-AWVO)
	G-WIKI	Europa XS	J. Greenhaigh
	G-WILB	Ultramagic M-105 balloon	A. S. Davidson, B. N. Trowbridge & W. C. Bailey
	G-WILD	Pitts S-1T Special	The Wild Bunch
	G-WILG	PZL-104 Wilga 35	M. H. Bletsoe-Brown (G-AZYJ)
	G-WILT	Ikarus C42 FB80	A. E. Lacy-Hulbert
	G-WIMP	Colt 56A balloon	T. & B. Chamberlain
	G-WINE	Thunder Ax7-77Z balloon ★	Balloon Preservation Group/Lancing
	G-WINH	EV-97 TeamEurostar UK	H. M. Wooldridge
	G-WINI	SA Bulldog Srs.120/121 (XX546:03)	A. Bole (G-CBCO)
	G-WINK	AA-5B Tiger	B. St. J. Cooke
	G-WINN	Stolp SA.300 Starduster Too	H. Feeney
	G-WINR	Robinson R22	Heli Air Ltd (G-BTHG)
	G-WINS	PA-32 Cherokee Six 300	Cheyenne Ltd
	G-WINV	Eurocopter EC155 B1	Starspeed Ltd (G-WJCJ)
	G-WIRL	Robinson R22 Beta	Rivermead Aviation Ltd/Switzerland
	G-WISE	PA-28-181 Archer III	M. Arnold
	G-WISZ	Steen Skybolt	G. S. Reid
	G-WIWI	Sikorsky S-76C	Air Harrods Ltd
	G-WIXI	Avions Mudry CAP-10B	A. R. Harris
	G-WIZI	Enstrom 280FX	AAA Pest Control GmbH
	G-WIZR	Robinson R22 Beta II	Physio Supplies Ltd
	G-WIZS	Mainair Pegasus Quik	P. J. Hopkins
	G-WIZY	Robinson R22 Beta	Subacoustech Ltd (G-BMWX)
	G-WIZZ	Agusta-Bell 206B JetRanger 2	Rivermead Aviation Ltd
	G-WJAC	Cameron TR-70 balloon	S. J. & J. A. Bellaby
	G-WJAN	Boeing 757-21K	Thomas Cook Airlines Ltd
	G-WJCM	CASA 1.131E Jungmann 2000 (S5+B06)	G. W. Lynch (G-BSFB)
	G-WKNS	Shaw Europa XS	A. L. Wickens
	G-WLAC	PA-18 Super Cub 150	White Waltham Airfield Ltd (G-HAHA/G-BSWE)
	G-WLDN	Robinson R44 Raven	Fly Executive Ltd
	G-WLGC	PA-28-181 Archer III	E. F. Mangion (G-FLUX)
	G-WLKI	Lindstrand LBL-105A balloon	C. Wilkinson
	G-WLKS	Schleicher ASW-20L	S. E. Wilks (G-IUMB)
	G-WLLS	Rolladen-Schneider LS8-18	L & A Wells
	G-WLMS	Mainair Blade 912	G. Zerrun
	G-WLSN	Best Off Skyranger 912S (1)	A. Wilson & ptnrs
	G-WMAS	Eurocopter EC 135T1	Bond Air Services Ltd
	G-WMTM	AA-5B Tiger	Falcon Flying Group
	G-WNCH	Beech B200 Super King Air	Winch Air Ltd (G-OMGI)
	G-WNSF	Sikorsky S-92A	CHC Scotia Ltd
	G-WNSG	Sikorsky S-92A	CHC Scotia Ltd
	G-WNSH	Sikorsky S-92A	CHC Scotia Ltd
	G-WNSI	Sikorsky S-92A	CHC Scotia Ltd
	G-WNSO	Eurocopter EC.225LP Super Puma	CHC Scotia Ltd (G-PNEO)
	G-WNTR	PA-28-161 Warrior II	Fleetlands Flying Group (G-BFNJ)
	G-WOCO	Waco YMF-5C	Classic Aviation Ltd
	G-WOFM	Agusta A109E Power	Quinnasette Ltd (G-NWRR)
	G-WOLF	PA-28 Cherokee 140	G-WOLF Ltd
	G-WONE	Schempp-Hirth Ventus 2cT	J. P. Wright
	G-WONN	Eurocopter EC135 T2	Bond Air Services Ltd
	G-WOOD	Beech 95-B55A Baron	M. S. Choskey (G-AYID)
	G-WOOF	Enstrom 480	Netcopter.co.uk Ltd & Curvature Ltd
	G-WOOL	Colt 77A balloon	Whacko Balloon Group
	G-WOOO	CZAW Sportcruiser	J. J. Nicholson
	G-WORM	Thruster T.600N	C. Childs
	G-WOSY	MBB Bö.105DBS/4	Redwood Aviation Ltd (G-PASD/G-BNRS)
	G-WOTW	Ultramagic M-77 balloon	Window on the World Ltd
	G-WOWI	Van's RV-7	P. J. Wood

Reg.	Type	Owner or Operator	Notes
G-WPAS	MDH MD-900 Explorer	Police Aviation Services Ltd	
G-WPDA	Eurocopter EC135 P1	WPD Helicopter Unit	
G-WPDB	Eurocopter EC135 P1	WPD Helicopter Unit	
G-WPDC	Eurocopter EC135 P1	WPD Helicopter Unit	
G-WPDD	Eurocopter EC135 P1	WPD Helicopter Unit	
G-WPIE	Enstrom 280FX Shark	Wrights Pies (Shelton) Ltd (G-RCAR/G-BXRD)	
G-WREN	Pitts S-2A Special	Modi Aviation Ltd	
G-WRFM	Enstrom 280C-UK Shark	A. J. Clark (G-CTSI/G-BKIO)	
G-WRIT	Thunder Ax7-77A balloon	G. Pusey	
G-WRLY	Robinson R22 Beta	Burman Aviation Ltd (G-OFJS/G-BNXJ)	
G-WRWR	Robinson R22 Beta II	MFH Helicopters Ltd	
G-WSKY	Enstrom 280C-UK-2 Shark	B. J. Rutterford (G-BEEK)	
G-WSMW	Robinson R44	M. Wass (G-SGPL)	
G-WSSX	Ikarus C42 FB100	J. M. Crane	
G-WTAV	Robinson R44 II	William Taylor Aviation Ltd	
G-WTEC	Cirrus SR22	B. J. White	
G-WTWO	Aquila AT01	J. P. Wright	
G-WUFF	Shaw Europa	W. H. Bliss	
G-WULF	WAR Focke-Wulf Fw.190 (8+)	S. Laver	
G-WVBF	Lindstrand LBL-210A balloon	Virgin Balloon Flights Ltd	
G-WVIP	Beech B.200 Super King Air	Capital Air Charter Ltd	
G-WWAL	PA-28R Cherokee Arrow 180	White Waltham Airfield Ltd (G-AZSH)	
G-WWAY	Piper PA-28-181 Archer II	R. A. Witchell	
G-WWBC	Airbus A.330-243	bmi british midland	
G-WWBD	Airbus A.330-243	bmi british midland	
G-WWBM	Airbus A.330-243	bmi british midland	
G-WWLF	Extra EA.300/L	P. Sapignoli	
G-WWZZ	CZAW Sportcruiser	L. Hogan	
G-WYAT	CFM Streak Shadow Srs SA	N. L. Phillips	
G-WYDE	Schleicher ASW-20BL	461 Syndicate	
G-WYKD	Tanarg/Ixess 15 912S(2)	D. L. Turner	
G-WYND	Wittman W.8 Tailwind	R. S. Marriott	
G-WYNE	BAe 125 Srs 800B	Global Flight Solutions Ltd (G-CJAA/G-HCFR/ G-SHEA/G-BUWC)	
G-WYNT	Cameron N-56 balloon	A. G. Jenkins	
G-WYPA	MBB Bö.105DBS/4	Police Aviation Services Ltd	
G-WYSZ	Robin DR.400/100	Exavia Ltd (G-FTIM)	
G-WYVN	DG Flugzeugbau DG-1000S	Army Gliding Association	
G-WZOL	RL.5B LWS Sherwood Ranger	D. Lentell (G-MZOL)	
G-WZOY	Rans S.6-ES Coyote II	S. P. Read	
G-WZRD	Eurocopter EC 120B Colibri	Conductia Enterprises Ltd	
G-XAIM	Ultramagic H-31 balloon	G. Everett	
G-XALT	PA-38-112 Tomahawk	P. J. Crowther	
G-XALZ	Rans S6S-116 Super Six	M. R. McNeil	
G-XARV	ARV Super 2	C. M. Rose (G-OPIG/G-BMSJ)	
G-XASH	Schleicher ASH-31	R. C. Wilson	
G-XAVB	Cessna 510 Citation Mustang	Aviation Beauport Ltd	
G-XAVI	PA-28-161 Warrior II	J. R. Santamaria (G-SACZ)	
G-XAVV	Schempp-Hirth Ventus 2c	A. J. McNamara & O. Walters	
G-XAYR	Raj Hamsa X'Air 582 (6)	P. Jordanou	
G-XBAL	Skyringer Nynja 912S(1)	W. G. Gill & N. D. Ewer	
G-XBCI	Bell 206B JetRanger 3	BCI Helicopter Charters Ltd	
G-XBEL	Cessna 560XL Citation XLS	Aviation Beauport Ltd	
G-XBGA	Glaser-Dirks DG500/22 Elan	N. Kelly	
G-XBJT	Aerotechnik EV-97 Eurostar	B. J. Tyre (G-WHOA/G-DATH)	
G-XBLD	MBB Bo.105DB	PLM Dollar Group Ltd	
G-XBLU	Cessna 680 Citation Sovereign	Datel Holdings Ltd	
G-XBOX	Bell 206B JetRanger 3	Castle Air Ltd (G-OOHO/G-OCHC/G-KLEE/ G-SIZL/G-BOSW)	
G-XCBI	Schweizer 269C-1	B. Durkan	
G-XCCC	Extra EA.300/L	P. T. Fellows	

Notes	Reg.	Type	Owner or Operator
	G-XCII	Sikorsky S-92A	Bristow Helicopters Ltd
	G-XCIT	Alpi Pioneer 300	A. Thomas
	G-XCRJ	Van's RV-9A	R. Jones
	G-XCUB	PA-18 Super Cub 150	M. C. Barraclough
	G-XDEA	Diamond DA.42 Twin Star	Diamond Executive Aviation Ltd
	G-XDUO	Schempp-Hirth Duo Discus xT	G-XDUO Group
	G-XDWE	P & M Quik GT450	R. J. Harper
	G-XELA	Robinson R44 II	A. Yew
	G-XELL	Schleicher ASW-27-18E	S. R. Ell
	G-XENA	PA-28-161 Warrior II	P. Brewer
	G-XERO	CZAW Sportcruiser	M. R. Mosley
	G-XFLY	Lambert Mission M212-100	Lambert Aircraft Engineering BVBA
	G-XHOT	Cameron Z-105 balloon	S. F. Burden
	G-XIII	Van's RV-7	Icarus Flying Group
	G-XIIX	Robinson R22 Beta ★	(Static exhibit)/Blackbushe
	G-XINE	PA-28-161 Warrior II	P. Tee (G-BPAC)
	G-XIOO	Raj Hamsa X'Air 133 (1)	M. Ridgway
	G-XIXI	Evektor EV-97 TeamEurostar UK	J. A. C. Cockfield
	G-XIXX	Glaser-Dirks DG-300 Elan	S. D. Black
	G-XJCB	Sikorsky S-76C	J. C. Bamford Excavators Ltd
	G-XJET	Learjet 45	CEGA Air Ambulance UK Ltd (G-IZAP/G-OLDK)
	G-XJJM	P & M Pegasus Quik	Mainair Microlight Centre Ltd
	G-XJON	Schempp-Hirth Ventus 2b	J. C. Bastin
	G-XKKA	Diamond KH36 Super Dimona	G-XKKA Group
	G-XLAM	Best Off Skyranger 912S	X-LAM Skyranger Syndicate
	G-XLEA	Airbus A.380-841	British Airways PLC
	G-XLEB	Airbus A.380-841	British Airways PLC
	G-XLEC	Airbus A.380-841	British Airways PLC
	G-XLGB	Cessna 560XL Citation Excel	Tosh Air Ltd
	G-XLII	Schleicher ASW-27-18E	P. M. Wells
	G-XLLL	AS.355F1 Twin Squirrel	MW Helicopters Ltd (G-PASF/G-SCHU)
	G-XLNT	Zenair CH.601XL	Zenair G-XLNT Group
	G-XLTG	Cessna 182S	T. I. M. Paul
	G-XLXL	Robin DR.400/160	L. R. Marchant (G-BAUD)
	G-XMGO	Aeromot AMT-200S Super Ximango	G. McLean & R. P. Beck
	G-XOAR	Schleicher ASW-27-18E	R. A. Browne
	G-XOIL	AS.355N Twin Squirrel	Firstearl Marine and Aviation Ltd (G-LOUN)
	G-XONE	Canadair CL600-2B16	Gama Aviation Ltd
	G-XPBI	Letov LK-2M Sluka	R. M. C. Hunter
	G-XPDA	Cameron Z-120 balloon	M. Cowling
	G-XPII	Cessna R.172K	The Hawk Flying Group (G-DIVA)
	G-XPWW	Cameron TR-77 balloon	Chalmers Ballong Corps/Sweden
	G-XPXP	Aero Designs Pulsar XP	B. J. Edwards
	G-XRAF	Raj Hamsa X'Air 582(5)	J. Ryan
	G-XRAY	Rand-Robinson KR-2	R. S. Smith
	G-XRED	Pitts S-1C Special	J. E. Rands (G-SWUN/G-BSXH)
	G-XRLD	Cameron A-250 balloon	The Cotswold Balloon Co.Ltd
	G-XRVB	Van's RV-8	P. G. Winters
	G-XRVX	Van's RV-10	N. K. Lamping
	G-XRXR	Raj Hamsa X'Air 582 (1)	R. J. Philpotts
	G-XSAM	Van's RV-9A	D. G. Lucas & S. D. Austen
	G-XSDJ	Europa XS	D. N. Joyce
	G-XSEA	Van's RV-8	H. M. Darlington
	G-XSEL	Silence Twister	Skyview Systems Ltd
	G-XSRF	Europa XS	R. L. W. Frank
	G-XTEE	Edge XT912-B/Streak III	Airborne Australia UK
	G-XTHT	Edge XT912-B/Streak III-B	H. A. Taylor
	G-XTME	Xtremeair XA42	Xtreme Aerobatics Ltd

Reg.	Type	Owner or Operator	Notes
G-XTNI	AirBorne XT912-B/Streak	A. J. Parry	
G-XTOR	BN-2A Mk III-2 Trislander	Aurigny Air Services Ltd (G-BAXD)	
G-XTRA	Extra EA.230	C. Butler	
G-XTUN	Westland-Bell 47G-3B1 (XT223)	P. A. Rogers (G-BGZK)	
G-XVAX	Tecnam P2006T	J. Byrne	
G-XVOM	Van's RV-6	A. Baker-Munton	
G-XWEB	Best Off Skyranger 912 (2)	K. B. Woods	
G-XWON	Rolladen-Schneider LS8-18	P. K Carpenter	
G-XXBH	Agusta-Bell 206B JetRanger 3	Coln Aviation Ltd (G-BYBA/G-BHXV/G-OWJM)	
G-XXEB	Sikorsky S-76C	The Queen's Helicopter Flight	
G-XXIV	Agusta-Bell 206B JetRanger 3	Castle Air Ltd	
G-XXIX	Schleicher ASW-18E	P. R. & A. H. Pentecost	
G-XXRG	Avid Speed Wing Mk.4	R. J. Grainger (G-BWLW)	
G-XXRS	Bombardier BD-700 Global Express	TAG Aviation (UK) Ltd	
G-XXRV	Van's RV-9	D. R. Gilbert & D. Slabbert	
G-XXTB	SOCATA TB20 Trinidad	N. Schaefer (G-KPTT)	
G-XXTR	Extra EA.300/L	Shoreham Extra Group (G-ECCC)	
G-XXVB	Schempp-Hirth Ventus b	R. Johnson	
G-XXZZ	Learjet 60	Gama Aviation Ltd	
G-XYAK	IDA Bacau Yakovlev Yak-52 (69 blue)	R. Davies	
G-XYJY	Best Off Skyranger 912 (2)	A. V. Francis	
G-XYZT	Aeromot AMT-200S Super Ximango	S. Marriott	
G-XZXZ	Robinson R44 II	Ashley Martin Ltd	
G-YAAK	Yakovlev Yak-50	R. J. Luke (G-BWJT)	
G-YADA	Ikarus C42 FB100	Ikarus Flying Syndicate (Carlisle)	
G-YAKA	Yakovlev Yak-50	M. Chapman	
G-YAKB	Aerostar Yakovlev Yak-52	M. J. Gadsby	
G-YAKC	Yakovlev Yak-52	C. L. Jones	
G-YAKE	Yakovlev Yak-52	D. J. Hopkinson (G-BVVA)	
G-YAKF	Aerostar Yakovlev Yak-52	P. C. Henry	
G-YAKG	Yakovlev Yak-18T	A. Dunk	
G-YAKH	IDA Bacau Yakovlev Yak-52	Plus 7 minus 5 Ltd	
G-YAKI	IDA Bacau Yakovlev Yak-52 (100 blue)	Yak One Ltd	
G-YAKK	Yakovlev Yak-50	A. P. Wilson	
G-YAKM	IDA Bacau Yakovlev Yak-50 (61 red)	Airborne Services Ltd	
G-YAKN	IDA Bacau Yakovlev Yak-52 (66 red)	Airborne Services Ltd	
G-YAKP	Yakovlev Yak-9	M. V. Rijkse & N. M. R. Richards	
G-YAKR	IDA Bacau Yakovlev Yak-52 (03 white)	G-YAKR Group	
G-YAKT	IDA Bacau Yakovlev Yak-52	G-YAKT Group	
G-YAKU	IDA Bacau Yakovlev Yak-50 (49 red)	D. J. Hopkinson (G-BXND)	
G-YAKV	IDA Bacau Yakovlev Yak-52 (31 grey)	P. D. Scandrett	
G-YAKX	IDA Bacau Yakovlev Yak-52 (27 red)	The X-Flyers Ltd	
G-YAKY	Aerostar Yakovlev Yak-52	W. T. Marriott	
G-YAKZ	IDA Bacau Yakovlev Yak-50 (33 red)	Airborne Services Ltd	
G-YANK	PA-28-181 Archer II	G-YANK Flying Group	
G-YARR	Mainair Rapier	D. Yarr	
G-YARV	ARV Super 2	A. M. Oliver (G-BMDO)	
G-YAWW	PA-28RT-201T Turbo Arrow IV	Barton Aviation Ltd	
G-YBAA	Cessna FR.172J	A. Evans	
G-YCII	LET Yakovlev C-11 (11 yellow)	R. W. Davies	
G-YCKF	Dassault Falcon 900EX	Execujet (UK) Ltd	
G-YCUB	PA-18 Super Cub 150	F. W. Rogers	
G-YCUE	Agusta A109A	Oldham Broadway Developments Ltd	
G-YDEA	DA-42 Twin Star	Diamond Executive Aviation Ltd	
G-YEHA	Schleicher ASW-27	B. L. Cooper	
G-YELL	Murphy Rebel	A. H. Godfrey	
G-YELO	Rotorsport UK MT-03	M. Black	
G-YELP	RL5A Sherwood Ranger ST	James Blunt Ltd	
G-YEOM	PA-31-350 Navajo Chieftain	A. B. Yeoman	
G-YEWS	Rotorway Executive 152	R. Turrell & P. Mason	

Notes	Reg.	Type	Owner or Operator
	G-YFUT	Yakovlev Yak-52	R. Oliver
	G-YFZT	Cessna 172S	AB Integro
	G-YIII	Cessna F.150L	Merlin Flying Club Ltd
	G-YIPI	Cessan FR.172K	A. J. G. Davis
	G-YIRO	Campbell Cricket Mk.4	R. Boese (G-KGED)
	G-YJET	Montgomerie-Bensen B.8MR	A. Shuttleworth (G-BMUH)
	G-YKSO	Yakovlev Yak-50	Russian Radials Ltd
	G-YKSS	Yakovlev Yak-55	T. Ollivier
	G-YKSZ	Aerostar Yakovlev Yak-52 (01 yellow)	Tzarina Group
	G-YKYK	Aerostar Yakovlev Yak-52	K. J. Pilling
	G-YMFC	Waco YMF	S. J. Brenchley
	G-YMMA	Boeing 777-236ER	British Airways
	G-YMMB	Boeing 777-236ER	British Airways
	G-YMMC	Boeing 777-236ER	British Airways
	G-YMMD	Boeing 777-236ER	British Airways
	G-YMME	Boeing 777-236ER	British Airways
	G-YMMF	Boeing 777-236ER	British Airways
	G-YMMG	Boeing 777-236ER	British Airways
	G-YMMH	Boeing 777-236ER	British Airways
	G-YMMI	Boeing 777-236ER	British Airways
	G-YMMJ	Boeing 777-236ER	British Airways
	G-YMMK	Boeing 777-236ER	British Airways
	G-YMML	Boeing 777-236ER	British Airways
	G-YMMN	Boeing 777-236ER	British Airways
	G-YMMO	Boeing 777-236ER	British Airways
	G-YMMP	Boeing 777-236ER	British Airways
	G-YMMR	Boeing 777-236ER	British Airways
	G-YMMS	Boeing 777-236ER	British Airways
	G-YMMT	Boeing 777-236ER	British Airways
	G-YMMU	Boeing 777-236ER	British Airways
	G-YNOT	D.62B Condor	T. Littlefair (G-AYFH)
	G-YNYS	Cessna 172S Skyhawk	T. V. Hughes
	G-YOBI	Schleicher ASH-25	J. Kangurs
	G-YODA	Schempp-Hirth Ventus 2cT	A. Charlier
	G-YOGI	Robin DR.400/140B	M. M. Pepper (G-BDME)
	G-YOLK	P & M Aviation Quik GT450	M. Austin
	G-YORK	Cessna F.172M	EIMH-Flying Group
	G-YOTS	IDA Bacau Yakovlev Yak-52	G-YOTS Group
	G-YOYO	Pitts S-1E Special	P. M. Jarvis (G-OTSW/G-BLHE)
	G-YPDN	Rotorsport UK MT-03	T. M. Jones
	G-YPOL	MDH MD-900 Explorer	West Yorkshire Police Authority
	G-YPRS	Cessna 550 Citation Bravo	Executive Aviation Services Ltd (G-IPAC/G-IPAL)
	G-YPSY	Andreasson BA-4B	M. J. Sharp
	G-YRAF	RAF 2000 GTX-SE gyroplane	J. R. Cooper
	G-YRAX	Magni M-24C	C. M. Jones
	G-YRIL	Luscombe 8E Silvaire	C. Potter
	G-YRKS	Robinson R44	Storetec Services Ltd
	G-YROA	Rotorsport UK MTO Sport	J. P. R. McLaren
	G-YROC	Rotorsport UK MT-03	C. V. Catherall
	G-YROH	Rotorsport UK MTO Sport	J. W. G. Andrews
	G-YROI	Air Command 532 Elite	W. B. Lumb
	G-YROJ	RAF 2000 GTX-SE gyroplane	J. R. Mercer
	G-YROK	Magni M-16C	K. J. Yeadon
	G-YROM	Rotorsport UK MT-03	A. Wallace
	G-YRON	Magni M-16C Tandem Trainer	A. J. Brent & A. D. Mann
	G-YROO	RAF 2000 GTX-SE gyroplane	L. Mullin
	G-YROP	Magni M-16C Tandem Trainer	Magni Guernsey Flying Group
	G-YROR	Magni M.24C	R. M. Stanley
	G-YROX	Rotorsport UK MT-03	Surplus Art
	G-YROY	Montgomerie-Bensen B.8MR	S. S. Wilson
	G-YROZ	Rotorsport UK Calidus	C. J. Rose
	G-YRRO	AutoGyro Calidus	W. C. Walters
	G-YRUS	Jodel D.140E	W. E. Massam (G-YRNS)

Reg.	Type	Owner or Operator	Notes
G-YSMO	Mainair Pegasus Quik	F. Poirot	
G-YTLY	Rans S-6-ES Coyote II	Royal Aeronautical Society	
G-YUGE	Schempp-Hirth Ventus cT	E. P. Lambert (G-CFNN)	
G-YUGO	HS.125 Srs 1B/R-522 ★	Fire Section/Dunsfold (G-ATWH)	
G-YULL	PA-28 Cherokee 180E	C. J. Varley (G-BEAJ)	
G-YUMM	Cameron N-90 balloon	H. Stringer	
G-YUMN	Dassault Falcon 2000	Gama Aviation Ltd	
G-YUPI	Cameron N-90 balloon	MCVH SA/Belgium	
G-YURO	Shaw Europa ★	Yorkshire Air Museum/Elvington	
G-YVES	Alpi Pioneer 300	G-YVES Group	
G-YXLX	ISF Mistral C	R. R. Penman	
G-YYAK	Aerostar SA Yak-52	A. Bonnet	
G-YYRO	Magni M-16C Tandem Trainer	J. A. McGill	
G-YYYY	MH.1521C-1 Broussard	Aerosuperbatics Ltd	
G-YZYZ	Mainair Blade 912	P. G. Eastlake	
G-ZAAP	CZAW Sportcruiser	H. Page	
G-ZAAZ	Van's RV-8	P. A. Soper	
G-ZABC	Sky 90-24 balloon	P. Donnelly	
G-ZACE	Cessna 172S	Sywell Aerodrome Ltd	
G-ZACH	Robin DR.400/100	A. P. Wellings (G-FTIO)	
G-ZADA	Best Off Skyranger 912S(1)	B. Bisley	
G-ZAIR	Zenair CH 601HD	G-ZAIR Flying Group	
G-ZANY	Diamond DA40D Star	Altair Aviation Ltd	
G-ZAPH	Bell 206B JetRanger 3	WPD Helicopter Unit (G-DBMW)	
G-ZAPK	BAe 146-200QC	Titan Airways Ltd (G-BTIA/G-PRIN)	
G-ZAPN	BAe 146-200QC	Titan Airways Ltd (G-BPBT)	
G-ZAPO	BAe 146-200QC	Trident Aviation Leasing Services (Jersey) Ltd (G-BWLG/G-PRCS)	
G-ZAPV	Boeing 737-3Y0	Titan Airways Ltd (G-IGOC)	
G-ZAPW	Boeing 737-3L9	Titan Airways Ltd (G-BOZB/G-IGOX)	
G-ZAPX	Boeing 757-256	Titan Airways Ltd	
G-ZAPY	Robinson R22 Beta	Heli Air Ltd (G-INGB)	
G-ZAPZ	Boeing 737-33A	Titan Airways Ltd	
G-ZARI	AA-5B Tiger	MPFC Ltd (G-BHVY)	
G-ZARV	ARV Super 2	P. R. Snowden	
G-ZAVI	Ikarus C42 FB100	B. & J. M. Cooper	
G-ZAZA	PA-18 Super Cub 95	G. J. Harry, The Viscount Goschen	
G-ZAZZ	Lindstrand LBL-120A balloon	Idea Balloon SAS Di Stefano Travaglia and Co./Italy	
G-ZBED	Robinson R22 Beta	P. D. Spinks	
G-ZBJA	Boeing 787-836	British Airways PLC	
G-ZBJB	Boeing 787-836	British Airways PLC	
G-ZBJC	Boeing 787-836	British Airways PLC	
G-ZBJD	Boeing 787-836	British Airways PLC	
G-ZBLT	Cessna 182S Skylane	Cessna 182S Group/Ireland	
G-ZBOP	PZL-Bielsko SZD-36A Cobra 15	S. Bruce	
G-ZDEA	Diamond DA.42 Twin Star	Diamond Executive Aviation Ltd	
G-ZEBO	Thunder Ax8-105 S2 balloon	S. M. Waterton	
G-ZEBS	Aerospatiale ATR-42-320	Blue Islands Ltd	
G-ZEBY	PA-28 Cherokee 140	G. Gee (G-BFBF)	
G-ZECH	CZAW Sportcruiser	P. J. Reilly	
G-ZEIN	Slingsby T.67M Firefly 260	R. C. P. Brookhouse	
G-ZELE	Westland Gazelle HT.Mk.2	London Helicopter Centres Ltd (G-CBSA)	
G-ZENA	Zenair CH.701UL	A. N. Aston	
G-ZENI	Zenair CH.601HD Zodiac	P. P. Plumley	
G-ZENN	Schempp-Hirth Ventus 2cT	T. P. Jenkinson	
G-ZENR	Zenair CH.601HD Zodiac	N. L. Daniels (G-BRJB)	
G-ZENY	Zenair CH.601HD Zodiac	T. R. & B. K. Pugh	
G-ZEPI	Colt GA-42 gas airship	P. A. Lindstrand (G-ISPY/G-BPRB)	
G-ZERO	AA-5B Tiger	Emery-Little Insurance Brokers Ltd	
G-ZETA	Lindstrand LBL-105A balloon	S. Travaglia/Italy	
G-ZEXL	Extra EA.300/L	2 Excel Aviation Ltd	

Notes	Reg.	Type	Owner or Operator
	G-ZFOX	Denney Kitfox Mk.2	S. M. Hall
	G-ZGZG	Cessna 182T	J. Noble
	G-ZHKF	Escapade 912(2)	C. D. & C. M. Wills
	G-ZHWH	Rotorway Executive 162F	B. Alexander
	G-ZIGI	Robin DR.400/180	Aeroclub du Bassin D'Arcachon/France
	G-ZIGY	Europa XS	K. D. Weston
	G-ZIII	Pitts S-2B	W. A. Cruickshank (G-CDBH)
	G-ZINC	Cessna 182S	Zinc Ahead Ltd (G-VALI)
	G-ZINT	Cameron Z-77 balloon	D. Ricci
	G-ZIPA	Rockwell Commander 114A	M. R. Kelly (G-BHRA)
	G-ZIPE	Agusta A109E Power Elite	Noble Foods Ltd
	G-ZIPI	Robin DR.400/180	A. J. Cooper
	G-ZIPY	Wittman W.8 Tailwind	K. J. Nurcombe
	G-ZIRA	Z-1RA Stummelflitzer	D. H. Pattison
	G-ZITZ	AS.355F2 Twin Squirrel	Heli Aviation Ltd
	G-ZIZI	Cessna 525 CitationJet	Ortac Air Ltd
	G-ZIZZ	Agusta A.109 II	Fortis Property Investment LLP
	G-ZLLE	Aérospatiale SA.341G Gazelle	MW Helicopters Ltd
	G-ZLOJ	Beech A36 Bonanza	W. D. Gray
	G-ZMAM	PA-28-181 Archer II	Z. Mahmood (G-BNPN)
	G-ZMED	Learjet 35A	Air Medical Fleet Ltd, Argyll Ltd (G-JETL)
	G-ZODY	Zenair CH.601UL Zodiac	Sarum AX2000 Group
	G-ZOGT	Cirrus SR20	M. Banbury
	G-ZOIZ	Ultramagic M-105 balloon	British Telecommunications PLC
	G-ZONX	Moulai Sonex	FFFF Flyers Group
	G-ZOOG	Tecnam P2006T	Polarb Air Ltd
	G-ZOOH	Balony Kubicek BB20XR balloon	Balony Kubicek Spol Sro
	G-ZOOL	Cessna FA.152	W. J. D. Tollett (G-BGXZ)
	G-ZORO	Shaw Europa	N. T. Read
	G-ZOSA	Champion 7GCAA	R. McQueen
	G-ZRZZ	Cirrus SR22	EKM Systems Ltd
	G-ZSDB	PA-28-236 Dakota	Dakota Air Services LLP (G-BPCX)
	G-ZSIX	Schleicher ASW-27-18E	C. Cowley & C. J. Curtis
	G-ZSKD	Cameron Z-90 balloon	M. J. Gunston
	G-ZSKY	Best Off Sky Ranger Swift 912S(1)	J. E. Lipinski
	G-ZTED	Shaw Europa	J. J. Kennedy
	G-ZTWO	Staaken Z-2 Flitzer	S. J. Randle
	G-ZUMI	Van's RV-8	D. R. CairnsT
	G-ZVIP	Beech 200 Super King Air	Capital Air Charter Ltd (G-SAXN/G-OMNH)
	G-ZVKO	Edge 360	R. J. Allan, N. Jones & A. J. Maxwell
	G-ZWIP	Silence Twister	Zulu Glasstek Ltd (G-TWST)
	G-ZXCL	Extra EA.300/L	2 Excel Aviation Ltd
	G-ZXEL	Extra EA.300/L	2 Excel Aviation Ltd
	G-ZXLL	Extra EA.300/L	2 Excel Aviation Ltd
	G-ZXZX	Learjet 45	Gama Aviation Ltd
	G-ZYAK	IDA Bacau Yakovlev YAK-52	J. A. H. Van Rossom
	G-ZZAC	Aerotechnik EV-97 Eurostar	Cosmik Aviation Ltd
	G-ZZAJ	Schleicher ASH-26E	A. T. Johnstone
	G-ZZDD	Schweizer 269C	Fly 7 Helicopters LLP (G-OCJK)
	G-ZZDG	Cirrus SR20 G2	F13 Ltd
	G-ZZEL	Westland Gazelle AH.1	Tregenna Castle Hotel Ltd
	G-ZZIJ	PA-28-180 Cherokee C	G-ZZIJ Group (G-AVGK)
	G-ZZLE	Westland Gazelle AH.2	Estates (UK) Management Ltd (G-CBSE)
	G-ZZMM	Enstrom 480B	Fly 7 Helicopters LLP (G-TOIL)
	G-ZZOE	Eurocopter EC 120B	J. F. H. James
	G-ZZOW	Medway Eclipse	M. Belemet

Reg.	Type	Owner or Operator	Notes
G-ZZSA	Eurocopter EC.225LP Super Puma	Bristow Helicopters Ltd	
G-ZZSB	Eurocopter EC.225LP Super Puma	Bristow Helicopters Ltd	
G-ZZSC	Eurocopter EC.225LP Super Puma	Bristow Helicopters Ltd	
G-ZZSD	Eurocopter EC.225LP Super Puma	Bristow Helicopters Ltd	
G-ZZSE	Eurocopter EC.225LP Super Puma	Bristow Helicopters Ltd	
G-ZZSF	Eurocopter EC.225LP Super Puma	Bristow Helicopters Ltd	
G-ZZSG	Eurocopter EC.225LP Super Puma	Bristow Helicopters Ltd	
G-ZZSH	Eurocopter EC.225LP Super Puma	Bristow Helicopters Ltd	
G-ZZSI	Eurocopter EC.225LP Super Puma	Bristow Helicopters Ltd (G-CGES)	
G-ZZSK	Eurocopter EC.225LP Super Puma	Bristow Helicopters Ltd	
G-ZZSJ	Eurocopter EC.225LP Super Puma	Bristow Helicopters Ltd	
G-ZZSP	Eurocopter EC.225LP Super Puma	Bristow Helicopters Ltd	
G-ZZTT	Schweizer 269C	Heli Andaluz SL/Spain	
G-ZZXX	P & M Quik GT450	R. G. Street	
G-ZZZA	Boeing 777-236	British Airways	
G-ZZZB	Boeing 777-236	British Airways	
G-ZZZC	Boeing 777-236	British Airways	
G-ZZZS	Eurocopter EC.120B Colibri	London Helicopter Centres Ltd	

ISLE OF MAN REGISTER

Reg.	Type	Owner or Operator	Notes
M-AAAD	Bombardier CL600-2B16 Challenger	Gulf Wings (IOM) Ltd	
M-AAAL	Bombardier BD700-1A10 Global Express	ALM Jet Ltd	
M-AAES	Bombardier CL600-2B16 Challenger	Eliston Enterprises Ltd	
M-ABCD	Dassault Falcon 2000	ASP Aviation Ltd	
M-ABCM	Bombardier BD100-1A10 Challenger 300	Cameron Industries Inc	
M-ABCU	Bombardier CL600-2B16 Challenger	MeHoria Ltd	
M-ABDL	Hawker 4000	SB Leasing Ireland Ltd	
M-ABDP	Hawker 800XP	Kitlan Ltd	
M-ABDQ	Eurocopter EC.135 P2+	Knightspeed Ltd	
M-ABEB	Dassault Falcon 900EX	Dassault Aviation SA	
M-ABEC	Embraer EMB-135BJ Legacy 600	Carys Investment Group Ltd	
M-ABEH	Bombardier CL600-2B16 Challenger	Barclays Bank PLC	
M-ABEI	Bombardier CL600-2B16 Challenger	Barclays Bank PLC	
M-ABEU	Learjet 45	Aviation Leasing (IOM) Ltd	
M-ABEV	Aerospatiale ATR-72-212A	Hubli Aircraft Leasing Ltd	
M-ABEW	Aerospatiale ATR-72-212A	Hubli Aircraft Leasing Ltd	
M-ABFC	Aerospatiale ATR-72-212A	KP Aero	
M-ABFD	Aerospatiale ATR-72-212A	KP Aero	
M-ABFE	Aerospatiale ATR-72-212A	KP Aero	
M-ABFI	Aerospatiale ATR-72-212A	Plateau Aviation Ltd	
M-ABFJ	Aerospatiale ATR-72-212A	Plateau Aviation Ltd	
M-ABFL	Airbus A.330-223	Swiss International Air Lines Ltd	
M-ABFM	Dassault Falcon 7X	Dassault Aviation SA	
M-ABFO	Hawker 400XP	Porto Mediterranean Investments Ltd	
M-ABFQ	Bombardier BD700-1A10 Global 6000	AGT International GmbH	
M-ABFR	Bombardier BD700-1A10 Global 6000	AGT International GmbH	
M-ABFU	Boeing 737-83N	Celestial Aviation Trading 41 Ltd	
M-ABFV	Boeing 737-83N	Celestial Aviation Trading 41 Ltd	
M-ACHO	Bombardier CL600-2B16 Challenger	Zeta Aviation Ltd	
M-ACPT	BAe. 125 Srs.1000	Remo Investments Ltd	
M-ACRO	Eurocopter AS.350B3 Ecureuil	F. Allani	
M-ADAM	Pilatus PC-12/47	ADAM Aircraft Services Ltd	
M-ADEL	Bombardier CL600-2B16 Challenger	Blue Nightingale Trading Ltd	
M-AFAJ	Dassault Falcon 900EX	Elan Finance Management SA	
M-AGGY	Cessna 550 Citation II	Maudib GmbH Deutschland	
M-AGIC	Cessna 680 Citation Sovereign	Trustair Ltd	
M-AIRS	Learjet 60	Maiton Air LLP	
M-AIRU	Bombardier CL600-2B16 Challenger	Setfair Holdings Ltd	
M-AJDM	Cessna 525A Citationjet CJ2	Mazia Investments Ltd	
M-AJOR	Hawker 900XP	INEOS Aviation LLP	
M-AJWA	Bombardier BD700-1A11 Global Express	Global Express Management Ltd	
M-AKAK	Embraer EMB-135BJ Legacy	AAK Company	
M-AKAR	Sikorsky S-76C	Starspeed Ltd	
M-AKOL	Dassault Falcon 7X	Elise Continental Ltd	
M-AKVI	Bombardier BD100-1A10 Challenger 300	AK VI Ltd	
M-ALAY	Gulfstream VP	Stonefel Trade & Invest Ltd	

Notes	Reg.	Type	Owner or Operator
	M-ALBA	Hawker 900XP	Madis Management Ltd
	M-ALCB	Pilatus PC-12/47E	M. S. Bartlett
	M-ALEX	Learjet 60	Berta Finance Ltd
	M-ALMA	Dassault Falcon 7X	Armad Ltd
	M-ALRV	Dassault Falcon 2000EX	Lodgings 2000 LP
	M-ALUN	BAe 125 Srs.700A	Briarwood Products Ltd
	M-AMAN	Pilatus PC-12	Pilatus PC-12 Centre UK Ltd
	M-AMND	Dassault Falcon 2000EX	Doha Capital Ltd
	M-AMRT	Bombardier CL600-2B16 Challenger	Eastern Heights Corporation
	M-ANGA	Embraer EMB-135BJ Legacy 600	Max Air Ltd
	M-ANGO	Bombardier CL600-2B16 Challenger	Waylawn Ltd
	M-ANIE	Gulfstream 550	Pobedy Corporation
	M-ANTA	Bombardier CL600-2B190 Challenger 85	Tathra International Holdings Inc
	M-APLE	Embraer EMB-505 Phenom 300	Poseidon Finance Ltd
	M-ARAE	Gulfstream 450	Global Pipeline Services Ltd
	M-ARCH	Cessna 750 Citation X	Archildsa International Inc.
	M-ARIE	Pilatus PC-12/47E	Guernsey PC-12 Ltd
	M-ARKZ	Bombardier CL600-2B16 Challenger	Markz Jet Ltd
	M-ARRJ	Bombardier BD700-1A10 Global Express	Sentonan Investments Ltd
	M-ARTY	Pilatus PC-12/47E	Creston (UK) Ltd
	M-ASHI	Bombardier CL600-2B16 Challenger	Beckett Holding Ltd
	M-ASRI	Bombardier BD700-1A10 Global Express	YYA Aviation Ltd
	M-ASRY	Bombardier BD100-1A10 Challenger 300	Celina Aviation Ltd
	M-ATAK	Bombardier BD700-1A10 Global 5000	Greenway Investment Assets Ltd
	M-ATAR	Bombardier BD700-1A10 Global	AV West Aircraft Pty.Ltd
	M-ATHS	Pilatus PC-12/47E	Altis Partners (Aviation) Ltd
	M-ATOS	Dassault Falcon 900EX	Banton Overseas Ltd
	M-ATPS	Gulfstream V-SP	Tarona Ltd
	M-AXIM	CessnaT.206H Turbo Stationair	C. D. B. Cope
	M-AYRU	Bombardier CL600-2B16 Challenger	Setfair Aviation Ltd
	M-AZAG	BAe.125 Srs.800B	Mazag
	M-AZIZ	Boeing 737-505	Azizi Group Ltd
	M-AZKL	Agusta A109S Grand	Azikel Dredging Nigeria Ltd
	M-BEST	Cessna 750 Citation X	Lanara Ltd
	M-BETS	Rockwell Commander 695A	Aldersey Aviation Ltd
	M-BETY	Dornier Do.328-310	Funfte XR-GmbH
	M-BIGG	Bombardier CL600-2B16 Challenger	Signal Aviation Ltd
	M-BISA	Pilatus PC-12/47 ★	Pilatus PC-12 Centre UK Ltd
	M-BJEP	Gulfstream 550	M-BJEP Ltd
	M-BLUE	Bombardier BD700-1A11 Global 5000	Tetran Assets Ltd
	M-BONO	Cessna 172N Skyhawk II	J. McCandless
	M-BTAR	Bombardier BD700-1A10 Global Express	AVWest Aircraft Pty.Ltd
	M-BTLT	Bombardier BD100-1A10 Challenger 300	Bombardier Transportation GmbH
	M-BXRH	Cessna 185A	R. E. M. Holmes
	M-CCCP	Bombardier BD700-1A11 Global 5000	Heda Airlines Ltd
	M-CELT	Dassault Falcon 7X	Cravant Ltd
	M-CHEM	Dassault Falcon 200EX	Hampshire Aviation LLP
	M-CHLG	Bombardier CL600-1A11 Challenger	Albion Holdings Ltd
	M-CICO	Dassault Falcon 50	BZ Air Ltd
	M-CIMO	Dassault Falcon 2000EX	Dassault Aviation SA
	M-CLAB	Bombardier BD100-1A10 Challenger 300	Shamrock Trading Ltd
	M-CMAF	Embraer EMB-135BJ	ATS 1011 Leasing Ltd
	M-COOL	Cessna 510 Citation Mustang	E. Keats
	M-CRCR	Bombardier CL600-2B16 Challenger	Prophiol Holdings Ltd
	M-CSTB	Hawker 850XP	Credit Suisse AG
	M-DADI	Dassault Falcon 900DX	Rubicon Capital Consulting Co.Ltd
	M-DARA	Dassault Falcon 200LX	Trident Investment Ltd
	M-DAVE	Pilatus PC-12/47E	Pilatus PC-12 Centre UK Ltd
	M-DBOY	Agusta A.109C	Herair Ltd
	M-DEJB	Dassault Falcon 200	Baron Aircraft Management SA
	M-DKVL	Gulfstream 450	Fiordani Holding Ltd
	M-DMMH	Cessna 680 Citation Sovereign	Heerenknecht Aviation GmbH
	M-DRIL	Pilatus PC-12/47E	Drilling Systems Ltd
	M-DSCL	Embraer 135BJ Legacy	Legacy Aviation Ltd

Reg.	Type	Owner or Operator	Notes
M-DWSF	Bell 430	Dave Whelan Sports Ltd	
M-DWWW	Bombardier CL600-2B19 Challenger	Dragon Asset Global Investment Group Ltd	
M-EAGL	Dassault Falcon 900EX	Faycroft Finance	
M-EANS	Bombardier BD100-1A10 Challenger 300	YH Aviation Ltd	
M-ECJI	Dassault Falcon 10	Fleet International Aviation and Finance Ltd	
M-EGGA	Beech B200 Super King Air	Langley Aviation Ltd	
M-ELON	Cessna 525B Citationjet CJ3	Sleepwell Aviation Ltd	
M-EMCT	Cessna 560 Citation V	Control Techniques Ltd	
M-EMLI	Agusta A109E Power	Tycoon Aviation Ltd	
M-ERCI	Bombardier CL600-2B16 Challenger	J & S Holding Ltd	
M-ERIL	Pilatus PC-12/47E	Confidentia Aviation Ltd	
M-ERRY	Sikorsky S-76B	Trustair Ltd	
M-ESGR	Embraer ERJ135 Legacy	Hermes Executive Aviation Ltd	
M-EVAN	Bombardier BD100-1A10 Challenger 300	Marcus Evans (Aviation) Ltd	
M-EXPL	Eurocopter AS.355N Ecureuil 2	Select Plant Hire Co.Ltd	
M-FAHD	Boeing 727-76	Prime Air Corporation	
M-FALC	Falcon 900EX	Noclaf Ltd	
M-FASH	Dassault Falcon 900B	Al Hokair Aviation Ltd	
M-FBVZ	Bombardier CL600-2B16 Challenger	Qaltin Enterprises Ltd	
M-FINK	BAe. 125 Srs.1000B	B. T. Fink	
M-FIVE	Beech B300 Super King Air 350	Larvotto LP	
M-FLYI	Beech B300 Super King Air 350	Avtrade Ltd	
M-FOUR	Beech G36 Bonanza	Quadra Aviation LP	
M-FROG	Beech 390 Premier 1	White and Cope Aviation LLP	
M-FRZN	Hawker 850XP	Iceland Foods Ltd	
M-FTOH	Boeing 727-269A	Strong Aviation (BVI) Ltd	
M-FUAD	Gulfstream 550	Future Pipe Aviation Ltd	
M-FWIN	Pilatus PC-12/47E	DW Consulting GmbH & Co KG	
M-FZMH	Bombardier CL600-2B19 Global Express	AK VI Ltd	
M-GACB	Dassault Falcon 10	Valiant Aviation Ltd	
M-GASG	Gulfstream 150	PIV Global Holding Ltd	
M-GBAL	Bombardier BD700-1A10 Global Express	Noclaf Ltd	
M-GCCC	Beech B.350i King Air	NG2 SA	
M-GDRS	Beech 390 Premier 1	G. de Rooy	
M-GFOR	Gulfstream IV	Star Oriental International Ltd	
M-GLEX	Bombardier BD700-1A10 Global Express	Pytonian Trade & Invest SA	
M-GLOB	Bombardier BD700-1A10 Global Express	Colvic Investment Holdings Ltd	
M-GOLF	Cessna FR.182RG	P. R. Piggin & C. J. Harding	
M-GPIK	Dassault Falcon 50EX	Dassault Falcon Leasing Ltd	
M-GRAN	Bombardier BD700-1A11 Global 5000	Starflight Investments Ltd	
M-GSKY	Bombardier BD700-1A10 Global Express	Jerand Holdings Ltd	
M-GVSP	Gulfstream 550	Business Universe Ltd	
M-GYQM	Bombardier BD700-1A10 Global Express	Head Win Group Ltd	
M-GZOO	Gulfstream 200	Sentrus Overseas Ltd	
M-HARP	Pilatus PC-12/47E	Harpin Ltd	
M-HAWK	Hawker 800XP	INEOS Aviation LLP	
M-HDAM	BAe 125 Srs.800B	ABG Air Ltd	
M-HELI	Eurocopter EC.155-B1	Flambards Ltd	
M-HHHH	Airbus A.318-112CJ	Kutus Ltd	
M-HLAN	Bombardier CL600-2B19 Challenger 850	Wonder Air International Ltd	
M-HOIL	Learjet 60	Begal Air Ltd	
M-HOTB	Gulfstream V SP	Darwin Air Ltd	
M-HSNT	Bombardier BD100-1A10 Challenger 300	Unisky Ltd	
M-HSXP	Hawker 800XP	HEWE Ltd	
M-IABU	Airbus A.340-313	Klaret Aviation Ltd	
M-IBAA	Aerospatiale ATR-72-212A	KF Turbo Leasing Ltd	
M-IBAC	Aerospatiale ATR-72-212A	K F Turbo Ltd	
M-ICKY	Pilatus PC12/45	Saxon Logistics Ltd	
M-ICRO	Cessna 525A	Pektron Ltd	
M-IDAS	Agusta A109E Power	Trustair Ltd	
M-IFES	Bombardier CL600-1A11 Challenger	Inflite Aviation (IOM) Ltd	
M-IFLY	Pilatus PC-12/47E	N. J. Vetch	

Notes	Reg.	Type	Owner or Operator
	M-IGHT	Learjet 60	High Wing Aviation Ltd
	M-IGOR	Learjet 60	Condamine Enterprises Ltd
	M-IGWT	Bombardier BD700-1A11 Global 5000	Cartek Development Inc
	M-IKAT	Dassault Falcon 2000EX	F2000 LX Ltd
	M-IKEL	Dassault Falcon 2000LX	Second Aircraft Co.Ltd
	M-ILTD	Gulfstream 200	Flash Sky Ltd
	M-IMAK	Embraer EMB-135BJ Legacy 600	Donard Trading Ltd
	M-INOR	Hawker 900XP	INEOS Aviation LLP
	M-IPHS	Gulfstream 550	Islands Aviation Ltd
	M-IRNE	Hawker 850XP	R. N. Edmiston
	M-ISKY	Cessna 550 Citation Bravo	MYSKY LLP
	M-ISLE	Cessna 680 Citation Sovereign	Bakewell Industries Ltd
	M-IVSP	Gulfstream IV SP	Travcorp Air Transportation Ltd
	M-IWPS	Cessna 525A Citationjet CJ2	Schneider Warenvertriebsgesellschaft mbH
	M-JACK	Beech B200GT King Air	Jetstream Aviation Ltd
	M-JANP	Bombardier BD700-1A10 Global Express	Joannou and Paraskevaides (Aviation) Ltd
	M-JCBA	Sikorsky S-76C	J C Bamford Excavators Ltd
	M-JCPO	HS.125 Srs.700A	Saucar Ltd
	M-JETI	BAe 125 Srs 800B	Cassel Invest Ltd
	M-JETT	Dassault Falcon 200	Piraeus Leasing Chrimatodotikes Mishoseis SA
	M-JETZ	Dassault Falcon 2000EX	Avtorita Holdings Ltd
	M-JIGG	Gulfstream 550	Hermes Executive Aviation Ltd
	M-JJTL	Pilatus PC-12/47E	L. Uggia, J. P. Huth & K. Giannamore
	M-JMMM	Dassault Falcon 900B	Executive Aviation (SPV) Ltd
	M-JNJL	Bombardier BD700-1A11 Global Express	Global Thirteen Worldwide Resources Ltd
	M-JOLY	Hawker 900XP	Rooksmead Capital Ltd
	M-JSMN	Bombardier BD700-1A11 Global 5000	Jasmin Aviation Ltd
	M-JSTA	Bombardier CL600-2B16 Challenger	Jetsteff Aviation Ltd
	M-KATE	Airbus A.319-100	Sophar Property Holding
	M-KELY	Embraer EMB-500 Phenom 100	Kelly Air Ltd
	M-KENF	Hawker 4000 Horizon	Avalanche Aviation Ltd
	M-KING	Beech C.90A King Air	Villocq Investments Ltd
	M-KPCO	Embraer EMB-135BJ Legacy	M-KPCO Holding Co.Ltd
	M-KRRR	Learjet 55	R. Rogner
	M-LCJP	Hawker 900XP	Yolenal Ltd
	M-LEFB	Cessna 550	Patagonia Assets Ltd
	M-LEKT	Robin DR.400/180	T. D. Allan, P. & J. P. Bromley
	M-LENR	Beech B.200GT Super King Air	BAE Systems Marine Ltd
	M-LEYS	Beech C.90A King Air	Heres Aviation Ltd
	M-LIFE	Bombardier BD100-1A10 Challenger 300	NY Jets Transporter Ltd
	M-LILY	Bombardier CL600-2B19 Challenger 850	Bright Loysal Ltd/Offshore Incorporations (Cayman) Ltd
	M-LION	Hawker 900XP	Lion Invest and Trade Ltd
	M-LJGI	Dassault Falcon 2000Easy	Ven Air
	M-LOOK	Bombardier CL600-2B16 Challenger	Kennington Ltd
	M-LRJT	Learjet 40	Chemiplastica Aviation Ltd
	M-LUNA	Eurocopter MBB BK-117C-2	Flambards Ltd
	M-LVIA	Eurocopter AS.365N3 Dauphin 2	Flambards Ltd
	M-LWSA	Bombardier BD700-1A10 305 Global Express	Lynx Aviation (Isle of Man) Ltd
	M-MACH	Embraer EMB-500 Phenom 100	Mach Air Ltd
	M-MANX	Cessna 425 Conquest	Suas Investments Ltd
	M-MARI	Learjet 60XR	Rumit Aviation Ltd
	M-MDDE	CL-600-2B16 Challenger	Fielding Overseas Ltd
	M-MDMH	Embraer EMB-505 Phenom 300	Herrenknecht Aviation GmbH
	M-MHAC	Learjet 60	Trans Aviation Ltd
	M-MHDH	Cessna 510 Citation Mustang	Herrenknecht Aviation GmbH
	M-MHFZ	Embraer EMB-135BJ Legacy	AK VI Ltd
	M-MHMH	Cessna 525B Citationjet CJ3	Herrenknecht Aviation GmbH
	M-MIDO	Raytheon Hawker 800XP	Barbican Holdings Ltd
	M-MIKE	Cessna 525B Citationjet CJ3	M. F. Jacobson
	M-MMAA	Bombardier BD700-1A10 Global Express	JAPAT AG (Isle of Man)
	M-MNAA	Bombardier BD700-1A10 Global Express	JAPAT AG (Isle of Man)
	M-MNBB	Dassault Falcon 7X	JAPAT AG (Isle of Man)
	M-MNCC	Dassault Falcon 7X	JAPAT AG (Isle of Man)
	M-MNDD	Dassault Falcon 900EX	JAPAT AG (Isle of Man)
	M-MOMO	Gulfstream V SP	Fayair (Jersey) Co Ltd

Reg.	Type	Owner or Operator	Notes
M-MOON	Cessna 750	Bambara Holding SA	
M-MRBB	Learjet 45	Boultbee Aviation 3 LLP	
M-MSGG	Gulfstream G200	ARTOC Prague	
M-MTPO	Bombardier CL600-2A12 Challenger	Marimax Jets Ltd	
M-NALE	Bombardier BD700-1A10 Global Express	Jover Ltd	
M-NGSN	Pilatus PC-12/47E	N. Stolt-Nielsen	
M-NHOI	Bombardier CL600-2B16 Challenger	Hatta Investments Ltd	
M-NICE	Gulfstream 200	M-NICE Ltd	
M-NIKO	Dassault Falcon 2000	Halkin Jet SRL	
M-NINE	Beech G58 Baron	Larvotto LP	
M-NJSS	Embraer EMB-135BJ Legacy	Saby Finance Ltd	
M-NLYY	PA-42-1000 Cheyenne 400LS	Factory Leasing Ltd	
M-NOEL	Bombardier BD100-1A10 Challenger	ABS Service Ltd	
M-NSJS	Cessna 525C Citationjet CJ4	Ferncroft Ltd	
M-ODKZ	Dassault Falcon 900EX	Skylane LP	
M-OGUL	Agusta A109S Grand	Medway Leasing Ltd	
M-OIWA	Bombardier BD100-1A10 Challenger	Delta A/S	
M-OLAR	Liberty XL-2	C. Partington	
M-OLEG	Embraer 135BJ Legacy	Hermitage Air Ltd	
M-OLLE	Hawker 750	Dunard Engineering Ltd	
M-OLLY	Cessna 525 Citationjet CJ1	MBK Maschinenbau GmbH/Bohnet GmbH	
M-OLTT	Pilatus PC-12/47E	One Luxury Travel LLP	
M-OMAN	Dassault Falcon 7X	RUWI Ltd	
M-ONAV	Hawker 900XP	Monavia Ltd	
M-ONDE	Eurocopter MBB BK.117C2	Peyton Ltd	
M-ONEM	Gulfstream 550	G550 Ltd	
M-ONTY	Sikorsky S-76C	Trustair Ltd	
M-OODY	Cessna 525B Citationjet CJ3	Futures Aviation Services Ltd	
M-OOSE	PA-46-500TP Malibu Meridian	Global Domain Names Ltd	
M-OPAL	Pilatus PC-12/47E	G-GYC Ltd	
M-OPED	PA-32-301XTC Saratoga	Hock Lai Cham	
M-ORAD	Dassault Falcon 2000EX	Swift Aviation Ltd	
M-OSPB	Gulfstream G200	G200 Ltd	
M-OTOR	Beech C90A King Air	Pektron Group Ltd	
M-OUSE	Cessna 510 Citation Mustang	Mouse (IOM) Ltd	
M-OUTH	Diamond DA.42 Twin Star	Sky Fly LP Inc	
M-OZZA	Bombardier BD100-1A10 Challenger 300	Casam International Ltd	
M-PACF	Eurocopter EC135 P2+	Starspeed Ltd	
M-PBKI	Gulfstream IV SP	GIV-SP Air Service Ltd	
M-PCPC	Pilatus PC-12/45	Treetops Aviation LLP	
M-PHML	American General AG-5B Tiger	I. J. Ross & J. R. Shannon	
M-PMPM	Embraer EMB-135BJ Legacy 600	Airstar Leasing Ltd	
M-POWR	Beech C.90A King Air	Northside Aviation Ltd	
M-PREI	Raytheon RB390 Premier 1	Craft Air SA	
M-PRVT	Cessna 750 Citation X	Unifox Holdings Ltd	
M-PZPZ	Gulfstream IV	A. I. Eze	
M-RBUS	Airbus A.319-115CJ	Belville Investment Ltd	
M-RCCG	Embraer EMB-135BJ Legacy 650	Russian Copper Co. Holdings Ltd	
M-RIDE	BD-700-1A11 Global 5000	Jesper Continental SA	
M-RKAY	Raytheon 390 Premier 1A	Sunseeker Corporate Aviation Ltd	
M-RLDR	Pilatus PC-12/45	RDLR Air Ltd	
M-RLIV	Bombardier CL600-2B16 Challenger	Mobyhold Ltd	
M-ROLL	Dassault Falcon 7X	Pacelli Beteiligungs GmbH and Co KG	
M-ROMA	Learjet 45	ArtJet Ltd	
M-RONE	Dassault Falcon 2000EX	Ocean Sky Aircraft Management Ltd	
M-ROWL	Dassault Falcon 900EX	M. Rowley	
M-RSKL	Bombardier BD700-1A10 Global Express	Angel Aviation Ltd	
M-RUAT	Bombardier BD700-1A10 Global Express	Vipjet Ltd	
M-RURU	Falcon 900B	Rozita Ltd	
M-SAHA	Embraer EMB-135BJ Legacy	ATT Aviation Ltd	
M-SAIL	Pilatus PC-12/47E	G. G. & L. G. Gordon	
M-SAIR	Falcon 900B	W. A. Developments International Ltd	
M-SAPL	Bombardier CL600-2B16 Challenger	Sapetro Aviation Ltd	
M-SAPT	Hawker 900XP	Sapetro Aviation Ltd	
M-SBAH	Embraer ERJ190ECJ Lineage 1000	National Lineage M-SBAH Holding Co.Ltd	
M-SCMG	Dassault Falcon 7X	BlueSky International Management Ltd	
M-SEAS	Bombardier BD700-1A11 Global 5000	Jana Aviation Ltd	
M-SFAM	McDonnell Douglas MD-87	Montavachi Ltd	

BRITISH CIVIL REGISTRATIONS

Notes	Reg.	Type	Owner or Operator
	M-SFRI	Bombardier CL600-2B16 Challenger	King Fontaine Ltd
	M-SGCR	Cessna 550 Citation Bravo	Labraid Ltd
	M-SHEP	SOCATA TBM-850	L. W. & J. K. Shephard
	M-SHLA	Bombardier CL600-2B16 Challenger	Barclays Bank PLC
	M-SITM	BAe 125-800SP	SITM Jet Ltd
	M-SKSM	Bombardier BD700-1A11 Global	Tesker Management Ltd
	M-SMKM	Cirrus SR20	K. Mallet
	M-SNAP	Dassault Falcon 2000EASy	Aviation Holding Services Ltd
	M-SNER	Dassault Falcon 2000EX	Wincor Aviation Establishment
	M-SNSS	Dassault Falcon 50EX	Brookline Holdings Ltd
	M-SPEC	Beech B350 Super King Air	Specsavers Aviation Ltd
	M-SPEX	Beech B350 Super King Air	Specsavers Aviation Ltd
	M-SPOR	Beech B200 King Air	Select Plant Hire Co.Ltd
	M-SQAR	Gulfstream V-SP	M Square Aviation Ltd
	M-SRNE	Eurocopter MBB-BK.117C-2	Serena Aviation Ltd
	M-SSSR	Bombardier BD700-1A10 Global Express	VipJet Ltd
	M-STAR	Boeing 727-2X8	Starling Aviation Ltd
	M-STCO	Dassault Falcon 2000LX	STC IOM Ltd
	M-STEP	Gulfstream G150	ArtJet Ltd
	M-SVGN	Cessna 680 Citation Sovereign	Vocalion Ltd
	M-SWAN	IAI Gulfstream 200	Falcon Crest Resources Inc.
	M-SYGB	Beech B.200GT Super King Air	Rialus Ltd
	M-TAKE	Bombardier CL600-2B19 Challenger 850	Caropan Company SA
	M-TEAM	Cessna 525B Citationjet CJ1+	Mistral Aviation Ltd
	M-TKFR	Gulfstream V SP	Tele-Fonika Kable Sp
	M-TNTJ	Learjet 55	TNT Airways SA
	M-TOMS	Pilatus PC-12/47E	C J Airways Ltd
	M-TOPI	Bombardier CL600-2B16 Challenger	Gladiator Flight Ltd
	M-TRBS	Bombardier CL600-2B16 Challenger	Arrow Management Property Corp
	M-TSRI	Beech C.90GTI King Air	Timpson Ltd
	M-UKHA	Hawker 800XP	Nebula III Ltd
	M-UNIS	Bombardier BD700-1A10 Global Express	Lapwing Ltd
	M-UPCO	Cessna 525B CitationJet CJ3	Ulla Popken GmbH
	M-URKA	Sikorsky S-76B	Starspeed Ltd
	M-URUS	Boeing 737-7GC	Ingram Services Ltd
	M-USBA	Gulfstream V	Shukra Ltd
	M-USCA	SOCATA TBM-850	Sterna Aviation Ltd
	M-USHY	Cessna 441 Conquest	Flying Dogs Ltd
	M-USTG	Cessna 510 Citation Mustang	OSM Aviation Ltd
	M-UTIN	Pilatus PC-12/45	Myriel Aviation SA
	M-VANG	Bombardier BD700-1A10 Global Express	Elderberry Ltd
	M-VBPO	Beech 390 Premier 1A	Asia Universal Jet Ltd
	M-VGIN	Dassault Falcon 50EX	Charter Air Ltd
	M-VITO	Hawker 800XP	Beratex Group Ltd
	M-VQBI	Bombardier BD700-1A10 Global Express	Altitude X3 Ltd
	M-VRNY	Gulfstream 550	Mirtos Ltd
	M-VSSK	Bombardier CL600-2B16 Challenger	Clear Horizon Ltd
	M-WATJ	Beech B.200GT Super King Air	Saxonhenge Ltd
	M-WHAT	Eurocopter EC.135T2+	Starspeed Ltd
	M-WING	Dassault Falcon 900EX	Certeco Aviation Ltd
	M-WINT	Pilatus PC-12/43E	Air Winton Ltd
	M-WLLM	Beech C.90GTI King Air	Wilpot Ltd
	M-WMWM	Cessna 525A Citationjet CJ2	Standard Aviation Ltd
	M-WOOD	Cessna 550 Citation Bravo	Horizon Air LLP
	M-XHEC	Eurocopter EC155B	Flambards Ltd
	M-XJOB	Cessna 560XL Citation XLS	AMS Ltd
	M-YAIR	Hawker 390 Premier 1A	RB209 IOM Ltd
	M-YBBJ	Boeing 737-7HE BBJ	Hamilton Jets Ltd
	M-YBJK	Gulfstream 550	AC Executive Aircraft (2011) Ltd
	M-YBST	Bombardier CL600-2B16 Challenger	Kilmarnock Management Ltd
	M-YCEF	Hawker 800XP	Spirit Ltd
	M-YCUP	Embraer EMB-135BJ Legacy	Reatex Invest SA
	M-YEDC	Cessna 525B CitationJet CJ3	Air Charter Scotland Ltd
	M-YEDT	Gulfstream 100	Opal Consulting LLC
	M-YFLY	Bombardier BD700-1A10 Global Express	Glenn Eagles Research LLP
	M-YGIV	Gulfstream IV	Al-Sahab Ltd
	M-YGLK	Gulfstream 450	Overseas Operation Ltd

Reg.	Type	Owner or Operator	Notes
M-YHOP	Agusta A109S Grand	Lemsage Ltd	
M-YJET	Dassault Falcon 2000Easy	My Jet Ltd	
M-YLEO	Pilatus PC-12/47E	Guernsey PC-12 Ltd	
M-YNNS	Dassault Falcon 7X	NS Falcon Ltd	
M-YONE	Bombardier CL600-2B16 Challenger	Inflite Aviation (IOM) Ltd	
M-YORK	Falcon 7X	Lead Universal Ltd	
M-YRGN	Aerospatiale ATR-72-212A	Turbo 72-500 Leasing Ltd	
M-YRGO	Embraer ERJ-170-200LR	ECC Leasing Co.Ltd	
M-YRGP	Embraer ERJ-170-200LR	ECC Leasing Co.Ltd	
M-YRGR	Airbus A.310-324F	Nilgiri Hills Leasing Ltd	
M-YRGS	Airbus A.310-324F	Kaveri Leasing Ltd	
M-YRGT	Airbus A.310-324F	Godvari Leasing Ltd	
M-YSAI	Bombardier BD700-1A10 Global 5000	Capital Investment Worldwide	
M-YSKY	Raytheon 390 Premier 1A	RB209 IOM Ltd	
M-YTAF	Beech B.36TC Bonanza	FBS Aviation Ltd	
M-YTOY	Embraer EMB-500 Phenom 100	TD Aviation IOM Ltd	
M-YULI	Bombardier BD700-1A11 Global Express	Primevalue Trading Ltd	
M-YUNI	Bombardier CL600-2B16 Challenger	Unitrans Management Ltd	
M-YWAU	Airbus A.320-211	South Jet One Ltd	
M-YWAY	Gulfstream IV SP	Blue Sky Leasing Ltd	
M-YZZT	Cirrus SR22T	Stamp Aviation Ltd	
M-ZELL	Cessna 208 Caravan	Ridler Verwaltungs und Vermittlungs GmbH	
M-ZUMO	Pilatus PC-12/47	C. C. H. Way Ltd	

G-AEEG M.3A Falcon Skysport. *Tom Cole*

G-ANZT Thruxton Jackaroo. *Peter R. March*

G-ATBU Beagle A.61 Terrier 2. *Peter R. March*

G-BMSL FRED Srs.1. *Peter R. March*

G-BTDE Cessna C-165 Airmaster. *Peter R. March*

G-BVVG Nanchang CJ-6R/68. *Peter R. March*

G-BWWT Dornier 328-100 of Flybe. *Allan S. Wright*

G-BYTM Dyn'Aero MCR-01. *Peter R. March*

G-CBLZ Rutan LongEz. *Tom Cole*

G-CZCZ Avions Mudry CAP-10B. *Peter R. March*

G-GATT Robinson R44 II. *Allan S. Wright*

G-HATZ Hatz CB-1. *Peter R. March*

G-KFLY Flight Design CTSW. *Peter R. March*

G-RCKT Harmon Rocket II. *Tom Cole*

G-RJXI Embraer RJ145EP of bmi regional. *Allan S. Wright*

G-TSOL EAA Acrosport 1. *Allan S. Wright*

G-UPFS Waco UPS-7. Peter R. March

G-VIIL Boeing 777-236 of British Airways. *Allan S. Wright*

G-ZEBS Aerospatiale ATR-42-320 of Blue Islands. *Allan S. Wright*

M-BETS Rockwell Commander 695A. *Peter R. March*

322

M-JETZ Falcon 2000EX. *Allan S. Wright*

Military to Civil Cross-Reference

Serial carried	Civil identity	Serial carried	Civil identity
001	G-BYPY	1373 (Portuguese AF)	G-CBJG
1	G-BPVE	1377 (Portuguese AF)	G-BARS
6G-ED (Luftwaffe)	G-BZOB	1747 (Portuguese AF)	G-BGPB
9 (Soviet AF)	G-OYAK	2345 (RFC)	G-ATVP
09 (DOSAAF)	G-BVMU	3066	G-AETA
10 (DOSAAF)	G-BTZB	3072:72 (USN)	G-TEXN
10 (DOSAAF)	G-CBMD	3349 (RCAF)	G-BYNF
11 (Soviet AF)	G-YCII	3397:174 (USN)	G-OBEE
26 (USAAC)	G-BAVO	4034 (Luftwaffe)	G-CDTI
26 (DOSAAF)	G-BVXK	4406:12 (USN)	G-ONAF
27 (Soviet AF)	G-YAKX	4513:1 (French AF)	G-BFYO
27 (USN)	G-BRVG	5964 (RFC)	G-BFVH
27 (USAAC)	G-AGYY	6136:205 (USN)	G-BRUJ
27 (Soviet AF)	G-YAKX	7198/18 (Luftwaffe)	G-AANJ
42 (Soviet AF)	G-CBRU	7797 (USAAF)	G-BFAF
43:SC (USAF)	G-AZSC	8178:FU-178 (USAF)	G-SABR
44 (DOSAAF)	G-BXAK	8449M (RAF)	G-ASWJ
49 (USAAF)	G-KITT	9917	G-EBKY
50 (DOSAAF)	G-CBPM	01420 (Polish AF but in Korean colours)	G-BMZF
50 (DOSAAF)	G-CBRW	14863 (USAAF)	G-BGOR
50 (DOSAAF)	G-EYAK	16693:693 (RCAF)	G-BLPG
52 (DOSAAF)	G-BWVR	18013:013 (RCAF)	G-TRIC
55 (DOSAAF)	G-BVOK	18393:393 (RCAF)	G-BCYK
67 (DOSAAF)	G-CBSL	18671:671 (RCAF)	G-BNZC
68 (Chinese AF)	G-BVVG	20310:310 (RCAF)	G-BSBG
69 (Russian AF)	G-XYAK	21261:261 (RCAF)	G-TBRD
78 (French Army)	G-BIZK	21509 (US Army)	G-UHIH
82:8 (French AF)	G-CCVH	24550 (US Army)	G-PDOG
93 (DOSAAF)	G-JYAK	24582 (US Army)	G-VDOG
100 (DOSAAF)	G-YAKI	28521:TA-521 (USAF)	G-TVIJ
112 (USAAC)	G-BSWC	30146 (Yugoslav Army)	G-BSXD
113 (Kuwait AF)	G-CFBK	30149 (Yugoslav Army)	G-SOKO
118 (USAAC)	G-BSDS	31145:G-26 (USAAF)	G-BBLH
124 (French Army)	G-BOSJ	3-1923 (USAAF)	G-BRHP
143 (French AF)	G-MSAL	31952 (USAAF)	G-BRPR
156 (French AF)	G-NIFE	39624:D-39 (USAAF)	G-BVMH
161 (Irish Air Corps)	G-CCCA	40467:19 (USN)	G-BTCC
168 (RFC)	G-BFDE	56321:U-AB (Royal Norwegian AF)	G-BKPY
174 (Royal Netherlands Navy)	G-BEPV	80105 (US Air Service)	G-CCBN
177 (Irish Air Corps)	G-BLIW	80425:WT-4 (USN)	G-RUMT
311 (Singapore AF)	G-MXPH	111836:JZ-6 (USN)	G-TSIX
347	G-AWYI	115042:TA-042 (USAF)	G-BGHU
354	G-BZNK	115227 (USN)	G-BKRA
379 (USAAC)	G-ILLE	115302:TP (USMC)	G-BJTP
422/15 (Luftwaffe)	G-AVJO	115373 (USAAF)	G-AYPM
423 / 427 (Royal Norwegian AF)	G-AMRK	115684 (USAAF)	G-BKVM
425 (Oman AF)	G-SOAF	121714:201-B (USN)	G-RUMM
441 (USN)	G-BTFG	124485:DF-A (USAAF)	G-BEDF
450/17 (Luftwaffe)	G-BVGZ	126922:503 (USN)	G-RADR
503 (Hungarian AF)	G-BRAM	150225:123 (USMC)	G-AWOX
540 (USAAF)	G-BCNX	18-2001 (USAAF)	G-BIZV
669 (USAAC)	G-CCXA	18-5395:CDG (French Army)	G-CUBJ
781-32 (Spanish AF)	G-BPDM	238410:A-44 (USAAF)	G-BHPK
854 (USAAC)	G-BTBH	314887 (USAAF)	G-AJPI
897:E (USN)	G-BJEV	315509:W7-S (USAAF)	G-BHUB
99+26 (Luftwaffe)	G-BZGL	329405:A-23 (USAAF)	G-BCOB
99+32 (Luftwaffe)	G-BZGK	329417 (USAAF)	G-BDHK
1018 (Polish AF)	G-ISKA	329471:F-44 (USAAF)	G-BGXA
1102:102 (USN)	G-AZLE	329601:D-44 (USAAF)	G-AXHR
1104 (Royal Saudi AF)	G-SMAS	329854:R-44 (USAAF)	G-BMKC
1125 (Kuwaiti AF)	G-CFBK	329934:B-72 (USAAF)	G-BCPH
1130 (Royal Saudi AF)	G-VPER	330238:A-24 (USAAF)	G-LIVH
1164:64 (USAAC)	G-BKGL	330485:C-44 (USAAF)	G-AJES
1211(North Korean AF)	G-MIGG	343251:27 (USAAF)	G-NZSS
1342 (Soviet AF)	G-BTZD	413521:5Q-B (USAAF)	G-MRLL
1363 (Portuguese AF)	G-DHPM	413704: 87-H (USAAF)	G-BTCD

Serial carried	Civil identity	Serial carried	Civil identity
413926: E2-S (USAAF)	G-CGOI	F235:B	G-BMDB
414419:LH-F (USAAF)	G-MSTG	F904	G-EBIA
433915 (USAAF)	G-PBYA	F938	G-EBIC
436021 (USAAF)	G-BWEZ	F943	G-BIHF
454467:J-44 (USAAF)	G-BILI	F943	G-BKDT
454537:J-04 (USAAF)	G-BFDL	F5447:N	G-BKER
461748:Y (USAF)	G-BHDK	F5459:Y	G-INNY
472035 (USAAF)	G-SIJJ	F8010:Z	G-BDWJ
472216:HO-M (USAAF)	G-BIXL	F8614	G-AWAU
474008:VF-R (USAAF)	G-PSIR	G-48-1 (Class B)	G-ALSX
479744:M-49 (USAAF)	G-BGPD	J-1573 (Swiss AF)	G-VICI
479766:D-63 (USAAF)	G-BKHG	J-1605 (Swiss AF)	G-BLID
479897:JD(USAAF)	G-BOXJ	J-1632 (Swiss AF)	G-VNOM
480015:M-44 (USAAF)	G-AKIB	J-1758 (Swiss AF)	G-BLSD
480133:B-44 (USAAF)	G-BDCD	J-4021 (Swiss AF)	G-HHAC
480173:57-H (USAAF)	G-RRSR	J-4083 (Swiss AF)	G-EGHH
480321:H-44 (USAAF)	G-FRAN	J7326	G-EBQP
480480:E-44 (USAAF)	G-BECN	J9941:57	G-ABMR
480636:A-58 (USAAF)	G-AXHP	K1786	G-AFTA
480723:E5-J (USAAF)	G-BFZB	K1930	G-BKBB
480752:E-39 (USAAF)	G-BCXJ	K2048	G-BZNW
493209 (US ANG)	G-DDMV	K2050	G-ASCM
542447 (USAF)	G-SCUB	K2059	G-PFAR
2632019 (Chinese AF)	G-BXZB	K2075	G-BEER
41-13297/284 (USAAC)	G-CDWH	K2227	G-ABBB
41-33275:CE (USAAF)	G-BICE	K2567	G-MOTH
42-10855 (USAAF)	G-KITT	K2572	G-AOZH
42-25068:WZ (USAAF)	G-CDVX	K2585	G-ANKT
42-35870:129 (USN)	G-BWLJ	K2587	G-BJAP
42-58678:IY (USAAF)	G-BRIY	K3241	G-AHSA
42-78044 (USAAF)	G-BRXL	K3661	G-BURZ
42-84555:EP-H (USAAF)	G-ELMH	K3731	G-RODI
43-35943 (USN)	G-BKRN	K4259:71	G-ANMO
44-79609:44-S (USAAF)	G-BHXY	K5054	G-BRDV
44-80594 (USAAF)	G-BEDJ	K5414:XV	G-AENP
44-83184 (USAAF)	G-RGUS	K5600	G-BVVI
51-7692 (French AF)	G-TROY	K5673	G-BZAS
51-11701A:AF258 (USAF)	G-BSZC	K5674	G-CBZP
51-15319 (USAAF)	G-FUZZ	K7985	G-AMRK
54-2445 (USAF)	G-OTAN	K8203	G-BTVE
69-16011 (USAAF)	G-OHGA	K8303:D	G-BWWN
A-10 (Swiss AF)	G-BECW	L2301	G-AIZG
A11-301 (RAN)	G-ARKG	L6906	G-AKKY
A16-199:SF-R (RAAF)	G-BEOX	N-294 (RNeth AF)	G-KAXF
A17-48 (RAAF)	G-BPHR	N500	G-BWRA
A-57 (Swiss AF)	G-BECT	N1854	G-AIBE
A-806 (Swiss AF)	G-BTLL	N1977:8 (French AF)	G-BWMJ
A8226	G-BIDW	N3200	G-CFGJ
B595:W	G-BUOD	N3788	G-AKPF
B1807	G-EAVX	N4877:MK-V	G-AMDA
B2458:R	G-BPOB	N5182	G-APUP
B6401	G-AWYY	N5195	G-ABOX
C1904:Z	G-PFAP	N5199	G-BZND
C3009	G-BFWD	N5719	G-CBHO
C3011:S	G-SWOT	N5903:H	G-GLAD
C4918	G-BWJM	N6-766 (Royal Australian Navy)	G-VYPO
C4994	G-BLWM	N6290	G-BOCK
C5430	G-CCXG	N6452	G-BIAU
C9533:M	G-BUWE	N6466	G-ANKZ
D-692	G-BVAW	N6537	G-AOHY
D5397/17 (Luftwaffe)	G-BFXL	N6720:VX	G-BYTN
D7889	G-AANM	N6797	G-ANEH
D8084	G-ACAA	N6847	G-APAL
D8096:D	G-AEPH	N6965:FL-J	G-AJTW
E-15 (Royal Netherlands AF)	G-BIYU	N9191	G-ALND
E3B-143 (Spanish AF)	G-JUNG	N9192:RCO-N	G-DHZF
E3B-153:781-75 (Spanish AF)	G-BPTS	P2902:DX-X	G-ROBT
E3B-350:05-97 (Spanish AF)	G-BHPL	P6382:C	G-AJRS
E449	G-EBJE	P9374	G-MKIA
E3273	G-ADEV	P9398	G-CEPL
E8894	G-CDLI	R-151 (RNethAF)	G-BIYR
F141:G	G-SEVA	R-163 (RNethAF)	G-BIRH

Serial carried	Civil identity	Serial carried	Civil identity
R-167 (RNethAF)	G-LION	DG590	G-ADMW
R1914	G-AHUJ	EM720	G-AXAN
R3821:UX-N	G-BPIV	EN224	G-FXII
R4118:UP-W	G-HUPW	EP120:AE-A	G-LFVB
R4922	G-APAO	ES.1-4 (Spanish AF)	G-BUTX
R4959:59	G-ARAZ	FB226:MT-A	G-BDWM
R5136	G-APAP	FE695:94	G-BTXI
R5172:FIJ-E	G-AOIS	FE788	G-CTKL
R5250	G-AODT	FH153	G-BBHK
S1287	G-BEYB	FJ777 (RCAF)	G-BIXN
S1579:571	G-BBVO	FR886	G-BDMS
S1581:573	G-BWWK	FS628	G-AIZE
T5854	G-ANKK	FT391	G-AZBN
T5879:RUC-W	G-AXBW	FX301:FD-NQ	G-TXAN
T6562	G-ANTE	FZ626:YS-DH	G-AMPO
T6953	G-ANNI	HB275	G-BKGM
T7230	G-AFVE	HB751	G-BCBL
T7281	G-ARTL	HD-75 (R Belgian AF)	G-AFDX
T7290	G-ANNK	HG691	G-AIYR
T7793	G-ANKV	HM580	G-ACUU
T7794	G-ASPV	JV579:F	G-RUMW
T7798	G-ANZT	KB889:NA-I	G-LANC
T7842	G-AMTF	KD345:130-A	G-FGID
T7909	G-ANON	KF584:RAI-X	G-RAIX
T8191	G-BWMK	KF729	G-BJST
T9707	G-AKKR	KG651	G-AMHJ
T9738	G-AKAT	KK116	G-AMPY
T9768	G-AIUA	KN353	G-AMYJ
U-0247 (Class B identity)	G-AGOY	LB264	G-AIXA
U-80 (Swiss AF)	G-BUKK	LB312	G-AHXE
U-95 (Swiss AF)	G-BVGP	LB323	G-AHSD
U-99 (Swiss AF)	G-AXMT	LB367	G-AHGZ
U-108 (Swiss AF)	G-BJAX	LB375	G-AHGW
U-110 (Swiss AF)	G-PTWO	LF858	G-BLUZ
V-54 (Swiss AF)	G-BVSD	LZ766	G-ALCK
V3388	G-AHTW	MB293	G-CFGI
V7497	G-HRLI	MH434:ZD-B	G-ASJV
V9312	G-CCOM	MJ627:9G-P	G-BMSB
V9367:MA-B	G-AZWT	ML407:OU-V	G-LFIX
V9673:MA-J	G-LIZY	MP425	G-AITB
W2718	G-RNLI	MS824 (French AF)	G-AWBU
W5856:A2A	G-BMGC	MT197	G-ANHS
W9385:YG-L	G-ADND	MT438	G-AREI
X4276	G-CDGU	MT818	G-AIDN
X4650	G-CGUK	MV268:JE-J	G-SPIT
Z2033:N/275	G-ASTL	MW401	G-PEST
Z5140:HA-C	G-HURI	MW763:HF-A	G-TEMT
Z5207	G-BYDL	NJ633	G-AKXP
Z5252:GO-B	G-BWHA	NJ673	G-AOCR
Z7015:7-L	G-BKTH	NJ695	G-AJXV
Z7197	G-AKZN	NJ719	G-ANFU
Z7288	G-AHGD	NJ889	G-AHLK
AB196	G-CCGH	NL750	G-AOBH
AP506	G-ACWM	NL985	G-BWIK
AP507:KX-P	G-ACWP	NM181	G-AZGZ
AR213:PR-D	G-AIST	NX534	G-BUDL
AR501:NN-A	G-AWII	NX611:LE-C/DX-C	G-ASXX
BB697	G-ADGT	PL965:R	G-MKXI
BB807	G-ADWO	PL983	G-PRXI
BE505:XP-L	G-HHII	PS853:C	G-RRGN
BI-005 (RNethAF)	G-BUVN	PT462:SW-A	G-CTIX
BM597:JH-C	G-MKVB	PT879	G-BYDE
CW-BG (Luftwaffe)	G-BXBD	RG333	G-AIEK
DE208	G-AGYU	RG333	G-AKEZ
DE470	G-ANMY	RH377	G-ALAH
DE623	G-ANFI	RK855	G-PIXY
DE673	G-ADNZ	RL962	G-AHED
DE992	G-AXXV	RM221	G-ANXR
DF112	G-ANRM	RN218:N	G-BBJI
DF128:RCO-U	G-AOJJ	RR232	G-BRSF
DF155	G-ANFV	RT486:PF-A	G-AJGJ
DF198	G-BBRB	RT520	G-ALYB

Serial carried	Civil identity	Serial carried	Civil identity
RT610	G-AKWS	WD331:J	G-BXDH
RX168	G-BWEM	WD363:5	G-BCIH
SM520:KJ-1	G-ILDA	WD373:12	G-BXDI
SM969:D-A	G-BRAF	WD379:K	G-APLO
SX336:105-VL	G-KASX	WD390:68	G-BWNK
TA634:8K-K	G-AWJV	WD413	G-VROE
TA719:6T	G-ASKC	WE569	G-ASAJ
TA805:FX-M	G-PMNF	WE724:062	G-BUCM
TD248:CR-S	G-OXVI	WF118	G-DACA
TE184:D	G-MXVI	WF877	G-BPOA
TE517	G-JGCA	WG308:8	G-BYHL
TJ534	G-AKSY	WG316	G-BCAH
TJ569	G-AKOW	WG321:G	G-DHCC
TJ652	G-AMVD	WG348	G-BBMV
TJ672:TS-D	G-ANIJ	WG350	G-BPAL
TJ704:JA	G-ASCD	WG407:67	G-BWMX
TS798	G-AGNV	WG422:16	G-BFAX
TW439	G-ANRP	WG465	G-BCEY
TW467	G-ANIE	WG469:72	G-BWJY
TW501	G-ALBJ	WG472	G-AOTY
TW511	G-APAF	WG655	G-CHFP
TW536:TS-V	G-BNGE	WG719	G-BRMA
TW591:N	G-ARIH	WJ358	G-ARYD
TW641	G-ATDN	WJ368	G-ASZX
TX213	G-AWRS	WJ945:21	G-BEDV
TX310	G-AIDL	WK163	G-BVWC
VF512:PF-M	G-ARRX	WK436	G-VENM
VF516	G-ASMZ	WK512:A	G-BXIM
VF526:T	G-ARXU	WK514	G-BBMO
VF581	G-ARSL	WK517	G-ULAS
VL348	G-AVVO	WK522	G-BCOU
VL349	G-AWSA	WK549	G-BTWF
VM360	G-APHV	WK577	G-BCYM
VN799	G-CDSX	WK585	G-BZGA
VP955	G-DVON	WK586:V	G-BXGX
VP981	G-DHDV	WK590:69	G-BWVZ
VR192	G-APIT	WK609:93	G-BXDN
VR249:FA-EL	G-APIY	WK611	G-ARWB
VR259:M	G-APJB	WK624	G-BWHI
VS356	G-AOLU	WK628	G-BBMW
VS610:K-L	G-AOKL	WK630	G-BXDG
VS623	G-AOKZ	WK633:A	G-BXEC
VV612	G-VENI	WK640:C	G-BWUV
VX113	G-ARNO	WK642:94	G BXDP
VX118	G-ASNB	WL626:P	G-BHDD
VX147	G-AVIL	WM167	G-LOSM
VX281	G-RNHF	WP308:572CU	G-GACA
VX927	G-ASYG	WP321	G-BRFC
VZ638:HF	G-JETM	WP788	G-BCHL
VZ728	G-AGOS	WP790:T	G-BBNC
WA576	G-ALSS	WP795:901	G-BVZZ
WA577	G-ALST	WP800:2	G-BCXN
WA591:FMK-Q	G-BWMF	WP803	G-HAPY
WB565:X	G-PVET	WP805:D	G-MAJR
WB569:R	G-BYSJ	WP808	G-BDEU
WB585:M	G-AOSY	WP809:78 RN	G-BVTX
WB588:D	G-AOTD	WP857:24	G-BDRJ
WB615:E	G-BXIA	WP859:E	G-BXCP
WB652:V	G-CHPY	WP860:6	G-BXDA
WB654:U	G-BXGO	WP896	G-BWVY
WB671:910	G-BWTG	WP901:B	G-BWNT
WB697:95	G-BXCT	WP903	G-BCGC
WB702	G-AOFE	WP925:C	G-BXHA
WB703	G-ARMC	WP928:D	G-BXGM
WB711	G-APPM	WP929:F	G-BXCV
WB726:E	G-AOSK	WP930:J	G-BXHF
WB763:14	G-BBMR	WP970:12	G-BCOI
WD286	G-BBND	WP971	G-ATHD
WD292	G-BCRX	WP983:B	G-BXNN
WD305	G-ARGG	WP984:H	G-BWTO
WD310:B	G-BWUN	WR360:K	G-DHSS
WD327	G-ATVF	WR410:N	G-BLKA

Serial carried	Civil identity	Serial carried	Civil identity
WR410	G-DHUU	XN637:03	G-BKOU
WR421	G-DHTT	XP242	G-BUCI
WR470	G-DHVM	XP254	G-ASCC
WT333	G-BVXC	XP279	G-BWKK
WT933	G-ALSW	XP282	G-BGTC
WV198:K	G-BJWY	XP355	G-BEBC
WV318:D	G-FFOX	XP907	G-SROE
WV322:Y	G-BZSE	XP924	G-CVIX
WV372:R	G-BXFI	XR240	G-BDFH
WV493:29	G-BDYG	XR241	G-AXRR
WV740	G-BNPH	XR246	G-AZBU
WV783	G-ALSP	XR267	G-BJXR
WZ507:74	G-VTII	XR486	G-RWWW
WZ662	G-BKVK	XR537:T	G-NATY
WZ711	G-AVHT	XR538:01	G-RORI
WZ847:F	G-CPMK	XR595:M	G-BWHU
WZ868:H	G-ARMF	XR673:L	G-BXLO
WZ872:E	G-BZGB	XR724	G-BTSY
WZ879	G-BWUT	XR944	G-ATTB
WZ882:K	G-BXGP	XR991	G-MOUR
XA880	G-BVXR	XS111	G-TIMM
XD693:Z-Q	G-AOBU	XS165:37	G-ASAZ
XE489	G-JETH	XS235	G-CPDA
XE685:861/VL	G-AII	XS587	G-VIXN
XE856	G-DUSK	XS765	G-BSET
XE956	G-OBLN	XT223	G-XTUN
XF114	G-SWIF	XT420:606	G-CBUI
XF597:AH	G-BKFW	XT435:430	G-RIMM
XF603	G-KAPW	XT634	G-BYRX
XF690	G-MOOS	XT671	G-BYRC
XF785	G-ALBN	XT787	G-KAXT
XF836:J-G	G-AWRY	XT788:316	G-BMIR
XG160:U	G-BWAF	XV134:P	G-BWLX
XG194:A	G-PRII	XV137	G-CRUM
XG452	G-BRMB	XV268	G-BVER
XH134	G-OMHD	XW289:73	G-JPVA
XH558	G-VLCN	XW293:Z	G-BWCS
XJ389	G-AJJP	XW310	G-BWGS
XJ398	G-BDBZ	XW324:K	G-BWSG
XJ615	G-BWGL	XW325:E	G-BWGF
XJ729	G-BVGE	XW333:79	G-BVTC
XJ771	G-HELV	XW354	G-JPTV
XK417	G-AVXY	XW422:3	G-BWEB
XK895:19/CU	G-SDEV	XW423:14	G-BWUW
XK896	G-RNAS	XW433	G-JPRO
XK940:911	G-AYXT	XW613	G-BXRS
XL426	G-VJET	XW635	G-AWSW
XL500	G-KAEW	XW784:VL	G-BBRN
XL502	G-BMYP	XW853	G-IBNH
XL571:V	G-HNTR	XW854:46/CU	G-TIZZ
XL573	G-BVGH	XW858:C	G-ONNE
XL577:V	G-BXKF	XW866:E	G-BXTH
XL587	G-HPUX	XX406:P	G-CBSH
XL602	G-BWFT	XX432	G-CDNO
XL621	G-BNCX	XX467:86	G-TVII
XL714	G-AOGR	XX513:10	G-CCMI
XL809	G-BLIX	XX514	G-BWIB
XL929	G-BNPU	XX515:4	G-CBBC
XL954	G-BXES	XX518:S	G-UDOG
XM223:J	G-BWWC	XX521:H	G-CBEH
XM370:10	G-BVSP	XX522:06	G-DAWG
XM424	G-BWDS	XX524:04	G-DDOG
XM479:54	G-BVEZ	XX525:8	G-CBJJ
XM553	G-AWSV	XX528:D	G-BZON
XM575	G-BLMC	XX534:B	G-EDAV
XM655	G-VULC	XX537:C	G-CBCB
XM685:513/PO	G-AYZJ	XX538:O	G-TDOG
XM819	G-APXW	XX543:F	G-CBAB
XN351	G-BKSC	XX546:03	G-WINI
XN437	G-AXWA	XX549:6	G-CBID
XN441	G-BGKT	XX550:Z	G-CBBL
XN498	G-BWSH	XX551:E	G-BZDP

Serial carried	Civil identity	Serial carried	Civil identity
XX554	G-BZMD	XZ937:Y	G-CBKA
XX561:7	G-BZEP	ZA250	G-VTOL
XX611:7	G-CBDK	ZA634:C	G-BUHA
XX612:A, 03	G-BZXC	ZA652	G-BUDC
XX614:V	G-GGRR	ZA730	G-FUKM
XX619:T	G-CBBW	ZB500	G-LYNX
XX621:H	G-CBEF	ZB627:A	G-CBSK
XX622:B	G-CBGZ	ZB646:59/CU	G-CBGZ
XX624:E	G-KDOG	2+1:7334 Luftwaffe)	G-SYFW
XX626:02, W	G-CDVV	3+ (Luftwaffe)	G-BAYV
XX628:9	G-CBFU	4+ (Luftwaffe)	G-BSLX
XX629:V	G-BZXZ	4-97/MM52801 (Italian)	G-BBII
XX630:5	G-SIJW	07 (Russian AF)	G-BMJY
XX631:W	G-BZXS	8+ (Luftwaffe)	G-WULF
XX636:Y	G-CBFP	F+IS (Luftwaffe)	G-BIRW
XX638	G-DOGG	BU+CC (Luftwaffe)	G-BUCC
XX658:07	G-BZPS	BU+CK (Luftwaffe)	G-BUCK
XX667:16	G-BZFN	CF+HF (Luftwaffe)	EI-AUY
XX668:1	G-CBAN	DM+BK (Luftwaffe)	G-BPHZ
XX692:A	G-BZMH	GM+AI (Luftwaffe)	G-SCTH
XX693:07	G-BZML	LG+01 (Luftwaffe)	G-AYSJ
XX694:E	G-CBBS	LG+03 (Luftwaffe)	G-AEZX
XX695:3	G-CBBT	KG+EM (Luftwaffe)	G-ETME
XX698:9	G-BZME	NJ+C11 (Luftwaffe)	G-ATBG
XX699:F	G-CBCV	S4+A07 (Luftwaffe)	G-BWHP
XX700:17	G-CBEK	S5+B06 (Luftwaffe)	G-WJCM
XX702:P	G-CBCR	6J+PR (Luftwaffe)	G-AWHB
XX704	G-BCUV	57-H (USAAC)	G-AKAZ
XX707:4	G-CBDS	97+04 (Luftwaffe)	G-APVF
XX885	G-HHAA	+14 (Luftwaffe)	G-BSMD
XZ239	G-BZYD	146-11083 (5)	G-BNAI
XZ934:U	G-CBSI		

G-BPHR/A17-48 (RAAF) DH.82A Tiger Moth. *Allan S. Wright*

Republic of Ireland Civil Registrations

Reg.	Type (†False registration)	Owner or Operator	Notes
EI-ABI	DH.84 Dragon	Aer Lingus Charitable Foundation (EI-AFK)	
EI-AED	Cessna 120	E. McNeill & P. O'Reilly	
EI-AEE	Auster 3/1 Autocrat	B. J. Hogan	
EI-AEF	Cessna 120	J. Halligan	
EI-AFE	Piper J3C-65 Cub	4 of Cubs Flying Group	
EI-AFF	B.A. Swallow 2	J. J. Sullivan & ptnrs	
EI-AGD	Taylorcraft Plus D	B. & K. O'Sullivan	
EI-AGJ	Auster J/1 Autocrat	T. G. Rafter	
EI-AHI	DH.82A Tiger Moth	High Fidelity Flyers	
EI-AII	Cessna 150F	L. Bagnell	
EI-AKM	Piper J-3C-65 Cub	J. A. Kent	
EI-ALP	Avro 643 Cadet	J.C. O'Loughlin (stored)	
EI-AMK	Auster J/1 Autocrat	Iona National Airways	
EI-ANT	Champion 7ECA Citabria	T. Croke & ptnrs	
EI-ANY	PA-18 Super Cub 95	Bogavia Group	
EI-AOB	PA-28 Cherokee 140	Knock Flying Group	
EI-APS	Schleicher ASK.14	E. Shiel & ptnrs	
EI-ARW	Jodel D.R.1050	J. Davy	
EI-AST	Cessna F.150H	Ormond Flying Club	
EI-ATJ	B.121 Pup Srs 2	L. O'Leary	
EI-AUM	Auster J/1 Autocrat	T. G. Rafter	
EI-AUO	Cessna FA.150K Aerobat	S. Burke & L. Bagnell	
EI-AVM	Cessna F.150L	Tojo Air Leasing	
EI-AWH	Cessna 210J	Rathcoole Flying Club	
EI-AWP	DH.82A Tiger Moth	A. P. Bruton	
EI-AWR	Malmö MFI-9 Junior	C. O'Shea	
EI-AYB	GY-80 Horizon 180	J. B. Smith	
EI-AYI	MS.880B Rallye Club	J. McNamara	
EI-AYN	BN-2A-8 Islander	Aer Arann	
EI-AYR	Schleicher ASK-16	B. O'Broin & ptnrs	
EI-AYT	MS.894A Rallye Minerva	K. A. O'Connor	
EI-AYY	Evans VP-1	R. Dowd	
EI-BAJ	Stampe SV.4C	Dublin Tiger Group	
EI-BAT	Cessna F.150M	K. Kacprzak	
EI-BAV	PA-22 Colt 108	E. Finnamore	
EI-BBC	PA-28 Cherokee 180C	Vero Beach	
EI-BBE	Champion 7FC Tri-Traveler (tailwheel)	P. Ryan	
EI-BBI	MS.892 Rallye Commodore	Ossory Flying & Gliding Club	
EI-BBV	Piper J-3C-65 Cub	F. Cronin	
EI-BCE	BN-2A-26 Islander	Aer Arann	
EI-BCF	Bensen B.8M	P. Flanagan	
EI-BCJ	Aeromere F.8L Falco 1 Srs 3	M. P. McLoughlin	
EI-BCK	Cessna F.172N II	K. A. O'Connor	
EI-BCM	Piper J-3C-65 Cub	M. Bergin & Partners	
EI-BCN	Piper J-3C-65 Cub	H. Diver	
EI-BCP	D.62B Condor	T. Delaney	
EI-BDL	Evans VP-2	P. Buggle	
EI-BDR	PA-28 Cherokee 180	Cherokee Group	
EI-BEN	Piper J-3C-65 Cub	Capt. J. J. Sullivan	
EI-BHI	Bell 206B JetRanger 2	G. Tracey	
EI-BHV	Champion 7EC Traveler	P. O'Donnell & ptnrs	
EI-BIB	Cessna F.152	Sligo Aeronautical Club Ltd	
EI-BID	PA-18 Super Cub 95	S. Coghlan & P. Ryan	
EI-BIK	PA-18 Super Cub 180	Dublin Gliding Club	
EI-BIO	Piper J-3C-65 Cub	H. Duggan & Partners	
EI-BIR	Cessna F.172M	Figile Flying Group	
EI-BIV	Bellanca 8KCAB	Atlantic Flight Training Ltd	
EI-BJB	Aeronca 7AC Champion	A. W. Kennedy	
EI-BJC	Aeronca 7AC Champion	A. E. Griffin	
EI-BJK	MS.880B Rallye 110ST	M. Keenen	
EI-BJM	Cessna A.152	K. A. O'Connor	
EI-BJO	Cessna R.172K	The XP Group	
EI-BKC	Aeronca 15AC Sedan	G. Hendrick & M. Farrell	
EI-BKK	Taylor JT.1 Monoplane	R. Klimcke	
EI-BMI	SOCATA TB9 Tampico	A. Breslin	
EI-BMN	Cessna F.152 II	K. A. O'Connor	

Notes	Reg.	Type	Owner or Operator
	EI-BMU	Monnet Sonerai IIL	N. O'Donnell
	EI-BNL	Rand-Robinson KR-2	K. Hayes
	EI-BNU	MS.880B Rallye Club	J. Cooke
	EI-BOE	SOCATA TB10 Tobago	Tobago Group
	EI-BOV	Rand-Robinson KR-2	G. O'Hara & G. Callan
	EI-BPL	Cessna F.172K	Phoenix Flying
	EI-BPP	Quicksilver MX	J. A. Smith
	EI-BRS	Cessna P.172D	P. Mathews
	EI-BRU	Evans VP-1	C. O'Shea
	EI-BSB	Wassmer Jodel D.112	S. Byrne
	EI-BSC	Cessna F.172N	M. Foreman
	EI-BSG	Bensen B.80	J. Todd
	EI-BSK	SOCATA TB9 Tampico	T. Drury
	EI-BSL	PA-34-220T Seneca III	P. Sreenan
	EI-BSN	Cameron O-65 balloon	C. O'Neill & T. Hooper
	EI-BSO	PA-28 Cherokee 140B	S. Brazil
	EI-BSW	Solar Wings Pegasus XL-R	E. Fitzgerald
	EI-BUA	Cessna 172M	K. A. O'Connor
	EI-BUC	Jodel D.9 Bébé	B. Lyons & M. Blake
	EI-BUE	Boeing 737-348	Mistral Air
	EI-BUF	Cessna 210N	210 Group
	EI-BUG	SOCATA ST.10 Diplomate	J. Cooke
	EI-BUL	Whittaker MW5 Sorcerer	J. Culleton
	EI-BUN	Beech 76 Duchess	K. A. O'Connor
	EI-BUT	MS.893A Commodore 180	T. Keating
	EI-BVJ	AMF Chevvron 232	A. Dunn
	EI-BVK	PA-38-112 Tomahawk	B. Lowe
	EI-BVT	Evans VP-2	P. Morrison
	EI-BVY	Zenith 200AA-RW	J. Matthews & M. Skelly
	EI-BYG	SOCATA TB9 Tampico	M. McGinn
	EI-BYL	Zenith CH.250	M. McLoughlin
	EI-BYO	Aérospatiale ATR-42-310	Aer Arann
	EI-BYX	Champion 7GCAA	P. J. Gallagher
	EI-BYY	Piper J-3C-85 Cub	The Cub Club
	EI-CAC	Grob G.115A	C. Phillips
	EI-CAD	Grob G.115A	C. Phillips
	EI-CAE	Grob G.115A	O. O'Reilly
	EI-CAN	Aerotech MW5 Sorcerer	V. A. Vaughan
	EI-CAP	Cessna R.182RG	K. K. Skorupski
	EI-CAU	AMF Chevvron 232	J. Tarrant
	EI-CAX	Cessna P.210N	K. A. O'Connor
	EI-CBK	Aérospatiale ATR-42-310	Aer Arann
	EI-CCF	Aeronca 11AC Chief	G. McGuinness
	EI-CCM	Cessna 152 II	E. Hopkins
	EI-CDF	Boeing 737-548	Jetscope Aviation Ireland/Pulkovo Airlines
	EI-CDG	Boeing 737-548	Nordic Aviation Contractor (Ireland) Ltd/Pulkovo Airlines
	EI-CDH	Boeing 737-548	Jetscope Aviation Ireland/Pulkovo Airlines
	EI-CDP	Cessna 182L	Irish Parachute Club
	EI-CDV	Cessna 150G	K. A. O'Connor
	EI-CEG	MS.893A Rallye 180GT	M. Jarrett
	EI-CES	Taylorcraft BC-65	G. Higgins & Partners
	EI-CFF	PA-12 Super Cruiser	J. & T. O'Dwyer
	EI-CFG	CP.301B Emeraude	F. Doyle
	EI-CFH	PA-12 Super Cruiser	G. Treacy
	EI-CFO	Piper J-3C-65 Cub	J. T. Wilson & ptnrs
	EI-CFP	Cessna 172P (floatplane)	K. A. O'Connor
	EI-CFY	Cessna 172N	K. A. O'Connor
	EI-CGD	Cessna 172M	G. Cashman
	EI-CGF	Luton LA-5 Major	P. White
	EI-CGH	Cessna 210N	J. Smith
	EI-CGP	PA-28 Cherokee 140C	L. A. Tattan
	EI-CHR	CFM Shadow Srs BD	B. Kelly
	EI-CIF	PA-28 Cherokee 180C	AA Flying Group
	EI-CIG	PA-18 Super Cub 150	K. A. O'Connor
	EI-CIM	Avid Flyer Mk IV	P. Swan
	EI-CIN	Cessna 150K	K. A. O'Connor
	EI-CJJ	Slingsby T-31M	J. J. Sullivan
	EI-CJR	SNCAN Stampe SV.4A	P. McKenna
	EI-CJS	Jodel D.120A	A. Flood
	EI-CJT	Slingsby Motor Cadet III	J. Tarrant

Reg.	Type	Owner or Operator	Notes
EI-CKH	PA-18 Super Cub 95	G. Brady	
EI-CKI	Thruster TST Mk 1	S. Woodgates	
EI-CKJ	Cameron N-77 balloon	A. F. Meldon	
EI-CKZ	Jodel D.18	J. O'Brien	
EI-CLA	HOAC Katana DV.20	J. Cooke	
EI-CLQ	Cessna F.172N	E. Finnamore	
EI-CMB	PA-28 Cherokee 140	K. Furnell & Partners	
EI-CML	Cessna 150M	P. Donohoe	
EI-CMN	PA-12 Super Cruiser	A. McNamee & ptnrs	
EI-CMR	Rutan LongEz	F. & C. O'Caoimh	
EI-CMT	PA-34-200T Seneca II	Atlantic Flight Training	
EI-CMU	Mainair Mercury	Bill O'Neill	
EI-CMV	Cessna 150L	K. A. O'Connor	
EI-CMW	Rotorway Executive	B. McNamee	
EI-CNC	TEAM mini-MAX	A. M. S. Allen	
EI-CNG	Air & Space 18A gyroplane	P. Joyce	
EI-CNU	Pegasus Quantum 15-912	M. Ffrench	
EI-COT	Cessna F.172N	Tojo Air Leasing	
EI-COY	Piper J-3C-65 Cub	W. Flood	
EI-COZ	PA-28 Cherokee 140C	L. A. Tattan	
EI-CPE	Airbus A.321-211	Aer Lingus St Enda	
EI-CPG	Airbus A.321-211	Aer Lingus St Aidan	
EI-CPH	Airbus A.321-211	Aer Lingus St Dervilla	
EI-CPI	Rutan LongEz	D. J. Ryan	
EI-CPP	Piper J-3C-65 Cub	E. Fitzgerald	
EI-CPT	Aérospatiale ATR-42-320	Aer Arann	
EI-CPX	I.I.I. Sky Arrow 650T	M. McCarthy	
EI-CRB	Lindstrand LBL-90A balloon	J. & C. Concannon	
EI-CRG	Robin DR.400/180R	D. & B. Lodge	
EI-CRR	Aeronca 11AC Chief	L. Maddock & ptnrs	
EI-CRU	Cessna 152	W. Reilly	
EI-CRV	Hoffman H-36 Dimona	The Dimona Group	
EI-CRX	SOCATA TB-9 Tampico	Hotel Bravo Flying Club	
EI-CSG	Boeing 737-8AS	CIT Aerospace International	
EI-CTL	Aerotech MW-5B Sorcerer	M. Wade	
EI-CUA	Boeing 737-4K5	Aerco Ireland/Blue Panorama	
EI-CUD	Boeing 737-4Q8	Castle 2003-2 Ireland/Blue Panorama	
EI-CUJ	Cessna 172N	M. Nally	
EI-CUM	Airbus A.320-232	Wilmington Trust SP Services (Dublin) Ltd/Windjet	
EI-CUN	Boeing 737-4K5	Aerco Ireland/Blue Panorama	
EI-CUS	AB-206B JetRanger 3	R. Lyons	
EI-CUT	Maule MX-7-180A	Cosair	
EI-CUW	BN-2B-20 Islander	Aer Arann	
EI-CVA	Airbus A.320-214	Aer Lingus St Schira	
EI-CVB	Airbus A.320-214	Aer Lingus St Mobhi	
EI-CVC	Airbus A.320-214	Aer Lingus St Kealin	
EI-CVL	Ercoupe 415CD	V. O'Rourke	
EI-CVM	Schweizer S.269C	Helicopter Support Ireland Ltd	
EI-CVW	Bensen B.8M	F. Kavanagh	
EI-CXC	Raj Hamsa X'Air 502T	R. Dunleavy	
EI-CXE	Boeing 737-76N	Celestial Aviation Trading 6 Ltd	
EI-CXF	Airbus A.330-223	Calliope Ltd	
EI-CXG	Airbus A.330-223	Calliope Ltd	
EI-CXK	Boeing 737-4S3	Transaero	
EI-CXN	Boeing 737-329	Transaero	
EI-CXO	Boeing 767-3G5ER	Blue Panorama	
EI-CXR	Boeing 737-329	Transaero	
EI-CXS	Sikorsky S-61N	CHC Ireland Ltd	
EI-CXV	Boeing 737-8CX	MASL Ireland(14)Ltd/MIAT Mongolian Airlines	
EI-CXY	Evektor EV-97 Eurostar	G. Doody & ptnrs	
EI-CXZ	Boeing 767-216ER	Transaero	
EI-CZA	ATEC Zephyr 2000	M. Higgins & Partners	
EI-CZC	CFM Streak Shadow Srs II	M. Culhane & D. Burrows	
EI-CZD	Boeing 767-216ER	Transaero	
EI-CZH	Boeing 767-3G5ER	Blue Panorama	
EI-CZK	Boeing 737-4Y0	Transaero	
EI-CZN	Sikorsky S-61N	CHC Ireland	
EI-CZP	Schweizer 269C-1	T. Ng Kam	
EI-DAA	Airbus A.330-202	Aer Lingus St Keeva	
EI-DAC	Boeing 737-8AS	Ryanair	
EI-DAD	Boeing 737-8AS	Ryanair	
EI-DAE	Boeing 737-8AS	Ryanair	

Notes	Reg.	Type	Owner or Operator
	EI-DAF	Boeing 737-8AS	Ryanair
	EI-DAG	Boeing 737-8AS	Ryanair
	EI-DAH	Boeing 737-8AS	Ryanair
	EI-DAI	Boeing 737-8AS	Ryanair
	EI-DAJ	Boeing 737-8AS	Ryanair
	EI-DAK	Boeing 737-8AS	Ryanair
	EI-DAL	Boeing 737-8AS	Ryanair
	EI-DAM	Boeing 737-8AS	Ryanair
	EI-DAN	Boeing 737-8AS	Ryanair
	EI-DAO	Boeing 737-8AS	Ryanair
	EI-DAP	Boeing 737-8AS	Ryanair
	EI-DAR	Boeing 737-8AS	Ryanair
	EI-DAS	Boeing 737-8AS	Ryanair
	EI-DBF	Boeing 767-3Q8ER	Transaero
	EI-DBG	Boeing 767-3Q8ER	Transaero
	EI-DBH	CFM Streak Shadow SA-11	M. O'Mahony
	EI-DBI	Raj Hamsa X'Air Mk.2 Falcon	E. Hamilton
	EI-DBJ	Huntwing Pegasus XL Classic	P. A. McMahon
	EI-DBK	Boeing 777-243ER	Alitalia
	EI-DBL	Boeing 777-243ER	Alitalia
	EI-DBM	Boeing 777-243ER	Alitalia
	EI-DBO	Air Creation Kiss 400	E. Spain
	EI-DBP	Boeing 767-35H	Alitalia
	EI-DBU	Boeing 767-37EER	Transaero
	EI-DBV	Rand Kar X' Air 602T	S. Scanlon
	EI-DBW	Boeing 767-201	Transaero
	EI-DCA	Raj Hamsa X'Air	S. Cahill
	EI-DCF	Boeing 737-8AS	Ryanair
	Ei-DCG	Boeing 737-8AS	Ryanair
	EI-DCH	Boeing 737-8AS	Ryanair
	EI-DCI	Boeing 737-8AS	Ryanair
	EI-DCJ	Boeing 737-8AS	Ryanair
	EI-DCK	Boeing 737-8AS	Ryanair
	EI-DCL	Boeing 737-8AS	Ryanair
	EI-DCM	Boeing 737-8AS	Ryanair
	EI-DCN	Boeing 737-8AS	Ryanair
	EI-DCO	Boeing 737-8AS	Ryanair
	EI-DCP	Boeing 737-8AS	Ryanair
	EI-DCR	Boeing 737-8AS	Ryanair
	EI-DCW	Boeing 737-8AS	Ryanair
	EI-DCX	Boeing 737-8AS	Ryanair
	EI-DCY	Boeing 737-8AS	Ryanair
	EI-DCZ	Boeing 737-8AS	Ryanair
	EI-DDA	Robinson R44 II	Eirecopter Helicopters Ltd
	EI-DDC	Cessna F.172M	Trim Flying Club
	EI-DDD	Aeronca 7AC	J. Sullivan & M. Quinn
	EI-DDH	Boeing 777-243ER	Alitalia
	EI-DDI	Schweizer S.269C-1	B. Hade
	EI-DDJ	Raj Hamsa X'Air 582	J. P. McHugh
	EI-DDK	Boeing 737-4S3	Transaero
	EI-DDP	Southdown International microlight	M. Mannion
	EI-DDW	Boeing 767-3S1ER	Alitalia
	EI-DDX	Cessna 172S	Atlantic Flight Training
	EI-DDY	Boeing 737-4Y0	Transaero
	EI-DEA	Airbus A.320-214	Aer Lingus St Fidelma
	EI-DEB	Airbus A.320-214	Aer Lingus St Nathy
	EI-DEC	Airbus A.320-214	Aer Lingus St Fergal
	EI-DEE	Airbus A.320-214	Aer Lingus St Fintan
	EI-DEF	Airbus A.320-214	Aer Lingus St Declan
	EI-DEG	Airbus A.320-214	Aer Lingus St Fachtna
	EI-DEH	Airbus A.320-214	Aer Lingus St Malachy
	EI-DEI	Airbus A.320-214	Aer Lingus St Kilian
	EI-DEJ	Airbus A.320-214	Aer Lingus St Oliver Plunkett
	EI-DEK	Airbus A.320-214	Aer Lingus St Eunan
	EI-DEL	Airbus A.320-214	Aer Lingus St Ibar
	EI-DEM	Airbus A.320-214	Aer Lingus St Canice
	EI-DEN	Airbus A.320-214	Aer Lingus St Kieran
	EI-DEO	Airbus A.320-214	Aer Lingus St Senan
	EI-DEP	Airbus A.320-214	Aer Lingus St Eugene
	EI-DER	Airbus A.320-214	Aer Lingus St Mel
	EI-DES	Airbus A.320-214	Aer Lingus St Pappin
	EI-DEZ	Airbus A.319-112	Meridiana

Reg.	Type	Owner or Operator	Notes
EI-DFA	Airbus A.319-112	Meridiana	
EI-DFM	Evektor EV-97 Eurostar	G. Doody	
EI-DFO	Airbus A.320-211	Windjet	
EI-DFP	Airbus A.319-112	Meridiana	
EI-DFS	Boeing 767-33AER	Transaero	
EI-DFX	Air Creation Kiss 400	L. Daly	
EI-DFY	Raj Hamsa R100 (2)	P. McGirr & R Gillespie	
EI-DGA	Urban Air UFM-11UK Lambada	Dr. P. & D. Durkin	
EI-DGG	Raj Hamsa X'Air 582	P. A. Weldon	
EI-DGH	Raj Hamsa X'Air 582	M. Garvey & T. McGowan	
EI-DGJ	Raj Hamsa X'Air 582	N. Brereton	
EI-DGK	Raj Hamsa X'Air 133	B. Chambers	
EI-DGP	Urban Air UFM-11 Lambada	R. Linehan	
EI-DGT	Urban Air UFM-11UK Lambada	P. Walsh & Partners	
EI-DGV	ATEC Zephyr 2000	K. Higgins	
EI-DGW	Cameron Z-90 balloon	J. Leahy	
EI-DGX	Cessna 152 II	K. A. O'Connor	
EI-DGY	Urban Air UFM-11 Lambada	D. McMorrow	
EI-DHA	Boeing 737-8AS	Ryanair	
EI-DHB	Boeing 737-8AS	Ryanair	
EI-DHC	Boeing 737-8AS	Ryanair	
EI-DHD	Boeing 737-8AS	Ryanair	
EI-DHE	Boeing 737-8AS	Ryanair	
EI-DHF	Boeing 737-8AS	Ryanair	
EI-DHG	Boeing 737-8AS	Ryanair	
EI-DHH	Boeing 737-8AS	Ryanair	
EI-DHL	Airbus A.300B4-203F	European Air Transport/DHL	
EI-DHN	Boeing 737-8AS	Ryanair	
EI-DHO	Boeing 737-8AS	Ryanair	
EI-DHP	Boeing 737-8AS	Ryanair	
EI-DHR	Boeing 737-8AS	Ryanair	
EI-DHS	Boeing 737-8AS	Ryanair	
EI-DHT	Boeing 737-8AS	Ryanair	
EI-DHV	Boeing 737-8AS	Ryanair	
EI-DHW	Boeing 737-8AS	Ryanair	
EI-DHX	Boeing 737-8AS	Ryanair	
EI-DHY	Boeing 737-8AS	Ryanair	
EI-DHZ	Boeing 737-8AS	Ryanair	
EI-DIA	Solar Wings Pegasus XL-Q	P. Byrne	
EI-DIF	PA-31-350 Navajo Chieftain	Flightwise Aviation Ltd & Partners	
EI-DIP	Airbus A.330-202	Alitalia	
EI-DIR	Airbus A.330-202	Alitalia	
EI-DIY	Van's RV-4	J. A. Kent	
EI-DJL	Boeing 767-330ER	Blue Panorama	
EI-DJM	PA-28-161 Warrior II	Waterford Aero Club	
EI-DJY	Grob G.115	Atlantic Flight Training	
EI-DJZ	Lindstrand LBL-31A Cloudhopper	M. E. White	
EI-DKC	Solar Wings Quasar	K. Daly	
EI-DKE	Air Creation Kiss 450-582	J. Bennett	
EI-DKI	Robinson R22 Beta	P. Gilboy	
EI-DKJ	Thruster T.600N	C. Brogan	
EI-DKK	Raj Hamsa X'Air Jabiru	M. Tolan	
EI-DKN	ELA Aviacion ELA-07 gyrocopter	S. Brennan	
EI-DKT	Raj Hamsa X'Air 582 (11)	S. O'Reilly	
EI-DKU	Air Creation Kiss 450-582 (1)	P. Kirwan	
EI-DKW	Evektor EV-97 Eurostar	Ormand Flying Club	
EI-DKY	Raj Hamsa X'Air 582	M. Clarke	
EI-DKZ	Reality Aircraft Escapade 912 (1)	J. Deegan	
EI-DLB	Boeing 737-8AS	Ryanair	
EI-DLC	Boeing 737-8AS	Ryanair	
EI-DLD	Boeing 737-8AS	Ryanair	
EI-DLE	Boeing 737-8AS	Ryanair	
EI-DLF	Boeing 737-8AS	Ryanair	
EI-DLG	Boeing 737-8AS	Ryanair	
EI-DLH	Boeing 737-8AS	Ryanair	
EI-DLI	Boeing 737-8AS	Ryanair	
EI-DLJ	Boeing 737-8AS	Ryanair	
EI-DLK	Boeing 737-8AS	Ryanair	
EI-DLL	Boeing 737-8AS	Ryanair	
EI-DLM	Boeing 737-8AS	Ryanair	
EI-DLN	Boeing 737-8AS	Ryanair	
EI-DLO	Boeing 737-8AS	Ryanair	

Notes	Reg.	Type	Owner or Operator
	EI-DLR	Boeing 737-8AS	Ryanair
	EI-DLS	Boeing 737-8AS	Ryanair
	EI-DLT	Boeing 737-8AS	Ryanair
	EI-DLV	Boeing 737-8AS	Ryanair
	EI-DLW	Boeing 737-8AS	Ryanair
	EI-DLX	Boeing 737-8AS	Ryanair
	EI-DLY	Boeing 737-8AS	Ryanair
	EI-DLZ	Boeing 737-8AS	Ryanair
	EI-DMA	MS.892E Rallye 150	J. Lynn & Partners
	EI-DMB	Best Off Skyranger 912S (1)	Fun 2 Fly Ltd
	EI-DMC	Schweizer 269C-1	B. Hade
	EI-DMG	Cessna 441	Dawn Meats Group
	EI-DMR	Boeing 737-436	Air One
	EI-DMU	Whittaker MW6S Merlin	M. Heaton
	EI-DNM	Boeing 737-4S3	Transaero
	EI-DNN	Bede BD-5G	H. John & E. M. Cox
	EI-DNO	Bede BD-5G	R. A. Gardiner
	EI-DNP	Airbus A.320-212	Wind Jet
	EI-DNR	Raj Hamsa X'Air 582 (5)	N. Furlong & J. Grattan
	EI-DNV	Urban Air UFM-11UK Lambada	F. Maughan
	EI-DNW	Skyranger J2.2 (1)	M. Kerrison
	EI-DOB	Zenair CH-701	D. O'Brien
	EI-DOH	Boeing 737-31S	Transaero
	EI-DOP	Airbus A.320-232	Wind Jet
	EI-DOT	Bombardier CL-600-2D24	Air One
	EI-DOU	Bombardier CL-600-2D24	Air One
	EI-DOW	Mainair Blade 912	G. D. Fortune
	EI-DOX	Solar Wings XL-R	T. Noonan
	EI-DOY	PZL Koliber 150A	V. O'Brien & Partners
	EI-DPA	Boeing 737-8AS	Ryanair
	EI-DPB	Boeing 737-8AS	Ryanair
	EI-DPC	Boeing 737-8AS	Ryanair
	EI-DPD	Boeing 737-8AS	Ryanair
	EI-DPE	Boeing 737-8AS	Ryanair
	EI-DPF	Boeing 737-8AS	Ryanair
	EI-DPG	Boeing 737-8AS	Ryanair
	EI-DPH	Boeing 737-8AS	Ryanair
	EI-DPI	Boeing 737-8AS	Ryanair
	EI-DPJ	Boeing 737-8AS	Ryanair
	EI-DPK	Boeing 737-8AS	Ryanair
	EI-DPL	Boeing 737-8AS	Ryanair
	EI-DPM	Boeing 737-8AS	Ryanair
	EI-DPN	Boeing 737-8AS	Ryanair
	EI-DPO	Boeing 737-8AS	Ryanair
	EI-DPP	Boeing 737-8AS	Ryanair
	EI-DPR	Boeing 737-8AS	Ryanair
	EI-DPS	Boeing 737-8AS	Ryanair
	EI-DPT	Boeing 737-8AS	Ryanair
	EI-DPV	Boeing 737-8AS	Ryanair
	EI-DPW	Boeing 737-8AS	Ryanair
	EI-DPX	Boeing 737-8AS	Ryanair
	EI-DPY	Boeing 737-8AS	Ryanair
	EI-DPZ	Boeing 737-8AS	Ryanair
	EI-DRA	Boeing 737-852	Aeromexico
	EI-DRC	Boeing 737-852	Aeromexico
	EI-DRD	Boeing 737-852	Aeromexico
	EI-DRE	Boeing 737-752	Aeromexico
	EI-DRH	Mainair Blade	J. McErlain
	EI-DRI	Bombardier CL-600-2D24	Air One
	EI-DRJ	Bombardier CL-600-2D24	Air One
	EI-DRK	Bombardier CL-600-2D24	Air One
	EI-DRL	Raj Hamsa X'Air Jabiru	J. O'Connor
	EI-DRM	Urban Air UFM-10 Samba	M. Tormey
	EI-DRT	Air Creation Tanarg 912	L. Daly
	EI-DRU	Tecnam P92/EM Echo	P. Gallogly
	EI-DRW	Evektor EV-97R Eurostar	Eurostar Flying Club
	EI-DRX	Raj Hamsa X'Air 582 (5)	M. Sheelan & D. McShane
	EI-DSA	Airbus A.320-216	Alitalia
	EI-DSB	Airbus A.320-216	Alitalia
	EI-DSC	Airbus A.320-216	Alitalia
	EI-DSD	Airbus A.320-216	Alitalia
	EI-DSE	Airbus A.320-216	Alitalia

Reg.	Type	Owner or Operator	Notes
EI-DSF	Airbus A.320-216	Alitalia	
EI-DSG	Airbus A.320-216	Alitalia	
EI-DSH	Airbus A.320-216	Alitalia	
EI-DSI	Airbus A.320-216	Alitalia	
EI-DSJ	Airbus A.320-216	Alitalia	
EI-DSK	Airbus A.320-216	Alitalia	
EI-DSL	Airbus A.320-216	Alitalia	
EI-DSM	Airbus A.320-216	Alitalia	
EI-DSN	Airbus A.320-216	Alitalia	
EI-DSO	Airbus A.320-216	Alitalia	
EI-DSP	Airbus A.320-216	Alitalia	
EI-DSR	Airbus A.320-216	Alitalia	
EI-DSS	Airbus A.320-216	Alitalia	
EI-DST	Airbus A.320-216	Alitalia	
EI-DSU	Airbus A.320-216	Alitalia	
EI-DSV	Airbus A.320-216	Alitalia	
EI-DSW	Airbus A.320-216	Alitalia	
EI-DSX	Airbus A.320-216	Alitalia	
EI-DSY	Airbus A.320-216	Alitalia	
EI-DSZ	Airbus A.320-216	Alitalia	
EI-DTA	Airbus A.320-216	Alitalia	
EI-DTB	Airbus A.320-216	Alitalia	
EI-DTC	Airbus A.320-216	Alitalia	
EI-DTD	Airbus A.320-216	Alitalia	
EI-DTE	Airbus A.320-216	Alitalia	
EI-DTF	Airbus A.320-216	Alitalia	
EI-DTG	Airbus A.320-216	Alitalia	
EI-DTH	Airbus A.320-216	Alitalia	
EI-DTI	Airbus A.320-216	Alitalia	
EI-DTJ	Airbus A.320-216	Alitalia	
EI-DTK	Airbus A.320-216	Alitalia	
EI-DTL	Airbus A.320-216	Alitalia	
EI-DTM	Airbus A.320-216	Alitalia	
EI-DTN	Airbus A.320-216	Alitalia	
EI-DTO	Airbus A.320-216	Alitalia	
EI-DTR	Robinson R44	R & M Quarries Ltd	
EI-DTS	PA-18 Super Cub	P. Dunne, K. Synnott & M. Murphy	
EI-DTT	ELA-07 R-100 Gyrocopter	N. Steele	
EI-DTV	Boeing 737-5Y0	Transaero	
EI-DTW	Boeing 737-5Y0	Transaero	
EI-DTX	Boeing 737-5Q8	Transaero	
EI-DUA	Boeing 757-256	Kras Air/AiRUnion	
EI-DUC	Boeing 757-256	Kras Air/AiRUnion	
EI-DUD	Boeing 757-256	Kras Air/AiRUnion	
EI-DUH	Scintex CP.1310C3 Emeraude	W. Kennedy	
EI-DUJ	Evektor EV-97 Eurostar	E. Fitzpatrick	
EI-DUK	Bombardier CL-600-2D24	myAir	
EI-DUL	Alpi Aviation Pioneer	J. Hackett	
EI-DUO	Airbus A.330-203	Aer Lingus	
EI-DUS	Boeing 737-32B	Mistral Air	
EI-DUV	Beech 55	J. Given	
EI-DUZ	Airbus A.330-203	Aer Lingus	
EI-DVA	Boeing 737-33A	Mistral Air	
EI-DVC	Boeing 737-33A	Mistral Air	
EI-DVD	Airbus A.319-113	WindJet SpA	
EI-DVE	Airbus A.320-214	Aer Lingus	
EI-DVF	Airbus A.320-214	Aer Lingus	
EI-DVG	Airbus A.320-214	Aer Lingus	
EI-DVH	Airbus A.320-214	Aer Lingus	
EI-DVI	Airbus A.320-214	Aer Lingus	
EI-DVJ	Airbus A.320-214	Aer Lingus	
EI-DVK	Airbus A.320-214	Aer Lingus	
EI-DVL	Airbus A.320-214	Aer Lingus	
EI-DVM	Airbus A.320-214	Aer Lingus	
EI-DVN	Airbus A.320-214	Aer Lingus	
EI-DVO	Barnett J4B2	T. Brennan	
EI-DVP	CL-600-2D24	Air One	
EI-DVR	CL-600-2D24	Air One	
EI-DVS	CL-600-2D24	Air One	
EI-DVT	CL-600-2D24	Air One	
EI-DVU	Airbus A.319-113	WindJet SpA	
EI-DVZ	Robinson R44 II	D. McAuliffe	

Notes	Reg.	Type	Owner or Operator
	EI-DWA	Boeing 737-8AS	Ryanair
	EI-DWB	Boeing 737-8AS	Ryanair
	EI-DWC	Boeing 737-8AS	Ryanair
	EI-DWD	Boeing 737-8AS	Ryanair
	EI-DWE	Boeing 737-8AS	Ryanair
	EI-DWF	Boeing 737-8AS	Ryanair
	EI-DWG	Boeing 737-8AS	Ryanair
	EI-DWH	Boeing 737-8AS	Ryanair
	EI-DWI	Boeing 737-8AS	Ryanair
	EI-DWJ	Boeing 737-8AS	Ryanair
	EI-DWK	Boeing 737-8AS	Ryanair
	EI-DWL	Boeing 737-8AS	Ryanair
	EI-DWM	Boeing 737-8AS	Ryanair
	EI-DWO	Boeing 737-8AS	Ryanair
	EI-DWP	Boeing 737-8AS	Ryanair
	EI-DWR	Boeing 737-8AS	Ryanair
	EI-DWS	Boeing 737-8AS	Ryanair
	EI-DWT	Boeing 737-8AS	Ryanair
	EI-DWV	Boeing 737-8AS	Ryanair
	EI-DWW	Boeing 737-8AS	Ryanair
	EI-DWX	Boeing 737-8AS	Ryanair
	EI-DWY	Boeing 737-8AS	Ryanair
	EI-DWZ	Boeing 737-8AS	Ryanair
	EI-DXA	Ikarus C42	M. Kirrane
	EI-DXC	Boeing 737-4Q8	Air One
	EI-DXL	CFM Shadow	F. Lynch
	EI-DXM	Raj Hamsa X'Air 582	B. Nugent
	EI-DXN	Zenair CH.601HD	N. Gallagher
	EI-DXP	Cyclone AX3/503	J. McCann
	EI-DXS	CFM Shadow	R. W. Frost
	EI-DXT	UrbanAir UFM-10 Samba	N. Irwin
	EI-DXV	Thruster T.600N	P. Higgins
	EI-DXX	Raj Hamsa X'AIR 582(5)	D. Hanly & C. Wright
	EI-DXY	Airbus A.320-212	Rossiya
	EI-DXZ	UrbanAir UFM-10 Samba	D. O'Leary
	EI-DYA	Boeing 737-8AS	Ryanair
	EI-DYB	Boeing 737-8AS	Ryanair
	EI-DYC	Boeing 737-8AS	Ryanair
	EI-DYD	Boeing 737-8AS	Ryanair
	EI-DYE	Boeing 737-8AS	Ryanair
	EI-DYF	Boeing 737-8AS	Ryanair
	EI-DYH	Boeing 737-8AS	Ryanair
	EI-DYI	Boeing 737-8AS	Ryanair
	EI-DYJ	Boeing 737-8AS	Ryanair
	EI-DYK	Boeing 737-8AS	Ryanair
	EI-DYL	Boeing 737-8AS	Ryanair
	EI-DYM	Boeing 737-8AS	Ryanair
	EI-DYN	Boeing 737-8AS	Ryanair
	EI-DYO	Boeing 737-8AS	Ryanair
	EI-DYP	Boeing 737-8AS	Ryanair
	EI-DYR	Boeing 737-8AS	Ryanair
	EI-DYS	Boeing 737-8AS	Ryanair
	EI-DYT	Boeing 737-8AS	Ryanair
	EI-DYV	Boeing 737-8AS	Ryanair
	EI-DYW	Boeing 737-8AS	Ryanair
	EI-DYX	Boeing 737-8AS	Ryanair
	EI-DYY	Boeing 737-8AS	Ryanair
	EI-DYZ	Boeing 737-8AS	Ryanair
	EI-DZA	Colt 21A balloon	P. Baker
	EI-DZB	Colt 21A balloon	P. Baker
	EI-DZE	UrbanAir UFM-10 Samba	P. Keane
	EI-DZF	Pipistrel Sinus 912	Light Sport Aviation Ltd
	EI-DZH	Boeing 767-3Q8ER	Rossiya
	EI-DZK	Robinson R22B2 Beta	Skywest Aviation Ltd
	EI-DZL	Urban Air Samba XXL	M. Tormey
	EI-DZM	Robinson R44 II	A. & G. Thomond Builders Ltd
	EI-DZN	Bell 222	B. McCarty & A. Dalton
	EI-DZO	Dominator Gyroplane Ultrawhite	P. O'Reilly
	EI-DZR	Airbus A.320-212	Rossiya
	EI-DZS	BRM Land Africa	M. Whyte
	EI-EAC	Airbus A.300B4-203F	European Air Transport/DHL
	EI-EAD	Airbus A.300B4-203F	European Air Transport/DHL

338

Reg.	Type	Owner or Operator	Notes
EI-EAG	Pipistrel Virus 912	R. Armstrong	
EI-EAJ	RAF-2000GTX-SE	J. P. Henry	
EI-EAK	Airborne Windsports Edge XT	M. O'Brien	
EI-EAM	Cessna 172R	Atlantic Flight Training Ltd	
EI-EAP	Mainair Blade	H. D. Lynch	
EI-EAR	Boeing 767-3Q8ER	Rossiya	
EI-EAV	Airbus A.330-302	Aer Lingus	
EI-EAX	Raj Hamsa X'Air 582 (2)	M. Murphy	
EI-EAY	Raj Hamsa X'Air 582 (5)	R. Smith	
EI-EAZ	Cessna 172R	Atlantic Flight Training Ltd	
EI-EBA	Boeing 737-8AS	Ryanair	
EI-EBB	Boeing 737-8AS	Ryanair	
EI-EBC	Boeing 737-8AS	Ryanair	
EI-EBD	Boeing 737-8AS	Ryanair	
EI-EBE	Boeing 737-8AS	Ryanair	
EI-EBF	Boeing 737-8AS	Ryanair	
EI-EBG	Boeing 737-8AS	Ryanair	
EI-EBH	Boeing 737-8AS	Ryanair	
EI-EBI	Boeing 737-8AS	Ryanair	
EI-EBK	Boeing 737-8AS	Ryanair	
EI-EBL	Boeing 737-8AS	Ryanair	
EI-EBM	Boeing 737-8AS	Ryanair	
EI-EBN	Boeing 737-8AS	Ryanair	
EI-EBO	Boeing 737-8AS	Ryanair	
EI-EBP	Boeing 737-8AS	Ryanair	
EI-EBR	Boeing 737-8AS	Ryanair	
EI-EBS	Boeing 737-8AS	Ryanair	
EI-EBT	Boeing 737-8AS	Ryanair	
EI-EBV	Boeing 737-8AS	Ryanair	
EI-EBW	Boeing 737-8AS	Ryanair	
EI-EBX	Boeing 737-8AS	Ryanair	
EI-EBY	Boeing 737-8AS	Ryanair	
EI-EBZ	Boeing 737-8AS	Ryanair	
EI-ECB	Boeing 767-3Q8ER	ILFC Ireland	
EI-ECC	Cameron Z-90 balloon	J. J. Daly	
EI-ECG	BRM Land Africa	J. McGuinness	
EI-ECK	Raj Hamsa X'Air Hawk	N. Geh	
EI-ECP	Raj Hamsa X'Air Hawk	R. Gillespie & Partners	
EI-ECR	Cessna 525	Aircraft International Renting Ltd	
EI-ECV	Raj Hamsa X'Air Hawk	D. P. Myers	
EI-ECW	BRM Land Africa	Seosamh Mac Eochgain	
EI-ECX	Airbus A.319-132	ILFC Ireland Ltd	
EI-ECY	Airbus A.319-132	ILFC Ireland Ltd	
EI-ECZ	Raj Hamsa X'Air Hawk	M. Tolan	
EI-EDA	Raj Hamsa X'Air Hawk	A. Clarke	
EI-EDB	Cessna 152	K. O'Connor	
EI-EDC	Cessna FA.152	K. O'Connor	
EI-EDI	Ikarus C42	M. Owens	
EI-EDJ	CZAW Sportcruiser	Croftal Ltd	
EI-EDP	Airbus A.320-214	Aer Lingus	
EI-EDR	PA-28R Cherokee Arrow 200	Dublin Flyers	
EI-EDS	Airbus A.320-214	Aer Lingus	
EI-EDY	Airbus A.330-302	Aer Lingus	
EI-EDZ	Boeing 737-8K5	Transaero	
EI-EEA	Boeing 737-8K5	Transaero	
EI-EEB	Boeing 737-73S	AIRES Colombia	
EI-EED	Boeing 767-31AER	Blue Panorama	
EI-EEH	BRM Land Africa	P. Higgins	
EI-EEO	Van's RV-7	A. Butler	
EI-EES	ELA-07R	D. Doyle & Partners	
EI-EEU	Osprey II	P. Forde & S. Coughlan	
EI-EEV	Boeing 737-73S	AIRES Colombia	
EI-EEW	Boeing 737-375	Blue Panorama	
EI-EEZ	Bombardier CL-600-2B19	Airlink Airways Ltd	
EI-EFA	Boeing 737-8AS	Ryanair	
EI-EFB	Boeing 737-8AS	Ryanair	
EI-EFC	Boeing 737-8AS	Ryanair	
EI-EFD	Boeing 737-8AS	Ryanair	
EI-EFE	Boeing 737-8AS	Ryanair	
EI-EFF	Boeing 737-8AS	Ryanair	
EI-EFG	Boeing 737-8AS	Ryanair	
EI-EFH	Boeing 737-8AS	Ryanair	

Notes	Reg.	Type	Owner or Operator
	EI-EFI	Boeing 737-8AS	Ryanair
	EI-EFJ	Boeing 737-8AS	Ryanair
	EI-EFK	Boeing 737-8AS	Ryanair
	EI-EFL	Boeing 737-8AS	Ryanair
	EI-EFM	Boeing 737-8AS	Ryanair
	EI-EFN	Boeing 737-8AS	Ryanair
	EI-EFO	Boeing 737-8AS	Ryanair
	EI-EFP	Boeing 737-8AS	Ryanair
	EI-EFR	Boeing 737-8AS	Ryanair
	EI-EFS	Boeing 737-8AS	Ryanair
	EI-EFT	Boeing 737-8AS	Ryanair
	EI-EFV	Boeing 737-8AS	Ryanair
	EI-EFW	Boeing 737-8AS	Ryanair
	EI-EFX	Boeing 737-8AS	Ryanair
	EI-EFY	Boeing 737-8AS	Ryanair
	EI-EFZ	Boeing 737-8AS	Ryanair
	EI-EGA	Boeing 737-8AS	Ryanair
	EI-EGB	Boeing 737-8AS	Ryanair
	EI-EGC	Boeing 737-8AS	Ryanair
	EI-EGD	Boeing 737-8AS	Ryanair
	EI-EHG	Robinson R22 Beta	G. Jordan
	EI-EHH	Aerospatiale ATR-42-300	Aer Arran
	EI-EHK	Magni Gyro M-22 Voyager	M. Concannon
	EI-EHL	Air Creation Tanarg/Ixess 15 912S	S. Woods
	EI-EHM	Rand KR-2T	A. Lagun
	EI-EHP	Robinson R44	P. Tallis
	EI-EHV	CZAW Sportcruiser	G. Doody & Partners
	EI-EHY	Urban Air Samba XXL	J. K. Woodville
	EI-EIA	Airbus A.320-216	Alitalia
	EI-EIB	Airbus A.320-216	Alitalia
	EI-EIC	Airbus A.320-216	Alitalia
	EI-EID	Airbus A.320-216	Alitalia
	EI-EIE	Airbus A.320-216	Alitalia
	EI-EIG	Airbus A.320-216	Alitalia
	EI-EJG	Airbus A.330-202	Alitalia
	EI-EJH	Airbus A.330-202	Alitalia
	EI-EJI	Airbus A.330-202	Alitalia
	EI-EJJ	Airbus A.330-202	Alitalia
	EI-EJK	Airbus A.330-202	Alitalia
	EI-EJL	Airbus A.330-202	Alitalia
	EI-EJM	Airbus A.330-202	Alitalia
	EI-EJN	Airbus A.330-202	Alitalia
	EI-EJO	Airbus A.330-202	Alitalia
	EI-EJP	Airbus A.330-202	Alitalia
	EI-EKA	Boeing 737-8AS	Ryanair
	EI-EKB	Boeing 737-8AS	Ryanair
	EI-EKC	Boeing 737-8AS	Ryanair
	EI-EKD	Boeing 737-8AS	Ryanair
	EI-EKE	Boeing 737-8AS	Ryanair
	EI-EKF	Boeing 737-8AS	Ryanair
	EI-EKG	Boeing 737-8AS	Ryanair
	EI-EKH	Boeing 737-8AS	Ryanair
	EI-EKI	Boeing 737-8AS	Ryanair
	EI-EKJ	Boeing 737-8AS	Ryanair
	EI-EKK	Boeing 737-8AS	Ryanair
	EI-EKL	Boeing 737-8AS	Ryanair
	EI-EKM	Boeing 737-8AS	Ryanair
	EI-EKN	Boeing 737-8AS	Ryanair
	EI-EKO	Boeing 737-8AS	Ryanair
	EI-EKP	Boeing 737-8AS	Ryanair
	EI-EKR	Boeing 737-8AS	Ryanair
	EI-EKS	Boeing 737-8AS	Ryanair
	EI-EKT	Boeing 737-8AS	Ryanair
	EI-EKV	Boeing 737-8AS	Ryanair
	EI-EKW	Boeing 737-8AS	Ryanair
	EI-EKX	Boeing 737-8AS	Ryanair
	EI-EKY	Boeing 737-8AS	Ryanair
	EI-EKZ	Boeing 737-8AS	Ryanair
	EI-ELA	Airbus A.330-302	Aer Lingus
	EI-ELB	Raj Hamsa X'Air 582 (1)	G. McLaughlin
	EI-ELC	Ikarus C42B	R. Maclaughlin
	EI-ELG	Airbus A.340-311	ILFC Ireland Ltd

Reg.	Type	Owner or Operator	Notes
EI-ELL	Medway Eclipser	P. McMahon	
EI-ELM	PA-18-95 Super Cub	S. Coughlan	
EI-ELV	Pegasus XL-R	D. Minnock	
EI-ELZ	Boeing 737-4Q8	Mistral Air	
EI-EMA	Boeing 737-8AS	Ryanair	
EI-EMB	Boeing 737-8AS	Ryanair	
EI-EMC	Boeing 737-8AS	Ryanair	
EI-EMD	Boeing 737-8AS	Ryanair	
EI-EME	Boeing 737-8AS	Ryanair	
EI-EMF	Boeing 737-8AS	Ryanair	
EI-EMH	Boeing 737-8AS	Ryanair	
EI-EMI	Boeing 737-8AS	Ryanair	
EI-EMJ	Boeing 737-8AS	Ryanair	
EI-EMK	Boeing 737-8AS	Ryanair	
EI-EML	Boeing 737-8AS	Ryanair	
EI-EMM	Boeing 737-8AS	Ryanair	
EI-EMN	Boeing 737-8AS	Ryanair	
EI-EMO	Boeing 737-8AS	Ryanair	
EI-EMP	Boeing 737-8AS	Ryanair	
EI-EMR	Boeing 737-8AS	Ryanair	
EI-EMT	PA-16 Clipper	J. Dolan	
EI-EMU	Cessna F.152	K. O'Connor	
EI-EMV	CZAW Sportcruiser	L. Doherty & partners	
EI-ENA	Boeing 737-8AS	Ryanair	
EI-ENB	Boeing 737-8AS	Ryanair	
EI-ENC	Boeing 737-8AS	Ryanair	
EI-ENE	Boeing 737-8AS	Ryanair	
EI-ENF	Boeing 737-8AS	Ryanair	
EI-ENG	Boeing 737-8AS	Ryanair	
EI-ENH	Boeing 737-8AS	Ryanair	
EI-ENI	Boeing 737-8AS	Ryanair	
EI-ENJ	Boeing 737-8AS	Ryanair	
EI-ENK	Boeing 737-8AS	Ryanair	
EI-ENL	Boeing 737-8AS	Ryanair	
EI-ENM	Boeing 737-8AS	Ryanair	
EI-ENN	Boeing 737-8AS	Ryanair	
EI-ENO	Boeing 737-8AS	Ryanair	
EI-ENP	Boeing 737-8AS	Ryanair	
EI-ENR	Boeing 737-8AS	Ryanair	
EI-ENS	Boeing 737-8AS	Ryanair	
EI-ENT	Boeing 737-8AS	Ryanair	
EI-ENV	Boeing 737-8AS	Ryanair	
EI-ENW	Boeing 737-8AS	Ryanair	
EI-ENX	Boeing 737-8AS	Ryanair	
EI-ENY	Boeing 737-8AS	Ryanair	
EI-ENZ	Boeing 737-8AS	Ryanair	
EI-EOA	Raj Hamsa X'Air Jabiru	B. Lynch Jnr	
EI-EOB	Cameron Z-69 balloon	J. Leahy	
EI-EOC	Van's RV-6	D. McCann	
EI-EOE	Boeing 737-505	Engaly Ltd	
EI-EOF	Jabiru SP430	J. Bermingham	
EI-EOH	BRM Land Africa	P. J. Piling	
EI-EOI	Take Off Merlin 1100	N. Fitzmaurice	
EI-EOJ	Boeing 737-8BK	Air Italy Polska	
EI-EOO	Ikarus C42 FB UK	B. Gurnett & Partners	
EI-EOU	Evektor EV-97 Eurostar SL	E. McEvoy	
EI-EOW	Flight Design CTSW	J. Moriarty	
EI-EOZ	Boeing 737-3Q8	Celestial Aviation Trading 21 Ltd	
EI-EPA	Boeing 737-8AS	Ryanair	
EI-EPB	Boeing 737-8AS	Ryanair	
EI-EPC	Boeing 737-8AS	Ryanair	
EI-EPD	Boeing 737-8AS	Ryanair	
EI-EPE	Boeing 737-8AS	Ryanair	
EI-EPF	Boeing 737-8AS	Ryanair	
EI-EPG	Boeing 737-8AS	Ryanair	
EI-EPH	Boeing 737-8AS	Ryanair	
EI-EPI	Medway Hybred 44XLR	H. J. Long	
EI-EPJ	Mainair/Gemini Flash IIA	L. Flannery	
EI-EPK	Pegasus Quantum 15-912	R. A. Atkinson	
EI-EPN	Jodel DR.1050	Conor Airpark Developments Ltd	
EI-EPP	PA-22-160	P. McCabe	
EI-EPR	Airbus A.319-111	Aer Lingus	

Notes	Reg.	Type	Owner or Operator
	EI-EPS	Airbus A.319-111	Aer Lingus
	EI-EPW	MXP-740 Savannah Jabiru(5)	L. Reilly
	EI-EPY	UFM-11 Lambada	P. Kearney
	EI-EPZ	Jodel DR.1050M1	A. Dunne & Partners
	EI-ERD	Boeing 737-36N	Aircraft Finance Trust Ireland Ltd
	EI-ERE	Pegasus Quantum 15-912	M. Carter
	EI-ERF	Boeing 757-256	I-Fly
	EI-ERH	Airbus A.320-232	Avia Nova
	EI-ERI	Air Creation Clipper/Kiss 400-582(1)	E. Redmond
	EI-ERJ	Southdown Raven X	M. Hanley
	EI-ERL	Best Off Sky Ranger 912	B. Chambers
	EI-ERM	Ikarus C42B	C42 Club
	EI-ERO	Pegasus XL-R	M. Doyle
	EI-ERP	Boeing 737-3S3	Transaero
	EI-ERV	Airbus A.320-214	Jet-I 566 Ltd
	EI-ERZ	Flight Design CT-2K	M. Bowden
	EI-ESB	Urban Air Samba XXL	G. Creegan
	EI-ESC	BRM Land Africa	D. Killian
	EI-ESD	Mainair Blade	O. Farrell
	EI-ESE	Zenair CH.601XL Zodiac	O. Haslett & Partners
	EI-ESF	PA-22-160	J. Dolan
	EI-ESL	Boeing 737-8AS	Ryanair
	EI-ESM	Boeing 737-8AS	Ryanair
	EI-ESN	Boeing 737-8AS	Ryanair
	EI-ESO	Boeing 737-8AS	Ryanair
	EI-ESP	Boeing 737-8AS	Ryanair
	EI-ESR	Boeing 737-8AS	Ryanair
	EI-ESS	Boeing 737-8AS	Ryanair
	EI-EST	Boeing 737-8AS	Ryanair
	EI-ESV	Boeing 737-8AS	Ryanair
	EI-ESW	Boeing 737-8AS	Ryanair
	EI-ESX	Boeing 737-8AS	Ryanair
	EI-ESY	Boeing 737-8AS	Ryanair
	EI-ESZ	Boeing 737-8AS	Ryanair
	EI-ETB	Ikarus C42B	S. Ryan & Partners
	EI-ETD	Raj Hamsa X'Air Hawk	T. McDevitt
	EI-ETE	MS.880B Rallye	L. Murray
	EI-ETF	Samba XXL	V. Vaughan
	EI-ETH	Airbus A.321-211	Wilmington Trust SP Services (Dublin) Ltd
	EI-ETI	Airbus A.330-322	Constitution Aircraft Leasing (Ireland) 3 Ltd
	EI-ETJ	Airbus A.321-231	Kolavia
	EI-ETK	Airbus A.321-231	Kolavia
	EI-ETL	Airbus A.321-231	Kolavia
	EI-ETN	Airbus A.319-112	Rossiya
	EI-ETO	Airbus A.319-112	Rossiya
	EI-ETP	Airbus A.319-111	Rossiya
	EI-ETT	Boeing 737-4K5	Mistral Air
	EI-ETU	Ikarus C42 FB UK	A. Leadley
	EI-ETV	Raj Hamsa X'Air Hawk	P. Higgins & Partners
	EI-ETX	Boeing 737-7Q8	Wilmington Trust SP Services (Dublin) Ltd
	EI-EUA	Airbus A.320-232	New Livingston
	EI-EUB	Airbus A.320-232	Palma Aviation Ltd
	EI-EUL	Airbus A.320-232	ILFC Ireland Ltd
	EI-EUS	Airbus A.320-232	ILFC Ireland Ltd
	EI-EUW	Boeing 737-7Q8	Transaero
	EI-EUX	Boeing 737-7Q8	Transaero
	EI-EUY	Boeing 737-7Q8	Transaero
	EI-EUZ	Boeing 737-7Q8	Transaero
	EI-EVA	Boeing 737-8AS	Ryanair
	EI-EVB	Boeing 737-8AS	Ryanair
	EI-EVC	Boeing 737-8AS	Ryanair
	EI-EVD	Boeing 737-8AS	Ryanair
	EI-EVE	Boeing 737-8AS	Ryanair
	EI-EVF	Boeing 737-8AS	Ryanair
	EI-EVG	Boeing 737-8AS	Ryanair
	EI-EVH	Boeing 737-8AS	Ryanair
	EI-EVI	Boeing 737-8AS	Ryanair
	EI-EVJ	Boeing 737-8AS	Ryanair
	EI-EVK	Boeing 737-8AS	Ryanair
	EI-EVL	Boeing 737-8AS	Ryanair
	EI-EVM	Boeing 737-8AS	Ryanair
	EI-EVN	Boeing 737-8AS	Ryanair

Reg.	Type	Owner or Operator	Notes
EI-EVO	Boeing 737-8AS	Ryanair	
EI-EVP	Boeing 737-8AS	Ryanair	
EI-EVR	Boeing 737-8AS	Ryanair	
EI-EVS	Boeing 737-8AS	Ryanair	
EI-EVT	Boeing 737-8AS	Ryanair	
EI-EVV	Boeing 737-8AS	Ryanair	
EI-EVW	Boeing 737-8AS	Ryanair	
EI-EVX	Boeing 737-8AS	Ryanair	
EI-EVY	Boeing 737-8AS	Ryanair	
EI-EVZ	Boeing 737-8AS	Ryanair	
EI-EWB	Ikarus C42B	E. Maguire	
EI-EWG	Airbus A.330-223	Nightjar Ltd	
EI-EWH	Airbus A.330-223	Skua Ltd	
EI-EWI	Boeing 717-2BL	Volotea Airlines	
EI-EWJ	Boeing 717-2BL	Volotea Airlines	
EI-EWO	Airbus A.320-232	Sunflower Aircraft Leasing Ltd	
EI-EWT	Boeing 757-28A	I-Fly	
EI-EWV	Ikarus C42 FB100 VLA	D. Parke	
EI-EWX	Aeropro Eurofox	J. L. Pearson	
EI-EWY	Van's RV-6A	D. Horan & Partners	
EI-EWZ	MB-2 Colibri	Colibri Group	
EI-EXA	Boeing 717-2BL	Volotea Airlines	
EI-EXB	Boeing 717-2BL	Volotea Airlines	
EI-EXD	Boeing 737-8AS	Ryanair	
EI-EXE	Boeing 737-8AS	Ryanair	
EI-EXF	Boeing 737-8AS	Ryanair	
EI-EXI	Boeing 717-2BL	Volotea Airlines	
EI-EXJ	Boeing 717-2BL	Volotea Airlines	
EI-EXK	Airbus A.320-232	New Livingston	
EI-EXR	Airbus A.300-B4622RF	ILFC Ireland Ltd	
EI-EXY	Urban Air Samba XXL	M. Tormey	
EI-EXZ	Airbus A.319-131	Balfour Aviation Ltd	
EI-EYI	PA-28-181	C. Rooney	
EI-EYJ	Cessna F.172N	M. Harvey & Partners	
EI-EYK	Airbus A.300B4-622R	ILFC Ireland Ltd	
EI-EYL	Airbus A.319-111	Rossiya	
EI-EYM	Airbus A.319-111	Rossiya	
EI-EYO	Airbus A.330-243	Continuity Air Finance (Ireland) 1 Limited	
EI-EYR	Airbus A.320-214	Rossiya	
EI-EYS	Airbus A.320-214	Rossiya	
EI-EYT	Ikarus C42B	Croom C42 Club	
EI-EYW	Thruster T600N 450	M. O'Carroll	
EI-EYY	Aerospatiale ATR-72-212A	Aircraft International Renting (A.I.R.) Ltd	
EI-EZA	Airbus A.320-214	B&B Air Funding 888 Leasing Ltd	
EI-EZB	Boeing 737-8Z9	Killick Aerospace Ltd	
EI-EZE	Airbus A.320-214	Celestial Aviation Trading 68 Ltd	
EI-EZF	Airbus A.320-214	Celestial Aviation Trading 68 Ltd	
EI-EZH	Boeing 737-8Z9	Killick Aerospace Ltd	
EI-EZL	Airbus A.330-223	CIT Aerospace International Ltd	
EI-EZN	Airbus A.320-232	Meridiana	
EI-EZO	Airbus A.320-232	Meridiana	
EI-EZR	Airbus A.320-214	Meridiana	
EI-EZS	Airbus A.320-214	Meridiana	
EI-EZT	Airbus A.320-214	Meridiana	
EI-FAB	Eurocopter EC.120B	Billy Jet Ltd	
EI-FII	Cessna 172RG	K. O'Connor	
EI-FXA	Aérospatiale ATR-42-300	Air Contractors (Ireland) Ltd	
EI-FXB	Aérospatiale ATR-42-300	Air Contractors (Ireland) Ltd	
EI-FXC	Aérospatiale ATR-42-300	Air Contractors (Ireland) Ltd	
EI-FXD	Aérospatiale ATR-42-300	Air Contractors (Ireland) Ltd	
EI-FXE	Aérospatiale ATR-42-300	Air Contractors (Ireland) Ltd	
EI-FXG	Aérospatiale ATR-72-202	Air Contractors (Ireland) Ltd	
EI-FXH	Aérospatiale ATR-72-202	Air Contractors (Ireland) Ltd	
EI-FXI	Aérospatiale ATR-72-202	Air Contractors (Ireland) Ltd	
EI-FXJ	Aérospatiale ATR-72-202	Air Contractors (Ireland) Ltd	
EI-FXK	Aérospatiale ATR-72-202	Air Contractors (Ireland) Ltd	
EI-GCE	Sikorsky S-61N	CHC Ireland Ltd	
EI-GDL	Gulfstream GV-SP (G550)	Westair Aviation	
EI-GER	Maule MX7-180A	R. Lanigan & J.Patrick	
EI-GJL	AS.365N3	Anglo Beef Processors Ireland	
EI-GLA	Schleicher ASK-21	Dublin Gliding Club Ltd	
EI-GLB	Schleicher ASK-21	Dublin Gliding Club Ltd	

Notes	Reg.	Type	Owner or Operator
	EI-GLC	Centrair 101A Pegase	Dublin Gliding Club Ltd
	EI-GLD	Schleicher ASK-13	Dublin Gliding Club Ltd
	EI-GLF	Schleicher K-8B	Dublin Gliding Club Ltd
	EI-GLG	Schleicher Ka 6CR	C. Sinclair
	EI-GLH	AB Sportine LAK-17A	S. Kinnear
	EI-GLL	Glaser-Dirks DG-200	P. Denman & C. Craig
	EI-GLM	Schleicher Ka-6CR	P. Denman, C. Craig & J. Finnan
	EI-GLN	Glasflugel H201 Standard Libelle	S. Coveney
	EI-GLO	Scheibe Zugvogel IIIB	J. Walsh, J. Murphy & N. Short
	EI-GLP	Olympia 2B	J. Cashin
	EI-GLS	Rolladen-Schneider LS-7	M. McHugo
	EI-GLT	Schempp-Hirth Discus b	D. Thomas
	EI-GLU	Schleicher Ka-6CR	K. Cullen & Partners
	EI-GLV	Schleicher ASW-19B	C. Sinclair & B. O'Neill
	EI-GMB	Schleicher ASW-17	ASW-17 Group
	EI-GMC	Schleicher ASK-18	The Eighteen Group
	EI-GMD	Phoebus C	F. McDonnell & Partners
	EI-GMF	Schleicher ASK-13	Dublin Gliding Club Ltd
	EI-GML	Grob G.103 Twin Astir	D. McCarthy
	EI-GMN	DG Flugzeugbau DG-808C	K. Houlihan
	EI-GPT	Robinson R22 Beta	Treaty Plant & Tool (Hire & Sales)
	EI-GSE	Cessna F.172M	K. A. O'Connor
	EI-GSM	Cessna 182S	Westpoint Flying Group
	EI-GVM	Robinson R22 Beta	G. V. Maloney
	EI-GWY	Cessna 172R	Atlantic Flight Training
	EI-HCS	Grob G.109B	H. Sydner
	EI-HUM	Van's RV-7	G. Humphreys
	EI-IAN	Pilatus PC-6/B2-H4	Irish Parachute Club
	EI-ICG	Sikorsky S-92A	CHC Ireland Ltd
	EI-IGN	Boeing 737-84P	Air Italy
	EI-IGP	Boeing 737-7GL	Air Italy
	EI-IGR	Boeing 737-36N	Air Italy
	EI-IGS	Boeing 737-36N	Air Italy
	EI-IGT	Boeing 737-73V	Air Italy
	EI-IGU	Boeing 737-73V	Air Italy
	EI-IKB	Airbus A.320-214	Alitalia
	EI-IKF	Airbus A.320-214	Alitalia
	EI-IKG	Airbus A.320-214	Alitalia
	EI-IKL	Airbus A.320-214	Alitalia
	EI-IKU	Airbus A.320-214	Alitalia
	EI-ILS	Eurocopter EC.135T2+	Irish Helicopters Ltd
	EI-IMB	Airbus A.319-112	Alitalia
	EI-IMC	Airbus A.319-112	Alitalia
	EI-IMD	Airbus A.319-112	Alitalia
	EI-IME	Airbus A.319-112	Alitalia
	EI-IMF	Airbus A.319-112	Alitalia
	EI-IMG	Airbus A.319-112	Alitalia
	EI-IMH	Airbus A.319-112	Alitalia
	EI-IMI	Airbus A.319-112	Alitalia
	EI-IMJ	Airbus A.319-112	Alitalia
	EI-IML	Airbus A.319-112	Alitalia
	EI-IMM	Airbus A.319-112	Alitalia
	EI-IMN	Airbus A.319-111	Alitalia
	EI-IMO	Airbus A.319-112	Alitalia
	EI-IMP	Airbus A.319-111	Alitalia
	EI-IMR	Airbus A.319-111	Alitalia
	EI-IMS	Airbus A.319-111	Alitalia
	EI-IMT	Airbus A.319-111	Alitalia
	EI-IMU	Airbus A.319-111	Alitalia
	EI-IMW	Airbus A.319-111	Alitalia
	EI-ING	Cessna F.172P	21st Century Flyers
	EI-ISA	Boeing 777-243ER	Alitalia
	EI-ISB	Boeing 777-243ER	Alitalia
	EI-ISD	Boeing 777-243ER	Alitalia
	EI-ISE	Boeing 777-243ER	Alitalia
	EI-ISO	Boeing 777-243ER	Alitalia
	EI-IXB	Airbus A.321-112	Alitalia
	EI-IXC	Airbus A.321-112	Alitalia
	EI-IXD	Airbus A.321-112	Alitalia
	EI-IXF	Airbus A.321-112	Alitalia
	EI-IXG	Airbus A.321-112	Alitalia
	EI-IXH	Airbus A.321-112	Alitalia

Reg.	Type	Owner or Operator	Notes
EI-IXI	Airbus A.321-112	Alitalia	
EI-IXJ	Airbus A.321-112	Alitalia	
EI-IXO	Airbus A.321-112	Alitalia	
EI-IXU	Airbus A.321-112	Alitalia	
EI-IXV	Airbus A.321-112	Alitalia	
EI-IXZ	Airbus A.321-112	Alitalia	
EI-JIM	Urban Air Samba XLA	J. Smith	
EI-JIV	L.382G-44K-30 Hercules	Air Contractors (Ireland)	
EI-JOR	Robinson R44 II	Skywest Aviation Ltd	
EI-JPK	Tecnam P2002-JF	Limerick Flying Club (Coonagh) Ltd	
EI-KDH	PA-28-181 Archer II	K. O'Driscoll & D. Harris	
EI-KEL	Eurocopter EC.135T2+	Bond Air Services (Ireland) Ltd	
EI-KEV	Raj Hamsa X'Air Jabiru(3)	P. Kearney	
EI-LAD	Robinson R44 II	J. Harney & Partners	
EI-LAX	Airbus A.330-202	Aer Lingus St Mella	
EI-LCM	TBM-700N	G. Power	
EI-LEM	SOCATA TB9 Tampico	M. Fleing	
EI-LFC	Tecnam P.2002-JF	Limerick Flying Club (Coonagh) Ltd	
EI-LIR	Airbus A.319-132	Belle Air	
EI-LIS	Airbus A.320-214	Belle Air	
EI-LOW	AS.355N	Executive Helicopter Maintenance Ltd	
EI-LSA	Cub Crafters CC11-160	Directsky Aviation Ltd	
EI-MCF	Cessna 172R	K. O'Connor	
EI-MCG	Cessna 172R	Galway Flying Club	
EI-MED	Cessna 550	Airlink Airways Ltd	
EI-MIK	Eurocopter EC 120B	Executive Helicopter Maintenance Ltd	
EI-MIP	SA.365N Dauphin 2	CHC Ireland	
EI-MIR	Roko Aero NG 4HD	H. Goulding	
EI-MJC	Cessna 525B	Munster Jet Partnership Ltd	
EI-MPW	Robinson R44	Connacht Helicopters	
EI-MSG	Agusta A.109E	Beckdrive Ltd	
EI-MTZ	Urban Air Samba XXL	M. Motz	
EI-NFW	Cessna 172S	Galway Flying Club	
EI-NJA	Robinson R44 II	Nojo Aviation Ltd	
EI-NVL	Jora spol S. R. O. Jora	A. McAllister & partners	
EI-ODD	Bell 206B JetRanger	Dwyer Nolan Developments Ltd	
EI-OFM	Cessna F.172N	C. Phillips	
EI-OOR	Cessna 172S	Sligo Flying Schol Ltd	
EI-OZD	Airbus A.300B4-203F	Air Contractors/DHL	
EI-OZE	Airbus A.300B4-203F	Air Contractors/DHL	
EI-OZF	Airbus A.300B4-203F	Air Contractors/DHL	
EI-OZH	Airbus A.300B4-203F	Air Contractors/DHL	
EI-OZI	Airbus A.300B4-203F	Air Contractors/DHL	
EI-OZJ	Airbus A.300B4-622R	Air Contractors	
EI-PCI	Bell 206B JetRanger	Malcove Ltd	
EI-PJD	AS.350B2 Twin Squirrel	New World Plant	
EI-PMI	Agusta-Bell 206B JetRanger III	Eirland Ltd	
EI-POP	Cameron Z-90 balloon	The Travel Department	
EI-RCA	Roko Aero NG4UL	Racecrest Ltd	
EI-RCG	Sikorsky S-61N	CHC Ireland	
EI-RDA	Embraer ERJ170-200LR	Alitalia Cityliner	
EI-RDB	Embraer ERJ170-200LR	Alitalia Cityliner	
EI-RDC	Embraer ERJ170-200LR	Alitalia Cityliner	
EI-RDD	Embraer ERJ170-200LR	Alitalia Cityliner	
EI-RDE	Embraer ERJ170-200LR	Alitalia Cityliner	
EI-RDF	Embraer ERJ170-200LR	Alitalia Cityliner	
EI-RDG	Embraer ERJ170-200LR	Alitalia Cityliner	
EI-RDH	Embraer ERJ170-200LR	Alitalia Cityliner	
EI-RDI	Embraer ERJ170-200LR	Alitalia Cityliner	
EI-RDJ	Embraer ERJ170-200LR	Alitalia Cityliner	
EI-RDK	Embraer ERJ170-200LR	Alitalia Cityliner	
EI-RDL	Embraer ERJ170-200LR	Alitalia Cityliner	
EI-RDM	Embraer ERJ170-200LR	Alitalia Cityliner	
EI-REH	Aérospatiale ATR-72-201	Aer Arann	
EI-REI	Aérospatiale ATR-72-201	Aer Arann	
EI-REJ	Aérospatiale ATR-72-201	Air Contractgors (Ireland) Ltd	
EI-REL	Aerospatiale ATR-72-212	Aer Arann	
EI-REM	Aerospatiale ATR-72-212	Aer Arann	
EI-REO	Aerospatiale ATR-72-212	Aer Arann	
EI-REP	Aerospatiale ATR-72-212	Aer Arann	
EI-REX	Learjet 60	Airlink Airways	
EI-RHM	Bell 407	A. Morrin	

Notes	Reg.	Type	Owner or Operator
	EI-RJA	Avro RJ85	Cityjet
	EI-RJB	Avro RJ85	Cityjet Bere Island
	EI-RJC	Avro RJ85	Cityjet
	EI-RJD	Avro RJ85	Cityjet
	EI-RJE	Avro RJ85	Cityjet
	EI-RJF	Avro RJ85	Cityjet
	EI-RJG	Avro RJ85	Cityjet
	EI-RJH	Avro RJ85	Cityjet
	EI-RJI	Avro RJ85	Cityjet
	EI-RJJ	Avro RJ85	Cityjet
	EI-RJN	Avro RJ85	Cityjet
	EI-RJO	Avro RJ85	Cityjet
	EI-RJR	Avro RJ85	Cityjet
	EI-RJS	Avro RJ85	Cityjet Dursey Island
	EI-RJT	Avro RJ85	Cityjet
	EI-RJU	Avro RJ85	Cityjet
	EI-RJW	Avro RJ85	Cityjet Garinish Island
	EI-RJX	Avro RJ85	Cityjet
	EI-RJY	Avro RJ85	Cityjet
	EI-RJZ	Avro RJ85	Cityjet
	EI-RMC	Bell 206B JetRanger	Westair Aviation
	EI-RNA	Embraer ERJ190-100STD	Alitalia Cityliner
	EI-RNB	Embraer ERJ190-100STD	Alitalia Cityliner
	EI-RNC	Embraer ERJ190-100STD	Alitalia Cityliner
	EI-RND	Embraer ERJ190-100STD	Alitalia Cityliner
	EI-RNE	Embraer ERJ190-100STD	Alitalia Cityliner
	EI-ROB	Robin R.1180TD	Extras Ltd
	EI-ROK	Roko Aero NG 4UL	K. Harley
	EI-RUA	Boeing 737-86J	Transaero
	EI-RUB	Boeing 737-85P	Transaero
	EI-RUC	Boeing 737-86R	Transaero
	EI-RUD	Boeing 737-86R	Transaero
	EI-RUE	Boeing 737-85P	Transaero
	EI-RUF	Boeing 737-85P	Transaero
	EI-RUG	Boeing 737-86N	Transaero
	EI-RUY	Boeing 767-3Q8ER	Transaero
	EI-RUZ	Boeing 767-3Q8ER	Transaero
	EI-SAC	Cessna 172P	Sligo Aero Club
	EI-SAF	Airbus A.300B4-203F	European Air Transport/DHL
	EI-SAI	Eurocopter SA.330J	Heavylift Charters Ltd
	EI-SAR	Sikorsky S-61N	CHC Ireland
	EI-SEA	SeaRey	J. Brennan
	EI-SKB	PA-44-180 Seminole	Shemburn Ltd
	EI-SKC	PA-44-180 Seminole	Shemburn Ltd
	EI-SKE	Robin DR400/140B	Shemburn Ltd
	EI-SKR	PA-44-180 Seminole	Shemburn Ltd
	EI-SKS	Robin R.2160	Shemburn Ltd
	EI-SKT	PA-44-180 Seminole	Shemburn Ltd
	EI-SKV	Robin R.2160	Shemburn Ltd
	EI-SKW	PA-28-161 Warrior II	Shemburn Ltd
	EI-SLA	Aérospatiale ATR-42-310	Air Contractors (Ireland) Ltd
	EI-SLF	Aérospatiale ATR-72-201	Air Contractors (Ireland) Ltd
	EI-SLG	Aérospatiale ATR-72-202	Air Contractors (Ireland) Ltd
	EI-SLH	Aerospatiale ATR-72-202	Air Contractors (Ireland) Ltd
	EI-SLJ	Aerospatiale ATR-72-201	Air Contractors (Ireland) Ltd
	EI-SLK	Aerospatiale ATR-72-212	Air Contractors (Ireland) Ltd
	EI-SLL	Aerospatiale ATR-72-212	Air Contractors (Ireland) Ltd/Aer Arran
	EI-SLN	Aerospatiale ATR-72-212	Air Contractors (Ireland) Ltd/Aer Arran
	EI-SMK	Zenair CH701	S. King
	EI-SPB	Cessna T206H	P. Morrissey
	EI-STA	Boeing 737-31S	Air Contractors (Ireland) Ltd/Europe Airpost
	EI-STB	Boeing 737-476F	Air Contractors (Ireland) Ltd
	EI-STC	Boeing 737-476	Air Contractors (Ireland) Ltd
	EI-STT	Cessna 172M	Trim Flying Club
	EI-SYM	Van's RV-7	E. Symes
	EI-TAB	Airbus A.320-233	Wilmington Trust SP Services/TACA
	EI-TAG	Airbus A.320-233	Wilmington Trust SP Services/TACA
	EI-TDV	Dassault Falcon 2000LX	Herodias Executive Aircraft
	EI-TIM	Piper J-5A	N. & P. Murphy
	EI-TKI	Robinson R22 Beta	J. McDaid
	EI-TON	M. B. Cooke 582 (5)	T. Merrigan

Reg.	Type	Owner or Operator	Notes
EI-UFO	PA-22 Tri-Pacer 150 (tailwheel)	W. Treacy	
EI-UNA	Boeing 767-3P6ER	Transaero	
EI-UNB	Boeing 767-3P6ER	Transaero	
EI-UNC	Boeing 767-319ER	Transaero	
EI-UND	Boeing 767-2P6ER	Transaero	
EI-UNE	Boeing 767-3Q8ER	Transaero	
EI-UNF	Boeing 767-3P6ER	Transaero	
EI-UNG	Boeing 737-524	Transaero	
EI-UNH	Boeing 737-524	Transaero	
EI-UNI	Robinson R44 II	Unipipe (Irl) Ltd	
EI-UNJ	Boeing 737-86J	Transaero	
EI-UNK	Boeing 737-86J	Transaero	
EI-UNL	Boeing 777-312	Transaero	
EI-UNM	Boeing 777-312	Transaero	
EI-UNN	Boeing 777-312	Transaero	
EI-UNP	Boeing 777-312	Transaero	
EI-UNR	Boeing 777-212ER	Transaero	
EI-UNS	Boeing 777-212ER	Transaero	
EI-UNT	Boeing 777-212ER	Transaero	
EI-UNU	Boeing 777-222ER	Transaero	
EI-UNV	Boeing 777-222ER	Transaero	
EI-UNW	Boeing 777-222	Transaero	
EI-UNX	Boeing 777-222	Transaero	
EI-UNY	Boeing 777-222	Transaero	
EI-UNZ	Boeing 777-222	Transaero	
EI-VII	Vans RV-7	B. Sheane	
EI-VLN	PA-18A-150	D. O'Mahony	
EI-WAC	PA-23 Aztec 250E	Westair Aviation	
EI-WAT	Tecnam P.2002-JF	Waterford Aero Club Ltd	
EI-WAV	Bell 430	Westair Aviation	
EI-WFD	Tecnam P.2002-JF	Waterford Aero Club Ltd	
EI-WFI	Bombardier CL600-2B16 Challenger	Midwest Atlantic/Westair	
EI-WIG	Sky Ranger 912	M. Brereton	
EI-WMN	PA-23 Aztec 250F	Westair Aviation	
EI-WOT	Currie Wot	D. Doyle & Partners	
EI-WWI	Robinson R44 II	J. Murtagh	
EI-WXA	Avro RJ85	Cityjet Ltd	
EI-WXB	Avro RJ85	Cityjet Ltd	
EI-WXP	Hawker 800XP	Westair Aviation Ltd	
EI-XLA	Urban Air Samba XLA	K. Dardis	
EI-XLB	Boeing 747-446	Transaero	
EI-XLC	Boeing 747-446	Transaero	
EI-XLD	Boeing 747-446	Transaero	
EI-XLE	Boeing 747-446	Transaero	
EI-XLF	Boeing 747-446	Transaero	
EI-XLG	Boeing 747-446	Transaero	
EI-XLH	Boeing 747-446	Transaero	
EI-XLI	Boeing 747-446	Transaero	
EI-XLJ	Boeing 747-446	Transaero	
EI-XLK	Boeing 747-412	Transaero	
EI-XLL	Boeing 747-412	Transaero	
EI-XLM	Boeing 747-412	Transaero	
EI-XLN	Boeing 747-412	Transaero	
EI-XLO	Boeing 747-412	Transaero	
EI-XLP	Boeing 777-312	Transaero	
EI-XLS	Cessna 560XL	Airlink Airways Ltd	
EI-XLZ	Boeing 747-444	Transaero	
EI-YLG	Robin HR.200/120B	Leinster Aero Club	
EI-ZZZ	Bell222	Executive Helicopter Maintenance Ltd	

EI-CXN Boeing 737-329 of Transaero. *Allan S. Wright*

EI-LSA Cub Crafter CC11-160. *Allan S. Wright*

AP-BGY Boeing 777-240LR of Pakistan International Airlines. *Allan S. Wright*

Overseas Airliner Registrations

(Aircraft included in this section are those most likely to be seen at UK and nearby European airports or overflying UK airspace.)

Reg.	Type	Owner or Operator	Notes

A6 (Arab Emirates)

Reg.	Type	Owner or Operator	Notes
A6-AFA	Airbus A.330-343X	Etihad Airways	
A6-AFB	Airbus A.330-343X	Etihad Airways	
A6-AFC	Airbus A.330-343X	Etihad Airways	
A6-AFD	Airbus A.330-343X	Etihad Airways	
A6-AFE	Airbus A.330-343X	Etihad Airways	
A6-AFF	Airbus A.330-343X	Etihad Airways	
A6-EAD	Airbus A.330-243	Emirates Airlines	
A6-EAE	Airbus A.330-243	Emirates Airlines	
A6-EAF	Airbus A.330-243	Emirates Airlines	
A6-EAG	Airbus A.330-243	Emirates Airlines	
A6-EAH	Airbus A.330-243	Emirates Airlines	
A6-EAI	Airbus A.330-243	Emirates Airlines	
A6-EAJ	Airbus A.330-243	Emirates Airlines	
A6-EAK	Airbus A.330-243	Emirates Airlines	
A6-EAM	Airbus A.330-243	Emirates Airlines	
A6-EAO	Airbus A.330-243	Emirates Airlines	
A6-EAP	Airbus A.330-243	Emirates Airlines	
A6-EAQ	Airbus A.330-243	Emirates Airlines	
A6-EAR	Airbus A.330-243	Emirates Airlines	
A6-EAS	Airbus A.330-243	Emirates Airlines	
A6-EBA	Boeing 777-31HER	Emirates Airlines	
A6-EBB	Boeing 777-36NER	Emirates Airlines	
A6-EBC	Boeing 777-36NER	Emirates Airlines	
A6-EBD	Boeing 777-31HER	Emirates Airlines	
A6-EBE	Boeing 777-36NER	Emirates Airlines	
A6-EBF	Boeing 777-31HER	Emirates Airlines	
A6-EBG	Boeing 777-36NER	Emirates Airlines	
A6-EBH	Boeing 777-31HER	Emirates Airlines	
A6-EBI	Boeing 777-36NER	Emirates Airlines	
A6-EBJ	Boeing 777-36NER	Emirates Airlines	
A6-EBK	Boeing 777-31HER	Emirates Airlines	
A6-EBL	Boeing 777-31HER	Emirates Airlines	
A6-EBM	Boeing 777-31HER	Emirates Airlines	
A6-EBN	Boeing 777-36NER	Emirates Airlines	
A6-EBO	Boeing 777-36NER	Emirates Airlines	
A6-EBP	Boeing 777-31HER	Emirates Airlines	
A6-EBQ	Boeing 777-36NER	Emirates Airlines	
A6-EBR	Boeing 777-31HER	Emirates Airlines	
A6-EBS	Boeing 777-31HER	Emirates Airlines	
A6-EBT	Boeing 777-31HER	Emirates Airlines	
A6-EBU	Boeing 777-31HER	Emirates Airlines	
A6-EBV	Boeing 777-31HER	Emirates Airlines	
A6-EBW	Boeing 777-36NER	Emirates Airlines	
A6-EBX	Boeing 777-31HER	Emirates Airlines	
A6-EBY	Boeing 777-36NER	Emirates Airlines	
A6-EBZ	Boeing 777-31HER	Emirates Airlines	
A6-ECA	Boeing 777-36NER	Emirates Airlines	
A6-ECB	Boeing 777-31HER	Emirates Airlines	
A6-ECC	Boeing 777-36NER	Emirates Airlines	
A6-ECD	Boeing 777-36NER	Emirates Airlines	
A6-ECE	Boeing 777-31HER	Emirates Airlines	
A6-ECF	Boeing 777-31HER	Emirates Airlines	
A6-ECG	Boeing 777-31HER	Emirates Airlines	
A6-ECH	Boeing 777-31HER	Emirates Airlines	
A6-ECI	Boeing 777-31HER	Emirates Airlines	
A6-ECJ	Boeing 777-31HER	Emirates Airlines	
A6-ECK	Boeing 777-31HER	Emirates Airlines	
A6-ECL	Boeing 777-31NER	Emirates Airlines	
A6-ECM	Boeing 777-31NER	Emirates Airlines	
A6-ECN	Boeing 777-31NER	Emirates Airlines	
A6-ECO	Boeinb 777-31NER	Emirates Airlines	
A6-ECP	Boeing 777-31NER	Emirates Airlines	

Notes	Reg.	Type	Owner or Operator
	A6-ECQ	Boeing 777-31HER	Emirates Airlines
	A6-ECR	Boeing 777-31HER	Emirates Airlines
	A6-ECS	Boeing 777-31HER	Emirates Airlines
	A6-ECT	Boeing 777-31HER	Emirates Airlines
	A6-ECU	Boeing 777-31HER	Emirates Airlines
	A6-ECV	Boeing 777-31HER	Emirates Airlines
	A6-ECW	Boeing 777-31HER	Emirates Airlines
	A6-ECX	Boeing 777-31HER	Emirates Airlines
	A6-ECY	Boeing 777-31HER	Emirates Airlines
	A6-ECZ	Boeing 777-31HER	Emirates Airlines
	A6-EDA	Airbus A.380-861	Emirates Airlines
	A6-EDB	Airbus A.380-861	Emirates Airlines
	A6-EDC	Airbus A.380-861	Emirates Airlines
	A6-EDD	Airbus A.380-861	Emirates Airlines
	A6-EDE	Airbus A.380-861	Emirates Airlines
	A6-EDF	Airbus A.380-861	Emirates Airlines
	A6-EDG	Airbus A.380-861	Emirates Airlines
	A6-EDH	Airbus A.380-861	Emirates Airlines
	A6-EDI	Airbus A.380-861	Emirates Airlines
	A6-EDJ	Airbus A.380-861	Emirates Airlines
	A6-EDK	Airbus A.380-861	Emirates Airlines
	A6-EDL	Airbus A.380-861	Emirates Airlines
	A6-EDM	Airbus A.380-861	Emirates Airlines
	A6-EDN	Airbus A.380-861	Emirates Airlines
	A6-EDO	Airbus A.380-861	Emirates Airlines
	A6-EDP	Airbus A.380-861	Emirates Airlines
	A6-EDQ	Airbus A.380-861	Emirates Airlines
	A6-EDR	Airbus A.380-861	Emirates Airlines
	A6-EDS	Airbus A.380-861	Emirates Airlines
	A6-EDT	Airbus A.380-861	Emirates Airlines
	A6-EDU	Airbus A.380-861	Emirates Airlines
	A6-EDV	Airbus A.380-861	Emirates Airlines
	A6-EDW	Airbus A.380-861	Emirates Airlines
	A6-EDX	Airbus A.380-861	Emirates Airlines
	A6-EDY	Airbus A.380-861	Emirates Airlines
	A6-EDZ	Airbus A.380-861	Emirates Airlines
	A6-EEA	Airbus A.380-861	Emirates Airlines
	A6-EEB	Airbus A.380-861	Emirates Airlines
	A6-EEC	Airbus A.380-861	Emirates Airlines
	A6-EED	Airbus A.380-861	Emirates Airlines
	A6-EEE	Airbus A.380-861	Emirates Airlines
	A6-EEF	Airbus A.380-861	Emirates Airlines
	A6-EEG	Airbus A.380-861	Emirates Airlines
	A6-EFD	Boeing 777-21H	Emirates Airlines
	A6-EFE	Boeing 777-21H	Emirates Airlines
	A6-EFF	Boeing 777-21H	Emirates Airlines
	A6-EFG	Boeing 777-21H	Emirates Airlines
	A6-EFH	Boeing 777-21H	Emirates Airlines
	A6-EFI	Boeing 777-21H	Emirates Airlines
	A6-EGA	Boeing 777-31HER	Emirates Airlines
	A6-EGB	Boeing 777-31HER	Emirates Airlines
	A6-EGC	Boeing 777-31HER	Emirates Airlines
	A6-EGD	Boeing 777-31HER	Emirates Airlines
	A6-EGE	Boeing 777-31HER	Emirates Airlines
	A6-EGF	Boeing 777-31HER	Emirates Airlines
	A6-EGG	Boeing 777-31HER	Emirates Airlines
	A6-EGH	Boeing 777-31HER	Emirates Airlines
	A6-EGI	Boeing 777-31HER	Emirates Airlines
	A6-EGJ	Boeing 777-31HER	Emirates Airlines
	A6-EGK	Boeing 777-31HER	Emirates Airlines
	A6-EGL	Boeing 777-31HER	Emirates Airlines
	A6-EGM	Boeing 777-31HER	Emirates Airlines
	A6-EGN	Boeing 777-31HER	Emirates Airlines
	A6-EGO	Boeing 777-31HER	Emirates Airlines
	A6-EGP	Boeing 777-31HER	Emirates Airlines
	A6-EGQ	Boeing 777-31HER	Emirates Airlines
	A6-EGR	Boeing 777-31HER	Emirates Airlines
	A6-EGS	Boeing 777-31HER	Emirates Airlines
	A6-EGT	Boeing 777-31HER	Emirates Airlines
	A6-EGU	Boeing 777-31HER	Emirates Airlines
	A6-EGV	Boeing 777-31HER	Emirates Airlines
	A6-EGW	Boeing 777-31HER	Emirates Airlines

Reg.	Type	Owner or Operator	Notes
A6-EGX	Boeing 777-31HER	Emirates Airlines	
A6-EGY	Boeing 777-31HER	Emirates Airlines	
A6-EGZ	Boeing 777-31HER	Emirates Airlines	
A6-EHA	Airbus A.340-541	Etihad Airways	
A6-EHB	Airbus A.340-541	Etihad Airways	
A6-EHC	Airbus A.340-541	Etihad Airways	
A6-EHD	Airbus A.340-541	Etihad Airways	
A6-EHE	Airbus A.340-642	Etihad Airways	
A6-EHF	Airbus A.340-642	Etihad Airways	
A6-EHH	Airbus A.340-642	Etihad Airways	
A6-EHI	Airbus A.340-642	Etihad Airways	
A6-EHJ	Airbus A.340-642	Etihad Airways	
A6-EHK	Airbus A.340-642	Etihad Airways	
A6-EHL	Airbus A.340-642	Etihad Airways	
A6-EKQ	Airbus A.330-243	Emirates Airlines	
A6-EKR	Airbus A.330-243	Emirates Airlines	
A6-EKS	Airbus A.330-243	Emirates Airlines	
A6-EKT	Airbus A.330-243	Emirates Airlines	
A6-EKU	Airbus A.330-243	Emirates Airlines	
A6-EKV	Airbus A.330-243	Emirates Airlines	
A6-EKW	Airbus A.330-243	Emirates Airlines	
A6-EKX	Airbus A.330-243	Emirates Airlines	
A6-EKY	Airbus A.330-243	Emirates Airlines	
A6-EMD	Boeing 777-21H	Emirates Airlines	
A6-EME	Boeing 777-21H	Emirates Airlines	
A6-EMF	Boeing 777-21H	Emirates Airlines	
A6-EMG	Boeing 777-21HER	Emirates Airlines	
A6-EMH	Boeing 777-21HER	Emirates Airlines	
A6-EMI	Boeing 777-21HER	Emirates Airlines	
A6-EMJ	Boeing 777-21HER	Emirates Airlines	
A6-EMK	Boeing 777-21HER	Emirates Airlines	
A6-EML	Boeing 777-21HER	Emirates Airlines	
A6-EMM	Boeing 777-31H	Emirates Airlines	
A6-EMN	Boeing 777-31H	Emirates Airlines	
A6-EMO	Boeing 777-31H	Emirates Airlines	
A6-EMP	Boeing 777-31H	Emirates Airlines	
A6-EMQ	Boeing 777-31H	Emirates Airlines	
A6-EMR	Boeing 777-31H	Emirates Airlines	
A6-EMS	Boeing 777-31H	Emirates Airlines	
A6-EMT	Boeing 777-31H	Emirates Airlines	
A6-EMU	Boeing 777-31H	Emirates Airlines	
A6-EMV	Boeing 777-31H	Emirates Airlines	
A6-EMW	Boeing 777-31H	Emirates Airlines	
A6-EMX	Boeing 777-31H	Emirates Airlines	
A6-ENA	Boeing 777-31HER	Emirates Airlines	
A6-ENB	Boeing 777-31HER	Emirates Airlines	
A6-ENC	Boeing 777-31HER	Emirates Airlines	
A6-END	Boeing 777-31HER	Emirates Airlines	
A6-ENE	Boeing 777-31HER	Emirates Airlines	
A6-ENF	Boeing 777-31HER	Emirates Airlines	
A6-ENG	Boeing 777-31HER	Emirates Airlines	
A6-ENH	Boeing 777-31HER	Emirates Airlines	
A6-ENI	Boeing 777-31HER	Emirates Airlines	
A6-ENJ	Boeing 777-31HER	Emirates Airlines	
A6-ERA	Airbus A.340-541	Emirates Airlines	
A6-ERB	Airbus A.340-541	Emirates Airlines	
A6-ERC	Airbus A.340-541	Emirates Airlines	
A6-ERD	Airbus A.340-541	Emirates Airlines	
A6-ERE	Airbus A.340-541	Emirates Airlines	
A6-ERF	Airbus A.340-541	Emirates Airlines	
A6-ERG	Airbus A.340-541	Emirates Airlines	
A6-ERH	Airbus A.340-541	Emirates Airlines	
A6-ERI	Airbus A.340-541	Emirates Airlines	
A6-ERJ	Airbus A.340-541	Emirates Airlines	
A6-ERM	Airbus A.340-313X	Emirates Airlines	
A6-ERN	Airbus A.340-313X	Emirates Airlines	
A6-ERO	Airbus A.340-313X	Emirates Airlines	
A6-ERP	Airbus A.340-313X	Emirates Airlines	
A6-ERS	Airbus A.340-313X	Emirates Airlines	
A6-ERT	Airbus A.340-313X	Emirates Airlines	
A6-ETA	Boeing 777-3FXER	Etihad Airways	
A6-ETB	Boeing 777-3FXER	Etihad Airways	

Notes	Reg.	Type	Owner or Operator
	A6-ETC	Boeing 777-3FXER	Etihad Airways
	A6-ETD	Boeing 777-3FXER	Etihad Airways
	A6-ETE	Boeing 777-3FXER	Etihad Airways
	A6-ETF	Boeing 777-3FXER	Ethiad Airways
	A6-ETG	Boeing 777-3FXER	Ethiad Airways
	A6-ETH	Boeing 777-3FXER	Etihad Airways
	A6-ETI	Boeing 777-3FXER	Ethiad Airways
	A6-ETJ	Boeing 777-3FXER	Etihad Airways
	A6-ETK	Boeing 777-3FXER	Etihad Airways
	A6-ETL	Boeing 777-3FXER	Ethiad Airways
	A6-ETM	Boeing 777-3FXER	Etihad Airways
	A6-ETN	Boeing 777-3FXER	Ethiad Airways
	A6-EWA	Boeing 777-21HLR	Emirates Airlines
	A6-EWB	Boeing 777-21HLR	Emirates Airlines
	A6-EWC	Boeing 777-21HLR	Emirates Airlines
	A6-EWD	Boeing 777-21HLR	Emirates Airlines
	A6-EWE	Boeing 777-21HLR	Emirates Airlines
	A6-EWF	Boeing 777-21HLR	Emirates Airlines
	A6-EWG	Boeing 777-21HLR	Emirates Airlines
	A6-EWH	Boeing 777-21HER	Emirates Airlines
	A6-EWI	Boeing 777-21HER	Emirates Airlines
	A6-EWJ	Boeing 777-21HLR	Emirates Airlines
	A6-EYD	Airbus A.330-243	Etihad Airways
	A6-EYE	Airbus A.330-243	Etihad Airways *Blue Moon Rising*
	A6-EYF	Airbus A.330-243	Etihad Airways
	A6-EYG	Airbus A.330-243	Etihad Airways
	A6-EYH	Airbus A.330-243	Etihad Airways
	A6-EYI	Airbus A.330-243	Etihad Airways
	A6-EYJ	Airbus A.330-243	Ethiad Airways
	A6-EYK	Airbus A.330-243	Etihad Airways
	A6-EYL	Airbus A.330-243	Ethiad Airways
	A6-EYM	Airbus A.330-243	Etihad Airways
	A6-EYN	Airbus A.330-243	Etihad Airways
	A6-EYO	Airbus A.330-243	Etihad Airways
	A6-EYP	Airbus A.330-243	Etihad Airways
	A6-EYQ	Airbus A.330-243	Etihad Airways
	A6-EYR	Airbus A.330-243	Ethiad Airways
	A6-EYS	Airbus A.330-243	Ethiad Airways
	A6-HAZ	Airbus A.300B4-622RF	Maximus Air Cargo
	A6-NIN	Airbus A.300B4-622RF	Maximus Air Cargo
	A6-SUL	Airbus A.300B4-622RF	Maximus Air Cargo

A7 (Qatar)

Notes	Reg.	Type	Owner or Operator
	A7-ACA	Airbus A.330-202	Qatar Airways *Al Wajba*
	A7-ACB	Airbus A.330-202	Qatar Airways *Al Majida*
	A7-ACC	Airbus A.330-202	Qatar Airways *Al Shahaniya*
	A7-ACD	Airbus A.330-202	Qatar Airways *Al Wusell*
	A7-ACE	Airbus A.330-202	Qatar Airways *Al Dhakira*
	A7-ACF	Airbus A.330-202	Qatar Airways *Al Kara'anah*
	A7-ACG	Airbus A.330-202	Qatar Airways *Al Wabra*
	A7-ACH	Airbus A.330-202	Qatar Airways *Al Mafjar*
	A7-ACI	Airbus A.330-202	Qatar Airways *Muathier*
	A7-ACJ	Airbus A.330-202	Qatar Airways *Zikreet*
	A7-ACK	Airbus A.330-202	Qatar Airways
	A7-ACL	Airbus A.330-202	Qatar Airways
	A7-ACM	Airbus A.330-202	Qatar Airways
	A7-AEA	Airbus A.330-302	Qatar Airways *Al Muntazah*
	A7-AEB	Airbus A.330-302	Qatar Airways *Al Sayliyah*
	A7-AEC	Airbus A.330-302	Qatar Airways *Al Markhiya*
	A7-AED	Airbus A.330-302	Qatar Airways *Al Nu'uman*
	A7-AEE	Airbus A.330-302	Qatar Airways *Semaisma*
	A7-AEF	Airbus A.330-302	Qatar Airways *Al Rumellah*
	A7-AEG	Airbus A.330-302	Qatar Airways *Al Duhell*
	A7-AEH	Airbus A.330-302	Qatar Airways
	A7-AEI	Airbus A.330-302	Qatar Airways
	A7-AEJ	Airbus A.330-302	Qatar Airways
	A7-AEM	Airbus A.330-302	Qatar Airways
	A7-AEN	Airbus A.330-302	Qatar Airways
	A7-AEO	Airbus A.330-302	Qatar Airways
	A7-AFL	Airbus A.330-202	Qatar Airways *Al Messilah*
	A7-AFM	Airbus A.330-202	Qatar Airways *Al Udaid*
	A7-AFP	Airbus A.330-202	Qatar Airways *Al Shamal*

Reg.	Type	Owner or Operator	Notes
A7-AGA	Airbus A.340-642	Qatar Airways	
A7-AGB	Airbus A.340-642	Qatar Airways	
A7-AGC	Airbus A.340-642	Qatar Airways	
A7-AGD	Airbus A.340-642	Qatar Airways	
A7-BAA	Boeing 777-3DZ ER	Qatar Airways	
A7-BAB	Boeing 777-3DZ ER	Qatar Airways	
A7-BAC	Boeing 777-3DZ ER	Qatar Airways	
A7-BAE	Boeing 777-3DZ ER	Qatar Airways	
A7-BAF	Boeing 777-3DZ ER	Qatar Airways	
A7-BAG	Boeing 777-3DZ ER	Qatar Airways	
A7-BAH	Boeing 777-3DZ ER	Qatar Airways	
A7-BAI	Boeing 777-3DZ ER	Qatar Airways	
A7-BAJ	Boeing 777-3DZ ER	Qatar Airways	
A7-BAK	Boeing 777-3DZ ER	Qatar Airways	
A7-BAL	Boeing 777-3DZ ER	Qatar Airways	
A7-BAM	Boeing 777-3DZ ER	Qatar Airways	
A7-BAN	Boeing 777-3DZ ER	Qatar Airways	
A7-BAO	Boeing 777-3DZ ER	Qatar Airways	
A7-BAP	Boeing 777-3DZ ER	Qatar Airways *Al Qattard*	
A7-BAQ	Boeing 777-3DZ ER	Qatar Airways	
A7-BAS	Boeing 777-3DZ ER	Qatar Airways	
A7-BAW	Boeing 777-3DZ ER	Qatar Airways	
A7-BAX	Boeing 777-3DZ ER	Qatar Airways	
A7-BAY	Boeing 777-3DZ ER	Qatar Airways	
A7-BAZ	Boeing 777-3DZ ER	Qatar Airways	
A7-BBA	Boeing 777-2DZ LR	Qatar Airways	
A7-BBB	Boeing 777-2DZ LR	Qatar Airways	
A7-BBC	Boeing 777-2DZ LR	Qatar Airways	
A7-BBD	Boeing 777-2DZ LR	Qatar Airways	
A7-BBE	Boeing 777-2DZ LR	Qatar Airways	
A7-BBF	Boeing 777-2DZ LR	Qatar Airways	
A7-BBG	Boeing 777-2DZ LR	Qatar Airways	
A7-BBH	Boeing 777-2DZ LR	Qatar Airways *A.Calall*	
A7-BBI	Boeing 777-2DZ LR	Qatar Airways *Jaow Alsalam*	
A7-BBJ	Boeing 777-2DZ LR	Qatar Airways	
A7-BCA	Boeing 787-8	Qatar Airways	
A7-BCB	Boeing 787-8	Qatar Airways	
A7-BCC	Boeing 787-8	Qatar Airways	
A7-BCK	Boeing 787-8	Qatar Airways	
A7-BCL	Boeing 787-8	Qatar Airways	
A7-BEA	Boeing 777-3DZ ER	Qatar Airways	

A9C (Bahrain)

A9C-KA	Airbus A.330-243 (501)	Gulf Air	
A9C-KB	Airbus A.330-243 (502)	Gulf Air	
A9C-KC	Airbus A.330-243 (503)	Gulf Air	
A9C-KD	Airbus A.330-243 (504)	Gulf Air	
A9C-KE	Airbus A.330-243 (505)	Gulf Air	
A9C-KF	Airbus A.330-243 (506)	Gulf Air *Aldafra*	
A9C-KG	Airbus A.330-243	Gulf Air	
A9C-KH	Airbus A.330-243	Gulf Air	
A9C-KI	Airbus A.330-243	Gulf Air	
A9C-KJ	Airbus A.330-243	Gulf Air	

A40 (Oman)

A40-DA	Airbus A.330-243	Oman Air	
A40-DB	Airbus A.330-343	Oman Air	
A40-DC	Airbus A.330-243	Oman Air	
A40-DD	Airbus A.330-343	Oman Air	
A40-DE	Airbus A.330-343	Oman Air	
A40-DF	Airbus A.330-243	Oman Air	
A40-DG	Airbus A.330-243	Oman Air	

AP (Pakistan)

AP-BDZ	Airbus A.310-308	Pakistan International Airlines	
AP-BEB	Airbus A.310-308	Pakistan International Airlines	

Notes	Reg.	Type	Owner or Operator
	AP-BEC	Airbus A.310-308	Pakistan International Airlines
	AP-BEG	Airbus A.310-308	Pakistan International Airlines
	AP-BEU	Airbus A.310-308	Pakistan International Airlines
	AP-BGJ	Boeing 777-240ER	Pakistan International Airlines
	AP-BGK	Boeing 777-240ER	Pakistan International Airlines
	AP-BGL	Boeing 777-240ER	Pakistan International Airlines
	AP-BGY	Boeing 777-240LR	Pakistan International Airlines
	AP-BGZ	Boeing 777-240LR	Pakistan International Airlines
	AP-BHV	Boeing 777-340ER	Pakistan International Airlines
	AP-BHW	Boeing 777-340ER	Pakistan International Airlines
	AP-BHX	Boeing 777-240ER	Pakistan International Airlines
	AP-BID	Boeing 777-340ER	Pakistan International Airlines
	AP-EDE	Airbus A.340-313X	AirBlue
	AP-EDF	Airbus A.340-313X	AirBlue

B (China/Taiwan/Hong Kong)

	B-HKE	Boeing 747-412	Cathay Pacific Airways
	B-HKF	Boeing 747-412	Cathay Pacific Airways
	B-HKJ	Boeing 747-412BCF	Cathay Pacific Airways
	B-HKT	Boeing 747-412BCF	Cathay Pacific Airways
	B-HKU	Boeing 747-412	Cathay Pacific Airways
	B-HKV	Boeing 747-412	Cathay Pacific Airways
	B-HKX	Boeing 747-412BCF	Cathay Pacific Airways
	B-HOP	Boeing 747-467	Cathay Pacific Airways
	B-HOR	Boeing 747-467	Cathay Pacific Airways
	B-HOS	Boeing 747-467	Cathay Pacific Airways
	B-HOV	Boeing 747-467	Cathay Pacific Airways
	B-HOW	Boeing 747-467	Cathay Pacific Airways
	B-HOY	Boeing 747-467	Cathay Pacific Airways
	B-HOZ	Boeing 747-467BCF	Cathay Pacific Airways
	B-HUA	Boeing 747-467	Cathay Pacific Airways
	B-HUB	Boeing 747-467	Cathay Pacific Airways
	B-HUE	Boeing 747-467	Cathay Pacific Airways
	B-HUF	Boeing 747-467	Cathay Pacific Airways
	B-HUG	Boeing 747-467	Cathay Pacific Airways
	B-HUH	Boeing 747-467F (SCD)	Cathay Pacific Airways
	B-HUI	Boeing 747-467	Cathay Pacific Airways
	B-HUJ	Boeing 747-467	Cathay Pacific Airways
	B-HUK	Boeing 747-467F (SCD)	Cathay Pacific Airways
	B-HUL	Boeing 747-467F (SCD)	Cathay Pacific Airways
	B-HUO	Boeing 747-467F (SCD)	Cathay Pacific Airways
	B-HUP	Boeing 747-467F (SCD)	Cathay Pacific Airways
	B-HUQ	Boeing 747-467F (SCD)	Cathay Pacific Airways
	B-HXA	Airbus A.340-313X	Cathay Pacific Airways
	B-HXB	Airbus A.340-313X	Cathay Pacific Airways
	B-HXC	Airbus A.340-313X	Cathay Pacific Airways
	B-HXD	Airbus A.340-313X	Cathay Pacific Airways
	B-HXE	Airbus A.340-313X	Cathay Pacific Airways
	B-HXF	Airbus A.340-313X	Cathay Pacific Airways
	B-HXG	Airbus A.340-313X	Cathay Pacific Airways
	B-HXH	Airbus A.340-313X	Cathay Pacific Airways
	B-HXI	Airbus A.340-313X	Cathay Pacific Airways
	B-HXJ	Airbus A.340-313X	Cathay Pacific Airways
	B-HXK	Airbus A.340-313X	Cathay Pacific Airways
	B-KAE	Boeing 747-412BCF	Cathay Pacific Airways
	B-KAF	Boeing 747-412BCF	Cathay Pacific Airways
	B-KAI	Boeing 747-412BCF	Cathay Pacific Airways
	B-KPA	Boeing 777-367ER	Cathay Pacific Airways
	B-KPB	Boeing 777-367ER	Cathay Pacific Airways
	B-KPC	Boeing 777-367ER	Cathay Pacific Airways
	B-KPD	Boeing 777-367ER	Cathay Pacific Airways
	B-KPE	Boeing 777-367ER	Cathay Pacific Airways
	B-KPF	Boeing 777-367ER	Cathay Pacific Airways
	B-KPG	Boeing 777-367ER	Cathay Pacific Airways
	B-KPH	Boeing 777-367ER	Cathay Pacific Airways
	B-KPI	Boeing 777-367ER	Cathay Pacific Airways
	B-KPJ	Boeing 777-367ER	Cathay Pacific Airways
	B-KPK	Boeing 777-367ER	Cathay Pacific Airways
	B-KPL	Boeing 777-367ER	Cathay Pacific Airways
	B-KPM	Boeing 777-367ER	Cathay Pacific Airways

Reg.	Type	Owner or Operator	Notes
B-KPN	Boeing 777-367ER	Cathay Pacific Airways	
B-KPO	Boeing 777-367ER	Cathay Pacific Airways	
B-KPP	Boeing 777-367ER	Cathay Pacific Airways	
B-KPQ	Boeing 777-367ER	Cathay Pacific Airways	
B-KPR	Boeing 777-367ER	Cathay Pacific Airways	
B-KPS	Boeing 777-367ER	Cathay Pacific Airways	
B-KPT	Boeing 777-367ER	Cathay Pacific Airways	
B-KPU	Boeing 777-367ER	Cathay Pacific Airways	
B-KPV	Boeing 777-367ER	Cathay Pacific Airways	
B-KPW	Boeing 777-367ER	Cathay Pacific Airways	
B-KPX	Boeing 777-367ER	Cathay Pacific Airways	
B-KPY	Boeing 777-367ER	Cathay Pacific Airways	
B-KPZ	Boeing 777-367ER	Cathay Pacific Airways	
B-KQA	Boeing 777-367ER	Cathay Pacific Airways	
B-KQB	Boeing 777-367ER	Cathay Pacific Airways	
B-KQC	Boeing 777-367ER	Cathay Pacific Airways	
B-KQD	Boeing 777-367ER	Cathay Pacific Airways	
B-KQE	Boeing 777-367ER	Cathay Pacific Airways	
B-KQF	Boeing 777-367ER	Cathay Pacific Airways	
B-LIA	Boeing 747-467ERF	Cathay Pacific Airways	
B-LIB	Boeing 747-467ERF	Cathay Pacific Airways	
B-LIC	Boeing 747-467ERF	Cathay Pacific Airways	
B-LID	Boeing 747-467ERF	Cathay Pacific Airways	
B-LIE	Boeing 747-467ERF	Cathay Pacific Airways	
B-LIF	Boeing 747-467ERF	Cathay Pacific Airways	
B-LJA	Boeing 747-867F	Cathay Pacific Airways	
B-LJB	Boeing 747-867F	Cathay Pacific Airways	
B-LJE	Boeing 747-867F	Cathay Pacific Airways	
B-LJF	Boeing 747-867F	Cathay Pacific Airways	
B-LJG	Boeing 747-867F	Cathay Pacific Airways	
B-LJH	Boeing 747-867F	Cathay Pacific Airways	
B-LJI	Boeing 747-867F	Cathay Pacific Airways	
B-LJJ	Boeing 747-867F	Cathay Pacific Airways	
B-2385	Airbus A.340-313X	Air China	
B-2386	Airbus A.340-313X	Air China	
B-2387	Airbus A.340-313X	Air China	
B-2388	Airbus A.340-313X	Air China	
B-2389	Airbus A.340-313X	Air China	
B-2390	Airbus A.340-313X	Air China	
B-2409	Boeing 747-412F (SCD)	Air China Cargo	
B-2453	Boeing 747-412BCF	Air China Cargo	
B-2455	Boeing 747-412BCF	Air China Cargo	
B-2456	Boeing 747-4J6BCF	Air China Cargo	
B-2457	Boeing 747-412BCF	Air China Cargo	
B-2458	Boeing 747-4J6BCF	Air China Cargo	
B-2460	Boeing 747-4J6BCF	Air China Cargo	
B-2475	Boeing 747-4FTF (SCD)	Air China Cargo	
B-2476	Boeing 747-4FTF (SCD)	Air China Cargo	
B-2477	Boeing 747-433SF	Air China Cargo	
B-2478	Boeing 747-433SF	Air China Cargo	
B-5902	Airbus A.330-243	China Eastern Airlines	
B-5903	Airbus A.330-243	China Eastern Airlines	
B-5908	Airbus A.330-243	China Eastern Airlines	
B-6070	Airbus A.330-243	Air China	
B-6071	Airbus A.330-243	Air China	
B-6072	Airbus A.330-243	Air China	
B-6073	Airbus A.330-243	Air China	
B-6075	Airbus A.330-243	Air China	
B-6076	Airbus A.330-243	Air China	
B-6079	Airbus A.330-243	Air China	
B-6080	Airbus A.330-243	Air China	
B-6081	Airbus A.330-243	Air China	
B-6082	Airbus A.330-243	China Eastern Airlines	
B-6090	Airbus A.330-243	Air China	
B-6091	Airbus A.330-243	Air China	
B-6092	Airbus A.330-243	Air China	
B-6093	Airbus A.330-243	Air China	
B-6099	Airbus A.330-243	China Eastern Airlines	
B-6113	Airbus A.330-243	Air China	
B-6115	Airbus A.330-243	Air China	
B-6117	Airbus A.330-243	Air China	
B-6121	Airbus A.330-243	China Eastern Airlines	

Notes	Reg.	Type	Owner or Operator
	B-6122	Airbus A.330-243	China Eastern Airlines
	B-6123	Airbus A.330-243	China Eastern Airlines
	B-6130	Airbus A.330-243	Air China
	B-6131	Airbus A.330-243	Air China
	B-6132	Airbus A.330-243	Air China
	B-6505	Airbus A.330-243	Air China
	B-6515	Airbus A.330-223	China Southern Airlines
	B-6516	Airbus A.330-223	China Southern Airlines
	B-6526	Airbus A.330-223	China Southern Airlines
	B-6528	Airbus A.330-223	China Southern Airlines
	B-6531	Airbus A.330-223	China Southern Airlines
	B-6532	Airbus A.330-223	China Southern Airlines
	B-6533	Airbus A.330-243	Air China
	B-6536	Airbus A.330-243	Air China
	B-6537	Airbus A.330-243	China Eastern Airlines
	B-6538	Airbus A.330-243	China Eastern Airlines
	B-6540	Airbus A.330-243	Air China
	B-6541	Airbus A.330-243	Air China
	B-6542	Airbus A.330-223	China Southern Airlines
	B-6543	Airbus A.330-243	China Eastern Airlines
	B-6545	Airbus A.330-243	China Eastern Airlines
	B-6546	Airbus A.330-243	China Eastern Airlines
	B-6547	Airbus A.330-223	China Southern Airlines
	B-6548	Airbus A.330-223	China Southern Airlines
	B-6549	Airbus A.330-243	Air China
	B-16401	Boeing 747-45E	EVA Air Cargo
	B-16402	Boeing 747-45E	EVA Air Cargo
	B-16406	Boeing 747-45E	EVA Air Cargo
	B-16407	Boeing 747-45E	EVA Air Cargo
	B-16462	Boeing 747-45E	EVA Air Cargo
	B-16463	Boeing 747-45E	EVA Air Cargo
	B-16481	Boeing 747-45E	EVA Air Cargo
	B-16482	Boeing 747-45E	EVA Air Cargo
	B-16483	Boeing 747-45E	EVA Air Cargo
	B-16701	Boeing 777-35EER	EVA Airways
	B-16702	Boeing 777-35EER	EVA Airways
	B-16703	Boeing 777-35EER	EVA Airways
	B-16705	Boeing 777-35EER	EVA Airways
	B-16706	Boeing 777-35EER	EVA Airways
	B-16707	Boeing 777-35EER	EVA Airways
	B-16708	Boeing 777-35EER	EVA Airways
	B-16709	Boeing 777-35EER	EVA Airways
	B-16710	Boeing 777-35EER	EVA Airways
	B-16711	Boeing 777-35EER	EVA Airways
	B-16712	Boeing 777-35EER	EVA Airways
	B-16713	Boeing 777-35EER	EVA Airways
	B-16715	Boeing 777-35EER	EVA Airways
	B-16716	Boeing 777-35EER	EVA Airways
	B-16717	Boeing 777-35EER	EVA Airways

C (Canada)

	C-FCAB	Boeing 767-375ER (681)	Air Canada
	C-FCAE	Boeing 767-375ER (682)	Air Canada
	C-FCAF	Boeing 767-375ER (683)	Air Canada
	C-FCAG	Boeing 767-375ER (684)	Air Canada
	C-FDAT	Airbus A.310-308 (305)	Air Transat
	C-FITL	Boeing 777-333ER (731)	Air Canada
	C-FITU	Boeing 777-333ER (732)	Air Canada
	C-FITW	Boeing 777-3Q8ER (733)	Air Canada
	C-FIUA	Boeing 777-233LR (701)	Air Canada
	C-FIUF	Boeing 777-233LR (702)	Air Canada
	C-FIUJ	Boeing 777-233LR (703)	Air Canada
	C-FIUL	Boeing 777-333ER (734)	Air Canada
	C-FIUR	Boeing 777-333ER (735)	Air Canada
	C-FIUV	Boeing 777-333ER	Air Canada
	C-FIUW	Boeing 777-333ER	Air Canada
	C-FIVK	Boeing 777-233LR	Air Canada
	C-FIVM	Boeing 777-333ER	Air Canada
	C-FIVQ	Boeing 777-333ER	Air Canada
	C-FIVR	Boeing 777-333ER	Air Canada

OVERSEAS AIRLINERS

C/CN

Reg.	Type	Owner or Operator	Notes
C-FIVS	Boeing 777-333ER	Air Canada	
C-FMWP	Boeing 767-333ER (631)	Air Canada	
C-FMWQ	Boeing 767-333ER (632)	Air Canada	
C-FMWU	Boeing 767-333ER (633)	Air Canada	
C-FMWV	Boeing 767-333ER (634)	Air Canada	
C-FMWY	Boeing 767-333ER (635)	Air Canada	
C-FMXC	Boeing 767-333ER (636)	Air Canada	
C-FNND	Boeing 777-233LR	Air Canada	
C-FNNH	Boeing 777-233LR	Air Canada	
C-FOCA	Boeing 767-375ER (640)	Air Canada	
C-FPCA	Boeing 767-375ER (637)	Air Canada	
C-FRAM	Boeing 777-333ER	Air Canada	
C-FTCA	Boeing 767-375ER (638)	Air Canada	
C-FXCA	Boeing 767-375ER (639)	Air Canada	
C-GBZR	Boeing 767-38EER (645)	Air Canada	
C-GCTS	Airbus A.330-342	Air Transat	
C-GDUZ	Boeing 767-38EER (646)	Air Canada	
C-GEOQ	Boeing 767-375ER (647)	Air Canada	
C-GEOU	Boeing 767-375ER (648)	Air Canada	
C-GFAF	Airbus A.330-343X (931)	Air Canada	
C-GFAH	Airbus A.330-343X (932)	Air Canada	
C-GFAJ	Airbus A.330-343X (933)	Air Canada	
C-GFAT	Airbus A.310-304 (301)	Air Transat	
C-GFUR	Airbus A.330-343X (934)	Air Canada	
C-GGTS	Airbus A.330-243 (101)	Air Transat	
C-GHKR	Airbus A.330-343X (935)	Air Canada	
C-GHKW	Airbus A.330-343X (936)	Air Canada	
C-GHKX	Airbus A.330-343X (937)	Air Canada	
C-GHLA	Boeing 767-35HER (656)	Air Canada	
C-GHLK	Boeing 767-35HER (657)	Air Canada	
C-GHLM	Airbus A.330-343X (938)	Air Canada	
C-GHLQ	Boeing 767-333ER (658)	Air Canada	
C-GHLT	Boeing 767-333ER (659)	Air Canada	
C-GHLU	Boeing 767-333ER (660)	Air Canada	
C-GHLV	Boeing 767-333ER (661)	Air Canada	
C-GHOZ	Boeing 767-375ER (685)	Air Canada	
C-GHPD	Boeing 767-3Y0ER (687)	Air Canada	
C-GHPE	Boeing 767-33AER	Air Canada	
C-GHPN	Boeing 767-33AER	Air Canada	
C-GITS	Airbus A.330-243 (102)	Air Transat	
C-GKTS	Airbus A.330-342 (100)	Air Transat	
C-GLAT	Airbus A.310-308 (302)	Air Transat	
C-GLCA	Boeing 767-375ER (641)	Air Canada	
C-GPAT	Airbus A.310-308 (303)	Air Transat	
C-GPTS	Airbus A.330-243 (103)	Air Transat	
C-GSAT	Airbus A.310-308 (304)	Air Transat	
C-GSCA	Boeing 767-375ER (642)	Air Canada	
C-GTSD	Airbus A.330-343	Air Transat	
C-GTSF	Airbus A.310-304 (345)	Air Transat	
C-GTSH	Airbus A.310-304 (343)	Air Transat	
C-GTSI	Airbus A.330-243	Air Transat	
C-GTSJ	Airbus A.330-243	Air Transat	
C-GTSN	Airbus A.330-243	Air Transat	
C-GTSO	Airbus A.330-342	Air Transat	
C-GTSR	Airbus A.330-243	Air Transat	
C-GTSW	Airbus A.310-304	Air Transat	
C-GTSX	Airbus A.310-304	Air Transat	
C-GTSY	Airbus A.310-304 (344)	Air Transat	
C-GTSZ	Airbus A.330-243	Air Transat	

Note: Airline fleet number when carried on aircraft is shown in parentheses.

CN (Morocco)

CN-NMA	Airbus A.320-214	Air Arabia Maroc	
CN-NMB	Airbus A.320-214	Air Arabia Maroc	
CN-NME	Airbus A.320-214	Air Arabia Maroc	
CN-NMF	Airbus A.320-214	Air Arabia Maroc	
CN-RGA	Boeing 747-428	Royal Air Maroc	
CN-RGE	Boeing 737-86N	Royal Air Maroc	
CN-RGF	Boeing 737-86N	Royal Air Maroc	
CN-RGG	Boeing 737-86N	Royal Air Maroc	

Notes	Reg.	Type	Owner or Operator
	CN-RGH	Boeing 737-86N	Royal Air Maroc
	CN-RGI	Boeing 737-86N	Royal Air Maroc
	CN-RGJ	Boeing 737-8B6	Royal Air Maroc
	CN-RGK	Boeing 737-8B6	Royal Air Maroc
	CN-RNJ	Boeing 737-8B6	Royal Air Maroc
	CN-RNK	Boeing 737-8B6	Royal Air Maroc
	CN-RNL	Boeing 737-7B6	Royal Air Maroc
	CN-RNM	Boeing 737-7B6	Royal Air Maroc
	CN-RNP	Boeing 737-8B6	Royal Air Maroc
	CN-RNQ	Boeing 737-7B6	Royal Air Maroc
	CN-RNR	Boeing 737-7B6	Royal Air Maroc
	CN-RNS	Boeing 767-3B6ER	Royal Air Maroc
	CN-RNT	Boeing 767-3B6ER	Royal Air Maroc
	CN-RNU	Boeing 737-8B6	Royal Air Maroc
	CN-RNV	Boeing 737-7B6	Royal Air Maroc
	CN-RNW	Boeing 737-8B6	Royal Air Maroc
	CN-RNZ	Boeing 737-8B6	Royal Air Maroc
	CN-ROA	Boeing 737-8B6	Royal Air Maroc
	CN-ROB	Boeing 737-8B6	Royal Air Maroc
	CN-ROC	Boeing 737-8B6	Royal Air Maroc
	CN-ROD	Boeing 737-7B6	Royal Air Maroc
	CN-ROE	Boeing 737-8B6	Royal Air Maroc
	CN-ROH	Boeing 737-8B6	Royal Air Maroc
	CN-ROJ	Boeing 737-8B6	Royal Air Maroc
	CN-ROK	Boeing 737-8B6	Royal Air Maroc
	CN-ROL	Boeing 737-8B6	Royal Air Maroc
	CN-ROP	Boeing 737-8B6	Royal Air Maroc
	CN-ROR	Boeing 737-8B6	Royal Air Maroc
	CN-ROS	Boeing 737-8B6	Royal Air Maroc
	CN-ROT	Boeing 737-8B6	Royal Air Maroc
	CN-ROU	Boeing 737-8B6	Royal Air Maroc
	CN-ROV	Boeing 767-3Q8ER	Royal Air Maroc
	CN-ROW	Boeing 767-343ER	Royal Air Maroc
	CN-ROY	Boeing 737-8B6	Royal Air Maroc
	CN-ROZ	Boeing 737-8B6	Royal Air Maroc

CS (Portugal)

	CS-TFS	Boeing 767-3YOER	Euro Atlantic Airways
	CS-TFT	Boeing 767-3YOER	Euro Atlantic Airways
	CS-TFW	Airbus A.340-542	Arik Air
	CS-TFX	Airbus A.340-542	Arik Air Captain Bob Hayes, OON
	CS-TFZ	Airbus A.330-243	HiFly/Livingston
	CS-TGU	Airbus A.310-304	SATA International Terceira
	CS-TGV	Airbus A.310-304	SATA International
	CS-TJE	Airbus A.321-211	TAP Portugal Pero Vaz de Caminha
	CS-TJF	Airbus A.321-211	TAP Portugal Luis Vaz de Camoes
	CS-TJG	Airbus A.321-211	TAP Portugal Amelia Rodrigues
	CS-TKJ	Airbus A.320-212	SATA International Pico
	CS-TKK	Airbus A.320-214	SATA International Corvo
	CS-TKL	Airbus A.320-214	SATA International Sao Jorge
	CS-TKM	Airbus A.310-304	SATA International Autonomia
	CS-TKN	Airbus A.310-325	SATA International Macaronesia
	CS-TKO	Airbus A.320-214	SATA International
	CS-TLO	Boeing 767-383ER	Euro Atlantic Airways/Cubana
	CS-TMW	Airbus A.320-214	TAP Portugal Luisa Todi
	CS-TNG	Airbus A.320-214	TAP Portugal Mouzinho da Silveira
	CS-TNH	Airbus A.320-214	TAP Portugal Almada Negreiros
	CS-TNI	Airbus A.320-214	TAP Portugal Aquilino Ribiera
	CS-TNJ	Airbus A.320-214	TAP Portugal Florbela Espanca
	CS-TNK	Airbus A.320-214	TAP Portugal Teofilo Braga
	CS-TNL	Airbus A.320-214	TAP Portugal Vitorino Nermesio
	CS-TNM	Airbus A.320-214	TAP Portugal Natalia Correia
	CS-TNN	Airbus A.320-214	TAP Portugal Gil Vicente
	CS-TNP	Airbus A.320-214	TAP Portugal Alexandre O'Neill
	CS-TNQ	Airbus A.320-214	TAP Portugal Jose Regio
	CS-TNR	Airbus A.320-214	TAP Portugal
	CS-TNS	Airbus A.320-214	TAP Portugal D.Alfonso Henriques
	CS-TNT	Airbus A.320-214	TAP Portugal
	CS-TNU	Airbus A.320-214	TAP Portugal
	CS-TNV	Airbus A.320-214	TAP Portugal ✓

Reg.	Type	Owner or Operator	Notes
CS-TOA	Airbus A.340-312	TAP Portugal *Fernao Mendes Pinto*	
CS-TOB	Airbus A.340-312	TAP Portugal *D Joao de Castro*	
CS-TOC	Airbus A.340-312	TAP Portugal *Wenceslau de Moraes*	
CS-TOD	Airbus A.340-312	TAP Portugal *D Francisco de Almeida*	
CS-TOE	Airbus A.330-223	TAP Portugal *Pedro Alvares Cabal*	
CS-TOF	Airbus A.330-223	TAP Portugal *Infante D Henrique*	
CS-TOG	Airbus A.330-223	TAP Portugal *Bartolomeu de Gusmão*	
CS-TOH	Airbus A.330-223	TAP Portugal *Nuno Gongalves*	
CS-TOI	Airbus A.330-223	TAP Portugal *Damiao de Gois*	
CS-TOJ	Airbus A.330-223	TAP Portugal *D.Ja-o II 'O Principe Perfeito*	
CS-TOK	Airbus A.330-223	TAP Portugal *Padre Antonio Vieira*	
CS-TOL	Airbus A.330-202	TAP Portugal *Joao Goncalves Zarco*	
CS-TOM	Airbus A.330-202	TAP Portugal *Vasco da Gama*	
CS-TON	Airbus A.330-202	TAP Portugal *Ja-o XXI*	
CS-TOO	Airbus A.330-202	TAP Portugal *Fernao de Magalhaes*	
CS-TOP	Airbus A.330-202	TAP Portugal *Pedro Nunes*	
CS-TQD	Airbus A.320-214	TAP Portugal	
CS-TQL	Airbus A.340-312	HiFly	
CS-TQP	Airbus A.330-202	HiFly	
CS-TQS	Airbus A.320-211	White Airways	
CS-TQU	Boeing 737-8K2	Euro Atlantic Airways	
CS-TQV	Airbus A.310-304	White Airways	
CS-TRI	Airbus A.330-322	HiFly	
CS-TTA	Airbus A.319-111	TAP Portugal *Vieira da Silva*	
CS-TTB	Airbus A.319-111	TAP Portugal *Gago Coutinho*	
CS-TTC	Airbus A.319-111	TAP Portugal *Fernando Pessoa*	
CS-TTD	Airbus A.319-111	TAP Portugal *Amadeo de Souza-Cardoso*	
CS-TTE	Airbus A.319-111	TAP Portugal *Francisco d'Ollanda*	
CS-TTF	Airbus A.319-111	TAP Portugal *Calouste Gulbenkian*	
CS-TTG	Airbus A.319-111	TAP Portugal *Humberto Delgado*	
CS-TTH	Airbus A.319-111	TAP Portugal *Antonio Sergio*	
CS-TTI	Airbus A.319-111	TAP Portugal *Eca de Queiros*	
CS-TTJ	Airbus A.319-111	TAP Portugal *Eusebio*	
CS-TTK	Airbus A.319-111	TAP Portugal *Miguel Torga*	
CS-TTL	Airbus A.319-111	TAP Portugal *Almeida Garrett*	
CS-TTM	Airbus A.319-111	TAP Portugal *Alexandre Herculano*	
CS-TTN	Airbus A.319-111	TAP Portugal *Camilo Castelo Branco*	
CS-TTO	Airbus A.319-111	TAP Portugal *Antero de Quental*	
CS-TTP	Airbus A.319-111	TAP Portugal *Josefa d'Obidos*	
CS-TTQ	Airbus A.319-112	TAP Portugal *Agostinho da Silva*	
CS-TTR	Airbus A.319-112	TAP Portugal	
CS-TTS	Airbus A.319-112	TAP Portugal *Guilhermina Suggia*	

CU (Cuba)

CU-T1250	Ilyushin IL-96-300	Cubana	
CU-T1251	Ilyushin IL-96-300	Cubana	
CU-T1254	Ilyushin IL-96-300	Cubana	

D (Germany)

D-AALA	Boeing 777-FZN	AeroLogic	
D-AALB	Boeing 777-FZN	AeroLogic	
D-AALC	Boeing 777-FZN	AeroLogic	
D-AALD	Boeing 777-FZN	AeroLogic	
D-AALE	Boeing 777-FZN	AeroLogic	
D-AALF	Boeing 777-FZN	AeroLogic	
D-AALG	Boeing 777-FZN	AeroLogic	
D-AALH	Boeing 777-FZN	AeroLogic	
D-AALI	Boeing 777-FZN	AeroLogic	
D-AALJ	Boeing 777-FZN	AeroLogic	
D-AALK	Boeing 777-FZN	AeroLogic	
D-AALL	Boeing 777-FZN	AeroLogic	
D-AALM	Boeing 777-FZN	AeroLogic	
D-AALN	Boeing 777-FZN	AeroLogic	
D-AALO	Boeing 777-FZN	AeroLogic	
D-AALP	Boeing 777-FZN	AeroLogic	
D-AALQ	Boeing 777-FZN	AeroLogic	
D-AALR	Boeing 777-FZN	AeroLogic	
D-ABAF	Boeing 737-86J	Air Berlin	

Notes	Reg.	Type	Owner or Operator
	D-ABAG	Boeing 737-86J	Air Berlin
	D-ABBG	Boeing 737-86J	Air Berlin
	D-ABBJ	Boeing 737-86Q	Air Berlin
	D-ABBK	Boeing 737-8BK	Air Berlin
	D-ABBS	Boeing 737-76N	Air Berlin
	D-ABBT	Boeing 737-76N	Air Berlin
	D-ABBV	Boeing 737-7Q8	Air Berlin
	D-ABBX	Boeing 737-808	Air Berlin
	D-ABBY	Boeing 737-808	Air Berlin
	D-ABCA	Airbus A.321-211	Air Berlin
	D-ABCB	Airbus A.321-211	Air Berlin
	D-ABCC	Airbus A.321-211	Air Berlin
	D-ABCF	Airbus A.321-211	Air Berlin
	D-ABCG	Airbus A.321-211	Air Berlin
	D-ABCH	Airbus A.321-211	Air Berlin
	D-ABCI	Airbus A.321-231	Air Berlin
	D-ABCJ	Airbus A.321-231	Air Berlin
	D-ABCK	Airbus A.321-231	Air Berlin
	D-ABDB	Airbus A.320-214	Air Berlin
	D-ABDP	Airbus A.320-214	Air Berlin
	D-ABDQ	Airbus A.320-214	Air Berlin
	D-ABDR	Airbus A.320-214	Air Berlin
	D-ABDS	Airbus A.320-214	Air Berlin
	D-ABDU	Airbus A.320-214	Air Berlin
	D-ABDW	Airbus A.320-214	Air Berlin
	D-ABDY	Airbus A.320-214	Air Berlin
	D-ABEA	Boeing 737-330	Lufthansa *Saarbrücken*
	D-ABEB	Boeing 737-330	Lufthansa *Xanten*
	D-ABEC	Boeing 737-330	Lufthansa *Karlsruhe*
	D-ABED	Boeing 737-330	Lufthansa *Hagen*
	D-ABEE	Boeing 737-330	Lufthansa *Ulm*
	D-ABEF	Boeing 737-330	Lufthansa *Weiden i.d.Obf.*
	D-ABEH	Boeing 737-330	Lufthansa *Bad Kissingen*
	D-ABEI	Boeing 737-330	Lufthansa *Bamberg*
	D-ABEK	Boeing 737-330	Lufthansa *Wuppertal*
	D-ABEN	Boeing 737-330	Lufthansa *Neubrandenburg*
	D-ABET	Boeing 737-330	Lufthansa *Gelsenkirchen*
	D-ABEU	Boeing 737-330	Lufthansa *Goslar*
	D-ABEW	Boeing 737-330	Lufthansa *Detmold*
	D-ABFA	Airbus A.320-214	Air Berlin
	D-ABFC	Airbus A.320-214	Air Berlin
	D-ABFE	Airbus A.320-214	Air Berlin
	D-ABFF	Airbus A.320-214	Air Berlin
	D-ABFG	Airbus A.320-214	Air Berlin
	D-ABFK	Airbus A.320-214	Air Berlin
	D-ABFN	Airbus A.320-214	Air Berlin
	D-ABFO	Airbus A.320-214	Air Berlin
	D-ABFP	Airbus A.320-214	Air Berlin
	D-ABFT	Airbus A.320-214	Air Berlin
	D-ABFU	Airbus A.320-214	Air Berlin
	D-ABFY	Airbus A.320-214	Air Berlin
	D-ABFZ	Airbus A.320-214	Air Berlin
	D-ABGS	Airbus A.319-111	Air Berlin
	D-ABIA	Boeing 737-530	Lufthansa *Greifswald*
	D-ABIB	Boeing 737-530	Lufthansa *Esslingen*
	D-ABIC	Boeing 737-530	Lufthansa *Krefeld*
	D-ABID	Boeing 737-530	Lufthansa *Aachen*
	D-ABIE	Boeing 737-530	Lufthansa *Hildesheim*
	D-ABIF	Boeing 737-530	Lufthansa *Landau*
	D-ABIH	Boeing 737-530	Lufthansa *Bruchsal*
	D-ABII	Boeing 737-530	Lufthansa *Lörrach*
	D-ABIK	Boeing 737-530	Lufthansa *Rastatt*
	D-ABIL	Boeing 737-530	Lufthansa *Memmingen*
	D-ABIM	Boeing 737-530	Lufthansa *Salzgitter*
	D-ABIN	Boeing 737-530	Lufthansa *Langenhagen*
	D-ABIO	Boeing 737-530	Lufthansa *Wesel*
	D-ABIP	Boeing 737-530	Lufthansa *Oberhausen*
	D-ABIR	Boeing 737-530	Lufthansa *Anklam*
	D-ABIS	Boeing 737-530	Lufthansa *Rendsburg*
	D-ABIT	Boeing 737-530	Lufthansa *Neumünster*
	D-ABIU	Boeing 737-530	Lufthansa *Limburg a.d. Lahn*
	D-ABIW	Boeing 737-530	Lufthansa *Bad Nauheim*

Reg.	Type	Owner or Operator	Notes
D-ABIX	Boeing 737-530	Lufthansa *Iserlohn*	
D-ABIY	Boeing 737-530	Lufthansa *Lingen*	
D-ABJB	Boeing 737-530	Lufthansa *Rheine*	
D-ABKA	Boeing 737-82R	Air Berlin	
D-ABKB	Boeing 737-86J	Air Berlin	
D-ABKC	Boeing 737-86J	Air Berlin	
D-ABKD	Boeing 737-86J	Air Berlin	
D-ABKJ	Boeing 737-86J	Air Berlin	
D-ABKK	Boeing 737-86J	Air Berlin	
D-ABKM	Boeing 737-86J	Air Berlin	
D-ABKN	Boeing 737-86J	Air Berlin	
D-ABKP	Boeing 737-86J	Air Berlin	
D-ABKQ	Boeing 737-86J	Air Berlin	
D-ABKS	Boeing 737-86J	Air Berlin	
D-ABKT	Boeing 737-86J	Air Berlin	
D-ABKU	Boeing 737-86J	Air Berlin	
D-ABKW	Boeing 737-86J	Air Berlin	
D-ABKY	Boeing 737-86J	Air Berlin	
D-ABLA	Boeing 737-76J	Air Berlin	
D-ABLB	Boeing 737-76J	Air Berlin	
D-ABLC	Boeing 737-76J	Air Berlin	
D-ABLD	Boeing 737-76J	Air Berlin	
D-ABLE	Boeing 737-76J	Air Berlin	
D-ABLF	Boeing 737-76J	Air Berlin	
D-ABMB	Boeing 737-86J	Air Berlin	
D-ABMC	Boeing 737-86J	Air Berlin	
D-ABMD	Boeing 737-86J	Air Berlin	
D-ABME	Boeing 737-86J	Air Berlin	
D-ABMF	Boeing 737-86J	Air Berlin	
D-ABMG	Boeing 737-86J	Air Berlin	
D-ABMH	Boeing 737-86J	Air Berlin	
D-ABMI	Boeing 737-86J	Air Berlin	
D-ABMJ	Boeing 737-86J	Air Berlin	
D-ABMK	Boeing 737-86J	Air Berlin	
D-ABML	Boeing 737-86J	Air Berlin	
D-ABNA	Airbus A.320-214	Air Berlin	
D-ABNB	Airbus A.320-214	Air Berlin	
D-ABNC	Airbus A.320-214	Air Berlin	
D-ABOA	Boeing 757-330	Condor	
D-ABOB	Boeing 757-330	Condor	
D-ABOC	Boeing 757-330	Condor	
D-ABOE	Boeing 757-330	Condor	
D-ABOF	Boeing 757-330	Condor	
D-ABOG	Boeing 757-330	Condor	
D-ABOH	Boeing 757-330	Condor	
D-ABOI	Boeing 757-330	Condor	
D-ABOJ	Boeing 757-330	Condor	
D-ABOK	Boeing 757-330	Condor	
D-ABOL	Boeing 757-330	Condor	
D-ABOM	Boeing 757-330	Condor	
D-ABON	Boeing 757-330	Condor	
D-ABQA	DHC.8Q-402 Dash Eight	Air Berlin	
D-ABQB	DHC.8Q-402 Dash Eight	Air Berlin	
D-ABQC	DHC.8Q-402 Dash Eight	Air Berlin	
D-ABQD	DHC.8Q-402 Dash Eight	Air Berlin	
D-ABQE	DHC.8Q-402 Dash Eight	Air Berlin	
D-ABQF	DHC.8Q-402 Dash Eight	Air Berlin	
D-ABQG	DHC.8Q-402 Dash Eight	Air Berlin	
D-ABQH	DHC.8Q-402 Dash Eight	Air Berlin	
D-ABQI	DHC.8Q-402 Dash Eight	Air Berlin	
D-ABQJ	DHC.8Q-402 Dash Eight	Air Berlin	
D-ABTA	Boeing 747-430 (SCD)	Lufthansa *Sachsen*	
D-ABTD	Boeing 747-430 (SCD)	Lufthansa *Hamburg*	
D-ABTE	Boeing 747-430 (SCD)	Lufthansa *Sachsen-Anhalt*	
D-ABTF	Boeing 747-430 (SCD)	Lufthansa *Thüringen*	
D-ABTH	Boeing 747-430 (SCD)	Lufthansa *Duisburg*	
D-ABTK	Boeing 747-430 (SCD)	Lufthansa *Kiel*	
D-ABTL	Boeing 747-430 (SCD)	Lufthansa *Dresden*	
D-ABUA	Boeing 767-330ER	Condor	
D-ABUB	Boeing 767-330ER	Condor	
D-ABUC	Boeing 767-330ER	Condor	
D-ABUD	Boeing 767-330ER	Condor	

Notes	Reg.	Type	Owner or Operator
	D-ABUE	Boeing 767-330ER	Condor
	D-ABUF	Boeing 767-330ER	Condor
	D-ABUH	Boeing 767-330ER	Condor
	D-ABUI	Boeing 767-330ER	Condor
	D-ABUK	Boeing 767-343ER	Condor
	D-ABUL	Boeing 767-31BER	Condor
	D-ABUM	Boeing 767-31BER	Condor
	D-ABUZ	Boeing 767-330ER	Condor
	D-ABVC	Boeing 747-430	Lufthansa *Baden-Württemberg*
	D-ABVD	Boeing 747-430	Lufthansa *Bochum*
	D-ABVE	Boeing 747-430	Lufthansa *Potsdam*
	D-ABVF	Boeing 747-430	Lufthansa *Frankfurt am Main*
	D-ABVH	Boeing 747-430	Lufthansa *Düsseldorf*
	D-ABVK	Boeing 747-430	Lufthansa *Hannover*
	D-ABVL	Boeing 747-430	Lufthansa *Muenchen*
	D-ABVM	Boeing 747-430	Lufthansa *Hessen*
	D-ABVN	Boeing 747-430	Lufthansa *Dortmund*
	D-ABVO	Boeing 747-430	Lufthansa *Mulheim a.d.Ruhr*
	D-ABVP	Boeing 747-430	Lufthansa *Bremen*
	D-ABVR	Boeing 747-430	Lufthansa *Koln*
	D-ABVS	Boeing 747-430	Lufthansa *Saarland*
	D-ABVT	Boeing 747-430	Lufthansa *Rheinland Pfalz*
	D-ABVU	Boeing 747-430	Lufthansa *Bayern*
	D-ABVW	Boeing 747-430	Lufthansa *Wolfsburg*
	D-ABVX	Boeing 747-430	Lufthansa *Schleswig-Holstein*
	D-ABVY	Boeing 747-430	Lufthansa *Nordrhein Westfalen*
	D-ABVZ	Boeing 747-430	Lufthansa *Niedersachsen*
	D-ABXA	Airbus A.330-223	Air Berlin
	D-ABXB	Airbus A.330-223	Air Berlin
	D-ABXC	Airbus A.330-243	Air Berlin
	D-ABXD	Airbus A.330-223	Air Berlin
	D-ABXL	Boeing 737-330	Lufthansa *Neuss*
	D-ABXM	Boeing 737-330	Lufthansa *Herford*
	D-ABXS	Boeing 737-330	Lufthansa *Sindelfingen*
	D-ABXU	Boeing 737-330	Lufthansa *Seeheim-Jugenheim*
	D-ABXW	Boeing 737-330	Lufthansa *Hanau*
	D-ABXX	Boeing 737-330	Lufthansa *Bad Homburg v.d. Höhe*
	D-ABXY	Boeing 737-330	Lufthansa *Hof*
	D-ABXZ	Boeing 737-330	Lufthansa *Bad Mergentheim*
	D-ABYA	Boeing 747-830	Lufthansa
	D-ABYC	Boeing 747-830	Lufthansa
	D-ABYD	Boeing 747-830	Lufthansa
	D-ABYE	Boeing 747-830	Lufthansa
	D-ABYF	Boeing 747-830	Lufthansa
	D-ABYG	Boeing 747-830	Lufthansa
	D-ABYH	Boeing 747-830	Lufthansa
	D-ABYI	Boeing 747-830	Lufthansa
	D-ABYJ	Boeing 747-830	Lufthansa
	D-ABYK	Boeing 747-830	Lufthansa
	D-ACGA	Boeing 747-409F	Air Cargo Germany
	D-ACGB	Boeing 747-409F	Air Cargo Germany
	D-ACGC	Boeing 747-412BCF	Air Cargo Germany
	D-ACGD	Boeing 747-412BCF	Air Cargo Germany
	D-ACKA	Canadair CRJ900ER	Lufthansa Regional *Pfaffenhofen a.d.ilm*
	D-ACKB	Canadair CRJ900ER	Lufthansa Regional *Schliersee*
	D-ACKC	Canadair CRJ900ER	Lufthansa Regional *Mettmann*
	D-ACKD	Canadair CRJ900ER	Lufthansa Regional *Wittlich*
	D-ACKE	Canadair CRJ900ER	Lufthansa Regional *Weningerode*
	D-ACKF	Canadair CRJ900ER	Lufthansa Regional *Prenzlau*
	D-ACKG	Canadair CRJ900ER	Lufthansa Regional *Glucksburg*
	D-ACKH	Canadair CRJ900ER	Lufthansa Regional *Radebuel*
	D-ACKI	Canadair CRJ900ER	Lufthansa Regional *Tuttlingen*
	D-ACKJ	Canadair CRJ900ER	Lufthansa Regional *Ilmenau*
	D-ACKK	Canadair CRJ900ER	Lufthansa Regional *Furstenwalde*
	D-ACKL	Canadair CRJ900ER	Lufthansa Regional *Bad Bergzabern*
	D-ACNA	Canadair CRJ900ER	Lufthansa Regional
	D-ACNB	Canadair CRJ900ER	Lufthansa Regional
	D-ACNC	Canadair CRJ900ER	Lufthansa Regional
	D-ACND	Canadair CRJ900ER	Lufthansa Regional
	D-ACNE	Canadair CRJ900ER	Lufthansa Regional
	D-ACNF	Canadair CRJ900ER	Lufthansa Regional
	D-ACNG	Canadair CRJ900ER	Lufthansa Regional

Reg.	Type	Owner or Operator	Notes
D-ACNH	Canadair CRJ900ER	Lufthansa Regional	
D-ACNI	Canadair CRJ900ER	Lufthansa Regional	
D-ACNJ	Canadair CRJ900ER	Lufthansa Regional	
D-ACNK	Canadair CRJ900ER	Lufthansa Regional	
D-ACNL	Canadair CRJ900ER	Lufthansa Regional	
D-ACNM	Canadair CRJ900ER	Lufthansa Regional	
D-ACNN	Canadair CRJ900ER	Lufthansa Regional	
D-ACNO	Canadair CRJ900ER	Lufthansa Regional	
D-ACNP	Canadair CRJ900ER	Lufthansa Regional	
D-ACNQ	Canadair CRJ900ER	Lufthansa Regional	
D-ACNR	Canadair CRJ900ER	Lufthansa Regional	
D-ACNT	Canadair CRJ900ER	Lufthansa Regional	
D-ACNU	Canadair CRJ900ER	Lufthansa Regional	
D-ACNV	Canadair CRJ900ER	Lufthansa Regional	
D-ACNW	Canadair CRJ900ER	Lufthansa Regional	
D-ACNX	Canadair CRJ900ER	Lufthansa Regional	
D-ACPA	Canadair CRJ700ER	Lufthansa Regional *Westerland/Sylt*	
D-ACPB	Canadair CRJ700ER	Lufthansa Regional *Rudesheim a. Rhein*	
D-ACPC	Canadair CRJ700ER	Lufthansa Regional *Espelkamp*	
D-ACPD	Canadair CRJ700ER	Lufthansa Regional *Vilshofen*	
D-ACPE	Canadair CRJ700ER	Lufthansa Regional *Belzig*	
D-ACPF	Canadair CRJ700ER	Lufthansa Regional *Uhingen*	
D-ACPG	Canadair CRJ700ER	Lufthansa Regional *Leinfelden-Echterdingen*	
D-ACPH	Canadair CRJ700ER	Lufthansa Regional *Eschwege*	
D-ACPI	Canadair CRJ700ER	Lufthansa Regional *Viernheim*	
D-ACPJ	Canadair CRJ700ER	Lufthansa Regional *Neumarkt i. d. Oberpfalz*	
D-ACPK	Canadair CRJ700ER	Lufthansa Regional *Besigheim*	
D-ACPL	Canadair CRJ700ER	Lufthansa Regional *Halberstadt*	
D-ACPM	Canadair CRJ700ER	Lufthansa Regional *Heidenheim an der Brenz*	
D-ACPN	Canadair CRJ700ER	Lufthansa Regional *Quedlinburg*	
D-ACPO	Canadair CRJ700ER	Lufthansa Regional *Spaichingen*	
D-ACPP	Canadair CRJ700ER	Lufthansa Regional *Torgau*	
D-ACPQ	Canadair CRJ700ER	Lufthansa Regional *Lübbecke*	
D-ACPR	Canadair CRJ700ER	Lufthansa Regional *Weinheim an der Bergstrasse*	
D-ACPS	Canadair CRJ700ER	Lufthansa Regional *Berchtesgarten*	
D-ACPT	Canadair CRJ700ER	Lufthansa Regional *Altötting*	
D-ADHA	DHC.8Q-402 Dash Eight	Lufthansa Regional	
D-ADHB	DHC.8Q-402 Dash Eight	Lufthansa Regional	
D-ADHC	DHC.8Q-402 Dash Eight	Lufthansa Regional	
D-ADHD	DHC.8Q-402 Dash Eight	Lufthansa Regional	
D-ADHE	DHC.8Q-402 Dash Eight	Lufthansa Regional	
D-ADHP	DHC.8Q-402 Dash Eight	Lufthansa Regional	
D-ADHQ	DHC.8Q-402 Dash Eight	Lufthansa Regional	
D-ADHR	DHC.8Q-402 Dash Eight	Lufthansa Regional	
D-ADHS	DHC.8Q-402 Dash Eight	Lufthansa Regional	
D-ADHT	DHC.8Q-402 Dash Eight	Lufthansa Regional	
D-AEAC	Airbus A.300B4-622R	EAT Leipzig/DHL	
D-AEAD	Airbus A.300B4-622R	EAT Leipzig/DHL	
D-AEAE	Airbus A.300B4-622R	EAT Leipzig/DHL	
D-AEAG	Airbus A.300B4-622R	EAT Leipzig/DHL	
D-AEAH	Airbus A.300B4-622R	EAT Leipzig/DHL	
D-AEAK	Airbus A.300B4-622R	EAT Leipzig/DHL	
D-AEAL	Airbus A.300B4-622R	EAT Leipzig/DHL	
D-AEAN	Airbus A.300B4-622R	EAT Leipzig/DHL	
D-AEAO	Airbus A.300B4-622R	EAT Leipzig/DHL	
D-AEAP	Airbus A.300B4-622R	EAT Leipzig/DHL	
D-AEAQ	Airbus A.300B4-622R	EAT Leipzig/DHL	
D-AEAR	Airbus A.300B4-622R	EAT Leipzig/DHL	
D-AEAT	Airbus A.300B4-622R	EAT Leipzig/DHL	
D-AEBA	Embraer ERJ190-200LR	Lufthansa Regional	
D-AEBB	Embraer ERJ190-200LR	Lufthansa Regional	
D-AEBC	Embraer ERJ190-200LR	Lufthansa Regional	
D-AEBD	Embraer ERJ190-200LR	Lufthansa Regional	
D-AEBE	Embraer ERJ190-200LR	Lufthansa Regional	
D-AEBF	Embraer ERJ190-200LR	Lufthansa Regional	
D-AEBG	Embraer ERJ190-200LR	Lufthansa Regional	
D-AEBH	Embraer ERJ190-200LR	Lufthansa Regional	
D-AEBI	Embraer ERJ190-200LR	Lufthansa Regional	
D-AEBJ	Embraer ERJ190-200LR	Lufthansa Regional	
D-AEBK	Embraer ERJ190-200LR	Lufthansa Regional	
D-AEBL	Embraer ERJ190-200LR	Lufthansa Regional	
D-AEBM	Embraer ERJ190-200LR	Lufthansa Regional	

Notes	Reg.	Type	Owner or Operator
	D-AEBN	Embraer ERJ190-200LR	Lufthansa Regional
	D-AEBO	Embraer ERJ190-200LR	Lufthansa Regional
	D-AEBP	Embraer ERJ190-200LR	Lufthansa Regional
	D-AEBQ	Embraer ERJ190-200LR	Lufthansa Regional
	D-AEBR	Embraer ERJ190-200LR	Lufthansa Regional
	D-AEBS	Embraer ERJ190-200LR	Lufthansa Regional
	D-AECA	Embraer ERJ190-100LR	Lufthansa Regional *Deidesheim*
	D-AECB	Embraer ERJ190-100LR	Lufthansa Regional *Meiben*
	D-AECC	Embraer ERJ190-100LR	Lufthansa Regional *Eisleben*
	D-AECD	Embraer ERJ190-100LR	Lufthansa Regional *Schkeuditz*
	D-AECE	Embraer ERJ190-100LR	Lufthansa Regional *Kronach*
	D-AECF	Embraer ERJ190-100LR	Lufthansa Regional
	D-AECG	Embraer ERJ190-100LR	Lufthansa Regional
	D-AECH	Embraer ERJ190-100LR	Lufthansa Regional
	D-AECI	Embraer ERJ190-100LR	Lufthansa Regional
	D-AEMA	Embraer ERJ190-200LR	Lufthansa Regional
	D-AEMB	Embraer ERJ190-200LR	Lufthansa Regional
	D-AEMC	Embraer ERJ190-200LR	Lufthansa Regional
	D-AEMD	Embraer ERJ190-200LR	Lufthansa Regional
	D-AEME	Embraer ERJ190-200LR	Lufthansa Regional
	D-AEMF	Embraer ERJ190-100LR	Lufthansa Regional
	D-AEMG	Embraer ERJ190-100LR	Lufthansa Regional
	D-AERQ	Airbus A.330-322	Air Berlin
	D-AFKA	Fokker 100	OLT Express/Swiss
	D-AFKB	Fokker 100	OLT Express
	D-AFKC	Fokker 100	OLT Express
	D-AFKD	Fokker 100	OLT Express
	D-AFKE	Fokker 100	OLT Express
	D-AFKF	Fokker 100	OLT Express
	D-AGEC	Boeing 737-76J	Air Berlin
	D-AGEL	Boeing 737-75B	Germania
	D-AGEN	Boeing 737-75B	Air Berlin
	D-AGEP	Boeing 737-75B	Germania
	D-AGEQ	Boeing 737-75B	Germania
	D-AGER	Boeing 737-75B	Germania
	D-AGES	Boeing 737-75B	Germania
	D-AGET	Boeing 737-75B	Germania
	D-AGEU	Boeing 737-75B	Germania
	D-AGPH	Fokker 100	OLT Express/Swiss
	D-AGPK	Fokker 100	OLT Express/Swiss
	D-AGWA	Airbus A.319-132	Germanwings
	D-AGWB	Airbus A.319-132	Germanwings
	D-AGWC	Airbus A.319-132	Germanwings
	D-AGWD	Airbus A.319-132	Germanwings
	D-AGWE	Airbus A.319-132	Germanwings
	D-AGWF	Airbus A.319-132	Germanwings
	D-AGWG	Airbus A.319-132	Germanwings
	D-AGWH	Airbus A.319-132	Germanwings
	D-AGWI	Airbus A.319-132	Germanwings
	D-AGWJ	Airbus A.319-132	Germanwings
	D-AGWK	Airbus A.319-132	Germanwings
	D-AGWL	Airbus A.319-132	Germanwings
	D-AGWM	Airbus A.319-132	Germanwings
	D-AGWN	Airbus A.319-132	Germanwings
	D-AGWO	Airbus A.319-132	Germanwings
	D-AGWP	Airbus A.319-132	Germanwings
	D-AGWQ	Airbus A.319-132	Germanwings
	D-AGWR	Airbus A.319-132	Germanwings
	D-AGWS	Airbus A.319-132	Germanwings
	D-AGWT	Airbus A.319-132	Germanwings
	D-AGWU	Airbus A.319-132	Germanwings
	D-AGWV	Airbus A.319-132	Germanwings
	D-AGWW	Airbus A.319-132	Germanwings
	D-AGWX	Airbus A.319-132	Germanwings
	D-AHFA	Boeing 737-8K5	Air Berlin
	D-AHFH	Boeing 737-8K5	TUIfly
	D-AHFI	Boeing 737-8K5	TUIfly
	D-AHFM	Boeing 737-8K5	TUIfly
	D-AHFO	Boeing 737-8K5	Air Berlin
	D-AHFP	Boeing 737-8K5	TUIfly
	D-AHFR	Boeing 737-8K5	TUIfly
	D-AHFS	Boeing 737-86N	Air Berlin

Reg.	Type	Owner or Operator	Notes
D-AHFT	Boeing 737-8K5	TUIfly	
D-AHFV	Boeing 737-8K5	TUIfly	
D-AHFW	Boeing 737-8K5	TUIfly	
D-AHFX	Boeing 737-8K5	TUIfly	
D-AHFY	Boeing 737-8K5	TUIfly	
D-AHFZ	Boeing 737-8K5	TUIfly	
D-AHHA	Airbus A.319-111	Hamburg Airways	
D-AHHB	Airbus A.319-112	Hamburg Airways	
D-AHHC	Airbus A.320-214	Hamburg Airways	
D-AHHD	Airbus A.320-214	Hamburg Airways	
D-AHHE	Airbus A.319-112	Hamburg Airways	
D-AHIA	Boeing 737-73S	Air Berlin	
D-AHIL	Airbus A.319-112	Germania	
D-AHIM	Airbus A.319-112	Germania	
D-AHLK	Boeing 737-8K5	TUIfly	
D-AHXA	Boeing 737-7K5	Air Berlin	
D-AHXB	Boeing 737-7K5	Air Berlin	
D-AHXC	Boeing 737-7K5	Air Berlin	
D-AHXD	Boeing 737-7K5	Air Berlin	
D-AHXE	Boeing 737-7K5	Air Berlin	
D-AHXF	Boeing 737-7K5	Air Berlin	
D-AHXG	Boeing 737-7K5	Air Berlin	
D-AHXH	Boeing 737-7K5	Air Berlin	
D-AHXJ	Boeing 737-7K5	Air Berlin	
D-AIAA	Airbus A.321-211	Condor	
D-AIBA	Airbus A.319-114	Lufthansa	
D-AIBB	Airbus A.319-114	Lufthansa	
D-AIBC	Airbus A.319-114	Lufthansa	
D-AIBD	Airbus A.319-114	Lufthansa Pirmasens	
D-AIBE	Airbus A.319-114	Lufthansa Schonfeld	
D-AIBF	Airbus A.319-112	Lufthansa	
D-AIBG	Airbus A.319-112	Lufthansa	
D-AIBH	Airbus A.319-112	Lufthansa	
D-AIBI	Airbus A.319-112	Lufthansa	
D-AIBJ	Airbus A.319-112	Lufthansa	
D-AICA	Airbus A.320-212	Condor	
D-AICC	Airbus A.320-212	Condor	
D-AICD	Airbus A.320-212	Condor	
D-AICE	Airbus A.320-212	Condor	
D-AICF	Airbus A.320-212	Condor	
D-AICG	Airbus A.320-212	Condor	
D-AICH	Airbus A.320-212	Condor	
D-AICI	Airbus A.320-212	Condor	
D-AICJ	Airbus A.320-212	Condor	
D-AICK	Airbus A.320-212	Condor	
D-AICL	Airbus A.320-212	Condor	
D-AICN	Airbus A.320-214	Condor	
D-AIDA	Airbus A.321-231	Lufthansa	
D-AIDB	Airbus A.321-231	Lufthansa	
D-AIDC	Airbus A.321-231	Lufthansa	
D-AIDD	Airbus A.321-231	Lufthansa	
D-AIDE	Airbus A.321-231	Lufthansa	
D-AIDF	Airbus A.321-231	Lufthansa	
D-AIDG	Airbus A.321-231	Lufthansa	
D-AIDH	Airbus A.321-231	Lufthansa	
D-AIDI	Airbus A.321-231	Lufthansa	
D-AIDJ	Airbus A.321-231	Lufthansa	
D-AIDK	Airbus A.321-231	Lufthansa	
D-AIDL	Airbus A.321-231	Lufthansa	
D-AIDM	Airbus A.321-231	Lufthansa	
D-AIDN	Airbus A.321-231	Lufthansa	
D-AIDO	Airbus A.321-231	Lufthansa	
D-AIDP	Airbus A.321-231	Lufthansa	
D-AIDQ	Airbus A.321-231	Lufthansa	
D-AIDT	Airbus A.321-231	Lufthansa	
D-AIDU	Airbus A.321-231	Lufthansa	
D-AIDV	Airbus A.321-231	Lufthansa	
D-AIFA	Airbus A.340-313X	Lufthansa Dorsten	
D-AIFC	Airbus A.340-313X	Lufthansa Gander/Halifax	
D-AIFD	Airbus A.340-313X	Lufthansa Giessen	
D-AIFE	Airbus A.340-313X	Lufthansa Passau	
D-AIFF	Airbus A.340-313X	Lufthansa Delmenhorst	

Notes	Reg.	Type	Owner or Operator
	D-AIGB	Airbus A.340-311	Lufthansa *Recklinghausen*
	D-AIGC	Airbus A.340-311	Lufthansa *Wilhelmshaven*
	D-AIGD	Airbus A.340-311	Lufthansa *Remscheid*
	D-AIGF	Airbus A.340-311	Lufthansa *Gottingen*
	D-AIGH	Airbus A.340-311	Lufthansa *Koblenz*
	D-AIGI	Airbus A.340-311	Lufthansa *Worms*
	D-AIGL	Airbus A.340-313X	Lufthansa *Herne*
	D-AIGM	Airbus A.340-313X	Lufthansa *Görlitz*
	D-AIGN	Airbus A.340-313X	Lufthansa *Solingen*
	D-AIGO	Airbus A.340-313X	Lufthansa *Offenbach*
	D-AIGP	Airbus A.340-313X	Lufthansa *Paderborn*
	D-AIGS	Airbus A.340-313X	Lufthansa *Bergisch-Gladbach*
	D-AIGT	Airbus A.340-313X	Lufthansa *Viersen*
	D-AIGU	Airbus A.340-313X	Lufthansa *Castrop-Rauxei*
	D-AIGV	Airbus A.340-313X	Lufthansa *Dinslaken*
	D-AIGW	Airbus A.340-313X	Lufthansa *Gladbeck*
	D-AIGX	Airbus A.340-313X	Lufthansa *Duren*
	D-AIGY	Airbus A.340-313X	Lufthansa *Lünen*
	D-AIGZ	Airbus A.340-313X	Lufthansa *Villingen-Schwenningen*
	D-AIHA	Airbus A.340-642	Lufthansa *Nurnberg*
	D-AIHB	Airbus A.340-642	Lufthansa *Bremerhaven*
	D-AIHC	Airbus A.340-642	Lufthansa *Essen*
	D-AIHD	Airbus A.340-642	Lufthansa *Stuttgart*
	D-AIHE	Airbus A.340-642	Lufthansa *Leverkusen*
	D-AIHF	Airbus A.340-642	Lufthansa *Lübeck*
	D-AIHH	Airbus A.340-642	Lufthansa
	D-AIHI	Airbus A.340-642	Lufthansa
	D-AIHK	Airbus A.340-642	Lufthansa
	D-AIHL	Airbus A.340-642	Lufthansa
	D-AIHM	Airbus A.340-642	Lufthansa
	D-AIHN	Airbus A.340-642	Lufthansa
	D-AIHO	Airbus A.340-642	Lufthansa
	D-AIHP	Airbus A.340-642	Lufthansa
	D-AIHQ	Airbus A.340-642	Lufthansa
	D-AIHR	Airbus A.340-642	Lufthansa
	D-AIHS	Airbus A.340-642	Lufthansa
	D-AIHT	Airbus A.340-642	Lufthansa
	D-AIHU	Airbus A.340-642	Lufthansa
	D-AIHV	Airbus A.340-642	Lufthansa
	D-AIHW	Airbus A.340-642	Lufthansa
	D-AIHX	Airbus A.340-642	Lufthansa
	D-AIHY	Airbus A.340-642	Lufthansa
	D-AIHZ	Airbus A.340-642	Lufthansa
	D-AIKA	Airbus A.330-343X	Lufthansa *Minden*
	D-AIKB	Airbus A.330-343X	Lufthansa *Cuxhaven*
	D-AIKC	Airbus A.330-343X	Lufthansa *Hamm*
	D-AIKD	Airbus A.330-343X	Lufthansa *Siegen*
	D-AIKE	Airbus A.330-343X	Lufthansa *Landshut*
	D-AIKF	Airbus A.330-343X	Lufthansa *Witten*
	D-AIKG	Airbus A.330-343X	Lufthansa *Ludwigsburg*
	D-AIKH	Airbus A.330-343X	Lufthansa
	D-AIKI	Airbus A.330-343X	Lufthansa
	D-AIKJ	Airbus A.330-343X	Lufthansa
	D-AIKK	Airbus A.330-343X	Lufthansa
	D-AIKL	Airbus A.330-343X	Lufthansa
	D-AIKM	Airbus A.330-343X	Lufthansa
	D-AIKN	Airbus A.330-343X	Lufthansa
	D-AIKO	Airbus A.330-343X	Lufthansa
	D-AIKP	Airbus A.330-343X	Lufthansa
	D-AIKQ	Airbus A.330-343X	Lufthansa
	D-AIKR	Airbus A.330-343X	Lufthansa
	D-AILA	Airbus A.319-114	Lufthansa *Frankfurt (Oder)*
	D-AILB	Airbus A.319-114	Lufthansa *Lutherstadt Wittenburg*
	D-AILC	Airbus A.319-114	Lufthansa *Russelsheim*
	D-AILD	Airbus A.319-114	Lufthansa *Dinkelsbühl*
	D-AILE	Airbus A.319-114	Lufthansa *Kelsterbach*
	D-AILF	Airbus A.319-114	Lufthansa Italia
	D-AILH	Airbus A.319-114	Lufthansa Italia *Norderstedt*
	D-AILI	Airbus A.319-114	Lufthansa Italia *Roma*
	D-AILK	Airbus A.319-114	Lufthansa *Landshut*
	D-AILL	Airbus A.319-114	Lufthansa *Marburg*
	D-AILM	Airbus A.319-114	Lufthansa *Friedrichshafen*

Reg.	Type	Owner or Operator	Notes
D-AILN	Airbus A.319-114	Lufthansa Idar-Oberstein	
D-AILP	Airbus A.319-114	Lufthansa Tubingen	
D-AILR	Airbus A.319-114	Lufthansa Tegernsee	
D-AILS	Airbus A.319-114	Lufthansa Heide	
D-AILT	Airbus A.319-114	Lufthansa Straubing	
D-AILU	Airbus A.319-114	Lufthansa Verden	
D-AILW	Airbus A.319-114	Lufthansa Donaueschingen	
D-AILX	Airbus A.319-114	Lufthansa Feilbach	
D-AILY	Airbus A.319-114	Lufthansa Schweinfurt	
D-AIMA	Airbus A.380-841	Lufthansa Frankfurt am Main	
D-AIMB	Airbus A.380-841	Lufthansa	
D-AIMC	Airbus A.380-841	Lufthansa	
D-AIMD	Airbus A.380-841	Lufthansa	
D-AIME	Airbus A.380-841	Lufthansa Johannesburg	
D-AIMF	Airbus A.380-841	Lufthansa Zurich	
D-AIMG	Airbus A.380-841	Lufthansa	
D-AIMH	Airbus A.380-841	Lufthansa	
D-AIMI	Airbus A.380-841	Lufthansa	
D-AIMJ	Airbus A.380-841	Lufthansa Brussel	
D-AIMK	Airbus A.380-841	Lufthansa	
D-AIPA	Airbus A.320-211	Lufthansa Buxtehude	
D-AIPB	Airbus A.320-211	Lufthansa Heidelberg	
D-AIPC	Airbus A.320-211	Lufthansa Braunschweig	
D-AIPD	Airbus A.320-211	Lufthansa Freiburg	
D-AIPE	Airbus A.320-211	Lufthansa Kassel	
D-AIPF	Airbus A.320-211	Lufthansa Deggendorf	
D-AIPH	Airbus A.320-211	Lufthansa Munster	
D-AIPK	Airbus A.320-211	Lufthansa Wiesbaden	
D-AIPL	Airbus A.320-211	Lufthansa Ludwigshafen am Rhein	
D-AIPM	Airbus A.320-211	Lufthansa Troisdorf	
D-AIPP	Airbus A.320-211	Lufthansa Starnberg	
D-AIPR	Airbus A.320-211	Lufthansa Kaufbeuren	
D-AIPS	Airbus A.320-211	Lufthansa Augsburg	
D-AIPT	Airbus A.320-211	Lufthansa Cottbus	
D-AIPU	Airbus A.320-211	Lufthansa Dresden	
D-AIPW	Airbus A.320-211	Lufthansa Schwerin	
D-AIPX	Airbus A.320-211	Lufthansa Mannheim	
D-AIPY	Airbus A.320-211	Lufthansa Magdeburg	
D-AIPZ	Airbus A.320-211	Lufthansa Erfurt	
D-AIQA	Airbus A.320-211	Lufthansa Mainz	
D-AIQB	Airbus A.320-211	Lufthansa Bielefeld	
D-AIQC	Airbus A.320-211	Lufthansa Zwickau	
D-AIQD	Airbus A.320-211	Lufthansa Jena	
D-AIQE	Airbus A.320-211	Lufthansa Gera	
D-AIQF	Airbus A.320-211	Lufthansa Halle (Saale)	
D-AIQH	Airbus A.320-211	Lufthansa Dessau	
D-AIQK	Airbus A.320-211	Lufthansa Rostock	
D-AIQL	Airbus A.320-211	Lufthansa Stralsund	
D-AIQM	Airbus A.320-211	Lufthansa Nordenham	
D-AIQN	Airbus A.320-211	Lufthansa Laupheim	
D-AIQP	Airbus A.320-211	Lufthansa Suhl	
D-AIQR	Airbus A.320-211	Lufthansa Lahr/Schwarzwald	
D-AIQS	Airbus A.320-211	Lufthansa Eisenach	
D-AIQT	Airbus A.320-211	Lufthansa Gotha	
D-AIQU	Airbus A.320-211	Lufthansa Backnang	
D-AIQW	Airbus A.320-211	Lufthansa Kleve	
D-AIRA	Airbus A.321-131	Lufthansa Finkenwerder	
D-AIRB	Airbus A.321-131	Lufthansa Baden-Baden	
D-AIRC	Airbus A.321-131	Lufthansa Erlangen	
D-AIRD	Airbus A.321-131	Lufthansa Coburg	
D-AIRE	Airbus A.321-131	Lufthansa Osnabrueck	
D-AIRF	Airbus A.321-131	Lufthansa Kempten	
D-AIRH	Airbus A.321-131	Lufthansa Garmisch-Partenkirchen	
D-AIRK	Airbus A.321-131	Lufthansa Freudenstadt/Schwarzwald	
D-AIRL	Airbus A.321-131	Lufthansa Kulmbach	
D-AIRM	Airbus A.321-131	Lufthansa Darmstadt	
D-AIRN	Airbus A.321-131	Lufthansa Kaiserslautern	
D-AIRO	Airbus A.321-131	Lufthansa Konstanz	
D-AIRP	Airbus A.321-131	Lufthansa Lüneburg	
D-AIRR	Airbus A.321-131	Lufthansa Wismar	
D-AIRS	Airbus A.321-131	Lufthansa Husum	
D-AIRT	Airbus A.321-131	Lufthansa Regensburg	

Notes	Reg.	Type	Owner or Operator
	D-AIRU	Airbus A.321-131	Lufthansa *Würzburg*
	D-AIRW	Airbus A.321-131	Lufthansa *Heilbronn*
	D-AIRX	Airbus A.321-131	Lufthansa *Weimar*
	D-AIRY	Airbus A.321-131	Lufthansa *Flensburg*
	D-AISB	Airbus A.321-231	Lufthansa *Hamein*
	D-AISC	Airbus A.321-231	Lufthansa *Speyer*
	D-AISD	Airbus A.321-231	Lufthansa *Chemnitz*
	D-AISE	Airbus A.321-231	Lufthansa *Neustadt an der Weinstrasse*
	D-AISF	Airbus A.321-231	Lufthansa *Lippstadt*
	D-AISG	Airbus A.321-231	Lufthansa *Dormagen*
	D-AISH	Airbus A.321-231	Lufthansa
	D-AISI	Airbus A.321-231	Lufthansa
	D-AISJ	Airbus A.321-231	Lufthansa
	D-AISK	Airbus A.321-231	Lufthansa
	D-AISL	Airbus A.321-231	Lufthansa *Arnsberg*
	D-AISN	Airbus A.321-231	Lufthansa *Goppingen*
	D-AISO	Airbus A.321-231	Lufthansa
	D-AISP	Airbus A.321-231	Lufthansa
	D-AISQ	Airbus A.321-231	Lufthansa
	D-AISR	Airbus A.321-231	Lufthansa
	D-AIST	Airbus A.321-231	Lufthansa
	D-AISU	Airbus A.321-231	Lufthansa *Nordlingen*
	D-AISV	Airbus A.321-231	Lufthansa *Bingen*
	D-AISW	Airbus A.321-231	Lufthansa
	D-AISX	Airbus A.321-231	Lufthansa
	D-AISZ	Airbus A.321-231	Lufthansa
	D-AIZA	Airbus A.320-214	Lufthansa
	D-AIZB	Airbus A.320-214	Lufthansa
	D-AIZC	Airbus A.320-214	Lufthansa
	D-AIZD	Airbus A.320-214	Lufthansa
	D-AIZE	Airbus A.320-214	Lufthansa
	D-AIZF	Airbus A.320-214	Lufthansa
	D-AIZG	Airbus A.320-214	Lufthansa
	D-AIZH	Airbus A.320-214	Lufthansa
	D-AIZI	Airbus A.320-214	Lufthansa
	D-AIZJ	Airbus A.320-214	Lufthansa
	D-AIZK	Airbus A.320-214	Lufthansa
	D-AIZL	Airbus A.320-214	Lufthansa
	D-AIZM	Airbus A.320-214	Lufthansa
	D-AIZN	Airbus A.320-214	Lufthansa
	D-AIZO	Airbus A.320-214	Lufthansa
	D-AIZP	Airbus A.320-214	Lufthansa
	D-AIZQ	Airbus A.320-214	Lufthansa
	D-AKNK	Airbus A.319-112	Germanwings
	D-AKNL	Airbus A.319-112	Germanwings
	D-AKNM	Airbus A.319-112	Germanwings
	D-AKNN	Airbus A.319-112	Germanwings
	D-AKNO	Airbus A.319-112	Germanwings
	D-AKNP	Airbus A.319-112	Germanwings
	D-AKNQ	Airbus A.319-112	Germanwings
	D-AKNR	Airbus A.319-112	Germanwings *Spirit of T-Com*
	D-AKNS	Airbus A.319-112	Germanwings *Spirit of T Mobile*
	D-AKNT	Airbus A.319-112	Germanwings *City of Hamburg*
	D-AKNU	Airbus A.319-112	Germanwings
	D-AKNV	Airbus A.319-112	Germanwings
	D-ALCA	McD Douglas MD-11F	Lufthansa Cargo
	D-ALCB	McD Douglas MD-11F	Lufthansa Cargo
	D-ALCC	McD Douglas MD-11F	Lufthansa Cargo
	D-ALCD	McD Douglas MD-11F	Lufthansa Cargo
	D-ALCE	McD Douglas MD-11F	Lufthansa Cargo
	D-ALCF	McD Douglas MD-11F	Lufthansa Cargo
	D-ALCG	McD Douglas MD-11F	Lufthansa Cargo
	D-ALCH	McD Douglas MD-11F	Lufthansa Cargo
	D-ALCI	McD Douglas MD-11F	Lufthansa Cargo
	D-ALCJ	McD Douglas MD-11F	Lufthansa Cargo
	D-ALCK	McD Douglas MD-11F	Lufthansa Cargo
	D-ALCL	McD Douglas MD-11F	Lufthansa Cargo
	D-ALCM	McD Douglas MD-11F	Lufthansa Cargo
	D-ALCN	McD Douglas MD-11F	Lufthansa Cargo
	D-ALCO	McD Douglas MD-11F	Lufthansa Cargo
	D-ALCP	McD Douglas MD-11F	Lufthansa Cargo
	D-ALCR	McD Douglas MD-11F	Lufthansa Cargo

Reg.	Type	Owner or Operator	Notes
D-ALCS	McD Douglas MD-11F	Lufthansa Cargo	
D-ALEA	Boeing 757-236SF	EAT Leipzig/DHL	
D-ALEB	Boeing 757-236SF	EAT Leipzig/DHL	
D-ALEC	Boeing 757-236SF	EAT Leipzig/DHL	
D-ALED	Boeing 757-236SF	EAT Leipzig/DHL	
D-ALEE	Boeing 757-236SF	EAT Leipzig/DHL	
D-ALEF	Boeing 757-236SF	EAT Leipzig/DHL	
D-ALEG	Boeing 757-236SF	EAT Leipzig/DHL	
D-ALEH	Boeing 757-236SF	EAT Leipzig/DHL	
D-ALEI	Boeing 757-236SF	EAT Leipzig/DHL	
D-ALEJ	Boeing 757-23APF	EAT Leipzig/DHL	
D-ALEK	Boeing 757-236SF	EAT Leipzig/DHL	
D-ALIN	BAe 146-300	WDL Aviation	
D-ALPA	Airbus A.330-223	Air Berlin	
D-ALPB	Airbus A.330-223	Air Berlin	
D-ALPC	Airbus A.330-223	Air Berlin	
D-ALPD	Airbus A.330-223	Air Berlin	
D-ALPE	Airbus A.330-223	Air Berlin	
D-ALPF	Airbus A.330-223	Air Berlin	
D-ALPG	Airbus A.330-223	Air Berlin	
D-ALPH	Airbus A.330-223	Air Berlin	
D-ALPI	Airbus A.330-223	Air Berlin	
D-ALPJ	Airbus A.330-223	Air Berlin	
D-ALSA	Airbus A.321-211	Air Berlin	
D-ALSB	Airbus A.321-211	Air Berlin	
D-ALSC	Airbus A.321-211	Air Berlin	
D-ALTE	Airbus A.320-214	Air Berlin	
D-ALTK	Airbus A.320-214	Air Berlin	
D-ALTL	Airbus A.320-214	Air Berlin	
D-AMAJ	BAe 146-200	WDL Aviation	
D-AMGL	BAe 146-200	WDL Aviation	
D-AOLB	SAAB 2000	OLT Express	
D-AOLC	SAAB 2000	OLT Express	
D-AOLG	Fokker 100	OLT Express	
D-AOLH	Fokker 100	OLT Express	
D-AOLT	SAAB 2000	OLT Emden	
D-APBB	Boeing 737-8FH	PrivatAir/Lufthansa	
D-APBC	Boeing 737-8BK	PrivatAir/Lufthansa	
D-APBD	Boeing 737-8BK	PrivatAir/Lufthansa	
D-ASTA	Airbus A.319-112	Gambia Bird	
D-ASTB	Airbus A.319-112	Germania	
D-ASTC	Airbus A.319-112	Germania	
D-ASTX	Airbus A.319-112	Germania	
D-ASTY	Airbus A.319-112	Germania	
D-ASTZ	Airbus A.319-112	Germania	
D-ATUA	Boeing 737-8K5	TUIfly	
D-ATUB	Boeing 737-8K5	TUIfly	
D-ATUC	Boeing 737-8K5	TUIfly	
D-ATUD	Boeing 737-8K5	TUIfly	
D-ATUE	Boeing 737-8K5	TUIfly	
D-ATUF	Boeing 737-8K5	TUIfly	
D-ATUG	Boeing 737-8K5	TUIfly	
D-ATUH	Boeing 737-8K5	TUIfly	
D-ATUI	Boeing 737-8K5	TUIfly	
D-ATUJ	Boeing 737-8K5	TUIfly	
D-ATUK	Boeing 737-8K5	TUIfly	
D-ATUL	Boeing 737-8K5	TUIfly	
D-AWBA	Bae 146-300	WDL Aviation	
D-AWUE	BAe 146-200	WDL Aviation	
D-CCAS	Short SD3-60-300	Night Express	
D-CRAS	Short SD3-60-300	Night Express	
D-IEXB	Beech 99	Night Express	

EC (Spain)

EC-ELT	BAe 146-200QT	Pan Air/TNT Airways	
EC-FCB	Airbus A.320-211	Iberia Express	
EC-FDA	Airbus A.320-211	Iberia Express	
EC-FDB	Airbus A.320-211	Iberia Express	
EC-FGR	Airbus A.320-211	Iberia Express	
EC-FGV	Airbus A.320-211	Iberia Express	

EC

Notes	Reg.	Type	Owner or Operator
	EC-FLP	Airbus A.320-211	Iberia Express
	EC-FNR	Airbus A.320-211	Iberia Express
	EC-FQY	Airbus A.320-211	Iberia Express
	EC-FVY	BAe 146-200QT	Pan Air/TNT Airways
	EC-FZE	BAe 146-200QT	Pan Air/TNT Airways
	EC-GGS	Airbus A.340-313	Iberia Concha Espina
	EC-GHX	Airbus A.340-313	Iberia Rosalia de Castro
	EC-GJT	Airbus A.340-313	Iberia Rosa Chacel
	EC-GLE	Airbus A.340-313	Iberia Concepcion Arenal
	EC-GPB	Airbus A.340-313X	Iberia Teresa de Avila
	EC-GQO	BAe 146-200QT	Pan Air/TNT Airways
	EC-GRH	Airbus A.320-211	Vueling Airlines
	EC-GUP	Airbus A.340-313X	Iberia Agustina De Aragon
	EC-GUQ	Airbus A.340-313X	Iberia Beatriz Galindo
	EC-GVE	Swearingen SA227AC Metro III	Aeronova
	EC-HCH	Swearingen SA227AC Metro III	Aeronova
	EC-HDH	BAe 146-200QT	Pan Air/TNT Airways
	EC-HDS	Boeing 757-256	Iberia Paraguay
	EC-HDT	Airbus A.320-214	Iberia Museo Guggenheim Bilbao
	EC-HEK	Canadair CRJ200ER	Air Nostrum/Iberia Regional
	EC-HGR	Airbus A.319-111	Iberia Ribeira Sacra
	EC-HGS	Airbus A.319-111	Iberia Bardenas Reales
	EC-HGT	Airbus A.319-111	Iberia Icnitas de Enciso
	EC-HGU	Airbus A.340-313X	Iberia Maria de Molina
	EC-HGV	Airbus A.340-313X	Iberia Maria Guerrero
	EC-HGZ	Airbus A.320-214	Iberia Boi Taull
	EC-HHA	Airbus A.320-214	Vueling Airlines
	EC-HHI	Canadair CRJ200ER	Air Nostrum/Iberia Regional
	EC-HJH	BAe 146-200QT	Pan Air/TNT Airways
	EC-HJP	Boeing 737-85P	Air Europa
	EC-HJQ	Boeing 737-85P	Air Europa
	EC-HKO	Airbus A.319-111	Iberia Gorbia
	EC-HQI	Airbus A.320-214	Vueling Airlines Merce Sune
	EC-HQJ	Airbus A.320-214	Vueling Airlines
	EC-HQL	Airbus A.320-214	Vueling Airlines Click on Vueling
	EC-HTB	Airbus A.320-214	Iberia Playa de las Americas
	EC-HTC	Airbus A.320-214	Iberia Alpujarra
	EC-HTD	Airbus A.320-214	Vueling Airlines Unos Vuelan,otros Vueling
	EC-HUH	Airbus A.321-211	Iberia Benidorm
	EC-HUI	Airbus A.321-211	Iberia Comunidad Autonoma de la Rioja
	EC-HUJ	Airbus A.320-214	Iberia Express
	EC-HUK	Airbus A.320-214	Iberia Laguna Negra
	EC-HUL	Airbus A.320-214	Iberia Monasterio de Rueda
	EC-HYC	Airbus A.320-214	Iberia Ciudad de Ceuta
	EC-HYD	Airbus A.320-214	Iberia Maspalomas
	EC-HZH	Swearingen SA227AC Metro III	Aeronova
	EC-HZS	Boeing 737-86Q	Air Europa
	EC-IBM	Canadair CRJ200ER	Air Nostrum/Iberia Regional
	EC-ICF	Airbus A.340-313X	Iberia Maria Zambrano
	EC-ICQ	Airbus A.320-211	Vueling Airlines Iker Ochandorena
	EC-ICR	Airbus A.320-211	Vueling Airlines
	EC-ICS	Airbus A.320-211	Vueling Airlines
	EC-ICT	Airbus A.320-211	Vueling Airlines
	EC-IDA	Boeing 737-86Q	Air Europa
	EC-IDC	Canadair CRJ200ER	Air Nostrum/Iberia Regional
	EC-IDF	Airbus A.340-313X	Iberia Mariana Pineda
	EC-IDT	Boeing 737-86Q	Air Europa
	EC-IEF	Airbus A.320-214	Iberia Castillo de Loarre
	EC-IEG	Airbus A.320-214	Iberia Costa Brava
	EC-IEI	Airbus A.320-214	Iberia Monasterio de Valldigna
	EC-IGK	Airbus A.321-211	Iberia Costa Calida
	EC-IGO	Canadair CRJ200ER	Air Nostrum/Iberia Regional
	EC-IIG	Airbus A.321-211	Iberia Ciudad de Siguenza
	EC-IIH	Airbus A.340-313X	Iberia Maria Barbara de Braganza
	EC-III	Boeing 737-86Q	Air Europa
	EC-IJE	Canadair CRJ200ER	Air Nostrum/Iberia Regional
	EC-IJN	Airbus A.321-211	Iberia Merida
	EC-ILO	Airbus A.321-211	Iberia Cueva de Nerja
	EC-ILP	Airbus A.321-211	Iberia Peniscola
	EC-ILR	Airbus A.320-214	Iberia San Juan de la Pena
	EC-ILS	Airbus A.320-214	Iberia Sierra de Cameros
	EC-INO	Airbus A.340-642	Iberia Gaudi

Reg.	Type	Owner or Operator	Notes
EC-INZ	Airbus A.320-214	Orbest	
EC-IOB	Airbus A.340-642	Iberia *Julio Romanes de Torres*	
EC-IRI	Canadair CRJ200ER	Air Nostrum/Iberia Regional	
EC-IQR	Airbus A.340-642	Iberia *Salvador Dali*	
EC-ISN	Boeing 737-86Q	Air Europa	
EC-ITN	Airbus A.321-211	Iberia *Empuries*	
EC-IXD	Airbus A.321-211	Iberia *Vall d'Aran*	
EC-IZD	Airbus A.320-214	Vueling Airlines	
EC-IZH	Airbus A.320-214	Iberia *San Pere de Roda*	
EC-IZP	Canadair CRJ200ER	Air Nostrum/Iberia Regional	
EC-IZR	Airbus A.320-214	Iberia *Urkiola*	
EC-IZX	Airbus A.340-642	Iberia *Mariano Benlliure*	
EC-IZY	Airbus A.340-642	Iberia *I. Zuloaga*	
EC-JAP	Boeing 737-85P	Air Europa	
EC-JAZ	Airbus A.319-111	Iberia *Las Medulas*	
EC-JBA	Airbus A.340-642	Iberia *Joaquin Rodrigo*	
EC-JBJ	Boeing 737-85P	Air Europa	
EC-JBK	Boeing 737-85P	Air Europa	
EC-JBL	Boeing 737-85P	Air Europa	
EC-JCG	Canadair CRJ200ER	Air Nostrum/Iberia Regional	
EC-JCL	Canadair CRJ200ER	Air Nostrum/Iberia Regional	
EC-JCM	Canadair CRJ200ER	Air Nostrum/Iberia Regional	
EC-JCO	Canadair CRJ200ER	Air Nostrum/Iberia Regional	
EC-JCU	Swearingen SA227AC Metro III	Aeronova	
EC-JCY	Airbus A.340-642	Iberia *Andrés Segovia*	
EC-JCZ	Airbus A.340-642	Iberia *Vicente Aleixandre*	
EC-JDL	Airbus A.319-111	Iberia *Los Llanos de Aridane*	
EC-JDM	Airbus A.321-211	Iberia *Cantabria*	
EC-JDR	Airbus A.321-211	Iberia	
EC-JEE	Canadair CRJ200ER	Air Nostrum/Iberia Regional	
EC-JEF	Canadair CRJ200ER	Air Nostrum/Iberia Regional	
EC-JEI	Airbus A.319-111	Iberia *Xátiva*	
EC-JEJ	Airbus A.321-211	Iberia *Rio Frio*	
EC-JFF	Airbus A.320-214	Vueling Airlines *Vueling the world*	
EC-JFG	Airbus A.320-214	Iberia Express	
EC-JFH	Airbus A.320-214	Iberia Express	
EC-JFN	Airbus A.320-214	Iberia *Sirrea de las Nieves*	
EC-JFX	Airbus A.340-642	Iberia *Jacinto Benavente*	
EC-JGM	Airbus A.320-214	Vueling Airlines *The joy of vueling*	
EC-JGS	Airbus A.321-211	Iberia *Guadelupe*	
EC-JHK	Boeing 737-85P	Air Europa	
EC-JHL	Boeing 737-85P	Air Europa	
EC-JHP	Airbus A.330-343X	Orbest	
EC-JLE	Airbus A.340-642	Iberia *Santiago Ramon y Cajal*	
EC-JLI	Airbus A.321-211	Iberia *Delta del Llobregrat*	
EC-JMR	Airbus A.321-211	Iberia *Aranjuez*	
EC-JNB	Canadair CRJ900ER	Air Nostrum/Iberia Regional	
EC-JNF	Boeing 737-85P	Air Europa *Mutua Madrileqa*	
EC-JNI	Airbus A.321-211	Iberia *Palmeral de Eiche*	
EC-JNQ	Airbus A.340-642	Iberia *Antonio Machado*	
EC-JPF	Airbus A.330-202	Air Europa	
EC-JPU	Airbus A.340-642	Iberia *Pio Baroja*	
EC-JQG	Airbus A.330-202	Air Europa *Estepona – Costa del Sol*	
EC-JQQ	Airbus A.330-202	Air Europa	
EC-JQZ	Airbus A.321-211	Iberia *Generalife*	
EC-JRE	Airbus A.321-211	Iberia *Villa de Uncastillo*	
EC-JSB	Airbus A.320-214	Iberia *Benalmadena*	
EC-JSK	Airbus A.320-214	Iberia Express	
EC-JSY	Airbus A.320-214	Vueling Airlines	
EC-JTQ	Airbus A.320-214	Vueling Airlines *Vueling, que es gerundio*	
EC-JTR	Airbus A.320-214	Vueling Airlines *No Vueling no party*	
EC-JTS	Canadair CRJ900ER	Air Nostrum/Iberia Regional	
EC-JTT	Canadair CRJ900ER	Air Nostrum/Iberia Regional	
EC-JTU	Canadair CRJ900ER	Air Nostrum/Iberia Regional	
EC-JUF	McD Douglas MD-83	Swiftair	
EC-JUG	McD Douglas MD-83	Swiftair	
EC-JVE	Airbus A.319-111	Iberia *Puerto de la Cruz*	
EC-JXJ	Airbus A.319-111	Iberia	
EC-JXV	Airbus A.319-111	Iberia *Concejo de Cabrales*	
EC-JXZ	Canadair CRJ900ER	Air Nostrum/Iberia Regional	
EC-JYA	Canadair CRJ900ER	Air Nostrum/Iberia Regional	
EC-JYV	Canadair CRJ900ER	Air Nostrum/Iberia Regional	

Notes	Reg.	Type	Owner or Operator
	EC-JYX	Airbus A.320-214	Vueling Airlines *Elisenda Masana*
	EC-JZI	Airbus A.320-214	Vueling Airlines *Vueling in love*
	EC-JZL	Airbus A.330-202	Air Europa
	EC-JZM	Airbus A.321-211	Iberia *Águila Imperial Ibérica* ✓
	EC-JZQ	Airbus A.320-214	Vueling Airlines *I want to Vueling*
	EC-JZS	Canadair CRJ900ER	Air Nostrum/Iberia Regional
	EC-JZT	Canadair CRJ900ER	Air Nostrum/Iberia Regional
	EC-JZU	Canadair CRJ900ER	Air Nostrum/Iberia Regional
	EC-JZV	Canadair CRJ900ER	Air Nostrum/Iberia Regional
	EC-KBJ	Airbus A.319-111	Iberia *Lince Iberico*
	EC-KBU	Airbus A.320-214	Vueling Airlines
	EC-KBX	Airbus A.319-111	Iberia *Oso Pardo*
	EC-KCG	Boeing 737-85P	Air Europa
	EC-KCL	Airbus A.340-311	Iberia
	EC-KCU	Airbus A.320-216	Vueling Airlines
	EC-KDG	Airbus A.320-214	Vueling Airlines
	EC-KDH	Airbus A.320-214	Vueling Airlines *Ain't no Vueling high enough*
	EC-KDI	Airbus A.319-111	Iberia *Cigu-a Negra*
	EC-KDT	Airbus A.320-216	Vueling Airlines
	EC-KDX	Airbus A.320-216	Vueling Airlines *Francisco Jose Ruiz Cortizo*
	EC-KFI	Airbus A.320-216	Vueling Airlines
	EC-KFT	Airbus A.319-111	Iberia *Nutria*
	EC-KHM	Airbus A.319-111	Iberia *Buho Real*
	EC-KHN	Airbus A.320-216	Vueling Airlines
	EC-KJD	Airbus A.320-216	Vueling Airlines
	EC-KKS	Airbus A.319-111	Iberia *Halcon Peregrino*
	EC-KKT	Airbus A.320-214	Vueling Airlines *Vueling Together*
	EC-KLB	Airbus A.320-214	Vueling Airlines *Vuela Punto*
	EC-KLR	Boeing 737-3Q8	Swiftair
	EC-KLT	Airbus A.320-214	Vueling Airlines
	EC-KMD	Airbus A.319-111	Iberia *Petirrojo*
	EC-KMI	Airbus A.320-216	Vueling Airlines *How are you? I'm Vueling!*
	EC-KOH	Airbus A.320-214	Iberia
	EC-KOM	Airbus A.330-202	Air Europa
	EC-KOU	Airbus A.340-313	Iberia
	EC-KOY	Airbus A.319-111	Iberia *Vencejo*
	EC-KRH	Airbus A.320-214	Vueling Airlines *Vueling me softly*
	EC-KRJ	Embraer RJ190-200SR	Air Europa
	EC-KSE	Airbus A.340-313X	Iberia
	EC-KSM	Boeing 747-412	Pullmantur Air
	EC-KTG	Airbus A.330-203	Air Europa
	EC-KTZ	Boeing 737-375	Swiftair
	EC-KUB	Airbus A.319-111	Iberia
	EC-KVD	Boeing 737-306	Swiftair
	EC-KXD	Embraer RJ190-200SR	Air Europa
	EC-KYO	Embraer RJ190-200SR	Air Europa
	EC-KYP	Embraer RJ190-200SR	Air Europa
	EC-KYZ	Airbus A.320-214	Orbest
	EC-KZG	Airbus A.320-214	Orbest
	EC-KZI	Airbus A.340-642	Iberia *Miguel Hernandez*
	EC-LAA	Airbus A.320-214	Vueling Airlines
	EC-LAB	Airbus A.320-214	Vueling Airlines
	EC-LAC	Boeing 737-3M8	Swiftair
	EC-LAJ	Airbus A.320-214	Orbest
	EC-LCQ	Embraer ERJ190-20LR	Air Europa
	EC-LCZ	Airbus A.340-642	Iberia
	EC-LEA	Airbus A.320-214	Iberia *Formentera*
	EC-LEI	Airbus A.319-111	Iberia *Vison Europeo*
	EC-LEK	Embraer ERJ190-200LR	Air Europa
	EC-LEQ	Airbus A.330-343E	Orbest
	EC-LEU	Airbus A.340-642	Iberia
	EC-LEV	Airbus A.340-642	Iberia
	EC-LEY	McD Douglas MD-83	Swiftair
	EC-LFS	Airbus A.340-642	Iberia
	EC-LHM	Airbus A.340-313X	Iberia
	EC-LIN	Embraer ERJ190-200LR	Air Europa
	EC-LJI	Boeing 737-301F	Swiftair
	EC-LJR	Canadair CRJ1000ER	Air Nostrum/Iberia Regional
	EC-LJS	Canadair CRJ1000ER	Air Nostrum/Iberia Regional
	EC-LJT	Canadair CRJ1000ER	Air Nostrum/Iberia Regional
	EC-LJX	Canadair CRJ1000ER	Air Nostrum/Iberia Regional
	EC-LKE	Airbus A.330-243	Air Europa

Reg.	Type	Owner or Operator	Notes
EC-LKF	Canadair CRJ1000ER	Air Nostrum/Iberia Regional	
EC-LKG	Airbus A.320-214	Iberia *Santiago de Compostela*	
EC-LKM	Embraer ERJ190-200LR	Air Europa	
EC-LKS	Airbus A.340-313	Iberia *Placido Domingo*	
EC-LKX	Embraer ERJ190-200LR	Air Europa	
EC-LLJ	Airbus A.320-216	Vueling Airlines *Luke-SkyVueling*	
EC-LLM	Airbus A.320-216	Vueling Airlines *Be happy, be Vueling*	
EC-LLR	Embraer ERJ190-200LR	Air Europa	
EC-LLX	Airbus A.320-214	Orbest	
EC-LML	Airbus A.320-216	Vueling Airlines	
EC-LMN	Airbus A.330-243	Air Europa	
EC-LMR	BAe 146-300QT	Panair/TNT Airways	
EC-LNH	Airbus A.330-243	Air Europa	
EC-LOB	Airbus A.320-232	Vueling Airlines	
EC-LOC	Airbus A.320-232	Vueling Airlines *Vueling on heaven's door*	
EC-LOF	BAe 146-300QT	Panair/TNT Airways	
EC-LOJ	Canadair CRJ1000ER	Air Nostrum/Iberia Regional	
EC-LOP	Airbus A.320-214	Vueling Airlines	
EC-LOV	Canadair CRJ1000ER	Air Nostrum/Iberia Regional	
EC-LOX	Canadair CRJ1000ER	Air Nostrum/Iberia Regional	
EC-LPG	Canadair CRJ1000ER	Air Nostrum/Iberia Regional	
EC-LPQ	Boeing 737-85P	Air Europa	
EC-LPR	Boeing 737-85P	Air Europa	
EC-LQJ	Airbus A.320-232	Vueling Airlines	
EC-LQK	Airbus A.320-232	Vueling Airlines	
EC-LQL	Airbus A.320-232	Vueling Airlines	
EC-LQM	Airbus A.320-232	Vueling Airlines	
EC-LQN	Airbus A.320-232	Vueling Airlines	
EC-LQO	Airbus A.330-243	Air Europa	
EC-LQP	Airbus A.330-243	Air Europa	
EC-LQX	Boeing 737-85P	Air Europa	
EC-LQZ	Airbus A.320-232	Vueling Airlines	
EC-LRA	Airbus A.320-232	Vueling Airlines	
EC-LRE	Airbus A.320-232	Vueling Airlines	
EC-LRG	Airbus A.320-214	Iberia Express	
EC-LRM	Airbus A.320-232	Vueling Airlines	
EC-LRN	Airbus A.320-214	Vueling Airlines	
EC-LRS	Airbus A.319-112	Vueling Airlines	
EC-LRT	Airbus A.320-214	Orbest	
EC-LRY	Airbus A.320-232	Vueling Airlines	
EC-LRZ	Airbus A.319-112	Vueling Airlines	
EC-LSA	Airbus A.320-214	Vueling Airlines	
EC-LTO	Boeing 737-301F	Swiftair	
EC-LTV	McD Douglas MD-83	Swiftair	
EC-LUC	Airbus A.320-214	Iberia Express	

EK (Armenia)

EK-32008	Airbus A.320-211	Armavia	

EP (Iran)

EP-IBA	Airbus A.300B4-605R	Iran Air	
EP-IBB	Airbus A.300B4-605R	Iran Air	
EP-IBC	Airbus A.300B4-605R	Iran Air	
EP-IBD	Airbus A.300B4-605R	Iran Air	
EP-IBK	Airbus A.310-304	Iran Air	

ER (Moldova)

ER-AXP	Airbus A.320-211	Air Moldova	
ER-AXV	Airbus A.320-211	Air Moldova	
ER-ECB	Embraer ERJ190-100AR	Air Moldova	

ES (Estonia)

ES-ACB	Canadair CRJ900ER	Estonian Air	
ES-ACC	Canadair CRJ900ER	Estonian Air	

Notes	Reg.	Type	Owner or Operator
	ES-ACD	Canadair CRJ900ER	Estonian Air
	ES-AEA	Embraer ERJ170-100LR	Estonian Air
	ES-AEB	Embraer ERJ170-100LR	Estonian Air
	ES-AEC	Embraer ERJ170-100LR	Estonian Air
	ES-AED	Embraer ERJ170-100LR	Estonian Air

ET (Ethiopia)

	ET-AJS	Boeing 757-260PF	Ethiopian Airlines
	ET-AJX	Boeing 757-260F	Ethiopian Airlines
	ET-AKC	Boeing 757-260	Ethiopian Airlines
	ET-AKE	Boeing 757-260	Ethiopian Airlines
	ET-AKF	Boeing 757-260	Ethiopian Airlines
	ET-ALC	Boeing 767-33AER	Ethiopian Airlines
	ET-ALH	Boeing 767-3BGER	Ethiopian Airlines
	ET-ALJ	Boeing 767-360ER	Ethiopian Airlines
	ET-ALL	Boeing 767-3BGER	Ethiopian Airlines
	ET-ALO	Boeing 767-360ER	Ethiopian Airlines
	ET-ALP	Boeing 767-360ER	Ethiopian Airlines
	ET-ALZ	Boeing 757-231	Ethiopian Airlines
	ET-AME	Boeing 767-306ER	Ethiopian Airlines
	ET-AMF	Boeing 767-3BGER	Ethiopian Airlines
	ET-AMG	Boeing 767-3BGER	Ethiopian Airlines
	ET-AMK	Boeing 757-28A	Ethiopian Airlines
	ET-AML	McD Douglas MD-11F	Ethiopian Airlines
	ET-AMQ	Boeing 767-33AER	Ethiopian Airlines
	ET-AMT	Boeing 757-23N	Ethiopian Airlines
	ET-AMU	Boeing 757-23N	Ethiopian Airlines
	ET-AND	McD Douglas MD-11F	Ethiopian Airlines
	ET-ANU	Boeing 767-3Q8ER	Ethiopian Airlines
	ET-AQG	Boeing 767-306ER	Ethiopian Airlines

EW (Belarus)

	EW-100PJ	Canadair CRJ200LR	Belavia
	EW-250PA	Boeing 737-524	Belavia
	EW-251PA	Boeing 737-5Q8	Belavia
	EW-252PA	Boeing 737-524	Belavia
	EW-253PA	Boeing 737-524	Belavia
	EW-254PA	Boeing 737-3Q8	Belavia
	EW-276PJ	Canadair CRJ200ER	Belavia
	EW-277PJ	Canadair CRJ200ER	Belavia
	EW-282PA	Boeing 737-3Q8	Belavia
	EW-283PA	Boeing 737-3Q8	Belavia
	EW-290PA	Boeing 737-5Q8	Belavia
	EW-294PA	Boeing 737-505	Belavia
	EW-303PJ	Canadair CRJ200LR	Belavia
	EW-308PA	Boeing 737-3K2	Belavia
	EW-336PA	Boeing 737-3Q8	Belavia
	EW-340PO	Embraer ERJ170-200LR	Belavia
	EW-341PO	Embraer ERJ170-200LR	Belavia

EZ (Turkmenistan)

	EZ-A010	Boeing 757-23A	Turkmenistan Airlines
	EZ-A011	Boeing 757-22K	Turkmenistan Airlines
	EZ-A012	Boeing 757-22K	Turkmenistan Airlines
	EZ-A014	Boeing 757-22K	Turkmenistan Airlines

F (France)

	F-GEXB	Boeing 747-4B3	Air France Cargo
	F-GFKH	Airbus A.320-211	Air France *Ville de Bruxelles*
	F-GFKJ	Airbus A.320-211	Air France *Pays de Roissy*
	F-GFKR	Airbus A.320-211	Air France *Ville de Barceloune*
	F-GFKS	Airbus A.320-211	Air France *Ville de Marseilles*
	F-GFKV	Airbus A.320-211	Air France *Ville de Bordeaux*
	F-GFKY	Airbus A.320-211	Air France *Ville de Toulouse*

Reg.	Type	Owner or Operator	Notes
F-GHQE	Airbus A.320-211	Air France	
F-GHQG	Airbus A.320-211	Air France	
F-GHQJ	Airbus A.320-211	Air France	
F-GHQK	Airbus A.320-211	Air France	
F-GHQL	Airbus A.320-211	Air France	
F-GHQM	Airbus A.320-211	Air France	
F-GHQO	Airbus A.320-211	Air France	
F-GHQP	Airbus A.320-211	Air France	
F-GHQQ	Airbus A.320-211	Air France	
F-GISC	Boeing 747-428	Air France	
F-GITD	Boeing 747-428	Air France	
F-GITE	Boeing 747-428	Air France	
F-GITF	Boeing 747-428	Air France	
F-GITH	Boeing 747-428	Air France	
F-GITI	Boeing 747-428	Air France	
F-GITJ	Boeing 747-428	Air France	
F-GIUA	Boeing 747-428ERF (SCD)	Air France Cargo	
F-GIUC	Boeing 747-428ERF (SCD)	Air France Cargo	
F-GIUD	Boeing 747-428ERF (SCD)	Air France Cargo	
F-GJVB	Airbus A.320-211	Air France	
F-GJVF	Airbus A.320-211	Aigle Azur	
F-GJVG	Airbus A.320-211	Air France	
F-GJVW	Airbus A.320-211	Air France	
F-GKHK	Airbus A.320-212	XL Airways France	
F-GKXA	Airbus A.320-211	Air France	
F-GKXC	Airbus A.320-214	Air France	
F-GKXD	Airbus A.320-214	Air France	
F-GKXE	Airbus A.320-214	Air France	
F-GKXF	Airbus A.320-214	Air France	
F-GKXG	Airbus A.320-214	Air France	
F-GKXH	Airbus A.320-214	Air France	
F-GKXI	Airbus A.320-214	Air France	
F-GKXJ	Airbus A.320-214	Air France	
F-GKXK	Airbus A.320-214	Air France	
F-GKXL	Airbus A.320-214	Air France	
F-GKXM	Airbus A.320-214	Air France	
F-GKXN	Airbus A.320-214	Air France	
F-GKXO	Airbus A.320-214	Air France	
F-GKXP	Airbus A.320-214	Air France	
F-GKXQ	Airbus A.320-214	Air France	
F-GKXR	Airbus A.320-214	Air France	
F-GKXS	Airbus A.320-214	Air France	
F-GKXT	Airbus A.320-214	Air France	
F-GKXU	Airbus A.320-214	Air France	
F-GKXV	Airbus A.320-214	Air France	
F-GKXY	Airbus A.320-214	Air France	
F-GKXZ	Airbus A.320-214	Air France	
F-GLZC	Airbus A.340-312	Air France	
F-GLZH	Airbus A.340-312	Air France	
F-GLZI	Airbus A.340-312	Air France	
F-GLZJ	Airbus A.340-313X	Air France	
F-GLZK	Airbus A.340-313X	Air France	
F-GLZL	Airbus A.340-313X	Air France	
F-GLZM	Airbus A.340-313X	Air France	
F-GLZN	Airbus A.340-313X	Air France	
F-GLZO	Airbus A.340-313X	Air France	
F-GLZP	Airbus A.340-313X	Air France	
F-GLZR	Airbus A.340-313X	Air France	
F-GLZS	Airbus A.340-313X	Air France	
F-GLZU	Airbus A.340-313X	Air France	
F-GMZA	Airbus A.321-111	Air France	
F-GMZB	Airbus A.321-111	Air France	
F-GMZC	Airbus A.321-111	Air France	
F-GMZD	Airbus A.321-111	Air France	
F-GMZE	Airbus A.321-111	Air France	
F-GNII	Airbus A.340-313X	Air France	
F-GPEK	Boeing 757-236	Open Skies	
F-GPMA	Airbus A.319-113	Air France	
F-GPMB	Airbus A.319-113	Air France	
F-GPMC	Airbus A.319-113	Air France	
F-GPMD	Airbus A.319-113	Air France	
F-GPME	Airbus A.319-113	Air France	

F

Notes	Reg.	Type	Owner or Operator
	F-GPMF	Airbus A.319-113	Air France
	F-GRGA	Embraer RJ145EU	Regional Airlines/Air France
	F-GRGB	Embraer RJ145EU	Regional Airlines/Air France
	F-GRGC	Embraer RJ145EU	Regional Airlines/Air France
	F-GRGD	Embraer RJ145EU	Regional Airlines/Air France
	F-GRGE	Embraer RJ145EU	Regional Airlines/Air France
	F-GRGF	Embraer RJ145EU	Regional Airlines/Air France
	F-GRGG	Embraer RJ145EU	Regional Airlines/Air France
	F-GRGH	Embraer RJ145EU	Regional Airlines/Air France
	F-GRGI	Embraer RJ145EU	Regional Airlines/Air France
	F-GRGJ	Embraer RJ145EU	Regional Airlines/Air France
	F-GRGK	Embraer RJ145EU	Regional Airlines/Air France
	F-GRGL	Embraer RJ145EU	Regional Airlines/Air France
	F-GRGM	Embraer RJ145EU	Regional Airlines/Air France
	F-GRHA	Airbus A.319-111	Air France
	F-GRHB	Airbus A.319-111	Air France
	F-GRHC	Airbus A.319-111	Air France
	F-GRHD	Airbus A.319-111	Air France
	F-GRHE	Airbus A.319-111	Air France
	F-GRHF	Airbus A.319-111	Air France
	F-GRHG	Airbus A.319-111	Air France
	F-GRHH	Airbus A.319-111	Air France
	F-GRHI	Airbus A.319-111	Air France
	F-GRHJ	Airbus A.319-111	Air France
	F-GRHK	Airbus A.319-111	Air France
	F-GRHL	Airbus A.319-111	Air France
	F-GRHM	Airbus A.319-111	Air France
	F-GRHN	Airbus A.319-111	Air France
	F-GRHO	Airbus A.319-111	Air France
	F-GRHP	Airbus A.319-111	Air France
	F-GRHQ	Airbus A.319-111	Air France
	F-GRHR	Airbus A.319-111	Air France
	F-GRHS	Airbus A.319-111	Air France
	F-GRHT	Airbus A.319-111	Air France
	F-GRHU	Airbus A.319-111	Air France
	F-GRHV	Airbus A.319-111	Air France
	F-GRHX	Airbus A.319-111	Air France
	F-GRHY	Airbus A.319-111	Air France
	F-GRHZ	Airbus A.319-111	Air France
	F-GRJG	Canadair CRJ100ER	Brit Air/Air France
	F-GRJJ	Canadair CRJ100ER	Brit Air/Air France
	F-GRJK	Canadair CRJ100ER	Brit Air/Air France
	F-GRJL	Canadair CRJ100ER	Brit Air/Air France
	F-GRJM	Canadair CRJ100ER	Brit Air/Air France
	F-GRJN	Canadair CRJ100ER	Brit Air/Air France
	F-GRJO	Canadair CRJ100ER	Brit Air/Air France
	F-GRJP	Canadair CRJ100ER	Brit Air/Air France
	F-GRJQ	Canadair CRJ100ER	Brit Air/Air France
	F-GRJR	Canadair CRJ100ER	Brit Air/Air France
	F-GRJT	Canadair CRJ100ER	Brit Air/Air France
	F-GRJU	Canadair CRJ100ER	Brit Air/Air France
	F-GRSQ	Airbus A.330-243	XL Airways France
	F-GRXA	Airbus A.319-111	Air France
	F-GRXB	Airbus A.319-111	Air France
	F-GRXC	Airbus A.319-111	Air France
	F-GRXD	Airbus A.319-111	Air France
	F-GRXE	Airbus A.319-111	Air France
	F-GRXF	Airbus A.319-111	Air France
	F-GRXJ	Airbus A.319-115LR	Air France
	F-GRXK	Airbus A.319-115LR	Air France
	F-GRXL	Airbus A.319-111	Air France
	F-GRXM	Airbus A.319-111	Air France
	F-GRZA	Canadair CRJ700	Brit Air/Air France
	F-GRZB	Canadair CRJ700	Brit Air/Air France
	F-GRZC	Canadair CRJ700	Brit Air/Air France
	F-GRZD	Canadair CRJ700	Brit Air/Air France
	F-GRZE	Canadair CRJ700	Brit Air/Air France
	F-GRZF	Canadair CRJ700	Brit Air/Air France
	F-GRZG	Canadair CRJ700	Brit Air/Air France
	F-GRZH	Canadair CRJ700	Brit Air/Air France
	F-GRZI	Canadair CRJ700	Brit Air/Air France
	F-GRZJ	Canadair CRJ700	Brit Air/Air France

Reg.	Type	Owner or Operator	Notes
F-GRZK	Canadair CRJ700	Brit Air/Air France	
F-GRZL	Canadair CRJ700	Brit Air/Air France	
F-GRZM	Canadair CRJ700	Brit Air/Air France	
F-GRZN	Canadair CRJ700	Brit Air/Air France	
F-GRZO	Canadair CRJ700	Brit Air/Air France	
F-GSEU	Airbus A.330-243	XL Airways France	
F-GSPA	Boeing 777-228ER	Air France	
F-GSPB	Boeing 777-228ER	Air France	
F-GSPC	Boeing 777-228ER	Air France	
F-GSPD	Boeing 777-228ER	Air France	
F-GSPE	Boeing 777-228ER	Air France	
F-GSPF	Boeing 777-228ER	Air France	
F-GSPG	Boeing 777-228ER	Air France	
F-GSPH	Boeing 777-228ER	Air France	
F-GSPI	Boeing 777-228ER	Air France	
F-GSPJ	Boeing 777-228ER	Air France	
F-GSPK	Boeing 777-228ER	Air France	
F-GSPL	Boeing 777-228ER	Air France	
F-GSPM	Boeing 777-228ER	Air France	
F-GSPN	Boeing 777-228ER	Air France	
F-GSPO	Boeing 777-228ER	Air France	
F-GSPP	Boeing 777-228ER	Air France	
F-GSPQ	Boeing 777-228ER	Air France	
F-GSPR	Boeing 777-228ER	Air France	
F-GSPS	Boeing 777-228ER	Air France	
F-GSPT	Boeing 777-228ER	Air France	
F-GSPU	Boeing 777-228ER	Air France	
F-GSPV	Boeing 777-228ER	Air France	
F-GSPX	Boeing 777-228ER	Air France	
F-GSPY	Boeing 777-228ER	Air France	
F-GSPZ	Boeing 777-228ER	Air France	
F-GSQA	Boeing 777-328ER	Air France	
F-GSQB	Boeing 777-328ER	Air France	
F-GSQC	Boeing 777-328ER	Air France	
F-GSQD	Boeing 777-328ER	Air France	
F-GSQE	Boeing 777-328ER	Air France	
F-GSQF	Boeing 777-328ER	Air France	
F-GSQG	Boeing 777-328ER	Air France	
F-GSQH	Boeing 777-328ER	Air France	
F-GSQI	Boeing 777-328ER	Air France	
F-GSQJ	Boeing 777-328ER	Air France	
F-GSQK	Boeing 777-328ER	Air France	
F-GSQL	Boeing 777-328ER	Air France	
F-GSQM	Boeing 777-328ER	Air France	
F-GSQN	Boeing 777-328ER	Air France	
F-GSQO	Boeing 777-328ER	Air France	
F-GSQP	Boeing 777-328ER	Air France	
F-GSQR	Boeing 777-328ER	Air France	
F-GSQS	Boeing 777-328ER	Air France	
F-GSQT	Boeing 777-328ER	Air France	
F-GSQU	Boeing 777-328ER	Air France	
F-GSQV	Boeing 777-328ER	Air France	
F-GSQX	Boeing 777-328ER	Air France	
F-GSQY	Boeing 777-328ER	Air France	
F-GSTA	Airbus A.300-608ST Beluga (1)	Airbus Transport International	
F-GSTB	Airbus A.300-608ST Beluga (2)	Airbus Transport International	
F-GSTC	Airbus A.300-608ST Beluga (3)	Airbus Transport International	
F-GSTD	Airbus A.300-608ST Beluga (4)	Airbus Transport International	
F-GSTF	Airbus A.300-608ST Beluga (5)	Airbus Transport International	
F-GTAD	Airbus A.321-211	Air France	
F-GTAE	Airbus A.321-211	Air France	
F-GTAH	Airbus A.321-211	Air France	
F-GTAI	Airbus A.321-211	Air France	
F-GTAJ	Airbus A.321-211	Air France	
F-GTAK	Airbus A.321-211	Air France	
F-GTAL	Airbus A.321-211	Air France	
F-GTAM	Airbus A.321-211	Air France	
F-GTAN	Airbus A.321-211	Air France	
F-GTAO	Airbus A.321-211	Air France	
F-GTAP	Airbus A.321-212	Air France	
F-GTAQ	Airbus A.321-211	Air France	
F-GTAR	Airbus A.321-211	Air France	

Notes	Reg.	Type	Owner or Operator
	F-GTAS	Airbus A.321-211	Air France
	F-GTAT	Airbus A.321-211	Air France
	F-GTAU	Airbus A.321-211	Air France
	F-GTAV	Airbus A.321-211	Air France
	F-GTAX	Airbus A.321-211	Air France
	F-GTAY	Airbus A.321-211	Air France
	F-GTAZ	Airbus A.321-211	Air France
	F-GTUI	Boeing 747-422	Corsair
	F-GUAA	Airbus A.321-211	Aigle Azur
	F-GUAM	Embraer RJ145MP	Regional Airlines/Air France
	F-GUBC	Embraer RJ145MP	Regional Airlines/Air France
	F-GUBD	Embraer RJ145MP	Regional Airlines/Air France
	F-GUBE	Embraer RJ145MP	Regional Airlines/Air France
	F-GUBF	Embraer RJ145MP	Regional Airlines/Air France
	F-GUBG	Embraer RJ145MP	Regional Airlines/Air France
	F-GUEA	Embraer RJ145MP	Regional Airlines/Air France
	F-GUFD	Embraer RJ145MP	Regional Airlines/Air France
	F-GUGA	Airbus A.318-111	Air France
	F-GUGB	Airbus A.318-111	Air France
	F-GUGC	Airbus A.318-111	Air France
	F-GUGD	Airbus A.318-111	Air France
	F-GUGE	Airbus A.318-111	Air France
	F-GUGF	Airbus A.318-111	Air France
	F-GUGG	Airbus A.318-111	Air France
	F-GUGH	Airbus A.318-111	Air France
	F-GUGI	Airbus A.318-111	Air France
	F-GUGJ	Airbus A.318-111	Air France
	F-GUGK	Airbus A.318-111	Air France
	F-GUGL	Airbus A.318-111	Air France
	F-GUGM	Airbus A.318-111	Air France
	F-GUGN	Airbus A.318-111	Air France
	F-GUGO	Airbus A.318-111	Air France
	F-GUGP	Airbus A.318-111	Air France
	F-GUGQ	Airbus A.318-111	Air France
	F-GUGR	Airbus A.318-111	Air France
	F-GUOB	Boeing 777-F28	Air France Cargo
	F-GUOC	Boeing 777-F28	Air France Cargo
	F-GUPT	Embraer RJ145MP	Regional Airlines/Air France
	F-GVHD	Embraer RJ145MP	Regional Airlines/Air France
	F-GXAH	Airbus A.319-132	Aigle Azur
	F-GYAJ	Airbus A.321-211	Air Mediterranée
	F-GYAN	Airbus A.321-111	Air Mediterranée
	F-GYAP	Airbus A.321-111	Air Mediterranée
	F-GYAQ	Airbus A.321-211	Air Mediterranée
	F-GYAR	Airbus A.321-211	Air Mediterranée
	F-GYAZ	Airbus A.321-111	Air Mediterranée
	F-GZCA	Airbus A.330-203	Air France
	F-GZCB	Airbus A.330-203	Air France
	F-GZCC	Airbus A.330-203	Air France
	F-GZCD	Airbus A.330-203	Air France
	F-GZCE	Airbus A.330-203	Air France
	F-GZCF	Airbus A.330-203	Air France
	F-GZCG	Airbus A.330-203	Air France
	F-GZCH	Airbus A.330-203	Air France
	F-GZCI	Airbus A.330-203	Air France
	F-GZCJ	Airbus A.330-203	Air France
	F-GZCK	Airbus A.330-203	Air France
	F-GZCL	Airbus A.330-203	Air France
	F-GZCM	Airbus A.330-203	Air France
	F-GZCN	Airbus A.330-203	Air France
	F-GZCO	Airbus A.330-203	Air France
	F-GZHA	Boeing 737-8GJ	Transavia France
	F-GZHB	Boeing 737-8GJ	Transavia France
	F-GZHC	Boeing 737-8GJ	Transavia France
	F-GZHD	Boeing 737-8K2	Transavia France
	F-GZHE	Boeing 737-8K2	Transavia France
	F-GZHF	Boeing 737-8HX	Transavia France
	F-GZHN	Boeing 737-8K2	Transavia France
	F-GZHV	Boeing 737-85H	Transavia France
	F-GZNA	Boeing 777-328ER	Air France
	F-GZNB	Boeing 777-328ER	Air France
	F-GZNC	Boeing 777-328ER	Air France

Reg.	Type	Owner or Operator	Notes
F-GZND	Boeing 777-328ER	Air France	
F-GZNE	Boeing 777-328ER	Air France	
F-GZNF	Boeing 777-328ER	Air France	
F-GZNG	Boeing 777-328ER	Air France	
F-GZNH	Boeing 777-328ER	Air France	
F-GZNI	Boeing 777-328ER	Air France	
F-GZNJ	Boeing 777-328ER	Air France	
F-GZNK	Boeing 777-328ER	Air France	
F-GZNL	Boeing 777-328ER	Air France	
F-GZNN	Boeing 777-328ER	Air France	
F-GZNO	Boeing 777-328ER	Air France	
F-HAVI	Boeing 757-26D	Open Skies *Violette*	
F-HAVN	Boeing 757-230	Open Skies	
F-HAXL	Boeing 737-8Q8	XL Airways France	
F-HBAB	Airbus A.321-211	Aigle Azur	
F-HBAF	Airbus A.321-211	Aigle Azur	
F-HBAL	Airbus A.319-111	Aigle Azur	
F-HBAO	Airbus A.320-214	Aigle Azur	
F-HBAP	Airbus A.320-214	Aigle Azur	
F-HBII	Airbus A.320-214	Aigle Azur	
F-HBIL	Airbus A.330-243	Corsair	
F-HBLA	Embraer RJ190-100LR	Regional Airlines/Air France	
F-HBLB	Embraer RJ190-100LR	Regional Airlines/Air France	
F-HBLC	Embraer RJ190-100LR	Regional Airlines/Air France	
F-HBLD	Embraer RJ190-100LR	Regional Airlines/Air France	
F-HBLE	Embraer RJ190-100LR	Regional Airlines/Air France	
F-HBLF	Embraer RJ190-100LR	Regional Airlines/Air France	
F-HBLG	Embraer RJ190-100LR	Regional Airlines/Air France	
F-HBLH	Embraer RJ190-100LR	Regional Airlines/Air France	
F-HBLI	Embraer RJ190-100LR	Regional Airlines/Air France	
F-HBLJ	Embraer RJ190-100LR	Regional Airlines/Air France	
F-HBMI	Airbus A.319-114	Aigle Azur	
F-HBNA	Airbus A.320-214	Air France	
F-HBNB	Airbus A.320-214	Air France	
F-HBNC	Airbus A.320-214	Air France	
F-HBND	Airbus A.320-214	Air France	
F-HBNE	Airbus A.320-214	Air France	
F-HBNF	Airbus A.320-214	Air France	
F-HBNG	Airbus A.320-214	Air France	
F-HBNH	Airbus A.320-214	Air France	
F-HBNI	Airbus A.320-214	Air France	
F-HBNJ	Airbus A.320-214	Air France	
F-HBNK	Airbus A.320-214	Air France	
F-HBNL	Airbus A.320-214	Air France	
F-HBNM	Airbus A.320-214	Air France	
F-HBNN	Airbus A.320-214	Air France	
F-HBXA	Embraer RJ170-100LR	Regional Airlines/Air France	
F-HBXB	Embraer RJ170-100LR	Regional Airlines/Air France	
F-HBXC	Embraer RJ170-100LR	Regional Airlines/Air France	
F-HBXD	Embraer RJ170-100LR	Regional Airlines/Air France	
F-HBXE	Embraer RJ170-100LR	Regional Airlines/Air France	
F-HBXF	Embraer RJ170-100LR	Regional Airlines/Air France	
F-HBXG	Embraer RJ170-100LR	Regional Airlines/Air France	
F-HBXH	Embraer RJ170-100LR	Regional Airlines/Air France	
F-HBXI	Embraer RJ170-100LR	Regional Airlines/Air France	
F-HBXJ	Embraer RJ170-100LR	Regional Airlines/Air France	
F-HBXK	Embraer RJ170-100LR	Regional Airlines/Air France	
F-HBXL	Embraer RJ170-100LR	Regional Airlines/Air France	
F-HBXM	Embraer RJ170-100LR	Regional Airlines/Air France	
F-HBXN	Embraer RJ170-100LR	Regional Airlines/Air France	
F-HBXO	Embraer RJ170-100LR	Regional Airlines/Air France	
F-HBXP	Embraer RJ170-100LR	Regional Airlines/Air France	
F-HCAI	Airbus A.321-111	Aigle Azur	
F-HCAT	Airbus A.330-243	Corsair	
F-HCOA	Boeing 737-5L9	Air Mediterranee	
F-HCZI	Airbus A.319-112	Aigle Azur	
F-HEPA	Airbus A.320-214	Air France	
F-HEPB	Airbus A.320-214	Air France	
F-HEPC	Airbus A.320-214	Air France	
F-HEPD	Airbus A.320-214	Air France	
F-HEPE	Airbus A.320-214	Air France ✓	
F-HJER	Boeing 737-86N	XL Airways France	

Notes	Reg.	Type	Owner or Operator
	F-HJUL	Boeing 737-8Q8	XL Airways France
	F-HKIS	Boeing 747-422	Corsair
	F-HLOV	Boeing 747-422	Corsair
	F-HMLA	Canadair CRJ1000	Brit Air/Air France
	F-HMLC	Canadair CRJ1000	Brit Air/Air France
	F-HMLD	Canadair CRJ1000	Brit Air/Air France
	F-HMLE	Canadair CRJ1000	Brit Air/Air France
	F-HMLF	Canadair CRJ1000	Brit Air/Air France
	F-HMLG	Canadair CRJ1000	Brit Air/Air France
	F-HMLH	Canadair CRJ1000	Brit Air/Air France
	F-HMLI	Canadair CRJ1000	Brit Air/Air France
	F-HMLJ	Canadair CRJ1000	Brit Air/Air France
	F-HMLK	Canadair CRJ1000	Brit Air/Air France
	F-HMLL	Canadair CRJ1000	Brit Air/Air France
	F-HMLM	Canadair CRJ1000	Brit Air/Air France
	F-HMLN	Canadair CRJ1000	Brit Air/Air France
	F-HPJA	Airbus A.380-861	Air France
	F-HPJB	Airbus A.380-861	Air France
	F-HPJC	Airbus A.380-861	Air France
	F-HPJD	Airbus A.380-861	Air France
	F-HPJE	Airbus A.380-861	Air France
	F-HPJF	Airbus A.380-861	Air France
	F-HPJG	Airbus A.380-861	Air France
	F-HPJH	Airbus A.380-861	Air France
	F-HPJI	Airbus A.380-861	Air France
	F-HPJJ	Airbus A.380-861	Air France
	F-HPJK	Airbus A.380-861	Air France
	F-HSEA	Boeing 747-422	Corsair
	F-HSKY	Airbus A.330-343	Corsair
	F-HSUN	Boeing 747-422	Corsair
	F-HXLF	Airbus A.330-303	XL Airways France
	F-OHGV	Airbus A.320-232	Royal Jordanian *Irbid*
	F-OHGX	Airbus A.320-232	Royal Jordanian *Madaba*
	F-OMRA	Airbus A.320-214	Middle East Airlines
	F-OMRB	Airbus A.320-214	Middle East Airlines
	F-OMRC	Airbus A.320-214	Middle East Airlines
	F-OMRN	Airbus A.320-232	Middle East Airlines
	F-OMRO	Airbus A.320-232	Middle East Airlines
	F-ORAD	Airbus A.320-233	Belle Air
	F-ORAE	Airbus A.320-233	Belle Air
	F-ORAG	Airbus A.319-132	Belle Air
	F-ORAH	Airbus A.319-132	Belle Air
	F-ORMA	Airbus A.330-243	Middle East Airlines
	F-ORMG	Airbus A.321-231	Middle East Airlines

HA (Hungary)

	HA-LKE	Boeing 737-86Q	Travel Service Airlines
	HA-LPD	Airbus A.320-233	Wizz Air
	HA-LPE	Airbus A.320-233	Wizz Air
	HA-LPF	Airbus A.320-233	Wizz Air
	HA-LPI	Airbus A.320-233	Wizz Air
	HA-LPJ	Airbus A.320-232	Wizz Air
	HA-LPK	Airbus A.320-231	Wizz Air
	HA-LPL	Airbus A.320-232	Wizz Air
	HA-LPM	Airbus A.320-232	Wizz Air
	HA-LPN	Airbus A.320-232	Wizz Air
	HA-LPO	Airbus A.320-232	Wizz Air
	HA-LPQ	Airbus A.320-232	Wizz Air
	HA-LPR	Airbus A.320-232	Wizz Air
	HA-LPS	Airbus A.320-232	Wizz Air
	HA-LPT	Airbus A.320-232	Wizz Air
	HA-LPU	Airbus A.320-232	Wizz Air
	HA-LPV	Airbus A.320-232	Wizz Air
	HA-LPW	Airbus A.320-232	Wizz Air
	HA-LPX	Airbus A.320-232	Wizz Air
	HA-LPY	Airbus A.320-232	Wizz Air
	HA-LPZ	Airbus A.320-232	Wizz Air
	HA-LWA	Airbus A.320-232	Wizz Air
	HA-LWB	Airbus A.320-232	Wizz Air
	HA-LWC	Airbus A.320-232	Wizz Air

Reg.	Type	Owner or Operator	Notes
HA-LWD	Airbus A.320-232	Wizz Air	
HA-LWE	Airbus A.320-232	Wizz Air	
HA-LWF	Airbus A.320-232	Wizz Air	
HA-LWG	Airbus A.320-232	Wizz Air	
HA-LWH	Airbus A.320-232	Wizz Air	
HA-LWI	Airbus A.320-214	Wizz Air	
HA-LWJ	Airbus A.320-214	Wizz Air	
HA-LWK	Airbus A.320-232	Wizz Air	
HA-LWL	Airbus A.320-232	Wizz Air	
HA-LWM	Airbus A.320-232	Wizz Air	
HA-LWN	Airbus A.320-232	Wizz Air	
HA-LWO	Airbus A.320-232	Wizz Air	
HA-LWP	Airbus A.320-232	Wizz Air	
HA-LWQ	Airbus A.320-232	Wizz Air	

HB (Switzerland)

Reg.	Type	Owner or Operator	Notes
HB-AEO	Dornier Do.328-110	Sky Work Airlines	
HB-AER	Dornier Do.328-110	Sky Work Airlines	
HB-AES	Dornier Do.328-110	Sky Work Airlines	
HB-AEV	Dornier Do.328-110	Sky Work Airlines	
HB-AEY	Dornier Do.328-130	Sky Work Airlines	
HB-IHX	Airbus A.320-214	Edelweiss Air *Calvaro*	
HB-IHY	Airbus A.320-214	Edelweiss Air *Upali*	
HB-IHZ	Airbus A.320-214	Edelweiss Air *Viktoria*	
HB-IJB	Airbus A.320-214	Swiss International *Embrach*	
HB-IJD	Airbus A.320-214	Swiss International	
HB-IJE	Airbus A.320-214	Swiss International *Arosa*	
HB-IJF	Airbus A.320-214	Swiss International	
HB-IJH	Airbus A.320-214	Swiss International	
HB-IJI	Airbus A.320-214	Swiss International *Basodino*	
HB-IJJ	Airbus A.320-214	Swiss International *Les Diablerets*	
HB-IJK	Airbus A.320-214	Swiss International *Wissigstock*	
HB-IJL	Airbus A.320-214	Swiss International *Pizol*	
HB-IJM	Airbus A.320-214	Swiss International *Schilthorn*	
HB-IJN	Airbus A.320-214	Swiss International *Vanil Noir*	
HB-IJO	Airbus A.320-214	Swiss International *Lissengrat*	
HB-IJP	Airbus A.320-214	Swiss International *Nollen*	
HB-IJQ	Airbus A.320-214	Swiss International *Agassizhorn*	
HB-IJR	Airbus A.320-214	Swiss International *Dammastock*	
HB-IJS	Airbus A.320-214	Swiss International *Creux du Van*	
HB-IJU	Airbus A.320-214	Swiss International *Bietschhorn*	
HB-IJV	Airbus A.320-214	Edelweiss Air	
HB-IJW	Airbus A.320-214	Swiss International *Bachtel*	
HB-IJX	Airbus A.320-214	Swiss International *Davos*	
HB-IOC	Airbus A.321-111	Swiss International *Eiger*	
HB-IOD	Airbus A.321-111	Swiss International	
HB-IOF	Airbus A.321-111	Swiss International	
HB-IOH	Airbus A.321-111	Swiss International *Piz Palu*	
HB-IOK	Airbus A.321-111	Swiss International *Biefertenstock*	
HB-IOL	Airbus A.321-111	Swiss International *Kaiseregg*	
HB-IOM	Airbus A.321-212	Swiss International	
HB-IOP	Airbus A.320-214	Air Berlin/Belair	
HB-IOQ	Airbus A.320-214	Air Berlin/Belair	
HB-IOR	Airbus A.320-214	Air Berlin/Belair	
HB-IOS	Airbus A.320-214	Air Berlin/Belair	
HB-IOW	Airbus A.320-214	Air Berlin/Belair	
HB-IOX	Airbus A.319-112	Air Berlin/Belair	
HB-IOZ	Airbus A.320-214	Air Berlin/Belair	
HB-IPR	Airbus A.319-112	Swiss International *Commune de Champagne*	
HB-IPS	Airbus A.319-112	Swiss International *Weiach*	
HB-IPT	Airbus A.319-112	Swiss International *Stadel*	
HB-IPU	Airbus A.319-112	Swiss International *Hochfelden*	
HB-IPV	Airbus A.319-112	Swiss International *Rumlang*	
HB-IPX	Airbus A.319-112	Swiss International *Steinmaur*	
HB-IPY	Airbus A.319-112	Swiss International *Hori*	
HB-IQI	Airbus A.330-223	Edelweiss Air *Kiburi*	
HB-IXN	Avro RJ100	Swiss European Airlines *Balmhorn 3699m*	
HB-IXO	Avro RJ100	Swiss European Airlines *Brisen 2404m*	
HB-IXP	Avro RJ100	Swiss European Airlines *Chestenberg 647m*	
HB-IXQ	Avro RJ100	Swiss European Airlines *Corno Gries 2969m*	

Notes	Reg.	Type	Owner or Operator
	HB-IXR	Avro RJ100	Swiss European Airlines *Hoho Winde 1204m*
	HB-IXS	Avro RJ100	Swiss European Airlines *Mont Velan 3731m*
	HB-IXT	Avro RJ100	Swiss European Airlines *Ottenberg 681m*
	HB-IXU	Avro RJ100	Swiss European Airlines *Pfannenstiel 853m*
	HB-IXV	Avro RJ100	Swiss European Airlines *Saxer First 2151m*
	HB-IXW	Avro RJ100	Swiss European Airlines *Shafarnisch 2107m*
	HB-IXX	Avro RJ100	Swiss European Airlines *Silberen 2319m*
	HB-IYQ	Avro RJ100	Swiss European Airlines *Piz Buin 3312m*
	HB-IYR	Avro RJ100	Swiss European Airlines *Vrenelisgärtli 2904m*
	HB-IYS	Avro RJ100	Swiss European Airlines *Churfirsten 2306m*
	HB-IYT	Avro RJ100	Swiss European Airlines *Bluemlisalp 3663m*
	HB-IYU	Avro RJ100	Swiss European Airlines *Rot Turm 2002m*
	HB-IYV	Avro RJ100	Swiss European Airlines *Pizzo Barone 2864m*
	HB-IYW	Avro RJ100	Swiss European Airlines *Spitzmeilen 2501m*
	HB-IYY	Avro RJ100	Swiss European Airlines *Titlis 3238m*
	HB-IYZ	Avro RJ100	Swiss European Airlines *Tour d'Ai 2331m*
	HB-JGA	DHC.8Q-402 Dash Eight	Sky Work Airlines
	HB-JHA	Airbus A.330-343	Swiss International
	HB-JHB	Airbus A.330-343	Swiss International *Sion*
	HB-JHC	Airbus A.330-343	Swiss International *Bellinzona*
	HB-JHD	Airbus A.330-343	Swiss International *St.Gallen*
	HB-JHE	Airbus A.330-343	Swiss International *Fribourg*
	HB-JHF	Airbus A.330-343	Swiss International
	HB-JHG	Airbus A.330-343	Swiss International *Glarus*
	HB-JHH	Airbus A.330-343	Swiss International *Neuchatel*
	HB-JHI	Airbus A.330-343	Swiss International *Geneve*
	HB-JHJ	Airbus A.330-343	Swiss International *Appenzell*
	HB-JHK	Airbus A.330-343	Swiss International
	HB-JHL	Airbus A.330-343	Swiss International
	HB-JHM	Airbus A.330-343	Swiss International
	HB-JHQ	Airbus A.330-343	Edelweiss Air *Chamsin*
	HB-JIJ	DHC.8Q-402 Dash Eight	Sky Work Airlines
	HB-JIK	DHC.8Q-402 Dash Eight	Sky Work Airlines
	HB-JLP	Airbus A.320-214	Swiss International *Allschwil*
	HB-JLQ	Airbus A.320-214	Swiss International *Bllach*
	HB-JLR	Airbus A.320-214	Swiss International
	HB-JLS	Airbus A.320-214	Swiss International
	HB-JMA	Airbus A.340-313X	Swiss International *Matterhorn*
	HB-JMB	Airbus A.340-313X	Swiss International *Zurich*
	HB-JMC	Airbus A.340-313X	Swiss International *Basel*
	HB-JMD	Airbus A.340-313X	Swiss International *Liestal*
	HB-JME	Airbus A.340-313X	Swiss International *Dom*
	HB-JMF	Airbus A.340-313X	Swiss International *Liskamm*
	HB-JMG	Airbus A.340-313X	Swiss International *Luzern*
	HB-JMH	Airbus A.340-313X	Swiss International *Chur*
	HB-JMI	Airbus A.340-313X	Swiss International *Schaffhausen*
	HB-JMJ	Airbus A.340-313X	Swiss International *City of Basel*
	HB-JMK	Airbus A.340-313X	Swiss International *Aarau*
	HB-JML	Airbus A.340-313X	Swiss International *Liestal*
	HB-JMM	Airbus A.340-313X	Swiss International
	HB-JMN	Airbus A.340-313X	Swiss International
	HB-JMO	Airbus A.340-313X	Swiss International
	HB-JOY	Airbus A.319-112	Air Berlin/Belair
	HB-JOZ	Airbus A.320-214	Air Berlin/Belair
	HB-JVC	Fokker 100	Helvetic Airways
	HB-JVE	Fokker 100	Helvetic Airways
	HB-JVF	Fokker 100	Helvetic Airways
	HB-JVG	Fokker 100	Helvetic Airways
	HB-JVH	Fokker 100	Helvetic Airways
	HB-JVI	Fokker 100	Helvetic Airways
	HB-JYA	Airbus A.320-214	easyJet Switzerland
	HB-JYB	Airbus A.319-111	easyJet Switzerland
	HB-JYC	Airbus A.319-111	easyJet Switzerland
	HB-JYD	Airbus A.320-214	easyJet Switzerland
	HB-JYE	Airbus A.320-214	easyJet Switzerland
	HB-JZF	Airbus A.319-111	easyJet Switzerland
	HB-JZI	Airbus A.319-111	easyJet Switzerland
	HB-JZJ	Airbus A.319-111	easyJet Switzerland
	HB-JZL	Airbus A.319-111	easyJet Switzerland
	HB-JZM	Airbus A.319-111	easyJet Switzerland
	HB-JZN	Airbus A.319-111	easyJet Switzerland
	HB-JZO	Airbus A.319-111	easyJet Switzerland

Reg.	Type	Owner or Operator	Notes
HB-JZP	Airbus A.319-111	easyJet Switzerland	
HB-JZQ	Airbus A.319-111	easyJet Switzerland	
HB-JZR	Airbus A.320-214	easyJet Switzerland	
HB-JZS	Airbus A.319-111	easyJet Switzerland	
HB-JZT	Airbus A.319-111	easyJet Switzerland	
HB-JZU	Airbus A.319-111	easyJet Switzerland	
HB-JZV	Airbus A.319-111	easyJet Switzerland	
HB-JZW	Airbus A.319-111	easyJet Switzerland	
HB-JZX	Airbus A.320-214	easyJet Switzerland	
HB-JZY	Airbus A.320-214	easyJet Switzerland	
HB-JZZ	Airbus A.320-214	easyJet Switzerland	

HL (Korea)

Reg.	Type	Owner or Operator	Notes
HL7400	Boeing 747-4B5F	Korean Air Cargo	
HL7402	Boeing 747-4B5	Korean Air	
HL7403	Boeing 747-4B5F	Korean Air Cargo	
HL7404	Boeing 747-4B5	Korean Air	
HL7413	Boeing 747-48EBCF	Asiana Airlines Cargo	
HL7414	Boeing 747-48EBCF	Asiana Airlines Cargo	
HL7415	Boeing 747-48EBCF	Asiana Airlines Cargo	
HL7417	Boeing 747-48EBCF	Asiana Airlines Cargo	
HL7419	Boeing 747-48EF (SCD)	Asiana Airlines Cargo	
HL7420	Boeing 747-48EF (SCD)	Asiana Airlines Cargo	
HL7434	Boeing 747-4B5F	Korean Air Cargo	
HL7436	Boeing 747-48EF (SCD)	Asiana Airlines Cargo	
HL7437	Boeing 747-4B5F	Korean Air Cargo	
HL7438	Boeing 747-4B5ERF	Korean Air Cargo	
HL7439	Boeing 747-4B5ERF	Korean Air Cargo	
HL7448	Boeing 747-4B5F (SCD)	Korean Air Cargo	
HL7449	Boeing 747-4B5F (SCD)	Korean Air Cargo	
HL7460	Boeing 747-4B5	Korean Air	
HL7461	Boeing 747-4B5	Korean Air	
HL7462	Boeing 747-4B5F	Korean Air Cargo	
HL7466	Boeing 747-4B5F	Korean Air Cargo	
HL7467	Boeing 747-4B5F	Korean Air Cargo	
HL7472	Boeing 747-4B5	Korean Air	
HL7473	Boeing 747-4B5	Korean Air	
HL7482	Boeing 747-4B5BCF	Korean Air Cargo	
HL7483	Boeing 747-4B5BCF	Korean Air Cargo	
HL7484	Boeing 747-4B5BCF	Korean Air Cargo	
HL7485	Boeing 747-4B5BCF	Korean Air Cargo	
HL7486	Boeing 747-4B5BCF	Korean Air Cargo	
HL7487	Boeing 747-4B5	Korean Air	
HL7489	Boeing 747-4B5	Korean Air	
HL7490	Boeing 747-4B5	Korean Air	
HL7491	Boeing 747-4B5	Korean Air	
HL7492	Boeing 747-4B5	Korean Air	
HL7493	Boeing 747-4B5	Korean Air	
HL7494	Boeing 747-4B5	Korean Air	
HL7495	Boeing 747-4B5	Korean Air	
HL7498	Boeing 747-4B5	Korean Air	
HL7499	Boeing 747-4B5ERF	Korean Air Cargo	
HL7500	Boeing 777-28EER	Asiana Airlines	
HL7526	Boeing 777-2B5ER	Korean Air	
HL7530	Boeing 777-2B5ER	Korean Air	
HL7531	Boeing 777-2B5ER	Korean Air	
HL7574	Boeing 777-2B5ER	Korean Air	
HL7575	Boeing 777-2B5ER	Korean Air	
HL7596	Boeing 777-28EER	Asiana Airlines	
HL7597	Boeing 777-28EER	Asiana Airlines	
HL7598	Boeing 777-2B5ER	Korean Air	
HL7600	Boeing 747-4B5ERF	Korean Air Cargo	
HL7601	Boeing 747-4B5ERF	Korean Air Cargo	
HL7602	Boeing 747-4B5ERF	Korean Air Cargo	
HL7603	Boeing 747-4B5ERF	Korean Air Cargo	
HL7605	Boeing 747-4B5ERF	Korean Air Cargo	
HL7608	Boeing 747-4B5BCF	Korean Air Cargo	
HL7616	Boeing 747-446F	Asiana Airlines Cargo	
HL7618	Boeing 747-446F	Asiana Airlines Cargo	
HL7620	Boeing 747-419F	Asiana Airlines Cargo	

Notes	Reg.	Type	Owner or Operator
	HL7700	Boeing 777-28EER	Asiana Airlines
	HL7714	Boeing 777-2B5ER	Korean Air
	HL7715	Boeing 777-2B5ER	Korean Air
	HL7721	Boeing 777-2B5ER	Korean Air
	HL7732	Boeing 777-28EER	Asiana Airlines
	HL7733	Boeing 777-2B5ER	Korean Air
	HL7734	Boeing 777-2B5ER	Korean Air
	HL7739	Boeing 777-28EER	Asiana Airlines
	HL7742	Boeing 777-28EER	Asiana Airlines
	HL7743	Boeing 777-2B5ER	Korean Air
	HL7750	Boeing 777-2B5ER	Korean Air
	HL7751	Boeing 777-2B5ER	Korean Air
	HL7752	Boeing 777-2B5ER	Korean Air
	HL7755	Boeing 777-28EER	Asiana Airlines
	HL7756	Boeing 777-28EER	Asiana Airlines
	HL7764	Boeing 777-2B5ER	Korean Air
	HL7765	Boeing 777-2B5ER	Korean Air
	HL7766	Boeing 777-2B5ER	Korean Air
	HL7775	Boeing 777-28EER	Asiana Airlines
	HL7782	Boeing 777-3B5ER	Korean Air
	HL7783	Boeing 777-3B5ER	Korean Air
	HL7784	Boeing 777-3B5ER	Korean Air
	HL7791	Boeing 777-28EER	Asiana Airlines
	HL8208	Boeing 777-3B5ER	Korean Air
	HL8209	Boeing 777-3B5ER	Korean Air
	HL8210	Boeing 777-3B5ER	Korean Air
	HL8216	Boeing 777-3B5ER	Korean Air
	HL8217	Boeing 777-3B5ER	Korean Air
	HL8218	Boeing 777-3B5ER	Korean Air
	HL8250	Boeing 777-3B5ER	Korean Air
	HL8251	Boeing 777-FB5	Korean Air Cargo
	HL8252	Boeing 777-FB5	Korean Air Cargo
	HL8254	Boeing 777-28EER	Asiana Airlines
	HL8274	Boeing 777-3B5ER	Korean Air
	HL8275	Boeing 777-3B5ER	Korean Air

HS (Thailand)

	HS-TGA	Boeing 747-4D7	Thai Airways International *Srisuriyothai*
	HS-TGB	Boeing 747-4D7	Thai Airways International *Si Satchanulai*
	HS-TGF	Boeing 747-4D7	Thai Airways International *Sri Ubon*
	HS-TGG	Boeing 747-4D7	Thai Airways International *Pathoomawadi*
	HS-TGK	Boeing 747-4D7	Thai Airways International *Alongkorn*
	HS-TGL	Boeing 747-4D7	Thai Airways International *Theparat*
	HS-TGM	Boeing 747-4D7	Thai Airways International
	HS-TGN	Boeing 747-4D7	Thai Airways International *Simongkhon*
	HS-TGO	Boeing 747-4D7	Thai Airways International *Bowonrangsi*
	HS-TGP	Boeing 747-4D7	Thai Airways International *Thepprasit*
	HS-TGR	Boeing 747-4D7	Thai Airways International *Siriwatthana*
	HS-TGT	Boeing 747-4D7	Thai Airways International *Watthanothai*
	HS-TGW	Boeing 747-4D7	Thai Airways International *Visuthakasatriya*
	HS-TGX	Boeing 747-4D7	Thai Airways International *Sirisobhakya*
	HS-TGY	Boeing 747-4D7	Thai Airways International *Dararasmi*
	HS-TGZ	Boeing 747-4D7	Thai Airways International *Phimara*
	HS-TLD	Airbus A.340-541	Thai Airways International
	HS-TNA	Airbus A.340-642	Thai Airways International *Watthana Nakhon*
	HS-TNB	Airbus A.340-642	Thai Airways International *Saraburi*
	HS-TNC	Airbus A.340-642	Thai Airways International *Chon Buri*
	HS-TND	Airbus A.340-642	Thai Airways International *Phetchaburi*
	HS-TNE	Airbus A.340-642	Thai Airways International *Nonthaburi*
	HS-TNF	Airbus A.340-642	Thai Airways International
	HS-TUA	Airbus A.380-841	Thai Airways International
	HS-TUB	Airbus A.380-841	Thai Airways International
	HS-TUC	Airbus A.380-841	Thai Airways International

HZ (Saudi Arabia)

	HZ-AK11	Boeing 777-368ER	Saudi Arabian Airlines
	HZ-AK12	Boeing 777-368ER	Saudi Arabian Airlines
	HZ-AK13	Boeing 777-368ER	Saudi Arabian Airlines

Reg.	Type	Owner or Operator	Notes
HZ-AK14	Boeing 777-368ER	Saudi Arabian Airlines	
HZ-AK15	Boeing 777-368ER	Saudi Arabian Airlines	
HZ-AK16	Boeing 777-368ER	Saudi Arabian Airlines	
HZ-AK17	Boeing 777-368ER	Saudi Arabian Airlines	
HZ-AKA	Boeing 777-268ER	Saudi Arabian Airlines	
HZ-AKB	Boeing 777-268ER	Saudi Arabian Airlines	
HZ-AKC	Boeing 777-268ER	Saudi Arabian Airlines	
HZ-AKD	Boeing 777-268ER	Saudi Arabian Airlines	
HZ-AKE	Boeing 777-268ER	Saudi Arabian Airlines	
HZ-AKF	Boeing 777-268ER	Saudi Arabian Airlines	
HZ-AKG	Boeing 777-268ER	Saudi Arabian Airlines	
HZ-AKH	Boeing 777-268ER	Saudi Arabian Airlines	
HZ-AKI	Boeing 777-268ER	Saudi Arabian Airlines	
HZ-AKJ	Boeing 777-268ER	Saudi Arabian Airlines	
HZ-AKK	Boeing 777-268ER	Saudi Arabian Airlines	
HZ-AKL	Boeing 777-268ER	Saudi Arabian Airlines	
HZ-AKM	Boeing 777-268ER	Saudi Arabian Airlines	
HZ-AKN	Boeing 777-268ER	Saudi Arabian Airlines	
HZ-AKO	Boeing 777-268ER	Saudi Arabian Airlines	
HZ-AKP	Boeing 777-268ER	Saudi Arabian Airlines	
HZ-AKQ	Boeing 777-268ER	Saudi Arabian Airlines	
HZ-AKR	Boeing 777-268ER	Saudi Arabian Airlines	
HZ-AKS	Boeing 777-268ER	Saudi Arabian Airlines	
HZ-AKT	Boeing 777-268ER	Saudi Arabian Airlines	
HZ-AKU	Boeing 777-268ER	Saudi Arabian Airlines	
HZ-AKV	Boeing 777-268ER	Saudi Arabian Airlines	
HZ-AKW	Boeing 777-268ER	Saudi Arabian Airlines	
HZ-ANA	McD Douglas MD-11F	Saudi Arabian Airlines Cargo	
HZ-ANB	McD Douglas MD-11F	Saudi Arabian Airlines Cargo	
HZ-ANC	McD Douglas MD-11F	Saudi Arabian Airlines Cargo	
HZ-AND	McD Douglas MD-11F	Saudi Arabian Airlines Cargo	

I (Italy)

Reg.	Type	Owner or Operator	Notes
I-AIGH	Boeing 767-23BER	Air Italy	
I-AIGI	Boeing 767-23BER	Air Italy	
I-BIKA	Airbus A.320-214	Alitalia *Johann Sebastian Bach*	
I-BIKC	Airbus A.320-214	Alitalia *Zefiro*	
I-BIKD	Airbus A.320-214	Alitalia *Maestrale*	
I-BIKE	Airbus A.320-214	Alitalia *Franz Liszt*	
I-BIKI	Airbus A.320-214	Alitalia *Girolamo Frescobaldi*	
I-BIKO	Airbus A.320-214	Alitalia *George Bizet*	
I-BIMA	Airbus A.319-112	Alitalia *Isola d'Elba*	
I-BIXA	Airbus A.321-112	Alitalia *Piazza del Duomo Milano*	
I-BIXE	Airbus A.321-112	Alitalia *Piazza di Spagna Roma*	
I-BIXK	Airbus A.321-112	Alitalia *Piazza Ducale Vigevano*	
I-BIXL	Airbus A.321-112	Alitalia *Piazza del Duomo Lecce*	
I-BIXM	Airbus A.321-112	Alitalia *Piazza di San Franceso Assisi*	
I-BIXN	Airbus A.321-112	Alitalia *Piazza del Duomo Catania*	
I-BIXP	Airbus A.321-112	Alitalia *Carlo Morelli*	
I-BIXQ	Airbus A.321-112	Alitalia *Domenico Colapietro*	
I-BIXR	Airbus A.321-112	Alitalia *Piazza dell Campidoglio-Roma*	
I-BIXS	Airbus A.321-112	Alitalia *Piazza San Martino-Lucca*	
I-DISU	Boeing 777-243ER	Alitalia *Madonna di Campiglio*	
I-EEZF	Airbus A.320-214	Meridiana Fly	
I-EEZG	Airbus A.320-214	Meridiana Fly	
I-EEZH	Airbus A.320-214	Meridiana Fly	
I-EEZI	Airbus A.320-214	Meridiana Fly	
I-EEZK	Airbus A.320-214	Meridiana Fly	
I-EEZM	Airbus A.330-223	Meridiana Fly	
I-EEZP	Airbus A.320-233	Meridiana Fly	
I-EEZQ	Airbus A.319-112	Meridiana Fly	
I-NEOS	Boeing 737-86N	Neos	
I-NEOT	Boeing 737-86N	Neos	
I-NEOU	Boeing 737-86N	Neos	
I-NEOW	Boeing 737-86N	Neos	
I-NEOX	Boeing 737-86N	Neos	
I-NEOZ	Boeing 737-86N	Neos *Monte Rosa*	
I-NDMJ	Boeing 767-306ER	Neos	
I-NDOF	Boeing 767-306ER	Neos	
I-SMEB	McD Douglas MD-82	Meridiana Fly	

Notes	Reg.	Type	Owner or Operator
	I-SMEL	McD Douglas MD-82	Meridiana Fly
	I-SMEM	McD Douglas MD-82	Meridiana Fly
	I-SMEN	McD Douglas MD-83	Meridiana Fly
	I-SMEP	McD Douglas MD-82	Meridiana Fly
	I-SMER	McD Douglas MD-82	Meridiana Fly
	I-SMES	McD Douglas MD-82	Meridiana Fly
	I-SMET	McD Douglas MD-82	Meridiana Fly
	I-SMEV	McD Douglas MD-82	Meridiana Fly
	I-SMEZ	McD Douglas MD-82	Meridiana Fly
	I-WEBA	Airbus A.320-214	Air One
	I-WEBB	Airbus A.320-214	Air One

JA (Japan)

	JA01KZ	Boeing 747-481F	Nippon Cargo Airlines
	JA02KZ	Boeing 747-481F	Nippon Cargo Airlines
	JA03KZ	Boeing 747-4KZF	Nippon Cargo Airlines
	JA04KZ	Boeing 747-4KZF	Nippon Cargo Airlines
	JA05KZ	Boeing 747-4KZF	Nippon Cargo Airlines *NCA Apollo*
	JA06KZ	Boeing 747-4KZF	Nippon Cargo Airlines
	JA07KZ	Boeing 747-4KZF	Nippon Cargo Airlines *NCA Andromeda*
	JA08KZ	Boeing 747-4KZF	Nippon Cargo Airlines *NCA Aries*
	JA13KZ	Boeing 747-8KZF	Nippon Cargo Airlines
	JA14KZ	Boeing 747-8KZF	Nippon Cargo Airlines
	JA15KZ	Boeing 747-8KZF	Nippon Cargo Airlines
	JA731A	Boeing 777-381ER	All Nippon Airways
	JA731J	Boeing 777-346ER	Japan Airlines
	JA732A	Boeing 777-381ER	All Nippon Airways
	JA732J	Boeing 777-346ER	Japan Airlines
	JA733A	Boeing 777-381ER	All Nippon Airways
	JA733J	Boeing 777-346ER	Japan Airlines
	JA734A	Boeing 777-381ER	All Nippon Airways
	JA734J	Boeing 777-346ER	Japan Airlines
	JA735A	Boeing 777-381ER	All Nippon Airways
	JA735J	Boeing 777-346ER	Japan Airlines
	JA736A	Boeing 777-381ER	All Nippon Airways
	JA736J	Boeing 777-346ER	Japan Airlines
	JA737J	Boeing 777-346ER	Japan Airlines
	JA738J	Boeing 777-346ER	Japan Airlines
	JA739J	Boeing 777-346ER	Japan Airlines
	JA740J	Boeing 777-346ER	Japan Airlines
	JA741J	Boeing 777-346ER	Japan Airlines
	JA742J	Boeing 777-346ER	Japan Airlines
	JA743J	Boeing 777-346ER	Japan Airlines
	JA777A	Boeing 777-381ER	All Nippon Airways
	JA778A	Boeing 777-381ER	All Nippon Airways
	JA779A	Boeing 777-381ER	All Nippon Airways
	JA780A	Boeing 777-381ER	All Nippon Airways
	JA781A	Boeing 777-381ER	All Nippon Airways
	JA782A	Boeing 777-381ER	All Nippon Airways
	JA783A	Boeing 777-381ER	All Nippon Airways
	JA784A	Boeing 777-381ER	All Nippon Airways
	JA785A	Boeing 777-381ER	All Nippon Airways
	JA786A	Boeing 777-381ER	All Nippon Airways
	JA787A	Boeing 777-381ER	All Nippon Airways
	JA788A	Boeing 777-381ER	All Nippon Airways
	JA789A	Boeing 777-381ER	All Nippon Airways

JY (Jordan)

	JY-AGM	Airbus A.310-304	Royal Jordanian *Princess Alia bin Al-Hussein*
	JY-AGQ	Airbus A.310-304F	Royal Jordanian Cargo
	JY-AGR	Airbus A.310-304F	Royal Jordanian Cargo
	JY-AIE	Airbus A.330-223	Royal Jordanian *Jordan River*
	JY-AIF	Airbus A.330-223	Royal Jordanian *Prince Ali bin Al Hussein*
	JY-AIG	Airbus A.330-223	Royal Jordanian *Prince Feisal Ibn Al-Hussein*
	JY-AYJ	Airbus A.321-231	Royal Jordanian *Ramtha*
	JY-AYK	Airbus A.321-231	Royal Jordanian
	JY-AYL	Airbus A.319-132	Royal Jordanian
	JY-AYM	Airbus A.319-132	Royal Jordanian *Ma'an*

Reg.	Type	Owner or Operator	Notes
JY-AYN	Airbus A.319-132	Royal Jordanian	
JY-AYP	Airbus A.319-132	Royal Jordabian *Ajloun*	
JY-AYQ	Airbus A.320-232	Royal Jordanian *Mount Nebo*	
JY-AYR	Airbus A.320-232	Royal Jordanian	
JY-AYS	Airbus A.320-232	Royal Jordanian	
JY-AYT	Aitbus A.320-232	Royal Jordanian	
JY-AYU	Airbus A.320-232	Royal Jordanian	
JY-AYV	Airbus A.321-231	Royal Jordanian *Madaba*	
JY-AYW	Airbus A.320-232	Royal Jordanian	

LN (Norway)

Reg.	Type	Owner or Operator	Notes
LN-BRE	Boeing 737-405	SAS *Haakon V Magnusson*	
LN-BRH	Boeing 737-505	SAS *Haakon den Gode*	
LN-BRI	Boeing 737-405	SAS *Harald Haarfagre*	
LN-BRQ	Boeing 737-405	SAS *Harald Graafell*	
LN-BRV	Boeing 737-505	SAS *Haakon Sverresson*	
LN-BRX	Boeing 737-505	SAS *Sigurd Munn*	
LN-BUC	Boeing 737-505	SAS *Magnus Erlingsson*	
LN-BUD	Boeing 737-505	SAS *Inge Krokrygg*	
LN-BUE	Boeing 737-505	SAS *Erling Skjalgsson*	
LN-BUG	Boeing 737-505	SAS *Oystein Haraldsson*	
LN-DYA	Boeing 737-8JP	Norwegian Air Shuttle *Erik Bye*	
LN-DYB	Boeing 737-8JP	Norwegian Air Shuttle *Bjornstjerne Bjornson*	
LN-DYC	Boeing 737-8JP	Norwegian Air Shuttle Max Manus	
LN-DYD	Boeing 737-8JP	Norwegian Air Shuttle *Hans Christian Andersen*	
LN-DYE	Boeing 737-8JP	Norwegian Air Shuttle *Arne Jacobsen*	
LN-DYF	Boeing 737-8JP*M*	Norwegian Air Shuttle *Fridtjof Nansen*	
LN-DYG	Boeing 737-8JP	Norwegian Air Shuttle *Jenny Lind*	
LN-DYH	Boeing 737-8JP	Norwegian Air Shuttle *Soren Kierkegaard*	
LN-DYI	Boeing 737-8JP	Norwegian Air Shuttle *Aasmund Olavson Vinje*	
LN-DYJ	Boeing 737-8JP	Norwegian Air Shuttle *Georg Brandes*	
LN-DYK	Boeing 737-8JP	Norwegian Air Shuttle *Karl Larsson*	
LN-DYL	Boeing 737-8JP	Norwegian Air Shuttle *Amalie Skram*	
LN-DYM	Boeing 737-8JP	Norwegian Air Shuttle *Andre Bjerke*	
LN-DYN	Boeing 737-8JP	Norwegian Air Shuttle *Karen Blixen*	
LN-DYO	Boeing 737-8JP	Norwegian Air Shuttle *Otto Sverdrup*	
LN-DYP	Boeing 737-8JP	Norwegian Air Shuttle *Aksel Sandemose*	
LN-DYQ	Boeing 737-8JP	Norwegian Air Shuttle *Helge Ingstad*	
LN-DYR	Boeing 737-8JP	Norwegian Air Shuttle *Peter C Asbjornsen/Jorgen Moe*	
LN-DYS	Boeing 737-8JP	Norwegian Air Shuttle *Niels Henrik Abel*	
LN-DYT	Boeing 737-8JP	Norwegian Air Shuttle *Kirsten Flagstad*	
LN-DYU	Boeing 737-8JP	Norwegian Air Shuttle *Jorn Utzon*	
LN-DYV	Boeing 737-8JP	Norwegian Air Shuttle *Elsa Beskow*	
LN-DYW	Boeing 737-8JP	Norwegian Air Shuttle	
LN-DYX	Boeing 737-8JP	Norwegian Air Shuttle	
LN-DYY	Boeing 737-8JP	Norwegian Air Shuttle	
LN-DYZ	Boeing 737-8JP	Norwegian Air Shuttle	
LN-KHA	Boeing 737-31S	Norwegian Air Shuttle	
LN-KHB	Boeing 737-31S	Norwegian Air Shuttle	
LN-KHC	Boeing 737-31S	Norwegian Air Shuttle	
LN-KKD	Boeing 737-33V	Norwegian Air Shuttle	
LN-KKJ	Boeing 737-36N	Norwegian Air Shuttle *Sonja Henie*	
LN-KKL	Boeing 737-36N	Norwegian Air Shuttle *Roald Amundsen*	
LN-KKM	Boeing 737-3Y0	Norwegian Air Shuttle *Thor Heyerdahl*	
LN-KKN	Boeing 737-3Y0	Norwegian Air Shuttle *Sigrid Undset*	
LN-KKW	Boeing 737-3K9	Norwegian Air Shuttle	
LN-KKX	Boeing 737-33S	Norwegian Air Shuttle	
LN-NGA	Boeing 737-8JP	Norwegian Air Shuttle	
LN-NGB	Boeing 737-8JP	Norwegian Air Shuttle	
LN-NGC	Boeing 737-8JP	Norwegian Air Shuttle	
LN-NGD	Boeing 737-8JP	Norwegian Air Shuttle	
LN-NGE	Boeing 737-8JP	Norwegian Air Shuttle	
LN-NGF	Boeing 737-8JP	Norwegian Air Shuttle	
LN-NGG	Boeing 737-8JP	Norwegian Air Shuttle	
LN-NGH	Boeing 737-8JP	Norwegian Air Shuttle	
LN-NGI	Boeing 737-8JP	Norwegian Air Shuttle	
LN-NGJ	Boeing 737-8JP	Norwegian Air Shuttle	
LN-NIA	Boeing 737-86JP	Norwegian Air Shuttle	
LN-NIB	Boeing 737-86J	Norwegian Air Shuttle *Helmer Hanssen*	

Notes	Reg.	Type	Owner or Operator
	LN-NOB	Boeing 737-8FZ	Norwegian Air Shuttle *Edward Grieg*
	LN-NOC	Boeing 737-81Q	Norwegian Air Shuttle *Ole Bull*
	LN-NOD	Boeing 737-8Q8	Norwegian Air Shuttle *Sonje Henie*
	LN-NOE	Boeing 737-8Q8	Norwegian Air Shuttle *Henrik Wergeland*
	LN-NOF	Boeing 737-86N	Norwegian Air Shuttle *Edvard Munch*
	LN-NOG	Boeing 737-86N	Norwegian Air Shuttle *Henrik Ibsen*
	LN-NOH	Boeing 737-86N	Norwegian Air Shuttle *Selma Lagerlof*
	LN-NOI	Boeing 737-86N	Norwegian Air Shuttle *Sam Eyde*
	LN-NOJ	Boeing 737-86N	Norwegian Air Shuttle *Tycho Brahe*
	LN-NOL	Boeing 737-8Q8	Norwegian Air Shuttle
	LN-NOM	Boeing 737-86N	Norwegian Air Shuttle *Greta Garbo*
	LN-NON	Boeing 737-86N	Norwegian Air Shuttle *Anders Celcius*
	LN-NOO	Boeing 737-86Q	Norwegian Air Shuttle *Gustav Vigeland*
	LN-NOP	Boeing 737-86N	Norwegian Air Shuttle *Camilla Collett*
	LN-NOQ	Boeing 737-86N	Norwegian Air Shuttle *Kristian Birkeland*
	LN-NOR	Boeing 737-86N	Norwegian Air Shuttle *Povel Ramel*
	LN-NOT	Boeing 737-8JP	Norwegian Air Shuttle *Piet Hein*
	LN-NOU	Boeing 737-8FZ	Norwegian Air Shuttle *Carl von Linne*
	LN-NOV	Boeing 737-8FZ	Norwegian Air Shuttle *Evart Taube*
	LN-NOW	Boeing 737-8JP	Norwegian Air Shuttle *Oda Krohg*
	LN-NOX	Boeing 737-8JP	Norwegian Air Shuttle *Christian Krohg*
	LN-NOY	Boeing 737-8JP	Norwegian Air Shuttle
	LN-NOZ	Boeing 737-8JP	Norwegian Air Shuttle
	LN-RCN	Boeing 737-883	SAS *Hedrun Viking*
	LN-RCT	Boeing 737-683	SAS *Fridlev Viking*
	LN-RCU	Boeing 737-683	SAS *Sigfrid Viking*
	LN-RCW	Boeing 737-683	SAS *Yngvar Viking*
	LN-RCX	Boeing 737-883	SAS *Hottur Viking*
	LN-RCY	Boeing 737-883	SAS *Eylime Viking*
	LN-RCZ	Boeing 737-883	SAS *Glitne Viking*
	LN-RGA	Boeing 737-883	SAS
	LN-RGB	Boeing 737-883	SAS
	LN-RGC	Boeing 737-883	SAS
	LN-RGD	Boeing 737-883	SAS
	LN-RGE	Boeing 737-883	SAS
	LN-RGF	Boeing 737-883	SAS
	LN-RGG	Boeing 737-883	SAS
	LN-RGH	Boeing 737-883	SAS
	LN-RGI	Boeing 737-883	SAS
	LN-RKF	Airbus A.340-313X	SAS *Godfred Viking*
	LN-RKG	Airbus A.340-313X	SAS *Gudrod Viking*
	LN-RKH	Airbus A.330-343X	SAS *Emund Viking*
	LN-RKI	Airbus A.321-231	SAS *Gunnhild Viking*
	LN-RKK	Airbus A.321-231	SAS *Viger Viking*
	LN-RKM	Airbus A.330-343	SAS
	LN-RKN	Airbus A.330-343	SAS
	LN-RLE	McD Douglas MD-82	SAS *Ketiil Viking*
	LN-RML	McD Douglas MD-82	SAS *Aud Viking*
	LN-RMM	McD Douglas MD-82	SAS *Blenda Viking*
	LN-RMO	McD Douglas MD-82	SAS *Bergljot Viking*
	LN-RMR	McD Douglas MD-82	SAS *Olav Viking*
	LN-RMS	McD Douglas MD-82	SAS *Nial Viking*
	LN-RMT	McD Douglas MD-82	SAS *Jarl Viking*
	LN-RNL	Canadair CRJ900ER	SAS *Fafner Viking*
	LN-RNN	Boeing 737-783	SAS *Borgny Viking*
	LN-RNO	Boeing 737-783	SAS *Gjuke Viking*
	LN-RNU	Boeing 737-783	SAS *Hans Viking*
	LN-RNW	Boeing 737-783	SAS *Granmar Viking*
	LN-ROP	McD Douglas MD-82	SAS *Bjoern Viking*
	LN-ROT	McD Douglas MD-82	SAS *Ingjaid Viking*
	LN-RPA	Boeing 737-683	SAS *Arnljot Viking*
	LN-RPB	Boeing 737-683	SAS *Bure Viking*
	LN-RPE	Boeing 737-683	SAS *Edla Viking*
	LN-RPF	Boeing 737-683	SAS *Frede Viking*
	LN-RPG	Boeing 737-683	SAS *Geirmund Viking*
	LN-RPH	Boeing 737-683	SAS *Hamder Viking*
	LN-RPJ	Boeing 737-783	SAS *Grimhild Viking*
	LN-RPK	Boeing 737-783	SAS *Heimer Viking*
	LN-RPL	Boeing 737-883	SAS *Svanevit Viking*
	LN-RPM	Boeing 737-883	SAS *Frigg Viking*
	LN-RPN	Boeing 737-883	SAS *Bergfora Viking*
	LN-RPO	Boeing 737-883	SAS *Thorleif Viking*

Reg.	Type	Owner or Operator	Notes
LN-RPR	Boeing 737-883	SAS Ore Viking	
LN-RPS	Boeing 737-683	SAS Gautrek Viking	
LN-RPT	Boeing 737-683	SAS Ellida Viking	
LN-RPU	Boeing 737-683	SAS Ragna Viking	
LN-RPW	Boeing 737-683	SAS Alvid Viking	
LN-RPX	Boeing 737-683	SAS Nanna Viking	
LN-RPY	Boeing 737-683	SAS Olof Viking	
LN-RPZ	Boeing 737-683	SAS Bera Viking	
LN-RRA	Boeing 737-783	SAS Steinar Viking	
LN-RRB	Boeing 737-783	SAS Cecilia Viking	
LN-RRC	Boeing 737-683	SAS Sindre Viking	
LN-RRD	Boeing 737-683	SAS Embla Viking	
LN-RRE	Boeing 737-883	SAS Knut Viking	
LN-RRF	Boeing 737-883	SAS Froydis Viking	
LN-RRG	Boeing 737-883	SAS Einar Viking	
LN-RRH	Boeing 737-883	SAS Freja Viking	
LN-RRJ	Boeing 737-883	SAS Frida Viking	
LN-RRK	Boeing 737-883	SAS Gerud Viking	
LN-RRL	Boeing 737-883	SAS Jarlabanke Viking	
LN-RRM	Boeing 737-783	SAS Erland Viking	
LN-RRN	Boeing 737-783	SAS Solveig Viking	
LN-RRO	Boeing 737-683	SAS Bernt Viking	
LN-RRP	Boeing 737-683	SAS Vilborg Viking	
LN-RRR	Boeing 737-683	SAS Torbjorn Viking	
LN-RRS	Boeing 737-883	SAS Ymir Viking	
LN-RRT	Boeing 737-883	SAS Lodyn Viking	
LN-RRU	Boeing 737-883	SAS Vingolf Viking	
LN-RRW	Boeing 737-883	SAS Saga Viking	
LN-RRX	Boeing 737-683	SAS Ragnfast Viking	
LN-RRY	Boeing 737-683	SAS Signe Viking	
LN-RRZ	Boeing 737-683	SAS Gisla Viking	
LN-TUA	Boeing 737-705	SAS Ingeborg Eriksdatter	
LN-TUD	Boeing 737-705	SAS Margrete Skulesdatter	
LN-TUF	Boeing 737-705	SAS Tyra Haraldsdatter	
LN-TUH	Boeing 737-705	SAS Margrete Ingesdatter	
LN-TUI	Boeing 737-705	SAS Kristin Knudsdatter	
LN-TUJ	Boeing 737-705	SAS Eirik Blodoks	
LN-TUK	Boeing 737-705	SAS Inge Bardsson	
LN-TUL	Boeing 737-705	SAS Haakon IV Haakonson	
LN-TUM	Boeing 737-705	SAS Oystein Magnusson	
LN-WDE	DHC.8-402 Dash Eight	Wideroe's Flyveselskap	
LN-WDF	DHC.8-402 Dash Eight	Wideroe's Flyveselskap	
LN-WDG	DHC.8-402 Dash Eight	Wideroe's Flyveselskap	
LN-WDH	DHC.8-402 Dash Eight	Wideroe's Flyveselskap	
LN-WDI	DHC.8-402 Dash Eight	Wideroe's Flyveselskap	
LN-WDJ	DHC.8-402 Dash Eight	Wideroe's Flyveselskap	
LN-WDK	DHC.8-402 Dash Eight	Wideroe's Flyveselskap	
LN-WDL	DHC.8-402 Dash Eight	Wideroe's Flyveselskap	
LN-WFC	DHC.8-311 Dash Eight	Wideroe's Flyveselskap	
LN-WFD	DHC.8-311 Dash Eight	Wideroe's Flyveselskap	
LN-WFH	DHC.8-311 Dash Eight	Wideroe's Flyveselskap	
LN-WFO	DHC.8Q-311 Dash Eight	Wideroe's Flyveselskap	
LN-WFP	DHC.8Q-311 Dash Eight	Wideroe's Flyveselskap	
LN-WFS	DHC.8Q-311 Dash Eight	Wideroe's Flyveselskap	
LN-WFT	DHC.8Q-311 Dash Eight	Wideroe's Flyveselskap	
LN-WFU	DHC.8Q-311 Dash Eight	Wideroe's Flyveselskap	

LX (Luxembourg)

Reg.	Type	Owner or Operator	Notes
LX-ACV	Boeing 747-4B5BCF	Cargolux	
LX-DCV	Boeing 747-4B5CF	Cargolux	
LX-KCV	Boeing 747-4R7F (SCD)	Cargolux City of Dudelange	
LX-LGA	DHC.8Q-402 Dash Eight	Luxair	
LX-LGE	DHC.8Q-402 Dash Eight	Luxair	
LX-LGF	DHC.8Q-402 Dash Eight	Luxair	
LX-LGG	DHC.8Q-402 Dash Eight	Luxair	
LX-LGH	DHC.8Q-402 Dash Eight	Luxair	
LX-LGI	Embraer RJ145LU	Luxair	
LX-LGJ	Embraer RJ145LU	Luxair	
LX-LGM	DHC.8Q-402 Dash Eight	Luxair	
LX-LGN	DHC.8Q-402 Dash Eight	Luxair	

Notes	Reg.	Type	Owner or Operator
	LX-LGQ	Boeing 737-7C9	Luxair *Chateau de Burg*
	LX-LGR	Boeing 737-7C9	Luxair *Chateau de Fischbach*
	LX-LGS	Boeing 737-7C9	Luxair *Chateau de Senningen*
	LX-LGT	Boeing 737-8K5	Luxair
	LX-LGU	Boeing 737-8C9	Luxair
	LX-LGW	Embraer RJ145LU	Luxair
	LX-LGX	Embraer RJ145LU	Luxair
	LX-LGY	Embraer RJ145LU	Luxair
	LX-LGZ	Embraer RJ145LU	Luxair
	LX-OCV	Boeing 747-4R7F (SCD)	Cargolux *City of Differdange*
	LX-RCV	Boeing 747-4R7F (SCD)	Cargolux *City of Schengen*
	LX-SCV	Boeing 747-4R7F (SCD)	Cargolux *City of Niederanven*
	LX-TCV	Boeing 747-4R7F (SCD)	Cargolux *City of Sandweiler*
	LX-UCV	Boeing 747-4R7F (SCD)	Cargolux *City of Bertragne*
	LX-VCA	Boeing 747-8R7F	Cargolux
	LX-VCB	Boeing 747-8R7F	Cargolux *City of Esch-sur-Aizette*
	LX-VCC	Boeing 747-8R7F	Cargolux
	LX-VCD	Boeing 747-8R7F	Cargolux *City of Luxembourg*
	LX-VCE	Boeing 747-8R7F	Cargolux
	LX-VCF	Boeing 747-8R7F	Cargolux *City of Grevenmacher*
	LX-VCG	Boeing 747-8R7F	Cargolux
	LX-VCH	Boeing 747-8R7F	Cargolux
	LX-VCI	Boeing 747-8R7F	Cargolux
	LX-VCV	Boeing 747-4R7F (SCD)	Cargolux *City of Walferdange*
	LX-WAD	BAe ATP	West Air Europe
	LX-WAE	BAe ATP	West Air Europe
	LX-WAF	BAe ATP	West Air Europe
	LX-WAK	BAe ATP	West Air Europe
	LX-WAL	BAe ATP	West Air Europe
	LX-WAM	BAe ATP	West Air Europe
	LX-WAN	BAe ATP	West Air Europe
	LX-WAO	BAe ATP	West Air Europe
	LX-WAP	BAe ATP	West Air Europe
	LX-WAS	BAe ATP	West Air Europe
	LX-WAT	BAe ATP	West Air Europe
	LX-WAV	BAe ATP	West Air Europe
	LX-WAW	BAe ATP	West Air Europe
	LX-WAX	BAe ATP	West Air Europe
	LX-WCV	Boeing 747-4R7F (SCD)	Cargolux *City of Petange*
	LX-YCV	Boeing 747-4R7F	Cargolux *City of Contem*

LY (Lithuania)

	LY-AQX	Boeing 737-322	Small Planet Airlines
	LY-FLC	Boeing 737-31S	Small Planet Airlines
	LY-FLE	Boeing 737-3L9	Small Planet Airlines
	LY-FLH	Boeing 737-382	Small Planet Airlines
	LY-FLJ	Boeing 737-3K2	Small Planet Airlines
	LY-SKA	Boeing 737-35B	Aurela
	LY-SKW	Boeing 737-382	Aurela
	LY-VEU	Airbus A.319-112	Avion Express
	LY-VEV	Airbus A.320-211	Avion Express
	LY-VEX	Airbus A.320-212	Avion Express
	LY-VEY	Airbus A.320-212	WOW Air
	LY-VEZ	Airbus A.320-212	Avion Express

LZ (Bulgaria)

	LZ-BHC	Airbus A.320-212	BH Air
	LZ-BHD	Airbus A.320-212	BH Air
	LZ-BHE	Airbus A.320-211	BH Air
	LZ-BUR	Embraer ERJ190-100IGW	Bulgaria Air
	LZ-FBA	Airbus A.319-112	Bulgaria Air
	LZ-FBB	Airbus A.319-112	Bulgaria Air
	LZ-FBC	Airbus A.320-214	Bulgaria Air
	LZ-FBD	Airbus A.320-214	Bulgaria Air
	LZ-FBE	Airbus A.320-214	Bulgaria Air
	LZ-FBF	Airbus A.319-111	Bulgaria Air
	LZ-LDC	McD Douglas MD-82	Bulgarian Air Charter
	LZ-LDG	McD Douglas MD-83	Bulgarian Air Charter

Reg.	Type	Owner or Operator	Notes
LZ-LDK	McD Douglas MD-82	Bulgarian Air Charter	
LZ-LDM	McD Douglas MD-82	Bulgarian Air Charter	
LZ-LDN	McD Douglas MD-82	Bulgarian Air Charter	
LZ-LDP	McD Douglas MD-82	Bulgarian Air Charter	
LZ-LDW	McD Douglas MD-82	Bulgarian Air Charter	
LZ-LDY	McD Douglas MD-82	Bulgarian Air Charter	
LZ-MDA	Airbus A.320-232	Air VIA	
LZ-MDB	Airbus A.320-232	Air VIA	
LZ-MDC	Airbus A.320-232	Air VIA	
LZ-MDD	Airbus A.320-232	Air VIA	
LZ-MDR	Airbus A.320-232	Air VIA/WOW Air	
LZ-PLO	Embraer ERJ190-100STD	Bulgaria Air	
LZ-SOF	Embraer ERJ190-100IGW	Bulgaria Air	
LZ-VAR	Embraer ERJ190-100IGW	Bulgaria Air	

N (USA)

Reg.	Type	Owner or Operator	Notes
N104UA	Boeing 747-422	United Airlines	
N105UA	Boeing 747-451	United Airlines	
N107UA	Boeing 747-422	United Airlines	
N116UA	Boeing 747-422	United Airlines	
N117UA	Boeing 747-422	United Airlines	
N118UA	Boeing 747-422	United Airlines	
N119UA	Boeing 747-422	United Airlines	
N120UA	Boeing 747-422	United Airlines	
N121UA	Boeing 747-422	United Airlines	
N122UA	Boeing 747-422	United Airlines	
N127UA	Boeing 747-422	United Airlines	
N128UA	Boeing 747-422	United Airlines	
N152DL	Boeing 767-3P6ER	Delta Air Lines	
N153DL	Boeing 767-3P6ER	Delta Air Lines	
N154DL	Boeing 767-3P6ER	Delta Air Lines	
N155DL	Boeing 767-3P6ER	Delta Air Lines	
N156DL	Boeing 767-3P6ER	Delta Air Lines	
N169DZ	Boeing 767-332ER	Delta Air Lines	
N171DN	Boeing 767-332ER	Delta Air Lines	
N171DZ	Boeing 767-332ER	Delta Air Lines	
N171UA	Boeing 747-422	United Airlines	
N172AJ	Boeing 757-223ET	American Airlines	
N172DN	Boeing 767-332ER	Delta Air Lines	
N172DZ	Boeing 767-332ER	Delta Air Lines	
N173AN	Boeing 757-223ET	American Airlines	
N173DZ	Boeing 767-332ER	Delta Air Lines	
N174AA	Boeing 757-223ET	American Airlines	
N174DN	Boeing 767-332ER	Delta Air Lines	
N174DZ	Boeing 767-332ER	Delta Air Lines	
N174UA	Boeing 747-422	United Airlines	
N175AN	Boeing 757-223ET	American Airlines	
N175DN	Boeing 767-332ER	Delta Air Lines	
N175DZ	Boeing 767-332ER	Delta Air Lines	
N175UA	Boeing 747-422	United Airlines	
N176AA	Boeing 757-223ET	American Airlines	
N176DN	Boeing 767-332ER	Delta Air Lines	
N176DZ	Boeing 767-332ER	Delta Air Lines	
N177AN	Boeing 757-223ET	American Airlines	
N177DN	Boeing 767-332ER	Delta Air Lines	
N177DZ	Boeing 767-332ER	Delta Air Lines	
N177UA	Boeing 747-422	United Airlines	
N178AA	Boeing 757-223ET	American Airlines	
N178DN	Boeing 767-332ER	Delta Air Lines	
N178DZ	Boeing 767-332ER	Delta Air Lines	
N178UA	Boeing 747-422	United Airlines	
N179AA	Boeing 757-223ET	American Airlines	
N179DN	Boeing 767-332ER	Delta Air Lines	
N179UA	Boeing 747-422	United Airlines	
N180DN	Boeing 767-332ER	Delta Air Lines	
N180UA	Boeing 747-422	United Airlines	
N181AN	Boeing 757-223ET	American Airlines	
N181DN	Boeing 767-332ER	Delta Air Lines	
N181UA	Boeing 747-422	United Airlines	
N182AN	Boeing 757-223ET	American Airlines	

Notes	Reg.	Type	Owner or Operator
	N182DN	Boeing 767-332ER	Delta Air Lines
	N182UA	Boeing 747-422	United Airlines
	N183AN	Boeing 757-223ET	American Airlines
	N183DN	Boeing 767-332ER	Delta Air Lines
	N184AN	Boeing 757-223ET	American Airlines
	N184DN	Boeing 767-332ER	Delta Air Lines
	N185AN	Boeing 757-223ET	American Airlines
	N185DN	Boeing 767-332ER	Delta Air Lines
	N186AN	Boeing 757-223ET	American Airlines
	N186DN	Boeing 767-332ER	Delta Air Lines
	N187AN	Boeing 757-223ET	American Airlines
	N187DN	Boeing 767-332ER	Delta Air Lines
	N188AN	Boeing 757-223ET	American Airlines
	N188DN	Boeing 767-332ER	Delta Air Lines
	N189AN	Boeing 757-223ET	American Airlines
	N189DN	Boeing 767-332ER	Delta Air Lines
	N190AA	Boeing 757-223ET	American Airlines
	N190DN	Boeing 767-332ER	Delta Air Lines
	N191AN	Boeing 757-223ET	American Airlines
	N191DN	Boeing 767-332ER	Delta Air Lines
	N192AN	Boeing 757-223ET	American Airlines
	N192DN	Boeing 767-332ER	Delta Air Lines
	N193AN	Boeing 757-223ET	American Airlines
	N193DN	Boeing 767-332ER	Delta Air Lines
	N194AA	Boeing 757-223ET	American Airlines
	N194DN	Boeing 767-332ER	Delta Air Lines
	N195AN	Boeing 757-223ET	American Airlines
	N195DN	Boeing 767-332ER	Delta Air Lines
	N196AA	Boeing 757-223ET	American Airlines
	N196DN	Boeing 767-332ER	Delta Air Lines
	N197AN	Boeing 757-223ET	American Airlines
	N197DN	Boeing 767-332ER	Delta Air Lines
	N197UA	Boeing 747-422	United Airlines
	N198AA	Boeing 757-223ET	American Airlines
	N198DN	Boeing 767-332ER	Delta Air Lines
	N199AN	Boeing 757-223ET	American Airlines
	N199DN	Boeing 767-332ER	Delta Air Lines
	N199UA	Boeing 747-422	United Airlines
	N200UU	Boeing 757-2B7	US Airways
	N201UU	Boeing 757-2B7	US Airways
	N202UW	Boeing 757-2B7	US Airways
	N203UW	Boeing 757-23N	US Airways
	N204UA	Boeing 777-222ER	United Airlines
	N204UW	Boeing 757-23N	US Airways
	N205UW	Boeing 757-23N	US Airways
	N206UA	Boeing 777-222ER	United Airlines
	N206UW	Boeing 757-2B7	US Airways
	N209UA	Boeing 777-222ER	United Airlines
	N216UA	Boeing 777-222ER	United Airlines
	N217UA	Boeing 777-222ER	United Airlines
	N218UA	Boeing 777-222ER	United Airlines
	N219CY	Boeing 767-383ER	ABX Air/DHL
	N220CY	Boeing 767-383ER	ABX Air/DHL
	N219UA	Boeing 777-222ER	United Airlines
	N220UA	Boeing 777-222ER	United Airlines
	N221UA	Boeing 777-222ER	United Airlines
	N222UA	Boeing 777-222ER	United Airlines
	N223UA	Boeing 777-222ER	United Airlines
	N224UA	Boeing 777-222ER	United Airlines
	N225UA	Boeing 777-222ER	United Airlines
	N226UA	Boeing 777-222ER	United Airlines
	N227UA	Boeing 777-222ER	United Airlines
	N228UA	Boeing 777-222ER	United Airlines
	N229UA	Boeing 777-222ER	United Airlines
	N245AY	Boeing 767-201ER	US Airways
	N246AY	Boeing 767-201ER	US Airways
	N248AY	Boeing 767-201ER	US Airways
	N249AU	Boeing 767-201ER	US Airways
	N250AY	Boeing 767-201ER	US Airways
	N251AY	Boeing 767-2B7ER	US Airways
	N252AU	Boeing 767-2B7ER	US Airways
	N253AY	Boeing 767-2B7ER	US Airways

Reg.	Type	Owner or Operator	Notes
N255AY	Boeing 767-2B7ER	US Airways	
N256AY	Boeing 767-2B7ER	US Airways	
N270AY	Airbus A.330-323X	US Airways	
N271AY	Airbus A.330-323X	US Airways	
N271WA	McD Douglas MD-11 (271)	World Airways	
N272AY	Airbus A.330-323X	US Airways	
N272WA	McD Douglas MD-11 (272)	World Airways	
N273AY	Airbus A.330-323X	US Airways	
N273WA	McD Douglas MD-11 (273)	World Airways	
N274AY	Airbus A.330-323X	US Airways	
N275AY	Airbus A.330-323X	US Airways	
N276AY	Airbus A.330-323X	US Airways	
N277AY	Airbus A.330-323X	US Airways	
N278AY	Airbus A.330-323X	US Airways	
N279AY	Airbus A.330-243	US Airways	
N280AY	Airbus A.330-243	US Airways	
N281AY	Airbus A.330-243	US Airways	
N282AY	Airbus A.330-243	US Airways	
N283AY	Airbus A.330-243	US Airways	
N284AY	Airbus A.330-243	US Airways	
N285AY	Airbus A.330-243	US Airways	
N301UP	Boeing 767-34AFER	United Parcel Service	
N302UP	Boeing 767-34AFER	United Parcel Service	
N303UP	Boeing 767-34AFER	United Parcel Service	
N304UP	Boeing 767-34AFER	United Parcel Service	
N305UP	Boeing 767-34AFER	United Parcel Service	
N306UP	Boeing 767-34AFER	United Parcel Service	
N307UP	Boeing 767-34AFER	United Parcel Service	
N308UP	Boeing 767-34AFER	United Parcel Service	
N309UP	Boeing 767-34AFER	United Parcel Service	
N310UP	Boeing 767-34AFER	United Parcel Service	
N311UP	Boeing 767-34AFER	United Parcel Service	
N312UP	Boeing 767-34AFER	United Parcel Service	
N313UP	Boeing 767-34AFER	United Parcel Service	
N314UP	Boeing 767-34AFER	United Parcel Service	
N315UP	Boeing 767-34AFER	United Parcel Service	
N316UP	Boeing 767-34AFER	United Parcel Service	
N317UP	Boeing 767-34AFER	United Parcel Service	
N318UP	Boeing 767-34AFER	United Parcel Service	
N319UP	Boeing 767-34AFER	United Parcel Service	
N320UP	Boeing 767-34AFER	United Parcel Service	
N322UP	Boeing 767-34AFER	United Parcel Service	
N323UP	Boeing 767-34AFER	United Parcel Service	
N324UP	Boeing 767-34AFER	United Parcel Service	
N325UP	Boeing 767-34AFER	United Parcel Service	
N326UP	Boeing 767-34AFER	United Parcel Service	
N327UP	Boeing 767-34AFER	United Parcel Service	
N328UP	Boeing 767-34AFER	United Parcel Service	
N329UP	Boeing 767-34AER	United Parcel Service	
N330UP	Boeing 767-34AER	United Parcel Service	
N331UP	Boeing 767-34AER	United Parcel Service	
N332UP	Boeing 767-34AER	United Parcel Service	
N334UP	Boeing 767-34AER	United Parcel Service	
N335UP	Boeing 767-34AF	United Parcel Service	
N336UP	Boeing 767-34AF	United Parcel Service	
N337UP	Boeing 767-34AF	United Parcel Service	
N338UP	Boeing 767-34AF	United Parcel Service	
N339UP	Boeing 767-34AF	United Parcel Service	
N340UP	Boeing 767-34AF	United Parcel Service	
N341UP	Boeing 767-34AF	United Parcel Service	
N342AN	Boeing 767-323ER	American Airlines	
N342UP	Boeing 767-34AF	United Parcel Service	
N343AN	Boeing 767-323ER	American Airlines	
N343UP	Boeing 767-34AF	United Parcel Service	
N344AN	Boeing 767-323ER	American Airlines	
N344UP	Boeing 767-34AF	United Parcel Service	
N345AN	Boeing 767-323ER	American Airlines	
N345UP	Boeing 767-34AF	United Parcel Service	
N346AN	Boeing 767-323ER	American Airlines	
N346UP	Boeing 767-34AF	United Parcel Service	
N347AN	Boeing 767-323ER	American Airlines	
N347UP	Boeing 767-34AF	United Parcel Service	

Notes	Reg.	Type	Owner or Operator
	N348AN	Boeing 767-323ER	American Airlines
	N348UP	Boeing 767-34AF	United Parcel Service
	N349AN	Boeing 767-323ER	American Airlines
	N349UP	Boeing 767-34AF	United Parcel Service
	N350AN	Boeing 767-323ER	American Airlines
	N350UP	Boeing 767-34AF	United Parcel Service
	N351AA	Boeing 767-323ER	American Airlines
	N351UP	Boeing 767-34AF	United Parcel Service
	N352AA	Boeing 767-323ER	American Airlines
	N352UP	Boeing 767-34AF	United Parcel Service
	N353AA	Boeing 767-323ER	American Airlines
	N353UP	Boeing 767-34AF	United Parcel Service
	N354AA	Boeing 767-323ER	American Airlines
	N354UP	Boeing 767-34AF	United Parcel Service
	N355AA	Boeing 767-323ER	American Airlines
	N355UP	Boeing 767-34AF	United Parcel Service
	N356UP	Boeing 767-34AF	United Parcel Service
	N357AA	Boeing 767-323ER	American Airlines
	N357UP	Boeing 767-34AF	United Parcel Service
	N358AA	Boeing 767-323ER	American Airlines
	N358UP	Boeing 767-34AF	United Parcel Service
	N359AA	Boeing 767-323ER	American Airlines
	N360AA	Boeing 767-323ER	American Airlines
	N361AA	Boeing 767-323ER	American Airlines
	N362AA	Boeing 767-323ER	American Airlines
	N363AA	Boeing 767-323ER	American Airlines
	N366AA	Boeing 767-323ER	American Airlines
	N368AA	Boeing 767-323ER	American Airlines
	N369AA	Boeing 767-323ER	American Airlines
	N370AA	Boeing 767-323ER	American Airlines
	N371AA	Boeing 767-323ER	American Airlines
	N372AA	Boeing 767-323ER	American Airlines
	N373AA	Boeing 767-323ER	American Airlines
	N374AA	Boeing 767-323ER	American Airlines
	N376AN	Boeing 767-323ER	American Airlines
	N377AN	Boeing 767-323ER	American Airlines
	N378AN	Boeing 767-323ER	American Airlines
	N379AA	Boeing 767-323ER	American Airlines
	N380AN	Boeing 767-323ER	American Airlines
	N380WA	McD Douglas MD-11F	World Airways
	N381AN	Boeing 767-323ER	American Airlines
	N381WA	McD Douglas MD-11F (381)	World Airways
	N382AN	Boeing 767-323ER	American Airlines
	N382WA	McD Douglas MD-11F	World Airways
	N383AN	Boeing 767-323ER	American Airlines
	N383WA	McD Douglas MD-11F	World Airways
	N384AA	Boeing 767-323ER	American Airlines
	N385AM	Boeing 767-323ER	American Airlines
	N386AA	Boeing 767-323ER	American Airlines
	N387AM	Boeing 767-323ER	American Airlines
	N388AA	Boeing 767-323ER	American Airlines
	N389AA	Boeing 767-323ER	American Airlines
	N390AA	Boeing 767-323ER	American Airlines
	N391AA	Boeing 767-323ER	American Airlines
	N392AN	Boeing 767-323ER	American Airlines
	N393AN	Boeing 767-323ER	American Airlines
	N394AN	Boeing 767-323ER	American Airlines
	N394DL	Boeing 767-324ER	Delta Air Lines
	N395AN	Boeing 767-323ER	American Airlines
	N396AN	Boeing 767-323ER	American Airlines
	N397AN	Boeing 767-323ER	American Airlines
	N398AN	Boeing 767-323ER	American Airlines
	N399AN	Boeing 767-323ER	American Airlines
	N408MC	Boeing 747-47UF	Atlas Air/Emirates SkyCargo
	N412MC	Boeing 747-47UF	Atlas Air
	N415MC	Boeing 747-47UF	Atlas Air
	N418MC	Boeing 747-47UF	Atlas Air
	N419MC	Boeing 747-48EF	Atlas Air
	N429MC	Boeing 747-481	Atlas Air
	N458MC	Boeing 747-446BCF	Atlas Air
	N459MC	Boeing 747-446BCF	Atlas Air
	N475MC	Boeing 747-47U	Atlas Air

Reg.	Type	Owner or Operator	Notes
N476MC	Boeing 747-47U	Atlas Air	
N477MC	Boeing 747-47U	Atlas Air	
N491EV	Boeing 747-412F	Evergreen International Airlines	
N492EV	Boeing 747-446BCF	Evergreen International Airlines	
N493EV	Boeing 747-4H6F	Evergreen International Airlines	
N496MC	Boeing 747-47UF	Atlas Air	
N497MC	Boeing 747-47UF	Atlas Air	
N498MC	Boeing 747-47UF	Atlas Air	
N499MC	Boeing 747-47UF	Atlas Air/Polar Air Cargo	
N517MC	Boeing 747-243F (SCD)	Atlas Air	
N521FE	McD Douglas MD-11F	Federal Express	
N522FE	McD Douglas MD-11F	Federal Express	
N523FE	McD Douglas MD-11F	Federal Express	
N524FE	McD Douglas MD-11F	Federal Express	
N525FE	McD Douglas MD-11F	Federal Express	
N527FE	McD Douglas MD-11F	Federal Express	
N528FE	McD Douglas MD-11F	Federal Express	
N529FE	McD Douglas MD-11F	Federal Express	
N572FE	McD Douglas MD-11F	Federal Express	
N573FE	McD Douglas MD-11F	Federal Express	
N574FE	McD Douglas MD-11F	Federal Express	
N575FE	McD Douglas MD-11F	Federal Express	
N576FE	McD Douglas MD-11F	Federal Express	
N577FE	McD Douglas MD-11F	Federal Express	
N578FE	McD Douglas MD-11F	Federal Express *Stephen*	
N579FE	McD Douglas MD-11F	Federal Express *Nash*	
N580FE	McD Douglas MD-11F	Federal Express *Ashton*	
N582FE	McD Douglas MD-11F	Federal Express *Jamie*	
N583FE	McD Douglas MD-11F	Federal Express *Nancy*	
N584FE	McD Douglas MD-11F	Federal Express *Jeffrey Wellington*	
N585FE	McD Douglas MD-11F	Federal Express *Katherine*	
N586FE	McD Douglas MD-11F	Federal Express *Dylan*	
N587FE	McD Douglas MD-11F	Federal Express *Jeanna*	
N588FE	McD Douglas MD-11F	Federal Express *Kendra*	
N589FE	McD Douglas MD-11F	Federal Express *Shaun*	
N590FE	McD Douglas MD-11F	Federal Express	
N591FE	McD Douglas MD-11F	Federal Express *Giovanni*	
N592FE	McD Douglas MD-11F	Federal Express *Joshua*	
N593FE	McD Douglas MD-11F	Federal Express *Harrison*	
N594FE	McD Douglas MD-11F	Federal Express	
N595FE	McD Douglas MD-11F	Federal Express *Avery*	
N596FE	McD Douglas MD-11F	Federal Express	
N597FE	McD Douglas MD-11F	Federal Express	
N598FE	McD Douglas MD-11F	Federal Express	
N599FE	McD Douglas MD-11F	Federal Express *Mariana*	
N601FE	McD Douglas MD-11F	Federal Express *Jim Riedmeyer*	
N602FE	McD Douglas MD-11F	Federal Express *Malcolm Baldridge 1990*	
N603FE	McD Douglas MD-11F	Federal Express *Elizabeth*	
N604FE	McD Douglas MD-11F	Federal Express *Hollis*	
N605FE	McD Douglas MD-11F	Federal Express *April Star*	
N606FE	McD Douglas MD-11F	Federal Express *Charles & Theresa*	
N607FE	McD Douglas MD-11F	Federal Express *Christina*	
N608FE	McD Douglas MD-11F	Federal Express *Karen*	
N609FE	McD Douglas MD-11F	Federal Express *Scott*	
N610FE	McD Douglas MD-11F	Federal Express *Marisa*	
N612FE	McD Douglas MD-11F	Federal Express *Alyssa*	
N613FE	McD Douglas MD-11F	Federal Express *Krista*	
N614FE	McD Douglas MD-11F	Federal Express *Christy Allison*	
N615FE	McD Douglas MD-11F	Federal Express *Max*	
N616FE	McD Douglas MD-11F	Federal Express *Shanita*	
N617FE	McD Douglas MD-11F	Federal Express *Travis*	
N618FE	McD Douglas MD-11F	Federal Express *Justin*	
N619FE	McD Douglas MD-11F	Federal Express *Lyndon*	
N620FE	McD Douglas MD-11F	Federal Express	
N621FE	McD Douglas MD-11F	Federal Express *Connor*	
N623FE	McD Douglas MD-11F	Federal Express *Meghan*	
N624FE	McD Douglas MD-11F	Federal Express	
N625FE	McD Douglas MD-11F	Federal Express	
N628FE	McD Douglas MD-11F	Federal Express	
N631FE	McD Douglas MD-11F	Federal Express	
N641UA	Boeing 767-322ER	United Airlines	
N642FE	McD Douglas MD-11F	Federal Express	

Notes	Reg.	Type	Owner or Operator
	N642UA	Boeing 767-322ER	United Airlines
	N643FE	McD Douglas MD-11F	Federal Express
	N643UA	Boeing 767-322ER	United Airlines
	N644FE	McD Douglas MD-11F	Federal Express
	N644UA	Boeing 767-322ER	United Airlines
	N645FE	McD Douglas MD-11F	Federal Express
	N646UA	Boeing 767-322ER	United Airlines
	N647UA	Boeing 767-322ER	United Airlines
	N648UA	Boeing 767-322ER	United Airlines
	N649UA	Boeing 767-322ER	United Airlines
	N651UA	Boeing 767-322ER	United Airlines
	N652UA	Boeing 767-322ER	United Airlines
	N653UA	Boeing 767-322ER	United Airlines
	N654UA	Boeing 767-322ER	United Airlines
	N655UA	Boeing 767-322ER	United Airlines
	N656UA	Boeing 767-322ER	United Airlines
	N657UA	Boeing 767-322ER	United Airlines
	N658UA	Boeing 767-322ER	United Airlines
	N659UA	Boeing 767-322ER	United Airlines
	N660UA	Boeing 767-322ER	United Airlines
	N661UA	Boeing 767-322ER	United Airlines
	N662UA	Boeing 767-322ER	United Airlines
	N663UA	Boeing 767-322ER	United Airlines
	N702TW	Boeing 757-2Q8	Delta Air Lines
	N703TW	Boeing 757-2Q8	Delta Air Lines
	N704CK	Boeing 747-246F	Kalitta Air
	N704X	Boeing 757-2Q8	Delta Air Lines
	N705TW	Boeing 757-231	Delta Air Lines
	N706TW	Boeing 757-2Q8	Delta Air Lines
	N707TW	Boeing 757-2Q8	Delta Air Lines
	N709TW	Boeing 757-2Q8	Delta Air Lines
	N710TW	Boeing 757-2Q8	Delta Air Lines
	N711ZX	Boeing 757-231	Delta Air Lines
	N712TW	Boeing 757-2Q8	Delta Air Lines
	N713TW	Boeing 757-2Q8	Delta Air Lines
	N717AN	Boeing 777-323ER	American Airlines
	N717TW	Boeing 757-231	Delta Air Lines
	N718AN	Boeing 777-323ER	American Airlines
	N718TW	Boeing 757-231	Delta Air Lines
	N719AN	Boeing 777-323ER	American Airlines
	N720AN	Boeing 777-323ER	American Airlines
	N721AN	Boeing 777-323ER	American Airlines
	N721TW	Boeing 757-231	Delta Air Lines
	N722AN	Boeing 777-323ER	American Airlines
	N722TW	Boeing 757-231	Delta Air Lines
	N723AN	Boeing 777-323ER	American Airlines
	N723TW	Boeing 757-231	Delta Air Lines
	N724AN	Boeing 777-323ER	American Airlines
	N725AN	Boeing 777-323ER	American Airlines
	N726AN	Boeing 777-323ER	American Airlines
	N727TW	Boeing 757-231	Delta Air Lines
	N740CK	Boeing 747-4H6BCF	Kalitta Air
	N740WA	Boeing 747-4H6F	World Airways
	N741CK	Boeing 747-4H6F	Kalitta Air
	N742CK	Boeing 747-446BCF	Kalitta Air
	N743CK	Boeing 747-446BCF	Kalitta Air
	N742WA	Boeing 747-412F	World Airways
	N744CK	Boeing 747-446BCF	Kalitta Air
	N745CK	Boeing 747-446BCF	Kalitta Air
	N746CK	Boeing 747-246B	Kalitta Air
	N748CK	Boeing 747-221F	Kalitta Air
	N750AN	Boeing 777-223ER	American Airlines
	N751AN	Boeing 777-223ER	American Airlines
	N752AN	Boeing 777-223ER	American Airlines
	N753AN	Boeing 777-223ER	American Airlines
	N754AN	Boeing 777-223ER	American Airlines
	N755AN	Boeing 777-223ER	American Airlines
	N756AM	Boeing 777-223ER	American Airlines
	N757AN	Boeing 777-223ER	American Airlines
	N758AN	Boeing 777-223ER	American Airlines
	N759AN	Boeing 777-223ER	American Airlines
	N760AN	Boeing 777-223ER	American Airlines

Reg.	Type	Owner or Operator	Notes
N761AJ	Boeing 777-223ER	American Airlines	
N762AN	Boeing 777-223ER	American Airlines	
N765AN	Boeing 777-223ER	American Airlines	
N766AN	Boeing 777-223ER	American Airlines	
N767AJ	Boeing 777-223ER	American Airlines	
N768AA	Boeing 777-223ER	American Airlines	
N768UA	Boeing 777-222	United Airlines	
N769UA	Boeing 777-222	United Airlines	
N770AN	Boeing 777-223ER	American Airlines	
N771AN	Boeing 777-223ER	American Airlines	
N771UA	Boeing 777-222	United Airlines	
N772AN	Boeing 777-223ER	American Airlines	
N772UA	Boeing 777-222	United Airlines	
N773AN	Boeing 777-223ER	American Airlines	
N773UA	Boeing 777-222	United Airlines	
N774AN	Boeing 777-223ER	American Airlines	
N774UA	Boeing 777-222	United Airlines	
N775AN	Boeing 777-223ER	American Airlines	
N775UA	Boeing 777-222	United Airlines	
N776AN	Boeing 777-223ER	American Airlines	
N776UA	Boeing 777-222	United Airlines	
N777AN	Boeing 777-223ER	American Airlines	
N777UA	Boeing 777-222	United Airlines	
N778AN	Boeing 777-223ER	American Airlines	
N778UA	Boeing 777-222	United Airlines	
N779AN	Boeing 777-223ER	American Airlines	
N779UA	Boeing 777-222	United Airlines	
N780AN	Boeing 777-223ER	American Airlines	
N780UA	Boeing 777-222	United Airlines	
N781AN	Boeing 777-223ER	American Airlines	
N781UA	Boeing 777-222	United Airlines	
N782AN	Boeing 777-223ER	American Airlines	
N782CK	Boeing 747-4HQF	Kalitta Air	
N782UA	Boeing 777-222ER	United Airlines	
N783AN	Boeing 777-223ER	American Airlines	
N783UA	Boeing 777-222ER	United Airlines	
N784AN	Boeing 777-223ER	American Airlines	
N784UA	Boeing 777-222ER	United Airlines	
N785AN	Boeing 777-223ER	American Airlines	
N785UA	Boeing 777-222ER	United Airlines	
N786AN	Boeing 777-223ER	American Airlines	
N786UA	Boeing 777-222ER	United Airlines	
N787AL	Boeing 777-223ER	American Airlines	
N787UA	Boeing 777-222ER	United Airlines	
N788AN	Boeing 777-223ER	American Airlines	
N788UA	Boeing 777-222ER	United Airlines	
N789AN	Boeing 777-223ER	American Airlines	
N790AN	Boeing 777-223ER	American Airlines	
N791AN	Boeing 777-223ER	American Airlines	
N791UA	Boeing 777-222ER	United Airlines	
N792CK	Boeing 747-212F	Kalitta Air	
N792AN	Boeing 777-223ER	American Airlines	
N792UA	Boeing 777-222ER	United Airlines	
N793AN	Boeing 777-223ER	American Airlines	
N793UA	Boeing 777-222ER	United Airlines	
N794AN	Boeing 777-223ER	American Airlines	
N794CK	Boeing 747-222B	Kalitta Air	
N794UA	Boeing 777-222ER	United Airlines	
N795AN	Boeing 777-223ER	American Airlines	
N795CK	Boeing 747-251B	Kalitta Air	
N795UA	Boeing 777-222ER	United Airlines	
N796AN	Boeing 777-223ER	American Airlines	
N796UA	Boeing 777-222ER	United Airlines	
N797AN	Boeing 777-223ER	American Airlines	
N797UA	Boeing 777-222ER	United Airlines	
N798AN	Boeing 777-223ER	American Airlines	
N798UA	Boeing 777-222ER	United Airlines	
N799AN	Boeing 777-223ER	American Airlines	
N799UA	Boeing 777-222ER	United Airlines	
N801NW	Airbus A.330-323X	Delta Airlines	
N802NW	Airbus A.330-323X	Delta Airlines	
N803NW	Airbus A.330-323X	Delta Air Lines	

Notes	Reg.	Type	Owner or Operator
	N804NW	Airbus A.330-323X	Delta Air Lines
	N805NW	Airbus A.330-323X	Delta Air Lines
	N806NW	Airbus A.330-323X	Delta Air Lines
	N807NW	Airbus A.330-323X	Delta Air Lines
	N808NW	Airbus A.330-323X	Delta Air Lines
	N809NW	Airbus A.330-323E	Delta Air Lines
	N810NW	Airbus A.330-323E	Delta Air Lines
	N811NW	Airbus A.330-323E	Delta Air Lines
	N812NW	Airbus A.330-323E	Delta Air Lines
	N813NW	Airbus A.330-323E	Delta Air Lines
	N814NW	Airbus A.330-323E	Delta Air Lines
	N815NW	Airbus A.330-323E	Delta Air Lines
	N816NW	Airbus A.330-323E	Delta Air Lines
	N817NW	Airbus A.330-323E	Delta Air Lines
	N818NW	Airbus A.330-323E	Delta Air Lines
	N819NW	Airbus A.330-323E	Delta Air Lines
	N820NW	Airbus A.330-323E	Delta Air Lines
	N821NW	Airbus A.330-323E	Delta Air Lines
	N825MH	Boeing 767-432ER (1801)	Delta Air Lines
	N826MH	Boeing 767-432ER (1802)	Delta Air Lines
	N827MH	Boeing 767-432ER (1803)	Delta Air Lines
	N828MH	Boeing 767-432ER (1804)	Delta Air Lines
	N829MH	Boeing 767-432ER (1805)	Delta Air Lines
	N830MH	Boeing 767-432ER (1806)	Delta Air Lines
	N831MH	Boeing 767-432ER (1807)	Delta Air Lines
	N832MH	Boeing 767-432ER (1808)	Delta Air Lines
	N833MH	Boeing 767-432ER (1809)	Delta Air Lines
	N834MH	Boeing 767-432ER (1810)	Delta Air Lines
	N835MH	Boeing 767-432ER (1811)	Delta Air Lines
	N836MH	Boeing 767-432ER (1812)	Delta Air Lines
	N837MH	Boeing 767-432ER (1813)	Delta Air Lines
	N838MH	Boeing 767-432ER (1814)	Delta Air Lines
	N839MH	Boeing 767-432ER (1815)	Delta Air Lines
	N840MH	Boeing 767-432ER (1816)	Delta Air Lines
	N841MH	Boeing 767-432ER (1817)	Delta Air Lines
	N842MH	Boeing 767-432ER (1818)	Delta Air Lines
	N843MH	Boeing 767-432ER (1819)	Delta Air Lines
	N844MH	Boeing 767-432ER (1820)	Delta Air Lines
	N845MH	Boeing 767-432ER (1821)	Delta Air Lines
	N850FD	Boeing 777-2S2LRF	Federal Express
	N851FD	Boeing 777-2S2LRF	Federal Express
	N851NW	Airbus A.330-223	Delta Air Lines
	N852FD	Boeing 777-2S2LRF	Federal Express
	N852NW	Airbus A.330-223	Delta Air Lines
	N853FD	Boeing 777-2S2LRF	Federal Express
	N853NW	Airbus A.330-223	Delta Air Lines
	N854FD	Boeing 777-2S2LRF	Federal Express
	N854NW	Airbus A.330-223	Delta Air Lines
	N855FD	Boeing 777-2S2LRF	Federal Express
	N855NW	Airbus A.330-223	Delta Air Lines
	N856FD	Boeing 777-2S2LRF	Federal Express
	N856NW	Airbus A.330-223	Delta Air Lines
	N857FD	Boeing 777-2S2LRF	Federal Express
	N857NW	Airbus A.330-223	Delta Air Lines
	N858FD	Boeing 777-2S2LRF	Federal Express
	N858NW	Airbus A.330-223	Delta Air Lines
	N859FD	Boeing 777-2S2LRF	Federal Express
	N859NW	Airbus A.330-223	Delta Air Lines
	N860FD	Boeing 777-2S2LRF	Federal Express
	N860NW	Airbus A.330-223	Delta Air Lines
	N861FD	Boeing 777-2S2LRF	Federal Express
	N861NW	Airbus A.330-223	Delta Air Lines
	N862FD	Boeing 777-2S2LRF	Federal Express
	N863FD	Boeing 777-2S2LRF	Federal Express
	N864FD	Boeing 777-2S2LRF	Federal Express
	N880FD	Boeing 777-2S2LRF	Federal Express
	N882FD	Boeing 777-2S2LRF	Federal Express
	N883FD	Boeing 777-2S2LRF	Federal Express
	N884FD	Boeing 777-2S2LRF	Federal Express
	N885FD	Boeing 777-2S2LRF	Federal Express
	N886FD	Boeing 777-2S2LRF	Federal Express
	N887FD	Boeing 777-2S2LRF	Federal Express

Reg.	Type	Owner or Operator	Notes
N889FD	Boeing 777-2S2LRF	Federal Express	
N890FD	Boeing 777-2S2LRF	Federal Express	
N892FD	Boeing 777-2S2LRF	Federal Express	
N901FD	Boeing 757-2B7	Federal Express	
N903FD	Boeing 757-2B7	Federal Express	
N915FD	Boeing 757-236	Federal Express	
N916FD	Boeing 757-2B7	Federal Express	
N917FD	Boeing 757-23A	Federal Express	
N918FD	Boeing 757-23A	Federal Express	
N919FD	Boeing 757-23A	Federal Express	
N922FD	Boeing 757-23A	Federal Express	
N923FD	Boeing 757-204	Federal Express	
N937UW	Boeing 757-2B7	US Airways	
N938UW	Boeing 757-2B7	US Airways	
N939UW	Boeing 757-2B7	US Airways	
N940UW	Boeing 757-2B7	US Airways	
N941UW	Boeing 757-2B7	US Airways	
N942UW	Boeing 757-2B7	US Airways	
N1200K	Boeing 767-332ER (200)	Delta Air Lines	
N1201P	Boeing 767-332ER (201)	Delta Air Lines	
N1501P	Boeing 767-3P6ER (1501)	Delta Air Lines	
N1602	Boeing 767-332ER (1602)	Delta Air Lines	
N1603	Boeing 767-332ER (1603)	Delta Air Lines	
N1604R	Boeing 767-332ER (1604)	Delta Air Lines	
N1605	Boeing 767-332ER (1605)	Delta Air Lines	
N1607B	Boeing 767-332ER (1607)	Delta Air Lines	
N1608	Boeing 767-332ER (1608)	Delta Air Lines	
N1609	Boeing 767-332ER (1609)	Delta Air Lines	
N1610D	Boeing 767-332ER (1610)	Delta Air Lines	
N1611B	Boeing 767-332ER (1611)	Delta Air Lines	
N1612T	Boeing 767-332ER (1612)	Delta Air Lines	
N1613B	Boeing 767-332ER (1613)	Delta Air Lines	
N7375A	Boeing 767-323ER	American Airlines	
N12109	Boeing 757-224	United Airlines	
N12114	Boeing 757-224	United Airlines	
N12116	Boeing 757-224	United Airlines	
N12125	Boeing 757-224	United Airlines	
N13110	Boeing 757-224	United Airlines	
N13113	Boeing 757-224	United Airlines	
N13138	Boeing 757-224	United Airlines	
N14102	Boeing 757-224	United Airlines	
N14106	Boeing 757-224	United Airlines	
N14107	Boeing 757-224	United Airlines	
N14115	Boeing 757-224	United Airlines	
N14118	Boeing 757-224	United Airlines	
N14120	Boeing 757-224	United Airlines	
N14121	Boeing 757-224	United Airlines	
N16065	Boeing 767-332ER (1606)	Delta Air Lines	
N17104	Boeing 757-224	United Airlines	
N17105	Boeing 757-224	United Airlines	
N17122	Boeing 757-224	United Airlines	
N17126	Boeing 757-224	United Airlines	
N17128	Boeing 757-224	United Airlines	
N17133	Boeing 757-224	United Airlines	
N17139	Boeing 757-224	United Airlines	
N18112	Boeing 757-224	United Airlines	
N18119	Boeing 757-224	United Airlines	
N19117	Boeing 757-224	United Airlines	
N19130	Boeing 757-224	United Airlines	
N19136	Boeing 757-224	United Airlines	
N19141	Boeing 757-224	United Airlines	
N20904	Boeing 787-8	United Airlines	
N21108	Boeing 757-224	United Airlines	
N26123	Boeing 757-224	United Airlines	
N26902	Boeing 787-8	United Airlines	
N27901	Boeing 787-8	United Airlines	
N26902	Boeing 787-8	United Airlines	
N27903	Boeing 787-8	United Airlines	
N26906	Boeing 787-8	United Airlines	
N27015	Boeing 777-224ER	United Airlines	
N27910	Boeing 787-8	United Airlines	
N29124	Boeing 757-224	United Airlines	

Notes	Reg.	Type	Owner or Operator
	N29129	Boeing 757-224	United Airlines
	N33103	Boeing 757-224	United Airlines
	N33132	Boeing 757-224	United Airlines
	N34131	Boeing 757-224	United Airlines
	N34137	Boeing 757-224	United Airlines
	N37018	Boeing 777-224ER	United Airlines
	N39356	Boeing 767-323ER	American Airlines
	N39364	Boeing 767-323ER	American Airlines
	N39365	Boeing 767-323ER	American Airlines
	N39367	Boeing 767-323ER	American Airlines
	N41135	Boeing 757-224	United Airlines
	N41140	Boeing 757-224	United Airlines
	N45905	Boeing 787-8	United Airlines
	N48127	Boeing 757-224	United Airlines
	N57016	Boeing 777-224ER	United Airlines
	N57111	Boeing 757-224	United Airlines
	N58101	Boeing 757-224	United Airlines
	N59053	Boeing 767-424ER	United Airlines
	N66051	Boeing 767-424ER	United Airlines
	N66056	Boeing 767-424ER	United Airlines
	N66057	Boeing 767-424ER	United Airlines
	N67052	Boeing 767-424ER	United Airlines
	N67058	Boeing 767-424ER	United Airlines
	N67134	Boeing 757-224	United Airlines
	N67157	Boeing 767-224ER	United Airlines
	N68061	Boeing 767-424ER	United Airlines
	N68155	Boeing 767-224ER	United Airlines
	N68159	Boeing 767-224ER	United Airlines
	N68160	Boeing 767-224ER	United Airlines
	N69020	Boeing 777-224ER	United Airlines
	N69059	Boeing 767-424ER	United Airlines
	N69063	Boeing 767-424ER	United Airlines
	N69154	Boeing 767-224ER	United Airlines
	N73152	Boeing 767-224ER	United Airlines
	N74007	Boeing 777-224ER	United Airlines
	N76010	Boeing 777-224ER	United Airlines
	N76021	Boeing 777-224ER	United Airlines
	N76054	Boeing 767-424ER	United Airlines
	N76055	Boeing 767-424ER	United Airlines
	N76062	Boeing 767-424ER	United Airlines
	N76064	Boeing 767-424ER	United Airlines
	N76065	Boeing 767-424ER	United Airlines
	N76151	Boeing 767-224ER	United Airlines
	N76153	Boeing 767-224ER	United Airlines
	N77006	Boeing 777-224ER	United Airlines
	N77012	Boeing 777-224ER	United Airlines
	N77014	Boeing 777-224ER	United Airlines
	N77019	Boeing 777-224ER	United Airlines
	N77022	Boeing 777-224ER	United Airlines
	N77066	Boeing 767-424ER	United Airlines
	N78001	Boeing 777-224ER	United Airlines
	N78002	Boeing 777-224ER	United Airlines
	N78003	Boeing 777-224ER	United Airlines
	N78004	Boeing 777-224ER	United Airlines
	N78005	Boeing 777-224ER	United Airlines
	N78008	Boeing 777-224ER	United Airlines
	N78009	Boeing 777-224ER	United Airlines
	N78013	Boeing 777-224ER	United Airlines
	N78017	Boeing 777-224ER	United Airlines
	N78060	Boeing 767-424ER	United Airlines
	N79011	Boeing 777-224ER	United Airlines

OD (Lebanon)

	OD-MEA	Airbus A.330-243	Middle East Airlines
	OD-MEB	Airbus A.330-243	Middle East Airlines
	OD-MEC	Airbus A.330-243	Middle East Airlines
	OD-MRL	Airbus A.320-232	Middle East Airlines
	OD-MRM	Airbus A.320-232	Middle East Airlines
	OD-MRR	Airbus A.320-232	Middle East Airlines
	OD-MRS	Airbus A.320-232	Middle East Airlines

Reg.	Type	Owner or Operator	Notes
OD-MRT	Airbus A.320-232	Middle East Airlines	
OD-RMH	Airbus A.321-231	Middle East Airlines	
OD-RMI	Airbus A.321-231	Middle East Airlines	
OD-RMJ	Airbus A.321-231	Middle East Airlines	
OD-TMA	Airbus A.300F4-605R	TMA – Trans Mediterranean Airways	

OE (Austria)

OE-IAT	Boeing 737-4MO	TNT Airways	
OE-IHA	Embraer ERJ190-100LR	Niki *Samba*	
OE-IHB	Embraer ERJ190-100LR	Niki *Lambada*	
OE-IHC	Embraer ERJ190-100LR	Niki *Bossa Nova*	
OE-IHD	Embraer ERJ190-100LR	Niki *Calypso*	
OE-IHE	Embraer ERJ190-100LR	Niki *Rumba*	
OE-IHF	Embraer ERJ190-100LR	Niki *Salsa*	
OE-IHG	Embraer ERJ190-100LR	Niki *Tango*	
OE-LAE	Boeing 767-3Z9ER	Austrian Airlines *Malaysia*	
OE-LAT	Boeing 767-31AER	Austrian Airlines *Enzo Ferrari*	
OE-LAW	Boeing 767-3Z9ER	Austrian Airlines *China*	
OE-LAX	Boeing 767-3Z9ER	Austrian Airlines *Thailand*	
OE-LAY	Boeing 767-3Z9ER	Austrian Airlines *Japan*	
OE-LAZ	Boeing 767-3Z9ER	Austrian Airlines *India*	
OE-LBA	Airbus A.321-111	Austrian Airlines *Salzkammergut*	
OE-LBB	Airbus A.321-111	Austrian Airlines *Pinzgau*	
OE-LBC	Airbus A.321-111	Austrian Airlines *Sudtirol*	
OE-LBD	Airbus A.321-111	Austrian Airlines *Steirisches Weinland*	
OE-LBE	Airbus A.321-111	Austrian Airlines *Wachau*	
OE-LBF	Airbus A.321-111	Austrian Airlines *Wien*	
OE-LBI	Airbus A.320-214	Austrian Airlines *Marchfeld*	
OE-LBN	Airbus A.320-214	Austrian Airlines *Osttirol*	
OE-LBO	Airbus A.320-214	Austrian Airlines *Pyhrn-Eisenwurzen*	
OE-LBP	Airbus A.320-214	Austrian Airlines *Neusiedler See*	
OE-LBQ	Airbus A.320-214	Austrian Airlines *Wienerwald*	
OE-LBR	Airbus A.320-214	Austrian Airlines *Frida Kahle*	
OE-LBS	Airbus A.320-214	Austrian Airlines *Waldviertel*	
OE-LBT	Airbus A.320-214	Austrian Airlines *Worthersee*	
OE-LBU	Airbus A.320-214	Austrian Airlines *Muhlviertel*	
OE-LBV	Airbus A.320-214	Austrian Airlines *Weinviertel*	
OE-LBW	Airbus A.320-214	Austrian Airlines	
OE-LBX	Airbus A.320-214	Austrian Airlines	
OE-LDA	Airbus A.319-112	Austrian Airlines *Sofia*	
OE-LDB	Airbus A.319-112	Austrian Airlines *Bucharest*	
OE-LDC	Airbus A.319-112	Austrian Airlines *Kiev*	
OE-LDD	Airbus A.319-112	Austrian Airlines *Moscow*	
OE-LDE	Airbus A.319-112	Austrian Airlines *Baku*	
OE-LDF	Airbus A.319-112	Austrian Airlines *Sarajevo*	
OE-LDG	Airbus A.319-112	Austrian Airlines *Tbilisi*	
OE-LEA	Airbus A.320-214	Niki *Rock 'n Roll*	
OE-LEB	Airbus A.320-214	Niki *Polka*	
OE-LEC	Airbus A.320-214	Niki *Flamenco*	
OE-LEE	Airbus A.320-214	Niki *Reggae*	
OE-LEF	Airbus A.320-214	Niki *Sirtaki*	
OE-LEG	Airbus A.320-214	Niki *Bolero*	
OE-LEH	Airbus A.320-214	Niki *Gospel*	
OE-LEL	Airbus A.320-214	Niki	
OE-LES	Airbus A.321-211	Niki *Boogie Woogie*	
OE-LET	Airbus A.321-211	Niki *Heavy Metal*	
OE-LEU	Airbus A.320-214	Niki *Cancan*	
OE-LEW	Airbus A.321-211	Niki *Cancan*	
OE-LEX	Airbus A.320-214	Niki *Jazz*	
OE-LEZ	Airbus A.321-211	Niki *Blues*	
OE-LFG	Fokker 70	Austrian Airlines *Innsbruck*	
OE-LFH	Fokker 70	Austrian Airlines *Salzburg*	
OE-LFI	Fokker 70	Austrian Airlines *Klagenfurt*	
OE-LFJ	Fokker 70	Austrian Airlines *Graz*	
OE-LFK	Fokker 70	Austrian Airlines *Wien*	
OE-LFL	Fokker 70	Austrian Airlines *Linz*	
OE-LFP	Fokker 70	Austrian Airlines *Wels*	
OE-LFQ	Fokker 70	Austrian Airlines *Dornbirn*	
OE-LFR	Fokker 70	Austrian Airlines *Steyr*	
OE-LGA	DHC.8Q-402 Dash Eight	Austrian Airlines *Karnten*	

Notes	Reg.	Type	Owner or Operator
	OE-LGB	DHC.8Q-402 Dash Eight	Austrian Airlines *Tirol*
	OE-LGC	DHC.8Q-402 Dash Eight	Austrian Airlines *Salzburg*
	OE-LGD	DHC.8Q-402 Dash Eight	Austrian Airlines *Steiermark*
	OE-LGE	DHC.8Q-402 Dash Eight	Austrian Airlines *Oberosterreich*
	OE-LGF	DHC.8Q-402 Dash Eight	Austrian Airlines *Niederosterreich*
	OE-LGG	DHC.8Q-402 Dash Eight	Austrian Airlines *Budapest*
	OE-LGH	DHC.8Q-402 Dash Eight	Austrian Airlines *Vorarlberg*
	OE-LGI	DHC.8Q-402 Dash Eight	Austrian Airlines *Eisenstadt*
	OE-LGJ	DHC.8Q-402 Dash Eight	Austrian Airlines *St Pölten*
	OE-LGK	DHC.8Q-402 Dash Eight	Austrian Airlines *Burgenland*
	OE-LGL	DHC.8Q-402 Dash Eight	Austrian Airlines *Altenrhein*
	OE-LGM	DHC.8Q-402 Dash Eight	Austrian Airlines *Villach*
	OE-LGN	DHC.8Q-402 Dash Eight	Austrian Airlines *Gmunden*
	OE-LNK	Boeing 737-8Z9	Austrian Airlines *Falco*
	OE-LNP	Boeing 737-8Z9	Austrian Airlines *George Harrison*
	OE-LNR	Boeing 737-8Z9	Austrian Airlines *Frank Zappa*
	OE-LOA	Airbus A.319-112	Niki
	OE-LOB	Airbus A.319-112	Niki
	OE-LOC	Airbus A.319-112	Niki
	OE-LOD	Airbus A.319-112	Niki
	OE-LOE	Airbus A.319-112	Niki
	OE-LPA	Boeing 777-2Z9	Austrian Airlines *Melbourne*
	OE-LPB	Boeing 777-2Z9	Austrian Airlines *Sydney*
	OE-LPC	Boeing 777-2Z9ER	Austrian Airlines *Donald Bradman*
	OE-LPD	Boeing 777-2Z9ER	Austrian Airlines *America*
	OE-LVA	Fokker 100	Austrian Airlines *Riga*
	OE-LVB	Fokker 100	Austrian Airlines *Vilnius*
	OE-LVC	Fokker 100	Austrian Airlines *Tirana*
	OE-LVD	Fokker 100	Austrian Airlines *Belgrade*
	OE-LVE	Fokker 100	Austrian Airlines *Zagreb*
	OE-LVF	Fokker 100	Austrian Airlines *Yerevan*
	OE-LVG	Fokker 100	Austrian Airlines *Krakow*
	OE-LVH	Fokker 100	Austrian Airlines *Minsk*
	OE-LVI	Fokker 100	Austrian Airlines *Prague*
	OE-LVJ	Fokker 100	Austrian Airlines *Bratislava*
	OE-LVK	Fokker 100	Austrian Airlines *Timisoara*
	OE-LVL	Fokker 100	Austrian Airlines *Odessa*
	OE-LVM	Fokker 100	Austrian Airlines *Krasnodar*
	OE-LVN	Fokker 100	Austrian Airlines *Dnepropetrovsk*
	OE-LVO	Fokker 100	Austrian Airlines *Chisinau*

OH (Finland)

	OH-BLG	Boeing 717-2CM	Blue 1
	OH-BLH	Boeing 717-2CM	Blue 1
	OH-BLI	Boeing 717-2CM	Blue 1
	OH-BLJ	Boeing 717-23S	Blue 1
	OH-BLM	Boeing 717-23S	Blue 1
	OH-BLN	Boeing 717-2K9	Blue 1
	OH-BLO	Boeing 717-2K9	Blue 1
	OH-BLP	Boeing 717-23S	Blue 1
	OH-BLQ	Boeing 717-2K9	Blue 1
	OH-LBO	Boeing 757-2Q8	Finnair
	OH-LBR	Boeing 757-2Q8	Finnair
	OH-LBS	Boeing 757-2Q8	Finnair
	OH-LBT	Boeing 757-2Q8	Finnair
	OH-LEI	Embraer RJ170-100STD	Finnair
	OH-LEK	Embraer RJ170-100STD	Finnair
	OH-LGC	McD Douglas MD-11F	Nordic Global Airlines
	OH-LGD	McD Douglas MD-11F	Nordic Global Airlines
	OH-LKE	Embraer RJ190-100LR	Finnair
	OH-LKF	Embraer RJ190-100LR	Finnair
	OH-LKG	Embraer RJ190-100LR	Finnair
	OH-LKH	Embraer RJ190-100LR	Finnair
	OH-LKI	Embraer RJ190-100LR	Finnair
	OH-LKK	Embraer RJ190-100LR	Finnair
	OH-LKL	Embraer RJ190-100LR	Finnair
	OH-LKM	Embraer RJ190-100LR	Finnair
	OH-LKN	Embraer RJ190-100LR	Finnair
	OH-LKO	Embraer RJ190-100LR	Finnair
	OH-LKP	Embraer RJ190-100LR	Finnair

Reg.	Type	Owner or Operator	Notes
OH-LKR	Embraer RJ190-100LR	Finnair	
OH-LQA	Airbus A.340-311	Finnair	
OH-LQB	Airbus A.340-313X	Finnair	
OH-LQC	Airbus A.340-313E	Finnair	
OH-LQD	Airbus A.340-313E	Finnair	
OH-LQE	Airbus A.340-313E	Finnair	
OH-LQF	Airbus A.340-313X	Finnair	
OH-LQG	Airbus A.340-313X	Finnair	
OH-LTM	Airbus A.330-302	Finnair	
OH-LTN	Airbus A.330-302	Finnair	
OH-LTO	Airbus A.330-302	Finnair	
OH-LTP	Airbus A.330-302	Finnair	
OH-LTR	Airbus A.330-302	Finnair	
OH-LTS	Airbus A.330-302	Finnair	
OH-LTT	Airbus A.330-302	Finnair	
OH-LTU	Airbus A.330-302	Finnair	
OH-LVA	Airbus A.319-112	Finnair	
OH-LVB	Airbus A.319-112	Finnair	
OH-LVC	Airbus A.319-112	Finnair	
OH-LVD	Airbus A.319-112	Finnair	
OH-LVG	Airbus A.319-112	Finnair	
OH-LVH	Airbus A.319-112	Finnair	
OH-LVI	Airbus A.319-112	Finnair	
OH-LVK	Airbus A.319-112	Finnair	
OH-LVL	Airbus A.319-112	Finnair	
OH-LXA	Airbus A.320-214	Finnair	
OH-LXB	Airbus A.320-214	Finnair	
OH-LXC	Airbus A.320-214	Finnair	
OH-LXD	Airbus A.320-214	Finnair	
OH-LXF	Airbus A.320-214	Finnair	
OH-LXH	Airbus A.320-214	Finnair	
OH-LXI	Airbus A.320-214	Finnair	
OH-LXK	Airbus A.320-214	Finnair	
OH-LXL	Airbus A.320-214	Finnair	
OH-LXM	Airbus A.320-214	Finnair	
OH-LZA	Airbus A.321-211	Finnair	
OH-LZB	Airbus A.321-211	Finnair	
OH-LZC	Airbus A.321-211	Finnair	
OH-LZD	Airbus A.321-211	Finnair	
OH-LZE	Airbus A.321-211	Finnair	
OH-LZF	Airbus A.321-211	Finnair	
OH-NGA	McD Douglas MD-11F	Nordic Global Airlines	
OH-NGB	McD Douglas MD-11F	Nordic Global Airlines	

OK (Czech Republic)

Reg.	Type	Owner or Operator	Notes
OK-ASA	Let L410UVP-E	Citywing	
OK-CEC	Airbus A.321-211	CSA Czech Airlines *Nove Mesto nad Metuji*	
OK-CED	Airbus A.321-211	CSA Czech Airlines *Havlikuv Brod*	
OK-DGL	Boeing 737-55S	CSA Czech Airlines *Tabor*	
OK-HCA	Airbus A.320-214	Holidays Czech Airlines	
OK-HCB	Airbus A.320-214	Holidays Czech Airlines	
OK-LEE	Airbus A.320-214	Holidays Czech Airlines	
OK-LEF	Airbus A.320-214	Holidays Czech Airlines	
OK-LEG	Airbus A.320-214	Holidays Czech Airlines	
OK-MEH	Airbus A.320-214	CSA Czech Airlines	
OK-MEI	Airbus A.320-214	CSA Czech Airlines	
OK-MEJ	Airbus A.320-214	CSA Czech Airlines	
OK-MEK	Airbus A.319-112	CSA Czech Airlines	
OK-MEL	Airbus A.319-112	CSA Czech Airlines	
OK-NEM	Airbus A.319-112	CSA Czech Airlines	
OK-NEN	Airbus A.319-112	CSA Czech Airlines	
OK-NEO	Airbus A.319-112	CSA Czech Airlines	
OK-NEP	Airbus A.319-112	CSA Czech Airlines	
OK-OER	Airbus A.319-112	CSA Czech Airlines	
OK-PET	Airbus A.319-112	CSA Czech Airlines	
OK-RDA	Let L410UVP-E9	Citywing	
OK-REQ	Airbus A.319-112	CSA Czech Airlines	
OK-SWT	Boeing 737-7Q8	Smart Wings	
OK-SWW	Boeing 737-7Q8	Smart Wings	
OK-SWX	Boeing 737-33A	Smart Wings	

Notes	Reg.	Type	Owner or Operator
	OK-TCA	Let L410UVP-E	Citywing
	OK-TVB	Boeing 737-8CX	Travel Service Airlines
	OK-TVD	Boeing 737-86N	Travel Service Airlines
	OK-TVF	Boeing 737-8FH	Travel Service Airlines
	OK-TVG	Boeing 737-8Q8	Travel Service Airlines
	OK-TVJ	Boeing 737-8Q8	Travel Service Airlines
	OK-TVK	Boeing 737-86N	Travel Service Airlines
	OK-TVL	Boeing 737-8FN	Travel Service Airlines
	OK-TVM	Boeing 737-8FN	Travel Service Airlines
	OK-TVO	Boeing 737-8CX	Travel Service Airlines
	OK-TVP	Boeing 737-8K5	Smart Wings
	OK-TVS	Boeing 737-86N	Travel Service Airlines
	OK-TVT	Boeing 737-86N	Travel Service Airlines
	OK-TVU	Boeing 737-86N	Travel Service Airlines
	OK-TVV	Boeing 737-86N	Travel Service Airlines
	OK-TVW	Boeing 737-86Q	Smart Wings
	OK-XGA	Boeing 737-55S	CSA Czech Airlines
	OK-XGB	Boeing 737-55S	CSA Czech Airlines *Olomouc*
	OK-XGC	Boeing 737-55S	CSA Czech Airlines *Ceske Budejovice*
	OK-XGD	Boeing 737-55S	CSA Czech Airlines *Poprad*
	OK-XGE	Boeing 737-55S	CSA Czech Airlines *Kosice*

OM (Slovakia)

	OM-AEX	Boeing 737-4YO	AirExplore
	OM-BEX	Boeing 737-382	AirExplore
	OM-CEX	Boeing 737-436	AirExplore
	OM-SAA	Boeing 737-476	Samair
	OM-TVA	Boeing 737-86N	Travel Service Airlines
	OM-TVR	Boeing 737-86N	Travel Service Airlines

OO (Belgium)

	OO-DWA	Avro RJ100	Brussels Airlines
	OO-DWB	Avro RJ100	Brussels Airlines
	OO-DWC	Avro RJ100	Brussels Airlines
	OO-DWD	Avro RJ100	Brussels Airlines
	OO-DWE	Avro RJ100	Brussels Airlines
	OO-DWF	Avro RJ100	Brussels Airlines
	OO-DWG	Avro RJ100	Brussels Airlines
	OO-DWH	Avro RJ100	Brussels Airlines
	OO-DWI	Avro RJ100	Brussels Airlines
	OO-DWJ	Avro RJ100	Brussels Airlines
	OO-DWK	Avro RJ100	Brussels Airlines
	OO-DWL	Avro RJ100	Brussels Airlines
	OO-JAA	Boeing 737-8BK	Jetairfly
	OO-JAD	Boeing 737-8K5	Jetairfly
	OO-JAF	Boeing 737-8K5	Jetairfly
	OO-JAH	Boeing 737-8K5	Jetairfly *Perspective*
	OO-JAM	Boeing 737-46J	Jetairfly
	OO-JAN	Boeing 737-76N	Jetairfly
	OO-JAO	Boeing 737-7K5	Jetairfly
	OO-JAP	Boeing 767-38EER	Jetairfly
	OO-JAQ	Boeing 737-8K5	Jetairfly *Vision*
	OO-JAR	Boeing 737-7K5	Jetairfly
	OO-JAS	Boeing 737-7K5	Jetairfly
	OO-JAT	Boeing 737-5K5	Jetairfly
	OO-JAX	Boeing 737-8K5	Jetairfly
	OO-JBG	Boeing 737-8K5	Jetairfly *Gerard Brack*
	OO-JBV	Boeing 737-8K5	Jetairfly
	OO-JDL	Boeing 787-8K5	Jetairfly
	OO-JLO	Boeing 737-8K5	Jetairfly
	OO-JPT	Boeing 737-8K5	Jetairfly
	OO-LTM	Boeing 737-3M8	Brussels Airlines
	OO-SFM	Airbus A.330-301	Brussels Airlines
	OO-SFN	Airbus A.330-301	Brussels Airlines
	OO-SFO	Airbus A.330-301	Brussels Airlines
	OO-SFV	Airbus A.330-322	Brussels Airlines
	OO-SFW	Airbus A.330-322	Brussels Airlines
	OO-SFY	Airbus A.330-223	Brussels Airlines

Reg.	Type	Owner or Operator	Notes
OO-SFZ	Airbus A.330-223	Brussels Airlines	
OO-SNA	Airbus A.320-214	Brussels Airlines	
OO-SNB	Airbus A.320-214	Brussels Airlines	
OO-SNC	Airbus A.320-214	Brussels Airlines	
OO-SND	Airbus A.320-214	Brussels Airlines	
OO-SNF	Airbus A.320-214	Brussels Airlines	
OO-SNG	Airbus A.320-214	Brussels Airlines	
OO-SSA	Airbus A.319-111	Brussels Airlines	
OO-SSB	Airbus A.319-111	Brussels Airlines	
OO-SSC	Airbus A.319-112	Brussels Airlines	
OO-SSD	Airbus A.319-112	Brussels Airlines	
OO-SSG	Airbus A.319-112	Brussels Airlines	
OO-SSK	Airbus A.319-112	Brussels Airlines	
OO-SSM	Airbus A.319-112	Brussels Airlines	
OO-SSN	Airbus A.319-112	Brussels Airlines	
OO-SSP	Airbus A.319-112	Brussels Airlines	
OO-SSQ	Airbus A.319-112	Brussels Airlines	
OO-SSR	Airbus A.319-112	Brussels Airlines	
OO-SSU	Airbus A.319-111	Brussels Airlines	
OO-SSV	Airbus A.319-111	Brussels Airlines	
OO-SSW	Airbus A.319-111	Brussels Airlines	
OO-TAD	BAe 146-300QT	TNT Airways	
OO-TAF	BAe 146-300QT	TNT Airways	
OO-TAH	BAe 146-300QT	TNT Airways	
OO-TAJ	BAe 146-300QT	TNT Airways	
OO-TAS	BAe 146-300QT	TNT Airways	
OO-TAU	BAe 146-200QT	TNT Airways	
OO-TAW	BAe 146-200QT	TNT Airways	
OO-TCH	Airbus A.320-214	Thomas Cook Airlines Belgium *experience*	
OO-TCI	Airbus A.320-214	Thomas Cook Airlines Belgium *relax*	
OO-TCJ	Airbus A.320-214	Thomas Cook Airlines Belgium *inspire*	
OO-TCP	Airbus A.320-214	Thomas Cook Airlines Belgium *desire*	
OO-TCS	Airbus A.319-132	Thomas Cook Airlines Belgium	
OO-TFA	Boeing 757-28A	TNT Airways	
OO-THA	Boeing 747-4HAERF	TNT Airways	
OO-THB	Boeing 747-4HAERF	TNT Airways	
OO-THC	Boeing 747-4HAERF	TNT Airways/Emirates Airlines	
OO-THD	Boeing 747-4HAERF	TNT Airways/Emirates Airlines	
OO-TNA	Boeing 737-3T0F	TNT Airways	
OO-TNB	Boeing 737-3T0F	TNT Airways	
OO-TNC	Boeing 737-3T0F	TNT Airways	
OO-TNL	Boeing 737-34SF	TNT Airways	
OO-TNN	Boeing 737-45D	TNT Airways	
OO-TNO	Boeing 737-49RF	TNT Airways	
OO-TNP	Boeing 737-45D	TNT Airways	
OO-TNQ	Boeing 737-4MOF	TNT Airways	
OO-TNR	Boeing 737-4MOF	TNT Airways	
OO-TNS	Boeing 737-4MOF	TNT Airways	
OO-TNT	Boeing 737-4MOF	TNT Airways	
OO-TSA	Boeing 777-FHT	TNT Airways	
OO-TSB	Boeing 777-FHT	TNT Airways	
OO-TSC	Boeing 777-FHT	TNT Airways	
OO-TUC	Boeing 767-341ER	TUI Airlines Belgium *Discover*	
OO-VAC	Boeing 737-8BK	TUI Airlines Belgium *Rising Sun*	
OO-VEN	Boeing 737-36N	Brussels Airlines	
OO-VLF	Fokker 50	Cityjet	
OO-VLI	Fokker 50	Cityjet	
OO-VLJ	Fokker 50	Cityjet	
OO-VLL	Fokker 50	Cityjet	
OO-VLM	Fokker 50	Cityjet	
OO-VLN	Fokker 50	Cityjet	
OO-VLO	Fokker 50	Cityjet	
OO-VLP	Fokker 50	Cityjet	
OO-VLQ	Fokker 50	Cityjet	
OO-VLS	Fokker 50	Cityjet	
OO-VLY	Fokker 50	Cityjet	
OO-VLZ	Fokker 50	Cityjet	

OY (Denmark)

| OY-BJP | Swearingen SA.227AC Metro III | Benair | |

Notes	Reg.	Type	Owner or Operator
	OY-JJB	Dornier 328-300 JET	Sun-Air
	OY-JRU	McD Douglas MD-87	Danish Air Transport
	OY-JTA	Boeing 737-33A	Jet Time
	OY-JTB	Boeing 737-3Y0	Jet Time
	OY-JTC	Boeing 737-3L9	Jet Time
	OY-JTD	Boeing 737-3Y0	Jet Time
	OY-JTE	Boeing 737-3L9	Jet Time
	OY-JTF	Boeing 737-382	Jet Time
	OY-JTH	Boeing 737-3YO	Jet Time
	OY-JTU	Boeing 737-7L9	Jet Time
	OY-JTV	Boeing 737-7L9	Jet Time
	OY-JTW	Boeing 737-7L9	Jet Time
	OY-JTY	Boeing 737-7Q8	Jet Time
	OY-JTZ	Boeing 737-73S	Jet Time
	OY-KAL	Airbus A.320-232	SAS
	OY-KBA	Airbus A.340-313X	SAS *Adalstein Viking*
	OY-KBB	Airbus A.321-231	SAS *Hjorulf Viking*
	OY-KBC	Airbus A.340-313X	SAS *Fredis Viking*
	OY-KBD	Airbus A.340-313X	SAS *Toste Viking*
	OY-KBE	Airbus A.321-231	SAS *Emma Viking*
	OY-KBF	Airbus A.321-231	SAS *Skapti Viking*
	OY-KBH	Airbus A.321-231	SAS *Sulke Viking*
	OY-KBI	Airbus A.340-313X	SAS *Rurik Viking*
	OY-KBK	Airbus A.321-231	SAS *Arne Viking*
	OY-KBL	Airbus A.321-231	SAS *Gynnbjorn Viking*
	OY-KBM	Airbus A.340-313X	HiFly
	OY-KBO	Airbus A.319-131	SAS *Christian Valdemar Viking*
	OY-KBP	Airbus A.319-131	SAS *Viger Viking*
	OY-KBR	Airbus A.319-132	SAS *Finnboge Viking*
	OY-KBT	Airbus A.319-131	SAS *Ragnvald Viking*
	OY-KFA	Canadair CRJ900ER	SAS *Johan Viking*
	OY-KFB	Canadair CRJ900ER	SAS *Alfhild Viking*
	OY-KFC	Canadair CRJ900ER	SAS *Bertil Viking*
	OY-KFD	Canadair CRJ900ER	SAS *Estrid Viking*
	OY-KFE	Canadair CRJ900ER	SAS *Ingemar Viking*
	OY-KFF	Canadair CRJ900ER	SAS *Karl Viking*
	OY-KFG	Canadair CRJ900ER	SAS *Maria Viking*
	OY-KFH	Canadair CRJ900ER	SAS *Ella Viking*
	OY-KFI	Canadair CRJ900ER	SAS *Rolf Viking*
	OY-KFK	Canadair CRJ900ER	SAS *Hardeknud Viking*
	OY-KFL	Canadair CRJ900ER	SAS *Regin Viking*
	OY-KGT	McD Douglas MD-82	SAS *Hake Viking*
	OY-KHE	McD Douglas MD-82	SAS *Saxo Viking*
	OY-KHG	McD Douglas MD-82	SAS *Alle Viking*
	OY-KHN	McD Douglas MD-82	SAS *Dan Viking*
	OY-KKS	Boeing 737-683	SAS *Ramveig Viking*
	OY-NCA	Dornier 328-100	Sun-Air/British Airways
	OY-NCL	Dornier 328-300 JET	Sun-Air/British Airways
	OY-NCM	Dornier 328-300 JET	Sun-Air/British Airways
	OY-NCN	Dornier 328-300 JET	Sun-Air/British Airways
	OY-NCO	Dornier 328-300 JET	Sun-Air
	OY-NCP	Dornier 328-300 JET	Sun-Air/British Airways
	OY-NCT	Dornier 328-300 JET	Sun-Air
	OY-PBH	Let L410UVP-E20	Benair
	OY-PBI	Let L410UVP-E20	Benair
	OY-PSA	Boeing 737-8Q8	Primera Air Scandinavia
	OY-PSB	Boeing 737-8Q8	Primera Air Scandinavia
	OY-PSC	Boeing 737-86N	Primera Air Scandinavia
	OY-PSD	Boeing 737-86N	Primera Air Scandinavia
	OY-PSE	Boeing 737-809	Primera Air Scandinavia
	OY-PSF	Boeing 737-7Q8	Primera Air Scandinavia
	OY-PSG	Boeing 737-7BX	Primera Air Scandinavia
	OY-RCC	Avro RJ100	Atlantic Airways
	OY-RCD	Avro RJ85	Atlantic Airways
	OY-RCE	Avro RJ85	Atlantic Airways
	OY-RCG	Airbus A.319-115	Atlantic Airways
	OY-RUE	McD Douglas MD-83	Danish Air Transport
	OY-SRF	Boeing 767-219 (SF)	Star Air
	OY-SRG	Boeing 767-219 (SF)	Star Air
	OY-SRH	Boeing 767-204 (SF)	Star Air
	OY-SRI	Boeing 767-25E (SF)	Star Air
	OY-SRJ	Boeing 767-25E (SF)	Star Air

Reg.	Type	Owner or Operator	Notes
OY-SRK	Boeing 767-204 (SF)	Star Air	
OY-SRL	Boeing 767-232 (SF)	Star Air	
OY-SRM	Boeing 767-25E (SF)	Star Air	
OY-SRN	Boeing 767-219 (SF)	Star Air	
OY-SRO	Boeing 767-25E (SF)	Star Air	
OY-SRP	Boeing 767-232 (SF)	Star Air	
OY-VKA	Airbus A.321-211	Thomas Cook Airlines	
OY-VKB	Airbus A.321-211	Thomas Cook Airlines	
OY-VKC	Airbus A.321-211	Thomas Cook Airlines	
OY-VKD	Airbus A.321-211	Thomas Cook Airlines	
OY-VKE	Airbus A.321-211	Thomas Cook Airlines	
OY-VKF	Airbus A.330-243	Thomas Cook Airlines	
OY-VKG	Airbus A.330-343X	Thomas Cook Airlines	
OY-VKH	Airbus A.330-343X	Thomas Cook Airlines	
OY-VKI	Airbus A.330-343X	Thomas Cook Airlines	
OY-VKM	Airbus A.320-214	Thomas Cook Airlines	
OY-VKS	Airbus A.320-214	Thomas Cook Airlines	
OY-VKT	Airbus A.321-211	Thomas Cook Airlines	

P4 (Aruba)

Reg.	Type	Owner or Operator	Notes
P4-EAS	Boeing 757-2G5	Air Astana	
P4-FAS	Boeing 757-2G5	Air Astana	
P4-GAS	Boeing 757-2G5	Air Astana	
P4-KCA	Boeing 767-306ER	Air Astana	
P4-KCB	Boeing 767-306ER	Air Astana	
P4-KCU	Boeing 767-23N	Air Astana	
P4-MAS	Boeing 757-28A	Air Astana	

PH (Netherlands)

Reg.	Type	Owner or Operator	Notes
PH-AHQ	Boeing 767-383ER	TUI Airlines Nederland/Arkefly	
PH-AHX	Boeing 767-383ER	TUI Airlines Nederland/Arkefly	
PH-AKA	Airbus A.330-303	KLM *Times Square – New York*	
PH-AKB	Airbus A.330-303	KLM *Piazza Navona-Roma*	
PH-AKD	Airbus A.330-303	KLM *Plaza de la Catedral-La Habana*	
PH-AOA	Airbus A.330-203	KLM *Dam – Amsterdam*	
PH-AOB	Airbus A.330-203	KLM *Potsdamer Platz – Berlin*	
PH-AOC	Airbus A.330-203	KLM *Place de la Concorde – Paris*	
PH-AOD	Airbus A.330-203	KLM *Plazza del Duomo – Milano*	
PH-AOE	Airbus A.330-203	KLM *Parliament Square – Edinburgh*	
PH-AOF	Airbus A.330-203	KLM *Federation Square – Melbourne*	
PH-AOH	Airbus A.330-203	KLM *Senaatintori/Senate Square-Helsinki*	
PH-AOI	Airbus A.330-203	KLM *Plaza de la Independencia-Madrid*	
PH-AOK	Airbus A.330-203	KLM *Radhuspladsen-Kobenhavn*	
PH-AOL	Airbus A.330-203	KLM *Picadilly Circus – London*	
PH-AOM	Airbus A.330-203	KLM	
PH-BCA	Boeing 737-8K2	KLM *Flamingo*	
PH-BCB	Boeing 737-8BK	KLM *Grote Pijlstormvogel/Great Shearwater*	
PH-BCC	Boeing 737-8BK	KLM	
PH-BCD	Boeing 737-8BK	KLM	
PH-BCE	Boeing 737-8BK	KLM	
PH-BCG	Boeing 737-8BK	KLM	
PH-BFA	Boeing 747-406	KLM *City of Atlanta*	
PH-BFB	Boeing 747-406	KLM *City of Bangkok*	
PH-BFC	Boeing 747-406 (SCD)	KLM *City of Calgary*	
PH-BFD	Boeing 747-406 (SCD)	KLM *City of Dubai*	
PH-BFE	Boeing 747-406 (SCD)	KLM *City of Melbourne*	
PH-BFF	Boeing 747-406 (SCD)	KLM *City of Freetown*	
PH-BFG	Boeing 747-406	KLM *City of Guayaquil*	
PH-BFH	Boeing 747-406 (SCD)	KLM *City of Hong Kong*	
PH-BFI	Boeing 747-406 (SCD)	KLM *City of Jakarta*	
PH-BFK	Boeing 747-406 (SCD)	KLM *City of Karachi*	
PH-BFL	Boeing 747-406	KLM *City of Lima*	
PH-BFM	Boeing 747-406 (SCD)	KLM *City of Mexico*	
PH-BFN	Boeing 747-406	KLM *City of Nairobi*	
PH-BFO	Boeing 747-406 (SCD)	KLM *City of Orlando*	
PH-BFP	Boeing 747-406 (SCD)	KLM *City of Paramaribo*	
PH-BFR	Boeing 747-406 (SCD)	KLM *City of Rio de Janeiro*	
PH-BFS	Boeing 747-406 (SCD)	KLM *City of Seoul*	

Notes	Reg.	Type	Owner or Operator
	PH-BFT	Boeing 747-406 (SCD)	KLM *City of Tokyo*
	PH-BFU	Boeing 747-406 (SCD)	KLM *City of Beijing*
	PH-BFV	Boeing 747-406	KLM *City of Vancouver*
	PH-BFW	Boeing 747-406	KLM *City of Shanghai*
	PH-BFY	Boeing 747-406	KLM *City of Johannesburg*
	PH-BGA	Boeing 737-8K2	KLM *Tureluur/Redshank*
	PH-BGB	Boeing 737-8K2	KLM *Whimbrel/Regenwulg*
	PH-BGC	Boeing 737-8K2	KLM *Pijlstaart/Pintail*
	PH-BGD	Boeing 737-706	KLM *Goldcrest/Goadhaantje*
	PH-BGE	Boeing 737-706	KLM *Ortolan Bunting/Ortolaan*
	PH-BGF	Boeing 737-7K2	KLM *Great White Heron/Grote Ziverreiger*
	PH-BGG	Boeing 737-706	KLM *King Eider/Koening Seider*
	PH-BGH	Boeing 737-7K2	KLM *Grutto/Godwit*
	PH-BGI	Boeing 737-7K2	KLM *Vink/Finch*
	PH-BGK	Boeing 737-7K2	KLM *Noordse Stormvogel/Fulmar*
	PH-BGL	Boeing 737-7K2	KLM *Rietzangler/Warbler*
	PH-BGM	Boeing 737-7K2	KLM *Aabscholver/Cormorant*
	PH-BGN	Boeing 737-7K2	KLM *Jan van Gent/Gannet*
	PH-BGO	Boeing 737-7K2	KLM *Paradijsvogel/Bird of Paradise*
	PH-BGP	Boeing 737-7K2	KLM *Pelikaan/Pelican*
	PH-BGQ	Boeing 737-7K2	KLM *Wielewaal/Golden Oriole*
	PH-BGR	Boeing 737-7K2	KLM *Zwarte Wouw/Black Kite*
	PH-BGT	Boeing 737-7K2	KLM *Zanglijster/Song Thrush*
	PH-BGU	Boeing 737-7K2	KLM *Koekoek/Cuckoo*
	PH-BGW	Boeing 737-7K2	KLM
	PH-BGX	Boeing 737-7K2	KLM *Scholekster/Oystercatcher*
	PH-BQA	Boeing 777-206ER	KLM *Albert Plesman*
	PH-BQB	Boeing 777-206ER	KLM *Borobudur*
	PH-BQC	Boeing 777-206ER	KLM *Chichen-Itza*
	PH-BQD	Boeing 777-206ER	KLM *Darjeeling Highway*
	PH-BQE	Boeing 777-206ER	KLM *Epidaurus*
	PH-BQF	Boeing 777-206ER	KLM *Ferrara City*
	PH-BQG	Boeing 777-206ER	KLM *Galapagos Islands*
	PH-BQH	Boeing 777-206ER	KLM *Hadrian's Wall*
	PH-BQI	Boeing 777-206ER	KLM *Iguazu Falls*
	PH-BQK	Boeing 777-206ER	KLM *Mount Kilimanjaro*
	PH-BQL	Boeing 777-206ER	KLM *Litomysl Castle*
	PH-BQM	Boeing 777-206ER	KLM *Macchu Picchu*
	PH-BQN	Boeing 777-206ER	KLM *Nahanni National Park*
	PH-BQO	Boeing 777-206ER	KLM *Old Rauma*
	PH-BQP	Boeing 777-206ER	KLM *Pont du Gard*
	PH-BVA	Boeing 777-306ER	KLM *National Park De Hoge Veluwe*
	PH-BVB	Boeing 777-306ER	KLM *Fulufjallet National Park*
	PH-BVC	Boeing 777-306ER	KLM *National ParkSian Ka'an*
	PH-BVD	Boeing 777-306ER	KLM *Amboseli National Park*
	PH-BVF	Boeing 777-306ER	KLM *Yakushima*
	PH-BVG	Boeing 777-306ER	KLM
	PH-BVI	Boeing 777-306ER	KLM *Nationaal Park Vuurland*
	PH-BVK	Boeing 777-306ER	KLM
	PH-BXA	Boeing 737-8K2	KLM *Zwaan/Swan*
	PH-BXB	Boeing 737-8K2	KLM *Valk/Falcon*
	PH-BXC	Boeing 737-8K2	KLM *Korhoen/Grouse*
	PH-BXD	Boeing 737-8K2	KLM *Arend/Eagle*
	PH-BXE	Boeing 737-8K2	KLM *Harvik/Hawk*
	PH-BXF	Boeing 737-8K2	KLM *Zwallou/Swallow*
	PH-BXG	Boeing 737-8K2	KLM *Kraanvogel/Crane*
	PH-BXH	Boeing 737-8K2	KLM *Gans/Goose*
	PH-BXI	Boeing 737-8K2	KLM *Zilvermeeuw*
	PH-BXK	Boeing 737-8K2	KLM *Gierzwallou/Swift*
	PH-BXL	Boeing 737-8K2	KLM *Sperwer/Sparrow*
	PH-BXM	Boeing 737-8K2	KLM *Kluut/Avocet*
	PH-BXN	Boeing 737-8K2	KLM *Merel/Blackbird*
	PH-BXO	Boeing 737-9K2	KLM *Plevier/Plover*
	PH-BXP	Boeing 737-9K2	KLM *Meerkoet/Crested Coot*
	PH-BXR	Boeing 737-9K2	KLM *Nachtegaal/Nightingale*
	PH-BXS	Boeing 737-9K2	KLM *Buizerd/Buzzard*
	PH-BXT	Boeing 737-9K2	KLM *Zeestern/Sea Tern*
	PH-BXU	Boeing 737-8BK	KLM *Albatros/Albatross*
	PH-BXV	Boeing 737-8K2	KLM *Roodborstje*
	PH-BXW	Boeing 737-8K2	KLM *Patrijs/Partridge*
	PH-BXY	Boeing 737-8K2	KLM *Fuut/Grebe*
	PH-BXZ	Boeing 737-8K2	KLM *Uil/Owl*

Reg.	Type	Owner or Operator	Notes
PH-CKA	Boeing 747-406ERF	KLM Cargo/Martinair *Eendracht*	
PH-CKB	Boeing 747-406ERF	KLM Cargo/Martinair *Leeuwin*	
PH-CKC	Boeing 747-406ERF	KLM Cargo/Martinair *Oranje*	
PH-CKD	Boeing 747-406F	KLM Cargo/Martinair *Wapen van Amsterdam*	
PH-EZA	Embraer ERJ190-100STD	KLM CityHopper	
PH-EZB	Embraer ERJ190-100STD	KLM CityHopper	
PH-EZC	Embraer ERJ190-100STD	KLM CityHopper	
PH-EZD	Embraer ERJ190-100STD	KLM CityHopper	
PH-EZE	Embraer ERJ190-100STD	KLM CityHopper	
PH-EZF	Embraer ERJ190-100STD	KLM CityHopper	
PH-EZG	Embraer ERJ190-100STD	KLM Cityhopper	
PH-EZH	Embraer ERJ190-100STD	KLM Cityhopper	
PH-EZI	Embraer ERJ190-100STD	KLM CityHopper	
PH-EZK	Embraer ERJ190-100STD	KLM CityHopper	
PH-EZL	Embraer ERJ190-100STD	KLM CityHopper	
PH-EZM	Embraer ERJ190-100STD	KLM CityHopper	
PH-EZN	Embraer ERJ190-100STD	KLM CityHopper	
PH-EZO	Embraer ERJ190-100STD	KLM CityHopper	
PH-EZP	Embraer ERJ190-100STD	KLM CityHopper	
PH-EZR	Embraer ERJ190-100STD	KLM CityHopper	
PH-EZS	Embraer ERJ190-100STD	KLM CityHopper	
PH-EZT	Embraer ERJ190-100STD	KLM CityHopper	
PH-EZU	Embraer ERJ190-100STD	KLM CityHopper	
PH-EZV	Embraer ERJ190-100STD	KLM CityHopper	
PH-EZW	Embraer ERJ190-100STD	KLM CityHopper	
PH-EZX	Embraer ERJ190-100STD	KLM CityHopper	
PH-HSA	Boeing 737-8K2	Transavia	
PH-HSB	Boeing 737-8K2	Transavia	
PH-HSC	Boeing 737-8K2	Transavia	
PH-HSD	Boeing 737-8K2	Transavia	
PH-HSE	Boeing 737-8K2	Transavia	
PH-HSF	Boeing 737-8K2	Transavia	
PH-HSG	Boeing 737-8K2	Transavia	
PH-HZD	Boeing 737-8K2	Transavia	
PH-HZE	Boeing 737-8K2	Transavia	
PH-HZF	Boeing 737-8K2	Transavia	
PH-HZG	Boeing 737-8K2	Transavia	
PH-HZI	Boeing 737-8K2	Transavia	
PH-HZJ	Boeing 737-8K2	Transavia	
PH-HZK	Boeing 737-8K2	Transavia	
PH-HZL	Boeing 737-8K2	Transavia	
PH-HZN	Boeing 737-8K2	Transavia	
PH-HZO	Boeing 737-8K2	Transavia	
PH-HZV	Boeing 737-8K2	Transavia	
PH-HZW	Boeing 737-8K2	Transavia	
PH-HZX	Boeing 737-8K2	Transavia	
PH-JCH	Fokker 70	KLM CityHopper	
PH-JCT	Fokker 70	KLM CityHopper	
PH-KCA	McD Douglas MD-11	KLM *Amy Johnson*	
PH-KCB	McD Douglas MD-11	KLM *Maria Montessori*	
PH-KCC	McD Douglas MD-11	KLM *Marie Curie*	
PH-KCD	McD Douglas MD-11	KLM *Florence Nightingale*	
PH-KCE	McD Douglas MD-11	KLM *Audrey Hepburn*	
PH-KCK	McD Douglas MD-11	KLM *Marie Servaes*	
PH-KZA	Fokker 70	KLM CityHopper	
PH-KZB	Fokker 70	KLM CityHopper	
PH-KZC	Fokker 70	KLM CityHopper	
PH-KZD	Fokker 70	KLM CityHopper	
PH-KZE	Fokker 70	KLM CityHopper	
PH-KZF	Fokker 70	KLM CityHopper	
PH-KZG	Fokker 70	KLM CityHopper	
PH-KZH	Fokker 70	KLM CityHopper	
PH-KZI	Fokker 70	KLM CityHopper	
PH-KZK	Fokker 70	KLM CityHopper	
PH-KZL	Fokker 70	KLM CityHopper	
PH-KZM	Fokker 70	KLM CityHopper	
PH-KZN	Fokker 70	KLM CityHopper	
PH-KZO	Fokker 70	KLM CityHopper	
PH-KZP	Fokker 70	KLM CityHopper	
PH-KZR	Fokker 70	KLM CityHopper	
PH-KZS	Fokker 70	KLM CityHopper	
PH-KZT	Fokker 70	KLM CityHopper	

Notes	Reg.	Type	Owner or Operator
	PH-KZU	Fokker 70	KLM Cityhopper
	PH-KZV	Fokker 70	KLM Cityhopper
	PH-KZW	Fokker 70	KLM CityHopper
	PH-MCP	McD Douglas MD-11CF	Martinair Cargo
	PH-MCR	McD Douglas MD-11CF	Martinair Cargo
	PH-MCS	McD Douglas MD-11CF	Martinair Cargo
	PH-MCT	McD Douglas MD-11CF	Martinair Cargo
	PH-MCU	McD Douglas MD-11F	Martinair Cargo
	PH-MCW	McD Douglas MD-11CF	Martinair Cargo
	PH-MPS	Boeing 747-412BCF	Martinair Cargo
	PH-OYE	Boeing 767-304ER	TUI Airlines Nederland/Arkefly
	PH-OYI	Boeing 767-304ER	TUI Airlines Nederland/Arkefly
	PH-OYJ	Boeing 767-304ER	TUI Airlines Nederland/Arkefly
	PH-TFA	Boeing 737-8FH	TUI Airlines Nederland/Arkefly
	PH-TFB	Boeing 737-8K5	TUI Airlines Nederland/Arkefly
	PH-TFC	Boeing 737-8K5	TUI Airlines Nederland/Arkefly
	PH-TFD	Boeing 737-86N	TUI Airlines Nederland/Arkefly
	PH-TFF	Boeing 737-86N	TUI Airlines Nederland/Arkefly
	PH-WXA	Fokker 70	KLM CityHopper
	PH-WXC	Fokker 70	KLM CityHopper
	PH-WXD	Fokker 70	KLM CityHopper
	PH-XRA	Boeing 737-7K2	Transavia *Leontien van Moorsel*
	PH-XRB	Boeing 737-7K2	Transavia
	PH-XRC	Boeing 737-7K2	Transavia
	PH-XRD	Boeing 737-7K2	Transavia
	PH-XRE	Boeing 737-7K2	Transavia
	PH-XRV	Boeing 737-7K2	Transavia
	PH-XRW	Boeing 737-7K2	Transavia
	PH-XRX	Boeing 737-7K2	Transavia
	PH-XRY	Boeing 737-7K2	Transavia
	PH-XRZ	Boeing 737-7K2	Transavia

PP/PR/PT (Brazil)

	PT-MUA	Boeing 777-32WER	TAM Linhas Aereas
	PT-MUB	Boeing 777-32WER	TAM Linhas Aereas
	PT-MUC	Boeing 777-32WER	TAM Linhas Aereas
	PT-MUD	Boeing 777-32WER	TAM Linhas Aereas
	PT-MUE	Boeing 777-32WER	TAM Linhas Aereas
	PT-MUF	Boeing 777-32WER	TAM Linhas Aereas
	PT-MUG	Boeing 777-32WER	TAM Linhas Aereas
	PT-MUH	Boeing 777-32WER	TAM Linhas Aereas
	PT-MVA	Airbus A.330-223	TAM Linhas Aereas
	PT-MVB	Airbus A.330-223	TAM Linhas Aereas
	PT-MVC	Airbus A.330-223	TAM Linhas Aereas
	PT-MVD	Airbus A.330-223	TAM Linhas Aereas
	PT-MVE	Airbus A.330-223	TAM Linhas Aereas
	PT-MVF	Airbus A.330-203	TAM Linhas Aereas
	PT-MVG	Airbus A.330-203	TAM Linhas Aereas
	PT-MVH	Airbus A.330-203	TAM Linhas Aereas
	PT-MVK	Airbus A.330-203	TAM Linhas Aereas
	PT-MVL	Airbus A.330-203	TAM Linhas Aereas
	PT-MVM	Airbus A.330-223	TAM Linhas Aereas
	PT-MVN	Airbus A.330-223	TAM Linhas Aereas
	PT-MVO	Airbus A.330-223	TAM Linhas Aereas
	PT-MVP	Airbus A.330-223	TAM Linhas Aereas
	PT-MVQ	Airbus A.330-223	TAM Linhas Aereas
	PT-MVR	Airbus A.330-223	TAM Linhas Aereas
	PT-MVS	Airbus A.330-223	TAM Linhas Aereas
	PT-MVT	Airbus A.330-223	TAM Linhas Aereas
	PT-MVU	Airbus A.330-223	TAM Linhas Aereas
	PT-MVV	Airbus A.330-223	TAM Linhas Aereas

RA (Russia)

	RA-61701	Antonov An-148-100B	Rossiya
	RA-61702	Antonov An-148-100B	Rossiya
	RA-61703	Antonov An-148-100B	Rossiya
	RA-61704	Antonov An-148-100B	Rossiya
	RA-61705	Antonov An-148-100B	Rossiya

Reg.	Type	Owner or Operator	Notes
RA-61706	Antonov An-148-100B	Rossiya	
RA-82042	An-124	Volga-Dnepr	
RA-82043	An-124	Volga-Dnepr	
RA-82044	An-124	Volga-Dnepr	
RA-82045	An-124	Volga-Dnepr	
RA-82046	An-124	Volga-Dnepr	
RA-82047	An-124	Volga-Dnepr	
RA-82068	An-124	Polet	
RA-82074	An-124	Volga-Dnepr	
RA-82075	An-124	Polet	
RA-82077	An-124	Polet	
RA-82078	An-124	Volga-Dnepr	
RA-82079	An-124	Volga-Dnepr	
RA-82080	An-124	Polet	
RA-82081	An-124	Volga-Dnepr	

S2 (Bangladesh)

Reg.	Type	Owner or Operator	Notes
S2-ACO	Douglas DC-10-30	Bangladesh Biman *City of Shah Makhdum (R.A.)*	
S2-ACR	Douglas DC-10-30	Bangladesh Biman *The New Era*	
S2-ADF	Airbus A.310-325	Bangladesh Biman *City of Chittagong*	
S2-ADK	Airbus A.310-324	Bangladesh Biman	
S2-AFO	Boeing 777-3E9ER	Bangladesh Biman	
S2-AFP	Boeing 777-3E9FR	Bangladesh Biman	
S2-AFT	Airbus A.310-325	Bangladesh Biman	

S5 (Slovenia)

Reg.	Type	Owner or Operator	Notes
S5-AAD	Canadair CRJ200LR	Adria Airways	
S5-AAE	Canadair CRJ200LR	Adria Airways	
S5-AAF	Canadair CRJ200LR	Adria Airways	
S5-AAG	Canadair CRJ200LR	Adria Airways	
S5-AAJ	Canadair CRJ200LR	Adria Airways	
S5-AAK	Canadair CRJ900LR	Adria Airways	
S5-AAL	Canadair CRJ900LR	Adria Airways	
S5-AAN	Canadair CRJ900LR	Adria Airways	
S5-AAO	Canadair CRJ900LR	Adria Airways	
S5-AAP	Airbus A.319-132	Adria Airways	
S5-AAR	Airbus A.319-132	Adria Airways	
S5-AAS	Airbus A.320-231	Adria Airways	

SE (Sweden)

Reg.	Type	Owner or Operator	Notes
SE-DIK	McD Douglas MD-82	SAS *Stenkil Viking*	
SE-DIN	McD Douglas MD-82	SAS *Eskil Viking*	
SE-DIR	McD Douglas MD-82	SAS *Nora Viking*	
SE-DIS	McD Douglas MD-82	SAS *Sigmund Viking*	
SE-DMB	McD Douglas MD-82	SAS *Bjarne Viking*	
SE-DNX	Boeing 737-683	SAS *Torvald Viking*	
SE-DOR	Boeing 737-683	SAS *Elisabeth Viking*	
SE-DTH	Boeing 737-683	SAS *Vile Viking*	
SE-DZK	Boeing 737-804	TUIfly Nordic	
SE-DZN	Boeing 737-804	TUIfly Nordic	
SE-DZV	Boeing 737-804	TUIfly Nordic	
SE-LGY	BAe ATP	West Air Sweden	
SE-LNY	BAe ATP	West Air Sweden	
SE-MAF	BAe ATP	West Air Sweden	
SE-MAH	BAe ATP	West Air Sweden	
SE-MAR	BAe ATP	West Air Sweden	
SE-MAY	BAe ATP	West Air Sweden	
SE-RDN	Airbus A.321-231	Novair Airlines	
SE-RDO	Airbus A.321-231	Novair Airlines	
SE-RDP	Airbus A.321-231	Novair Airlines	
SE-REE	Airbus A.330-343X	SAS *Sigrid Viking*	
SE-RER	Boeing 737-7BX	SAS	
SE-RES	Boeing 737-7BX	SAS	
SE-RET	Boeing 737-76N	SAS	
SE-REU	Boeing 737-76N	SAS	
SE-REX	Boeing 737-76N	SAS	

Notes	Reg.	Type	Owner or Operator
	SE-REY	Boeing 737-76N	SAS
	SE-REZ	Boeing 737-76N	SAS
	SE-RFR	Boeing 767-38AER	TUIfly Nordic
	SE-RFS	Boeing 767-304ER	TUIfly Nordic
	SE-RFT	Boeing 737-8K5	TUIfly Nordic
	SE-RFU	Boeing 737-8K5	TUIfly Nordic
	SE-RFV	Boeing 737-86N	TUIfly Nordic
	SE-RFX	Boeing 737-8K5	TUIfly Nordic
	SE-RJE	Airbus A.320-232	SAS
	SE-RJF	Airbus A.320-232	SAS
	SE-RJH	McD Douglas MD-82	SAS

SP (Poland)

Notes	Reg.	Type	Owner or Operator
	SP-ENA	Boeing 737-4Q8	Enter Air
	SP-ENB	Boeing 737-4Q8	Enter Air
	SP-ENC	Boeing 737-4Q8	Enter Air
	SP-ENE	Boeing 737-4Q8	Enter Air
	SP-ENF	Boeing 737-4C9	Enter Air
	SP-ENH	Boeing 737-405	Enter Air
	SP-ENI	Boeing 737-43Q	Enter Air
	SP-ENK	Boeing 737-46J	Enter Air
	SP-ENW	Boeing 737-86J	Enter Air
	SP-ENX	Boeing 737-8Q8	Enter Air
	SP-ENY	Boeing 737-86N	Enter Air
	SP-ENZ	Boeing 737-85F	Enter Air
	SP-LDA	Embraer RJ170 100ST	LOT
	SP-LDB	Embraer RJ170 100ST	LOT
	SP-LDC	Embraer RJ170 100ST	LOT
	SP-LDD	Embraer RJ170 100ST	LOT
	SP-LDE	Embraer RJ170 100LR	LOT
	SP-LDF	Embraer RJ170 100LR	LOT
	SP-LDG	Embraer RJ170 100LR	LOT
	SP-LDH	Embraer RJ170 100LR	LOT
	SP-LDI	Embraer RJ170 100LR	LOT
	SP-LDK	Embraer RJ170 100LR	LOT
	SP-LIA	Embraer RJ170-200STD	LOT
	SP-LIB	Embraer RJ170-200STD	LOT
	SP-LIC	Embraer RJ170-200STD	LOT
	SP-LID	Embraer RJ170-200STD	LOT
	SP-LIE	Embraer RJ170-200STD	LOT
	SP-LIF	Embraer RJ170-200STD	LOT
	SP-LII	Embraer RJ170-200STD	LOT
	SP-LIK	Embraer RJ170-200STD	LOT
	SP-LIL	Embraer RJ170-200STD	LOT
	SP-LIM	Embraer RJ170-200STD	LOT
	SP-LIN	Embraer RJ170-200STD	LOT
	SP-LIO	Embraer RJ170-200STD	LOT
	SP-LKE	Boeing 737-55D	LOT
	SP-LKF	Boeing 737-55D	LOT
	SP-LLC	Boeing 737-45D	LOT
	SP-LLE	Boeing 737-45D	LOT
	SP-LLF	Boeing 737-45D	LOT
	SP-LLG	Boeing 737-45D	LOT
	SP-LLK	Boeing 737-4Q8	LOT
	SP-LNA	Embraer RJ190-200LR	LOT
	SP-LNB	Embraer RJ190-200LR	LOT
	SP-LNC	Embraer RJ190-200LR	LOT
	SP-LND	Embraer RJ190-200LR	LOT
	SP-LNE	Embraer RJ190-200LR	LOT
	SP-LPB	Boeing 767-35DER	LOT *Gdansk*
	SP-LPE	Boeing 767-341ER	LOT
	SP-LPG	Boeing 767-306ER	LOT

SU (Egypt)

Notes	Reg.	Type	Owner or Operator
	SU-GAC	Airbus A.300B4-203F	EgyptAir Cargo *New Valley*
	SU-GAS	Airbus A.300F4-622RF	EgyptAir Cargo *Cheops*
	SU-GAY	Airbus A.300B4-622RF	EgyptAir Cargo *Seti I*
	SU-GBR	Boeing 777-266ER	EgyptAir *Nefertari*

Reg.	Type	Owner or Operator	Notes
SU-GBS	Boeing 777-266ER	EgyptAir *Tyie*	
SU-GBT	Airbus A.321-231	EgyptAir *Red Sea*	
SU-GBU	Airbus A.321-231	EgyptAir	
SU-GBV	Airbus A.321-231	EgyptAir	
SU-GBW	Airbus A.321-231	EgyptAir *The Nile*	
SU-GBX	Boeing 777-266ER	EgyptAir *Neit*	
SU-GBY	Boeing 777-266ER	EgyptAir *Titi*	
SU-GCE	Airbus A.330-243	EgyptAir	
SU-GCF	Airbus A.330-243	EgyptAir	
SU-GCG	Airbus A.330-243	EgyptAir	
SU-GCH	Airbus A.330-243	EgyptAir	
SU-GCI	Airbus A.330-243	EgyptAir	
SU-GCJ	Airbus A.330-243	EgyptAir	
SU-GCK	Airbus A.330-243	EgyptAir	
SU-GDL	Boeing 777-36NER	EgyptAir	
SU-GDM	Boeing 777-36NER	EgyptAir	
SU-GDN	Boeing 777-36NER	Egyptair	
SU-GDO	Boeing 777-36NER	Egyptair	
SU-GDP	Boeing 777-36NER	Egyptair	
SU-GDR	Boeing 777-36NER	Egyptair	
SU-GDS	Airbus A.330-343X	Egyptair	
SU-GDT	Airbus A.330-343X	Egyptair	
SU-GDU	Airbus A.330-343X	Egyptair	
SU-GDV	Airbus A.330-343X	Egyptair	

SX (Greece)

Reg.	Type	Owner or Operator	Notes
SX-BHR	Boeing 737-5L9	Hermes Airlines	
SX-BHS	Airbus A.321-111	Air Mediterranee	
SX-BHV	Airbus A.320-211	Air Mediterranee	
SX-BRM	Fokker 50	Minoan Air	
SX-BRS	Fokker 50	Minoan Air	
SX-BRV	Fokker 50	Minoan Air	
SX-DGA	Airbus A.321-231	Aegean Airlines	
SX-DGB	Airbus A.320-232	Aegean Airlines	
SX-DGC	Airbus A.320-232	Aegean Airlines	
SX-DGD	Airbus A.320-232	Aegean Airlines	
SX-DGE	Airbus A.320-232	Aegean Airlines	
SX-DGF	Airbus A.319-132	Aegean Airlines	
SX-DGG	Airbus A.319-132	Aegean Airlines	
SX-DVG	Airbus A.320-232	Aegean Airlines *Ethos*	
SX-DVH	Airbus A.320-232	Aegean Airlines *Nostos*	
SX-DVI	Airbus A.320-232	Aegean Airlines *Kinesis*	
SX-DVJ	Airbus A.320-232	Aegean Airlines *Kinesis*	
SX-DVK	Airbus A.320-232	Aegean Airlines	
SX-DVL	Airbus A.320-232	Aegean Airlines	
SX-DVM	Airbus A.320-232	Aegean Airlines	
SX-DVN	Airbus A.320-232	Aegean Airlines	
SX-DVO	Airbus A.321-232	Aegean Airlines *Philoxenia*	
SX-DVP	Airbus A.321-232	Aegean Airlines	
SX-DVQ	Airbus A.320-232	Aegean Airlines	
SX-DVR	Airbus A.320-232	Aegean Airlines	
SX-DVS	Airbus A.320-232	Aegean Airlines	
SX-DVT	Airbus A.320-232	Aegean Airlines	
SX-DVU	Airbus A.320-232	Aegean Airlines *Pheidias*	
SX-DVV	Airbus A.320-232	Aegean Airlines *Cleisthenes*	
SX-DVW	Airbus A.320-232	Aegean Airlines	
SX-DVX	Airbus A.320-232	Aegean Airlines	
SX-DVY	Airbus A.320-232	Aegean Airlines	
SX-DVZ	Airbus A.321-232	Aegean Airlines	

TC (Turkey)

Reg.	Type	Owner or Operator	Notes
TC-AAE	Boeing 737-82R	Pegasus Airlines *Hayirli*	
TC-AAH	Boeing 737-82R	Pegasus Airlines	
TC-AAI	Boeing 737-82R	Pegasus Airlines	
TC-AAJ	Boeing 737-82R	Pegasus Airlines	
TC-AAL	Boeing 737-82R	Pegasus Airlines	
TC-AAN	Boeing 737-82R	Pegasus Airlines *Merve*	
TC-AAO	Boeing 737-86N	Pegasus Airlines	

Notes	Reg.	Type	Owner or Operator
	TC-AAR	Boeing 737-86N	Pegasus Airlines
	TC-AAS	Boeing 737-82R	Pegasus Airlines
	TC-AAT	Boeing 737-82R	Pegasus Airlines
	TC-AAU	Boeing 737-82R	Pegasus Airlines *Duru*
	TC-AAV	Boeing 737-82R	Pegasus Airlines
	TC-AAY	Boeing 737-82R	Pegasus Airlines
	TC-AAZ	Boeing 737-82R	Pegasus Airlines *Mina*
	TC-ABK	Airbus A.300B4-203F	ULS Cargo *Adiyaman*
	TC-ABP	Boeing 737-82R	Pegasus Airlines *Nisa*
	TC-ACE	Airbus A.300B4-203F	myCargo Airlines
	TC-ACF	Boeing 747-481F	myCargo Airlines
	TC-ACG	Boeing 747-481F	myCargo Airlines
	TC-ACP	Boeing 737-82R	Pegasus Airlines
	TC-ACU	Airbus A.300B4-203F	myCargo Airlines
	TC-ACZ	Airbus A.300B4-103F	myCargo Airlines
	TC-ADP	Boeing 737-82R	Pegasus Airlines *Nisa Nur*
	TC-AEP	Boeing 737-82R	Pegasus Airlines
	TC-AGK	Airbus A.300B4-203F	ULS Cargo
	TC-AGP	Boeing 737-82R	Pegasus Airlines *Sebnem*
	TC-AHP	Boeing 737-82R	Pegasus Airlines *Iram Naz*
	TC-AIP	Boeing 737-82R	Pegasus Airlines *Hante*
	TC-AIS	Boeing 737-82R	Pegasus Airlines *Sevde Nil D*
	TC-AJP	Boeing 737-82R	Pegasus Airlines *Masal*
	TC-AMP	Boeing 737-82R	Pegasus Airlines *Nil*
	TC-ANP	Boeing 737-82R	Pegasus Airlines *Sena*
	TC-APD	Boeing 737-42R	Pegasus Airlines
	TC-APH	Boeing 737-8S3	Pegasus Airlines
	TC-APR	Boeing 737-4Y0	Pegasus Airlines
	TC-ARP	Boeing 737-82R	Pegasus Airlines *Nehir*
	TC-ASP	Boeing 737-82R	Pegasus Airlines
	TC-ATB	Airbus A.321-211	Atlasjet Airlines
	TC-ATE	Airbus A.321-211	Atlasjet Airlines
	TC-ATF	Airbus A.321-211	Atlasjet Airlines
	TC-ATH	Airbus A.321-231	Atlasjet Airlines
	TC-ATJ	Airbus A.320-233	Atlasjet Airlines
	TC-ATK	Airbus A.320-232	Atlasjet Airlines
	TC-ATM	Airbus A.320-232	Atlasjet Airlines
	TC-ATO	Airbus A.321-231	Atlasjet Airlines
	TC-AVP	Boeing 737-82R	Pegasus Airlines
	TC-AZP	Boeing 737-82R	Pegasus Airlines *Maya*
	TC-CBP	Boeing 737-82R	Pegasus Airlines
	TC-CCP	Boeing 737-86J	Pegasus Airlines
	TC-CPA	Boeing 737-82R	Pegasus Airlines *Sena*
	TC-CPB	Boeing 737-82R	Pegasus Airlines *Doge*
	TC-CPC	Boeing 737-82R	Pegasus Airlines *Oyku*
	TC-CPD	Boeing 737-82R	Pegasus Airlines *Berra*
	TC-CPE	Boeing 737-82R	Pegasus Airlines *Bade*
	TC-CPF	Boeing 737-82R	Pegasus Airlines
	TC-CPG	Boeing 737-82R	Pegasus Airlines
	TC-CPI	Boeing 737-82R	Pegasus Airlines
	TC-ETF	Airbus A.321-211	Atlasjet Airlines
	TC-ETH	Airbus A.321-211	Atlasjet Airlines
	TC-ETJ	Airbus A.321-211	Atlasjet Airlines
	TC-ETM	Airbus A.321-131	Atlasjet Airlines
	TC-ETN	Airbus A.321-131	Atlasjet Airlines
	TC-ETV	Airbus A.321-211	Atlasjet Airlines
	TC-FBG	Airbus A.321-131	Freebird Airlines
	TC-FBH	Airbus A.320-214	Freebird Airlines
	TC-FBJ	Airbus A.320-232	Freebird Airlines
	TC-FBO	Airbus A.320-214	Freebird Airlines
	TC-FBR	Airbus A.320-232	Freebird Airlines
	TC-FBT	Airbus A.321-131	Freebird Airlines
	TC-FBV	Airbus A.320-214	Freebird Airlines
	TC-JAI	Airbus A.320-232	Turkish Airlines
	TC-JBI	Airbus A.320-232	Turkish Airlines
	TC-JCT	Airbus A.310-304F	Turkish Airlines *Samsun*
	TC-JCY	Airbus A.310-304F	Turkish Airlines *Coruh*
	TC-JCZ	Airbus A.310-304F	Turkish Airlines *Ergene*
	TC-JDG	Boeing 737-4Y0	Turkish Airlines *Marmaris*
	TC-JDH	Boeing 737-4Y0	Turkish Airlines *Amasra*
	TC-JDJ	Airbus A.340-311	Turkish Airlines *Istanbul*
	TC-JDK	Airbus A.340-311	Turkish Airlines *Diyarbakir*

Reg.	Type	Owner or Operator	Notes
TC-JDL	Airbus A.340-311	Turkish Airlines *Ankara*	
TC-JDM	Airbus A.340-311	Turkish Airlines *Izmir*	
TC-JDN	Airbus A.340-313X	Turkish Airlines *Adana*	
TC-JDT	Boeing 737-4Y0	Turkish Airlines *Alanya*	
TC-JFC	Boeing 737-8F2	Turkish Airlines *Diyarbakir*	
TC-JFD	Boeing 737-8F2	Turkish Airlines *Rize*	
TC-JFE	Boeing 737-8F2	Turkish Airlines *Hatay*	
TC-JFF	Boeing 737-8F2	Turkish Airlines *Afyon*	
TC-JFG	Boeing 737-8F2	Turkish Airlines *Mardi*	
TC-JFH	Boeing 737-8F2	Turkish Airlines *Igdir*	
TC-JFI	Boeing 737-8F2	Turkish Airlines *Sivas*	
TC-JFJ	Boeing 737-8F2	Turkish Airlines *Agri*	
TC-JFK	Boeing 737-8F2	Turkish Airlines *Zonguldak*	
TC-JFL	Boeing 737-8F2	Turkish Airlines *Ordu*	
TC-JFM	Boeing 737-8F2	Turkish Airlines *Nigde*	
TC-JFN	Boeing 737-8F2	Turkish Airlines *Bitlis*	
TC-JFO	Boeing 737-8F2	Turkish Airlines *Batman*	
TC-JFP	Boeing 737-8F2	Turkish Airlines	
TC-JFR	Boeing 737-8F2	Turkish Airlines	
TC-JFT	Boeing 737-8F2	Turkish Airlines *Kastamonu*	
TC-JFU	Boeing 737-8F2	Turkish Airlines *Elazig*	
TC-JFV	Boeing 737-8F2	Turkish Airlines *Tunceli*	
TC-JFY	Boeing 737-8F2	Turkish Airlines *Manisa*	
TC-JFZ	Boeing 737-8F2	Turkish Airlines *Bolu*	
TC-JGA	Boeing 737-8F2	Turkish Airlines	
TC-JGB	Boeing 737-8F2	Turkish Airlines *Eskisehir*	
TC-JGC	Boeing 737-8F2	Turkish Airlines *Kocaeli*	
TC-JGD	Boeing 737-8F2	Turkish Airlines *Nevsehir*	
TC-JGF	Boeing 737-8F2	Turkish Airlines *Ardahan*	
TC-JGG	Boeing 737-8F2	Turkish Airlines *Erzincan*	
TC-JGH	Boeing 737-8F2	Turkish Airlines *Tokat*	
TC-JGI	Boeing 737-8F2	Turkish Airlines *Siirt*	
TC-JGJ	Boeing 737-8F2	Turkish Airlines	
TC-JGK	Boeing 737-8F2	Turkish Airlines	
TC-JGL	Boeing 737-8F2	Turkish Airlines	
TC-JGM	Boeing 737-8F2	Turkish Airlines	
TC-JGN	Boeing 737-8F2	Turkish Airlines	
TC-JGO	Boeing 737-8F2	Turkish Airlines	
TC-JGP	Boeing 737-8F2	Turkish Airlines *Bartin*	
TC-JGR	Boeing 737-8F2	Turkish Airlines *Usak*	
TC-JGS	Boeing 737-8F2	Turkish Airlines *Kahramanmaras*	
TC-JGT	Boeing 737-8F2	Turkish Airlines *Avanos*	
TC-JGU	Boeing 737-8F2	Turkish Airlines *Bodrum*	
TC-JGV	Boeing 737-8F2	Turkish Airlines *Cesme*	
TC-JGY	Boeing 737-8F2	Turkish Airlines *Managvat*	
TC-JGZ	Boeing 737-8F2	Turkish Airlines *Midyat*	
TC-JHA	Boeing 737-8F2	Turkish Airlines *Mudanya*	
TC-JHB	Boeing 737-8F2	Turkish Airlines *Safranbolu*	
TC-JHC	Boeing 737-8F2	Turkish Airlines *Iskenderun*	
TC-JHD	Boeing 737-8F2	Turkish Airlines *Serik*	
TC-JHE	Boeing 737-8F2	Turkish Airlines *Burhaniye*	
TC-JHF	Boeing 737-8F2	Turkish Airlines *Ayvalik*	
TC-JHG	Boeing 737-8GJ	AnadoluJet	
TC-JHH	Boeing 737-8GJ	AnadoluJet	
TC-JHI	Boeing 737-8FH	AnadoluJet	
TC-JHJ	Boeing 737-86Q	AnadoluJet	
TC-JHK	Boeing 737-8F2	Turkish Airlines *Yesilkoy*	
TC-JHL	Boeing 737-8F2	Turkish Airlines *Unye*	
TC-JHM	Boeing 737-8F2	Turkish Airlines *Burgaz*	
TC-JHN	Boeing 737-8F2	Turkish Airlines	
TC-JHO	Boeing 737-8F2	Turkish Airlines	
TC-JIH	Airbus A.340-313X	Turkish Airlines *Kocaeli*	
TC-JII	Airbus A.340-313X	Turkish Airlines *Mersin*	
TC-JJE	Boeing 777-3F2ER	Turkish Airlines *Dolmabahce*	
TC-JJF	Boeing 777-3F2ER	Turkish Airlines *Beylerbeyi*	
TC-JJG	Boeing 777-3F2ER	Turkish Airlines *Yildiz*	
TC-JJH	Boeing 777-3F2ER	Turkish Airlines *Rumeli*	
TC-JJI	Boeing 777-3F2ER	Turkish Airlines *Ede*	
TC-JJJ	Boeing 777-3F2ER	Turkish Airlines *Erzurum*	
TC-JJK	Boeing 777-3F2ER	Turkish Airlines *Akdeniz*	
TC-JJL	Boeing 777-3F2ER	Turkish Airlines *Karadeniz*	
TC-JJM	Boeing 777-3F2ER	Turkish Airlines *Mamara*	

Notes	Reg.	Type	Owner or Operator
	TC-JJN	Boeing 777-3F2ER	Turkish Airlines *Anadolu*
	TC-JJO	Boeing 777-3F2ER	Turkish Airlines *Istanbul*
	TC-JJP	Boeing 777-3F2ER	Turkish Airlines *Ankara*
	TC-JKJ	Boeing 737-752	Turkish Airlines *Eyup*
	TC-JKK	Boeing 737-752	Turkish Airlines *Fatih*
	TC-JKL	Boeing 737-76N	AnadoluJet
	TC-JKM	Boeing 737-76N	AnadoluJet
	TC-JKN	Boeing 737-752	Turkish Airlines *Besiktas*
	TC-JKO	Boeing 737-752	Turkish Airlines *Kadikoy*
	TC-JKP	Boeing 737-7GL	AnadoluJet
	TC-JKR	Boeing 737-7GL	AnadoluJet
	TC-JLJ	Airbus A.320-232	Turkish Airlines *Sirnak*
	TC-JLK	Airbus A.320-232	Turkish Airlines *Kirklareli*
	TC-JLL	Airbus A.320-232	Turkish Airlines *Duzce*
	TC-JLM	Airbus A.319-132	Turkish Airlines *Sinop*
	TC-JLN	Airbus A.319-132	Turkish Airlines *Karabuk*
	TC-JLO	Airbus A.319-132	Turkish Airlines *Ahlat*
	TC-JLP	Airbus A.319-132	Turkish Airlines *Koycegiz*
	TC-JLR	Airbus A.319-132	Turkish Airlines
	TC-JLS	Airbus A.319-132	Turkish Airlines *Salihli*
	TC-JLT	Airbus A.319-132	Turkish Airlines *Adilcevaz*
	TC-JLU	Airbus A.319-132	Turkish Airlines
	TC-JLV	Airbus A.319-132	Turkish Airlines
	TC-JLY	Airbus A.319-132	Turkish Airlines *Bergama*
	TC-JLZ	Airbus A.319-132	Turkish Airlines
	TC-JMH	Airbus A.321-232	Turkish Airlines *Didim*
	TC-JMI	Airbus A.321-232	Turkish Airlines *Milas*
	TC-JMJ	Airbus A.321-232	Turkish Airlines *Tekirdag*
	TC-JMK	Airbus A.321-232	Turkish Airlines *Uskudar*
	TC-JML	Airbus A.321-231	Turkish Airlines *Eminonu*
	TC-JMM	Airbus A.321-232	Turkish Airlines
	TC-JMN	Airbus A.321-232	Turkish Airlines
	TC-JMO	Airbus A.321-232	Turkish Airlines
	TC-JMP	Airbus A.321-232	Turkish Airlines
	TC-JNA	Airbus A.330-203	Turkish Airlines *Gaziantep*
	TC-JNB	Airbus A.330-203	Turkish Airlines *Konya*
	TC-JNC	Airbus A.330-203	Turkish Airlines *Bursa*
	TC-JND	Airbus A.330-203	Turkish Airlines *Antalya*
	TC-JNE	Airbus A.330-203	Turkish Airlines *Kayseri*
	TC-JNF	Airbus A.330-203	Turkish Airlines *Canakkale*
	TC-JNG	Airbus A.330-203	Turkish Airlines *Eskisehir*
	TC-JNH	Airbus A.330-343X	Turkish Airlines *Topkapi*
	TC-JNI	Airbus A.330-343X	Turkish Airlines *Konak*
	TC-JNJ	Airbus A.330-343X	Turkish Airlines *Kapadokya*
	TC-JNK	Airbus A.330-343X	Turkish Airlines *Sanliurfa*
	TC-JNL	Airbus A.330-343E	Turkish Airlines *Trabzon*
	TC-JNM	Airbus A.330-343X	Turkish Airlines *Samsun*
	TC-JNN	Airbus A.330-343	Turkish Airlines *Manisa*
	TC-JNO	Airbus A.330-343	Turkish Airlines
	TC-JNP	Airbus A.330-343	Turkish Airlines *Gokceada*
	TC-JNR	Airbus A.330-343	Turkish Airlines
	TC-JPA	Airbus A.320-232	Turkish Airlines *Mus*
	TC-JPB	Airbus A.320-232	Turkish Airlines *Rize*
	TC-JPC	Airbus A.320-232	Turkish Airlines *Erzurum*
	TC-JPD	Airbus A.320-232	Turkish Airlines *Isparta*
	TC-JPE	Airbus A.320-232	Turkish Airlines *Gumushane*
	TC-JPF	Airbus A.320-232	Turkish Airlines *Yozgat*
	TC-JPG	Airbus A.320-232	Turkish Airlines *Osmaniye*
	TC-JPH	Airbus A.320-232	Turkish Airlines *Kars*
	TC-JPI	Airbus A.320-232	Turkish Airlines *Dogubeyazit*
	TC-JPJ	Airbus A.320-232	Turkish Airlines *Edremit*
	TC-JPK	Airbus A.320-232	Turkish Airlines *Erdek*
	TC-JPL	Airbus A.320-232	Turkish Airlines *Goreme*
	TC-JPM	Airbus A.320-232	Turkish Airlines *Harput*
	TC-JPN	Airbus A.320-232	Turkish Airlines *Sarikamis*
	TC-JPO	Airbus A.320-232	Turkish Airlines *Kemer*
	TC-JPP	Airbus A.320-232	Turkish Airlines *Harran*
	TC-JPR	Airbus A.320-232	Turkish Airlines *Kusadasi*
	TC-JPS	Airbus A.320-232	Turkish Airlines *Adilcevaz*
	TC-JPT	Airbus A.320-232	Turkish Airlines *Urgup*
	TC-JPU	Airbus A.320-214	Turkish Airlines *Salihli*
	TC-JPV	Airbus A.320-214	Turkish Airlines *Sisli*

Reg.	Type	Owner or Operator	Notes
TC-JPY	Airbus A.320-214	Turkish Airlines *Beykoz*	
TC-JRA	Airbus A.321-231	Turkish Airlines *Kutayha*	
TC-JRB	Airbus A.321-231	Turkish Airlines *Sanliurfa*	
TC-JRC	Airbus A.321-231	Turkish Airlines *Sakarya*	
TC-JRD	Airbus A.321-231	Turkish Airlines *Balikesir*	
TC-JRE	Airbus A.321-231	Turkish Airlines *Trabzon*	
TC-JRF	Airbus A.321-231	Turkish Airlines *Fethiye*	
TC-JRG	Airbus A.321-231	Turkish Airlines *Finike*	
TC-JRH	Airbus A.321-231	Turkish Airlines *Yalova*	
TC-JRI	Airbus A.321-232	Turkish Airlines *Adiyaman*	
TC-JRJ	Airbus A.321-232	Turkish Airlines *Corum*	
TC-JRK	Airbus A.321-231	Turkish Airlines *Batman*	
TC-JRL	Airbus A.321-231	Turkish Airlines *Tarsus*	
TC-JRM	Airbus A.321-232	Turkish Airlines *Afyonkarahisar*	
TC-JRN	Airbus A.321-232	Turkish Airlines *Sariyer*	
TC-JRO	Airbus A.321-231	Turkish Airlines *Uludag*	
TC-JRP	Airbus A.321-231	Turkish Airlines *Urgup*	
TC-JRR	Airbus A.321-231	Turkish Airlines *Emirgan*	
TC-JRS	Airbus A.321-231	Turkish Airlines *Datca*	
TC-JRT	Airbus A.321-231	Turkish Airlines *Alacati*	
TC-JRU	Airbus A.321-231	Turkish Airlines	
TC-JRV	Airbus A.321-232	Turkish Airlines	
TC-JRY	Airbus A.321-232	Turkish Airlines	
TC-JRZ	Airbus A.321-232	Turkish Airlines	
TC-JSA	Airbus A.321-232	Turkish Airlines	
TC-JSB	Airbus A.321-231	Turkish Airlines	
TC-JSC	Airbus A.321-231	Turkish Airlines	
TC-JSD	Airbus A.321-231	Turkish Airlines	
TC-JUA	Airbus A.319-132	Turkish Airlines	
TC-JUB	Airbus A.319-132	Turkish Airlines	
TC-JUD	Airbus A.319-132	Turkish Airlines	
TC-JYA	Boeing 737-9F2ER	Turkish Airlines *Amasya*	
TC-JYB	Boeing 737-9F2ER	Turkish Airlines *Debizli*	
TC-JYC	Boeing 737-9F2ER	Turkish Airlines *Eregu*	
TC-JYD	Boeing 737-9F2ER	Turkish Airlines	
TC-JYE	Boeing 737-9F2ER	Turkish Airlines	
TC-JYF	Boeing 737-9F2ER	Turkish Airlines	
TC-JYG	Boeing 737-9F2ER	Turkish Airlines	
TC-JYH	Boeing 737-9F2ER	Turkish Airlines	
TC-JYI	Boeing 737-9F2ER	Turkish Airlines	
TC-JYJ	Boeing 737-9F2ER	Turkish Airlines	
TC-KZV	Airbus A.300B4-103F	ULS Cargo	
TC-LER	Airbus A.310-308F	ULS Cargo *Aras*	
TC-MCA	Airbus A.300B4-605R	MNG Cargo	
TC-MCB	Airbus A.300B4-203F	MNG Cargo	
TC-MCF	Boeing 737-4K5F	MNG Cargo	
TC-MNJ	Airbus A.300B4-203F	MNG Cargo	
TC-MNV	Airbus A.300B4-605R	MNG Cargo	
TC-OAL	Airbus A.321-231	Onur Air	
TC-OAN	Airbus A.321-231	Onur Air	
TC-OBD	Airbus A.320-232	Onur Air	
TC-OBE	Airbus A.320-232	Onur Air	
TC-OBF	Airbus A.321-231	Onur Air	
TC-OBG	Airbus A.320-233	Onur Air	
TC-OBH	Airbus A.320-233	Onur Air	
TC-OBI	Airbus A.320-233	Onur Air	
TC-OBJ	Airbus A.321-231	Onur Air	
TC-OBK	Airbus A.321-231	Onur Air	
TC-OBL	Airbus A.320-232	Onur Air	
TC-OBM	Airbus A.320-232	Onur Air	
TC-OBN	Airbus A.320-232	Onur Air	
TC-OBO	Airbus A.320-232	Onur Air	
TC-OBP	Airbus A.320-232	Onur Air	
TC-OBR	Airbus A.321-231	Onur Air	
TC-OBS	Airbus A.320-232	Onur Air	
TC-OBU	Airbus A.320-231	Onur Air ✓	
TC-OBV	Airbus A.321-231	Onur Air	
TC-OBY	Airbus A.321-231	Onur Air	
TC-ONJ	Airbus A.321-131	Onur Air	
TC-ONS	Airbus A.321-131	Onur Air	
TC-SAC	Boeing 737-76N	AnadoluJet	
TC-SAD	Boeing 737-76N	AnadoluJet	

Notes	Reg.	Type	Owner or Operator
	TC-SAE	Boeing 737-76N	AnadoluJet
	TC-SAF	Boeing 737-73V	AnadoluJet
	TC-SAG	Boeing 737-73V	AnadoluJet
	TC-SAI	Boeing 737-8AS	AnadoluJet
	TC-SAJ	Boeing 737-8AS	AnadoluJet
	TC-SAK	Boeing 737-8AS	AnadoluJet
	TC-SAL	Boeing 737-76N	AnadoluJet
	TC-SNE	Boeing 737-8HX	SunExpress
	TC-SNF	Boeing 737-8HC	SunExpress
	TC-SNG	Boeing 737-8HC	SunExpress
	TC-SNH	Boeing 737-8FH	SunExpress
	TC-SNI	Boeing 737-8FH	SunExpress
	TC-SNJ	Boeing 737-86J	SunExpress
	TC-SNL	Boeing 737-86N	SunExpress
	TC-SNM	Boeing 737-8BK	SunExpress
	TC-SNN	Boeing 737-8HC	SunExpress
	TC-SNO	Boeing 737-8HC	SunExpress
	TC-SNP	Boeing 737-8HC	SunExpress
	TC-SNR	Boeing 737-8HC	SunExpress
	TC-SNT	Boeing 737-8HC	SunExpress
	TC-SNU	Boeing 737-8HC	SunExpress
	TC-SNV	Boeing 737-86J	SunExpress
	TC-SUI	Boeing 737-8CX	SunExpress
	TC-SUL	Boeing 737-85F	SunExpress
	TC-SUM	Boeing 737-85F	SunExpress
	TC-SUO	Boeing 737-86Q	SunExpress
	TC-SUU	Boeing 737-86Q	SunExpress
	TC-SUV	Boeing 737-86N	SunExpress
	TC-SUY	Boeing 737-86N	SunExpress
	TC-SUZ	Boeing 737-8HX	SunExpress
	TC-TJB	Boeing 737-3Q8	Corendon Air
	TC-TJE	Boeing 737-4YO	Corendon Air
	TC-TJF	Boeing 737-4YO	Corendon Air
	TC-TJG	Boeing 737-86J	Corendon Air
	TC-TJH	Boeing 737-86J	Corendon Air
	TC-TJI	Boeing 737-8S3	Corendon Air
	TC-TJJ	Boeing 737-8S3	Corendon Air
	TC-TJK	Boeing 737-8GQ	Corendon Air
	TC-TLA	Boeing 737-4Q8	Tailwind Airlines
	TC-TLB	Boeing 737-4Q8	Tailwind Airlines
	TC-TLC	Boeing 737-4Q8	Tailwind Airlines
	TC-TLD	Boeing 737-4Q8	Tailwind Airlines
	TC-TLE	Boeing 737-4Q8	Tailwind Airlines
	TC-VEL	Airbus A.310-308F	ULS Cargo

TF (Iceland)

Notes	Reg.	Type	Owner or Operator
	TF-AAA	Boeing 747-236F	Air Atlanta Icelandic/Saudi Arabian Airlines
	TF-AAC	Boeing 747-481	Air Atlanta Icelandic/Saudi Arabian Airlines
	TF-AAD	Boeing 747-4H6	Air Atlanta Icelandic/Saudi Arabian Airlines
	TF-AAE	Boeing 747-4H6	Air Atlanta Icelandic/Saudi Arabian Airlines
	TF-AAF	Boeing 747-446	Air Atlanta Icelandic/Saudi Arabian Airlines
	TF-AME	Boeing 747-312	Air Atlanta Icelandic/Saudi Arabian Airlines
	TF-AMF	Boeing 747-412BCF	Air Atlanta Icelandic/Saudi Arabian Airlines
	TF-AMI	Boeing 747-412BCF	Air Atlanta Icelandic/Saudi Arabian Airlines
	TF-AMP	Boeing 747-481BCF	Air Atlanta Icelandic/Saudi Arabian Airlines
	TF-AMS	Boeing 747-481	Air Atlanta Icelandic/Saudi Arabian Airlines
	TF-AMT	Boeing 747-481	Air Atlanta Icelandic/Saudi Arabian Airlines
	TF-AMU	Boeing 747-48E	Air Atlanta Icelandic/Saudi Arabian Airlines
	TF-AMV	Boeing 747-412	Air Atlanta Icelandic/Saudi Arabian Airlines
	TF-AMX	Boeing 747-441BCF	Air Atlanta Icelandic/Saudi Arabian Airlines
	TF-BBD	Boeing 737-3Y0F	Bluebird Cargo/TNT Airways
	TF-BBE	Boeing 737-36EF	Bluebird Cargo/Swiftair
	TF-BBF	Boeing 737-36EF	Bluebird Cargo
	TF-BBG	Boeing 737-36EF	Bluebird Cargo/TNT Airways
	TF-BBH	Boeing 737-4YO	Bluebird Cargo/TNT Airways
	TF-FIA	Boeing 757-256	Icelandair
	TF-FIC	Boeing 757-23N	Icelandair
	TF-FID	Boeing 757-23APF	Icelandair Cargo
	TF-FIE	Boeing 757-23APF	Icelandair Cargo/TNT Airways
	TF-FIG	Boeing 757-23APF	Icelandair Cargo

Reg.	Type	Owner or Operator	Notes
TF-FIH	Boeing 757-208PCF	Icelandair Cargo/TNT Airways	
TF-FII	Boeing 757-208	Icelandair	
TF-FIJ	Boeing 757-208	Icelandair Surtsey	
TF-FIN	Boeing 757-208	Icelandair Bryndis	
TF-FIO	Boeing 757-208	Icelandair Valdis	
TF-FIP	Boeing 757-208	Icelandair Leifur Eiriksson	
TF-FIR	Boeing 757-256	Icelandair	
TF-FIU	Boeing 757-256	Icelandair	
TF-FIV	Boeing 757-208	Icelandair Gudridur Porbjarnardottir	
TF-FIX	Boeing 757-308	Icelandair Snorri Porfinnsson	
TF-FIY	Boeing 757-256	Icelandair	
TF-FIZ	Boeing 757-256	Icelandair	
TF-ISL	Boeing 757-223	Icelandair	
TF-IST	Boeing 757-256	Icelandair	
TF-LLX	Boeing 757-256	Icelandair	
TF-TNM	Boeing 737-34SF	Bluebird Cargo/TNT Airways	

TS (Tunisia)

Reg.	Type	Owner or Operator	Notes
TS-IMB	Airbus A.320-211	Tunis Air Fahrat Hached	
TS-IMC	Airbus A.320-211	Tunis Air 7 Novembre	
TS-IMD	Airbus A.320-211	Tunis Air Khereddine	
TS-IME	Airbus A.320-211	Tunis Air Tabarka	
TS-IMF	Airbus A.320-211	Tunis Air Djerba	
TS-IMG	Airbus A.320-211	Tunis Air Abou el Kacem Chebbi	
TS-IMH	Airbus A.320-211	Tunis Air Ali Belhaouane	
TS-IMI	Airbus A.320-211	Tunis Air Jughurta	
TS-IMJ	Airbus A.319-114	Tunis Air El Kantaoui	
TS-IMK	Airbus A.319-114	Tunis Air Kerkenah	
TS-IML	Airbus A.320-211	Tunis Air Gafsa el Ksar	
TS-IMM	Airbus A.320-211	Tunis Air Le Bardo	
TS-IMN	Airbus A.320-211	Tunis Air Ibn Khaldoun	
TS-IMO	Airbus A.319-114	Tunis Air Hannibal	
TS-IMP	Airbus A.320-211	Tunis Air La Galite	
TS-IMQ	Airbus A.319-114	Tunis Air Alyssa	
TS-IMR	Airbus A.320-211	Tunis Air Habib Bourguiba	
TS-IMS	Airbus A.320-214	Tunis Air Dougga	
TS-IMT	Airbus A.320-214	Tunis Air	
TS-INA	Airbus A.320-214	Nouvelair	
TS-INB	Airbus A.320-214	Nouvelair	
TS-INC	Airbus A.320-214	Nouvelair	
TS-INF	Airbus A.320-212	Nouvelair	
TS-INH	Airbus A.320-214	Nouvelair	
TS-INI	Airbus A.320-212	Nouvelair	
TS-INL	Airbus A.320-212	Nouvelair	
TS-INN	Airbus A.320-212	Libyan Airlines	
TS-INO	Airbus A.320-214	Nouvelair	
TS-INP	Airbus A.320-214	Libyan Airlines	
TS-IOG	Boeing 737-5H3	Tunis Air Sfax	
TS-IOH	Boeing 737-5H3	Tunis Air Hammamet	
TS-IOI	Boeing 737-5H3	Tunis Air Mahida	
TS-IOJ	Boeing 737-5H3	Tunis Air Monastir	
TS-IOK	Boeing 737-6H3	Tunis Air Kairouan	
TS-IOL	Boeing 737-6H3	Tunis Air Tozeur-Nefta	
TS-IOM	Boeing 737-6H3	Tunis Air Carthage	
TS-ION	Boeing 737-6H3	Tunis Air Utique	
TS-IOP	Boeing 737-6H3	Tunis Air El Jem	
TS-IOQ	Boeing 737-6H3	Tunis Air Bizerte	
TS-IOR	Boeing 737-6H3	Tunis Air Tahar Haddad	
TS-IPA	Airbus A.300B4-605R	Tunis Air Sidi Bou Said	
TS-IPB	Airbus A.300B4-605R	Tunis Air Tunis	
TS-IPC	Airbus A.300B4-605R	Tunis Air Amilcar	
TS-IQA	Airbus A.321-211	Nouvelair	
TS-IQB	Airbus A.321-211	Nouvelair	

UK (Uzbekistan)

Reg.	Type	Owner or Operator	Notes
UK-31002	Airbus A.310-324	Uzbekistan Airways Fergana	
UK-31003	Airbus A.310-324	Uzbekistan Airways Bukhara	
UK-67001	Boeing 767-33PER	Uzbekistan Airways	

Notes	Reg.	Type	Owner or Operator
	UK-67002	Boeing 767-33PER	Uzbekistan Airways
	UK-67003	Boeing 767-33PER	Uzbekistan Airways
	UK-67004	Boeing 767-33PER	Uzbekistan Airways
	UK-67005	Boeing 767-33PER	Uzbekistan Airways
	UK-75701	Boeing 757-23P	Uzbekistan Airways
	UK-75702	Boeing 757-23P	Uzbekistan Airways

UN (Kazakhstan)

Note: Air Astana operates P4- registered Boeing 757s and 767s.

UR (Ukraine)

UR-GAH	Boeing 737-32Q	Ukraine International *Mayrni*
UR-GAK	Boeing 737-5Y0	Ukraine International
UR-GAN	Boeing 737-36N	Ukraine International
UR-GAO	Boeing 737-4Z9	Ukraine International
UR-GAP	Boeing 737-4Z9	Ukraine International
UR-GAQ	Boeing 737-33R	Ukraine International
UR-GAS	Boeing 737-528	Ukraine International
UR-GAU	Boeing 737-5Y0	Ukraine International
UR-GAV	Boeing 737-4C9	Ukraine International
UR-GAW	Boeing 737-5Y0	Ukraine International
UR-GAX	Boeing 737-4Y0	Ukraine International
UR-GAZ	Boeing 737-55D	Ukraine International
UR-GBA	Boeing 737-36N	Ukraine International
UR-PSA	Boeing 737-8HX	Ukraine International
UR-PSB	Boeing 737-8HX	Ukraine International
UR-PSC	Boeing 737-8HX	Ukraine International
UR-PSD	Boeing 737-89P	Ukraine International
UR-PSE	Boeing 737-84R	Ukraine International
UR-PSF	Boeing 737-84R	Ukraine International
UR-WUA	Airbus A.320-232	Wizz Air Ukraine
UR-WUB	Airbus A.320-232	Wizz Air Ukraine
UR-82007	Antonov An-124	Antonov Airlines
UR-82008	Antonov An-124	Antonov Airlines
UR-82009	Antonov An-124	Antonov Airlines
UR-82027	Antonov An-124	Antonov Airlines
UR-82029	Antonov An-124	Antonov Airlines
UR-82060	Antonov An-225	Antonov Airlines
UR-82072	Antonov An-124	Antonov Airlines
UR-82073	Antonov An-124	Antonov Airlines

V5 (Namibia)

V5-NME	Airbus A.340-311	Air Namibia
V5-NMF	Airbus A.340-311	Air Namibia

V8 (Brunei)

V8-BLA	Boeing 777-212ER	Royal Brunei Airlines
V8-BLB	Boeing 777-212ER	Royal Brunei Airlines
V8-BLC	Boeing 777-212ER	Royal Brunei Airlines
V8-BLF	Boeing 777-212ER	Royal Brunei Airlines

VH (Australia)

VH-OQA	Airbus A.380-841	QANTAS
VH-OQB	Airbus A.380-841	QANTAS
VH-OQC	Airbus A.380-841	QANTAS
VH-OQD	Airbus A.380-841	QANTAS
VH-OQE	Airbus A.380-841	QANTAS
VH-OQF	Airbus A.380-841	QANTAS
VH-OQG	Airbus A.380-841	QANTAS
VH-OQH	Airbus A.380-841	QANTAS
VH-OQI	Airbus A.380-841	QANTAS
VH-OQJ	Airbus A.380-841	QANTAS

Reg.	Type	Owner or Operator	Notes
VH-OQK	Airbus A.380-841	QANTAS	
VH-OQL	Airbus A.380-841	QANTAS	
VH-OQM	Airbus A.380-841	QANTAS	
VH-OQN	Airbus A.380-841	QANTAS	

VN (Vietnam)

VN-A141	Boeing 777-2Q8ER	Vietnam Airlines	
VN-A142	Boeing 777-2Q8ER	Vietnam Airlines	
VN-A143	Boeing 777-26KER	Vietnam Airlines	
VN-A144	Boeing 777-26KER	Vietnam Airlines	
VN-A145	Boeing 777-26KER	Vietnam Airlines	
VN-A146	Boeing 777-26KER	Vietnam Airlines	
VN-A147	Boeing 777-2Q8ER	Vietnam Airlines	
VN-A149	Boeing 777-2Q8ER	Vietnam Airlines	
VN-A150	Boeing 777-2Q8ER	Vietnam Airlines	
VN-A151	Boeing 777-2Q8ER	Vietnam Airlines	

VP-B/VP-Q (Bermuda)

VP-BAV	Boeing 767-36NER	Aeroflot Russian International L. Tolstoy	
VP-BAX	Boeing 767-36NER	Aeroflot Russian International F. Dostoevsky	
VP-BAY	Boeing 767-36NER	Aeroflot Russian International I. Turgenev	
VP-BAZ	Boeing 767-36NER	Aeroflot Russian International N. Nekrasov	
VP-BDC	Airbus A.321-211	Aeroflot Russian International	
VP-BDD	Airbus A.330-343	Aeroflot Russian International	
VP-BDE	Airbus A.330-343	Aeroflot Russian International	
VP-BDI	Boeing 767-38AER	Aeroflot Russian International A. Pushkin	
VP-BDK	Airbus A.320-214	Aeroflot Russian International G. Sviridov	
VP-BDM	Airbus A.319-111	Aeroflot Russian International A. Borodin	
VP-BDN	Airbus A.319-111	Aeroflot Russian International A. Dargomyzhsky	
VP-BDO	Airbus A.319-111	Aeroflot Russian International I. Stravinsky	
VP-BDP	McD Douglas MD-11F	Aeroflot Cargo	
VP-BDQ	McD Douglas MD-11F	Aeroflot Cargo	
VP-BDR	McD Douglas MD-11F	Aeroflot Cargo	
VP-BID	Airbus A.320-214	Aeroflot Russian International	
VP-BIQ	Airbus A.319-111	Rossiya	
VP-BIT	Airbus A.319-111	Rossiya	
VP-BIU	Airbus A.319-114	Rossiya	
VP-BKC	Airbus A.320-214	Aeroflot Russian International	
VP-BKX	Airbus A.320-214	Aeroflot Russian International G. Sedov	
VP-BKY	Airbus A.320-214	Aeroflot Russian International M. Rostropovich	
VP-BLX	Airbus A.330-243	Aeroflot Russian International E. Svetlanov	
VP-BLY	Airbus A.330-243	Aeroflot Russian International	
VP-BME	Airbus A.320-214	Aeroflot Russian International N. Mikluho-Maklay	
VP-BMF	Airbus A.320-214	Aeroflot Russian International G. Shelihov	
VP-BPA	Boeing 737-5K5	Transaero	
VP-BPD	Boeing 737-5K5	Transaero	
VP-BQP	Airbus A.320-214	Aeroflot Russian International A. Rublev	
VP-BQR	Airbus A.321-211	Aeroflot Russian International I. Repin	
VP-BQS	Airbus A.321-211	Aeroflot Russian International I. Kramskoi	
VP-BQT	Airbus A.321-211	Aeroflot Russian International I. Shishkin	
VP-BQU	Airbus A.320-214	Aeroflot Russian International A. Nikitin	
VP-BQV	Airbus A.320-214	Aeroflot Russian International V. Vasnetsov	
VP-BQW	Airbus A.320-214	Aeroflot Russian International V. Vereshchagin	
VP-BQX	Airbus A.321-211	Aeroflot Russian International I. Ayvazovsky	
VP-BRW	Airbus A.321-211	Aeroflot Russian International	
VP-BRX	Airbus A.320-214	Aeroflot Russian International V. Surikov	
VP-BRY	Airbus A.320-214	Aeroflot Russian International K. Brulloff	
VP-BRZ	Airbus A.320-214	Aeroflot Russian International V. Serov	
VP-BUE	Boeing 767-3CBER	Uzbekistan Airways	
VP-BUF	Boeing 767-33PER	Uzbekistan Airways	
VP-BUH	Boeing 757-231	Uzbekistan Airways	
VP-BUI	Boeing 757-231	Uzbekistan Airways	
VP-BUJ	Boeing 757-231	Uzbekistan Airways	
VP-BUK	Airbus A.319-111	Aeroflot Russian International Yuri Senkevich	
VP-BUM	Airbus A.321-211	Aeroflot Russian International A.Deineka	
VP-BUN	Airbus A.319-112	Aeroflot Russian International	
VP-BUO	Airbus A.319-111	Aeroflot Russian International K. Malevich	
VP-BUP	Airbus A.321-211	Aeroflot Russian International	

Notes	Reg.	Type	Owner or Operator
	VP-BWA	Airbus A.319-111	Aeroflot Russian International S. Prokofiev
	VP-BWD	Airbus A.320-214	Aeroflot Russian International A. Aliabiev
	VP-BWE	Airbus A.320-214	Aeroflot Russian International H. Rimsky-Korsakov
	VP-BWF	Airbus A.320-214	Aeroflot Russian International D. Shostakovich
	VP-BWG	Airbus A.319-111	Aeroflot Russian International A. Aleksandrov
	VP-BWH	Airbus A.320-214	Aeroflot Russian International M. Balakirev
	VP-BWI	Airbus A.319-111	Aeroflot Russian International A. Glazunov
	VP-BWJ	Airbus A.319-111	Aeroflot Russian International A. Shnitke
	VP-BWK	Airbus A.319-111	Aeroflot Russian International S. Taneyev
	VP-BWL	Airbus A.319-111	Aeroflot Russian International A. Grechaninov
	VP-BWM	Airbus A.320-214	Aeroflot Russian International S. Rakhmaninov
	VP-BWN	Airbus A.321-211	Aeroflot Russian International A. Skriabin
	VP-BWO	Airbus A.321-211	Aeroflot Russian International P. Chaikovsky
	VP-BWP	Airbus A.321-211	Aeroflot Russian International M. Musorgsky
	VP-BWW	Boeing 767-306ER	Aeroflot Russian International S. Esenin
	VP-BWX	Boeing 767-306ER	Aeroflot Russian International A. Blok
	VP-BYI	Boeing 737-524	Transaero
	VP-BYJ	Boeing 737-524	Transaero
	VP-BYN	Boeing 737-524	Transaero
	VP-BYO	Boeing 737-524	Transaero
	VP-BYP	Boeing 737-524	Transaero
	VP-BYQ	Boeing 737-524	Transaero
	VP-BYT	Boeing 737-524	Transaero
	VP-BZO	Airbus A.320-214	Aeroflot Russian International V. Bering
	VP-BZP	Airbus A.320-214	Aeroflot Russian International E. Habarov
	VP-BZQ	Airbus A.320-214	Aeroflot Russian International Yu. Lisiansky
	VP-BZR	Airbus A.320-214	Aeroflot Russian International F. Bellinsgauzen
	VP-BZS	Airbus A.320-214	Aeroflot Russian International M. Lazarev
	VQ-BAQ	Airbus A.319-112	Rossiya
	VQ-BAR	Airbus A.319-112	Rossiya
	VQ-BAS	Airbus A.319-112	Rossiya
	VQ-BAT	Airbus A.319-112	Rossiya
	VQ-BAU	Airbus A.319-112	Rossiya
	VQ-BAV	Airbus A.319-112	Rossiya
	VQ-BAX	Airbus A.320-214	Aeroflot Russian International G. Nevelskoy
	VQ-BAY	Airbus A.320-214	Aeroflot Russian International S. Krasheninnikov
	VQ-BAZ	Airbus A.320-214	Aeroflot Russian International V. Obruchev
	VQ-BBA	Airbus A.319-112	Aeroflot Russian International S. Cheliuskin
	VQ-BBB	Airbus A.320-114	Aeroflot Russian International Yu. Gagarin
	VQ-BBC	Airbus A.320-214	Aeroflot Russian International
	VQ-BBD	Airbus A.319-112	Aeroflot Russian International V. Golovnin
	VQ-BBE	Airbus A.330-243	Aeroflot Russian International I. Brodsky
	VQ-BBF	Airbus A.330-243	Aeroflot Russian International A. Griboedov
	VQ-BBG	Airbus A.330-243	Aeroflot Russian International N. Gogol
	VQ-BBM	Airbus A.320-214	Rossiya
	VQ-BCM	Airbus A.320-214	Aeroflot Russian International
	VQ-BCN	Airbus A.320-214	Aeroflot Russian International
	VQ-BCO	Airbus A.319-111	Aeroflot Russian International
	VQ-BCP	Airbus A.319-112	Aeroflot Russian International D. Mendeleev
	VQ-BCQ	Airbus A.330-343	Aeroflot Russian International
	VQ-BCU	Airbus A.330-343	Aeroflot Russian International W. Majakowski
	VQ-BCV	Airbus A.330-343	Aeroflot Russian International
	VQ-BDQ	Airbus A.320-214	Rossiya
	VQ-BDR	Airbus A.320-214	Rossiya
	VQ-BDY	Airbus A.320-214	Rossiya
	VQ-BEA	Airbus A.321-211	Aeroflot Russian International I. Michurin
	VQ-BED	Airbus A.321-211	Aeroflot Russian International
	VQ-BEE	Airbus A.321-211	Aeroflot Russian International
	VQ-BEF	Airbus A.321-211	Aeroflot Russian International
	VQ-BEG	Airbus A.321-211	Aeroflot Russian International
	VQ-BEH	Airbus A.320-214	Aeroflot Russian International
	VQ-BEI	Airbus A.321-211	Aeroflot Russian International
	VQ-BEJ	Airbus A.320-214	Aeroflot Russian International
	VQ-BEK	Airbus A.330-343	Aeroflot Russian International A. Tvardovsky
	VQ-BEL	Airbus A.330-343	Aeroflot Russian International
	VQ-BHK	Airbus A.321-211	Aeroflot Russian International
	VQ-BHL	Airbus A.320-214	Aeroflot Russian International
	VQ-BHM	Airbus A.321-211	Aeroflot Russian International
	VQ-BHN	Airbus A.320-214	Aeroflot Russian International N. Lobachevsky
	VQ-BIR	Airbus A.320-214	Aeroflot Russian International
	VQ-BIT	Airbus A.320-214	Aeroflot Russian International
	VQ-BIU	Airbus A.320-214	Aeroflot Russian International

Reg.	Type	Owner or Operator	Notes
VQ-BIV	Airbus A.320-214	Aeroflot Russian International *A. Kolmogorov*	
VQ-BIW	Airbus A.320-214	Aeroflot Russian International *V. Glushko*	
VQ-BKS	Airbus A.320-214	Aeroflot Russian International *A. Chizhevsky*	
VQ-BKT	Airbus A.320-214	Aeroflot Russian International *V. Vernadsky*	
VQ-BKU	Airbus A.320-214	Aeroflot Russian International	
VQ-BMV	Airbus A.330-343	Aeroflot Russian International	
VQ-BMX	Airbus A.330-343	Aeroflot Russian International	
VQ-BMY	Airbus A.330-343	Aeroflot Russian International *Ilya Frank*	
VQ-BNS	Airbus A.330-343	Aeroflot Russian International *A. Bakulev*	
VQ-BOH	Airbus A.321-211	Aeroflot Russian International	
VQ-BOI	Airbus A.321-211	Aeroflot Russian International	
VQ-BPI	Airbus A.330-343	Aeroflot Russian International	
VQ-BPJ	Airbus A.330-343	Aeroflot Russian International	
VQ-BPK	Airbus A.330-343	Aeroflot Russian International	
VQ-BQX	Airbus A.330-343	Aeroflot Russian International	
VQ-BQY	Airbus A.330-343X	Aeroflot Russian International *M. Sholohov*	
VQ-BQZ	Airbus A.330-343	Aeroflot Russian International	
VQ-BRD	Airbus A.320-214	Rossiya	
VQ-BRF	Boeing 737-5Q8	Transaero	

VT (India)

Reg.	Type	Owner or Operator	Notes
VT-ALA	Boeing 777-237LR	Air-India *State of Andhra Pradesh*	
VT-ALB	Boeing 777-237LR	Air-India *Arunachal Pradesh*	
VT-ALC	Boeing 777-237LR	Air-India *State of Assam*	
VT-ALD	Boeing 777-237LR	Air-India *Gujarat*	
VT-ALE	Boeing 777-237LR	Air India *Haryana*	
VT-ALF	Boeing 777-237LR	Air India *Jharkhand*	
VT-ALG	Boeing 777-237LR	Air India *Kerala*	
VT-ALH	Boeing 777-237LR	Air India *Maharashtra*	
VT-ALJ	Boeing 777-337ER	Air India *Bihar*	
VT-ALK	Boeing 777-337ER	Air India *Chattisgarh*	
VT-ALL	Boeing 777-337ER	Air-India *State of Assam*	
VT-ALM	Boeing 777-337ER	Air India *Himachel Pradesh*	
VT-ALN	Boeing 777-337ER	Air India *Jammu & Kashmir*	
VT-ALO	Boeing 777-337ER	Air India *Karnataka*	
VT-ALP	Boeing 777-337ER	Air India *Madhya Pradesh*	
VT-ALQ	Boeing 777-337ER	Air India *Manpur*	
VT-ALR	Boeing 777-337ER	Air India *Meghalaya*	
VT-ALS	Boeing 777-337ER	Air India *Mizoram*	
VT-ALT	Boeing 777-337ER	Air India *Nagaland*	
VT-ALU	Boeing 777-337ER	Air India *Orissa*	
VT-ALV	Boeing 777-337ER	Air India	
VT-ALW	Boeing 777-337ER	Air India	
VT-ALX	Boeing 777-337ER	Air India	
VT-JEG	Boeing 777-35RER	Jet Airways	
VT-JEH	Boeing 777-35RER	Jet Airways	
VT-JEK	Boeing 777-35RER	Jet Airways	
VT-JEL	Boeing 777-35RER	Jet Airways	
VT-JEM	Boeing 777-35RER	Jet Airways	
VT-JWE	Airbus A.330-243	Jet Airways	
VT-JWF	Airbus A.330-243	Jet Airways	
VT-JWG	Airbus A.330-243	Jet Airways	
VT-JWH	Airbus A.330-302	Jet Airways	
VT-JWJ	Airbus A.330-203	Jet Airways	
VT-JWK	Airbus A.330-203	Jet Airways	
VT-JWL	Airbus A.330-203	Jet Airways	
VT-JWM	Airbus A.330-202	Jet Airways	
VT-JWN	Airbus A.330-203	Jet Airways	
VT-JWP	Airbus A.330-203	Jet Airways	
VT-JWQ	Airbus A.330-203	Jet Airways	
VT-JWR	Airbus A.330-302	Jet Airways	
VT-JWS	Airbus A.330-302	Jet Airways	

XA (Mexico)

Reg.	Type	Owner or Operator	Notes
XA-EAP	Boeing 767-25D	Aeromexico	
XA-FRJ	Boeing 767-283	Aeromexico	
XA-JBC	Boeing 767-284	Aeromexico	
XA-OAM	Boeing 767-2B1	Aeromexico	

Notes	Reg.	Type	Owner or Operator
	XA-TOJ	Boeing 767-283	Aeromexico

YL (Latvia)

YL-BBD	Boeing 737-53S	Air Baltic
YL-BBE	Boeing 737-53S	Air Baltic
YL-BBI	Boeing 737-33A	Air Baltic
YL-BBJ	Boeing 737-36Q	Air Baltic
YL-BBK	Boeing 737-33V	Air Baltic
YL-BBL	Boeing 737-33V	Air Baltic
YL-BBM	Boeing 737-522	Air Baltic
YL-BBN	Boeing 737-522	Air Baltic
YL-BBO	Boeing 737-33V	Air Baltic
YL-BBP	Boeing 737-522	Air Baltic
YL-BBQ	Boeing 737-522	Air Baltic
YL-BBR	Boeing 737-31S	Air Baltic
YL-BBS	Boeing 737-31S	Air Baltic
YL-BBX	Boeing 737-36Q	Air Baltic
YL-BBY	Boeing 737-36Q	Air Baltic

YR (Romania)

YR-ASA	Airbus A.318-111	Tarom
YR-ASB	Airbus A.318-111	Tarom
YR-ASC	Airbus A.318-111	Tarom
YR-ASD	Airbus A.318-111	Tarom
YR-BAE	Boeing 737-46N	Blue Air
YR-BAG	Boeing 737-5L9	Blue Air
YR-BAJ	Boeing 737-430	Blue Air
YR-BAK	Boeing 737-430	Blue Air
YR-BAM	Boeing 737-4Q8	Blue Air
YR-BAN	Boeing 737-4Q8	Blue Air
YR-BAO	Boeing 737-42C	Blue Air
YR-BGA	Boeing 737-38J	Tarom *Alba Iulia*
YR-BGB	Boeing 737-38J	Tarom *Bucuresti*
YR-BGD	Boeing 737-38J	Tarom *Deva*
YR-BGE	Boeing 737-38J	Tarom *Timisoara*
YR-BGF	Boeing 737-78J	Tarom *Braila*
YR-BGG	Boeing 737-78J	Tarom *Craiova*
YR-BGH	Boeing 737-78J	Tarom *Hunedoara*
YR-BGI	Boeing 737-78J	Tarom *Iasi*
YR-BGS	Boeing 737-8GJ	Tarom
YR-HBD	McD Douglas MD-83	Medallion Air
YR-HBE	McD Douglas MD-83	Medallion Air
YR-HBY	McD Douglas MD-83	Medallion Air
YR-LCA	Airbus A.310-325	Tarom

YU (Serbia and Montenegro)

YU-AND	Boeing 737-3H9	JAT Airways *City of Krusevac*
YU-ANF	Boeing 737-3H9	JAT Airways
YU-ANI	Boeing 737-3H9	JAT Airways
YU-ANK	Boeing 737-3H9	JAT Airways
YU-ANL	Boeing 737-3H9	JAT Airways
YU-ANV	Boeing 737-3H9	JAT Airways
YU-ANW	Boeing 737-3H9	JAT Airways
YU-AON	Boeing 737-3Q4	JAT Airways

ZK (New Zealand)

ZK-OKA	Boeing 777-219ER	Air New Zealand
ZK-OKB	Boeing 777-219ER	Air New Zealand
ZK-OKC	Boeing 777-219ER	Air New Zealand
ZK-OKD	Boeing 777-219ER	Air New Zealand
ZK-OKE	Boeing 777-219ER	Air New Zealand
ZK-OKF	Boeing 777-219ER	Air New Zealand
ZK-OKG	Boeing 777-219ER	Air New Zealand
ZK-OKH	Boeing 777-219ER	Air New Zealand

Reg.	Type	Owner or Operator	Notes
ZK-OKM	Boeing 777-319ER	Air New Zealand	
ZK-OKN	Boeing 777-319ER	Air New Zealand	
ZK-OKO	Boeing 777-319ER	Air New Zealand	
ZK-OKP	Boeing 777-319ER	Air New Zealand	
ZK-OKQ	Boeing 777-319ER	Air New Zealand	

ZS (South Africa)

ZS-SLF	Airbus A.340-211	South African Airways	
ZS-SNA	Airbus A.340-642	South African Airways	
ZS-SNB	Airbus A.340-642	South African Airways	
ZS-SNC	Airbus A.340-642	South African Airways	
ZS-SND	Airbus A.340-642	South African Airways	
ZS-SNE	Airbus A.340-642	South African Airways	
ZS-SNF	Airbus A.340-642	South African Airways	
ZS-SNG	Airbus A.340-642	South African Airways	
ZS-SNH	Airbus A.340-642	South African Airways	
ZS-SNI	Airbus A.340-642	South African Airways	
ZS-SXA	Airbus A.340-313E	South African Airways	
ZS-SXB	Airbus A.340-313E	South African Airways	
ZS-SXC	Airbus A.340-313E	South African Airways	
ZS-SXD	Airbus A.340-313E	South African Airways	
ZS-SXE	Airbus A.340-313E	South African Airways	
ZS-SXF	Airbus A.340-313E	South African Airways	
ZS-SXG	Airbus A.340-313X	South African Airways	
ZS-SXH	Airbus A.340-313X	South African Airways	
ZS-SXU	Airbus A.330-243	South African Airways	
ZS-SXV	Airbus A.330-243	South African Airways	
ZS-SXW	Airbus A.330-243	South African Airways	
ZS-SXX	Airbus A.330-243	South African Airways	
ZS-SXY	Airbus A.330-243	South African Airways	
ZS-SXZ	Airbus A.330-243	South African Airways	

3B (Mauritius)

3B-NAU	Airbus A.340-312	Air Mauritius *Pink Pigeon*	
3B-NAY	Airbus A.340-313X	Air Mauritius *Cardinal*	
3B-NBD	Airbus A.340-313X	Air Mauritius *Parakeet*	
3B-NBE	Airbus A.340-313X	Air Mauritius *Paille en Queue*	
3B-NBI	Airbus A.340-313E	Air Mauritius *Le Flamboyant*	
3B-NBJ	Airbus A.340-313E	Air Mauritius *Le Chamarel*	

4K (Azerbaijan)

4K-AZ03	Airbus A.319-111	Azerbaijan Airlines	
4K-AZ04	Airbus A.319-111	Azerbaijan Airlines	
4K-AZ05	Airbus A.319-111	Azerbaijan Airlines	
4K-AZ11	Boeing 757-22L	Azerbaijan Airlines	
4K-AZ12	Boeing 757-22L	Azerbaijan Airlines	
4K-AZ38	Boeing 757-256	Azerbaijan Airlines	
4K-AZ43	Boeing 757-2M6	Azerbaijan Airlines	
4K-AZ54	Airbus A.320-214	Azerbaijan Airlines	
4K-AZ77	Airbus A.320-214	Azerbaijan Airlines	
4K-AZ78	Airbus A.320-214	Azerbaijan Airlines	
4K-AZ79	Airbus A.320-214	Azerbaijan Airlines	
4K-AZ80	Airbus A.320-214	Azerbaijan Airlines	
4K-AZ81	Boeing 767-32LER	Azerbaijan Airlines	
4K-AZ83	Airbus A.320-214	Azerbaijan Airlines	
4K-AZ84	Airbus A.320-214	Azerbaijan Airlines	

4O (Montenegro)

4O-AOA	Embraer ERJ190-200LR	Montenegro Airlines	
4O-AOB	Embraer ERJ190-200LR	Montenegro Airlines	
4O-AOC	Embraer ERJ190-200LR	Montenegro Airlines	
4O-AOK	Fokker 100	Montenegro Airlines	
4O-AOM	Fokker 100	Montenegro Airlines	
4O-AOP	Fokker 100	Montenegro Airlines	

Notes	Reg.	Type	Owner or Operator
	4O-AOT	Fokker 100	Montenegro Airlines

4R (Sri Lanka)

	4R-ADA	Airbus A.340-311	SriLankan Airlines
	4R-ADB	Airbus A.340-311	SriLankan Airlines
	4R-ADC	Airbus A.340-311	SriLankan Airlines
	4R-ADE	Airbus A.340-313X	SriLankan Airlines
	4R-ADF	Airbus A.340-313X	SriLankan Airlines
	4R-ADG	Airbus A.340-313X	SriLankan Airlines
	4R-ALA	Airbus A.330-243	SriLankan Airlines
	4R-ALB	Airbus A.330-243	SriLankan Airlines
	4R-ALC	Airbus A.330-243	SriLankan Airlines
	4R-ALD	Airbus A.330-243	SriLankan Airlines
	4R-ALG	Airbus A.330-243	SriLankan Airlines
	4R-ALH	Airbus A.330-243	SriLankan Airlines
	4R-ALJ	Airbus A.330-243	SriLankan Airlines

4X (Israel)

	4X-ABF	Airbus A.320-232	Israir
	4X-ABG	Airbus A.320-232	Israir
	4X-AXL	Boeing 747-245F (SCD)	El Al Cargo
	4X-EAJ	Boeing 767-330ER	El Al
	4X-EAK	Boeing 767-3Q8ER	El Al
	4X-EAL	Boeing 767-33AER	El Al
	4X-EAM	Boeing 767-3Q8ER	El Al
	4X-EAP	Boeing 767-3Y0ER	El Al
	4X-EAR	Boeing 767-352ER	El Al
	4X-ECA	Boeing 777-258ER	El Al *Galilee*
	4X-ECB	Boeing 777-258ER	El Al *Negev*
	4X-ECC	Boeing 777-258ER	El Al *Hasharon*
	4X-ECD	Boeing 777-258ER	El Al *Carmel*
	4X-ECE	Boeing 777-258ER	El Al *Sderot*
	4X-ECF	Boeing 777-258ER	El Al *Kiryat Shmona*
	4X-EHA	Boeing 737-958ER	El Al
	4X-EHB	Boeing 737-958ER	El Al
	4X-EHC	Boeing 737-958ER	El Al
	4X-EHD	Boeing 737-958ER	El Al
	4X-EKA	Boeing 737-858	El Al *Tiberias*
	4X-EKB	Boeing 737-858	El Al *Eilat*
	4X-EKC	Boeing 737-858	El Al *Beit Shean*
	4X-EKD	Boeing 737-758	El Al *Ashkelon*
	4X-EKE	Boeing 737-758	El Al *Nazareth*
	4X-EKF	Boeing 737-858	El Al *Kinneret*
	4X-EKH	Boeing 737-85P	El Al *Yarden*
	4X-EKI	Boeing 737-86N	El Al
	4X-EKJ	Boeing 737-85P	El Al *Degania*
	4X-EKL	Boeing 737-85P	El Al *Nahalal*
	4X-EKM	Boeing 737-804	El Al
	4X-EKO	Boeing 737-86Q	El Al
	4X-EKP	Boeing 737-8Q8	El Al
	4X-EKR	Boeing 737-804	El Al
	4X-EKS	Boeing 737-8Q8	El Al *Caesarea*
	4X-EKT	Boeing 737-8BK	El Al
	4X-EKU	Boeing 737-8Z9	El Al
	4X-ELA	Boeing 747-458	El Al *Tel Aviv-Jaffa*
	4X-ELB	Boeing 747-458	El Al *Haifa*
	4X-ELC	Boeing 747-458	El Al *Beer Sheva*
	4X-ELD	Boeing 747-458	El Al *Jerusalem*
	4X-ELE	Boeing 747-458	El Al *Rishon Letsion*
	4X-ELF	Boeing 747-412F	El Al Cargo
	4X-ELH	Boeing 747-412	El Al

5B (Cyprus)

	5B-DBB	Airbus A.320-231	Cyprus Airways *Akamas*
	5B-DCF	Airbus A.319-132	Cyprus Airways *Larnaka*
	5B-DCG	Airbus A.320-232	Cyprus Airways *Aphrodite*

5B-DCH	Airbus A.320-232	Cyprus Airways *Lefkosia*	
5B-DCJ	Airbus A.320-232	Cyprus Airways *Amathus*	
5B-DCK	Airbus A.320-232	Cyprus Airways *Pafos*	
5B-DCL	Airbus A.320-232	Cyprus Airways *Pentadaktylos*	
5B-DCM	Airbus A.320-232	Cyprus Airways *Troodos*	
5B-DCN	Airbus A.319-132	Cyprus Airways *Limassol*	
5B-DCO	Airbus A.321-231	Cyprus Airways	
5B-DCP	Airbus A.321-231	Cyprus Airways	

5N (Nigeria)

5N-MJN	Boeing 737-86N	Arik Air	
5N-MJO	Boeing 737-86N	Arik Air	
5N-MJP	Boeing 737-8JE	Arik Air	
5N-MJQ	Boeing 737-8JE	Arik Air	

5Y (Kenya)

5Y-KQS	Boeing 777-2U8ER	Kenya Airways	
5Y-KQT	Boeing 777-2U8ER	Kenya Airways	
5Y-KQU	Boeing 777-2U8ER	Kenya Airways	
5Y-KQX	Boeing 767-36NER	Kenya Airways	
5Y-KQY	Boeing 767-36NER	Kenya Airways	
5Y-KQZ	Boeing 767-36NER	Kenya Airways	
5Y-KYV	Boeing 767-3Q8ER	Kenya Airways	
5Y-KYW	Boeing 767-319ER	Kenya Airways	
5Y-KYX	Boeing 767-3P6ER	Kenya Airways	
5Y-KYZ	Boeing 777-2U8ER	Kenya Airways	

7T (Algeria)

7T-VJG	Boeing 767-3D6ER	Air Algerie	
7T-VJH	Boeing 767-3D6ER	Air Algerie	
7T-VJI	Boeing 767-3D6ER	Air Algerie	
7T-VJJ	Boeing 737-8D6	Air Algerie *Jugurtha*	
7T-VJK	Boeing 737-8D6	Air Algerie *Mansourah*	
7T-VJL	Boeing 737-8D6	Air Algerie *Illizi*	
7T-VJM	Boeing 737-8D6	Air Algerie	
7T-VJN	Boeing 737-8D6	Air Algerie	
7T-VJO	Boeing 737-8D6	Air Algerie	
7T-VJP	Boeing 737-8D6	Air Algerie	
7T-VJQ	Boeing 737-6D6	Air Algerie *Kasbah d'Alger*	
7T-VJR	Boeing 737-6D6	Air Algerie	
7T-VJS	Boeing 737-6D6	Air Algerie	
7T-VJT	Boeing 737-6D6	Air Algerie	
7T-VJU	Boeing 737-6D6	Air Algerie	
7T-VJV	Airbus A.330-202	Air Algerie *Tinhinan*	
7T-VJW	Airbus A.330-202	Air Algerie *Lalla Setti*	
7T-VJX	Airbus A.330-202	Air Algerie *Mers el Kebir*	
7T-VJY	Airbus A.330-202	Air Algerie *Monts des Beni Chougrane*	
7T-VJZ	Airbus A.330-202	Air Algerie *Teddis*	
7T-VKA	Boeing 737-8D6	Air Algerie	
7T-VKB	Boeing 737-8D6	Air Algerie	
7T-VKC	Boeing 737-8D6	Air Algerie	
7T-VKD	Boeing 737-8D6	Air Algerie	
7T-VKE	Boeing 737-8D6	Air Algerie	
7T-VKF	Boeing 737-8D6	Air Algerie	
7T-VKG	Boeing 737-8D6	Air Algerie	
7T-VKH	Boeing 737-8D6	Air Algerie	
7T-VKI	Boeing 737-8D6	Air Algerie	
7T-VKJ	Boeing 737-8D6	Air Algerie	

9A (Croatia)

9A-CTF	Airbus A.320-211	Croatia Airlines *Rijeka*	
9A-CTG	Airbus A.319-112	Croatia Airlines *Zadar*	
9A-CTH	Airbus A.319-112	Croatia Airlines *Zagreb*	
9A-CTI	Airbus A.319-112	Croatia Airlines *Vukovar*	

Notes	Reg.	Type	Owner or Operator
	9A-CTJ	Airbus A.320-214	Croatia Airlines *Dubrovnik*
	9A-CTK	Airbus A.320-214	Croatia Airlines *Split*
	9A-CTL	Airbus A.319-112	Croatia Airlines *Pula*

9H (Malta)

Notes	Reg.	Type	Owner or Operator
	9H-AEF	Airbus A.320-214	Air Malta
	9H-AEG	Airbus A.319-112	Air Malta
	9H-AEH	Airbus A.319-111	Air Malta *Floriana*
	9H-AEJ	Airbus A.319-111	Air Malta *San Pawl il-Bahar*
	9H-AEK	Airbus A.320-214	Air Malta *San Giljan*
	9H-AEL	Airbus A.319-111	Air Malta *Marsaxlokk*
	9H-AEM	Airbus A.319-111	Air Malta *Birgu*
	9H-AEN	Airbus A.320-214	Air Malta
	9H-AEO	Airbus A.320-214	Air Malta
	9H-AEP	Airbus A.320-214	Air Malta
	9H-AEQ	Airbus A.320-214	Air Malta

9K (Kuwait)

Notes	Reg.	Type	Owner or Operator
	9K-ADE	Boeing 747-469 (SCD)	Kuwait Airways *Al-Jabariya*
	9K-AMA	Airbus A.300B4-605R	Kuwait Airways *Failaka*
	9K-AMB	Airbus A.300B4-605R	Kuwait Airways *Burghan*
	9K-AMC	Airbus A.300B4-605R	Kuwait Airways *Wafra*
	9K-AMD	Airbus A.300B4-605R	Kuwait Airways *Wara*
	9K-AME	Airbus A.300B4-605R	Kuwait Airways *Al-Rawdhatain*
	9K-ANA	Airbus A.340-313	Kuwait Airways *Warba*
	9K-ANB	Airbus A.340-313	Kuwait Airways *Bayan*
	9K-ANC	Airbus A.340-313	Kuwait Airways *Meskan*
	9K-AND	Airbus A.340-313	Kuwait Airways *Al-Riggah*
	9K-AOA	Boeing 777-269ER	Kuwait Airways *Al-Grain*
	9K-AOB	Boeing 777-269ER	Kuwait Airways *Garouh*

9M (Malaysia)

Notes	Reg.	Type	Owner or Operator
	9M-MNA	Airbus A.380-841	Malaysian Airlines
	9M-MNB	Airbus A.380-841	Malaysian Airlines
	9M-MNC	Airbus A.380-841	Malaysian Airlines
	9M-MND	Airbus A.380-841	Malaysian Airlines
	9M-MNE	Airbus A.380-841	Malaysian Airlines
	9M-MNF	Airbus A.380-841	Malaysian Airlines
	9M-MPK	Boeing 747-4H6	Malaysian Airlines *Johor Bahru*
	9M-MPL	Boeing 747-4H6	Malaysian Airlines *Penang*
	9M-MPM	Boeing 747-4H6	Malaysian Airlines *Melaka*
	9M-MPN	Boeing 747-4H6	Malaysian Airlines *Pangkor*
	9M-MPP	Boeing 747-4H6	Malaysian Airlines *Putrajaya*
	9M-MPQ	Boeing 747-4H6	Malaysian Airlines *Kuala Lumpur*
	9M-MPR	Boeing 747-4H6F	Malaysian Airlines Cargo
	9M-MPS	Boeing 747-4H6F	Malaysian Airlines Cargo
	9M-MRA	Boeing 777-2H6ER	Malaysian Airlines
	9M-MRB	Boeing 777-2H6ER	Malaysian Airlines
	9M-MRC	Boeing 777-2H6ER	Malaysian Airlines
	9M-MRD	Boeing 777-2H6ER	Malaysian Airlines
	9M-MRE	Boeing 777-2H6ER	Malaysian Airlines
	9M-MRF	Boeing 777-2H6ER	Malaysian Airlines
	9M-MRG	Boeing 777-2H6ER	Malaysian Airlines
	9M-MRH	Boeing 777-2H6ER	Malaysian Airlines
	9M-MRI	Boeing 777-2H6ER	Malaysian Airlines
	9M-MRJ	Boeing 777-2H6ER	Malaysian Airlines
	9M-MRK	Boeing 777-2H6ER	Malaysian Airlines
	9M-MRL	Boeing 777-2H6ER	Malaysian Airlines
	9M-MRM	Boeing 777-2H6ER	Malaysian Airlines
	9M-MRN	Boeing 777-2H6ER	Malaysian Airlines
	9M-MRO	Boeing 777-2H6ER	Malaysian Airlines
	9M-MRP	Boeing 777-2H6ER	Malaysian Airlines
	9M-MRQ	Boeing 777-2H6ER	Malaysian Airlines

9V (Singapore)

Reg.	Type	Owner or Operator	Notes
9V-SCB	Boeing 747-412F	Singapore Airlines Cargo	
9V-SFD	Boeing 747-412F	Singapore Airlines Cargo	
9V-SFF	Boeing 747-412F	Singapore Airlines Cargo	
9V-SFG	Boeing 747-412F	Singapore Airlines Cargo	
9V-SFJ	Boeing 747-412F	Singapore Airlines Cargo	
9V-SFK	Boeing 747-412F	Singapore Airlines Cargo	
9V-SFL	Boeing 747-412F	Singapore Airlines Cargo	
9V-SFM	Boeing 747-412F	Singapore Airlines Cargo	
9V-SFN	Boeing 747-412F	Singapore Airlines Cargo	
9V-SFO	Boeing 747-412F	Singapore Airlines Cargo	
9V-SFP	Boeing 747-412F	Singapore Airlines Cargo	
9V-SFQ	Boeing 747-412F	Singapore Airlines Cargo	
9V-SKA	Airbus A.380-841	Singapore Airlines	
9V-SKB	Airbus A.380-841	Singapore Airlines	
9V-SKC	Airbus A.380-841	Singapore Airlines	
9V-SKD	Airbus A.380-841	Singapore Airlines	
9V-SKE	Airbus A.380-841	Singapore Airlines	
9V-SKF	Airbus A.380-841	Singapore Airlines	
9V-SKG	Airbus A.380-841	Singapore Airlines	
9V-SKH	Airbus A.380-841	Singapore Airlines	
9V-SKI	Airbus A.380-841	Singapore Airlines	
9V-SKJ	Airbus A.380-841	Singapore Airlines	
9V-SKK	Airbus A.380-841	Singapore Airlines	
9V-SKL	Airbus A.380-841	Singapore Airlines	
9V-SKM	Airbus A.380-841	Singapore Airlines	
9V-SKN	Airbus A.380-841	Singapore Airlines	
9V-SKP	Airbus A.380-841	Singapore Airlines	
9V-SKQ	Airbus A.380-841	Singapore Airlines	
9V-SKR	Airbus A.380-841	Singapore Airlines	
9V-SKS	Airbus A.380-841	Singapore Airlines	
9V-SKT	Airbus A.380-841	Singapore Airlines	
9V-SWA	Boeing 777-312ER	Singapore Airlines	
9V-SWB	Boeing 777-312ER	Singapore Airlines	
9V-SWD	Boeing 777-312ER	Singapore Airlines	
9V-SWE	Boeing 777-312ER	Singapore Airlines	
9V-SWF	Boeing 777-312ER	Singapore Airlines	
9V-SWG	Boeing 777-312ER	Singapore Airlines	
9V-SWH	Boeing 777-312ER	Singapore Airlines	
9V-SWI	Boeing 777-312ER	Singapore Airlines	
9V-SWJ	Boeing 777-312ER	Singapore Airlines	
9V-SWK	Boeing 777-312ER	Singapore Airlines	
9V-SWL	Boeing 777-312ER	Singapore Airlines	
9V-SWM	Boeing 777-312ER	Singapore Airlines	
9V-SWN	Boeing 777-312ER	Singapore Airlines	
9V-SWO	Boeing 777-312ER	Singapore Airlines	
9V-SWP	Boeing 777-312ER	Singapore Airlines	
9V-SWQ	Boeing 777-312ER	Singapore Airlines	
9V-SWR	Boeing 777-312ER	Singapore Airlines	
9V-SWS	Boeing 777-312ER	Singapore Airlines	
9V-SWT	Boeing 777-312ER	Singapore Airlines	

9Y (Trinidad and Tobago)

Reg.	Type	Owner or Operator	Notes
9Y-LGW	Boeing 767-316ER	Caribbean Airlines	
9Y-LHR	Boeing 767-316ER	Caribbean Airlines	

D-AEAG Airbus A.300-622RF of DHL. *Tom Cole*

HA-LPW Airbus A.320-232 of WizzAir. *Allan S. Wright*

SE-RFS Boeing 767-304ER of Tuifly. *Allan S. Wright*

YR-BAM   Boeing 737-4Q8 of Blue Air. *Allan S. Wright*

S5-AAP Airbus A.319-432 of Adria Airways. *Tom Cole*

9K-ANB Airbus A.340-313 of Kuwait Airways. *Allan S. Wright*

Radio Frequencies

The frequencies used by the larger airfields/airports are listed below. Abbreviations used: TWR – Tower, APP – Approach, A/G – Air-Ground advisory. It is possible that changes will be made from time to time with the frequencies allocated, all of which are quoted in Megahertz (MHz).

Airfield	TWR	APP	A/G
Aberdeen	118.1	119.05	
Alderney	125.35	128.65	
Andrewsfield			130.55
Barton			120.25
Barrow			123.2
Beccles			120.375
Belfast International	118.3	128.5	
Belfast City	130.75	130.85	
Bembridge			123.25
Biggin Hill	134.8	129.4	
Birmingham	118.3	118.05	
Blackbushe			122.3
Blackpool	118.4	119.95	
Bodmin			122.7
Bourn			124.35
Bournemouth	125.6	119.475	
Breighton			129.80
Bristol/Filton	132.35	122.725	
Bristol/Lulsgate	133.85	127.25	
Bruntingthorpe			122.825
Caernarfon			122.25
Cambridge	122.2	123.6	
Cardiff	125.0	126.625	
Carlisle	123.6		
Clacton			118.15
Compton Abbas			122.7
Conington			129.725
Cosford	128.65	135.875	
Coventry	124.8	119.25	
Cranfield	134.925	122.85	
Cumbernauld	120.6		
Denham			130.725
Doncaster RHA	128.775	126.225	
Dundee	122.9		
Dunkeswell			123.475
Durham Tees Valley	119.8	118.85	
Duxford			122.075
Earls Colne			122.425
Edinburgh	118.7	121.2	
Elstree			122.4
Exeter	119.8	128.975	
Fairoaks			123.425
Farnborough	122.5	134.35	
Fenland			122.925
Fowlmere			135.7
Gamston			130.475
Gatwick	124.225	126.825	
Glasgow	118.8	119.1	
Gloucester/Staverton	122.9	128.55	
Goodwood			122.45
Guernsey	119.95	128.65	
Haverfordwest			122.2
Hawarden	124.95	123.35	
Henstridge			130.25
Headcorn			122.0
Heathrow	118.5	119.725	
Hethel			122.35
Hucknall			130.8
Humberside	124.9	119.125	
Inverness			122.6
Jersey	119.45	120.3	
Kemble			118.9
Land's End	120.25		
Lasham			125.25
Leeds Bradford	120.3	123.75	
Leicester			122.125
Liverpool	126.35	119.85	
London City	118.075	132.7	
Luton	132.55	129.55	
Lydd			120.7
Manchester	118.625	119.575	
Manston	119.925	126.35	
Netherthorpe			123.275
Newcastle	119.7	124.375	
Newquay	123.4	128.725	
North Denes			123.4
North Weald			123.525
Norwich	124.25	119.35	
Nottingham EMA	124.0	134.175	
Old Warden			130.7
Oxford	133.425	125.325	
Penzance			118.1
Perth	119.8		
Popham			129.8
Prestwick	118.15	120.55	
Redhill	119.6		
Rochester			122.25
Ronaldsway IOM	118.9	120.85	
Sandown			119.275
Sandtoft			130.425
Scilly Isles	123.825		
Seething			122.6
Sheffield City			128.525
Sherburn			122.6
Shipdham			132.25
Shobdon			123.5
Shoreham	125.4	123.15	
Sibson			122.3
Sleap			122.45
Southampton	118.2	128.85	
Southend	127.725	130.775	
Stansted	123.8	120.625	
Stapleford			122.8
Sumburgh	118.25	131.3	
Swansea			119.7
Sywell			122.7
Tatenhill			124.075
Thruxton			130.45
Tollerton			134.875
Wellesbourne			124.025
Welshpool			128.0
White Waltham			122.6
Wick			119.7
Wickenby			122.45
Wolverhampton			123.3
Woodford	120.7	130.75	
Woodvale	119.75	121.0	
Wycombe Air Park			126.55
Yeovil	125.4	130.8	

Airline Flight Codes

Those listed below identify many of the UK and overseas carriers appearing in the book

Code	Airline		Code	Airline		Code	Airline	
AAF	Aigle Azur	F	BZH	Brit Air	F	IRM	Mahan Air	EP
AAG	Atlantic Air Transport	G	CAI	Corendon Airlines	TC	ISS	Meridianafly	I
AAL	American Airlines	N	CAL	China Airlines	B	IWD	Orbest	EC
AAR	Asiana Airlines	HL	CCA	Air China	B	IYE	Yemenia	7O
ABD	Air Atlanta Icelandic	TF	CES	China Eastern	B	JAI	Jet Airways	VT
ABQ	AirBlue	AP	CFG	Condor	D	JAL	Japan Airlines	JA
ABR	Air Contractors	EI	CKS	Kalitta Air	N	JAT	JAT Airways	YU
ACA	Air Canada	C	CLH	Lufthansa CityLine	D	JKK	Spanair	EC
ADB	Antonov Airlines	UR	CLX	Cargolux	LX	JXX	Iceland Express	TF
ADH	Air One	I	COA	Continental Airlines	N	JOR	Blue Air	YR
ADR	Adria Airways	S5	CPA	Cathay Pacific	B	JTG	Jet Time	OY
AEA	Air Europa	EC	CRB	Air Astana	UN	KAC	Kuwait Airways	9K
AEE	Aegean Airlines	SX	CRL	Corsair	F	KAL	Korean Air	HL
AEY	Air Italy	I	CSA	CSA Czech Airlines	OK	KBR	Koral Blue	AP
AFL	Aeroflot	RA	CTN	Croatia Airlines	9A	KLC	KLM CityHopper	PH
AFR	Air France	F	CUB	Cubana	CU	KLM	KLM	PH
AHY	Azerbaijan Airlines	4K	CWC	Centurion Air Cargo	N	KQA	Kenya Airways	5Y
AIC	Air-India	VT	CYP	Cyprus Airways	5B	KZR	Air Astana	UN
AJA	Anadolujet	TC	DAH	Air Algerie	7T	KZU	Kuzu Airlines Cargo	TC
AKL	Air Kilroe	G	DAL	Delta Air Lines	N	LBT	Nouvelair	TS
ALK	SriLankan Airlines	4R	DBK	Dubrovnik Airline	9A	LDA	Lauda Air	OE
AMC	Air Malta	9H	DHL	DHL Express	D/G/N	LGL	Luxair	LX
AMT	ATA Airlines	N	DLH	Lufthansa	D	LLC	Small Planet Airlines	LY
ANA	All Nippon Airways	JA	DTR	Danish Air Transport	OY	LOG	Loganair	G
ANE	Air Nostrum	EC	EDW	Edelweiss Air	HB	LOT	Polish Airlines (LOT)	SP
ANZ	Air New Zealand	ZK	EIA	Evergreen International	N	LSK	Aurela	LY
ARA	Arik Air	5N	EIN	Aer Lingus	EI	LZB	Bulgaria Air	LZ
ATN	Air Transport International	N	ELL	Estonian Air	ES	MAH	Malev	HA
AUA	Austrian Airlines	OE	ELY	El Al	4X	MAS	Malaysian Airlines	9M
AUI	Ukraine International	UR	ETD	Etihad Airways	A6	MAU	Air Mauritius	3B
AUR	Aurigny A/S	G	ETH	Ethiopian Airlines	ET	MEA	Middle East Airlines	OD
AWC	Titan Airways	G	EUK	Air Atlanta Europe	TF	MGX	Montenegro Airlines	4O
AZA	Alitalia	I	EVA	EVA Airways	B	MLD	Air Moldova	ER
AZE	Arcus Air	D	EWG	Eurowings	D	MMZ	Euro Atlantic Airways	CS
AZW	Air Zimbabwe	Z	EXS	Jet2	G	MNB	MNG Airlines	TC
BAW	British Airways	G	EZE	Eastern Airways	G	MON	Monarch Airlines	G
BBC	Biman Bangladesh	S2	EZS	easyJet Switzerland	HB	MPH	Martinair	PH
BBD	Bluebird Cargo	TF	EZY	easyJet	G	MSR	EgyptAir	SU
BCS	European A/T	OO	FDX	Federal Express	N	NAX	Norwegian Air Shuttle	LN
BCY	CityJet	EI	FHE	Hello	HB	NCA	Nippon Cargo Airlines	JA
BDI	BenAir A/S	OY	FHY	Freebird Airlines	TC	NEX	Northern Executive	G
BEE	Flybe	G	FIF	Air Finland	OH	NLY	Niki	OE
BEL	Brussels Airlines	OO	FIN	Finnair	OH	NMB	Air Namibia	V5
BER	Air Berlin	D	FLI	Atlantic Airways	OY	NOA	Olympic Air	SX
BGA	Airbus Tpt International	F	GEC	Lufthansa Cargo	D	NOS	Neos	I
BGH	Balkan Holidays	LZ	GFA	Gulf Air	A9C	NPT	Atlantic Airlines	G
BHP	Belair	HB	GHA	Ghana Airways	9G	NVR	Novair Airlines	SE
BID	Binair	D	GMI	Germania	D	OAE	Omni Air International	N
BIE	Air Mediterranée	F	GTI	Atlas Air	N	OAS	Oman Air	A40
BIH	CHC Scotia	G	GWI	Germanwings	D	OAW	Helvetic Airways	HB
BLC	TAM Linhas Aereas	PT	GWL	Great Wall Airlines	B	OBS	Orbest	CS
BLF	Blue 1	OH	GXL	XL Airways Germany	D	OGE	Atlasjet	TC
BMR	bmi regional	G	HAY	Hamburg Airways	D	OHY	Onur Air	TC
BOS	Open Skies	F	HCC	Holidays Czech Airlines	OK	OLT	OLT	D
BOX	AeroLogic	D	HFY	HiFly	CS	PAC	Polar Air Cargo	N
BPA	Blue Panorama	I	HVN	Vietnam Airlines	VN	PGT	Pegasus Airlines	TC
BRT	BA Citiexpress	G	IBE	Iberia	EC	PIA	Pakistan International A/L	AP
BRU	Belavia	EW	ICB	Islandsflug	TF	PLK	Rossiya	RA
BTI	Air Baltic	YL	ICE	Icelandair	TF	POT	Polet	RA
BUC	Bulgarian Air Charter	LZ	IOS	Isles of Scilly Skybus	G	PRI	Primera Airlines	OY
BWA	Caribbean Airlines	9Y	IRA	Iran Air	EP	PTG	PrivatAir	D

G-PERB Agusta AW.139. *Allan S. Wright*

British Aircraft Preservation Council Register

The British Aircraft Preservation Council was formed in 1967 to co-ordinate the works of all bodies involved in the preservation, restoration and display of historical aircraft. Membership covers the whole spectrum of national, Service, commercial and voluntary groups, and meetings are held regularly at the bases of member organisations. The Council is able to provide a means of communication, helping to resolve any misunderstandings or duplication of effort. Every effort is taken to encourage the raising of standards of both organisation and technical capacity amongst the member groups to the benefit of everyone interested in aviation. To assist historians, the B.A.P.C. register has been set up and provides an identity for those aircraft which do not qualify for a Service serial or inclusion in the UK Civil Register.

Aircraft on the current B.A.P.C. Register are as follows:

Reg.	Type	Owner or Operator	Notes
1	Roe Triplane Type 4 (replica)	Shuttleworth Collection as G-ARSG (not carried)	
2	Bristol Boxkite (replica)	Shuttleworth Collection as G-ASPP (not carried)	
6	Roe Triplane Type IV (replica)	Manchester Museum of Science & Industry	
7	Southampton University MPA	Solent Sky, Southampton	
8	Dixon ornithopter	The Shuttleworth Collection	
9	Humber Monoplane (replica)	Midland Air Museum/Coventry	
10	Hafner R.II Revoplane	Museum of Army Flying/Middle Wallop	
12	Mignet HM.14	Museum of Flight/East Fortune	
13	Mignet HM.14	Brimpex Metal Treatments	
14	Addyman Standard Training Glider	A. Lindsay & N. H. Ponsford	
15	Addyman Standard Training Glider	The Aeroplane Collection	
16	Addyman ultra-light aircraft	N. H. Ponsford	
17	Woodhams Sprite	BB Aviation/Canterbury	
18	Killick MP Gyroplane	A. Lindsay & N. H. Ponsford	
20	Lee-Richards annular biplane (replica)	Visitor Centre Shoreham Airport	
21	Thruxton Jackaroo	M. J. Brett	
22	Mignet HM.14 (G-AEOF)	Aviodome/Netherlands	
23	SE-5A Scale Model	Newark Air Museum	
24	Currie Wot (replica)	Newark Air Museum	
25	Nyborg TGN-III glider	Midland Air Museum	
28	Wright Flyer (replica)	Corn Exchange/Leeds	
29	Mignet HM.14 (replica) (G-ADRY)	Brooklands Museum of Aviation/Weybridge	
32	Crossley Tom Thumb	Midland Air Museum	
33	DFS.108-49 Grunau Baby IIb	–	
34	DFS.108-49 Grunau Baby IIb	D. Elsdon	
35	EoN primary glider	–	
36	Fieseler Fi 103 (V-1) (replica)	Kent Battle of Britain Museum/Hawkinge	
37	Blake Bluetit (G-BXIY)	The Shuttleworth Collection/Old Warden	
38	Bristol Scout replica (A1742)	K. Williams & M. Thorn	
39	Addyman Zephyr sailplane	A. Lindsay & N. H. Ponsford	
40	Bristol Boxkite (replica)	Bristol City Museum	
41	B.E.2C (replica) (6232)	Yorkshire Air Museum/Elvington	
42	Avro 504 (replica) (H1968)	Yorkshire Air Museum/Elvington	
43	Mignet HM.14	Newark Air Museum/Winthorpe	
44	Miles Magister (L6906)	Museum of Berkshire Aviation (G-AKKY)/ Woodley	
45	Pilcher Hawk (replica)	Stanford Hall Museum	
46	Mignet HM.14	Stored	
47	Watkins Monoplane	National Museum of Wales	
48	Pilcher Hawk (replica)	Glasgow Museum of Transport	
49	Pilcher Hawk	Royal Scottish Museum/East Fortune	
50	Roe Triplane Type 1	Science Museum/South Kensington	
51	Vickers Vimy IV	Science Museum/South Kensington	
52	Lilienthal glider	Science Museum Store/Hayes	
53	Wright Flyer (replica)	Science Museum/South Kensington	
54	JAP-Harding monoplane	Science Museum/South Kensington	
55	Levavasseur Antoinette VII	Science Museum/South Kensington	
56	Fokker E.III (210/16)	Science Museum/South Kensington	
57	Pilcher Hawk (replica)	Science Museum/South Kensington	
58	Yokosuka MXY7 Ohka II (15-1585)	F.A.A. Museum/Yeovilton	
59	Sopwith Camel (replica) (D3419)	Aerospace Museum/Cosford	

Notes	Reg.	Type	Owner or Operator
	60	Murray M.1 helicopter	The Aeroplane Collection Ltd
	61	Stewart man-powered ornithopter	Lincolnshire Aviation Museum
	62	Cody Biplane (304)	Science Museum/South Kensington
	63	Hurricane (replica) (P3208)	Kent Battle of Britain Museum/Hawkinge
	64	Hurricane (replica) (P3059)	Kent Battle of Britain Museum/Hawkinge
	65	Spitfire (replica) (N3289)	Kent Battle of Britain Museum/Hawkinge
	66	Bf 109 (replica) (1480)	Kent Battle of Britain Museum/Hawkinge
	67	Bf 109 (replica) (14)	Kent Battle of Britain Museum/Hawkinge
	68	Hurricane (replica) (H3426)	Midland Air Museum
	69	Spitfire (replica) (N3313)	Kent Battle of Britain Museum/Hawkinge
	70	Auster AOP.5 (TJ398)	North East Aircraft Museum/Usworth
	71	Spitfire (replica) (P8140)	Norfolk & Suffolk Aviation Museum
	72	Hurricane (model) (V6779)	Gloucestershire Aviation Collection
	73	Hurricane (replica)	–
	74	Bf 109 (replica) (6357)	Kent Battle of Britain Museum/Hawkinge
	75	Mignet HM.14 (G-AEFG)	N. H. Ponsford
	76	Mignet HM.14 (G-AFFI)	Yorkshire Air Museum/Elvington
	77	Mignet HM.14 (replica) (G-ADRG)	Lower Stondon Transport Museum
	78	Hawker Hind (K5414) (G-AENP)	The Shuttleworth Collection/Old Warden
	79	Fiat G.46-4B (MM53211)	British Air Reserve/France
	80	Airspeed Horsa (KJ351)	Museum of Army Flying/Middle Wallop
	81	Hawkridge Dagling	Russavia Collection
	82	Hawker Hind (Afghan)	RAF Museum/Hendon
	83	Kawasaki Ki-100-1b (24)	Aerospace Museum/Cosford
	84	Nakajima Ki-46 (Dinah III)(5439)	Aerospace Museum/Cosford
	85	Weir W-2 autogyro	Museum of Flight/East Fortune
	86	de Havilland Tiger Moth (replica)	Yorkshire Aircraft Preservation Society
	87	Bristol Babe (replica) (G-EASQ)	Bristol Aero Collection/Kemble
	88	Fokker Dr 1 (replica) (102/17)	F.A.A. Museum/Yeovilton
	89	Cayley glider (replica)	Manchester Museum of Science & Industry
	90	Colditz Cock (replica)	Imperial War Museum/Duxford
	91	Fieseler Fi 103 (V-1)	Lashenden Air Warfare Museum
	92	Fieseler Fi 103 (V-1)	RAF Museum/Hendon
	93	Fieseler Fi 103 (V-1)	Imperial War Museum/Duxford
	94	Fieseler Fi 103 (V-1)	Aerospace Museum/Cosford
	95	Gizmer autogyro	F. Fewsdale
	96	Brown helicopter	North East Aircraft Museum
	97	Luton L.A.4A Minor	North East Aircraft Museum
	98	Yokosuka MXY7 Ohka II (997)	Manchester Museum of Science & Industry
	99	Yokosuka MXY7 Ohka II (8486M)	Aerospace Museum/Cosford
	100	Clarke Chanute biplane gliderr	RAF Museum/Hendon
	101	Mignet HM.14	Newark Air Museum/Winthorpe
	102	Mignet HM.14	Not completed
	103	Hulton hang glider (replica)	Personal Plane Services Ltd
	104	Bleriot XI	Sold in France
	105	Blériot XI (replica)	Arango Collection/Los Angeles
	106	Blériot XI (164)	RAF Museum/Hendon
	107	Blériot XXVII	RAF Museum/Hendon
	108	Fairey Swordfish IV (HS503)	RAF Restoration Centre/Wyton
	109	Slingsby Kirby Cadet TX.1	RAF Museum/Henlow store
	110	Fokker D.VII replica (static) (5125)	Stored
	111	Sopwith Triplane replica (static) (N5492)	F.A.A. Museum/Yeovilton
	112	DH.2 replica (static) (5964)	Museum of Army Flying/Middle Wallop
	113	S.E.5A replica (static) (B4863)	Stored
	114	Vickers Type 60 Viking (static) (G-EBED)	Brooklands Museum of Aviation/Weybridge
	115	Mignet HM.14	Norfolk & Suffolk Aviation Museum/Flixton
	116	Santos-Dumont Demoiselle (replica)	Cornwall Aero Park/Helston
	117	B.E.2C (replica)(1701)	Stored Hawkinge
	118	Albatros D.V (replica) (C19/18)	North Weald Aircraft Restoration Flight
	119	Bensen B.7	North East Aircraft Museum
	120	Mignet HM.14 (G-AEJZ)	South Yorkshire Aviation Museum/Doncaster
	121	Mignet HM.14 (G-AEKR)	South Yorkshire Aviation Society
	122	Avro 504 (replica) (1881)	Stored

Reg.	Type	Owner or Operator	Notes
123	Vickers FB.5 Gunbus (replica)	A. Topen (stored)/Cranfield	
124	Lilienthal Glider Type XI (replica)	Science Museum/South Kensington	
126	D.31 Turbulent (static)	Midland Air Museum/Coventry	
127	Halton Jupiter MPA	The Shuttleworth Collection	
128	Watkinson Cyclogyroplane Mk IV	IHM/Weston-super-Mare	
129	Blackburn 1911 Monoplane (replica)	Cornwall Aero Park/Helston store	
130	Blackburn 1912 Monoplane (replica)	Yorkshire Air Museum	
131	Pilcher Hawk (replica)	C. Paton	
132	Blériot XI (G-BLXI)		
133	Fokker Dr 1 (replica) (425/17)	Kent Battle of Britain Museum/Hawkinge	
134	Pitts S-2A static (G-CARS)	Toyota Ltd/Sywell	
135	Bristol M.1C (replica) (C4912)	Stored	
136	Deperdussin Seaplane (replica)	National Air Race Museum/USA	
137	Sopwith Baby Floatplane (replica) (8151)	Stored	
138	Hansa Brandenburg W.29 Floatplane (replica) (2292)	Stored	
139	Fokker Dr 1 (replica) 150/17	Stored	
140	Curtiss 42A (replica)	Stored	
141	Macchi M39 (replica)	Switzerland	
142	SE-5A (replica) (F5459)	Stored	
143	Paxton MPA	R. A. Paxton/Gloucestershire	
144	Weybridge Mercury MPA	Cranwell Gliding Club	
145	Oliver MPA	Stored	
146	Pedal Aeronauts Toucan MPA	Stored	
147	Bensen B.7	Norfolk & Suffolk Aviation Museum/Flixton	
148	Hawker Fury II (replica) (K7271)	High Ercall Aviation Museum	
149	Short S.27 (replica)	F.A.A. Museum (stored)/Yeovilton	
150	SEPECAT Jaguar GR.1 (replica) (XX728)	RAF M & R Unit/St. Athan, RAF Marketing & Recruitment Unit/St. Athan	
151	SEPECAT Jaguar GR.1 (replica) (XZ363)	RAF M & R Unit/St. Athan	
152	BAe Hawk T.1 (replica) (XX227)	RAF M & R Unit/Bottesford	
153	Westland WG.33	IHM/Weston-super-Mare	
154	D.31 Turbulent	Lincolnshire Aviation Museum/E. Kirkby	
155	Panavia Tornado GR.1 (model) (ZA556)	RAF M & R Unit/St. Athan	
156	Supermarine S-6B (replica)	National Air Race Museum/USA	
157	Waco CG-4A(237123)	Yorkshire Air Museum/Elvington	
158	Fieseler Fi 103 (V-1)	Defence Ordnance Disposal School/Chattenden	
159	Yokosuka MXY7 Ohka II	Defence Ordnance Disposal School/Chattenden	
160	Chargus 18/50 hang glider	Museum of Flight/East Fortune	
161	Stewart Ornithopter Coppelia	Bomber County Museum	
162	Goodhart MPA	Science Museum/Wroughton	
163	AFEE 10/42 Rotabuggy (replica)	Museum of Army Flying/Middle Wallop	
164	Wight Quadruplane Type 1 (replica)	Solent Sky, Southampton	
165	Bristol F.2b (E2466)	RAF Museum/Hendon	
166	Bristol F.2b (D7889)	Stored	
167	Bristol SE-5A	Stored	
168	DH.60G Moth (static replica)	Stored Hawkinge (G-AAAH)	
169	BAC/Sepecat Jaguar GR.1 (XX110)	RAF Training School/Cosford	
170	Pilcher Hawk (replica)	A. Gourlay/Strathallan	
171	BAe Hawk T.1 (model) (XX308)	RAF Marketing & Recruitment Unit/Bottesford	
172	Chargus Midas Super 8 hang glider	Science Museum/Wroughton	
173	Birdman Promotions Grasshopper	Science Museum/Wroughton	
174	Bensen B.7	Science Museum/Wroughton	
175	Volmer VJ-23 Swingwing	Manchester Museum of Science & Industry	
176	SE-5A (replica) (A4850)	South Yorks Aviation Society/Firbeck	
177	Avro 504K (replica) (G-AACA)	Brooklands Museum of Aviation/Weybridge	
178	Avro 504K (replica) (E373)	Bygone Times Antique Warehouse/Eccleston, Lancs	
179	Sopwith Pup (replica) (A7317)	Midland Air Museum/Coventry	
180	McCurdy Silver Dart (replica)	Reynolds Pioneer Museum/Canada	
181	RAF B.E.2b (replica) (687)	RAF Museum/Hendon	
182	Wood Ornithopter	Manchester Museum of Science & Industry	

Notes	Reg.	Type	Owner or Operator
	183	Zurowski ZP.1 helicopter	Newark Air Museum/Winthorpe
	184	Spitfire IX (replica) (EN398)	Fighter Wing Display Team/North Weald
	185	Waco CG-4A (243809)	Museum of Army Flying/Middle Wallop
	186	DH.82B Queen Bee (LF789)	de Havilland Heritage Museum
	187	Roe Type 1 biplane (replica)	Brooklands Museum of Aviation/Weybridge
	188	McBroom Cobra 88	Science Museum/Wroughton
	189	Bleriot XI (replica)	Stored
	190	Spitfire (replica) (K5054)	P. Smith/Hawkinge
	191	BAe Harrier GR.7 (model) (ZH139)	RAF M & R Unit/St. Athan
	192	Weedhopper JC-24	The Aeroplane Collection
	193	Hovey WD-11 Whing Ding	The Aeroplane Collection
	194	Santos Dumont Demoiselle (replica)	RAF Museum Store/RAF Stafford
	195	Moonraker 77 hang glider	Museum of Flight/East Fortune
	196	Sigma 2M hang glider	Museum of Flight/East Fortune
	197	Scotkites Cirrus III hang glider	Museum of Flight/East Fortune
	198	Fieseler Fi 103 (V-1)	Imperial War Museum/Lambeth
	199	Fieseler Fi 103 (V-1)	Science Museum/South Kensington
	200	Bensen B.7	K. Fern Collection/Stoke
	201	Mignet HM.14	Caernarfon Air Museum
	202	Spitfire V (model) (MAV467)	Maes Artro Craft Centre
	203	Chrislea LC.1 Airguard (G-AFIN)	The Aeroplane Collection
	204	McBroom hang glider	Newark Air Museum
	205	Hurricane (replica) (Z3427)	RAF Museum/Hendon
	206	Spitfire (replica) (MH486)	RAF Museum/Hendon
	207	Austin Whippet (replica) (K.158)	South Yorkshire Aviation Museum/Doncaster
	208	SE-5A (replica) (D276)	Prince's Mead Shopping Precinct/Farnborough
	209	Spitfire IX (replica) (MJ751)	Museum of D-Day Aviation/Shoreham
	210	Avro 504J (replica) (C4451)	Solent Sky, Southampton
	211	Mignet HM.14 (replica) (G-ADVU)	North East Aircraft Museum
	212	Bensen B.8	IHM/Weston-super-Mare
	213	Vertigo MPA	IHM/Weston-super-Mare
	214	Spitfire prototype (replica) (K5054)	Tangmere Military Aviation Museum
	215	Airwave hang-glider prototype	Solent Sky, Southampton
	216	DH.88 Comet (replica) (G-ACSS)	de Havilland Heritage Museum/London Colney
	217	Spitfire (replica) (K9926)	RAF Museum/Bentley Priory
	218	Hurricane (replica) (P3386)	RAF Museum/Bentley Priory
	219	Hurricane (replica) (L1710)	RAF Memorial Chapel/Biggin Hill
	220	Spitfire 1 (replica) (N3194)	RAF Memorial Chapel/Biggin Hill
	221	Spitfire LF.IX (replica) (MH777)	RAF Museum/Northolt
	222	Spitfire IX (replica) (BR600)	RAF Museum/Uxbridge
	223	Hurricane 1 (replica) (V7467)	RAF Museum/Coltishall
	224	Spitfire V (replica) (BR600)	Ambassador Hotel/Norwich
	225	Spitfire IX (replica) (P8448)	RAF Museum/Cranwell
	226	Spitfire XI (replica) (EN343)	RAF Museum/Benson
	227	Spitfire 1A (replica) (L1070)	RAF Museum/Turnhouse
	228	Olympus hang-glider	North East Aircraft Museum/Usworth
	229	Spitfire IX (replica) (MJ832)	RAF Museum/Digby
	230	Spitfire (replica) (AA550)	Eden Camp/Malton
	231	Mignet HM.14 (G-ADRX)	South Copeland Aviation Group
	232	AS.58 Horsa I/II	de Havilland Heritage Museum/London Colney
	233	Broburn Wanderlust sailplane	Museum of Berkshire Aviation/Woodley
	234	Vickers FB.5 Gunbus (replica)	RAF Manston Museum
	235	Fieseler Fi 103 (V-1)	Eden Camp Wartime Museum
	236	Hurricane (replica) (P2793)	Eden Camp Wartime Museum
	237	Fieseler Fi 103 (V-1)	RAF Museum Store/RAF Stafford
	238	Waxflatter ornithopter	Personal Plane Services Ltd
	239	Fokker D.VIII 5/8 scale replica	Norfolk & Suffolk Aviation Museum/Flixton
	240	Messerschmitt Bf.109G (replica)	Yorkshire Air Museum/Elvington
	241	Hurricane 1 (replica) (L1679)	Tangmere Military Aviation Museum
	242	Spitfire Vb (replica) (BL924)	Tangmere Military Aviation Museum
	243	Mignet HM.14 (replica) (G-ADYV)	P. Ward
	244	Solar Wings Typhoon	Museum of Flight/East Fortune
	245	Electraflyer Floater hang glider	Museum of Flight/East Fortune
	246	Hiway Cloudbase hang glider	Museum of Flight/East Fortune
	247	Albatross ASG.21 hang glider	Museum of Flight/East Fortune

BRITISH AIRCRAFT PRESERVATION

Reg.	Type	Owner or Operator	Notes
248	McBroom hang glider	Museum of Berkshire Aviation/Woodley	
249	Hawker Fury 1 (replica) (K5673)	Brooklands Museum of Aviation/Weybridge	
250	RAF SE-5A (replica) (F5475)	Brooklands Museum of Aviation/Weybridge	
251	Hiway Spectrum hang glider (replica)	Manchester Museum of Science & Industry	
252	Flexiform Wing hang glider	Manchester Museum of Science & Industry	
253	Mignet HM.14 (G-ADZW)	H. Shore/Sandown	
254	Hawker Hurricane (P3873)	Yorkshire Air Museum/Elvington	
255	NA P-51D Mustang (replica) (463209)	American Air Museum/Duxford	
256	Santos Dumont Type 20 (replica)	Brooklands Museum of Aviation/Weybridge	
257	DH.88 Comet (G-ACSS)	The Galleria/Hatfield	
258	Adams balloon	British Balloon Museum	
259	Gloster Gamecock (replica)	Jet Age Museum Gloucestershire	
260	Mignet HM280	–	
261	GAL Hotspur (replica)	Museum of Army Flying/ Middle Wallop	
262	Catto CP-16	Museum of Flight/East Fortune	
263	Chargus Cyclone	Ulster Aviation Heritage/Langford Lodge	
264	Bensen B.8M	IHM/Weston-super-Mare	
265	Spitfire 1 (P3873)	Yorkshire Air Museum/Elvington	
266	Rogallo hang glider	Ulster Aviation Heritage	
267	Hurricane (model)	Duxford	
268	Spifire (model)	–	
269	Spitfire (model) USAF	Lakenheath	
270	DH.60 Moth (model)	Yorkshire Air Museum	
271	Messerschmitt Me 163B	Shuttleworth Collection/Old Warden	
272	Hurricane (model)	Kent Battle of Britain Museum/Hawkinge	
273	Hurricane (model)	Kent Battle of Britain Museum/Hawkinge	
274	Boulton & Paul P.6 (model)	Boulton & Paul Aircraft Heritage Project	
275	Bensen B.7 gyroglider	Doncaster Museum	
276	Hartman Ornithopter	Science Museum/Wroughton	
277	Mignet HM.14	Visitor Centre Shoreham Airport	
278	Hurricane (model)	Kent Battle of Britain Museum/Hawkinge	
279	Airspeed Horsa	Shawbury	
280	DH.89A Dragon Rapide (model)	–	
281	Boulton & Paul Defiant (model)	–	
282	Manx Elder Duck	Isle of Man Airport Terminal	
283	Spitfire (model	Jurby, Isle of Man	
284	Gloster E.28/39 (model)	Lutterworth Leics	
285	Gloster E.28/39 (model)	Farnborough	
286	Mignet HM.14	Caernarfon Air Museum	
287	Blackburn F.2 Lincock (model)	Street Life Museum/Hull	
288	Hurricane (model)	Wonderland Pleasure Park, Mansfield	
289	Gyro Boat	IHM Weston-super-Mare	
290	Fieseler Fi 103 (V1) (model)	Dover Museum	
291 Kent	Hurricane (model)	National Battle of Britain Memorial, Capel-le-Ferne,	
292	Eurofighter Typhoon (model)	RAF Museum/Hendon	
293	Spitfire (model)	RAF Museum/Hendon	
294	Fairchild Argus (model)	Visitor Centre, Thorpe Camp, Woodhall Spa	
295	Da Vinci hang glider (replica)	Skysport Engineering	
296	Army Balloon Factory NuIII (replica)	RAF Museum, Hendon	
297	Spitfire (replica)	Kent Battle of Britain Museum/Hawkinge	
298	Spitfire IX (Model)	RAF Cosford Parade Ground	
299 Kent	Spitfire 1 (model).	National Battle of Britain Memorial, Capel-le-Ferne,	
300	Hummingbird (replica)	Shoreham Airport Historical Association	
301	Spitfire V FSM (replica)	Thornaby Aerodrome Memorial, Thornaby-on-Tees	
302	Mignet HM.14 reproduction	Shoreham Airport Historical Association	
303	Goldfinch 161 Amphibian	Norfolk and Suffolk Aviation Museum, Flixton	
305	Mersnier pedal powered airship Reproduction	British Balloon Museum and Library	
306	Lovegrove Autogyro trainer	Norfolk and Suffolk Aviation Museum, Flixton	

Note: Registrations/Serials carried are mostly false identities.
MPA = Man Powered Aircraft, IHM = International Helicopter Museum. The aircraft, listed as 'models' are generally intended for exhibition purposes and are not airworthy although they are full scale replicas.
However, in a few cases the machines have the ability to taxi when used for film work

Future Allocations Log

The grid provides the facility to record future registrations as they are issued or seen. To trace a particular code, refer to the left hand column which contains the three letters following the G prefix. The final letter can be found by reading across the columns headed A to Z. For example, the box for G-CIFT is located 6 rows down (CIF) and then 19 across to the T column.

G-	A	B	C	D	E	F	G	H	I	J	K	L	M	N	O	P	R	S	T	U	V	W	X	Y	Z
CIA																									
CIB																									
CIC																									
CID																									
CIE																									
CIF																									
CIG																									
CIH																									
CII																									
CIJ																									
CIK																									
CIL																									
CIM																									
CIN																									
CIO																									
CIP																									
CIR																									
CIS																									
CIT																									
CIU																									
CIV																									
CIW																									
CIX																									
CIY																									
CIZ																									
CJA																									
CJB																									
CJC																									
CJD																									
CJE																									
CJF																									
CJG																									
CJH																									
	A	B	C	D	E	F	G	H	I	J	K	L	M	N	O	P	R	S	T	U	V	W	X	Y	Z

Credit: *Wal Gandy*